Handbook of Latin American Studies: No. 37

A SELECTIVE AND ANNOTATED GUIDE TO RECENT PUBLICATIONS IN ANTHROPOLOGY, ECONOMICS, EDUCATION, GEOGRAPHY, GOVERNMENT AND POLITICS, INTERNATIONAL RELATIONS, AND SOCIOLOGY

VOLUME 38 WILL BE DEVOTED TO THE HUMANITIES: ART, CINEMA, FOLKLORE, HISTORY, LANGUAGE, LITERATURE, MUSIC, AND PHILOSOPHY

EDITORIAL NOTE

Comments concerning the *Handbook of Latin American Studies,* should be sent directly to the Editor, *Handbook of Latin American Studies,* Latin American, Portuguese, and Spanish Division, Library of Congress, Washington, D.C. 20540.

Advisory Board

Charles Gibson, *University of Michigan,* CHAIRMAN
Cole Blasier, *University of Pittsburgh*
Pauline P. Collins, *University of Massachusetts*
Frank N. Dauster, *Rutgers University, New Brunswick*
William P. Glade, Jr., *University of Texas*
Joseph Grunwald, *The Brookings Institution*
Javier Malagón, *General Secretariat, Organization of American States*
Betty J. Meggers, *Smithsonian Institution*
James R. Scobie, *Indiana University, Bloomington*
Kempton E. Webb, *Columbia University*
Bryce Wood, *Social Science Research Council*

Administrative Officers • The Library of Congress

Daniel J. Boorstin, *Librarian of Congress*
Alan M. Fern, *Director, Department of Research*
Mary Ellis Kahler, *Chief, Latin American, Portuguese, and Spanish Division*

Representative of the University of Florida

William B. Harvey, *Director, University of Florida Press*

Handbook Editorial Staff

Assistant Editor
  Dolores Moyano Martin
Assistant to the Editor
  Alfredda H. Payne
  Janice M. Herd
Editorial Assistants
  Jane L. Lowe
  Kim B. Wallace

HANDBOOK OF LATIN AMERICAN STUDIES
No. 37

Prepared by
A NUMBER OF SCHOLARS
for
the Latin American,
Portuguese, and Spanish Division
of
The Library of Congress

54056

Edited by
DONALD E. J. STEWART

•

SOCIAL SCIENCES

MEMPHIS
THEOLOGICAL SEMINARY
LIBRARY
168 EAST PARKWAY SOUTH
MEMPHIS, TN. 38104

UNIVERSITY OF FLORIDA PRESS
GAINESVILLE
1975

L. C. Card Number: 36-32633

ISBN 0-8130-0552-3

A UNIVERSITY OF FLORIDA PRESS BOOK

COPYRIGHT © 1975 BY THE BOARD OF REGENTS
OF THE STATE OF FLORIDA

PRINTED BY ROSE PRINTING CO.
TALLAHASSEE, FLORIDA

Contributing Editors

Richard E.W. Adams, *University of Texas, San Antonio*, ANTHROPOLOGY
*Earl M. Aldrich, Jr., *University of Wisconsin, Madison*, LITERATURE
Fuat Andic, *University of Puerto Rico, Rio Piedras*, ECONOMICS
Suphan Andic, *University of Puerto Rico, Rio Piedras*, ECONOMICS
John J. Bailey, *Georgetown University*, GOVERNMENT AND POLITICS
*Arnold Bauer, *University of California, Davis*, HISTORY
*Gerald Béhague, *University of Texas at Austin*, MUSIC
R. Albert Berry, *University of Toronto*, ECONOMICS
Robert L. Bennett, *University of Maryland, College Park*, ECONOMICS
*Rolando E. Bonachea, *Boise State University*, HISTORY
Leslie Ann Brownrigg, *Northwestern University*, ANTHROPOLOGY
Ripley P. Bullen, *The Florida State Museum, Gainesville*, ANTHROPOLOGY
*E. Bradford Burns, *University of California, Los Angeles*, HISTORY
*David Bushnell, *University of Florida*, HISTORY
*Edward E. Calnek, *University of Rochester*, HISTORY
*D. Lincoln Canfield, *Southern Illinois University at Carbondale*, LATIN AMERICAN LANGUAGES
*Thomas E. Case, *San Diego State University*, LITERATURE
*Donald E. Chipman, *North Texas State University, Denton*, HISTORY
Lambros Comitas, *Columbia University*, ANTHROPOLOGY
*Edith B. Couturier, *Evanston, Illinois*, HISTORY
José Fabio Barbosa-Dasilva, *University of Notre Dame*, SOCIOLOGY
*Frank Dauster, *Rutgers University, New Brunswick*, LITERATURE
*Ralph E. Dimmick, *General Secretariat, Organization of American States*, LITERATURE
Clinton R. Edwards, *University of Wisconsin, Milwaukee*, GEOGRAPHY
Robert C. Eidt, *University of Wisconsin, Milwaukee*, GEOGRAPHY
Clifford Evans, *Smithsonian Institution*, ANTHROPOLOGY
Yale H. Ferguson, *Rutgers University, Newark*, INTERNATIONAL RELATIONS
*Rubén A. Gamboa, *Mills College*, LITERATURE
*Naomi M. Garrett, *West Virginia State College*, LITERATURE
Marion H. Gillim, *Eastern Kentucky University*, ECONOMICS
*Roberto González Echevarría, *Cornell University*, LITERATURE
*Richard E. Greenleaf, *The Tulane University*, HISTORY
Robert A. Halberstein, *University of Miami*, ANTHROPOLOGY
*Michael T. Hamerly, *Archivo Histórico del Guayas, Ecuador*, HISTORY
John R. Hebert, *Library of Congress*, GEOGRAPHY
Pedro F. Hernández, *Loyola University*, SOCIOLOGY
Bruce Herrick, *University of California, Los Angeles*, ECONOMICS
Mario Hiraoka, *Millersville State College*, GEOGRAPHY
John M. Hunter, *Michigan State University*, ECONOMICS
John M. Ingham, *University of Minnesota*, ANTHROPOLOGY
Thomas B. Irving, *University of Tennessee*, LITERATURE
Lovell S. Jarvis, *University of California, Berkeley*, ECONOMICS
Quentin Jenkins, *Louisiana State University*, SOCIOLOGY
*Harvey L. Johnson, *University of Houston*, LITERATURE
Nora Scott Kinzer, *Purdue North Central University*, SOCIOLOGY
Asunción Lavrin, *Howard University*, HISTORY

Seth Leacock, *University of Connecticut,* ANTHROPOLOGY
*Luis Leal, *University of Illinois, Urbana-Champaign,* LITERATURE
Fred D. Levy, Jr., *International Bank for Reconstruction and Development,* ECONOMICS
*Santiago Luppoli, *New York University,* LITERATURE
*James B. Lynch, Jr., *University of Maryland, College Park,* ART
*Colin MacLachlan, *The Tulane University,* HISTORY
Tom L. Martinson, *Ball State University,* GEOGRAPHY
Betty J. Meggers, *Smithsonian Institution,* ANTHROPOLOGY
*Carolyn Morrow, *University of Utah,* LITERATURE
John V. Murra, *Cornell University,* HISTORY
*José Neistein, *Brazilian American Cultural Institute, Washington,* ART
*Betty T. Osiek, *Southern Illinois University at Edwardsville,* LITERATURE
*Vincent C. Peloso, *Howard University,* HISTORY
Lisandro Pérez, *Louisiana State University,* SOCIOLOGY
*Humberto M. Rasi, *Andrews University,* LITERATURE
*Daniel R. Reedy, *University of Kentucky,* LITERATURE
*Donald Robertson, *The Tulane University,* ART
*Mario Rodríguez, *University of Southern California,* HISTORY
C. Neale Ronning, *New School for Social Research,* INTERNATIONAL RELATIONS
*Gordon C. Ruscoe, *University of Louisville,* EDUCATION
Jorge Salazar-Carrillo, *The Brookings Institution,* ECONOMICS
*Arturo Santana, *University of Puerto Rico, Río Piedras, Puerto Rico,* HISTORY
*Merle E. Simmons, *Indiana University, Bloomington,* FOLKLORE
Hobart A. Spalding, Jr., *Brooklyn College,* HISTORY
John Strasma, *University of Wisconsin, Madison,* ECONOMICS
Andrés Suárez, *University of Florida,* GOVERNMENT AND POLITICS
Philip B. Taylor, Jr., *University of Houston,* GOVERNMENT AND POLITICS
*Juan Carlos Torchia-Estrada, *General Secretariat, Organization of American States,* PHILOSOPHY
Agnes E. Toward, *San Diego State University,* EDUCATION
Alan C. Wares, *Instituto Lingüístico de Verano, México,* ANTHROPOLOGY
Kempton E. Webb, *Columbia University,* GEOGRAPHY
Hasso von Winning, *Southwest Museum, Los Angeles,* ANTHROPOLOGY
Jan Peter Wogart, *Institut für Weltwirtschaft, Universität Kiel,* ECONOMICS
*Benjamin M. Woodbridge, *University of California, Berkeley,* LITERATURE
*Winthrop R. Wright, *University of Maryland, College Park,* HISTORY

Foreign Corresponding Editors

Dr. Wilhelm Stegmann, *Ibero-Amerikanisches Institut, Berlin-Lankwich, Federal Republic of Germany,* GERMAN LANGUAGE MATERIAL
Marcello Carmagnani, *Università di Torino, Italy,* ITALIAN LANGUAGE MATERIAL

---

*Contributing Editors to Handbook no. 38 (Humanities), scheduled for publication in 1976.

Wolf Grabendorff, *Lateinamerikareferat, Stiftung Wissenschaft und Politik, Ebenhausen/Isar,* SOCIAL SCIENCES
Manfred Kossok, *Karl-Marx-Universitaet, Leipzig, German Democratic Republic,* GERMAN LANGUAGE MATERIAL
Magnus Mörner, *Ibero-Amerikanska Institutet i Stockholm, Stockholm, Sweden,* SCANDINAVIAN LANGUAGE MATERIAL
Daniel Pécaut, *Ecole Pratique des Hautes Etudes, Paris, France,* FRENCH LANGUAGE MATERIAL
R.A.M. van Zantwijk, *Universiteit van Amsterdam, The Netherlands,* DUTCH LANGUAGE MATERIAL

Special Contributing Editors

T. Stephen Cheston, *Georgetown University,* SLAVIC LANGUAGES
Georgette M. Dorn, *Library of Congress,* GERMAN AND HUNGARIAN LANGUAGES
Hans J. Hoyer, *George Mason University,* GERMAN LANGUAGE
Maurice A. Lubin, *Howard University,* HAITIAN MATERIAL
Carmelo Mesa-Lago, *University of Pittsburgh,* CUBAN MATERIAL
Anita R. Navon, *Library of Congress,* SLAVIC LANGUAGES
Arnold H. Price, *Library of Congress,* GERMAN LANGUAGE
Renata V. Shaw, *Library of Congress,* SCANDINAVIAN LANGUAGES

Contents

	PAGE
CHANGES IN VOLUME 37................................	xii

BIBLIOGRAPHY AND GENERAL
WORKS .... *Donald E.J. Stewart*	3
Journal Abbreviations: Bibl. & Gen. Works..........................	17

ANTHROPOLOGY

GENERAL..	18
ARCHAEOLOGY	
MESOAMERICA............................... *Hasso von Winning*	25
and *Richard E.W. Adams*	
THE CARIBBEAN .... *Ripley P. Bullen*	48
SOUTH AMERICA .... *Betty J. Meggers* and *Clifford Evans*	52
ETHNOLOGY	
MIDDLE AMERICA................................ *John M. Ingham*	84
WEST INDIES .... *Lambros Comitas*	98
SOUTH AMERICA LOWLANDS............................ *Seth Leacock*	115
SOUTH AMERICA HIGHLANDS.................... *Leslie Ann Brownrigg*	126
LINGUISTICS.. *Alan C. Wares*	151
PHYSICAL ANTHROPOLOGY................ *Robert A. Halberstein*	168
Journal Abbreviations: Anthropology...............................	202

ECONOMICS

GENERAL.. *John M. Hunter*	208
MEXICO... *Robert L. Bennett*	233
CENTRAL AMERICA/WEST INDIES	
(except Puerto Rico and Cuba).................... *Marion H. Gillim*	240
Cuba.................... *Handbook of Latin American Studies Staff*	248
SPANISH SOUTH AMERICA	
COLOMBIA, ECUADOR, AND THE GUIANAS .... *R. Albert Berry*	251
VENEZUELA.. *Jorge Salazar-Carrillo*	260
BOLIVIA, CHILE, PARAGUAY, PERU	
AND URUGUAY..................... *John Strasma* and *Bruce Herrick*	266
ARGENTINA... *Lovell S. Jarvis*	275
BRAZIL .... *Fred D. Levy, Jr.* and *Jan Peter Wogart*	286
Journal Abbreviations: Economics	311

EDUCATION

LATIN AMERICA (except Brazil) .... Gordon C. Ruscoe	314
BRAZIL .... Agnes E. Toward	333
Journal Abbreviations: Education....................................	355

GEOGRAPHY

GENERAL .... *Clinton R. Edwards*	357
MIDDLE AMERICA............................... *Tom L. Martinson*	364
SOUTH AMERICA (except Brazil) ... *Robert C. Eidt* and *Mario Hiraoka*	379
BRAZIL.. *Kempton E. Webb*	408
CARTOGRAPHY .... *John R. Hébert*	421
Journal Abbreviations: Geography	436

GOVERNMENT AND POLITICS

GENERAL .... *John J. Bailey; Philip B. Taylor, Jr.*	439
and *Andrés Suárez*	
MEXICO, CENTRAL AMERICA, THE CARIBBEAN,	
THE GUIANAS..................................... *Andrés Suárez*	455
SOUTH AMERICA WEST COAST .... *John J. Bailey*	471
EAST COAST................ *Philip B. Taylor, Jr.*	491
Journal Abbreviations: Government and Politics	520

INTERNATIONAL RELATIONS

GENERAL .... *Yale H. Ferguson*	524
and *C. Neale Ronning*	
MEXICO, CENTRAL AMERICA, THE	
CARIBBEAN .... *Yale H. Ferguson*	537
SOUTH AMERICA.............................. *C. Neale Ronning*	544
Journal Abbreviations: International Relations	552

SOCIOLOGY

GENERAL .... *Quentin Jenkins; Lisando Pérez*	555
and *Pedro F. Hernández*	
MEXICO, CENTRAL AMERICA, THE	
CARIBBEAN and THE GUIANAS............... *Pedro F. Hernández*	565
SOUTH AMERICA: ANDEAN COUNTRIES .... *Quentin Jenkins*	578
and *Lisandro Pérez*	
SOUTH AMERICA: THE RIVER PLATE........... *Nora Scott Kinzer*	586
BRAZIL .... *José Fábio Barbosa-Dasilva*	590
Journal Abbreviations: Sociology......................................	605

INDEXES

ABBREVIATIONS AND ACRONYMS 611
TITLE LIST OF JOURNALS INDEXED 616
SUBJECT INDEX... 630
AUTHOR INDEX 651

Changes In Volume 37

The various changes introduced over the past few years have become standardized and there have been only a few additional refinements to improve the format. To adjust to the increased quantity of material being published, another contributor was added to the Brazil-Economics section and the Sociology-South America: River Plate section was established.

The Title List of Journals Indexed has become a permanent feature of the *Handbook*. The Subject Index headings are generally based on those of *HLAS 35,* in an effort to maintain consistency and to establish a uniform system for future volumes.

Only material received from the Contributing Editors before May 31, 1975, has been included in this volume. Adherence to this cutoff date makes it possible for the editorial staff to cope with the increased workload.

Changes in the roster of Contributing Editors are noted below:

Anthropology: Dr. Robert A. Halberstein (University of Miami) assumed sole responsibility for the preparation of the Physical Anthropology section.

Economics: Dr. R. Albert Berry (University of Toronto) prepared the Colombia, Ecuador, and the Guianas section. Dr. Lovell S. Jarvis (University of California, Berkeley) prepared the Argentina section. Dr. Jan Peter Wogart (Institut für Weltwirtschaft, Universität Kiel) joined Dr. Fred D. Levy, Jr., in the preparation of the Brazil section.

Geography: Dr. Mario Hiraoka (Millersville State College) joined Dr. Robert C. Eidt in the preparation of the South America (except Brazil) section.

Sociology: Dr. Nora Scott Kinzer (Purdue North Central University) prepared the South America: River Plate section.

Administrative changes within the editorial staff of the *Handbook of Latin American Studies* are reflected on the title page of the present volume.

Donald E. J. Stewart

Washington, D.C.
December 1975

Handbook of Latin American Studies

Bibliography and General Works

Donald E.J. Stewart
Editor
Handbook of Latin American Studies

GENERAL BIBLIOGRAPHY

1. *Boletín de la Sociedad Mexicana de Geografía y Estadística.* Vol. III, 1972- México.

A listing of bibliographies compiled in Mexico and of bibliographies prepared elsewhere with significant references to Mexico published between 1950 and 1970.

2. Bonfanti, Celestino and **Arabia Teresa Cova.** Bibliografía de humanidades y ciencias sociales del profesorado de la U.C.V.: 1967-1970. Caracas, Univ. Central de Venezuela, Consejo de Desarrollo Científico y Humanístico, 1973. 101 p., bibl. (Proyecto de investigación, CH-4)

Compilation according to schools of the Univ. Central de Venezuela. Only fully published works, these and dissertations, and published conference works are listed. Includes subject and author indexes. Useful unannotated work.

Cardozo G., Armando; Julio Rea C.; and **Irma A. de Viscarra.** Bibliografía de la Quinua y la Cañahua. See item 6822.

3. City University of New York, *New York.* **Brooklyn College. Institute of Puerto Rican Studies.** The Puerto Rican people: a selected bibliography for use in social work education. N.Y., Council on Social Work Education, 1973. 54 p.

A selective, annotated bibliography aimed at presenting a broad view of the historical, economic, and cultural factors that have had an influence on Puerto Ricans.

4. Escamilla González, Gloria. Manual de metodología y técnica bibliográficas. México, UNAM, Instituto de Investigaciones Bibliográficas, 1973. 112 p., bibl. (Instrumenta bibliographica, 1)

Calls for a standardized methodology in the preparation of all bibliography. Work is based on the Anglo-American cataloging rules published in 1967.

5. Gill, Michael E. Planning meeting on national bibliographies of the English-speaking Caribbean (UNESCO/BL, 28:6, Nov./Dec. 1974, p. 308-310)

Report on the developments planned for the immediate future in the bibliographic control of publications in the Commonwealth Caribbean and relates these developments to the ideal of universal bibliographic control in the whole region.

6. *Ibero-Americana.* Institute of Latin American Studies *for the* Scandinavian Association for Research on Latin America (NOSALF). Vol. 4, No. 1, 1974- . Stockholm.

In addition to news and acquisitions, edition includes an article by Miguel Benito, Latin America in the Swedish bibliography, 1972 to 1973. See *HLAS 36:55*.

7. Millares Carlo, Agustín. Prontuario de bibliografía general (UCAB/M, 2, 1973, p. 7-144, facsims.)

Organized by century: 1) XVI, 2) XVII, 3) XVIII; and 4) XIX and XX. Includes combined author and title index. Good reference work.

8. The New York Public Library, *New York.* **The Branch Library System. The Office of Adult Services.** Borinquen: lista bilingüe de libros, películas y discos sobre la experiencia puertorriqueña (A bilingual list of books, films, and records on the Puerto Rican experience). N.Y., 1974. 32 p.

Subtitle is self-explanatory. Includes general works, history, social sciences, literature, language, arts, biography, films, and records. Annotated, useful.

9. North American Congress on Latin America, *New York.* NACLA's bibliography on Latin America. N.Y., 1975. 48 p.

The expectation of this work is to sharpen the ideological and political struggle between the imperialist and anti-imperialist forces of the world on two inter-related levels: providing access to information and analysis for political battles; and suggesting sources for ongoing analysis. Makes "no pretense of bourgeois scholarly neutrality."

10. Sánchez de Meazzi, Stella Maris; Hilda Zulama Guglielmone; and María Elvira Zimmermann de Ferreyra. Contribución para una bibliografía sobre Córdoba: artículos de revistas existentes en la Biblioteca Mayor de la Universidad Nacional de Córdoba, 1860-1970. Córdoba, Arg., Univ. Nacional de Córdoba, Biblioteca Mayor, 1974. 147 l.

Compilation of periodical articles on Cordoba between 1860 and 1970. Materials are arranged by subject.

COLLECTIVE AND PERSONAL BIBLIOGRAPHY

Biblioteca Nacional, *Rio.* Nordeste brasileiro: catálogo da exposição. See item 7067.

11. Cabral Mejía, Tobías E. Indice de *Clío* y del *Boletín del Archivo General de la Nación.* Santo Domingo, Editora del Caribe, 1972. 288 p. bibl. (Academia Dominicana de la Historia, 32)

Clío is published by the Academia Dominicana de la Historia and the *Boletín* is self explanatory. Material listed alphabetically by author and subjects. Includes subject and author index, bibliography of materials published by Academy of the Archivo. Useful reference.

12. Calvo de Elcoro, Miren Zorkunde. Contribución a la bibliografía de Fernando Paz Castillo: 1893. Caracas, Univ. Católica Andrés Bello, Escuela de Letras, Centro de Investigaciones Literarias, 1974. 332 p., plate (Col. Bibliografías, 11)

Work is divided into seven major categories: 1) bibliographic references; 2) major works; 3) miscellaneous; 4) various works; 5) published letters; 6) biography and criticism; and 7) appendix. Includes a brief chronology of major events in Paz Castillo's life.

13. Comas, Juan. Cien años de Congresos Internacionales de Americanistas: ensayo histórico-crítico y bibliográfico. México, UNAM, Instituto de Investigaciones Históricas, Instituto de Investigaciones Antropológicas, 1974. 542 p., bibl., plates.

History and development of Congress. Lists various Americanist societies, the principal motions of recommendations that have been made, a bibliography of all Congress proceedings published, a bibliography of works published listed by subject, and an author index. Useful reference.

14. Dabbs, Jack Autrey. The Mariano Riva Palacio Archives: a guide. México, Editorial Jus *for* Univ. of Texas, Institute of Latin American Studies, 1972. v. 3 (p. 839-1149) (Independent Mexico in documents: independence, empire, and republic, 2)

Description of documents in the archive. Includes useful explanatory notes.

15. *La Educación.* Organización de los Estados Americanos, Departamento de Asuntos Educativos. Año 16, No. 59, enero/abril 1971- . Washington.

The index to the first 58 issues (1956-1970). See item 6014.

Evelyn, Shirley *ed.* and *comp.* West Indian social sciences index: an index to *Moko, New World Quarterly, Savacou, Tapia,* 1963-1972. See item 1230a.

16. Hasler, Juan A. Bibliografía americanística brevis. Medellín, Colo., Univ. de Antioquia, 1973. 170 p., map.

Arranged alphabetically by subject and geographically. Unannotated, but useful compilation.

17. Lange de Cabrera, María Zoraida; Hilda Margarita Pellicer; Ziona de Fischbach; and **Lil Barceló Sifontes.** Contribución a la bibliografía de Arturo Uslar Pietri: 1906. Caracas, Univ. Católica Andrés Bello, Escuela de Letras, Centro de Investigaciones Literarias, 1973. 396 p., bibl., plates (Col. Bibliografías, 10)

Divided into five major sections: bibliographic references; major works in turn subdivided into the novel, short story, essay, bibliographies, and theater; miscellaneous works, various works; and biography and criticism. Unannotated, but useful. There is a brief chronology of major events in Uslar Pietri's life.

18. Rey Fajardo, José del. Biobibliografía de los jesuitas en la Venezuela colonial. Caracas, Univ. Católica Andrés Bello, Instituto de Investigaciones Históricas, 1974. 590 p.

Information is arranged alphabetically by person. Highlights each person's life and lists what each wrote.

Serracino Inglott, George comp. Bibliografía por autor: departamento El Loa, provincia de Antofagasta, Chile. See item 948.

19. Universidad de los Andes, Mérida, Ven. **Facultad de Humanidades y Educación. Centro de Investigaciones Literarias.** Diccionario general de la literatura venezolana: autores. Mérida, Ven., 1974. 829 p., bibl.

The biography, bibliography, and criticism of Venezuelan authors. Excellent reference.

20. Villas-Bôas, Pedro. Notas de bibliografia sul-rio-grandense: autores. Pôrto Alegre, Bra., A Nação em co-edição com o Instituto Estadual do Livro, 1974. 615 p.

Biography of authors of Rio Grande do Sul. Useful reference.

ACQUISITIONS, LIBRARY HOLDINGS AND CATALOGS

21. Biblioteca Nacional José Martí, La Habana. **Hemeroteca e Información Humanística.** Indices de las revistas cubanas: *Verbum, Espuela de Plata, Nadio Parecía, Clavileño, Poeta, Orígenes,* and *Ciclón,* t. 1. La Habana, 1969. 293 p.

Indices for all by subject, author and title except *Verbum* which has only an author and subject index. Excellent reference.

22. Bohorquez C., José Ignacio. Catálogo del Centro de Documentación (INCOMEX): publicaciones registradas en el período 1 agosto 1973—30 abril 1974. Bogotá, Instituto Colombiano de Comercio Exterior, Centro de Documentación, 1974. 415 p.

Prepared for the II Reunión de la Red Colombiana de Información y Documentación Económica, *Bogotá, 1974.*

23. *Boletím da Biblioteca da Câmara dos Deputados.* Vol. 20, Nos. 1/3, jan./dez. 1971- . Brasília.

Lists recent acquisitions by type: monographs and pamphlets; reference works; periodicals; Universal Decimal Classification. There is also a bibliography of environmental pollution. The next issue of this bulletin will be entitled *Documentação e Informação na Câmara dos Deputados.*

24. Briceño Perozo, Mario. La hemeroteca de la Academia Nacional de la Historia. Caracas, Academia Nacional de la Historia, 1972. 79 p., facsims. (Biblioteca venezolana de historia, 17)

Description of the newspaper holdings and history of the Venezuelan press.

25. Companhia Vale do Rio Doce, Rio. **Centro de Informações Técnicas.** Catálogo coletivo de livros e folhetos: 1966-1970. Rio, 1971. 1 v. (Various pagings) (Serie 1: catálogos, 1)

Compilation of holdings in company library arranged by subject. Includes author and title indexes.

26. Fundación para la Educación Superior y el Desarrollo (FEDESARROLLO), Bogotá. **Biblioteca.** Bibliografía de publicaciones: materias y autores. Bogotá, 1974. 28 p.

Bibliography organized by subject by the library of the Fundación para la Educación Superior y el Desarrollo, a nonprofit Colombian entity. Useful. For more publications by FEDESARROLLO, see items 4460, 4461, 4462, 4471, 4482, 4486, 4490, 4499, 4505, and 4520.

27. García y García, J. Jesús. Guía de archivos: contiene material de interés para el estudio del desarrollo socioeconómico de México. México, UNAM, Instituto de Investigaciones Sociales, 1972. 185 p.

A description of the organization, holdings, and sources for each archive arranged by chapter which include: executive, judicial, legislative, private or autonomous educational institutions, church, state, and cultural and scientific archives. Excellent reference.

28. Gelfand, Morris A. Política de aquisição em bibliotecas universitárias: planos e programas, individuais e cooperativos, de formação de acervos (*Revista de Biblioteconomia de Brasília,* 2:2, julho/dez. 1974, p. 155-165, bibl.)

In view of the rising volume of publication and the mounting costs throughout the world of library materials, academic libraries should join and support cooperative acquisition programs.

29. **Hernández de Caldas, Angela** and **Inés Alvarez de la Cruz.** Publicaciones periódicas del CIEB. Bogotá, Cámara de Comercio de Bogotá, Centro de Informática Económica, 1974. 1 v. (Various pagings)

Study presented at the II Reunión de la Red Colombiana de Información y Documentación Económica, Bogotá. In addition to listing the holdings there are geographic and subject indexes.

30. **Instituto de Estudios Ibero-Americanos,** *Stockholm* and **La Oficina Central de Estadística de Suecia,** *Stockholm.* Statistical sources on Latin America available at Institute of Latin American Studies and National Central Bureau of Statistics. Stockholm, 1974. 62 p.

"List of publications available in the two libraries of the Latinamerika-institutet i Stockholm and the Statistiska Centralbyrån with national statistical information of the Latin American countries."

31. **Instituto Nacional del Libro Español,** *Madrid?* Catálogo de los libros conmemorativos: año internacional del libro. Madrid?, 1972. 117 p.

32. **Jackson, William Vernon** *ed.* Latin American collections. Nashville, Tenn., The Author, 1974. 142 p.

Excellent historiography of collections in the various major institutions with L.A. holdings. Describes means of acquisition, problems of maintenance and expansion, strengths and weaknesses and all the myriad attendant considerations surrounding major research collections. Excellent reference. Distributed by Vanderbilt Univ. Bookstore.

33. Latin America: a catalog of dissertations. Ann Arbor, Mich., Xerox Univ. Microfilms, 1974. 70 p.

Lists selected dissertations available through the Xerox Univ. Microfilms. Most were written recently, but earlier ones are included to provide an historical overview. Entries are listed by country according to discipline. Excellent reference.

34. Livros recém-adquiridos: dezembro de 1973/junho de 1974 (Boletim Bibliográfico [Serviço Social do Comérico, Divisão de Documentação e Intercâmbio, Seção de Documentação. Rio] 12, dez. 1974, p. 127-176)

Lists acquisitions made between Dec. 1973 and June 1974 by subject.

Lizana V., María Victoria. Catálogo de informes inéditos. See item 6856.

35. **Monte-Mór, Jannice.** Microfilmagem de jornais da Biblioteca Nacional (Revista de Biblioteconomia de Brasília, 2:2, julho/dez. 1974, p. 143-153, bibl.)

Microfilming started with the *Jornal do Comercio* collection of 1841 to 1956. Other libraries have cooperated with the program, but not publishers. A Brazilian newspapers union catalog is available in national and foreign institutions and the Ford Foundation has provided a grant to microfilm newspapers in the National Library.

36. **Musso Ambrosi, Luis Alberto.** Archivos del Uruguay. Montevideo, Estado Mayor del Ejército, Depto. de Estudios Históricos, División Histórica, 1974. 49 p.

Guide and description of Uruguayan archives. Excellent reference.

37. **Peru. Oficina Nacional de Desarrollo Cooperativo. Biblioteca.** Catálogo de publicaciones periódicas: 1965-1970. Lima, 1971. 41 p. (CENACOOP. Serie bibliográfica, 4)

List of periodicals received by La Oficina Nacional de Desarrollo Cooperativo in Peru arranged by subject.

38. **Rede de Bibliotecas de Amazônia** (REBAM), *Belém, Bra.* Documentação amazônica: catálogo coletivo. Belém, Bra., 1974. 543 p.

Work intended to gather all possible material, information, documents, and bibliographies concerning the region. Organized by subject, and printed out on cut-out cards that could be used for a card catalog. Includes 650 works. Excellent reference.

39. **Reunión de Publicaciones Periódicas,** *I, Bogotá, 1973.* Memorias de la primera reunión de publicaciones periódicas. Bogotá, Ministerio de Educación Nacional, Instituto Colombiano para el Fomento de la Educación Nacional (ICFES), Instituto Colombiano para el Fomento de la Educación Superior, División de Documentación y Fomento Bibliotecario, 1973. 184 p., illus.

Conference held to iron out problems encountered while compiling the *Catálogo Colectivo Nacional de Publicaciones Periódicas.* Informative.

40. **Robredo, Jaime; Yone Sepúlveda Chastinet;** and **Claudia de Amorim Ponce.** Metodologia para a elaboração da lista básica dos periódicos nacionais em ciências agrícolas e estudo da dispersão da literatura agrícola brasileira (Revista de Biblioteconomia de

Brasília, 2:2, julho/dez. 1974, p. 119-142, bibl., tables)

Based on periodicals indexed in *Bibliografía Brasileira de Ciências Agrícolas* of 1969 and 1972/73. Added were other periodicals of a scientific and technical scientific level.

41. Rubio, Mañé, J. Ignacio. El Archivo General de la Nación: México, Distrito Federal, Estados Mexicanos. 2. ed. México, Talleres Gráficos de la Nación, 1973. 69 p., illus.

Updates 1st ed. by including section on the period 1940 to 1973. Excludes three sections from the original work: description of facilities; publications; and the index.

42. Universidad Boliviana Mayor Tomás Frías, *Potosí, Bol.* **División de Extensión Universitaria.** Catálogo del libro potosino. Potosí, Bol., 1973. 42 p.

Lists relevant works by library; therefore a work may appear more than once. Includes author index.

43. Universidad de la República, *Montevideo.* Catálogo colectivo de publicaciones periódicas existentes en las bibliotecas universitarias del Uruguay. t. 1, A-G. t.2, H-Z. Montevideo, 1970. 2 v. (696 p.) (Continuous pagination)

Preliminary compilation to be followed by corrected and enlarged edition. Includes materials received by all universities. Useful reference.

44. Universidad de los Andes, *Bogotá.* **Comité de Investigaciones.** Catálogo de tesis: 1960-1973. Bogotá, 1973? 41 p.

Compiled by authors. Includes subject index. Useful.

45. Universidad Federal do Paraná, *Curitiba, Bra.* **Instituto de Letras e Artes. Centro de Estudos Brasileiros.** Catálogo coletivo de literatura história e geografia do Paraná. Curitiba, Bra., 1972. 327 p., bibl.

Compilation of literary works authored by persons born or living in Paraná, and of history and geography of Paraná regardless of author's domicile. Lists libraries consulted; bibliography of works is arranged alphabetically; and there is a list of Univ. Federal do Paraná publications and theses. Useful reference.

Waller, Helen *comp.* Bibliografia do Summer Institute of Linguistics. See item 1954.

LIBRARY SCIENCE AND SERVICES

46. The American Library Association; The Library of Congress; The Library Association; and The Canadian Library Association. Reglas de catalogación angloamericanas. Washington, Organización de los Estados Americanos, Depto. de Asuntos Culturales, Programa de Fomento de Bibliotecas, 1970. 395 p. (Manuales del bibliotecario, 7)

Spanish version of the *Anglo-American Cataloging Rules.*

47. Associação Paulista de Bibliotecários *São Paulo.* **Bibliotecários Biomédicos.** Normas para catalogação de publicações seriadas nas bibliotecas especializadas. São Paulo, Editôra Polígono, 1972. 121 p. p.

Self explanatory title.

48. _____, _____. Grupo de Trabalho de Bibliotecas de Ciências Sociais e Humanas. Guia de bibliotecas de ciências sociais e humanas do Estado de São Paulo. São Paulo. São Paulo, 1973. 44 l.

Guide intended to foster increased contact among the various libraries. Gives brief summary of staff, holdings, and other information. Good reference.

49. _____, _____. Grupo de Trabalho em Technologia. Comissão de Levantamento de Bibliotecas da Area Tecnológica. Levantamento de bibliotecas da área tecnológica. Rio, Instituto Brasileiro de Bibliografía e Documentação, 1974. 418 p.

Compilation of information on Brazilian technical libraries. Includes copies of questionnaires sent to the libraries. Useful reference.

50. *Bibliotecas y Archivos.* Escuela Nacional de Biblioteconomía y Archivonomía. No. 4, 1973- . México.

Deals with seven library science topics: 1) library school programs; 2) reorganization of library services Instituto Politécnico Nacional; 3) archive terminology; 4) primary school libraries; 5) information science in library schools; 6) the library as a service institution; 7) standards for library school accreditation to American Library Association.

51. Bloch, Thomas. Education for management in Central America: the role of the library of the Instituto Centroamericano de Administración de Empresas (UNESCO/BL, 27:4, July/Aug. 1973, p. 219-221, 227)

History and future of the Instituto Centroamericano de Administración de Empresas. Library is run by a staff of five and has holdings of over 4000 volumes and receives 300 periodicals.

52. Bohorquez, José Ignacio. Estado actual de las bibliotecas en Colombia. Bogotá, Fondo Colombiano de Investigaciones Científicas, Proyectos Especiales Francisco José de Caldas, 1972. 82 p., tables (Serie Bibliotecología y documentación, 2)

Limited study but useful. Concludes there is great need for more funds, joint ventures, greater coordination, library science training program, cooperation, and standardization of training and services.

53. Castro, Astréa de Moraes e. Arquivo no Brasil e na Europa. Rio, Ministério da Justiça, Arquivo Nacional, 1973. 124 p.

Description of archival functions and responsibilities. Discusses preservation, training, and the historical archive of the Chamber of Deputies.

54. Córdova de Castillo, Nora. La biblioteca de Ocopa: su historia y organización (FENIX, 23, 1973, p. 71-127)

Thorough work on one of the earliest libraries in America.

55. Figueiredo, Nice. Evolução e avaliação do serviço de referência (Revista de Biblioteconomia de Brasília, 2:2, julho/dez. 1974, p. 175-197, bibl.)

Surveys literature on the concepts, the development of services and the use of computers in library reference. Describes the methodology, for quantifying and evaluating reference services and information retrieval systems.

56. Lemos, Antônio Agenor Briquet de and **Vera Amália Amarante Macedo.** A posição da biblioteca na organização operacional da universidade (Revista de Biblioteconomia de Brasília, 2:2, julho/dez. 1974, p. 167-174, bibl.)

The diversity of university library organizations in Brazil is a reflex of the university decision making process characterized by an inarticulate agglomeration of previously separate institutions. Calls for reorganization in accordance with the principles laid down by the University Reform Act.

57. Litton, Gaston L. El bibliotecario. B.A., Bowker Editores Argentina, 1973. 242 p., bibl. (Breviarios del bibliotecario, 13)

Discusses training, responsibilities, and life of a librarian. Chatty and personal in approach.

58. _____. La biblioteca especializada. B.A.,Bowker Editores Argentina, 1974. 208 p. (Breviarios del bibliotecario, 18)

Discusses the role, function, and organizational makeup of specialized libraries. Feels that since these libraries cater to scientists and technical specialists to help prevent costly duplication of effort in research they generally attract the best trained and most able librarians.

59. _____ La biblioteca pública. B.A., Bowker Editores Argentina, 1973. 210 p., bibl. (Breviarios del bibliotecario, 14)

Discusses the importance of public libraries as book depositories and sources of information to all sectors of a community. Points out that they are the cornerstone of the library system.

60. _____. La biblioteca universitaria. B.A., Bowker Editores Argentina, 1974. 213 p., bibl. (Breviarios del bibliotecario, 17)

Feels that this is the most important of the libraries. To be effective it must have a well trained librarian in addition to a proper collection and buildings.

61. _____. Bibliotecas escolares. B.A., Bowker Editores Argentina, 1974. 207 p., bibl. (Breviarios del bibliotecario, 16)

Suggests that good primary and secondary school libraries should help train the student to exploit the full resources of libraries in the higher educational systems. If this is done the university and other advanced institutional libraries will contribute more to the educational system.

62. _____. Bibliotecas infantiles. B.A., Bowker Editores Argentina, 1973. 225 p. (Breviarios del bibliotecario, 15)

Considers a good children's library within the public library system to be essential for instilling knowledge of library resources in users at the earliest age possible a must.

63. McCarthy, Cavan. Developing libraries in Brazil: with a chapter on Paraguay. Metuchen, N.J., The Scarecrow Press, 1975. 207 p., bibl.

Analyzes librarianship and the Brazilian environment with the contrasts created by the unique pattern of library organization and the forces that brought them into being. Information on all types of libraries, librarians, and their problems. Discusses outside influences, as well as Brazilian contributions. Brief chapter on libraries in Paraguay.

64. Moraes, Jomar. Guía histórica da Biblioteca Pública Benedito Leite. São Luís, Bra., Fundação Cultural do Maranhão (FUNC), 1973. 63 p., bibl.

History, description and organization of the institution.

65. Naylor, Bernard; Laurence Hallewell; and Colin Steele. Directory of libraries and special collections on Latin America and West Indies. London, Univ. of London, The Athlone Press, 1975. 161 p.

Libraries are listed by city. Services and information provided by each library are listed. Excellent reference source.

66. Penna, Carlos Víctor. The interaction between education, libraries and mass communication, as seen by a librarian (UNESCO/BL, 28:6, Nov./Dec. 1974, p. 311-314, 324)

Recommendations made concerning the functions of rural libraries as a focal part of mass communication media, and the need for centers for educational interaction.

67. _____. Inter-American Seminar on integrated information services of libraries, archives and documentation centres in Latin American and the Caribbean (UNESCO/BL, 27:3, May/June 1973, p. 152-154)

Meeting of archivists, librarians, and documentalists to discuss problems of common interest: information exchange; improvement of services; integrated national plan for services, aims, and coordination of information centres.

68. Reipert, Herman José. História da Biblioteca Pública Municipal Mário de Andrade. São Paulo, Prefeitura do Município de São Paulo, Secretaria de Educação e Cultura, Depto. de Cultura, Divisão de Bibliotecas, 1972. 72 p., facsims.

History, information and statistics of this institution.

69. Robinson, Joyce L. Rural library development in Jamaica (UNESCO/BL, 27:4, July/Aug. 1973, p. 213-218, plates, tables)

Describes organization and services over the past 23 years of the rural libraries existence.

70. Russo, Laura Garcia Moreno. Estado de São Paulo: bibliotecas públicas municipais, situação e sugestões. São Paulo, Federação Brasileira de Associações de Bibliotecários (FEBAB), 1973. 90 p., maps.

Describes the state's public library organization which is divided into eleven regions.

71. Segunda Reunión del Grupo de Trabajo para el Desarrollo de los Servicios Bibliotecarios y de Información Científica y Técnica de los Países Signatarios del convenio *Andrés Bello* (FENIX, 23, 1973, p. 225-239)

Organization and resolutions made at the meeting held in Medellín, Bogotá, and Río Negro, Colo., 19-25 Nov. 1972.

72. Seminar on the Acquisition of Latin American library Materials (SALALM), *XVII, Amherst, Mass., 1972.* Final report and working papers. Amherst, Mass., Univ. of Massachusetts Library [and] Organization of American States, General Secretariat, 1975. 2 v. (Various pagings)

The theme of the seminar was "Education and training of librarians for area collections". This report deals with the five areas covered: 1) Executive Board meetings, 2) business sessions, 3) committee meetings, 4) workshops, and 5) other reports.

73. Seminar on the Acquisition of Latin American Library Materials (SALALM), *XVIII, Port-of-Spain, 1973.* Final report and working papers. Port-of-Spain, Library Association of Trinidad and Tobago, Univ. of the West Indies [and] Organization of American States, General Secretariat, 1975. 456 p., bibl.

The seminar theme was "National, regional, and international planning for library services in Latin America". The format of the report follows the same pattern used for SALALM XVII.

74. Seminario Interamericano sobre la Integración de los Servicios de Información de Archivos, Bibliotecas y Centros de Documentación en América Latina y el Caribe, *Washington, 1972.* Informe final. Washington, 1973. 143 p.

Sponsored by UNESCO, OAS, US Dept. of State, US Commission for UNESCO, the American Library Association and the Council of Library Resources. Compiled by Carlos Víctor Penna in cooperation with Eleanor Mitchell and Marietta Daniels Shepard.

75. Seminário sobre Documentação e Informática, *Rio, 1971.* Da documentação à informática. Rio, Fundação Getúlio Vargas, Instituto de Documentação, Serviço de Publicações, 1974. 240 p.

Proceedings of INDOC Seminar of 24-27 Nov. 1971, dealing with information retrieval and computers.

76. Shepard, Marietta Daniels. Planeamiento nacional de servicios bibliotecarios. v. 1, La infraestructura bibliotecologica de los sistemas nacional de información. Washington, Organización de los Estados Americanos, Secretaría General, Secretaría Ejecutiva para la Educación, la Ciencia y la Cultura, Depto. de Asuntos Culturales, 1972. 136 p. (Estudios bibliotecarios, 8) (UP/0.2 II/II.8.I)

Deals with library infrastructure and the various national information systems.

77. Socorro del Hoyo Briones, María del. Catálogo abreviado de libros y folletos manuscritos en el Instituto Tecnológico y de Estudios Superiores de Monterrey. Monterrey, Mex., Instituto Tecnológico y de Estudios Superiores de Monterrey, 1971. 64 p. (Serie: catálogos de biblioteca, 4)

Summary of the library's catalog organized into three sections for cataloging purposes; books and pamphlets; documents; and correspondence. Dewey decimal classification system is used.

78. Sperandio, Liliana. Histórico da biblioteca pública do Paraná (Revista de Biblioteconomia de Brasília, 2:2, julho/dez. 1974, p. 199-202)

A brief history of the institution from its founding in 1975 to the present.

79. Tavares, Denise Fernandes. A biblioteca escolar: conceituação, organização e funcionamento, orientação do leitor e do professor. São Paulo, Libros Irradiates (LISA) *em convênio com o* Ministerio de Educação e Cultura, Instituto Nacional do Livro, 1973. 161 p., bibl., illus.

Manual on how to organize a school library when there is no librarian.

80. Universidad Mayor de San Andrés, La Paz. Centro Nacional de Documentación Científica y Tecnológica. Guía de bibliotecas, centros y servicios documentarios de Bolivia: 1973. La Paz, 1973. 113 p.

Lists libraries by city giving specialty, hours of operation, services holdings, organization, staff and date founded.

NATIONAL BIBLIOGRAPHY

Bibliografie van Suriname. See item 1209.

81. Bissainthe, Max. Dictionnaire de bibliographie haitienne: premier supplement. Metuchen, N.J., The Scarecrow Press, 1973. 269 p., bibl.

Intended to provide a key to users of the *Dictionnaire de Bibliographie Haitienne*. Organized alphabetically by author for each year between 1950 and 1970. Includes appendix listing works published prior to 1950. Excellent reference and research work.

82. *Boletín Nicaragüense de Bibliografía y Documentación.* Banco Central de Nicaragua. Vol. 1/5, julio 1974/julio 1975- . Managua.

Purpose is to establish the foundation for a national bibliography originally started in the 1940's in the *Biblioteca Americana Rubén Darío*, Managua, and to begin a methodical inventory of Nicaraguan culture. Each of the first five numbers includes an informative essay on some phase of scholarly interest, i.e. archeology, primitive civilizations, etc.

83. Fenoy, Gerard. Colombia contemporánea: elementos para una bibliografía (PUJ/UH, 3, julio 1972, p. 261-277)

Organized into six major subject areas: 1) history; 2) economics; 3) sociology; 4) the church, army, and university; 5) politics; and 6) political trends. Unannotated, but excellent work.

84. Fernández Robaina, Tomás comp. Bibliografía de bibliografías cubanas: 1859-1972. Compilación, prólogo y notas por. . . La Habana, Biblioteca Nacional José Martí, Depto. de Hemeroteca e Información de Humanidades, 1973. 340 p., bibl.

Excellent, annotated work. Divided into 19th and 20th centuries. Includes three descriptive essays on: 19th century bibliographies; 20th century, 1900-1937; and 20th century 1937-1958. Also includes author and subject index and a periodical title index.

85. García, Miguel Angel. Anuario bibliográfico hondureño: 1961-1971. Tegucigalpa, Banco Central de Honduras, 1973? 512 p.

Works are listed by year and within each year works are listed by subject, alphabetically by author.

86. ──────. Bibliografía hondureña: 1620-1930, v. 2. Tegucigalpa, Banco Central de Honduras, 1971. 486 p.

Vol. 2 of *HLAS 35:50*. Works are arranged by year of publication and divided into governmental and non governmental publications.

87. Guttentag Tichauer, Werner. Bibliografía boliviana del año 1973, con datos biográficos, suplementos de 1962 a 1972; bibliografía de mapas. Literatura agrícola de Bolivia [de] Armando Cardozo. Cochabamba, Bol., Editorial Los Amigos del Libro, 1974. 171 p., bibl.

Excellent compilation in series begun by the author in 1962. With this edition, biographic data on each author is included: date and place of birth, profession, etc. Includes a bibliography of maps as well as an updating of works previously omitted. See *HLAS 33:59* and *HLAS 34:50.*

Nagelkerke, G.A. *comp.* Literatuur-overzicht van de Nederlandse Antillen vanaf de 17e eeuw tot 1970. See item 1272.

————. ————. Literatuur-overzicht van Suriname tot 1940. See item 1273.

————. ————. Literatuur-overzicht van Suriname 1940 tot 1970. See item 1274.

REFERENCE WORKS AND RESEARCH

88. Archila, Ricardo. Diccionario biográfico de médicos venezolanos: ensayo. Letra A. Caracas, Tipografía Vargas, 1974. 105 p.

Initial attempt to compile a medical biography. Author is not pleased with the results but hopes to continue. If completed, it could become a useful work.

89. Association of Universities and Colleges of Canada, Ottawa. Directory of scholars in Latin American teaching and research in Canada: 1969-1970. Ottawa, 1970? 36 p.

A Canadian equivalent to the National Directory of Latin Americanists.

90. Brazil. Congresso. Senado. Subsecretaria de Taquigrafia. Manual de autoridades e siglas. Brasília, 1973. 370 p.

Primarily for shorthand. However, excellent source of acronyms (258 p.).

91. Cabral, Álvaro and **Eva Nick.** Dicionário técnico de psicologia. São Paulo, Editôra Cultrix, 1974. 406 p., table.

Attempts to use the most up to date definitions. Useful reference.

92. Cámara de Comercio de Bogotá. Organismos económicos internacionales y sus siglas. Bogotá, 1971. 70 p.

Organized into three sections: 1) international economic organizations; 2) geographic index by continent; and international economic organizations by speciality. Useful compilation of acronyms.

93. Comma, Carlton N. *ed.* and *comp.* Who's who in Trinidad and Tobago. 2. ed. Port of Spain, n.p., 1973. 470 p., illus.

In addition to some 1000 biographic entries, there is a commercial and industrial index on the leading enterprises and their management.

94. Diccionario de sinónimos, antónimos e ideas afines. Una selección rigurosa de palabras equivalentes y opuestas de acuerdo al uso en vigor. B.A., Editorial Andina, 1973. 213 p.

Updates the language. Excellent reference.

95. Dicionário de sociologia. Pôrto Alegre, Bra., Editôra Glóbo, 1974. 377 p.

Attempts to update terminology. Uses encyclopedic style. Useful reference.

96. La empresa del libro en América Latina: guía seleccionada de editoriales distribuidores y librerías de América Latina. 2. ed. B.A., Bowker Editores Argentina, 1974. 307 p. (Col. Guías de Bowker, 1)

Selected listing with basic information on presses and book dealers arranged alphabetically by country and by city. Includes index of cities and firms cited. Useful references for acquisitions.

97. Foster, David William *ed.* Latin American government leaders. 2. ed. Tempe, Arizona State Univ., Center for Latin American Studies, 1975. 135 p.

Leaders are listed alphabetically by country. Information deals exclusively with each persons role as a leader without any bio data. Excellent reference.

98. Martins, Manuel J. Dicionário português-inglês. Pôrto, Portugal, Editorial Domingos Barreira, 1971? 1039 p.

Compiled according to the principles used for US British, and Portuguese dictionaries.

99. Meirinho, Jali and **Theobaldo Costa Jamunda.** Nomes que ajudaram a fazer Santa Catarina, v. 1. Florianópolis, Bra., Editôra Empreendimentos Educacionais (EDEME), 1973? 104 p., illus.

Biographical reference work.

100. 1973 [Mil novecientos setenta y tres] directorio nacional de profesionales. Bogotá, Economistas, Consultores, Contadores, Editores (ECOC), 1973. 140 p., illus., plates.

Includes listing of universities and individuals by profession.

Polisenský, Josef and **Lubomír Vebr.** La iberoamericanística en la Europa Occidental, la Unión Soviética y los países socialistas: 1964-1967. See item 6045.

101. Quem é quem no Pará. Belém, Bra., Editôra Persona, 1970. 552 p., plates.

Portrait of current and future personalities of the state.

102. Ramos, Dulce Helena Alvares Pessôa. Levantamento das pesquisas sobre assuntos brasileiros feitos em universidades americanas: 1960-1970 (USP/RH, julho/set. 1974, p. 281-308)

Surveys Brazilian studies in US universities, listing titles. Finds greatest emphasis to be on contemporary problems and analyzes support that appears to have been given Latin American studies by foundations and the US government. Economics is the major discipline with history, sociology, and literature (in equal proportions) and political science also represented. Notes that North Americans have covered many subjects yet untreated by Brazilians. [M.E. Kahler]

Relações de publicaçes de Lourenço Filho em psicologia. See item 6340.

103. Rubin Zamora, Lorenzo. Diccionario biográfico cultural del Estado Guarico. Caracas, Gráficas Herpa, 1974. 364 p.

Biography of native sons and daughters who have received recognition of one sort or another. Quaint.

104. Sociedade brasileira: 1974. Rio, Livraria São José, 1974. 177 p.

Lists government and state officials, members of the Brazilian Academy of Letters, Brazil's diplomatic corps overseas, accredited diplomatic corps in Brasília, international organizations represented in Brazil, and who's who in Brasília. Marginal reference work.

105. Súmulas biográficas de cidadãos prestantes. São Paulo, Ensil Publicações Culturais, 1975. 1258 p., plates.

Presents an unusual who's who of prominent immigrants to Brazil. Its utility is somewhat diminished by the fact that the main alphabetization is by first names, rather than patronymics. There is, however, an alphabetical index of patronymics at the end of the book. [G.M. Dorn]

106. Who's notable in Mexico, v. 1. México, Imprenta Nuevo Mundo, 1972. 250 p.

Listing of those who have distinguished themselves in their specialty. Intended as reference for public libraries and universities and will be periodically updated.

107. Zarubezhnye Tsentry po izuchentiiu Latinskoi Ameriki: v. 1/2 (Foreign centers for the study of Latin America: v. 1/2). Moskva, Nauka, Institut Latinskoi Ameriki, 1970. 2 v. (185, 159 p.)

Two-volume Soviet guide to research centers and data sources on Latin America. V. 1 lists names and addresses of such centers in Latin America itself. V. 2 lists those in Western Europe. Titles of the centers are in Spanish, French, and Portuguese as well as Russian. Annotations are in Russian. Handy set. [T.S. Cheston]

SUBJECT BIBLIOGRAPHY

108. *Bibliografia Brasileira de Botânica: 1971/72.* Vol. 6/7, 1973- . Rio.

Uses KWIC and KWAC systems. Bibliographies are prepared by individual discipline. This serial began publication in 1957. Vol. 1 covers material from 1950 to 1955. Published by the Instituto Brasileiro de Bibliografia e Documentação.

109. Bibliography of selected statistical sources of the American nations (Bibliografía de fuentes estadísticas escogidas de las naciones americanas). Detroit, Mich., Blaine Ethridge, 1974. 689 p.

"A guide to the principal statistical materials of the 22 American nations, including data, analyses, methodology, and laws and organization of statistical agencies." A reprinting of the 1947 ed. See *HLAS 13:436.*

110. Bicalho, Maria Dias and **Maria das Graças Moreira Ferreira** *comps.* Bibliografia de ciências florestais. Viçosa, Bra., Univ. Federal de Viçosa, Biblioteca Central, Seção de Bibliografia e Documentação, 1973. 188 p., bibl. (Série Bibliografias especializadas, 2)

Compilation of holdings in the Central Library of the Univ. Federal de Viçosa on forestry arranged by subject. Works prepared by the faculty of the Univ. are annotated, but other works are not.

111. Bowker Editores Argentina, *Buenos Aires.* Libros universitarios: bibliografía de ciencias exactas y naturales. B.A., 1974. 1 v. (Unpaged)

Compilation of material published in Spanish since 1967. Arranged by subject in accordance with the Dewey decimal system. Includes author, title, and publishers indexes.

Bustelo, Ana Margarita *comp.* Monografías y tesis universitarias sobre industrialización en el Uruguay: 1937-1972. See item 4668.

112. *Ciência e Cultura.* Sociedade Brasileira para o Progresso da Ciência (SBPC). Vol. 26, No. 7, julho 1974- . São Paulo.

Special massive supplement (685 p.) to the journal *Ciência e Cultura* published by the Brazilian Assn. for the Advancement of Science and as a result of its XXVI Annual Meeting. Consists of an annotated bibliography of Brazilian research in both the natural and social sciences. Excellent reference.

113. Cosío Villegas, Daniel. Ultima bibliografía política de la historia moderna de Mexico (CN/M, 7:1, 1970, p. 41-222)

Lists 1858 items of secondary sources on modern Mexico. Useful reference.

114. *Cuadernos de Bibliotecología y Documentación.* Univ. de Chile, Facultad de Filosofía y Educación, Escuela de Bibliotecología. No. 1, marzo 1970- . Santiago?

Cunha, Alda das Mercês Moreira da; Maria Thereza Alves; Clara Maria Galvão; and **Saphyra Farias Leitão** *comps.* Geografia da Amazônia: bibliografia. See item 7099.

Desarrollo económico y planificación en la República Argentina: selección bibliográfica, 1930-1972. See item 4707.

Dexter, Byron *ed.* and *comp.* The foreign-affairs 50-year bibliography: new evaluations of significant books in international relations, 1920-1970. See item 8717.

Fallah, Skaidrite Maliks *comp.* A selected bibliography on urban insurgency and urban unrest in Latin America and other areas. See item 8041.

Ferrari, Gustavo. Bibliografía de base sobre política exterior argentina. See item 8881.

115. Florén Lozano, Luis *comp.* Bibliografía bibliotecológica colombiana: 1966-1970. Medellín, Colo., Univ. de Antioquia, Escuela Interamericana de Bibliotecología, 1971. 119 l. (Serie bibliografía, 2. Manuales de bibliografía y documentación colombiana, 1)

Compilation of works published from 1966 to 1970. Complements previous bibliographies. Good reference.

Hellmuth, Nicholas M. *comp.* The Olmec civilization, art and archaeology: an introductory bibliography. See item 635.

Holm, Olaf *comp.* Bibliografía de autores nacionales y extranjeros, relacionada con temas antropológicos ecuatorianos. See item 512.

Kendall, Aubyn. The art of pre-columbian Mexico: an annotated bibliography of works in English. See item 639.

Lambert, Levindo Furquim. Bibliografia de uma cidade mineira. See item 7131.

MacDonald Escobedo, Eugenio. Una aproximación al conocimiento turístico: bibliografía, su lectura y localización. See item 6685.

116. McDowell, Robert E. Bibliography of literature from Guyana. Arlington, Tex., Sable Publishing Corp., 1975. 117 p., bibl.

A catalog of works by earlier Guyanese writers of memoirs, history, anthropology, newspaper articles, and travel books. Material is listed alphabetically by author. Because of dearth of bibliographies on Guyana, this is a highly useful reference work.

McGlynn, Eileen A. Middle American anthropology: directory, bibliography, and guide to the UCLA Library Collections. See item 515.

Mareski, Sofía and **Oscar Humberto Ferraro** *comps.* Bibliografía sobre datos y estudios económicos en el Paraguay. See item 4636.

_____ and _____ *comps.* Bibliografía sobre datos y estudios etnográficos y antropológicos del Paraguay. See item 1363.

117. Miquel i Vergés, José María. Diccionario de insurgentes. México, Editorial Porrúa, 1969. 623 p., plates.

Biographies of over four thousand Mexicans who participated in its war of independence. Excellent reference and research work.

Montañé M., Julio C. *comp.* Bibliografía de antropología chilena VII, 1969-1970. See item 517.

Müller, María S. Bibliografía para el estudio de la población de la Argentina. See item 6790.

Nodal, Roberto *comp.* A preliminary bibliography on African cultures and black peoples of the Caribbean and Latin America. See item 1276.

Peña, Hugo A. Bibliografía geológica de Tucumán. See item 6792.

118. Pérez-Embid, Florentino and **Francisco Morales Padrón.** Bibliografía española de historia marítima: 1932-1962. Sevilla, Spain, Consejo Superior de Investigaciones Científicas, Escuela de Estudios Hispano-Americanos, 1970. 155 p. (Publicaciones, 188)

Includes small section on the Americas.

119. Piedrahita P., Dora comp. Indice económico colombiano: 1967-1970. Medellín, Colo., Univ. de Antioquia, Escuela Interamericana de Bibliotecología, 1973. 131 p., bibl. (Serie Bibliografías, 23)

Updates the 1960-1966 listing prepared by María Cristina Suaza. Material is arranged by subject. Includes author index, list of journals surveyed, and a bibliography of material consulted.

120. Pinilla Aguilar, José I. Antología artística colombiana. Bogotá, Editor-Distribuidora Escorial, 1973. 272 p., plates.

General who's who arranged alphabetically without reference to art specialty. However, there is a 45 p. section on composers. Informative.

121. Pino, Frank. Mexican Americans: a research bibliography. East Lansing, Mich., Michigan State Univ., Latin American Studies Center, 1974. 2 v. (631, 727 p.)

A comprehensive, unannotated bibliography. Because of the absence of any other similar work, it is a basic research tool and essential to anyone doing work on Mexican Americans.

Pinto. Aloisio de Arruda and **Maria das Graças Moreira Ferreira.** Bibliografia de bibliografias agrícolas do Brasil. See item 7164

122. Ramírez Vargas, María Teresa. Documentación periodística de Bogotá. Bogotá, Fundación Univ. de América, Escuela de Ciencias de la Comunicación Social, 1973. 129 p.

Compilation of works on the press, radio, television, and film used for mass media and communication. Handy reference.

123. Recursos humanos: bibliografía (Boletim Bibliográfico [Serviço Social do Comércio, Divisão de Documentação e Intercâmbio, Seção de Documentação, Rio.] 12, dez. 1974, p. 9-117)

Lists alphabetically by author publications on human resources published between 1965 and 1974. Each citation is followed by an acronym to identify the library which has the item. There is also a title list of journals indexed. Useful reference.

Ríos, Jorge Martínez. Tenencia de la tierra y desarrollo agrario en México: bibliografía selectiva y comentada; 1522-1968. See item 4312.

124. Rodríguez Escalonilla, Arturo. Bibliografía sobre los problemas del trabajo en América Latina: 1960-1970; Bibliographie sur les problèmes du travail en Amérique Latine: 1960-1970; Bibliography on labour problems in Latin America: 1960-1970. Geneva, Instituto Internacional de Estudios Laborales, Servicio Internacional de Intercambio de Documentación para la Enseñanza, 1971? 132 p., bibl.

Compilation of works in Spanish, English, Portuguese and French, arranged by country with subject subdivisions. Includes a bibliography and an author index. Unannotated, but useful reference.

Russell, Charles A., James A. Miller; and **Robert E. Hildner.** The urban guerrilla in Latin America: a select bibliography. See item 8099.

Santamarina, Estela Barbieri de; Alicia I. García; and **Hilda M. Díaz.** Nueva bibliografía geográfica de Tucumán. See item 6799.

Serracino Inglott, George comp. Referencias bibliográficas, yacimientos precerámicos, departamento El Loa. See item 948a.

Superintendência do Desenvolvimento da Região Sul (SUDESUL), *Pôrto Alegre, Bra.* **Divisão de Documentação.** Bibliografia de educação e assuntos correlatos: material bibliográfico existente na Divisão de Documentação da SUDESUL. See item 6365.

125. United Nations. International Labour Organization (ILO), *Geneva.* **International Institute for Labour Studies.** Bibliografía sobre los movimientos obreros en la América Latina: 1950-1964. [Bibliography on trade movements in Latin America: 1950-1964] Geneva, 1965. 74 p.

126. Universidade Federal de Viçosa, Bra. Biblioteca Central. Seção de Bibliografia e Documentação. Bibliografia do café: 1952-1972. Viçosa, Bra., 1973. 124 p. (Série bibliografias especializadas, 3)

Compilation of books and articles divided into 1) books, 2) journal articles, and 3) technical journals; and organized within each category by subject.

University of Wisconsin, Madison. Land Tenure Center *comp.* Agrarian reform in Latin America: an annotated bibliography. See item 6557.

Valdés, Nelson P. *ed.* and *comp.* A bibliography on Cuban women in the twentieth century. See item 8246.

Vaughan, Denton R. *comp.* Urbanization in twentieth century Latin America: a working bibliography. See item 6558.

Wagner, Erika *comp.* Bibliografía antropológica reciente sobre Venezuela. See item 524.

──────. *comp.* Segunda bibliografía antropológica reciente sobre Venezuela. See item 525.

GENERAL WORKS

127. Bailey, Samuel L. and **Ronald T. Hyman** *eds.* Perspectives on Latin America. N.Y., Macmillan, 1974. 105 p., maps, plates.

Six essays from the point of view of an anthropologist, historian, economist, political scientist, research physicist, and a professor of education. Purpose is to focus the student on the realities of Latin America and approach any study without preconceived prejudices.

128. Benton, William. The voice of Latin America. Westport, Conn., Greenwood Press, 1974. 204 p., map, plates, tables.

Reprint of work which first appeared in 1961. See *HLAS* 24:2802.

129. Brazil 71: cultural aspects. Rio, Sindicato Nacional dos Editores de Livros, 1971. 1 v. (Unpaged) illus., plates.

Well illustrated work on Brazil's art, literature, music, theater, cinema and television, education and technology, and publishing business. For the beginner.

130. Carrera Andrade, Jorge. Libros hispanoamericanos editados en París antes de la Primera Guerra Mundial (RIB, 23:4, oct./dic. 1973, p. 447-450)

Discusses the attraction and impact of Paris on Latin American men of letters.

131. Cayman Islands handbook and businessman's guide. George Town, Northwester, 1973. 282 p., illus., map, tables.

Intended primarily for businessmen. Includes business and finance, government information, and reference section covering all types of information. Informative. Useful reference.

Centro de Investigaciones Sociales y Socio-Religiosas (CISOR), *Caracas.* Anuario de la Iglesia Católica en Venezuela. See item 8515b.

132. Colombia: trayectoria de un pueblo. t. 1. Bogotá, Editora Arco, 1974. 73 p., maps, plates, tables.

Richly illustrated work on the culture, geography, social and economic development, and other aspects of Colombian life.

133. Cozean, Jon D. Latin America: 1974. Washington, Stryker-Post Publications, 1974. 87 p., illus., maps.

Annual, almanac-like information on each country and dependency. Includes brief sketch of early civilizations, history and government, and items of current interest. Excellent reference.

Economie antillaise. See item 4339.

134. Ellis, Joseph A. Latin America: its peoples and institutions. 2. ed. Beverly Hills, Calif., Glencoe Press *a division of* Benziger Bruce & Glencoe, 1975. 300 p., bibl., maps, plates, tables.

Introductory textbook. Each of the first nine chapter has list of selected references in paperback in addition to a subject/chronological bibliography.

135. Fitzgibbon, Russell H. *ed.* and *comp.* Brazil: a chronology and fact book, 1488-1973. Dobbs Ferry, N.Y., Oceana Publications, 1974. 150 p., bibl. (World chronology series)

In addition to the chronology there is a list of 1) some of the most important documents affecting Brazil since 1494 to 1969, 2) Brazil's rulers since 1808, 3) eminent Brazilians, and 4) area and population.

136. Gardner, Mary A. The press of Latin America: a tentative and selected bibliography in Spanish and Portuguese. Austin, Univ. of Texas at Austin, Institute of Latin American Studies, 1973. 34 p. (Guides and bibliographies, 4)

Bibliography of works available at Michigan State Univ., the Univ. of Minnesota, and the Univ. of Texas at Austin. With few exceptions English editions of works are omitted. Excellent reference work.

137. Guyana Manufacturers Association, *Georgetown.* Guyana handbook:

industry, tourism, commerce. Georgetown, 1974. 215 p., illus.

Welcome addition to the limited collection of informational and reference material available.

138. Hilton, Ronald. The Latin Americans: their heritage and their destiny. N.Y., J.B. Lippincott, 1973. 253 p., bibl.

A synthesis of the major disciplines which attempts to deal with the fundamental issues confronting the area. Good general work which author hopes will stimulate discussion.

139. Hurwitz, Samuel Justin and **Edith F. Hurwitz.** Jamaica: a historical portrait. N.Y., Praeger, 1971. 273 p., bibl.

Account of the economic, political and social development of Jamaica from its origins to the present. Good bibliography.

140. Imagem do Brasil e da América Latina: 1973. São Paulo, Editôra Banas, 1973. 187 p., illus.

Almanac on Brazil and the rest of the Americas except the U.S. and Canada. The Brazilian section is in the greatest detail. Useful reference.

141. Instituto de Estudios Ibero-Americanos, *Stockholm.* Actividades durante el año laboral de 1973-1974. Stockholm, 1974. 26 p. (Publicaciones, serie C. Informes anuales, 5)

The Institute's annual report.

142. Jamaica. Department of Statistics. History and government. Kingston, 1973. 42 p., tables (Facts on Jamaica)

An historical review from the time of discovery to the present. This eries forms part of an annual yearbook soon to be introduced. Useful reference.

143. Lewald, Herald Ernest. Latinoamérica: sus culturas y sociedades. N.Y., McGraw-Hill, 1973. 436 p., plates.

An attempt to explore the origins and cultural evolution of the various Latin American societies. Uses several of the social sciences methodologies.

144. Lux, William. Historical dictionary of the British Caribbean. Metuchen, N.J., The Scarecrow Press, 1975. 266 p. (Latin American historical dictionaries, 12)

Information is by individual political unit. Includes general information section for data dealing with more than one unit. There is a good bibliography. Useful reference.

145. Niskier, Arnaldo. Nosso Brasil. 2. ed. Rio, Bloch Editores, 1973. 224 p., bibl., maps, plates (Série Estudos de problemas brasileiros, 5)

Another almanac on the geography, infrastructure, economic development, socioeconomics, political problems, and national security. Useful reference.

146. Paraíba (state), *Bra.* **Secretaria da Educação e Cultura. Conselho Estadual de Cultura.** Paraíba cultural. Paraíba, Bra., 1971? 54 p.

Includes cultural calendar showing events chronologically by day under each month but without regard to the year. There is a chapter on Pará cultural institutions.

147. Reed, Irving B.; Jaime Suchlicki; and Dodd L. Harvey. The Latin American scene of the seventies: a basic fact book. Coral Gables, Fla., Univ. of Miami, Center for Advanced International Studies, 1972. 220 p., maps (Monographs in international affairs)

Basic information arranged by country with emphasis on the economy, politics and social structures. Also lists by country each American firm in each and names the parent U.S. firm. Good reference work.

148. Sánchez-Pérez, J.M. The hispanico: a new concept of Pan-Americanism. N.Y., Exposition Press, 1974. 98 p.

". . . an intense examination of the values and traditions of the countries whose cultural achievements must continue to exist and progress." Interesting for its point of view.

149. West, Robert C. and **John P. Augelli.** Middle America: its lands and peoples. 2. ed. Englewood Cliffs, N.J., Prentice-Hall, 1976. 494 p., bibl., illus., maps, plates.

Emphasizes the cultural and historical approach to the geography of Middle America while at the same time presenting the economic, political, and social problems that confront the area. Excellent introductory work.

150. The Year Book of World Affairs: 1975. N.Y., Praeger *under the auspices of* The London Institute of World Affairs, 1975. 384 p.

Series of chapters prepared by contributors on topics of global scope. The thrust is analysis and not instant information. Specific chapters on Latin America are one on the Andean Common Market, on Argentina, and Chile. Excellent work.

151. *Zeitschrift für Kulturaustausch.* Institut für Auslandsbeziehungen. Vol. 22, No. 2, 1972-   . Stuttgart, FRG.

Contains several well-written essays concerning contemporary Brazil, the pedagogical method of Paulo Freire, German contribution to the development of Brazil, the Brazilian independence movement and German artistic expressions in colonial Chile. [H.J. Hoyer]

JOURNAL ABBREVIATIONS

CN/M	Memoria de El Colegio Nacional. México.
FENIX	Fénix. Biblioteca Nacional. Lima.
RIB	Revista Interamericana de Bibliografía [Inter-American Review of Bibliography]. Organization of American States. Washington.
UCAB/M	Montalban. Univ. Católica Andrés Bello, Facultad de Humanidades y Educación, Institutos Humanísticos de Investigación. Caracas.
UNESCO/BL	Unesco Bulletin for Libraries. United Nations Education, Scientific and Cultural Organization. Paris.
USP/RH	Revista de História. Univ. de São Paulo, Faculdade de Filosofia, Ciências e Letras, Depto. de História [and] Sociedade de Estudos Históricos. São Paulo.

Anthropology

GENERAL

500. Abreu, Aurélio M. G. de. Civilizações perdidas das Américas. Rio, Edição de Nosso Brasil, 1973. 227 p., bibl., maps, plates.

Uses archaeological and historical evidence in order to write a popular book on the injustices done to the indigenous civilizations by Europeans. Mixes observations on earlier cultures with a lot of fantasy and poor anthropology: such as pygmies in South America, system of ventilation for Chavín de Huantar construction of El Castillo, and the Lost Cities of El Dorado in Brazil. [C. Evans]

501. Alcina Franch, José. La antropología americanista en España: 1950-1970 (UM/REAA, 7, 1972, p. 17-58, bibl., illus.)

Review of contributions to New World anthropology by Spanish investigators and institutions; concludes that although the number of original works has increased, interest in theory and method is minimal. [B. J. Meggers]

502. Anton, Ferdinand. Die Frauen der Azteken-Maya-Inka-Kultur. Stuttgart, FRG, W. Kohlhammer-Verlag, 1973. 86 p. illus., maps, plates.

Comments on women's role in each precolumbian group on the basis of their depiction in pottery, stone, codices, and textiles from Aztec, Maya and Inca cultures. [C. Evans]

503. Antropologia do açúcar: curso sôbre antropologia do açúcar promovido pelo Museu do Açúcar nos meses de maio-junho de 1971. Recife, Bra., Instituto do Açúcar e do Alcool, Museu do Açúcar, 1972. 111 p., bibl., plate.

Study on the economics of sugar plantations. Includes chapters on slavery, sickness related to sugar-cane activity, rum and its problems, treatment of Negro slaves in Brazil, nutrition, etc. Does not compare Brazil with other sugar-producing countries. [C. Evans]

504. Benítez, Ana M. de. Cocina prehispánica; Pre-Hispanic cooking. México, Ediciones Euroamericanas (EURAM), 1974. 133 p., bibl., illus.

Recipes in Spanish and English of precolumbian dishes from region today known as Mexico. [C. Evans]

505. Clastres, Pierre. Éléments de démographie amérindienne (EPHE/H, 13:1/2, jan./juin 1973, p. 23-26, bibl.)

Cites documentary evidence in support of the estimate of one and a half million Guarani-speaking Indians in 1530 and upholds those who place the population of precolumbian America between 80 and 100 million. [B. J. Meggers]

Comas, Juan. Hipótesis transatlántica sobre el poblamiento de América: caucasoides y negroides. See item 2006.

──────. Transatlantic hypothesis on the peopling of America: Caucasoids and Negroids. See item 2007.

Congreso Internacional de Americanistas, XL, Roma-Genova, 1972. See item 513.

506. Eisleb, Dieter. Abteilung amerikanische Archäologie (MV/BA, 21, 1973, p. 175-217, illus., plates, table)

Celebration of the 100th anniversary of the Museum für Völkerkunde, Berlin, FRG, with comments on history of the archaeological collections from the Americas, including photos of exhibit halls, collections, field work. [C. Evans]

507. García Cisneros, Florencio. Maternity in pre-Columbian art (La maternidad en el arte precolombiano). N.Y., Cisneros Gallery of New York, 1970. 147 p., plates.

English and Spanish texts explain 95 plates which illustrate motherhood in pottery figurines from various cultures of precolumbian Mexico, Central America, and South America, especially Peru and Ecuador. [C. Evans]

508. González-Wippler, Migene. Santería: African magic in Latin America. N.Y., The Julian Press, 1973. 181 p., bibl., plates.

Santería is the Spanish term for Latin American magic, the practice of which originated in Nigeria. It was brought to the New World by slaves over 400 years ago. It is believed that over 100 million persons throughout Latin America (including large communities of over five million and of Latin American origin in N.Y. and Miami) still practice it. Santería is the Spanish name, the Portuguese names are different in Brazil, and in the French-speaking islands of the West Indies it is known by its negative aspect or voodoo. Study offers detailed comparison with Yoruba myths and magic, and comments on the role of magic spells and witchcraft in controlling human life. A profound study but written for a popular audience. [C. Evans]

509. Haekel, Josef und **Anton Lukesch.** Einführung in die Ethnologie Südamerikas. Wien, Univ. Wien, Institut für Völkerkunde, 1972. 158 p., bibl., map (Studia culturalia, 1)

Summary of the ethnology of South America at time of European conquest with brief mention of archaeological forerunners in some areas. [C. Evans]

510. Hawkes, Jacquetta *ed.* Atlas of ancient archaeology. N.Y., McGraw Hill, 1974. 272 p., illus., maps, tables.

Popular approach with maps and architectural plans for major sites. Norman Hammond contributed section on South America (only 10 p. out of a book 270 p. long) which unfortunately is very weak. Ruins of San Agustín, Chavín de Huantar, Tiahuanaco, Chan Chan, Machu Picchu and Cuzco depicted. Unfortunately, there is nothing on Moseley and his team's recent work in Chan Chan section. [C.Evans]

511. Heath, Dwight B. *ed.* Contemporary cultures and societies of Latin America: a reader in the social anthropology of Middle and South America. 2. ed. N.Y., Random House, 1974. 572 p., bibl., tables.

Second ed. of a reader in social anthropology consisting of 34 articles about contemporary Latin America, only five of which are original and especially prepared for this volume: Casagrande on Indians of highland Ecuador; Dobyns on the Cornell Peru project in Vicos; Whitten on the ecology of race relations in northwest Ecuador, S.Z. Stone on power distribution in Costa Rica; and Aron-Schaar on local government in Bolivia. The others have been edited, improved and corrected and, in a few cases, abridged but without affecting their meaning. This volume together with Olien's (item 518) would make a good English language introduction to Latin America. [C. Evans]

Helms, Mary W. Middle America: a culture history of heartland and frontiers. See item 1142.

512. Holm, Olaf *comp.* Bibliografía de autores nacionales y extranjeros, relacionada con temas antropológicos ecuatorianos (CCE/CHA, 22:39, 1972, p. 234-260)

Bibliography on ethnology and archaeology of Ecuador on any subject after 1960, plus a few additional earlier (1950's) entries that did not appear in Larrea's bibliographic compendium (see *HLAS 31:46*). Holms date of compilation is 1972. [C. Evans]

513. International Congress of Americanists, *XL, Roma-Genova, 1972.* Atti. v. 1, Parte generale, antropologia fisica, prehistoria, archeologia, scrittura e calendario in Mesoamerica, Archeologia del Quintana Roo; v. 2, Problemi generali, teoria e metodologia, etnologia, transformazione culturale volontaria tra gli indiani del Nord America, struttura culturale e sociale dei popoli di lingua caribica; v. 3, Linguistica, folklore, storia americana: conflitti culturali, colonia, independenza, sociologia: modernizzazione e modificazioni culturali recenti. Genova, Italy, Casa Editrice Tilgher, 1973. 3 v. (509, 677, 556 p.) bibl., illus., maps, plates, tables.

G.F. De Stefano, J.J. Molieri "Contributo per uno Studio Antropologico Comparativo delle Popolazioni del Nicaragua" p. 3-10
H. Lagrange de Castillo "Odontometría y Morfología Dental de los Guajiros" p. 11-16
B. Méndez de Pérez "Odontometría y Morfología Dental de los Irapa" p. 17-22
L. Miraglia "Notizie Antropologiche ed Etnologiche sugli Acce-Guayaki" p. 23-32
J. Schobinger "Nuevos Hallazgos de Puntas 'Colas de Pescado' y Consideraciones en Torno al Origen y Dispersión de la Cultura de Cazadores Superiores Toldense (Fell I) en Sudamérica" p. 33-50
Pedro I. Porras Garcés "Supervivencia de Tradición Cerámica Común a las Culturas del Alto Amazonas y de Manera Especial a las de la Zona Oriental del Ecuador: Secuencia Seriada de los artefactos de Piedra Pulida de la Fase de Cosanga en el Oriente, Ceja de Montaña, del Ecuador, en Suramérica" p. 51-58
Pedro I. Porras Garcés "Secuencia Seriada de los artefactos de Piedra Pulida de la Fase de Cosanga en el Oriente, Ceja de Montaña, del Ecuador, Suramérica" p. 59-66

W.W. Taylor "Emic Attributes and Normative Theory in Archaeology" p. 67-70
A. Hitchcock "The Use of Archaeological Attributes in the Museum" p. 71-76
R.C. Euler "Attributes of Prehistoric Pueblo Settlement Patterns on Black Mesa, Arizona" p. 77-82
G.J. Gumerman "A Rural-Urban Continuum for the Prehistoric Pueblo Southwest: Black Mesa and Chaco Canyon" p. 83-88
W. Marschall "Exploration of Glen Helen Mound" p. 89-98
H.S. Petersen "The Koster Expedition in the Lower Illinois River Valley" p. 99-102
D.W. Chase, H.A. Huscher "The Muskhogean Cultural Area of the Southern Apalachian Piedmont: a Regional Cultural Sub-Climax" p. 103-104
C. Serrano "La Llamada 'Trepanación Suprainiana' en Mesoamérica y sus Implicaciones Arqueológicas" p. 105-108
D. Heyden "What is the Significance of the Mexica Pyramid?" p. 109-116
N. Castillo Tejero "Cerámica Pintada en Mesoamérica como Marcador de Horizontes" p. 117-122
H. von Winning "Mexican Figurines Attached to Pallets and Cradles" p. 123-132
G.F. Ekholm "The Archaeological Significance of Mirrors in the New World" p. 133-136
G. Tibón "La Festa della Pubertá Femminile nell'Archeologia Mesoamericana" p. 137-146
E. Pasztory "The Gods of Teotihuacan: a Synthetic Approach in Teotihuacan Iconography" p. 147-160
W. Tommasi de Magrelli "La Nueva Zona Arqueológica de Teotenango y su Cerámica" p. 161-166
W. Jiménez Moreno "La Migración Mexica" p. 167-172
Mary Elizabeth King "A New Textile Technique from Oaxaca, Mexico" p. 173-178
N. Hammond "Maya Settlement Patterns: A Byzantine Parallel" p. 179-180
G. Weber "Unos Nuevos Problemas Arqueológicos de la Región de Las Palmas, Chiapas" p. 181-188
J. Hairs "Operación Rescate: Guatemala's Answer to the Problems of Plundering of Ancient Maya Sites" p. 189-194
R. Girard "Nuevas Esculturas Líticas en el Area Maya" p. 195-202
L.A. Parsons "Iconographic Notes on a New Izapan Stela from Abaj Takalik, Guatemala" p. 203-212
D. Stone "El Dios-Hacha de Jadeita en la América Central: su Localización Geográfica y su Lugar en Tiempo" p. 213-218
L. Laurencich and L. Minelli "La Fase Aguas Buenas en la Región de San Vito de Java, Costa Rica: Informe Preliminar" p. 219-224
R.P. Bullen and M. Mattioni "Some Ceramic Variations at Vivé, Martinique" p. 225-230
M. Mattioni "Découverte d'une Sépulture Arawak du II Siècle à la Martinique" p. 231-238
E. Wagner "Nueva Evidencia Arqueológica deVenezuela Oriental: el Yacimiento de Campoma" p. 239-246
M. Sanoja Obediente and I. Vargas "Niveles de Integración Sociopolítica de las Comunidades Precolombinas del Orinoco y la Costa Oriental de Venezuela" p. 247-254
M. Sanoja Obediente "Projecto 72" p. 255-260
A. Zucchi "Tropical Forest Groups of the Venezuelan Savannas: Archaeological Evidence" p. 261-268
H. Bischof "The Origins of Pottery in South America: Recent Radiocarbon Dates from Southwest Ecuador" p. 269-282

H. Bischof "The Stratygraphy of Valdivia, Ecuador: New Evidence" p. 283-24
U. Bankmann "Bemerkungen zu einigen skulpturen aus dem nordperuanischen Hochland" p. 285-292
Luciana Pallestrini "Metodi di Scavi Adattati a Zone Archeologiche Brasiliane" p. 293-302
L.C. Alfaro de Lanzone "La Figura Humana Dentro del Arte Rupestre del Area Puneña, Argentina" p. 303-312
H. Trimborn "Nuevas Fechas Radiocarbónicas para Algunos Monumentos y Sitios Prehispánicos de la Costa Peruana" p. 313-316
F.X. Grollig "Pikillaeta Incaie Precursor" p. 317-324
P.C. Sestieri "Seavi a Cajamarquilla' Peru" p. 325-328
C. Cavatrunci "L'Influsso Wari nella Ceramica di Stile Nievería Proveniente dalla Huaca Tello a Cajamarquilla" p. 329-332
H. Trimborn "Investigaciones Arqueológicas en el Departamento de Tacna, Perú" p. 333-336
A. Kendall "A Method for Analysis of Inca Architectural Remains: Introducing a List of Activity Requirements to Generate Functional Solutions to Forms" p. 337-342
M. Polia "Le Rovine di Aypate. Relazione della loro Scoperta e Studio Preliminare" p. 343-352
M. Rivera Dorado "Aspectos Tipológicos de la Cerámica Cuzqueña del Período Intermedio Tardío" p. 353-362
D.E. Thompson "Archaeological Investigations in the Eastern Andes of Northern Peru" p. 363-372
C.E. Dibble "The Syllabic-Alphabetic Trend in Mexican Codices" p. 373-378
J. de Durand Forest "Chimalpahin et l'Histoire de la Vallée de Mexico" p. 379-388
B. Riese "Objetivos y Estado de la Investigación de la Escritura Maya" p. 389-398
A.L. Vollemaere "Catalogue des Glyphes et Éléments Graphiques des Codex Mayas" p. 399-408
A.L. Vollemaere "Nouveaux Déchiffrements Mayas" p. 409-412
F.J. Hochleitner "The Correlation between the Mayan and the Julian Calendar" p. 413-418
A.L. Vollemaere "Problémes des Calendriers Mayas et de Corrélation" p. 419-426
F.J. Hochleitner "A Inscriçâo Hieroglífica Maia de Dos Pilas" p. 427-430
M. Kudlek "A Statistical Analysis of Dates on Maya Monuments to Find Astronomical Inscriptions" p. 431-432
A. Digby "Evidence in Mexican Glyphs and Sculpture for a Hitherto Unrecognised Astronomical Instrument" p. 433-442
C.A. Burland "A Calendar of Fate: Life and Death in two Mexican Codices in the Vatican Library" p. 443-446
H.J. Prem "The 'Map of Chichimec History.' Identified" p. 447-454
J.A. Sabloff and W.L. Rathje "A Study of Changing Precolumbian Commercial Patterns on the Island of Cozumel, Mexico" p. 455-464
A.G. Miller "The Mural Painting in Structure 12 at Tancah and in Structures 5 at Tulum, Quintana Roo, Mexico: Implications of their Style and Iconography" p. 465-472
A.P. Andrews "A Preliminary Study of the Ruins of Xcaret and a Reconnaissance of other Archaeological Sites on the Central Coast of Quintana Roo, Mexico" p. 473-478
P.D. Harrison "Precolumbian Settlement Distributions and External Relationships in Southern Quintana Roo, P. 1: Architecture" p. 479-486

R.E. Fry "The Archaeology of Southern Quintana Roo: Ceramics" p. 487-494
P.D. Harrison "The Lintels of Tzibanche, Quintana Roo" p. 495-501

V. 2, *Problemi generali, teoria e metodologia, etnologia, struttura culturale e sociale dei popoli di lingua caribica:*

A. Rivas Salmón "El Cometa Halley visto por los Indígenas de America" p. 9-10
A. Rivas Salmón "La Contabilidad de los Pueblos Mesoamericanos no es Vigesimal ni de Origen Dígito sino Astronómica y Veintiunitaria" p. 11-12
M. Cuesta Domingo "Las Islas Molucas en la Cartografía" p. 13-24
H.A. Huscher "Pre-Columbian Trans-Atlantic Contacts Recorded in Material Culture Vocabularies" p. 25-30
R. Tekiner "Trans-Pacific Contact: the Evidence of the Panpipe" p. 31-38
J.M. Gomez-Tabanera "En Torno a la Introduccíon en Europa del Zea Mays y su Posible Difusión desde el Noroeste Hispánico" p. 39-54
R. Mańkowska and A. Krzanowski "Polish Ethnographical and Archaeological Collections from South America" p. 55-60
A.B. Hellbom "The 'Image' of the Latin American Indians in a Westernized World. an Example of National and International Discrimination" p. 61-68
C. Irwin-Williams "The Seasonal Strategy in the Development of Sedentary Life" p. 69-76
S.N. Gerber; S.M. Greenfield; and W.E. Wright "Fieldwork, Categorial Bias, and Understanding Socio-cultural Reality: some Philosophical Considerations" p. 77-84
I. Tudela Herrero and S. Cano de Santayana "Las Guías de Americanistas por las Bibliotecas y Museos de Europa" p. 85-86
B. Riese and O. Smailus "CILA: Centro de Investigaciones Latinoamericanas — Universidad de Hamburgo" p. 87-90
J. García-Bárcena G. "Obsidian Hydration Dating in Central Mexico: Preliminary Results" p. 91-98
J.R. Galván García and E. Sánchez Montañés "Aplicación de las Técnicas de Microscopía Electrónica y Difracción de Rayos X, al Estudio de Cerámicas Arqueológicas Peruanas" p. 99-106
F.H. Eikaas "How Reliable are Census Data: a Look at a New York Reservation" p. 107-112
K.H. Schlesier "The Strategy of Southern Cheyenne: Action Anthropology" p. 113-118
O. Stavrakis Puleston and D.E. Puleston "A Processual Model for the Rise of Classic Maya Civilization in the Southern Lowlands" p. 119-124
P. Masson "Problemas de un Análisis Secundario Diacrónico de 'Cultura Normativa' " p. 125-132
G. Johnson and G. Marzano "A Preliminary Eidochronic Analysis of Bororo Myth" p. 133-142
U. Schlenther "Eduar Seler Laudatio" p. 143-146
L. Makarius Levi "Significato del Trickster in America Settentrionale" p. 147-152
I. Signorini "Transvestitism and Institutionalized Homosexuality in North America" p. 153-164
N.H.H. Graburn "A Preliminary Analysis of Symbolism in Eskimo Art and Culture" p. 165-170
B. Cox "Environmental Disturbances in Northern Peoples' Lands" p. 171-182
T.F. Kehoe "Stone 'Medicine Wheel' Monuments in the Northern Plains of North America" p. 183-190

G. Mazzoleni "Buffoni Rituali ed Integrazione Culturale nel Sud-Ovest: Ipotesi" p. 191-196
M.E. Smith "A Comparative Reconstruction of Tiwa Governing Systems" p. 197-202
R.A. Jairazbhoy "Egyptian Gods in Mexico" p. 203-212
T.D. Sullivan "Tlaloc: a New Etymological Interpretation of the God's Name and what it Reveals of his Essense and Nature" p. 213-220
T.J.J. Leyenaar "Ulama, Supervivencia de un Juego de Pelota Precolombino" p. 221-230
B. Bittmann Simons "El Empleo del Zacate como Elemento Ceremonial en el México Prehispanico" p. 231-240
R. Escalante H. and A. López G. "Hongos Sagrados de los Matlatzincas" p. 243-250
E. Hinz "Operating Criteria for Aztec Philology" p. 251-256
U. Köhler "Huitzilopochtli und die präkolumbische Einteilung des Kosmos in links und rechts. Eine Kritik gängiger Lehrmeinungen" p. 257-272
V. Piho "La Jerarquía Militar Azteca" p. 273-288
M. Arioti "Evolution of Mayan Settlements from Preclassic to Postclassic Eras" p. 289-294
J.M. Collins "Kinship Behavior and Terminology of the Yucatecac Maya" p. 295-308
J. Arias " 'Relatedness terms' as Trigger to Elucidate some Cultural Categories of the Pedrano in the Highlands of Chiapas, Mexico" p. 309-320
U. Köhler "Grundzüge des religiösen Denkens der Pableros im Hochland von Chiapas, Mexiko" p. 321-328
S. Cosminsky "Utilization of a Health Clinic in a Guatemalan Community" p. 329-338
O. Smailus "The Social and Sociolinguistic Situation in Belize, British Honduras" p. 339-348
A. Seiler-Baldinger "Ein seltener Hängemattentypus und seine Verbreitung in Amerika" p. 349-356
A. Ghidinelli and R. Terranova "Relazione Preliminare sull'Applicazione dei Test Mentali Carta-Matita all'Analisi dei Fenomeni Provocati dalla Acculturazione nell'Area Pokomam, Guatemala" p. 357-364
C. Sáenz de Santa María "Lo Cristiano en los Libros Indígenas del Altiplano Guatemalteco" p. 365-370
L. Laurencich de Minelli "Un Grupo de Indios Guaymí en la Región Sur de Costa Rica. Notas Etnograficas, Lingüísticas, Antropológicas" p. 371-380
M.M. Suárez "Enfermedades Populares, Causas y Tratamientos: el Caso de el Morro en los Andes Venezolanos" p. 381-386
O. Zerries "Besessenheit und Geisterbesuch. Parapsychologische Erscheinungen unter den Mahekodo-tedi, einer Yanoama-Gruppe am oberen Orinoco" p. 387-390
H. Bischoff "Una Colección Etnográfica de la Sierra Nevada de Santa Marta, Colombia, — Siglo XVII" p. 391-398
V.D. Stähle "Medien des sozialen wandels bei Tikunaindianern im Kolumbischen Amazonasgebiet-Schule, Landfunk und Tourismus" p. 399-412
J. Contreras Hernández "La Adivinación por la Coca en Chinchero, Cuzco, Peru" p. 413-420
M. Ballesteros-Gaibrois "Etnohistoria de la Sierra Peruana, Chinchero" p. 421-432
A. Seiler-Baldinger "Der Federmantel der Tupinamba im Museum für Völkerkunde, Basel" p. 433-438
G. Bamonte "Da un Trabalho do Campo do Autor: Localizaçao de Aldeias Macus na area do Rio Tiqué, Alto Rio Negro-Amazonas" p. 439-446
A. Lukesch "Erster Kontakt und crstes Zusam-

menleben mit einer Stammesgruppe am rechten Ufer des Xingú, die Asuriní vom Ipiaçaba" p. 447-456
H. Schindler "Die Stellung der Carijona im Kulturareal Nordwestamazonien" p. 457-468
G. Guariglia "Gli Xavante del Mato Grosso in fase acculturativa" p. 469-478
M. Münzel "Die Aché-Guayaki in Paraguay" p. 479-482
H. Burgos-Guevara "La Población del Ecuador en la Encrucijada de los Siglos XVI y XVII" p. 483-488
J. Golte "El Trabajo y la Distribución de Bienes en el Runa Simi del Siglo XVI" p. 489-506
I. Terrades Saborit "Organización Económica y Virginidad: Conceptos para una Correlación; Caso Andino-Circummediterráneo" p. 507-510
E. Choy "Estructuras de Amortiguación y Lucha de Clases en el Sistema Esclavista Incaico" p. 511-514
S. Palomino Flores "Un Puente Colgante Inka en la Comunidad de Sarhua, Peru" p. 515-520
M.E. King "Mythological Figures in Textiles from Ocucaje, Peru" p. 521-530
C. Bolton and R. Bolton "Techniques of Socialization among the Qolla" p. 531-540
R. Bolton "Kallawaya Sorcery: Description of a Session'" p. 541-554
J.J. Honigmann "Introductory Remarks" p. 555-556
F.N. Ferguson "Change from without and within: Navajo Indians' Response to an Alcoholism Treatment Program in Terms of Social Stake" p. 557-566
E.S. Rogers and J. Shawana "Programme for Ontario Indians: Action and Reactions" p. 567-578
T. Weaver "Social and Economic Change in the Context of Pima-Maricopa History" p. 579-592
J.S. Matthiasson "Caught in the Middle: two Cree Communities and the Southern Indian Lake Hidro-Electric Power Controversy" p. 593-602
A. McElroy "The Origins and Development of Inuit, Eskimo, Alliance Movements in the Eastern Canadian Arctic" p. 603-612
W.W. Koolage Jr. "Relocation and Culture Change: a Canadian Subarctic Case Study" p. 613-618
D. Savoie "Etude des Dimensions Sociales et Politiques de Deux Projects de Développement dans le Nord Canadien" p. 619-628
E.B. Basso "The Kalapalo Dietary System" p. 629-638
P.G. Rivière "Some Problems in the Comparative Study of Carib Societies" p. 639-644
J.P. Dumont "Of Dogs and Men: Naming among the Panare Indians" p. 645-652
H. Schindler "Some Critical Remarks on Dumont's Paper about Naming among the Panare" p. 653-656
N. Arvelo-Jiménez "A Study on the Process of Village Formation in Ye'cuana Society" p. 657-664
B.J. Hoff "Linguistic Change in Carib Society." p. 665-669

V. 3, *Linguistica, folklore, storia americana: conflitti culturali, colonia, independenza, sociologia: modernizzazioni modificazioni culturali recenti:*

V.J. Gilbert "The Importance of the South-American Toponomy and Faunal Nomenclature as Evidence of the World-Wide Diffusion of a Common Ancestral Tongue" p. 9-22
M.R. Wise "Some Recent Advances in Tagmemic Theory: Illustration from Amerindian Languages" p. 23-30
R. Hartmann "En Torno a las Ediciones más, Recientes de los Textos Quechuas Recogidos por Francisco de Avila" p. 31-42
R. Hartmann "Observaciones Críticas acerca de la Nueva Edición de la *Gramática keshua* de Ernst W. Middendorf" p. 43-44
M. Kudlek "Computer Programs for Generating and Analyzing Quiché Verb Phrases" p. 45-46
G. Regni Cassinis "Practical 'Bribri' " p. 55-68
M. Durbin and H. Seijas "The Phonological Structure of the Western Carib Languages of the Sierra de Perijá, Venezuela" p. 69-78
M. Gnerre "L'utilizzazione delle Fonti Documentarie dei Secoli XVI e XVII per la Storia Linguistica Jíbaro" p. 79-86
A.M. D'Ans "Etude Glottochronologique de Neuf Langues Pano" p. 87-98
I. Pozzi-Escot "Plan para la Castellanización de los Niños Quechua-Hablantes en el Perú" p. 99-106
A. Bausani "Nuovi Materiali sulla Lingua Chono" p. 107-118
T. Engl and L. Engl "Pishtaku oder Nakak. Kultur-und sozialkritische Fragen zu einem gespenstischen Phänomen in Peru" p. 119-126
E.M. Merino de Zela "Moderna 'Extirpación de Idolatrías': el Caso de Lambayeque, Peru" p. 127-134
A. García "Le Manichéisme dans les Romans de José María Arguedas" p. 135-142
J. Cáceres Freyre "Los Elementos Nacionales en el Arte Popular Argentino" p. 143-156
A. Pollak-Eltz "The Double-Soul Concept among Afroamericans" p. 157-164
D. Ramos Pérez "Viaje Realizado para Localizar el Lugar en el que Colón, en 1494, Tomó Posesión de la Tierra Continental de América del Sur" p. 165-172
F.J. Hochleitner "Eine neue Interpretation des 370 Légua Meridians im Vertrag von Tordesillas, 1494" p. 173-176
P. Hernández Aparicio "Una Instrucción Inédita de 1559 para Nuevos Descubrimientos y Poblaciones" p. 177-184
C. Aguilera de Litvak "The Styles in the Illustrations of Book IX of the Florentine Codex" p. 185-194
E.W. Palm "Estilo Cartográfico y Tradición Humanista en las Relaciones Geográficas de 1579-1581" p. 195-204
A. Borges "Contribución del Archipiélago Canario a la Empresa Indiana en el siglo XVI" p. 205-214
B. Escandell Bonet "Sobre la Peculiarización Americana de la Inquisición Española en Indias" p. 215-222
P. Castañeda Delgado "Implicaciones Etico-Morales de la Tributación Indiana: Siglos XVI y XVII" p. 223-229
A. Muro Orejón and J. Llavador Mira "Cedulario Americano del Siglo XVIII" p. 231-234
P. Sanchiz Ochoa "La Sociedad Guatemalteca en el Siglo XVI: Contribución Metodológica al Análisis del Sistema de Valores" p. 235-242
S. Rodríguez-Becerra "Metodología y Fuentes para el Estudio de la Población de Guatemala en el Siglo XVI" p. 243-254
M.A.E. Martínez "El Asiento de La Alcabala en el Nuevo Reino de Granada, siglo XVI" p. 255-258
H. Storni "Breve Biobibliografía del P. Diego de Torres Bollo SI" p. 259-264
J. Gil-Bermejo García " La Isla de Santo Domingo en el Siglo XVII: Problemas del Situado" p. 265-270
E. Vila Vilar "Algunas Consideraciones en Torno a las Fortificaciones de Puerto Rico" p. 271-276
M.C. García Bernal "La Visita del Obispo de Yucatán,

Fray Luis de Cifuentes Sotomayor, 1669" p. 277-284
E. Fidente "Due Proposte per la Difesa di Buenos Aires: 1672-1679" p. 285-290
L. Díaz-Trechuelo "El Primer Conde de Revillagigedo, Virrey de Nueva España" p. 291-294
A. Gimeno "La Expedición del General Flores al Ecuador, como Síntoma" p. 295-302
J. Chenu "La Deuxième Création du Consulado de Cartagena de Indias: Rôle et Activité de José Ignacio de Pombo" p. 303-310
C.H. Guerrero "San Juan en su Ayuda a la Campaña del Perú" p. 311-316
J. Santos Sanz "Notas para un Estudio Demográfico de Cuzco" p. 317-320
C. Minguet "Les Récits de Voyages Européens en Amérique Espagnole et Portugaise aux 18 et 19e Siècles" p. 321-324
G. Judde "Un Témoignage Inédit d'un Voyageur Français dans la République de l'Equateur au 19e siècle" p. 325-336
J. Fisher "Silver Production and the Economic Crisis of the Viceroyalty of Peru, 1776-1821" p. 337-346
J.J. Vega "Los Trabajadores de las Minas Andinas en la Epoca de Túpac Amaru, 1780" p. 347-350
O. Baulny "Les Immigrants Italiens et leur Rôle dans l'Histoire du Rio de la Plata à l'Aube du XIXe Siècle" p. 351-356
M. Brignole "Il Contributo della Danimarca alla Formazione della Nazione Groenlandese: L'Originale Rapporto di Simbiosi Politico-Sociale fra la Danimarca e la Groenlandia" p. 357-364
J. Lafaye "Les Processus d'Integration Nationale au Mexique" p. 365-370
A. Valdez "La Dotación de Tierras a Comunidades Indígenas en Venezuela: Desde la Colonia hasta Nuestros Dias" p. 371-376
H. Kellenbenz "Die frühen Kredit-und Bankverhältnisse in Iberoamerika" p. 377-384
R. Luraghi "Strutture Sociali pre-Capitalistiche nel Sud degli Stati Uniti e in America Latina" p. 385-390
J. Fox Przeworski "The Entrance of North American Capital into the Chilean Copper Industry and the Role of Government, 1904-1916" p. 391-416
M. Kossok "Aufklärung in Lateinamerika: Mythos oder Realität?" p. 417-422
M.J. Sarabia Viejo "La Esclavitud Indígena en la Gobernación de Pánuco" p. 423-428
M.C. Borrego Pla "Palenques de Negros Cimarrones en Cartagena de Indias" p. 429-432
E.G. Peralta Rivera "Informe Preliminar al Estudio de la Tributación de Negros Libres Mulatos y Zambahigos en el Siglo XVII Peruano" p. 433-438
B. Torres "La Compañía Gaditana de Negros" p. 439-444
J. Llavador Mira "Modificación y Límites de la Esclavitud" p. 445-452
N. Scott Kinzer "Myths and Misinterpretations of the Latin America Female" p. 453-458
P. Singelmann "Campesino Movements in Latin America: Converging Theoretical Perspectives" p. 459-468
M.L. Carlos "Traditional and Modern Forms of Compadrazgo among Mexicans and Mexican-Americans: a Survey of Continuities and Changes" p. 469-484
G. Clarac N. "Alcance del Desarrollo Indígena Venezolano Mediante la Reforma Agraria, Dentro de las Perspectivas Latinoamericanas" p. 485-494
G. Krause "La Función de un Mercado en la Economía del Valle del Mantaro: La Feria Dominical de Huancayo" p. 495-498
F. Del Pino Diaz "Migración y Adaptación: el caso de los Serranos en el Departamento Selvático de Madre de Dios, Perú" p. 499-510
J. Nash "Dependency and the Failure of Feedback: the Case of Bolivian Mining Communities" p. 511-532
H.E. Agüero Zahnd; M. Perez; and L. Quiroga "Problemas Ocupacionales de la Mujer en San Juan, Argentina" p. 533-542
E. Timo "Determinadas Pervivencias de Transfeudalización en Iruya, Provincia de Salta, Republica Argentina" p. 543-549

Karst, Kenneth; Murray L. Schwartz; and Audrey J. Schwartz. The evolution of law in the barrios of Caracas. See item 8521a.

514. Katz, Friedrich. The ancient American civilizations. Translated by K. M. Lois Simpson. N.Y., Praeger, 1972. 386 p., bibl., maps.

Discussion of precolumbian history south of Mexican border; two thirds of which deals with Mesoamerica. Chapters on Aztecs and Incas describe daily life, religion, militarism, technological advances in metallurgy and pottery, social change, etc. Last chapters compare these two civilizations. Includes up-to-date bibliography and uses references, but lacks illustrations. Only three maps. [C. Evans]

515. McGlynn, Eileen A. Middle American anthropology: directory, bibliography, and guide to the UCLA Library Collections. Los Angeles, Univ. of California, Latin American Center and University Library, 1975. 131 p., illus., map.

A handy reference work, intended to facilitate and encourage library research. It is a model in organization and will be most useful to all persons engaged in Mesoamerican studies at UCLA or other specialized libraries. Includes index. [H. von Winning]

516. Marroquín, Alejandro Dagoberto. Balance del indigenismo: informe sobre la política indigenista en América. México, Instituto Indigenista Iteramericano (III), Sección de Investigaciones Antropológica, 1972. 300 p., bibl., illus., tables (Ediciones especiales, 62)

History of native American Indian. Also describes developments and movements in Americas with details about six countries (Mexico, Guatemala, Ecuador, Peru, Brazil and Bolivia). Concludes with comments on those that failed and those that succeeded. [C. Evans]

Martínez Crovetto, Raúl. Distribución de algunos juegos de hilo entre los aborígenes sudamericanos. See *HLAS 36:768.*

517. Montañé M., Julio C. *comp.* Bibliografía de antropología chilena VII, 1969-1970 (Noticiario Mensual [Museo Nacional de Historia Natural, Santiago] 16:189, abril, 1972, p. 3-7)

Journals, monographs and general articles on Chile dated 1969 and 1970, with a few 1968 not listed previously. [C. Evans]

Neel, James V. Control of disease among Amerindians in cultural transition. See item 2243.

518. Olien, Michael D. Latin Americans: contemporary peoples and their cultural traditions. N.Y., Holt, Rinehart & Winston, 1973. 408 p., bibl., illus., maps, plates, tables.

Excellent introductory book on the anthropology of Latin America designed to give the student and general reader an understanding of the temporal, spatial and cultural setting of the region. Has 75 pages of excellent bibliography divided into a variety of useful categories for additional reading. [C. Evans]

519. Palerm, Angel. Historia de la etnología: los precursores. México, Instituto Nacional de Antropología e Historia, Centro de Investigaciones Superiores, 1974. 319 p. (Historia de la etnología, 1)

History of anthropological thought, especially ethnology, from standpoint of classic writers, travelers, missionaries, etc. Includes original quotations (translated to Spanish from other languages when necessary). Divides book and such material into four sections: Exponents of classical world (such as Herodotus, Aristotle, Estrabón, Tacitus); travelers and discoveries in the era of exploration (such as Marco Polo, Columbus, Cabeza de Vaca, Carvejal, Pinto); missionaries and officials during colonization (such as Sahagún, Landa, Oviedo, and Acosta); and utopians and insurgents of the revolutionary period (such as Las Casas, Bacon, Rousseau). Most interesting time depth approach to history of ethnology. Although author states he wrote it for students rather than colleagues, it is interesting reading for the professional. [C. Evans]

Portal, Marta. El maíz: grano sagrado de América. See *HLAS 36:1430.*

520. Ramos, Arthur. As culturas européias: introdução à antropologia brasileira. Rio, Libraria Editôra da Casa do Estudante do Brasil, (CEB), 1973. 379 p., bibl., illus., maps, plates, tables (Col. Arthur Ramos, 4)

Reprint of Ramos' articles on European or Europeanized cultures in Brazil: Portuguese, Spanish, French, Anglo-Saxons, Italians, Germans, Dutch, Negro slaves, Syrians and Lebanese, gypsies, Jews, Japanese and Chinese. [C. Evans]

Schaden, Egon and Gioconda Mussolini. Povos e trajes da América Latina. See *HLAS 36:774.*

521. Séjourné, Laurette. América Latina. v. 1, Antiguas culturas precolombinas. México, Siglo XXI Editores, 1971. 331 p., bibl., illus., maps, plates, tables (Historia universal, 21)

Briefly outlines precolumbian cultures of Mexico, Central America, Caribbean, and South America, in terms of a time sequence of development, discussing in some detail (although without recent bibliography) the archeology of Peru and Mesoamerica. Also includes generalizations on the socio-political and religious systems of these cultures. [C. Evans]

Stewart, T. Dale. The people of America. See item 2018.

522. Tovar Pinzón, Hermes. Notas sobre el modo de producción precolombino. Bogotá, Aquelarre, 1974. 119 p., illus., maps, plates.

Consists of observations on the socio-political life, economic controls and way of life of precolumbian societies, based chiefly on precolumbian cultures of Colombia, with some reference to South America as a whole. [C. Evans]

523. Wagley, Charles *ed.* Man in the Amazon. Gainesville, Fla., The University Presses of Florida, 1974. 330 p., bibl., maps (A University of Florida book)

Study is the result of the XXXIII Annual Latin American Conference on the Brazilian Amazon and current development therein, held at the Univ. of Florida in Feb. 1973. Consists of 15 chapters by different contributors from the US and Brazil whose Portuguese articles were translated into English. Offers a current summary of the geopolitics, public health, transmittable diseases, the highway system based on a solid knowledge of geography, soils, ecology, and agricultural development as well as its effect on various peoples from the indigenous to the caboclo and modern population. [C. Evans]

524. Wagner, Erika comp. Bibliografía antropológica reciente sobre Venezuela (AVAC/ACV, 23, 1972, p. 52-54).

Reference materials on Venezuelan anthropology (archaeology, ethnology, linguistics, and physical anthropology). [C. Evans]

525. _____. (Segunda bibliografía antropológica reciente sobre Venezuela) (AVAC/ACV, 24, 1973, p. 68-70).

Reference materials dated 1970-73 of importance to Venezuelan anthropology (archaeology, ethnology, linguistics and physical anthropology), not previously listed, see item 524. [C. Evans]

526. Zubrow, Ezra B. W.; Margaret C. Fritz; and John M. Fritz eds. New world archaeology: theoretical and cultural transformations. San Francisco, Calif., W. H. Freeman, 1974. 335 p., bibl., illus., maps, plates, tables (Readings from *Scientific American*)

Reprint of 33 articles originally published in *Scientific American* of which the oldest (1968) is Roberts' on salvage archaeology and the most recent (1972) Hammond's on the Maya ceremonial center of Lubaantún in British Honduras. Editors arranged articles to reflect theoretical shifts in New World archaeology. Section topics are: the romantic vision, time-space systematics; reconstruction of events, of sequences, and of strategies; analysis of systems and processes; and an epilogue on contemporary issues of salvage archaeology and the modern day surviving American Indian by La Farge. Editors introduce each section noting relevant articles and commenting on objectives, theoretical perspectives, methods, disadvantages and advantages, and wider relevance of each approach. [C. Evans]

ARCHAEOLOGY: MESOAMERICA

RICHARD E. W. ADAMS
Professor of Anthropology
University of Texas
San Antonio

HASSO VON WINNING
Consultant in Mesoamerican Archaeology
Southwest Museum

ONE OF MESOAMERICAN ARCHAEOLOGY'S PRINCIPAL PROBLEMS has long been one of inadequacy of information sample in both quality and quantity. Reviewing the past two year's publications, one can see that a definite shift has set in toward greater control over more areas within the whole field. More regions are being worked and more topics are being confronted. Several trends can be noted in the publications. One is that smaller, more specialized and highly focused conferences are being held which are producing interesting results, if not consensus. Another trend is that more site and regional reports are appearing which link the previously isolated bodies of information produced by older work. Mesoamerican archaeology has become old and sophisticated enough that it is developing an interest in its own intellectual history. Republication of important older works has been of great aid to the scholar and to interested persons. The usual photographic essays with commentary continue to appear but some are approaching a high degree of sophistication and are distinct contributions to the field.

Taking matters first by archaeological stages, it is interesting to note that no significant publication in early man studies appeared during the last two years. This is highly regrettable. Reevaluation of the El Chayal site (item 777) is the only related study of importance. On the other hand, the Formative of Mesoamerica is well treated in quality if not quantity. Grove's study of the Morelos Early Formative material is valuable (item 718), and a major advance in understanding of highland formative chronology.

The classic stage is well treated. Perhaps the major publication event is the appearance of Millon's Teotihuacan map, excellently presented and published in several scales (item 659). Miller's well produced book on the Teotihuacan murals reinforces the map with vast amounts of new graphic data. Tajin, long inadequately published, has at last received some intensive treatment through Kampen's study of its sculptures (item 638). Winter's article on Monte Albán residences anticipates major information forthcoming on that highly urbanized site (item 792). The end of the Maya classic receives intense scrutiny in a major volume of papers from a conference (item 612). A rather surprising and sweeping reevaluation of classic Maya culture is included in the book as well as a complex model of the collapse itself.

The postclassic periods receive less attention. A major paper by Ball on northern Yucatan combines ethnohistoric and archaeological material in a convincing manner (item 603). Diehl's work at Tula is published in a new series, and begins to make a more intelligible picture of Toltec culture. One of the most important publications of the last two years (and perhaps 20 years) is that of Di Peso's first three volumes on Casas Grandes in Chihuahua (item 613). While dealing with a regional sequence, the major portion of the site's history is postclassic and Toltec connected.

Topically, there are some very interesting writings. Basic site and regional reports of importance include Casas Grandes, already mentioned (item 613), the site of Los Naranjos, Honduras (item 690), Tonina in the Guatemalan highlands (item 691), the Rio Bec region of the Maya lowlands (item 683), the northern area of British Honduras (item 724), Palo Gordo on the Guatemalan Pacific coast (item 786), Dzibilchaltun in northern Yucatan (items 643, 672 and 739), several reports in Oaxaca (items 696-698 and 783), Tula (item 705), Chalchuapa, Honduras (item 776), and the Middle Grijalva (item 741). It is noteworthy that most of these reports are from the Maya area, although we are not sure that this has any particular implication. Particularly noteworthy are the Oaxacan reports from the Nochixtlan Valley north of the Valley of Oaxaca and from the coastal and Miahuatlan areas to the south of it. These lend perspective to the intensive work underway in the Valley itself.

Individual papers still make major contributions. Turner's revolutionary report on intensive agriculture among the classic lowland Maya is an example (item 678). On the other hand, major works of traditional scholarship continue to demonstrate their worth as in the excellent study of the jades of the Chichen cenote by Proskouriakoff (item 762).

An important book on Maya cities by Andrews, an architect, makes a major contribution to Maya archaeology by offering a different perspective (item 685). Gendrop's sumptuous book on Mesoamerican art brings an up-to-date perspective to the field of precolumbian art.

Epigraphy is well represented with two major groups of papers appearing on Maya hieroglyphic writing (items 797 and 813) both resulting from conferences. Dütting publishes two individual papers of importance (items 801 and 802). Barthel and Kelley support the idea of Southeast Asian derivation of Mesoamerican calendars (items 794, 796 and 806). A volume on archaeoastronomy, just published by the Univ. of Texas, will be included in *HLAS 39*.

West Mexico was brought forward a giant step by publication of several items, notably the conference volume edited by Bell (item 605), the paper by Meighan (item 744), and the volume on shaft tomb figures by von Winning (item 788). Materials bearing on the area from other parts of Mesoamerica also enhance its understanding (e.g. Grove's Morelos work (item 718).

A group of important although diverse papers stem from the Cambri Univ. conference (item 633). A very important book on Mesoamerican religions, edited by Litvak and Tejero, consists of 91 papers largely ethnohistorical in content but of great interest to archaeologists.

The history of Mesoamerican archaeology is treated briefly by Sabloff and Willey in their more broadly focused book (item 633). Brunhouse publishes an anecdotally oriented book (item 799). It is apparent that Mesoamerican archaeology still needs a definitive intellectual history.

The republication of Maudslay is a major event (item 653) as is to a lesser degree the book of essays by Seler, Sapper and their colleagues (item 798).

The several photographic essay books were led by a first rate one on Copan published by a dentist (item 669).

Culbert's non-technical book on classic Maya civilization merits special mention for its readability and interest (item 611).

We regret having to mention the deaths of the following scholars during the past two years:

Pedro Bosch-Gimpera in 1974. Great Spanish prehistorian whose major work was done in the Old World but who did publish on rock art in Mesoamerica.

Carl Guthe in 1975. Pioneer worker with S. G. Morley at Tayasal in the 1920s, who later abandoned Maya archaeology, and became eminent in North American archaeology. One of the founders of the Society for American Archaeology.

Joaquin Meade in 1971. Scholar who worked most of his life in the Huasteca and produced the only major book on the area.

Anna O. Shepard in 1973. Chiefly noted for her petrographic work with tempers of archaeological pottery. Her study of plumbate ware is the major example of her life time activity. Trained as a geologist and petrographer.

Mathew W. Stirling in 1975. Discoverer of the Olmecs whose monuments and culture he largely documented. His work laid the basis for the later quantum jumps in understanding of both the Olmec and Mesoamerican cultures in general. Longtime Chief of the Bureau of American Ethnology and active until his death. (REWA)

GENERAL

600. Adams, Richard E.W. The classic Maya collapse: a correction (SAA/AA, 39:3, July 1974, p. 397).

Sabloff attributes agreement by Adams to his interpretation of evidence from the Pasion River. Adams still dissents on evidential grounds and offers an alternative. [REWA]

601. ──────. A trial estimation of classic Maya palace populations at Uaxactun (*in* Hammond, Norman *ed.* Mesoamerican Archaeology: new approaches [see item 633] p. 285-296, tables.

Using measured sleeping spaces in residential palaces, an estimate is arrived at of about 184 elite persons at Uaxactun, or one to two percent of the total late classic population. [REWA]

602. Andrews, George F. Maya cities: placemaking and urbanization. Norman, Univ. of Oklahoma Press, 1974. 468 p., illus., maps.

Major and important book on Maya architecture, the first really original study since George Totten's. Somewhat lacking in awareness of archaeological literature but more than compensated for by the unique perspective that Andrews brings as an architect and one who has made maps of two Maya sites. Lavishly illustrated studies of 20 Maya cities, mostly in the lowlands. Architectural analysis of each and an attempt at a theoretical interrelation of their functional features. Andrews' theory of urbanism is tied to a technical and conceptual base not yet entirely clear, but his studies of the individual buildings are worth the whole book. Excellent reconstruction and analytical drawings. Includes 351 figures. [REWA]

603. Ball, Joseph W. A coordinate approach to northern Maya prehistory: AD 700-1200 (SAA/AA, 39:1, Jan. 1974, p. 85-93)

"In the present paper a trial coordination of the accumulated archaeological and ethnohistoric materials dealing with the eighth through 12th centuries A.D. is presented, and a culture historic framework for this period is suggested." The problems of the classic Maya collapse and the identification and intrusions of the Itzá are convincingly dealt with. [REWA]

604. Becker, Marshall Joseph. Archaeological evidence for occupational specialization among the classic period Maya at Tikal, Guatemala (SAA/AA, 38:3, July 1973, p. 396-406)

Direct evidence for stratified occupational specialization is presented from Tikal. Six specialties are defined including stoneworkers, potters, woodcarvers, and dentists. Important. [REWA]

605. Bell, Betty *ed.* The archaeology of West Mexico. Ajijic, Mex., Sociedad de Estudios Avanzados del Occidente de México, 1974. 252 p., bibl., illus., maps, tables.

Contains the following papers, the majority of which derive from the Society for American Archaeology symposia on West Mexico in 1970-71:
Otto Schöndube Baumbach "Introducción: Algunas Consideraciones sobre la Arqueología del Occidente de México" p. 1-5
Henry B. Nicholson and Clement W. Meighan "The UCLA Department of Anthropology Program in West Mexican Archaeology-Ethnohistory, 1956-1970" p. 6-18
J. Charles Kelley "Speculations on the Culture History of Northwestern Mesoamerica" p. 19-39
Beatriz Braniff "Oscilación de la Frontera Septentrional Mesoamericana" p. 40-50
Stuart D. Scott "Archaeology and the Estuary: Researching Prehistory and Paleoecology in the Marismas Nacionales, Sinaloa and Nayarit, Mexico" p. 51-56
J. Richard Shenkel "Quantitative Analysis and Population Estimates of the Shell Mounds of the Marismas Nacionales, West Mexico" p. 57-67
Rosemary Sweetman "Prehistoric Pottery from Coastal Nayarit" p. 68-82
George W. Gill "Toltec-Period Burial Customs within the Marismas Nacionales of Western Mexico" p. 83-105
Joseph B. Mountjoy "San Blas Complex Ecology" p. 106-119
Phil C. Weigand "The Ahualulco Site and the Shaft-Tomb Complex of the Etzatlan Area" p. 120-131
Peter R. Furst "Some Problems in the Interpretation of West Mexican Tomb Art" p. 132-146
Betty Bell "Excavations at El Cerro Encantado, Jalisco" p. 147-167

Otto Shöndube Baumbach "Deidades Prehispánicas en el Area de Tamazula-Tuxpan-Zapotlan en el Estado de Jalisco" p. 168-181
José Oliveros "Nuevas Exploraciones en El Opeño, Michoacan" p. 182-201
Eduardo Matos and Isabel Kelly "Una Vasija que Sugiere Relaciones entre Teotihuacan y Colima" p. 202-205
Isabel Kelly "Stirrup Pots from Colima: some Implications" p. 206-211
Louise Fish "Figurines with Up-tilted Noses from Colima, Mexico" p. 212-214
R.E. Taylor "Archaeometric Studies in West Mexican Archaeology" p. 215-224
Lawrence H. Feldman "Archaeomolluscan Species of Northwest Mesoamerica: Patterns of Natural and Cultural Distribution" p. 225-239
Robert B. Pickering "A Preliminary Report on the Osteological Remains from Alta Vista, Zacatecas" p. 240-248. [HvW]

606. Berger, Rainer; Suzzane De Atley; Reiner Protsch; and Gordon R. Willey. Radiocarbon chronology for Seibal, Guatemala (NWJS, 252, 6 Dec. 1974, p. 472-473, table)

Six Carbon-14 dates fit well with the ceramic sequence and comprehend a span from 900 BC to 1050 AD. [REWA]

607. Bernal, Ignacio. Tenochtitlan en una isla. México, Secretaría de Educación Pública, 1972. 159 p., bibl., illus., plates (SepSetentas, 39)

Modified version of first ed. 1959 (see *HLAS 22:508*) which appeared in English 1963 (*Mexico Before Cortés*, see *HLAS 27:198*). [HvW]

608. Callen, E.O. Dietary patterns in Mexico between 6500 BC and 1580 AD (*in* International Botanical Congress, XI, Seattle, Wash., 1969. Man and his foods. University, Univ. of Alabama Press, 1973, p. 29-49, illus.)

Presents chronological summaries, based on data from Tehuacan and Tamaulipas, of consumption of food plants evident in coprolites. See also in the above, *Man and his foods,* the article by Lawrence Kaplan, "Ethnobotanical and Nutritional Factors in the Domestication of American Beans" (p. 75-85). [HvW]

609. Clewlow, Carl William, Jr. A stylistic chronological study of Olmec monumental sculpture. Berkeley, Univ. of California Archaeological Research Facility, 1974. 229 p., bibl., illus., plates, tables (Contributions, 19)

Up-to-date descriptive inventory of 211 monuments arranged by categories (colossal heads, anthropomorphic and animal figures, altars, relief panels, etc.) from the Veracruz-Tabasco heartland and other regions. Ample discussions of the stylistic and chronological development. See also item 713. [HvW]

610. Craven, Roy C. Ceremonial centers of the Maya. Introduction by William R. Bullard, Jr. Site descriptions by Michael E. Kampen. Gainesville, The University Presses of Florida, 1974. 152 p., illus., maps, plates.

Includes 24 in good photographs in black and white and color of 14 Maya centers, accompanied by commentary by Kampen. Bullard's introduction is first-class. Commentary and captions are marred by minor spelling and factual errors, but these do not detract from the major pictorial goals of the book. [REWA]

611. Culbert, T. Patrick. The lost civilization: the story of the classic Maya. N.Y., Harper & Row, 1974. 123 p., illus., maps.

Lively, interesting account of classic Maya Lowland civilization from the perspective of the southern lowlands and especially from Tikal data. Review of the preclassic background and the characteristics of classic civilization is followed by a summary presentation of the collapse model developed by the 1970 Santa Fe Conference. Culbert draws timely parallels between the Club of Rome projections and the collapse model. [REWA]

612. _____ed. The classic Maya collapse. Albuquerque, Univ. of New Mexico Press, School of American Research, 1973. 549 p., bibl., illus., maps, plates, tables.

A carefully integrated series of 18 papers prepared for an advanced seminar on the collapse of Maya civilization. A background is laid and reviewed in three papers, followed by nine others which are principally data oriented, followed by five interpretative ones, and the volume is rounded off by the concluding synthesis paper based on discussions at the five-day conference. They are as valuable for the reassessment of Maya civilization presented as for the new model of the collapse. Content of the papers can be surmised by their titles which are given in sequence below:
T. Patrick Culbert "Introduction: a Prologue to Classic Maya Culture and the Problem of its Collapse" p. 3-20
Richard E. W. Adams "The Collapse of Maya Civilization: a Review of Previous Theories" p. 21-34
Jeremy A. Sabloff "Major Themes in the Past Hypotheses of the Maya Collapse" p. 35-42
Robert L. Rands "The Classic Collapse in the Southern Maya Lowlands" p. 43-62
T. Patrick Culbert "The Maya Downfall at Tikal" p. 63-92
Gordon R. Willey "Certain Aspects of the Late Classic to Postclassic Periods in the Belize Valley" p. 93-106
Jeremy A. Sabloff "Continuity and Disruption during Terminal Late Classic Times at Seibal: Ceramic and other Evidence" p. 107-132
Richard E. W. Adams "Maya Collapse: Transformation and Termination in the Ceramic Sequence at the Altar de Sacrificios" p. 133-164
Robert L. Rands "The Classic Maya Collapse: Usumacinta Zone and the Northwestern Periphery" p. 165-206
John A. Graham "Aspects of the Non-Classic Pres-

ences in the Inscriptions and Sculptural Art of Seibal" p. 207-220
William R. Bullard, Jr. "Postclassic Culture in Central Petén and Adjacent British Honduras" p. 221-242
E. Wyllys Andrews, IV "The Development of Maya Civilization after the Abandonment of the Southern Cities" p. 243-268
Demitri B. Shimkin "Models for the Downfall: some Ecological and Culture-Historical Considerations" p. 269-300
Frank P. Saul "Disease in the Maya Area: the Pre-Columbian Evidence" p. 301-324
William T. Sanders "The Cultural Ecology of the Lowland Maya: A Reevaluation" p. 325-366.

613. Di Peso, Charles C. Casas Grandes, a fallen trading center of the Gran Chichimeca. Edited by Gloria J. Fenner. Illustrations by Alice Wesche. Dragoon, Ariz., The Amerind Foundation, 1974. 3 v. (1103 p.) (Continuous pagination) bibl., illus., maps.

Lavishly illustrated "narrative description" of the results of the Joint Casas Grandes Expedition to northern Mexico, initiated 1958. V. 1 *The Preceramic, Plainware, and Viejo Periods* covers the cultural history to AD 1060. V. 2 *The Medio Period,* comprising the years 1060-1340, contains references to contemporary Mesoamerican history. V. 3 *The Tardio and Españoles Periods* covers 1340-1821. V. 4/8 (in preparation) will "contain the detailed source material and basic scientific data upon which the evaluation and conclusions in the first three volumes are based." The historical narrative is interspersed by appropriate caricature-like drawings, accompanied by copious notes and references, and contains a wealth of information presented in a novel, imaginative approach. Includes index, notes, and charts. [HvW]

614. Doehring, Donald O. and Joseph H. Butler. Hydrogeologic constraints on Yucatan's development (AAAS/S, 186:4164, 15 Nov. 1974, p. 591-595, illus., maps)

Description and analysis of Yucatan's potable water supplies and their present vulnerability to rapid contamination and the spread of water-borne diseases. Relevant to the prehistoric past. [REWA]

615. Echánove Trujillo, Carlos A. ¡Esas pobres ruinas mayas maravillosas! Xp'uhil, Chican-na, Becán (Campeche), Cobá, Xelhá, Tancah, Tulum, El Caracol (Quintana-Róo), Etzná (Campeche), Chichén Itzá (Yucatán), Palenque (Chiapas), Copán (Honduras), Uxmal (Yucatán). México, B. Costa-Amic Editor, 1973. 197 p., fold. maps, illus., plates, tables.

A travel book filled with inaccuracies and journalistic questions, albeit ingenuously interesting. [REWA]

616. Eisleb, Dieter. Alt-Amerika: Führer durch die Ausstellung der Abteilung amerikanische Archäologie. Berlin, FRG, Museum für Völkerkunde, 1974. 190 p., bibl., illus., maps.

Well-illustrated guide to the Mesoamerican and South American exhibits in the Berlin Museum, with concise culture historical explanations. [HvW]

617. ———. Hundert Jahre Museum für Völkerkunde Berlin: Abteilung amerikanische Archäologie (MV/BA, 21, 1973, p. 175-217, illus.)

A history of the centenarian Berlin Museum which contains formidable collections from the Americas. [HvW]

618. Flannery, Kent V. The origins of agriculture (Annual Review of Anthropology [Annual Reviews Inc., Palo Alto, Calif.] 2, 1973, p. 271-310)

Includes a discussion on recent theories on the origin of maize in Mesoamerica. [HvW]

619. Fry, R. E. and S. C. Cox. The structure of ceramic exchange at Tikal, Guatemala (World Archaeology [London] 6:2, 1974, p. 209-225, map, tables)

"Two models of Lowland Maya socio-economic organization are tested using ceramic data from Tikal, Guatemala. The data tend to support [an] 'inward-looking' model of site organization, while also indicating possible boundaries of the Late Classic sustaining area around Tikal." [REWA]

620. Fuente, Beatriz de la. Arte prehispánico funerario: el occidente de México. México, UNAM, 1974. 61 p., plates. (Col. de Arte, 27)

Introduction to the figural art of Colima, Jalisco and Nayarit with emphasis on stylistic and aesthetic qualities. Covers materials in Mexican museums. Includes 90 plates. [HvW]

621. Garcés Contreras, Guillermo. Bonampak: una visión sincrónica. México, Editorial Arana, 1972. 125 p., illus., plates.

Comparisons are drawn between the Bonampak murals and those of the rest of Mesoamerica, the Far East, India, Southeast Asia, the Arab world, Egypt, and with Europe. More an uninformed appreciation than a rigorous study. Includes 20 plates. [REWA]

622. García Payón, José. Chac y Tlaloc: orígenes y evolución (CAM, 34:198, enero/feb. 1975, p. 137-170, illus.)

Recapitulates iconographic interpretations of pan-mesoamerican rain god representations and describes Tlaloc sculptures from Veracruz. Points out regional and temporal variations in characteristic features. [HvW]

623. Gendrop, Paul. A guide to architecture in ancient Mexico. México, Minutiae Mexicana, 1974. 128 p., bibl., illus., maps.

Review of the development of Mesoamerican architecture, with reference to its major regional styles and outstanding examples. [P. Gendrop]

624. ———— and **Doris Heyden.** Architettura mesoamericana. Milano, Italy, Electa Editrice, 1973. 340 p., bibl., illus. (Col. Storia universale dell'architettura, 13)

Each chapter presents two complementary approaches: cultural antecedents (by D. Heyden) and analyses of the main developmental phases of Mesoamerican architecture (by P. Gendrop). Profusely illustrated. An English ed. *Precolumbian architecture of Mesoamerica.* (N.Y., Abrams) is in press, and both German and Spanish editions are in preparation. [P. Gendrop]

625. **Ghidinelli, Azzo.** The alimentation of the Maya (SEM/E, 36:1/4, 1971, p. 23-32)

Somewhat naive and secondary source article on Maya food sources and nutrition. [REWA]

626. **Gifford, James C.** Recent thought on the interpretation of Maya prehistory (*in* Hammond, Norman *ed.* Mesoamerican archaeology: new approaches [see item 633] p. 77-98, illus.)

Somewhat intuitive and mystical final statement of a gifted scholar on the nature of Maya civilization and its historical course. Gifford discusses a number of important ideas. [REWA]

627. **González Aparicio, Luis.** Plano reconstructivo de la región de Tenochtitlan. México, INAH, 1973. 1 v. (Various pagings) map.

A comprehensive study of the planning and layout of the ancient Aztec capital with special reference to lake borders, hydraulic works, roads, towns and settlements in the Valley of Mexico. Includes a separate large map. [HvW]

628. **Gorenstein, Shirley** *ed.* Prehispanic America. N.Y., St. Martin's Press, 1974. 192 p., bibl., illus.

"Describes the culture history of Mesoamerica and South America and interprets the rise of civilizations. Authors discuss the effects of the contact between the Old and the New Worlds and define current controversies concerning the descriptions of prehistoric life through culture change, and the reasons behind those changes." [HvW]

629. **Graham, John A.** *ed.* Studies in ancient Mesoamerica. Berkeley, Univ. of California, Dept. of Anthropology, 1973. 207 p., illus. (Contributions of the Archaeological Research Facility, 18)

Contains the following articles:
R.E.W. Adams "Fine Orange Pottery as a Source of Ethnological Information" p. 1-9
Jacinto Quirarte "Izapan and Mayan Traits in Teotihuacan III Pottery" p. 11-29
Frank P. Saul and Norman Hammond "A Classic Maya Tooth Cache from Lubaantun, British Honduras" p. 31-35
S. Jeffrey K. Wilkerson "An Archaeological Sequence from Santa Luisa, Veracruz, Mexico" p. 37-49
Christopher Corson "Iconographic Survey of Some Principal Figurine Subjects from the Mortuary Complex of Jaina, Campeche" p. 51-75
Lawrence H. Feldman "Languages of the Chiapas Coast and Interior in the Colonial Period 1525-1820" p. 77-85
Lawrence H. Feldman "Stones for the Archaeologist" p. 87-103
Lawrence H. Feldman "Chiapas in 1774" p. 105-135
Arthur G. Miller "Archaeological Investigations of the Quintana Roo Mural Project: A Preliminary Report of the 1973 Season" p. 137-147
John P. Silva and Thomas R. Hester "Archaeological Materials from a Nonceramic Site in Eastern Durango, Mexico" p. 149-165
Thomas R. Hester; Robert N. Jack; and Alice Benfer "Trace Element Analyses of Obsidian from Michoacan, Mexico: Preliminary Results" p. 167-175
Robert J. Sharer and David W. Sedat "Monument 1, El Portón, Guatemala and the Development of Maya Calendrical and Writing Systems" p. 177-193
John A. Graham "The Dating of Stela 4 at Ixtutz" p. 195-197
Robert F. Heizer "An Unusual Olmec Figurine" p. 199-201
J. Eric S. Thompson "The Maya Glyph for Capture or Conquest and an Iconographic Representation of Itzam Na on Yucatecan Facades" p. 203-207.
[HvW]

630. **Gumerman, George J.** and **James A. Neely.** Película infrarroja en trabajos arquelógicos (INAH/B, 2:4, enero/marzo 1973, p. 51-54, illus.)

Advantages and pitfalls in the application of infrared color photography in the Tehuacan Valley. [HvW]

631. **Hammond, Norman.** The distribution of late classic Maya major ceremonial centres in the Central Area (*in* Hammond, Norman *ed.* Mesoamerican archaeology: new approaches [see item 633], p. 313-334, maps, table)

Important and sophisticated expansion of settlement pattern theory examining alternatives ranging from "central place" and economic matrix explanations for Maya ceremonial center distribution. Thiessen polygons, nearest-neighbor contouring, and statistics are used. Packing of centers in northeastern Peten are best explained by demographic-political factors. Social circumscription theory is suggested by Hammond as partly explaining the rise of Maya civilization. [REWA]

632. _____. Preclassic to postclassic in northern Belize (AT/A, 48:191, Sept. 1974, p. 177-189, illus., maps, plates)

Summary of the preliminary results of the Corozal Project including a regional ceramic sequence of six complexes ranging from middle preclassic to protohistoric. The protoclassic is suggested to be a regional Belize development perhaps dependent on cacao trade for its wealth. See also item 724. [REWA]

633. _____ ed. Mesoamerican archaeology: new approaches. Austin, Univ. of Texas Press, 1974. 474 p., bibl., illus., maps, plates, tables.

Papers presented in a symposium on Mesoamerican archaeology at Cambridge (England), Aug. 1972. Contents:
Thomas A. Lee, Jr. "The Middle Grijalva Regional Chronology and Ceramic Relationships: a Preliminary Report" p. 1-20 (see item 741)
Glyn Williams "External Influence and the Upper Rio Verde Drainage Basin at Los Altos, West Mexico" p. 21-50
Robert L. Rands "The Ceramic Sequence at Palenque, Chiapas" p. 51-75 (see item 766)
James C. Gifford "Recent Thought Concerning the Interpretation of Maya Prehistory" p. 77-98 (see item 626)
Ronald A. Grennes-Ravitz "The Olmec Presence at Iglesia Vieja, Morelos" p. 99-108
David C. Grove "The Highland Olmec Manifestation: a Consideration of What Is and Isn't" p. 109-128
Lawrence H. Feldman "Shells from Afar: 'Panamic' Molluscs in Mayan Sites" p. 129-133 (see item 711)
David H. Kelley "Eurasian Evidence and the Mayan Calendar Correlation Problem" p. 135-143 (see item 806)
Henry B. Nicholson "Tepepolco, the Locale of the First State of Fray Bernardino de Sahagún's Great Ethnographic Project: Historical and Cultural Notes" p. 145-154
Gordon Brotherston "Huitzilopochtli and What Was Made of Him" p. 155-166
Arthur G. Miller "The Iconography of the Painting in the Temple of the Diving God, Tulum, Quintana Roo: the Twisted Cords p. 167-186 (see item 656)
Peter R. Furst "Morning Glory and Mother Goddess at Tepantitla, Teotihuacan: Iconography and Analogy in Pre-Columbian Art" p. 187-216
Gary H. Gossen "A Chamula Calendar Board from Chiapas, Mexico" p. 217-254
Alexander Marshack "The Chamula Calendar Board: an Internal and Comparative Analysis" p. 255-270
Adrian Digby "Crossed Trapezes: a Pre-Columbian Astronomical Instrument" p. 271-284
R.E.W. Adams "A Trial Estimation of Classic Maya Palace Populations at Uaxactun" p. 285-296 (see item 601)
J. Eric S. Thompson " 'Canals' of the Rio Calendaria Basin, Campeche, Mexico" p. 297-302 (see item 674)
Dennis E. Puleston "Intersite Areas in the Vicinity of Tikal and Uaxactun" p. 303-311 (see item 763)
Norman Hammond "The Distribution of Late Classic Maya Major Ceremonial Centres in the Central Area" p. 313-334 (see item 631)
René Millon "The study of Urbanism at Teotihuacan, Mexico p. 335-362
George Cowgill: Quantitative Studies of Urbanization at Teotihuacan" p. 363-396
Jeremy A. Sabloff and others "Trade and Power in Postclassic Yucatan: Initial Obervations" p. 397-416 (see item 771)
Gordon R. Willey "The Classic Maya Hiatus: a 'Rehearsal' for the Collapse?" p. 417-430
John P. Molloy and William L. Rathje "Sexploitation among the Late Classic Maya" p. 431-444 (see item 661)
Barbara J. Price "The Burden of the *Cargo*: Ethnographic Models and Archaeological Inference" p. 445-466 (see item 666). [HvW]

634. Hartung, Horst. Alte Stadt in Mexiko: Monte Alban (Deutsche Bauzeitung [Stuttgart, FRG] 2, 1974, p. 152-159, illus.)

Offers new insights in the architectural planning. Proposes a developmental sequence based on compositional aspects of space and volume. [HvW]

635. Hellmuth, Nicholas M. comp. The Olmec civilization, art and archaeology: an introductory bibliography. Providence, R.I., Foundation for Latin American Anthropological Research, 1974. 1 v. (Various pagings) (Anthropological publication series, 3)

636. The iconography of Middle American sculpture. N.Y., The Metropolitan Museum of Art, 1973. 167 p., bibl., illus., maps, tables.

Contains the following symposium papers presented Oct. 1970 on occasion of the Museum's exhibition "Before Cortés" and is the companion volume to the Catalogue (see *HLAS 33:657*):
Michael D. Coe "The Iconology of Olmec Art" p. 1-12
Ignacio Bernal "Stone Reliefs in the Dainzú Area" p. 13-23
George Kubler "Iconographic Aspects of Architectural Profiles at Teotihuacan and in Mesoamerica" p. 24-39
Gordon F. Ekholm "The Eastern Gulf Coast" p. 41-51
J. Eric S. Thompson "Maya Rulers of the Classic Period and the Divine Right of Kings" p. 52-71
Henry B. Nicholson "The Late Pre-Hispanic Central Mexican (Aztec) Iconographic System" p. 72-97
Peter T. Furst "West Mexican Art: Secular or Sacred?" p. 98-133
Haberland Wolfgang "Stone Sculpture from Southern Central America" p. 134-152
Gordon R. Willey "Mesoamerican Art and Iconography and the Integrity of the Mesoamerican Ideological System" p. 153-162
George Kubler "Science and Humanism among Americanists" p. 163-167. [HvW]

637. Ivanoff, Pierre. Monuments of civilization: Maya. Foreword by Miguel Angel Asturias. N.Y., Madison Square Press [and] Grosset & Dunlap, 1973. 190 p., plates, tables.

Somewhat pedestrian photographic survey of Maya ceremonial centers. Text is sprinkled with eccentricities and errors (e.g., Dos Pilas is labeled Dos Pozos). Published in Italian as *Città Maya* by Arnoldo Mondadori Editore. [REWA]

638. Kampen, Michael Edwin. The sculptures of El Tajín, Veracruz, Mexico. Gainesville, Univ. of Florida Press, 1972. 195 p., bibl., illus., plates.

Detailed interpretative study of sculptural techniques, decorative forms, style characteristics, and iconography of the monumental sculptures and numerous architectural reliefs which depict mainly sequences of sacrificial and pulque ceremonies and scroll patterns, accompanied by a descriptive catalogue with excellent line drawings. [HvW]

639. Kendall, Aubyn. The art of pre-columbian Mexico: an annotated bibliography of works in English. Austin, Univ. of Texas at Austin, Institute of Latin American Studies, 1973. 115 p., bibl. (Guides and bibliographies series, 5)

Includes 653 items with brief annotations and value judgments as well as illustrations of Mexican pottery in the Museum of the Institute of Latin American Studies at the Univ. of Texas, Austin. [HvW]

640. Keshishian, John M. Reproduction of Mayan stelae using fast-curing RTV silicones (EJ, 51:3, Sept. 1972, p. 172-175, plates)

Significantly improved method of reproducing sculptured surfaces. [REWA]

641. Kirkby, Anne V.T. The use of land and water resources in the past and present Valley of Oaxaca, Mexico. v. 1, Prehistory and human ecology of the Valley of Oaxaca. Kent V. Flannery, General Editor. Ann Arbor, Univ. of Michigan, 1973. 174 p., bibl., illus., maps (Memoirs of the Museum of Anthropology, 5)

Based on present population density, settlement patterns, area of agricultural land, and archaeological evidence, a model is presented for prehispanic developmental stages between 1300 BC and AD 900. Includes Spanish summary and appendices. [HvW]

642. Krickeberg, Walter. Altmexikanische Kulturen: Mit einem Anhang über die Kunst Altmexikos von Gerdt Kutscher. Berlin, FRG, Safari-Verlag, 1971. 644 p., illus., maps, plates.

Reprinting of the original edition of 1956, see *HLAS 20:55*. [REWA]

643. Kurjack, Edward B. Prehistoric lowland Maya community and social organization: a case study at Dzibilchaltun, Yucatan, Mexico. New Orleans, La., Tulane Univ., Middle American Research Institute, 1974. 105 p., illus., maps, tables (Publication, 38)

Settlement pattern study of medium-sized northern site. Kurjack discusses the history of such studies in the Maya lowlands. Evidence is presented for social stratification and barrio and neighborhood divisions. The core of Dzib. is three square kilometers and is interpreted as a "preindustrial city." E. Wyllys Andrews V wrote the preface and in it abandons the 12.9 correlation and the black-on-cream period at the site. [REWA]

644. Lamberg-Karlovsky, C.C. and Jeremy A. Sabloff. The rise and fall of civilizations: modern archaeological approaches to ancient cultures: selected readings. Menlo Park, Calif., Cummings, 1974. 485 p., bibl., illus., maps.

Contains the following reprinted articles on Mesoamerican archaeology:

Richard S. MacNeish "Speculations about how and why Food Production and Village Life Developed in the Tehuacan Valley, Mexico" p. 43-54 (see *HLAS 35:585*)
Michael D. Coe and Kent V. Flannery "Microenvironments and Mesoamerican Prehistory" p. 55-63 (see *HLAS 27:205* and *HLAS 35:530*)
Kent V. Flannery "The Olmec and the Valley of Oaxaca: a Model for Interregional Interaction in Formative Times" p. 64-83 (see *HLAS 31:1064*)
William L. Rathje "The Origin and Development of Lowland Classic Maya Civilization" p. 84-94 (see *HLAS 33:593*)
Gordon R. Willey "Commentary on the Emergence of Civilization in the Maya Lowlands" p. 95-103 (see *HLAS 33:555*)
Gordon R. Willey and Demitri B. Shimkin "The Collapse of Classic Maya Civilization in the Southern Lowlands: a Symposium Summary Statement" p. 104-118 (see *HLAS 33:612*)
William T. Sanders "Hydraulic Agriculture, Economic Symbiosis, and the Evolution of States in Central Mexico" p. 119-133 (see *HLAS 35:608*)
Gordon R. Willey "Precolumbian Urbanism: the Central Mexican Highlands and the Lowland Maya" p. 134-144
Geoffrey W. Conrad "Toward a Systemic View of Mesoamerican Prehistory: Inter-Site Sociopolitical Organization" p. 145-156 (first printing)
Gordon R. Willey "The Early Great Styles and the Rise of Pre-Columbian Civilizations" p. 157-169. [HvW]

645. Lees, Susan H. Sociopolitical aspects of canal irrigation in the Valley of Oaxaca. Ann Arbor, Univ. of Michigan, Museum of Anthropology, 1973. 141 p., bibl., illus., maps, tables (Memoirs of the Museum of Anthropology, 6)

Summary of irrigation practices and water use in Prehispanic times (p. 89-97). Includes Spanish abstract. [HvW]

646. Litvak King, Jaime. Algunas observaciones acera del clásico de Xochicalco, México (UNAM/AA, 11, 1974, p. 9-17)

Assessment of the importance of classic Xochiacalco in the Teotihuacan dominated network of trade routes. Their modification, after the fall of Teotihuacan, bypassed Xochicalco and led to its abandonment. [HvW]

647. ———. Los patrones de cambio de estadío en el Valle de Xochicalco (UNAM/AA, 10, 1973, p. 93-110)

Theoretical-methodological discussion of the established eight-phase sequence. Proposes, on the basis of quantitative data analyses, an earlier beginning and a later end of the classic period in this region. [HvW]

648. ——— and **Noemi Castillo Tejero** eds. Religión en Mesoamérica. México, Sociedad Mexicana de Antropología 1972. 632 p., bibl., illus. (Mesa Redonda, 12)

Includes 91 papers, presented at the Round Table Conference, Cholula, Mex., 1972, dealing mainly with prehispanic religious concepts and their manifestation in art, architecture, rituals, funerary practices, etc., and also covering a wide range of related topics. [HvW]

649. Lumholtz, Carl. Unknown Mexico: a record of five years' exploration among the tribes of the Western Sierra Madre; in the tierra caliente of Tepic and Jalisco; and among the Tarascos of Michoacan. With a new introduction by Evon Z. Vogt. N.Y., AMS Press *for* Harvard Univ., Peabody Museum of Archaeology and Ethnology, 1973. 2 v. (530, 487 p.), facsims., fold. map, illus., maps, plates, tables.

Reprint of the 1902 ed., a classic report containing the first illustrations of West Mexican shaft tomb figures. [HvW]

650. McVicker, Donald E. Variation in protohistoric Maya settlement pattern (SAA/AA, 39:4, Oct. 1974, p. 546-556, maps, tables)

Late prehistoric site patterns in the Chiapas highlands reflect two systems, one internally and the other externally oriented. McVicker presents data and suggests that early classic lowland Maya fell into the first category and in the late classic changed to the second. [REWA]

651. Márquez, Pedro José. Sobre lo bello en general y dos monumentos de arquitectura mexicana: Tajín y Xochicalco. Estudio y edición de Justino Fernández. México, UNAM, 1972. 208 p., plates.

Biobibliographical study of P. J. Márquez, S.J. (1741-1820) by J. Fernández, a facsimile (1804, in Italian) and Spanish translation of descriptions of El Tajín and Xochicalco. Both are based on J. Antonio Alzate's 1785 and 1791 articles. [HvW]

652. Matos Moctezuma, Eduardo. Manuel Gamio y la arqueología mexicana (III/AI, 33:4, oct./dic. 1973, p. 959-965)

Reviews the contributions of one of the pioneers in Mexican archaeologic research. With English summary. [HvW]

653. Maudslay, Alfred Percival. Archaeology: biologia Centrali-Americana. Introduction by Francis Robicsek. Appendix by J.T. Goodman. N.Y., Mulpatron Publishing Co., 1974. 6 v. in 4 (Unpaged, unpaged, 38, 149 p.) illus., fold. maps, maps, plates, tables (Contributions to the knowledge of the fauna and flora of Mexica and Central America)

Excellently reproduced facsimile ed. of Maudslay's indispensable and monumental work originally published in 1889-1902. The quality of the photographs, drawings, and the utility of Goodman's tables all make for enduring value to Mayanists and Mesoamericanists. Emphasis is on monumental acrhitecture and inscriptions of Copan, Quirigua, Yaxchilan, Chichen Itza, Tikal, Palenque. Long out of print and unavailable. Pt. 1 of this reprint comprises the original v. 1/2; pt. 2 includes the original v. 3/4; pt. 5 corresponds to v. 5 and pt. 6 to v. 6. V. 1 consists of 119 maps and plates; v. 2 of 98 maps and plates; v. 3 of 82 maps and plates; v. 4 of 93 maps and plates; v. 5 of 38 p. of text; v. 6 of the Appendix, 149 p. long, and 133 tables. [REWA]

654. Mendoza, Angela. Anfänge der Urbanisierung in Michoacan (*in* International Congress of Americanists, XXXVIII, Stuttgart-München, FRG, 1968. Verhandlungen [see *HLAS 33:510*] v. 4, p. 27-32)

Outlines the elements which contributed to urbanization of the Tarascan capital Tzintzuntzan. [HvW]

655. Meyer, Karl E. The plundered past. N.Y., Atheneum Press, 1973. 353 p., illus., plates.

Extraordinarily important book with the first systematic study of the international illegal traffic in prehistoric art. Ch. 1 comments directly on Maya sculpture and other artifacts stolen from countries of origin. Appendix A is a list of looted sites in the Peten district of Guatemala with notes on the present whereabouts of the stelae. Valuable collection of the pertinent legislation, both US and foreign, and of the international agreements relating to antiquities. Exposes the world of shabby subterfuges of art dealers, collectors, and scholars of ambivalent ethics. [REWA]

656. Miller, Arthur G. The iconography of the painting in the Temple of the Diving God, Tulum, Quintana Roo, Mexico: the twisted cords (*in* Hammond, Norman ed. Mesoamerican archaeology: new approaches [see item 633] p. 167-186, illus.)

Interpretation of a Tulum mural twisted cord motif as

representing an umbilical cord. In turn, the cord represents several important concepts including lineage, and a mystical connection of the human with the supernatural world. Miller traces the symbolism back to Izapa times. [REWA]

657. _____. The mural painting of Teotihuacan. Drawings by Felipe Dávalos G. Appendix by R. Littmann. Washington, Dumbarton Oaks Research Library and Collections, Harvard Univ. Trustees, 1973. 193 p., facsims., illus., plates, tables.

A comprehensive collection of the polychrome wall paintings, presented in their architectural contexts and discussed in terms of their pictorial composition and style characteristics. Littmann deals with the physical aspects. Excellent photographs, many in color, with accompanying line drawings and reconstructions constitutethe bulk of the volume which represents a primary source for the study of Teotihuacan art and iconography. [HvW]

658. Millon, Clara. Painting, writing, and polity in Teotihuacan, Mexico (SAA/AA, 38:3, July 1973, p. 294-314, illus.)

Interpretation of the "Tassel headdress glyph" as hierarchical insignia of leadership. [HvW]

659. Millon, René ed. Urbanization at Teotihuacan, Mexico. v. 1, The Teotihuacan map: pt. 1, by René Millon; pt. 2, by René Millon, R. Bruce Dewitt, and George L. Cogwill. Austin, Univ. of Texas Press, 1973. 154 p., bibl., fold. maps, illus., plates.

The first volume of a series in preparation contains detailed photogrammetric maps of the ancient city, covering 38 sq. km. at a scale of 1:2000, based on extensive field surveys to determine the layout and maximum boundaries. Pt. 1 describes field procedures and contains architectural interpretations, various related topics, a phase-by-phase development of the city's expansion, and preliminary conclusions (which will be elaborated in v. 2). It is accompanied by large photographs of architectural and decorative features. Pt. 2 consists of three large fold-out maps (in pocket) and 147 pairs of maps (topographic field data with transparent overlays indicating interpretations). Includes indices. [HvW!]

660. Mitchell, Robert W.; James Reddell; Mark Rowland; and **David McKenzie.** Report on invertebrate zoology (The Museum Quarterly [The West Texas Museum Association, Lubbock] Oct./Dec. 1974, p. 6-11, illus.)

Zoologists working in several Yucatec caves found ancient pottery, an example of which is illustrated. [REWA]

661. Molloy, John P. and **William L. Rathje.** Sexploitation among the late classic Maya (*in* Hammond, Norman ed. Mesoamerican archaeology: new approaches [see item 633] p. 431-444, map)

The core/buffer zone model of Rathje (*HLAS 33:593*) is summarized, elaborated, and discussed. Buffer zone centers were able to compete with core centers after the hiatus. Core centers attempted to retain control by warfare and by less expansive royal marriages. An examination is made of the exceedingly detailed dynastic information now available on Tikal, Yaxchilan, Copan, Quirigua, and Altar de Sacrificios which seems to support the thesis that Tikal used this means to try to dominate the whole lowlands. [REWA]

662. Moser, Christopher L. Human decapitation in ancient Mesoamerica. Washington, Dumbarton Oaks Research Library and Collections, Harvard Univ. Trustees, 1973. 72 p., bibl., illus., tables (Studies in precolumbian art and archaeology, 11)

Compilation of abundant archaeological and ethnohistorical data, from the Formative to Contact, of decapitation scenes, severed, shrunken, and trophy heads, with a discussion of their sociopolitical and religious significance. Seven major aspects of the "head complex" are distinguished, which indicates that the importance of this pan-Mesoamerican trait is far greater than previously recognized. [HvW]

663. Nowotny, Karl A. Beiträge zur Geschichte des Weltbildes: Farben und Weltrichtungen. Horn-Wien, Austria, Verlag Ferdinand Berger, 1970. 263 p., bibl., illus., map (Wiener Beiträge zur Kulturgeschichte und Linguistik, 17)

A compendium, drawn from a vast store of sources, concerning the connections between colors and world directions in the Orient, classical antiquity, Mexico, Central and North America. An indispensable reference for comparative Old and New World cosmological studies. [HvW]

664. Palerm, Angel. Agricultura y sociedad en Mesoamérica. México, Editorial Porrúa, 1972. 198 p.

Contains six articles, published 1954-70, discussing theories of Asian hydraulic societies and their relevance for investigations of the development of Mesoamerican agricultural and civilization. See also William P. Mitchell "The Hydraulic Hypothesis: A Reappraisal" in *Current Anthropology* (14:5, Dec. 1973, p. 532-534). [HvW]

665. _____. Obras hidráulicas prehispánicas en el sistema lacustre del Valle de México. México, INAH, 1973. 244 p., bibl., maps.

Compilation of data from post-conquest literary sources pertaining to late prehispanic water control systems with reference to their political and agricultural context. [HvW]

666. Price, Barbara J. The burden of the

cargo: ethnographical models and archaeological inference (*in* Hammond, Norman ed. Mesoamerican archaeology: new approaches [see item 633] p. 445-465)

Lengthy and detailed discussion of the use of ethnographic analogy and the theoretical implications of applying the cargo system of present day to the archaeological past. Sophisticated in logic. Price argues that past cargo systems have been class-oriented and contributed to economic status for elite class benefit. [REWA]

667. Reinhold, Robert. Theft and vandalism: an archaeological disaster (UMUP/E, 15:4, Summer 1973, p. 2-6, plates)

Examination of the various facets of the illegal export of Maya and other antiquities. For a thorough study of the contraband traffic in antiquities, see item 655. [REWA]

668. Rivera Dorado, Miguel. Hipótesis sobre relaciones entre Mesoamérica y el área andina septentrional (UM/REAA, 7:2, 1972, p. 19-31, map)

Outlines the methodology for assessment of north to south diffusion of Mesoamerican traits and of their selective regional adaptation, attributed to sporadic sea voyages from Guatemala to Ecuador and Colombia. [HvW]

669. Robicsek, Francis. Copan: home of the Mayan gods. Foreword by Gordon Ekholm. N.Y., Museum of the American Indian, Heye Foundation, 1972. 168 p., bibl., illus., maps, plates, tables.

Beautiful photographic study of Copan sculpture and architecture. Excellently produced (with 297 color plates! and 123 black-and-white illustrations). Some inaccuracies in the informally written text and captions, but these detract little from a major accomplishment in recording and publishing much at Copan which had never before been adequately recorded or available. Valuable and exhaustive bibliography on the site. [REWA]

670. Sanders, William T. and Joseph W. Michaels. Kaminaljuyu. State College, Pennsylvania State Univ., Dept. of Anthropology, 1971. 1 v. (Unpaged) fold. map.

Topographic map of the major site located on the edges of Guatemala City. [REWA]

671. Simposio Internacional sobre Posibles Relaciones Transatlánticas Precolombinas, *I, Las Palmas, Spain, 1971.* Comunicaciones. Madrid, Patronato de la Casa de Colón, 1971. 572 p., bibl., fold. map, illus., maps, plates, tables (Anuario de Estudios Atlánticos, 17)

Entire issue of *Anuario de Estudios Atlánticos* (Madrid, No. 17, 1971) devoted to the Simposio which was directed by Luis Pericot and José Alcina. Contents are:
Carmelo García Cabrera "Interrelaciones entre las Faunas Marinas de las Antillas y Canarias" p. 37-55
Joaquín Meco and Emiliano Aguirre: Las Canarias en la Filogenia y Migración de Moluscos Cuaternarios" p. 57-63
Carmelo Lisón Tolosana "Difusión y Evolución: Estado de la Cuestión en Antropología" p. 67-94
Lionel Balout "Canarias y Africa en los Tiempos Prehistóricos y Protohistóricos" p. 95-102
José Alcina Franch "El (Formativo) Americano a la Luz de los Posibles Influjos Recibidos por el Atlántico" p. 103-149
Claudio Esteva Fábregat "El Circummediterráneo y sus Relaciones con la América Prehispánica: ¿Difusión o Paralelismo?" p. 151-197
Alfredo Jiménez Núñez "Matrimonio entre Hermanos: ¿ difusión o Paralelismo?" p. 199-217
Juan Bosch Millares "Problemas de Paleopatología Osea en los Indígenas Prehispánicos de Canarias: su Similitud con Casos Americanos" p. 221-244
Juan Comas Camps "La Supuesta Difusión Trasatlántica de la Trepanación Prehistórica" p. 245-261
Manuel Pellicer Catalán and Pilar Acosta "Estratigrafías Arqueológicas Canarias: la Cueva del Barranco de la Arena, Tenerife" p. 265-279
Antonio Beltrán Martínez "El Arte Rupestre Canario y las Relaciones Atlánticas" p. 281-306
Federico Pérez Castro "La Inscripción Fenicio-Cananea de Paraíba, Brasil: La Polémica Gordon/Friedrich-Cross, Estado de la Cuestión" p. 307-333
Manuel Ballesteros Gaibrois "La Idea de la Atlántida en el Pensamiento de los Diversos Tiempos y su Valoración como Realidad Geográfica" p. 337-346
Juan Schobinger "El Mito Platónico de la Atlántida, Frente a la Teoría de las Vinculaciones Trasatlánticas Prehistóricas entre el Viejo Mundo y América" p. 347-362
Johanna Schmidt "Jenseits der Sauler des Herakles" p. 365-368
Raymond Mauny "Hypothèses Concernant les Rélations Précolombiennes entre l'Afrique et l'Amerique" p. 369-389
Elías Serra Rafols "La Navegación Primitiva en el Atlántico Africano" p. 391-399
Juan Vernet "Textos Arabes de Viajes por el Atlántico" p. 401-427
Francisco Morales Padrón "Los Descubrimientos en los Siglos XIV y XV, y los Archipiélagos Atlánticos" p. 429-465
Demetrio Ramos Pérez "Los Contactos Trasatlánticos Decisivos, como Precedentes del Viaje de Colon" p. 467-532
Antonio Rumeu de Armas "Cristóbal Colón, Cronista de las expediciones Atlánticas p. 533-560
Enrique Marco Dorta "Viajes Accidentales a América" p. 561-572. [HvW]

Spence, Michael W. Residential practices and the distribution of skeletal traits in Teotihuacan, Mexico. See item 2016.

672. Stewart, T. Dale. Human skeletal remains from Dzibilchaltun, Yucatan, Mexico, with a review of cranial deformity types in the Maya region

(TUMARI/P, 31, 1974, p. 199-225, illus.)

Reports on the 10 skulls from Dzibilchaltun, surveys the literature on Maya skull deformation, and suggests cultural patterns perhaps responsible for the various classes of deformities. [REWA]

673. Stingl, Miloslav. Tajemstvi indianskych pyramid. 2. ed. rev. Praha, Orbis, 1974. 277 p., illus., maps, plates.

A description of Mayan art and architecture, and the stories of the discoveries of the Mayan monuments, based on the authors' researches and travels. A postscript includes a discussion of Mayology and a short description of the current state of research in Mayan studies in the socialist countries. [A.R. Navon]

674. Thompson, J. Eric S. "Canals" of the Rio Candelaria basin, Campeche, Mexico (*in* Hammond, Norman ed. Mesoamerican archaeology: new approaches [see item 633] p. 297-302, map)

Argues from ethnohistorical evidence that "canals" detected by Siemens and Puleston were actually fish ponds. Important. [REWA]

675. Trautmann, Wolfgang. Die Agrarregionen Mexicos vor der Conquista (MV/BA, 20, 1972, p. 173-198, map)

Maps the main production areas for maize, chianhuauhtli (Salvia and amaranth), maguey-nopal, chile, cotton and cacao, and comments on their significance for trade and tribute. [HvW]

676. _____. Formen der Landnutzung im Präkolonialen Mexiko (JGSWGL, 10, 1973, p. 1-15)

Reviews prehispanic agricultural systems and distinguishes two methods of construction of chinampas. Includes Spanish summary. [HvW]

677. Tschohl, Peter and Herbert J. Nickel. Catálogo arqueológico y etnohistórico de Puebla-Tlaxcala, México. v. 1, A-C. Puebla, Mex., Fundación Alemana para le Investigación Científica, 1972. 573 p., bibl., illus., maps, tables (Proyecto Puebla-Tlaxcala)

Alphabetical (A-C) site catalogue with detailed descriptions of archaeological remains, comparative notes, references, interpretations and ethnohistorical data. Prefaced by a 150 p. introduction (in Spanish and German) describing organization and methodology. [HvW]

678. Turner, B.L. Prehistoric intensive agriculture in the Mayan lowlands (AAAS/S, 185:4146, 12 July 1974, p. 118-124, illus., maps)

Data developed during the 1973 Rio Bec Ecological Project is presented as evidence that the Maya in that zone began practising various forms of intensive agriculture perhaps as early as 400 AD. Hillside terracing, field walls, swamp (bajo) drainage, and the use of raised fields are all extensive during the late classic and correlate with high density population. Crucial. [REWA]

679. Willey, Gordon R. The classic Maya hiatus: a rehearsal for the collapse? (*in* Hammond, Norman ed. Mesoamerican Archaeology: new approaches [see item 633] p. 417-430)

Discussion of the 60-80 year gap in Maya historical records on stelae. Cultural change and reorientation followed the hiatus. During the hiatus there was limited population decline. Illuminating comparisons between late classic collapse and the hiatus. A causal factor in both events is presented as being the severance of symbiotic relationships between the Maya lowlands and the rest of Mesoamerica. [REWA]

680. Zehnder, Wiltraut. La dualidad en el mundo prehispánico (ARMEX, 20:173, 1975, p. 1-92, bibl., illus.)

Illustrates a wide range of dualistic manifestations in clay and stone sculpture from Mexico (bicephalous figures, life and death masks, fertility themes, etc.) and discusses their magico-religious significance. Text in Spanish and English. [HvW]

EXCAVATIONS AND ARTIFACTS

681. Acosta, Jorge R. Nuevos descubrimientos en Zaachila, 1971 (INAH/B, 2:3, oct./dic. 1972, p. 22-31, illus.)

Exploration of two masonry tombs containing abundant early Mixtec pottery and an elaborately embossed gold disc with turquoise mosaic. [HvW]

682. Adams, Richard E.W. Fine Orange pottery as a source of ethnological information (UCARF/C, 18, 1973, p. 1-9)

Review of distributional and chronological evidence; interpretation of the major scene categories; comments on glyphic notations; discussion of Thompson's Putun Maya hypothesis. [REWA]

683. _____ ed. Preliminary reports on archaeological investigations in the Río Bec Area, Campeche, Mexico 9TUMARI/P, 31, 1974, p. 103-146, illus., maps)

Contains short summary papers from the 1969-71 work. Ingolf Vogeler "The Cultural Ecological Setting of Southeastern Campeche;" Joseph W. Ball "A Regional Ceramic Sequence for the Rio Bec Area;" D.F. Potter "Architectural Style at Becan during the Maya Late Classic Period;" D.L. Webster "The Fortifications of Becan, Campeche, Mexico;" Irwin Rovner "Implications of the Lithic Analysis at Becan;" Jack D. Eaton "Chicanna: an Elite Center in the Rio Bec Region;" P.M. Thomas, Jr. "Prehistoric Settlement at Becan: a Preliminary report." The Ceramic sequence runs from Mamon-like pottery (ca 500 BC) to early postclassic (1200 AD). Fortifications are at least early classic in date and possibly late preclassic. Teotihuacan influence is strong in early classic. [REWA]

684. Alvarez de Williams, Anita. Five rock art sites in Baja California south of the 29th parallel (Quarterly [Pacific Coast Archaeological Society, Costa Mesa, Calif.] 9:4, Oct. 1973, p. 37-46, illus.)

Description of cliff paintings and petroglyphs with human, animal, and geometric motifs. [HvW]

685. Andrews, E. Wyllys, IV and **Irwin Rovner.** Archaeological evidence on social stratification and commerce in the northern Maya lowlands: two mason's tool kits from Muna and Dzibilchaltun, Yucatan (TUMARI/P, 31, 1974, p. 81-102, illus.)

Specialty tools were found in two caches, including banana-shaped smoothers, pestles, chisels, and abraders. [REWA]

686. _____; **M.P. Simmons; E.S. Wing;** and **E. Wyllys Andrews, V.** Excavation of an early shell midden on Isla Cancun, Quintana Róo, Mexico (TUMARI/P, 31, 1974, p. 147-197, illus.)

Account of a late preclassic midden. Chiefly valuable for its sample of regionalized Chicanel sphere ceramics, and for the sample of marine food resources. Appendix by J.M. Andrews. [REWA]

687. L'art olmeque: source des arts classiques du Méxique. Paris, Musée Rodin, 1972. 1 v. (Unpaged) plates.

Includes 53 illustrations of Olmec stone and clay sculptures and objects from classic Veracruz, Monte Alban, and Mezcala, in Mexican collections. [HvW]

688. Ball, Joseph W. A Teotihuacan-style cache from the Maya Lowlands (AIA/A, 27:1, Jan./March 1974, p. 2-9, illus., maps)

Well-illustrated article showing spectacular Teotihuacan vessel and hollow figurine containing smaller figurines found at Becan. Comparisons with similar caches from Teotihuacan itself. [REWA]

689. _____ and **Irwin Rovner.** Protohistoric Putun trade patterns: evidence from two graves at Atasta, Campeche, Mexico (SSC/K, 3:2, 1973, p. 40-46)

Reassessment of two grave lots from Atasta proved the ceramics of both to be one variety and the obsidian blades in both graves to have come from the same core indicating contemporaneity. Inferences are drawn to the effect that the Putun (at Xicalango) indeed operated as middlemen in highland-lowland trade. [REWA]

690. Baudez, Claude F. and **Pierre Becquelin.** Archéologie de Los Naranjos, Honduras. México, Mission Archéologique et Ethnologique Française au Mexique, 1973. 438 p., fold. maps, illus., maps, tables (Etudes mesoaméricaines, 2)

A major site report and interpretation of data from the site of Los Naranjos on the southeast Mesoamerican frontier. Sequence runs from an Olmec-related phase (800 BC) to an early postclassic phase (to 1250 AD). Mound building and major defensive ditches characterize and distinguish the site from middle preclassic times on. Important implications for the role of warfare in the rise of Mesoamerican civilizations. Well-illustrated, thorough description, careful interpretation. [REWA]

691. Becquelin, Pierre and **Claude F. Baudez.** Recherches archéologiques a Toniná, Chiapas, Mexique (SA/J, 61, 1973, p. 255-257, illus.)

Summary of the 1973 second season at the important highland site of Toniná. See item 692 for more complete summary. [REWA]

692. _____ and _____. Toniná: une cité maya de l'âge classique (ARCHEO, 80, mars 1975, p. 10-22, illus., maps)

Excavations in 1972-73 revealed a sequence of late preclassic through early postclassic at this highland Maya city. All of the characteristics of lowland civilization were found, but are stylistically distinct. Stelae, for example, are freestanding statues. Toniná may have been brought down by a quick raid. A short postclassic occupation followed. Well-illustrated and important. [REWA]

693. Beecher, Graciella and **Robert Beecher.** Danzantes engraved on two jade placques (AIA/A, 27:2, April 1974, p. 130-132, illus.)

Description of two Olmec carvings reportedly acquired near Monte Alban in 1898. John F. Scott (*Archaeology*, 27:4, Oct. 1974, p. 281) declares them to be fakes. [HvW]

694. Bernal, Ignacio. Esculturas asociadas del Valle de Oaxaca. [Ilustraciones por] Andy Seuffert. México, INAH, 1973. 26 p., bibl., plates (Corpus antiquitatum americanensium, 6)

Excellent drawings of relief carvings now mostly incorporated in walls of churches and houses at Macuilxochitl and Tlacochahuaya. Consists of a portfolio of 26 p. and 13 plates with explanatory text in Spanish and English. [HvW]

695. Boggs, Stanley H. Pre-Maya costumes and coiffures (OAS/AM, 25:2, Feb. 1973, p. 19-24, plates)

Analysis of the Bolinas style of Olmec-affiliated figurines from Salvador. Suggested uses were in curing and in public narration. [REWA]

696. Brockington, Donald L. Archaeological investigations at Miahuatlan, Oaxaca. Nashville, Tenn., Vanderbilt Univ., 1973. 89 p., bibl., illus. (Publications in anthropology, 7)

Analysis of Mixtec pottery at Miahuatlan and adjacent coastal sites with a reevaluation of origin and spread of the Mixtec ceramic tradition in Oaxaca. [HvW]

697. _____ **and J. Robert Long.** The Oaxaca Coast Project reports: pt. 2. Nashville, Tenn., Vanderbilt Univ., 1974. 98 p., illus., maps (Publications in anthropology, 9)

Continuation of pt. 1, see item 698. Brockington describes the 124 individual sites with maps of some, and artifactual illustration. Long deals with the late classic and early postclassic ceramics, describing them by the type-variety system. Long interprets the presence of fine wares (orange, black and grey) as evidence of a Maya migration from Tabasco to southeast Oaxaca about the end of the late classic period. [REWA]

698. _____; **Maria Jorrin; and J. Robert Long.** The Oaxaca Coast Project reports: pt. 1. Nashville, Tenn., Vanderbilt Univ., 1974. 97 p., illus., maps (Publications in anthropology, 8)

Systematic reconnaissance of the coast is reported in this, pt. 1, pt. 2 (item 697) and in item 696. Brockington gives the general aims and accomplishments of the project. 124 sites were located, 13 tested, 48 carved monuments found, and a long ceramic sequence established. Jorrin describes the carved monuments in detail, and Long and Brockington deal descriptively with the stone artifacts. Valuable. [REWA]

699. Charlton, Thomas H. Population trends in the Teotihuacan Valley, AD 1400-1969 (World Archaeology [London] 4:1, 1972, p. 106-123)

Aztec pottery styles, contrary to previous assumptions, continue into the 17th century, while post-conquest population decline was gradual rather than dramatic. [HvW]

700. *Comunicaciones del Proyecto Puebla-Tlaxcala.* Fundación Alemana para la Investigación Científica. No. 9, 1973- . Puebla, Mex.

Includes the following articles on archaeology:
Joerg Aufdermauer, "Aspectos de la Cronologia del Preclásico en la Cuenca de Puebla-Tlaxcala: Nueva Evidencia de Moyotzingo, Pue.," p. 11-24 (reprinted in *Katunob,* 8:3, Feb. 1973, p. 11-24)
Angel García Cook "Algunos Descubrimientos en Tlalancaleca, Edo. de Puebla," p. 25-34 (reprinted in *Katunob,* 8:3, Feb. 1973, p. 25-34)
Abascal M. Rafael "Un Monolito en Cacaxtla, Edo. de Tlaxcala," p. 35-38, fold. map.
Angel García Cook "Una Punta Acanalada en el Estado de Tlaxcala, México," p. 39-42, fold. map. [HvW]

701. _____. _____. No. 10, 1974- Puebla, Mex.

Articles on archaeology:
Carmen Aguilera "La Estela-Elemento 7—de Tlalancaleca" p. 1-4
Angel García Cook "Una Secuencia Cultural para Tlaxcala" p. 5-22 (outlines evidence of settlements, ceramics, and exterior relationships for seven cultural phases, 1700? BC-AD 1519)
Angel García Cook and Raziel Mora López "Tetepetla: un Sitio Fortificado del 'Clásico' en Tlaxcala" p. 23-30. [HvW]

702. _____. _____. No. 11, 1974- Puebla, Mex.

Contains thefollowing articles on archaeology:
Klaus Heine "Sobre la Disposición y Antigüedad de las Terrazas de la Ladera Poniente del Cerro Xochitecatl, Tlaxcala, México" p. 5-6
Noemí Castillo Tejero "La Llamada Cerámica Policroma Mixteca no es un Producto Mixteco" p. 7-10
Peter J. Schmidt "San Luis Coyotzingo, Puebla: una Pirámide del Post-Clásico y un Nuevo Chacmool" p. 11-18
Raziel Mora and Jonathan Guevara "Hallazgo de un 'Yugo' de Piedra, Liso, en el Estado de Tlaxcala" p. 19-26
Angel García Cook and Leonor Merino C. "Malacates de Tlaxcala: Intento de una Secuencia Evolutiva" p. 27-36
Franz Tichy "Explicación de las Redes de Poblaciones y Terrenos como Testimonio de la Ocupación y Planificación del Altiplano Central en el México Antiguo" p. 41-52. [Hvw]

703. Corona Núñez, José. Estudios antropológicos en el occidente de México. Xalapa, Mex., Univ. Veracruzana, Escuela de Antropología, 1972. 85 p., bibl., illus. (Memoria, 1)

Reprint of seven articles on West Mexican archaeology, ethnohistory, and ethnology, published 1952-71. [Hvw]

704. DeBloois, Evan I. Archaeological researches in Northern Campeche, Mexico. Ogden, Utah, Weber State College, Dept. of Sociology and Anthropology, 1970. 119 p., illus., maps, plates, tables.

Reports on work at the Chenes sites of Santa Rosa Xtampak and Dzibilnocac, with special emphasis on the chultuns at the former site. Apparent lack of early classic at both sites, after a strong preclassic and a following late classic, is of special interest. [REWA]

705. Diehl, Richard A. *ed.* Studies of ancient Tollan: a report of the University of Missouri Tula Archaeological Project. Columbia, Univ. of Missouri, 1974. 220 p., bibl., illus., maps, tables (Monographs in anthropology, 1)

Contains 14 chapters by various participants and a summary by R.A. Diehl. Covers excavations and surveys 1970-72 to complement INAH's investigations and to clarify chronology, settlement and community patterns, economy, ceramics, social and political organization, and religion. "The chapters are tentative and preliminary statements on their respective topics and (the Summary and Conclusions) are equally tentative." [HvW]

706. _____; **Roger Lomas**; and **Jack T. Wynn**. Toltec trade with Central America, new light and evidence (AIA/A, 27:3, July 1974, p. 182-187, illus.)

A cache in a dwelling at Tula contained complete plumbate and Papagayo (Nicoya polychrome) vessels, indicative of trade with Costa Rica and Nicaragua. [HvW]

707. Digby, Adrian. Maya jades. London, Trustees of the British Museum, Dept. of Ethnography [and] Univ. of Oxford Press, 1972. 32 p., bibl., illus., plates.

Short study of Maya jades in the British Museum set in the perspective of technological and functional interpretation. [REWA]

708. Eaton, Jack D. Jaina figurines (Museum [Museum of Science, Miami, Fla.] 6:10, Feb. 1975, p. 15-18, 23, illus.)

Eaton characterizes the spectacular figurines from the burials on Jaina Island. Jaina was not just a burial island, but has major structures. Eaton suggests that it may have been a cult center for the Moon Goddess, Ix Chel. [REWA]

709. _____. Shell celts from coastal Yucatan, Mexico. (TAS/B, 45, 1974, p. 197-208, illus., map, table)

On the coasts of Yucatan, shell celts replaced their stone counterparts elsewhere and were used from middle preclassic into early colonial times. A workshop site of middle preclassic times was located. Good illustrations showing manufacture techniques and probable use. [REWA]

710. Ekholm-Miller, Susanna. The Olmec rock carving at Xoc, Chiapas, Mexico. Provo, Utah, Brigham Young Univ., 1974. 28 p., illus., maps (New World Archaeological Foundation paper, 32)

Important publication of the only Olmec carving discovered so far in the Maya lowlands. The now-destroyed seven-foot man-bird was carved striding across a cliff face. Possibly La Venta horizon in date. [REWA]

711. Feldman, Lawrence H. Shells from afar: "Panamic" molluscs in Mayan sites (*in* Hammond, Norman ed. Mesoamerican archaeology: new approaches [see item 633] p. 129-133, tables)

Diagnostic marine shells from Maya sites are listed and compared to the distribution of the same species found in other Mesoamerican centers. [REWA]

712. Field, Frederick V. Prehispanic Mexican stamp designs. N.Y., Dover, 1974. 208 p., bibl., illus.

Impressions in natural size of 602 ceramic stamps in the author's collection, from Olmec to Aztec cultures, with commentaries on their symbolism. [HvW]

713. Fuente, Beatriz de la. Escultura monumental olmeca: catálogo. Con la colaboración de Nelly Gutiérrez Solana. México, UNAM, Instituto de Investigaciones Estéticas, 1973. 352 p., bibl., illus., plates (Cuadernos de historia del arte, 1)

Detailed descriptive catalogue of 248 Olmec stone sculptures from Veracruz and Tabasco, with line drawings and photographs. [HvW]

714. García Moll, Roberto. Rara muestra de cestería del preclásico medio (INAH/B, 2:3, oct./dic. 1972, p. 23-26, illus.)

Impression of a coiled basket fragment with polychrome layers, from Tlatilco. [HvW]

715. García Payón, José. Los enigmas de El Tajín: pt. 1, La ciudad sagrada; pt. 2, Chacmol en la apoteosis del pulque. México, INAH, 1973. 57 p., illus. (Col. Científica, 3. Arqueología)

Contains two articles: 1) a report on an architectural complex northeast of Tajín Chico, the layout of which is in the shape of a stepped fret (xicalcoliuhqui). Occurrences of this motif at El Tajín are discussed; and 2) an interpretation of the pulque ceremonies on panels of the South Ball Court. For detailed drawings see item 638. [HvW]

716. Gendrop, Paul. Nueva zona arqueológica cerca de San Felipe Los Alzati, Michoacan (BBAA, 25:1, 1972, p. 91-94, illus.)

Reconnaissance of a large, late postclassic, six stages high pyramid with stone sculptures. [HvW]

717. González Rul, Francisco. Sobre las minas de obsidiana del Cerro Pelón, Hidalgo (INAH/B, 2:3, oct./dic. 1972, p. 11-16, illus.)

Availability of good quality obsidian to the peoples in the Valley of Mexico resulted, from earliest times on, in extensive manufacture of artifacts, and is considered a contributing factor in the tardy development of metal tools. [HvW]

718. Grove, David C. San Pablo, Nexpa, and the early formative archaeology of Morelos, Mexico. Nashville, Tenn., Vanderbilt Univ., 1974. 88 p., illus., maps, tables (Publications in anthropology, 12)

Very important report giving data from Nexpa excavations which confirm the previous Morelos early formative sequence published by Grove (*HLAS 33:670*). Tolstoy and Paradis' revision of the Valley of Mexico formative sequence is also confirmed (*HLAS 33:773*). Grove sees diffusion of traits from South America into West Mexico about 1600 BC thence and into the central highlands. There is also interaction between West Mexico, the Gulf Coast, and the Central Highlands during the early formative. No evidence is seen for the origins of Olmec coastal culture in the highlands. A differential trade and status borrowing pattern seems to best explain the variable appearance of Olmec traits in the early formative highland sites. [REWA]

719. ———— and Jorge Angulo V. Chalcatzingo: un sitio excepcional en el estado de Morelos (INAH/B, 2:4, enero/marzo 1973, p. 21-26, illus.)

Ceremonial structures, water control systems, and a cemetery were excavated in 1972. The ceramic stratigraphy indicates a middle preclassic occupation of the site (ca. 900-800 BC), which places its Olmec rock carvings later than San Lorenzo, perhaps contemporaneously with La Venta. [HvW]

720. Gussinyer, Jordi. Rescate de un adoratorio azteca en México, DF; Una base para brasero ceremonial tenochca; Rescate de un adoratorio circular mexica (INAH/B, 2:2, julio/sept. 1972, p. 21-30, illus.; 2:3, oct./dic. 1972, p. 17-22, illus.; 2:4, enero/marzo 1973, p. 27-32, illus.)

Three articles in three different issues of INAH's *Boletin* on salvage of masonry structures during Metro excavations in Mexico City. [HvW]

721. Haberland, Wolfgang. Gold in Alt-Amerika. 2. ed. rev. Hamburg, FRG, Museum für Völkerkunde, 1972. 48 p., bibl., illus., maps, plates (Wegweiser zur Völkerkunde, 4)

Guide to the Museum's collection of gold artifacts from Mexico to Peru, with description of the manufacturing techniques. [HvW]

722. ————. Zentral-Mexiko: ein kulturgeschichtlicher Abriss. Hamburg, FRG, Museum für Völkerkunde, 1974. 97 p., bibl., illus., plates, table (Wegweiser zur Völkerkunde, 15)

Concise introduction to the cultural history of Central Highland Mexico. Includes glossary and chronological chart. [HvW]

723. Hammond, Norman. Maya sites in northern Belize: pts. 1/2 (ILN, 2899, Dec. 1974, p. 107-108, illus.; 2900, Jan. 1975, p. 53-55, illus.)

Results of the 1973-74 British Museum/Cambridge Univ. expedition reported in two parts in two different issues of *The Illustrated London News*. Pt. 1 concerns the Corozal and Orange Walk Districts investigation of the emergence of the classic; pt. 2 describes discoveries at Nohmul, a classic ceremonial site with pre- and postclassic occupation. [HvW]

724. ———— ed. British Museum-Cambridge University Corozal Project: 1973 interim report. Cambridge, England, Cambridge Univ., Centre of Latin American Studies, 1974. 92 p., illus., maps, tables.

Data-stuffed preliminary report on a very active field project in northern British Honduras (Belize). The goals are to build a regional sequence; do a settlement pattern study; and make a site-location/soil and resource survey. An examination of the protoclassic problem is a special topical focus. Reconnaissance, mapping, excavation and resource survey made up field activities, and the bulk of the volume consists of reports on them. Includes 88 figures. [REWA]

725. Harrison, Peter D. Archaeology in southwestern Quintana Roo: interim report. Peterborough, Canada, Trent Univ., Dept. of Anthropology, 1974. 19 p., illus., map.

In 1972 and 1973, 110 sites were surveyed which are only a fraction of the total in southwestern Quintana Roo. Extensive populations occupied the region in classic and late postclassic times. The periodic swamps (bajos) were anciently used for a system of intensive agriculture. See also item 678. [REWA]

726. Hartung, Horst. Lambityeco und Mitla: präkolumbische Architektur in Oaxaca (Antike Welt: Zeitschrift für Archäologie und Urgeschichte [Zürich, Switzerland] 4, 1973, p. 14-23)

Discusses dominant architectural features in the Valley of Oaxaca. Also in this special issue on "Altamerika:" David M. Pendergast "Die Maya stadt der Sonne" p. 24-40 (see *HLAS 33:733-734*)
Gerd-Dieter Moss "Gewebte Götterbilder aus dem alten Peru" p. 45-49
Peter Pleuss "Zwei Goldstatuetten aus dem Schatz von Frias [No. Peru]" p. 50-56. [HvW]

727. Haviland, William A. Occupational specialization at Tikal, Guatemala: stoneworking-monument carving (SAA/AA, 39:3, July 1974, p. 494-496)

Artifactual evidence is presented for stoneworking and monument carving being confined to a single family within a lineage at Tikal. [REWA]

728. Hawley, Henry. Classic Veracruz sculptures (Bulletin of the Cleveland Museum of Art [Cleveland, Ohio] 51:10, Dec. 1974, p. 321-330, illus.)

Description of a palma and a yoke, both exceptionally fine sculptures with relief decoration, recently acquired by the Museum. Both sculptures were published previously. [HvW]

729. Healan, Dan M. Residential architecture at Tula (The Southern Anthropologist [Newsletter of the Southern Anthropological Association, Univ. of New Orleans, La.] 3:1, 1973, p. 2-8)

Included in item 705.

730. Healy, Paul F. The Cuyamel Caves: preclassic sites in northeast Honduras (SAA/AA, 39:3, July 1974, p. 435-447, illus., map)

Ceramics from the Cuyamel Caves show strong affinities to Olmec and later preclassic pottery in Mesoamerica. Healy suggests that eastern Honduras was tied to the rest of Mesoamerica by long distance trade, possibly in cacao. See also item 690. [REWA]

731. Heizer, Robert F. Charcoal collecting at La Venta for radiocarbon dating (Research Reports: 1967 Projects [National Geographic Society, Washington] 1974, p. 149-152)

1957 carbon dates were revised in 1964 and 1967. Published also in 1968 (see *HLAS 31:1228*). See also R.F. Heizer and John A. Graham "Olmec Colossal Stone Heads" in this issue (p. 153-157) also published in 1967 (see *HLAS 31:1036*).

732. Hester, Thomas R. The re-use of obsidian blade cores in Mesoamerica (SM/M, 47:4, Oct./Dec. 1973, p. 149-152, illus.)

Suggested secondary function as a burnishing tool, with comparative notes. [HvW]

733. _____; Robert N. Jack; and **Alice Benfer.** Trace element analyses of obsidian from Michoacán, Mexico: preliminary results (UCARF/C, 18, Aug. 1973, p. 167-176, illus., table)

Sources of obsidian and distribution of artifacts are discussed with reference to gray specimens from Tula. [HvW]

734. Heyden, Doris. ¿ Un Chicomoztoc en Teotihuacán? La cueva bajo la Pirámide del Sol (INAH/B, 2:6, sept. 1973, p. 3-18, illus.)

Comments on the ritualistic-mythological significance of a natural tunnel leading to four cave chambers, discovered 1971 beneath the Sun Pyramid. [HvW]

735. _____. Xiuhtecutli: investidor de soberanos (INAH/B, 2:3, oct./dic. 1972, p. 3-10, illus.)

Iconographic study of a statue believed to represent a ruler attired for his investiture. [HvW]

736. Hopkins, Joseph. Ceramics of La Cañada, Mexico. Nashville, Tenn., Vanderbilt Univ., 1973. 31 p., bibl., illus. (Publications in anthropology, 6)

Description of surface sherds from southern Puebla and northern Oaxaca and from limited excavations near Cuicatlán. [HvW]

737. Hyslop, John. The petroglyphs of Cerro del Chivo (AIA/A, 28:1, Jan. 1975, p. 38-45, illus.)

Description with comparative notes of four groups of motifs (spirals, faces, stairways, miscellaneous) on a hilltop in southern Guanajuato, believed to date AD 750-1500. [HvW]

738. Isphording, Wayne C. and **Eugene M. Wilson.** The relationship of "volcanic ash," *sak lu'um,* and palygorskite in northern Yucatan Maya ceramics (SAA/AA, 39:3, July 1974, p. 483-488, table)

Misidentification of temper in certain northern Maya ceramics as volcanic ash has led to many interpretative difficulties. These are eased by the discovery that the tempering in question was actually palygorskite, widespread in the peninsula. [REWA]

739. Joesink-Mandeville, LeRoy V. Yucatan and the Chenes during the formative: a comparative synthesis (SSC/K, 8:2, 1973, p. 1-38, illus., maps, tables)

Major paper on a major northern Maya lowland preclassic regional sequence. Three phases run from middle preclassic to protoclassic times. Comparative statements are included. Reevaluation is made of Brainerd's pioneering sequence. [REWA]

740. Krotser, G. Ramón. El agua ceremonial de los olmecas (INAH/B, 2:6, sept. 1973, p. 43-48, illus.)

Exploration, in 1968, of a long and complex aqueduct built with capped trough stones, for ritual purposes, at San Lorenzo. [HvW]

741. Lee, Thomas A., Jr. The Middle Grijalva regional chronology and ceramic relations: a preliminary report (*in* Hammond, Norman *ed.* Mesoamerican archaeology: new approaches [see item 633] p. 1-20, tables)

A ceramic sequence of 13 phases is based on reconnaissance and excavations at 105 sites and runs from ca. 1500 BC to 1821 AD, bolstered by C14 dates. Each phase and ceramic complex is generally described with pertinent comparative commentary. The first two phases show strong Olmec linkages, while later complexes show close connections with Maya preclassic ceramics. Important and useful. [REWA]

742. _____. Mound 4 excavations at San Isidro, Chiapas, Mexico. Provo, Utah, Brigham Young Univ., 1974. 88 p., illus., maps (New World Archaeological Foundation paper, 34)

Well-organized report on one part of an important Middle Grijalva site. Mound 4 produced refuse lots, cached and burial vessels and architectural remains; middle preclassic to early postclassic. Site sequence is longer (mds. 1, 2, and 20 were also dug). See item 741. Stratigraphy, type-variety analysis of ceramics are presented. Includes good illustrations, comparative statements, plans and sections. Important. [REWA]

743. Lehmann, Henri and **Alain Ichon.** Les *Sarcophages* de pierre de San Andres Sajcabaja, Guatemala (MH/OM, 13:1, Printemps 1973, p. 35-46, illus., map, plates, table)

Massive stone boxes discovered in the Western Guatemalan highlands are interpreted as sarcophagi and dated as late classic and early postclassic. Stela fragments and carved stone boxes are reported on from La Lagunita. [REWA]

744. Meighan, Clement W. Prehistory of West Mexico (AAAS/S, 184:4143, 21 June 1974, p. 1254-1261, illus.)

Concise and up-to-date overview of the culture history of Sinaloa, Nayarit, Jalisco, Colima and Michoacan from the preceramic period (2000 BC) to the 16th century. [HvW]

745. Michaels, Joseph W. El Chayal, Guatemala: a chronological and behavioral reassessment (SAA/AA, 40:1, Jan. 1975, p. 103-106)

Obsidian dating results suggest that the El Chayal chipping station probably dates to the early postclassic period (AD 1000-1200) and certainly no earlier than AD 900. Independent of and complementary of item 777. [REWA]

746. Milton, George and **Roberto Gonzalo.** Jaguar cult—Down's syndrome—were-jaguar (UMUP/E, 16:4, Summer 1974, p. 33-37, illus.)

Olmec figures of were-jaguar babies may represent infants afflicted by Down's syndrome (Mongolism, mental retardation) rather than the mythical offspring from the union of a jaguar and a woman. [HvW]

747. Mirambell, Lorena. El hombre en Tlapacoya desde hace unos 20 mil años (INAH/B, 2:4, enero/marzo 1973, p. 3-8, illus.)

Summary of excavations since 1965 at this lakeshore site in the southeastern Valley of Mexico. Preliminary report on discoveries includes a human skull (7000 BC) and lithic artifacts carbon-dated 20,000 BC. [HvW]

748. Mora López, Raziel. Las pinturas rupestres de Atlihuetzían, Tlaxcala, México (UNAM/AA, 11, 1974. p. 89-108, illus.)

Describes and illustrates semi-naturalistic and symbolic pictographs in Tlaxcala, attributed to nomadic hunters and incipient agriculturists, and discusses their probable dates. [HvW]

749. Mountjoy, Joseph B. Some hypotheses regarding the petroglyphs of West Mexico. Carbondale, Ill., Southern Illinois Univ., University Museum, Research Records, 1974. 36 p., bibl., illus., maps, table (Mesoamerican studies, 9)

Interpretative description of rock art in Nayarit and other sites in Mexico. [HvW]

750. _____ and **David Petersen.** Man and land at prehispanic Cholula. Nashville, Tenn., Vanderbilt Univ., 1973. 155 p., bibl., illus., tables (Publications in anthropology, 4)

Excavations 1969-71 east of the Pyramid, at the construction site of the new campus of the Univ. of the Americas, for the study of prehispanic land use. [HvW]

751. Muller, Florencia. El origen de los barrios de Cholula (INAH/B, 2:5, abril/junio 1973, p. 35-42, illus.)

Outline of the prehispanic ceramic sequence as evidence of population and settlement changes to determine the antiquity of ten barrios in the town of Cholula. [HvW]

752. Muser, Curt. Impressions of two molds (Indian Notes [Museum of the American Indian, N.Y.] 10:1, Winter 1974, p. 9-17, 28, illus.)

Description of two Teotihuacan-style pectorals made from the same mold, and of two vessels of different size and provenience (Oaxaca and Teotihuacan) with relief decoration made from a Tajin-style mold. [HvW]

753. Navarrete, Carlos. The Olmec rock carvings at Pijijiapan, Chiapas, Mexico. Provo, Utah, Brigham Young Univ., 1974. 26 p., illus., map (New World Archaeological Foundation paper, 35)

Translation and combination of papers previously published in Spanish (*HLAS 33:720-721*) with some additional material. [REWA]

754. Nelson, Fred W., Jr. Archaeological investigations at Dzibilnocac, Campeche, Mexico. Provo, Utah, Brigham Young Univ., 1973. 142 p., illus., maps, tables (New World Archaeological Foundation paper, 33)

Valuable report on a Chenes region, lowland Maya site. A new map, brief architectural notes, observations on the hydrology, and descriptions and analyses of new sculpture (including a phallic statue) precede the description of excavations. 20 test pits were dug resulting in pottery organized into ceramic groups and four phases. The latter form a middle preclassic to late classic sequence with a weak early classic phase. Stone artifacts are described. [REWA]

755. Noguera, Eduardo. Las funciones del momoztli (UNAM/AA, 10, 1973, p. 111-122, illus.)

Comments on form, distribution in time and space, and on the ritualistic significance of small masonry platforms. [HvW]

756. _____. Sitios de ocupación en la periferia de Tenochtitlan y su significado histórico-arqueológico (UNAM/AA, 11, 1974, p. 53-88, illus., map)

Describes numerous settlements surrounding Tenochtitlan and their role as satellites, comparable to suburbs of modern Mexico City. [HvW]

757. Ochoa Salas, Lorenzo. El culto fálico y la fertilidad en Tlatilco, México (UNAM/AA, 10, 1973, p. 123-139, illus.)

Interprets certain Tlatilco figurines as phallic representations and discusses the preclassic fertility cult. [HvW]

758. _____. Las pinturas rupestres en la Cueva de la Malinche (INAH/B, 2:5, abril/junio 1973, p. 3-14, illus.)

Comments on various human and abstract postpreclassic cave paintings in Hidalgo. [HvW]

759. Pasztory, Esther. The iconography of the Teotihuacan Tlaloc. Washington, Dumbarton Oaks, Trustees for Harvard Univ., 1974. 22 p., bibl., illus., plates (Studies in precolumbian art and archaeology, 15)

A reassessment of Tlaloc imagery "to differentiate those figures that may represent the equivalent of the Postclassic Tlaloc from the other supernaturals in Teotihuacan iconography." [HvW]

760. Piña Chan, Román. Teotenango prehispánico (INAH/B, 2:2, julio/sept. 1972, p. 17-20, illus.)

Exploration and restauration of an extensive early postclassic fortified hilltop site, near Toluca, with a ball court and pyramidal platforms. [HvW]

761. Precolumbian art of Mexico and Central America: exhibition catalog. Santa Ana, Calif., The Bowers Museum, 1974. 1 v. (Unpaged) illus.

Annotated catalogue of 380 objects with summary of cultural history, by Hasso von Winning. Contains following articles: Charles N. Irwin "Conch Shell Trumpets in Mesoamerica" and "Bone Artifacts from Nayarit" and Hasso von Winning "Prehispanic Contacts between the Old World and the New World." [HvW]

762. Proskouriakoff, Tatiana. Jades from the Cenote of Sacrifice, Chichen Itza, Yucatan. Cambridge, Mass., Harvard Univ., 1974. 217 p., bibl., illus., maps, plates (Memoirs of the Peabody Museum, 10:1)

Major study presenting results of analysis of nearly 20,000 jade items from the pilgrimage well at Chichen Itza. The artifacts date from 600 BC to 1200 AD and come from all over Mesoamerica. Most items are classic period from the southern Maya lowlands or early postclassic in Toltec-Maya style from Chichen. Proskouriakoff discusses the material and manufacturing techniques and then proceeds to discuss the major stylistic and functional classes. Perceptive and interesting discussions of sociopolitical, comparative, trade, iconographic and other implications enhance the text. Includes frontispiece, 86 plates, 15 figures, and four color plates. Well-illustrated and important. [REWA]

763. Puleston, Dennis E. Intersite areas in the vicinity of Tikal and Uaxactun (*in* Hammond, Norman *ed*. Mesoamerican archaeology: new approaches [see item 633] p. 303-311, maps, table)

Late classic ancient population at Tikal was significantly concentrated within earthworks which define the site limits, an area of 120 km^2. Densities may have reached figures as high as 900 persons per km^2. [REWA]

764. Quirarte, Jacinto. Izapan and Maya traits in Teotihuacan III pottery (UCARF/C, 18, Aug. 1973, p. 11-29, illus.)

Suggests that the long-lipped head motif (Kidder's "Serpent X") originated in Chiapas and the Guatemalan highlands. [HvW]

765. Ramos, Luis J. La serpiente y el jaguar: su interpretación en una escultura cholulteca (UM/REAA, 5, 1970, p. 179-196, illus.)

A stone sculpture from the Cholula Pyramid, which portrays a jaguar fighting with a serpent, is interpreted as the only known depiction showing how Tezcatlipoca lost his foot, an episode deleted in the sequence in Codex Borgia 35. [HvW]

766. Rands, Robert L. The ceramic sequence at Palenque, Chiapas (*in* Hammond, Norman E. *ed*. Mesoamerican archaeology: new approaches [see item 633] p. 51-75, illus.)

Thoughtful, useful, and well-illustrated summary of the highly regionalized sequence which is distinct from any other in the Maya lowlands. Rands' methodology in reconstructing the horrifyingly poorly preserved ceramic evidence is of special interest. [REWA]

767. Reyna Robles, Rosa María. Las figurillas preclásicas: tesis. Mexico, Escuela Nacional de Antropología, 1971. 427 p., bibl., illus.

Reclassifies the preclassic figurines from the Valley of Mexico and adjacent regions, maintaining Vaillant's typology, into complexes, traditions, types and variants that reflect cultural changes through style variations. Useful for its copious illustrations. [HvW]

768. Rice, Don Stephen. The archaeology of British Honduras: a review and synthesis. Greeley, Colo., Univ. of Northern Colorado, Museum of Anthropology, 1974. 159 p., illus., maps, tables (Occasional publications in anthropology. Archaeology series, 6)

Attempt to comprehensively bring together all data available up to 1970. Useful, but unfortunately flawed by too many errors to be used by any but persons who already have extensive knowledge of the area. [REWA]

769. Ritter, Eric W. Prehistoric hunting patterns inferred from rock art in central Baja California (Quarterly [Pacific Coast Archaeological Society, Costa Mesa, Calif.] 10:1, Jan. 1974, p. 13-18, illus.)

Discussion of deer motifs. Other articles in this "Special Baja California Number" are:
Lee G. Massey "Jesuits and Indians: a Brief Evaluation of Three Early Descriptions of Baja California" p. 1-12
Peveril Meigs "Field Notes on the Sh'un and Jat'am, Manteca, Baja California" p. 19-28, illus.
E.W. Ritter "A Magico-Religious Wooden Tablet from Bahia Concepción, Baja California Sur" p. 29-36, illus.
Ralph C. Michelson "Ethnographic Notes on Agave Fiber Cordage" p. 39-47, illus. [HvW]

770. Rovner, Irwin. Evidence for a secondary obsidian workshop at Mayapan, Yucatan (Newsletter of Lithic Technology [Washington State Univ., Laboratory of Anthropology, Pullman, Wash.] 3:2, 1974, p. 19-26, illus.)

Rejuvenation techniques used on obsidian cores at Mayapan indicate local scarcity perhaps due to trade difficulties. Various techniques are defined. [REWA]

771. Sabloff, Jeremy A. and others. Trade and power in postclassic Yucatan: initial observations (*in* Hammond, Norman *ed.* Mesoamerican archaeology: new approaches [see item 633] p. 397-416, tables)

Cozumel Island work was oriented toward an examination of the emergence of a merchant elite culture in the early postclassic. Field work was organized to test hypotheses related to this premise. Summary settlement pattern and ceramic data presented in an interpretative form with comparisons to Mayapan. Cozumel is presented as a probable port of trade which later converted to a "free port." [REWA]

772. Schöndube Baumbach, Otto. Tamazula-Tuxpan-Zapotlan, pueblos de la frontera septentrional de la antigua Colima: tésis. México, Escuela Nacional de Antropología, 1973-1974, 2 v. (295 p., Unpaged) bibl., illus., maps.

Study of the cultural history of a region in Jalisco which was once part of the Tarascan domain, with detailed descriptions and copious illustrations of ceramics and lithic artifacts. Infers the early existence of a complex pantheon with rituals, similar to those of the Valley of Mexico. [HvW]

773. Schoenwetter, James. Pollen records of Guila Naquitz Cave (SAA/AA, 39:2, April 1974, p. 292-303, illus., table)

Pollen sediments from Oaxaca include those of a plant closely related to modern maize and suggest that the people, without being farmers, "had the technical knowledge to support a farming economy by 7000 BC." Includes figures. [HvW]

774. Segovia, Víctor. La pirámide de Kohunlich (UY/R, 12:67 enero/feb. 1970, p. 97-105, plates)

Summary account of the excavations and restoration of the pyramid at Kohunlich with its extraordinary masks. [REWA]

775. Seuffert, Andy. El *Templo B*, redescubierto en la zona de Río Bec (INAH/B, 2:8, enero/marzo 1974 [i.e. 1975] p. 3-18, illus., map)

Inaccurate, anecdotal, and illustrated account of the relocation of Rio Bec B, 60 years after its discovery by Merwin. [REWA]

776. Sharer, Robert J. The prehistory of the southeastern Maya periphery (UC/CA, 15, 1974, p. 165-187, illus., map, tables)

Summary of intensive work in an unknown area. Ceramic sequence runs from ca. 1200 BC to about 1400 AD. A remarkable preclassic development (including Olmec linkages) led to a very complex sculpture, architecture, etc., a trend truncated by volcanic eruptions in the region. Thereafter, Chalchuapa became truly peripheral to major Maya events. Attempts to link linguistic and ethnic groups to archaeological phases. Important. Includes commentary by 19 scholars. [REWA]

777. Sheets, Payson D. A reassessment of the precolumbian obsidian industry of El Chayal, Guatemala (SAA/AA, 40:1, Jan. 1975, p. 98-103)

Coe and Flannery's assessment of El Chayal as an archaic obsidian industry is refuted here by comparative study of the artifacts. At Chalchuapa in El Salvador, the artifacts are mainly 800-1500 AD in date; postclassic. [REWA]

778. Silva, John P. and Thomas R. Hester. Archaeological materials from a nonceramic site in eastern Durango, Mexico (UCARF/C, 18, Aug. 1973, p. 149-165, illus.)

Description of surface collection, mostly of projectile points, from a large site south of Torreon. Includes appendix. [HvW]

779. Simposio del Proyecto Puebla-Tlaxcala, *I, Puebla, Mex., 1973.* Proyecto Puebla-Tlaxcala. Puebla, Mex., Fundación Alemana para la Investigación Científica, 1973. 64 p., bibl., illus., maps (Comunicaciones, 8)

Includes following articles on archaeology:
Wilhelm Lauer "Diez Años de Investigación Científica en la Región Puebla-Tlaxcala" p. 9-14
Diana Dávila and Patricio Dávila "Resultados Preliminares de Investigaciones Arqueológicas en el Area de Cuauhtinchan" p. p. 15-18
Florencia Muller "La Extensión Arqueológica de Cholula a Través del Tiempo" p. 19-22. [HvW]

780. Sisson, Edward B. Second annual report of the Coxcatlan Project. Andover, Mass., Philips Academy, Robert S. Peabody Foundation for Archaeology, 1974. 55 p., bibl., illus. (Tehuacan Project reports, 4)

The third (1973) season in the Tehuacan Valley included excavations at three architectural complexes, surface surveys, and continued investigation of material culture of contemporary Coxcatlan. For first report see *HLAS 35:703*. [HvW]

781. Smith, A. Ledyard. Uaxactun: a pioneering excavation in Guatemala. Reading, Mass., Addison-Wesley, 1972. 42 p., illus., maps, tables (Addison-Wesley module in anthropology, 40)

Interesting retrospective summary of the Uaxactun project and its principal accomplishments by its major director. Comparisons are made with later Maya projects and practicalities of field work are discussed. Includes sections and plans. [REWA]

782. Smith, Harvey P., Jr. A ballplayer from Mexico's past (SM/M, 49:1, Jan./March 1975, p. 30-33, illus.)

Description of a preclassic figurine, probably from Tlapacoya, Valley of Mexico. [HvW]

783. Spores, Ronald. Stratigraphic excavations in the Nochixtlan Valley, Oaxaca. Nashville, Tenn., Vanderbilt Univ., 1974. 79 p., illus., maps, plates, tables (Publications in anthropology, 11)

Presents the basic regional sequence in the form of five phases beginning at 1300 BC and ending 1820 AD. Physical evidence for seriation and sequencing is emphasized with information on sampling controls. Basic. [REWA]

784. Stern, Jean. A carved spindle whorl from Nayarit (SM/M, 47:4, Oct./Dec. 1973, p. 143-148, illus.)

Description of the feathered serpent design in Mixteca-Puebla style. [HvW]

785. Supplement to the *Handbook of the Robert Woods Bliss Collection of precolumbian art.* Washington, Dumbarton Oaks, Trustees for Harvard Univ., 1969. 1 v. (Unpaged) plates.

Describes items 426-461 (Olmec, Veracruz, Maya, Peru). The *Handbook* was published 1963 with numerous plates. [HvW]

786. Termer, Franz. Palo Gordo: Ein Beitrag zur Archäologie des pazifischen Guatemala. English summary by Hasso von Winning. München, FRG, Kommissionverlag Klaus Renner, 1973. 251 p., bibl., illus., map, plates (Monographien zur Völkerkunde. Hamburgischesn Museum für Völkerkunde, 8)

Report on the excavations at a Pacific slope site in Guatemala. 31 mounds at the site include a ball court. 22 sculptures, at least some from the late preclassic and the rest from various other periods. Ceramic sequence runs from early preclassic to early Spanish colonial. Probable political relationships are indicated with El Baúl and Bilbao during the classic. Last work of a distinguished German scholar. Includes 144 figures and 24 plates. [REWA]

787. Torres Guzmán, Manuel. Hallazgos en el Zapotal, Veracruz: informe preliminar, segunda temporada (INAH/B, 2:2, julio/sept. 1972, p. 3-8, illus.)

Exploration of a late classic cemetery in central Veracruz. Notable is an altar with a large death god sculpture of unfired clay and smiling face figures. [HvW]

788. von Winning, Hasso. The shaft tomb figures of West Mexico. Los Angeles, Calif., Southwest Museum, 1974. 183 p., bibl., illus., maps, plates, tables (Southwest Museum papers, 24)

Style characteristics of the clay figures from Colima, Jalisco and Nayarit are defined and these are classified by themes, with comparative notes. Cultural background and previous research are outlined. Covers material (355 photographs) in private collections in California. See also "A Duck Hunter from West Mexico" in *The Masterkey* (48:2, April/June 1974, p. 72-73). [HvW]

789. ———. The tumpline in prehispanic figures (SM/M, 48-3, julio/sept. 1974, p. 108-114, illus.)

Notes on the use of the head strap for carrying burdens in Mesoamerica and the Southwest. [HvW]

790. Whitley, Glenn R. The Muscovy duck in Mexico (AAC/AJ, 11:2, 1973, p. 2-8, illus.)

Concludes that the Wind God's mask and Ehecatl's facial features are derived from the tame or domesticated Muscovy duck, native to Meso- and South American forests. [HvW]

791. Wilkerson, S. Jeffrey K. An archaeological sequence from Santa Luisa, Veracruz, Mexico (UCARF/C, 18, Aug. 1973, p. 37-50)

Presents a long sequential list of pottery types and artifacts from a coastal site near El Tajín, with conclusions on population trends. Includes chart. [HvW]

792. Winter, Marcus C. Residential patterns at Monte Alban, Oaxaca, Mexico (AAAS/S, 186:4186, 13 Dec. 1974, p. 981-987, illus.)

Developments of household clusters from Period IA through IIIB and their sociological implication, based on 1972-73 excavations. [HvW]

793. Zubryn, Emil. Mystery of the Mayan mask (Westways [Automobile Association of Southern California, Los Angeles] Jan. 1975, p. 27-29, 69, illus.)

Somewhat inaccurate but lively account of the recovery and restoration of the giant sun-god mask now in the Museum of Anthropology in Mexico. [REWA]

NATIVE SOURCES

794. Barthel, Thomas S. Informationsverschlüsselungen im Codex Laud (MLV/T, 22, 1973, p. 95-166)

Following his earlier study *(HLAS 35:721)*, Barthel found much additional evidence for southeast Asian-derived components (mainly Khmer or preceding Funan and Chenla cultures. He discovered that placement of figures and occurrences of attributes (which have numerical value: gold bead = one, knot = 10, rope = 20, etc.) convey, beyond the pictorial face value, an impressive amount of coded information relating to calendric periods, planetary revolutions, and deities. Several complete and interlocking code systems are deciphered which expose sino-hinduistic ideology underlying Mesoamerican concepts and thereby distinguish Codex Laud as a repository of intellectual achievement of unsuspected depth. [HvW]

795. ———. Neue Lesungen zur Mayaschrift (MLV/T, 23, Nov. 1974, p. 175-211, illus.)

Presents new or alternative interpretations of select passages in Codex Dresden with a comparative analysis of the phonemic values of glyphs, based on linguistic data and the writings of Eric Thompson, Knorosow, and others. Points out subtleties in the composition of glyph compounds which reflect the acumen of the Maya scribes. [HvW]

796. ———. Ein Transformationsproblem für asiatisch-amerikanische Serien (DGV/ZE, 98:1, 1973, p. 30-35)

Shows, by arithmetic progression, the parallels and astronomical significance between the Mesoamerican 20-day series and a 35-day series of southeastern Asia, still operational in Java/Bali. Suggests that the former, a better-calibrated system, was derived from the latter and presents a model of its transformation. [HvW]

797. Benson, Elizabeth P. *ed.* Mesoamerican writing systems: a Conference at Dumbarton Oaks, October 30th and 31st, 1971. Washington, Dumbarton Oaks Research Library and Collections, Trustees for Harvard Univ., 1973. 226 p., bibl., illus., plates.

Contains the following papers:
H.B. Nicholson "Phoneticism in the late Pre-Hispanic Central Mexican Writing System" p. 1-46
Mary Elizabeth Smith "The Relationship between Mixtec Manuscript Painting and the Mixtec Language: a Study of Some personal Names in Codices Muro and Sánchez Solís" p. 47-98
Floyd G. Lounsbury "On the Derivation and Reading of the 'Ben-Ich' Prefix" p. 99-143
George Kubler "The Clauses of Classic Maya Inscriptions" p. 145-164
Tatiana Proskouriakoff "The 'Hand-Grasping-Fish' and Associated Glyphs on Classic Maya Monuments" p. 165-178
David H. Kelley and K. Ann Kerr "Mayan Astronomy and Astronomical Glyphs" p. 179-215
Bodo Spranz "Late Classic Figurines from Tlaxcala, Mexico, and their Possible Relation to the Codex Borgia-Group" p. 217-226. [HvW]

798. Bowditch, Charles P. *ed.* Mexican and Central American antiquities: Calendar systems and history; twenty-four papers by Eduard Seler, E. Förstemann, Paul Schellhas, Carl Sapper, and E.P. Dieselldorff. Translated from the German under the supervision of . . . Detroit, Mich., Blaine-Ethridge Books, 1975. 682 p., bibl., facsims., illus., maps, plates, tables (Smithsonian Institution, Bureau of American Ethnology. Bulletin, 28)

Reprint of an exceedingly important group of studies by German scholars. Useful today, and long out of print. The facsimile edition is adequate although the plates are somewhat dimmer than the originals. [REWA]

799. Brunhouse, Robert L. In search of the Maya: the first archaeologists, Albuquerque, Univ. of New Mexico Press, 1973. 243 p., illus., maps.

Eight early explorers and scholars are treated in an anecdotal and occasionally inaccurate manner. Adequate, but unfortunately not the intellectual and personality history needed. [REWA]

800. Coe, Michael D. The Maya scribe and his world. N.Y., The Grolier Club, 1973. 160 p., bibl., plates, tables.

Magnificent publication from an exhibit of an extraordinary selection of hitherto unpublished Maya ceramics, sculpture, and a possibly authentic fourth Maya codex. Coe adopts a unitary theory of interpretation of the scenes and texts. He argues that all refer to Popol Vuh-related material, especially the underworld adventures of the Hero Twins. The theory is worth considering, but is surely not the interpretative key to all Maya funerary iconography. Unfortunately, nearly all of the items are from private collections and lack archaeological context which could give interpretative alternatives. Coe determinedly ignores all contrary evidence. Valuable, important, and stimulating with first class illustrations, 88 in total, six of them in color. [REWA]

801. Dütting, Dieter. Hieroglyphic miscellanea (DGV/ZE, 97:2, 1972, p. 220-256, bibl., plates)

Continuation of Dütting's previous paper (*HLAS 35:723*) on main sign T360, the "procreation" glyph. By contextual analysis formal and linguistic decipherments are made. Main signs T502, T281, T505, and T585 are also attempted by formal, linguistic, and contextual analysis. [REWA]

802. _____. Sorcery in Maya hieroglyphic writing (DGV/ZE, 99:1/2, 1974, p. 2-62, bibl., illus.)

Scrutinizes the widespread occurrences of glyphs T758 and T565 and of their compounds in codices, stone and pottery inscriptions. Demonstrates their significance in sorcery, and that sorcery and magic have not only malevolent but also highly benevolent aspects. Includes translations of numerous graphemes, thereby contributing substantially to the understanding of their meaning in Maya inscriptions. Includes four appendices. [HvW]

804. Gay, Carlo T.E. Olmec hieroglyphic writing: the probable background and meaning of an incised stone tablet from Ahuelican, Guerrero, Mexico (AIA/A, 26:4, Oct. 1973, p. 278-288, illus.)

Interpretation of a four-glyph column carved on a small tablet attributed to 600-400 BC and claimed to be the "earliest coherent hieroglyphic text known in the Western Hemisphere." [Hvw]

805. Hochleitner, Franz Joseph. Decifração semântica de 70 hieróglifos Maya de sentido astronômico (USP/RA, 17/20:1, 1969/1972, p. 189-207, tables)

Attempt at deciphering 70 astronomical glyphs. [REWA]

806. Kelley, David H. Eurasian evidence and the Mayan calendar correlation problem (*in* Hammond, Norman ed. Mesoamerican archaeology: new approaches [see item 633] p. 135-143, table)

Argues that Mesoamerican calendar system was based on Indo-Greek science during Hellenistic times, citing Asian aparallels in a number of selected elements, such as the use of zero. Difficult to assess, but seems unlikely at the moment. [REWA]

807. Knorozov, Yuri V. Notes on the Maya calendar: a general survey [Sovetskaia Etnografiia [Moskva] 2, 1971, p. 77-86; 3, 1971, p. 33-39)

808. Kubler, George. Climate and iconography in Palenque sculpture (*in* King, Mary Elizabeth and Idris R. Taylor, Jr. eds. Art and environment in native America. Lubbock, Texas Technological Univ., 1974, p. 103-113, illus., table)

Stimulating paper suggesting that certain Palenque tablets depict the same two individuals, one of whom may be from Teotihuacan. Both persons may be involved in commemoration rites for the ruler "Sun Shield," buried in the Temple of the Inscriptions tomb. [REWA]

809. Malmstrom, Vincent H. Origin of the Mesoamerican 260-day calendar (AAAS/S, 181:4103, 7 Sept. 1973, p. 939-941)

Suggests that for astronomical-geographical reasons the sacred calendar originated near a latitude of 15° North. [HvW]

810. Marcus, Joyce. The iconography of power among the classic Maya (World Archaeology [London] 6:1, 1974, p. 83-94, illus.)

"The paper is restricted to three topics: the way the Maya ruling class used iconography and writing to establish its credentials; the way they contrasted conqueror and conquered; and the way realism was employed to distinguish the ruler and the ruled. Comparisons are made with the Zapotec centre of Monte Alban which emphasize that other archaic Mesoamerican states displayed themes of militarism and power." [REWA]

812. Prem, Hanns J. A tentative classification of non-Maya inscriptions in Mesoamerica (Indiana [Ibero-Amerikanisches Institut, Berlin, FRG] 1, 1973, p. 29-58, illus.)

Presents stylistic criteria to distinguish five different but related writing systems. Outlines their temporal and spatial distribution, characteristics, calendrical use, and relationships. [HvW]

813. Robertson, Merle Greene ed. Primera Mesa Redonda de Palenque. Pebble Beach, Fla., Robert Louis Stevenson School, 1974. 2 v. (173, 143 p.) bibl., fold. map, illus., maps, plates, tables.

Loosely related series of 22 papers principally concerned with the art, iconography and dynastic history of Palenque, but covering some other matters as well. The papers vary greatly in quality and are the product of a conference. The major highlights are in the suggested Palenque dynastic history. These controversial interpretations (the arguments are extraordinarily complex) have at least the virtue of stimulating debate and perhaps leading to new advances in decipherment and interpretation. Well-illustrated and generally free of errors.
V. 1:
G.G. Griffin "Early Travelers to Palenque" p. 9-34
R.L. Rands "A Chronological Framework for Palenque" p. 35-39
L. Schele "Observations on the Cross Motif at Palenque" p. 41-61
P. Mathews and L. Schele "Lords of Palenque: the Glyphic Evidence" p. 63-75
M. Greene Robertson "The Quadripartite Badge—a Badge of Rulership" p. 77-93
M. Cohodas "The Iconography of the Panels of the [Temples of the] Sun, Cross, and Foliated Cross at Palenque" p. 95-107
E.P. Benson "Gestures and Offerings" p. 109-120
J. H. Bowles "Notes on a Floral Form Represented in Maya Art and its Iconographic Implications" p. 121-127
J. Quirarte "Terrestrial/Celestial Polymorphs as Narrative Frames in the Art of Izapa and Palenque" p. 129-135
E.W. Andrews V "Some Architectural Similarities between Dzibilchaltun and Palenque" p. 137-147
Jeffrey H. Miller "Notes on a Stelae Pair Probably from Calakmul, Campeche, Mexico" p. 149-173
V. 2:
F.G. Lounsbury "The Inscription of the Sarcophagus Lid at Palenque" p. 5-19
C.H. Smiley "Dates on the Palenque Sarcophagus Cover" p. 21-22
G. Kubler "Mythological Ancestries in Classic Maya Inscriptions" 23-43
A.G. Miller "West and East in Maya Thought: Death and Rebirth at Palenque and Tulum" p. 45-49
M.D. Coe "A Carved Wooden Box from the Classic Maya Civilization" p. 51-58
M. Foncerrada de Molina "Reflexiones en Torno a Palenque como Necrópolis" p. 77-79
P. Gendrop "Consideraciones sobre la Arquitectura de Palenque" p. 81-87
D. Robertson "Some Remarks on Stone Relief Sculpture at Palenque" p. 103-124
M. Morales M. "The 'Pais de Pacal'" p. 125-143. [REWA]

814. Romanov, M.A.; Norman Hammond; and Joyce Marcus. On the "square" model of Maya territorial organization (AAAS/S, 183:4127, 1 March 1974, p. 875-877)

Commentary by two scholars on Marcus' paper (item 810) with a reply by Marcus. Discussion revolves around the use of central place theory, the quality of evidence, etc. [REWA]

815. Schulz-Friedemann, Ramón. The Nine Lords of the Night: Survival of ancient beliefs among the Zapotec of Loxicha, Oaxaca (MVW/AV, 26, 1972, p. 197-203)

Correlates the Aztec and Maya series of the Lords of the Night with a calendar still operational on the Isthmus of Tehuantepec in the 1950s which apparently originated there among the Olmecs in the first millennium BC. [HvW]

ARCHAEOLOGY: CARIBBEAN AREA

RIPLEY F. BULLEN
Curator Emeritus, Florida State Museum
University of Florida

DURING 1973 AND 1974 FIELD WORK continued in Central American but on a somewhat reduced basis. Except for a few journal articles little of the work started in the two previous years has reached publication. In Panama attention has been turned to rock shelters and Formative sites with important results. These are summarized by Olga F. Linares in the "Current Research" section of *American Antiquity* (38:2, April/June 1973, p. 234-5).

In the Antilles during the last two years, three issues of the *Boletín del Museo del Hombre Dominicano* in Santo Domingo and two issues of the *Proceedings of the International Congress for the Study of the Pre-Columbian Cultures of the Lesser Antilles* have been published. The most important news is the delineation of preceramic blade cultures followed by those with grinding stones and ground tools from Cuba eastward into Antigua. Much of the present data is included in the publications just mentioned. The VI Congress was held in Guadeloupe in July 1975 and publication may be expected early in 1976.

Ronald V. Taylor has replaced the late Neville Connell as Director of the Barbados Museum and we understand that Gary S. Vercelius is now Archaeologist of the American Virgin Islands. We also wish to welcome Pierre Verin—an ethnological-archaeologist—who has recently started teaching at the new Univ. on Guadeloupe after teaching for some years in Madagascar.

CENTRAL AMERICA

816. Aguilar, Carlos H. Guayabo de Turrialba: arqueología de un sitio indígena prehispánico. San José, The Author, 1972. 192 p., bibl., illus., maps, plates, tables.

Good preliminary report on this very large and complicated site.

817. Andrews, E. Wyllys, V. Nota sobre excavaciones preliminares en Quelepa, El Salvador (MNDJA/A, 11:37/41, 1963/1967, p. 53-57, facsims., plates)

Discusses work at Quelepa in terms of periods I, II, and III correlating with pre-classic and early classic.

818. Brizuela, Gladys C. Investigaciones arqueológicas en la provincia de Veraguas (UNCIA/HC, 2:3, dic. 1972, p. 119-137)

Summary of work in Veraguas Prov., Pan. Pottery is extremely well illustrated. Brizuela concludes that much of it is pre-classic extends further back in time than usually considered to be the case.

819. Contreras, José del C. ¿Por qué los objetos culturales son patrimonios de la nación? (LNB/L, 202, sept. 1972, p. 58-61)

Short article covering the antiquity laws of Panama.

820. Dawson, Frank Griffith. Barrack revolt: Costa Rican style (EJ, 50:2, June 1972, p. 93-99, plates)

An account of the National Museum of Costa Rica with pictures and brief comments on some of their special exhibited specimens.

821. Guardia, Roberto de la; Arturo Barbería; and Luis Máximo Miranda. El complejo de Santa Cruz (LNB/L, 182, enero 1971, p. 34-37, illus.)

Illustrates and describes six rather unique pottery vessels and figurines from near Santa Cruz, Pan.

822. Haberland, Wolfgang. El cementerio indígena de Los Angeles, Nicaragua (Antiquitas [B.A.] 12/13, 1971, Unpaged)

Important account of excavation of 35 burials on the island of Ometepe, Nic., with good illustrations of accompanying ceramics.

823. Heath, Dwight B. Economic aspects of commercial archaeology in Costa Rica (SAA/AA, 38:3, July 1973, p. 259-265)

A fairly detailed analysis of the illicit digging and export of Amerindian specimens from Costa Rica.

824. Miranda G., Luis Máximo. Una excavación en el sitio arqueológico denominado el Cacao-Chiriquí (LNB/L, 199, junio 1972, p. 56-65, illus.)

Description of a burial vault and neighboring excavations. Stone axes and a drill as well as pottery are illustrated. The latter is compared with that from San Lorenzo.

825. Rivero de la Calle, Manuel; Ercillo Vento; and Orlando Soles. La cueva funeraria de Las Cazuelas, Canimar, Matanzas (UCLV/I, 41, enero/abril 1972, p. 55-80, bibl., maps, plates)

Report of cave excavations producing a fair number of burials with pottery which authors date to 14th century.

Stewart, Robert. Evidencias geológicas del hombre primitivo en Panamá. See item 2017.

826. Thieck, Frederic. Idolos de Nicaragua. León, Nic., Univ. Nacional Autónoma de Nicaragua, Depto. de Arqueología y Antropología, 1971. 218 p., map, plates (Album, 1)

Well illustrated album of carved stone statues of Nicaragua, arranged by areas. Includes Squier's "Idols of Zapatera."

827. Torres de Araúz, Reina. Arte precolombino de Panamá. Panama, Instituto Nacional de Cultura y Deportes, Dirección de Patrimonio Histórico, 1972. 95 p., bibl., plates.

Covers all fields of archaeological art, some illustrations in color. Valuable for comparisons.

WEST INDIES

828. Barbotin, Maurice. Archéologie caraïbe et chroniqueurs (SHG/B, 15/16, 1971, p. 53-67, illus.)

Discussion of Carib life on Marie Galante combining ethnology and archaeology.

829. Boletín del Museo del Hombre Dominicano. Instituto de Cultura Dominicana. No. 3, oct. 1973- Santo Domingo.

Includes following seven reports in Spanish and one in English:
Marcio Veloz; Elpidio Ortega; Renato O. Rímoli; and Fernando Calderón "Estudio Comparativo y Preliminar de Dos Cementerios Neo-Indios: La Cucama y La Union, República Dominicana" p. 11-47
Bernardo Vega "Material Pre-Cerámico de la Hispaniola en el Instituto Smithsonian" p. 53-63
Marcio Veloz "La Athebeanenequen: Evidencia de Sacrificio Humano entre los Tainos" p. 64-69
Elpidio Ortega; Marcio Veloz; Fernando L. Calderón; and R. Rímoli "Informe sobre Tres Nuevos Precerámicos de la República Dominicana" p. 105-134
Marcio Veloz; Elpidio Ortega; and Plinio Pina "Fechas de Radio-carbón para el Período Ceramista en la República Dominicana" p. 138-198
Elpidio Ortega and Marcio Veloz "Plaza de Yuboa" p. 227-229
Janusz K. Kozloski "Industrial Lítica de 'Aguas Verdes' Baracoa, Oriente, Cuba" p. 300-314
Ripley P. Bullen and Adelaide K. Bullen "Settlement Pattern and Environment in [Pre-] Columbian Eastern Dominican Republic" p. 315-324.

829a. _____. _____, No. 4, 1974- Santo Domingo.

This issue includes of the following articles of interest to archeologists:
Elpidio Ortega "La 'Mayólica' Hallada en las Ruinas de San Francisco" p. 67-80
Dorothy W. Pike "Primer Sitio de Elaboración del Pedernal Encontrado en Puerto Rico" p. 97-107
P. O. B. Harris "Resumen sobre la Arquelogía de Trinidad, 1973" p. 108-120.

829b. _____. _____. No. 5, 1974- Santo Domingo.

Includes one article of archaeological interest, Gordon R. Wiley "Un Modelo de Difusión-Aculturación" (p. 73-92). First part of this issue will be of interest to ethnologists.

830. Bullen, Ripley P. and **Adelaide K. Bullen.** Tests at Hacienda Grande, Puerto Rico (Boletín Informativo [Fundación Arqueológica, Antropológica e Histórica de Puerto Rico, San Juan] 1, agosto 1974, p. 1-14, plates, tables)

Presents results of two tests at Hacienda Grande documenting occupation by four sequential culture groups.

830a. _____ and **Mario Mattioni.** Some ceramic variations at Vivé, Martinique (in International Congress of Americanists, XL, Roma-Genova, 1972. Atti [see item 513] v. 1, p. 225-229, plate, table)

Illustrates ceramic differences between two cultural layers separated by a thick zone of volcanic ash including radiocarbon dates.

831. Bulletin de Liaison et de Recherche Archéologique. Musée Départamental de la Martinique. Nos. 1 [through] 4, 1974- . Fort-de-France, Antilles Françaises.

New bulletin published by the Musée Départamental de la Martinique, directed by Mario Mattioni. It was designed to serve, in between biennial meetings, as a means of communication among members of the International Congress for the Study of Pre-Columbian Cultures (see items 837 and 838). Articles of special archaeological interest include in issue No. 1: Henri Petitjean-Roget "Identification of Vestiges of Terminal Saladoid in Martinique" and Mario Mattioni's account of a ceremonial burial at Vivé, Martinique; in issue No. 2: Alfredo E. Figueredo "Current Research in the Virgin Islands" and José Oliver's communication on newly found petroglyphs at La Mina, P.R.; and in issue No. 4: Pierre Verin's communications on salvage archaeology at the Schoelcher site in Martinique and Edgar Clerc's study of traces of bitumen on bases and sides of three pointer stones found in Guadeloupe.

832. Cartagena Portalatin, Aída. Dos técnicas cerámicas indoantillanas: diagnóstico de origen de los yacimientos de las Antillas Mayores. Santo Domingo, Univ. Autónoma de Santo Domingo, Facultad de Humanidades, Instituto Dominicano de Antropología, 1972? 22 p., plates (Boletín Informativo del Museo de Antropología-Arqueología, 10)

Undated study (probably published 1972) gives a brief but adequate description of the typology of Hispaniola pottery.

833. Clerc, Edgar. Les trois-pointes des sites précolombiens de la cote nord-est de la Grande-Terre (SHG/B, 15/16, 1971, p. 41-52, illus., plates)

A good discussion of shell and stone three-pointers with special emphasis on those found on Guadeloupe.

834. Cordero Michel, Emilio. Economía pre-colonial de la isla La Española (El Pequeño Universo [Univ. Autónoma de Santo Domingo, Facultad de Humanidades] 2, oct./dic. 1972, p. 37-51, plates)

Author discusses precolumbian agriculture on Hispaniola (Dominican Republic and Haiti).

835. Decal, Ramón. Moluscos marinos y terrestres presentes en el sitio arquelógico "Aguas Verdes," Nibuján, Oriente, Cuba. La Habana, Univ. de La Habana, Centro de Información Científica y Técnica, 1973. 41 p., map, tables (Serie Ciencias, 9. Antropologia y prehistoria, 2)

Describes and compares mollusks from Aguas Verdes and Cueva Funche.

836. Figueredo, Alfredo E. The British Virgin Islands Archeological Survey: first season (Indian Notes [Museum of the American Indian, N.Y.] 8:4, 1972, p. 131-135, illus., map)

Popular account of two weeks' survey netting seven sites. Sherds collected suggest occupation from Insular Saladoid times around the time of Christ to Chicoid or Esperanza times immediately before the arrival of the Spanish.

837. International Congress for the Study of the Pre-Columbian Cultures of the Lesser Antilles, *IV, St. Lucia, 1971.* Proceedings. Edited by Ripley P. Bullen. Gainesville, Fla., Univ. of Florida, Florida State Museum, 1973. 216 p., bibl., illus., maps, tables.

Contains 31 papers of which the first eight cover petroglyps of the Antilles and the next three comparative data from eastern Costa Rica, the Orinoco region of Venezuela and Guyana. Eight articles discuss stone specimens of the Antilles (including three-pointers) with special emphasis on preceramic sites. Three papers in French by Jacques and Henri Petitjean-Roget are outstanding in their analyses of complicated geometric designs on pottery vessels from Martinique. Routes and times for the peopling of the Antilles are discussed by Raggi in Spanish and by Olsen in English. Also includes papers on tests made on Guadeloupe, St. Lucia, and Union Island in the Grenadines.

838. _____, *V, Antigua, 1973.* Proceedings. Edited by Ripley P. Bullen. Gainesville, Fla., Univ. of Florida, Florida State Museum, 1973. 178 p., bibl., illus., maps, tables.

Contains 21 scientific papers, four of which were not presented at the Congress. Topics discussed are: Salvage archaeology at Villa Taina, Puerto Rico; a flint workshop on Puerto Rico; the Archaic occupations of Antigua; a possible preceramic site on Martinique; a possible ball court on Antigua; excavations at Tower Hill, Jamaica, compared with those on St. Martin; an archaeological survey of St. Kitts; shell work on Guadeloupe; excavations at Indian Creek, Antigua, and Parquemar, Martinique; ceramic pastes from Martinique; precolumbian dogs of Puerto Rico and Martinique; los indios lucahios; Cayo pottery from St. Vincent; a tentative correlation between certain petroglyphs and precolumbian cultures; excavations at Ceru Noka, Aruba, and at Pointe Gravier, Guyane Française; and a summary of Trinidad archaeology.

839. Kozlowski, Janusz K. Industria lítica de "Aguas Verdes," Baracoa, Oriente, Cuba. La Habana, Univ. de La Habana, Centro de Información Científica y Técnica, 1972, 11 p., illus.

(Serie Ciencias, 9. Antropología y prehistoria, 1)

In Spanish with English abstract. Covers blade industry from Baracoa. See also item 839a.

839a. _____. Preceramic cultures in the Caribbean. Kraków, Poland, Uniw. Jagiellónskiego, 1974. 106 p., bibl., illus., map, tables (Prace acheológiczne, 20)

Important summary and discussion of blades industries of Cuba with comparisons with those of neighboring areas. Written in English, typology follows European usage.

840. Mattioni, Mario and M. Nicolas. Art précolombien de la Martinique. Fort-de-France, Antilles Françaises, Musée Départamental de la Martinique, 1972. 89 p., illus.

Contains spectacular pictures of pottery and other artifacts from Martinique with an introductory text.

841. Olsen, Fred. Indian Creek: Arawak site on Antigua, West Indies, 1973 excavation by Yale University and the Antigua Archeological Society. Norman, Univ. of Oklahoma Press, 1974. 58 p., plates.

Description of excavations with illustrations of some artifacts. This preliminary report is of interest as it will probably be some years before final report is written on this very important site.

841a. _____. On the trail of the Arawaks. Norman, Univ. of Oklahoma Press, 1974. 406 p., bibl., illus., maps, plates.

A personalized account of archaeological work in the Antilles and northeastern South America. Contains theoretical considerations, tentative conclusions, and first report on Yale-Antigua Archeological Society excavations at large Indian Creek site on Antigua, lesser Antigua.

842. Rey, Estrella. Las peculiaridades de la desintegración de las comunidades primitivas cubanas. La Habana, Academia de Ciencias de Cuba, Depto. de Antropología, 1969. 22 p. (Serie antropología, 5)

Of interest to those dealing with historical archaeology and the termination of the Amerindian cultures.

843. Sellon, Michael. Exploring the enigmatic tri-point (Indian Notes [Museum of the American Indian, N.Y.] 9:2, 1973, p. 51-64, illus., plates)

Gives a fairly detailed classification of shell and stone three-pointers from the Antilles. Closes with a discussion of the de Hostos, Lovén, and Olsen theories regarding their origin and symbolism.

844. Serie Arqueológica. 1- . La Habana, Academia de Ciencias de Cuba, Instituto de Arqueología, 1972-

New monographic series published by the Cuban Academy of Sciences. Four studies were issued in 1972-74: Nos. 1/2 by José M. Guarch "Excavaciones en el Extremo Oriental de Cuba" and "La Cerámica Taína de Cuba" (including Ostiones and Santa Elena traits), No. 3 was not available at HLAS press time; and No. 4, also by Guarch, "Ensayo de Reconstrucción Etno-histórica del Taíno de Cuba."

845. Veloz Maggiolo, Marcio. Arqueología prehistórica de Santo Domingo. Singapore, McGraw Hill Far Eastern Publishers, 1972. 383 p., bibl., illus., plates.

Published in Singapore, this important book is marred by incorrect interpretation of author's name on cover. Excellently illustrated, Veloz's valuable compilation brings up to date the archaeology of the Dominican Republic.

845a. _____ and **Elpidio Ortega.** El precerámico de Santo Domingo, nuevos lugares, y su posible relación con otros puntos del área antillana. Santo Domingo, Editora Cultural Dominicana, 1973? 61 p., illus., maps, plates (Museo del Hombre Dominicano. Papeles ocasionales, 1)

Well illustrated and containing comparisons with Trinidad materials, this booklet is of special interest to those studying preceramic cultures in the area. Originally a paper presented at the I Puerto Rican Symposium on Archaeology of the Caribbean Area, held in Santurce, P.R., 20-30 Jan. 1973, by the Fundación Arqueológica, Antropológica e Histórica de Puerto Rico.

ARCHAEOLOGY: SOUTH AMERICA

CLIFFORD EVANS
Curator—South American Archaeology
Department of Anthropology
Smithsonian Institution

BETTY J. MEGGERS
Research Associate
Department of Anthropology
Smithsonian Institution

SOME INTERESTING SHIFTS IN ENTRIES OCCURRED these past two years. Uruguay, after many years with only two or three entries, rose to 10 items as the result of the I Congreso Nacional de Arqueología held 20-23 Dec. 1972, under the auspices of the Museo Municipal de Historia Natural de Río Negro in Fray Bentos, Uruguay. Some of this interest may reflect the influence of Pedro Ignacio Schmitz of the Univ. Federal do Rio Grande do Sul in Pôrto Alegre, Bra., who is assisting some of the Uruguayans in field work, as well as instruction in the standardized ceramic terminology established among Brazilian archaeologists in recent years.

The two other countries with outstanding increase in entries (see *HLAS 35,* p. 50, table I for comparative figures for previous years) are Chile and Ecuador. Peru slid from a high in *HLAS 33* of 136 items to 107 items in *HLAS 35,* to only 77 here, but retained the balance of about 50-50 between national and foreign authors reached in *HLAS 35.* This decline is difficult to explain because publications resulting from the long-range program of the Peabody Museum of Harvard Univ. at the urban center of Chan Chan on North Coast Peru are beginning to appear and the second issue of a new scientific journal *Anales Científicos de la Universidad del Centro del Perú,* Huancayo, was published in 1973.

The increase in entries for Chile is largely due to the appearance in early 1974 of the *Actas del VI Congreso de Arqueología Chilena,* held in October 1971 in Santiago under the auspices of the Sociedad Chilena de Arqueología, Univ. de Chile, Santiago, and to the creation of two new journals: *Serie Arqueología* under the auspices of the Facultad de Arte, Educación y Ciencias Humanas, Univ. del Norte, Antofagasta, and *Estudios Atacameños* by the Museu de Arqueología in San Pedro de Atacama and the Univ. del Norte. Another encouraging factor is the continuation of established publication series by the Museo de la Serena, the Museo Regional de Iquique, el Depto. de Antropología of the Univ. del Norte in Arica, and the Instituto de la Patagonia in Punta Arenas.

The increase in items on Ecuador (up to 24 after a drop last time to 15) is not attributable to a congress, new journal, or other collection of articles but rather a variety of individual contributions. Most significant are two volumes by Pedro Ignacio Porras Garcés. One, dealing with the *Historia y arqueología de la ciudad española Baeza de los Quijos* (item 978a), initiates a series on the Oriente of Ecuador published by the Pontificia Univ. Católica del Ecuador in Quito. The other, *El Encanto* (item 978), is No. 5 in the series "Huancavilca" sponsored by the Museo Francisco Piana in Guayaquil. It describes a large, ring-shaped shell midden of the Valdivia period and contributes significant new evidence on this early culture and its subsequent dispersal. The monograph is noteworthy not only for its scientific data, but because the quality of the paper and illustrations is superior to that generally associated with archaeological monographs in South America.

The appearance of a new series and a new serial in Brazil reaffirms the growing interest in archaeology: *Inventário Arqueológico do Estado de Goiás* published by the Museu da Univ. Católica de Goiás, Goiânia (item 898), and the *Revista do CEPA* (Centro de Ensino e Pesquisas Arqueológicas) of the Faculdade de Filosofia, Ciências e Letras, Santa Cruz do Sul, Rio Grande do Sul (item 922).

Hombre y Cultura, a journal dealing primarily with Panamá and published by the Centro de Investigaciones Antropológicas, Univ. Nacional de Panamá, completed its first decade in 1972. Beginning with Tomo 2, No. 4, 1973, it was converted into a journal of Latin American anthropology as a contribution to the growing need for communication within this region. The first international issue contains three items relevant to South American archaeology. One is a settlement pattern and ecological study of a preceramic site at the mouth of the Río Loa in northern Chile, by Lautaro Núñez Atencio, Viera Zlater M., and Patricio Núñez H. (item 942b). The other is a two-part study of the pottery of the present-day Indians of the Río Curaray, eastern Ecuador. Pedro Ignacio Porras Garcés describes the ethnographic details (item 978d and 978e) and Owen S. Rye analyzes the raw materials and methods of manufacture from the standpoint of a ceramic technologist (item 979).

Two major syntheses of regional cultural development deserve special attention. *Antiguas formaciones y modos de producción venezolanos* by Mario Sanoja Obediente and Iraida Vargas (item 1062a) is a pioneering analysis of Venezuelan society from the peopling of the region to the present time, employing an ecological and cultural evolutionary point of view that produces new insights applicable to the present as well as the past. *Peoples and cultures of ancient Peru* by Luis G. Lumbreras (item 1026a) is an updated revision of a book originally published in Spanish (see *HLAS 33:1177*) with numerous new maps and photographs selected to complement the text and to present specimens and sites not previously published. As the only comprehensive up-to-date description of Peruvian prehistoric cultural development, it is an essential reference for scholars as well as a book that armchair archaeologists and art historians can enjoy.

GENERAL

846. Bryan, Alan L. Paleoenvironments and cultural diversity in Late Pleistocene South America (Quatenary Research [Academic Press, N.Y.] 3:2, Aug. 1973, p. 237-256, bibl.)

Summary assessment of certain selected Paleo-Indian sites in South America discussed in terms of reconstruction of paleo environmental situation. Reevaluates the Taima-Taima site in Venezuela where animals, now extinct, were killed with El Jobo-like points about 13,000 years ago. Indicates presence of at least four different traditions of bifacially flaked-stone projectile points in widely separated and environmentally diverse parts of America, 11,000 to 13,000 years ago. They suggest that cultural antecedents of these were essentially independent of one another. Author argues for several flaked-stone point traditions developing indigenously in America.

847. Diessl, Wilhelm G Zur Kinematik der Boleadora (MVW/AV/ 25, 1971, p. 23-41, illus.)

Very detailed study of the bola from standpoint of kinetics, the branch of dynamics that treats of the changes of motion produced by forces.

Eisleb, Dieter. Alt-Amerika: Führer durch die Ausstellung der Abteilung amerikanische Archäologie. See item 616.

848. *El Dorado.* A newsletter-bulletin on South American anthropology. Univ. of Northern Colorado. Vol. 1, No. 1, Aug. 1973- . Greeley, Colo.

Edited and published by George E. Fay, this new bulletin (77 p.) includes a variety of articles, notes, information on field work, general comments, etc., as would a newsletter that only covers South America. Also includes reprints of articles published elsewhere, such as *Science*, papers delivered at annual meetings, especially the XXXVIII Annual Meeting of the Society for American Archaeology, held in May 1973 at San Francisco. A new medium of interchange for South American specialists, at present in mimeographed form.

849. Fantin, Mario. Mistici scalatori di vette eccelse (IGM/U, 51:6, nov./dic. 1971, p. 1225-1256, bibl., illus., maps, plates)

Summarizes between five-6000 m. elevation; ruins and human sacrifices of precolumbian cultures, probably Inca from 1884-1969, including most recent and famous ones of Cerro El Toro, Sierra de Famatina, Nevado Pichu Picchu.

Gorenstein, Shirley *ed.* Prehispanic America. See item 628.

850. Gross, Daniel R. *ed.* Peoples and cultures of native South America: an anthropological reader. N.Y., Doubleday, Natural History Press *for* The American Museum of Natural History, 1973. 566 p., bibl., maps.

Reader on South America ranging from archaeological interpretative materials to ethnology of Indians of tropical forest, Andean area, as well as a reconstruction of life during Inca times. Of 25 articles only six are originals: Siskind on Sharanahua of Upper Purús, Gregor on the Mehinacu of central Brazil, da Matta on the Apinaye, Sorensen on South American linguistics at the turn of 1970s, Tavener on the Karajá, and Saloman on the Otavalo.

851. Hébert-Stevens, François. L'art ancien de l'Amérique du Sud. Réalisation et photographs de Claude Arthaud et . . . Préface de Jacques Soustelle. Paris, B. Arthaud, 1972. 247 p., bibl., illus., maps, plates, tables.

Pt. 1 discusses and illustrates sculpture, pottery, textiles, metal work principally of Quimbaya, San Agustín, Esmeraldas, Chavin, Mochica, Chimu, Paracas, Nazca, Tiahuanaco, Huari, and Inca. Pt. 2 compares their interpretation of motifs such as doubleheads, tongues, steps, spirals, horizontal and vertical, heraldry, meanders, etc., and geometric lines with those of other world cultures to show symmetry of various structures.

852. Lynch, Thomas F. The antiquity of man in South America (Quaternary Research [Academic Press, N.Y.] 4, 1974, p. 356-377, bibl.)

Summarizes the antiquity of man in South America as he perceives it from literature. Sees weak evidence for the Biface and Chopper tradition (pre-projectile points) and stronger evidence for a flake tradition, but does not believe in possibility that this might precede use of projectile points. Cautions about radiocarbon and terrace dating. Favors man's entry into South America as a big-game hunter of late Pleistocene fauna using projectile points in a way of life similar to Paleo-Indian in North America.

853. Pedersen, Ashjorn. Aspectos de la metalurgia indígena americana prehispánica: la huyara y su empleo en el proceso de fundición (UCEIA/H, 7:1, 1969/1970, p. 35-50, bibl.)

Uses literature of early chroniclers and data from northwest Argentina to comment on metallurgical techniques and especially the precolumbian use of pottery furnace to extract metals from ores.

854. Pericot, Luis. El problema de los contactos prehistóricos afroamericanos (IGFO/RI, 31:123/124, enero/junio 1971, p. 173-181, bibl.)

Suggests need for serious study of possible contacts between African continent and precolumbian America, directly or through the Canary Islands.

855. Pierson, Donald and others. O homem no Vale do São Francisco. Rio, Superintendência do Vale do São Francisco (SUVALE), 1972. 3 v. (361, 638, 503 p.), bibl., illus., tables.

Three-vol. work on man and his way of life in San Francisco Valley (states of Minas Gerais, Bahia and Pernambuco, Bra.). V. 1 describes the geography, climate, native flora and fauna as well as ethnographic data on Indian tribes at time of European contact including the introduction of other ethnic and racial groups. V. 2 is a sociological study of the Valley's present-day people, their way of life, food, subsistence, housing, mobility, clothing, hygiene, health, and land-use. V. 3 deals with society and culture with detailed information on family, rituals, ceremonies, sociopolitical structure and the individual life cycle from birth to death. The final chapter makes suggestions for further investigation and social planning in terms of official Brazilian development programs. Thorough scholarship and extensive bibliography make these three volumes a basic reference for any research on this vast river drainage in northeastern Brazil.

856. Rivera Dorado, Miguel. Relaciones prehispánicas entre Mesoamérica y el área andina septentrional. Madrid, The Author, 1973. 46 p., bibl.

Extract of author's doctoral thesis presented to the Univ. in Madrid. Shows that from preclassic times onward, contacts by water could have occurred from Guatemala's Pacific coast and nearby regions to Ecuador's northern and Colombia's southern coasts.

857. Schobinger, Juan. Nuevos hallazgos de puntas "colas de pescado," y consideraciones en torno al origen y dispersión de la cultura de cazadores superiores toldense—Fell I—en Sudamérica (*in* International Congress of Americanists, XL, Roma-Genova, 1972. Atti [see item 513] v. 1, p. 33-50, bibl., illus., map)

Fishtail projectile points found in Uruguay, southern Brazil, Argentina, Chile, Ecuador, and Peru link a Paleo-Indian culture complex in South America.

858. Tekiner, Roselle. Transpacific contact: the evidence of the panpipe (*in* International Congress of Americanists, XL, Roma-Genova, 1972. Atti [see item 513] vs. 2, p. 31-38, bibl., illus.)

Gives background to problem, proposes a system of recording data on scale, pitch and metric measurements of panpipes and plotting for easy comparisons.

859. Viteri Gamboa, Julio. Vocabulario de arqueología. Guayaquil, Ecua., The Author, 1974. 33 p., bibl., illus.

Terminology of importance to archaeology from author's point of view and mostly referring to Ecuador. A mixture of proper names, persons, geological terms, pottery and stone terminology, etc. For popular usage only.

860. Willey, Gordon R. The early great styles and the rise of pre-columbian civilizations (*in* Sabloff, Jeremy A. and C.C. Lamberg-Karlovsky eds. The rise and fall of civilizations [see item 644] p. 157-169, bibl.)

Reprint. See *HLAS 25:333a* for comment on original.

ARGENTINA

861. Aguerra, Ana M.; Alicia A. Fernández Distel; and Carlos A. Aschero. Hallazgo de un sitio acerámico en la Quebrada de Inca Cueva, Provincia de Jujuy (SAA/R, 7, 1973, p. 197-235, bibl., illus., map)

In Quebrada de Inca Cueva, sites of early ceramic, classic Huamahuaca and Huamahuaca Inca compare with sites from Quebrada de Huamahuaca and Huachichocana, but underneath all this is a nonceramic comparison of importance in Site IC-c. 7 of Quebrada de Inca Cueva and site CH.III (level three) from Quebrada de Huachichocana of late preceramic materials. The preservation of skins, basketry, textiles, gourds, and objects of wood and bone from IC-c-7 is outstanding. Compares with Chile and Peru material and estimates date at somewhere at least 2000 BC.

862. Alfaro de Lanzone, Lidia C. La figura humana dentro del arte rupestre del área puneña, Argentina (*In* International Congress of Americanists, XL, Roma-Genova, 1972. Atti [see item 513] v. 1, p. 303-312, bibl., illus.)

Representations of human figures—some precolumbian, others clearly showing contact with Spanish—in pictographs and petroglyphs of the Argentine Puna.

862a. ———. Yacimiento precerámico de Vilama, Puna jujeña (UNCIA/H, 4, 1973, p. 69-93, bibl., illus., map)

Describes nonceramic sites around the borders of lakes in the Argentine Andes, Jujuy prov. Classifies lithic material as belonging to the Ayampitin complex, estimates dating at between 7000-3000 BC and gives geologists' opinions that the lakes, now at around 4000 m. altitude, have risen from 2000 m. altitude over the last 9000 years, due to rapid tectonic uplift after last glacial advance. Believes this explains a more favorable environment for hunting of deer, llama, guanaco.

863. Aschero, Carlos A. Los motivos laberínticos en América (SAA/R, 7, 1973, p. 259-275, bibl., illus.)

Discusses symbolism of labyrinths in precolumbian America; leans heavily on earlier works of Schuster (see *HLAS 23:15*)

864. Austral, Antonio Gerónimo. El yacimiento arqueológico Badal en el departamento de Chadileo, provincia de la Pampa (UNC/AAE, 26, 1971, p. 99-109, bibl., illus., map)

Defines pottery and lithic material from the site and places it in "Estadio Ceramolítico" (see *HLAS 35:764*)

865. Berberián, Eduardo E. Las primeras contribuciones a la arqueología de Córdoba (ANC/B, 49, 1972, p. 147-152, bibl.)

History of archaeological research carried out in Córdoba, Arg., from 1875 to 1900, especially by H. Weyenbergh and Florentino Ameghino.

866. Borrello, María Angélica. Un nuevo sitio incaico en el Valle de Abaucán, depto. de Tinogasta, Catamàrca (Actualidad Antropológica [Suplemento de *Etnía,* Museo Etnográfico Municipal Dámaso Arce, Olavarría, Arg.] 11, julio/dic. 1972, p. 1-7, bibl., illus.)

Site showing 12 percent of total ceramics as Inca mixed with local wares; no Spanish colonial material.

867. Caggiano, María.; Eduardo M. Cigliano; and Rodolfo A. Raffino. Consideraciones sobre la arqueología de Salto Grande, provincia de Entre Rios (UNC/AAE, 26, 1971, p. 53-68, bibl., illus., map)

Presents the archaeology of this region from preceramic to Late Guarani in historical times. Shows geographic associations and cultural relationships with Rio Grande do Sul, Bra., materials.

868. Cardich, Augusto; Lucio Adolfo Cardich; and Adán Hajduk. Secuencia arqueológica y cronología radiocarbónica de la Cueva 3 de Los Toldos, Santa Cruz, Argentina (SAA/R, 7, 1973, p. 85-123, bibl., illus., map)

Reports on recent research on nonceramic site begun in

1933 which also has a large number of pictographs on cave walls. Carbon dates are: a) For middle level No. 7: 7260±350 BP; b) For level No. 9: 8750±480 BP; and c) For level No. 11, near bottom: 12,600 ± 600 BP. Describes definitive artefacts and illustrates them from each cultural level in the 1.35 m. deposit. Stone materials of extreme importance to Paleo-Indian experts for in Level No. 11 they define a new horizon earlier than Toldense.

869. Ceruti, Carlos and Roberto Crowder. La presencia de cerámica en los cordones conchiles litorales de la provincia de Buenos Aires, Argentina: un sitio nuevo (*in* Congreso del Museo Municipal de Historia Natural de Río Negro, Fray Bentos, Uru., 1973. Antecedentes y anales. Fray Bentos, Uru., Museo Municipal de Historia Natural de Río Negro, 1973, p. 55-103, bibl., illus., map)

Site of La Maza I is in the same geological situation as Cigliano's Palo Blanco site on old shell bar, and with same type of pottery (see *HLAS 31:1417*). Could be same age. Site has two clearcut occupation levels, this earlier one related to Palo Blanco, and a late Tupiguarani of 1545 AD based on Carbon-14 dates

870. Cigliano, Eduardo M. and Rodolfo A. Raffino. Tastil: un modelo cultural de adaptación, funcionamiento y desarrollo de una sociedad urbana prehistórica (SAA/R, 1973, p. 159-181, bibl., illus., map)

Short article of larger monograph on 14th-century urban center in Salta prov., at altitude of 3200 m., estimated to have had about 2000 population (see *HLAS 35:769a*).

871. D'Antoni, Héctor Luis. Extracción de muestras de sedimentos para análisis de polen: nota técnica (Actualidad Antropológica [Suplemento de *Etnía*, Museo Etnográfico Municipal Dámaso Arce, Olavarría, Arg.] 12, enero/junio 1973, p. 9-11, illus.)

Simple description of a tool for collecting soil samples from archaeological sites for pollen study.

871a. ———. Hacia una paleoecología en arqueología (MEMDA/E, 18, julio/dic. 1973, p. 21-30, bibl., illus.)

Using Argentine examples shows why an ecological point of view is useful to archaeology in this area, especially from the standpoint of reconstructing past climates. Illustrates procedure with charts.

872. Deambrosis, María Susana and Mónica de Lorenzi. La influencia incaica en la Puna y Quebrada de Humahuaca, República Argentina (UNCIA/R, 4, 1973, p. 129-139, bibl., illus., map)

Based on typical Inca decorative elements on pottery and form, shows the strong Inca impact on sites in this extreme northwest point of Argentina.

873. De La Fuente, Nicolás R. Informe arqueológico sobre el valle de Vinchina, provincia de la Rioja (UNCIA/R, 4, 1973, p. 96-127, bibl., illus., map)

Brief summary of archaeology of area from earliest preceramic hunting cultures to Inca and Spanish occupation. Stresses a geographical approach. Illustrates and describes in detail the lithic complexes, as well as some peculiar stone walls and pavements, in area known as La Estrella near town of Vinchina.

873a. ———. El yacimiento arqueológico de Guandacol, provincia de la Rioja (UNCIA/R, 4, 1973, p. 151-167, bibl., illus.)

Restudy of the site in San Juan prov. first visited by Debenedetti in 1916. Site is a pure example of Sanagasta culture distributed throughout three provinces: the south of Catamarca; central, west and south of La Rioja; and north of San Juan. Divides culture at this site into two phases: most recent one showing Inca influence with habitation sites being constructed of adobe, and later one showing relationships to the Chilean culture called Coquimbo.

874. Dougherty, Bernardo. Un nuevo yacimiento con construcciones tumuliformes de piedra: Agua Hedionda (MEMDA/E, 16, julio/dic. 1972, p. 20-29, bibl., illus., map)

Describes site with stone mounds and how only extensive excavation will solve all the problematical statements that have been made in the past about such structures in Jujuy prov. Will not assign a cultural period at this time. Appears to be similar to Tastil, but on smaller scale (see *HLAS 35:769a* and item 870).

875. Fernández, Jorge. La edad de piedra en la Puna de Atacama. Tucumán, Arg., Univ. Nacional de Tucumán, Facultad de Filosofía y Letras, Instituto de Antropología, 1971. 136 p., bibl., illus., maps, plates (Revista del Instituto de Antropología, 1)

Monograph on regional and chronological study of man's occupation of the Puna de Atacama, Arg., and its Paleo-Indian materials. Emphasizes how geography is the only science that can fully aid the archaeologist in interpreting the way of life of these hunters and why they lived there in past millennia. Excellent illustrations.

875a. ———. La Gruta del Inca: nueva contribución al estudio de la evolución de las culturas en el noroeste argentino (AINA/C, 7, 1968/1971, bibl., illus., map)

Site located in quebrada of a minor tributary of the Humahuaca, Jujuy prov., produced preceramic artefacts, especially points, along with corncobs, fibers, etc. Few sherds found in upper levels of shelter only. Relates material to Ayampitin complex.

876. González, Alberto Rex. Arte, estructura y arqueología: análisis de figuras duales y anatrópicas del N.O. Argentino. B.A., Ediciones Nueva Visión, 1974. 151 p., bibl., illus.)

Study of dual and/or inverted animal and bird figures made of wood or metal or precolumbian pottery in Northwest Argentina. Also discusses their meaning in the iconography of the cultures.

876a. _____ and Humberto A. Lagiglia. Registro nacional de fechadas radiocarbónicas: necesidad de su creación (SAA/R, 7, 1973, p. 291-312, bibl.)

Proposes the establishment, through a committee, of a national registry of Argentine radiocarbon dates of importance to archaeology and early man. Suggests form for such a registry and requests comment. In the meantime publishes here all known dates from Argentina with lab numbers and reference up to June 1973.

877. Gradin, Carlos J. La piedra pintada de Manuel Choique, provincia de Río Negro [(SAA/R, 7, 1973, p. 145-157, bibl., illus.)

Describes the pictographs on this rock face and tries to relate the geometric patterns to various cultures in Argentina, especially the engraved plaques from provinces of Río Negro and Chubut.

878. Greslebin, Héctor. Una nueva representación de la figura humana draconiana (AINA/C, 7, 1968/1971, p. 71-109, bibl., illus.)

Pottery vessel and other artifacts in private collection of Sr. Cafferata believed to be from La Aguada, Catamarca prov., with new elements in the whole problem of dragon representations on pottery. Discusses this motif and his philosophical points of view; does not believe they show any relationships to feline elements.

879. Hunziker, Armando T. Sobre un nuevo hallazgo de *Amaranthus Caudatus* en tumbas indígenas de Argentina (Kurtziana [Córdoba, Arg.] 6, julio 1971, p. 63-67, bibl., illus.)

Important find of Amaranths in precolumbian tomb at Gruta del Indio del Rincón del Atuel, San Rafael dept., Mendoza prov., dated by four Carbon-14 samples at c. 2000 years BP.

880. Krapovickas, Pedro. Arqueología de Yavi Chico, provincia de Jujuy, República Argentina (UNCIA/R, 4, 1974, p. 1-22, bibl., illus., map)

Describes excavations and pottery and defines certain unique polychrome styles. Believes site to be end of Middle period or beginning of Late with some Incaic sherds on surface.

881. Lorandi de Gieco, Ana María and Delia Magda Lovera. Economía y patrón de asentamiento en la provincia de Santiago del Estero (SAA/R, 6, 1972, p. 173-191, bibl., illus., map)

On the basis of archaeological work, 1967-72, discusses settlement pattern and subsistence pattern of the various sites through periods from Paleo-Indian hunters, but especially from 800-1500 AD.

882. Madrazo, Guillermo B. Síntesis de arqueología pampeana. (MEMDA/E, 17, enero/junio 1973, p. 13-25, bibl.)

Good summary of the archaeology of the pampas from earliest known materials to Spanish colonial.

883. Menghin, Osvaldo F.A. Prehistoria de los indios canoeros del extremo sur de América (UNC/AAE, 26, 1971, p. 5-51, bibl., illus., map)

Translation of author's article "Urgeschichte der Kanuindianer des sudlichsten Amerika" published in 1960 with introduction and appendix by Amalia Sanguinetti de Bórmida, and text notes and supplemental bibliography by Juan Schobinger. First translation into Spanish of this article about the archaeology of Patagonia updates Menghin's point of view by adding new material.

883a. _____ and Carlos J. Gradin. La piedra calada de las plumas, provincia del Chubut, República Argentina (CAEP/AP, 11, 1972, p. 13-63, bibl., illus., map)

Results of researches made 1955, 1956, 1959 and 1968 of this important petroglyph area of Patagonia. Illustrates the various motifs and attempts to explain them in magico-religious terms. Estimates date at somewhere from 500-1000 AD.

884. Morresi, Eldo S. Las ruinas del Km. 75 y Concepción del Bermejo: primera etapa de una investigación de arqueología histórica regional. Resistencia, Arg., Univ. Nacional del Nordeste, Facultad de Humanidades, Instituto de Historia, 1971. 184 p., bibl., illus., maps, plates, tables.

Historical archaeology of the town of Concepción del Bermejo (Km. 75, Chaco prov., northern Arg.) including Carbon-14, ethnohistorical data, and identification of archaeological artefacts, proves that the site was founded by the Spanish in 1585. An excellent historical-archaeological report.

885. Núñez Regueiro, Víctor A. La cultura alamito de la subárea valliserrana del noroeste argentino (SA/J, 60, 1971, p. 7-64, bibl., illus., map)

Discussion of the ecology, settlement pattern, architecture, subsistence pattern, artefacts, pottery seriation and discussion of Alamito cultures and their relationships with Argentine and Chilean cultures. Extremely important article.

885a. _____ **and Beatriz N. Núñez Regueiro de De Lorenzi.** Arqueología histórica del norte de la provincia de Corrientes (UNCIA/R, 4, 1974, p. 23-68, bibl., illus.)

In correlation with PRONAPA research program in Brazil authors sought relationships to contact period sites in southern Brazil and northeast Argentina. Provides good ecological approach, describes ceramic materials, establishes sequences by seriation, and applies ethnohistorical documents of founding of missions to correlate the material into historic periods. Also has Tupiguarani and non-Tupiguarani traditions as well as European ones. A highly significant article.

886. Palanca, Floreal; Liliana Gau; and Aldo Pankonin. Yacimiento Estancia La Moderna, partido de Azul, provincia de Buenos Aires (MEMDA/E, 17, enero/junio 1973, p. 1-12, bibl., illus., map)

Additional comments on same site previously discussed in *HLAS 35:791*. Reports on quartz and quartzite chips, flakes and artefacts found in association with extinct megafauna, such as glyptodon and closely related fauna.

887. Palma, Néstor Homero. Transfiguraciones antropológicas de la puna argentina (UNLPM/R, 7:48 [Antropología] 18 oct. 1972, p. 239-296, bibl.)

From ecological approach, discusses the value of the term *puna* both as a geographical and cultural concept. Describes prehispanic roots and their carry-over into Spanish colonial and modern times as well as the demographic situation which has been created by the

888. Pelissero, Norberto. Las pictografías de Abra de Lagunas, depto. de Rinconada, prov. de Jujuy (SAA/R, 7, 1973, p. 187-195, bibl., illus.)

Describes pictographs and then tries to divide the motifs and use of color among various periods based on comparison with pottery motifs from nearby Quebrada de Huamahuaco sites.

889. Raffino, Rodolfo A. Agricultura hidráulica y simbiosis económica demográfica en la Quebrada del Toro, Salta, Argentina (UNLPM/R, 7:49 [Antropología] 22 marzo 1973, p. 297-332, illus., maps, plates, tables)

For a better understanding of the archaeological context of the area, suggests a study of the present ecological adjustment and shows that in late periods (13th to 15th centuries) the introduction of artifical irrigation, control of land erosion and use of fertilizers increased population and allowed urban centers to develop.

889a. _____ **and Eduardo M. Cigliano.** La Alumbrera, Antofagasta de la Sierra: un modelo de ecología cultural prehispánica (SAA/R, 7, 1973, p. 241-258, bibl., illus., map)

Based on Murra's "vertical adaptation" theories, authors suggest possibility of applying these ecosystems of highland situations and their relationships to archaeological situations of the lowlands, coast, and plateau such as the Valle de Hualfin and Antofagasta de la Sierra.

890. Rodríguez, Amílcar. Notas relacionadas con los sitios arqueológicos relevados en Salto Grande, depto. Federación, prov. de Entre Ríos, Argentina (Revista [Comisión Municipal de Cultura, Depto. de Antropología y Folklore, Concordia, Arg.] 2:2, 1971, p. 13-16, ilus.)

Description of ceramic and lithic remains from shell midden Carbon-14 dated between 860 and 1180 AD. Pottery decoration is limited to a row of nicks a or punctates on the flat or rounded lip of simple, open, deep bowls.

891. Rolandi de Perrot, Diana Susana. Ikat en Tastil, provincia de Salta (SAA/R, 7, 1973, p. 183-185, bibl.)

First time in Argentina that ikat painting (negative) technique is clearly associated with Late period (1400 AD) materials from Tastil site (see item 870 and *HLAS 35:769a*).

892. Schobinger, Juan. Una punta de tipo "cola de pescado" de La Crucecita, Mendoza (UNC/AAE, 26, 1971, p. 89-97, bibl., illus.)

Describes fishtail projectile point of fine-grained basalt and other lithic artefacts of small points, scrapers, bifacial artefacts, etc., and compares this style with others from Brazil, Uruguay, Argentina and Chile.

893. Sempe de González Llanes, María Carlota. Ultimas etapas del desarrollo cultural indígena, 1480-1690, en el Valle de Abaucán, Tinogasta, provincia de Catamarca (UNLPM/R, 8:50 [Antropología] 1 agosto 1973, p. 1-46, bibl., illus., maps, plates, tables)

Series of sites excavated by author in 1969-71 extending from Inca period to early Spanish colonial in the Abaucán valley of southwest part of Catamarca prov. Combines archaeological and ethnohistorical accounts.

894. Togo, José. Prospeccion arqueológica en el departamento Santa Victoria, provincia de Salta (Actualidad Antropológica [Suplemento de *Etnía*, Museo Etnográfico Municipal Dámasco Arce, Olavarría,

Arg.] 12, enero/junio 1973, p. 1-8, bibl., map)

Surface survey and stratigraphic testing revealed four sites with pottery of late complex probably related to what Bennett called Iruya complex.

BOLIVIA

895. Ibarra Grasso, Dick Edgar. Prehistoria de Bolivia. 2. ed. rev. La Paz, Editorial Los Amigos del Libro, 1973. 427 p., bibl., illus., plates, tables (Enciclopedia boliviana)

Rev. 2. ed. (see *HLAS 29:1068*) of pocket book about Bolivian archaeology from earliest Paleo-Indian horizon to Inca period. Extensive bibliography.

896. Riester, Jürgen. Felszeichnungen und-gravierungen in Ostbolivien (DGV/ZE, 97:1, 1972, p. 74-102, illus., maps, plates)

Pictographs of eastern Bolivian provinces: Velasco, Chiquitos, Ñuflo de Chavez, Cordillera and Sara.

897. Wassén, S. Henry. Ethnobotanical follow-up of Bolivian Tiahuanacoid tomb material, and of Peruvian shamanism, psychotropic plant constituent, and espingo seeds (EM/A, 1972, p. 35-47, bibl.)

Attempts to identify espingo seeds described by author in sorcerer's grave lot (see *HLAS 34:1236* and *HLAS 35:821*). Includes appendix by Wolmar E. Bondeson "Anatomical Notes on Espingo and Seeds of Quararibea" (p. 48-52) which microscopically and anatomically compares espingo seeds with those of the Quararibea species of Bombacaceae genera.

BRAZIL

898. Baiocchi, Mari de Nazaré. Inventário arqueológico do Estado de Goiás: esboço de pesquisas que continuam . . . Goiânia, Bra., Oriente, 1972. 31 p., bibl., illus., maps, plates.

Brief geographical description of Goiás and what little is known of its archaeology (mostly petroglyphs, lithic material, pictographs, and very little ceramic material), noting regions to be studied, and plotting the known sites in a good map of the state.

899. Becker-Donner, Etta. Geriefte Keramik des Río Negro: Gebietes aus den Jahren 1830-1831 (MVW/AV, 24, 1970, p. 1-19, bibl., illus.

Although not archaeology, this study of a large collection in Vienna's Museum für Volkerkunde—assembled in 1830-31 by Johann Natter from Barcelos on Rio Negro and from Baniva tribe on lower Rio Içana—is of extreme importance for comparative data. During the 1830s, the last of the Manao tribe lived at Barcelos; both Baniva and Manao were Arawak-speaking. Study of pottery techniques, including chemical data by W.P. Bauer, is of interest to archaeologist because excised techniques and designs resemble materials from Rio Napo and are distributed down the Amazon as far as Marajó in Meggers and Evans' Horizon III. Suggests modern survival of old techniques.

900. Beltrão, Maria da Conceição de M. Coutinho and **Edina Gabizo de Faria.** Acampamentos Tupiguarani para coleta de moluscos (MP/R, 19, 1970/1971, p. 97-135, bibl., illus., maps, plates)

Description and seriation of complexes attributed to the Tupiguarani in Guanabara state. Nomenclature does not correlate with previously described phases, nor do all sites produce pottery of the type defined as Tupiguarani by others; comparison with other archaeological findings is consequently hampered.

901. Blasi, Oldemar. Cultura do índio pré-histórico: Vale do Iapó, Tibagi, Paraná, Brasil (MP/A, 6, 1972, p. 1-20, bibl., illus., map)

Correlates pictographs of animals with existing fauna and describes the lithic materials stratigraphically excavated from a rockshelter in area known as Floriano.

902. Brochado, José Proenza. Migraciones que defundieron la tradición alfarera tupíguaraní (SAA/R, 7, 1973, p. 7-39, bibl., maps)

An excellent summary, with complete bibliography of the Tupiguarani ceramic tradition based on 52 Carbon-14 dates and archaeology of PRONAPA program in Brazil. Proposes two great migrations to explain complicated pattern of diffusion of culture in lowland South America. Two centers, one located in Alto Paraná and another in Alto Uruguay river valleys. First began about 500-700 AD, other ca. 1300 AD onward.

902a. ———. Pesquisas arqueológicas no escudo cristalino do Rio Grande do Sul (*in* Programa Nacional de Pesquisas Arqueológicas. Resultados preliminares do quinto ano: 1969-1970. Belém, Bra., Museu Paraense Emílio Goeldi, 1974, p. 25-52, bibl., illus., map [Publicações avulsas, 26])

Studies areas in uplands of the right-bank tributaries of Rio Camaquã and on coastal plain adjacent to Laguna dos Patos in southeastern Rio Grande do Sul. Coastal plain dominated by small mounds consists of two components: one with lithic artifacts; other with pottery, a few sherds of which show relationships to Vieira Phase. Upland forested area produced four phases. Two are clearly of Tupiguarani tradition, Corrugated subtradition (Camaquã and Canguçu Phases), one possibly showing trade or imitation of Tupiguarani tradition (Piratini) and one Neobrazilian tradition (Faxinal Phase). Neobrazilian sites date into 20th century and estimate Tupiguarani phases as dating from 16th century or later.

903. Calderón, Valentín. Contribução para o conhecimento da arqueologia do recôncavo e do sul do Estado da Bahia (*in* Programa Nacional de Pesquisas Arqueológicas. Resultados preliminares do quinto ano: 1969-1970. Belém, Bra., Museu Paraense Emílio Goeldi, 1974, p. 141-154, bibl., illus., map [Publicações avulsas, 26])

Investigations defined sites representing the Periperi and Aratu traditions and Tupiguaranti tradition, but insufficient material available from latter to define the subtradition.

904. Chymz, Igor. Dados arqueológicos do Baixo Rio Paranapanema e do Alto Rio Paraná (*in* Programa Nacional de Pesquisas Arqueológicas. Resultados preliminares do quinto ano: 1969-1970. Belém, Bra., Museu Paraense Emílio Goeldi, 1974, p. 67-90, bibl., illus., map [Publicações avulsas, 26])

Studies 53 sites along lower Rio Paranapanema at its junction with the Rio Paraná and on the lower Rio Samambaia in adjacent Mato Grosso. Originally region dominated by tropical rain forest. Ten sites represent two nonceramic phases; rest four Tupiguarani phases, one to Painted subtradition, two to Corrugated subtradition, and one the Brushed subtradition. No Carbon-14 dates available but they can be related to previously recognized phases in Paraná.

905. Dias Júnior, Ondemar F. Nota prévia sobre as pesquisas arqueológicas em Minas Gerais (*in* Programa Nacional de Pesquisas Arqueológicas. Resultados preliminares do quinto ano: 1969-1970. Belém, Bra., Museu Paraense Emílio Goeldi, 1974, p. 105-116, bibl., illus., map [Publicações avulsas, 36])

Survey and testing in valley of Rio Grande and its tributaries in southern Minas Gerais in Brazilian Planalto produced 16 sites: 13 of non-Tupiguarani origin and one of Tupiguarani tradition, one of Neo-Brazilian and other pictographs.

905a. _____. Pesquisas arqueológicas no sudeste brasileiro (Boletim do Instituto de Arqueologia Brasileira [Centro de Estudos Arqueológicos, Rio] 1 [série especial] 1975, p. 1-31, bibl.)

Good brief summary of archaeological work over past seven years in states of Rio de Janeiro, Guanabara, and Goiás by author and staff of Instituto publishing this new series, the Patrimônio Histórico e Artístico Nacional, and PRONAPA.

906. Eble, Alroino B. Identificação arqueológica de padrões de povoamento e de subsistencia na região do Alto Vale do Itajaí, Santa Catarina, Brasil (Anais do Museu de Antropologia [Univ. Federal do Santa Catarina, Florianópolis, Bra.] 6:6, dez. 1973, p. 63-74, bibl.)

In order to solve the problem of the Xokleng Indians' settlement patterns, proposes going backward in time through archaeological evidence in the Itajaí Valley, especially since there is written information on this group and what has been happening in their reservations since 1914. Stresses the ecological approach, especially environmental niches.

906a. _____. Problemas arqueológicos da região do Alto Valle do Itajaí (Anais do Museu de Antropologia [Univ. Federal do Santa Catarina, Florianópolis, Bra.] 6:6, dez. 1973, p. 41-50, bibl.)

From the original 19 sites found by Piazza in Valley of Itajaí, Eble extended the study in 1972-73 and found 93 sites, gathering collections from each. This new data covers all the previously found phases and extends our knowledge of them as well as of material from sites recently occupied by the acculturated Xokleng Indians.

906b. _____ and **Sérgio Schmitz.** Sitio cerâmico sôbre dunas: SC-LL-70 (Anais do Museu de Antropologia [Univ. Federal de Santa Catarina, Florianópolis, Bra.] 5:5, dez. 1971, p. 29-56, bibl., illus.)

Site of Guaiúba in the município of Laguna in Santa Catarina state produced pottery which was typed and described. Compares with Miller's material from Rio Grande do Sul and relates it to Maquiné phase, Tupiguarani tradition.

907. Evans, Clifford and Betty J. Meggers. Introdução (*in* Programa Nacional de Pesquisas Arqueológicas. Resultados preliminares do quinto ano: 1969-1970. Belém, Bra., Museu Paraense Emílio Goeldi, 1974, p. 7-10, bibl. [Publicações avulsas, 26])

Brief statement of the fifth report and final official year of the cooperative research program. For individual authors and their specific contributions see items 902a, 903, 904, 905, 910, 913, 916, 918, 919, 921, and 925.

908. Hurt, Wesley R. The interrelationships between the natural environment and four sambaquís: coast of Santa Catarina, Brazil. Bloomington, Indiana Univ. Museum, 1974. 23 p., bibl., illus., maps (Occasional papers and monographs, 1)

This report on fieldwork conducted in 1966 stresses only the relationships between the four sites and their habitat, reserving for future discussion the artifacts and their stratigraphic associations. Divides chronology of shell middens of Santa Catarina into VII periods from first of ca. 18,000-5800 years ago to most recent of 2000-1600 BP. Four sites were in three different environmental situations. Good photos and profile drawings and charts thoroughly explain the ecological situation.

909. Kneip, Lina Maria. Pescadores e

coletores do litoral: sugestões para um projeto de pesquisas (MP/R, 19, 1970/1971, p. 137-145, bibl.)

Proposes that a research program be designed around a social anthropological interpretation of the archaeological data on fishermen and gatherers along coast of state of Guanabara and Rio de Janeiro in shell midden sites.

910. Maranca, Silvia. Relatório das atividades do quarto e quinto anos do PRONAPA no estado de São Paulo (*in* Programa Nacional de Pesquisas Arqueológicas. Resultados preliminares do quinto ano: 1969-1970. Belém, Bra., Museu Paraense Emílio Goeldi, 1974, p. 117-126, bibl., illus., map [Publicações avulsas, 26])

Studies two widely separated areas in São Paulo state: 1) Rio Itararé in south, the principal left-bank tributary of the Rio Paranapanema, which produced eight sites, among them one lithic and another representing two phases of the Tupiguarani tradition, Painted subtradition; and 2) the Ilha Solteira region on the Rio Paraná (studied because of the forthcoming hydroelectric dam construction) which yielded eight sites but insufficient material to define cultural phases.

911. Meggers, Betty J. and Clifford Evans. A reconstitução da pré-história amazônica: algumas considerações teóricas (MPEG/PA, 20, 1973, p. 51-69, bibl., maps)

Biologists established forest refuges in the Amazonian basin which show that there was a change of climate over past history of man's occupation of area, especially the last arid period of from 3500—2000 years ago. Comparisons with their findings suggest that some correlation can occur with language distributions. Unfortunately, one cannot draw final interpretation because archaeology and linguistic studies of Amazon are still relatively unknown in areas of these refugia. However, we can suggest directions of future research and how it should take into consideration these climatic fluctuations.

912. Mendes, Josué Camargo. Conheça a pré-história brasileira. São Paulo, Editôra Polígono da Univ. de São Paulo, 1970. 153 p., illus., maps, plates, tables.

History from late Pleistocene times to various cultures, such as Santarem, existing when European arrived. Devotes excessive amount of space to shell mounds, Lagôa Santa and Marajó without referring to other areas. Makes no mention of recent program (PRONAPA) of archaeological research. His training as a paleontologist is reflected in emphasis given certain subjects.

913. Miller, Eurico Th. Pesquisas arqueológicas em abrigos-sob-rocha no nordeste do Rio Grande do Sul (*in* Programa Nacional de Pesquisas Arqueológicas. Resultados preliminares do quinto ano: 1969-1970. Belém, Bra., Museu Paraense Emílio Goeldi, 1974, p. 11-24, bibl., illus., maps [Publicações avulsas, 26])

Investigates 50 sites along the lower escarpment of Rio Grande do Sul between 10 and 300 m. elevation. Analysis includes other rock shelter sites from previous work, but open sites are left out for future reports. Five phases: two ceramic (Taquara phase of the Taquara tradition and Monjolo phase of Neobrazilian tradition) and three preceramic (Umbu, Itapui and Camboatá), representing two subtraditions. Earliest prior to 6000 BP with lanceolate points and later with stemmed points imply two chronological phases of 6000-4000 BP and 4000-1000 (?) BP.

914. Myazaki, Nobue and Desidério Aytai. A aldea prehistórica de Monte Mór. Campinas, Bra., Pontifícia Univ. Católica de Campinas, 1974. 33 p., illus. (Publicações avulsas)

Concerns materials gathered in stratigraphic excavation at a site on the left side of the Rio Capivari-Mirim, São Paulo state. Without using established terminology for Brazil's pottery types, develops different classifications by surface color, thickness and weight of sherds per level.

915. Myers, Thomas P. Toward the reconstruction of prehistoric community patterns in the Amazon basin (*in* Lathrap, Donald W. and Jody Douglas eds. Variations in anthropology: essays in honor of John C. McGregor. Urbana, Illinois Archaeological Survey, 1973, p. 233-252, bibl.)

Using data on Amazonian settlement patterns from ethnographic information and archaeology of Meggers, Evans, Simões, and Hilbert, reconstructs precolumbian picture. Then compares this with Lathrap's data on central Ucayali in eastern Peru and observes that this information is inadequate. Author does not believe large societies developed first in Marajó, Rio Napo or Ucayali. Suggests that one may have to look outside the tropical forest for the origin of Amazonian complex societies but notes prior need to learn more about tropical forest area.

916. Nasser, Nássaro A. de Souza. Nova contribuição à arqueologia do Rio Grande do Norte (*in* Programa Nacional de Pesquisas Arqueológicas. Resultados preliminares do quinto ano: 1969-1970. Belém, Bra., Museu Paraense Emílio Goeldi, 1974, p. 155-163, bibl., illus., map [Publicações avulsas, 26])

Investigations concentrated on east coast produced a site where surface and upper levels were of Tupiguarani tradition whereas below was Papeba phase, the first non-Tupiguarani phase reported for Rio Grande do Norte. This phase had lots of shell and small mammal bones in refuse and no evidence of agriculture.

917. Pallestrini, Luciana. Metodi de scavi adattati a zone archeologiche brasiliane (*in* International Congress of Americanists, XL, Roma-Genova, 1972. Atti [see item 513 v. 1, p. 293-301, bibl., illus., map)

Explains how she adapts the excavation technique of Prof. Leroi-Gourhan of France to a variety of sites in São Paulo state, ranging from shell middens to urn burials of Tupiguarani tradition.

918. Perota, Celso. Resultados preliminares sobre a arqueolgia da região central do estado do Espírito Santo (*in* Programa Nacional de Pesquisas Arqueológicas. Resultados preliminares do quinto ano: 1969-1970. Belém, Bra., Museu Paraense Emílio Goeldi, 1974, p. 127-139, bibl., illus., map [Publicações avulsas, 26])

Area studied covers the Valley of the Rio Doce and the shore between the river and the town of Vitória. There were 47 sites representing five phases and three traditions. Two phases of the Tupiguarani tradition, Painted subtradition were defined, and two phases of the Aratu tradition were identified as well as six sites of the Una tradition. Carbon-14 dates for area show Tupiguarani tradition sites to be earlier than Aratu tradition.

919. Piazza, Walter F. Dados à arqueológia do litoral norte e do planalto de Canoinhas (*in* Programa Nacional de Pesquisas Arqueológicas. Resultados preliminares do quinto ano: 1969-1970. Belém, Bra., Museu Paraense Emílio Goeldi, 1974, p. 53-66, bibl., illus., map [Publicações avulsas, 26])

Two distinct environments produced sites: 1) coastal marine zone yielded 61 sites with three nonceramic and three ceramic phases (two non-Tupiguarani tradition and one Tupiguarani tradition, Corrugated subtradition); and 2) highland area produced six sites all belonging to the nonceramic Itaió phase, dating by Carbon-14 at 1290-1660 AD.

920. Prous-Poirier, André. Os objetos zoomorfos do litoral do sul do Brasil e do Uruguai (Anais do Museo de Antropologia [Univ. Federal de Santa Catarina, Florianópolis, Bra.] 5:5, dez. 1971, p. 57-102, bibl., illus.)

Pulls together the literature with descriptive material and photos of the polished-stone zoomorphic artifacts found over last century in shell midden sites along Brazilian and Uruguayan coast. Concludes that they were not utilitarian objects but involved in social life of people and that because of their significance were often traded beyond coastal area. Unfortunately, too few have good provenience data or information on associations.

921. Rauth, José Wilson. Nota prévia sobre a escavação arqueológica do sambaqui do Rio Jacarei (*in* Programa Nacional de Pesquisas Arqueológicas. Resultados preliminares do quinto ano: 1969-1979. Belém, Bra., Museu Paraense Emílio Goeldi, 1974, p. 91-104, bibl., illus., map [Publicações avulsas, 26])

Results of excavation of shell-midden Jacarei with brief description of artefacts, predominantly pounders and choppers with a few stemmed projectile points. Predominantly mangrove oyster and *Anomalocardia* with lots of animal bones and very few fish bones. Three badly preserved human burials found in refuse. Artefacts and geological situation suggest it is more recent than others in area, with closest resemblances to Saquarema, Gomes, and Macedo which date between 2937 and 1356 BC.

922. Ribeiro, Pedro Augusto Mentz. Os abrigos-sob-rocha do Virador, no estado do Rio Grande do Sul, Brasil: nota prévia (Revista do CEPA [Associação Pró-Ensino em Santa Cruz do Sul, Bra.] 2, 1975, p. 1-25, bibl., illus., map)

Virador I rockshelter is largest with Taquara tradition sherds in upper 80 cm., dated 630 ± 250 BP from 50-60 cm. depth. Virador II shelter has the same tradition. Eight extended burials from this shelter represent one adult male, three adult females, and four sub-adults.

922a. _____. Novos petróglifos na encosta centro-oriental da Serra Geral, Rio Grande do Sul, Brasil: nota prévia (Antropologia [Museu do Colégio Mauá, Santa Cruz do Sul, Bra.] 2, 1973, p. 2-28, bibl., illus. map)

Describes 10 groups of petroglyphs on east central slope of the Serra Geral and tries to correlate with known archaeological phases.

922b. _____. Os petróglifos de Cerro Alegre, Santa Cruz do Sul, Rio Grande do Sul, Brasil (Revista do CEPA [Associação Pró-Ensino em Santa Cruz do Sul, Bra.] 1, 1974, p. 2-15, bibl., illus., map)

Petroglyphs in the form of a tree or fish backbone suggest they might be related to Itapuí phase.

922c. _____. Petróglifos do sítio RS-T-14: Morro do Sobrado, Montenegro, RS, Brasil (Iheringia [Antropologia. Pôrto Alegre, Bra.] 2, 1972, p. 3-14, bibl., illus.)

Petroglyphs on a sandstone slab include steps, "bird tracks," a "bridge," a tree, and a "star."

922d. _____. Primeiras datações pelo método do Carbon-14 para o Vale do Rio Caí, Rio Grande do Sul (Revista do CEPA [Associação Pró-Ensino em Santa Cruz do Sul, Bra.] 1, 1974, p. 16-22, bibl.)

Comments on six Carbon-14 dates furnished by Smithsonian laboratory, from various phases in Valle do Rio Caí, Rio Grande do Sul. Of interest to specialist are the full details on the phases.

922e. _____. Sítio RS-C-4: Bom Jardim Velho—Abrigo sob rocha: nota prévia (Iheringia [Antropologia. Pôrto Alegre, Bra.] 2, 1972, p. 15-58, bibl., illus.)

Excavations in a rock shelter in the Rio Caí drainage revealed two habitation layers. The upper 10 cm. produced pottery, bone points, stone tools, shell and tooth ornaments, and food remains; it belongs to the Taquara tradition. The lower 35 cm. produced only stone, bone and tooth artefacts and food remains.

923. Schmitz, Pedro Ignacio. Cronología de las culturas del sudeste de Rio Grande do Sul, Brasil (*in* Congreso del Museo Municipal de Historia Natural de Río Negro, Fray Bentos, Uru., 1973. Antecedentes y anales. Fray Bentos, Uru., Museo Municipal de Historia Natural de Río Negro, 1973, p. 105-117, bibl.)

Brief, but useful summary of archaeological sequences for southeast Brazil. Includes chart.

923a. _____. Programa arqueológico de Goiás (Anuário de Divulgação Científica [Goiânia, Bra.] 1:1, 1974, p. iii-iv, map)

Statement of the official archaeological research program in Goiás, the Cabinete de Arqueologia of the Univ. Católica de Goiás.

923b. _____. Projecto Alto Araguaia: relatório prévio (Anuário de Divulgação Científica [Goiânia, Bra.] 1:1, 1974, p. 39-43, bibl., map)

Survey of archaeological sites on upper Rio Araguaia between Rio Vermelho and Rio Claro defines Tupiguarani tradition and Uru tradition, as well as petroglyphs.

923c. _____; Irmilhild Wüst; Altair Sales Barbosa; and Itale Irene Basile Becker. Projecto Alto Tocantins, Goiás: comunicação prévia (Anuário de Divulgação Científica [Goiânia, Bra.] 1:1, 1974, p. 1-38, bibl., illus.)

First serious archaeology of this area reveals possibility of showing a carryover of archaeological horizons into actual living Indian populations, where they still survive relatively unacculturated. Defines several different ceramic traditions: Tupiguarani, Painted subtradition, and Uru, a new one probably recent posterior to European conquest. Includes charts.

924. Silva, Mauricio Paranhos da. La culture marajoara (ARCHEO, 58, May 1973, 31-37, plates)

Review of history of investigation of the Marajoara culture at the mouth of the Amazon. No new data; illustrations include pottery vessels from the Musée d'Ethnographie de Genève.

925. Simões, Mário F. Contribuição à arqueologia dos arredores do Baixo Rio Negro, Amazonas (*in* Programa Nacional de Pesquisas Arqueológicas. Resultados preliminares do quinto ano: 1969-1970. Belém, Bra., Museu Paraense Emílio Goeldi, 1974, p. 165-188, bibl., illus., map [Publicações avulsas, 26])

Ten sites in the vicinity of the junction of the Rio Negro with the Amazon produced ceramics that could be identified as representing three phases already defined by Hilbert (*HLAS 31:1500*) as the Paredão, Guarita and Itacoatiara, as well as three new ones. Only one site was pure with a single occupation. Simões' work expands distribution and phase definitions of Hilbert's work. New phases are Apuaú which resembles Guarita but is distinguishable by paste, vessel shapes and some decorative techniques; Umari phase which is predominantly incised, punctate, fingernail-marked with some red slipping and red on white; and Pajurá phase which is a red slipped, punctate and incised tradition. Supports and redefines Hilbert's Guarita tradition into the Guarita subtradition of the Polychrome tradition in the Amazon basin.

925a. _____; Conceição G. Corrêa; and Ana Lucia Machado. Achados arqueológicos no Baixo Rio Fresco, Pará (MPEG/PA, 20, 1973, p. 113-138, bibl., illus., map)

On the Rio Fresco, a tributary of the Rio Xingú, geologists surveyed the area and found a habitation site and made surface collections and a stratigraphic cut. Sherds classify into a distinct culture complex, the Carapaná phase, representing a semipermanent sedentary agricultural group of tropical-forest type receiving some influences or trade of Tupiguarani tradition.

CHILE

926. Alaniz Carvajal, Jaime. Excavaciones arqueológicas en un conchal precerámico: La Herraura, provincia de Coquimbo, Chile (Boletín [Museo Arqueológico de La Serena, Chile] 15, 1973, p. 189-213, bibl., illus., map)

Upper levels produce Diaguita material related to earlier work of Bird and Iribarren; lower levels a nonceramic horizon of gatherers and fishermen. Dates lower levels tentatively at 3700 years ago.

927. Ampuero Brito, Gonzalo and Mario A. Rivera D. Síntesis interpretativa de la arqueología del Norte Chico (*in* Congreso Nacional de Arqueología Chilena, VI, Arica, 1971. Actas. Santiago,

Sociedad Chilena de Arqueología [and] Univ. de Chile, Depto. de Ciencias Antropológicas y Arqueología, 1971, p. 339-343)

Summary provides sequence and Carbon dates (see item 947b).

928. Bate Petersen, Luis Felipe. Apuntes para la arqueología de los primeros poblamientos del extremo sur americano. Santiago, Instituto Nacional de Antropología e Historia, Depto. de Prehistoria, 1974. 200 p., bibl., illus., map (Cuadernos de trabajo, 3)

Excellent summary of all the information available on the early cultures in Patagonia, with an effort to put it into a theoretical framework. Extensive bibliography.

928a. _____. Primeras investigaciones sobre el arte rupestre de la Patagonia chilena: segundo informe (Anales del Instituto de la Patagonia [Punta Arenas, Chile] 2:1/2, 1971, p. 33-41, bibl.)

Describes pictographs in Patagonia area and suggests a new stylistic classification needed to take into account the more extensive finds encountered since Menghin's 1957 classification.

929. Bergholz W., Hans and Walter Bergholz M. Estudios arqueológicos en el Litoral de Atacama (Boletín [Museo Arqueológico de La Serena, Chile] 15, 1973, p. 165-174, illus.)

Brief description of artefacts from tombs along coast in area of Obispito, Atacama prov., which relate to Inca period.

930. Checura Jeria, Jorge. La importancia de la conservación de los bienes culturales. Iquique, Chile, Museo Regional de Iquique, 1974. 10 p. (Cuadernos de investigaciones históricas y antropológicas, 4)

Continuation of discussion in item 930a.

930a. _____. Problemas de conservación de los bienes culturales en el área andina. Iquique, Chile, Museo Regional de Iquique, 1974. 7 p., bibl. (Cuadernos de investigaciones históricas y antropológicas, 3)

Brief comments on problem of conservation of cultural objects in such a variety of climates from such a variety of soil conditions.

931. Dauelsberg, Percy. Excavaciones arqueológicas en Quiani, provincia de Tarapacá, depto. de Arica, Chile (Revista Chungara [Univ. del Norte, Depto. de Antropología, Arica, Chile] 4, dic. 1974, p. 7-38, bibl., illus., map)

Excavation of seven tombs, description and classification of their contents, and comparison with previous excavations and materials obtained from the area by Uhle, Bird, Niemeyer and Schiappacasse. Puts site and its complexes into broader picture for coastal Chile. The preceramic Conanoxa phase, a part of the Quiani complex, has Carbon-14 dates of 3740 to 4020 BP; the Camarones complex is associated with hunters with Carbon-14 date of 6170 BP.

931a. _____. Tambores precolombinos procedentes de Playa Miller (Revista Chungara [Univ. del Norte, Depto. de Antropología, Arica, Chile] 4, dic. 1974, p. 61-63, bibl., illus.)

Drums of pottery, whalebone and wood, with the skin drumhead still in place or visible, from Playa Miller just south of Arica; from Gentilar phase dating from 1200-1350 AD.

932. Espoueys, Oscar. Metodología para el trabajo de cementerios y ordenamiento de bodegas en museos de la zona norte de Chile (Revista Chungara [Univ. del Norte, Depto. de Antropología, Arica, Chile] 2, 1973, p. 24-55)

Outlines a plan to systematize cemetery excavations and analysis of North Chilean materials and how to catalog them in museum store-rooms.

932a. _____. Tipificación de keros de madera de Arica (Revista Chungara [Univ. del Norte, Depto. de Antropología, Arica, Chile] 4, dic. 1974, p. 39-54, bibl., illus.)

Establishes a standard for description, classification, and measurement of wooden keros from their first introduction into Chile during Tiahuanacoid times to those showing Spanish influence.

933. Focacci, Guillermo and Sergio Erices. Excavaciones en túmulos de San Miguel de Azapa, Arica, Chile (*in* Congreso de Arqueología Chilena, VI, Arica, 1971. Actas. Santiago, Sociedad Chilena de Arqueología [and] Univ. de Chile, Depto. de Ciencias Antropológicas y Arqueología, 1971, p. 47-62, bibl., illus.)

Burial mounds contain: mutilated bodies without heads, and one with a trophy head in a cloth bag; spear throwers; and textiles in good condition whose style suggests acculturation period of this area from highland Tiahuanacoid culture.

934. Fonck Sieveking, Oscar. Rapa Nui: el último refugio, el origen de los pascuenses. Santiago, Editorial Zig-Zag, 1974. 314 p., bibl., illus., maps, plates, tables (Libros de bolsillo Zig-Zag, 22)

Sensational, uncritical handling of all ideas about origins of Easter Island culture without using any of the monographic studies written over last 15 years. Entirely based on romantic and popular writings.

935. Iribarren Charlín, Jorge. La arqueología en el departamento de Combarbalá, provincia de Coquimbo, Chile (Boletín [Museo Arqueológico de La Serena, Chile] 15, 1973, p. 7-115, bibl., illus., map)

Summary of many years' work in Corbambalá by Museo de La Serena. Establishes a sequence from Late Agricultural periods into Inca times (although only slightly). Notes that main occupation is the El Molle culture. Includes good line drawings of modeled pottery adornos, miscellaneous polished-stone artefacts, chipped projectile points, and other lithic artefacts.

935a. _____. Pictografías en las provincias de Atacama y Coquimbo, Chile (Boletín [Museo Arqueológico de La Serena, Chile] 15, 1973, p. 115-159, bibl., illus.)

Paper originally delivered at II Simposio Internacional de Arte Rupestre in Peru, 1967. Since lack of funds did not permit publication of its proceedings, this article is printed here without revision. Summary type of report of distribution and description of pictographs in these two provinces.

936. Laming-Emperaire, Annette. Los sitios arqueológicos de los archipiélagos de Patagonia occidental (Anales [Instituto de la Patagonia, Punta Arenas, Chile] 3:1/2, 1972, p. 87-96, bibl., map)

Summarizes literature on archaeology of archipelago of Chiloé, as well as Kaltwasser's unpublished notes, concluding that area is still practically unknown. Studies area occupied by Alakaluf and suggests extensive future work by interdisciplinary teams and widespread excavations to determine village-site differences and identify remains of great ceremonial huts.

937. Lanning, Edward P. Burin industries in the Pleistocene of the Andes (Estudios Atacameños [Univ. del Norte, Museo de Arqueología, San Pedro de Atacama, Chile] 1, 1973, p. 21-38, bibl., illus., map)

On the basis of Andean materials proposes: spread of a typical upper Paleolithic technology and toolkit into North America; arrival of this tradition into Andes about 15,000-16,000 years ago; progressive impoverishment of burin and blade technologies; and their replacement shortly after 14,000 years ago with a Biface tradition.

938. Le Paige, Gustavo. El yacimiento de Tchaputchayna (Estudios Atacameños [Univ. del Norte, Museo de Arqueología, San Pedro de Atacama, Chile] 2, 1974, p. 59-74, illus.)

Reports on work of many years at site in desert area about 6.5 km. south of San Pedro de Atacama. Describes lithic materials from surface areas of site and a cemetary which can be defined as having communal tombs, producing 68 skeletons from 38 excavations. Tabulates finds from graves of pottery, bone artefacts, copper, etc. Another part of site has mounds producing mostly incised black polished ware.

938a. _____. El valor arqueológico del Museo San Pedro de Atacama (Estudios Atacameños [Univ. del Norte, Museo de Arqueología, San Pedro de Atacama, Chile] 1, 1973, p. 7-20)

Lists the sites and number of their Paleo-Indian artefacts and materials from Chile, Bolivia, Peru, Argentina, and Venezuela, catalogued in the Museo de San Pedro de Atacama. Using author's European terminology also lists materials from more recent periods (Mesolithic and Neolithic), as well as pictographs and petroglyph sites.

938b. _____ and **George Serracino Inglott.** Informes de trabajo: Proyecto Tulan (Estudios Atacameños [Univ. del Norte, Museo de Arqueología, San Pedro de Atacama, Chile] 1, 1973, p. 43-46)

In order to develop an ecological approach to the study of man's occupation of San Pedro de Atacama area, this site at its extreme north was chosen to contrast it with Guatín (see item 948c) at the extreme south. Authors believe that a possible ceremonial structure was related at this site to Paleo-Indian horizon but needed intensive work to prove point.

939. Matson, R.G. and **D.L. True.** Site relationships at Quebrada Tarapacá, Chile: a comparison of clustering and scaling techniques (SAA/AA, 39:1, Jan. 1974, p. 51-74, bibl., map)

Applies and compares the results of a variety of clustering methods and two multidimensional scaling techniques on data from archaeological sites in northern Chile. In general concludes that relative frequency analysis is superior to the presence/absence.

940. Montané M., Julio and **Raúl Bahamondes B.** Un nuevo sitio paleo-indio en la provincia de Coquimbo, Chile (Boletín [Museo Arqueológico de La Serena, Chile] 15, 1973, p. 215-222, bibl., map)

In addition to mentioning new Paleo-Indian Program of Smithsonian and its agreement with Museo de La Serena as well as a brief summary of Paleo-Indian situation in Chile, describes new site of Queredo three km. south of Los Vilos port on a peninsula called Punta de Lobos. Chipped materials found in association with Pleistocene fauna. Relating situation to Tagua Tagua (see *HLAS 31:1534, 1548* and *HLAS 33:1054*) suggests a date of 11,000-15,000 for lowest level of site.

941. Niemeyer Fernández, Hans. Cementerio diaguita incaico del Alto de Carmen, depto. de Huasco, prov. de Atacama, Chile (UC/BPC, 3:4, 1971, p. 69-86, bibl., illus., map)

Description with good drawings of Diaguiata-Incaic materials.

941a. _____. Las pinturas indígenas rupestres de la Sierra de Arica. San Felipe, Chile, Editorial Jerónimo de Vivar, 1972? 114 p., bibl., illus., maps, plates (Enciclopedia moderna de Chile, 3)

Most complete study of pictographs from Sierra de Arica region of north Chile. Well-illustrated, with appendices describing pottery and stone artefacts from some sites in an effort to date the rock paintings.

942. Núñez Atencio, Lautaro. La agricultura prehistórica en los Andes meridonales. Santiago, Editorial Orbe, 1974. 195 p., bibl., illus., map.

Agriculture in precolumbian times discussed according to highland and coastal problems in southern and central Andean chain. Good popular account of region's archaeological background.

942a. _____. Seminario de integración local y regional de las actividades arqueológicas: sedes Universidad del Norte y Universidad de Chile. Antofagasta, Chile, Univ. del Norte, 1973. 73 p. (Serie arqueología, 1)

Series of recommendations proposed at a meeting to stress: 1) the need for integrating local and national research in archaeology with museology, 2) the protection of the national patrimony, and 3) the importance of archaeology to ecological studies and modern development plans.

942b. _____; **Viera Zlatar;** and **Patricio Núñez H.** Caleta Huelén-42: una aldea temprana en el norte de Chile, nota preliminar (UNCIA/HC, 2:5, 1974, p. 67-103, bibl., illus.)

Preceramic site at mouth of Río Loa, north Chile with stratified materials showing a village of 75-100 living structures of semicircular plan, depending exclusively on sea resources for food. Occupation dates from about 4780 to 3780 years BP. One of a few settlement patterns and human ecological studies of preceramic-sites for area. Typical artefacts illustrated. Of interest to expert.

942c. _____; _____; and _____. Reciente prospección de sitios arqueológicos componentes de un circuito trashumántico entre la costa y el borde occidental de Pampa de Tamarugal, norte de Chile (MEMDA/E, 16, julio/dic. 1972, p. 1-6, bibl.; 17, enero/junio 1973, p. 26-31, illus.)

Proposes hunting-gathering cycle of pre-agricultural groups in vertical sense from higher to lower valleys, on basis of North Chile archaeological survey of Pisagua Viejo, Punta Pichalo and the Pampa de Tamarugal.

943. Ochsenius P., Claudio. Observaciones geoecológicas en la Puna de Atacama, Chile (UC/BPC, 3:4, 1971, p. 27-48, bibl., illus., map)

Establishes the geoecology of the arid piedmont (the transitional zone between the Bolivian plateau and the Atacama desert) from standpoint of potential use and human resources in present day, but data useful to archaeologist working in area.

944. Orellana Rodríguez, Mario. Informe de las excavaciones de Loa Oeste 3 (UC/BPC, 3:4, 1971, p. 3-25, illus., map)

Archaeological excavations near pueblo of Chiu-Chiu, Loa dept., Antofagasta prov. Describes the stone materials in detail and gives the occurence by levels in strata. Includes charts.

945. Ortiz Troncoso, Omar R. Antecedentes históricos y prospección arqueológica de las Islas Isabel, Santa Marta, Magdalena y Contramestre, Estrecho de Magallanes (Anales [Instituto de la Patagonia, Punta Arenas, Chile] 2:1/2, 1971, p. 20-27, bibl., illus., map)

Documents of the 16th and 17th century discuss the importance of these Straits-of-Magellan islands in supplying food for seagoing expeditions. Now archaeology demonstrates that the Alakaluf entered the area, their easternmost penetration.

945a. _____. Arqueología de los poblados hispánicos de la Patagonia austral: segunda etapa de excavaciones en Rey Don Felipe y nuevos antecedentes sobre Nombre de Jesús (Anales [Instituto de la Patagonia, Punta Arenas, Chile] 2:1/2. 1971, p. 3-19, bibl., illus., map)

See *HLAS 35:982* for first phase of the report. To date only actual ruins of the Church found but extensive sherd refuse suggests outlines of occupation. Appendices have detailed studies of bones, shells and sherds from the excavation of this historical site which dates from 1584 to abandonment before 1587.

945b. _____. Artefactos de silex de una tumba de Morro Philippi, valle medio del Rió Gallegos, prov. de Santa Cruz, Rep. Argentina (Anales [Instituto de la Patagonia, Punta Arenas, Chile] 4:1/3, 1973, p. 131-139, illus.)

Site, some 67 km. from coast in Patagonia, produced artefacts made of quartz and not recent. Describes and illustrates ten of them. Without stratigraphic proof believes tools to be old, but author does not commit himself to actual number of years.

945c. _____. Aspectos arqueológicos de

la península de Brunswick, Patagonia austral (Anales [Instituto de la Patagonia, Punta Arenas, Chile] 4:1/3, 1973, p. 109-129, bibl., illus., map)

Defines by archaeology two distinct occupations in history of maritime nomadism in Straits of Magellan. Excellent drawings and data on nonceramic lithic materials.

945d. _____. Material lítico de Patagonia austral: seis yacimientos de superficie (Anales [Instituto de la Patagonia, Punta Arenas, Chile] 3:1/2, 1972, p. 49-65, bibl., illus., map)

Study of 602 lithic materials from six sites in southernmost Patagonia plus collections from private owners. Good descriptions, drawings and photographs of bolas, bi- and unifacial artefacts, points, scrapers, etc. Makes brief comparisons with other materials from region but, lacking stratigraphic digging in these six sites, cannot define an exact time period.

945e. _____. Nota sobre yacimiento arqueológico en el archipiélago del Cabo de Hornos (Anales [Instituto de la Patagonia, Punta Arenas, Chile] 3:1/2, 1972, p. 83-85, bibl., map)

Most southernmost site recorded to date in Patagonia is at Caleta Marcial, Herschel Island, belonging to the Cape Horn group, could be the most southern penetration of Canoe Indians.

945f. _____. Reconocimiento arqueológico del Fiordo Parry, Tierra del Fuego (Anales [Instituto de la Patagonia, Punta Arenas, Chile] 2:1/2, 1971, p. 28-32, bibl., illus., map)

Archaeological testing of the Parry Fiord revealed some historical house foundations of aborigines when they had adopted glass for making tools. It is possible that older sites exist on old marine terraces now covered by dense vegetation.

946. Reymond, Jacquelin. Cementerio araucano de Membrillo (UC/BPC, 3:4, 1971, p. 87-107, bibl., illus., map)

Araucanian cemetery with material-goods associates from end of 18th century to beginning of 19th. Interesting historical archaeology for this region, northeast of Cholchol, Cautin prov., south-central Chile.

947. Rivera, Mario A. Bases para planificar la investigación antropológica-arqueológica en el Norte Grande chileno: esquema metodológico (Revista Chungara [Univ. del Norte, Depto. de Antropología, Arica, Chile] 2, 1973, p. 4-23, bibl.)

Outlines an ecological approach to study of area using archaeology, ethnology, ethnohistory and modern social anthropology.

947a. _____. Nuevos enfoques de la teoría arqueológica aplicada al Norte Chico (*in* Congreso Nacional de Arqueología Chilena, VI, Arica, 1971. Actas. Santiago, Sociedad Chilena de Arqueología [and] Univ. de Chile, Depto. de Ciencas Antropológicas y Arqueología, 1971, p. 295-309, bibl., illus.)

Discusses concept of the Formative period in Norte Chico area of Chile, with special emphasis on botanical evidences of three different specialized races of corn at a date of ca. 4700 BP and three varieties of beans, all previously known from early Peruvian sites.

947b. _____. Nuevos fechados radiocarbónicos para la arqueología del Norte Chico (UCIA/R, 4, 1972, p. 1-6, bibl.)

Comments on 11 Carbon dates and the sequence and how the most recent of these (five from Isotopes) clarify the picture of lithic hunting and gathering of Pichasca 1, Strata III of 7970 years ago to Molle culture dates of 310 and 665 years ago.

948. Serracino Inglott, George *comp.* Bibliografía por autor: departamento El Loa, provincia de Antofagasta, Chile. San Pedro de Atacama, Chile, Univ. del Norte, Museo de Arqueología, 1974. 1 v. (Unpaged) (Documentos para la investigación, 1)

General reference bibliography of Loa dept. of significance to the region, alphabetically arranged by author and consisting of 473 regular entries plus 11 in an addendum.

948a. _____ *comp.* Referencias bibliográficas, yacimientos precerámicos, departamento El Loa. San Pedro de Atacama, Chile, Univ. del Norte, Museo de Arqueología, 1974. 33 p. (Documentos para la investigación, 5)

Specialized bibliography on nonceramic sites of Loa Dept., arranged by site names and then by author and title.

948b. _____ and **Carlos Thomas Winter.** Excavación del yacimiento Confluencia 1: informe preliminar. (UC/BPC, 3:4, 1971, p. 49-68, illus.)

Description of lithic complex of a nonceramic site in Río Salado area of Antafagasta prov.

948c. _____ and **Rubén Stehberg.** Investigaciones arqueológicas en Guatín, San Pedro de Atacama: 2° informe (Estudios Atacameños [Univ. del Norte, Museo de Arqueología, San Pedro de Atacama, Chile] 2, 1974, p. 7-57, bibl., illus., map)

Serracino and another author discuss the settlement pattern while Stehberg deals with the architecture. From an ecological approach, authors reconstruct way of life from preceramic to recent times through various pottery-agricultural phases. They also reconstruct various adaptations to region's way of life at different times.

948d. _____; _____; and **Gloria Liberman.** Informes de trabajo: proyecto Guatín (Estudios Atacameños [Univ. del Norte, Museo de Arqueología, San Pedro de Atacama, Chile] 1, 1973, p. 39-42)

Study of site of Guatín in zone of San Pedro de Atacama in effort to reconstruct the paleoenvironment as well as the way of life of the peoples who produced the lithic artefacts of this area.

949. Urrejola Dittborn, Carlos. Isla Grande de Tierra del Fuego, Bahía Inútil: informe arqueológico (UC/BPC, 3:4, 1971, p. 121-133, bibl., illus.)

Survey of sites in this part of Patagonia causes author to conclude that all of the area's archaeology must take into consideration the past geographical situation when man lived there. Lists sites worthy of further study.

950. Von Borries, Edgar. Sitios arqueológicos precerámicos y agroalfareros en la precordillera de la zona central (UC/BPC, 3:4, 1971, p. 109-119, illus., map)

Survey of sites along border of Santiago and Aconcagua provs. describes lithic materials in greater detail than pottery.

COLOMBIA

951. Banco de la República, *Bogotá*. El Dorado. Bogotá, Museo del Oro [and] Litografía Arco, 1973. 1 v. (Unpaged) bibl., illus., map, plates, tables.

Gold Museum as it was reorganized in 1973 with color photos of some of its new and also most famous pieces.

952. Bischof, Henning. Die Tairona-Kultur: Untersuchungen zur Indianischen Kulturgeschichte Nord-Kolumbens (BGAEU/M, 2:2, 1969 [i.e., 1972] p. 53-68, bibl., illus.)

Brief comment on small excavation at the Pueblito site of the Tairona culture and discussion of chronology and correlations with Mesoamerica.

953. Broadbent, Sylvia M. Reconocimientos arqueológicos de la Laguna de Herrera (ICA/RCA, 15, 1970/1971, p. 171-213, illus., tables)

Describes sites and their pottery in survey of the Laguna de Herrera area which lies in the southern part of the Bogotá Sabana. Materials relate to that found at other sites in Chibcha territory, such as Tocanicipa, by Haury and Cubillos.

954. Caldas, Ana María de; Alvaro Chaves Mendoza; and **Marina Villamizar.** Las tumbas del Valle de El Dorado. Bogotá Ediciones de la Univ. de los Andes, 1972. 29 p., bibl., illus., map (Antropología, 5)

Antechambered shaft tombs in Municipio of Yotoco and Restrepo, Valle de Cauca dept., produced pottery of the Sonso phase dated around 1235-1580 AD by Carbon-14.

955. Duque Gómez, Luis. Arte lítico monumental en San Agustín (ESP, 125, sept./dic. 1972, p. 5-48, map, plates)

Description and commentary on stone sculptures of San Agustín. See *HLAS 29:1174* for greater details in a full-length monograph on this culture and site.

955a. _____ and **Pascal Hinous.** Les geants qui sortent de terre en Colombie (CA, 252, fev. 1973, p. 46-55, illus., plates)

Illustration of a sample of more than 300 stone sculptures from San Agustín, Huila dept., associated with tombs dating between 500 BC and 1200 AD.

956. Jijón y Caamaño, Jacinto. Las culturas andinas de Colombia. Bogotá, Banco Popular, 1974. 307 p., bibl., illus., maps, plates, tables (Biblioteca Banco Popular, 60)

Author's original edition based on his notes on precolumbian cultures of Colombia, was published in 1956, six years after his death. This is a reprint.

957. Preuss, Konrad Theodor. Arte monumental prehistórico: excavaciones hechas en el Alto Magdalena y San Agustín, Colombia; comparación arqueológica con las manifestaciones artísticas de las demás civilizaciones americanas. Traducción del alemán por Hermann Walde-Waldegg y César Uribe Piedrahita. Edición y notas a cargo de Eugenio Barney Cabrera y Pablo Gamboa Hinestrosa. Fotografías de Pablo Gamboa Hinestrosa. 3. ed. Bogotá, Univ. Nacional de Colombia, Dirección de Divulgación Cultural, 1974. 503 p., bibl., illus., maps, plates, tables.

Spanish translation including excellent reproduction of Preuss' original 1931 plates, with additional photos and comments by Pablo Gamboa Hinestrosa.

958. Reichel-Dolmatoff, Gerardo. Contribuciones al conocimiento de la estratigrafía cerámica de San Agustín, Colombia. Bogotá, Banco Popular, 1975. 157 p., bibl., illus., map (Biblioteca Banco Popular)

Results of seven stratigraphic excavations by author in

1966-68 in San Agustín, which produced 150,000 sherds. Establishes three major periods: 1) Horqueta and Primavera complexes before zero AD; 2) Isnos complex up to around 400 AD; and 3) the Sombrerillos complex. Of importance to Colombian archaeology. Shows the extensive village refuse through long periods and probably indicates a large population in the area at any one time.

958a. _____. **The cultural context of early fiber-tempered pottery in northern Colombia** (UASD/R, 2:4, julio/dic. 1972, p. 123-130, illus.)

Type site for fiber-tempered pottery is Puerto Hormiga. Summarizes the situation of this small community of shellfish gatherers and fishermen with Early Formative period pottery. See *HLAS 25:305* for more detailed discussion.

959. Rodríguez Lamus, Luis Raúl and **Vidal Antonio Rozo. Museo Arqueológico Casa del Marqués de San Jorge.** Bogotá, Museo Arqueológico Casa del Marqués de San Jorge, 1974. 110 p., bibl., illus., map.

Catalog of pottery specimens in the new archaeological museum. Some pieces heretofore unpublished. Interesting Tumaco material once again illustrates the error of considering it a culture separate from that found in northern Ecuador, Esmeraldas prov. In a recently restored colonial house, this museum now owns a pottery collection of over 10,000 pieces from all parts of Colombia.

960. Sampson, E.H.; S.J. Fleming; and **W. Bray. Thermoluminescent dating of Colombian pottery in the Yotoco style** (Archaeometry [Oxford Univ., Research Laboratory for Archaeology in the History of Art, London] 14:1, Feb. 1972, p. 119-126, bibl., illus., map)

Specimens collected during field work in 1964 and from sites in floodplain of Cauca Valley, Colombian Andes, close to city of Buga. Thermoluminescent studies on two unrelated chronological problems. Experts should read article for interesting correlations occur with TL dates and Carbon-14. Yotoco style by TL gives mean dates of 900 AD and by Carbon-14 1100 AD, but the dating errors of the two techniques explain this. The recent TL date of the pottery crucible is possibly explicable in terms of the peculiar collecting conditions, which were not scientific. See *HLAS 35:859* for more on Buga area.

961. Schlenther, Ursula. Im Reiche el Dorados: eine Kulturgeschichte der Indianer in Kolumbien. Leipzig, GDR, Urania-Verlag, 1973. 182 p., bibl., plates.

Summary of the culture history of Indian groups up to Spanish conquest of Colombia with archaeological data stressed when available.

962. Schuler-Schömig, Immina von. Patrizen im Goldschmiedhandwerk der Muisca kolumbiens (MV/BA, 22, 1974, p. 1-22, bibl., illus.)

Description with excellent photographs of the stone counterdie upon which the gold was pressed to form certain designs of the Muisca culture.

ECUADOR

963. Agro, Robert J. Algunas sugerencias ambientales determinantes que se relacionan con la geografía política del Perú pre-incáico y del sur del Ecuador (CCE/CHA, 32:39, 1972, p. 186-209, bibl., maps)

Compares the ecological situation on Peru's coast where political and military control and competition for land and irrigation water lead to a sociopolitical situation different from that of coastal and highland Ecuador where author sees easy movement back and forth, plenty of water due to rainfall and no great problems of control needed for land or irrigation. However, he admits no hard proof is available for his ideas.

964. Alcina Franch, José. El proyecto de arqueología de Esmeraldas, Ecuador (EANH/B, 56:121, enero/julio 1973, p. 55-76, bibl.)

Outlines an interdisciplinary program for Esmeraldas region of coastal Ecuador from 1970-75.

965. Athens, J. Stephen and **Alan J. Osborn. Archaeological investigations at two ceramic period sites in the highlands of northern Ecuador** (*in* Archaeological investigations in the highlands of northern Ecuador: two preliminary reports. Otavalo, Ecua., Instituto Otavaleño de Antropología, 1974, p. 1-9, illus., map [Series: Archaeology, 1:1])

Excavation results at La Chimba site, 3160 m. altitude on slopes of Mt. Cayambe in northern Pichincha prov.; and Otavalo mounds and Site Im ll in Imbabura prov. Tabulates sherds and lithic artifacts, but their descriptions are not conventional, and no effort is made to use known periods of pottery terminology of Ecuador. Carbon-14 dates put sites in 730-760 AD horizon. Includes unnumbered pages of 21 figures and appendices.

966. Bischof, Henning. Una investigación estratigráfica en Valdivia, Ecuador: primeros resultados (Indiana [Ibero-Amerikanischen Institut, Berlin, FRG] 1, 1973, p. 157-164, bibl., illus.)

Proposes new ceramic complex based on 27 sherds from lowest levels of the Valdivia site. San Pedro pottery is well made, decorated with incision, and believed intrusive into the non-ceramic community occupying the site.

966a. _____. **The origins of pottery in

South America: recent radiocarbon dates from Southwest Ecuador (*in* International Congress of Americanists, XL, Roma-Genova, 1972. Atti [see item 513] v. 1, p. 269-281, bibl.)

On the basis of dates from 11 samples from four different sites of Valdivia period, reconstructs version of Valdivia history different than Meggers, Evans and Estrada's (SEE *HLAS 29:1203.*) Also discusses Colombian materials, especially Puerto Hormiga and Canapote, noting need for more work on the country's early sites. Since presentation of this paper at the 1972 Americanists Congress other dates have been obtained that would tend to reconfirm the Meggers, Evans and Estrada sequence and time period rather than Bishof's.

967. Capua, Constanza di. Analisis morfológico y estético de algunos fragmentos de la cultura Valdivià (EANH/B, 56:121, enero/julio 1973, p. 102-114, bibl., illus.)

Extremely detailed analysis of Valdivia pottery figurines from standpoint of technique of manufacture and decoration motifs.

968. Crespo Toral, Hernán. Queros ecuatorianos (UCEIA/H, 7:1, 1969/1970, p. 7-34, bibl., plates)

Describes 17 wooden keros in collections with information on condition, ownership, size, and known provenience to demonstrate Inca domination of Ecuador area. Useful compilation with good photographs.

969. Holm, Olaf. La casa precolombina. Guayaquil, Ecua., Casa de la Cultura Ecuatoriana, Núcleo del Guayas, Sección de Antropología Cultural, 1974. 12 p., illus. (La pieza del mes, 1)

Booklet about a special exhibition held at the Anthropology Section of the Casa de la Cultura's center in Guayaquil, Ecua. Part of a series entitled "The Piece of the Month," the booklet concerns house models from various precolumbian cultures of the Ecuadorian coast, from Chorrera period upward. Special piece is called Chorrera, but because of its negative painting it would be more correct to assign it to Tejar period.

969a. ———. La cultura Chorrera. Guayaquil, Ecua., Casa de la Cultura Ecuatoriana, Núcleo del Guayas, Sección de Antropología Cultural, 1974. 11 p., illus. (La pieza del mes, 2)

For the special exhibition (see item 969) a polychrome (red, yellow with dark brown or black) Chorrera period specimen gave the opportunity to summarize the Chorrera culture in a small booklet will illustrations of typical pieces.

969b. ———. Monedas primitivas del Ecuador prehistórico. Guayaquil, Ecua., Casa de la Cultura Ecuatoriana, Núcleo del Guayas, Sección de Antropología Cultural, 1975. 15 p., illus., map (La pieza del mes, 5)

Briefly summarizes the occurrence of different types of copper ax-money found on Ecuador's coast in Milagro-Quevedo and Huancavilca-Manteño cultures. Occurrence of 3,000 pieces of ax-money in one burial and of over 13,000 pieces in another indicates a precolumbian concept of accumulation of riches for economic purposes.

970. Lubensky, Earl H. Los cementerios del Anllulla: informe preliminar sobre una excavación arqueológica (EANH/B, 58:123, enero/julio 1974, p. 16-23, bibl., illus., map)

In Hacienda Ayalan (Anllulla peninsula, east of Estero Salado, Gulf of Guayaquil) there are a series of urn burials with multiple secondary burials. Metal and other objects therein suggest Milagro-Quevedo phase and Southern Manteño phase. Includes description and sketches of urns. As the work began, Dr. Ubelaker, Physical Anthropologist of the Smithsonian, joined Lubensky and continues working at the site.

971. Marcos, Jorge G. Tejidos hechos en telar en el contexto Valdivia Tardío (CEE/CHA, 23:40, 1973, p. 163-184, bibl., illus., map)

Impression on piece of clay from Sitio Real Alto in Chanduy from Late Valdivia Horizon of loomed textile.

972. Molestina Zaldumbide, M. Carmen. Toctiuco, un sitio arqueológico en las faldas del Pinchincha (EANH/B, 57:122, julio/dic. 1973, p. 124-152, illus., map)

Describes pottery, but unfortunately the comparisons run all over Ecuador without regard to time period making it almost impossible to conclude what culture or exact time period is represented in this Quito area site. Includes a very complex form designation in letters and numbers.

973. Myers, Thomas P. Evidence of prehistoric irrigation in northern Ecuador (Journal of Field Archaeology [Boston Univ., Mass] 1:3/4, 1974, p. 309-313, illus., map)

Evidence of irrigation in region of artificial mounds between Mira and Guayllabamba rivers, in Imbabura and Pichincha provs., leads author to reinterpretation of pre-Inca cultures of area. Sees a larger population engaged in construction of special architecture directed by and for use of elite as well as a landed economy of intensive agriculture which facilitated Inca control of the region.

974. Osborn, Alan J. and J. Stephen Athens. Prehistoric earth mounds in the highlands of Ecuador: a preliminary report (*in* Archaeological investigations in the highlands of northern Ecuador:

two preliminary reports. Otavalo, Ecua., Instituto Otaveleño de Antropología, 1974, p. 1-22, bibl., illus., map)

Excavation at several sites of artificially constructed earth mounds in Imbabura and Pichincha provs. and a study of other mounds leads author to generalize that the complex of each group consists of platform mound for ceremonial purposes and that smaller hemispherical mounds around it were house platforms and burial tumuli.

975. Parducci Z., Resfa and **Ibrahim Parducci Z.** Artefactos de piedra, concha y hueso: fase Guayaquil (CCE/CHA, 32:39, 1972, p. 97-185, bibl., illus., plates)

Continuation of description of site's archaeological materials, determined as Guayaquil phase (see *HLAS 33:1114*), strictly concerns stone, shell and bone artefacts with measurements, line drawings and photographs.

976. Parsons, James J. Campos de cultivos prehistóricos con camellones paralelos, en la cuenca de Río Guayas, Ecuador (CCE/CHA, 23:40, 1973, p. 185-202, bibl., illus., map)

Spanish translation of article in English, see *HLAS 33:1115*.

977. Paulsen, Allison C. The thorny oyster and the voice of god: spondylus and strombus in Andean prehistory (SAA/AA, 39:4 [pt. 1] Oct. 1974, p. 597-607, bibl., illus., map)

Exchange network of long-distance export of spondylus and strombus, native to Ecuador, unites highlands and coast of both this country and Peru. Traces such trade through three periods, beginning with earliest of 2800-1100 BC. Sees both mollusks used in Chavín as symbols of the oracles.

978. Porras Garcés, Pedro Ignacio. El Encanto, La Puna: un sitio insular de la fase Valdivia asociado a un conchero anular. Guayaquil, Ecua., Museo Francisco Piana, 1973. 167 p., bibl., illus., map, plates, tables (Huancavilca, 5. Serie La Puna, 1)

Describes site, techniques of excavation, classification of artefacts from a ring shaped-shell midden on Puna Island in Gulf of Guayaquil. From study of 9,847 sherds, 300 stone artefacts and 27 non lithic artefacts from 980 cubic m. of stratigraphically dug refuse, author defines the occupation as Valdivia period B and C, based on comparison with sequence of Meggers, Evans and Estrada (see *HLAS 29:1203*). Carbon-14 dates range from 2455 BC in lowest seriated levels to 1590 BC in upper, corresponding to time range previously published. First Valdivia site in Ecuador of period B and C to show ring shaped-shell midden arrangement of Ford's Colonial Formative (see *HLAS 31:984*). Excellent illustrations, and line drawings of vessel shapes, artefacts, figurines, etc. Of major importance in expansion of knowledge of Early Formative cultures in Ecuador and their relationship to South America.

978a. ———. Historia y arqueología de la ciudad española Baeza de los Quijos, siglo XVI. Quito, Pontificia Univ. Católica del Ecuador, Centro de Publicaciones, 1974. 219 p., bibl., illus., maps (Estudios científicos sobre el oriente ecuatoriana, 1)

Pt. 1 concerns Spanish history of settlement of the region in the 16th century with all the archival documentation. Pt. 2 describes excavation of town of Baeza de los Quijos, founded in 1559, and problems of relating the location of the first city with documents on Quijos Indians and various indigenous groups at time of Spanish contact during 16th century. Excellent use of historical documents combined with archaeology.

978b. ———. Una plataforma convexa de lajas de esquisto, varias de estas esculpidas en forma de arabescos con motivos zoológicos y asociadas a cerámica del Carchi y de Cosanga, Quijos, se descubre en Pimampiro, provincia de Imbabura (CCE/CHA, 22:39, 1972, p. 210-233, bibl., illus.)

Platform with carved motifs relates site to Carchi and Cosanga phases, and author believes it possible that such platforms are related to drying of coca. More excavation of site and survey of whole area are needed to relate it to other known highland and sub-Andean, as well as lowland Ecuadorian areas.

978c. ———. Secuencia seriada de los artefactos de piedra pulida de la fase Cosanga en el Oriente, Ceja de Montaña, del Ecuador, Suramérica (*in* International Congress of Americanists XL, Roma-Genova, 1972. Atti [see item 513] v. 1, p. 59-63)

Time span of 17 different types of polished-stone tools, especially axes, but also bark beaters, mauls, mortar and pestles, etc., in Cosanga phase from circa 400 BC to 1100 AD. Includes charts.

978d. ———. Sobrevivencia de tradición cerámica común a las culturas del Alto Amazonas y de manera especial a las de la zona oriental del Ecuador en Suramérica (*in* International Congress of Americanists, XL, Roma-Genova, 1972. Atti [see item 513] v. 1, p. 51-57, illus.)

Modern survival of pottery techniques among Indians of eastern Ecuador, especially on Río Curaray. See also items 978e and 979, for greater details.

978e. ———. Supervivencia de tradición cerámica común en las culturas del Alto Amazonas y de manera especial a las de la zona oriental del Ecuador en Sudamérica (UNCIA/HC, 2:5, sept. 1974, p. 17-39, illus., plates)

Observations of pottery making in traditional ways among Curaray Indians of Eastern Ecuador with excellent photos and explanation of procedures from ethnographic standpoint. Should be read in conjunction with Rye's technological studies of materials, see item 979.

979. Rye, Owen S. Technological analysis of pottery making materials and procedures (UNCIA/HC, 2:5, sept. 1974, p. 41-62, bibl., illus.)

Should be read in conjunction with item 978e. This is the technical analysis of the raw material and of the Curaray Indian pottery technology by a ceramics expert. Includes clay composition, firing temperatures, and understanding of coloring materials. Valuable demonstration to ethnologist of how archaeologist can observe Indians' pottery-making and of how an expert's analysis can establish the Indians' excellent knowledge of ceramic technology. Very important.

980. Salazar, Ernesto. Chinchiloma: Análisis tipológico del material de superficie (CCE/RA, 5, 1974, p. 1-69, bibl., illus.)

Site, sometimes known as Chinchín, located southeast of Ilaló, near Merced of the Quito Canton, produced preceramic materials. Study of two separate collections; comparative material is principally with El Inga site with which it is most closely affiliated. New artefact types and burin technology described for first time. Suggests region was center of a burin tradition dating around 3000 years BC. Good line drawings of artefact types.

981. Sánchez Montañés, Emma. Introducción al estudio de la fauna de la costa de Esmeraldas a través de sus representaciones (UM/REAA, 7:2, 1972, p. 75-93, bibl., illus.)

Pottery figurines from Esmeraldas region can be typed into zoomorphic, anthropozoomorphic, and fantastic or mythical. Compares figurines with actual fauna of region. Finds that amphibians and reptiles are represented less than mammals and birds. Notes the absence of fish and invertebrates but points out that they appear, although infrequently, in collections not available to her at the time of her study. Because so many are tropical forest creatures and the region is within tropical forest distribution, author proposes that there has been a degradation of area's forest.

982. Sarma, Akkaraju V.N. Evidences of post-pleistocene dessication in south west Ecuador and northern Peru (KNGMG/GM, 1973, p. 33-34, bibl., illus., map)

Same information as in item 982a.

982a. ———. Holocene paleoecology of south coastal Ecuador (APS/P, 118:1, Feb. 1974, p. 93-134, bibl., map)

From study of shells from archaeological sites in Santa Elena peninsula southwestern Ecuador, author suggests paleoecological changes in region during recent times. What is today a semiarid region was wetter during 6500-5000 BC, became dry during 5000-2650 BC, turned wet again from 2650-1600 BC and then very dry from 1600-1000 BC. Author correlates these changes with archaeological data to show occupation, movement out of and back into area. Moreover, he correlates climatic data with other information on South America as a whole. Insists that all past cultural occupations must be interpreted in terms of a reconstruction of past climatic situations, without consideration of present conditions, since they may be totally irrelevant to the aboriginal situation.

983. Torre Barba, Joaquín Gómez de la. Motivos indígenas ecuatorianos. Quito, Artes Gráficas, 1971. 55 p., bibl., illus.

Besides describing a variety of art motifs from stamps, spindle whorls, figurines, etc., his most interesting contribution is the interpretation of some of the designs on roller stamps and flat, tablet-form stamps which he feels are a form of codices with a written message, or a form of mnemonic device (like a quipu) for recalling certain events or interpretive symbols in mythology and religion.

984. Wilbert, Johannes. The thread of life: symbolism of miniature art from Ecuador. Washington, Dumbarton Oaks Research Library and Collections, 1974. 112 p., bibl., illus. (Studies in precolumbian art and archaeology, 12)

Study of about 8000 spindle whorls from Ecuador, especially the Guangala and Manteño cultures, allows classification into decorative motifs which author discusses from an ideological standpoint. Also has a good section on technical process of spinning and role of spindle whorl. Excellent rollout drawings of motifs in 157 figures give most complete coverage of this material in any single book.

PERU

985. Alcina Franch, José. Chinchero, village Inca (ARCHEO, 66, jan. 1974, p. 58-65, facsim., illus., plates)

Results of several seasons of archaeological work at the Inca site of Chinchero, Cuzco dept.

986. Angles Vargas, Víctor. Machupijchu: enigmática ciudad inka. Lima, Industrial, 1972. 445 p., bibl., plates.

After studying the literature and chronicles of Machu Picchu, author concludes that city was a unit of itself controlling an area around it and not the last surviving city of Incas, nor the city of Vitcos where Manco Inca lived. Many pictures, but color reproduction poor, and good architectural plans of site as well as of other important area Inca sites.

987. Anton, Ferdinand. The art of ancient Peru. English translation by Mary Whittall. 2. ed. rev. N.Y., G.P. Putnam's Sons, 1972. 368 p., bibl., illus., maps, plates, tables.

First English translation of 1962 German original (see *HLAS 25:367*), but revised and enlarged. Arty presentation of artefacts from various culture periods from Chavín through Inca. Includes pottery, stone, textiles, wood, metal, shell artefacts. Most specimens from European collections.

988. Arnold, Dean E. Ceramic ecology of the Ayacucho basin, Peru: implications for prehistory (UC/CA, 16:2, June 1975, p. 183-206)

Study of modern ceramic specialization in village of Quinua, Ayacucho dept., and of how these observations allow certain authors some theoretical points on development of ceramic specialization in Middle Horizon from 600-800 AD. Stresses the importance of population size and density which increases the demand for pottery and forces the potter out of agricultural zone into drier area where he can become a full-time specialist.

988a. _____. Mineralogical analyses of ceramic materials, department of Ayacucho, Peru (Archaeometry [Oxford Univ., Research Laboratory for Archaeology in the History of Art, London] 14:1, Feb. 1972, p. 93-101, bibl.)

Study of present-day sources of ceramic materials from vicinity of Quinua shows that these same resources could have also supported a tradition of several Polychrome styles of Middle Horizon from 600-800 AD. Also shows variability of resources in precolumbian materials and how modern differences in pastes, tempered and not tempered by potter, can also apply to ancient pottery although notion of temper as "nonplastics" needs redefinition.

989. Arqueología peruana: precursores. Selección, introducción, comentario y notas de Duccio Bonavia [and] Rogger Ravines. Lima, Casa de la Cultura del Perú, 1970. 240 p., illus.

Reprinting of various articles by famous writers of past several centuries on Peruvian archaeology with commentary by compilers. Includes persons such as Wiener, Bandelier, Squier, José Toribio Polo, Middendorf, Antonio de Ulloa, to mention just a few. Only of historical interest.

990. Avalos de Matos, Rosalía and Rogger Ravines. Las antigüedades peruanas y su protección legal (PEMN/R, 40, 1974, p. 363-485)

Discusses problem of protection of national patrimony (artistic and historic, works of man and nature). Examines future and present needs by publishing 42 copies of original documents, from 1822 to 1971. Extremely useful compilation of archaeological monuments, regulations prohibiting export of archaeological objects, etc.

991. Bankmann, Ulf. Bemerkungen zu einigen Skulpturen aus dem nordperuanischen Hochland (*in* International Congress of Americanists, XL, Roma-Genova, 1972. Atti [see item 513] v. 1, p. 285-291, bibl., illus.)

Shows relationship between Mochica and Recuay cultures in the sculptures of human faces.

992. Benson, Elizabeth P. Death-associated figures on Mochica pottery (*in* Benson, Elizabeth P. *ed.* Death and the afterlife in pre-columbian America. Washington, Dumbarton Oaks Research Library and Collections, 1975, p. 105-144, bibl., illus.)

Uses a large number of photographs and rollout drawings of all sorts of Mochica figures, buildings, pottery shapes, musical instruments, etc., to show the role of death. Some new and interesting ideas about associations and the complex hierarchy of the other world and its relation to the living one during Mochica times.

992a. _____. A man and a feline in Mochica art. Washington, Dumbarton Oaks Research Library and Collections, 1974. 31 p., bibl., illus. (Studies in pre-columbian art and archaeology, 14)

Describes a new acquisition of a turquoise carving, with pyrite inlay, of a human being with a feline in back whose mouth is on human's head. Author goes into general subject of motif combination of both elements in Mochica artefacts of all sorts and compares them to those of other Andean cultures. Believes that, at least in Mochica IV times, the myth and ritual of man and feline related to an actual event of a prisoner of war being offered to feline as a proxy-diety as part of ritual, religion, warfare and conquest of new lands.

993. Bonavia, Duccio and Rogger Ravines. El precerámico andino: evolución y problemas (PEMN/R, 38, 1972, p. 23-60, bibl.)

Lists principal preceramic sites of Peru by valleys, bays, depts., etc., with site numbering system, brief description, discoverer and bibliographic reference, with a short comment on history of preceramic finds in Peru.

994. Cardich, Augusto. Excavaciones en la Caverna de Huargo, Perú (PEMN/R, 39, 1973, p. 11-47, bibl., illus.)

Provides detailed description of finds from an excavated site in a cave with deep deposits, located in Dos de Mayo prov., Huánuco dept. Middle levels date by Carbon-14 at 11,510±700 BC. Pottery from upper levels, with a Carbon-14 date of 1,610±230 BC. Additional appendices analyze site's bone materials and the sedimentology of the deposits. Includes charts and plans.

994a. _____. Los yacimientos de la etapa agrícola de Lauricocha, Perú y los límites superiores del cultivo (SAA/R, 8, 1974, p. 27-48, bibl., illus., map)

Explains by paleoclimatology the expansion of both population and areas under cultivation in highlands around Lauricocha area. The expansion was most intensive in the Early Intermediate period of 200 BC-700 AD and in the Late Intermediate period of 1100-1460 AD. Believes the change over the last 30-40 years of areas that can be cultivated and are intensively so were the result of retreating glaciers in Andes.

995. Cavatrunci, Claudio. L'influsso Wari nella ceramica di stile Nievería proveniente dalla Huaca a Cajamarquilla (*in* International Congress of Americanists, XL, Roma-Genova, 1972. Atti [see item 513] v. 1, p. 329-332, bibl.)

Influence of Wari empire as seen by Nievería style pottery found at Huaca Tello in Cajamarquilla site.

996. Collier, Donald. The central Andes (*in* Lamberg-Karlovsky, C.C. and Jeremy A. Sabloff eds. The rise and fall of civilizations [see item 644] p. 170-181, bibl., map)

Reprint. See *HLAS 25:372* for comment on original.

997. Cossío del Pomar, Felipe. The art of ancient Peru. Drawings by Emilio Sánchez. N.Y., Wittenborn, 1971. 219 p., bibl., plates.

Although author states this is an up-to-date version of 1949 ed., references in chapter bibliographies date to 1952 and occasionally 1954. Uses Rowe's old terminology for periods. Very poor color reproductions. For a single arty presentation with a better range of objects, layman should use Anton (item 987).

998. Craig, Alan K. and Norbert P. Psuty. Studies in marine desert ecology: reconnaissance report. Boca Ratón, Fla., Florida Atlantic Univ., Dept. of Geography, 1968. 196 p., bibl., illus., maps (The Paracas papers, 1:1. Occasional publication, 1)

Very useful volume with good charts, diagrams and illustrations of the marine desert ecology off the Peruvian coast, especially the south coast from Río Pisco to Río Ica. Of basic significance to any archaeologist working on coastal Peru.

999. Cuesta Domingo, Mariano. El sistema militarista de los mochicas (UM/REAA, 7:2, 1972, p. 269-307, bibl., illus.)

Excellent breakdown of motifs from Mochica pottery into details of warriors dress and armaments — caps, helmets, shields, face painting, arms, bags or purses, tattoo, prisoners, techniques of combat, and similar subjects.

1000. Day, Kent C. Walk-in wells and water management at Chanchán, Peru (*in* Lamberg-Karlovsky, C.C. and Jeremy A. Sabloff eds. The rise and fall of civilizations [see item 644] p. 182-190, bibl.)

Problem of permanent water supply to city of Chanchán was solved by the society's digging walk-in wells, which remained adequate as long as extensive irrigation systems were maintained in city's upslope area. Wells were dug, controlled, maintained and expanded by those with the status and power to make and enforce public decisions. Inca domination of Chimú city of Chanchán was probably related to disruption of irrigation system or its lack of maintenance.

1001. Deboer, Warren R. Ceramic longevity and archaeological interpretation: an example from the upper Ucayali, Peru (SAA/AA, 39:2 [pt. 1] April 1974, p. 335-343, bibl., illus., map)

Using modern ethnographic comparative data on frequency of Conibo vessel forms, compares them with archaeological data of midden refuse, and shows how estimates of village population size and duration are not always realistic. Suggests archaeologists make study of ethnographic situation before all groups are totally acculturated.

1002. Disselhoff, Hans Dietrich. Vicús: eine neue Entdeckte Altperuanische Kultur. Berlin, FRG, Gebr. Mann Verlag, 1971. 57 p., illus., tables (Monumenta Americana. Herausgegeben von Ibero-Amerikanischen Institut Preussischer Kulturbesitz, 7)

The only scientific report to date on Vicus culture in North Peru which has been so badly looted by grave robbers. In an effort to salvage what was possible, author reconstructs grave shafts with good drawings, measurements, etc., of the shaft and chambered tombs and associations of objects. Appendix on analysis of metal by George Peterson G., and textiles by Irene Emery and Elizabeth King. Carbon-14 dates of 1490±40 BP and 1485±35 BP. Excellent photos of this documented Vicus collection make possible the cultural evaluation of other pieces that have reached art market and private collections.

1003. Dollfus, O. and Danièle Lavellée. Ecología y ocupación del espacio en los Andes tropicales durante los últimos veinte milenios (IFEA/B, 2:3, 1973, p. 75-92, bibl.)

Geographers comment on need to view Andean area from standpoint of human ecology and of microenvironments available to man over last 20,000 years.

1004. Donnan, Christopher B. A precolumbian smelter from northern Peru (AIA/A, 26:4, Oct. 1973, p. 289-297, illus.)

Ceramic vessel said to be from Moche cemetery in Nepeña Valley depicts a scene which shows metalworking procedures and use of smelter. Author compares copper ingots from Moche burials with that obtained from cuprite ore, the only one that yields copper whose composition is similar to that of precolumbian ingots. Very important contribution to knowledge of precolumbian metal-working techniques.

1005. Dwyer, Jane Powell and **Edward B. Dwyer.** The Paracas cemeteries: mortuary patterns in a Peruvian south coastal tradition (*in* Benson, Elizabeth P. ed. Death and the afterlife in pre-columbian America. Washington, Dumbarton Oaks Research Library and Collections, 1975, p. 145-161, bibl., illus.)

Report on research begun in 1968 and continued until present on Paracas mummy bundles and their contents from collections both in Peru and US museums, including Tello's voluminous notes. Sees Paracas sites as covering a long period of time with a large population that can be ordered into a developmental sequence. Work concentrated on elite from south coast cemeteries.

1006. Engel, Frédéric. La Gorge de Huarangal: ébauche d'une monographie de géographie humaine préhistorique (IFEA/B, 2:2, 1973, p. 1-26, bibl., illus.)

Study of human occupation of dry-river drainage of Huarangal, part of the Río Chilca area, leads to data on area use over last 10,000 years. Of especial importance are the lomas (see item 1005) the settlement pattern at various early agricultural, preceramic stages.

1006a. _____. Las Lomas de Iguanil y el Complejo de Haldas. Lima, Univ. Nacional Agraria La Molina, Depto. de Publicaciones, 1970. 58 p., bibl., illus., maps, plates, tables.

Ecological and precolumbian agricultural studies based on preliminary work at Las Lomas de Iguanil and el Complejo de Haldas. Describes and illustrates pottery of Formative periods (pre-Chavín and Chavinoid). Useful charts correlate cultures with sea level changes and climatology.

1006b. _____. New facts about pre-columbian life in the Andean lomas (UC/CA, 14:3, June 1973, p. 271-280, bibl., illus.)

Extensive and intensive investigations reveal that occupation of the "lomas" of the central and south Peruvian coast concentrates in three periods: preagricultural, archaic agricultural, and late intensive agricultural. All equate with periods of marine transgression and warmer climate, suggesting drought may have caused abandonment. Description and sample community maps summarize data obtained from more than 1000 settlements in this type of environmental setting, giving the best overview to date.

1007. Fernández Baca, Jenaro. Motivos de ornamentación de la cerámica inca-Cuzco. t. 1 Lima, Librería Studium, 1973? 262 p., plates.

Includes 199 color plates with his classification of 735 design motifs shown taken from Cuzco-Inca pottery. V. 1 deals only with geometric design motifs; v. 2 in preparation will cover naturalistic design motifs.

1008. Fung Pineda, Rosa. Análisis tecnológico de encajes del antiguo Perú: período Tardío (Cuadernos Culturales de la Industria Textil Peruana [Lima] 1, 1974, p. 1-8, bibl., illus.)

Originally presented in 1958 and later revised and enlarged with illustrations in 1972. Discusses "lace" from Peru's central coast from Chancay collections in Amano Museum and Museum of Lima's San Marcos Univ. Technique also called knotted-weft wrapping (sujeción de trama anudada). Illustrations and diagrams explain techniques.

1008a. _____ and **Víctor Pimentel Gurmendi.** Chakillo (PEMN/R, 39, 1973, p. 71-80, bibl., illus.)

Chankillo is a complex of archaeological sites in Casma Valley, known locally as Castillo de San Rafael and in archaeological literature as Castillo de las Calaveras as well as Chanquillo. Principal structure is a hilltop covered with round structures encircled by defensive walls with special entrances. No sherds found. Carbon-14 date on wood indicates 342 BC which would place it in Chavin expansionistic period. Offers possibility that it might belong instead to Casma culture which coexists with Moche in the north.

1008b. _____; **Carlos F. Cenzano Z.**; and **Amaro Zavaleta G.** El taller lítico de Chivateros, Valle del Chillón (PEMN/R, 38, 1972, p. 61-72, bibl., illus., map)

Discusses a preceramic workshop site. Describes and illustrates typical bifacial artifacts and includes analysis of soil and petroglyphic analysis of stone. Soil profiles show no climatic change from the present. Estimates occupation at ca. 10,000 but without absolute proof.

1009. García Rosell, César. Diccionario arqueológico del Perú. Lima, Sociedad Geográfica de Lima [and] Sociedad Peruana de Espeleología, Centro de Estudios Históricos Militares, 1968. 406 p., plates.

Most useful for tracking down proper names, especially Quechua ones, not found in most sources. No current usage of archaeological terminology.

1010. González del Río, Concepción. La columna estratigráfica en la parte baja de Tablada de Lurín (PUCIRA/BSA, 13:85, enero/dic. 1972, p. 31-36)

Geological explanation of strata in Lurín valley (see also item 1039).

1011. Grobman, Alex and **Rogger Ravines.** Maíz prehispánico del Valle de Cajamarca, Perú (PEMN/R, 40, 1974, p. 135-138, bibl.)

Describes corn grains from site of Iscoconga, Río Chonta, near Cajamarca from Cajamarca I period of Reichlen, ca. 500-100 BC. Sees type as intermediate strain between Confite Chavinense and present-day race of Huayleño.

1012. Grollig, Francis Xavier. Pikillacta: Incaic precursor (*in* International Congress of Americanists, XL, Roma-Genova, 1972. Atti [see item 513] v. 1, p. 317-324, bibl.)

Stone architecture city of Pikillacta, just a few km. south of Cuzco, is in the Huari (Wari) empire of ca. 1000 AD. Although first cleared and partially studied in 1924 little new work has been done. Offers idea that many of the elaborate architectural features of Machu Picchu have their antecedents at Pikillacta.

1013. Grossman, Joel W. An ancient gold worker's tool kit: the earliest metal technology in Peru (AIA/A, 25:4, Oct. 1972, p. 270-275, illus.)

Excavations at site of Waywaka, in Andahuaylas prov., produced an early ceramic complex, known as Muyu Moqo, with Carbon-14 date of ca. 1490 BC. (uncorrected). This early level yielded gold-foil and lapis-lazuli beads, as well as two soft stone bowls containing stone gold-working tools such as an anvil and three hammers. If this foil was made locally, as suggested by the metalworking tools, then gold is a thousand years earlier than Chavín in this south highland area of Peru. The earliest reported gold to date is Chongoyape style, from Peru's north coast and related to Chavín.

1014. Hastings, C. Mansfield and **M. Edward Moseley.** The abodes of Huaca del Sol and Huaca de la Luna (SAA/AA, 40:2 [pt. 1] April 1975, p. 196-203, bibl., illus.)

The mud bricks in these two massive sites differ in soil composition, dimensions, mold marks and makers' marks. Such differences reflect conditions of brick production and use and some variables are chronologically significant. Due to looters' destruction of some site units, the sample is small and holes or core of mounds are not visible. However, author's approach is extremely interesting and has important socio-political interpretations for coastal Peruvian archaeology.

1015. Isbell, William H. Ecología de la expansión de los Quechua-hablantes (PEMN/R, 40, 1974, p. 139-155, bibl.)

Studies the dispersion of a plain, utilitarian pottery of a special color and shape and correlates it with distribution of Quechua. Attempts to show how archaeology and linguistics can assist each other in discussing the Inca Empire as determined by distribution of Quechua speakers.

1016. Jiménez Borja, Arturo and **Lorenzo Alberto Samaniego Román.** Guía de Sechín, Casma. Lima, Instituto Nacional de Cultura, Comisión de Reconstrucción y Rehabilitación de la Zona Afectada, 1973. 50 p., maps.

Excellent guide booklet to Sechin ruins of Formative period in Casma valley, Peru. Includes charts as well as maps.

1017. Keatinge, Richard W. Chimu rural administrative centres in the Moche Valley, Peru (World Archaeology [London] 6:1, June 1974, p. 66-82, bibl., maps)

Recent fieldwork in Moche Valley has focused attention on the socio-economic organization of the valley during Chimu occupation of the city of Chan Chan in Late Intermediate period of 1000-1476 AD. Describes three Chimu rural administrative centers and offers functional interpretation that they represented "state-presence" in non-metropolitan areas of the valley whose primary function was the maintenance of state control over land, water, and labor resources.

1017a. ——— and Kent C. Day. Chan Chan: a study of precolumbian urbanism and the management of land and water resources in Peru (AIA/A, 27:4, Oct. 1974, p. 228-235, illus.)

Popular version of item 1017b.

1017b. ——— and ———. Socio-economic organization of the Moche Valley, Peru, during the Chimu occupation of Chan Chan (UNM/JAR, 29:4, Winter 1973, p. 275-295, bibl., map)

Analysis of the architecture, settlement distribution and geography of The Chimu city of Chan Chan and attendant sites makes it possible to discuss the administration of land, water, and labor resources and the production and distribution of goods as primary socio-economic factors in the maintenance of a hierarchical social organization. Special U-shaped structures in urban and rural settings are crucial to interpretation of the Chimu administration of production, distribution and storage of goods. Given the Peruvian coastal environment, this interpretation provides an insight into the structure of urban-rural relations during the Chimu occupation of the Moche Valley.

1018. Kellers, James. A dusty cache of Peruvian history (Rutgers Alumni Magazine [Rutgers Univ., New Brunswick N.J.] Spring 1974, p. 1-6, illus., map)

Some Peruvian pieces (most of them Mochica, Chimu and Inca) which were brought to the Rutgers Univ. Geological Museum ca. 1887 were recently found in the collections. Author also describes Spanish colonial piece by Indian sculptors, about which he is seeking further information.

1019. Kendall, Ann. Architecture and planning at the Inca sites in the

Cusichaca Area (MV/BA, 22, 1974, p. 73-137, bibl., illus., map)

Study made in 1968 of architectural remains of site halfway between Machu Picchu and Ollantaytambo shows an extensive pre-Inca occupation as far back as Chanapata period. Excellent architectural drawings and plans as well as details of settlement pattern of this residential administrative unit. On the basis of her detailed work, author suggests that distinctions in Inca architecture at various sites are so clear cut that they could be seriated in order to develop a chronology.

1019a. _____. A method of analysis of Inca architectural remains: introducing a list of activity requirements to generate functional solution to forms (*in* International Congress of Americanists, XL, Roma-Genova, 1972. Atti [see item 513] v. 1, p. 337-342, bibl.)

This study of Inca structures uses architectural techniques and approaches and is based on work done at Cusichaca. Discusses how Inca cultural activities can be deduced from the various elements of construction.

1020. King, Mary Elizabeth. Mythological figures in textiles from Ocucaje, Peru (*in* International Congress of Americanists, XL, Roma-Genova, 1972. Atti [see item 513] v. 2, p. 521-529, bibl., illus.)

Detailed analysis of a large collection of Paracas textiles from Hacienda Ocucaje now in Washington's Textile Museum and N.Y.'s American Museum of Natural History. Uses a method of design interpretation which combines typology with distribution, borrowing heavily from linguistic analysis.

1021. Kornfield, Guillermo. Significado de la industria lítica de Paiján (PUCIRA/BSA, 13:85, enero/dic. 1972, p. 52-141, bibl., illus., map)

Rafael Larco Hoyle and Junius Bird found lithic materials and declared them to be important in an area from km. 600 to 650 of the Carretera Panamericana Norte, Pampas de Paiján, north of Chicama. Author describes and illustrates materials found in ceramic and lithic sites therein which he relates to materials from El Inga in Ecuador and Laurichocha in Peru.

1022. Lathrap, Donald W. Gifts of the cayman: some thoughts on the subsistence base of Chavín (*in* Lathrap, Donald W. and Jody Douglas *eds*. Variations in anthropology: essays in honor of John C. McGregor. Urbana, Illinois Archeological Survey, 1973, p. 91-105, bibl., illus.)

Author believes that the most important plant depicted on Tello obelisk at Chavín de Huantar (the Great Cayman deity) is manioc. This adds evidence to his theme that Chavín affiliations lie to east in moist tropics of Amazon basin.

1023. Lavallée, Danièle. Estructura y organización del habitat en los Andes centrales durante el período intermedio tardío (PEMN/R, 39, 1973, p. 91-116, illus., map)

Complex of sites in an area known as the Territory of Asto, one of the principal pre-Incaic political entities in the area between Río Mantaro and Río Vilca (Vilcamayo). Carbon dates and other factors date complex from 980-1200 AD with Inca and Spanish colonial overlay. Very interesting architectural features, especially the cellular structures grouped together in units not only for living but for storage as well, e.g. silo-like warehouses for crops, probably tubers (potatoes).

1023a. _____ and **Michèle Julien.** Villages et paysans des Andes avant la conquete espagnole: lumières sur la communauté des Asto (ARCHEO, 71, juin 1974, p. 30-39, bibl., illus., map, plates)

Interdisciplinary study of Andean communities (between Vilca, Cuenca, Moya and Conaica, from 3000-5000 m.) from earliest Paleo-Indian occupation through Inca and Spanish domination to present.

1024. Lechtman, Heather. El dorado de metales en el Perú precolombino (PEMN/R, 40, 1974, p. 87-110, bibl., illus.)

Uses metallurgical methods to study gilding (covering surface with goldleaf, mise-en-couleur, goldplating by fusion or alloying) on certain artifacts. Then makes effort to correlate these detailed studies to comments made by Spanish chroniclers of metal-working in precolumbian cultures.

1025. Linares Málaga, Eloy. Anotaciones sobre cuatro modalidades de arte rupestre en Arequipa (UNCP/AC, 2, 1973, p. 133-267, bibl., illus., maps)

Describes occurrence in Arequipa dept. of: pictographs, petroglyphs, mobile rock art (stones small enough to carry) and geoglyphs (figures made on ground by clearing off rocks and outlining figure). Also includes description and sketches of lithic materials from a variety of nonceramic sites.

1026. Lumbreras, Luis Guillermo. Los estudios sobre Chavín. Peru (PEMN/R, 38, 1972, p. 74-92, bibl., illus.)

Brief but good summary of Chavin period materials from highlands as well as coast with present opinion on sequence, dates and relationships.

1026a. _____. The peoples and cultures of ancient Peru. 2. ed. rev. Translated by Betty J. Meggers. Washington, Smithsonian Institution Press, 1974. 248 p., bibl., illus., maps, plates.

Translation of *HLAS 33:1177* brought up to date and completely revised with an entirely new selection of photographs and art work which is now correlated to the text. There are maps in each chapter as well as chronological tables organized into the following periods: Lithic, Archaic, Formative, Regional Developmental, Wari Empire, Regional States, and Empire of Tawantisuyu (Inca). The only up-to-date publication on precolumbian Peru in either English or Spanish with such excellent and numerous illustrations (232 plates) as well as figures and maps. Most useful reference.

1026b. _____. Los reinos post-Tiwanaku en el área altiplánica (PEMN/R, 40, 1974, p. 55-85, bibl., illus.)

Summarizes the post-Tiahuanaco cultures by following divisions: the Titicaca altiplano, the culture of Mollo and Churajón, the cultures of the coast, and other regions. A very useful summary.

1027. Matos Mendieta, Ramiro. Ataura: un centro Chavín en el Valle del Mantaro (PEMN/R, 38, 1972, p. 93-108, bibl., illus., map)

Ataura in the Mantaro valley is not only a Chavín center but a village or town of agriculturists who also made great use of animals in their diet. It has both classic Chavín and Chavinoid materials. Sees closer relationships to coastal Chavín than to highland centers, although the highland ones are clearly demonstrated with relationships to Ofrendas phase at Chavín de Huantar.

1027a. _____. Wakan y Wamalli: estudio arqueológico de dos aldeas rurales (in Ortiz de Zúñiga, Iñigo. Visita de la provincia de León de Huánuco [see HLAS 34:1200] p. 369-382, bibl., illus.)

As part of the study of provincial Inca life directed by Murra, Matos conducted in 1965 an investigation of two sites: 1) Wakan, an Inca agricultural community (near present-day town of Tangor, Paucar district, Pasco dept.); and 2) Wamalli, an Inca herding community (near present-day town of Mito, Punchao district, Huánuco dept.). The objective of this study was to correlate both sites with communities mentioned by Ortiz de Zúñiga in his 1560 visita. Although he only visited Wamalli, he described other pottery-making agricultural communities very similar to Wakan.

1028. Matsuzawa, Tsugio. Excavation at Las Haldas on the coast of central Peru (Proceedings of the Department of Humanities [Univ. of Tokyo, College of General Education, Series of Cultural Anthropology, Tokyo] 59:2, 1974, p. 3-44, bibl., illus., map)

Description in Japanese (includes a five-p. English summary) of the architecture of Las Haldas ruins, especially the temple. Attempts to determine how and if temple was constructed during preceramic period. Concludes that it is not related to preceramic horizon as originally thought but that, at least, a section of it was begun during early part of Chavín period. Also, tends to view center more as a religious one of the Chavín period rather than a large settlement.

1029. Mejía Xesspe, Toribio. Patrimonio cultural de Julio Tello (PEMN/R, 38, 1972, p. 119-124)

After Julio Tello's death in 1947 all of his notes, books, and archives were made part of the national cultural heritage of Peru through a bequest to Univ. Nacional Mayor de San Marcos. The materials date to 1909 when Tello began his career and contain invaluable information on Peruvian history, ethnohistory, and archaeology.

1030. Morris, Craig. El almacenaje en dos aldeas de los Chuapaychu (in Ortiz de Zúñiga, Iñigo. Visita de la provincia de León de Huánuco [see HLAS 34:1200] p. 385-404, bibl.)

As part of the study of Inca provincial life directed by Murra, Morris conducted field work between 1963-66 of which this is a summary chapter. Uses archaeology and the documents of the 1560 visita to describe the Inca storage-warehouse system.

1030a. _____. Establecimientos estatales en el Tawantinsuyu: una estrategia de urbanismo obligado (PEMN/R, 39, 1973, p. 127-141, bibl.)

Development of administrative centers in Andes, obligatory for successful Inca administrative control of area, had antecedents in region for several hundred years. Much of this data was gathered as part of the program directed from 1963-66 by John Murra on the study of provincial Inca life under auspices of Institute of Andean Research.

1030b. _____. El muestreo en la excavación de sitios urbanos; el caso de Huánuco-Pampa (PEMN/R, 40, 1974, p. 111-132, bibl., illus.)

The problem of the archaeologist in sampling and studying an urban site as demonstrated from the archaeological project of Huánuco-Pampa, the Inca administrative center.

1030c. _____ and **Donald E. Thompson.** Huánuco Viejo; an Inca administrative center (in Lamberg-Karlovsky, C.C. and Jeremy A. Sabloff eds. The rise and fall of civilizations [see item 644] p. 191-208, bibl.)

Reprint of HLAS 33:1199.

1031. Moseley, Michael Edward. Chan Chan: Andean alternative of the preindustrial city (AAAS/S, 187, 24 Jan. 1975, p. 219-225, illus.)

Summary of general conclusions of a project in progress for several years to study the imperial capital of the Chimor state, subjugated about 1470 by the Inca and incorporated into their empire. Compares it with Old World pre-industrial cities. Chan Chan was political center for controlling area's irrigation, labor taxes due the royal dynasties, and the distribution of goods and food. Civic facilities were intended to serve the aristocracy and the state but not the common citizenry.

Nuclear settlement covered about six square km. with buildings over more than 20 sq. kms.

1031a. _____. Prehistoric principles of labor organization in the Moche Valley, Peru (SAA/AA, 40:2 [pt. 1] April 1975, p. 191-196, bibl., illus.)

Believes that labor-tax obligation permitted the mobilization and coordination of the large number of individuals required to build prehistoric projects of Moche Valley.

1031b. _____. Subsistence and demography: an example of interaction from prehistoric Peru (UNM/SWJA, 28:1, Spring 1972, p. 25-49, bibl., map)

Studies series of basic changes in subsistence pattern among prehistoric cultures of Ancón and Chillón valleys off Peruvian coast. Describes role of desert, sandy and rocky-coast shoreline, and lomas as well as the relatively slow change in technology and social organization until canal irrigation of desert opened up new areas for intensive agriculture. Explains that some of these changes were due to demographic growth. Also discusses resource rights.

1031c. _____ and **Carol J. Mackey.** Twenty-four architectural plans of Chan-Chan, Peru. Cambridge, Mass., Peabody Museum of Archaeology and Ethnology, Harvard Univ., 1974. 1 v. (Unpaged) bibl., fold. maps.

Detailed architectural studies of the urban center of Chan Chan with 24 folded maps. (see item 1031).

1031d. _____ and **Gordon R. Willey.** Aspero, Peru: a reexamination of the site and its implications (SAA/AA, 38:4, Oct. 1973, p. 452-468, bibl., map)

Large preceramic site of Aspero near town of Puerto de Supe previously studied by Uhle, Willey and Corbett. They did not recognize sizeable artificial platform mounds demonstrating need for "corporate labor activity." Propose that the preadaptation toward corporate labor society expedited the rapid transference from a marine economy to an agricultural one at close of the Cotton preceramic period of about 2000-1800 BC.

1031e. _____ and **Luis Watanabe.** The abode sculpture of Huaca de los Reyes: imposing art work from coastal Peru (AIA/A, 27:3, July 1974, p. 154-161, illus.)

Huaca de los Reyes, the best preserved structure within the Caballo Muerto Complex in Moche River drainage, has elaborate sculpture of abode in friezes. Falls within style of Cupisnique art on coast and shows importance of this cultural center at this time, independent of Chavín de Huantar in highlands.

1032. Moser, Christopher L. Ritual decapitation in Moche art (AIA/A, 27:1, Jan. 1974, p. 30-37, illus.)

Designs on pottery or molded vessels suggest human decapitation was a central ritual act in the Moche culture and that the Fanged Being, most probably a principal diety of earth or moon fertility in the Moche pantheon, was associated in important ways with the practice of beheading. Excellent pictures.

1033. Muelle, Jorge C. Arqueología peruana después de Tello (PEMN/R, 38, 1972, p. 11-22, bibl.)

This issue of *Revista del Museo Nacional* marked its 40th year of continuous publication and, with a series of articles, was dedicated to Tello and Valcárcel. The various trends in the archaeology of Peru, in terms of South America as a whole and during recent years, are outlined in the summary.

1033a. _____ and **Rogger Ravines.** Los estratos precerámicos de Ancón (PEMN/R, 39, 1973, p. 49-70, bibl., illus., map)

Excavations in 1959 uncovered preceramic materials at Ancón, central coast Peru, and continued off and on until 1973. Artifacts of nets and fishhooks and shell remains suggest strong dependence on sea for food with approximately 325 years of this way of life until pottery introduced. Appendices discuss a series of Carbon-14 dates from 1835 and 1860 BC up to 2270 BC, as well as human skeletal remains and artifacts of shell, wood, stone, and textiles and fibers.

1034. Onuki, Yoshio and **Tatsuhiko Fujii.** Excavations at La Pampa, Peru (Proceedings of the Department of Humanities [Univ. of Tokyo, College of General Education, Series of Cultural Anthropology,] 59:2, 1974, p. 45-104, bibl., illus., map)

La Pampa site is at 1650 m. altitude on left bank of Río Manta, a tributary of Río Santa in Ancash dept. excavated by Tokyo Univ. Scientific Expedition in 1969. Large site has occupation materials from Chavín Horizon up into Inca period. La Pampa phase has pre-Chavin materials resembling same periods at Kotosh, but major occupation is Chavín de Huantar type of materials and Kotosh Chavín period material. Although in Japanese, the excellent photos and drawings make report useful with the six-p. English summary.

1035. Orellana Valeriano, Simeón. Huacjlasmarca: un pequeño poblado huanca (UNCP/AC, 2, 1973, p. 69-132, bibl., illus., map, plates)

First study of the history of architecture in the Mantaro Valley of districts of Juaja, Concepción and Huancayo in Junín dept. One of the few basic studies of the Huancas culture, and urban development in pre-Inca, Inca and colonial times.

1036. Parsons, Jeffrey R. and **Norbert P. Psuty.** Agricultura de chacras hundidas en el antiguo Peru (PEMN/R, 40, 1974, p. 31-54, bibl., illus., map)

Detailed study of sunken gardens on coast of Peru from

pre-columbian times into early part of the 17th century. Of extreme importance to anyone studying area's agricultural techniques and ecological picture.

1037. Polia, Mario. La rovine di Aypate, relazione della loro scoperta e studio preliminare (*in* International Congress of Americanists, XL, Roma-Genova, 1972. Atti [see item 513] v. 1, p. 343-352, bibl., illus.)

Correlates archaeology of Aypate, Ayabaca area in Piura dept. with the ethnohistorical documents of expansion of Inca empire under Tupac Yupanqui. Relates these stone structure, pyramids, and complexes to other classic stone Inca structures.

1038. Proulx, Donald A. Archaeological investigations in the Nepeña Valley, Peru. Amherst, Univ. of Massachusetts, Dept. of Anthropology, 1973. 292 p., bibl., illus., maps, plates, tables (Research reports, 13)

Report on 1971 field work from preceramic through Inca, in Nepeña Valley. Special chapters describe roads, defense walls, ancient canals, irrigation, and the valley's petroglyphs as well as 110 sites and five site-complexes.

1039. Ramos de Cox, Josefina. Estratos marcadores y niveles de ocupación en Tablada de Lurín, Lima: 25J/PV 48-11 (PUCIRA/BSA, 13:85, enero/dic. 1972, p. 7-30, bibl.)

Stratigraphic excavation of terrace in Valley of Lurín yielded evidence of human occupation from early non-ceramic period to present day, showing a column of about 12,000 years, based on comparison with Carbon-14 date for Chivateros. Includes charts.

1040. Ravines, Rogger. Conchales del Río Zarumilla, Perú (PEMN/R, 39, 1973, p. 81-90, bibl., illus.)

Rió Zarumilla is present-day frontier between El Oro prov., Ecuador, and Zarumilla prov. in Tumbes dept., Peru. Shell middens with pottery, especially Loma Saavedra, excavated. Even though possible that site is contemporaneous with Jambelli culture of Ecuador in El Oro prov., sees little resemblance to ceramic materials but notes an affiliation with Garbanzal phase from Tumbes area. This point difficult to understand in many ways because both phases are very closely related and, in the opinion of Evans and Meggers, indistinguishable. Designated as independent culture phases only because of different excavators working at different times in two countries.

1041. Richardson, James B. The pre-ceramic sequence and the Pleistocene and Post-Pleistocene climate of northwest Peru (*in* Lathrap, Donald D. and Jody Douglas *eds.* Variations in anthropology: essays in honor of John C. McGregor. Urbana, Illinois Archaeological Survey, 1973, p. 199-211, bibl., map)

Northwest Peru, from Talara region along the Río Chira drainage, presents unique opportunity to study man's culture adaptation to fluctuations in climatic conditions and progressive dessication over past 8000 years. Such change may be the direct result of northern countercurrent (El Niño) whose movement inward toward shore used to be seasonal but is now periodic, every seven to ten years. Dessication occurred as the current moved from tablazo surfaces to terraces within the ravines and along the coast.

1042. Rivera Dorado, Miguel. Aspectos tipológicos de la cerámica cuzqueña del período Intermedio Tardío (*in* International Congress of Americanists, XL, Roma-Genova, 1972. Atti [see item 513] v. 1, p. 353-362, illus., bibl.)

Archaeological Spanish Mission in Chinchero area, Urubamba prov., Cuzco dept., 1968-70, produced large pottery collections from site of Cancha-Cancha. Illustrates, describes and places types in Late Intermediate period.

1043. Roe, Peter. A further exploration of the Rowe Chavín seriation and its implications for North Central Coast chronology. Washington, Dumbarton Oak Research Library and Collections, 1974. 80 p., bibl., illus. (Studies in precolumbian art and archaeology, 13)

Author uses the human figure and snake motif in his seriation, which had not been used by Rowe. Illustrates little known pieces of Chavín art. Feels the spread of the Chavín cult was not always peaceful. Adds much to the coherence of the late periods of Chavín art style, but nothing new on origins. Useful to specialists in Andean archaeology.

1044. Rostworoski de Diez Canseco, María. Plantaciones pre-hispánicas de coca en la vertiente del Pacífico (PEMN/R, 39, 1973, p. 193-224, bibl., illus.)

Extremely detailed study of the precolumbian custom of growing coca on the eastern slopes of the Andes which does not intend to be exhaustive on coca-growing in tropical forest. Makes extensive use of chroniclers as well as archaeological materials such as actual finds and scenes on Mochica and Nasca pottery.

1045. Samaniego Román, Lorenzo Alberto. Los nuevos trabajos arqueológicos en Sechín, Casma, Perú. Trujillo, Peru, Ediciones Lersen, 1973. 97 p., bibl., illus., map.

History of archaeological investigations in Sechín from 1937-69 including recent work begun as a result of the earthquake of 31 May 1970. Excellent summary of different architectural phases of building, etc. Although pottery not clearly associated with the stone part of the temple, justifies assignment of site to construction in Early Formative period. Sees relationships to Temples of Punkuri and Cerro Blanco in Nepeña valley.

1046. Sestieri, Pellegrino Claudio. Scavi a Cajamarquilla, Peru (*in* International Congress of Americanists, XL, Roma-Genova, 1972. Atti [see item 513] v. 1, p. 325-327)

Summary comments about Italian Archaeological Mission's excavations at Cajamarquilla, 1962-71.

1047. Stephens, S. G. Cotton remains from archaeological sites in central coastal Peru (AAAS/S, 180:4082, April 1973, p. 186-188, plates, tables)

Compares archaeological cotton remains from sites, representing 2500-1000 BC, with living wild and cultivated Gossypium barbadense L. Although these archaeological forms are not the earliest cottons recorded for the New World, they are primitive forms of this genus and species and represent the earliest stages of recorded cotton domestication.

1048. Thompson, Donald E. Archaeological investigations in the eastern Andes of northern Peru (*in* International Congress of Americanists, XL, Roma-Genova, 1972. Atti [see item 513] bv. 1, p. 363-369, bibl., illus.)

Results of field work in 1970 of late prehispanic occupation of the area around Uchucmarca, east of Marañon, Libertad dept. Interested in communities in existence at time of incorporation into Inca empire. Combines ethnohistorical study of early Spanish documents with social anthropological study of present-day communities. Believes data shows area was more intensively populated then than now, with more sites in puna and on saddle ridges, mostly of Late Intermediate period to early Colonial period. Indicates that these groups' origin was more than one in Upper Marañon area and that their subsistence was on many microclimates from lower area where maize was exploited to higher regions for potatoes, etc., and that there was trade with coast.

1048a. _____. Arquitectura y patrones de establecimiento en el Valle de Casma (PEMN/R, 40, 1974, p. 9-29, bibl., illus., map)

Summarizes results of a settlement-pattern study based on field work in the Casma Valley in 1956 and done in the style of Willey's Viru Valley project (see *HLAS 19:488*) by periods. Formative period also used the upper reaches of the valley; Tiahuanaco period shows the greatest architectural buildings therein; and Inca period shows very little evidence of Inca occupation.

1048b. _____. Investigaciones arqueológicas en los Andes orientales del norte del Perú (PEMN/R, 39, 1973, p. 117-125, bibl., illus.)

Archaeological survey and excavations in 1970 of Upper Marañón produced information on settlement pattern, architecture, etc. to suggest that area was more extensively and intensively occupied in past than today. All sites date from Late Intermediate to Early Colonial, and area shows strong influence from various regions with an economic exploitation and trade with lowlands as well as coast (also see item 513).

1048c. _____ and **Rogger Ravines.** Tinyash, a prehispanic village in the Andean puna (AIA/A, 26:2, April 1973, p. 94-100, illus.)

Stone-wall compounds with interior rooms and aboveground funerary chambers (chullpas) are characteristic of a relatively large site on the puna dating probably between 1000-1476 AD.

1049. Trimborn, Hermann. Investigaciones arqueológicas en el departamento de Tacna, Peru (*in* International Congress of Americanists, XL, Roma-Genova, 1972. Atti [see item 513] v. 1, p. 333-335)

Summarizes field work of 1970-72 in Tacna dept., Peru.

1049a. _____. Nuevas fechas radiocarbónicas para algunos monumentos y sitios prehispánicos de la costa peruana (*in* International Congress of Americanists, XL, Roma-Genova, 1972. Atti [see item 513] v. 1, p. 313-315)

Includes 24 carbon dates on materials from late Urban period of massive architectural constructions. Of interest to expert are dates from Apurlec in Lambayeque dept., and pyramid sites near Túcume called Huaca El Mirador, Huaca Alargada, Huaca de las Estacas in the north; sites of the Huaycán area in the Valle del Rimac; and various sites in south in the extreme southern Peruvian valleys in Tacna dept.

1050. Usera Mata, Luis de. Una colección de cerámica del Valle de Huara, Perú (UM/REAA, 7:2, 1972, p. 191-234, bibl., illus.)

Report on material left on surface of looted cemetery located in Huara Valley, 130 km. north of Lima near main town of Huacho, along Pan American highway. Excellent description and drawings of pottery. In addition to Chancay White and Chancay Black-on-White, material shows Huari influence. Dates occupation of area from ca. 900-1470 AD.

1051. Wassén, S. Henry. A problematic metal object from northern Peru (EM/A, 1972, p. 29-33, bibl., plate, table)

Ceremonial plate armor of metal, mainly copper, said to be from precolumbian grave near Sipán, 25 km. north of Chiclayo.

URUGUAY

1052. Baeza, Jorge E. and **Emilio Peláez.**

Un proyecto de estudio y levantamiento arqueológico nacional (*in* Congreso Nacional de Arqueología, I, Fray Bentos, Uru., 1973. Antecedentes y anales. Fray Bentos, Uru., Museo Municipal de Historia Natural de Río Negro, 1973, p. 173-178, map)

Propose a national system for recording archaeological sites (numerical, symbols, maps, aerial photos, etc.) and discuss its relevance to the protection of the national patrimony.

1052a. _____; **Carlos Echeverry;** and **José L. Barone.** Un yacimiento paraneolitizado en Las Marías, depto. de Cerro Largo (*in* Congreso Nacional de Arqueología, I, Fray Bentos, Uru., 1973. Antecedentes y anales. Fray Bentos, Uru., Museo Municipal de Historia Natural de Río Negro, 1973, p. 123-146, bibl., illus., map)

Describes surface materials from a site, ranging from nonceramic (such as some types of stone artifacts similar to Bird's Patagonia period IV materials) to Tupiguarani pottery.

1053. Berroa Belén, Carlos and **René Boretto Ovalle.** El uso de espículas de esponjas en la cerámica indígena (*in* Congreso Nacional de Arqueología, I, Fray Bentos, Uru., 1973. Antecedentes y anales. Fray Bentos, Ur., Museo Municipal de Historia Natural de Río, Negro, 1973, p. 119-122)

Emphasizes importance of noting use of fresh water-sponge spicules in Uruguay's aboriginal pottery.

1054. Boretto Ovalle, René; Rosendo Bernal Romero; Pedro Ignacio Schmitz; and **Itala Irene Basile Becker.** Arqueología del departamento de Río Negro: esquema tentativa de una secuencia cronológica para sitios del Río Uruguay y Río Negro (*in* Congreso Nacional de Arqueología, I, Fray Bentos, Uru., 1973. Antecedentes y anales. Fray Bentos, Uru., Museo Municipal de Historia Natural de Río Negro, 1973, p. 147, bibl., map)

Results of study based on only two-years field work of 80 ceramic samples representing 20,000 sherds and seriated into a sequence of two phases (Yeguada and Vizcaíno).

1055. Femenias, Jorge. Informe preliminar sobre en yacimiento epiprotolítico en la zona de Salto Grande, Uruguay (*in* Congreso Nacional de Arqueología, I, Fray Bentos, Uru., 1973. Antecedentes y anales. Fray Bentos, Uru., Museo Municipal de Historia Natural de Río Negro, 1973, p. 19-40, bibl., illus., map)

Nonceramic site with flakes, artifacts, and choppers, which unfortunately is given name from European terminology. Shows relationship to Saltogradense lithic complex.

1056. Flangini, Tabaré. Un yacimiento precerámico en la zona de Playa Verde, depto. de Maldonado. Montevideo, Centro de Estudios Arqueológicos, 1972. 15 p., bibl., illus., map (Publicaciones, 2)

Describes over 600 lithic materials from nonceramic site clearly related to those from southern Brazil and northern Argentina though author gives no date or comparative data.

1057. Peláez Castello, Emilio. El yacimiento pictográfico del Cerro Pan de Azúcar (*in* Congreso Nacional de Arqueología, I, Fray Bentos, Uru., 1973. Antecedentes y anales. Fray Bentos, Ur., Museo Municipal de Historia Natural de Río Negro, 1973, p. 41-50, bibl., illus., map)

Reconstructs designs of badly eroded and defaced pictographs near Piriápolis, known since 1878.

Prous-Poirier, André. Os objetos zoomorfos do litoral do sul do Brasil e do Uruguai. See item 920.

1058. Rodríguez Saccone, Osvaldo. Communicación preliminar acerca de una industria basáltica en el Río Negro medio, depto. de Durazno (*in* Congreso Nacional de Arqueología, I, Fray Bentos, Uru., 1973. Antecedentes y anales. Fray Bentos, Uru., Museo Municipal de Historia Natural de Río Negro, 1973, p. 179-191, bibl., map)

Typology of 42 different types of extra large chipped basalt artifacts from three sites in central part of country on middle course of Río Negro.

1059. Rouco, Cristina; Antonio Días; and **Jorge E. Baeza.** Métodos modernos aplicados en la cerámica del sitio arqueológico Cerrito Vizcaíno, delta del Río Negro, Uruguay (*in* Congreso Nacional de Arqueología, I, Fray Bentos, Uru., 1973. Antecedentes y anales. Fray Bentos, Uru., Museo Municipal de Historia Natural de Río Negro, 1973, p. 4-17, bibl., illus.)

Analysis of archaeological pottery by differential thermal studies and X-ray diffraction.

1060. Silva, Luis Angel. Presentación arqueológica del departamento de Colonia, Uruguay (*in* Congreso Nacional de Arqueología, I, Fray Bentos, Uru., 1973. Antecedentes y anales. Fray Bentos, Uru., Museo Municipal de Historia Natural de Río Negro, 1973, p. 51-54, map)

Summarizes the archaeological situation of this part of Uruguay studied by author for ten years.

VENEZUELA

1061. Peñalver Gómez, Henriqueta. Correspondientes a las actividades realizadas durante los años 1968-1971 (Boletín [Instituto de Antropología e Historia del Estado de Carabobo, Museo de Arte e Historia, Valencia, Ven.] 3/4, 1972? p. 7-42, illus.)

Shows work from several ceramic periods underway at Los Cerritos, Morro de Guacara, Puerto Cabello district, and La Iguana. Important paleotological excavations which deal with Pleistocene fauna, mastodon and glyptodon. Includes charts, field diagrams and illustrations.

1062. Sanoja Obediente, Mario. Proyecto 72 (*in* International Congress of Americanist, XL, Roma-Genova, 1972. Atti [see item 513] v. 1, p. 255-260, illus.)

Describes Caño Grande phase on the southwest side of Lake Maracaibo and by relating it to Zancudo material believes it began about 500-600 AD. Also sees connections with Early Tairona and other Colombian cultures.

1062a. _____ **and Iraida Vargas.** Antiguas formaciones y modos de producción venezolanos: notas para el estudio de los procesos de integración de la sociedad venezolana 12.000 A.C.-1.900 B.C. Caracas, Monte Avila Editores, 1974. 290 p., bibl., illus., plates (Col. Temas venezolanos)

Reconstruction and interpretation of the various processes that determined the evolution and development of aboriginal Venezuelan cultures. Begins with prehistory, continues into the Spanish conquest and the emergence of a colonial mestizo society, and culminates in the modern period. Combines an archaeological and ecological approach with an historical, social, and economic interpretation of the cultural processes involved. This unique time-depth approach to understanding modern Venezuela is thought-provoking. Possibly only archaeologists can examine the development of various cultures through time without the emotional involvement that social anthropologists and ethnologists have with the people they study.

1062b. _____ **and** _____. Niveles de integración sociopolítica de las comunidades precolumbinas del Orinoco y la costa oriental de Venezuela (*in* International Congress of Americanists, XL, Roma-Genoa, 1972. Atti [see item 513] v. 1, p. 247-253, bibl.)

Discusses the precolumbian cultural development of Lower Orinoco and coast of Venezuela in terms of evolution of a socio-political system for the best exploitation of natural resources.

1063. Sujo Volsky, Jeannine. El estudio del arte rupestre en Venezuela: su literatura, su problemática y una nueva propuesta metodológica (UCAB/M, 4, 1975, p. 709-928, bibl., illus.)

Extensive coverage of literature on rock art (pictographs and petroglyphs) of Venezuela, with good illustrations, catalog listing and bibliography. Comments on need for field work and suggests computer analysis.

1064. Wagner, Erika. Nueva evidencia arqueológica de Venezuela Oriental: el yacimiento de Campoma (*in* International Congress of Americanists, XL, Roma-Genova, 1972. Atti [see item 513] v. 1, p. 239-245, bibl. illus., map.)

Describes material that leads to definition of a new phase, or perhaps better seen as now part of a Series Campomoide to which Campoma, Punta Arenas and possibly Cabrantica belong. Time period from Carbon-14 dates put it in Period IV (1000-1500 AD) of Rouse and Cruxent.

1064a. _____. Prehistory of the Venezuelan Andes (AVAC/ACV, 23:3, 1972, p. 181-184, bibl., tables)

Establishes two cultural patterns for Venezuelan Andes: Andean and sub-Andean based on cultural ecology and ethnohistorical and archaeological study of Carache and Mucuchíes regions.

1064b. _____. La protohistoria e historia inicial de Boconó, Estado Trujillo (SCNLS/A, 33, 1972, p. 39-60, bibl., illus., map, table)

Summary of archaeology of Boconó region divided into three phases from Periods III-IV in Rouse's and Cruxent s regional chronology, or from ca. 300-1500 AD.

1065. Zucchi, Alberta. Aboriginal earth structures of the western Venezuelan llanos (ICS/CJS, 12:1/2, June 1972, p. 95-106, bibl., illus., map)

Using principally La Betania site, but also others, comments on artificial earth constructions and causeways in western Venezuelan llanos, dating about 500 AD. See also item 1065a.

1065a. _____. Prehistoric human occupations of the western Venezuelan llanos (SAA/AA, 38:2, April 1973, p. 182-190, bibl., illus., map)

Describes maize cultivation dated at from 920 BC to 500 AD in flooded savannas of western Venezuela, from detailed work in Hato de la Calzada near Caño del Oso, where a complex of mound sites are connected by a causeway. Author suggests manioc (evidence not given of what data causes this positive identification) is older than maize in area and that such agricultural system developed in Amazon. Follows Lathrap's viewpoint rather than Steward, Meggers or Evans' of tropical-forest agricultural systems deriving from Formative period in Andean area and moving into tropical forest.

1065b. _____. Recent research on the prehistory of the western Venezuelan llanos (AVAC/ACV, 23:3, 1972, p. 185-187, bibl., map)

From work in Barinas area dates polychrome pottery at 2870 ± 170 years BP suggesting it is older here than in any other part of South America, Caribbean or Central America. Artificial earth mound construction is late and intrusive into area, probably adopted from Arququinoid peoples who had inhabited the Orinoco llanos from Period III-IV of the Cruxent and Rouse periods.

1065c. _____. Tropical forest groups of the Venezuelan savannas: archeological evidence (*in* International Congress of Americanists, XL, Roma-Genova, 1972. Atti [see item 513] v. 1, p. 261-267, illus., map, bibl.)

In spite of title, article is in Spanish about recent finds at the site of Caño Caroni, Barinas state, and others nearby and their relationship to savanna cultures.

ETHNOLOGY: MIDDLE AMERICA

JOHN M. INGHAM
Associate Professor of Anthropology
University of Minnesota

RECENT YEARS HAVE WITNESSED THEORETICAL ORIGINALITY and methodological sophistication in anthropological research in Middle America. Forsaking the community study for problem-oriented approaches, scholars are applying a variety of methodological techniques to varied ethnographic questions.

Investigators have sought more precise specification of the structure and function of *compadrazgo* under differing socioeconomic conditions (items 1116 and 1188-1189). Other aspects of social organization, including kinship (item 1103), barrio-chapel systems (items 1123 and 1187), and social deviance (item 1182), have received fruitful attention. Women's roles—too long a lacuna in the ethnographic literature—are now matters of serious interest. Elmendorf (item 1129) has fashioned vivid portraits of women in Chan Kom, and Chiñas (item 1118) has provided us with a monograph on Zapotec women. Studies of education (item 1166), household membership (item 1184), and economic innovation (item 1151) have also brought women's roles into clearer perspective. While earlier work on folk medicine tended to concentrate on its metaphorical representation of social values, current research has broadened to include biomedical questions of diagnosis and effectiveness (items 1130, 1157 and 1167).

Anthropologists working in Michoacán have debated the relative weight of cultural/psychological factors versus economic opportunity as determinants of rural economic innovation (items 1101, 1132 and 1170). While this type of argument cannot easily be resolved, work presented here clearly shows that rural communities do respond to economic opportunities (items 1115, 1149 and 1178). In a particularly pertinent study of twenty-four communities in Michoacán, Moone finds that traditionalism (Tarascan language, civil-religious hierarchies, etc.) does not substantially interfere with a community's socioeconomic integration into the national society (item 1167). Beals suggests that Middle American Indians characteristically wish both to preserve their *costumbres* and to improve the material aspects of their lives. He observes, however, that arguments about the interrelationship of cultural and economic integration may eventually prove to be moot, as population pressures and scarce resources undermine traditional community life in any case (item 1106).

A noteworthy development during the last few years has been an increasing concern with the interdependence of religion and politics. Scholars have shown that religious images may serve as patrons for political movements (item 1195), that religious organization may be reflected in political organization (item 1200), and that particular religious sects may be associated with particular political factions (item 1131). Turner's (item 1195) penetrating essay on Hidalgo and the *via crucis* theme in Mexican history and culture reveals unsuspected cultural patterning, and readers may find that his treatment of historical dialectics resonates with Bricker's stimulating discussions of ritual conflict between Indian and Ladino (items 1114 and 1114a).

The following interpretative synopsis, suggested in part by my own research in northeastern Morelos, may indicate the manifold implications of the recent accounts of folk religions.

In Bricker's study, which focuses on highland Chiapas, a central representation of the Ladino is the Blackman, a malevolent, devil-like, oversexed (he has a six-foot-long, death-dealing, red penis) demon previously described by Blaffer (see *HLAS 35:1035*). What is doubtless the same monster appears as Satan in central Mexico (depicted with red skin, tail, and black dress, like a Spaniard). Here, he is associated with harmful winds and with unsavory supernatural figures (e.g., *naguales,* La Llorona, Rainbow, and others) who inhabit barrancas and caves. Satan's precolumbian predecessor would appear to have been the wind god Quetzalcóatl (black body; long, red snout) or the black Tezcatlipoca (also a wind god). Cortés, the prototype of the greedy Spaniard, was identified with Quetzalcóatl at the time of the Conquest, and a parallel connection holds between La Malinche, Cortés' mistress, and Cihuacoatl, a sinister female deity who may have been a forerunner of La Llorona (see item 1152). This set of evil figures contrasts with the sun god and the gods of fertility, who in various parts of Middle America have been identified with Christ and the Virgin (see items 1114a and 1195).

Thus evil figures are aligned with violent weather (such as wind, and possibly hail and excess rain), with hypersexuality, and with death, while an opposing set of more benevolent deities is associated with agricultural fertility, rain, virginity, and rebirth. Wind spirits cause *aire,* the symptoms of which—analgesia, neuralgia, seizures, paralyses, deafness, etc.—are reminiscent of conversion hysteria; other evil figures occasion *susto* (fright), an ailment which encompasses anxiety and depression. The threats posed by Middle American monsters appear to reinforce social codes, particularly with respect to female sexuality (see items 1144 and 1186), and it may well be that occurrences of *susto* and *aire* in turn reflect the emotional repercussions of the political and sexual suppression of women (hysteria is generally thought to afflict women more than men, and it is now well established that more women than men suffer from *susto;* but see item 1196). Blackman, then, is a multivocal symbol that reflects the Middle American countryman's concern with Ladino-Indian relations, agricultural fertility, and wifely chastity. Structuralism illuminates the formal qualities of the Blackman symbol, but it does not account for its importance in Middle American culture. A complete anthropological exorcism of the prince of darkness will require a magic of a different sort.

1101. Acheson, James M. Reply to Mary Lee Nolan (AAA/AA, 76:1, March 1974, p. 49-53, bibl.)

Takes exception to Nolan's emphasis on the role of socioeconomic factors in economic development, and discusses several ambiguities in her paper. In particular, she is faulted for not controlling economic variables and for failing to delineate the precise nature of economic opportunities.

1102. Aguirre Beltrán, Gonzalo. Applied anthropology in Mexico (SAA/HO, 33:1, Spring 1974, p. 1-7)

Indigenismo has origins in the transformations brought about by the emergence of industrialization in the late 19th century. Mexican anthropology since Clavijero has had the goal of an integrated nation, although the theory and praxis of this goal were clearly enunciated for the first time by Manuel Gamio: anthropological community studies would furnish knowledge about acculturation, and this knowledge would guide the formation of rural schools and cultural missions which would stimulate the incorporation of marginal groups into the nation. Present-day INI emphasis on interdisciplinary and regional programs rests on analytical principles laid down in *Regiones de refugio.* Following the events of 1968, some younger anthropologists expressed criticism of indigenismo. These critics have been given responsible government positions in the hope that they will confront the moral necessity of integration and development.

1103. Arizpe S., Lourdes. Parentesco y economía en una sociedad nahua: Nican Pehua Zacatipán. México, Secretaría de Educación Pública, Instituto Nacional Indigenista, 1973. 225 p., bibl., illus., maps, plates, tables.

A solid grasp of social anthropology enhances this sophisticated analysis of economy and family in a Nahua community. Demography, ecology, and agricultural production receive comprehensive coverage. The developmental cycle of domestic groups is skillfully analyzed in terms of socioeconomic status and labor requirements. A componential analysis of the kinship terminology, in conjuction with other evidence, establishes the cognatic nature of the kinship system. The author finds that cargo service is not an individual responsibility but one shared by an entire family. The persistence of civil-religious cargo systems, then, may depend on the perpetuation of traditional patterns of patrilocality and parental authority, which in this case have been undermined by the increasing importance of a cash economy. The study concludes with a critique of attempts to impose African models of unilineal descent on Middle American data.

1104. Beals, Ralph Leon. Cherán: A sierra Tarascan village. 2. ed. rev. Prepared in conjunction with the U.S. State Dept. as a project of the Interdepartmental Committee on Cultural and Scientific Cooperation. N.Y., Cooper Square Publishers, 1973. 225 p., bibl., illus., maps, plates, tables (Smithsonian Institution, Institute of Social Anthropology. Publication, 2. Library of Latin American history and culture)

Reprint of the original published in Washington, U.S. Government Printing Office, 1946, see *HLAS 12:201*.

1105. _____. Ethnology of the Western Mixe. N.Y., Cooper Square Publishers, 1973. 175 p., plates (Library of Latin American history and culture)

Reprint of the original published in Berkeley, Univ. of California Press, 1945 (Publications in American archaeology and ethnology, 42:1), see *HLAS 11:243*.

1106. _____. Mexico's persistent Indians (CUH, 66:393, May 1974, p. 204-207, 231-232)

A balanced summary of controversies concerning the cultural and economic assimilation of Mexico's Indian communities. Indians themselves, as illustrated by the Mayo, may prefer to retain traditional customs while improving their economic situation. In the long run, assimilationist and pluralist policies may make little difference, as Indian communities disintegrate under the impact of population pressure and scarce resources.

1107. Beaucage, Pierre. Comunidades indígenas de la Sierra Norte de Puebla (UNAM/RMS, 36:1, enero/marzo 1974, p. 11-147, bibl.)

Borrowing a metaphor from Leach, Beaucage avers that previous work on the cultural dimensions of Middle American communities has amounted to little more than ethnographic butterfly collection; only historical materialism can bring Middle American anthropology to a scientific plane. The Marxist reorientation should concentrate on relations between actual communities and centers of domination, while attending to the various syntheses (as determined by local conditions) of local-level, semi-feudal modes of production with agrarian capitalism and capitalist industry and finance at regional and national levels. To illustrate this approach, the mode of agricultural production in six communities in the highlands of northern Puebla is subjected to detailed analysis. The prevailing stress on coffee production is explicated in terms of historical, demographic, climatic, and technological factors; and the relation of social stratification to production at both regional and local levels is described.

1108. Benítez, Fernando. Historia de un chamán cora. México, Ediciones Era, 1973. 142 p., plate (Serie popular Era, 24)

Many facets of Cora cosmology, folk medicine, and everyday experience are educed by means of a life history of a Cora shaman.

1109. Benzi, Marino. Le mythe de l'ancêtre des Huichol, Huatakáme: contribution à l'étude de la mythologie Huichol (SA/J, 60, 1971, p. 177-190, bibl., plates)

French and Spanish versions of the myth of Huatakáme follow a brief description of the narrator.

1110. Berlin, Brent; Dennis E. Breedlove; and **Peter H. Raven.** Principles of Tzeltal plant classification: an introduction to the botanical ethnography of a Mayan-speaking people of highland Chiapas. N.Y., Academic Press, 1974. 660 p., bibl., maps, illus., plates, tables (Series in language, thought, and culture)

This clearly written and copiously illustrated compendium should interest the general student of Middle America as well as the specialist in ethnoscience. The cognitive principles underlying Tzeltal plant classification are presented and explained with reference to general and comparative features of folk systematics. The terminology used by the Tzeltal in describing and discussing the structure and growth of plants is amply described, and detailed attention is given to the cultural significance of plants, as in agriculture, food types, house-building, and other areas of material culture. All known Tzeltal plant classes receive precise ethnobotanical definition in terms of basic and extended ranges of meaning.

1111. Bonilla P., Janina. Dicen de don Manuel Tucurrique (III/AI, 34:2, abril/junio 1974, p. 423-426)

Transcription of several tales (anecdotes?) about Manuel Tucurrique, the last Indian chief of Tucurrique, C.R.

1112. Bozzoli de Wille, María E. Situación de una frontera agrícola y una frontera política: ticos, guaymíes e italianos en el cantón Coto Brus (III/AI, 34:2, abril/junio 1974, p. 381-418, table)

Relates in diary-like fashion the author's impressions of agricultural colonization in Coto Brus, Punta Arenas, by Costa Ricans, Italians, and Guaymí. Notes on Guaymí culture and a table showing the composition of 30 Guaymí households are included. The article concludes with comments on population pressure and land utilization.

1113. Bremmé de Santos, Ida. El compadrazgo en Mixco (Estudios [Guatemala] 4, 1971, p. 87-100, bibl.)

Principal features of *compadrazgo* are extracted from a review of several representative studies of the institution. Ladinos' views of their co-parent relations with Ladinos and Indians in Mixco are illustrated with case material. The data shed light on informants' perceptions of economic interests in *compadrazgo* relationships.

1114. Bricker, Victoria Reifler. Ritual humor in highland Chiapas. Austin, Univ. of Texas Press, 1973. 257 p., bibl., illus., maps, plates (Texas Pan American series)

Describes in scholarly detail the patterns of ritual humor in Zinacantan, Chamula, and Chenalhó. Ritual humor occurs during the Christmas-New Year season and the fiesta of San Sebastián (Zinacantan) and during Carnival (all three communities). Costumed persons portray bullfighters, Spanish ladies and gentlemen, Monkey, Jaguar, Blackman, Plumed Serpent, and others. Comic reversals of moral code effected by these ribald figures may actually serve to reinforce the moral code by ridiculing exceptions to it. Includes a provocative survey of ritual conflict between good and evil, Christian and Moor, and Spaniard and Indian. For folklorist's comment see *HLAS 36:967.*

1114a. ———. Algunas consecuencias religiosas y sociales del nativismo maya del siglo XIX (III/AI, 33:2, abril/junio 1973, p. 327-348, bibl.)

In highland Chiapas, Chamula is unique with respect to cargo systems in having two separate cults—one for saints and another for "Nuestro Padre" ("El Señor del Cielo"). Although this second cult superficially refers to the crucifixion of Christ, it has numerous elements that originated with the Caste War of 1867-70; among these is the apparent commemoration of the sacrifice of an Indian Christ who served as a patron for the insurgent Indians. In fact, ethnic conflict is clearly portrayed in contemporary Chamula ritual by means of humorous costumed figures. The peculiar structure of the Chamula cargo system may be traced, then, to the leading role that Chamula played in the Caste War.

1115. Cancian, Frank. Change and uncertainty in a peasant economy: the Maya corn farmers of Zinacantan. Stanford, Calif., Stanford Univ. Press, 1972. 208 p., bibl., illus., maps, plates, tables.

Excellent, tightly-written study examines the response of Zinacanteco corn-farmers to economic opportunities resulting from new roads and a government corn-buying program. New roads enabled Zinacantecos to expand production by renting Ladino fields in the lowlands; aspects of this development—planting practices, work groups, crop yields, tenure arrangements, and marketing—are described in detail. While price supports stabilized and eventually increased incomes, there was initial uncertainty about market reactions. Under these conditions, Zinacantecos could not have acted in accordance with an abstract principle of economic rationality. Actually, they seem to have used what knowledge they had to enhance or preserve social status. Intricate, a priori reasoning suggests a model of positive, negative, and curvilinear effects of social status on innovation. Predictions derived from the model appear to fit the empirical evidence.

1116. Carlos, Manuel L. Fictive kinship and modernization in Mexico (CUA/AQ, 46:2, April 1973, p. 75-91, bibl., table)

Survey of rural and urban patterns and trends in *compadrazgo*, with reference to modernization. In traditional Indian communities *compadrazgo* is an individual and group mutual-aid mechanism; types of *compadrazgo* are numerous and their extensions are pervasive. Modernization initially promotes the selection of Ladinos as godparents. In more heterogeneous communities, types of *compadrazgo* are fewer, while godparents are selected within and outside a community. In modern urban settings, the types of *compadrazgo* are few and either kin or individuals of similar socioeconomic background are selected.

1117. Carmack, Robert M. and others. La pre y protohistoria de Santiago Momostenango (GIIN/GI, 7:4, oct./dic. 1972, p. 5-21)

Summarizes extant prehistorical and ethnohistorical information about a contemporary Guatemalan community.

Chapman, Anne M. Chamanisme et magie des ficelles chez les Tolupan—Jicaque—du Honduras. See *HLAS 36:895.*

1118. Chiñas, Beverly. The Isthmus Zapotecs: women's roles in cultural context. Foreword by Louise and George Spindler. N.Y., Holt, Rinehart and Winston, 1973. 122 p., bibl., illus., map, plates (Case studies in cultural anthropology)

Isthmus Zapotec women supplement family income by selling in local markets. Marketing, however, merely complements the more prestigious work of men and does not give women significant advantages. Life cycle, marriage, *compadrazgo*, and fiesta system are described with reference to the social position of women. While resonating with other Middle American ethnographies, the material includes interesting local nuances (e.g., prolonged female mourning and behavior and public announcement of the consummation of marriage). Informal aspects of women's roles are also noted (e.g., women mediate conflict, serve as messengers, and assist one another in rape prevention). Zapotec values and styles of masculinity and femininity are compared and contrasted with mestizo patterns.

1119. Colby, B.N. and **L.M. Colby.** Two

Ixil myths: Guatemala (AI/A, 69:1/2, 1974, p. 216-223, bibl.)

The eidochronic component of a myth or tale concerns the sequence of events or circumstances, that is, the plot, which can be expressed as an abbreviated synopsis. A large corpus of data is required to establish an eidon inventory and rules of composition; here, two myths—"The abode of the mountain deities" and "The fish merchant"—merely illustrate the approach. Analysis reveals that these two manifestly different stories actually share a similar narrative structure and such eidons as "wrongdoing," "transport," "interrogation," etc.

1120. Collier, Jane Fishburne. Law and social change in Zinacantan. Stanford, Calif., Stanford Univ. Press, 1973. 281 p., bibl., map, plates, tables.

This study of Zinacanteco conflict-management focuses on the uncertainty of law, the fallibility of individuals who manipulate it, and the cultural stereotypes which rationalize behavior. Zinacanteco law and society are viewed as a feedback system, in which type of claim influences legal procedures, which influence outcomes, which influence future claims. Disputes and claims, depending on content and parties involved, require one or more mechanisms of resolution (e.g., curing ceremonies, begging formal pardon, mediation by hamlet elder, or mediation by the *presidente* in the town hall). A cultural premise—misdeeds evoke both supernatural sanction and anger in the heart of the victim, which calls out for vengeance—reinforces the private nature of quarrels and restrains mediators from imposing their own solutions. Detailed chapters cover witchcraft, aggressive acts, marital disputes, courtship disputes, disagreements between neighbors, and disputes between an individual and the community. A dramatistic sense of social action is skillfully combined with the exegesis of key Zinacanteco concepts.

1121. Cone, Cynthia A. Perception of occupations in a newly industrializing region of México (SAA/HO, 32:2, Summer 1973, p. 143-151, bibl., tables)

The role of factory worker, a novel occupation in the region of a new industrial town, is affecting attitudes about traditional occupations. Farmers and shopkeepers have devalued their own occupations, while developing positive evaluations of factory work. These changes in attitude have not affected job preference, but they are reflected in aspirations for sons' occupations. The political ramifications of this situation are considered.

1122. Cook, Scott. Stone tools for steelage Mexicans? Aspects of production in a Zapotec stoneworking industry (AAA/AA, 75:5, Oct. 1973, p. 1485-1503, bibl., plates, tables)

The technology, social organization, and quarry tenure of stonework production in the Valley of Oaxaca are described in detail. Following Marx, the suggestion is made that the concept of production is a key to the integration of interests in economy, cultural ecology, and cultural evolution.

1123. Cortés Ruiz, Efraín C. San Simón de la Laguna: la organización familiar y lo mágico-religioso en el culto al oratorio. México, Secretaría de Educación Pública, Instituto Nacional Indigenista, 1972. 165 p., bibl., illus., maps, plates (Col. SEP-INI)

An intriguing Mazahua chapel-cross complex is analyzed within the context of a religious system which includes household altars and community saints. The crosses are distinct in being malevolent; they cause illnesses and require propitiatory offerings of candels and copal. Although situated on individual house sites, the chapels are supported by groups of families which show a marked tendency toward agnation. Fiestas accompany chapel repairs and periodic replacements of old crosses with new crosses. These fiestas are reminiscent of baptism; the chapels have godparents, who are coparents to the owners of the chapels. The alliance between families that are formed by this type of *compadrazgo* are hereditary, unless dreams dictate the selection of new godparents.

1124. Coy, Peter. An elementary structure of ritual kinship: a case of prescription in the compadrazgo (RAI/M, 9:3, Sept. 1974, p. 470-479, bibl., tables)

Selection of marriage sponsors in a Mexican community is discussed with reference to status, kinship relationship, and previous *compadrazgo* ties. A prerogative to become baptismal sponsor also tends to reinforce and perpetuate the relationship between marriage sponsor and procreation group.

Crumrine, N. Ross. Ritual drama and cultural change. See *HLAS 36:969*.

1125. Dehouve, Danièle. L'influence de l'état dans la transformation du système des charges d'une communaté indienne mexicaine (EPHE/H, 14:2, avril/juin 1974, p. 87-108, tables)

Systems of civil-religious offices in Mexican Indian communities form prestige hierarchies. As illustrated by the case of Xalpatlahuac (Guerrero, Mex.), they also regulate relations with the government. New civil offices created at the end of the 19th century were absorbed and disrupted by the traditional office system.

1126. Dennis, Philip A. The Oaxacan village president as political middleman (UP/E, 12:4, Oct. 1973, p. 419-427, bibl.)

Describes the several strategies used by village presidents in the delicate task of mediating civil disputes.

1127. Dobyns, Henry F. The Papago people. Phoenix, Ariz., Indian Tribal Series, 1972. 106 p., bibl., maps, plates.

Brief history of the Papago from the colonial period to the present.

1128. Early, John D. Education via radio

among Guatemalan highland Maya (SAA/HO, 32:3, Fall 1973, p. 221-229, bibl., tables)

Population and pressure change in national law concerning land titles have rendered most of the Santiago Atitlán families incapable of self-sufficiency in food production. This has led to increased integration into the national economy and has resulted in the emergence of a felt need for literacy. With the sponsorship of the Catholic Diocese of Oklahoma, a radio school was established with the aim of developing literacy, useful mathematical skills, and Western consciousness of social structure and the physical universe.

1129. Elmendorf, Mary Lindsay. The Mayan woman and change. Cuernavaca, Mex., Centro Intercultural de Documentación (CIDOC) 1972. 1 v. (Various pagings) bibl., (CIDOC cuaderno, 81)

In this empathetic enquiry into womanhood in the Maya community of Chan Kom intimate portraits of nine women depict the range of female experience while short sections treat marriage, family, children, self-image, economy, and religion. Attitudes about work and love receive particularly perceptive discussion—love in Chan Kom is a collective concept, a matter of living together, working together, being together; work is viewed as a means of creative self-expression. Women welcome and initiate change—even against the wishes of men—when it benefits their children, but in general they prefer to preserve the traditional fabric of their lives. The author herself has a deeply felt sense of the rewards of peasant life and expresses strong misgivings about modernization.

1130. Fábrega, Horacio and Daniel B. Silver. Illness and shamanistic curing in Zinacantan: an ethnomethodological analysis. Stanford, Calif., Stanford Univ. Press, 1973. 285 p., bibl., illus., map, tables.

Rigorous experimental study of shamanic curing in Zinacantan focuses on native perceptions of symptoms and biomedical states. Zinacanteco shamans are socially and psychologically similar to others but somewhat less constricted in their interpersonal relationships and thought processes. Shamans' reputations depend more on aspects of role-performance than on their folk-medical knowledge. The native typology of illness conforms only slightly to the western biomedical model, and Zinacantecos do not stress specificity in the association of symptom and type of illness; rather, they seem to be more concerned with the spiritual and social aspects of illness. According to Zinacantecos, illness involves the patient's emotional state and his relationships with supernatural figures and other Zinacantecos. Shamanistic ceremonies mediate these relationships. Sick persons are treated with private ceremonies; droughts and epidemics are prevented with public ceremonies. The cognitive and symbolic aspects of these ceremonies receive little attention.

1131. Falla, Ricardo. Evolución político-religiosa del indígena rural en Guatemala, 1945-1965 (Estudios Sociales Centroamericanos [San José] 1:1, enero/abril 1972, p. 27-43, bibl., map)

A survey of eight Guatemalan communities shows that religious orientations have been associated with political preferences. Traditionalists have supported the *cofradía* system in opposition to proponents of voluntary service. Protestants have allied themselves with poor, radical Ladinos in opposition to wealthy Ladinos. New Catholic groups—AC and the Third Order—have fomented a divisive opposition to communism.

1132. Foster, George M. Limited Good or Limited Goods: observations on Acheson (AAA/AA, 76:1, March 1974, p. 53-57, bibl.)

In reply to the charge that he has ignored economic determinants of change, Foster observes that he has insisted all along that actual innovation entails an interplay of economic opportunity (as created by infrastructure, technical guidance, etc.) and cultural-psychological factors. Much of the discussion between Foster and Acheson turns on the interpretation of government-sponsored community development programs.

1133. ———. A second look at Limited Good (CUA/AQ, 45:2, April 1972, p. 57-64, bibl.)

Aspects of the world view of Limited Good are summarized and clarified: 1) Limited Good may occur to a certain extent in various societies, but it is particularly apparent in traditional peasant societies; 2) it is an analytical model; 3) the world view of Limited Good obtains despite the fact that peasant communities are part-societies; and 4) it is not assumed that the model applies to all domains of experience.

1134. Friedlander, Judith. Being Indian in Hueyapan: a study of forced identity in contemporary Mexico. N.Y., St. Martin's Press, 1975. 205 p., bibl., illus., plates, tables.

Examines the meanings of "Indian" in a Nahuatl-speaking community. Being Indian in Hueyapan means being poor, oppressed, and denigrated. A descriptive treatment of life in Hueyapan, particularly as represented by one family, reveals that little Indian culture survives. What does survive—in language, cooking, weaving, curing, and ritual—shows much European influence. Even these elements of Indian culture are best interpreted as boundary-maintaining mechanisms or as expressions of identification with national culture (e.g., while the Dance of the Christians and the Moors tends to persist in Indian communities, the villagers of Hueyapan, at least, clearly identify with the Spaniards, not the Moors). "Indian" is a derogatory term that reflects what people cannot do or do not have; to be non-Indian is to have "culture," money, beds, tables, radios, etc. The villagers are pawns in a game of conflicting middle-class ideologies concerning the value of Indian and mestizo cultures. The political process and the educational system proclaim the image of an integrated mestizo society, while they actually perpetuate the Indian's self-identification as Indian. Cultural extremists, wishing to revive Nahuatl culture, have shown little sensitivity to the harsh realities faced by Indians.

1135. Fuente, Julio de la. Educación, antropología y desarrollo de la comunidad. Introducción de Gonzalo Aguirre Beltrán. México, Instituto Nacional Indigenista, 1973. 315 p., table (Serie de antropología social. Col. SEP/INI, 4)

A collection of 24 of Julio de la Fuente's earlier papers on rural education, applied anthropology, and community development. In an introductory essay Dr. Gonzalo Aguirre Beltrán reviews some of the history of rural education in Mexico and explores a variety of issues concerning the interrelationship of rural education and *indigenismo*.

Galbis, Ricardo. Métodos de curación entre los cuná y los otomí: estudio comparativo. See item 2224.

1136. Gann, Thomas. Ancient cities and modern tribes: exploration and adventure in Maya lands. 2. ed. N.Y., Benjamin Blom, 1972. 256 p., plates.

Personal travel account with interesting ethnographic anecdotes. First published in 1926.

1137. Goldkind, Victor. Anthropologists, informants and the achievement of power in Chan Kom (SOCIOL, 20:1, 1970, p. 17-41, bibl.)

Anthropologists working in the Maya village of Chan Kom have favored one informant to the disadvantage of other villagers. The key informant's association with Americans increased his own prestige and power within the community, and this development raises a series of ethical and methodological questions. Cross-cultural data reveal the biases which may result from excessive use of key informants.

1138. Gossen, Gary H. Chamulas in the world of the sun: time and space in Maya oral tradition. Cambridge, Mass., Harvard Univ. Press, 1974. 382 p., bibl., illus., maps, tables.

Chamula world view is thoroughly and insightfully presented through an ethnography of speaking. Chamula conceptions of time and space form a coherent system in which the sun, light, warmth, "up," and seniority have primacy. These time-space principles of Chamula cosmology are elucidated with detailed accounts of the content, style, and setting of various genres of speech and ritual. These include jokes, tales, riddles, historical narratives, games, prayers, songs, and myths. Appended is a large corpus of narrative texts.

1139. Greenfield, Patricia Marks. Comparing dimensional categorization in natural and artificial contexts: a developmental study among the Zinacantecos of Mexico (JSP, 93:2, Aug. 1974, p. 157-171, bibl., illus., tables)

This study, which examines the effects of object-familiarity on categorization, employs three-dimensional objects (flowers and rods) as familiar and unfamiliar stimuli; it thereby avoids the difficulties of previous studies that have confounded object and mode of representation. Sorting and resorting abilities are found to develop with age in schooled and unschooled Zinacantecos; sorting is not facilitated by familiarity with objects.

1140. Gregory, James R. Image of Limited Good, or expectation of reciprocity? (UC/CA, 16:1, March 1975, p. 73-92, bibl.)

Behavior patterns suggest that the Mopán Maya's (southern Belize) world-view of Limited Good is better understood in terms of a principle of "expectation of circumstantially balanced reciprocity." Article includes comments and reply.

Griffith, James. Cáhitan *Pascola* masks. See *HLAS 36:976*.

1141. Heijmerink, J.J.M. La tenencia de la tierra en las comunidades indígenas en el estado de Oaxaca, el caso de Santo Tomás Ocotepec en la región de la Mixteca Alta (UNAM/ RMS, 35:4, oct./dic. 1973, p. 289-299)

As a result of abuses initiated by local caciques, confidence in the communal land system has been undermined and communal plots are being sold and subdivided. These findings question the accuracy of government information about the agrarian situation in Indian communities.

1142. Helms, Mary W. Middle America: a culture history of heartland and frontiers. Englewood Cliffs, N.J., Prentice-Hall, 1975. 367 p., bibl., illus., maps, plates, tables (The Prentice-Hall series in anthropology)

A comprehensive culture history of Middle and Central America from the prehistoric period to the present with emphasis on the influence of traditional culture and institutions on the process of nation-building.

1143. Higgins, Cheleen Mahar. Integrative aspects of folk and Western medicine among the urban poor of Qaxaca (CUA/AQ, 48:1, Jan. 1975, p. 31-37, bibl.)

Definitions of illness takes into account general symptoms which are shared by folk and Western illness. Specific diagnoses depend on type of causation—natural or supernatural—and specific symptoms, although this latter aspect of diagnostic procedure is obscure. Informants seem to differentiate folk and Western medicine only with respect to cure; folk curers can treat some illnesses, while doctors can treat others.

1144. Holland, William R. and Roland

G. Tharp. Psicoterapia en las tierras altas mayas (ICACH, 5/6:23/24 [2. época] enero/dic. 1972, p. 57-69, bibl.)

Evaluates the psychotherapeutic aspects of the Tzotzil curing ceremony for soul-loss. Disorders of the spirit, which include various physical complaints, are seen as supernatural retribution for a lack of proper sociality. Unlike Western psychotherapy, which places greater emphasis on emotional catharsis and transference, Tzotzil shamanic curing actively and authoritatively manipulates the supernatural in a manner which symbolically and actually reaffirms social solidarity.

1145. Hollenbach, Elena E. de. El parentesco entre los Triques de Copala, Oaxaca (III/AI, 33:1, 1. trimestre 1973, p. 167-186)

Consanguineal kinship terminology among the Trique of Copala is essentially Hawaiian, although siblings and cousins may be distinguished with descriptive terms. Terms of reference for consanguines of ego's spouse and terms of address for ego's consanguines are defined by relative age. Several types of *compadrazgo* are recognized, and co-parent terms are Spanish loanwords; mestizos are commonly chosen as godparents. The many terms for address are extended to non-relatives and include only a few of the terms for reference. A comparison of Copala and Chicahuaxtla Trique shows that consanguineal systems are the same while affinal systems differ, with the Trique of Chicahuaxtla using generation rather than relative age to define terms of reference for spouse's consanguines.

1146. Horcasitas de Barros, María Luisa. La artesanía, con a raíces prehispánicas, de Santa Clara del Cobre. México, Secretaría de Educación Pública, 1973. 186 p., bibl., maps, plates (SepSetentas, 87)

Traces the art of hammering copper from the precolumbian era to the present, with particular attention to the industry's current economic problems.

1147. Hunn, Eugene. The Tenejapa Tzeltal version of the animal kingdom (CUA/AQ, 48:1, Jan. 1975, p. 15-30, bibl., tables)

Description of folk zoological classification among Tzeltal-speaking Indians of Tenejapa, highland Chiapas. Principles of animal classification parallel those adduced by Berlin *et al* for Tzeltal plant classification: generic taxa predominate; unique beginners are ambiguously named; life form taxa are rare; intermediate taxa are seldom labelled; generic taxa outnumber specific taxa; and specific and varietal taxa occur in contrast sets of few members.

1148. Hurtado, Juan José. Algunas ideas para un modelo estructural de las creencias en relación con la enfermedad en el altiplano de Guatemala (GIIN/GI, 8:1, enero/marzo 1973, p. 9-22)

Illness categories in traditional folk medicine are grouped according to cause (e.g., emotional disequilibrium; mechanical disequilibrium; imbalance of hot and cold; soul-loss; supernatural influence; and parasitic infestation). Medical practitioners are likely to receive better cooperation from rural patients if diagnoses are explained in terms of the appropriate folk-medical principles of causation. For example, if an infant is presented as having *la mollera caída*, a mechanical condition, then in this instance the physician may wish to attribute mechanical efficacy to his use of modern medicines.

1149. Iszaevich, Abraham. Modernización de una comunidad oaxaqueña del Valle. México, Secretaría de Educación Pública, 1973. 182 p., bibl., maps, plates, tables (SepSetentas, 109)

Describes economic modernization—and attendant continuity and change in social and religious spheres—in Las Margaritas, Oaxaca. Following elimination of the haciendas and the traditional system of water distribution, the cultivation of sugar cane and wheat were replaced by modern dairy farming. Las Margaritas demonstrates that Mexican communities—even when characterized by population pressure, scarce lands, and lack of credit—can develop productive, market-oriented economies. An optimistic outlook among the people of Las Margaritas can be attributed to the following factors: an ejido; dairy farming; seasonal and permanent migration; socioeconomic mobility; and an absence of a compulsory mayordomia system.

1150. Jones, Grant D. Revolution and continuity in Santa Cruz Maya society (American Ethnologist [American Anthropological Assn., Washington] 1:4, Nov. 1974, p. 659-683, bibl.)

Differences in political organization between the Santa Cruz Maya (1850-63) and their descendants, the X-Cacal group (1935-36), are elucidated by a history of the disputes between the priestly leadership of the cult of the talking cross and the secular military authorities.

1151. Jopling, Carol F. Women's work: a Mexican case study of low status as a tactical advantage (UP/E, 13:2, April 1974, p. 187-195, bibl., table)

Scarcity and erosion of farmland in Yalálag, Oaxaca, have led to greater dependence on craft industries as sources of income. Unlike the traditional men's occupation of *huarache*-making, shirtmaking, a women's occupation, has had considerable economic success, possibly as a consequence of women's lower social status. A man's status depends as much on adherence to conventions of reciprocity as on competitiveness, and thus *huarache* production and marketing are embedded in status relations which do not permit unmitigated interest in profit. The low status and low visibility of women, on the other hand, insulate them from social and political restrictions on entrepreneurship.

1152. Kearney, Michael. The winds of Ixtepeji: world view and society in a Zapotec town. Foreword by George and Louise Spindler. N.Y., Holt, Rinehart and Winston, 1972. 140 p., bibl., maps, plates (Case studies in cultural anthropology)

World view in the Zapotec town of Ixtepeji is a response to actual, and worsening, conditions of material scarcity and insecurity. The life-worlds of the Ixtepejanos are filled with expressions of anger, envy, and deceit, and individuals feel resigned to unremitting hard work, suffering, and frustration. The folk medical notion of *aire* is interpreted as a metaphor for the manifold threats to the individual, and the logical coherence of *aire* with beliefs in other supernatural phenomena is elucidated, albeit somewhat inconclusively. There are perceptive observations on the enculturation of world view, and the treatment of the myth about La Llorona, an aire-like creature, is interpreted in terms of child training and male-female relations. Social drinking is seen as a temporary release from sadness and defensive individualism. The prospects for change are briefly considered.

1153. Kemper, Robert V. Anthropologists and the study of urbanization: an example from Mexico (KAS/P, 45/46, Fall 1972, p. 1-17, bibl.)

Brief overview of anthropological approaches to urbanization in Mexico, with notes on difficulties encountered by the author in Mexico City while studying a scattered group of migrants from Tzintzuntzan, Michoacán.

1154. _____. Family and household organization among Tzintzuntzan migrants in Mexico City (*in* Cornelius, Wayne A. and Felicity M. Trueblood *eds.* Anthropological perspectives on Latin American urbanization [see item 9625] v. 4, p. 23-45, bibl.)

Emphasizes the positive adjustments of Tzintzuntzan migrant families in Mexico City. Matrifocal families are uncommon, and the nuclear family remains the norm. Family relations become more symmetrical and democratic, as the traditional roles of *macho* and *mujer abnegada* are reinterpreted, and as children are raised in an atmosphere that stresses achievement and independence rather than obedience. A combination of economic security and the absence of the husband's mother may account for these trends. Value orientations of urban Tzintzuntzeños are illustrated with several Thematic Apperception Test stories.

1155. Laurencich de Minelli, Laura. Un grupo de indios guaymí en Costa Rica (III/AI, 34:2, abril/junio, 1974, p. 369-380, tables)

Concludes from ethnographic, linguistic, and anthropometric evidence that the Guaymi show a mixture of sub-Andean and Mexican influences. The Spanish Conquest brought about a decline of Guaymí culture (and commerce) and necessitated retreat to a jungle habitat.

1156. Logan, Michael H. Digestive disorders and plant medicinals in highland Guatemala (AI/A, 68:3/4, 1973, p. 537-547, bibl.)

Describes use of herbal medicines by Ladino peasants in various communities in the highlands of Guatemala. Of 122 medicinal species collected, 34 percent are used in treatments of digestive-intestinal disorders. This high percentage reflects actual medical problems in Guatemala—dysentery, diarrhea, and intestinal parasites are the major causes of death in Guatemala.

1157. _____. Humoral medicine in Guatemala and peasant acceptance of modern medicine (SAA/HO, 32:4, Winter 1973, p. 385-395, bibl., tables)

A review of Hippocratic medicine is followed by an excellent delineation of principles of hot/cold classification in highland Guatemala. The data were gathered from a large number of informants using such eliciting techniques as term-frame construction, named information-slips, and triads test. Classification of modern drugs according to the hot/cold framework results in their rejection as suitable remedies for certain illnesses. Comparative Puerto Rican data are described and tabled along with the Guatemalan material.

1158. Lomnitz, Larissa. The social and economic organization of a Mexican shantytown (*in* Cornelius, Wayne A. and Felicity M. Trueblood *eds.* Latin American urban research [see item 9625] v. 4, 135-155, bibl., tables)

The biographies of residents of a Mexico City shantytown reveal that city and intracity migration are generally kin-mediated. Shantytown residents in fact depend on networks of *confianza* and reciprocity among kin and neighbors for security. When urbanization and modernization are regarded dialectically, it is apparent that the creation of a skilled proletariat is accompanied by the formation of surplus labor and marginal groups. Such people, as exemplified by these shantytown dwellers, manage to survive by means of mutual assistance; they exchange information, job assistance, loans, and moral and emotional support.

López Austin, Alfredo. Ideas etiológicas en la medicina náhuatl. See *HLAS 36:986.*

1159. López de Piza, Eugenia. Xirinachs de Zent: una comunidad cabécar de Costa Rica (III/AI, 34:2, abril/junio 1974, p. 440-453, illus., plates, tables)

Concise ethnographic survey, with information on demography, material culture, economy, social organization, health, and acculturation. The subsistence economy is based on swidden agriculture, fishing, and hunting; matrilateral cross-cousin marriage is preferred. Isolated from urban influence, the Cabécar are not peasants; but new roads and the lumber industry have exacerbated their economic exploitation by non-Indians.

Lowell, Edith S. A comparison of Mexican and Seri Indian versions of the

Legend of Lola Casanova. See *HLAS 36:988*.

1160. McCosker, Sandra Smith. The lullabies of the San Blas Cuna Indians of Panama. Göteborg, Sweden, Göteborgs Etnografiska Museum, 1974. 190 p., bibl., maps, music, tables (Ethnologiska studier, 33)

A general description of music in Cuna culture is followed by a detailed analysis of the melodic and nonmelodic features of Cuna lullabies.

1161. McCullough, John M. Human ecology, heat adaptation, and belief systems: the hot-cold syndrome of Yucatán (UNM/JAR, 29, 1973, p. 32-36, bibl.)

Suggests that the hot-cold system of food classification among the Maya of Yucatán may be a biocultural adaptation that helps to prevent heatstroke and heat cramps.

1162. McMahon, David F. Antropología de una presa: los mazatecos y el proyecto del Papaloapan. México, Secretaría de Educación Pública, Instituto Nacional Indigenista, 1973. 174 p., bibl., maps, plates, tables (Col. SEP-INI, 19)

Assesses the impact of the Papaloapan Project on the Mazatec area of Ixcatlán; various government-sponsored community development programs are shown to have had salutary effects.

Manrique Castañeda, Leonardo. El sistema de salud en el agua puerca, San Luis Potosí. See *HLAS 36:991*.

1163. Margain, Carlos R. Los lacandones de Bonampak. 2. ed. México, Secretaría de Educación Pública, 1972. 132 p., map, plates (SepSetentas, 34)

A personal account of the Lacandon of Bonampak. First published in 1951.

1164. Mayers, Marvin K. and **Miriam McNeilly.** Pocomchi corn origin tales (LING, 104, 15 May 1973, p. 74-94, map, table)

Versions of corn origin tales told by three dialect groups of Pocomchi (Guat.) are compared. A student's independent analysis of the tales conforms with the anthropologist's description of their respective communities. That is, the presence, absence, and content of elements, which are segregated by narrative junctures, are shown to reflect such general features of community life as economic prosperity, social cohesion, and Latin influence.

1165. Mejía Fernández, Miguel. La tenencia de la tierra entre los grupos indígenas de México (III/AI, 33:4, oct./dic. 1973, p. 1071-1094, tables)

A variety of population and agricultural census data are used to delineate the size of the Indian population in Mexico and its pattern of landholding. Data indicate that in 1960 50 percent of Indian land was communal land, 28.8 percent was private land, and 21.2 percent was ejido land. Indians comprised 16 percent of the agricultural sector, but they possessed only 8.2 percent of the nation's ejido land. Recent land reform policies may be improving the Indian situation.

1166. Modiano, Nancy. Indian education in the Chiapas Highlands. Foreword by George and Louise Spindler. N.Y., Holt, Rinehart and Winston, 1973. 150 p., bibl., illus., maps, plates, tables (Case studies in education and culture)

Overview of history and culture in highland Chiapas introduces a study of child rearing and formal education in Tzotzil and Tzeltal communities. Informal education stresses economic skills and a strong work ethic; bilingual INI-sponsored schools have had more success than all-Spanish (state and federal) schools in such areas as reading in Spanish, adult education, female enrollment, and community improvement.

Montoya, B., José de Jesús and **Gabriel Moedano N.** Esbozo analítico de la estructura socioeconómica y el folklore de Xochitlán, Sierra Norte de Puebla. See *HLAS 36:994*.

1167. Moone, Janet Ruth. Desarrollo tarasco: integración nacional en el occidente de México. México, Instituto Indigenista Interamericano, Sección de Investigaciones Antropológicas, 1973. 211 p., bibl., maps, tables (Ediciones especiales, 67)

Examines the development and national integration of 22 communities in the region of Lake Pátzcuaro, Michoacán. Economic systems, community organization, regional integration, and patterns of response to development programs are described in detail. The Guttman scalogram technique is used to rank the 22 communities on four dimensions of development and national integration: 1) infrastructure, 2) social structure, 3) economy, and 4) values. A combined index of integration based on the first three indices shows that when community size and resources are controlled, the traditional Tarascan communities manifest the same, or nearly the same, degree of national integration as those communities that have nationalized sociocultural institutions and values. That is to say, the persistence of local culture (e.g. Tarascan language, the system of civil-religious offices, etc.) is compatible with socioeconomic integration into the national society.

1168. Moore, Alexander. Life cycles in Atchalán: the diverse careers of certain Guatemalans. Forword by Solon Kimball. N.Y., Teachers College Press, 1973. 220 p., bibl., illus., maps, plates, tables (Anthropology & education series)

With a fine sense for the imprint of Hispanic tradition on home, street, and plaza, the community is depicted as a theater in which Indian and Ladino men and women play their contrasting parts. The careers of Indian and Ladino men are especially different: an Indian man, in concert with others, passes through a series of offices which enhance his prestige and validate community values; the careers of Ladinos center on individual wealth, power, patronage, monumental tombs, and distinguished bloodlines. Traditional schooling, an accessory to clientage and patronage, has had more relevance for Ladinos than Indians. Modernization, however, is creating new educational needs for both Indians and Ladinos. Alternate educational schemes—a government literacy program, chantry catechism classes, and an Indian literacy movement—are critically evaluated.

1169. Myerhoff, Barbara G. Peyote hunt: the sacred journey of the Huichol Indians. Foreword by Victor Turner. Ithaca, N.Y., Cornell Univ. Press, 1974. 285 p., bibl., plates (Series in symbol, myth, and ritual)

This extraordinary and exemplary study is a major contribution to Middle American scholarship. The Huichol pantheon, the symbolism of the Deer-Maize-Peyote complex, and the peyote hunt itself are empathetically described. Concludes that the pilgrims, who return to Wirikuta as the Ancient Ones, do everything backward, thereby enacting their original sacred condition. While interpreting facets of the pilgrimage with the ideas of Freud, Jung, Geertz, Turner, and Lévi-Strauss, the author insists—with grace and ease—on the peyote hunt's element of irreducible mystery and subjectivity.

1170. Nolan, Mary Lee. The reality of differences between small communities in Michoacán, México (AAA/AA, 76:1, March 1974, p. 47-49, bibl.)

Comparison of seven Tarascan towns reveals the existence of inter-town variation within a single ethnographic region. The variety of responses to economic opportunities shown by these towns can be attributed to sociocultural factors and to economic constraints.

1171. Noval, Joaquín. Resumen etnográfico de Guatemala. 2. ed. Guatemala, Univ. de San Carlos de Guatemala, 1972. 180 p., bibl. (Estudios universitarios, 8)

This readable ethnographic overview of the various Indian and Ladino groups in Guatemala critically examines Ladino economic and political domination. A thorough discussion of issues attendant to acculturation and national integration points to the need for land reform, income distribution, social welfare measures, and greater intercultural understanding.

1172. Paulat Legorreta, Jorge. Una crónica de la condición humana: la historia de la discriminación del indio. México, Academia Nacional de Ciencias, 1972. 266 p., bibl.

A history of political and social discrimination against the Mexican Indian, from the early colonial period to the present.

Pennington, Campbell W. Plantas medicinales utilizadas por el pima montañés de Chihuahua. See item. 2248.

1173. Quigley, Carroll. Mexican national character and circum-Mediterranean personality structure (AAA/AA, 75:1, Feb. 1973, p. 319-322, bibl.)

Quigley argues that Mexican national character is a variant of the widespread Mediterranean personality type, which is characterized by low self-esteem, fatalism, defeatism, distrust, preoccupation with death, machismo, emphasis on honor, low respect for manual labor, etc.

1174. Redfield, Robert. Tepoztlán: a Mexican village. Chicago, Ill., Midway Reprints, 1973. 247 p., bibl., illus., map, plates.

Reprint of the original published by the Univ. of Chicago, 1930.

1175. Reina, Rubén and Norman B. Schwartz. The structural context of religious conversion in Petén, Guatemala: status, community, and multicommunity (American Ethnologist [American Anthropological Assn., Washington] 1:1, Feb. 1974, p. 157-191, bibl., tables, plates)

Comparison of four communities indicates the manifold determinants (e.g., forest/modern world orientations, migration, socioeconomic differentiaiton, and ethnic complexity) of conversion to Protestantism.

1176. Roberts, Bryan R. The interrelationships of city and provinces in Peru and Guatemala (in Cornelius, Wayne A. and Felicity M. Trueblood eds. Latin American urban research [see item 9625]. v. 4, p. 207-235, bibl.)

Compares and contrasts the styles of economic organization and sociality of urban migrants in Peru and Guatemala. The greater organizational capacity of poor people in Peru—as reflected in the perpetuation of rural patterns of fiesta organization contexts—is said to be due to the greater strength of rural-urban relationships in Peru and to Peru's history of rural development.

1177. Rodríguez Rouanet, Francisco. Concepción del mundo sobrenatural y costumbres funerarias entre los indígenas (GIIN/GI, 7:4, oct./dic. 1972, p. 161-186)

Funeral practices and conceptions of soul and afterlife among ancient and contemporary Guatemalan Maya are briefly illustrated with examples from existing literature.

1178. Rollwagen, Jack R. Mediation and

rural-urban migration in Mexico: a proposal and a case study (*in* Cornelius, Wayne A. and Felicity M. Trueblood *eds.* Anthropological perspectives on Latin American urbanization [see item 9625]. v. 4, p. 47-63, bibl.)

Presents a previously unreported type of cultural and economic mediation between city and rural community. Following entry into the local popsicle-ice cream business in 1946, villagers from Mexticacan, Jalisco, eventually captured a sizable segment of the national market, opening *paleterías* (ice cream factories) in various cities. *Paleta* entrepreneurs initially hired fellow villagers from Mexticacan as factory workers, but later they abandoned the role of mediator on finding the single-stranded relationships with unknown employees more convenient and profitable than multi-stranded ones with fellow villagers. The entrepreneurs were transformed into national-level businessmen and were assimilated into urban life; as the patron-client, mediator-mediated relationships disappeared, many workers returned from the cities to Mexticacan. These findings show the salience of historical perspective in any assessment of the effects of business enterprise and economic mobility on traditional patterns of social relations.

1179. Saquic Calel, Rosalío. La mujer indígena guatemalteca (GINN/GI, 8:1, enero/marzo 1973, p. 81-110)

Examines cultural aspects of the life cycle of women in Santa Lucía Utatlán, Sololá.

1180. Schulz Friedemann, Ramón P.C. The Nine Lords of the Night: survival of ancient beliefs among the Zapotecs of Loxicha, Oaxaca, Mexico (MVW, AV, 26, 1972, p. 197-203, bibl.)

Remnants of a system of Nine Lords are juxtaposed with corresponding Aztec and Maya beliefs in order to clarify the general features of the series. In addition to the Loxicha material, a prognostic cycle of nine days found in Coatlan is described.

1181. Schwartz, Norman B. Dreaming and managing the future: notes on a Guatemalan Ladino (non-Indian) theorie [sic] of dreams (SOCIOL, 24:1, 1974, p. 16-36, bibl.)

In the dream theory of San Martineros, the "soul" (*anima* or *alma*) does the dreaming. Dreams are used to predict good and bad fortune, although bad dreams may be prevented or mitigated. Confronted with an uncertain world and an atomistic society, San Martineros trust themselves and consult their dreams.

1182. Selby, Henry A. Zapotec deviance: the convergence of folk and modern sociology. Foreword by Howard S. Becker. Austin, Univ. of Texas Press, 1974. 166 p., bibl., illus., maps, tables.

In this application of the so-called labelling or interactionist theory of deviance to a Zapotec Indian community, the author shows that social position structures labelling more than the personal traits of putative deviants. Moreover, the villagers themselves view deviance in terms more sociological than psychological. An illuminating discussion of the native meanings of "respect," "trust," "humility," and "envy" relates the attribution and display of these attitudes to social/kinship distance (e.g., the recognition and handling of homicide, extramarital relations, and witchcraft are a function of social distance). The value system implied by these terms is said to reinforce symbolic exchange, the essence of communal relations. These interpretations are supported with interview data, case studies, and an earthy, perceptive portrayal of everyday life.

1183. Sitton, Salomón Nahmad. Resumen de la política y la acción del Instituto Nacional Indigenista de México (III/A, 32, dic. 1972, p. 99-132, tables)

Reviews the efforts of INI's Centros Coordinadores in the areas of education, health, agriculture, forestry, and the creation of Conasupo-INI stores in Mexico's "refuge regions." The article concludes with a series of suggestions for improving INI's programs. These suggestions reaffirm the importance of developing extension programs in accordance with the findings of continuing anthropological research.

1184. Stern, Lilo. Inter-household movement in a ladino village of southern Mexico (RAI/M, 8:3, Sept. 1973, p. 393-415, bibl., tables)

Beginning with a delightful and lucid exposition of the case of Lidia—an unmarried widow who runs off with Pedro for the third time—Stern shows that household membership is highly unstable. Inter-household movements are multidimensional and reversible, and in many instances they are not attributable to the developmental cycle of domestic groups. Rather, household dissociations result from disputes over inheritance, contradictory implications in the double standard for sexual behavior, and from tensions between independence and conformity. Recombinations of household membership nonetheless follow definite rules of recruitment.

1185. Stoll, Otto. La posición étnica del indio tz'utujil de Guatemala (USCG/ES, 3, 1969, p. 59-90, tables)

Historical and linguistic data clarify the ethnic position of the Tz'utujil: at the time of the Spanish Conquest the Tz'utujil formed an independent state; and yet linguistically, they are very similar to their neighbors, the Northern Cakchiquel.

1186. Stross, Brian. Social structure and role allocation in Tzeltal oral literature (AFS/JAF, 86:340, April/June 1973, p. 95-113, plates)

Oral tradition of the Tenejapa Tzeltal reflects aspects of social structure (e.g., the civil-religious hierarchy, the system of patron saints, and the relations between Ladino and Indian, male and female, and older brother and younger brother). Various and sundry Ladino-like demons—Black Demon, Backwards Foot, Tree Moss, Janus Face, *et al*—mete out punishments on behalf of the ancestor gods for infractions of the social code.

Tzeltal tales, by associating improper conduct with monsters and danger, thus facilitate the socialization of children. For folklorist comment, see *HLAS 36:1006*.

1187. Thomas, Norman D. Un estudio comparativo de la estructura de las asociaciones ermita de los indios zoques en dos comunidades (ICACH, 7/8:25/26 [2. época] enero/dic. 1973, p. 19-27, bibl.)

Postulates a model of structured conflict for the Zoque neighborhood chapel system. The many neighborhood chapels are each supported by a group of some six families, which are usually partilineally extended and agnatically related. Brothers, however, are prone to quarrel over land, whereas envy is common among neighbors. Dialectical tension between association and conflict is reflected in the fact that each family maintains its own religious image within the chapel. This system may be an unsuitable mechanism for structuring conflict in urban contexts; the chapel complex in Tuxtla, a one-time Zoque community, has greatly deteriorated.

1188. Thompson, Richard A. A theory of instrumental social networks (UNM/JAR, 29:4, Winter 1973, p. 244-265, bibl., table)

Study explores in a highly theoretical fashion the implications of network theory for a special theory about the instrumental uses of asymmetric alliances in contexts of social change. In a modernizing Yucatec town, agriculturalists are somewhat more likely than non-agriculturalists to form asymmetric co-parent relationships. However, those non-agriculturalists and economically mobile persons who have *compadres* of high status are significantly more likely than agriculturalists and non-mobile persons to have multiplied their asymmetric *compadrazgo* ties. Although these findings are admittedly inconclusive, they imply that the structure and function of asymmetric alliances undergo modification with modernization.

1189. _____. The winds of tomorrow: social change in a Maya town. Chicago, Ill., The Univ. of Chicago Press, 1974. 182 p., bibl., tables.

This well-constructed study analyzes social change in a Yucatec town which is becoming increasingly industrial and middle class. Ethnographic chapters consider kinship, residence, ritual kinship, gremio participation, occupational activities, ethnicity, and social hierarchy. Biographical portrayals of mobility are combined with a statistical analysis of mobility patterns. Social mobility is found to have been more frequent at the lower levels of the social hierarchy. Finally, a stochastic model purports to predict future changes in the status structure.

1191. Torres de Araúz, Reina. La leyenda de los indios blancos del Darién y su influencia en la etnografía istemeña y en la historia política nacional (UNCIA/HC, 2:4, sept. 1973, p. 5-68, bibl., plates)

Recounts the scholarly and political ramifications of Richard O. Marsh's investigations among the Cuna.

1192. _____. Tendencias de la antropología aplicada en Panamá: un ejemplo concreto (UNCIA/HC, 2:3, dic. 1972, p. 77-91, bibl., map, plates)

A review of the current status of ethnic groups in Panama illustrates the need for an applied anthropology.

1193. Torres Trueba, Henry. Nahuat factionalism (UP/E, 12:4, Oct. 1973, p. 463-474, bibl.)

Analyzes conflict between monolingual and bilingual factions in Xalacapan, Puebla. The bilingual faction is motivated by economic and political gain; the monolingual faction concentrates on control of public and private religious ceremonies, which monolinguals perceive as sources of supernatural power. In Xalacapan, then, factionalism represents different responses to acculturation, and in some respects the presence of factions in turn promotes political innovation and economic entrepreneurship.

1194. Turner, Paul R. The Highland Chontal. Foreword by George and Louise Spindler. N.Y., Holt, Rinehart and Winston, 1972. 96 p., illus., maps, plates (Case studies in cultural anthropology)

Descriptive treatment of the social, cultural, and personality systems of the Highland Chontal. Noteworthy are a componential analysis of kinship terminology, a discussion of socialization, and unusual private rituals involving cut sticks and eggs. Chontal personality patterns are portrayed by means of life histories and thematic analyses of folktales.

1195. Turner, Victor. Dramas, fields, and metaphors: symbolic action in human society. Ithaca, N.Y., Cornell Univ. Press, 1974. 309 p., bibl., maps, tables (Series in symbol, myth and ritual)

Professor Turner employs to analytical advantage the concepts of social drama, political field, and metaphor in these wide-ranging studies of communitas and liminality. Two essays are of particular interest to students of Middle America. In a remarkable piece, Hidalgo is seen as a symbol of communitas, while the Hidalgo Insurrection is viewed as an initiatory process that repeated deep-rooted mythic patterns. In another essay, Mexican pilgrimages are also interpreted as initiatory processes, that is, as expressions of normative communitas.

1196. Uzzell, Douglas. *Susto* revisited: illness as strategic role (American Ethnologist [American Anthropological Assn. Washington] 1:2, May 1974, p. 369-378, bibl.)

Proposes that *susto* is not necessarily indicative of stress or mental disorder. Ambiguous diagnostic criteria permit the condition to function as a role, as a means of manipulating interpersonal relations. This theoretical construction is rather weakly supported with material gathered in a village in Oaxaca.

1197. Vandervelde, Marjorie. Moonchildren of San Blas Islands (UMUP/E, 15:4, Summer 1973, p. 15-24, plates)

There is a high rate of albinism among San Blas Cuna. Known as Moon-children, albinos are thought to sin less and to have special relations with the spirit world. Charcoal is taken internally by pregnant women as a preventative measure, and some albino infants are eliminated by means of infanticide.

Vela, David. Danzas y primeras manifestaciones dramáticas del indígena mayaquiché. See *HLAS 36:1009*.

1198. Villa Rojas, Alfonso. Notas sobre los zoques de Chiapas (III/AI, 33:4, oct./dic. 1973, p. 1031-1070, bibl., plates, tables)

Reviews and assesses present knowledge of the Zoque. Various scholarly publications have considered Zoque prehistory, folklore, and textiles, but only one anthropologist (Norman D. Thomas) has undertaken a modern community study. The article briefly discusses prehistory, the colonial period, the current size and distribution of the Zoque population, Zoque linguistic affiliations, economic conditions, and social and cultural patterns in contemporary Zoque communities. Barrio organizations seem to be deteriorating, although beliefs in *naguales* and the deities of the four directions still survive. Thus opportunities for research on traditional religious beliefs may still exist in the more conservative communities.

1199. Vírvez, Donató and others. Santa Eulalia: tierra de nuestros antepasados y esperanza para nuestros hijos. Prólogo por Epáminondas Quintana. Guatemala, Instituto Indigenista Nacional, 1968? 86 p., maps, plates.

In this unusual and informative book the people of Santa Eulalia (i.e., a committee of leaders), assisted by a North American anthropologist, give a comprehensive account of their own community. Topics covered range from traditional beliefs and customs to the contemporary economic situation.

1200. Vogt, Evon Z. Gods and politics in Zinacantan and Chamula (UP/E, 12:2, April 1973, p. 99-113, bibl., table)

Zinacantan has a differentiated system of sacred places and ancestral deities, whereas Chamula religion focuses on the sun god and the Church of San Juan in Chamula Center. Just as the Zinacanteco religious system is decentralized, political power in Zinacantan is distributed among civil and religious office-holders in the Zinacantan Center, the shamans, and the lineage heads in the hamlets. Similarly, a parallelism between the organization of gods and politics occurs in Chamula—political power is concentrated in the hands of an oligarchy of caciques in Chamula Center. The greater impact of roads and highways on Zinacantan and problems of social integration posed by Chamula's barrio system and large population may have entered into the formation of the differences between the two communities.

1201. Westphalen, Wilfried. Lacandonia: ein Volk stirbt im Dschungel. Zürich, Switzerland, Flamberg Verlag, 1972. 175 p., bibl., map, plates.

Fascinating account of an expedition to the land of the Lacandones, descendants of the Mayas in southern Mexico. Includes beautiful photographs. [H.J. Hoyer]

1202. Williams García, Roberto. Mitos tepehuas. México, Secretaría de Educación Pública, 1972. 156 p., bibl., illus. (SepSententas, 27)

The author describes Tepehua socioeconomic organization, political institutions, ceremonial cycle, and beliefs; he then presents various Tepehua myths in order to evoke the emotive color and syncretic integrity of Tepehua world view. The work concludes with reflections on hermeneutics: above all, myth is language, the sacred, transcendental word—the native's comprehension of the world.

1202a. Wilson, Carter. Crazy February: death and life in the Mayan highlands of Mexico. Berkeley, Univ. of California Press, 1974. 253 p.

This novel conveys ethnographic information through the telling of a story, somewhat in the manner of Oscar Lewis. It involves the reader in the dynamics of life of the Maya of Chamula in the mountains of southeastern Mexico. Good case history of cultural change in the mid-20th century. [G.M. Dorn]

1203. Wilson, Jack L. El verdadero origen de la tierra y el mar, relatado por los bribris (III/AI, 34:2, abril/junio 1974, p. 419-421)

Presentation—without commentary or analysis—of a myth about the origins of Earth and Sea.

ETHNOLOGY: WEST INDIES

LAMBROS COMITAS
*Professor of Anthropology and Education
Teachers College, Columbia University*

IN MY INTRODUCTION TO THIS SECTION in *HLAS 35*, I argued that Caribbean anthropology appeared to have become more eclectic, to be very much in a state of transition and, given the volatile nature of determining factors external to the discipline, it was likely to remain in flux and uncertainty for some time to come. Two years later, I find no reason to change this assessment in any substantial fashion. The cursory review which follows is essentially in support of this position.

Utilizing the scheme developed in my last introduction, anthropological scholarship on the West Indies can be conveniently divided into three gross categories: *Continuities*, that is, research and publications dealing with theoretical, methodological, and problem themes, or population segments, which have received considerable attention or development in the past and which have persisted to the present; *Newer Thrusts*, or research which, in terms of problem or subject matter, departs from past experience; and *Consolidations*, or bibliographic work, collections of essays by single authors, and readers.

During the current review period, two more or less traditional themes continue to be of interest to Caribbeanists: East Indian studies (see items 1211, 1228-1129, 1248 and 1253-1254) and Amerindian-Bush Negro studies (see items 1217, 1230, 1237, 1246, 1249, 1282-1283 and 1290). It is of more than passing moment to note that East Indian studies, with only few exceptions, appear to be increasingly a specialization of Trinidadian and Guyanese East Indian scholars trained in disciplines other than anthropology. This is in sharp contrast with the period no more than a decade ago when this particular field of inquiry was dominated by North American anthropologists. On the other hand, Amerindian-Bush Negro studies continue to be almost exclusively the province of Dutch, French, British, and occasional American anthropologists. In any case, other traditional areas of research in the West Indies, such as family organization, religious behavior and micro-economics of black, lower-class Antilleans have not fared well during this period. There also has been little recent, substantive work on the nature of West Indian society, a theme which held great promise for social scientists and which generated considerable scholarly excitement after the ground-breaking work of M.G. Smith, Lloyd Braithwaite, R.A.J. van Lier, R.T. Smith, H. Hoetink, and Leo Despres.

Several new, or not too deeply rooted, research themes appear to be developing. One is centered on social and cultural descriptions and analyses of coastal Creole populations of Surinam and, to a lesser extent, of the Netherlands Antilles by Dutch sociologists and anthropologists (see items 1216, 1251-1252, 1263, 1269, 1278, 1286, 1298-1300, 1303-1304 and 1306-1307). Much of this research has been stimulated by the social science faculties of the Universities of Leiden and Amsterdam. Another trend, perhaps only an artifact of publishing vagaries, is the dispersal of North American anthropologists to the smaller and lesser known islands of the Caribbean archipelago and away from territories long studied and politically more sensitive (see items 1233, 1242, 1256-1259, 1277, 1297 and 1305). A third and perhaps more important new focus is on the systematic study of West Indian migrants abroad (see items 1205, 1212-1214, 1223 and 1243). Held in Amsterdam, a recent two-day symposium on the adaptation of migrants from the Caribbean in the European and American metropolis confirmed that considerable research was underway on West Indians in the United Kingdom, in France, and in the Netherlands and that there was growing interest in the US. We might expect a dramatic increase in publications on this complex topic in the near future.

Bibliographies, readers and collections of essays by single authors consolidate the scholarship on a region and help to focus pertinent theoretical and methodological issues. An unusually large number of such works has appeared during this review period. Bastide, for example, edited a volume on women of color in Latin America; Price has brought together a unique collection of essays on Maroon societies; and Mintz has organized his principal articles on slavery, plantation systems, peasantries and Caribbean nationhood into one volume. In addition, a comprehensive bibliography on

Surinam (see item 1209) has been produced by the Netherlands Foundation for Cultural Cooperation with Surinam and the Netherlands Antilles; Mevis has compiled an overview of social research on the Caribbean by Antillean, Dutch and Surinamese scholars during the period 1945-73; Nagelkerke has compiled three bibliographies, one on the Netherlands Antilles from the 17th century to 1970, another on Surinam from its colonization to 1940 and the last on Surinam from 1940 to 1970; and finally, Evelyn has compiled a useful social science index for the radical Commonwealth Caribbean publications *Moko, New World Quarterly, Savacou* and *Tapia.*

1204. Abrahams, Roger D. Deep the water, shallow the shore: three essays on shantying in the West Indies. Austin, Univ. of Texas Press, 1974. 125 p., bibl. (American Folklore Society memoir series, 60)

Sea shanties, their sociocultural context and music, in three British West Indian communities: Newcastle, Nevis; Plymouth, Tobago; and Barouallie, St. Vincent. Of particular interest is the chapter on Barouallie where whaling is still a significant occupation and where the tradition of sea shanties appears to be flourishing.

1205. Alers, M. H. Taalproblemen van Surinaamse kinderen in Nederland. Amsterdam, Univ. van Amsterdam, Antropologisch-Sociologisch Centrum, Afdeling Culturele Antropologie, 1974. 51 p., bibl., tables (Uitgave, 4)

Survey of language problems of Surinamese children (third grade or higher) in Dutch schools (two elementary, schools in Amsterdam) based on written language use in essays and a language test. Dutch children are used as controls. Language use of Surinamese is different from Dutch because of bilingual background. Surinamese utilize a different form of ABN (General Civilized Dutch) which might be called Surinamese Dutch as well as Sranan Tongo. In school, the Surinamese are obliged to use ABN and not Surinamese Dutch. The differences between the latter and ABN are especially difficult for the lower-class Surinamese to grasp and partially as a result of this they have less of a chance at higher education. The author urges additional help in education for the Surinamese child in the Netherlands.

1206. Ashcraft, Norman. The early British settlement in the Bay of Honduras (Journal of Belizean Affairs [Belize City] 2, Dec. 1973, p. 51-65, bibl.)

The economic characteristics of Belize began early in the country's history and were well established by the end of the 19th century. Land, labor, and all significant economic activity were in the control of a small number of merchant houses. The total control of the legislature by the forestry merchant group effectively prevented changes in the mono-economy.

1207. ———. The internal marketing system of Belize (Journal of Belizean Affairs [Belize City] 3, June 1974, p. 30-37, bibl.)

The economy of Belize continues to be dominated by external trade, and production for domestic consumption is negligible. "There has been no 'dual economy' in Belize. In contrast, the traditional 'peasant' sector has been intimately involved in or at least influenced by the capitalistic sector."

1208. Bastide, Roger ed. La femme de couleur en Amérique Latine. Paris, Editions Anthropos, 1974. 265 p., bibl., tables.

Popular literature exalted black male virility and depicted black women as objects of pleasure, submissive and readily available. Intermixture in multiracial societies also functioned as a form of systematic color genocide and the desire to "lighten the race" was internalized into the value system of black women, subordinated by sex and class as well as by race. The articles in this volume provide historical, demographic, economic, social, cultural and psychological analyses of the position of black women in Latin America and raises questions for research. Practically all deal directly or indirectly with the circum-Caribbean region:
Roger Bastide "Introduction" p. 9-48
Roger Bastide "Les Données Statistiques: Brésil" p. 49-74
Gisèle Cossard-Binon "Le Role de la Femme de Couleur dans les Religions Afro-Brésiliennes" p. 75-96
Michel Simon "La Femme de Couleur dans la Chanson Brésilienne" p. 97-114
Sidney Mintz "Les Roles Economiques et la Tradition Culturelle" p. 115-148
Suzanne-Sylvain Comhaire "La Paysanne de la Région de Kenscoff (Haïti)" p. 149-170
Luciano Castillo; Ruben Silie; and Porfirio Hernández "Réflexions sur la Femme Noire en République Dominicaine" p. 171-192
Yolène de Vassoigne "La Femme Noire dans la Société Antillaise Française" p. 193-210
Françoise Morin "La Femme Haïtienne en Diaspora" p. 211-220
Angelina Pollak-Eltz "La Femme de Couleur au Vénézuéla" p. 221-246
Inès Reichel-Dolmatoff "Aspects de la Vie de la Femme Noire dans le Passé et de nos Jours en Colombie (Côte atlantique)" p. 247-265.

1209. Bibliografie van Suriname. Amsterdam, Nederlandse Stichting voor Culturele Samenwerking met Suriname en de Nederlandse Antillen, 1972. 255 p.

Comprehensive bibilography on Surinam produced by

the Netherlands Foundations for Cultural Cooperation with Surinam and the Netherlands Antilles. Coverage is through 1972 and includes sections on religion, social science, legal science, economy, natural science, applied sciences (medicine, mining, agriculture, plants, etc.), art, language and linguistics, geography, and history.

Boletín del Museo del Hombre Dominicano. See item 829b.

1210. Bolland, O. Nigel. Maya settlements in the upper Belize River valley and Yalbac Hills: an ethnohistorical view (Journal of Belizean Affairs [Belize City] 3, June 1974, p. 3-23, bibl.)

Aspects of 18th- and 19th-century Mayan ethnohistory of the upper Belize River valley and Yalbac Hills presented in order to establish a framework for the analysis of Maya-British relations in Belize in the 19th century. Sections on ancient Maya settlements, the approach of Europeans and Spaniards at Tipu, the arrival of British woodcutters, the anti-colonial activity of the Chichenha Maya, and Maya settlements and the colonization of Belize.

1211. Boodhoo, Ken I. The case of the missing majority (Caribbean Review [Hato Rey, P.R.] 6:2, April/May/June 1974, p. 3-7, plates)

General discussion on the nature of Caribbean society with particular reference to the Black Power Movement and the position of East Indians in Trinidad and Guyana. Stressing the need for the introduction of additional conceptual tools to facilitate analysis and "useful" concepts such as power, authority and minority status, the author concludes that "Caribbean societies, particularly Trinidad and Guyana, are composed of minorities without majorities."

1212. Bovenkerk, Frank. Emigratie uit Suriname. Amsterdam, Univ. van Amsterdam, Antropologisch-Sociologisch Centrum, Afdeling Culturele Antropologie, 1975. 88 p., bibl., tables (Uitgave, 6)

Review and analysis of publications on emigration from Surinam including descriptive data (migration histories) collected by the author on 115 Surinamese emigrants. Focuses on emigration motives of individual migrants. In general, it would appear that the differences between the Netherlands and Surinam in standard of living or level of development is the primary factor of migration (push-pull effect). Specific reasons for migration (e.g., education) appear to be less important now and migration to the Netherlands appears to be affecting all segments of Surinamese society.

1213. _____. Terug naar Suriname? Over de opnamecapaciteit van de Surinaamse arbeidsmarkt voor Surinaamse retourmigratie uit Nederland. Amsterdam, Univ. van Amsterdam, Antropologisch-Sociologisch Centrum, Afdeling Culturele Antropologie, 1973. 53 p., bibl., tables (Uitgave, 2)

Survey of Surinamese ministerial officials and executives in private enterprise on the capacity of the Surinamese labor market to absorb migrants who wish to return from the Netherlands. Concludes that large numbers of returning migrants will not find employment. Labor market lacks specialists and is overloaded with unskilled labor. Information flow concerning job openings in Surinam as well as in the Netherlands is clearly insufficient. There is a larger proportion of employers against employing returning Surinamese than those who take a positive or even neutral position on the question. In any case, although many Surinamese in the Netherlands wish to return only a few actually do. Return seems part of migrant ideology exacerbated by the worsening of their position in Dutch society.

1214. _____ and L. M. Bovenkerk-Teerink. Surinamers en Antillianen in de Nederlandse pers. Amsterdam, Univ. van Amsterdam, Antropologisch-Sociologisch Centrum, Afdeling Culturele Antropologie, 1972. 79 p., bibl., tables (Uitgave, 1)

Antilleans and Surinamese in the Netherlands often complain that the Dutch press is discriminatory, particularly with regard to alleged or real criminal activity. Purpose of the study (random selection of articles on crime in the Netherlands printed in five Dutch newspapers dealing with Antilleans and Surinamese, Dutch, Turks, and Moroccans) was to test this allegation. Results indicate that crime connected with Antilleans and Surinamese is reported twice more often than crime connected with Dutchmen. Articles about the criminal activities of Turks and Moroccans are published on the front page more often than articles about Dutchmen and Antilleans and Surinamese. On this point, there appears to be no discrimination against the latter groups. The fact of Turkish or Moroccan nationality is mentioned more often in the headlines than Dutch, Surinamese or Antillean origins.

1215. Brathwaite, Edward Kamau. The African presence in Caribbean literature (AAAS/D, 103:2, Spring 1974, p. 73-109, bibl.)

Author deals with what he considers the four kinds of written African literature in the Caribbean: rhetorical (when writer uses Africa as mask or signal); the literature of African survival ("inheres most surely and securely in the folk tradition—in folk tale, in folk songs, proverb, ..."); the literature of African expression ("in terms of literary craftmanship, ... a shift from rhetoric to involvement"); and, the literature of reconstruction.

1216. Buschkens, Willem F. L. The family system of the Paramaribo Creoles. The Hague, Martinus Nijhoff, 1974. 324 p., bibl., tables (Verhandelingen van het Koninklijk Instituut voor Taal-, Land- en Volkenkunde, 71)

Based on data derived from observation, interview and

questionnaire methods as well as through archival research, the author describes and analyses family life of lower-class Creoles in Paramaribo both historically and synchronically. Beginning with a discussion of West Indian family systems and a general socio-economic description of Surinam, the study deals with the early period of the settlement of Surinam up to the abolition of the slave trade in 1808; the period from 1808 up to emancipation in 1863; the post-emancipation period; the situation after World War II; the nature of marital unions and household structure; and, the functioning of the family system. It is stressed by the author that the development of the family system was necessary for the group survival of the slaves and their descendants, the lower-class Creoles. "Hence this institutionalization should also be regarded as a process of adaptation, or adjustment to totally new and almost invariably adverse circumstances, as a refined instrument whereby the slave/lower-class Creole was able to go on living, multiplying and perpetuating his particular subculture in the society of Surinam."

1217. Butt Colson, Audrey. Inter-tribal trade in the Guiana highlands (SCNLS/A, 34, 1973, p. 1-70, bibl., map, plates)

A study of the trading links in the 1950s of the Akawaio and Arekuna Indians of the upper Mazaruni basin in Guyana. Deals with the Akawaio view of neighboring tribes; goods traded (blowpipes, cassava graters, pots, gourds, cow horns, shaman equipment, songs, hammocks and dogs); Akawaio exports and ports of trade; and, the nature of traditional inter-tribal trade.

1218. Canet, Carlos. Lucumí: religión de los yorubas en Cuba. Miami, Fla., Talleres Air Publications Center, 1973. 187 p., bibl., illus., plates.

A description of Lucumí, a Yoruba religion in Cuba, by a Cuban practitioner who also visited Nigeria in order to better understand the roots of the religion, to demonstrate the changes that occurred in Cuba, and to correct misconceptions about the religion held by many non-believers. Separate sections devoted to the major gods (Olodumare, Obatalá, Ifá, etc.); spiritual gods and sacred trees; offerings; ceremonies (initiation, birth, marriage, funeral); music, possession, problems of language.

1219. Cohen, David W. and Jack P. Greene eds. Neither slave nor free: the freedmen of African descent in the slave societies of the New World. Baltimore, Md., The Johns Hopkins Univ. Press, 1972. 344 p., tables.

A volume generated by a symposium on "The Role of the Free Black and Free Mulatto in Slave Societies of the New World" at The Johns Hopkins Univ. 1970. A welcome addition to the growing body of literature on slave systems and their constituent elements. Eight of the contributed articles are by historians, one (Surinam and Curaçao—H. Hoetink) by a sociologist and another (Barbados—Handler and Sio) by an anthropologist and sociologist. Includes following articles:
David W. Cohen and Jack P. Greene "Introduction" p. 1-18
Frederick P. Bowser "Colonial Spanish America" p. 19-58
H. Hoetink "Surinam and Curaçao" p. 59-83
A. J. R. Russell-Wood "Colonial Brazil" p. 84-133
Léo Elisabeth "The French Antilles" p. 134-171
Gwendolyn Midlo Hall "Saint Domingue" p. 172-192
Douglas Hall "Jamacia" p. 193-213
Jerome S. Handler and Arnold A. Sio "Barbados" p. 214-257
Eugene D. Genovese "The Slave States of North America" p. 258-277
Franklin W. Knight "Cuba" p. 278-308
Herbert S. Klein "Nineteenth-Century Brazil" p. 309-334.

1220. Collymore, Frank A. Notes for a glossary of words and phrases of Barbadian dialect. Bridgetown, Advocate, 1970. 127 p.

First published in 1955, this fourth ed. includes a small number of additional words and phrases. A useful volume for Barbadian specialists.

1221. Conference on the Family in the Caribbean, II, Aruba, Netherlands Antilles, 1969. The family in the Caribbean: proceedings. Edited by Stanford N. Gerber. Río Piedras, Univ. of Puerto Rico, Institute of Caribbean Studies, 1973. 167 p., bibl., tables.

The two primary objectives of the II Conference on the Family in the Caribbean, held in Aruba, Dec. 1969, were to rethink prevalent concepts and notions concerning Caribbean households, domestic groups and family relationships and to suggest new modes of theoretical analysis for dealing with Caribbean—generated data. Includes the following articles:
Stanford N. Gerber "Introduction" p. 11-16
Vera Green "Methodological Problems Involved in the Study of the Aruban Family" p. 17-30
Sidney M. Greenfield "Dominance, Focality and the Characterization of Domestic Groups: Some Reflections on 'Matrifocality' in the Caribbean" p. 31-50
Anselme Remy "Some Reflections on Caribbean Anthropology with Special Reference to the Family" p. 51-64
Roy Simon Bryce-Laporte "Family, Household and Intergenerational Relations in a 'Jamaican' Village in Limón, Costa Rica" p. 65-94
Helen Icken Safa "Progress and Poverty: A Study of Relocated Shanty Town Families in Puerto Rico" p. 95-106
Annemarie De Waal Malefijt and Marcia Hellerman "Aruban Mating Patterns" p. 107-120
David Stea and James M. Blaut "Some Preliminary Observations on Spatial Learning in Puerto Rican School Children" p. 121-129
Stanford N. Gerber "Introduction" p. 133-136
Stanford N. Gerber and Howard R. Stanton "Ethnic Structure and Social Change in the U.S. Virgin Islands" p. 137-150
Helen Icken Safa "Assimilation vs. Pluralism: Two Models for the Integration of Ethnic Groups in the Americas" p. 151-165.

1222. Conference on the Implications of Independence for Grenada, *St. Augustine, T. and T., 1974.* Independence for Grenada: myth or reality? Proceedings. St. Augustine, T. and T., Univ. of the West Indies, Institute of International Relations, 1974. 159 p., bibl., tables.

Proceedings of a Conference on the Implications of Independence for Grenada sponsored by the Institute of International Relations and the Dept. of Government, Univ. of the West Indies, St. Augustine, Trinidad in January, 1974. The volume is divided into three sections: 1) Grenada, A Social and Political Profile; 2) Independence, Legal and Political Aspects; and 3) Role of Agriculture in the Economic Development of Grenada. And the sections consist of the following articles of interest and value to anthropologists:
Selwyn Ryan "Introduction" p. 1-3
Beverly Steel "Social Stratification in Grenada" p. 7-18
Richard Jacobs "The Movement Towards Grenadian Independence" p. 21-34
Archie Singham "Grenadian Independence in the Context of the New Imperialism" p. 39-42
Basil Ince "The Decolonization of Grenada in the UN" p. 43-52
Nugent Miller "The Scope to Monetary and Financial Independence" p. 57-64
Bernard Coard "The Meaning of Political Independence in the Commonwealth Caribbean" p. 69-76
Chuks Okpaluba "Fundamental Human Rights: The Courts and the Independent West Indian Constitutions" p. 79-90
Theodore Ferguson "The Potential for Increasing Agricultural Production in Grenada" p. 95-98
Curtis McIntosh and T. O. Osuji "Economic Aspects of Food Production in Grenada" p. 99-104
Winston Phillips "Market Prospects for Grenada's Major Export Crops" p. 105-118
George Sammy "Agro-Industries - Prospects for Grenada" p. 119-126.

1223. Corro, Berta Alicia. "Kolonialneger" und antillische "Chombos" in Panama (*in* Gräbener, Jürgen *comp.* Kassengesellschaft und Rassismus [see *HLAS 35:8268*] p. 105-112, bibl., tables)

Composition of the Negro population of Panama. Blacks, who were brought in during the Colonial period, acculturated, mixed with the majority segments of the population, and have been socially mobile. Antillean migrants, called "Chombos", came with the building of the railroad (mid-19th century) and the digging of the Canal. They are a distinct minority with their own culture, exhibit little social mobility, are considered a marginal group by the rest of the society ("illegal intruders") and are discriminated against, remaining an isolated group in Panamanian society.

1224. Crépeau, Pierre. Classifications raciales populaires et métissage: essai d'antropologie cognitive. Montreal, Canada, Univ. of Montreal, Center of Caribbean Research, 1973. 44 p., bibl., tables.

A description and comparison of folk racial classifications from St. Dominique in the 18th century, Grand Cayman, Mexico, and Brazil.

1225. DeCamp, David and Ian F. Hancock *eds.* **Pidgins and creoles: current trends and prospects.** Washington, Georgetown Univ. Press, 1974. 137 p., bibl., tables.

A collection of articles which represent "the summation of ideas exchanged at the pidgin and creole interest group session" at the Georgetown Univ. Round Table on Languages and Linguistics, 1972. Of particular interest to Caribbeanists are the following articles:
Jay Edwards "African Influences on the English of San Andrés Island, Colombia" p. 1-26
Marguerite Saint-Jacques Fauquenoy "Guyanese: A French Creole" p. 27-37
Richard R. Day "Decreolization: Coexistent Systems and the Post-Creole Continuum" p. 38-45
David DeCamp "Neutralizations, Iteratives, and Ideophones: The Locus of Language in Jamaica" p. 46-60
Paul Kay and Gillian Sankoff "A Language-Universals Approach to Pidgins and Creoles" p. 61-72
Gillian Sankoff and Suzanne Laberge "On the Acquisition of Native Speakers by a Language" p. 73-84
Charles-James N. Bailey "Some Suggestions for Greater Consensus in Creole Terminology" p. 88-91
John R. Rickford "The Insights of the Mesolect" p. 92-117
Sister Mary Canice Johnson "Two Morpheme Structure Rules in an English Proto-Creole" p. 118-129
Ian F. Hancock "Shelta: A Problem of Classification" p. 130-137.

1226. The Declaration of Barbados: for the liberation of the Indians (UC/CA, 14:3, June 1973, p. 267-270)

A statement issued by 14 Latin American anthropologists at the Symposium on Inter-Ethnic Conflict in South America which met in Barbados, 25-30 Jan., 1971. This declaration calls for the assumption of "unavoidable responsibilities" for immediate action in order to halt aggressions against aboriginal groups and cultures and for significant contributions to the process of Amerindian liberation. With regard to these objectives, the document delineates the specific responsibilities of the State, of Religious Missions, and of Anthropology.

1227. Desruisseaux, Jacques. La structure foncière de la Martinique. Montreal, Canada, Univ. of Montreal, Center of Caribbean Research, 1975. 49 p., bibl.

A study of land tenure in Martinique. It is argued that ownership of large properties devoted to the production of export crops is concentrated among several powerful families. Within a century after settlement, large sugar plantations became the dominant form of land tenure. Small properties, while never entirely absent, emerged after emancipation as freedman settled on the marginal peripheries of the estate. The history of land tenure has oscillated between two poles depending on the economic cycle. In periods of prosperity there is consolidation of estates and in times of crisis a parcelling of properties. Crises, however, have not changed the basic profile of the agrarian structure. Despite some increase of small properties they remain in marginal areas while the estates retain the best land, the most easily mechanized, with owners who possess the capital and technology for modernizing their economic activities.

1228. Durbin, Mridula Adenwala. Formal changes in Trinidad Hindi as a result of language adaptation (AAA/AA, 75:5, Oct. 1973, p. 1290-1304, bibl., table)

It is argued that changes and directions of change in the structure of Trinidad Hindi are best explained by sociocultural changes over time in the East Indian community of Trinidad. Five aspects of the sociocultural order are stressed: relationship between caste and language in India; the breaking down of caste structure among immigrants to Trinidad; development of a new network of communication; effect of this new network on the emerging code of Trinidadian East Indians; and, change in the functions of IKNDIC LANGUAGE AND ITS EFFECT ON THE EMERGING CODE*

1229. Ehrlich, Allen S. Ecological perception and economic adaptation in Jamaica (SAA/HO, 33:2, Summer 1974, p. 155-161, bibl., map, tables)

Article focuses on the adaptational responses of East Indians in Jamaica to the sugar plantation system as they moved from the status of indentured laborers, to part-time peasantry, and then to rural proletariat. For a lengthy period of time, sugar estate owners and Indian cane workers in western Jamaica perceived an environment composed of two ecological niches: flat dry lands suited for cane production and wet morass lands for rice cultivation. Up to 1959, the Indian laborer could work for the estate for wages and rent land for rice cultivation. When the sugar companies needed the wet lands for expansion of cane fields, East Indians were forced from part-time peasant status to that of full-time rural proletariat with deleterious social and economic effects.

1230. Elst, Dirk H. van der. The Coppename Kwinti: notes of an Afro-American tribe in Surinam (NWIG, 50:1, Jan. 1975, p. 7-17, map)

The first part of an ethnographic report on the Kwinti, smallest and least known of Surinam's Bush Negro tribes. Based on field data collected during a ten-weeks' pilot study in 1973, this section deals primarily with the history and development of the Kwinti. Particular attention is paid to the various Kwinti theories of tribal origins and settlement, to present-day population size, to language and language similarities with Sranan and to the relativity of tribal isolation and obscurity in Surinam.

1230a. Evelyn, Shirley *ed.* and *comp.* West Indian social sciences index: an index to *Moko, New World Quarterly, Savacou, Tapia,* 1963-1972. St. Augustine, T. and T., Univ. of the West Indies, 1974. 117 p. (mimeo)

Original purpose was to generate a record of the contents of a number of "little" newspapers and journals from the Caribbean. Original plan scaled down to two newspapers (*Moko* and *Tapia*) and two journals (*New World Quarterly* and *Savacou*). Author and subject index of all contents of the four publications as well as all their occasional publications.

1231. Foner, Nancy. Party politics in a Jamaican community (UPR/CS, 13:2, July 1973, p. 51-64)

Although modern two-party politics are operant in Jamaica and local party branches exist in rural towns the author's study indicates that the PNP and JLP do not provide rural Jamaicans with opportunities to achieve prestige, power, or any significant economic gain. Local political office leads neither to power nor prestige; political conflict on the village level is minimal; and rewards distributed locally by the parties do not permit occupational mobility. It is suggested that these conditions may well have implications for the future. "For if modern political institutions do not provide the means for rural villagers to express their aspirations or achieve desired goals, does this suggest that when they act politically they will do so outside of the formal political institutions of the society?" For political scientist comment, see item 8260.

1232. Fouchard, Jean. Langue et littérature des aborigènes d'Ayti. Paris, Editions de l'Ecole, 1972. 172 p. (Col. Histoire et littérature)

Utilizing diverse archival and historical sources, author attempts a general review of the problems of illuminating language and oral literature of Haitian aboriginals.

1233. Fraser, Thomas M. *ed.* Windward road: contributions to the anthropology of St. Vincent. Amherst, Univ. ov Massachusetts, Dept. of Anthropology, 1973. 164 p., bibl. (Research reports, 12)

A collection of student papers based on field research in St. Vincent sponsored by the Univ. of Massachusetts field-training course in cultural anthropology during the summer of 1970 and 1971. Includes the following articles:
Robert Ciski "Settlement and Land Use Patterns: Villo Point" p. 7-22
Michael A. Krasnow "Fishing in Calliaqua" p. 23-28
John J. Hourihan "Youth Employment: Stubbs" p. 29-34
Susan D. Marks "Occupational Alternatives: the Hotel Staff" p. 35-42
Deborah Laufer "The Population Problem on St. Vincent" p. 43-57
Carey D. Toran "Education in St. Vincent: Biabou" p. 58-72
Grace E. Morth "Commess: Traditional and Official Forms of Social Control" p. 73-79
Phillip S. Katz "Some Aspects of Gossip: Villo Point" p. 80-89
Susan C. Linsey "The Handicapped Person in Colonarie" p. 90-107
F. David Mulcahy "A Sketch of Vincentian-Portuguese Fold Botany and Medicine" p. 108-122
Paul E. Carlson "Cognition and Social Function in the West Indian Dialect" p. 123-147
Linda S. Stone "East Indian Adaptations on St. Vincent: Richland Park" p. 148-155.

1234. Fraser, Thomas M., Jr. Class and the changing bases of elite support in St. Vincent, West Indies (UP/E, 14:2, April 1975, p. 197-209, bibl., tables)

Analysis of changes taking place in social ranking, mobility and the validation of status with specific reference to elites in St. Vincent. Author distinguishes a traditional elite, a political elite and an emerging intellectual elite.

1235. Gerber, Stanford N. Reflections on the concept of matrifocality (Journal of Belizean Affairs [Belize City] 3, June 1974, p. 24-29)

A brief review of aspects of the literature on the West Indian family. Argument posed is that little evidence exists to support the generalization that the matrifocal family is representative or characteristic in the West Indies and that matrifocality is an "aberrant" structure which does not permit "proper" socialization of the child.

1236. Green, Vera M. Migrants in Aruba: interethnic integration. Assen, The Netherlands, Van Gorcum, 1974. 137 p., bibl., maps.

A study of interethnic integration in Aruba, Netherlands Antilles. After a short discussion of Aruban history, economy, government, religion, and education, the various ethnic groups are described and discussed: Dutch subjects (Antilleans, Surinamers, Netherlanders) and non-Dutch residents (U.S. citizens, French, Colombians, Dominicans, Chinese, Portuguese, Venezuelans, Jews). Types and roles of voluntary associations are delineated, followed by a discussion of the mechanisms of integration: language, marriage and kinship, voluntary associations, occupational specialization, religion, and the industrial complex.

1237. Groot, Silvia W. de. Surinaamse Granmans in Afrika. Utrecht, The Netherlands, Het Spectrum, 1974. 99 p., bibl., tables.

At the initiation of the government of Surinam, the author organized and supervised a trip to West Africa by four Bush Negro paramount chiefs (Djuka, Saramacca, Paramacca, and Matoeari). A description of the journey to and in Africa is given; a history of the West African states; the slave trade; history and culture of the Bush Negroes; reactions of the chiefs after the trip; similarities between the cultures, noted, etc.

1238. Guyana. Ministry of Information and Culture. Amerindian integration: a brief outline of the progress of integration in Guyana. Georgetown, Guyana Lithographic Co., 1970. 63 p., bibl., plates.

Government publication summarizing official policy of integrating the Amerindian population (approximately 32,000) of Guyana into the mainstream of Guyanese life. Short sections on the ways of integration (education, technical training, agriculture, self-help, communications, local government); on the Amerindian Lands Commission established in 1967; and on the Amerindian Conference held in Georgetown in 1969.

1239. Handler, Jerome S. The unappropriated people: freedmen in the slave society of Barbados. Baltimore, Md., The John Hopkins Univ. Press, 1974. 225 p., tables.

A study about the freedmen in Barbados focused on the period from the end of the 18th century to 1834. Based on data generated from manuscript collections and archival repositories in Barbados, London and Edinburgh, the author describes and analyzes questions related to manumission and free status; the politico-judicial system as it related to freedmen; the militia; the economic system and economic rewards; the religious system; the educational system; and, the position of freedmen in the Barbadian social order. The author "shows how the freedmen's struggle for civil rights was a collective effort to maximize their free status and to avoid a position of permanent intermediacy between whites and slaves."

1240. ———— and Lon Shelby eds. A seventeenth century commentary on labor and military problems in Barbados (BMHS/J, 34:3/ March 1973, p. 117-121)

An anonymously written manuscript of 1667 or 1668 titled "Some Observations on the Island Barbadoes." A detailing of labor difficulties and military dangers faced at a particularly critical juncture in the island's existence.

1241. Hanley, Eric R. Rice, politics and development in Guyana (in Oxaal, Ivar; Tony Barnett; and David Booth eds. Beyond the sociology of development: economy and society in Latin America and Africa. London, Routledge & Kegan Paul, 1975, p. 131-153, bibl.)

Description and analysis of the Guyanese rice industry and the applicability of Andre Gunder Frank's model of metropolitan/satellite relationships.

1242. Hannerz, Ulf. Caymanian politics: structure and style in a changing island society. Stockholm, Univ. of Stockholm, Dept. of Social Anthropology, 1974. 198 p., bibl., map (Stockholm studies in social anthropology, 1)

"An anthropologist's attempt to write political history within social history." Based on field research in the Cayman Islands between April and Aug. 1970, the author concentrates on a serious political crisis concerning the legislation of regulations that occured during the period of residence. A welcome publication on the Caymans, which have received only minimal attention, and on the political anthropology of the English-speaking Caribbean, a subject that only now is beginning to receive serious treatment.

1243. Hendricks, Glenn. The Dominican

diaspora: from the Dominican Republic to New York City, villagers in transition. N.Y., Teachers College Press, 1974. 171 p., bibl., illus., map, tables.

A study of the effects of the circulatory migration of Dominicans to and from N.Y. City. Utilizing the conceptual framework of social field and concentrating on the villagers from one Dominican pueblo, the author divides his book into three sections: the first deals with the Dominican national background and includes short statements on economy, demography, history, political process, race, and education, as well as a more detailed overview of the study village and the interaction of the village to N.Y. City; the second is involved with the migration process itself with interesting material on US immigration laws, the process of obtaining a visa, employment prospects, types of visas, and illegal entry and residence; the third sector is devoted to the N.Y. experience, the adaptations in household, marriage, and role patterns, non-kin activities, and the implications of this form of migration for the schools.

1244. Herskovits, Melville J. Life in a Haitian valley. Introduction by Edward Brathwaite. Garden City, N.Y., Doubleday, 1971. 371 p.

A re-issue of Herskovits' classic study of a small, rural Haitian community in the Artibonite valley. In the words of Edward Brathwaite, who eloquently introduces this new edition: "As it is, [Herskovits'] book, pathfinding in 1937, but almost forgotten, for long unavailable, is clearly more than ever relevant now, possessing as it does the intellectual framework, vision, and material information that the reader of today needs and can understand."

1245. Herzog, J.D. Father-absence and boys' school performance in Barbados (SAA/HO, 33:1, Spring 1974, p. 71-83, bibl., tables)

An examination of the relationships between father-absence and school performance in a small fishing and agricultural village on the south coast of Barbados. Results of the study do not support the usual prediction of a negative relationship between a child's performance in school and the absence of his father from home. The data indicate that paternal absence during the first two years of a child's life "seems modestly beneficial" to his late school performance, as does the presence of the father during the third through fifth years of the child's life. Results best explained through interactionist analysis: "In Barbados, it is good for a boy to have his father away during the earliest years of his life, because of what this is likely to mean for his relationship with his mother; it is equally good to have Dad return home after age two or three, because this usually means he has regular employment and will provide a needed input of (perhaps over strict) discipline and economic support."

1246. Hurault, Jean-Marcel. Français et indiens en Guyane: 1604-1972. Paris, Union Générale d'Editions, 1972. 438 p., maps, illus. (Série Inédit, 7)

Comprehensive analysis of ethnohistorical and ecological factors in social organization of coastal and interior Amerindians; impact of French conquest and colonization and the politics of assimilation; "civilizing" efforts of Jesuit missions; slavery; wage-labor; demographic and social effects of culture contact; present condition of coastal and interior Amerindians in French Guyana. Author utilizes historical documents extensively starting with material dating back to the end of the 16th century.

1247. Irving, Brian *ed.* Guyana: a composite monograph. Hato Rey, P.R., Inter American Univ. Press, 1972. 87 p., map, tables.

Results of a 1970 study of Guyana by the Caribbean Institute and Study Center for Latin America of Inter American Univ., P.R. Includes the following articles:
Brian Irving "A Brief History" p. 5-12
Harold A. Lutchman "A Review of Recent Political Developments" p. 13-31
Brian Wearing "Present Political Situation" p. 32-39
Yereth Knowles "Black Power?" p. 40-47
Ved P. Duggal "Economic Development Since Independence" p. 48-61
Della Walker "Problems in Amerindian Acculturation" p. 62-65
Alexander D. Acholonu "Wildlife and Pollution" p. 66-85.

1248. Jha, Jagdish Chandra. Indian heritage in Trinidad, West Indies. St. Augustine, T. and T., Univ. of the West Indies, 1974? 23 p. (mimeo.)

Review of Indian cultural retentions in Trinidad: derivation of migrants; religious backgrounds; festivals; the question of caste, development of surnames; social organization; language; foods; etc. Author concludes that the Indian heritage in Trinidad seems to have been largely retained and, in fact, some aspects of Indian culture which had been lost to westernization or modernization are now being revived. Factors which have contributed to this cultural persistence and renaissance cited.

1249. King, Johannes. Life at Maripaston. [Edited by H.F. de Ziel] The Hague, Martinus Nijhoff, 1973. 142 p. (Verhandelingen van het Koninklijk Instituut voor Taal-, Land- en Volkenkunde, 64)

One of the first original works in Sranan, Creole language of Surinam, written by a Matuari Bush Negro Johannes King (ca. 1830-98). English summary and Sranan text included. King, a Moravian convert and proselytizer of his fellow Bush Negroes, wrote in order to justify for posterity the reasons for his quarrel with his elder brother, the chief. There is no doubt that the claim that this book contributes to Surinamese church history and offers interesting insights into Bush Negro life is correct.

1250. Kramer, Jane. Letter from Guyana (The New Yorker, 16 Sept. 1974, p. 100-128, illus.)

Excellent journalistic account of political process, racial antagonisms, and economic maneuvering in Guyana. Provides interesting introduction for the neophyte in Guyanese or West Indian studies.

1251. Krimpen, A. van. Een onderzoek onder werknemers van een in Suriname gevestigd energiebedrijf, de OGEM. Amsterdam, Univ. van Amsterdam, Sociografisch Instituut FSW, 1974. 117 p., tables (Onderzoekprojekt Sociale Ontwikkelingsstrategie Suriname 1969, 8b)

Based on survey data collected from employees of OGEM, a Surinamese power company, the author attempts to answer the question whether trade unions play a dynamic role in the social and economic development of the country. Sample consists of members of the trendsetting company union which has managed to achieve relatively good labor conditions for its employees. Conclusions concerning the central question are ambiguous.

1252. ———. Verslag van een enquête onder leerlingen van Surinaamse scholen. Amsterdam, Univ. van Amsterdam, Sociografisch Instituut FSW, 1974. 117 p., tables (Onderzoekprojekt Sociale Ontwikkelingsstrategie Suriname 1969, 16)

Survey of Surinamese students at upper levels of elementary school and all grades of secondary school, to assess which students joined what kind of organization; the differences between joiners and non-joiners; and, differences in attitude between joiners and non-joiners. These data are compared descriptively with an earlier survey of 500 household heads.

1253. LaGuerre, John *ed.* Calcutta to Caroni: the East Indians of Trinidad. Port-of-Spain, Longman Caribbean, 1974. 111 p., bibl., tables.

Of considerable interest to anthropologists is this collection of studies by West Indian historians, political scientists and economists on the historical and contemporary experiences of the East Indian community of Trinidad. Includes the following articles:
L. E. S. Braithwaite "Foreword" p. vii-viii
John G. LaGuerre "Preface" p. xi-xiv
J. C. Jha "The Indian Heritage in Trinidad" p. 1-24
Bridget Brereton "The Experience of Indentureship: 1845-1917" p. 25-28
Kelvin Singh "East Indians and the Larger Society" p. 39-68
Winston Dookeran "East Indians and the Economy of Trinidad and Tobago" p. 69-83
Brinsley Samaroo "Politics and Afro-Indian Relations in Trinidad" p. 84-97
John G. LaGuerre "The East Indian Middle Class Today" p. 98-107.

Lamur, H. E. The demographic evolution of Surinam, 1920-1970: a sociodemographic analysis. See item 2047.

1254. Landis, Joseph B. Racial attitudes of Africans and Indians in Guyana (UWI/SES, 22:4, Dec. 1973, p. 426-439, bibl., tables)

A survey of 456 East Indians and 372 Afro-Guyanese on racial attitudes. Results indicate that East Indians tend to have superordinate racial attitudes towards Afro-Guyanese while Afro-Guyanese tend to show defensive attitudes towards East Indians. The East Indian racialism is based on the belief they are thriftier or more ambitious than the Afro-Guyanese and that their racial characteristics are superior. This racialism is restrained "by a norm of nonracialism and by a fairly strong commitment to integration." Afro-Guyanese defensive racialism revolves around stereotypes of Indian thriftiness and ambition, and an awareness of Indian superordinate racialism. Major correlates of Indian superordinate racialism are religion and education while those of African defensive racialism are occupation and area of residence.

1255. León, Argeliers. Presencia del africano en la cultura cubana (UCLV/I, 41, enero/abril 1972, p. 155-169)

Preceded by a short history of African migration into Cuba, the author briefly notes Africanisms in Cuban culture (Santería, musical instruments, songs, dances, etc.).

1256. MacDonald, Judy Smith. In-law terms and affinal relations in a Grenadian fishing community (UPR/CS, 12:4, Jan. 1973, p. 44-75)

Description and analysis of in-law terms and their contexts of utterance. In-law terminology does not distinguish between legal and non-legal mating relationships; they can encompass both stable, long-term residential unions without children and unions of various kinds with children. In addition, in-law terminology may cover past as well as present mating links of the stable or child-producing types.

1257. Manning, Frank E. Black clubs in Bermuda: ethnography of a play world. Ithaca, N. Y., Cornell Univ. Press, 1973. 277 p., bibl., tables, plates.

A study of the meaning and context of play in Bermuda and the first major anthropological research on that island. Stimulated in part by Johan Huizinga's seminal writing on *Homo ludens* and in part by modern symbolic anthropological scholarship, the author describes the black club of Bermuda. The volume opens with a short but useful statement on demography, political organization, and social structure followed by the historical and sociological dimensions of the club world (e.g., club ethos, relationship of club to Christian morality). Bulk of the volume is devoted to three linked concepts: the game ("as it pertains to agonistics"), the show ("as it pertains to entertainment") and the bar ("as it pertains to casual sociability that takes place around club bars."). The relationship between the play of the club world and the "holiday atmosphere" of Bermuda is examined. Concludes with a provocative discussion of the effects of tourism. In Bermuda the play and prosperity made possible by tourism do not function to denigrate the native tradition in favor of foreign substitutes. Nor do they inhibit progressive movements or sustain a racial inferiority complex. On the contrary, club play symbolizes a set of meanings that rejuvenate its indigenous cultural tradition and that promote the process of social change by making it comprehensible and appealing to the people."

1258. _____. Entertainment and black identity in Bermuda (*in* Fitzgerald, Thomas K. *ed.* Social and cultural identity. Athens, The Univ. of Georgia Press, 1974, p. 39-50, bibl.)

Description and analysis of entertainment at black sports and recreational clubs with particular reference to symbolization of racial-cultural identity. Two categories of symbolic expression are identified: Afro-American symbols (soul, black, mod, and Afro) and Afro-Caribbean (creole, carnival, and Gombey). In addition to symbols of identity, symbols of tone are delineated and discussed (i.e., symbols of elegance, sexuality, and exuberance). "These symbols encourage the audience to put aside their particularistic identity as colored Bermudians and to adopt a more universal identification which relates them to other peoples of African ancestry . . ."

1259. _____. Nicknames, and number plates in the British West Indies (AFS/JAF, 87:344, April/June 1974, p. 123-132)

Ethnographic description of nicknames and number plates as alternate forms of nomenclature in Bermuda and Barbados. Within their social structural context, their functions and cultural meaning are considered.

1260. Massajoli, Pierleone. Popoli e civiltá dell'America Centrale: i Caribi neri (IGM/U, 51:5, set./ott. 1971, p. 1121-1162, bibl., maps, plates)

Descriptive review of the anthropology of the Black Caribs of Central America (Belize, Honduras, Guatemala). Short sections on historical movements, physical anthropology, material life, food patterns, housing and construction, clothing and ornaments, navigation and transportation, life cycle, family structure, recreation, dance and music, religion and shamanism, behavior and psychological character, and language.

1261. Memmi, Albert. The impossible life of Frantz Fanon (TMR, 14:1, Winter 1973, p. 9-39)

A very interesting and provocative analysis of the life of Frantz Fanon by a writer trained in philosophy and psychology who like his subject was involved with and in the North African struggle for liberation from French colonialism. The author's thesis is psychological—Fanon's "true problem was neither how to be FKRENCH/ NOR HOW TO BE Algerian, but how to be West Indian. He refused to attempt a solution to this problem, or rather he discussed it once in *Black skins, white masks* and then did not concern himself with it any more." Memmi, from his perspective, traces out Fanon's life in psychological-philosophical terms: first, Fanon refuses his West Indian and black identity for a universalist humanism which was then embodied in France. Failure in this effort and rejection by the French lead him to select another role, that of the Algerian patriot. This leads to another universalism, embodied in Africa. "But this too was not the final stage. When he attacked Europe in *The wretched of the earth*, he did so not merely in the name of Africa, but in the name of 'the sweat and cadavers of Negroes, Arabs, Indians, and Orientals'. Soon thereafter he found himself both attacking Europe and wanting to save it; now he wanted to save all of humanity. It was no longer a matter of Algeria or even of Africa, but of Man and the entire world. To quote again the concluding lines of his final work: 'For Europe, for ourselves and for humanity, comrades, we must make a new beginning, develop new thought, try to create a new man'." Memmi raises some extraordinarily relevant issues not only about Fanon and the interpretation of Fanon's life and work but also about the colonial, post-colonial and neo-colonial condition.

1262. Mevis, René *comp.* Inventory of Caribbean studies: an overview of social research on the Caribbean conducted by Antillean, Dutch and Surinamese scholars in the period 1945-1973. Leiden, The Netherlands, Royal Institute of Linguistics and Anthropology, Caribbean Dept. 1974. 181 p., bibl.

A report commissioned by the Advisory Board of the Royal Institute of Linguistics and Anthropology, Leiden, which asked for an inventory of social science research and publications by Antillean, Dutch and Surinamese scholars on topics relating to the Caribbean. Caribbean is defined as the Greater and Lesser Antilles, Mexico, Central America, Colombia, Venezuela, and the Guianas. Includes an index of Caribbean specialists and a bibliography.

1263. Mijs, A. A. Onderwijs en ontwikkeling van Suriname. Amsterdam, Univ. van Amsterdam, Sociografisch Instituut FSW, 1974. 359 p., bibl., tables (Onderzoekprojekt Sociale Ontwikkelingsstrategie Suriname 1969, 7)

A sociological study of education and its relation to development in Surinam. The major objective is to isolate the positive and negative functions of education for the social and economic development of the country. The author provides a comprehensive overlook of all educational institutions; delineates the cultural and socio-economic factors which influence education; surveys the structure and activities of the Ministry of Education and National Development; and, describes the unequal participation of the different Surinamese ethnic groups in education.

1264. Miller, Errol L. Self evaluation among Jamaican high school girls (UWI/SES, 22:4, Dec. 1973, p. 407-426, bibl., tables)

Based on a stratified random sample drawn from seven of the eight girls' high schools in Kingston, the author tests the validity of his theoretical position that members of Jamaican society are socialized to evaluate self-worth habitually according to racial factors, debasing creole elements in the society, and class factors. In general, results provide strong support for theory being tested.

1265. Mintz, Sidney W. Afroamerikaner auf den Antillen (*in* Gra..bener, Ju..rgen comp. Kassengesellschaft und Rassimus [see *HLAS 35:8268*] p. 51-63, bibl.)

Important factors for the analysis of contemporary Caribbean society and Afroamericans in the region include the fact that many of the Antilles had and have exceptional ecological conditions for plantation production, that there are premature extermination of the aboriginal population and its substitution by African slaves, and that there was early development of agricultural enterprises and agricultural capitalism in the area. For a description and understanding of the complex sociology of the Caribbean, a four pronged approach is useful: racial distribution, ethnic distribution, subjective race, and languages and dialects in social context.

1266. ———. The Caribbean region (AAAS/D, 103:2, Spring 1974, p. 45-71, bibl.)

Within the context of a *Daedalus* issue devoted to "Slavery, Colonialism, and Racism," the author deals with the Caribbean concentrations on several critical features of its history which effect and help structure contemporary life: slavery, forced settlement of the region and the use of involuntary labor, the plantation system, colonial control, the development of a peasantry, increasing ethnic heterogeneity, the widening of Caribbean social, political and economic horizons, and the spread of Afro-Caribbean people to England, Europe, and the US. "The peculiar poignancy of these lands and peoples is still only imperfectly grasped, it seems. But someday their achievements will receive appropriate recognition—for nowhere else in the universe can one look with certainty into the past and discern the outlines of an undisclosed future."

1267. ———. Caribbean transformations. Chicago, Ill., Aldine Publishing Co., 1974. 355 p., bibl.

A collection of articles written by the author over the past two decades. Volume divided into three sections: Slavery, Forced Labor and the Plantation System; Caribbean Peasantries; Caribbean Nationhood. Articles have been revised and rewritten. Particularly useful are articles originally published in difficult to locate sources (e.g., "The Role of Forced Labour in Nineteenth-Century Puerto Rico," "The Question of Caribbean Peasantries: A Comment," and "The Historical Sociology of the Jamaican Church: Founded Free Village System").

1268. ———. Indiens de l'Inde aux Antilles (EPHE/H, 13:4, Oct./Dec. 1973, p. 142-146)

A short review of the social science literature on East Indians in the Antilles.

1269. Molen, G. van der. De rol van de mijnbouw en bosbouw in de Surinaamse ontwikkeling. Amsterdam, Univ. van Amsterdam, Sociografisch Instituut FSW, 1974. 131 p., bibl. (Onderzoekprojekt Sociale Ontwikkelingsstrategie Suriname 1969, 8a)

The role of mining and sylviculture in Surinamese development, a study based on data generated from annual balance sheets, import-export statements, production surveys, and statistics from various organizations involved with mining and sylviculture (corporations, governmental institutions and departments, unions, etc.). Included in the report is an extensive description of the organization and functions of SURALCO (Surinamese Aluminum Company), a subsidiary of ALCOA (Aluminum Company of America).

1270. Moore, Richard B. Caribs, "cannibals," and human relations: a revealing exposure of smears and stereotypes. Patchogue, N.Y., Pathway Publishers for the Afroamerican Institute, 1972. 38 p., bibl.

Essay devoted to correcting what the author claims is a common stereotype about Carib Indians, that they are frequent consumers of human flesh. The argument presented is that the notion of the savage Carib as cannibal, "who made war and hunted down other human beings in order to devour them" is patently incorrect and had been used in an attempt to justify their enslavement by European conquerors.

1271. Morbán Laucer, Fernando A. Pintura rupestre y petroglifos en Santo Domingo. Santo Domingo, Univ. Autónoma de Santo Domingo, Facultad de Humanidades, Instituto de Investigaciones Antropológicas, 1970. 233 p., bibl., map, plates (Univ. Autónoma de Santo Domingo, 147. Col. Historia y sociedad, 4)

Plates and brief analysis of precolumbian art (pictographs and petroglyphs) in the Dominican Republic researched by a team from the Institute of Anthropological Research of the Autonomous Univ. of Santo Domingo. It is claimed that before these investigations little was known about the subject in this Antillean nation except for brief references to paintings in Borbón and Samaná by Sir Robert Schomburgk and Alph Pinart in the latter part of the 19th century. Finds in caves in the provinces of San Cristóbal, San Pedro de Macorí, Juan Sánchez Ramírez, La Altagracia, Samaná, and in the National District now made the Dominican Republic unique in Antillean archaeology as no other area can claim artistic materials of similar nature and importance. For archaeologist's comment, see *HLAS 33:858*.

1272. Nagelkerke, G. A. *comp.* Literatuur-overzicht van de Nederlandse Antillen vanaf de 17e eeuw tot 1970. Leiden, The Netherlands, Bibliotheek Koninklijk Instituut voor Taal-, Land-en Volkenkunde, 1973. 147 p.

Bibliography of the Netherlands Antilles from the 17th Century to 1970. Includes only the holdings of the Royal Institute of Linguistics and Anthropology, Leiden. Alphabetical listing by author's name. Contains 1904 books and articles.

1273. ——— *comp.* Literatuur-overzicht

van Suriname tot 1940. Leiden, The Netherlands, Bibliotheek Koninklijk Instituut voor Taal-, Land- en Volkenkunde, 1972. 199 p.

Bibliography of Surinam until 1940. Includes only the holdings of the Library of the Royal Institute of Linguistics and Anthropology, Leiden. Alphabetical listing by author's name. Contains 2480 books and articles.

1274. _____ comp. Literatuur-overzicht van Suriname 1940 tot 1970. Leiden, The Netherlands, Bibliotheek Koninklijk Instituut voor Taal-, Land- en Volkenkunde, 1971. 96 p.

A bibliography of Surinam from 1940-70. Includes only the holdings of the Library of the Royal Institute of Linguistics and Anthropology, Leiden. Alphabetical listing by author's name. Contains 1479 books and articles.

1275. New Vision. No. 1, 1974- . San Juan, T. and T.

First issue of a new quarterly magazine, edited by Aknath Maharaj, and published in Trinidad and Tobago. Includes the following articles:
M. P. Alladin "Festivals of Trinidad and Tobago" p. 3-10
Brinsley Samaroo "Hindu Marriage in the Caribbean" p. 11-15
Allan Harris "Did you Know there Were Indentured Africans too?" p. 16-20
Aknath Maharaj "Is Hinduism Relevant to the 20th Century" p. 22-24
Merle Hodge "Male Attitudes in Caribbean Family Life" p. 25-29
Narsaloo Ramaya "A Comparison between Indian and Western Music" p. 30-32.

1276. Nodal, Roberto comp. A preliminary bibliography on African cultures and black peoples of the Caribbean and Latin America. Milwaukee, Univ. of Wisconsin, Dept. of Afro-American Studies, 1972. 33. p., bibl. (Afro-American studies report, 1) (mimeo)

Purpose is to present a list of materials essential for an understanding of the dynamics of African cultures, and of black people, in the Caribbean area and in Latin America. Bibliography, in 33 mimeographed pages, covers general Caribbean, Spanish America excluding Cuba, Brazil, and French Caribbean excluding Haiti. This short and in many ways inadequate list is not annotated.

Ortiz, Fernando. Hampa afrocubana: los negros brujos, apuntes para un estudio de etnología criminal. See HLAS 36:4255.

1277. Otterbein, Charlotte Swanson and **Keith F. Otterbein.** Believers and beaters: a case study of supernatural beliefs and child rearing in the Bahama Islands (AAA/AA, 75:5, Oct. 1973, p. 1670-1681, bibl., tables)

Based on field work in Congo Town, settlement district of Long Bay Cays, Andros Island, the authors tested the hypothesis that caretakers (mothers and grandmothers) who fear the supernatural will inflict more pain on the children in their charge than will those caretakers who do not fear the supernatural. Twenty caretakers were interviewed about their beliefs in the supernatural and about the training given to their 48 children and grandchildren. Derived from the major hypothesis, three specific hypotheses were field tested. Each of the three was supported by data generated by "the method of subsystem validation" allowing the authors to claim that the major hypothesis was confirmed.

1278. Oud, P. J. Coöperatives, waterschappen en ontwikkeling in Suriname. Amsterdam, Univ. van Amsterdam, Sociografisch Instituut FSW, 1974. 131 p., bibl. (Onderzoekprojekt Sociale Ontwikkelingsstrategie Suriname 1969, 8a)

Cooperatives, waterworks and development in Surinam. Because of the limited dispersal of cooperatives and their low level of functioning, this institutional form has not contributed to the social and economic uplifting of the country. Description of various situations and procedures which can cause success or failure of cooperatives in underdeveloped countries and the relevance of these data to the Surinamese case.

1279. Oxaal, Ivar. The dependency economist as grassroots politician in the Caribbean (in Oxaal, Ivar; Tony Barnett; and David Booth eds. Beyond the sociology of development: economy and society in Latin America and Africa. London, Routledge & Kegan Paul, 1975, p. 28-49, bibl.)

Description and analysis of the career of Lloyd Best, Trinidadian economist and political leader. In this context, the author deals with Naipaul's concept of West Indian "mimic men"; Lloyd Best and the New World Group; the founding of Tapia House, the development of dependency theory as a central critical thrust of West Indian economy; the critique of the economic thought of Sir Arthur Lewis; and anti-imperialism without Marxism.

Pierce, B. Edward. Status competition and personal networks: informal social organization among the Nengre of Paramaribo. See item 1378.

1280. Pollak-Eltz, Angelina. El concepto de múltiples almas y algunos ritos fúnebres entre los negros americanos. Caracas, Univ. Católica Andrés Bello, Instituto de Investigaciones Históricas, 1974. 52 p., bibl.

The multiple soul concept and funeral rites of black

Americans. Book deals specifically with the concept of soul following Christian doctrine; popular Iberian beliefs concerning the soul and funeral rites; concept of multiple soul in West Africa; soul concept and funeral rites among black Venezuelans and Bush Negroes; concept of triple soul and funeral rites of the black Caribs of Central America; soul concept and funeral rites among Black Mexicans, in Jamaica, in Haiti, in Trinidad, along the Colombian coasts, and in Cuba; concept of multiple soul and funeral rites in Brazil; and the double soul concept of US blacks.

1281. ———. Cultos afroamericanos. Caracas, Univ. Católica Andrés Bello, Facultad de Humanidades y Educación, Instituto de Investigaciones Históricas, 1972. 258 p., bibl.

Spanish language version of the Dutch publication *Afro-amerikaanse godsdiensten en culten*. Remains a useful review of Afroamerican religious groups with sections on the religions of West Africa (Gold Coast, Dahomey, Nigeria, Congo-Angola); the Afroamerican religious of Brazil (Candomblé, Batuque, Chango, Macumba, Pagelanca, Catimbo, Umbandá); the Afroamerican religions of the Antilles (Shango, Shouting Baptists, Myalism, Obeah, Convince Cult, Black Carib forms, Vodún, religion and magic in the French Antilles, African rites in Santo Domingo, Santería); Venezuela (Cult of María Lionza); Bush Negroes and Urban blacks in Surinam; and, Negro sects and popular cults in the US.

1282. Price, Richard *ed*. Maroon societies: rebel slave communities in the Americas. Garden City, N.Y., Anchor Press/Doubleday, 1973. 429 p., bibl., plates.

A collection of 21 essays on Maroons and *Marronage* in the New World. Edition blends modern scholarship on the subject with illuminating material written during the slave period. Geographical areas covered are the Spanish Americas (Cuba, Venezuela, Colombia, Mexico), the French Caribbean, Brazil, Jamaica, and the Guianas. A useful introduction and preface to each section are provided. Articles included are:
José L. Franco "Maroons and Slave Rebellions in the Spanish Territories" p. 35-48
Francisco Pérez de la Riva "Cuban *Palenques*" p. 49-59
Demoticus Philalethes "Hunting the Maroons with Dogs in Cuba" p. 60-63
Miguel Acosta Saignes "Life in a Venezuelan *Cumbe*" p. 64-73
Aquiles Escalante "*Palenques* in Colombia" p. 74-81
David M. Davidson "Negro Slave Control and Resistance in Colonial Mexico, 1519-1650" p. 82-104
Gabriel Debien "Marronage in the French Caribbean" p. 107-134
M. L. E. Moreau de Saint-Méry "The Border Maroons of Saint-Domingue: Le Maniel" p. 135-142
Yvan Debbasch "Le Maniel: Further Notes" p. 143-148
Herbert Aptheker "Maroons Within the Present Limits of the United States" p. 151-168
R. K. Kent "Palmares: An African State in Brazil" p. 170-190
Roger Bastide "The Other *Quilombos*" p. 191-201
Stuart B. Schwartz "The *Mocambo*: Slave Resistance in Colonial Bahia" p. 202-226
Bryan Edwards "Observations on . . . the Maroon Negroes of the Island of Jamaica" p. 230-245
Orlando Patterson "Slavery and Slave Revolts: A Sociohistorical Analysis of the First Maroon War, 1665-1740" p. 246-292
Johannes King "Guerrilla Warfare: A Bush Negro View" p. 298-304
Captain J. G. Stedman "Guerrilla Warfare: A European Soldier's View" p. 305-311
"Rebel Village in French Guiana: A Captive's Description" p. 312-319
A. J. F. Köbben "Unity and Disunity: Cottica Djuka Society as a Kinship System" p. 320-369
W. van Wetering "Witchcraft Among the Tapanahoni Djuka" p. 370-387
Silvia W. de Groot "The Bush Negro Chiefs Visit Africa: Diary of an Historic Trip" p. 389-398. For historian's comment see *HLAS 36:1516*.

1283. ——— **and Sally Price.** Kammbá: The ethnohistory of an Afro-American art (SCNLS/A, 32, 1972, p. 3-27, bibl., map, illus.)

Cicatrization, or ornamental body scarification, is examined as an art form among the Saramaka Bush Negroes in Surinam. It is argued that it is not a direct African retention or survival but it was developed in the early part of the 19th century. In style this art form was clearly distinct from African models. "And like the 'African-looking' art of woodcarving in Surinam, which also took shape only well into the 19th century, Saramaka civilization has gone through extensive stylistic development since that time. Saramaka cicatrization represents an imaginative extrapolation of West African aesthetic ideas and provides an excellent illustration of some of the ways that Afro-Americans have made African arts truly their own."

1284. Pullen-Burry, Bessie. Ethiopia in exile: Jamaica revisited. Freeport, N.Y., Books for Libraries Press, 1971. 288 p. (The Black heritage library collection)

First published in 1905, an Englishman's account of observations and impressions of a "somewhat prolonged" tour of Canada, the US, Cuba, and Jamaica. The book deals primarily with Jamaica (the conditions of the time, governmental structure, evils of slavery, the hurricane of 1903, praedial larceny, tourist sights, education and educational policy, religion and African superstitions, Jamaican women, obeah, etc.) and with the Negro in the US (Booker Washington, Southern education, race mixture, examples of Negro literature, comparison of Indian and Negro, justice in the North and in the South, Negro as soldier, government, the Negro Church in slavery, Tuskegee, position of the educated Negro in the South, etc.). "Having been favourably impressed with the condition of the blacks and coloured people under British rule during a former visit to Jamaica, I thought that an acquaintance with their more recently emancipated kinsfolk in the United States would not be without interest."

1285. Remy, Anselme. The unholy trinity (Caribbean Review [Hato Rey, P. R.] 6:2, April/May/June 1974, p. 14-18)

Focusing on Martinique, the author attempts to operationalize the concept of *ethno class*, "a product of the colonial nature of Caribbean societies." Given the unique Caribbean history and experience, an understanding of political behavior in the region requires concepts which incorporate the dynamic interaction of class and ethnicity. Factors which contribute to *ethno class* are race (or color), culture, and economics.

1286. Rest, C P. M. van. Het Department van Landbouw, Veeteelt en Visserij. Amsterdam, Univ. van Amsterdam, Sociografisch Instituut FSW, 1974. 142 p., tables. (Onderzoekprojekt Sociale Ontwikkelingsstrategie Suriname 1969, 3)

Description and analysis of the functions of the Surinamese Dept. of Agriculture, Cattle Breeding and Fishing with particular reference to the development of the country.

1287. *Revista Interamericana Review*. Inter-American Univ. of Puerto Rico. Vol. 3, No. 1, 1973- Hato Rey, P. R.

A special edition devoted to race in the Americas. Of particular interest to social scientists are articles by:
Eric Williams "The Blackest Thing in Slavery was not the Black Man" p. 1-23
Magnus Mörner "Legal Equality—Social Inequality: A Post-Abolition Theme" p. 24-41
T. Dale Stewart "The Indians of the Americas: Myths and Realities" p. 42-54
Ved P. Duggal "Relations Between Indians and Africans in Guyana" p. 55-60
Luis M. Díaz Soler "Relaciones Raciales en Puerto Rico" p. 61-72
R. Alfonso López Yustos "Racial Self-Perception of the Black Teacher in the Public Schools of Puerto Rico" p. 73-84
Herbert J. Muller "Educación para el Futuro" p. 85-95

1288. Rubin, Vera and Lambros Comitas. Ganja in Jamaica: a medical anthropological study of chronic marihuana use. The Hague, Mouton, 1975. 205 p., bibl., tables.

Report of team research (anthropological and medical) on the effects of chronic cannabis smoking among lower class Jamaicans. Volume is essentially divided into two sections: the first deals with the social and cultural setting of cannabis use in Jamaica with chapters on the ethnohistory of cannabis, *ganja* legislation, and acute effects of ganja smoking in a natural setting; the second is primarily concerned with the results of clinical studies of 30 chronic ganja smokers of 30 controls with chapters on respiratory function and hematology, psychiatry and electroencephalography, and psychological assessment. Concluding chapters deal with attitudes and reactions to ganja, cultural expectations and predisposition to ganja, and cannabis, society and culture. Results of the clinical tests indicate that the physical risk to the individual from chronic cannabis smoking is minimal and relate primarily to *smoking per se*. Psychiatric and psychological findings do not bear out any of the extreme allegations about the deleterious effects of chronic cannabis use on sanity, cerebral atrophy, brain damage or personality deterioration. Argument is presented that the ganja complex has developed and proliferated in Jamaican society and is well integrated into and serves multiple pragmatic purposes in working-class life.

1288a. _____ and Richard P. Schaedel eds. The Haitian potential: research and resources of Haiti. N.Y., Teachers' College Press, 1975. 308 p., bibl.

Revised papers originally presented at the Conference on Research and Resources of Haiti at the Research Institute for the Study of Man, N.Y.C. in 1967. Volume is divided into four substantive sections: demography and human resources; language and literacy; nutrition and health; and, institutions. Includes the following articles:
Richard P. Schaedel "Introduction" p. ix-xiv
Ernst T. Brea "Creation of a Research and Documentation Center for Haiti" p. xv-xxi
Robert Bazile "Demographic Statistics in Haiti" p. 3-10
Rémy Bastien "Social Anthropology: Recent Research and Recent Needs" p. 11-16
Caroline J. Legerman "Observations on Family and Kinship Organization in Haiti" p. 17-22
Richard P. Schaedel "The Concept of Community Development in Haiti and Venezuela" p. 23-37
Alan Lomax "Africanism in New World Negro Music" p. 38-60
Albert Valdman "The Language Situation in Haiti" p. 61-82
Paul Berry "Literacy and the Question of Creole" p. 83-113
Kléber Viélot "Primary Education in Haiti" p. 114-146
Kendall W. King "Nutrition Research in Haiti" p. 147-156
Pierre Noel "Recent Research in Public Health in Haiti" p. 157-166
Ari Kiev "Research and Resources in Psychiatry in Haiti" p. 173-182
Max H. Dorsinville "Haiti and its Institutions: From Colonial History to 1957" p. 183-220
François Latortue "Reflections on the Haitian Labor Force" p. 221-239
Serge Vieux "Research Problems and Perspectives of the Haitian Civil Service" p. 240-272.

1289. Ryan, Selwyn D. Race and nationalism in Trinidad and Tobago: a study of decolonization in a multiracial society. Toronto, Canada, Univ. of Toronto Press, 1972. 509 p., maps, plates, tables.

Detailed and thorough study of the transition of Trinidad from colony to nation and the examination of several key problems which it has faced since Independence in 1962. Monograph is divided into four substantive sections: 1) deals with the early years of the reform movement through 1955 when Eric Williams becomes its leader; 2) is concerned with the emergence of the People's National Movement in 1955-56, describes its organization and ideology; 3) covers the period Sept. 1956 to Aug. 1962, the "period that witnessed the consolidation of power by the Negro-dominated People's National Movement and the rally of opposition elements—mainly Hindu and European—in the Democratic Labour Party"; and 4) analyses and evaluates the extent to which the PNM reached the goals it stated in 1956. The last paragraph of the work gives a good sense of the author's general position: "Given the limits of traditional democratic politics, the size and location of the country, the nature of its resource base, and the sociological origins of the PNM leadership, the Party has perhaps succeeded as well as anyone could realistically expect. What Trinidad needs now is a new kind of decentralized and participatory political movement that can harness the frustrations of the people and direct them into constructive social and economic action, concerned not merely with fulfilling the statistical demands for economic growth but with the needs of the bottom levels of the society, the mass of dispossessed Indians and blacks. In short, what is now needed is a movement that can find new ways to implement the People's Charter which was launched with such optimism and hope in 1956." A major contribution to our understanding of the recent political history of Trinidad and Tobago.

1290. Sanders, Andrew. Family structure and domestic organization among coastal Amerindians in Guyana (UWI/SES, 22:4, Dec. 1973, p. 440-478, bibl., tables)

Perhaps the first study of coast-dwelling Amerindians, a creolized West Indian population. Acculturation and social change engendered by contact with creole culture and institutions have transformed coastal Amerindian family structure making it a variant of Caribbean lower-class creole family systems. Amerindians have assimilated aspects of white middle-class values on mating and domestic organization. Household often has a uterine bias in its composition but rarely is matrifocal, given the importance of men as money-earners. Some features of the transformed coastal Amerindian family system are "related to traditional Amerindian structures and differentiate them from other Creole family systems. Most notable are joint family households and the expectations of uxorilocal residence for young couples entering domestic unions." Considerable detail on kinship and friendship patterns, mating and domestic relationships, the household (including the developmental cycle), and household grouping.

1291. Sanford, Margaret. Revitalization movements as indicators of completed acculturation (CSSH, 16:4, Sept. 1974, p. 504-518)

Argues that "some revitalization movements, the return of a group to older, formerly discarded practices, are far from a negative sign, but indeed may be quite positive indications that acculturation may be completed or well on the way to accomplishment." The case presented as illustration of this point is a "revitalization movement" started in the early 1940s by T. V. Ramos among his black Carib brethren in British Honduras.

1292. ———. A socialization in ambiguity: child-lending in a British West Indian society (UP/E, 13:4, Oct. 1974, p. 393-400, bibl.)

A study of child-lending in British Honduras based on quantitative data generated in 1969 from sections of the city of Belize and from the rural town of Stann Creek. The argument posed is that the practice of lending children has consequences on the socialization and enculturation of these children. This pattern may explain "socialized ambivalence." "When socializers are multiple, then the 'slippage' in transmission of cultural models is proportionately greater. When to this is added an experience under a keeper of another culture, then the wide range of a cultural norm already absorbed may be widened further to include what to the observer appears as contradictory behaviors."

1293. Simpson, Joy M. A demographic analysis of internal migration in Trinidad and Tobago: a descriptive and theoretical orientation. Kingston, Univ. of the West Indies, Institute of Social and Economic Research, 1973. 63 p., maps, tables.

Descriptive demographic analysis of internal migration in Trinidad and Tobago during the periods 1931-46 and 1946-60. This short book deals with the intensity and main streams of internal migration; urbanization and population concentration in specially demarcated areas; distribution of migrants by industrial group, occupation group, and work status; and distribution of migrants by level of educational attainment. A final section provides a theoretical analysis of migrants using the Stochastic process and the Theory of Markov Chains.

1294. Smith, M.G. Race and stratification in the Caribbean (*in* Smith, M.G. Corporations and society: the social anthropology of collective action. Chicago, Ill., Aldine Publishing Co., 1975. p. 271-346, bibl., tables)

A new lengthy essay included in a collection of already published papers. ". . . in response to the social-psychological interpretation of Caribbean race relations advanced by H. Hoetink, [Smith] tried to analyse the conditions and development of the racial aspects of social stratification in West Indian societies, in order to clarify their corporate bases, forms and characterisitcs." Within the context of the argument, a wide range of ethnographic, sociological and statistical data is presented and utilized.

1295. Souffrant, Claude. La religion du paysan haïtien: de l'anathème au dialogue (FERES/SC, 19:4, 1972, p. 585-597)

Historically persecuted as a pagan African religion, the practice of Vodou in Haiti assumed a clandestine character. Vodou, however, is a form of living Christianity intermingling folk beliefs with elements of Catholicism and Protestantism. It is argued that the Catholicism of the Haitian peasant is similar to that of the French peasant in the Middle Ages and the peasants of Latin America. While these latter groups are and have been considered Catholics, Haitians who practice Vodou, have been anathematized as pagans. With the onset of national liberation movements which followed the 1915 American occupation, the impact of the 1957 Bandung Conference and the rapid decolonization of Africa and Asia a more tolerant ecumenical view of Vodou in Haiti was engendered. The resultant dialogue is not so much an exchange between two religions as it is a recognition of values previously anathematized that can lead to mutual enrichment.

1296. Stone, Carl. Class, race and political behaviour in urban Jamaica. Mona, Jam., Univ. of the West Indies, Institute of Social and Economic Research (ISER) 1973. 188 p., bibl.

Detailed study by political scientist on the nature of mass support for the political system of Jamaica and the forms of and reasons for political and social alienation among the urban population of its captial. Relying heavily on data generated through a sample survey of a stratified quota sample (605 respondents), the author describes and analyzes the growing relative deprivation in the nation which has led to "increased political apathy and alienation and intensified class and racial militancy among the subproletariat and lumpen proletariat".

1297. Thomas, Garry L. *ed.* Anthropological field reports from San Salvador Island. Corning, N.Y., College Center of the Finger Lakes, 1973. 119 p., bibl. (Island environmental studies reports 1973)

A collection of undergraduate field research reports in environmental studies sponsored by the College Center of the Finger Lakes. On invitation of the Bahamian Government, San Salvador Island was used as the site of this research. Collection includes:
Marc Tull "San Salvadorian Reactions to the American" p. 1-5
John Duckworth "An Inquiry into the African Origins of San Salvador Culture" p. 6-8
Sally Kentch and Heather Beverly "Agricultural Methods and Food Preparation on San Salvador" p. 9-24
Judith Daniels and Joan Margolis "Variations in Family Structure and Familial Role Expectation on San Salvador Island" p. 25-47
Stephanie Prete and Joan Hampton "The Children of San Salvador" p. 48-58
Marc Tull "Fun Take, Puttin'-in-Jail, Tracey, Ring Take and Knocks Hole: The Role Played by Marbles in Child Socialization on San Salvador" p. 59-68
Michele Hall "The Role of Religion on San Salvador" p. 69-76
Veronica Jenkins "Fertility and Birth Control on San Salvador" p. 77-81
Marc Tull and Bill Attride "Continuity of Cooperation in a Transitional Economy" p. 82-90
Leander Yeaton "Gambling: a Brief Case Study of Cultural Change" p. 91-94
Kathleen Jane Hanley "A Study of Incipient Class Structure on San Salvador" p. 95-98
Jim Erdle "Land Use Patterns and Systems of Land Tenure on San Salvador" p. 99-105
Charleen Arnett Darlington "A Brief Examination of Political Attitudes on San Salvador on the Eve of Political Independence" p. 106-109
Sharon Jacobs "San Salvador Island: From Culture Contact to Alienation" p. 110-119.

1298. Veen, L.J. van der. De funkties van banken en verzekeringsmaatschappijen voor de ontwikkeling van Suriname. Amsterdam, Univ. van Amsterdam, Sociografisch Instituut FSW, 1974. 130 p., bibl., tables (Onderzoekprojekt Sociale Ontwikkelingsstrategie Suriname 1969, 5)

Author deals with the functions of banks and insurance companies for the development of Surinam. Descriptive analysis deals with these functions (primarily credit and loans) in relation to the agrarian structure, mining and industry, import and export trade, government sector, etc. Secondary functions derived from primary ones, such as employment opportunities and increase of national income, are also considered in the context of the general economic development of the country.

1299. Vollers, J.L. De bestuurlijke struktuur van Suriname. Amsterdam, Univ. van Amsterdam, Sociografisch Instituut FSW, 1974. 194 p., bibl. (Onderzoekprojekt Sociale Ontwikkelingsstrategie Suriname 1969, 12)

A study dealing with the administrative structure of Surinam based on a comprehensive survey of all administrative organizations as to their functions and tasks. Special attention is given to: district-level administration and the institutional obstructions that hinder decentralization; employment mediation and employment opportunities and factors complicating the unemployment issue; and, the Guardians' Supervisory Board and its extraordinary position in a society where unstable household and male-female relationships are quite common.

1300. Vuijsje, H. Ontwikkelingsfunkties van religieuze organisaties in Suriname. Amsterdam, Univ. van Amsterdam, Sociografisch Instituut FSW, 1974. 84 p., bibl., tables (Onderzoekprojekt Sociale Ontwikkelingsstrategie Suriname 1969, 9)

Developmental functions of religious organizations in Surinam. Lists the existing Surinamese religious organizations, describes their activities, the structural and cultural factors that influence them, and how they materially influence the social development of the country.

1301. Walcott, Derek. The Caribbean: culture or mimicry? (UM/JIAS, 16:1, Feb. 1974, p. 3-13)

A noted West Indian poet and writer responds to the idea that Caribbean culture mimics that of the Old World and has created nothing new, an idea developed, in part, by Vidia Naupaul. He concludes with a more positive and hopeful perspective. "Poets and satirists are afflicted with the superior stupidity which believes that societies can be renewed, and one of the most nourishing sites for such a renewal, however visionary it may seem, is the American archipelago."

1302. Watson, G. Llewellyn. Social structure and social movements: the Black Muslims in the U.S.A. and the Ras-Tafarians in Jamaica (BJS, 24:2, June 1973, p. 188-204)

A comparison of two social movements in two

different social structures. One major implication of the "theoretical uniformities" of the two movements is that "the phenomena of the Rastas and the Muslims are a resultant of a complex of forces of which neocolonial racism, protracted class struggle and systematic exploitation are essential ingredients."

1303. Weker, H.N. Funkties van de massamedia in Suriname. Amsterdam, Univ. van Amsterdam, Sociografisch Instituut FSW, 1974. 118 p., bibl., tables (Onderzoekprojekt Sociale Ontwikkelingsstrategie Suriname 1969, 10)

Study of the functions of the mass media in Surinam. Based on interviews with key individuals in television, radio, newspapers and journals, the author attempts to assess the influence (positive, negative, neutral) of the manifest aims and unplanned side effects of the mass media on Surinamese development. Three areas are carefully examined: media as purveyor of news; position and role of mass media in the political system; and, the educational role of the mass media.

1304. Wengen, G.D. van. De Javanen in de Surinaamse samenleving. Amsterdam, Sticusa, 1971? 236 p., bibl.

An anthropological study of the Javanese in Surinam based on field work in 1962. Description of a Javanese agricultural community focusing on economic and social structure and patterns of communal life. Separate sections on Javanese migration and urbanization and the position of the Javanese in modern Surinamese society. Author argues that acculturation among young urban Javanese is increasing but since this ethnic group lags in social development there is a need for higher levels of educational attainment.

1305. Wilson, Peter J. Oscar: an inquiry into the nature of sanity. N.Y., Random House, 1974. 142 p.

A study of the relationship of Oscar Bryan, an extraordinary "mad" man and his society, Providencia. "Oscar is an extraordinary person, and his life is not to be taken as one that is typical of lives lived in the Caribbean. Yet it is, to paraphrase Oscar himself, only through the study of the extraordinary that we can come to some sort of understanding of the ordinary. In the events of Oscar's life there is, I think, the exaggeration of what passes unnoticed, though not unsuffered, in the lives of ordinary people." In a concluding chapter, the author further develops the concepts of respectability and reputation as the dual value orientation in the Caribbean.

1306. Wooding, Charles J. The Winti-Cult in the Para-district (UPR/CS, 12:1, April 1972, p. 51-78)

In essence, this paper summarizes the English much of the data on the *Winti* cult in the author's book *Winti: Een Afroamerikaanse Godsdienst in Suriname* (see item 1307). Dealt with are cult beliefs (the Winti pantheon, materialization of Gods and spirits, dwelling places of the Gods, the languages of the Gods, the concept of the soul, supernatural powers); magic and curing practices; and, worship and healing (complete treatment, less complicated treatment). The analysis delves into acculturation, economic effects of the cult, sociological effects, and psychological effects.

1307. ———. Winti: een Afroamerikaanse godsdienst in Suriname. Meppel, The Netherlands, Krips Repro B.V., 1972. 565 p., bibl., map, tables.

Detailed study of the religion and its social parameters in seven villages in the Para District, Surinam, and area where former slaves bought the plantations after the abolition of slavery in 1863. Argument presented is that due to the processes of social and cultural change their original West African institutions have undergone change and that their traditional religions have "ultimately integrated into a new religious system known as *Winti*". Tribal origins of slaves are traced and an analysis of their societies is presented from written sources. Field data deals with religion and the supernatural. Winti is defined as "an Afroamerican religion which centres round the belief in personified supernatural beings, who take possession of a human being, eliminate his consciousness, after which they unfold the past, the present and the future, and are able to cause and cure diseases of a supernatural origin". The author claims that Winti is a unique religion in the New World since it has not adopted elements from Christianity as have other Afroamerican religions. "Since mainly West African parallel institutions have integrated into Winti, the term syncretism cannot be used to denote this religious system. Hence for such a system the word *fromu* is introduced. Fromu then means the process in which homogeneous religious elements integrate into a new religious system with adoration and behaviour patterns that show great similarities with the original ones."

1308. Wouters, A.E. Suriname. Amsterdam, Allert de Lange, 1972. 157 p., maps, plates.

A general traveller's guide to Surinam with short sections on its history, geography, people, on Paramaribo, and on tourist sights.

ETHNOLOGY

SOUTH AMERICA: LOWLANDS

SETH LEACOCK
Associate Professor of Anthropology
University of Connecticut

ALTHOUGH IT IS UNDOUBTEDLY STILL TRUE that South America is the least known of the continents, ethnographically, the situation does continue to improve, however slowly. During the past two years several major monographs have appeared, as well as a number of excellent articles. Although the indigenous populations continue to disappear at a horrifying rate (see items 1315, 1342, 1370 and 1388), it is still possible that we will obtain a reasonably good sampling from most parts of lowland South America before the remaining tribal groups become extinct.

It is gratifying to report several detailed studies of the tribes of the Upper Xingu, a region about which we still know remarkably little. Basso's study of the Kalapalo (item 1320), although published in the Holt, Rinehart and Winston series of short ethnographies for undergraduates, is the most complete account yet published of an Upper Xingu tribe and is in every respect an excellent piece of work. In the area of kinship and marriage, Gregor's report on the Mehinacu (item 1348) very convincingly confirms Basso's claim of remarkable homogeneity in Xingu institutions. Two recent studies of tribes on the margins of the Xingu region by two Brazilian anthropologists from the Museu Goeldi should be noted. The first is a first-class monograph on the Jurúna by A.E. Oliveira (item 1373), and the second is a historical account of conflicts between the Xingu tribes and one of their long-time foes, the Ge-speaking Suiá, by the late Protásio Frikel (item 1342).

For other areas, the best monographs are those of Siskind on the Sharanahua (item 1399) and Riester on the Guarasug'wä (item 1388). Clastres has also brought together most of his already published material on the Guayaki in a single volume (item 1331).

For a few tribes, we are beginning to get some very impressive in-depth material from several observers. For the Warao, for example, the excellent studies of kinship by Heinen (items 1351 and 1352) raise questions about the interpretation provided earlier by Suárez (*HLAS 35:1323*). Lizot continues to provide comparative data on the Yanomamö (item 1357), as does Watson on the Goajiro (items 1407 and 1408).

As might be expected, several current interests in anthropology are reflected in the literature under review. The role of women is the focus of a work on the Mundurucú (item 1372) by Yolanda and Robert Murphy (based on fieldwork done in the 1950s), and Siskind also emphasizes the female perspective in her study of the Sharanahua (item 1399). Several studies deal with intra- and inter-tribal trade: Bodley (item 1321), Colson (item 1332), and Thomas (item 1401).

Students and scholars alike will find item 1400 of particular interest. In this collection of papers presented at a symposium in Bridgetown in 1971 will be found both an up-to-date list of all remaining indigenous populations in lowland South America, as well as a striking expression of the growing concern felt by many anthropologists for the welfare of the Indians.

1309. *América Indígena.* Instituto Indigenista Americano. Vol. 34, No. 1, enero/marzo 1974- . México.

In keeping with recent policy, this entire issue is devoted to the indigenous populations of a single country, in this case Venezuela. Most of the articles discuss broad political issues, but the following deal with the current situation of specific tribes:
Gilberto Antolínez "Sintesis de las Características Socioculturales de la Tribu Yaruro" p. 19-38
Luis Cocco "El Imperio Yanomamo de la Amazonas Venezolana" p. 39-62
Daniel Barandiarán "Civilizaciones Indias Actuales de la Guayana Venezolana" p. 63-72
Misión Santa María Erebato "Evolución y Situación de la Población Indígena Makiritare y Sanemá" p. 73-90
Gilberto Antolínez "Enseñanzas Útiles de la Agricultura Jirajara-Miku" p. 91-104
Nemesio Montiel Fernández "Nociones sobre los Guajiros Prehispánicos y su Procedencia" p. 105-112
Adelaida G. de Díaz Ungría "Microevolución en las Poblaciones Indígenas Yupa" p. 113-134.

1310. Amorim, Paulo Marcos de. Indios

camponeses: os potiguára de Baía de Traição (MP/R, 19, 1970/1971, p. 7-96, bibl., tables)

The Potiguára Indians live on a reservation on the northeast coast of Brazil. This study deals with their participation in the local economy as farmers and fishermen. Some historical data are also provided.

1311. d'Ans, André-Marcel. Les tribus indigénes du Parc National du Manú (*in* International Congress of Americanists, XXXIX, Lima, 1970. Actas y memorias [see *HLAS 35:510*] v. 4, p. 95-100)

Sketch of the location and present situation of the indigenous populations living in the Manú National Park in the Peruvian *montaña*.

1312. Arancibia, Ubén Gerardo. Vida y mitos del mundo mataco. B.A., Ediciones Depalma, 1973. 106 p., bibl., plates (Serie Conducta y comunicación, 4)

Myths collected from a group of missionized Mataco (western Chaco).

1313. Armellada, Cesáro de. Pemontón Taremurú: los tarén de los indios pemón. Caracas, Univ. Católica Andrés Bello, Instituto de Investigaciones Históricas, Centro de Lenguas Indígenas, 1972. 333 p. (Serie lenguas indígenas de Venezuela)

Remarkable collection of 110 elaborate spells used by the Pemón of eastern Venezuela to ward off danger and accomplish other ends. Each spell is part of a standardized story with myth-like characteristics. The compiler, a Franciscan-Capuchin missionary, gives both the Pemón text and a Spanish translation. His linguistic skill as well as his excellent rapport with the Indians is evident.

1314. Arnaud, Expedito. Aspectos da legislação sobre os índios do Brasil. Belém, Bra., Conselho Nacional de Pesquisas, Instituto Nacional de Pesquisas da Amazonia, Museu Paraense Emílio Goeldi, 1973. 45 p., bibl. (Publicações avulsas, 22)

Survey of major legislation concerning the Indians of Brazil from colonial times to the present (1970). Most detail is provided for the period since the founding of the *Serviço de Proteção aos Indios* (SPI) in 1910. Replacement of the SPI by the *Fundação Nacional do Indio* (FUNAI) in 1967 is discussed.

1315. _____ and **Ana Rita Alves.** A extinção dos índios karacaô (kayapó) Baixo Xingu, Pará (MPEG/B, 53, 26 junho 1974, p. 1-19, bibl., map)

Yet another tragic story of the extinction of a group of Brazilian Indians. In this case the Indian Service induced the Indians to leave their village and engage in the collection of Brazil nuts. Undernourished and demoralized, the Indians died of the usual diseases.

1316. Arvelo-Jiménez, Nelly. Estructura y funcionamiento del sistema político ye'cuana (AVAC/ACV, 23:3, 1972, p. 171-175, bibl.)

Brief description of Ye'cuana (Makiritare) political organization, dealing both with its internal and external manifestations. For a more complete account by the same author in English, see *HLAS 35:1224*.

1317. Baer, Gerhard. The pahotko masks of the Piro, Eastern Peru (SSA/B, 38, 1974, p. 7-16, illus.)

Describes gourd and clay masks used by the Piro and discusses some associated beliefs.

1318. Bamberger, Joan. Naming and the transmission of status in a central Brazilian society (UP/E, 13:4, Oct. 1974, p. 363-378, bibl., tables)

Elaborate analysis of the way in which ceremonial names are transmitted among the Kayapó. As among other Gê-speaking tribes, male names go to a sister's son, and female names to a brother's daughter. Name transmission is related to kinship and residence patterns. See item 1359.

1319. Bandeira, Maria de Lourdes. Os kariris de Mirandela: um grupo indígena integrado. Bahia, Bra., Univ. Federal da Bahia *em convênio com a* Secretaria de Educação e Cultura do Estado de Bahia, 1972. 171 p., bibl., music, plates, tables (Estudos baianos, 6)

Based on four months fieldwork, this study compares a group of acculturated Indians of eastern Brazil with their non-Indian neighbors. Religious beliefs, typical of rural areas in this part of Brazil, are described in detail. Also contains six myths, a list of herbal remedies, and 18 songs (words and music). For musicologist's comment, see *HLAS 36:4532*.

1320. Basso, Ellen B. The Kalapalo Indians of Central Brazil. N.Y., Holt, Rinehart and Winston, 1973. 157 p., bibl., illus., maps, plates, tables.

This excellent monograph is a major contribution to our understanding of the tribes of the Upper Xingu (central Brazil). It deals intensively with the kinship system, authority structure, and ceremonial life of the Carib-speaking Kalapalo, but it includes abundant comparative material on neighboring tribes. Focus is on the shared values and activities that unite the Xingú tribes into a single society, in spite of their linguistic diversity. See item 1348.

Becher-Donner, Etta. Geriefte Keramik des Río Negro: Gebietes aus den Jahren 1830-1831. See item 899.

1321. Bodley, John H. Deferred exchange among the Campa Indians (AI/A, 68:3/4, March 1973, p. 589-596, bibl.)

Brief description of patterns of intratribal trade among the Campa of eastern Peru. Trading partners exchange locally produced items as well as manufactured goods obtained from Peruvians. For other studies of indigenous trade, see items 1332 and 1401.

Boglár, Lajos. Aspects of story-telling among the Piaroa Indians. See *HLAS 36:1026.*

1322. ———. Häuptling und Medizinmann bei den Piaroa-Indianern: Venezuela (MVL/J, 28, 1972, p. 405-413)

German version of "Chieftainship and the Religious Leader" (see *HLAS 35:1230*).

1323. ———. Zur kulturgeschichtlichen Stellung der Nambiquara-Indianer (DGV/ZE, 96:2, 1971, p. 266-270)

Brief discussion of the various interpretations given the "primitive" characteristics of the Nambikuara of southern Mato Grosso, Bra. Conclusion is that formerly the Nambikuara were probably more dependent on agriculture.

1324. *Boletim Informativo FUNAI.* Ministério do Interior, Fundação Nacional do Indio (FUNAI). Ano 2, No. 7, Trimestre 2, [through] No. 8, Trimestre 3, 1973- . Brasília.

Bulletins of the new Brazilian Indian Service (FUNAI), obviously designed to improve the reputation of the organization. Most of the material is for the nonspecialist, but there are several reports of recent contacts with hitherto unknown indigenous populations, especially along the trans-Amazonian highway. Numerous photographs.

1325. Bormida, Marcelo and **Alejandra Siffredi.** Mitología de los tehuelches meridionales (UBAI/R, 12:1/2, 1969/1970, p. 199-245, bibl., tables)

Collection of myths obtained from some of the few surviving Tehuelche Indians of southern Patagonia. Several versions of myths about the culture hero Elal are presented; these are then compared with similar Ona myths. See also item 1398.

1326. Brazil. Ministério do Interior. Fundação Nacional do Indio (FUNAI). Estatuto do índio; The Indian statute; Le statut de l'Indien. Brasília, 1973. 15 p.

Laws passed in 1973 concerning the civil and political rights, and rights to land, of Brazilian Indians. In Portuguese, English, and French.

Camargo, Pedro Pablo and **Angelina de Coral.** La violación de derechos humanos en Colombia: el problema indígena, la justicia militar o de excepción, el trato a los presos políticos, el Concordato. See item 8306.

Cardozo, Luis and others. Bibliografía de la literatura indígena venezolana. See *HLAS 36:1027.*

1327. Carsten, Dietmar M. Letzte Inseln der Glückseligkeit: als Forscher unter den bedrohten Paradiesmenschen in Lateinamerika. Wien, Econ Verlag, 1973. 266 p., plates.

Account of travels among the Campa and Shipibo of Eastern Peru. Author also describes his efforts to enlist the aid of the UN and other agencies on behalf of South American Indians.

1328. Cavalcante, Paulo B. and **Protásio Frikel.** A farmacopéia tiriyó: estudo étno-botânico. Belém, Bra., Conselho Nacional de Pesquisas, Instituto Nacional de Pesquisas da Amazônia, Museu Paraense Emílio Goeldi, 1973. 145 p., map, tables (Publicações avulsas, 24)

Excellent study of plants utilized by the Tiriyó (Trio) of the Brazil-Surinam border in the treatment of disvase. For each of the 171 plants identified (out of 328 collected), information is presented concerning its name, preparation, use, and effect. Final chapter provides a useful summary and classification. See item 1343.

1329. Chrostowski, Marshall S. The ecogeographical characteristics of the Gran Pajonal and their relationships to some Campa Indian cultural patterns (*in* International Congress of Americanists, XXXIX, Lima, 1970. Actas y memorias [see *HLAS 35:510*] v. 4, p. 145-160)

Description of the physical geography and ecology of the area inhabited by the Campa of eastern Peru. Effect of Campa subsistence activities on the environment is also discussed. See item 1335.

1330. Civrieux, Marc de. Clasificación zoológica y botánica entre los makiritare y los kariña (FSCN/A, 36, 1973, p. 3-83, bibl., tables)

Preliminary report of study dealing with the classification of plants and animals by the Makiritare of southern Venezuela and the Kariña of eastern Venezuela. Only a few of the hundreds of names obtained are grouped into categories. See item 1350.

1331. Clastres, Pierre. Chronique des Indiens Guayaki: ce que savent les Aché, chasseurs nomades du Paraguay. Paris, Plon, 1972. 366 p., illus., plates (Terre humaine)

Graphic description of events experienced while studying the Guayaki of eastern Paraguay, used as a framework for presenting popular and sensationalized version of material on Guayaki culture published elsewhere (see *HLAS 31:2088* and *HLAS 33:1530-1531*). Many new details are included, but stress is on practices such as endocannibalism and polyandry which make the Guayaki unique among South American tribes. Not for the squeamish.

1332. Colson, Audrey Butt. Inter-tribal trade in the Guiana highlands. Caracas, Fundación La Salle de Ciencias Naturales, Instituto Caribe de Antropolgía y Sociología, 1973. 70 p., bibl., fold. map, illus., plates, tables (Antropológica, 34)

Based on fieldwork carried out in the 1950s, this article deals primarily with the Akawaio and Arekuna of the upper Mazaruni basin. Trading relationships with other tribes (Makiritare, Patamona, Kamarakoto, Taulebang, Makusi) are outlined. Items traded included graters, blowguns, pottery, and shamanistic paraphernalia. See item 1401.

1333. Cordeu, Edgardo J. Aproximación al horizonte mítico de los tobas (UBAIA/R, 12:1/2, 1969/1970, p. 67-176, bibl., tables)

Elaborate analysis of 87 myths collected from the Toba of the Argentine Chaco. Myths are examined for religious conceptions and for evidence of influence from other areab of South America. Comparisons are made with myths collected by Métraux and others. For folklorist's comment, see *HLAS 36:786*.

1334. Cowell, Adrian. The tribe that hides from man. London, The Bodley Head' 1973. 251 p., maps, plates.

Account of the 1968 expedition led by Cláudio Villas Boas to contact the Kreen-Akrore (Xingu region of Brazil), written by a British film maker. Presents many dramatic vignettes of life in the Xingu National Park and gives some useful data on tribal locations and history. See items 1320 and 1342.

1335. Denevan, William M. Campa subsistence in the Gran Pajonal, eastern Peru (*in* International Congress of Americanists, FXXIX, Lima, 1970. Actas y memorias [see *HLAS 35:510*] v. 4, p. 161-179)

Same as *HLAS 35:1248*.

1336. Dietschy, Hans. L'homme honteux et la femme-crampon (SSA/B, 38, 1974, p. 35-41)

Discusses some themes found in the mythology of the Carajá (central Brazil) and relates these to marriage practices.

1337. Diniz, Edson Soares. Mitos dos índios makuxí (SA/J, 60, 1971, p. 75-103, bibl.)

Twenty-six myths, in Portuguese, collected from the Carib-speaking Makuxí.

1338. _____. O xamanismo dos índios makuxí (SA/J, 60, 1971, p. 65-73, bibl., map)

Brief sketch of beliefs and techniques associated with shamanism among the Makuxi of the Brazil-Guyana border. Material obtainez primarily from one informant.

1339. Eibl-Eibesfeldt, Irenäus. Die Waruwádu (Yuwana) ein kürzlich entdeckter, noch unerforschter Indianerstamm Venezuelas (AI/A, 68:1/2, 1973, p. 137-144, bibl., maps, plates)

Report of a brief visit to hitherto unknown group of Indians recently (1970) contacted by missionaries on the upper Ventuari (southern Venezuela). Language said to be related to Piaroa.

Figueiredo, Napoleão and **Anaíza Vergolino e Silva.** Festas de santos e encantados. See *HLAS 36:852*.

1340. Forno, Mario. I Chavante: le armi (IGM/U, 52:3, maggio/giugno 1972, p. 485-526, bibl., plates, tables)

Description of weapons and hunting techniques used by the Chavante of central Brazil, based on data collected by Antonio Colbacchini.

1341. _____. I Chavente: sintesi culturale e storia dell'acculturazione (IGM/U, 52:6, Nov./Dic. 1972, p. 1237-1274, maps, plates)

Popular history of the Chavante of central Brazil, stressing the missionary activities of the Salesian Order led by the missionary-ethnographer P. Antonio Colbacchini.

1342. Frikel, Protásio. Migração e sobrevivência suiá (USP/RA, 17/20:1, 1969/1972, p. 105-136, bibl., map, tables)

Detailed account, based on traditional history, of the relationship between the Gê-speaking Suiá and other tribes of the Upper Xingu (central Brazil). Demographic data suggest that the 74 remaining Suiá may not survive as a separate tribe. See items 1320 and 1334.

1343. _____ and **Roberto Cortez.** Elementos demográficos do Alto Paru de Oeste, Tumucumaque brasileiro: índios ewarhoyána, kaxúyana e tiriyó. Belém, Bra., Conselho Nacional de Pesquisas, Instituto Nacional de Pesquisas da Amazônia, Museu Paraense Emílio Goeldi, 1972. 103 p., bibl., illus., maps, plates, tables (Publicações avulsas, 19)

Detailed demographic study of remnants of three

Carib-speaking tribes now living at a Franciscan mission in northern Brazil. Data collected by the late Protásio Frikel during the period 1959-70 include composition by age and sex, births, deaths, and spacing of children. Material on Tiriyó (Trio) kinship is included. See item 1328.

1344. Gade, Daniel W. Comercio y colonización en la zona de contacto entre la sierra y las tierras bajas del valle del Urubamba, Perú (*in* International Congress of Americanists, XXXIX, Lima, 1970. Actas y memorias [see *HLAS 35:510*] v. 4, p. 207-221, bibl.)

Historical account of contact between peoples of the highlands and those of the tropical forest from the time of the Inca Empire to the present. Contact situation is described for the Urubamba valley of eastern Peru.

1345. Gancedo, Omar Antonio. Cestería guayaquí (UNLPM/R, 7:42 [Antropología] 1971, p. 67-78, bibl., plates, tables)

Description of types of baskets and techniques of manufacture among the Guayaquí of eastern Paraguay. See item 1331.

1346. ———. Un elemento de alfarería caingua: la pipa (UNLPM/R, 7:47, 26 sept. 1972, p. 225-238, bibl., illus., plates)

Detailed description of pipes smoked by the acculturated Caingua of northern Argentina.

1347. García, Argimiro. Cuentos y tradiciones de los indios guaraúnos. Caracas, Univ. Católica Andrés Bello, Instituto de Investigaciones Históricas, Seminario de Lenguas Indígenas, 1971. 277 p.

These 69 myths, collected over many years by a Capuchin missionary from the Guaraúno (Warao) of the Orinoco delta, were originally published in the journal *Venezuela Misionera*.

1348. Gregor, Thomas A. Publicity, privacy, and Mehinacu marriage (UP/E, 13:4, Oct. 1974, p. 333-349, bibl., illus.)

As in other Xingu tribes, Mehinacu adults engage in frequent extra-marital sexual relationships. Distinctions between spouses and lovers are clearly maintained since spouses always interact in public and lovers only in private. See item 1320.

1349. Hanbury-Tenison, Robin. A question of survival for the Indians of Brazil. Foreword by H.R.H., the Duke of Edinburgh. N.Y., Charles Scribner, 1973. 272 p.

Report of two month survey of 28 tribes, made at the request of the Brazilian government. Presents brief but reasonably objective account of the present (1971) condition of the groups visited, together with a strong appeal for international involvement in Indian survival.

Hartmann, Günther. Die materielle Kultur der Xavante, Zentralbrasilien. See *HLAS 36:4546*.

1350. Hartmann, Thekla. Zur botanischen Nomenklatur der Bororo-Indianer (DGV/ZE, 96:2, 1971, p. 234-249)

Discusses the criteria used by the Bororo of central Brazil in classifying plants and compares the categories found in Bororo classification with those of the Guaraní of Paraguay. See item 1330.

1351. Heinen, H. Dieter. Economic factors in marriage alliance and kinship system among the Winikina-Warao (SCNLS/A, 32, 1972, p. 28-67, bibl., plates, tables)

Considering stated marriage rules, as well as actual patterns of marriage among Winikina sub-tribe of the Warao, author questions conclusion of Suárez (see *HLAS 35:1323*) that Warao once had a two-section system of marriage alliances. Features of kinship terminology that suggest such a system are said to be epiphenomena of residence patterns and economic activities. For material on Warao religion, see item 1413.

1352. ———. Residence rules and household cycles in a Warao subtribe: the case of the Winikina (SCNLS/A, 31, 1972, p. 21-86, illus., maps, tables)

Detailed analysis of post-marital residence patterns among the Warao (Orinoco delta). Although census data show less than half of married couples conforming to matrilocal rule, further analysis in terms of unstated but recognized alternatives explains most exceptions. Includes 48 p. of diagrams of actual households.

1353. ——— and **Kenneth Ruddle.** Ecology, ritual, and economic organization in the distribution of palm starch among the Warao of the Orinoco delta (UNM/JAR, 30:2, Summer 1974, p. 116-138, bibl., map, table)

Traditional Warao rituals all involve the sharing of food, especially palm starch. Authors argue that major rituals serve functions of channeling surplus food between subgroups and accumulating food for distribution during times of food scarcity.

Kensinger, Kenneth M. *Banisteriopsis* usage among the Peruvian Cashinahua. See item 2231.

1354. Knobloch, Franz. Geschichte der Missionen unter den Indianerstämmen des Rio-Negro-Tales (ZMR, 56:4, Okt. 1972, p. 283-304)

Brief historical account (to 1971) of Salesian missions in the upper Negro region of northwestern Brazil. Contains useful lists of missions and Indian villages, together with a classification of the many languages spoken in the area.

1355. Leopoldi, José Sávio. A linguagem social de um mito tenetehara (VOZES, 67:2, março 1973, p. 121-132, bibl.)

Structural analysis of a Tenetehara (eastern Brazil) myth, in which twins are said to be symbolic of society and the jaguar symbolic of nature.

1356. Lévi-Strauss, Claude. Tristes tropiques. Translated from the French by John and Doreen Weightman. N.Y., Atheneum, 1974. 425 p., illus., plates.

New English translation, including four chapters omitted from the 1961 first English ed. (see *HLAS 25:543*) of a classic first published in French in 1955 (see *HLAS 20:561*). Describes the author's travels and research in Brazil in the 1930s.

Levine, Robert M. The first Afro-Brazilian Congress: opportunities for the study of race in the Brazilian Northeast. See item 2049.

1357. Lizot, Jacques. Economie ou société? Quelques thèmes à propos de l'étude d'une communauté d'Amérindiens (SA/J, 60, 1971, p. 137-175, bibl., illus., map, plates, tables)

Primarily an account of the subsistence activities of the central Yanomami of southern Venezuela, this study also deals with demography, kinship, and village structure. Data on relative importance of crops and time spent on daily tasks are presented. Author has now published on all aspects of Yanomami culture except religion (see items 1358 and 1382 as well as *HLAS 33:1283-1285*).

1358. ———. Poisons Yanomami de chasse, de guerre et de pêche (SCNLS/A, 31, 1972, p. 3-20, plates, tables)

The preparation of *curare*, its use on arrow points, and beliefs and myths associated with it are described in detail. Fish poisons are also discussed.

Lucas, Theodore D. Songs of the Shipibo of the Upper Amazon. See *HLAS 36:4606*.

1359. Lukesch, Anton. Aspekte aus der indianischen Gefühlswelt: Kayapó-Ge (DGV/ZE, 97:2, 1972, p. 257-267, bibl.)

Rather superficial account of some of the values and attitudes of the Kayapó of central Brazil. Deals with marriage, children, death, strangers, and age classes, among other things. Based on fieldwork done in 1953-58. See item 1318.

1360. ———. Kontaktaufnahme mit Urwaldindianern—Brasilien—die Asuriní im Xingu-Gebiet (AI/A, 68:5/6, 1973, p. 801-814, bibl., map)

Account of two week stay with little known tribe on the upper Xingu (central Brazil). Group involved, probably Asuriní, will soon become better known, since Trans-Amazonian highway will pass nearby.

1361. Lyon, Patricia J. *ed.* Native South Americans: ethnology of the least known continent. Boston, Mass., Little, Brown, 1974. 433 p., bibl., fold. map, maps, plates, tables.

Excellent collection of articles intended for use in undergraduate courses in South American ethnology. Most articles deal with specific lowland tribes and are relatively recent. In addition to providing introductory comments and suggestions for further reading, editor has translated 12 articles originally published in Portuguese, Spanish and French. Table of contents follows:
Julian H. Steward "American Culture History in the Light of South America" p. 4-22
George Peter Murdock "South American Culture Areas" p. 22-39
John Howland Rowe "A Review of *Outline of South American Cultures*" p. 40-43
John Howland Rowe "Linguistic Classification Problems in South America" p. 43-50
Aryon Dall 'Igna Rodrigues "Linguistic Groups of Amazonia" p. 51-59
Max Schmidt "Comments on Cultivated Plants and Agricultural Methods of South American Indians" p. 60-72
Robert L. Carneiro "Slash-and-Burn Cultivation Among the Kuikuru and Its Implications for Cultural Development in the Amazon Basin" p. 73-91
William M. Denevan "Campa Subsistence in the Gran Pajonal, Eastern Peru" p. 92-110
Curt Nimuendajú "Farming Among the Eastern Timbira" p. 111-119
Fritz W. Up de Graff "Jivaro Field Clearing with Stone Axes" p. 120-121
Robert L. Carneiro "Hunting and Hunting Magic Among the Amahuaca of the Peruvian Montaña" p. 122-133
John Gillin "Barama River Carib Fishing" p. 134-137
Arthur P. Sorensen, Jr. "Multilingualism in the Northwest Amazon" p. 138-158
Walter Edmund Roth "Trade and Barter Among the Guiana Indians" p. 159-166
Darcy Ribeiro "Kadiwéu Kinship" p. 167-183
William H. Crocker "Extramarital Sexual Practices of the Ramkokamekra-Canela Indians: An Analysis of Socio-Cultural Factors" p. 184-194
Robert F. Murphy "Deviance and Social Control I: What Makes Warú Run?" p. 195-201
Robert F. Murphy "Deviance and Social Control II: Borai" p. 202-207
Mischa Titiev "Social Singing Among the Mapuche" p. 208-220
Niels Fock "Mataco Law" p. 221-225
Anthony Leeds "The Ideology of the Yaruro Indians in Relation to Socio-Economic Organization" p. 226-234
Juan Víctor Núñez del Prado B. "The Supernatural World of the Quechua of Southern Peru as Seen from the Community of Qotobamba" p. 238-250

Gerald Weiss "Campa Cosmology" p. 251-266
Julio Cezar Melatti "Myth and Shaman" p. 267-275
Michael J. Harner "The Sound of Rushing Water" p. 276-282
Kenneth M. Kensinger "Cashinahua Medicine and Medicine Men" p. 283-288
Gerardo Reichel-Dolmatoff "Funerary Customs and Religious Symbolism Among the Kogu" p. 289-301
Gertrude E. Dole "Endocannibalism Among the Amahuaca Indians" p. 302-308
Pierre Clastres "Guayaki Cannibalism" p. 309-322
Robert Charles Padeen "Cultural Change and Military Resistance in Araucanian Chile, 1550-1730" p. 327-342
M. Inez Hilger and Margaret Mondlock "Surnames and Time and Distance Measurements Among the Chilean Araucanians" p. 343-354
Udo Oberem "Trade and Trade Goods in the Ecuadorian Montaña" p. 346-257
Protásio Frikel "Notes on the Present Situation of the Xikrín Indians of the Rio Caeteté" p. 358-369
Roque de Barros Laraia " 'Polyandrous Adjustments' in Suruí Society" p. 370-372
Charles Wagley "The Effects of Depopulation upon Social Organization as Illustrated by the Tapirapé Indians" p. 373-376
Charles Wagley "Cultural Influences on Population: A Comparison of Two Tupí Tribes" p. 377-384
Herbert Baldus "Shamanism in the Acculturation of a Tupí Tribe of Central Brazil" p. 385-390
Elmer S. Miller "The Christian Missionary, Agent of Secularization" p. 391-396
José Alvarez "A New Tribe of Toyeri Savages" p. 397-400
"A Guide to the Bibliography of South American Ethnology" p. 401-402
"Bibliography" p. 403-432
"A Note on the Tribal Distribution Map" p. 433.

1362. Manzini, Giorgio Mario. Apuntes acerca de los iuko de la Serranía de Perijá (UA/U, 182, julio/sept. 1971, p. 407-422)

Based on three months fieldwork, this is a superficial account of the culture of the Iuko (Yuco) of northern Colombia. Data are presented relating to the remarkably short stature of the Iuko (men average 4 ft. 6 in.; women, 4 ft. 4 in.). See items 1391 and 1414.

1363. Mareski, Sofía and Oscar Humberto Ferraro comps. Bibliografía sobre datos y estudios etnográficos y antropológicos del Paraguay. Asunción, Centro Paraguayo de Estudios Sociológicos, Centro Paraguayo de Documentación Social, 1972. 143 1. (Documentos y estudios bibliiográficos) (mimeo)

Useful bibliography of studies devoted to the aboriginal populations of Paraguay.

1364. Matta, Roberto da. Ensaios de antropologia estrutural. Petrópolis, Bra., Editôra Vozes, 1973. 173 p., bibl. (Antropologia, 3)

Collection of essays, all previously published, in which structural analysis is applied to Gê myths, the concept of *panema*, a story by Poe, and *Carnaval*.

1365. Mayorga Martínez, Pedro. Costumbres y extinción de los indios del extremo austral. Santiago, Arancibia Hermanos, 1972. 171 p., illus., map, plates.

Popular history of the Indians of Tierra del Fuego, based on standard sources.

1366. Mélo, Veríssimo de. Ensaios de antropologia brasileira. Natal, Bra., Imprensa Universitária, 1973. 172 p., bibl.

Intended primarily for undergraduates, these short essays deal with a wide range of topics from folklore to the assimilation of Japanese into Brazilian society. Several essays contain data derived from author's research.

1367. Montoya Sánchez, Javier. Antología de creencias: mitos, teogonías, cosmogonías, leyendas y tradiciones de algunos grupos aborígenes colombianos. Medellín, Colo., Consejo de Medellín, 1973. 236 p., plates.

Myths collected from many different groups of Colombian Indians. Most of the myths were collected by missionaries and many have been published before.

Morase, Mario A.P. and G.M. Chaves. Onchoceriasis in Brazil: new findings among the Yanomama. See item 2241.

1368. Morey, Nancy C.; Robert V. Morey, Jr.; and Donald J. Metzger. Guahibo band organization (FSCN/A, 36, 1973, p. 83-95, bibl., map, illus.)

Description of the small, bilateral bands of the Guahibo of eastern Colombia. This form of organization is said to keep the population appropriately distributed in relation to the seasonal variation in resources. See item 1369.

1369. Morey, Robert V., Jr. Warfare patterns of the Colombian Guahibo (*in* International Congress of Americanists, XXXIX, Lima, 1970. Actas y memorias [see *HLAS 35:510*] v. 4, p. 59-68)

Analysis of band organization and warfare patterns among the Guahibo of eastern Colombia. Settled, horticultural groups were subject to attack by nomadic hunters, the latter seeking agricultural products, women, or Western trade goods. See item 1368.

1370. Münzel, Mark. The Aché Indians: genocide in Paraguay. Copenhagen, International Work Group for Indigenous Affairs, 1973. 82 p., plates (IWGIA Document, 11)

Firsthand account of the sometimes brutal methods used to force the Aché (Guayaki) of eastern Paraguay to live on reservations. See item 1331.

1371. _____. Notas preliminares sôbre os Kaborí: Makú entre o Rio Negro e o Japurá (USP/RA, 17/20:1, 1969/1972, p. 137-181, bibl., map, tables)

Superficial description of recent history and culture of the Kaborí, an acculturated tribe of northwestern Brazil. Matrilocal residence and high status of women are said to distinguish this group from typical Rio Negro tribes.

1372. Murphy, Yolanda and **Robert F. Murphy.** Women of the forest. N.Y., Columbia Univ. Press, 1974. 236 p., bibl.

Based on fieldwork conducted in 1952-53, this study of the role of women supplements earlier publications on the Mundurucú of central Brazil by Robert F. Murphy (see *Headhunter's heritage,* Berkeley, Univ. of California Press, 1960). Women in traditional villages are said to have relatively high status, even though they are excluded from most religious and political activity. Trappings of male dominance are said to mask male insecurity. Basically Freudian interpretation does not obscure useful ethnographic data on women's activities and attitudes.

Neel, James V. and **W.J. Schull.** Differential fertility and human evolution. See item 2051.

1373. Oliveira, Adélia Engrácia de. Os índios jurúna do Alto Xingu (USPMAE/D, 6:11/12, junho/dez. 1970, p. 7-291, bibl., illus., maps, plates, tables)

Historical and ethnographic account of the Jurúna, a Tupí-speaking tribe that over the last 300 years moved up the Xingu from the Amazon to the Xingu National Park (central Brazil). Especially good on kinship and material culture, monograph deals with all aspects of the culture of the 58 remaining Jurúna. Comparisons are made throughout with Upper Xingu tribes. See items 1320 and 1342.

1374. Oliveira, Roberto Cardoso de. Estruturalismo e estruturalistas na antropologia social (*in* Estruturalismo. 3. ed. Rio, Edições Tempo Brasileiro, 1973, p. 85-96, bibl. [Tempo brasileiro, 15/16]

Brief account, for the uninitiated, of the French structuralist approach in anthropology. Most of the major works by Brazilian anthropologists using this approach are cited.

1375. _____ and **L. de Castro Faria.** O contacto interétnico e o estudo de populações (USP/RA, 12/20:1, 1969/1972, p. 31-48, bibl., map, tables)

Classification of 211 Brazilian tribes both on a regional basis and in terms of whether or not they have remained relatively isolated. Intent is to provide a basis for future comparative studies, either cultural or biological.

1376. Palavecino, Enrique. Mitos de los indios tobas (UBAIA/R, 12, pts. 1/2, 1969/70, p. 177-197)

Eighteen short myths, translated into Spanish, collected over many years from the Toba of the western Chaco. For folklorist's comment, see *HLAS 36:802.*

Pellizzaro, Siro M. Cultura shuar: una civilización desconocida. See *HLAS 36:933.*

1377. Persson, Lars. Indianskt moleri fron Amazonas. Stockholm, Moderna Museet, 1973. 32 p., bibl., illus., plates.

Catalogue of exhibition of paintings by the Cubeo Indians from the Vaupés-Caquetá district of Colombia. Erroneously known as "bark paintings," they are painted on elastic sheets pounded from the oahómo tree. Colors used chiefly are: black (derived from coal), red (from a moharió-bush fruit), and yellow (from the toyolbó root). An integral part of the Indians' life, the paintings are highly symbolic. Author regrets lack of appreciation for them in Colombia and fears that when tribe becomes "civilized" their art will die. [Renata V. Shaw]

Peters, John Fred. Demography of the Shirishana. See item 2053.

1378. Pierce, B. Edward. Status competition and personal networks: informal social organization among the Nengre of Paramaribo (RAI/M, 8:4, Dec. 1973, p. 580-591, bibl.)

Description of patterns of social interaction among the Nengre (Creoles), the largest lower class ethnic group in Paramaribo, Surinam. Kinship is less important than friendship in this group, but upward mobility tends to restrict personal networks.

1379. Política indigenista del Brasil (III/A, 32, dic. 1972, p. 53-62, tables)

General and idealistic description of the operation of the Brazilian Indian Service (Fundação Nacional do Indio) as of 1972.

Pollak-Eltz, Angelina. El concepto de múltiples almas y algunos ritos fúnebres entre los negros americanos. See item 1280.

_____. Cultos afroamericanos. See item 1281.

1380. _____. María Lionza: mito y culto venezolano. Caracas, Univ. Católica Andrés Bello, Instituto de Investigaciones Históricas, 1972. 72 p., bibl.

Description and analysis of modern non-Christian mediumistic cult which is becoming increasingly popular in Venezuela, especially among the urban poor. Similar to Umbanda and other Afro-Brazilian religions, the cult of María Lionza has been strongly influenced by the Santería of Cuba. Interpretation offered stresses psychological functions.

Powlinson, Paul S. The application of Propp's functional analysis to a Yagua folktale. See *HLAS 36:771*.

1381. Pressel, Esther. Umbanda in São Paulo: religious innovation in a developing society (*in* Bourguignon, Erika ed. Religion, altered states of consciousness, and social change. Columbus, Ohio State Univ. Press, 1973, p. 264-318, bibl., plates)

Best description to date of Umbanda, a thriving mediumistic religous cult practiced throughout Brazil. Author analyzes the cult on several levels, relating its popularity both to social stresses and personality problems.

1382. Ramos, Alcida R. How the Sanumá acquire their names (UP/E, 13:2, April 1974, p. 171-185, bibl., tables)

Among the Sanúma (Yanomamö sub-tribe, southern Venezuela), children are given names of animals killed during a ritual hunt. Author relates this practice to kinship and other variables. See item 1357.

1383. Ramos, Arthur. Introdução à antropologia brasileira: as culturas indígenas. Rio, Casa do Estudante do Brasil, 1971? 316 p., bibl., illus., map, plate (Col. Arthur Ramos, 2)

Reissue of a book on Brazilian Indians that was first published over 30 years ago and is now sadly out of date.

1384. Raposo, Gabriel Viriato. Ritorno alla maloca: autobiografia di un indio Makuxí. Torino, Italy, Eidizioni Missioni Consolata, 1972. 123 p., plates (Col. Incontri, 6)

Brief autobiography of an acculturated Macuxí Indian of northern Brazil. Author discusses his military service, his role as chief, and his interaction with Catholic and Protestant missionaries.

1385. Reichel-Dolmatoff, Gerardo. The cultural context of an aboriginal hallucinogen: *Banisteriopsis Caapi* (*in* Furst, Peter T. ed. Flesh of the gods. N.Y., Praeger, 1972, p. 84-113)

Interesting interpretation of the use of *yajé* (*ayahuasca*) among the Tukano of eastern Colombia. Hallucinations produced by the drug are related to mythology and art motifs. Data are not always distinguishable from author's Freudian interpretation. See *HLAS 33:1618*.

1386. Ridgwell, W.M. The forgotten tribes of Guyana. London, Tom Stacey, 1972. 248 p., map.

Deals primarily with politics, but contains some information about treatment of Indians during the 1969 uprisings.

1387. Riester, Jürgen. Medizinmänner und Zauberer der Chiquitano-Indianer (DGV/ZE, 96:2, 1971, p. 250-265, illus., plates)

Although baptized Catholics, the Chiquitano of eastern Bolivia retain an elaborate set of beliefs relating to shamanism, curing, and sorcery. Author describes belief system and analyzes political authority that shamans often have. .

1388. _____. Die Pauserna-Guarašug ẁä: Monographie eines Tupí-Guaraní-Volkes in Ostbolivien. Bonn, Verlag des Anthropos-Instituts, 1972. 562 p., illus. (Col. Instituti Anthropos, 3)

Based on seven months' fieldwork, this monograph describes the material culture and religion of one of the last Tupí-speaking tribes in eastern Bolivia. Over 150 p. are devoted to myths. In 1970 the 50 inhabitants of the last Guarašug ẁä village scattered to neighboring towns, so in a sense this volume is a memorial. It is handsomely illustrated.

1389. Robinson, Scott S. Shamanismo entre los kofan (*in* International Congress of Americanists, XXXIX, Lima, 1970. Actas y memorias [see *HLAS 35:510*] v. 4, p. 89-93)

Brief sketch of the training and activities of the curer among the Kofan of the Colombia-Ecuador border. Using *ayahuasca* and manipulating magical arrows, the Kofan curer fits the typical montaña shamanistic pattern.

Rodrigues, José Carlos Sousa and **Rosine Perelberg.** Introdução bibliográfica: comentada à antropologia. See *HLAS 36:877*.

1390. Romero Moreno, María Eugenia. Algunos aspectos sobre la localización y situación de los grupos indígenas de la región oriental de Colombia (III/AI, 33:2, April/June 1973, p. 349-353)

Brief survey of surviving tribes of eastern Colombia (no sources are cited), together with an appeal for better treatment of the Indians.

1391. Ruddle, Kenneth. The hunting technology of the Maracá Indians (SCNLS/A, 25, 1970, p. 21-63, bibl., illus., plates)

Detailed descriptions of weapons and hunting techniques used by the Maracá (Yuco) of northeastern Colombia (Sierra de Perijá). Most animals and birds hunted are identified as to species. Data on supernatural beliefs associated with hunting are included. See item 1362.

1392. Salzano, Francisco M. and others. Problemas indígenas brasileiros (SBPC/CC, 24:11, nov. 1972, p. 1015-1023)

Author uses brief history of Brazilian Indian Service to support argument that concern for national development now outweighs most other considerations in dealing with Brazil's remaining Indians.

1393. Santos, Sílvio Coelho dos. Indios e brancos no sul do Brasil: a dramática experiência dos Xokleng. Florianópolis, Bra., EDEME, 1973. 313 p., bibl., maps, plates, tables.

Detailed history of a tribe made famous by Jules Henry in *Jungle people* (N.Y., Knopf, 1941). Once widespread in Santa Catarina and adjoining states, the Xokleng (Kaingáng) were in conflict with Brazilian settlers until 1910. Today they live impoverished on three reservations. Unfortunately their social system has been so modified that Santos was unable to verify or correct any of the bizarre details reported by Henry.

1394. ———. Sobrevivência e assistência de indígenas no sul do Brasil (Anais do Museu de Antropologia [n.p.] 4, dez. 1971, p. 5-24)

Author sketches the present condition of the few tribes remaining in the southernmost Brazilian states, then offers a number of highly specific suggestions for a policy that would improve the lot of the Indians.

Schauer, Stanley and others. Aspectos de la cultura material de grupos étnicos de Colombia. See item 1932.

1395. Schultz, Harald and **Vilma Chiara.** Mais lendas waurá (SA/J, 60, 1971, p. 105-135, bibl., illus.)

Portuguese translation of 13 myths collected by the late Harald Schultz from the Waurá of the Upper Xingu (central Brazil).

1396. Schwerin, Karl H. Arawak, Carib, Ge, Tupi: cultural adaptation and culture history in the tropical forest, South America (*in* International Congress of Americanists, XXXIX, Lima, 1970. Actas y memorias [see *HLAS 35:510*] v. 4, p. 39-57, bibl.)

Speculative reconstruction, based on early historical accounts and linguistic evidence, of the movements of major linguistic groups in precolumbian lowland South America.

1397. Seijas, Haydée. El susto como categoría etiológica (AVAC/ACV, 23:3, 1972, p. 176-178, bibl.)

Data from the Sibundoy of southern Colombia are used to support the argument that *susto* as an explanation of illness is more readily understood from a cultural than a psychological perspective. Good bibliography.

1398. Siffredi, Alejandra. Hierofanías y concepciones mítico-religiosas de los tehuelches meridionales (UBAIA/R, 12:1/2, 1969/1970, p. 247-271, bibl.)

Based both on historical sources and recent research, this useful attempt to systematize the religious beliefs of the Tehuelche must remain somewhat doubtful, since traditional Tehuelche culture has long since disappeared. See also item 1325. For folklorist's comment se *HLAS 36:809*.

1399. Siskind, Janet. To hunt in the morning. N.Y., Oxford Univ. Press, 1973. 214 p., illus., maps, plates, tables.

Highly personalized, somewhat popular account of fieldwork among the Sharanahua, a small Panoan-speaking group on the upper Purús (Peru-Brazil border). Describes subsistence activities, kinship system, male-female relationships, use of hallucinogenic drugs, and curing. Author lived intimately with her informants, presents the culture from the perspective of a few close friends. Good account of the effects of taking *ayahuasca*.

1400. La situación del indígena en América del Sur: aportes al estudio de la fricción inter-étnica en los indios noandinos. Montevideo, Biblioteca Científica, 1972. 510 p., bibl., maps, plates, tables.

Collection of papers presented at a symposium of anthropologists organized by the Institute of Ethnology, Univ. of Bern, and held in Bridgetown, Barbados, Jan. 1971. Each paper deals generally with the current status of indigenous populations in a given nation, then presents demographic data for all known tribes, together with their location. This very useful compilation is combined with a strong appeal for better treatment of the Indians, summed up in the "Declaration of Barbados" which has attracted international attention.

Soto Olguín, Alvaro. Mitos de los cubeo. See *HLAS 36:930*.

Spielman, Richard S.; E.C. Migliazza; and **James V. Neel.** Regional, linguistic and genetic differences among the Yanomama Indians. See item 2125.

Stahle, Vera-Dagny. Carreras ceremoniales con troncos entre indios brasileños. See *HLAS 36:883*.

1401. Thomas, David J. The indigenous trade system of southeast Estado Bolívar, Venezuela (SCNLS/A, 33, 1972, p. 3-37, bibl. map, tables)

Detailed analysis of trade relationships among the Pemon, Makiritare (Yecuana), and Makuxi. Focusing on the Pemon, author describes trade partnerships and the role of kinship in the movement of goods. Both indigenous items (canoes, graters) and trade goods (shotguns, beads) are involved. Parallels are drawn between the rules governing trade and those governing marriage. See item 1332.

1402. Varese, Stefano. The Forest Indians in the present political situation of Peru. Copenhagen, International Work

Group for Indigenous Affairs, 1972. 28 p., map, tables (IWGIA Document, 8)

General discussion of the present status of the estimated 220,000 Indians of eastern Peru, together with a few suggestions for involving them in the agrarian reform program. Map and list of tribes included.

1403. Villas Bôas, Orlando and **Cláudio Villas Bôas.** Indios do Xingu. Fotos de W. Jesco von Puttkamer. Ilustrações de José Lanzelotti. São Paulo, Gráficos Brunner, 1973. 43 p., illus., plates.

Short, general, popular book, with text in Portuguese and English. Excellent photographs.

1404. _____ and _____. Xingu: the Indians, their myths. Edited by Kenneth S. Brecher. Translated by Susana Hertelendy Rudge. Drawings by Wacupiá. N.Y., Farrar, Straus and Giroux, 1973. 270 p., illus., maps.

English translation of *Xingu: os indios, seus mitos*, see HLAS 35:1328.

1405. Vivante, Armando and **Omar Antonio Gancedo.** Nuevas observaciones sobre el arco y la flecha de los guayaquí (UNLPM/R, 7:44 [Antropología] 1972, p. 109-155, bibl., illus., plates, tables)

Description of the manufacture and use of bows and arrows among the Guayaquí of eastern Paraguay. See item 1331.

1406. Wallis, Ethel Emily. Aucas downriver, Dayuma's story today. N.Y., Harper & Row, 1973. 126 p., illus., plates.

Dramatic account of the continuing efforts to missionize the Aucas of eastern Ecuador. Provides insights into the motivation and procedures of the Wycliffe Bible Translators.

1407. Watson, Lawrence C. Defense mechanisms in Guajiro personality and culture (UNM/JAR, 30:1, Spring 1974, p. 17-34, bibl.)

Author uses psychological data from study of Guajiro (Guajira peninsula) to consider whether Freud's concept of defense mechanisms can be used in all societies. Concludes that such mechanisms have widespread occurrence in personality processes.

1408. _____. Marriage and sexual adjustment in Guajiro society (UP/E, 12:2, April 1973, p. 153-161, bibl.)

In spite of severe sexual socialization of Guajiro girls (see HLAS 35:1331), positive sexual adaptation to marriage is the rule. Data are used to question theory that negative fixation in children inevitably produces conflict and anxiety in adults.

1409. Watson-Franke, Maria-Barbara. Tradition und Urbanisation: Guajiro-Frauen in der Stadt. Wien, Univ. Wien, Institut für Völkerkunde, 1972. 154 p., bibl., (Acta ethnologica et linguistica, 26. Series Americana, 6)

Life histories of 40 Guajiro women who moved to a suburb of Maracaibo are discussed. Women in the city have lower status and less security than women living the traditional life, but they have more freedom and most adapt fairly readily to the new environment.

1410. _____. Zur Desintegration eines matrilinearen Verwandtschaftssystems: die Position des Mutterbruders bei den Guajiro (SCNLS/A, 25, 1970, p. 3-20, bibl.)

Changing role of the mother's brother is used to illustrate the breakdown of matrilineal institutions which follows the movement of Guajiro to the suburbs of Maracaibo, Ven.

1411. Weiss, Gerald. Campa cosmology (in International Congress of Americanists, XXXIX, Lima, 1970. Actas y memorias [see *HLAS 35:510*] v. 4, p. 189-206)

Same as HLAS 35:1333.

1412. _____. Campa organization (AAA/AE, 1:2, May 1974, p. 379-403, bibl., tables)

Sketch of the major institutions of Campa society (eastern Peru), presented as test of "theoretical model" for analysis of "cultural organization." See item 1321.

1413. Wilbert, Johannes. Tobacco and shamanistic ecstasy among the Warao Indians of Venezuela. (*in* Furst, Peter T. ed. Flesh of the gods. N.Y., Praeger, 1972, p. 55-83)

Detailed account of the unusually complex belief system associated with shamanism among the Warao (Orinoco delta). Tobacco is used in curing, sorcery, and initiation and is relied upon to produce trance and dreams. For material on Warao kinship, see items 1352 and 1353.

1414. Wustmann, Erich. Unterwegs zu Zwergindianern in Kolumbien. Wien, Verlag J. Neumann-Neudamm, 1973. 227 p., illus., plates.

Travel book describing visits to several tribes (Guajiro, Tairona, Arhuaco) of northern Colombia. The "dwarfs" of the title are the Yuco, whose unusually short stature is documented in a number of photographs. See items 1362 and 1391.

1415. Zerries, Otto and **Meinhard Schuster.** Mahekodotedi: monographie eines Dorfes der Waika-Indianer "Yanoama" am oberen Orinoco "Venezuela." Mit einem Beitrag von Kurt Reinhard. München, FRG, Renner Verlag, 1974. 443 p., illus., maps (Ergebnisse der Frobenius-Expedition nach Südost-Venezuela, 2)

Comprehensive, solidly-researched monograph, including drawings and pictures, of the life of the Waika Indians in the Upper Orinoco. [H.J. Hoyer]

ETHNOLOGY
SOUTH AMERICA: HIGHLANDS

LESLIE ANN BROWNRIGG
Consultant-Anthropologist
Ecuadorian-Peruvian Mixed Commission
for the Utilization of the Hydraulic
Binational Basins of Puyango-Tumbes
and Catamayo-Chira

SOCIOCULTURAL SYSTEMS ARE NO WHERE STATIC. An important theme of many selections in the present bibliographical review is analysis of the effects of macrosocial changes within national political economies at the level of local sociocultural systems.

Given the self-conscious change-oriented program, policies and innovative laws of several Andean nations, a major category is evaluations of government actions. Agrarian reform is preeminently assessed. In the cases from Bolivia, a time depth of over two decades since the promulgation of land reform in 1953 lends conclusiveness to observations. Instrumentation of a universal law was differentiated locally by ecological conditions, community forms and patterns of stratification as noted by Heath (item 1486), Heyduk (item 1489), Leons (in an unpublished dissertation which, together with others available from University Microfilms, is listed at the end of this introduction) Burke (item 1442), and Simmons (item 1534).

Social forms generated by land reform are presently well institutionalized in Bolivia. These include continuities in traditional structures, such as the perpetuation of landlords' power (see Graef item 1478), external domination (see Havet item 1485) and hierarchies of privilege among peasants (see Heyduk item 1488), as well as emergent phenomenon: syndicate organization (see McEwen item 1503), independent political status for ex-hacienda communities which bring about realignments and creations in the political and economic functions of towns (see Buechler item 1439, Guillet item 1480, Aaron-Schaar item 1426, and Burke item 1442 and Clark's unpublished dissertation).

From accounts of the Peruvian agrarian reform program after the 1969 law emerges only the proverbial description of an elephant by blindmen feeling one part of the beast. Skeptical opinions of the law's overall intentions or of its instrumentation by all too human agents see the program as an intensified exploitation of the peasantry (see Stein item 1539), a paternalistic imposition of the agricultural technician's preference for monocrop cultivation (see Conlin item 1456), a reassertion and intensification of hierarchies among employees and types of rural proletariat (see Horton items 1439 and 1492). In item 1507, Martínez explains a related 1970 law reorganizing peasant communities. The historical work of Davies (item 1460) is related in specifying governmental policy toward a cultural minority. Clearly the instrumentation of the 1969 agrarian reform law, which is itself tailored to diverse circumstances and not a universal law, is bringing unanticipated results. The critical tone of many reports appear addressed to the Peruvian government and testify to the observers' faith in the sincerity of the program, despite disparities between the ideal and its actualization.

Reports on the agrarian reform program of the Unidad Popular government of Chile (1970-73) include a film by the Chile Communications Project of FAO (item 1459) and a government document on the reform's impact on the Mapuche problem (item 1451).

Other studies which focus on the Mapuche are by Dowling (item 1464), Hilger (item 1490), Lomnitz (item 1502), Millape Canuiqueo (item 1513), San Martín Ferrari (item 1532), and Titiev (item 1543).

Stearman's article on colonization (item 1538) offers comments on that aspect of agrarian reform in Bolivia. Soles' unpublished dissertation on rural land invasions deals in part with Colombian agrarian reform. Brownrigg (item 1436) traces the alliance of Ecuador's agrarian elite with other interest groups to produce counter-reform as well as *coup d'états*.

Government sponsored change programs less holistic than agrarian reform have also inspired evaluation. Problems related to bilingual education are discussed by Dubly in item 1466 and by Vega-Cadima in his unpublished dissertation on schooling, acculturation and nationality. Núñez del Prado (item 1521) and McEwen (item 1504) describe government community development programs in Peru and Bolivia respectively.

A macrosocial change program of an important non-governmental agency, the Roman Catholic Church, to reevangelize in dialogue with native religious traditions is amply reflected. Marzal (item 1508) and Berthelot (item 1430) provide good general views of the social science and theological controversies regarding this movement, which contextualize the orientations of such studies of native religious practices as appear in *Allpanchis Phuturinqa* (items 1418-1421) including Barrionuevo (item 1427), Cáceres Olazo (item 1444), Casaverde Rojas (item 1448), Cayon Armelia (item 1449) Flores Ochoa (item 1473), Marzal (item 1509), Michaud (item 1511), Núñez del Prado (item 1522), and Tamayo Herrera (item 1542). Other studies of Andean religion not related to this reevangelization movement include those by Earls (item 1467), Ossio (item 1526) and Tortosa (item 1544), as well as unpublished dissertations: by Bastien on Qollahuaya ritual, Cole on the human soul in Aymara culture, Kagen on the Virgin of Bojaca, Custed on symbols and control in an Andean community, and Sharon on a Peruvian *curandero*.

Macrosocial changes which are reflected in governmental policy changes and particular institutional programs but which are of more diffuse ("superorganic") character are those in the political economies of the Andean nations. Changes triggered involved differentiations of roles, classes and status and redistributions of the population. Among the most obvious are physical migrations.

Urban-ward migration typically involves not only geographical but also social mobility and the modification of one set of economic and social strategies (such as in peasant agriculture and small-town commerce) in favor of adjustment to and the creation of strategies suitable in an urban environment. Studies which illuminate aspects of these urbanization processes include those by Brownrigg (item 1437), Andrews and Phillips (item 1423), Flinn (item 1470), Hargous-Vogel (item 1483), Harkness (item 1484), Jongkind (item 1496), Leeds (items 1499-1500), Nett (item 1520), Roberts (items 1176), M. Smith (item 1536), Uzzell (items 1545-1546) and Whiteford (item 1554). Three unpublished dissertations on rural to urban migration processes are by Ashton on the differential adaptation of two slum groups; Moles, on Quechua Spanish bilinguals in Peru; and Uzzell, on the adaptation of migrants in Lima.

Celestino (item 1450); Dipolo and Suárez (item 1461); and Escobar (item 1469) deal with outmigration from the perspective or rural communities. Two studies which discuss the ties of urban residents to their communities of origin are Myers (item 1518) and Roberts (item 1176).

Migration to the remaining frontiers within each Andean nation is accelerating, extending economic development, national culture and economic enclaves (e.g. petroleum fields, lumber operations and cattle ranches) into the remote Amazonian and Pacific littoral "jungle" regions. Whitten has made conceptually paired studies of the interaction of entrepreneurial settler *serranos* moving into both of these zones in Ecuador with the respective entrenched cultures of each. His work on the lowland Quechua in the Oriente Puyo area is still in manuscript form, but the study of the "gente morena" or "Blacks" of the northwest littoral are published (item 1555 and 1556). Varese's model of the types of contact between highland and Peruvian montaña peoples (item 1547) provides a general framework, which is validated by four case studies: of the Campa by Bodley (item 1432), of the Cuiva by Arcand (item 1425), of the Aguaruna by Siverts (item 1535), and of the Amuesha by Smith (item 1537). The latter were published by the International Work Group of Indigenous Affairs in Copenhagen, an outlet for advocate anthropologists concerned with the often tragic social and demographic consequences of the massive cultural change created by contact. The term ethnocide, which refers to the destruction from whatever intention of the lifeway of a distinct culture, keynotes the tone of their alarm. In the periodicals *Indígena* (P.O. Box 4073, Berkeley, Calif. 94704) and *Akwesasne Notes* (Mohawk Nation, via Rooseveltown, N.Y. 13683) appear brief articles of a similar theme, for the Andean Amazon as well as other South and Middle American regions (see items 1513 and 1528).

The adjustment of settler colonists in the new montaña or Amazonian environment creates special cultural patterns. Stearman (item 1538) discusses outposts of highland, national culture as do unpublished dissertations by Hawkins on Mitu, Colombia, and by McDaniel on culture and disease in a South American montaña settlement.

The cultural patterning of sex roles in society respond more subtly to macrosocial, political-economic changes. Cohen's studies of the first generation of Colombian university graduate professionally trained women (items 1452-1453); M. Smith's study of domestic service as a mobility tactic for young provincial women migrants to Lima (item 1536); Chaney's profile of women politicians emerging in Peru and Chile (item 8366a); and Harkness' comparison of the values of women among poor recent migrants and wealthier, longer-term residents in Bogotá (item 1484) all illustrate trends in the reinterpretation of the role of Latin women, as specified by class as well as gender. Unfortunately, there is an inadequate corpus of sex role studies in more traditional circumstances, against which new dynamics would become clearer. Some background is provided by DeGrys' unpublished dissertation on women's role in a Peruvian north coast fishing village, Flores Ochoa (item 1472), and Whitten (item 1557 and chapters in item 1555). A precise description of the role cooperation between men and women in the operation of the footplow by Gade (item 1476) constitutes data of this type as much as Bolton's report of the intercouple bonds among the Qolla (item 1433) or the articles in the Andean Life Cycle issue of *Allpanchis* (item 1420).

Beyond the topical theme of the intervention of national political economy in local socio-cultural systems, selections in this bibliography represent a continuity of some theoretical approaches to Andean culture and the introduction of relatively new approaches to the corpus.

The vertical ecology hypothesis (see *HLAS 35*, p. 106) rests behind studies by Browman (item 1435), Brush (item 1438), Webster (item 1551) and the Alberti and Meyer collection (item 1417). Unpublished dissertations concerned with the vertical ecology hypothesis include those by Brush on subsistence strategies; Custed on symbols and control; and Thomas on human adaptation.

Structural analysis underlies articles by Earls (items 1467-1468) and Isbell (item 1495) as well as both their unpublished dissertations: Earls' on Andean cosmology and Isbell's on Andean structures and activities.

Traditional community study style presentation and functionalist notions are represented by Celestino (item 1450), Escobar (item 1469), Núñez del Prado (item 1521), and Simmons (item 1534) as well as in the unpublished dissertations of Hooks on Pequín, Hutchinson on Acolla, and Oliver Smith on Yungay Norte. All of these community studies deal with social change situations and are diachronic, so enlivening with dynamics a highly sophisticated application of this methodology.

Psychological approaches to Andean culture, a relatively new trend, appear in Dobkin de Ríos (item 1462), Micklin, Durbin and Leon (item 1512), Gobeil (item 1477), and Naranjo (item 1519).

A basic controversy in developing in Andean literature over the theory suitable for the analysis of power minority groups, whose member status is marked by differences in language or social dialect, wealth, customary lifestyle, access to social and economic resources and/or phenotype. Stein in item 1539 argues convincingly for a framework of class analysis and the intrepretation of such differences as characteristics of class culture. Casagrande's item 1447 and Stutzman's unpublished dissertation adopt a concept of ethnicity and write in terms of inter-ethnic stratification.

Ethnicity theory is associated with anthropological studies of African, Southeast Asian, modern industrial European and North American societies, and of polities newly independent from colonial domination, especially British or Dutch administration which left "plural societies" in their wake. Ethnicity theory is applied where several named, generally group-conscious ethnolinguistic segments, which may display class stratification internally, are in interaction. This condition is best met in the Andean Amazon region, yet Varese's writings on such an area in Peru (item 1402, 1547 and 1548) recognize that inter-ethnic relations are also class relations.

In most Andean contexts reported there are only two "ethnic" groups in interaction—"Indians" and "mestizos;" *serranos* and *costeños*—and at best three, whether distinguished by language (Aymara, Quechua, Spanish) or social race (Indian, Black, White): see for example, Primov (item 1529) and Leons' unpublished dissertation. Greaves comments upon the rough fit of such theories in item 1479.

A theoretical perspective blending the two approaches or justly alternating between both yields fruitful analysis. Flores (item 1471) examines the tenacious assertion by *mistis* in a small Cuzco dept. town of the few minor traits which distinguish them from surrounding Indians. Orlove (item 1525) argues convincingly that rural craftsmen embedded in the social obligation of peasant communities are, in culture and in class affiliation, also peasants, whereas the interests and lifestyle of craftsmen practicing in a town center are integrated with those of the petty merchants. Stein (item 1539) inveighs that emphasis by anthropologists of the cultural differentness of Indians, devoid of an explanatory analysis rooted in the social relations of production, abets the ideological justification of superordination and mestizo/white domination of Indians.

Where "traditional" agrarian "internal colonial" social relations still flourish, status barriers between classes accentuate class culture. In the dynamic sites of social mobility, where local class cultures are in fluid formation, the concept of ethnicity is less useful. Miller (item 1514) describes a typical rural economic enclave. Having read other studies by William Stein, Javier Albó and Adrian de Wind in manuscript form on similar rural sites of rapid social change, I am convinced that studies of the economic enclaves represent an important strategy for resolving some of these theoretical issues.

I would like to thank those colleagues who responded to my request for citations and copies of their work: your care and participation has enriched the review process. I would also like to thank the students in the winter quarter 1975 course "Peoples of Latin America" at Northwestern Univ., who, as a collectivity, served as research assistants for this project. The names of those students who contributed individual reviews appear in parenthesis after their works.

Literature from, as well as about, the Andean nations is under-represented, reflecting only the difficulty of obtaining works published in journals and limited editions from South America in the US. *Nispa Ninchis* (Apartado 4771, Lima, or 515 Dryden Road, Ithaca, N.Y. 14850), which issues occasional bibliographic bulletins, is the only regular source, though citations appear in the *Newsletter of the AA Latin American Anthropology Group* (1703 New Hampshire Avenue, N.W., Washington, D.C. 20009), in the *Boletin de Antropologia Ecuatoriana* (Dept. of Anthropology, Univ. of Illinois, Urbana, Ill. 61801) as well as in the standard journals. Hopefully, your reviewer will be able to collect materials in Peru which will appear in the next volume, *HLAS 39*.

Finally, the bans on social science research in Chile have interrupted the career of many Chilean scholars. Zúñiga's "The Experimenting Society and Radical Reform: the Role of the Social Scientist in Chile's Unidad Popular Experience" (item 1559) as well as San Martín Ferrari's item 1532 give some idea of the contribution of social scientists during the Unidad Popular years.

Recent doctoral dissertations (1969-74) published through University Microfilms of interest in the field are listed below:

DOCTORAL DISSERTATIONS
(available from University Microfilms, Ann Arbor, Mich.)

1969-1974

Ailinger, Rita Louise. Illness referral system of Latin American immigrant families. The Catholic Univ. of America, 1974. (Microfilm Order No. 74-19409)
Ashton, Guy Theodore. The differential adaptation of two slum groups and working-

class segment to a housing project in Cali, Colombia. Univ. of Illinois at Urbana-Champaign, 1972. (Microfilm Order No. 73-9869)

Bastien, Joseph W. Qollahuaya ritual: an ethnographic account of the symbolic relation of man and land in an Andean village. Cornell Univ., 1973. (Microfilm Order No. 74-7168)

Brush, Stephen Bourne. Subsistence strategies and vertical ecology in an Andean community: Uchucmarca, Peru. Univ. of Wisconsin at Madison, 1973. (Microfilm Order No. 73-23056)

Clark, Evelyn Kiatipoff. Agrarian reform and developmental change in Parotani, Bolivia. Indiana Univ., 1970. (Microfilm Order No. 70-26912)

Cole, John Tafel. The human soul in the Aymara culture of Pumasara: an ethnographic study in the light of George Herbert Mead and Martin Buber. Univ. of Pennsylvania, 1969. (Microfilm Order No. 69-21336).

Custed, Harry Glynn, Jr. Symbols and control in a high altitude Andean community. Indiana Univ., 1973. (Microfilm Order No. 73-19737)

De Grys, Mary Schweitzer. Women's role in a north coast fishing village in Peru: a study in male dominance and female subordination. New School for Social Research, 1973. (Microfilm Order No. 74-19516)

Earls, John Charles. Andean continuum cosmology. Univ. of Illinois at Urbana-Champaign, 1973. (Microfilm Order No. 74-5557)

Forman, Sylvia Helen. Law and conflict in rural highland Ecuador. Univ. of California at Berkeley, 1972. (Microfilm Order No. 74-14344)

Hawkins, Harlan Glenn. Mitú, Colombia: a geographical analysis of an isolated border town. Univ. of Florida, 1972. (Microfilm Order No. 73-569)

Himes, James. The utilization of research for development: two case studies in rural modernization and agriculture in Peru. Princeton Univ., 1972. (Microfilm Order No. 72-24682)

Hooks, Paul. Pequín: land tenure and social organization in a northeastern Venezuelan village. Univ. of California at Los Angeles, 1973. (Microfilm Order No. 73-13144)

Hutchinson, William B. Sociocultural change in the Mantaro Valley region of Peru: Acolla, a case study. Indiana Univ., 1973. (Microfilm Order No. 74-9429)

Isbell, Billie Jean. Andean structures and activities: toward a study of transformations of traditional concepts in a central highland peasant community. Univ. of Illinois at Urbana-Champaign, 1973. (Microfilm Order No. 74-12052)

James, William. Household composition and domestic groups in a highland Colombian village. Univ. of Wisconsin at Madison, 1972. (Microfilm Order No. 72-23743)

Kagan, Harold. The Virgen of Bojacá: miracles and change in a Colombian peasant community. Univ. of California at Riverside, 1973. (Microfilm Order No. 73-23831)

Leons, William. Dimensions of pluralism in a changing Bolivian community. Pennsylvania State Univ., 1972. (Microfilm Order No. 73-14009)

McDaniel, John M. Culture and disease in a South American montaña settlement: a study of behavior and disease among La Gente and Los Serranos de Concepción, Peru. Univ. of Pennsylvania, 1972. (Microfilm Order No. 73-13434)

Mitchell, William P. The system of power in Quinua: a community of the central Peruvian highlands. Univ. of Pittsburgh, 1972. (Microfilm Order No. 73-1647)

Moles, Jerry Allen. Speak as you can: classification of and behavior toward other persons by Quechua-Spanish bilinguals in Peru. Stanford Univ., 1973. (Microfilm Order No. 73-14945)

Ocampo, Alfredo. Variations in value-orientations of elites and last year high school students in three provincial capitals of western Colombia. Columbia Univ., 1972. (Microfilm Order No. 73-29857)

Oliver-Smith, Anthony R. Yungay Norte: disaster and social change in the Peruvian highlands. Indiana Univ., 1973. (Microfilm Order No. 74-13533)

Soles, Roger Edward. Rural land invasions in Colombia: a study of the macro- and micro-conditions leading to peasant unrest. Univ. of Wisconsin, 1972. (Microfilm Order No. 73-7220)

Stutzman, Ronald Lee. Black Serranos: a study of the racial dimensions of social identity in highland Ecuador. Univ. of Washington, 1974. (Microfilm Order No. 74-22549)

Thomas, Randall Brooke. Human adaptation to high Andean energy flow system. Pennsylvania State Univ., 1972. (Microfilm Order No. 72-33211)

Uzzell, John Douglas. Bound for places I'm not known to: adaptation of migrants and residence in four irregular settlements in Lima, Peru. Univ. of Texas at Austin, 1972. (Microfilm Order No. 73-7665)

Vega-Cadima, Hugo Lizardo. Schooling, acculturation, and development of a sense of nationality among Indian school children in the Peruvian highlands. Univ. of Wisconsin, 1972. (Microfilm Order No. 73-9296)

Abelson, Andrew E.; T.S. Baker; and **Paul T. Baker.** Altitude, migration, and fertility in the Andes. See item 2192.

1416. Alberti, Giorgio. The breakdown of provincial urban power structure and the rise of peasant movements. Madison, Univ. of Wisconsin at Madison, Land Tenure Center, 1973. 22 p. (Reprint, 103)

The decay of Juaca's hacendado elite in terms of political control created power conditions favoring peasant movements. Declines followed the emergence of Huancayo as a commercial center and capital of a province carved from Jauca (1864); the establishment of an economic enclave by Cerro de Pasco (1902); formation of cattle-raising corporations between Lima interests and local hacendados and the destruction of Juaca's commercial elite (1929). The peons of Yanamarca, a hacienda leased to renter-patrons by the state, mobilized under initial influence from Apristas and the model of mine labor relations. After decades of struggles, they formalized a union (1960) and leased the hacienda themselves as a cooperative (1965).

1417. _____ and **Enrique Mayer.** Reciprocidad e intercambio en los Andes. Lima, Instituto de Estudios Peruanos, 1974. 375 p., bibl.

Collection of original essays by 13 authors on reciprocity and other forms of exchange in the Andes. Includes Isbell (see *HLAS 35:1422*); C. Fonesca Martel "Modalidades de la Minka;" Enrique Mayer "Las Reglas del Juego en la Reciprocidad;" Bolton "Tawanku" (see item 1433); R.E. Burchard's "Coca y Trueque de Alimentos": Glynn Custred "Llameros y Comercio Interregional"; Benjamin Orlove "Reciprocidad, Desigualdad y Dominación."

1418. *Allpanchis Phuturinqa.* Instituto de Pastoral Andina. Vol. 2, 1970- Cuzco, Peru.

This volume is the most thematicly integrated of any that have appeared (255 p., bibl., plates). All the articles deal with Andean cosmology or "vision of the Universe." Reprints *HLAS 35:1454* and includes the following original pieces:
Andree Michaud "La Religiosidad en Qollana" (see item 1511)
Mariano Cáceres Olazo "Apuntes sobre el Mundo Sobrenatural de Llavini" (see item 1444)
Manuel Marzal "La Imagen de Dios en Urcos" (see item 1509)
Juvenal Casaverde Rojas "El Mundo Sobrenatural en una Comunidad" (see item 1448)

José Tamayo Herrera "Algunos Conceptos Filosóficos de la Cosmovisión del Indigena Quechua" (see item 1542).

1419. _____. _____. Vol, 3, 1971- Cuzco, Peru.

This volume of "Germinating Earth" is largely devoted to folkloric formula descriptions of specific agricultural rites from single observances in a locale. Articles of this type report events, paraphernalia and often the texts of prayers or songs. Carlos A. Vivanco Flores reports on the *Suyunakuy* (maize or potato cultivation micro-rituals from Turpo district in Apurimac (p. 25-27); Luis Dalle on *la miska* (first planting of maize in a special plot to be consumed green) at Hacienda Wagarpap, Quiquijana district in Cuzco, based on observation 16 July 1970 (p. 28-33); and on the "new year" payment to the earth as *Mosoq Wata* the night of July 31 and day of Aug. 1 in Quiquijana (p. 34-44); Juan Antonio Manya describes the *sara tarpuy* maize sowing in the Vilcanota valley (p. 47-55); Carlos A. Vivanco Flores records the songs and ceremonies of the first potato weeding-hoeing *papa pajchay* in Ocobamba district, Apurimac (p. 56-58); Luis Dalle reports the same for the Kutipay or second maize hoeing in Accha district, Cuzco (p. 59-65); Mery Alinda Sánchez Gamarra describes the festival to San Isidro, patron of agriculturalists, held May 15 in Lamay district, Calca, Cuzco (p. 87-98); Faustino Mayta Medina concerns his description of the maize harvest in Yucay, Urubamba, Cuzco, not only with the ritual but with work organization (p. 101-112). The second section of the issue is devoted to the "cult to the animals" (p. 133-134, 163-201) especially round-up and marking rituals, again by various authors writing on specific observations. Other articles in the volume do not conform to the general format. There are several discussions of how such rites can be integrated into orthodox Catholicism (e.g. "Can a Christian Peasant Offer Payment to the Earth? p. 116-128 by Manuel María Marzal, S.J.). Three articles which are of special interest are reviewed separately.

1420. _____. _____. Vol. 4, 1972- Cuzco, Peru.

Special issue on the "Life Cycle of the Andean Family" consists of articles listed below, followed by a pastoral reflection by Father Rodrigo Sánchez Arjona, S.J. (p. 157-181) and a methodological statement by Father Manuel María Marzal, S.J. (p. 185-201):
Thomas M. Garr "La Familia Campesina y el Cosmos Sagrado" p. 7-19
Zulma Zamalloa González "Ciclo Vital en Sayllapata" p. 21-32
Carlos A. Vivanco Flores "El Matrimonio Indígena" p. 33-42
Guillermo Allen and Javier Albó "Costumbres y Ritos Aymaras" p. 43-68

Jean Louis Christinat "La Mortalidad en Chia" p. 69-84
Inocencio Salazar Recio "Unión Familiar y Salud" p. 85-100
Domingo Llanque Chana "La Mujer Campesina Aymara" p. 101-119
Henrique O. Urbano "Intercambio de Mujeres Estructuras Familiares" p. 121-1343
Daisy Núñez del Prado B. "La Reciprocidad como Ethos de la Cultura Quechua" p. 135-154.

1421. _____. _____. Vol. 5, 1973- Cuzco, Peru.

Like Vol. 4 (see item 1420), this issue is subtitled "Life Cycle in the Andean Family" though its major sections concern various aspects of Andean social organization and theological reflections. Also includes Spanish version of Pierre Van den Berghe's study "El Uso de Términos Etnicos" (p. 5-18). The following important articles are reviewed separately in this HLAS section:
I.N.D.I.C.E.P. "El Jilakata" p. 33-44
Jorge Flores O. "La Viudad y el Hijo del Soq'a Machu" (see item 1472)
Pierre van den Berghe "La Población de San Jerónimo" p. 57-66
Benjamin Orlove "Abigeato" (see item 1524)
Ralph Bolton "Explicando la Exogamia Andina" p. 83-120
Antoinette Fioravanti "Reciprocidad y Economía del Mercado" p. 121-130
David Gow "Reforma Agraria y Sistema de Cargos" p. 131-158
Rodrigo Sánchez-Arjona "El Compadrazgo" p. 167-183.

1422. *América Indígena.* Instituto Indigenista Interamericano. Vol. 33, No. 3, julio/sept. 1973- . Mexico.

Special issue of *América Indígena* focuses on the native Argentine peoples. Editor Gonzalo Rubio Orbe provides a general introduction, followed by selections on archaeology, ethnohistory and social anthropology of particular groups. For article on Argentine Andean peoples see item 1431.

1423. Andrews, Frank M. and George W. Phillips. The squatters of Lima: who they are and what they want (JDA, 4, Jan. 1970, p. 211-224, tables)

Report on the results of a sample interview survey conducted in 1967 by the Sample Survey Center in Lima (CISM) among 361 selected households in 59 geographical locations within 30 barriadas. Presents a composite portrait of an "average" family and its barriada context then goes on to report findings on the extent and intensity of dissatisfaction with 26 public and private sector services. High priority felt needs included more conveniently located medical services, secure property titles, better water and sewage services, paved streets, etc. Educational facilities were largely regarded as adequate. A sectoral analysis on the basis of sex, length of residence, age, income and location near services produced similar results. This sample survey is an important complement to more in-depth studies of individual barriadas, or the residents or groupings therein typical of anthropological approaches.

1424. Araúz, Reina Torres de. La cultura chocó: estudio etonológico e histórico. Panamá, Univ. de Panamá, Centro de Investigaciones Antropológicas, 1966. 207 p., bibl., map, plates (Publicación especial, 1)

The Chocó (Catío, Chamies, Noanamas, Embera) occupy settlements close to the rivers of the interior jungle of northwest South American from the Darien to the Colombian-Ecuadorian border. Arauz' fieldwork was concentrated in Panama and northern Colombia, but this formal ethnography—much in the style of the *Handbook of South American Indians*—draws freely on earlier studies by Henry Wassen, Paul River, Erland Nordenskiold and on archive material for every relevant subject. The emphasis is upon material culture and subsistence patterns and its technology. Ethnohistorical materials are excellent, discussions of religion and social organization, poor.

1425. Arcand, Bernard. The urgent situation of Cuiva Indians of Colombia. Copenhagen, International Work Group for Indigenous Affairs, 1972. 28 p., bibl., maps (IWGIA Document, 7)

The "Cuiva" (also known as the nomadic Guahibo) occupy plains east of the Andes in Colombia. Contact with Latin peoples began in 1531, beginning a period of exploration, hostilities and the first epidemics of European-introduced diseases. From 1650-1767 the Jesuits missionized some groups; after their expulsion, an era of settlement by Colombians began which continues to the present. Decimated by warfare, slave raids and epidemics, the remaining Cuiva are few. Arcand describes three bands. That of the Meta river has been reduced to begging, stealing and working as day laborers among the settlers who have overrun their territory. Although the Meta band adapted to sedentary agriculture, they were attacked by colonists. The Meta are considering a move to Cravo Norte, the principal Colombian-Venezuelan village. The Ariporo and Agua Clara bands have continued to move away from the advancing frontier, but Arcand projects that they will eventually be reduced to the Meta band's status. He suggests that the Cuiva be helped to buy their own land so as to operate with respect within the system of the settlers and secure legal protection from incursion as well as physical, though not cultural survival.

1426. Aron-Schaar, Adrianne. Local government in Bolivia: public administration and popular participation (*in* Heath, Dwight B. ed. Contemporary cultures and societies of Latin America [see item 1487] p. 495-501)

A case study of Coroico (pop. 2,000; mayor's salary: US$33.60) supported by data collected elsewhere in Bolivia by other researchers focuses on the practices through which civil authorities supplement their meagre salaries: "private enterprise." A taxonomy of graft and its semantics in local government is given. Concludes that although the power relationships have varied since the 1952 revolution, local government in Bolivia remains hierarchical and corrupt. [Jack Moyer]

1427. Barrionuevo, Alfonsina. Chiaraqe (IPA/AP, 3, 1971, p. 79-84)

Chiaraqe and Toqto are fields in the high puna (4500-4900 m. above sea level) in Kanas prov., Cuzco, where five times a year—Dec. 8, Jan. 1 and 20 (San Sebastian), Feb. 2 and the Day of Compadres (moveable, before Ash Wednesday)—opposing armies of allied communities' warriors meet in ritual battles. Their blood flows from wounds and deaths are regarded as offerings assuring fecundity. This account is journalistic, slick, based on some first person observation and apparently, published reports. For an account of a smaller scale, similar battle in Ecuador see *HLAS 35:1361 and 1417.* Author concurs that the rite involves manhood validation, the analysis of *HLAS 35:1361.*

1428. _____. Sirvinakuy: un ensayo sobre el matrimonio de prueba. Lima, The Author, 1973. 64 p., plates.

Contains a useful survey of the chronicles and modern ethnographies on the subject of "trial marriage": a literature which is spotty, anecdotal and oriented to curious customs. William E. Carter's still unpublished paper on Aymara marriage as a long-term process marked by a series of ceremonies is closer to the emerging ethnological understanding of the various customs. They come under the rubric of trial marriage relative to the formation of complex and stable affinal ties at the heart of community social organization. See item 1433.

1429. Bear, Audrey. Weaving llamas with Señora Sebastiana (Andean Times [Andean Air Mail and Peruvian Times, Lima] 34:1763, Oct. 1974, p. 14-15, plates)

Photo essay on an Aymara weaver in Sorata, Bol.

1430. Berthelot, Jean; Jean Louis Christinat; and **Olivier François Maillard.** Approaches sociologiques des communautés indiennes des Andes (Communautés [Entente Communautaire, Paris] 32, juillet/déc. 1972, p. 7-44, bibl., plates, tables)

A trilogy: Jean Louis Christinat, "Demographie et Developpement dans une Communauté Indienne du Pérou Andine," assembles records of mortality rates (1947-71) by month—confirming Aug. is the dying season—and interprets causes of death for Chia, Carabaya prov., Puno; Olivier François Maillard "Associationnismes et Développement dans les Communautés Indiennes des Andes Péruviennes," reflects upon the units treated as communities relative to French Mission applied anthropology in Andahuaylas; Jean Berthelot "Réligions et Développement dans les Communautés Indiennes des Andes Péruviennes," contrasts the dominant Roman Catholicism with the dominated native expressions and remarks upon the phenomenon represented by the Andean Pastoral Institute (IPA) of Cuzco.

1431. Biró de Stern, Ana. El medio social del habitante del altiplano jujeño (III/AI, 33:3, julio/sept. 1973, p. 771-781)

Describes the basic life cycle and certain customs (*compadrazgo,* burial rituals, the first hair cutting, house roofing) of the Indians (*coya*) and mestizos of the Argentine Andes puna zone. This folkloristic superficial treatment reflects the ethnocentric selectivity Stein (see item 1539) has identified as a syndrome: titillating reports of sexual courtship and surmises of prehispanic survivals which accomplish a cultural distancing.

1432. Bodley, John H. Tribal survival in the Amazon: Campa case. Copenhagen, International Work Group of Indigenous Affairs, 1972. 13 p., maps, tables (IWGIA Document, 5)

The Campa of the upper Ucayali in eastern Peru are presently ranged in three stages of acculturation. Only approximately 2,500 live in a traditional manner in a hunting and gathering society with some horticulture. Nearly 7,750 Campa have established debt labor relationships with settlers, who act as individual patrons, exchanging manufactured goods for labor or forest products (lumber, rubber). The majority, an estimated 10,750 persons, are termed the "market" Campa, assimilated into the cash economy as cash crop producers and wage laborers. Bodley sketches the history of contact and regards the Campa as typical of Amazonian montaña groups.

1433. Bolton, Ralph. *Tawanku:* intercouple bonds in a Qolla village, Peru (AI/A, 68:1/2, 1973, p. 145-155, bibl.)

In Incawatana, Peru, marriage norms construct monogamous family unites and an endogamous community. Each family unit is usually atomistic and suspicious of others. In contrast the rare *tawanku* institution relates two already married couples in sexual, social and economic interdependence for periods of time varying from months to a lifetime. Tawanku bonds provide emotional and physical security for those involved, although the relationship is not generally sanctioned. [J. Mikelson]

1434. _____. To kill a thief: a Kallawaya sorcery session in the Lake Titicaca region of Peru (AI/A, 69:1/2, 1974, p. 191-215, bibl.)

Records a Kallawaya sorcery session and the events which preceded it. The sorcery ritual is interpreted as bringing relief to a theft victim who has exhausted conventional means to obtain justice and as diminishing the interpersonal tension and potential conflict generated by the theft, as well as supplying "good theater" for the peasant village.

1435. Browman, David L. Pastoral nomadism in the Andes (UC/CA, 15:2, June 1974, p. 188-196, bibl.)

On the basis of statistical and observational data, Browman presents a generalized model for pastoralism in the central highlands, a summary of archaeological data for early herding groups and a survey of the ethnohistorical and ethnographic evidence documenting the present pattern of pastoralism in the Jauja-Huancayo basin in Peru. Hypothesizes that the Huari Empire redirected the primary economic dependence on pastoralism with secondary hunting and horticulture to agriculture, followed by an introduction of new trade goods, though camilid herding is argued to be more conducive to long-range population stabilization than agriculture. Since the Spanish conquest, nomadism has decreased. Highland pastoralists enjoy a nutritional advantage over lowland agriculturalists today, their system having developed and endured for at least 7,000 years. [Valerie Kalter]

1436. Brownrigg, Leslie Ann. Interest groups in regime changes in Ecuador (IAMEA, 28:1, Summer 1974, p. 3-17)

The commercial community, agrarian elite, salaried middle class, urban popular classes and foreign interests are identified as forces within the politically active minority in Ecuador. Their interplay and various alliances from 1960-73 provides the scenario for toppling regimes and counter-reform legislation.

1437. ———. The role of secondary cities in Andean urbanism: a bibliographic essay exploring urban process. With comments by Ronald Edari. Evanston, Ill., Northwestern Univ., Center for Urban Affairs, Comparative Urban Studies Program, 1974. 70 p., bibl., maps.

Changes in the settlement pattern of Chiclayo, Cuenca, Trujillo and Santa Cruz as the social stratification, economic relationship of the urban center to its own hinterland and to international spheres, and net population evolved during the recent domination of Andean national economics by international interests are traced especially in terms of elite precincts and "barriada" formation. The model is posed as the other side of the tendency of increased primacy, long analyzed as a pattern of dependency. (Multilith volume available from the Center for Urban Affairs, Northwestern Univ.)

1438. Brush, Stephen Bourne. A study of subsistence activities in Uchucmaraca, Peru (LTC Newsletter [Univ. of Wisconsin at Madison, Land Tenure Center] 40, April/June 1973, p. 10-18)

Exerpts from author's 1973 dissertation include list of crop zones, map locating the community, an agricultural annual calendar of activities and charts summarizing labor inputs in man-days/hectare, per crop and by monthly employment rates.

1439. Buechler, Hans C. The reorganization of counties in the Bolivian highlands: an analysis of rural-urban networks and hierarchies (*in* Eddy, Elizabeth M. *ed.* Urban anthropology: research perspectives and strategies. Athens, Univ. of Georgia Press [and] Southern Anthropological Society, 1968, p. 48-57, bibl.)

Although the authority of *canton* capitals has been bypassed by peasants through alternative hierarchies of syndicate *centrales* and peasant federations since the 1952 revolution, communities still vie for the prestige of capital status. The cases of Jank'o Amaya on Lake Titicaca, Cruz Loma as studied by Félix Mangudo in the Yungas, and Arapata, the subject of Madeline Leons 1966 dissertation illustrate the strategies of competition for this prestige change.

1440. ———. The social position of an ethnographer in the field (*in* Henry, Francis and Satish Saberwal *eds.* Stress and response in fieldwork. N.Y., Holt, Rinehart and Winston, 1968, p. 7-19)

Swiss-born, Bolivian educated anthropologist examines the development of his own relationship with the exhacienda community of Compi, fieldwork reported in *HLAS 35:1363 and 1364*. Turns in his status and acceptance came with the choice of an acknowledged "cultural broker" as interpreter, the entry of the author's anthropologist-wife, and the excitement generated by his ability to play and record native instruments: each of these opened wider channels of communication. Setbacks included the suspicion aroused by a briefly retained interpreter embarrassed by certain questions, by a medical student who joined them but did not accept their guidelines and by a survey team's payment for information in contrast to the Buechler's practice of rewarding favors.

1441. ——— and **Judith Maria Buechler.** El aymara boliviano y el cambio social: reevaluación del concepto de intermediario cultural (IBEAS/EA, 2:3, 1971/72, p. 137-147, bibl.)

Four culture brokers of Compi, La Paz, are assessed in terms of the networks of influence they manage which enable each to operate both within the post-reform exhacienda community and larger spheres of La Paz, national bureaucracies and various missions of foreign aid institutions.

1442. Burke, Melvin. Land reform in the Lake Titicaca region. Madison, Univ. of Wisconsin at Madison, Land Tenure Center, 1974. 41 p. (LTC Reprint, 110)

General view of Bolivian land reform, sample comparison of four Peruvian haciendas and four Bolivian ex-haciendas in Puno (Peru) and La Paz (Bol.) depts. is oriented to productivity evaluation. Despite dissimilar tenure conditions, poor economic performance was similar. Bolivian ex-*sayaña* holders earned more per capita than wage labor Peruvian *colonos;* Bolivia compared favorably in terms of high land productivity but unfavorably in lower labor productivity. Dates to 1964-65 research.

1443. Burton, J.H. Infant feeding habits causing malnutrition (Andean Times [Andean Air Mail and Peruvian Times, Lima] 34:1756, Sept. 1974, p. 14-15, plates)

Report of cultural and social factors contributing to the poor nutritional base of infant diets, is based on survey of Lima's Villa El Salvador (pop. 200,000).

1444. Cáceres Olazo, Mariano. Apuntes sobre el mundo sobre-natural de Llavini (IPA/AP, 2, 1970, p. 19-34)

Excerpt from a longer study of the Puno community of Llavini presents the problem of evil spirits of the Ukhu

Pacha: el Supay (wealthy older son of Jesus and Mary!), the *Anchacho* demon and the *condenados* (evil ghosts). Analysis of the theory of soul is made (*qhamasa*) and el ángel de la guarda located in the heart: each of these is subdivided into Father, Son and Holy Ghost sectors.

1445. Calvet de Villagómez, Marta; Víctor Daniel Bonilla; and Marie-Hélène Laraque. Colombia: the Coconuco struggle for life; massacre on the Llanos (Akwesasne Notes [Kanienkahake—Mohawk Nation—Middletown, Conn.] 5:4, Summer 1973, p. 28-29)

Report on invasions of Church owned haciendas in Coconuco.

1446. Camino D.C., Alejandro. Algunos factores del cambio socio-ecológico en el Alto Urubamba (IBEAS/EA, 3:3, 1973, p. 119-138, bibl.)

Cultural ecology of the Machiguengas of the Upper Urubamba, history of contacts with Andean inmigrants, description of change "factors" (era of rubber gathering, post World War II colonization) and the Summer Institute of Linguistics mission provide background for analysis of the group's process of social, cultural and economic change.

1447. Casagrande, Joseph B. Strategies for survival: the Indians of highland Ecuador (*in* Heath, Dwight B. *ed.* Contemporary cultures and societies of Latin America [see item 1487] p. 93-107)

Serious objection can be made to Casagrande's framework of analysis. He compares six Indian communities: 1) the Chimborazo freehold peasant villages of San Francisco; 2) those of Guabug who are also tied to the hacienda system; 3) the Cayambe canton exhacienda Atahualpa corporate agrarian cooperatives (but spatially at least, communities); 4) the Salasaca; and 5) Saraguru (these last two large groups organized in many distinct settlements); and 6) Peguche which is not described for itself but in terms of the Otavalos' status, generally in Ecuador. The view of Ecuadorian Indians as a dispossessed *strata* marked off by institutionalized racism is contradicted by the Indians' own perception that they are separate groups. The different adaptations of Indian groups to varied "ecological circumstances" interpreted in terms of dependency on and exchanges with the larger society and of each group's access to land, water, pasture and fuel, and the varied historical experience of the hacienda and obraje systems are simply not the full explanation. Casagrande ignores the strong socio-cultural differences among Ecuadorian Indians of pre-conquest origin, reinforced by different ecological strategies in John V. Murra's sense, which have shaped regionally distinct patterns of social race relations. Indeed, as the Otavalan textile industry and Saraguru territorial expansion into the Oriente illustrate, Indian groups are extrapolating their differentiation into a modern future as organized ethnic groups. While urban Ecuadorians may generalize about "Indians" from the most impoverished examples, anthropologists should better examine evidence to the contrary which is furnished even within this article.

1448. Casaverde Rojas, Juvenal. El mundo sobrenatural en una comunidad (IPA/AP,2, 1970, P. 121-244)

Describes Kuyo Grande, gives a calendar of major rituals and lists traditional religious authorities briefly. The supernatural world is analyzed in the following categories: I) Traditional Quechua Deities; 1) mountain spirits (*apu, ruwal, auki*), 2) the Pachamama, 3) the various types of *machu,* 4) personifications of nature (sun, moon, stars, lightning, wind, rain, rainbow; II) Demonic beings (the *supay, sirena* or *saqra, wa'ka, duendes,* flying heads-*quepque* and *nak'aq;* III); Deities of christian origin; IV) Spirits of the Living; V) Spirits of the Dead; VI) Magic, Magicians and Magical Rites. The whole is highly instructive, well-detailed and sensitive to cultural nuances.

1449. Cayón Armelia, Edgardo. El hombre y los animales en la cultura quechua (IPA/AP, 3, 1971, p. 135-162, bibl.)

Based on on-going ethnozoological study in the high altitude Andahuaylas, Apurimac communities of Huancabamba and Kakiabamba, this article is essentially a list of animals known. Spanish names in alphabetical order head commentaries which include Quechua name or names, symbolic associations evoked by the animal class, specific uses and taboos of its products and/or body parts and the meanings attached to its situational activities. It forms a useful glossary and introduction to the rich relationship between men and animals within Quechura culture.

1450. Celestino, Olinda. Migración y cambio estructural: la comunidad de Lampián. Lima, Instituto de Estudio Peruanos, 1972. 107 p., map, plates (Proyecto de estudios etnológicos del Valle de Chancay. Monografía, 2)

Excellent political anthropology of a democratic communal government is based on the remarkable social history of San Juan Bautista de Lampián at 2,400 m. above the Chancay valley. Disequilibrium between population and traditional exploitation of land resources led the communal assembly to expell 30 "rebel" *comuneros* in 1936, rather than allocate to them due usufruct plots. Exiling of the youth created a vacuum in the lower ranks of the civic-religious hierarchy and on communal work crews, contributing to the mounting internal crisis, further aggravated by lawsuits with neighbors and zooepidemics. Author traces careers of exiles, who were invited back after seven years. The political-ideological, legal economic and technological innovations the group applied from experiences outside the community rescued, revitalized, and realized a modern transformation of the agrarian communal economy. Stands as one of the finest IEP monographs from the Chancay series directed by José Matos Mar.

Chaney, Elsa M. Women in Latin American politics: the case of Chile and Peru. See item 8366a.

1451. Chile. Dirección de Asuntos

Indígenas. Oficina de Planificación Agrícola. Departamento de Programación. Chile: el problema mapuche (III/A, 32, dic. 1972, p. 75-98)

A dramatic account of Mapuche history and smatterings of socio-cultural insight are followed by a presentation of the Unidad Popular's program relative to the Chilean Indian minority. Concrete actions of the UP government are synopsized: restitution and increase of the Mapuche land base through Agrarian Reform, extension of technical assistance and credit and a massive compaign to improve education through primary school, training courses, adult education, newly created technical centers and by 1972, 6000 scholarships for Mapuches. "Great Lines of Action for the Future" were to be further land tenency security, reorganization of communities along cooperativistic lines and the integration of Mapuche people into the political process. As an official report of UP government agencies directly involved with delivering the promises of Allende's coalition regime to the Mapuche people, this document has special historical value. The culturally unique Mapuche character and their special oppression was recognized by this government, though its larger intentions were clearly assimilationist.

1452. Cohen, Lucy M. Las colombianas ante la renovación universitaria. Bogotá, Ediciones Tercer Mundo, 1971. 149 p., tables (Serie Tribuna libre)

Full report of Cohen's study of 100 of the initial women university graduates of Colombia based on interviews in Bogotá, Medellín and Cali. See item 1453.

1453. ——. Women's entry to the professions in Colombia: selected characteristics (WRU/JMF, 35, May 1973, p. 322-330, bibl., tables)

One hundred professional women largely residing in Bogotá, Medellín and Cali whose education was completed between 1940 and 1955 were interviewed. Characteristics reported include their family background (largely middle class), motivations in seeking professional education (encouragement by parents or significant others), present employment (69 percent of sample worked fulltime; 18 percent half or part time) and adjustment to the new social role in terms of family role (63 percent were married, etc.). The presentation is statistical and lacks the intimacy that a style quoting from the women interviewed might bring.

1454. Collier, David. Los pueblos jóvenes y la adaptación de los migrantes al ambiente urbano limeño (IBEAS/EA, 3:3, 1973, p. 25-49, bibl., map)

Compares attitudes of a sample of slum and "young town" residents on a scheduled questionnaire to conclude that differences between them are overdrawn though the latter invest more cash and energy in home and community improvement.

1455. Collin Delavaud, Claude. Les régions côtières du Pérou septentrional: occupation du sol, aménagement régional. Lima, Institut Français d'Etudes Andines, 1968. 600 p., bibl., illus., maps, plates, tables.

This thorough survey of the region of Tumbes, Piura and Lambayeque depts. is unmatched in the literature. Contains the history of land and water use, settlement patterns, development of industry and infrastructure of each geographically defined micro-region: the oases of Chao-Viru, Santa Catalina (Río Moche), Chicama, Jequetepeque, Lambayeque, Piura and Chira; the Sana valley, and the cities of Trujillo, Chiclayo and Piura and their specific hinterlands. The spatial, social, technological and financial organization of agriculture is detailed down to the major individual agribusiness plantations, many of which were nationalized after the completion of this study. Aerial photographs, charts summarizing population and economic data from Peruvian surveys and excellent land-use maps complement the analysis and provide basic background data for any researcher interested in this north coast region. Highly recommended!

1456. Conlin, Sean. Participation versus expertise (YU/IJCS, 15:3/4, Sept./Nov. 1974, p. 151-166, bibl.)

In his expert's role, a SINAMOS agricultural engineer vetoes field for field proposals for a plan of production suggested by members of a peasant cooperative recently formed out of six former estates in Cuzco dept., quelling objections to any crop but wheat. Peasant participation is reduced to rubber stamping his expertise on the commercial market as opposed to their years of experience with crop rotation. This case introduces a thoughtful discussion of dilemmas in the Peruvian "revolution." Expertise gained through formal education legitimates the higher status of bureaucrats and promoters, who dominate decision-making through prestige. Educational reform inculcates respect for the status of experts and offers only limited individual mobility. Participation, "the basis of the government's claim to be revolutionary," thus fosters incorporation rather than dialogue and becomes the mechanism for efficient conforming integration into a rational political machine. With a libertarian philosophical viewpoint and well-chosen examples, Conlin illuminates the ironic nature of the Peruvian revolution.

1457. Cotler, Julio. Actuales pautas de cambio en la sociedad rural del Perú (*in* Matos Mar, José *ed.* Dominación y cambios en el Perú rural: la micro-región del Valle de Chancay [see item 1510] p. 60-79)

Essay on social change interplays peasant politicization and syndicalism, rural out-migration and the decay of traditional plantation systems.

1458. ——. Alternativas de cambio en dos haciendas algodoneras (*in* Matos Mar, José *ed.* Dominación y cambios en el Perú rural: la micro-región del Valle de Chancay [see item 1510] p. 223-241)

The specific cases of two cotton plantations detail the role of peasant syndicates, changes in labor relations, presence or absence of subcontractors or freehold peasant communities in the process of de-yanaconization (distribution of usufruct plots to land-for-labor exchange yanacona workers) since the 1964 Agrarian Reform Law. The personal fatalism and disallegiance to the state (presumably Belaúnde-era) and its institutions, among the hacienda workers, are put in the context of change and in the direction of dysfunction rather than social improvement.

1459. Counterpoint of the Agrarian Reform: Chile, 1973. Contrapunto de la Reforma Agraria: Chile, 1973 (Motion picture) The Land Tenure Center, University of Wisconsin-Madison [c. 1973] Made by Chile Communications Project of the Food and Agricultural Organization of the United Nations. 42 min. sd. color. 16 mm. Spanish and Spanish with English overvoice.

Agrarian reform under the Frei and Allende governments is traced with interviews with officials, peasant leaders and scenes of the changes in community and production forms. Filmed in 1965 and 1973.

1460. Davies, Thomas M., Jr. Indian integration in Peru: a half century of experience, 1900-1948. Lincoln, Univ. of Nebraska, 1974. 204 p., bibl., maps, tables.

This study in historical political analysis can serve as a useful resource for ethnologists interested in Peruvian indigenous peoples. Describes various social programs and changes in legislation affecting Indians and evaluates how political support at the national level affected these programs' impact on the local level.

1461. Dipolo, Mario and María Matilde Suárez. History, patterns, and migration: a case study in the Venezuelan Andes (SAA/HO, 33:2, Summer 1974, p. 183-195, bibl., maps, tables)

Reconstructs the history of municipal migration for San Jacinto El Morro in the Venezuelan Andean state of Mérida from 1872-1971, interpreting migration rates in terms of the main national socio-economic events which created zones of attraction and repulsion. Describes three direct and two indirect migratory, and three counter-migratory spatial patterns, based on 186 cases of personal migration history obtained in scheduled interviews with residents.

1462. Dobkin de Ríos, Marlene. Banisteriopsis in witchcraft and healing activities in Iquitos, Peru (SEB/EB, 24:3, 1970, p. 296-300)

Emphasizes an aspect of *ayahuasca* use in the jungle urban slum of Belén outside Iquitos, to bewitch individuals by inducing an hallucinogenic state of paranoid delusion. Analysis is framed within folkloric witchcraft belief system and relative to known psychoactive effects of harmine. Contrast with item 1519.

1463. Dobyns, Henry F. The Cornell-Peru Project: experimental intervention in Vicos (*in* Heath, Dwight B. ed. Contemporary cultures and societies of Latin America [see item 1487] p. 201-210)

This historical outline of the 12-year Cornell-Peru Project of socio-economic intervention in Vicos discusses the methodology used to transform the highland hacienda of the Quechua Vicosinos from a "culture of repression" into a communally owned and operated commercial production unit. The theory and objectives of the project designer, Allan Holmberg, are sympatheticly treated, and the article positively evaluates the project. A good introduction but see also item 1540.

1464. Dowling Desmadryl, Jorge. Religión, chamanismo y mitología mapuches. Santiago, Editorial Universitaria, 1971. 148 p., bibl., plates. (Col. Imagen de Chile, 10)

Minimal and largely secondary ethnography and maximal speculation characterize this *Golden Bough* of Mapuche religion. "Affinities" between Mapuche deities and ancient Germanic, Polynesian and Turke-Tartar are emphasized. Pillán, a Mapuche high god aspect associated with volcanos and fire is said to be a tall blond Thor, for example. The only Andean analogy, to Choke Illapu (quoted from Tello and Mason) is considered on the page equating Pillan and the African Shango. Except for insisting the female or transvestite male *machis* (shamans) practice group hypnosis, there is little descriptive of shamanism, only a literal assertion of Eliade's thesis of a global preneolithic shamanistic religion. Mapuche are claimed to be Lake Baikal Turko-Tartars. The work is marred by unsophisticated macrodiffusionism and represents an ideological attempt to Indo-europeanize the Andean Mapuche. Dowling warns us more "proof" will appear in his forthcoming book: *The blond Mapuche of Boroa*.

1465. Drake, George F. Elites and voluntary associations: a study of community power in Manizales, Colombia. Madison, Univ. of Wisconsin at Madison, Land Tenure Center, 1973. 58 p., tables (Research paper, 52)

Study of the dynamics and membership of 234 voluntary organizations (charities, mutual benefits associations, social action centers) indicates that most are either directed by the elite or support their interests. The Manizales elite is largely a merchant class led by a clique (la rosca) of community decision-makers uniquely anti-labor and "anti-communist." Examples of the repression of organizations formed among non-oligarchs—labor unions, shanty-town support alliances and social justice Catholic action groups—completes the thesis of elitist, paternalistic structuring of community power through voluntary associations. Includes graphs, diagrams and statistical tables.

1466. Dubly, Alain. Una nueva alfabetización para la aculturación del campesino andino (III/AI, 33:1, 1. trimestre 1973, p. 45-63)

After a philosophical introduction to the problem of two cultures in the Andean nations, describes new approaches in literacy campaigns specified by the example of Ecuador's efforts in Chimborazo.

1467. Earls, John. La organización del poder en la mitología quechua (*in* Ossio A., Juan M. *ed.* Ideología mesiánica del mundo andino [see item 1526] p. 395-414, bibl.)

Based on original research in Sarhua, Huancasancos, (both in Ayacucho dept.) and interviews in other areas and on research by other scholars, the analysis presents the hierarchial structure of Quechua mythology. Below Viracocha and creator stem two groups: A) the Sun, Morning Star, Lord of the Earth and man; B) the Moon, Evening Star, Lady of the Sea and woman. The four levels of power (e.g. Sun-Moon; man-woman) have a modern-day interpretation; 1) the Sun or God, 2) Inka and President and his government, 3) the *Wamanis* and the *Mistis*, and 4) the common people. The highest level (God) and the lowest (common people) are no longer conceptually bifurcated.

1468. _____. The structure of modern Andean social categories (Journal of the Steward Anthropological Society [Urbana, Ill.] 3:1, 1971, p. 69-106, bibl.)

In a rich interpretation of Quechua kinship organization, the minimal/maximal lineages (*castas*) of Vicos (Ancash) as described by Mario C. Vázquez, and the ayllu, moiety and caste-like endogamic units of Sarhua (Ayacucho), Earls analyses alliance patterns as Arunta-like, separating patrilineal lines by at least five generations whenafter lineages are typically double-linked by sister exchange. The final section applies Van Foerster's equations as a thermodynamic model through which the kinship elements are used to formulate minimal entropy requirements of the system as an organization.

1469. Escobar, Gabriel. Sicaya: cambios culturales en una comunidad mestiza andina. Lima, Instituto de Estudios Peruanos, 1973. 185 p., bibl., plates.

Fieldwork in the mestizo commercial/craft center Sicaya, a town of the Montaro valley, was completed in 1945-46. The study rewritten in 1968 follows the compartmentalized "community study" format with chapters on Sicaya's geographical milieu; population and migration; social stratification and mobility; economic structure; family, marriage and life cycle; religion; social and political organization and history. Luis E. Valcárcel, Harry Tschopik, José María Arguedas and Allan R. Holmberg each guided phases of the work which emerges as an especially complete and sympathetic example of its (community study) genre. Change discussed is largely mestizaje as a process and urban influences from migrants' experiences.

Espinoza Bravo, Clodoaldo. Mitología del valle del Mantaro. See *HLAS 36:1014*.

Esteva Fabregat, Claudio. Medicina tradicional, curanderismo y brujería en Chinchero, Perú. See *HLAS 36:1015*.

1470. Flinn, William L. Rural and intra-urban migration in Colombia: two case studies in Bogotá (*in* Rabinovitz, Francine F. and Felicity M. Trueblood *eds.* Latin American urban research [see *HLAS 36:1716*] p. 83-93, bibl., tables)

Summarizes a rural-to-urban migration pattern through intra-urban steps similar to those described for Lima by Mangin. Interviews conducted in Barrios El Carmen and El Gavilán indicate steps through rented quarters in a decayed core slum to the peripheral *tugurio* shanty towns.

1471. Flores Ochoa, Jorge A. Mistis and Indians: their relations in a microregion of Cuzco (YU/IJCS, 15:3/4, Sept./Nov. 1974, p. 182-192, bibl.)

The settlement of Kaykay is a district capitol in Paucartambo, Cuzco. Most of its 287 residents are subsistence peasants in a *Qeshwa* zone, who prefer to speak Quechua but as self-conscious *mistis* (mestizos) cultivate proficiency in Spanish. Similar in culture, occupation and economic status to the surrounding Indians, *misti* superordination is expressed through asymmetrical *compadrazgo* of the vertical type, physical and verbal abuse of Indians, and demands that "their" Indians provide labor for public works. Flores suggests this type of ethnic ethos in the absence of class differences exists between townsmen and their surrounding Indians in several areas of the Vilcanota river region.

1472. _____. La viuda y el hijo del Soq'a Machu (IPA/AP, 5, 1973, p. 45-55, bibl.)

In "Población" a village of *mistis* referred to as *wiracochakuna* by the Indians in higher altitudes, a young widow claims she has been impregnated by a *Soq'a Machu*: a mythological figure also called *Nawpa Machu, Machula, Machu, Awki* as a masculine figure. Along with the female type of these *gentiles* (heathens) called *Soq'a Paya, Nawpa Paya, Awlay* and *Paya* both identified with the shriveled mummies living in little houses (tombs), the *Machus* cause all manner of harm. They are invigorated by assuming human form and cohabiting with unsuspecting humans. Although the widow's trading and itinerant labor takes her to many communities where her sexual adventures are well known, the *mistis* accept her explanation, for were they to admit her immoral behavior, she would be attributed with bringing calamity upon the town. She commits infanticide by exposing the new-born child to the cold wind the night after its birth. Its death is accepted as "proof" that it was indeed a Soq'a Machu's child, which are either born deformed or die soon after birth. The case is an interesting account of the interrelationship of mythology and social sanctions in a face-to-face community.

1473. _____. La Wak'a Awicha Anselma (IPA/AP, 3, 1971, p. 68-78, bibl.)

Flores presents a Quechua and Spanish version of a conversation with a village elder of Che'eqa Pupuja in José Domingo Choquewanka district, Puno, tape-recorded in 1971 and adds his comments. The account concerns the interpretation by villagers of changes in the weather caused by the removal of a monolith the wak'a (shrine) Awicha named Anselma and also

Patrona, removed by a schoolteacher to Pucará the decade before. A delegation was organized to free the image from "jail" and return it to a mountain shrine, attended by proper rituals and offerings. No sooner than they were carrying the heavy monolith back, did the desired weather begin . . .

Frisancho, A. Roberto and others. Adaptive significance of small body size under poor socio-economic conditions in southern Peru. See item 2200.

1474. Gade, Daniel W. Ethnobotany of Cañihua—Chenopodium pallidicaule: rustic seed crops of the altiplano (SEB/EB, 24:1, 1970, p. 55-61, bibl., plates)

Not an ethnobotany in the linguistic sense, this article is rather a presentation of the agricultural practices, uses and formal botanical characteristics of cañihua, a species related to the more widespread quinoa. Cañihua is adapted to a high (12-15,000 ft. above sea level) cold ecozone, and is an important food and forage crop in the Peruvian-Bolivian altiplano complex. Resistant to frost, drought, pest and saline soil, this amino acid rich seed the stalk of which is burned for the high calcium content of its ash, is an important "insurance" crop.

1475. ———. Grist milling with the horizontal water wheel in the central Andes (Technology and Culture [Society for the History of Technology, Detroit, Mich.] 12:1, 1971, p. 43-51, maps, plates)

The Old World horizontal water-powered grist mill known as the "Greek" and "Norse" has survived as an item of material technology into the 20th century in Andalusian Spain from where it was probably introduced to the Andes by 1539 as part of the complex surrounding wheat and barley. Gade describes the cultural use of mills of this type focusing on a group of mills along the Cachuma river, a tributary of the Vilcanota (Urubamba) in Cuzco. Milling begins before All Souls to prepare the flour for the bread offerings to the dead proper on this day and continues through March. Grain producers rent the use of mills from their owners. The description is concise, but ends with the unverified assumption that mills of this type will be abandoned as modernization sweeps the Andes in a temporarily unspecified but vaguely immediate future trend. For folklorist comment, see HLAS 36:2942.

1476. ——— and **Roberto Ríos.** Chaquitaclla: the native footplough and its persistence in central Andean agriculture (Tools and Tillage [G.E.C. Gad, Copenhagen] 2:1, 1972, p. 3-15, bibl., map, plates)

The chaquitaclla or taclla, regarded as an Inca era technological invention, is placed in archaeological, ethnohistorical, ethnographic and ecological context. Photographs, 16th-century manuscript sketches, diagrams and description give the variations of its forms and illustration of its use in work groups. Gade argues that taclla is closely associated with sod-breaking after field fallowing. Although the application of potato and tuber cultivation to other crops and field situations is generalized, taclla is essentially a man's tool and designed for use in a work team (masa) or form two-to-five people carrying out the yapuy or barbecho, one of which (rapa) turns to sod. Also gives contemporary distribution. For folklorist's comment, see HLAS 36:1016.

1477. Gobeil, Oliva. El susto: a descriptive analysis (IJSP, 19:1/2, Spring/Summer 1973, p. 38-43, bibl.)

Reviews Latin American susto literature, following a model developed by Sal y Rosas (see HLAS 27:1626 and HLAS 35:1485). Suggests that children and young women manifest their insecurity within geographically mobile families as susto for which paramedical attention from predominantly female curanderas is a specific "cure".

1478. Graeff, Peter. The effects of continued landlord presence in the Bolivian countryside during the post-reform era: lessons to be learned. Madison, Univ. of Wisconsin at Madison, Land Tenure Center, 1974. 36 p., bibl., tables (LTC, 103)

Discusses cases of continued landlord presence in Bolivia. Official research evaluations of land reform in ten selected Bolivian regions are culled from the National Agrarian Reform Service (LTC/CIDA-SNRA). Those landlords who received the generally prime hacienda lands through the reform either engaged in land speculation or easily reinstituted only slightly modified versions of the hacienda regime on their generous allocations. Concludes that continued hacienda landlord presence was highly detrimental to the goal of transforming the "feudal" system of land tenure and worker exploitation.

1479. Greaves, Thomas C. En busca de un pluralismo cultural en los Andes (IBEAS/EA, 3:1, 1973, p. 5-28, bibl.)

Reviews theories in North American literature which could be or have been used in Andean ethnography: Lewis' "Culture of Poverty" and its critiques, especially Valentine's; the concept of subcultures and refuge cultures á-la Beals, Fried, Mangin, Doughty; the concept of dual society (which I thought Stavenhagen—who is not cited—had axed as an erroneous thesis), class analysis, especially of the emerging rural proletariat. Suggests tactics such as the study of values, expressive culture, standards, individual status change and radical changes within Indian communites. Cites examples from Andean ethnographic literature throughout.

Grebe, María Ester. El kultrún mapuche: un microcosmo simbólico. See HLAS 36:4576.

1480. Guillet, David. Integración sociopolítica de las poblaciones nuevas en Bolivia: descripción de un caso y discusión (IBEAS/EA, 3:3, 1973, p. 111-128, bibl.)

Omereque, a canton of Campero province, Cochabamba was dominated by haciendas in the pre-revolutionary era. After agrarian reform, a slow steady stream of Quechua-speaking peasants migrated there to seek land and also escape a malarial epidemic along the Mizque river. Minor changes in the regional road and market system favored the development of two cash crops ecologically suited to the area: sugar-cane and the spice, cumin. Ad-hoc groups organized major public works, and the town attracted a small, but culturally significant migration of craftsmen, merchants and schoolteachers who encouraged a shift to urban, national values.

1481. Guzmán Arze, Humberto. Diagrama sociológico de Cochabamba. Cochabama, Bol., Corporación de Desarrollo de Cochabamba, 1971? 175 l., tables.

A broad diachronic view of Cochabamca city and valley's social stratification is particularized by historical and modern demographic statics. Thematically, the indigenous peasant strata is regarded as closed in social organization while mestizos, *"vallunos"* and *cholos* are treated as dynamic strata reflecting social change in each era. Includes a detailed 1967 urban occupational census with good raw data unanalyzed in this study. This rare monograph of a provincial city and its hinterland relationships is valuable.

1482. Hanna, Joel M. Coca leaf use in Southern Peru: some biosocial aspects (AAA/AA, 76:2, June 1974, p. 281-296, bibl., tables)

Well-documented presentation of experiments on the physiological effects of coca chewing confirms several native Indian claims concerning coca: that coca is non-addictive in the amounts consumed, that its use dulls sensations of fatigue and aids in the retention of body heat. Field studies were conducted in Nuñoa, a high altitude village in southern Peru, to determine rates and conditions of consumption; laboratory studies simulating certain climatic conditions were conducted at sea level. Studies of the economic and social implications of coca trade are cited. Coca use is interpreted as a response to biological stress and its trade as an integrating element in native and mestizo society. See also item 1506. For physical anthropologist's comment, see item 2201.

1483. Hargous-Vogel, Sabine. Urban problems, Peruvian style (UMUP/E, 15:4, Summer 1973, p. 25-31, plates)

Popular presentation of a broad spectrum of barriada research regards barriadas as urban, but "the final stage of the rural-urban continuum of marginality whose most characteristic trait is non-participation in national life." Three types of "squatters' villages" are distinguished by degree of isolation: 1) autonomous satellite urban embryos such as the Ciudad de Dios, 2) geographic regroupings prevented by some physical feature of the landscape from total fusion with the city such as San Cosme or El Augustino, and 3) assimilated barriadas receiving extensions of urban services such as San Martín de Porres. Also discusses the organization of land take-over, architecture, building phases, and the image of the barriadas as mediating transitional societies.

1484. Harkness, Shirley J. The pursuit of an ideal: migration, social class, and women's roles in Bogotá, Colombia (*in* Pescatello, Ann *ed.* Female and male in Latin America: essays. Pittsburgh, Pa., Univ. of Pittsburgh Press, 1973, p. 231-254, bibl., tables)

Sociologically phrased study in which the independent variables are socio-economic status (very poor, working class, lower middle class) and length of residence in Bogotá (-15 or $+15$ years). The dependent variables are women's role relationships in the institutional areas of politics, education, and family. Based on interviews with a 20 percent sample of the female residents (age 15-40) of Marco Fidel, a slum barrio settled by refugees from La Violencia, and Quiroga Central, a housing project completed in 1960. Contrary to the working hypothesis of differences in "modern" versus "traditional" values varying with socio-economic status, results indicate generally traditional conservative values. Poor recent arrivals (one extreme of the six categories formed by the independent variables) sought status within their reference group; long-resident lower middle class women (the opposite pole) sought middle class status, each reflecting conforming views.

1485. Havet, José. Estructura del poder en una zona rural boliviana (IBEAS/EA, 2:3, 1971/72, p. 65-87)

Charts and describes the domination of post-reform peasants in the Belisario Boeto prov. of northeast Chuquisaca, Bol., by outside political and economic institutions.

1486. Heath, Dwight B. New patrons for old: changing patron-client relationships in the Bolivian Yungas (UP/E, 12:1, Jan. 1973, p. 75-98, bibl.)

The pre-revolutionary local subculture of Aymara-speaking *colonos* on haciendas in the coca and coffee producing semi-tropics of Nor Yungas prov. cast the resident hacendado into a highly paternalistic role: mediating disputes, providing first aid, intervening with the legal system, coordinating activities, etc. Agrarian reform removed the ex-landlords. Neither wealthy nor cosmopolitan, most settled in the provincial capital or towns where many became market middlemen. Vertical *compadrazgo* ties cement bonds between ex-colono producers and ex-hacendado merchants, the latter functioning as patrons, supplying credit in exchange for purchase options. Virtually all ex-colonos were organized into syndicates representing each hacienda. Initially constituted as a medium to secure estate expropriation and titles, these syndicates also assumed paternalistic roles: coordinating public works projects, resolving interpersonal conflict among the peasants and serving as an intermediary to larger political institutions. The patron role of the syndicate is largely accrued to the person occupying the office of secretary-general, whose behavior is of course subject to members' control. A striking analysis of cultural continuity in social change, this example indicates the special anthropological contribution to studies of socioeconomic transformation of society. Also available as LTC **Rqnt** No. 101 with a 7-p. appendix of figures, Univ. of Wisconsin, Land Tenure Center, Madison.

1487. _____ ed. Contemporary cultures and societies of Latin America: a reader in the social anthropology of Middle and South America. 2. ed. N.Y., Random House, 1974. 572 p., bibl., tables.

Second ed. of standard textbook for Latin American anthropology courses includes large number of articles of interest to Andeanists. Those reviewed separately in this *HLAS* section are followed by item number.
Joseph B. Casagrande "Strategies for Survival: the Indians of Highland Ecuador" (see item 1447)
Solomon Miller "Proletarianization of Indian Peasants in Northern Peru" (see item 1514)
Henry F. Dobyns "The Cornell-Peru Project: Experimental Intervention in Vicos" (see item 1463)
Richard W. Patch "Serrano and Criollo: the Confusion of Race with Class" p. 307-316
Norman E. Whitten, Jr. "Ecology of Race Relations in Northwest Ecuador" (see item 1556)
Charles E. Erasmus "Agrarian Reform vs. Land Reform: Three Latin American Countries" p. 143-157
William Mangin "Latin American Squatter Settlements: a Problem and a Solution" p. 340-365
Daniel Goldrich "Political Organization and Politicization in the Poblador" p. 365-387
Richard M. Morse "The Claims of Tradition in Urban Latin America" (see item 1516)
Charles Nisbet "Interest Rates and Imperfect Competition in the Informal Credit Market" p. 1638
Adrianne Aron-Schaar "Local Government in Bolivia: Public Administration and Popular Participation" (see item 1426)
Camilo Torres "Message to Students" p. 525-526
William F. Whyte "Rural Peru: Peasants as Activists" p. 526-541.

1488. Heyduk, Daniel. Bolivia's land reform hacendados (IAMEA, 27:1, 1973, p. 87-96)

By allocating land in the Sucre-Tarija area to the tenants at the time of agrarian reform, "reform" reinforced the position of tenants over their sub-tenants, creating one "land reform hacendados" out of each three hacienda heads of family. Sub-tenants, in contrast, received no land and disparities in the size of plots rented by the tenants were not equalized, creating further hierarchization of post-reform land ownership.

1489. _____. The hacienda system and agrarian reform in highland Bolivia: a re-evaluation (UP/E, 13:1, Jan. 1974, p. 71-81, bibl.)

Contends the social order resulting from the agrarian reform law in Bolivia is an evolutionary rather than revolutionary process by examining four regions once dominated by the hacienda system: 1) the altiplano, 2) *yungas*, 3) Cochabamba valley, and the 4) Sucre, Tarija area. Demonstrates how differences in the hacienda structure of each region are reflected in the rural social organization after agrarian reform.

1490. Hilger, M. Inez and **Margaret Mondloch.** Surnames and time and distance measurements among the Chilean Araucanians (*in* Lyon, Patricia J. *ed.*

Native South Americans: ethnology of the least known continent [see item 1361] p. 343-345)

Notes on the influence of Chilean cultural concepts in each topic listed in the title. This article was originally published in the *Journal de la Société des Americanistes* (Paris, 55:1, 1966).

1491. Himes, James. Dos proyectos de desarrollo en el Perú: una evaluación de Vicos y de maíz (IBEAS/EA, 3:2, 1973, p. 71-86, bibl.)

Synopsis in Spanish of the results of author's Ph.D. dissertation.

1492. Horton, Douglas E. The effects of land reform on four haciendas in Peru (LTC Newsletter [Univ. of Wisconsin at Madison, Land Tenure Center] 38, Oct./Dec. 1972, p. 15-22)

Brief report in English and Spanish on the agrarian reform process on a system of four estates in Lambayeque and Cajamarca, owned by a family corporation before 1970 intervention, designates each by letters (A, B, C, D). Same estates as reported in items 1455 and 1493.

1493. _____. Haciendas and cooperatives: a preliminary study of latifundist agriculture and agrarian reform in northern Peru. Madison, Univ. of Wisconsin at Madison, Land Tenure Center, 1973. 96 p., maps, tables (Research paper, 53)

In-depth study of four recently cooperativized haciendas, formerly owned by a single family: Pomalca, a unionized factory-in-the-field Lambayeque sugar estate; Udima, the largest hacienda in Cajamarca, which produces cattle, wool and cheese; Monteseco, a *selva* coffee section and Espinal, organized in rice production under the *colonato* system. Social stratification and administrative organization of the estates is demonstrated to have changed only in the upper echelon where owners were replaced by upper level managers and hacienda cooperative leaders. Udima, Espinal and Monteseco colonos have resisted cooperativization. See item 1455 for further pre-reform data on Pomalca and item 1514 for an account of a relationship similar to that of Pomalca and Udima haciendas.

1494. *International Journal of Comparative sociology.* York Univ., Dept. of Sociology and Anthropology. Vol. 15, Nos. 3/4, Sept./Nov. 1974- . Toronto, Canada.

Special issue on "Class and Ethnicity in Peru" (211 p., including bibliographies, charts, glossary and maps). The editor, Pierre L. van den Berghe, contributes two bibliographic essays: 1) An "Introduction," where Marx's and especially Lenin's positions on the national question are seriously distorted, leading to a simplistic view of Latin "kitchen" Marxist traditions. Unsuccessfully attempts to apply the plural society model for recent post-colonial societies (formerly under British or Dutch rule) to Peru, a country which has experienced a "shift in international hegemony" (as current Peruvian textbooks describe their initial political independence from Spain) for a century and a half, 2) A bibliographic essay, "The Use of Ethnic Terms in the Peruvian Social Science Literature," where van den Berghe's spotlight is overly selective. Fortunately, the analytical tactics of contributing authors largely ignore the editor's framework. Their articles which are reviewed separately are followed by item numbers:

Douglas Uzzell "Cholos and Bureaus in Lima: Case History and Analysis" p. 143-150 (see item 1545)

Sean Conlin "Participation Versus Expertise" p. 151-166 (see item 1456)

George Primov "Aymara-Quechua Relations in Puno" (see item 1529).

Jorge A. Flores Ochoa "Mistis and Indians: their Relations in a Micro-Region of Cuzco" p. 182-192 (see item 1471)

Benjamin S. Orlove "Urban and Rural Artisans in Southern Peru" p. 193-210 (see item 1525).

1495. Isbell, Billie Jean. La influencia de los inmigrantes en los conceptos sociales y políticos tradicionales (IBEAS/EA, 3:3, 1973, p. 81-104, bibl.)

Structuralized analysis of the cosmology of Ayacucho migrants in Lima.

Jiménez Borja, Arturo. Imagen del mundo aborigen. See *HLAS 36:1018.*

1496. Jongkind, C.F. La supuesta funcionalidad de los clubes regionales en Lima, Perú (Boletín de Estudios Latinoamericanos [Univ. of Amsterdam, Centro de Estudios y Documentación Latinoamericanos (CEDLA)] 11, enero 1971, p. 1-14)

Identifies regional clubs in Lima and analyzes shifts in their activity patterns relative to length of residence in Lima.

1497. Klein, Harriet E. Manelis. Los urus: el extraño pueblo del altiplano (IBEAS/EA, 3:1, 1973, p. 129-150, bibl.)

Concise resumé of early colonial accounts concerning the "Urus"—a linguisticly and culturally distinct group located on islands in Lakes Titicaca and Poopó and along the Desaguadero river today, but once found in enclaves in the Atacama, Arequipa region and northern Argentina and reportedly elsewhere. The culture of the Urus is described from various sources. Extreme depopulation (over 8,000 Urus were listed in 1578 and 1596 *mita* rolls whereas by the 1940s, various accounts polled only scores of Urus), expulsion by other Indian groups and ecological disasters rent by natural changes in their aquatic niche are cited as causes for Uru deculturalization.

1498. Lafon, Ciro René. Estudio etnográfico comparativo de la subcultura humahuaqueña (UBAIA/R, 11:1/2, 1968, p. 7-69)

Monographs of superficial observations of the peasant subculture around Tilcara in the Argentian Andes searches for resemblances to Inka, Aymara and Peruvian Quechua communities circa the late 1940s. Pt. 1 surveys the historical influences on the area, especially the displacement of indigenous people by cattle ranches; pt. 2 attempts to reconstruct Inka era culture from survivals; and pt. 3 compares data from Miskin (1947) and Adams (1919?!) with the Humahuaca subculture.

1499. Leeds, Anthony. Housing-settlement types, arrangements for living, proletarianization, and the social structure of the city (*in* Cornelius, Wayne A. and Felicity M. Trueblood *eds.* Anthropological perspectives on Latin American urbanization [see item 9625] p. 67-99)

The physical apparatus of Lima, Bogotá and Santiago provide examples for a model based on Rio of the city as a lagging concretization of urban social order. Housing-settlement types are proposed: 1) rooming houses (cabeça de porco, casa de cômodo, casas subdividas); 2) 1/2 room units around a courtyard housing individuals or small families (avenida or vila proletaria, callejón, conventillo); 3) temporary government housing units assigned to families (parque proletario, villa de emergencia); 4) multi-unit rental complexes built by labor unions or other occupational associations; 5) "Levittown" style popular housing; 6) humble neighborhoods of separated private homes within the city (suburbios); 7) slums proper in areas of decaying, once-good housing and 8) "squatter" settlements on illegal or untitled land. Summarizes the following: Household maximization strategies in selecting among the alternative life arrangements and the advantages offered by each type; constraints on free choice (largely financial); and the nature of networks, solidarity groups and proletarian coalitions with elite elements characteristic of each generic housing-settlement types. Ideas in this article were first presented at LASA in 1967 by Leeds. Every researcher with an interest in Latin American urbanism should take heed of this important article, worth two or three monographs in precision and insight.

1500. ———. Political, economic and social effects of producer and consumer orientations toward housing in Brazil and Peru: a systems analysis (*in* Rabinowitz, Francine F. and Felicity M. Trueblood *eds.* National-local linkages: the interrelationships of urban and national policies in Latin America. Beverly Hills, Calif., Sage Publications, 1973, p. 181-215, bibl. [Latin American urban research, 3])

Leeds contrasts Peru's consumer-oriented strategy for promoting housing construction with Brazil's producer oriented provision of inflexibly designed ticky-tacky housing projects. The Peruvian policy harnesses the efforts of the state, private developers, cooperatives and individual households to provide appropriate physical structures adapted to culturally varied users' community and household forms. Squatter settlement house construction is cited as an extreme form of this "consumer-orientation," a less expensive adaptive if slow (15-30 years) process of committed investment and labor by house owner-occupants.

1501. Lindner-Emden, Hans. A Tyrolean village in the heart of the Andes (Andean Times [Andean Air Mail and Peruvian Times, Lima] 33:1726, Feb. 1974, p. 12-13, plates)

Photo essay on Pozuzo, upper jungle valley, settled by 300 Austro-Germans in 1859.

Lobb, C. Gary. El uso de la coca como manifestación de cultura indígena en las montañas occidentales de Sudamérica. See item 2235.

1502. Lomnitz, Larissa. Influencia de los cambios políticos y económicos en la ingestión del alcohol: el caso mapuche (III/AI, 33:1, 1. trimestre 1973, p. 133-150, bibl.)

Mapuche patterns of alcohol consumption in four historical periods are analyzed. During the conquest era (16th and 17th centuries) drinking to achieve ritual intoxication and to integrate congregated units (family, lineage, province) made alcohol of cohesive value. By the 18th century, drunkenness on distilled liquors at trading posts had become a symptom of cultural disintegration. Since their loss of independence new patterns, including abstention by women have further evolved. For historian's comment, see HLAS 36:2990.

Lyon, Patricia J. ed. Native South Americans: ethnology of the least known continent. See item 1361.

1503. McEwen, William. Los cambios políticos después de la revolución boliviana: el poder en una comunidad provincial (IBEAS/EA, 3:1, 1973, p. 91-110)

Micropolitical analysis of the rural town of Sorata in the La Paz Yungas emphasizes how the syndicates became an important base for the dominant MNR political party and the drastic realignments after that party's fall in 1965.

1504. _____. Comunidad: análisis y acción (IBEAS/EA, 3:2, 1973, p. 109-132, bibl.)

Data from community action programs in Coroico and Sorata (Yungas), Rreyes (Beni), Villa Abecia (Valle de Cinti), San Miguel and Compi (La Paz altiplano) is analyzed in terms of models provided by Clark in *Community structure and decision-making* (San Francisco, Calif., Chandler, 1968) and Goodenough in *Cooperation in change* (N.Y., Russel Sage Foundation, 1963) and discuss needs, problems of leadership for public works, construction and infrastructure development), etc. Meanwhile, the sky falls on the Bolivian revolution which created a wedge in the socioeconomic structure making all the minor victories of "progress" possible.

1505. McGee, T.G. Peasants in the cities: a paradox, a paradox, a most ingenious paradox (SAA/HO, 32:2, Summer, 1973, p. 135-142, bibl.)

Reaction to *HLAS 35:1435*.

1506. Martin, Richard T. The role of coca in the history, religion, and medicine of South American Indians (SEB/EB, 24:4, 1970, p. 422-437)

Reviews the importance of coca leaves especially in their role in indigenous medicine and religion, concluding, as scientific studies of coca use usually do, that it is highly integrated into Indian culture and attempts to suppress coca leaf use are part of an ethnocidal attack on indigenous lifestyle. See also item 1482.

1507. Martínez, Héctor. Perú: los comuneros no agrícolas (III/AI, 1. trimestre 1973, p. 125-131)

Discusses the implications of the Supreme Decree No. 395-70-AG of 6 Nov. 1970 which will allow a new category of membership in the Peruvian "peasant communities." Previously, members had to be agricultural peasants, heads of family born into or assimilated into each community. The new law allows workers native to an area or outsiders, or least five years resident who use the communal land and develop their work activities within the community, to be considered members of the collectivity, except with regard to landholding rights. The decree effectively opens peasant communities to artisans, vendors, miners, quarry workers, fishermen, transport workers, etc. Concludes that the apparent double standard in land rights is a just reflection of the division of complementary labor within the community.

1508. Marzal, Manuel María. ¿Es posible una iglesia indígena en el Perú? (III/AI, 33:1, 1. trimestre 1973, p. 107-123)

The positions assessed regarding a native Peruvian Catholic Church provide an important context for the recent outpouring of studies of native ritual practices and beliefs by Church-related scholars. Secularists argue that Indian involvement with agrarian ritual and involvement with nature—non-Christian emphases of cult folk Catholicism—will not survive modernization. Integrationists wish to combine the dual spheres of Spanish and Indian culture into a national church. The liberator school holds that a native church cannot arise until the Indian dependence on westernized society is broken. Marzal details his objections to each position and argues for a culturally tailored presentation of Catholicism affirming aspects of native belief and ritual, creating a psychological and organizational buffer against further ethnocide.

1509. _____. La imagen de Dios en Urcos (IPA/AP, 2, 1970, p. 35-56)

An analysis of a questionnaire concerning various conceptualizations of God administered to students, peasants and landowners of Urcos district, Peru, confirms a majority concensus of the Christian God concept. Syncretism with notions from the cults devoted to pantheons of local deities such as the Pachamama and the Apus is regarded as a "trait" characteristic of Andean religion.

1510. Matos Mar, José and others. Dominación y cambios en el Perú rural: la micro-región del Valle de Chancay. Lima, Instituto de Estudios Peruanos, 1969. 377 p., bibl., illus., plates.

Collection of essays by José Matos Mar, Julio Cotler, Giorgio Alberti, Fernando Fuenzalida V., William F. Whyte, Lawrence K. Williams, and J. Oscar Alers on conceptualization of pluralism, domination, social change, socio-economic development and field methodology in Peru. Articles by Matos Mar, Whyte, Cotler and Alers specify the plantation-dominated valley of Chancay context. Completed before the sweeping 1969 Agrarian Reform Law and other radical reorganizations of the military government, the focus of the theory and cases is microsociological and attitudinal, what we expect from Whyte and Matos Mar. A bootstrap mentalistic school of "solution" to underdevelopment prevails; Alers cites motivational preconditions for socio-economic development. The ideology of pluralism, a social organizational plan tutored by colonial and neo-colonial masters is the key concept. The exceptional essays are by Cotler, a Peruvian land reform anthropologist, and are reviewed separately, see items 1457-1458. An English translation was published in 1970 (Chicago, Ill., Aldine). For political scientist's comment, see *HLAS 35:7695.*

1511. Michaud, Andree. La religiosidad en Qollana (IPA/AP, 2, 1970, p. 7-18)

Preliminary report of religious life in the Puno community of Qollana, describes the hierarchy of cult specialists—*responsero* (an intermediary between the living and the dead) *maestro* (a mortician and funeral director) *Yachaq* (a diviner, curer and native priest)—tripartite division of universal time and the gods and spirits which intervene in human life: the Pachamama, the Sirena, Machu Wayra, Wa'ka Rumi and *condenados* (wandering dead souls). [Caroline Levy]

1512. Micklin, Michael; Marshall Durbin; and Carlos A. León. The lexicon for madness in a Colombian city: an exploration in semantic space (AAA/AE, 1:1, Feb. 1974, p. 143-156, bibl., tables)

Study demonstrates that two separate populations—laymen represented by a sample of 800 adult residents of Cali, from all socio-economic levels, and medical personnel, represented by 333 medical and paramedical technicians—use different paraphrasing to synonymize "*loco.*" Both groups characterize "*loco*"/crazy as a malfunction, exclusively mental among laymen but having both a mental and physical basis for the medical and paramedical respondents. Specifies a semantic domain and gives examples of the synonyms.

1513. Millape Caniuqueo, Antonio. Chilean war games: the Mapuche people (Akwesasne Notes [Kanienkahake—Mohawk Nation, Middletown, Conn.] 6:1, Spring 1974, p. 30-31)

President of National Mapuche Confederation outlines the organization, demands and actions of regional Mapuche associations and interprets the Sept. 1973 military coup as a desperate attempt to block the Popular Unity's revolution in which Mapuches were integral.

1514. Miller, Solomon. Proletarianization of Indian peasants in northern Peru (*in* Heath, Dwight B. ed. Contemporary cultures and societies of Latin America [see item 1487] p. 135-142)

Study from 1957 until 1959 of the process of proletarianization in "Ganadabamba," a highland hacienda and "Caña Azul," a coastal plantation. Movements between these communities and subsequent changes in lifestyle are categorized into three distinct phases: 1) the Peasant Phase, characterized by a stable peasant population with little pressure to shift location; 2) the Transitional Phase of oscillation between the sierra and the coast without strong communal ties in either location but the creation with the founding of families by cyclical migrant males; and 3) the Proletarian Phase, when Indians are established as a social group within plantation society. Miller effectively contrasts peasants owning land and deriving subsistence from it with landless proletarians paid in terms of measured time. Additional comparisons are made between hacienda and plantation life, between Indians and criollos. [Caroline Levy]

1515. Montaño Aragón, Mario. El hombre del suburbio: estudio de las areas periféricas de Oruro. La Paz, Editorial Don Bosco, 1972. 254 p., map, tables.

The interpretation of Bolivian social stratification, multiple elites, culture change, social race and cultural-economic imperialism is influenced by Marxism. The historical resumé from the Oruro area and Bolivian context breaks away from orthodox Morgan-Engels evolutionism (Incas as a tribe) to assert that Tahuatinsuyu and early Spanish colonial Bolivia were slave empires, with the *mitayos* as the slaves. Presentation of early prehistory—30,000 BC (?!) to 1100 AD remains conventional Ibarro Grasso, complete with Antarctic migrants and the Aymara caste as the Greeks of ancient America. The central study was based on a questionnaire on social, cultural, religious, economic and political "structure" administered to a 2.6 percent sample of Oruro's population. Subjects were classified by social race as indicated by language and dress custom: 57 percent were "cholos", the remainder Aymara, Quechua or Hispanic criollo. Charts and tables summarize answers to various interesting questions. Perceptions of the perpetrators of injustices, social reactions to wealth, the power of native deities and the Bolivian government vary according to social race. Analyses of natal origins into named neighborhoods, appendixed by a sociogram demonstrating distribution of family members into Oruro's major barrios, educational achievement levels and demographic information abound. We learn 55 percent of those interviewed—not all of whom were miners but disproportionately small businessmen and minor professionals—believe the demon "El Tío" "owns" the veins of minerals, and that 20 percent of the Aymara, 24 percent Quechua, 17 percent cholo and 13 percent criollo families practice family ultimogenitural inheritance.

Such nuggets of data which confirm or dispute analyses of Bolivian culture by other anthropological methodologies render Montaño Aragón's elaborate study a valuable contribution on the Bolivian mining sector. The presentation is lively and would make fascinating reading for the non-specialist.

1516. Morse, Richard M. The claims of tradition in urban Latin America (*in* Heath, Dwight B. ed. Contemporary cultures and societies of Latin America [see item 1487] p. 480-494, bibl.)

Morse, an urban historian (see *HLAS 34:1284* and two issues of *Latin American Research Review*, 6:1, Spring 1971 and 6:2, Summer 1971) designates the urban ethos of Latin America, idealism of city plan and macro-cultural functionalism. Lima, B.A. and São Paulo are compared. An analytical and philosophical break-through which should be required reading for all Latin Americanists.

1517. Moxley, Robert L. Family solidarity and quality of life in an agricultural Peruvian community (WRU/JMF, 35:3, Aug. 1973, p. 497-504, tables)

A neo-Guttman scale computed by Werner's scalogram program measured "family solidarity" in the peasant community of Chacan in Cuzco dept. scaling such items as "togetherness" (eating meals as a family), family "team performance" (serving visitors food), and economic planning, etc. Among the dependent variables tested (household construction complexity, possessions, language, land-ownership, etc.) only the medical practice scale high rating (eg. diverse strategies for seeking aid) correlated well with "family solidarity." A somewhat ethnocentric study all around.

1518. Myers, Sarah K. Lazos culturales de los habitantes de barriadas con su tierra andina (IBEAS/EA, 2:3, 1971/72, p. 115-136)

Residents of the "pueblos jóvenes" of Villa María del Perpetuo Socorro and El Planeta, Lima, are characterized as "cultural commuters." Patterns of step migration, continued ties to village of origin, and back migration are determined from interview data.

1519. Naranjo, Claudio. The healing journey: new approaches to consciouness. N.Y., Random House, 1975. 234 p. (Ballantine books)

A popular account of the psychiatrist-author's experimental application of shamanistic healing techniques to middle and upper-class Chilean patients presents a unique panoply of the psychological problems generated by Latin family and sex-role forms and of their expression in personal symbolism. Patient treatment with harmaline, a psychedelic substance common in *ayahuasca, yagé* and *caapi* formulae of several Amazon, Orinoco and montaña cultures, produced visions with content similar to the native cosmologies but modified by Euro-Latin experience. This famous experiment tends to support Jung's postulation of a collective unconscious and represents a rare cross-cultural experience. Includes index.

Naranjo, Plutarco. El cocaísmo entre los aborígenes de Sud América. See item 2242.

1520. Nett, Emily M. The servant class in a developing country: Ecuador (UM/JIAS, 8:3, 1966, p. 347-352)

Contrasts the Weberian theory of the contract basis of industrialized society and statistical shifts in the numbers of service workers employed in the US as domestics between 1870 and 1960 with the case of Ecuador, still a largely agrarian society. A cultural account of the varied origins and daily duties of the archetypical Ecuadorian servant in Quito, of the special quasi-kinship social relations between servants and the employing family and the larger societal reinforcement of a role for servants through the underdevelopment of extra-household services and household technology all reflect thorough familiarity with the situation. Employment as a servant is analyzed as an avenue of acculturation for rural migrants to urban Ecuador and as increasingly controlled by social legislation.

1521. Núñez del Prado, Oscar and William Foote Whyte. Kuyo-Chico: applied anthropology in an Indian community. Translated by Lucy Whyte Russo and Richard Russo. Chicago, Ill., The Univ. of Chicago Press, 1973. 162 p., map, plates.

Kuyo Chico is a dandy account of community development style applied anthropology, suitable for college teaching. The portrait of Kuyo Chico and its microregion along a side road up into the mountains from the Sunday market town of Pisaq, well-known to Cuzco tourists, recites a litany of pre-program Indian powerlessness before mestizo merchants, authorities, hacienda patrons, labor grabbers (*enganchadores*). Remarks on the spiritual world, synopsized from Núñez del Prado's depth studies (see *HLAS 35:1454* and item 1522) and family structure are sound, if brief. The applied program proceeded in a chain of "linked projects." House improvement led to the creation of a roof-tile craft industry for local use and for sale in Cuzco. The project expanded to ten other communities and its demonstration effect spured others into action. Its total cost was US$188,413 in staff salary wages and expenses: the estimated value of physical improvements tops a half million. Whyte contributes a positive evaluation of the project (p. 119-141) comparing values surveyed in its impact area with data from the Cornell-IEP Study of Change in Peruvian Communities. Both authors summarize lessons for applied anthropology. Like Vicos, Kuyo Chico could not be replicated for the mass of Peruvian Indians, until such time as structural political changes are made, national economic priorities are realigned and cadres of socially and culturally conscious Peruvian interventionists are trained.

1522. Núñez del Prado B., Juan Víctor. The supernatural world of the Quechua of southern Peru as seen from the community of Qotobamba (*in* Lyon, Patricia J. ed. Native South Americans:

ethnology of the least known continent [see item 1361] p. 238-250)

Builds upon *HLAS 35:1454* to present a conceptual and structural analysis of the native mythological world in which the universe is divided into the three estates: Hanaqpacha, Kaypacha and Ukhupacha. Mythological variation is treated, comparing texts of creation myths from Q'ero and Qotobamba. Concludes belief in mountain spirits is a universal in southern Peru, paralled and complemented by religious syncretism. [Carolin Levy]

1523. Oberem, Udo. Trade and trade goods in the Ecuadorian montaña (*in* Lyon, Patricia J. ed. Native South Americans: ethnology of the least known continent [see item 1361] p. 345-357, bibl.)

Diachronic description of trade among Yumbo (Kofan), Quijo, Jíbaro (Suara) and Canelo and between each of these Ecuadorian montaña groups and highland peoples. Emphasizes decisive shifts in dependency upon materials traded-in (e.g. when reliance upon trade goods led to disappearance of pre-contact manufacture as in the substitution of metal tools for stone) and the relative values of various items.

1524. Orlove, Benjamin S. Abigeato: la organización social de una actividad ilegal (IPA/AP, 5, 1973, p. 65-82, bibl.)

Revealed at last—the inner workings of the Robin Hood like gangs of rustlers working Canchis prov., Cuzco, who provide a counter-force to powerful expanding cattle haciendas: the favorite target for raids (*asaltos*) which net each member of the band 8-20,000 soles once the stolen cattle are sold.

1525. ———. Urban and rural artisans in southern Peru (YU/IJCS, 15:3/4, Sept./Nov. 1974, p. 193-211, bibl.)

The similar work and social organization of artisans and merchants in Sicuani is demonstrated to unite them as an urban, petit-bourgeois class, just as the rural seasonally practicing artisans are immeshed in familial and community obligations which integrate them in the Canchis prov. peasantry. A town carpenter and a country carpenter share a trade, not a class. Orlove argues convincingly for ascribing the urban/rural distinction to class; his strategic use of role types found in both contexts is elegant. Etic ethnographic detailing of the behavior of various types of artisans in their shop organization and work habits adds value apart from a well-argued thesis.

1526. Ossio A., Juan M. Ideología mesiánica del mundo andino. Lima, Ignacio Prado Pastor, 1973. 477 p., bibl., maps.

This fascinating, well-integrated collection exploring aspects of Andean mythology is introduced by the bold vision of its editor (p. xi-xlv). The theme of messianism is tracee through historical examples: Pachacuti as an "earth-remaking" religious leader (R.T. Zuidema, p. 3-33: the second representation) Guaman Poma as an interpreter of native thought categories (J.M. Ossio A., p. 153-213), indigenous rationalizations of the Spanish conquest (N. Wachtel, p. 35-82), the Taki Ongoy 16th century (Luis Millones, p. 83-94; 95-102) and Yanahuara 1596 (W. Espinoza S., p. 143-152) nativistic movements and the general relationship of rebellion to millenarianism (N. Wachtel, p. 103-142). Specific messianic myths, especially variants of the Inkarrí from Ayacucho, Cuzco, Puno, the barriadas of Lima and the jungle are given. The interpretative essays original to this volume include important analyses and are reviewed separately: John Earls "La Organización del Poder en la Mitología Quechua (see item 1467); Onorio Ferrero "Significado e Implicaciones Universales de un Mito Peruano." Collection also reprints José María Arguedas' "Mitos Quechua Post-Hispánicos" (p. 379-391) from *Amaru* (no. 3) and Franklin Pease G.Y.'s "El Mito de Inkarri y La Visión de los Vencidos" (p. 441-458) from *Los últimos incas del Cuzco.* An appendix gives two versions of Inkarrí myth in Spanish and in Quechua (pp. 461-477). Highly recommended.

1527. Palomino, Salvador. The hanging bridge of Sarhua (Andean Times [Andean Air Mail and Peruvian Times, Lima] 34:1742, May 1974, p. 12-14, plates)

Photo essay on the re-making of rope suspension bridge by two Sarhua, Ayacucho, ayllus.

1528. Peru: "you are no longer Indians . . you are now farmers" (Akwesasne Notes [Kanienkahke—Mohawk Nation—Middletown, Conn.] 5:5, Fall 1973, p. 27)

Report on the status and programs oriented to Peruvian Indians.

Preston, David A. Freeholding communities and rural development: the case of Bolivia. See *HLAS 36:2957.*

1529. Primov, George. Aymara-Quechua relations in Puno (YU/IJCS, 15:3/4, Sept./Nov. 1974, p. 167-181)

Ethnic relations in Puno dept. Peru are complex. There are three major linguistic groups: 1) the widespread Quechua, 2) the towncentric Spanish speaking *mistis*, and 3) the enclaved Aymara (including one minor group the Aymara-speaking *mitimae* of Ichu, traditionally viewed as relocated from Ecuador by the Incas). Other factors influencing ethnic relations are regional indentifications, cross-cutting language, such as the division between the altiplano Puno "Kolla" and the "cuzqueños," as well as the consolidating influence of community loyalties. This study also details types of mono-, bi-, and tri-lingualism, opportunities for language interaction and acquisition (markets, schools, army service, travel) rates and attitudes of personal interethnic contact in marriage and *compadrazgo* and a profile of mutual out-group stereotypes.

1530. Rawls, Joseph. El antisuyo de los incas (OAS/AM, 23:8, Aug., 1971, p. 15-25, plates)

Gives a general overview of the lifestyle of eastern

slope "tribes" which are, according to the author, "living descendants of the Incas."

Roberts, Bryan R. The interrelationships of city and provinces in Peru and Guatemala. See item 1176.

1531. Rubin, Vera *ed.* Cannabis and culture. The Hague, Mouton, 1975. 568 p., plates.

Includes: Roderick E. Burchard "Coca Chewing: A New Perspective;" William L. Partridge "Cannabis and Cultural Groups in a Colombian Municipio;" B.R. Elejalde "Marihuana and the Genetic Studies in Colombia: the Problem in the City and in the Country;" and Marlene Dobkin de Ríos "Man, Culture and Hallucinogens."

1532. San Martín Ferrari, Hernán. Los araucanos. Santiago, Editorial Nacional Quimantú, 1972. 98 p., illus., plates (Col. Nosotros los chilenos, 8. Serie: Hoy contamos)

Intended as a sympathetic introduction to the Indian ethnic groups for the general Chilean public, this Quimantú booklet is made beautiful with color photographs and poetry. The prehistory and history are just arbitrations of known archaeology and ethnohistorical reconstructions. Some statements on aboriginal social organization are disputed and are perhaps non-universal as is implied. The view of the modern Araucanian people is firmly based on demographic, economic and educational statistics. A plan for their integration in the nation as members of agrarian collectives, after a dynamic agrarian reform, completes the study.

1533. Schoop, Wolfgang. Vergleichende Untersuchungen zur Agrarirkolonisation der Hochlandindianer am Andeanabfall und im Tiefland Ostbolviens. Wiesbaden, FRG, Franz Steiner Verlag, 1970. 298 p., bibl., illus., maps, plates, tables (Aachener Geographische Arbeiten, 4)

The study is concerned with the settlement of highland Indians in the three most important new areas in Bolivia: Yungas, Chapare and Santa Cruz. Author distinguishes between spontaneous, independent, and directed colonization zones according to the degree of planning and support made available. Study recommends that a more rigidly controlled form of colonization ought to be implemented. But since directed colonization is too expensive for mass immigration, model colonies could be selected for more intensive support with the object of establishing in them focal points for socio-economic development measures. [Hans J. Hoyer]

1534. Simmons, Roger A. Palca and Pucara: a study of the effects of revolution on two Bolivian haciendas. Berkeley, Univ. of California Press, 1974. 212 p., bibl., maps (Publications in anthropology, 9)

Both a community study of the adjoining ex-haciendas of Palca and Pucara, canton Tiraque in the Cochabamba valley, and a study of the change process of land reform, this monograph concludes that the ingrained adaptive mechanisms which the peasants evolved under the hacienda system continue to hold them fixed in a technological-social plateau. Bureaucratic agents sponsored by the national government despise their peasant clients and avoid assigned extension work; peasant's political leaders advance their own careers.

1535. Siverts, Henning. Tribal survival in the Alto Marañón: the Aguaruna case. Copenhagen, International Work Group for Indigenous Affairs, 1972. 82 p., bibl., maps (IWGIA Document, 10)

The distinguished senior curator of the Historisk Museum of the Univ. of Bergen in Copenhagen, reports upon this division of the Jívaro-Suara whose territory of approximately 22,000 sq. km. is along the Marañón and its tributaries from the Pongo de Retema to the Río de Retema to the Río de Apaga in the Peruvian montaña. Government sponsored settler colonization into this area has introduced destructive ecological trends. Siverts emphasizes the specialized cultural ecological adaptation of the Aguaruna to the delicate environment, as opposed to the colonists' ruining of broad areas. Also measures undertaken by the Peruvian government which have had disastrous effects (such as a DDT campaign against malarial mosquitos which killed the Aguarunas' domestic animals, a prime source of protein given their shrinking hunting reserves, and which shortened the durability of thatch-rooves by two-thirds), and the general limitations imposed on traditional Aguaruna lifestyle. Five cases including the original appeals of various groups of Aguaruna to Peruvian authorities illustrate the displacement of Aguaruna by individual land speculators and Peruvian institutions. The essential thesis presented is that the influx of colonists has created a situation of overpopulation and incipient overtaxing of resources, which immediately create ethnocidal conditions for the Aguaruna and eventually lead to the failure of specific Peruvian settlement.

1536. Smith, Margo L. Domestic service as a channel of upward mobility for the lower-class woman: the Lima case (*in* Pescatello, Ann *ed.* Female and male in Latin America: essays. Pittsburgh, Pa., Univ. of Pittsburgh Press, 1973, p. 191-207, bibl., table)

An important capsule ethnography of the female domestic servants of Lima, who are largely young (15-24) migrants from the provinces and whose career typically spans a seven-year period after which time they devote themselves to their own family formation. An estimated 90,000 women occupied this status in Lima in 1970, 88 percent of the total servant population. Domestic service as a channel of upward mobility is emphasized: women migrants are often highly motivated, persue education while in service and undergo intensive acculturation. Their own children rarely repeat domestic service in their own careers.

1537. Smith, Richard Chase. The Amuesha people of Central Peru: their struggle to survive. Copenhagen, International Work Group for Indigenous Affairs, 1974. 44 p., bibl., maps (IWGIA Document, 16)

Documents the history of the Amuesha of the Quillazu valley along the Chorobamba river, a garden spot which the native inhabitants were able to defend until late in the last century, at which time the hacienda system, especially posing as Franciscan missions posts, was installed. The Belaúnde government of Peru generously allowed Amuesha to buy back land alienated from them; action has been at snail's pace under the present government's agrarian reform. An appendix details the tenure situation of 47 communities and 681 families.

1538. Stearman, Allyn MacLean. Colonization in eastern Bolivia: problems and prospects (SAA/HO, 32:3, Fall 1973, p. 285-294, bibl.)

Explanations for the low incidence of success of organized colonizations in the vast, unexploited eastern jungle zone of Bolivia, hailed by Bolivia as the panacea for problems of land pressure, are detailed in terms of case studies. Suggestions are made for the modification of colonization planning. This important study identifies an arena of human tragedy staged by a national myth.

1539. Stein, William W. Countrymen and townsmen in the Callejón de Huaylas, Peru: two views of Andean social structure. Buffalo, State Univ. of New York at Buffalo, Council on International Studies, 1974. 78 p., bibl.

The opposed views are: 1) racist-culturalist notion of a dual society (mestizo/Indian), and 2) class analysis of social relations of production and the traits which mark off class membership. Views correspond with first-person documentary statements by townsmen who exaggerate Indian differentness and minimize their exploitation of country people and by countrymen, Vicosinos with realistic perceptions of their subordination and the role of Spanish language fluency and literacy in the *mistis'* power position. Stein inveighs against anthropological service to romantic folkloristic myths which ultimately validate domination. Speculates that agrarian reform in Peru is creating ever more efficient peasant exploitation.

1540. _____. El peón que se negaba (IPA/AP, 6, 1974, p. 79-142)

Translation of item 1541.

1541. _____. The peon who wouldn't: a study of the hacienda at Vicos. Buffalo, State Univ. of New York at Buffalo, 1973. 55 p., bibl.

Contrasts methods of social control on "traditional" haciendas (*embargo, tarea* allotment, *temple* adjustments) with the methods instituted during Cornell Univ.'s leasing of Vicos (abolition of *embargo,* unrenumerated labor, patron profit and raising of *temple*) to conclude that the hacienda system "must be replaced, not reformed" because the network of internal exploitation remains intact even after the abolition of patron profit. Interviews with representatives from various points along the power spectrum ("town mestizo," *colonatos*-serfs, *mayorales*-straw bosses, vacos, etc.) reveal attitudes toward the traditional system and the Cornell reforms. A specific case of excessive colonato absenteeism is the catalyst for Stein's interviews; records and fieldnotes from the Cornell Vicos project elaborate his points. The article is a strong presentation of general hacienda techniques of labor control, the vocabulary of roles, rights and obligations and general hacienda structure. Forms part of Stein's ongoing re-analysis of the Vicos project, see *HLAS 35:1494.* [Toni Murray]

1542. Tamayo Herrera, José. Algunos conceptos filosóficos de la cosmovisión del indígena quechua (IPA/PA, 2, 1970, p. 245-254)

Somewhat superficial and highly philosophical essay takes the stand that the syncretism of native and Catholic religion is a superficial tactic allowing the clandestine survival of native ritual under the eye of the dominant culture. Data is based upon J. Casaverde Rojas and J.V. Núñez del Prado.

1543. Titiev, Mischa. Social singing among the Mapuche (*in* Lyon, Patricia J. *ed.* Native South Americans: ethnology of the least known continent [see item 1361] p. 208-220)

Texts and free translations of unaccompanied songs improvised at public gatherings ("assembly songs"). They were collected by J.M. Collio Huaiquilaf in 1948 in Mapuche reduccions and are interpreted as poetic, emotional outlets. For review of original, see *HLAS 16:420.*

1544. Tortosa, José M. Ritual and cultural lag: the feast of San Isidro in Tiraque, Bolivia (FERES/SC, 19:4, 1972, p. 613-616)

Ritual representation of hierarchial hacienda society in a local feast demonstrates a cultural lag between old and new labor systems. Generation of new forms within the folk religion are beginning to change the religious drama.

1545. Uzzell, Douglas. Cholos and bureaus in Lima: case history and analysis (KU/IJCS, 15:3/4, 1974, p. 143-150, bibl.)

The case of a group of 35 *colectivo* drivers residing in San Martín de Porras, who petition the government for approval of a new route for their collective taxis is analyzed in terms of the author's "play" concept, a variant of game theory. The drivers are defined as urban *cholos*, who supplicate, manipulate, bribe and rile a series of bureaucrats in their quest. These bureaucrats are presumably creoles, in that they operate the "creole-dominated existing institutions" which, as a group-defining trait, *cholos* avoid in favor of developing alternative institutions. It is unclear whether Uzzell envisions the *cholo-creole* distinction as one of the class, ethnicity power-holding or simply years of metropolitan experience.

1546. ———. The interaction of population and locality in the development of squatter settlements in Lima (*in* Cornelius, Wayne A. and Felicity M. Trueblood *eds.* Anthropological perspectives on Latin American urbanization [see item 9625] p. 113-132, bibl.)

Diachronic miniethnographies of four Lima settlements which differ in their tenure characteristics and developmental trajectories but which all fall under the general rubric of "squatter settlements," *barriadas, pueblo jóvenes*: the respective terms of social science, popular Peruvian parlance and Peruvian government euphemism respectively.

Varese, Stefano. The Forest Indians in the present political situation of Peru. See item 1402.

1547. ———. Las minorías étnicas de la montaña peruana: esquema para una antropología de urgencia (UNMSM/L, 40:80/81, 1968, p. 41-59, bibl.)

Documents the state of ignorance concerning the lower-altitude Peruvian montaña cultural groups and proposes an historical morphology of contacts between these groups and Peruvian society. The first type of contact, dating to precolumbian times, involves the technological changes and relatively minor population pressure brought through seasonal or spontaneous colonization of Andean highland people exploiting the zone as one in a system of vertical eco-islands. Mission influence constitutes another historically long-term relationship which subordinated and reorganized montaña societies. Rubber gatherings, especially during the early 20th-century boom, created dependencies as well as technological, economic and social changes. The last type is government stimulated formal colonization which forces interethnic contact, creates territorial boundaries and in general profoundly disrupts montaña social order. Varese ends with a plea for urgent anthropological studies in this zone to avoid the tragedies of ethnocide.

1548. ———. La nueva política peruana y las comunidades tribales (IBEAS/EA, 2:3, 1971/72, p. 89-113, map)

Spanish version of item 1402.

1549. Vellard, J. Contribución al estudio de las poblaciones indígenas de los yungas de La Paz, Bolivia (UBAIA/R, 12:1/2, 1969/1970, p. 329-361, bibl., plates, tables)

Resumé of ethnohistory, contemporary culture and physical anthropology (especially cephalic indices reported by age/sex groups in tables) of the Lecos or Yungas of Beni affluents, the lower Coroico and Guanay and of the Mostenes or Chunchos of the upper Beni river concentrated near old mission sites at Santa Ana de Huachi and Covendo. The photographs (20) are the best part of the article, even if most look like mug shots.

Vessuri, Hebe. Brujos y aprendices de brujos en una comunidad rural de Santiago del Estero. See *HLAS 36:814.*

1550. Villavicencio Rivadeneira, Gladys. Relaciones interétnicas en Otavalo: ¿una nacionalidad india en formación? México, Instituto Indigenista Interamericano, 1973. 315 p., bibl., plates, tables (Ediciones especiales, 65)

In his review of the book in *American Anthropologist* (76:4, Dec. 1974, p. 915-916), Antonio Ugalde states that eight chapters form a conventional "community study" of the history, geography, and social, political and religious systems of the town of Otavalo and its parish. A final chapter, curiously unrelated to the prior, denounces the segregation, abuse and inferior social services available to Indians. Exaggerations flaw the piece which concludes with recommendations to the Ecuadorian government that the integration of the Indian sector requires programs to reorient attitudes among the mestizo (town) population.

1551. Webster, Steven S. Native pastoralism in the southern Andes (UP/E, 12:2, 1973, p. 115-133, bibl.)

Summarizes the literature on the importance of camelid pastoralism and compares the pattern of Q'ero, with its diversified relatively self-sufficient vertical ecosystem, and that in the *puna* community of Alccavitoria, with its limited access to cultivable zones and consequent specialization in pastoralism and necessity of product exchange with other groups. The herding regime of Q'ero determines the location of primary domiciles; status, wealth, inheritance, and ritual have important bases in herding. The Feb. *Pa'chay* ritual at the time of alpaca rutting and just after maize planting and early middle altitude tuber harvests and the Aug.-Sept. *Ahata Uxuchichis* ritual after the maize harvest and major tuber planting are interpreted as marking the major cycles in the Q'ero pattern of pastoralism and transhumant agriculture.

1552. Whiteford, Andrew H. Aristocracy, oligarchy and cultural change in Colombia (*in* Field, A. *ed.* City and country in the Third World.

Cambridge, Mass., Schenkman, 1970, p. 63-91, bibl.)

The senior Whiteford presents an apology of the Colombian oligarchy, arguing from pan-Colombian statistics and recent history and data specifies from the Cauca Valley that the oligarchy is "far from monolithic," undergoes change and dissension, contains talented, well-educated professionals, elements of radical social justice vision as well as status-quo supporters and, in sum, constitutes "a kind of national resource" important for modernization.

1553. Whiteford, Michael B. Barrio Tulcan: fieldwork in a Colombian city (*in* Foster, G.M. and R.V. Kemper *eds*. Anthropologists in cities. Boston, Mass., Little, Brown, 1974, p. 41-62)

His household established in spacious quarters in central Popayán, the investigator motorcycled daily to his field site: "Barrio Tulcan," a green slum of lots parceled out from a former clay pit at the edge of the city. The article describes step-by-step fieldwork decisions and progress and closes with a brief summary of the ethnographic results. For other fieldwork confessions see item 1439.

1554. _____. Neighbors at a distance: life in a low income Colombian barrio (*in* Cornelius, Wayne A. and Felicity M. Trueblood *eds*. Anthropological perspectives on Latin American urbanization [see item 9625] p. 157-181)

Another account of life in Barrio "Tulcan" of Popayán Colombia emphasizing the social distance which the mobility in and out of the community creates.

1555. Whitten, Norman E., Jr. Black frontiersmen: a South American case. N.Y., John Wiley, 1974. 221 p., bibl., maps, plates.

Highly recommended general ethnography of the adaptations of "Afro-Hispanic" culture to the rain forest, mangrove sea-edge and mangrove swamp interior of the Chocó and wet Pacific littoral of the northwest coast of South America, this study expands upon the author's community study of San Lorenzo, Ecua. Interactions between black people (*gente morena*) in rural scattered dwellings and rural settlements and the aboriginal peoples (Cayapa, Chocó etc.) whose settlements interdigitate and who share a peasant subsistence strategy contrast sharply with the set of social relations between blacks and representatives of the dominant Colombian or Ecuadorian culture, with whom the blacks interact in the growing coastal towns or when they adopt proletarian strategies, such as lumbering under contract. Chapters on Afro-Hispanic secular and sacred rituals expand upon item 1557. Descriptions of kinship organization generalize from the San Lorenzo ethnography. The process of political and economic disenfranchisement and racism which accompany economic development are treated in a general view of the ethnic dimensions of blackness in northern South America. A resume of the history of Afro-Hispanic culture from secondary sources and geographical-ecological descriptions of the habitat are useful summaries.

1556. _____. Ecology of race relations in Northwest Ecuador (*in* Heath, Dwight B. *ed*. Contemporary cultures and societies of Latin America. [see item 1487] p. 327-340)

Revision and up-date of *HLAS 35:1507*.

1557. _____. Ritual enactment of sex roles in the Pacific lowlands of Ecuador-Colombia (UP/E, 13:2, April 1974, p. 129-143, bibl.)

Symbolic interactionist analysis examines the continuum of dyadic sex role enactments in secular and sacred ritual contexts and their relationship to social structure. Secular enactments occur in the *cantina* context (male dominated, competitive dyad), the saloon (cooperative male-male dyad) and the *currulao* or *marimba* damce (competitive male-female dyad). Sacred rituals occur in the contexts of adult death observances-*alabado novenario* (co-operative male-famale dyad), those of a child's death-*chigulo* (motherdead child dyad) and the propitiation of the saints (cooperative female-female dyad). [Deborah Bouck]

1558. Wilson, Peter J. Oscar: an inquiry into the nature of sanity. N.Y., Vintage Books, 1974. 142 p., maps.

By an accident of historic geopolitics, the Caribbean island three-by-five mi., off the coast of Nicaragua and its predominantly English-speaking, Protestant, black population are a *municipio* of Colombia. Thus Oscar was shipped to Colombia for a six-year stint in a mental institution when his attempt to build a family life and reputation first collapsed. Islanders eventually got Oscar back: this highly personal account describes the relationship between the islanders and their madman. Anthropologists are traditionally warned to avoid "the first native of the beach" (Oscar actually boated out to greet Wilson) as likely to be deviant. This popularly written story reveals the special insights and hosts of problems brought about by ignoring that conventional wisdom of field work.

1559. Zúñiga, Ricardo B. The experimenting society and radical social reform: the role of the social scientist in Chile's Unidad Popular experience (The American Psychologist [American Psychological Assn., Washington] 30:2, Feb. 1974, p. 99-115 bibl.)

Refugee social psychologist Zúñiga examines the special milieu and the role of social scientists within the Unidad Popular government of Chile, which he contextualizes as a self-consciously "experimenting" society of a type theorized by D. Campbell. The piece is a valuable insight in and of itself and important as background material for understanding anthropological work by Chileans in this era.

LINGUISTICS

ALAN C. WARES

Bibliographer
Summer Institute of Linguistics

LINGUISTIC DESCRIPTION IS BASIC to language classification and to linguistic theory if these are to have any validity. "A thorough description of a language is . . . the best testing ground for theoretical assumptions," writes Campbell (item 1827), who has drawn upon historical documentary evidence to determine relationships among Mayan languages of Guatemala.

Seven phonological descriptions have appeared in a second volume of studies of Colombian languages since the last report (item 1856), as well as a number of separate articles on phonology. The contrast of tone systems with stress systems is the subject of an informative article by Eunice Pike (item 1918), who also collaborated with other writers to describe the phenomenon of "terrace tone" in two dialects of Mixtec (items 1919 and 1920).

Two doctoral dissertations have been published as monographs in the S.I.L. linguistic series: Daly's description of Peñoles Mixtec syntax following a transformational model, and Peeke's description of Auca grammar, using a modified tagmemic model. Three volumes of *Série lingüística,* published by S.I.L. in Brazil, describe languages of that country, generally in terms of one or the other of the above models. Crofts' description of Mundurukú grammar is a monograph (vol. 2 in this series). Another monograph worthy of note is Schumann's description of the Tila dialect of Chol. Three descriptive analyses of Colombian languages have been published in microfiche form in S.I.L.'s *Language data* series (items 1808, 1864, and 1939).

Text material in indigenous languages has been compiled by the Saxtons in Papago, Mayers in Pocomchí, Fought in Chorti, Orr and Hudelson in Quichua, and by others in shorter published works. The fifth centennial of the death of the Aztec poet-king Netzahualcóyotl was the occasion for a number of books dealing with the man and his poetry (items 1831 and 1935), including texts in the Indian language.

Key's vocabulary of regional Spanish is not recent, but was overlooked in earlier *HLAS* listings. Among indigenous language dictionaries of recent date one might mention Landerman's of Quechua del Pastaza and Swisshelm's of Quechua de Huaraz; Miranda's of Aymara; Ortiz Mayans' of Guaraní; Aschmann's of Papantla Totonac and Reid and Bishop's of Xicotepec Totonac; and Pensinger's of Mixtec of Eastern Jamiltepec. Shorter vocabulary lists are included as separate articles or along with other works.

Two bibliographies of works by members of the Summer Institute of Linguistics have been published, one in Brazil (item 1954) and the other in Colombia (item 1955).

The classification of native languages has been the subject of several works. Campbell notes a previously unknown classification of Mayan languages made by Gatschet about 80 years ago (item 1824), which is of historical significance. Rensch places Huave in the Otomanguean langauge family, and Cazes discusses Matlatzinca as a member of the Otopamean subbranch of the same. Suárez writes about the Chon languages at the extreme south of the American continent, and Lastra de Suárez deals with languages classified as Utoaztecan. Bouroncle Carrión lists the indigenous language families of Peru, and Arroyo those of Costa Rica. Rona finds a typological classification more useful than a genealogical in arriving at the origin of a now extinct language of Paraguay.

An important contribution in the area of language classification is Casad's monograph describing techniques used in Mexico for determining the degree of intelligibility between dialects. The same techniques have been used for measuring bilingualism in a community.

Live issues in comparative studies include the source of palatalization in Quiché (item 1826), the reconstruction of complex stops in Proto-Quechua (items 1913 and 1921), and the relationship of Bolivian Chipaya to the Mayan languages of Mexico and

Central America (item 1823). Turner advocates comparative studies of grammar as well as of phonology and lexicon.

The mutual interaction of languages in contact is the topic of several studies. Hollenbach mentions the influence of Spanish on Trique in Mexico, Hensey that of English on Spanish in the southwestern US, Leander that of Aztec on the Spanish of Mexico, Cassano that of Guaraní on the Spanish of Paraguay, and Lopes that of Quichua on Portuguese of Brazil.

Sociolinguistic works include Garvin and Mathiot's on urbanization of Guaraní, the report on bilingual education in the Peruvian jungle (item 1910), and Paulston's "moral dilemma" concerning the use of indigenous languages in primary education. Gudschinsky's literacy manual, translated and published by Mexico's Ministry of Education, is designed to assist in the planning of literacy programs among preliterate peoples.

Works covering many other areas of linguistic interest need not be mentioned here, or the introduction will overbalance the bibliography listing itself. They include items on ethnolinguistics, generative theory, discourse analysis, semantics, case grammar, and kindred subjects.

1800. Alhajj M., Norman. Fundamentos contemporáneos de la filosofía del lenguaje (Lenguaje [Univ. del Valle, División de Humanidades, Cali, Colo.] 1:1/2, agosto 1972, p. 21-34, bibl.)

Brief summary of the development of structural linguistics both in Europe and in North America, and the generative linguistic theory of Chomsky. The new developments [transformationalism] deny the existence of universals in themselves (no existen en sí), and must be complemented by a theory of social communication.

1801. Arroyo, Víctor Manuel. Lenguas indígenas costarricenses. 2. ed. San José, Editorial Universitaria Centroamericana (EDUCA) 1972. 286 p., bibl., plates (Col. Aula)

Brief descriptions of phonology and grammar, with vocabularies, of Brunka, Terraba, Bribri, and Cabecar, Chibchan languages spoken by a relatively small number of inhabitants of southeastern Costa Rica.

1802. Aschmann, Herman Pedro *comp.* Diccionario totonaco de Papantla, Veracruz: totonaco—español, español-totonaco. Prólogo de Carlo Antonio Castro. México, Instituto Lingüístico de Verano, 1973. 268 p. (Serie de vocabularios y diccionarios indígenas Mariano Silva y Aceves, 16)

Dictionary of the dialect of Totonac spoken by some 25,000 Indians living in the region of Papantla, Veracruz, Mex.

1803. Baena Z., Luis A. Estructura semántica y transformaciones (Lenguaje [Univ. del Valle, División de Humanidades, Cali, Colo.] 1:1/2, agosto 1972, p. 35-41, bibl.)

Discusses deep structure and surface structure in grammar and the important role that culture plays in any particular language.

1804. Baptista, Patricia *ed.* Lenguas de Panamá. t. 1, Sistemas fonológicos. Prólogo de Reina Torres de Araúz. Panamá, Instituto Nacional de Cultura and Instituto Lingüístico de Verano, 1974. 94 p., bibl., illus., tables.

Descriptions of phonological systems of five indigenous languages of Panama by members of the Summer Institute of Linguistics. Contents include: Priscilla M. Baptista and Ruth B. Wallin "La Jerarquía Fonológica del Bayano Cuna" p. 5-16
Michael F. Kopesec and Bonnie M. Kopesec "La Jerarquía Fonológica del Guaymí" p. 17-30
Robert D. Gunn and Mary R. Gunn "Fonología Bocotá" p. 31-48
Carol Koontz and Joanne Anderson "Fonología Teribe" p. 49-69
Ronald G. Binder and Kathleen P. Binder "Fonología Waunana" p. 71-92.

1805. Baptista, Priscilla M. and Ruth B. Wallin. Baure vowel elision (LING, 38, April 1968, p. 5-11, table)

Speakers of Baure, an Arawakan language of northeastern Bolivia, optionally elide medial and final vowels of words, especially in rapid speech, resulting in consonant clusters and in consonantal allophones that do not otherwise occur in the language. Includes brief description of phonemes (12 consonants, two semi-consonants, four vowels) and stress, and a 66-item vocabulary.

1806. _____ and _____. La jerarquía fonológica del bayano cuna (*in* Baptista, Patricia *ed.* Lenguas de Panamá [see item 1804] t. 1, p. 5-16)

Describes phonological phrase and phonological word as well as the segmental phonemes of the Bayano dialect of Cuna, an indigenous language of Panama traditionally classified as Chibchan. Includes vocabulary list of 66 entries.

1807. Bastidas C., Alfonso. Reflexivos en español (Lenguaje [Univ. del Valle, División de Humanidades, Cali, Colo.] 1:1/2, agosto 1972, p. 43-70, bibl., illus.)

Application of principles of transformational grammar to reflexive pronouns of Spanish.

1808. Berg, Marie L. and **Isabel J. Kerr.** Cuiva language grammar. Santa Ana, Calif., Summer Institute of Linguistics, 1973. 105 p., bibl., maps, tables (Language data microfiche, Amerindian series, 1)

Presents grammar of Cuiva, a Guajiban language of the plains country of east and central Colombia, following the tagmemic model of K.L. Pike. Includes two texts and a Cuiva-English lexicon.

1809. Bernard, H. Russell. Otomi phonology and orthography (IU/IJAL, 39:3, July 1973, p. 180-184, bibl., tables)

Suggested revision of the practical orthography of Mezquital Otomi (Mexico) in order to minimize problems of tone, nasalization, and stops.

1810. _____. Otomi tones in discourse (IU/IJAL, 40:2, April 1974, p. 141-150)

Considers rising tone in Otomi to be a function of geminate vowels rather than a phonemically distinct feature, as maintained by Wallis (see *HLAS 31:2466*), and that writing of tone in a practical orthography is unnecessary for native speakers of the language. Includes sample text with free and literal translation. This is an Otomanguean language spoken in central Mexico.

1811. Binder, Ronald G. and **Kathleen P. Binder.** Fonología waunana (*in* Baptista, Patricia *ed*. Lenguas de Panamá [see item 1804] t. 1, 71-92)

Describes 20 consonant phonemes and 16 vowel phonemes (10 oral, 6 nasal) of Waunana, a Choco language of about 2,500 speakers located in southeastern Panama and along the Pacific coast of Colombia. Includes description of the syllable and the phonological word, and a vocabulary list of 66 items.

1812. Boswood, Joan. Algumas funções de participante nas orações Rikbaktsa (Série Lingüística [Summer Institute of Linguistics, Brasília] 3, 1974, p. 7-33, bibl., tables)

Analysis of semantic relationships in Rikbaktsa discourse, following the orientation of Fillmore and Chafe.

1813. _____. Citações no discurso narrativo da língua Rikbaktsa. Tradução de Mary L. Daniel (Serie Lingüística [Summer Institute of Linguistics, Brasília] 3, 1974, p. 99-129, tables)

Direct quotation in Rikbaktsa discourse is used for providing information about events, identifying participants, describing the setting of an action, telling about preceding events, evaluating, and giving collateral information. Mechanisms for indicating quotations are described, followed by a native text, illustrating the article.

1814. _____. Evidências para a inclusão do Aripaktsá no filo (Série Lingüística [see item 1936] p. 67-78, bibl., maps, tables)

Comparison of Aripaktsa (Rikbaktsa) a hitherto unclassified language of northern Mato Grosso, Bra., with reconstructed forms of Proto-Jê.

1815. Bouda, K. Zapotekische Studien: Das Zapotek and seine Beziehungen zu Sprachen in Mexico und Zentralamerika (CIDG/O, 22:1, 1973, p. 188-200)

Lists words from various Zapotec dialects and from other languages of Mexico for comparative purposes.

1816. Bouroncle Carrión, Alfonso. Idioma, lenguas y dialectos en el Perú (III/AI, 33:2, abril/junio 1973, p. 375-403, bibl., maps, tables)

Mentions variety of languages in pre-conquest Peru and their present distribution, based on census figures and on reports of the Summer Institute of Linguistics. In several depts. (political divisions of Peru), Quechua is spoken by about half the population, but there are fewer monolinguals now than there were in 1940. The same is true for tribes in the upper Amazon basin where bilingual schools have flourished for many years. Besides Quechua and Aymara, there are eight major groups of indigenous languages in Peru, namely: 1) Jíbaro, 2) Pano, 3) Arawakan, 4) Andean, 5) Huitotoan, 6) Macro Carib, 7) Tupí-Guaraní, and 8) Macro Tucanoan.

1817. Branks, Thomas and **Judith Branks.** Fonología del guambiano (*in* Gerdel, Florence and others. Sistemas fonológicos de idiomas colombianos [see item 1856] t. 2, p. 39-56, tables)

Phonemic system of Guambiano, a Chibchan language of 5,000 speakers in central Colombia, consists of 17 consonants, two semivowels, five vowels, and a phoneme of stress. A predominant feature of the language is its sibilants, which occur in native text with much greater frequency than sibilants in Spanish or English.

1818. Briggs, Janet R. Ayoré narrative analysis (IU/IJAL, 39:3, July 1973, p. 155-163, bibl.)

Ayoré narratives follow a pattern of title, event sequence, and coda. In the event sequence, the *complication and resolution* consists of temporally oriented *episodes,* each of which consists of *paragraphs,* with *periods* of semantically associated sentences at the lowest level of the structure. "Paragraphs are organized around an actor-reactor pattern of participant relations throughout the narrative." Case relations are Actor, Experiencer, Goal, Objective, Associative, and Benefactive. Repetition of elements is used for emphasis or continuing action. Ayoré is a Bolivian Indian language of uncertain classification.

1819. Brown, Cecil H. Formal semantic analysis of Huastec kinship terminology: a case for an unusual marriage role (IU/AL 15:6, Sept. 1973, p. 259-266, bibl., tables)

Lists Huastec kinship terms and their meaning and concludes that the pattern that emerges suggests that in the past Huastec speakers may have practiced ambilateral parallel-cousin marriage. Huastec is a Mayan language spoken in the states of Veracruz and San Luis Potosí, Mex.

1820. Burtch, Bryan and **Mary Ruth Wise.** Murui (Witotoan) clause structure (LING, 38, April 1968, p. 12-29, tables)

Tagmemic analysis of clause structure in Murui, a Witotoan language of Peru with some 200 speakers. Matrix charts present contrastive clause types and lower-level constructions.

1821. Cadogan, León. Ywyra Ñe'ery: fluye del árbol la palabra; sugestiones para el estudio de la cultura guaraní. Con un prólogo e ilustraciones de Bartomeu Meliá. Asunción, Univ. Católica Nuestra Señora de la Asunción, Centro de Estudios Antropológicos, 1971. 127 p., bibl., plates.

Comments on linguistic and ethnographic matters arising out of the texts in Guayakí which occupy the last half of the book. Guayakí is a Tupí-Guaraní language of Paraguay.

1822. Caicedo A., Antonio J. Conceptos fundamentales de la gramática transformacional (Lenguaje [Univ. del Valle, División de Humanidades, Cali, Colo.] 1:1/2, agosto 1972, p. 5-20, bibl.)

Presents linguistic theories of Noam Chomsky relating to how a child learns a language in order to arrive at an internalized generative grammar.

1823. Campbell, Lyle. Distant genetic relationships and the Maya-Chipaya hypothesis (IU/AL, 15:3, March 1973, p. 113-135, bibl.)

Reconsideration of data presented in support of the hypothesis of genetic relationship between Chipaya of Bolivia and the Mayan languages of Mexico and Central America, set forth by Olson in 1964-65 (see *HLAS 29:2304*). Criteria for correspondence are: a) a significant number of matchings in basic vocabulary, b) items matched should be of corresponding length, preferably CVC, and c) the forms must not be onomatopoetic in origin. On the basis of this reconsideration of Olson's articles in the *International Journal of American Linguistics,* the writer finds "very few examples which suggest a possible relationship between Uru-Chipayan and the Mayan family."

1824. ———. Gatschet's classification of Mayan languages (IU/IJAL, 39:4, Oct. 1973, p. 250-252)

Previously unknown classification of Mayan languages, discovered in the library of the Brigham Young Univ., is presented in its entirety and discussed briefly. "Gatschet's classification is an important stage in the history of Mayan studies. His insights should not be forgotten, and his errors should be understood."

1825. ———. The philological documentation of a variable rule in the history of Pokom and Kekchi (IU/IJAL, 39:3, July 1973, p. 133-134)

Historical evidence from colonial documents indicates that the phonological change from ¢ to s in Kekchi and Pokom (Pocomam and Pocomchí) occurred as a common innovation after the conquest, when the two language groups were already separate, and therefore should not be educed as evidence of their being members of a single subgroup of the Mayan family. All of these are Guatemalan languages.

1826. ———. Quichean palatalized velars (IU/IJAL, 40:2, April 1974, p. 132-168, table)

Presents evidence from historical documents to show that the palatalization rule formulated by James L. Grimes (see *HLAS 33:1732*) was not Proto-Quichean, but of later origin and diffused from west to east. Considers diffusion from Mamean languages as source of Quichean palatalization. Quichean and Mamean are subgroups of Mayan languages of Guatemala.

1827. ———. Theoretical implications of Kekchi phonology (IU/IJAL, 40:4, Oct. 1974, p. 269-278, tables)

Presents phonological rules of Cobán dialect of

Kekchí, a Mayan language of the Quichean subgroup in Guatemala. Considers rule ordering theory and cites external evidence (a word game and native reaction to borrowed words) in support of the phonological rules. Reasserts value of linguistic description.

1828. Casad, Eugene H. Dialect intelligibility testing. Norman, Univ. of Oklahoma, Summer Institute of Linguistics, 1974. 201 p., bibl., illus., maps, tables (Publications in linguistics and related fields, 38)

Reports techniques used in dialect surveys among indigenous groups in Mexico, with some details of results obtained, a general theory of intelligibility, and statistical measures used in testing intelligibility between speakers from different areas.

1829. Cassano, Paul V. Retention of certain hiatuses in Paraguayan Spanish (LING, 109, 1 Aug. 1973, p. 12-16)

Discusses the influence of Guaraní on Paraguayan Spanish, particularly in relation to the hiatus between contiguous vowels (as in *país*) which in some Spanish dialects is dropped, with the formation of a diphthong (as in *pais*).

1830. ———. The substrat theory in relation to the bilingualism of Paraguay: problems and findings (IU/AL, 15:9, Dec. 1973, p. 406-426)

Deviations from standard Spanish in Latin America have been attributed to the influence of the indigenous languages of the particular area where they occur. Theory tested by phonological comparison of Guaraní and Paraguayan Spanish.

1831. Castillo F., Víctor M. Nezahualcóyotl: crónica y pinturas de su tiempo. Texcoco, Mex., Gobierno del Estado de México, 1972. 195 p., facsims.

Reproductions of 144 drawings from 16th-century codices relating to the era of Nezahualcóyotl a century earlier. Accompanying the drawings are interpretive comments. Introduction includes a sketchy discussion of Aztec glyphs and their meanings.

1832. Cazes, Daniel. La lengua maclasinca de Nsampaanchu: San Francisco Oxtotilpan (SA/J, 60, 1971, p. 191-232, bibl., maps, tables)

Discusses classification of Matlatzinca (to use the more common spelling) within the Otopamean language family. Gives a sketch of the phonology and syntax, using tagmemic structural formulas for the letter. Bibliography of 483 items covers linguistic theory, general references, and works on Otopamean languages. The speakers of Matlatzinca, who are largely bilingual, live mainly in the state of Mexico, southeast of Toluca, the state capital.

1833. Crofts, Marjorie. Gramática mundurukú. Tradução de Mary L. Daniel. Prefácio de Loraine Irene Bridgeman. Brasília, Summer Institute of Linguistics, 1973. 192 p., facsims, tables (Série lingüística, 2)

Begins with description of discourse structure of Mundurukú (Tupí, Brazil) at paragraph level and continues to levels of sentence, clause, phrase, and word, within a tagmemic framework. Appendixes include 14-page text with Portuguese translation, tagmemic formulas, phonemic inventory and 341-item vocabulary, and list of abbreviations used.

1834. Crowell, Thomas H. Cohesion in Bororo discourse (LING, 104, 15 May 1973, p. 15-27, bibl.)

Presents hierarchical structure of discourse in Bororo, and independent linear organization that enables the listener to follow the theme of the discourse. This cohesion is provided by connectives and anaphoric phrases. Bororo is an as yet unclassified language spoken by some 300-400 Indians of central Mato Grosso, Bra.

1835. Daly, John P. A generative syntax of Peñoles Mixtec. Norman, Univ. of Oklahoma, Summer Institute of Linguistics, 1973. 90 p., bibl. (Publications in linguistics and related fields, 42)

Transformational grammar of a dialect of Mixtec using Chomsky's *Syntactic structures* as a model. The four chapters are: "Introduction," "Phrase Structure," "Transformational Structure," and "Lexicon." In the Appendix are an analyzed text and a sample of sentence generation. Mixtec is an Otomanguean language of southern Mexico.

D'Ans, André-Marcel. Reclasificación de las lenguas pano y datos glotocronológicos para la etnohistoria de la Amazonía peruana. See *HLAS 36:1388.*

1836. ———. Repertorios etno-botánico y etnozoológico amahuaca (PEMN/R, 38, 1972, p. 352-384, tables)

Lists names of plants and animals in Spanish and in Amahuaca, a Panoan language (2,000 speakers) of eastern Peru.

1837. Dobson, Rose. Notas sobre substantivos do Kayabí (Série Linguística [see item 1936] p. 30-56, tables)

Analysis in tagmemic terms of noun phrases of Kayabí, a Tupí language of about 250 speakers in Mato Grosso, Bra.

1838. Durbin, Mridula Adenwala. Formal changes in Trinidad Hindi as a result of language adaptation (AAA/AA, 75:5, Oct. 1973, p. 1290-1304, bibl., tables)

Immigrants to Trinidad from India from 1845 to 1917,

consisting of Hindus, Moslems, and Christians, spoke about a dozen languages and represented a variety of castes. Social, cultural, and psychological factors resulted in the development of Trinidad Hindustani, a creole language closely related to Bhojpuri Hindi. Discusses probable reasons for linguistic innovations as social relations within this heterogeneous group became more relaxed.

1839. Elliott, Raymond L. Notas sobre algunas características lingüísticas de idiomas indígenas guatemaltecos (GIIN/GI, 8:1, enero/marzo 1973, p. 70-80, tables)

Refutes popular misconception of Indian languages as consisting of animal-like sounds, few words, and indicating an inferior level of intelligence, by focusing on a verb phrase in Ixil (a Mayan language of Guatemala) which, with various affixes, is capable of more than six hundred billion ("seiscientos mil millones") permutations to express various shades of meaning of the verb.

1840. Elson, Benjamin and Velma Pickett. Introdução à morfologia e à sintaxe. Tradução de Aryon D. Rodrigues and others. Petrópolis, Bra., Editôra Vozes, 1973. 220 p., bibl., tables (Col. Perspectivas lingüísticas, 8)

Translation into Portuguese of a textbook on morphology and syntax that has been used for more than a decade in linguistic courses presented by the Summer Institute of Linguistics, which published the English ed.

1841. Escobar, Alberto. Problemática de las lenguas nacionales (UNMSM/L, 40:80/81, 1968, p. 1-11)

Regional, national, and supranational standards of Spanish cause problems in communication in Hispanic America. Basic education is needed in areas where substandard Spanish is spoken.

1842. Estrada D., Samuel. Fundamentos lingüísticos de la composición oral y escrita (Lenguaje [Univ. del Valle, División de Humanidades, Cali, Colo.] 1:1/2, agosto 1972, p. 87-110, bibl.)

Philosophical treatment of the relationship between thought and language, with practical suggestions for oral and written composition, using transformational methodology.

1843. Estrada Monroy, Agustín. Lenguas de 12 provincias de Guatemala en el siglo XVIII (GIIN/GI, 7:4, oct./dic. 1972, p. 23-70)

Documents from Parish churches, now in the national archives of Guatemala, provide the data for a list of indigenous languages spoken in Guatemala and in Chiapas during the 18th century.

1844. *Estudios de Cultura Maya.* UNAM, Facultad de Filosofía y Letras. Vol. 7, 1968- . México.

Collection of 20 papers presented at the I International Seminar for the Study of Mayan Writing, 4-10 Dec. 1966, in Mexico City. Most of these articles have to do with the decipherment of glyphs from Mayan codices and monuments, but two deal with Mayan phonology: Norman McQuown "La Estructura Tonal de las Silabas del Maya Yucateco," and Michael G. Owen "Yucatec Phonology and Mayan Glyph Values," and two give a general linguistic orientation to the subject: Mauricio Swadesh "Algunas Orientaciones Generales sobre la Escritura Maya," and Marshall Durbin "Linguistics and Writing Systems."

1845. Faust, Norma. Gramática cocama: lecciones para el aprendizaje del idioma cocama. Presentación de Martha Hildebrandt. Yarinacocha, Peru, Instituto Lingüístico de Verano, 1972. 173 p. (Serie lingüística peruana, 6)

Twenty lessons in Cocama for non-speakers of the language, many of whom are young people of the tribe who have abandoned their forefathers' language in favor of Spanish. Author's purpose is to give these young people an appreciation of the grammar of the language and to enable them to communicate more effectively with older members of the tribe. Cocama is a Tupí-Guaraní language of some 10,000 speakers in northern Peru.

1846. Fields, Harriet. Una identificación preliminar de los sufijos indicadores de referencia en mayoruna (*in* Loos, Eugene E. *ed.* Estudios panos 2 [see item 1896] p. 283-306)

Considers verb suffixes in Mayoruna that indicate tense relationships, focus, mood, and first person without attempting to describe the deep structure of each.

1847. Foris, David. Sochiapan Chinantec syllable structure (IU/IJAL, 39:4, Oct. 1973, p. 232-235)

Phonemes of the Sochiapan dialect of Chinantec (14 consonants, two laryngeals, seven vowels, three tones) are described with reference to their distribution in the syllable. Stress is described as ballistic vs. controlled, contrasting in syllables that have a 32 tone glide (i.e., a glide from tone level three to level two). This dialect of Chinantec is spoken by some 2,000 Mexican Indians living in the area of San Pedro Sochiapan, Oaxaca.

1848. Fortune, David Lee. Gramática karajá: um estudo preliminar em forma transformacional (Série Lingüística [see item 1936] p. 101-161, bibl., tables)

Transformational analysis of Karajá, a Jê language of the state of Goiás, Bra. Includes 25 phrase structure rules, text with free translation and analysis, 14 transformational rules, and a Karajá-Portuguese lexicon of well over 600 forms.

1849. Foster, David William. Análisis transformacional de SE español. Traducción de Tito Villa Villegas

(Lenguaje [Univ. del Valle, División de Humanidades, Cali, Colo.] 1:1/2, agosto 1972, p. 189-209)

Transformational rules for generating *se*, which has been called "one of the most ubiquitous morphs in the Spanish language." (The original article appeared in Linguistics, No. 64, 1970, p. 10-25).

1850. Fought, John G. Chorti (Mayan) texts. Edited by Sarah S. Fought. Philadelphia, Univ. of Pennsylvania Press, 1972. 566 p., illus., tables.

Brief outline of phonology and grammar of Chorti, a Guatemalan language of 20,000 or more speakers, followed by a variety of native texts.

1851. Frantz, Donald G. "Citaciones directas" (*in* Loos, Eugene E. *ed.* Estudios panos 1 [see item 1895] p. 9-21)

Transformational analysis of direct and indirect quotations in Spanish with parallel examples from Cashibo, a Panoan language of eastern Peru.

1852. García de León, Antonio. Los elementos del tzotzil colonial y moderno. México, UNAM, Coordinación de Humanidades, Centro de Estudios Mayas, 1971. 107 p., map (Serie cuadernos, 7)

Presents phonology and grammatical sketch of Tzotzil (Mayan, Mexico), with vocabulary of roots and a brief text from colonial times, with phonemic transcription and Spanish translation.

1853. Garvin, Paul L. and **Madeline Mathiot.** The urbanization of the Guaraní language (*in* Tilly, Charles *ed.* An urban world. Boston, Mass., Little, Brown, 1974, p. 152-159)

Applies criteria for a standard language to Paraguayan Guaraní, spoken almost exclusively in rural areas and practically on a par with Spanish in urban areas. Criteria include properties of a standard language (flexible stability and intellectualization), functions of a standard language (unifying, separatist, and prestige), and attitudes toward a standard language (language loyalty, pride, and awareness of the norm). Concludes that Guaraní is becoming a standard language, and speaking it is a good index of the overall urbanization of different segments of the population.

1854. Gerdel, Florence. Fonemas del páez (*in* Gerdel, Florence and others. Sistemas fonológicos de idiomas colombianos [see item 1856] t. 2, p. 7-37, tables)

Spanish version of item 1855.

1855. _____. Paez phonemes (LING, 104, 15 May 1973, p. 28-48, tables)

Describes phonemes of Páez, a Macro-Chibchan language of Colombia of approximately 40,000 speakers. In addition to four oral and four nasal vowels (i, u, e, a and their nasalized counterparts), there are three semivowels (w, y, and ?) and 25 consonants and a phoneme of stress.

1856. _____ and others. Sistemas fonológicos de idiomas colombianos. t. 2. Bogota, Ministerio de Gobierno, 1973. 132 p., tables.

Studies in the phonology of seven indigenous languages of Colombia, representing four language families: Chibcha, Chocó, Guahibo, and Eastern Tucanoan. (For earlier studies in this series, see *HLAS 35:1640a*.) Individual titles are:
Florence Gerdel "Fonemas del Páez" (see item 1854)
Thomas Branks and Judith Branks "Fonología del Guambiano (see item 1817)
Hubert P. Tracy and Martha Tracy "Fonemas del Ica (Arhuaco)" (see item 1951)
Eileen Rex and Mareike Schöttelndreyer "Sistema fonológico del Catio (see item 1926)
Isabel Kerr and Marie Berg "Fonoemas del Cuiba" (see item 1874)
James Klumpp and Deloris Klumpp "Sistema Fonológico del Piratapuyo" (see item 1876)
Ronald Metzger and Lois Metzger "Fonología del Carapana" (see item 1903).

1857. Goller, Theodore R.; Patricia L. Goller; and **Viola G. Waterhouse.** The phonemes of Orizaba Nahuatl (IU/IJAL, 40:2, April 1974, p. 126-131, illus., table)

Phonology of Orizaba Nahuatl illustrates characteristic symmetry of consonant system typical of Aztec languages. This dialect of one of the major Uto-Aztecan languages is spoken by some 100,000 Indians living in the vicinity of Orizaba, Veracruz, Mex.

1858. González Casanova, Pablo. Cuentos indígenas. 2. ed. México, UNAM, Instituto de Investigaciones Históricas, 1965. 118 p.

Fourteen folktales in Náhuatl and Spanish compiled by a Mexican linguist of a generation ago.

1859. Gudschinsky, Sarah C. Fragmentos de Ofaié: a descrição de uma língua extinta. Tradução de Miriam Lemle (Série Lingüística [Summer Institute of Linguistics, Brasília] 3, 1974, p. 177-249, bibl., tables)

Describes phonology and noun and verb morphology of Ofaié, with a vocabulary of well over 200 items; based on linguistic data obtained from the last surviving speaker of the language, a member of the Jê language family, formerly spoken in southern Mato Grosso, Bra. (see *HLAS 35:1546*).

1860. _____. Manual de alfabeticación para pueblos pre-alfabetas. Traducción de Celia Paschero y Miguel Donoso Pareja. Mexico, Secretaría de Educación Pública, 1974. 215 p., illus., tables (SepSetenta, 149)

Deals with literacy in indigenous languages in four sections: 1) "Introduction," 2) "Teaching of Reading," 3) "Constructing the First Reading Book," and 4) "Special Problems." In 1) total program of literacy and the preparation of vernacular literature are considered; 2) is devoted to teaching recognition of key words and function words, along with other classroom techniques; 3) to format and content of primers; and 4) to teaching of adults, planning and testing an orthography, and teaching bilinguals. Many illustrations are drawn from the author's wide experience in Latin America as well as other parts of the world.

1861. _____. Sistemas contrastivos de marcadores de pessoa em duas línguas Carib: Apalaí e Hixkaryana (Série Lingüística [see item 1936] p. 57-62, tables)

Comparison of personal prefix systems of transitive and intransitive verbs of Apalai and Hixkaryana, two Carib languages spoken by small indigenous groups (100 speakers or less) in the state of Pará, Bra.

Guevara, Darío. El castellano y el quichua en el Ecuador: historia, etimología y semántica. See *HLAS 36:3819.*

1862. Gunn, Robert D. and **Mary R. Gunn.** Fonología bocotá (*in* Baptista, Patricia ed. Lenguas de Panamá [see item 804] t. 1, p. 31-48)

Describes sentence, phrase, word, and syllable levels of Bocotá as well as the 20 consonant and ten vowel (segmental) phonemes of the language and the suprasegmental phoneme of stress. Bocotá is an indigenous language of some 1,500 speakers located in central Panama and divided ethnographically into two distinct cultures, one of them closely related to Guaymí, with which group there is considerable intermarriage.

1863. Hall de Loos, Betty and **Eugene E. Loos.** La estructura semántica y fonológica de los prefijos verbales en capanahua (*in* Loos, Eugene E. ed. Estudios panos 1 [see item 1895] p. 63-132)

Proposes an explanation, in terms of transformational theory, of the semantic structure of verbal prefixes in Capanahua and evaluates the implication of the proposal for the development of languages in general and Panoan languages (of which family Capanahua is a member) in particular. This language is spoken by about 400 Indians of east central Peru.

Harvey, H.R. The Relaciones Geográficas, 1579-1586: native languages. See *HLAS 36:1304.*

1864. Headland, Paul. The grammar of Tunebo. Huntington Beach, Calif., Summer Institute of Linguistics, 1973. 76 p., bibl., map, tables (Language data microfiche, Amerindian series, 2)

Grammatical analysis of Tunebo, a Chibchan language of Colombia, spoken by about 3,000 inhabitants of the eastern and northern slopes of the eastern range of the Andes. Follows tagmemic model and uses practical (rather than scientific) orthography for examples and texts.

1865. Hensey, Fritz. Grammatical variables in southwestern American speech (LING, 108, 15 July 1973, p. 5-26, illus.)

Study of deviations from Standard Spanish in a corpus of text gathered from Mexican-Americans in the area of El Paso, Tex. Follows transformational model.

1866. Hills, Robert A. and **William R. Merrifield.** Ayutla Mixtec, just in case (IU/IJAL, 40:4, Oct. 1974, p. 283-291)

Outlines way in which case relations are realized in (surface) syntactic structure of the Ayutla dialect of Mixtec, an Otomanguean language spoken in the state of Guerrero, Mex. Cases discussed are: Agent, Patient, Source and Goal, Instrument, and Experiencer.

1867. Hollenbach, Barbara E. Reduplication and anomalous rule ordering in Copala Trique (IU/IJAL, 40:3, July 1974, p. 176-181, illus.)

Copying rules, to account for reduplication of verb roots in Copala Trique (an Otomanguean language of the state of Oaxaca, Mex.), seem to follow the tone sandhi rule. Suggests four solutions to resolve the problem of anomalous ordering.

1868. Hollenbach, Olena E. de. La aculturación lingüística entre los triques de Copala, Oaxaca (III/AI, 33:1, enero/marzo 1973, p. 65-95, bibl.)

Four centuries of contact with Spanish has had an influence on the Copala dialect of Trique, a Mixtecan language of the state of Oaxaca, Mex. Lists loan words, extensions of native words, and descriptive phrases used in various areas of the culture, and discusses sound changes made when Spanish words were borrowed.

1869. Horcasitas, Fernando. Cambio y evolución en la antroponimia náhuatl (UNAM/AA, 10, 1973, p. 265-283, bibl., tables)

Discusses sources of Aztec personal names before and since the Conquest, and lists modern surnames of Aztec origin.

1870. Hyde, Sylvia Y. El verbo reflexivo del amahuaca (*in* Loos, Eugene E. ed. Estudios panos 2 [see item 1896] p. 9-5)

Proposes analysis of verb forms in Amahuaca (a Panoan language of Peru) to establish a basic form that will account for their variety.

1871. Idrobo, James E. Las oraciones de relativo en español (Lenguaje [Univ. del Valle, División de Humanidades, Cali, Colo.] 1:1/2, agosto 1972, p. 71-86, bibl., illus.)

Presents traditional analysis of relative pronouns and a transformational analysis of the same and concludes that the latter presents numerous advantages.

Isbell, William H. Ecología de la expansión de los Quechua-hablantes. See item 1015.

1872. Jaquith, James R. Ayn plotdiytshet obaytsay: a practical alphabet for Plattdeutsch in Spanish-speaking areas (IU/ALK/ 12:8, Nov. 1970, p. 293-303, bibl., tables)

Sketches background of Mennonite colonies in northern Mexico, Bolivia, and Paraguay, where the common speech is Plattdeutsch. Non-phonemic spelling has been used in the scanty amount of vernacular literature which is printed in traditional gothic characters. Suggests new alphabet based on roman characters as a step toward learning Spanish on the part of the less conservative element in the Mennonite colonies.

1873. Keller, Kathryn C. Additional Chontal classifiers (IU/IJAL, 40:3, July 1974, p. 248-249)

Adds 34 suffixial classifiers in Chontal to list of 78 previously published in *International Journal of American Linguistics* (21, 1955, p. 258-275). Chontal is a Myan language (not to be confused with the Hokan language of the same name) of from 30 to 40,000 speakers living in the state of Tabasco, Mex.

1874. Kerr, Isabel J. and Marie Berg L. Fonemas del cuiba (*in* Gerdel, Florence and others. Sistemas fonológicos de idiomas colombianos [see item 1856] t. 2, p. 89-103, tables)

Phonemic system of Cuiba consists of 14 consonants, two semivowels, and six vowels, with a suprasegmental phoneme of stress. Cuiba is a Guahiban language of some 400 speakers located in the plains of eastern Colombia.

1875. Key, Mary Ritchie de *comp.* Vocabulario castellano regional. Prefacio por Féliz Sattori Román. Riberalta, Bol., Instituto Lingüístico de Verano, 1966. 62 p. (Vocabularios bolivianos, 5)

Around 1,000 words or phrases occurring in the Spanish of Peru and/or Bolivia, many of them loan words from Indian languages of those countries, some being older forms of Spanish no longer in common use, and others common expressions with a semantic shift. Glosses are in Spanish and/or English.

1876. Klumpp, James and Deloris Klumpp. Sistema fonológico del piratapuyo (*in* Gerdel, Florence and others. Sistemas fonológicos de idiomas colombianos [see item 1856] t. 2, p. 107-120, tables)

Piratapuyo is an Eastern Tucanoan language of about 400 speakers living along the Papuri river and its tributaries in Colombia and Brazil. The language has ten consonant phonemes, two semivowels, and six vowels, as well as two tones (high and low) and nasalization.

1877. Kneeland, Harriet. La frase nominal relativa en mayoruna y la ambigüedad (*in* Loos, Eugene E. *ed.* Estudios panos 2 [see item 1896] p. 53-105)

Cultural taboos on the use of proper names force mayoruna speakers to use circumlocutions either in the form of kinship terms or as "free" relative phrases, i.e., those that lack the nuclear referent of the nominal phrase. Lists rules for arriving at deep structure of such phrases which, out of context, are frequently ambiguous. Mayoruna is a Panoan language of 2,000 speakers in eastern Peru.

1878. Koefoed, G. De eenlettergrepige engelse woorden in het Surinaams (KITLV/B, 129:2/3, 1973, p. 321-339, tables)

Monosyllabic English words correspond to either monosyllabic or bisyllabic words in Sranan, depending upon the canonical form of the syllable: words consisting of a consonant and a vowel, or consonant, vowel and nasal, remain monosyllabic, but those that are closed syllables, or that contain a consonant cluster, become bisyllabic. Sranan, the lingua franca of Surinam, and spoken by 80 percent of the population, is an English creole language.

1879. Koontz, Carol and Joanne Anderson. Fonología teribe (*in* Baptista, Patricia *ed.* Lenguas de Panamá [see item 1804] t. 1, p. 49-69)

Describes phonological levels from sentence to segmental phoneme of Teribe, a Chibchan language of northwestern Panama comprising about 1,000 speakers. Phonemic system includes 22 consonants and 13 vowels, and suprasegmental phonemes of stress and nasalization.

1880. Kopesec, Michael F. and Bonnie M. Kopesec. La jerarquía fonológica del guaymí (*in* Baptista, Patricia *ed.* Lenguas de Panamá [see item 1804] t. 1, p. 7-30)

Describes sentence, phrase, word, and syllable levels of Guaymí phonology in addition to the 18 consonant and eight vowel (segmental) phonemes of the language and suprasegmental phonemes of stress and nasalization. Guaymí is a Chibchan language spoken by some 35,000 Indians of western Panama.

1881. Landerman, Peter *comp.* Vocabulario quechua del Pastaza. Presentación de Martha Hildebrandt.

Prólogo de Pedro Landerman. Yarinacocha, Peru, Instituto Lingüístico de Verano, 1973. 114 p. (Serie lingüística peruana, 8)

Vocabulary of Inga, a dialect of Quechua spoken by Indians of Peru living along the Pastaza river and some of its tributaries in the Dept. of Loreto. Contains a pronunciation guide, a phonological summary, and grammatical notes.

1882. Larsen, Helen. Some grammatical features of legendary narrative in Ancash Quechua (*in* Brend, Ruth M. *ed.* Advances in tagmemics. Amsterdam, North-Holland 1974, p. 419-440, bibl. [North-Holland linguistic series, 9])

Legendary narrative is one of three classes of discourse in the Huaraz dialect of Quechua spoken in the dept. of Ancash, Peru, (other discourse types are personal account narrative and conversation). Narrative analysis is illustrated by ten pages of text with free translation.

1883. Lastra de Suárez, Yolanda. Panorama de los estudios de lenguas yutoaztecas (UNAM/AA, 10, 1973, p. 337-386, bibl., tables)

Lists classifications of Uto-Aztecan languages from 1800 to the present and descriptive works on individual languages, as well as tables showing geographical distribution, approximate number of speakers, classifications of extinct languages, and types of descriptive works.

1884. Leander, Birgitta. Herencia cultural del mundo náhuatl a través de la lengua. México, Secretaría de Educación Pública, 1972. 286 p., bibl. (SepSetentas, 35)

Discusses daily life of pre-conquest Aztecs and gives Spanish vocabulary items that have been borrowed from Nahuatl and that are in common use, particularly in Mexico.

1885. _____. In Xochitl in Cuicatl: Flor y Canto, la poesía de los aztecas. México, Secretaría de Educación Pública, Instituto Nacional Indigenista, 1972. 308 p., bibl., illus., plates (Col. Sep-INI, 14)

First section deals with function and character of classical Aztec poetry, was well as sources and investigators; second section is a collection of pre-conquest Aztec poems with Spanish translation; and third is a smaller collection of post-conquest poems.

1886. Leap, William L. Who were the Piro? (IU/AL, 13:7, Oct. 1971, p. 321-330, bibl., tables)

Comparison of several languages of the American Southwest tends to support the thesis that Piro, now extinct, was a Tanoan language. (This Piro is not to be confused with the Arawakan language of the same name still spoken in Peru.)

1887. Lemle, Miriam. El nuevo estructuralismo en lingüística: Chomsky. Traducido del portugués por Antonio J. Caicedo (Lenguaje [Univ. del Valle, División de Humanidades, Cali, Colo.] 1:1/2, agosto 1972, p. 211-227, illus.)

Discusses development of generative-transformational linguistic theory which regards traitional grammars as outmoded and linguistic developments during the first half of the present century as an interregnum during which certain positive values were stressed, such as the need for formal precision and adequate data. Generative grammar, which is still in process of formulation, is largely concerned with syntax and with "deep" structure of language as well as "surface" structure. The original article in Portuguese appeared in *Tempo Brasileiro*, Nos. 15/16, 1968, p. 51-64).

1888. *Lenguaje.* Univ. del Valle, División de Humanidades. Vol. 1, Nos. 1/2, agosto 1972- . Cali, Colo.

Various aspects of transformational grammar are dealt with in nine of the 11 articles in this volume. These are:
Antonio J. Caicedo A. "Conceptos Fundamentales de la Gramática Transformacional" (see item 1822)
Norman Alhajj M. "Fundamentos Contemporáneos de la Filosofía del Lenguaje" (see item 1800)
Luis A. Baena Z. "Estructura Semántica y Transformaciones" (see item 1803)
Alfonso Bastidas C. "Reflexivos en Español" (see item 1807)
James E. Idrobo F. "Las Oraciones de Relativo en Español" (see item 1871)
Samuel Estrada D. "Fundamentos Lingüísticos de la Composición Oral y Escrita" (see item 1842)
David William Foster "Análisis Transformacional del SE en Español" (see item 1849)
Miriam Lemle "El Nuevo Estructuralismo en Lingüística: Chomsky" (see item 1887)
J.P. Thorne "La Gramática Generativa y el Análisis Estilístico" (see item 1949).

1889. Liccardi, Millicent and Joseph Grimes. Itonama intonation and phonemes (LING, 38, April 1968, p. 36-41, tables)

Brief description of intonation contours, words, syllables, and phonemes of Itonama, an indigenous language of northeastern Bolivia, with short text and 66-item vocabulary.

1890. Lionnet, Andrés. Los elementos de la lengua tarahumara. Mexico, UNAM, Instituto de Investigaciones Históricas, 1972. 104 p., bibl., map (Serie antropológica, 13)

Pt. 1 sketches briefly the phonology and grammar of Tarahumara, a Uto-Aztecan language of northern Mexico; pt. 2 consists of tables of affixes and their combinations; pt. 3 is an inventory of Tarahumara "elements" (root morphemes); and pt. 4 is a brief Spanish-Tarahumara vocabulary.

1891. Lobsiger, Georges. Connaissance de la nature et classifications indiennes (SSA/B, 38, 1974, p. 55-64, bibl.)

Based on words from various Indian languages of South America, the claim is made that the indigenous peoples classified flora and fauna and used generic names for fish, reptiles, plants, etc.

1892. Loos, Eugene E. Algunas implicaciones de la reconstrucción de un fragmento de la gramática del proto-pano (*in* Loos, Eugene E. *ed.* Estudios panos 2 [see item 1896] p. 263-282)

Proposes transformational rules for deriving surface structures in modern Panoan languages from assumed deep structures of proto-Pano.

1893. _____. La construcción del reflexivo en los idiomas panos (*in* Loos, Eugene E. *ed.* Estudios panos 2 [see item 1896] p. 161-261)

Proposes a definition of reflexive in semantic structures to distinguish genuine reflexives from pseudo reflexives in Capanahua. Lists 12 rules to explain the different forms of the reflexive verb.

1894. _____. La señal de transitividad del sustantivo en los idiomas panos (*in* Loos, Eugene E. *ed.* Estudios panos 1 [see item 1895] p. 133-184)

Attempts to explain the various kinds of subject markers in Panoan languages by means of transformational rules. Languages of this family are spoken in Bolivia and Peru.

1895. _____ *ed.* Estudios panos 1. Presentación [de] Martha Hildebrandt. Yarinacocha, Peru, Instituto Lingüístico de Verano, 1973. 211 p., bibl., illus., tables (Serie lingüística peruana, 10)

Five articles by members of the Summer Institute of Linguistics in Peru on languages of the Panoan family of the upper Amazon:
Donald G. Frantz "Citaciones Directas" p. 9-21 (see item 1851)
Olive A. Shell "Los Modos del Cashibo y el Análisis del Performativo" p. 23-62 (see item 1938)
Betty Hall de Loos and Eugene Loos "La Estructura Semántica y Fonológica de los Prefijos Verbales en Capanahua" p. 63-132 (see item 1863)
Eugene Loos "La Señal de Transitividad del Sustantivo en los Idiomas Panos" p. 133-184 (see item 1894)
Eugene Scott and Donald G. Frantz "La Pregunta en Sharanahua y Constreñimientos Propuestos sobre la Permutación de la Pregunta" p. 185-209 (see item 1934).

1896. _____ *ed.* Estudios panos 2. Presentación [de] Martha Hildebrandt. Yarinacocha, Peru, Instituto Lingüístico de Verano, 1973. 313 p., bibl., illus., tables (Série lingüística peruana, 11)

Six articles on Panoan languages by members of the Summer Institute of Linguistics [see item 1895]. Contents are:
Sylvia Young de Hyde "El Verbo Reflexivo del Amahuaca" p. 9-51 (see item 1870)
Harriet Kneeland "La Frase Nominal Relativa en Mayoruna y la Ambigüedad" p. 53-105 (see item 1877)
Richard Montag "La Estructura Semántica de las Relaciones entre Frases Verbales en Cashinahua" p. 107-159 (see item 1905)
Eugene Loos "La Construcción del Reflexivo en los Idiomas Panos" p. 161-261 (see item 1893)
Eugene Loos "Algunas Implicaciones de la Reconstrucción de un Fragmento de la Gramática del Proto-Pano" p. 263-282 (see item 1892)
Harriet Fields "Una Identificación Preliminar de los Sufijos Indicadores de Referencia en Mayoruna" p. 283-306 (see item 1846).

1897. Lopes, Gildo. Caminos del quichua al Brasil. Quito, Editorial Casa de la Cultura Ecuatoriana, 1969. 94 p., illus.

Discusses Ecuador's linguistic influence on Brazil, where words of both Spanish and Quichua origin are in common use.

1898. López Austin, Alfredo. Un repertorio de los tiempos en idioma náhuatl (UNAM/AA, 10, 1973, p. 285-296)

Description of a kind of almanac handwritten on blank pages of a copy of Pedro de Gante's *Doctrina christiana en lengua mexicana,* published in 1553. Text, which appears to have been written by a native speaker of Nahuatl who did not speak Spanish, is transscribed and translated into Spanish, with notes on some of the misspellings and doubtful readings.

1899. Lozano, E. La mujer infiel (UNC/AIL, 10, 1970, p. 97-100)

Translation of a story in Vilela, an indigenous language of northern Argentina, related to the Guaicuruan languages of the Chaco.

1900. McLeod, Ruth. Fonemas xavánte. Tradução de Yonne de Freitas Leite (Série Lingüística [Summer Institute of Linguistics, Brasília] 3, 1974, p. 131-152, tables)

Describes six syllable patterns, ten consonant phonemes (p, t, c, ʔ, b, d, j, w, r, h), and 13 vowel phonemes (i, +, u, ĩ, e, ë o, ɛ̃, a, ɿ, ɛ̃, ã, ɿ̃) of Xavánte, a Jê language of eastern Mato Grosso, Bra.

1901. Mattos, Rinaldo de. Fonêmica xerente (Série Lingüística [see item 1936] p. 79-100, tables)

Ten consonants and 14 vowels (considering five nasalized vowels as distinct from their oral counterparts) form the phoneme inventory of Xavante, an digenous Jê language of the state of Goiás, Bra. Includes vocabulary list of more than 200 words, with phonemic and phonetic transcription.

1902. Mayers, Marvin K. and **Miriam McNeilly.** Pocomchi corn origin tales

(LING, 104, 15 May 1973, p. 74-94, map, table)

Comparison of three versions of a corn-origin tale told by Pocomchi Indians of Guatemala from different dialect areas.

1903. Metzger, Ronald and Lois Metzger. Fonología de carapana (*in* Gerdel, Florence and others. Sistemas fonológicos de idiomas colombianos [see item 1856] t. 2, p. 121-132, tables)

About 500 inhabitants of the tropical jungle in southeastern Colombia speak Carapana, an Eastern Tucanoan language of eight consonant phonemes, three semivowels, and six vowels. Tone and nasalization are the suprasegmental phonemes.

1904. Miranda S., Pedro. Diccionario breve castellano-aymara y aymara-castellano. La Paz, Editorial El Siglo, 1970. 311 p.

Dictionary of Aymara, the native language of well over a million inhabitants of the Andean highlands of Bolivia and Peru. About 2,500 entries in the Spanish-Aymara section and twice that number in the Aymara-Spanish. Uses orthography recommended by the III Inter-American Indian Congress (1954).

1905. Montag, Richard. La estructura semántica de las relaciones entre frases verbales en cashinahua (*in* Loos, Eugene E. *ed.* Estudios panos 2 [see item 1896] p. 107-159)

Proposes semantic structures to represent the relations between propositions in the deep structure of Cashinahua, and transformational rules to derive the surface structures from these. Cashinahua is a Panoan language of Peru and Brazil.

1906. Montes Giraldo, Juan Joaquín and María Luisa Rodríguez de Montes. El maíz en el habla y la cultura popular de Colombia: con notas sobre su origen y nombres en lenguas indígenas americanas. Bogotá, Instituto Caro y Cuervo, 1975. 187 p., bibl., illus., maps, plates, tables (Publicaciones, 33)

Considers various claims for the place of origin of Indian corn and lists names of the plant in various indigenous languages of the Americas. Ch. 3 lists words pertaining to corn and its use in the Spanish of Colombia, and Ch. 4 is a collection of popular refrains, sayings, and riddles connected with corn, and a discussion of the use of corn as a food and as medicine, along with popular beliefs and customs relating to corn.

1907. Moore, Bruce R. El sistema fonético del idioma colorado (Boletín de Informaciones Científicas Nacionales [Casa de la Cultura Ecuatoriana, Quito] 13:101/102 [3. época] enero/junio 1972, p. 72-78)

Describes phonology of Colorado, a Chibchan language spoken by about 1,000 inhabitants of the eastern jungles of Ecuador. Phonemic system includes 16 consonants and five vowels, besides nasalization, stress, intonation, and "a form of intersyllabic aspiration."

1908. Münzel, Mark. Kawre veja puku "Dejamos lejos al gran oso hormiguero:" notas preliminares sobre cinco canciones axé (Suplemento Antropológico [Univ. Católica, Asunción] 6:1/2, 1971, p. 177-259, bibl., plates)

Text and translation, with notes, of five songs in the language of the Axé, or Guayaki, a nomadic group of about 350 Indians of eastern Paraguay. The songs and a narrative in the vernacular were transcribed from tape recordings. Includes six plates.

1909. Navarrete N., Antonio. Lenguas y tambores (Lenguaje [Univ. del Valle, División de Humanidades, Cali. Colo.] 1:1/2, agosto 1972, p. 111-117, bibl.)

Many African tribes and several in South America use drums for sending messages over long distances. The "drum language" reproduces to some degree the tones and rhythm of the language spoken by the tribe that uses it. Witotos of Colombia use two drums, called male and female, to produce distinct tones.

1910. La obra del Instituto Lingüístico de Verano (SGL/B, 89, agosto 1969/agosto 1970, p. 49-55, map)

Brief account of history of the Summer Institute of Linguistics since its founding in 1935 and of the program of bilingual education among jungle Indians of Peru. Begun in 1952 in collaboration with the Peruvian Ministry of Education, by 1968 this program had trained 190 bilingual teachers who in turn had taught more than 6,000 indigenous children to read and write in Spanish as well as in their mother tongues and had given them basic instruction in agriculture, hygiene, and other subjects. Since 1964 a similar program has been carried on under the direction of Donald H. Burns among the Uuechua Indians of the highlands of Peru (see *HLAS 35:1515*).

1911. Orr D., Carolina and Juan E. Hudelson *eds.* and *comps.* Cuillurguna: cuentos de los quichuas del Oriente ecuatoriano. Quito, Houser Limitada, 1971. 95 p., illus.

Collection of 32 folktales in Quichua of Ecuador (Quechumaran language family), with Spanish translation.

1912. Ortiz Mayans, Antonio. Nuevo diccionario español-guaraní: guaraní-español. 10. ed. B.A., Platero Editorial, 1973. 986 p., map.

Dictionary of Guaraní, an indigenous language spoken in several areas of South America, but particularly in Brazil and Paraguay. Spanish-Guaraní section covers

728 p., Guaraní-Spanish, 277 p. Eight p. of "grammatical synthesis."

1913. Parker, Gary J. On the evidence for complex stops in Proto-Quechua (IU/IJAL, 39:2, April 1973, p. 106-110, bibl., tables)

Presents arguments against Proulx's reconstruction of aspirated stops in Proto-Quechua (see *HLAS 33:1802*). Evidence for reconstruction of complex stops in Proto-Quechua as proposed by Orr and Longacre (see *HLAS 31:2409*) is only tenuous at present, Parker considers.

1914. Paulston, Christina Bratt. Del dilema moral de un especialista en sociolingüística (III/AI, 33:1, 1. trimestre 1973, p. 97-105)

Deals with the use of other than the standard language or dialect in primary education and the contention that it is a political tool for maintaining the status quo. Mentions particularly the use of Quechua in Peru (see item 1910 and *HLAS 35:1515*) and non-standard English in schools in black communities in the US.

1915. Peeke, M. Catherine. Preliminary grammar of Auca. Norman, Univ. of Oklahoma, Summer Institute of Linguistics, 1973. 135 p., bibl., illus. (Publications in linguistics and related fields, 39)

Author follows a modified tagmemic model to describe the grammar of Auca, a language spoken by "a few hundred Indians whose hunting rights comprise approximately one hundred square miles of rain forest in eastern Ecuador." Although some have classified Auca as Zaparoan, "recent descriptive analyses of Auca and of Zaparo . . . show little structural or phonological similarity." Book's six chapters consist of: "Introduction;" "Discourse Constraints on Sentence Structure;" "Sentence Classification;" "Sentence Structure;" "Permutations;" and "Partial Lexicon."

1916. Pensinger, Brenda J. *comp.* Diccionario mixteco-español, español-mixteco. Mexico, Instituto Lingüístico de Verano, 1974. 159 p., illus., maps, tables (Serie de vocabularios y diccionarios indígenas Mariano Silva y Aceves, 18)

Dictionary of about 2,000 entries in a sub-dialect of Mixtec, an Otomanguean language of the State of Oaxaca, Mex. Words illustrated by usage in context. Includes grammatical sketch of dialect and explanation of the orthography.

1917. Pickering, Wilbur. Vocabulário Kaxarirí (Série Lingüística [see item 1936] p. 63-66, tables)

Word list gathered on a field trip to Amazonas, Bra., in 1962 is presented as evidence that Kaxarirí should be classified as a Pano language rather than Arawakan, as formerly believed.

1918. Pike, Eunice V. A multiple stress system versus a tone system (IU/IJAL, 40:3, July 1974, p. 169-175)

Discusses contrastive features of two language systems (multiple stress and tonal) that distinguish them from one another. Examples cited from many indigenous languages of Latin America.

1919. ———— and Kent Wistrand. Step-up terrace tone in Acatlán Mixtec, Mexico (*in* Brend, Ruth M. *ed.* Advances in tagmemics. Amsterdam, North Holland, 1974, p. 81-104, tables [North-Holland linguistic series, 9])

Process phoneme of terrace tone in the Acatlán dialect of Mixtec operates in the opposite direction from that in the Coatzospan dialect (see item 1920), in that high tones following the phoneme have a higher pitch than high tones preceding the phoneme. Tonal system described with 16 rules of tone sandhi. Segmental phonemes include 21 consonants and five oral and five nasal vowels.

1920. ———— and Priscilla Small. Downstepping terrace tone in Coatzospan Mixtec (*in* Brend, Ruth M. *ed.* Advances in tagmemics. Amsterdam, North Holland, 1974, p. 105-134, tables, bibl. [North-Holland linguistic series, 9])

Tonal system of the Coatzospan dialect of Mixtec (Otomanguean language family, Mexico) includes a process phoneme of "terrace tone" which exerts a lowering influence on a following high tone. Tone sandhi described by 18 rules, with illustrations from Mixtec.

1921. Proulx, Paul. Certain aspirated stops in Quechua (IU/IJAL, 40:3, July 1974, p. 257-262, table)

Considers Parker's evidence against reconstructing complex stops in Proto-Quechua (see item 1913 and *HLAS 33:1802*). Reaffirms validity of seven of the eight cognate sets originally presented, and adduces three more. Discards six of Parker's 23 cognate sets in which correspondence appears in the second syllable and presents evidence for the reshaping of 17 Cuzco words by analogy. The remaining five counter-examples are unexplained, but aspiration in the Cuzco words may be due to the influence of Aymara on that dialect of Quechua.

1922. Reichlen, Henry and Paule Reichlen. Le manuscrit Boscana de la Bibliothèque Nationale de Paris: relation sur les indiens Acâgchemem de la mission de San Juan Capistrano, Californie (SA/J, 60, 1971, p. 233-273, facsims.)

Complete text of an early 19th-century manuscript written by a Franciscan priest, Gerónimo Boscana, describing the folklore and manner of life of the Indians of San Juan Capistrano. Considered by the late A.L. Kroeber to be a most important ethnographic document on the Indians of California, the work has been translated in whole or in part into both English and French, but inconsistencies in content and lack of knowledge of the whereabouts of the Spanish original created what came to be known as the "Boscana mystery." Variant copies may have been made by the author; that published here is now in the National Library in Paris.

1923. Reid, Aileen A. and Ruth G. Bishop comps. Diccionario totonaco de Xicotepec de Juárez, Puebla: totonaco-castellano, castellano-totonaco. Mexico, Instituto Lingüístico de Verano, 1974. 418 p., bibl., illus., tables (Serie de vocabularios y diccionarios indígenas Mariano Silva y Aceves, 17)

Bilingual dictionary of some 4,000 words in a dialect of Totonac spoken by 10,000 or more inhabitants of the district of Xicotepec in the state of Puebla, Mex. Includes outline of the grammar as well as numerous phrases and sentences in Totonac illustrating the words in context.

1924. Relatório de atividades do Summer Institute of Linguistics, período de 1956 a 1973. Brasília, Summer Institute of Linguistics, 1973. 85 p., map, plates, table.

Lists works by S.I.L. authors working in Brazil, both published and archived in the National Museum. Describes bilingual education program and linguistic courses presented since 1969 in Rio and Brasília. Includes photos of Indians of various tribal groups.

1925. Rensch, Calvin R. Otomanguean isoglosses (in Sebeok, Thomas A. ed. Diachronic, areal, and typological linguistics. The Hague, Mouton, 1973, p. 295-316, bibl., map [Current trends in linguistics, 11])

Presents evidence for the inclusion of Huave in the Otomanguean family of languages (spoken mainly in Mexico), and discusses sound changes in their history within this language family.

1926. Rex, Eileen and Mareike Schötelndreyer. Sistema fonológico del Catío (in Gerdel, Florence and others. Sistemas fonológicos de idiomas colombianos [see item 1856] t. 2, p. 73-85, tables)

Close to 10,800 inhabitants of northwest Colombia speak Catío, a language of the Chocó family. Phonemic system consists of 13 consonants, three semi-vowels, and six vowels, with stress and nasalization as suprasegmental phonemes.

1927. Richards, Joan. Dificuldades na análise da possessão nominal na língua Waurá (Série Lingüística [see item 1936] p. 11-29, tables)

Waurá nouns fall into three classes: obligatorily non-possessed, obligatorily possessed, and optionally possessed. Possession is marked in some instances by a suffix, in others by nasalization or by stress change, and in some it is unmarked. Waurá is an Arawakan language spoken by 100-250 Indians of Brazil living in the Xingu National Park, Mato Grosso.

1928. Rona, José Pedro. Extensión del tipo chaqueño de lenguas (USP/RA, 17/20:1, 1969/1972, p. 93-103, illus.)

Considers typological classification of languages more useful than genealogical classification in determining the origin of the extinct Charrúa language, formerly spoken in the Paraguayan Chaco.

1929. Rowan, Orland. Some features of Paressí discourse structure (IU/AL, 14:4, April 1972, p. 131-146)

Describes narrative discourse of Paressi, with illustrations of this and three other discourse types: procedural, expository, and hortatory. Patterns found in development of discourse deal with operation of space settings, time settings, connective devices, and identification of participants. Paressí is an Arawakan language spoken by some 300 individuals in the state of Mato Grosso, Bra.

1930. Sánchez Labrador, José and Elke Unger. Familia guaycurú: vocabulario eyiguayegi, según el manuscrito del siglo XVIII; parte 2da.: Letras M-Z [and] Resumen etnográfico del vocabulario eyiguayegi-mbayá. Asunción, Museo Etnográfico Andrés Barbero, 1972. 1 v. (Various pagings) (Lenguas chaqueñas, 3)

Consists of two papers: José Sánchez Labrador "Vocabulario Eyiguayegi, Según el Manuscrito del Siglo XVIII ... Parte 2da: Letras M-Z," and Elke Unger "Resúmen Etnográfico del Vocabulario Eyiguayegi-Mbayá del P.J. Sánchez Labrador, S.I." The first is a continuation of a vocabulary begun in an earlier volume (see HLAS 35:1631), and the second a reorganization, under ethnographic subdivisions, of this vocabulary made by an 18th-century priest. Both vocabularies are from Spanish to the indigenous language. Eyiguayegi, or Guayaqui, an indigenous language of Paraguay, belongs to the Guarani branch of the Tupi-Guaraní language family.

1931. Saxton, Dean and Lucille Saxton comps. O'otham hoho'ok a'agitha: Legends and lore of the Papago and Pima Indians. Foreword by Bernard L. Fontana. Tucson, Univ. of Arizona Press, 1973. 441 p., bibl., illus.

Compilation of legends in Papago and English, the former written in a practical alphabet developed through tests with Papago speakers. Includes notes on legends and on the alphabet, and 50 p. of vocabulary. Papago is a Utoaztecan language of the southwestern US and northern Mexico.

1932. Schauer, Stanley and others Aspectos de la cultura material de grupos étnicos de Colombia. t. 1. Translated by Jorge Arbeláez G. Bogotá, Ministerio de Gobierno, 1973. 335 p., bibl., illus., map, plates.

Vocabulary items from various indigenous languages appear here and there in what is primarily a series of ethnographic studies of native peoples of Colombia prepared by members of the Summer Institute of Linguistics. Each chapter is written by a different author or pair of authors, and consists of a description of the culture of a particular ethnic group, illustrated by photographs and/or drawings of objects referred to in the text. The 20 chapters deal with the following groups: Yucuna, Huitoto, Tucano, Cubeo, Carapana, Desano, Cacua (Macú), Guanano, Southern Barasano, Siona, Emberá, Guahibo, Cuiba, Guajiro, Tunebo, Guambiano, Inga, Cogui, Malayo, and Arhuaco (Ica).

1933. Schumann G., Otto. La lengua chol de Tila, Chiapas. México, UNAM, Coordinación de Humanidades, Centro de Estudios Mayas, 1973. 113 p., bibl. (Serie cuadernos, 8)

Brief description of phonology, morphophonemics, and noun classes of a dialect of Chol (Mayan, Mexico), together with a Spanish-Chol and Chol-Spanish vocabulary and a brief chapter on the relationship of Chol to other Mayan languages.

1934. Scott, Eugene and **Donald G. Frantz.** La pregunta en sharanahua y constreñimientos propuestos sobre la permutación de la pregunta (*in* Loos, Eugene E. *ed.* Estudios panos 1 [see item 1895] p. 185-209)

Transformational analysis of interrogative sentences in Sharanahua (also called Marinahua), a Panoan language of eastern Peru.

1935. Selva, Salomón de la. Acolmixtli Nezahualcóyotl: poema en tres tiempos clásicos. Acroasis de Ernesto Mejía Sánchez. México, Gobierno del Estado de México, 1972. 121 p., illus.

Three-part poem in honor of Nezahualcóytl, prince of Texcoco who became emperor of the Aztecs during the century preceding the Spanish conquest. Presented to the President of Mexico in 1958, this last work of the Nicaraguan poet, Salomón de la Selva, was republished in 1972 on the fifth centennial of the death of the Aztec hero.

1936. *Série Lingüística.* Summer Institute of Linguistics. No. 1, 1973- Brasília.

Collection of linguistic articles on indigenous languages of Brazil, published by the branch of the Summer Institute of Linguistics working in that country, Titles of individual articles are:
Joan Richards "Dificuldades na Análise da Possessão Nominal na Língua Waurá" p. 11-29 (see item 1927)
Rose Dobson "Notas sobre Substantivos do Kayabí" p. 30-56 (see item 837)
Sarah C. Gudschinsky "Sistemas Contrastivos de Marcadores de Pessoa en Duas Línguas Carib: Apalí e Hixkaryána" p. 57-62 (see item 1861)
Wilbur Pickering "Vocabulário Kaxarirí" p. 63-66 (see item 1917)
Joan Boswood "Evidências para a Inclusão do Aripaksta no Filo Marco-Jê" p. 67-78 (see item 1814)
Rinaldo de Mattos "Fonêmica Xerente" p. 79-100 (see item 1901)
David Lee. Fortune "Gramática Karaja: un Estudo Preliminar em Forma Transformacional" p. 101-161 (see item 1848).

1937. Sheldon, Steven N. Some morphophonemic and tone perturbation rules in Mura-Pirahã (IU/IJAL, 40:4, Oct. 1974, p. 279-282, tables)

Presents six morphophonemic rules (three affecting tone and three affecting segmental phonemes) for noun-adjective and noun-verb sequences in Mura-Pirahã, a language isolate of Amazonas, Bra., of about 100 speakers. These deal with tone extension across word boundaries and within the noun, metathesis, deletion, vowel replacement, and tone replacement.

1938. Shell, Olive A. Los modos del Cashibo y el análisis del performativo (*in* Loos, Eugene E. *ed.* Estudios panos 1 [see item 1895] p. 23-62)

Analysis of surface structure of Cashibo sentences shows that performative verbs are implicit in the deep structure. Cashibo is a Panoan language of eastern Peru.

1939. Smith, Richard D. Southern Barasano grammar. Huntington Beach, Calif., Summer Institute of Linguistics, 1973. 75 p., bibl., tables (Language data microfiche. Amerindian series, 3)

Describes the southern dialect of Barasano, an Eastern Tucanoan language of 300-400 speakers living along the Piraparaná river and its tributaries in Colombia.

Spielman, Richard S.; E.C. Migliazza; and **James V. Neel.** Regional, linguistic and genetic differences among the Yanomama Indians. See item 2125.

1940. Stout, Mickey and **Ruth Thomson.** Fonêmica Txukuhamẽi, Kayapó. Tradução de Eunice Burgess (Série Lingüística [Summer Institute of Linguistics, Brasília] 3, 1974, p. 153-176, tables)

Succinct presentation of the 16 consonant and 17 vowel phonemes, and eight syllable types, of Kayapó, followed by word lists and charts illustrating distribution of allophones. Stress occurs normally on final syllable of word theme.

1941. _____ and _____. Modalidade em Kayapó (Série Lingüística [Summer Institute of Linguistics, Brasília] 3, 1974, p. 69-97, table)

Focuses on Fillmore's concept of modality as described in a previous article on Kayapó sentence structure (see item 1948). Orientation, connection, and concept are the three types of modality posited for this Jê language of 1,500 speakers living in northern Mato Grosso, Bra.

1942. Stross, Brian. Social structure and role allocation in Tzeltal oral literature (AFS/JAF, 86:340, April/June 1973, p. 95-113, plates)

Recommends study of folk tales as aid to ethnographic analysis of culture and presents ten such tales from Tenejapa Tzeltal, a Mayan language of southern Mexico. For folklorist comment see *HLAS 36:1006*.

1943. Suárez, Jorge A. Clasificación interna de la familia lingüística Chon (UNC/AIL, 10, 1970, p. 29-59, bibl., tables)

Discusses relationships among indigenous languages of the southern part of South America (Patagonia and Tierra del Fuego). These are difficult to establish with certainty, as some languages have become extinct and the only data from them are scanty word lists inadequately transcribed; the vocabulary of others has been affected by taboos that suppress the use of words which are also names of persons recently deceased.

1944. ─────. Macro-Pano-Tacanan (IU/IJAL, 39:3, July 1973, p. 137-154, bibl., tables)

Evidence of genetic relationships among language groups includes not only sound correspondences but resemblances in form and meaning among pronominal elements as well. Gives summary of phonemic systems of Proto-Panoan (according to Shell 1965), Proto-Tacanan (Key 1968; Girard 1970), Yuracare, Moseten, and Tehuelche, and sound correspondences based on a list of 208 cognate sets. The area covered by these languages includes parts of Peru, Bolivia, and Brazil.

1945. ─────. On Proto-Zapotec phonology (IU/IJAL, 39:4, Oct. 1973, p. 236-249, bibl., tables)

Reconsideration of the proto-Zapotec phonemic system proposed by María Teresa Fernández de Miranda, particularly her reconstruction of *c, *c, *3, *s, *z, and *r. Author considers fortis/lenis contrast as equivalent to that between geminate and simple consonants. Appends list of reconstructed forms.

1946. Swadesh, Mauricio; Maria Cristina Alvarez; and **Juan R. Bastarrachea.** Diccionario de elementos del maya yucateco colonial. Prólogo por Daniel Cazés. México, UNAM, Coordinación de Humanidades, Centro de Estudios Mayas, 1970. 137 p., bibl. (Cuaderno, 3)

Compilation of materials from several dictionaries of classical Mayan, with brief sketch of its phonology and grammar.

1947. Swisshelm, Germán. Un diccionario del quechua de Huaraz: quechua-castellano, castellano-quechua. Huaraz, Peru, n.p. 1972. 399 p. (Estudios culturales benedictinos, 2)

Detailed description of phonology and grammar precedes the vocabulary of a dialect of Quechua spoken in the Dept. of Ancash, Peru.

Thompson, J. Eric S. Sufijos numerales y medidas en yucateco. See *HLAS 36:1356*.

1948. Thomson, Ruth and **Mickey Stout.** Elementos proposicionais em orações Kayapó (Série Lingüística [Summer Institute of Linguistics, Brasília] 3, 1974, p. 35-67, bibl., tables)

Sentence structure of Kayapó (Jê, Brazil), analyzed according to a modified transformational-generative pattern.

1949. Thorne, J.P. La gramática generativa y el análisis estilístico. Traducción por Norman Alhajj y Eutiqio Leal (Lenguaje [Univ. del Valle, División de Humanidades, Cali, Colo.] 1:1/2, agosto 1972, p. 229-242)

Discusses generative rules that will result in "well-formed sentences." (Taken from Lyons, John ed. *New horizons in linguistics*, Baltimore, Md., Penguin Books, 1970.)

Torero, Alfredo. Lingüística e historia de la sociedad andina. See *HLAS 36:1443*.

1950. Tracy, Francis V. An introduction to Wapishana verb morphology (IU/IJAL, 40:2, April 1974, p. 120-125, table)

Five levels of structure are posited from root to word in the verb system of Wapishana, an Arawakan language of southern Guyana and northwestern Brazil with between 4,000 and 9,000 speakers Tagmemic formulas illustrate transitive, intransitive, and descriptive clauses.

1951. Tracy, Hubert P. and **Martha Tracy.** Fonemas del ica─arhuaco (*in* Gerdel, Florence and others. Sistemas fonológicos de idiomas colombianos [see item 1856] t. 2, p. 57-70, tables)

Ica words may have from one to five syllables, with stress generally falling on the penultimate. Phonemic system has 18 consonants and seven vowels. Ica is a language of the Chibchan family, spoken by about 3,000 inhabitants of the Sierra Nevada de Santa Marta, Colo.

1952. Turner, Paul R. Highland Chontal dialect survey (LING, 104, 15 May 1973, p. 95-104, map)

Discusses survey of the highland dialect of Tequistlatec (Oaxaca Chontal) and its implications for diachronic linguistics. Outlines procedure followed and presents phonological, lexical, and grammatical contrasts discovered. Concludes that comparative studies should not be limited to phonology and lexicon, but should include grammar. Oaxaca Chontal is a Hokan language spoken in the southeastern part of the state of Oaxaca, Mex.

1953. Uribe Villegas, Oscar. Monolingües indígenas de México: su distribución territorial y su dispersión sociolingüística (UNAM/RMS, 35:3, julio/sept. 1973, p. 585-600, tables)

Attempts to interpret census figures to determine location of monolingual Indians in Mexico and the responsibilities of individual states for the social development of various groups. Only 29 language names are identified, mutually unintelligible dialects are not distinguished, and two language names, Popoloca and Popoluca, are confused.

1954. Waller, Helen *comp.* Bibliografia do Summer Institute of Linguistics. Brasília, Summer Institute of Linguistics, 1973. 68 p.

Lists works by members of the Brazil branch of the Summer Institute of Linguistics under these categories: 1) linguistics and anthropology and 2) applied linguistics as well as 3) items that have been placed in the archives of the national museum in Rio. Works in press included in short appendix.

1955. Walton, James *comp.* Bibliografía del Instituto Lingüístico de Verano en Columbia, 1972. Prólogo por Antonio J. Arango. Bogoá, Ministerio de Gobierno, 1973. 27 p.

Lists linguistic and ethnographic works by members of the Summer Institute of Linguistics in Colombia and didactic materials that they have published in the indigenous languages of that country.

1956. Wasson, R. Gordon; George Cowan; Florence Cowan; and Willard Rhodes. María Sabina and her Mazatec mushroom velada. N.Y., Harcourt Brace Jovanovich, 1974. 282 p., illus., maps, music, plates (Ethnomycological studies, 3)

Text and translation of a shamanic ceremony in Mazatec, with accompanying recording and musical score. María Sabina was the shaman; she and the participants in the vigil (held in Huautla de Jiménez, Oaxaca, Mex., on the night of 12-13 July 1958) were under the influence of hallucinogenic mushrooms while the ceremony, performed for the benefit of a sick teenager, was recorded photographically and on magnetic tape. Excellent source of ethnographic and linguistic information about the Mazatecs, whose language belongs to the Otomanguean language family. Includes four cassette recordings and a 79-p. musical score.

1957. Wheatley, James. Knowledge, authority and individualism among the Cura, Bacairi (IU/AL, 15:8, Nov. 1973, p. 337-344)

Discusses individualism and political organization among the Curas (otherwise known as Bacairi) of Brazil, their attitude to authority, and their world view. Of great importance to them is the shaman who is essentially a healer rather than a sorcerer, and respected for his wisdom. The tribal name is from the first person plural pronoun, meaning "we, inclusive."

1958. ———. Pronouns and nominal elements in Bacairi discourse (LING, 104, 15 May 1973, p. 105-115)

Analysis of pronominal system of Bacairi, a Carib language of some 250 speakers in west central Brazil. Considers system to have four dimensions: thematization, focus, deictic scaling, and animateness; and discusses these in terms of Halliday's concept of theme and rheme.

1959. Wikander, Stig. Chichenitzá: an Altaic name (SL, 25:2, 1971, p. 129-130)

Name of Mayan ruins of Chichén Itzá presented in evidence to support claim that Mayan and Altaic are related language families (see *HLAS 31:2471*).

1960. Wise, Mary Ruth. Social roles, plot roles, and focal roles in a Nomatsiguenga Campa myth (*in* Brend, Ruth M. *ed.* Advances in tagmemics. Amsterdam, North Holland, 1974, p. 389-418, bibl., tables [North-Holland linguistic series, 9])

Analysis of one type of discourse in Nomatsiguenga Campa, an Arawakan language of about 1,000 speakers in eastern Peru. Kinship terms, rather than proper names, are often used in identifying the characters in the myths, who play three types of roles simultaneously. Illustrated by a deity myth with free and literal translation.

PHYSICAL ANTHROPOLOGY

ROBERT A. HALBERSTEIN

*Assistant Professor of Anthropology
Department of Anthropology and Department of Epidemiology
and Public Health
University of Miami*

THE FIELD OF PHYSICAL ANTHROPOLOGY is at once becoming increasingly unified and diversified. Theory construction in physical anthropology has traditionally involved the incorporation of numerous varied methods and findings which bear upon the understanding of the complexities of human evolution and biological variation. The recent trend toward a stronger unification of the field is reflected by the fact that no fewer than 16 new or revised general textbooks on physical anthropology were published between 1971 and 1974. It is an encouraging sign that many of these works draw upon several common bodies of data and manifest a broad consensus as to the identification and definition of the basic issues and problem areas addressed by the discipline. The 16 new books are listed in the initial section of this review; especially distinguished are the contributions by Lasker (1973), Kelso (1974), Hulse (1971), and Poirier (1974).

The increasing diversification of physical anthropology, on the other hand, is indicative of the ongoing growth and differentiation of the profession as its practitioners continually uncover and scrutinize more and newer sources of data relevant to the investigation of human variation and evolution. Today one can find physical anthropologists engaged in research on such assorted and disparate subjects as the dentition of fossil monkeys, human reproductive physiology at high altitudes, population differences in inherited blood factors, and age-changes in human skeletal maturation. Two significant recent developments exemplify the progressing expansion of the field: 1) the emergence of two new scientific journals since 1972—*Journal of Human Evolution* (Academic Press, New York) and *Annals of Human Biology* (Taylor and Francis Publishers, London), the latter serving as the official publication of the Society for the Study of Human Biology; 2) the appearance of a large number of doctoral dissertations on Latin American topics in physical anthropology and closely related sciences (also compiled below).

The present review of physical anthropological research in Latin America focuses upon the period 1973-74, although several important materials published between 1970 and 1972 are also included. The literature in this area has been substantially augmented and enriched over the past five years.

The annotated references are listed under six headings: Palaeoanthropology, Population Studies: Demography, Population Studies: Genetics, Growth and Nutrition, Human Adaptation, and Biomedical Studies. These categories are not mutually exclusive, and there is a good deal of overlap. For example, one can find studies on anthropometric variation, fertility, disease, and the genetically-influenced ability of humans to digest lactose (milk sugar) in three of the sections. Papers on drug use, aging, mortality, and growth are listed under at least two headings each.

PALEOANTHROPOLOGY

Several topics in palaeoanthropology in Latin America have received considerable attention over the past few years: 1) population variability in morphological traits and their measurements; 2) diseases, anomalies, deformities, and other pathologies in prehistoric and recent skeletal populations; 3) palaeodemographic indicators of population movements and evolutionary relationships; and 4) the reconstruction of past social structure and behavior from osteological evidence. Researchers in this area employ a variety of methods in order to test hypotheses—physical measurement, X-rays, electron microscopes and other devices to facilitate histological studies, elaborate statistical tests and computer techniques, and biomechanical analysis.

Several publications are concerned with population origins and the early colonization and habitation of Latin American regions, as ascertained from biological and cultural evidence. T.D. Stewart's new book, *The People of America* (item 2018), is an absorbing, up-to-date treatment of the general problem of the physical and cultural evolution of prehistoric New World populations. The extensive studies of Comas (items 2006 and 2007) deal with the controversial subject of precolumbian transatlantic contact between peoples of African and American ancestry. Comas states that insufficient anatomical or archaeological evidence exists to support the transatlantic hypothesis.

POPULATION STUDIES: DEMOGRAPHY

Demographic data are of direct relevance for physical anthropologists because they help to explain and predict microevolutionary changes in the biological composition of populations.

Recent demographic research in Latin America focuses upon variations in a number of different parameters—population structure, fertility, population growth and spatial distribution, mortality, population movement and migration patterns, and mate selection. The symposium and bibliography edited by Thomas (item 2025) is a useful general reference resource on population dynamics in Latin America. Sanders (item 2060) has assembled an informative collection of current demographic statistics on Mexico.

Investigations of migratory behavior have been conducted recently in numerous Latin American countries. The symposium edited by Elizaga and Macisco (item 2043) covers a broad range of topics in this area.

Current fertility studies in Latin American populations are mainly concerned with delineating and assessing the effects of the many cultural and biological factors that influence reproductive performance—contraceptive devices and other means of birth control, child spacing, sterilization, household size and composition, marital stability, level of pre-natal mortality, residential mobility, age at marriage, social and religious attitudes on family size, age at menarche, and seasonal differences in conception rates. Some papers summarize historical trends in achieved fertility in many Latin American countries, while others discuss the need for population policies designed to limit growth.

Several of the publications on mortality refer to socio-cultural and biological elements involved in the observed patterns of death and dying. The effects of diseases, nutritional status and dietary habits, birthweight, and local ecological conditions upon mortality levels, and the roles of sex, age, race, socio-economic status, and the quality and availability of medical facilities in differential mortality are examples of some of the problems which receive consideration. Arriaga (item 2022) and Puffer and Serrano (item 2056) provide basic overviews of the demographic aspects of mortality in Latin America.

There is an increasing emphasis upon the analysis of demographic transitions in historical perspective. Demographic changes in national and local populations have been charted in several Latin American and Caribbean countries—Mexico (items 2036, 2039 and 2048), Brazil (item 2042), Argentina (item 2027), Venezuela (item 2028), Surinam (item 2047), Jamaica (items 2031 and 2040), and Cuba (item 2035).

POPULATION STUDIES: GENETICS

A recent trend in the investigation of human biological evolution has been the increasing proliferation of comparative population genetic studies. The literature on microevolution and genetic variability in Latin American populations has grown appreciably over the past few years. A large number of polymorphic genetic markers have been utilized in the presently reviewed research reports—blood groups, serum proteins, red cell enzymes and proteins, dental traits, dermatoglyphics, abnormal hemoglobins, color vision, anthropometric measurements, lactase defiency, and inherited abnormalities such as polydactyly. The publications in this section represent work done in 17 different countries in South and Central America plus Cuba and the Dominican Republic.

Specialists in this area have explored a number of different problems in Latin American populations. There is an accelerating interest in comparing the genetic make-ups of "Indian", "Mestizo", and other ethnically identified populations inhabitating diverse geographic and ecological environments. Several investigations, such as those by Crawford and others (item 2078); Neel and Ward (item 2108); Neel, Rothhammer, and Lingoes (item 2109); Plato and others (item 2112); Spielman, Migliazza, and Neel (item 2125); Brown and others (item 2072); and De Stefano (item 2081) examine patterns of gene flow, hybridization, and genetic microdifferentiation among these groups and compare geographic, linguistic and biologic-genetic distances between and within the groups. The development and refinement of a battery of statistical measures of distance have greatly enhanced this work. Some descriptive papers report gene frequencies and distributions in specific Latin American populations, while other authors tap this growing storehouse of genetic data in order to reconstruct the ancestry and phylogenetic relationships of the populations.

Research on biological variability in Latin America continues to reveal a vast expanse of genetic heterogeneity. The important reviews by Neel (items 2105 and 2106) and Neel and Ward (item 2108) draw together a substantial amount of comparative material for South and Central American populations. Weitkamp and his colleagues (items 2130-2132) have contributed significantly to the understanding of the variations in serum albumin polymorphisms in Latin America. Salzano and co-workers have provided excellent articles on populational diversity with respect to blood groups, serum proteins, hemoglobins, immunoglobins, dermatoglyphics, and other inherited characters in South America (items 2115-2119).

A landmark text and reference volume on human population genetics appeared in 1973. *Methods and theories of anthropological genetics,* edited by M. H. Crawford and P. L. Workman (item 2077), comprises an essential synthesis of original research and theoretical assimilation which effectively paves the way for future work in this field. The provocative chapter by R. H. Ward, "Some Aspects of Genetic Structure in the Yañomama and Makiritare: Two Tribes of Southern Venezuela", is abstracted separately here.

GROWTH AND NUTRITION

Research on human development in Latin America employs data from an array of different sources, such as physical measurement, X-rays, biochemical analyses of blood and urine, histological studies, medical exams and histories, and dietary evaluations. Anthropometric indices and hand-wrist radiographs have been especially important in the assessment of variations in growth schedules. Results are usually compared with U.S. norms, international standards, or age-matched controls.

The review articles by Kardonsky (item 2161) and Stini (item 2186) contain many valuable insights regarding the clinical and evolutionary effects of nutritional stress upon human development in Latin America. The work of Prado (item 2177) in Brazil and Malpica (item 2168) in Peru are examples of solid, in-depth interpretations of the many facets of growth and nutrition in national populations.

The annotated references are addressed to an assortment of problems relevant to the evolutionary investigation of human growth and development. The effects of protein-calorie malnutrition are compared with those of vitamin, fat, and mineral deficiencies. Factors accentuating nutritional stress, such as insufficient nutrient intake or hormonal imbalances, are identified. Pathologies accompanying malnutrition are described, including metabolic disturbances, difficulties in absorptive functions, and adverse modifications in intestinal structure. Several papers are devoted to the interaction of physical and psychological development and the relationship of physical constitution and learning abilities, linguistic competence, and other behavioral patterns. A number of nutritionally-based disorders (cretinism, kwashiorkor, diarrhea, etc.) are studied from various aspects. Additional topics in this section include the following: 1) skeletal maturation compared with muscular development under conditions of nutritional deprivation; 2) age, sex, socioeconomic, and "racial" differences in nutritional adaptation; 3) the relationship of nutritional status and susceptibility to infectious diseases; 4) the phenomenon of "catch-up" improvement in growth during nutritional recuperation; 5) the possible role of maternal age and physical dimensions in childhood malnutrition, morbidity, and mortality; 6) weaning customs and infant nutrition; and 7) the association of birthweight and early mortality.

HUMAN ADAPTATION

The biological variability of human populations may be partly attributed to the evolutionary process of adaptation. The phenotypic diversity between and within populations living under varying environmental conditions may result from differences in the genetic structure of the populations due to natural selection, distinctive patterns of acclimatization, or differences in adaptive ontogenetic modifications among individuals.

Human adaptation to heat, cold, and high altitude are currently being examined in Latin America. Adaptation to disease-producing agencies is treated separately in the section entitled "Biomedical studies", although a series of investigations on abnormal hemoglobins in Jamaica and Brazil is included here (items 2197 and 2209-2211).

Over half of the abstracted items deal with adaptive mechanisms in high altitude populations in the Peruvian and Ecuadorian Andes. The general overviews written by Hurtado (items 2203 and 2204) establish a useful perspective and framework for the interpretation of the morphological, physiological, and biochemical means of adaptation and acclimatization to the stress of high altitude hypoxia. Respiratory function, work and exercise capacity, drug usage, metabolic and cardiovascular alterations, and aging are all discussed by the present authors. The influence of high altitude upon mortality and fertility is described in several of the papers. Birthweight, prematurity, reproductive wastage, sex drive, child spacing, and age at menarche are important variables affecting the adaptation process. Pathologies observed in high altitude populations are noted. Comparative research on upward versus downward migrants and on permanent high altitude residents versus acclimatized newcomers and sojourners from sea level helps to elucidate the efficacy of the various adaptive systems. Configurations of growth and maturation are especially important because there is strong evidence indicating that numerous high altitude adaptive modifications become established during the developmental period (items 2198-2200).

BIOMEDICAL STUDIES

The biomedical studies in this review have been conducted on aspects of ecology, epidemiology, and population biology in some 20 Latin American and Caribbean countries. Many of the findings are of direct value to physical anthropologists interested in natural selection and human adaptation in relation to disease. Three new publications issued by the Pan American Health Organization (items 2245-2247) define the boundaries of current research on health and disease in Latin America. Shiffer (item 2260) outlines past and present scientific projects supported by PAHO.

Two areas studied in the biomedical field serve as bridges between the social and biological sciences—drug use and cross-cultural medical practices. Articles on the latter subject deal with the behavior and materials of medical herbalists, the activities and paraphenalia of mid-wives and folk practitioners, sorcery, biological correlates of ritual magic, and popular medicine in both tribal and industrialized populations. The papers on patterns of drug use concentrate upon cocaine (ingested by chewing coca leaves), tobacco, marijuana, psychedelic mushrooms, and ayahuasca (a hallucinogenic brew used for ritual and medical purposes in Peru). The healing and magical properties of these substances are reported.

Epidemiologic reconnaissance in Latin America commonly involves the monitoring of ecological variables which mediate the contraction and contagion of human diseases—population size and density, age differences in susceptibility and immunity, population differences in biological traits affecting disease prevalence (antigens, antibodies, cholesterol levels, etc.), variations in the reservoirs and vectors of disease-producing micro-organisms, "risk factors" in degenerative disorders, and the possible evolutionary significance of increasing pollution problems. The penetrating analysis by Black and others (item 2216) illustrates the interaction of multiple demographic and ecological elements in the incidence of infectious diseases in small, isolated populations in the Amazonian Basin of Brazil. The perceptive observations of Neel (item 2243) help to demonstrate the impact of culture contact and acculturation upon disease and its management in indigenous South American peoples. Some of the abstracted publications contain information on recent progress in primary health care delivery, community medical programs, and mental health services in Latin American countries.

Recent textbooks (1971-74) and doctoral dissertations (1970-74) in the field are listed below:

RECENT TEXTBOOKS

(1971-74)

Barnouw, Victor. An introduction to anthropology. v. 1, Physical anthropology and archaeology. Homewood, Ill., Dorsey Press, 1971.

Birdsell, Joseph B. Human evolution: an introduction to the new physical anthropology. Chicago, Rand McNally, 1972.
Buettner-Janusch, John. Physical anthropology: a perspective. N.Y., Wiley, 1973.
Campbell, Bernard G. Human evolution: an introduction to man's adaptations. 2. ed. Chicago, Aldine, 1974.
Downs, James F. and Hermann K. Bleibtreu. Human variation: an introduction to physical anthropology. 2. ed. Beverly Hills, Calif., Glencoe Press, 1972.
Harrison, Richard J. and William Montagna. Man. 2. ed. N.Y., Appleton-Century-Crofts, 1973.
Hulse, Frederick S. The human species: an introduction to physical anthropology. 2. ed. N.Y., Random House, 1971.
Kelso, A. J. Physical anthropology: an introduction. 2. ed. Philadelphia, Pa., Lippincott, 1974.
Lasker, Gabriel W. Physical anthropology. N.Y., Holt, Rinehart, and Winston, 1973.
McKern, Sharon S. and Thomas W. McKern. Living prehistory: an introduction to physical anthropology and archaeology. Menlo Park, Calif., Cummings, 1974.
Pfeiffer, John E. The emergence of man. 2. ed. N.Y., Harper and Row, 1972.
Poirier, Frank E. In search of ourselves: an introduction to physical anthropology. Minneapolis, Minn., Burgess, 1974.
Stein, Philip L. and Bruce M. Rowe. Physical anthropology. N.Y., McGraw-Hill, 1974.
Washburn, Sherwood L. and Ruth Moore. Ape into man; a study of human evolution. Boston, Mass., Little, Brown, 1974.
Weiner, Joseph S. The natural history of man. N.Y., Universe, 1971.
Williams, B. J. Evolution and human origins: an introduction to physical anthropology. N.Y., Harper and Row, 1973.

RECENT DOCTORAL DISSERTATIONS

Physical Anthropology in Latin America

(1970-74)

Beaver, Steven E. A reinterpretation of demographic transition theory with an application to recent natality trends in Latin America. Stanford Univ., 1972.
Blanch, José-María. Differential fertility behavior in rural and semi-urban Costa Rica. Univ. of Southern California, 1973.
Bridges, Julian C. The population of Mexico: its composition and changes. Univ. of Florida, 1973.
Brown, Antoinette B. Bone stontium content as a dietary indicator in human skeletal populations. Univ. of Michigan, 1973.
Butler, Barbara H. The people of Casas Grandes: cranial and dental morphology through time. Southern Methodist Univ., 1971.
Carvalho, José Alberto de. Analysis of regional trends in fertility, mortality, and migration in Brazil: 1940-1970. London School of Economics, 1973.
Daud, Christián A. A. El bocio endémico en Tucumán: estado actual y profilaxis. Univ. Nacional de Tucumán, Argentina, 1970.
Dobkin de Rios Marlene. The use of hallucinogenic substances in Peruvian Amazonian folk healing. Univ. of California, Riverside, 1972.
Fitzsimmons, Charles I. Susto: an epidemiological study of stress adaptation. Univ. of Texas, 1974.
Fuller, Gary A. The spatial diffusion of birth control in Chile. Pennsylvania State Univ., 1972.
Garruto, Ralph M. Polycythemia as an adaptive response to chronic hypoxic stress. Pennsylvania State Univ., 1973.
Gill, George W. The prehistoric inhabitants of Northern Coastal Nayarit: skeletal analysis and description of burials. Univ. of Kansas, 1971.
Haas, Jere D. Altitudinal variation and infant growth and development in Peru. Pennsylvania State Univ., 1973.
Halberstein, Robert A. Evolutionary implications of the demographic structure of a transplanted population in Central Mexico. Univ. of Kansas, 1973.

Hoff, Charles J. Preliminary observations on altitudinal variations in the physical growth and development of Peruvian Quechua. Pennsylvania State Univ., 1972.
Jackson, Wilma J. Ecological factors affecting the nutritional adequacy of foods purchased by families in Cali, Colombia. Michigan State Univ., 1972.
Kietzman, Dale W. Indian survival in Brazil. Univ. of Southern California, 1972.
Martorell, Reynaldo. Illness and incremental growth in young Guatemalan children. Univ. of Washington, 1973.
McCullough, John M. A physiological test of the Bergmann and Allen rules among the Yucatec Maya. Univ. of Illinois, 1972.
McDaniel, John M. Culture and disease in a South American Montaña settlement: a study of behavior and disease among La Gente and Los Serranos of Concepcion, Peru. Univ. of Pennsylvania, 1972.
Miltzer, Stanley. Pleistocene man in Northern Chile. Colombia Univ., 1973.
Moore, Lorna. Red blood cell adaptation to high altitude: mechanisms of the 2,3 Diphosphoglycerate response. Univ. of Michigan, 1973.
Page, John W. Human evolution in Peru: 9,000—1,000 B. P. Univ. of Missouri, 1974.
Potrzebowski, Patricia W. A family study of dermatoglyphics and oral-facial clefts. Univ. of Pittsburgh, 1974.
Recchini de Lattes, Zulma L. The contributions of migration and natural increase to the growth of Buenos Aires, 1855-1960. Univ. of Pennsylvania, 1971.
Rico-Velasco, Jesús A. Modernization and fertility in Puerto Rico: an ecological analysis. Ohio State Univ., 1972.
Saul, Frank P. Disease and death in an ancient Maya community: an osteobiographic analysis. Harvard Univ., 1972.
Spence, Michael W. Skeletal morphology and social organization in Teotihuacan, Mexico. Southern Illinois Univ., 1971.
Spielman, Richard S. Anthropometric and genetic differences among Yanomama villages. Univ. of Michigan, 1971.
Thomas, R. Brooke. Human adaptation to a high Andean energy flow system. Pennsylvania State Univ., 1972.
Ward, Richard H. Micro-differentiation and genetic relationships of Yanomama villages. Univ. of Michigan, 1971.

PALAEOANTHROPOLOGY AND OSTEOLOGY

2000. Allison, Marvin J.; D. Mendoza; and A. Pezzia. Documentation of a case of tuberculosis in precolumbian America (ASTS/ARRD, 107:3, 1973, p. 985-991, bibl., plates)

Report on a case of tuberculosis in a child from the Nazca culture of southern Peru dated at approximately 700 A.D. The mummified boy, age eight-ten years at time of death, was affected by the disease in his lungs, pleura, liver, and kidneys.

2001. _____; _____; and _____. A radiographic approach to childhood illness in precolumbian inhabitants of southern Peru (AJPA, 40:3, May 1974, p. 409-416, bibl., plates, tables)

Study of 108 individuals from six different prehistoric cultures from southern Peru regarding skeletal indications of disease as revealed by X-rays. Frequency of Harris' Lines (bone-scars) lower in mountain peoples compared to coastal samples, suggesting possibility of healthier childhood in former groups. Survey of modern Peruvian population disclosed pattern of Harris' Lines similar to that found in Inca culture some 450 years ago.

2002. _____. and others. A case of Carrion's disease associated with human sacrifice from the Huari culture of southern Peru (AJPA, 41:2, Sept. 1974, p. 295-300, bibl., plates)

Carrion's disease, bacterial infection transmitted by sandflies, diagnosed in mummy from prehistoric Tiahuanaco culture of southern Peru. Individual had apparently expired through ritualized sacrifice.

2003. _____. and others. A case of hookworm infestation in a precolumbian American (AJPA, 41:1, July 1974, p. 103-106, bibl., plates)

Hookworm (Ancylostoma duodenale) infestation described for a Tiahuanco mummy from a gallery burial in coastal southern Peru dated at 890-950 A.D. Photographs, enlarged 100 to 1000 times by a scanning electron microscope, reveal worms embedded in intestines. This is the earliest evidence of hookworm in the New World, and it confirms previous hypothesis that the parasite existed in the Americas prior to the arrival of people of European and African ancestry.

2004. Chapman, F. H. Osteophytosis in prehistoric Brazilian populations (RAI/M, 8:1, March 1973, p. 93-99, map, table)

Three prehistoric Brazilian populations studied to investigate possible relationship of osteophytosis (bony lipping that projects from vertebral bodies) to environmental and secular factors. Varying ecological conditions did not seem to affect incidence in these samples. Significant differences found by age but not by sex. Results briefly compared to author's previous findings in other New World populations.

2005. Christmann, Federico; L. Pianzola; and **A. Poncet.** Osteopatías en los primitivos habitantes de nuestro país (ANC/B, 49, 1972, p. 119-146, bibl., plates, tables)

Re-evaluation and new analyses of all skeletal remains (several thousand pieces) of prehistoric Argentine populations housed in Univ. of La Plata science museum. Metrical, histological, and X-ray investigations assisted in diagnoses of osteological and dental pathologies, including injuries. Eight categories of disorders are established.

2006. Comas, Juan. Hipótesis transatlánticas sobre el poblamiento de América: caucasoides y negroides. México, Instituto de Investigaciones Históricas, 1972. 32 p., bibl., plates, tables (Cuadernos: serie antropológica, 26)

Osteological evidence suggests contact between American Indians and peoples of African origin probably did not occur until the arrival of Spanish explorers and colonists in the late 15th or early 16th century. There may have been a Paleolithic movement of European Caucasians into northeast North America, as suggested by presence of several "Caucasoid" osteological characteristics in some Indian populations, both past and present.

2007. _____. Transatlantic hypothesis on the peopling of America: Caucasoids and Negroids (Journal of Human Evolution [London] 2:2, March 1973, p. 75-92, bibl.)

Review of available evidence on question of possible precolumbian transatlantic immigration into the New World of Caucasoid and Negro groups. No proof exists in archaeological or anatomical data that people of African origin visited America prior to the time of the Spanish exploration and colonization beginning in the late 15th century.

2008. _____ and **Carlos V. Serrano.** Craneología Cora-Huichol, México (UNAM/AA, 10, 1973, p. 311-328, bibl., plates, tables)

Well-illustrated analysis of 17 prehistoric human skulls from Cora-Huichol region of the Sierra de Nayarit in northern Mexico. 12 metrical measurements and 11 anthropometric indices are calculated, and results of statistical tests are reported. Findings compared with data from previous craniometric studies on Indian groups from northwestern Mexico and Middle America.

2009. Correal Urrego, Gonzalo. Análisis craneométrico con los restos paleoindígenas del Tequendama, Colombia (Ethnia [Centro Colombiano Antropológico de Misiones, Bogotá] 8:43, mayo/junio 1973, p. 69-77, tables)

Analysis of prehistoric human skeletal and cultural remains from Colombian site of Tequendama, dated between 5,000-11,000 years ago. 21 burials are examined, and for seven of the best preserved skulls 36 standard anthropometric measurements and 21 cranial indices are computed. Archaeological data also briefly described, but results are not compared with other populations.

2010. Gill, George W. Prehistoric man in the coastal Marismas Nacionales, Sinaloa and Nayarit, Mexico (Graduate Studies on Latin America [Univ. of Kansas, Center of Latin American Studies, Lawrence] 1, 1973, p. 39-51, bibl.)

Analysis of 141 human burials and skeletal remains from a swamp-estuary from a prehistoric site in northwestern Mexico. Age, sex, pathology, tooth decoration, and artificial cranial deformation are studied in relation to effects of climate, disease, diet, population migration and gene flow, and cultural factors. Burial practices, ceramic forms, and associated fauna are also considered. Population appears to have been rather stable, well-adapted, and comprising a definable gene pool.

2011. Jaén Esquivel, María Teresa and **Luis A. Vargas Guadarrama.** El metopismo en cráneos prehispánicos y modernos de Tlatelolco (INAH/A, 2 [7. época] 1969 [i.e. 1971] p. 43-57, bibl., map, plates, tables)

Variability in closure of metopic suture of the skull, thought to be under genetic control, studied in series of prehistoric and modern crania from Federal District of Mexico. Three grades of metopism recognized for both sets of samples, and these are related to cephalic index and other cranial measurements. Sexual differences in the trait are noted.

2012. Lagunas R., Zaid. La variabilidad del agujero mentoniano en mandíbulas prehispánicas de México (INAH/A, 2 [7. época] 1969 [i.e. 1971] p. 101-121, bibl., plates, tables)

Variability of mental foramen (opening in lower-jaw bone) determined in examination of 74 pre-hispanic Mexican mandibles from archaeological site of Cholula, Puebla. Several types of foramina are identified based upon location on mandible body, relative position with respect to dentition and mandibular borders, and direction of the aperture. Sexual and ethnic differences are noted. Author speculates on possible adaptive significance of observed variability.

2013. López Alonso, Sergio. La escotadura ciática mayor en la determinación sexual de restos óseos prehispánicos de México (INAH/A, 2 [7. época] 1969 [i.e. 1971] p. 31-41, bibl., illus., tables)

In 112 pre-hispanic pelvic specimens from Cholula, Puebla, Mex., and 28 from Baja California sex was determined by measuring size, shape, and angle of greater sciatic notch. Three distinct configurations are delineated, and male and female characteristics are described. Criterion found to have practical utility.

Mirambell, Lorena. El hombre en Tlapacoya desde hace unos 20 mil años. See item 747.

2014. Pucciarelli, Héctor M. Relaciones entre huesos wormianos y otros rasgos neurocraneanos sobre un grupo racial homogéneo. La Plata, Arg., Sociedad Científica Argentina, 1972. 243 p., bibl., tables (Anales, 194:5/6)

Analysis of occipital wormian bones in 47 crania of contemporary Andido people of northern Argentina. Variability related to developmental differences in other cranial features. Contributing nutritional factors are suggested.

2016. Spence, Michael W. Residential practices and the distribution of skeletal traits in Teotihuacan, Mexico (RAI/M, 9:2, June 1974, p. 262-273, bibl.)

Study of distribution of various discrete, discontinuous morphological characteristics by sex and local population in prehistoric Teotihuacan, as reported in the literature. Results interpreted in terms of possible genetic relationships of populations and implications for social organization of the times.

2017. Stewart, Robert. Evidencias geológicas del hombre primitivo en Panamá (III/AI, 32:1, enero/marzo 1972, p. 31-36, bibl.)

Geological materials and radiocarbon dates prove that humans inhabited Panama at least 6,300 years ago, and probably as early as 8,000 years ago. The latter date roughly corresponds to the initial appearance of corn in the country.

Stewart, T. Dale. Human skeletal remains from Dzibilchaltun, Yucatan, Mexico, with a review of cranial deformity types in the Maya region. See item 672.

2018. ———. The people of America. N.Y., Chaes Scribner, 1973. 261 p., bibl., illus., maps, tables.

General coverage of origins, prehistoric development, and physical anthropology of native peoples of North, Central, and South America. Demography, disease patterns, physique, tool traditions, and skeletal pathologies (due to cultural practices of artificial deformation and trephination as well as disease and injury) of early New World peoples presented within evolutionary framework. Important work by a major authority on the subject. Also published in London, Weidenfeld and Nicolson, 1973.

2019. Vargas Guadarrama, Luis A.; M.E. Ramírez; and L. Flores. El dimorfismo sexual en fémures mexicanos modernos (UNAM/AA, 10, 1973, p. 329-336, bibl.)

Sex determination of skeletal remains is important for academic and legal problems, but main methods for doing so typically involve appreciable range of error. Applicability and accuracy of discriminant function analysis for this purpose is tested in an examination of 216 contemporary Mexican femurs. Possibility of error with this method found to be comparatively low (6.43 percent). Discriminant function approach described as more precise and objective than traditional forms of sex determination.

POPULATION STUDIES: DEMOGRAPHY

2020. Alvirez, David. The effects of formal church affiliation and religiosity on the fertility patterns of Mexican-American Catholics (PAA/D, 10:1, Feb. 1973, p. 19-36, bibl.)

The majority of Mexican-Americans are Catholic and exhibit high fertility. Study explores effects of religion upon contraceptive use, desired family size, and achieved fertility. Author states that church affiliation does not greatly influence fertility patterns or use of contraceptive devices among Mexican-Americans. Paper does not, however, adequately describe samples studied or fertility data itself.

2021. *Anuario de Epidemiologia y Estadistica Vital.* Ministerio de Sanidad y Asistencia Social. 1971 [through] 1974- . Caracas.

Documents on demographic trends in Venezuela including population size, natality, pre-natal and infant mortality, epidemiological aspects of infectious diseases, and forms of medical assistance.

2022. Arriaga, Eduardo E. Mortality decline and its demographic effects in Latin America. Berkeley, Univ. of California, Institute of International Studies, 1970. 232 p., bibl., tables (Population monograph series, 6)

Comprehensive and thorough documentation of mortality trends and associated demographic changes in Latin America over past 100 years. Mortality has declined dramatically during this period—in Mexico, for example, death rate has reduced by more than half since 1920. Fertility has been increasing recently in many Latin American localities. These factors help to explain the broad-based, youthful age structures of several present-day countries of Latin America. For geographer's comment, see *HLAS 33:5001*.

2023. Balakrishnan, T.R. A cost-benefit analysis of the Barbados Family Planning Programme (LSE/PS, 27:2, July 1973, p. 353-364, bibl.)

During past 10 years fertility has declined rapidly on Barbados and in 1970 the island exhibited the lowest fertility level in the Caribbean and one of the lowest in the world for countries of similar economic development. Author assesses role of island-wide family planning program in the fertility reductions and resultant cost and benefits. Trends in population size, number of live births and birth rate reconstructed for period 1946-70 from official documents. Number of births averted is estimated, as is demographic impact of family planning program.

2024. Cicourel, Aaron V. Theory and method in a study of Argentine fertility. N.Y., John Wiley, 1974. 212 p., bibl., maps, tables.

Extensive analysis of social, biological, and psychological factors affecting fertility in Argentina. Great deal of space devoted to methodological problems encountered in the field work and various issues in the conduct of field research. Author offers criticisms of his own study and its methods.

2025. Conference of Latin Americanist Geographers, II, Boston, Mass., 1971. Population dynamics of Latin America: a review and bibliography. Edited by Robert N. Thomas. East Lansing, Mich., CLAG Publications, 1973. 200 p., bibl., illus. (Publication series, 2)

Six articles dealing with general demographic aspects of the entire area of Latin America and case studies of the structure and dynamics of some specific populations in Honduras and Argentina. Focus is upon methodology, population geography and settlement patterns, migration, and differential fertility. An outstanding feature of the volume is the 75-page bibliography of population studies on Latin America compiled by the editor.

2026. Davidson, Maria. A comparative study of fertility in Mexico City and Caracas (Social Biology [Society for the Study of Social Biology, N.Y.] 20:4, Dec. 1973, p. 460-472, bibl.)

Compares reproductive behavior of married women from Mexico City and Caracas to learn possible effects of age at marriage, education, occupation, religious affiliation, and expressed desired family size upon variations in achieved fertility. Mexico City women found to be more fertile. Age at marriage and level of husband's occupation both inversely related to achieved fertility in each locality.

2027. *Desarrollo Económico.* Instituto de Desarrollo Económico y Social. Vol. 12, No. 48, enero/marzo 1973- . B.A.

Issue devoted to "Temas de Población de la Argentina: Aspectos Demográficos," consists of six papers outlining principal demographic changes in Argentina during the period 1870-1970. Relying primarily upon census data and vital statistics registers, authors reconstruct dominant trends and historical fluctuations in population size and composition, fertility, mortality, and population movement. Particularly strong is the contribution by Jorge L. Somoza, "La Mortalidad en la Argentina entre 1869 y 1970."

2028. Dipolo, Mario and **María M. Suárez.** History, patterns, and migration: a case study in the Venezuelan Andes (SAA/HO, 33:2, Summer 1972, p. 183-195, bibl., map, tables)

Historical patterns of migratory behavior in a municipality in the Venezuelan Andes are reconstructed from censuses covering the past century. Special attention given to geographic and temporal configurations of rural-urban migration. Specific generations distinct in observed patterns. Results are placed in context of urban growth and economic development in region.

2029. Early, John D. Revision of Ladino and Maya census populations of Guatemala, 1950 and 1964 (PAA/D, 11:1, Feb. 1974, p. 105-117, bibl.)

Author's comparison of census reports and vital statistics records for Guatemala for 1950 and 1964 reveals inconsistencies in the identification and enumeration of Ladino and Maya populations of the country. Problems in the Guatemalan census materials are analyzed, and revised versions of the 1950 and 1964 counts are presented, along with a corrected classification of Maya and Ladino.

2030. *Estadísticas Vitales y de la Salud.* Ministerio de Bienestar Social, Depto. de Estadísticas y Salud. Nos. 12 [and] 18, 1972- . B.A.

Important issues are No. 12, "Tendencia de la Mortalidad en Argentina," and No. 18, "Tendencia de la Mortalidad Infantil en Argentina."

2031. Eyre, L. Alan. Geographic aspects of population dynamics in Jamaica. Boca Raton, Florida Atlantic Univ. Press, 1972. 172 p., maps, plates, tables.

Economic and spatial elements of demographic dynamics on Jamaica placed in historical perspective. Patterns of population growth, density, and movement during past century related to observed geographic distribution of population on the island and various forms of economic behavior. For geographer's comment, see *HLAS 35:6650.*

2032. Freire-Maia, Newton. Population genetics and demography (HH, 24:2, 1974, p. 105-113, bibl.)

General article on interplay of genetics and the demographic structure of populations. Author illustrates many points with data on breeding patterns in Brazilian populations.

2033. Goldsmith, Alfredo; Gilda

Echeverría; and **Rona Goldberg.** Vasectomy in Colombia: a pilot study (Journal of Biosocial Science [Oxford, England] 5:4, Oct. 1973, p. 497-505, bibl., tables)

172 vasectomized men representing widely varied social and economic backgrounds were interviewed, and more than half expressed satisfaction with the operation because of its effectiveness and previous failures with other methods of birth control. Most reported sexual activity as unchanged or improved. Operation occurred relatively late in life in the sample (average of 38.9 years of age) and after a relatively large number of children (average of 5.9 offspring).

2034. _____; **Rona Goldberg;** and **Gilda Echeverría.** An in-depth study of vasectomized men in Latin America: a preliminary report (Journal of Reproductive Medicine [American Academy of Reproductive Medicine, Chicago, Ill.] 10:4, April 1973, p. 150-155, bibl.)

Vasectomy operations have only recently become available in Latin America. Interviews were conducted with 172 men from Colombia and 77 from Costa Rica who had been vasectomized for at least three months, and responses were elicited on the magnitude of any discomfort, psychological or behavioral changes, pain, or inconvenience caused by surgery. Over half of the sampled men reported little or no biological problem during and after the operation. Most expressed satisfaction and positive feelings regarding the outcome.

2035. González, Alfonso. The population of Cuba (UPR/CS, 11:2, July 1971, p. 74-84, bibl.)

Historical growth of Cuban population and recent demographic trends are synthesized. Racial composition, geography of population distribution, patterns of urbanization, and future population prospects are outlined from censuses. Cuba emerges as demographically unique because of its high population density, numerically small Negroid and Amerindian elements in comparison to other Latin American areas, and state of rapid demographic transition.

2036. Halberstein, Robert A.; Michael H. Crawford; and **Hugo G. Nutini.** Historical-demographic analysis of Indian populations in Tlaxcala, Mexico (Social Biology [Society for the Study of Social Biology, N.Y.] 20:1, March 1973, p. 40-50, bibl., maps, tables)

In charting historical changes in various demographic features of populations from state of Tlaxcala, Mex., for period 1519-1970 authors found that demographic conditions favoring different evolutionary processes have undergone modification during past four and a half centuries. Temporal trends in population size and structure, changes in fertility patterns, and Spanish military and colonial activities in 16th century all demonstrated to influence past and present microevolution of Tlaxcalan populations.

2037. Hall, M. Françoise. Male sexual behavior and use of contraceptives in Santiago, Chile (American Journal of Public Health [N.Y.] 62:5, May 1972, p. 700-709, bibl.)

Questionnaire on sexual behavior was administered to a large sample of Santiago men. Frequency of intercourse and type of contraception used was studied in relation to a number of socioeconomic and demographic factors. Good deal of overall and nonmarital sexual activity was reported.

2038. _____. Population growth: U.S. and Latin American views (LSE/PS, 27:3, Nov. 1973, p. 415-429, bibl.)

Latin American population has experienced an increment of well over 300 percent since 1920, representing a faster rate of growth than any other major world area. This article views the reactions of Latin American countries and the US to the situation with respect to economic and political programs, activities of private organizations, and social attitudes.

2039. Hicks, W. Whitney. Economic development and fertility change in Mexico, 1950-1970 (PAA/D, 11:3, Aug. 1974, p. 407-421, bibl.)

Paper charts effects of declining mortality and rapid economic growth in Mexico upon fertility changes during period 1950-1970. Identifies several factors as influencing differences in completed fertility recorded in censuses and vital statistics: income and wealth, education of mothers, ethnic background, and agricultural versus non-agricultural occupations. Mexican areas which experienced fertility reductions tended to be characterized by larger mortality declines and small proportion of population employed in agriculture.

2040. Higman, B.W. Household structure and fertility on Jamaican slave plantations: a nineteenth-century example (LSE/PS, 27:3, Nov. 1973, p. 527-550, bibl.)

Size and structure of slave households from two Jamaican sugar estates and a livestock pen in 1825 are reconstructed from historical documents. Fertility and age composition changes in slave population between 1817 and 1832 suggest that the most fertile women were those living with a mate and their children. About half of the 864 slaves in 1825 lived in such dwelling units. Findings support previously observed associations between marital instability and reduced fertility in the Caribbean.

2041. Hinshaw, Robert; P. Pyeatt; and **Jean-Pierre Habicht.** Environmental effects of child-spacing and population increase in highland Guatemala (UC/CA, 13:2, April 1972, p. 216-230, bibl.)

Historical trends in birth intervals, fecundity spans of females, and population growth are analyzed for three Indian populations of western Guatemala in order to ascertain cultural and environmental factors involved.

Extensive variability observed by generation and across the communities. Declining fertility and mortality rates discovered in all three populations, due mainly to recently increasing birth intervals. Interpopulation variation in level of population growth related to differences in reproductive constraints of postpartum amenorrhea and differences in concern over reproductive behavior expressed by inhabitants.

2042. Hugon, Paul. Demografia brasileira: ensaio de demoeconomia brasileira. São Paulo, Editôra Atlas, 1973. 342 p., bibl., illus., (Série demografia)

Statistical compilation and theoretical analysis of historical and recent Brazilian demographic data. National trends in population size are depicted for the period 1500-1970. Age and sex structure, scale of rural-urban migration, and geographic distribution of population are reviewed within the context of their possible social, economic, and demographic consequences.

2043. *The International Migration Review.* Center for Migration Studies. Vol. 6, No. 2, Summer 1972- . N.Y.

Whole issue of journal devoted to symposium on descriptive and theoretical analysis of migration in various parts of Latin American countries. Edited by Juan C. Elizaga and J.J. Macisco, Jr., and entitled "Internal Migration in Latin America." Main theme is impact of migratory patterns on differential population growth and redistribution. Migration found to be "selective" with respect to a number of demographic factors. Contents include:
Juan C. Elizaga "Internal Migration: an Overview" p. 121-146
Arthur M. Conning "Rural-Urban Destinations of Migrants and Community Differentiation in Rural Regions of Chile" p. 148-157
Waltraut Feindt and H.L. Browning "Return Migration: its Significance in an Industrial Metropolis and an Agricultural Town in Mexico" p. 158-165
Alan B. Simmons and R. Cardona G. "Rural-Urban Migration: Who Comes, Who Stays, Who Returns? The Case of Bogotá, Colombia, 1929-1968" p. 166-181
Dagmar Raczynski "A Note on Migration and Social Mobility in Chile" p. 182-199
George Martine "Migration, Natural Increase, and City Growth: the Case of Rio de Janeiro" p. 200-215
John J. Macisco, Jr. "Some Directions for Further Research on Internal Migration in Latin America" p. 216-223.

2044. Kemper, Robert V. Rural-urban migration in Latin America: a framework for the comparative analysis of geographic and temporal patterns (CMS/IMR, 5:1, Spring 1971, p. 36-47, bibl.)

General but sparse treatment of factors affecting form and extent of rural-urban migration in Latin America as a whole. Data on specific countries receive only brief mention. Actual numbers of migrants or frequency of movement are not analyzed. Article lacks clear purpose or conclusions.

2045. Kesseru, Esteban and others. Postcoital contraception with D-norgestrel (Contraception [Los Altos, Calif.] 7:5, May 1973, p. 367-379, bibl.)

Examination of results of large-scale clinical investigation of the effectiveness and various side effects of D-norgestrel, a contraceptive medication ingested in tablet form within three hours following sexual intercourse. Sample comprised of 4,631 lower-middle class women from Lima, who were healthy, of reproductive age, and had previously been pregnant.

2046. Kiser, Clyde V. Unresolved issues in research on fertility in Latin America (MMFQ, 49:3, July 1971, p. 379-388, bibl.)

Concise summary of needed research on topic of fertility in Latin America. Author suggests exploring the relationship of fertility in various populations and urbanization, level of economic development, church affiliation, incidence of abortion, and programs of family planning. Each area treated briefly.

2047. Lamur, H.E. The demographic evolution of Surinam, 1920-1970: a sociodemographic analysis. Translated by Dirk H. van der Elst. The Hague, Martinus Nijhoff, 1973. 207 p., bibl., maps, tables.

Useful compilation of data and interpretative comments on recent demographic transformations in Surinam. Author discusses how trends in births, deaths, and migration have differentially influenced the rapidly changing demographic structure of the country. Includes five appendices.

2048. Lebowitz, Michael D. Influence of urbanization and industrialization on birth and death rates (Social Biology [Society for the Study of Social Biology, N.Y.] 20:1, March 1973, p. 89-102, bibl.)

Article concerned with rapidly changing demographic characteristics of Japan and Mexico, especially as influenced by urbanization and socioeconomic variables. Censuses, vital statistics, and secondary sources are consulted. Since 1920 the two countries have both experienced sharp mortality reductions. During the same time, natality has decreased in Japan and increased in Mexico, notably in urban areas. The result is a younger population and a greater rate of natural increase in Mexico. Contrasting fertility and mortality rates in the two countries are traced to Japan's more advanced level of "modernization."

2049. Levine, Robert M. The first Afro-Brazilian Congress: opportunities for the study of race in the Brazilian Northeast (IRR/R, 15:2, Oct. 1973, p. 185-193, bibl.)

Report on conference on racial studies in northeastern Brazil containing contributions by physicians, psychologists, and anthropologists. In addition to studies on Afro-Brazilian folklore and culture, topics include mental illness among Brazilian blacks, mortality in different racial groups, patterns of drug use, and racial typology.

2050. Merrick, Thomas W. Interregional differences in fertility in Brazil, 1950-1970 (PAA/D, 10:3, Aug. 1974, p. 423-440, bibl.)

Moderate decline in fertility occurred in Brazil between 1950 and 1970 accompanied by increase in internal migration. During same period regional fertility differences within nation generally grew wider. Fertility trends cited for 11 regions suggest that the substantial interregional movement was a factor which contributed to increasing fertility differentials by altering population structures and promoting contact between peoples with varying reproductive behaviors.

2051. Neel, James V. and W. J. Schull. Differential fertility and human evolution (Evolutionary Biology [N.Y.] 6, 1972, p. 363-379, bibl.)

Informative theoretical article on effects of fertility variations upon evolutionary action in human populations. Instructive examples of various principles drawn from recent work on Xavante and Yanomama Indians of Brazil. Economic behavior in a culture seen as an important variable influencing achieved reproduction.

2052. Onaka, Alvin T. and D. Yaukey. Reproductive time lost due to sexual union dissolution in San José, Costa Rica (LSE/PS, 27:3, Nov. 1973, p. 457-465, bibl.)

Study of amount of reproductive time which Costa Rican females expend after or between sexual unions because of their dissolution through widowhood, separation, or divorce. Marital histories of 1,226 women obtained from 1964 fertility survey of San José, indicate that approximately 10 percent of their overall reproductive period was lost due to dissolution of sexual unions. Significantly greater amount of lost time found in consensual as compared to legal marriages. Reproductive time lost tended to be from the later, less fecund years of the reproductive period.

2053. Peters, John Fred. Demography of the Shirishana (Social Biology [Society for the Study of Social Biology, N.Y.] 21:1, Spring 1974, p. 58-69, bibl.)

Study of population structure and demographic dynamics of Shirishana, a small northern Brazilian group that had been relatively isolated until 1957. Data presented on child spacing, population growth, number of pregnancies per woman, incidence of reproductive wastage and infanticide, age at marriage, marriage forms, migration rates, and mortality. A number of unusual demographic features distinguish this population, including marked sexual differences in age at marriage, very high sex ratio, polyandrous marriages, and low percentage of fertile women.

2054. Plank, Stephen J. and M.L. Milanesi. Fertility in rural Chile (Social Biology [Society for the Study of Social Biology, N.Y.] 20:2, June 1973, p. 151-159, bibl.)

Report on demographic conditions and family planning practices present in 15 rural Chilean communities prior to dissemination of contraceptive education and materials in selected localities. Interviews with 3,528 women aged 15-44 yielded information on birth rates, fertility levels and differentials, prenatal mortality, and practices of contraception. Birth rates strongly affected by population structure, female emigration patterns, and birth control.

2055. Presser, Harriet B. Sterilization and fertility decline in Puerto Rico. Berkeley, Univ. of California, Institute of International Studies, 1973. 211 p., bibl., (Population monograph series, 13)

Puerto Rican women have recently shown increased interest in birth control, and many have chosen sterilization as a means of achieving this end. History of sterilization practices and techniques in Puerto Rico is outlined. Comparative study of demographic characteristics of sterilized versus non-sterilized women suggested that level of education and socioeconomic condition are important variables distinguishing the two groups. Relationship of emerging popularity of sterilization and declining fertility in country is discussed.

2056. Puffer, Ruth R. and Carlos V. Serrano. Patterns of mortality in childhood: report of the inter-American investigation of mortality in childhood. Washington, Pan American Health Organization (PAHO), 1973. 270 p., illus., (Scientific publication, 262)

Report on a well-designed, comprehensive field project concerned with infant and childhood mortality in the New World as they are affected by disease vectors, reproductive behavior, and socioeconomic variables. Results provide insights into the magnitude of early death in Latin America and the possible roles played by the following contributing factors: weaning customs, birthweight, nutritional status of mother and child, congenital abnormalities, infectious diseases, environmental variation, and differences in the structure and accessibility of medical practices.

2057. Ram, Bali and G.E. Ebanks. Stability of unions and fertility in Barbados (Social Biology [Society for the Study of Social Biology, N.Y.] 20:2, June 1973, p. 143-150, bibl.)

Article attempts to evaluate role of marital instability in reproductive behavior of 461 Barbados women, most of whom had used contraceptives and were of lower socioeconomic status. More than 75 percent of sample had been associated with more than one sex partner. Fertility of women with larger number of sex partners was generally, but not consistently, higher than women with few partners.

2058. Roberts, Robert F. Modernization and infant mortality in Mexico

(UC/EDCC, 21:4, July 1973, p. 655-669, bibl.)

Purpose of paper is to explore interrelationship between modernization, as measured by economic criteria, and the magnitude and distribution of mortality of children under one year of age. The "more modern" Mexican states tend to manifest lower infant mortality rates, and the underregistration of infant deaths is more pronounced in the "less modernized" areas.

2059. Rona, Roberto and **Gloria Pereira.** Factors that influence age of menarche in girls in Santiago, Chile (WSU/HB, 46:1, Feb. 1974, p. 33-42, bibl.)

In a stratified sample of 354 Santiago schoolgirls average age at menarche was found to be 12.6 years. Age at menarche was significantly earlier in girls representing lower socioeconomic statuses and in girls with fewest foreign-born grandparents. Direct relationship exists between age at menarche and amount of subcutaneous fat at several regions of the body. Results are generally comparable to findings from other Latin American populations.

2060. Sanders, Thomas G. Mexico, 1974: demographic patterns and population policy. Hanover, N.H., American Universities Field Staff Reports 1974. 28 p., bibl., maps, tables (North America series, 2:1)

Timely and useful summary and review of current demographic characteristics of Mexico. Topics covered include population size and structure, fertility, mortality, urbanization, migration patterns, socioeconomic structure, and population policies. Pertinent details given for each state. Excellent brief compilation of important features of Mexican demography.

2061. Siegel, Bernard J. Migration dynamics in the interior of Ceará, Brazil (UNM/SWJA, 27:3, Autumn 1971, p. 234-258, bibl., map, tables)

A behavioral adaptation of populations in semi-arid interior of state of Ceará in northeastern Brazil is extensive movement in times of recurrent drought. Populational mobility includes both large-scale forced emigration under severe conditions and almost continual movement from estate to estate corresponding to climatic variations. Demographic effects of migration patterns are considered.

2062. Simmons, Alan B. Ambivalence towards small families in rural Latin America (Social Biology [Society for the Study of Social Biology, N.Y.] 21:2, Summer 1974, p. 127-143)

Perceptions of advantages and disadvantages of different family sizes and factors affecting preferences examined in fertility survey by Centro Latinoamericano de Demografía in rural areas of Costa Rica, Colombia, Mexico, and Peru. A large proportion of the over 6,800 married women interviewed indicated a preference for large families which have traditionally characterized these countries.

2063. Thompson, Richard A. and **Michael C. Robbins.** Seasonal variation in conception in rural Uganda and Mexico (AAA/AA, 75:3, June 1973, p. 676-686, bibl.)

Multivariate statistical procedures utilized to ascertain multiple effects of cultural and climatic variables upon seasonal fluctuations in conception and childbirth. Mexican data consist of monthly birth records from highland community in state of Querétaro for period 1963-70. Significant seasonal variations discovered in conceptions. For Mexican materials, level of urban migration found to be more important than workloads in influencing conception and birthdate, in contrast to some previous investigations.

2064. Uhlenberg, Peter. Fertility patterns within the Mexican American population (Social Biology [Society for the Study of Social Biology, N.Y.] 20:1, March 1973, p. 30-39, bibl.)

Reproductive performance of Mexican American women, as recorded by the 1960 US census, is described. Mexican American females are more fertile overall than women of other ethnic groups in the US. Achieved fertility of the Mexican American sample is not as high as Mexican national averages, but is greater than US Caucasian women. Figures are broken down by age, marital status, and occupation of husband.

2065. van der Tak, Jean and **M. Gendell.** The size and structure of residential families, Guatemala City, 1964 (LSE/PS, 27:2, July 1973, p. 302-322)

Variations in size and structure of 4,898 households in Guatemala City ascertained from 1964 government census. Following characteristics of household head were important variables in residential structure: age, sex, education, marital status, presence or absence of spouse, and number of biological children. Mean size of dwelling units, 5.3 persons, is comparable to that noted for developing nations world-wide and nearly identical to figure for country of Guatemala as a whole in 1964 (5.2). Family structure is basically nuclear with non-nuclear relatives comprising only 17 percent of the households, even though 36.6 percent of the households contained at least one non-nuclear relative.

POPULATION STUDIES: GENETICS

2066. Alvarez Perelló, José de Jesús. Frecuencia en la República Dominicana de los fenotipos, genes y genotipos del sistema de grupos Rh-Hr, con especial referencia al problema de la eritroblastosis (Aula [Santo Domingo] 1:2/3, julio/dic. 1972, p. 156-173, bibl.)

Hereditary mechanics of Rh blood genotype and phenotype inheritance are reviewed, and statistics on prevalence of Rh hemolytic disease are presented for Dominican Republic. 6.5 percent of marriages involve Rh incompatibility, and erythroblastosis affects about one in 400 births in the country.

2067. Arends, Tulio and **María L. Gallango.** Alloalbuminemia: su distribución en poblaciones venezolanas (AVAC/ACV, 22:3, 1972, p. 191-195, bibl., plates, tables)

Study of albumin variants and their distribution in Venezuelan populations. Six types described in addition to normal (A), and all exhibit slower migration rates than Albumin A during electrophoresis. No clinical disorders detected in individuals homozygous for Albumin B or Albumin Caracas. Paper contains useful table summarizing location, electrophoretic characteristics, and estimated frequencies of known albumin polymorphisms.

2068. Azevedo, Tania F.S. de; Francisco M. Salzano; and E.S. Azevedo. Factors influencing anhaptoglobinemia from Salvador, Brazil (HH, 24:3, 1974, p. 300-305, bibl.)

Frequency of haptoglobin in cord blood of 505 Brazilian newborns was eight percent. An excess of the Hp 1-1 phenotype was observed. Presence of haptoglobin was unrelated to birth weight, ABO compatability, parity, or haptoglobin type of mothers.

2069. Benoist, Jean and **G. Dansereau.** Donnés qualitatives et quantitatives sur les dermatoglyphes digitaux et palmaires de Saint-Barthélemy, Antilles Françaises (SAP/BM, 12:9, juillet/sept. 1972, p. 165-176, bibl., tables)

Descriptive study of digital and palmar dermatoglyphic patterns in 149 individuals from Lorient, Saint Barthélemy, a relatively isolated population in the French West Indies.

2070. Blanco, Richardo A; Jean-Pierre Habicht; João Salomon; and **Cipriano Canosa.** Prevalence of brachymesophalangia V in Guatemalan rural children (WSU/HB, 45:4, Dec. 1973, p. 571-581, bibl., tables)

Brachymesophalangia, an inherited anomaly characterized by short and wide middle bones of the fingers, was investigated in a sample of Guatemalan children in order to examine the possible influence of age, sex, body size, and malnutrition upon the prevalence of the condition. Brachymesophalangia of the fifth finger was discovered in 5.1 percent of the 1,206 children, but the incidence of the anomaly was not significantly associated with age, sex, stature, weight, or bone cortical thickness.

2071. _____ and others. Análisis genético cuantitativo de cinco rasgos morfológicos dentarios (SMS/RMC, 101:3, 1973, p. 223-226, bibl.)

Data collected on heritability of five characteristics of dental morphology in Chilean Andean community of Socaire. Familial, sibling, and parent-child concordance rates described for each trait. Relative value and importance of these dental features in studying human microevolution and populational relationships is considered.

2072. Brown, Stephen M. and others. Genetic studies in Paraguay: blood group, red cell, and serum genetic patterns of the Guayakí and Ayore Indians, Mennonite settlers, and seven other Indian tribes of the Paraguayan Chaco (AJPA, 41:2, Sept. 1974, p. 317-344, bibl., maps, plates, tables)

Serological specimens from 540 Indians from nine tribes in Paraguay examined with respect to number of polymorphic traits. Samples from 57 Mennonite settlers in Gran Chaco region also screened. Local differentiation in gene frequencies explained as partially the result of genetic drift and founder effect.

2073. Cann, H.M. and others. Genetic structure of the HL-A system in a Nahua population in Mexico (Tissue Antigens [Copenhagen] 3:5, 1973, p. 364-372, bibl.)

HL-A phenotype and gene frequencies listed for sample of Nahua Indians from state of Tlaxcala, Mex. Frequencies resemble other American Indian groups and are different from those found in Caucasian, black, and Mongoloid populations. Variability in this system is generally more restricted in native peoples of the New World, and this observation is supported by the present data.

2074. Castilla, Eduardo and others. Polydactyly: a genetic study in South America (ASHG/J, 25:4, July 1973, p. 405-412, bibl., plates, tables)

Incidence, ethnic correlation, penetrance, and expressivity of polydactyly in Latin America are discussed, based upon examination of 188,704 live births at hospitals in Chile, Argentina, and Uruguay. The malformation was found in 188 of the babies (.1 percent). Highest frequencies seen in areas with most "Negro" ancestors.

2075. Castro, G.A.M. and **L.M. Snyder.** G-6—PD San José: a new variant characterized by NADPH inhibition studies (Humangenetik [Berlin, FRG] 21:4, April 1974, p. 361-363, bibl.)

New variant of red cell enzyme G-6-PD described for 23-year-old male Caucasian from Costa Rica. G-6-PD San Jose found to be very similar to G-6-PD A(-) in electrophoretic mobility, structure, and other biochemical characteristics.

2076. Cleve, H. The variants of the group-specific component: a review of their distribution in human populations (Israel Journal of Medical Sciences [Weizmann Institute, Jerusalem] 9:9/10, 1973, p. 1133-1146, bibl.)

Data and interpretation of distribution of four general categories of variants of three common group-specific components (Gc) among human populations. Allelic and genotypic frequencies given. Associations of the different types with disease are discussed. Genotype distribution in South American Indian populations presented diagrammatically.

2077. Crawford, Michael H. and P.L. Workman eds. Methods and theories of anthropological genetics. Albuquerque, Univ. of New Mexico Press, School of American Research, 1973. 509 p., bibl., illus., maps, tables (Advanced seminar series)

Distinguished collection of 19 authoritative and well-written papers on anthropological genetics by the top researchers in the field. Extremely important and significant contribution which effectively defines the scope and boundaries of current field and laboratory work in human population genetics. Some of the many topics include the effects of inbreeding on evolutionary processes, the use of genetic markers and gene frequency analyses, hybridization, genetic distance, computer simulation of population structure, historical demography, and genetic adaptation. Outstanding field studies of specific populations are also featured.

2078. _____ and others. Human biology in Mexico: pt. 2, A comparison of blood group, serum and red cell enzyme frequencies, and genetic distances of the Indian populations of Mexico (AJPA, 41:2, Sept. 1974, p. 251-268, bibl., map, tables)

Population genetic research on microevolutionary processes acting upon Indian and mestizo populations of Tlaxcala, Mex. Fifteen polymorphic genetic systems of the blood are analyzed for 395 individuals. Genetic distances estimated from allelic frequencies employing three techniques, and results are compared with geographic distances and previous biological data on Mexican populations. Rare Rh blood group phenotype reported for first time for American Indians. Excellent study provides useful model for reconstructing gene flow and hybridization, the genetic diversification of historically-related populations, and other evolutionary phenomena from data on genetic markers.

2079. Da Rocha, Fernando J.; Richard S. Spielman; and James V. Neel. A comparison of gene frequency and anthropometric distance matrices in seven villages of four Indian tribes (WSU/HB, 4:2, May 1974, p. 295-310, bibl., map, tables)

Genetic and anthropometric variability are compared for four South American Indian tribes. Methods of Cavalli-Sforza and Edwards, and of Mahalanobis, are employed. While some differences are noted, intertribal populational distances calculated from genetic markers and anthropometric measures are generally comparable.

2080. _____. and others. New studies on the heritability of anthropometric characteristics as ascertained from twins (IGM/AGMG, 21:1/2, 1972, P. 125-134, bibl.)

Sixteen anthropometric measurements were taken of 48 monozygotic and 51 dizygotic pairs of adult twins from South American populations in order to estimate the amount of variation due to genetic factors. The dizygotic sample was found to be two to three times more variable in stature and other metrical characters. Heritability values and F ratios were significant for 12 traits. Highest heritability estimates were discovered for stature, head breadth, and lip thickness.

2081. De Stefano, Gian Franco. A study of morphological and genetic distance among four Indian villages of Nicaragua (Journal of Human Evolution [London] 2:3, May 1973, p. 231-240, bibl.)

Phylogenetic relationships of four Indian populations from Nicaragua are calculated from a statistical study of anthropometric measurements. Findings are compared with biological distances determined from serological data. In contrast to other similar investigations, distance values derived from morphological and genetic characteristics were not closely correlated.

2082. Díaz Ungría, Adelaide G. de. Microevolución de las poblaciones indígenas yupa (III/AI, 34:1, enero/marzo 1974, p. 113-134, bibl.)

Presentation of demographic and genetic data collected among three groups of culturally and linguistically distinct Yupa Indians from Sierra de Perijá region of Venezuela. Populations are characterized by low fertility levels, low to moderate mortality, relatively youthful age structures, and increasing migration rates. Preliminary serological data on a number of genetic systems disclose an increasing amount and rate of gene flow and hybridization in the communities, corresponding largely to observed patterns of culture contact.

2083. Dill, James E. and others. Lactase deficiency in Mexican-American males (ASCN/J, 25:9, Sept. 1972, p. 869-870, bibl.)

Deficiency of enzyme lactase found in six of 11 Mexican-American subjects and in one of eight Caucasian controls. Attempt is made to draw conclusions concerning racial and ethnic differences in this condition, but minute sample size in present case would seem to impair generalizations about the Mexican-American population.

2084. Echavarría, A.R.; C.V. Molina; and C.I. Zapata. Hemoglobina A_2' (B_2) en asociación con beta talasemia y persistencia hereditaria de hemoglobina fetal: estudios en tres familias colombianas (Sangre [Barcelona] 18:2, 1973, p. 145-156, bibl.)

First evidence of abnormal hemoglobin A_2' in Colombia found in three Negro families. Two other abnormalities also present in populations sampled: beta thalassemia and post-natal persistence of fetal hemoglobin. Variants discussed with respect to following characteristics: hematological, clinical, electrophoretic, biochemical and genetic.

2085. _____; _____; and **G.C. Zúñiga.** Hemoglobina México en una familia colombiana (Sangre [Barcelona] 18:3, 1973, p. 277-282, bibl.)

Electrophoretic, genetic, and hematologic investigation of Colombian mestizo family carrying the abnormal hemoglobin Mexico. Five of the 12 family members possessed the defect. No evidence of gene flow or admixture in family's history suggests trait may be result of mutation which occurred independently of those in populations of Mexico where condition has been previously reported. No clinical alterations could be detected in affected parties.

2086. Escobar Gutiérrez, A.; C. Gorodezky; and **M. Salazar Mallen.** Distribution of some of the HL-A system lymphocyte antigens in Mexicans: pt. 2, studies in atopics and in lepers (SITS/VS, 25:2, 1973, p. 151-155, bibl.)

Lymphocytes from normal individuals, atopics, and lepers from Mexico City tested for seven HL-A antisera. Significant differences found across the samples in distribution of various HL-A antigens. Indianmestizo differences also noted.

2087. Freire-Maia, E.A. Chautard. Linkage relationships between 22 autosomal markers (UCGL/AHG, 38:2, Oct. 1974, p. 171-198, bibl.)

Linkage analysis using 22 autosomal polymorphic genetic markers collected from 770 families from northeastern Brazilian populations. Statistical tests suggest linkage between Se (Secretor) and Gm (immunoglobin) loci, and between PTC taste sensitivity and the Kell blood group system.

2088. Freire-Maia, Newton and others. The Poland syndrome: clinical and genealogical data, dermatoglyphic analysis, and incidence (HH, 23:2, 1973, p. 97-104, bibl.)

Two cases of Poland syndrome, an inherited disorder involving malformation of upper extremities, were detected in a survey of 60,000 inhabitants from the state of Minas Gerais, Bra. Incidence of the disease is sporadic throughout Brazil. Unusual dermatoglyphic patterns, similar in both the present cases, are described.

2089. Geerdink, Rolf A.; H.A. Bartstra; and **D.A. Hopkinson.** Phosphoglucomutase (PGM_2) variants in Trio Indians from Surinam (HH, 24:1, 1974, p. 40-44, bibl., plates, tables)

Two different PGM_2 variants discovered and identified electrophoretically in sample of 240 Trio Indians from Surinam, South America. No unusual PGM_1 variants detected. Genealogical data verifies genetic determination of the sub-types.

2090. _____; _____; and **J.M. Schillhorn van Heen.** Serum proteins and red cell enzymes in Trio and Wajana Indians from Surinam (ASHG/J,/ 26:5, Sept. 1974, p. 581-587, bibl.)

Population genetic data on four serum protein systems and four polymorphic red cell enzymes in relatively unacculutrated Indian populations from Surinam. Results of electrophoretic typing are presented.

2091. _____ and others. Blood groups and immunoglobin in Trio and Wajana Indians from Surinam (ASHG/J, 26:1,/ Jan. 1974, p. 45-53, bibl., map, tables)

800 blood samples were collected among Trio and Wajana Indian populations in order to calculate various gene frequencies and estimate evolutionary relationships. The two groups exhibit similarity at the ABO and Rh loci. MNS proportions largely conform to that expected by the Hardy-Weinberg principle. The value of the study is depreciated by the conclusion that the Trio and Wajana are "racially pure" tribes.

2092. Golubjatnikov, Rjurik and **M. Steadman.** Serum levels of immunoglobins in Mexican preschool children (JHU/AJE, 95:6, June 1972, p. 542-548, bibl.)

Age-specific levels of serum immunoglobins IgC, IgM, and IgA of random sample of 189 Mexican children presented. Levels of each immunoglobin showed changes by age of subjects. No differences in concentrations could be attributed to sex or to number of siblings.

2093. Halberstein, Robert A. and **Michael H. Crawford.** Anomalous color vision in three Mexican populations (AJPA, 41:1, July 1974, p. 91-94, bibl., table)

Frequencies of color vision anomalies in related Indian and mestizo populations from states of Mexico and Tlaxcala are compared with 31 other Latin American groups. Incidence of color blindness in Latin American males is variable (a range of 0-8 percent was found), and afflicted females are extremely rare. While no consistent patterns are seen in comparing ethnic groups or people practicing different forms of economy, the overall Latin American frequencies are generally lower than in populations of European ancestry. Ratio of protanopia to deuteronopia is consistent with global patterns. Results do not provide strong support for "selection relaxation" hypothesis which attempts to account for presence of highest frequencies in sedentary populations and lowest in nomadic hunters on worldwide basis as due to varying selection pressures influenced by different economic behaviors.

2094. Kirk, R.L. and others. Blood group, serum protein, and red cell enzyme groups of Amerindian populations in Colombia (AJPA, 41:2, Sept. 1974, p. 301-316, bibl., maps, plates, tables)

Compares 22 genetic systems of the blood for four

linguistically distinct Indian populations from Colombia. Results interpreted in light of previous work in native South American populations. While some systems showed little polymorphism and few abnormalities, several loci exhibited variability, and some genes served as "markers" for the different groups.

2095. Lalouel, Jean M. and **N.E. Morton.** Bioassay of kinship in a South American Indian population (ASHG/J, 25:1, Jan. 1973, p. 62-73, bibl.)

Genetic distance estimated for seven villages of Makiritare Indians of Brazil using 11 polymorphic systems. Kinship and hybridity declined with geographic distance. Results interpreted in light of history of population movement and mate selection.

2096. Lasker, Gabriel W. and **B.A. Kaplan.** Anthropometric variables in the offspring of isonymous marriages (WSU/HB, 46:4, Dec. 1974, p. 713-717, bibl.)

Analysis of possible effects of inbreeding, as measured by isonymy (marital surname concordance), upon anthropometric variation in 480 Mexican and 609 Peruvian individuals. Isonymy did not consistently influence the pattern of the 26 anthropometric indicators.

2097. Layrisse, Zulay and **Inés Malave.** Erythrocritic and gamma-globulin antibodies in Venezuelan Indian populations (AVAC/ACV, 23:3, 1972, p. 196-200, bibl., map, tables)

Communication of results of five year lab-study of various serological and immunological characteristics of Venezuelan Indian populations. Some traits found to be correlated with geographic factors and degree of breeding isolation. Patterns of blood group incompatibilities and immunological reactions in several systems are described.

2098. _____ and M. Layrisse. Cold reacting autoantibodies in Venezuelan populations (SITS/VS, 22, 1972, p. 457-468, bibl., map, tables)

Unusually high incidence of cold auto-haemagglutinins found in Yanomama, Makiritare, and Piaroa Indians confined to limited area in Venezuela. Same substances were absent in two of same ethnic groups situated in other environments.

2099. _____ and others. Histocompatibility antigens in a genetically isolated American Indian tribe (ASHG/J, 25:5, Sept. 1973, p. 493-509, bibl., map, tables)

Paper describes results of HL-A typing of 221 Yanomama Indians living on the Venezuela-Brazil border. Phenotypic and genotypic frequencies of the different specificities display wide variation among different village populations. When compared to other South American Indian groups, findings are suggestive of rather rapid microdifferentiation of the Yanomama.

2100. Lechin, Fuad and others. A study of some immunological and clinical characteristics of gastritis, gastric ulcer, and duodenal cancer in three racial groups of the Venezuelan population (AJPA, 39:3, Nov. 1973, p. 369-374, bibl.)

Immunological and histological differences associated with chronic gastritis, gastric ulcer, and duodenal ulcer compared in 248 Negro, Caucasian, and mestizo patients examined at gastroenterological clinic in Caracas. Study sample, similar in dietary and living habits, exhibited higher level of circulating gastric antibodies than in healthy controls. Negroes showed significantly lower proportion of gastric antibodies and higher tendency toward prepyloric ulcer, duodenal ulcer, and esophagitis than in other racial groups. Gastric ulcer, however, was most prevalent among the mestizo subjects and least common among the Negroes. Genetic factors in the differential susceptibility are postulated.

2101. Lisker, Rubén and others. Lactase deficiency in a rural area of Mexico (ASCN/J, 27:7, July 1974, p. 756-759, bibl.)

Lactase deficiency and lactose intolerance studies in mestizo and Indian subjects from state of Tlaxcala to ascertain prevalence and possible relationship to milk consumption, and many individuals classified as intolerant were able to digest milk with few difficulties.

2102. Luyken, R. and others. Lactose intolerance in Surinam (TGM, 23:1, 1971, p. 54-59, bibl.)

Lactose intolerance described for various subpopulations of the ethnically-heterogeneous Surinam. Intolerance is probably cause for widespread milk indigestion reported in country.

2103. Martínez, G.; H. Vidal; and **B. Colombo.** A further observation on the possible association between Haemoglobin G alpha-Philadelphia and alpha-Thalassaemia (HH, 23:2, 1973, p. 157-163, bibl., illus., tables)

Clinical data on Cuban family possessing hemoglobin G Philadelphia, an alpha-chain variant. Red-cell abnormalities are associated with condition. Findings support hypothesis that genes coding for hemoglobin G Philadelphia and alpha-thalassemia are closely linked.

2104. Muller, Aixa and **Tulio Arends.** Electrophoretic phenotypes of adenylate kinase in Venezuelan populations (ASHG/J, 23:5, Sept. 1971, p. 507-509, bibl.)

Analyzes 651 serological specimens from Indian and mestizo individuals from Venezuela with respect to adenylate kinase polymorphism frequencies. Indian-mestizo differences revealed that locus may be valuable in assessing amount of genetic admixture between Caucasian and Indian groups.

2105. Neel, James V. Diversity within and between South American Indian tribes (Israel Journal of Medical Science [Weizmann Institute, Jerusalem] 9:9/10, 1973, p. 1216-1224, bibl.)

Compares 12 Indian tribes from South America with respect to seven genetic loci. Substantial amount of genetic heterogeneity found within, as well as across, major ethnic groups. Matrix constructed for genetic distances, and phylogenetic dendrograms prepared by three different methods. Microdifferentiation of various tribes has been very rapid owing to widespread opportunity for evolutionary changes each generation.

2106. _____. "Private" genetic variants and their frequency of mutation among South American Indians: pt. 1 (NAS/P, 70:12 1973, p. 3311-3315, bibl.)

Electrophoretic analysis of 15 serum and red cell proteins obtained from 72 villages of six relatively unacculturated tribes from South America. Ten different "private" variants encountered in 131 of the more than 56,000 screened. Frequency of polymorphisms is described. Mutation rates are estimated from the data.

2107. _____ **and Richard H. Ward.** The genetic structure of a tribal population, the Yanomama Indians: pt. 6, Analysis by F-statistics; including a comparison with the Makiritare and Xavante (UT/G, 72:4, Dec. 1972, p. 639-666, bibl.)

Statistical study of population structure and mating patterns in three isolated tribes of South American Indians. An excess of consanguineous marriages over random expectation was found. Amount of genetic heterogeneity directly correlated with differences in breeding structure. Evidence for the action of natural selection in the populations is cited. For pts. 1-5 and 8 of this study, see *HLAS 35:1749, 1737, 1770-1772, 1768,* and *1761;* for pts. 7, 9, and 10, see items 2114, 2127 and 2109.

2108. _____ and _____. Village and tribal genetic distances among American Indians and the possible implications for human evolution (NAS/P, 65:2, Feb. 1970, p. 323-330, bibl., map, tables)

Pair-wise genetic distances calculated for 26 populations of Makiritare and Yanomama Indians of Brazil and Venezuela and for 12 other tribes from Central and South America, based upon six genetic systems in the blood. Tribal genetic distances found to be about 10-15 percent greater than inter-village distances. A common demographic occurrence in past New World Indian groups has been gene pool disjunction and population splintering, both of which accelerate a number of interrelated evolutionary processes.

2109. _____; **Francisco Rothhammer;** and **J.C. Lingoes.** The genetic structure of a tribal population, the Yanomama Indians: pt. 10, Agreement between representation of village distances based on different sets of characteristics (ASHG/J, 26:3, May 1974, p. 281-303, bibl.)

Genetic distances and phylogenetic relationships among different Yanomama populations are derived from statistical analyses of serological markers, dermatoglyphics, and anthropometric measurements. In most cases the results of the three sources of data showed significant correspondence. Positive correlation of biological and geographic distance was also statistically significant. Evolutionary implications interpreted in light of recent demographic trends in the tribe. For further information on other parts of this study, see item 2107.

2110. Newman, Marshall T. Palm and finger prints of Quechua Indians from Vicos in the north Central Peruvian Sierra (WSU/HB, 46:3, Sept. 1974, p. 519-530, bibl., map, tables)

Digital and palmar dermatoglyphic impressions collected from 230 male Quechua Indians from Vicos in northern Peru. Relative homogeneity observed in patterns explained as result of drift through the founder principle, and past and present inbreeding in the population of 2,500, as gene flow into the community has been mimimal. Figures compared to other American Indian groups.

2111. Pederneiras, M.P.; E. Karam, Jr.; and Newton Freire-Maia. Consanguineous marriages and umbilical tetanus in Brazilian populations (HH, 24:1, 1974, p. 75-81, bibl.)

Survey of 56,740 liveborn children from state of Minas Gerais, Bra., to determine possible relationship of death due to umbilical tetanus and parental consanguinity. Findings suggest no significant correlation. Mortality through umbilical tetanus probably more influenced by socioeconomic status than by racial differences or inbreeding level in a population.

2112. Plato, C.C. and others. Digital and palmar dermatoglyphic patterns among southern Peruvian Quechua (WSU/HB, 46:3, Sept. 1974, p. 495-518, bibl., map, tables)

Finger and palmar dermatoglyphics collected for 362 Peruvian Quechua Indians representing five populations. Although sample populations differed in altitude and other ecological variables, they exhibited high degree of dermatoglyphic similarity, with the exception of the Nuñoa group. Ethno-historical information and migration patterns suggest gene flow has been acting to maintain genetic continuity among the populations. Results compared to previous findings from other South American Indian populations.

2113. Reeves, W.C. and others. Differences in the prevalence of Hepatitis B antigen and antibody among Panamanian Indian populations (Journal of Infectious Diseases

[Chicago, Ill.] 128:3, Sept. 1973, p. 265-270, bibl., map, tables)

1,623 serological specimens from three major Indian tribes from Panama tested for Hepatitis B antigen, and tribal and local populational differences are discussed in terms of demographic factors.

2114. Rothhammer, Francisco and others. The genetic structure of a tribal population, the Yanomama Indians: pt. 7, Dermatoglyphic differences among villages (ASHG/J, 25:2, March 1973, p. 152-166, bibl.)

Based on statistical study of sample of Yanomama Indians of Venezuela and Brazil, considerable variation in dermatoglyphic configurations is seen among seven different villages. Sexual distinctions are noted, and the Yanomama are compared to other indigenous South American populations for 15 dermatoglyphic characteristics. For further information on other parts of this study, see item 2107.

2115. Salzano, Francisco M. Situação atual e perspectivas sôbre o melhoramento genético no Estado do Rio Grande do Sul (SBPC/CC, 24:8, agôsto 1972, p. 714-718)

Suggestions offered concerning genetic improvement of plants and animals in Brazilian state of Rio Grande do Sul through program of selective breeding. Steps outlined necessary for obtaining greater productivity in the state. Particular problems associated with different plant and animal species are mentioned.

2116. _____. and F.R. de Sá e Benevides F. Fingerprint quantitative variation and asymmetry in Brazilian whites and blacks (AJPA, 40:3, May 1974, p. 325-328, bibl.)

Dermatoglyphic characteristics compared in black and white subjects from state of Pôrto Alegre, Bra. No significant racial differences detected for pattern intensity, total ridge count, or degree of asymmetry in ridge counts. Sexual differences were significant for both sample populations in total ridge count, but significant only among the blacks in pattern intensity.

2117. _____; A.G. Steinberg; and M.A. Tepfenhart. Gm and Inv allotypes of Brazilian Cayapó Indians (ASHG/J, 25:2, March 1973, p. 167-177, bibl.)

Frequencies of different Gm and Inv phenotypes are presented for a sample of 440 individuals representing four Cayapó populations. Values are generally in accordance with those reported previously for South American Indians. Phylogenetic relationships of the populations are not clear from analysis of these loci alone.

2118. _____ and others. Alloalbuminemia in two Brazilian populations: a possible new variant (ASHG/J, 26:1, Jan. 1974, p. 54-58, bibl., plates)

1,628 plasma samples from Pôrto Alegre and 1,360 from Belém, Bra., were examined. Three albumin variants were discerned in the latter series. One of the polymorphisms is unique in comparison with the 22 which have been previously described.

2119. _____ and others. Blood groups, serum proteins, and hemoglobins of Brazilian Tiriyó Indians (WSU/HB, 46:1, Feb. 1974, p. 81-87, bibl.)

Population genetic investigation of tribe living near border between Brazil and Surinam. Analysis of 23 genetic markers from serological specimens revealed absence of marked heterogeneity within this group. Gene frequencies generally fall within ranges observed for South American Indians. Evidence indicates little admixture from outside populations.

2120. Seid-Akhavan, M. and others. Two more examples of Hb Pôrto Alegre in Belém, Brazil (HH, 23:2, 1973, p. 175-181, bibl., plate, tables)

The abnormal hemoglobin Pôrto Alegre was discovered in two individuals from a random sample of 1,369 surveyed in Belém, Bra. Electrophoretic patterns are described. The abnormality is very rare, having been previously found in only a few other South American individuals.

2121. Serrano S., Carlos. Los dermatoglifos digitales de la población masculina de Cholula, Puebla (INAH/A, 2 [7 época] 1969 [i.e. 1971] p. 59-66, bibl., illus., map, tables)

As part of more comprehensive field project, digital and palmar dermatoglyphics collected for 178 males from Cholulu in Mexican state of Puebla. Frequencies of various impressional designs, as well as indices derived from them, are tabulated. Results are compared with ranges previously established for Mexican populations.

2122. Silva, M.A. Pereira da. Les dermatoglyphes digitopalmaires des indiens alakaluf des archipels de Patagonie Occidentale (SAP/BM, 13:1, jan./mars 1974, p. 85-108, maps, plates, tables)

Dermatoglyphic analysis of 24 Alakaluf individuals. Several digital and palmar indices suggest biological affinity with other South American Indian groups.

2123. Speilman, Richard S. Differences among Yanomama Indian villages: do the patterns of allele frequencies, anthropometrics and map locations correspond? (AJPA, 39:3, Nov. 1973, p. 461-480, bibl.)

Evolutionary microdifferentiation among villages of Yanomama Indians of Brazil and Venezuela determined by assessing sets of multivariate observations on different biological characteristics. Significant correspondence discovered among geographic, anthropometric, and gene frequency distances in 19 villages. Results explained in terms of cultural and demographic aspects of the populations, which have a history of fragmentation and splitting. Elaborate statistical procedures receive considerable attention.

2124. _____. Do the natives all look alike? Size and shape components of anthropometric differences among Yanomama villages (American Naturalist [Essex Institute, Lancaster, Pa.] 107:957, Sept./Oct. 1973, p. 694-708, bibl.)

Statistical calculations of biological distances among 11 Yanomama villages utilizing anthropometric data. Distinctive within-village homogeneity in body shape discovered across the sexes. Marked morphological differentiation found between villages. Populational distances estimated through D^2 technique developed by Mahalanobis. Results discussed in light of previously collected genetic data on Yanomama. Cultural and biological facets of observed anthropometric variations considered in evolutionary terms.

2125. _____; E.C. Migliazza; and James V. Neel. Regional, linguistic and genetic differences among the Yanomama Indians (AAAS/S, 184:4137, May 1974, p. 637-644, bibl.)

Biological and cultural evolution of the relatively isolated Yanomama Indians of southern Venezuela are calibrated by examining gene frequency divergences and patterns of linguistic differentiation. The construction of dendrograms and phylogenetic trees indicates significant similarity and congruence between linguistic and genetic data in seven language areas. A chronological index is developed for measuring and estimating approximate rate of evolution in the Yanomama, both within and between tribes.

2126. Tanis, Robert J. and others. Albumin Yanomama-2, a "private" polymorphism of serum albumin (UCGL/AHG, 38:2, Oct. 1974, p. 179-190, bibl., map, plate, tables)

Albumin variant Yanomama-2 found widespread throughout Yanomama populations but not in other South American Indian tribes so far studied. Frequencies fall in geographic cline and range from 0 to 0.40 in individual villages with a mean of 0.08. Data support previous hypothesis that Yanomama have long been a genetically-isolated tribe.

2127. _____ and others. The genetic structure of a tribal population, the Yanomama Indians: pt. 9, Gene frequencies for 18 serum protein and erythrocyte enzyme systems in the Yanomama and five neighboring tribes: nine new variants (ASHG/J, 25:6, Nov. 1973, p. 655-676, bibl., map, plates, tables)

Several genetic polymorphisms in Yanomama populations are explored in serological studies. New variants in serum and red cell proteins are described along with electrophoretic patterns. Yanomama are relatively distinct when compared with 5 nearby tribes. For further information on other parts of this study, see item 2107.

2128. Ward, Richard H. Some aspects of genetic structure in the Yanomama and Makiritare: two tribes of southern Venezuela (*in* Crawford, Michael H. and P.L. Workman eds. Methods and theories of anthropological genetics. Albuquerque, Univ. of New Mexico Press, 1973, p. 367-388, bibl., illus., tables)

Theoretical analysis of genetic microdifferentiation and phylogenetic relationships among Indian tribal populations from Venezuela. Genetic networks are constructed for over 40 villages. Gene frequency distributions within and among the populations are described.

2129. Weinstein, B.I. de and others. A new unstable haemoglobin: Hb Buenos Aires (AHIJH, 50:6, 1973, p. 357-363, bibl.)

New hemoglobin variant found in four members of an Argentine family. All were heterozygous and all suffered from hemolytic anemia. This hemoglobin represents fifth example of an unstable variant resulting from a substitution involving the amino acid phenylalanine. Clinical aspects of condition are discussed.

2130. Weitkamp, Lowell R. The contributions of variations in serum albumin to the characterization of human populations (Israel Journal of Medical Science [Weizmann Institute, Jerusalem] 9:9/10, Sept./Oct. 1973, p. 1238-1248, bibl.)

Review of distribution and population genetics of 28 known electrophoretically distinguishable variants of serum albumin. Frequencies of polymorphic allotypes described for ‘New World Indian and mestizo populations.

2131. _____ and others. Additional data on the population distribution of human serum albumin genes: three new variants (UCGL/AHG, 37:2, Oct. 1973, p. 219-226, bibl.)

Further discussion of distribution of serum albumin variants in human populations including a comparison of three additional types, two of which occur in New World Indians. A total of 50 albumin variants are analyzed electrophoretically. Distinctive albumins observed in Brazilian populations receive special attention.

2132. _____ and others. Human serum albumin: twenty-three genetic variants and their population distribution (UCGL/AHG, 36:4, April 1973, p. 381-392, bibl., plate, table)

Survey of known serum albumin variants including

summary of individual frequencies and populational distributions. Some of the 23 varieties have been identified in Indians of the US, Mexico, and South America. The three clearly polymorphic variants all occur in peoples native to Latin America.

2133. Zegers, B.J.M.; Rolf A. Geerdink; and P.C. Sander. Serum immunoglobin levels in Trio and Wajana Indians of Surinam (SITS/VS, 24:5, 1973, p. 457-467, bibl.)

Levels of three serum immunoglobins reported for 62 Indian children and 12 adults from Surinam. Very high levels found in comparison with control samples. No significant differences according to sex; differences in mean levels between children and adults were statistically significant for two immunoglobins, but only among males. Unusual array of findings probably reflect small size of study group and sampling procedures.

GROWTH AND NUTRITION

2134. Acosta, Phyllis B. and others. Nutritional status of Mexican-American preschool children in a border town (ASCN/J, 27:12, Dec. 1974, p. 1359-1368, bibl.)

Study of developmental and nutritional status of 170 preschool children of Mexican descent living in California based upon physical measurements, dental examinations, biochemical analyses, dietary evaluations, and medical histories. One-third of the children were shorter than average US growth standards, and over one-fourth were underweight in the same respect. Over half of the children manifested iron deficiency, and some 90 percent of the children over three years of age were in need of dental care.

2135. Adrianzen T., Blanca; J.M. Baertl; and George C. Graham. Growth of children from extremely poor families (ASCN/J, 26:9, 1973, p. 926-930, bibl.)

Growth patterns depicted for 444 healthy siblings of children hospitalized for severe malnutrition. Sample represents 115 Peruvian mestizo families of extremely low socioeconomic condition. Some growth parameters showed delay in comparison with US and international standards.

2136. Alderman, Michael H. and others. A young-child nutrition programme in rural Jamaica (LANCET, 2:7813, 26 May 1973, p. 1166-1168, tables)

Report on development of recently instituted program designed to reduce high mortality and morbidity rates among rural Jamaican children. Anthropometric indices used to assess growth schedules. About half of Jamaican preschool children are underfed, and present program aims to alleviate the situation.

2137. Alvarado, Jorge and others. Vitamin B_{12} absorption in protein-calorie malnourished children and during recovery: influence of protein depletion and diarrhea (ASCN/J, 26:6, June 1973, p. 595-599, bibl.)

Studies 25 Guatemalan children with severe protein-calorie malnutrition to gain information of effects on vitamin B_{12} absorption. Findings indicate that absorption is depressed in malnutrition, especially when accompanied by diarrhea. Improvement observed in absorption of the vitamin during nutritional recovery.

2138. Ashcroft, M.T. and G.R. Serjeant. Body habitus of Jamaican adults with sickle-cell anemia (Southern Medical Journal [Birmingham, Ala.] 65:5, May 1972, p. 579-582, bibl.)

Anthropometric study of 121 Jamaican patients over age 20 with sickle-cell anemia. Compared to age-matched controls, subjects were taller and thinner, had higher ratio of limb length to trunk size, and had narrower pelvic and pectoral girdles.

2139. _____ ; _____; and P. Desai. Heights, weights, and skeletal age of Jamaican children with sickle-cell anemia (Archives of Diseases in Childhood [British Medical Association, London] 47:4, 1972, p. 519-524, bibl.)

Skeletal maturation, as determined by hand and wrist radiographs, and body size assessed in 99 Jamaican youths aged 12-21. Weight and skeletal age were less than in age-matched control samples, although average stature was not significantly different.

2140. Beghin, Ivan and others. Assessment of biological value of a new corn-soy-wheat noodle through recuperation of Brazilian malnourished children (ASCN/J, 26:3, March 1973, p. 246-258, bibl.)

Study of nutritional value of a pasta developed by a food company and introduced to Brazil as a food supplement for malnourished children. Results are compared with control group fed a normal balanced diet. Nutritional recuperation occurred in both groups, although anthropometric and chemical data indicate a better response in the control sample. Methodological considerations are discussed in detail.

2141. Blanco, Ricardo A. Sex differences in retardation of skeletal development in rural Guatemala (Pediatrics [American Academy of Pediatrics, Springfield, Ill.] 50:6, Dec. 1972, p. 912-915, bibl.)

Hand and wrist radiographs of 1,409 Guatemalan children under age seven showed significantly lower cortical thickness in boys. Both sexes had considerably lower mean values than in US children of same age.

2142. _____ and others. Height, weight, and lines of arrested growth in young Guatemalan children (AJPA, 40:1, Jan. 1974, p. 39-48, bibl.)

Patterns of human development examined in rural

Guatemalan area where malnutrition is common. Height, weight, and skeletal maturation studied in cross-sectional sample of 1,412 children under seven years of age from nine separate villages. Significant differences between study sample and well-nourished Guatemalan children becomes evident early in life. Authors point out that results provide further support for observation that adverse environmental effects on human growth tend to fall more heavily upon males than females.

2143. Brazleton, T.B. Implications of infant development among the Maya Indians of Mexico (Human Development [Basel, Switzerland] 15:2, 1972, p. 90-111, bibl.)

Examination of interrelationship of human physical and psychological development, child rearing practices, and environmental stresses among Zinacantec Indians from southeast Mexican state of Chiapas. Motor, mental, and social parameters suggest Mayan infants develop in similar fashion as US counterparts except for relative chronological delays. In first year of life, Zinacantec infants appeared to consistently lag behind US norms, but the lag did not increase with age. Malnutrition, frequency of infection, and hypoxia described as powerful influences upon fetal and infantile development.

2144. Brooke, O.G. Hypothermia in malnourished Jamaican children (Archives of Diseases in Childhood [British Medical Association, London] 47:4, 1972, p. 525-530, bibl.)

Study of body temperature and its changes in 137 malnourished Jamaican children averaging ten months of age. Hypothermia (low core temperature) occured in 19.7 percent of sample, more commonly in marasmus than in kwashiorkor.

2145. ———. Influence of malnutrition on the body temperature of children (BMA/J, 1:5796, Feb. 1972, p. 331-333, bibl.)

Effects of malnutrition and its treatment upon body temperature examined in Jamaican infants. Reduced temperature, found to accompany malnutrition, may be an adaptation which acts to conserve calories.

Cabanillas de Rodríguez, Berta. El puertorriqueño y su alimentación a través de su historia: siglos XVI al XIX. See *HLAS 36:2384.*

2146. Carluci, María Angélica. Observaciones antropométricas en el cretinismo endémico del Ecuador andino (III/AI, 34:3, julio/sept. 1974, p. 797-806, bibl.)

Descriptive work on the measurement of 34 Ecuadorian Indians suffering from congenital deficiency of thyroid hormone which has retarded mental and physical growth. Significant differences from control populations observed in corporal diameters, limb proportions, and some cranial and facial indices.

2147. Chase, H. Peter. Nutritional status of preschool Mexican-American migrant family children (American Journal of Diseases of Children [Chicago American Medical Association] 122:4, Oct. 1971, p. 316-324, bibl., plates, tables)

Diagnosis and evaluation of nutritional and medical problems encountered in examination of 300 preschool Mexican-American children from Colorado. High infant mortality rate discovered in population. Low nutrient levels, low birth weights, and wide range of pathologies characterize sample group. Study demonstrates close relationship between nutrition and health.

2148. Cook, J.D. and others. Nutritional deficiency and anemia in Latin America: a collaborative study (Blood [N.Y.] 38:5, Nov. 1971, p. 591-603, bibl.)

Lab studies of relationship of nutrition and anemia in seven Latin American countries. Among nearly 900 pregnant women studied, anemia found in 38.5 percent, iron deficiency in 48 percent, and vitamin B_{12} deficiency in 15 percent.

2149. Cravioto, Joaquín and E. DeLicardie. Environmental correlates of severe clinical malnutrition and language development in survivors of kwashiorkor and marasmus (OSP/B, 7:2, 1973, p. 50-70, bibl., plate, tables)

Longitudinal study of malnutrition and its effects upon growth, mental development, and learning abilities in a rural, agricultural population in Mexico. Variations in health care practices, size and age of mothers, socioeconomic status, infant mortality, and language development are considered. Population is young and life expectancy at birth is low, partly because of nutritional factors.

2150. Eveleth, Phyllis B.; Francisco M. Salzano; and P.E. de Lima. Child growth and adult physique in Brazilian Xingu Indians (AJPA, 41:1, July 1974, p. 95-102, bibl.)

19 anthropometric measurements taken for 267 children and 363 adults from several Xingu Indian tribes of Central Brazil. Sample exhibits short stature and sitting height compared to British standards. Adult height shows no significant decrease with age up to 50 years. Xingu adults are slightly taller than most South American Indians except the Xavante of Brazil.

2151. Fierro-Benítez, Rodrigo and others. Biopatología andina y nutrición (III/AI, 34:3, julio/sept. 1974, p. 777-793, bibl., maps, plates, tables)

Investigation of developmental effects of iodine in areas of Ecuadorian Andes where goiter is endemic. Correction of iodine deficiency effectively serves to prevent endemic cretinism. Physical and mental effects of iodine deficiency found to be variable in sample populations. Contribution of protein-calorie malnutrition and environmental factors are considered.

2152. _____ **and others. The clinical pattern of cretinism as seen in highland Ecuador** (ASCN/J, 27:5, May 1974, p. 531-543, bibl., plates, tables)

Various physical correlates of cretinism assessed in 94 subjects from Andean region of Ecuador. Following found to be adversely affected by the condition: hearing, speech, performance on intelligence tests, motor abilities, glandular functioning (especially thyroid), and growth and maturation. When compared to normal individuals, differences mainly quantitative rather than qualitative.

2153. Glass, R.L. and others. The prevalence of human dental caries and water-borne trace metals (Archives of Oral Biology [London] 18:9, Sept. 1973, p. 1099-1104, bibl.)

Comparative study of two isolated villages in Colombia which exhibited contrasting prevalences of dental caries even though diets were remarkably similar. Analyses of drinking water by emission spectroscopy revealed highly significant differences between the populations with respect to the concentrations of seven trace elements.

2154. Graham, George C. and Blanca Adrianzen T. Growth, inheritance and environment (Pediatric Research [Basel, Switzerland] 5:12, Dec. 1971, p. 691-697, bibl.)

15 Peruvian children hospitalized for severe malnutrition and their families followed for number of years and compared with healthy controls with respect to patterns of growth and development. "Catch-up" growth in height, weight, and head size observed to continue for many years after period of extreme malnutrition. According to authors, data indicate that adverse environmental influences affecting nutrition throughout growth and maturation period are probably as important as genetic factors in determining stature.

2155. _____ **and** _____. **Late "catch-up" growth after severe infantile malnutrition** (Johns Hopkins Medical Journal [Baltimore, Md.] 131:9, Sept. 1972, p. 204-211, bibl.)

Paper dealing with growth of eight malnourished children from poor families in Lima, and matched sample of controls. Clinical data on each child included. The eight subjects made dramatic gains in stature following improvement in physical surroundings.

2156. Greene, Lawrence S. Physical growth and development, neurological maturation, and behavioral functioning in two Ecuadorian Andean communities in which goiter is endemic; pt. 2: PTC taste sensitivity and neurological maturation (AJPA, 41:1, July 1974, p. 139-152, bibl.)

In two Ecuadorian Andean communities where goiter is endemic, study conducted on relationship between PTC tast sensitivity (a diallelic polymorphism) and neurological maturation in 264 children under age 16. Significant correlation found between ability to taste the chemical and visual-motor development in both sexes. Significant increase in taste sensitivity discovered by age. Tasters probably are at a selective advantage because they are more sensitive to bitter taste sensation of naturally occurring goiterogens prevalent in diet. Nontasters are not so equipped to avoid the metabolically harmful goiterogens, and thus the PTC system may have played an important role in the evolution of human nutritional adaptations.

2157. Habicht, Jean Pierre; J.A. Schwedes; G. Arroyave; and R.E. Klein. Biochemical indices of nutrition reflecting ingestion of a high protein supplement in rural Guatemalan children (ASCN/J, 26:10, Oct. 1973, p. 1046-1052, bibl.)

As part of a larger study of dietary supplementation and nutritional improvement among Guatemalan preschool children, present paper provides account of physiological level of nutrition in control villages and explores adequacy of food supplements selected. 19 children receiving supplement and 15 control children differed significantly with respect to certain standard indicators of protein and vitamin nutrition.

2158. Hildalgo, Carlos P. Recopilación sobre el consumo de nutrientes en diferentes zonas de México; pt. 2: Consumo de vitaminas y minerales (SLN/ALN, 23:3, sept. 1973, p. 293-304, bibl., map, tables)

Nutrient intake compared in several different Mexican areas. Findings indicate that rural areas are generally more prone to vitamin deficiency than low income urban area. Particularly adversely affected are southern and southeastern zones of the country. Preschool rural children showed especially low intake of vitamin A, riboflavin, and calcium.

2159. Hoeldtke, Robert D. and R.J. Wurtman. Excretion of catecholamines and catecholamine metabolites in kwashiorkor (ASCN/J, 26:2, Feb. 1973, p. 205-210, bibl.)

15 Guatemalan Indian children from poor families, being treated for kwashiorkor, were investigated in order to determine whether changes in catecholamine metabolism occur in conjunction with protein malnutrition. Results suggest that acute kwashiorkor alters the excretion of catecholamines metabolites in various directions.

2160. Johnston, Francis E.; Michael Borden; and Robert B. MacVean. Height, weight, and their growth velocities in Guatemalan private school children of high socioeconomic class (WSU/HB 45:4, Dec. 1973, p. 627-641, bibl., tables)

Presents data on amount and rate of growth in ght and

weight for a sample of 139 children of Guatemalan ancestry representing the highest socioeconomic levels of the country. The children, studied longitudinally since 1953, were free of infectious diseases or nutritional deficiencies. Since observed growth patterns differ from standards for US school children, authors believe that results might serve as a norm or standard for growth of Guatemalan people under optimal environment conditions. Includes graphs.

2161. Kardonsky C.V. and others. Efectos diferenciales de la desnutrición y la deprivación cultural en el desarrollo psicobiológico: un model de diseño y método de análisis (Cuadernos de Psicología [Univ. de Chile, Depto. de Psicología, Santiago] 2, 1972, p. 7-23, bibl., tables)

Excellent review article on effects of nutritional stress upon psychological and biological development. Experimental designs presented for actual and projected studies in Latin American populations. Basic terms are defined, and analytical methods and procedures are clearly outlined. Useful compilation of information on subject of malnutrition and its proper investigation.

2162. Klipstein, Frederick A. and others. Investigations concerning the prevalence of nutritional deficiencies and intestinal malabsorption among rural populations of the West Indies; pt. 1: Methodology (ASCN/J, 25:11, Nov. 1972, p. 1236-1242, bibl.)

Report on methodological strategies involved in long-term investigation to determine nutritional status and incidence of intestinal abnormalities among rural inhabitants of Puerto Rico and Dominican Republic. Sampling procedures and laboratory tests are described. Problems encountered in relating nutritional condition and intestinal function are discussed.

2163. _____ and others. Nutritional status and intestinal function among rural populations of the West Indies; pt. 2: Barrio Nuevo, Puerto Rico (Gastroenterology [Baltimore, Md.] 63:5, Nov. 1972, p. 758-767, bibl.)

Diet, nutrition, and intestinal structure and function evaluated in 96 Puerto Rican adults from rural barrio. Changes in intestinal morphology, nutritional deficiencies, and abnormalities all found to be uncommon.

2164. _____ and others. Nutritional status and intestinal function among rural populations of the West Indies; pt. 3, Barrio Cabreto, Dominican Republic (ASCN/J, 26:1, Jan. 1973, p. 87-95, bibl.)

Relationship of dietary intake, nutritional status, and intestinal structure and function evaluated in 42 residents of rural population in Dominican Republic. The people are poor and have no access to modern sanitary facilities. 47 percent of subjects were deficient in at least one nutrient, and multiple deficiencies were encountered in 27 percent. Abnormalities of intestinal structure and function present in 55 percent of the sample. Low dietary intake of protein, calories, and fat is characteristic of the population.

2165. Kohn de Brief, Fritzi and Betty Méndez de Pérez. Antropometria de los indios cariña. Caracas, Univ. Central de Venezuela, Facultad de Ciencias Económicas y Sociales, División de Publicaciones, 1972. 111 p., tables.

Descriptive anthropometric study of 100 male Carina Indians from two states in Venezuela. 18 different measures and indices suggest that the sample is relatively short in stature, low in body weight, brachycephalic in head shape, and extremely variable in facial structure and body proportions and morphology.

2166. Lugo de Rivera, C.; H. Rodríguez; and R. Torres Pinedo. Studies on the mechanism of sugar malabsorption in infantile infectious diarrhea (ASCN/J, 25:11, Nov. 1972, p. 1248-1253, bibl.)

Malabsorption of sugar is thought to play important role in contraction of diarrhea. Paper attempts to clarify differences in mechanics of sugar transport and absorption in normal and diseased intestines in 28 Puerto Rican infants. Absorption defects observed in diarrheal cases, possibly due to physical obstructions.

2167. Malina, R.M. and others. Skinfold thicknesses at seven sites in rural Guatemalan Ladino children from birth through seven years of age (WSU/HB, 46:3, Sept. 1974, p. 453-469, bibl.)

Skinfold thickness measured at seven locations on body in 1,119 Guatemalan children suffering from mild to moderate protein-calorie malnutrition. Skinfolds increase sharply between birth and three-six months of age, followed by a decrease to 18-21 months and another, slighter acceleration after 21-24 months. Sex differences described. Skinfolds small in comparison to other world populations.

2168. Malpica S.S., Carlos. Crónica del hambre en el Perú. 2. ed. corregida y actualizada. Lima, Moncloa-Campodónico Ediciones, 1970. 284 p. (Toda la realidad, 2. Ensayo)

Review of nutritional problems in Peru from ancient times to present. Reconstruction of past agricultural practices and diets indicate that recent problems have a long history. Nutritional deficiencies are shown to be related to geographic factors, dietary customs, unproductive agricultural activities, and problems of food distribution. Effects of nutritional status of various populations on birth rate, childhood mortality, and morbidity are discussed.

2169. Mata, Leonardo J.; María L. Mejicanos; and Franklin Jiménez. Studies on the indigenous gastrointestinal flora of Guatemalan children (ASCN/J, 25:12, Dec. 1972, p. 1380-1390, tables)

Deficient nutrition and susceptibility to infectious disease are highly interrelated in developing regions of Latin America. Present investigation explores this relationship in Guatemalan infants and preschool children from Indian families of low socioeconomic level. Long-term study revealed that intestinal flora developed early in life, remained stable during breast feeding period, and was remarkably similar in all subjects examined. Effect of intestinal bacteria on nutritional processes is still not clearly understood and requires further investigation.

2170. _____ and others. Gastrointestinal flora of children with protein-calorie malnutrition (AJCN/J, 25:10, Oct. 1972, p. 1118-1126, bibl.)

Study of gastrointestinal flora of 13 malnourished Guatemalan children undertaken to ascertain level of bacterial proliferation associated with acute malnutrition and its recovery period. High concentrations of bacteria detected in G-I system, especially small intestines. Significant decrease in bacterial population of stomach, duodenum, and jejunum observed during recuperation.

2171. _____ and others. Influence of recurrent infections on nutrition and growth of children in Guatemala (ASCN/J, 25:11, Nov. 1972, p. 1267-1275, bibl.)

Research on general effects of infections on nutritional processes and growth in rural Indian community of highland Guatemala. Fetal and post-natal development exhibited retardation. Problem of malnutrition began early in life and continued throughout preschool age. Poor diets of mother and child and widespread infectious diseases contributed to situation. Authors suggest that control of infections, as well as dietary modifications, are essential for improvement of nutrition and childhood growth in region.

2172. Mayoral, L.G. and others. Intestinal, functional, and morphologic abnormalities in severely protein-malnourished adults (ASCN/J, 25:10, Oct. 1972, p. 1084-1091, bibl., plates, tables)

Longitudinal investigation of intestinal malabsorption in 26 malnourished adults from the Cauca Valley, Colo. Abnormal bacterial colonization was observed in the small intestine, and defects were seen in the mucosal lining.

2173. O'Nell, C.W. Aging in a Zapotec community (Human Development [Basel, Switzerland] 15:5, 1972, p. 294-309, bibl.)

Various aspects of aging examined in 50 adults from Zapotec Indian community in Valley of Oaxaca, Mex. Significance of health and stress factors are considered. Article exemplifies fact that aging is an important topic for both physical and cultural anthropologists.

2174. Paige, David M. and others. Lactose intolerance in Peruvian children: effect of age and early nutrition (ASCN/J, 25:3, March 1972, p. 297-301, bibl.)

Study of lactose intolerance in 90 Peruvian mestizo children under age 17 in order to assess effects of breast feeding, subsequent habits of milk consumption, and previous episodes of nutritional diseases. High prevalence of lactose malabsorption was found, and above-named variables did not appear to contribute significantly to variations in tolerance levels. Incidence of malabsorption did, however, show increase with age.

2175. _____ and others. Response of lactose-intolerant children to different lactose levels (ASCN/J, 25:5, May 1972, p. 467-469, bibl.)

Experiments considering symptomatology changes with varying lactose doses in eight Peruvian mestizo children identified as intolerant. Results suggest little difference in ability to tolerate lactose load when small amounts are ingested. Symptoms of intolerance were present at lowest levels of lactose.

Parahym, Orlando da Cunha. Escola, alimentação e saúde. See item 6319.

2176. Plank, S.J. and **M.L. Milanesi.** Infant feeding and infant mortality in rural Chile (WHO/B, 48:2, 1973, p. 203-210, bibl.)

1,712 mothers from 15 rural populations of Chile were interviewed about dietary habits and mortality of their young children. Information was collected regarding duration of breast feeding, major components of postweaning diets, and rates of survival in first year of life. Also stresses importance of maternal age, parity, nutritional factors, and socioeconomic status.

2177. Prado, Carlos. Fatores sócio-econômicos da desidratação e desnutrição na infância. São Paulo, Impresa IPSIS, 1973. 273 p., illus.

High quality text on social and economic aspects of nutrition in Brazil. Following clinical descriptions of nutritional diseases and their varied causes and treatments, author discusses how several cultural and environmental factors are involved: agricultural practices, dietary habits, water sources, living conditions, and demographic stresses. Recommendations are offered for future improvement.

2178. Ramírez, Irma; Rafael Santini; José J. Corcino; and **P.J. Santiago.** Serum vitamin E levels in children and adults with tropical sprue in Puerto Rico (ASCN/J, 26:10, Oct. 1973, p. 1045, bibl.)

Possible criteria for diagnosis of tropical sprue, disease of unknown etiology which is endemic in the Caribbean, are stated. Authors point out that depressed vitamin E levels (about one-third normal) are also characteristic, according to examination of 30 Puerto Rican individuals with the disorder. Malabsorption of folic acid and vitamin B_{12} have been previously recorded.

2179. Rona, R. and **T. Pierret.** Genotipo y estatura en niñas adolescentes de Santiago (Revista Médica de Chile [Santiago] 101:3, 1973, p. 207-211, bibl.)

Investigation of stature differences among girls aged 10-17 from Santiago, who represented different socioeconomic statuses. Girls of higher statuses were significantly taller from about age 11.5 onwards. In higher-status sample, girls with larger number of foreign-born grandparents were also significantly taller. Figures compared with European and American statistics on stature in adolescent females.

2180. Santini, Rafael and **José J. Corcino.** Analysis of some nutrients of the Puerto Rican diet (ASCN/J, 27:8, Aug. 1974, p. 840-844, bibl.)

Nutritional appraisal of high and low cost diets that are typical in Puerto Rico. Significant differences found with respect to vitamin and protein content. Observations related to general picture of health in Puerto Rico.

2181. Schenk, Eric A.; Frederick A. Klipstein; and **J.T. Tomasini.** Morphologic characteristics of jejunal biopsies from asymptomatic Haitians and Puerto Ricans (ASCN/J, 25:10, Oct. 1972, p. 1080-1083, bibl.)

Morphological features of small bowel biopsies presented for random sample of 65 healthy Puerto Ricans and 18 Haitians. Types and degrees of structural abnormalities are summarized. Findings showed differences from samples representing temperate regions.

2182. Schneider, Roberto E. and **Fernando E. Viteri.** Morphological aspects of the duodenojejunal mucosa in protein-calorie malnourished children and during recovery (ASCN/J, 25:10, Oct. 1972, p. 1092-1102, bibl., plates, tables)

Longitudinal study of 11 Guatemalan children with severe protein-calorie malnutrition in order to obtain information on role of diarrhea, infection, and malnutrition in gastrointestinal pathogenesis. Three categories of morphological alterations in the intestine are described. Malnutrition is not the sole cause of the changes, and nonspecific diarrhea probably exerts considerable influence. Strong correlation between protein-calorie malnutrition and diarrhea found in study group.

2183. Sebrell, William H., Jr. and others. Nutritional status of middle and low-income groups in the Dominican Republic (SLN/ALN, 22 [special supplement] julio 1972, Unpaged)

Broad and comprehensive study of nutrition in 5,500 people from the Dominican Republic. Methodology included anthropometrics, dental exams, X-rays, nutriment analysis, clinical observations, dietery surveys, and biochemical tests on blood and urine. Most subjects had been chronically malnourished from birth. Vitamin, mineral, and protein deficiencies were common, and over one-half of sample were anemic. Growth and maturation retarded in childhood. Suggestions offered for improving the situation.

2184. Selowsky, Marcelo and **Lance Taylor.** The economics of malnourished children: an example of disinvestment in human capital (UC/EDCC, 22:1, Oct. 1973, p. 1730, bibl.)

Paper attempts to assess the economic impact of infantile malnutrition in Santiago. Since childhood malnutrition has long-range effects upon an individual's physical and intellectual development, it may exert strong pressure on an economic system. A number of demographic variables are compared for malnourished and "normal" Santiago children, and the economic benefits that would be derived from improving infant nutritional standards in Chile are mentioned.

2185. Smith, Frank R. and others. Serum vitamin A, retinol-binding protein, and prealbium concentrations in protein-calorie malnutrition; pt. 2: Treatment including supplemental vitamin A (ASCN/J, 26:9, Sept. 1973, p. 982-987, bibl.)

Eight Guatemalan children suffering from acute malnutrition monitored to find possible reasons for vitamin A deficiency which often accompanies protein calorie malnutrition. Present data implicate faulty serum retinol transport system.

2186. Stini, William A. Evolutionary implications of changing nutritional patterns in human populations (AAA/AA, 73:5, Oct. 1971, p. 1019-1030, bibl.)

Past and present human adaptations to nutritional stress are critically treated in order to throw light upon effects of varying dietary habits upon evolution of the species. Physical adjustments often occur during developmental period, when undernutrition has its most devastating results, and they may take the form of altered growth schedules or changes in patterns of sexual dimorphism. Hormonal responses and physiological factors are considered. Author's data on malnourished population from Heliconia, Colo., suggest nutritional adaptations tend to be effective, as seen in fact that adult body size proportions are similar regardless of nutritional circumstances. Paper represents worthwhile contribution to evolutionary study of human nutrition.

2187. ———. Malnutrition, body size and proportion (Ecology of Food and Nutrition [N.Y.] 1:1, 1972, p. 121-126, bibl.)

Stature, weight, and ponderal index described for protein-deficient Indian population of Heliconia, Colo., and compared with various other human groups in order to assess effects of malnutrition upon body size and proportion. Relatively low stature characterized both sexes. Measures and indices provide information on amount of sexual dimorphism and body proportions.

Population exhibits protracted, slow period of growth, especially pronounced in males.

2188. Stoopler, Mark; W. Frayer; and **Michael H. Alderman.** Prevalence and persistence of lactose malabsorption among young Jamaican children (ASCN/J, 27:7, July 1974, p. 728-732, bibl.)

Lactose absorption investigated in 94 rural Jamaican children under age four. Faulty absorption occurred in 53 of the subjects, and there was a significant decrease in proportion of children able to absorb lactose after first year of life. 21 percent of original malabsorbers manifested improvement in later examinations. Incidence or persistence of condition showed no consistent correlation with sex, anthropometric profile, patterns of milk consumption, symptoms of lactose intolerance, or duration of breast-feeding period.

2189. Torres-Pinedo, R.; C. Rivera; and **H. Rodríguez.** Intestinal absorptive defects associated with enteric infections in infants (NYAS/A, 174:4, 1971, p. 284-298, bibl.)

Puerto Rican infants with enteric infections such as diarrhea manifest defective sugar absorption by intestines. Present paper reviews faulty mechanisms involved. Impairment probably due to overall reduction in absorptive powers of intestinal mucosa.

2190. Villarejos, Víctor M. and others. Heights and weights of children in urban and rural Costa Rica (Journal of Tropical Pediatrics and Environmental Child Health [London] 17:1, March 1971, p. 32-43, bibl.)

Heights and weights of random sample of 11,829 Costa Rican children aged 0-18 years representing rural and urban areas of the country. Sample children measured shorter and lighter, on the average, than North American children of the same ages. Intra- and interpopulational disparities in growth and size are related to nutritional and socioeconomic factors.

2191. Viteri, Fernando E. and others. Intestinal malabsorption in malnourished children before and during recovery: relationship between severity of protein deficiency and the malabsorption process (American Journal of Digestive Diseases [N.Y.] 18:3, March 1973, p. 201-211, bibl.)

Intestinal absorption processes followed in 32 protein-calorie malnourished children from Guatemala through recovery period. Mechanics of direct relationship between degree of protein deficiency and adverse intestinal changes are described. Mucosal malfunction implicated as main cause of malabsorption.

HUMAN ADAPTATION

2192. Abelson, Andrew E.; T.S. Baker; and **Paul T. Baker.** Altitude, migration, and fertility in the Andes (Social Biology [Society for the Study of Social Biology, N.Y.] 21:1, Spring 1974, p. 12-27, bibl.)

Paper examines relationship between hyposia and reduced fertility characteristic of high altitude Andean populations of Peru. Variables which affect reproductive behavior in these areas include socioeconomic conditions, cultural practices, demography, and stresses of physical environment. Upward and downward migrants studied to assess influence of hypoxia on fertility. Data consists mainly of informant reports of reproductive life histories and censuses. Low altitude nonmigrant sample displayed high fertility, and the upward and downward migrants exhibited lower levels of achieved reproduction.

2194. Boyce, A.J. and others. Respiratory function in Peruvian Quechua Indians (Annals of Human Biology [London] 1:2, April 1974, p. 137-148, bibl.)

Data on respiratory function and body size obtained for sample of 686 males from high altitude and sea level Quechua Indian populations of Peru. Loss of respiratory function commonly accompanies increase in age. High altitude population exhibited higher lung volumes and lower rates of decline in function with age. Differences due to altitude are apparent from at least age 12 onward. Vital capacity and expiratory volume in Quechua among the largest ever recorded.

2195. Brooke, O.G.; M. Harris; and **C.B. Salvosa.** The response of malnourished babies to cold (Journal of Physiology [London] 233:1, Aug. 1973, p. 75-91, bibl.)

Experiments concerning reactions to cold stress in 12 severely malnourished Jamaican infants. Subjects displayed no increase in metabolic heat production, and core temperatures fell rapidly, indicating subnormal tolerance. Following successful hospital treatment, the children were able to maintain normal body temperatures upon exposure to identical cold stress, and heat production was increased by 20 percent through non-shivering thermogenesis. The mechanics of reduced cold tolerance in malnutrition are as yet unknown.

2196. Clegg, E.J. and **G.A. Harrison.** Reproduction in human high altitude populations (Hormones [Basel, Switzerland] 2:1, 1971, p. 13-25, bibl.)

Survey of literature and authors' own original research on reproduction at high altitude uncovers good evidence that fertility is strongly affected by prevailing environmental conditions, especially hypoxia—pregnancy is difficult and frequently interrupted, birth weights are low, and prematurity and reproductive wastage are appreciable. While high altitude appears to depress sex drive and impair successful conception, demographic data, drawn principally from Andean populations from Peru, suggest total fertility is often at least as high as in surrounding lowland communities. Two possible reasons are that high altitude has little adverse effect upon gametogenesis and high altitude women typically take fuller advantage of their reproductive periods in terms of child spacing.

2197. Ennis, J.T.; G.R. Serjeant; and H. Middlemiss. Homozygous sickle cell disease in Jamaica (British Journal of Radiology [London] 46:551, p. 943-950, bibl., plates, tables)

Radiological analysis of 61 Jamaican individuals with homozygous sickle-cell anemia. Abnormal appearances observed during skeletal survey are described. Bone marrow expansion and bone infarction were both prevalent, the latter increasing in frequency with age.

2198. Frisancho, A. Roberto. Influence of developmental adaptation on aerobic capacity at high altitude (Journal of Applied Physiology [American Physiological Society, Washington] 34:2, Feb. 1973, p. 176-180, bibl.)

High altitude natives and acclimatized sea-level residents from Peru were compared with respect to oxygen intake, ventilation, and work capacity. Lowland subjects acclimatized during the developmental period approached the level of adaptedness of high altitude natives more closely than did the lowlanders acclimatized as adults. Study provides additional evidence for the view that several respiratory adaptations to high altitude hypoxia develop during the growth and maturation period of life.

2199. _____; Tulio Velázquez; and Jorge Sánchez. Influence of developmental adaptation on lung function at high altitude (WSU/HB, 45:4, Dec. 1973, p. 583-594, bibl., tables)

A comparison of lung volume in high altitude residents of Peru with acclimatized adults and children from sea level indicates that the significantly larger lung-volume of the native peoples (advantageous because it permits the introduction of greater amounts of air to the body with each breath) is influenced by adaptations occurring during the developmental process. Authors suggest that increased lung volume, like many other morphological adaptations to high altitude, probably becomes established during period of growth and development.

2200. _____ and others. Adaptive significance of small body size under poor socio-economic conditions in southern Peru (AJPA, 39:2, Sept. 1973, p. 255-262, bibl.)

Relationship of body size, natural selection, and adaptation studied in Peruvian highland population of low socioeconomic and nutritional level. Demographic and anthropometric data collected to investigate survival rates in offspring of parents of varying body size representing 190 households. Shorter mothers in all age groups had significantly greater offspring survival, but association was not as pronounced in small fathers. Authors believe results demonstrate that smaller body size may be the most adaptive under poor socioeconomic conditions marked by nutritional restriction.

2201. Hanna, Joel M. Coca leaf use in southern Peru: some biosocial aspects (AAA/AA, 76:2, June 1974, p. 281-296, bibl.)

In many highland populations of the Peruvian Andes cocaine is ingested by chewing coca leaves. While amount of coca use is directly correlated with altitude, the contention that the addictive nature of the drug is mainly responsible for its widespread use in high altitude peoples is not well-substantiated. Patterns of consumption among Quechua Indians of Nuñoa in southern Peru are described. High level of coca use maintained because of social and economic motivations in addition to possible biological advantages in the face of the stresses of high altitudes. This paper reviews existing evidence on the topic but does not offer firm conclusions.

2202. _____ and Paul T. Baker. Comparative heat tolerance of Shipibo Indians and Peruvian mestizos (WSU/HB, 46:1, Feb. 1974, p. 69-80, bibl.)

Male Indians from Peruvian Amazon jungle are compared with acclimatized mestizo men with respect to heat tolerance during physical activity in the afternoon sun. Indian subjects generally experienced less cardiovascular stress, and they exhibited lower resting rectal temperatures, higher total sweat losses, and lower final heart rates. Sample differences were most noticeable during experimental periods of lighter activity, possibly because the mestizos had been accustomed to strenuous labor under hot conditions, and because the Indians tend to limit their activities in the hot parts of the day.

2203. Hurtado, Alberto. Aclimatación a la altura (OAS/CI, 14:1/2, enero/abril 1973, p. 2-11, bibl., tables)

Thorough and useful overview of human physiological adaptation to high altitude environments, based largely upon data collected in Peruvian Andes and control populations from lowland areas of Peru. Ventilatory and hematological characteristics of high altitude populations are discussed, as are effects of differing levels of physical activity of subjects. Various pathological aspects of high altitude populatios are pointed out. Large number of original studies are reviewed.

2204. _____. The influence of altitude on man (OSP/B, 6:3, 1972, p. 37-43, bibl.)

General article covering nature of high altitude environments and different forms of biological adaptations observed in human populations. Author's extensive investigations in Peruvian Andes suggest distinctive morphological, biochemical, and physiological mechanisms of genetic adaptation and short-term acclimatization. A number of well-defined adaptive processes favor efficient respiratory functions and prodigious capacity for physical work in indigenous high altitude people. Areas of insufficient knowledge and needed research are outlined.

2205. Little, Michael A.; R. Brooke Thomas; and James W. Larrick. Skin temperature and cold pressor responses of Andean Indians during hand immersion in water at 4 degrees C (WSU/HB, 45:4, Dec. 1973, p. 643-662, bibl., tables)

Hand skin tempratures, blood pressure, and heart rate were measured and compared for 22 highland Quechuan Indians and six Caucasians during immersion of hands in ice water. Indian subjects were found to be much better able to tolerate the cold stresses than the Caucasians, and they maintained significantly warmer skin temperatures. Possible contributing circulatory adaptations are discussed.

2206. McCullough, John M. Human ecology, heat adaptation, and belief systems: the hot-cold syndrome of Yucatan (UNM/JAR, 29:1, Spring 1973, p. 32-36, bibl.)

In study of native Yucatan populations, it was observed that properly balanced consumption of substances culturally perceived as "hot" and "cold" is a biobehavioral adaptation to heat stress. One important facet of the phenomenon is fact that salt is identified "hot" while water is visualized as "cold." Author found that judicious compliance with hot-cold rules consistently helped to decrease incidence of heat casualties among farmers routinely exposed to extreme stresses. This interesting study effectively demonstrates interaction of cultural and biological elements in human adaptation.

2207. Mazess, Richard B. and R. Larsen. Responses of Andean highlanders to night cold (International Journal of Biometeorology [Amsterdam] 16:2, March 1972, p. 181-192, bibl.)

Peruvians native to high altitudes, who commonly practice herding and some subsistence agriculture, must withstand extremely cold temperatures with simple clothing and unheated homes. Laboratory study of response to cold indicated that the skillful employment of skins and blankets was very effective in reducing stress. Highland Indians maintained warmer skin and rectal temperatures than Caucasian control subjects when exposed to cold experimentally. Authors believe that in this population clothing and bedding play important roles in resolving adaptive problems of cold stress.

2208. Monge, Carlos. Acclimatization in the Andes: historical confirmations of "climatic aggression" in the development of Andean man. Translated by Donald F. Brown. With a foreword by Isaiah Bowman. New preface for this edition by Paul T. Baker. Detroit, Mich., Blaine Ethridge, 1973. 130 p., bibl.

New edition of a classic work on human adaptation to high altitude by one of the modern pioneers in the field (1 ed., Baltimore, Md., Johns Hopkins Press, 1948). Contains historical accounts of the stresses of the Andean environment, discussions of the marked effects of high altitude upon human fertility and mortality, and a synthesis of data relating to morphological and physiological aspects of the genetic adaptation of populations and the acclimatization of individuals. Populational differences and individual variability are treated within an evolutionary framework. Author concludes that indigenous high altitude populations are rather distinct biologically. This basic and highly readable book has been widely cited in the literature on high altitude adaptation.

2209. Salzano, Francisco M.; Fernando J. Da Rocha; and G.V. Simões. Fertiflity of abnormal hemoglobin carriers in Pôrto Alegre, Brazil (HH, 23:1, 1973, p. 27-31, bibl., table)

In a malarial region of the state of Pôrto Alegre, Bra., the fertility of 123 couples having at least one carrier of Hemoglobin S or Hemoglobin C was compared with a like number of control couples in order to estimate fitness values. No significant differences were observed for mean number of pregnancies, number of live births, frequency of reproductive wastage, number of premature children, or childhood (pre-reproductive) mortality. The siblings of the two sample populations were also similar in reproductive parameters. Since the abnormal hemoglobins in heterozygote form do not appear to confer adaptive advantage, it is predicted that they should decrease or disappear entirely from the area through natural selection.

2210. Serjeant, G.R.; J.T. Ennis; and H. Middlemiss. Haemoglobin SC disease in Jamaica (British Journal of Radiology [London] 46:551, 1973, p. 935-942, bibl., plates, tables)

Radiological study of 84 Jamaican individuals with hemoglobin SC disease. Several skeletal abnormalities noted, including vascular lesions. Contributing factors are discussed. No clear association found between clinical severity of condition and degree of skeletal changes.

2211. _____; _____; and _____. Sickle cell Beta thalassemia in Jamaica (British Journal of Radiology [London] 46:551, 1973, p. 951-959, bibl., plates, tables)

Radiological investigation of 47 Jamaican patients with sickle-cell Beta thalassemia. Skeletal abnormalities are similar to those associated with hemoglobin SC disease and homozygous sickle-cell anemia. Bone marrow expansion and bone infarction in femoral and humeral heads were both common.

2211a. Sime, Francisco and others. Hypoxemia, pulmonary hypertension, and low cardiac output in newcomers at low altitude (Journal of Applied Physiology [American Physiological Society, Washington] 36:5, May 1974, p. 561-565, bibl.)

Eight male Peruvian subjects from low altitude studied with respect to cardiopulmonary function at rest and during exercise at sea level and at high altitude. Following were measured: cardiac output, blood pressure, oxygen uptake, and pulmonary artery pressure. High altitude environment observed to impede work capacity.

2212. Sorensen, Soren C. and others. Cerebral glucose metabolism and cerebral blood flow in high altitude residents (Journal of Applied Physiology [American Physiological Association, Washington] 37:3, Sept. 1974, p. 305-310, bibl.)

Glucose metabolism in brain and cerebral blood flow measured in 23 high altitude dwellers from La Paz. Slightly lowered blood flow may be a result of increased hematocrit. Regulation of respiration in subjects related to chronic hypoxia characteristic of high altitude natives.

2213. Vogel, James A.; L.H. Hartley; and J.C. Cruz. Cardiac output during exercise in altitude natives at sea level and high altitude (Journal of Applied Physiology [American Physiological Association, Washington] 36:2, Feb. 1974, p. 173-176, bibl.)

Study of cardiovascular changes in eight Peruvian subjects native to altitude of 4,350 meters who underwent exercise at that elevation and at sea level. During sea level episode, cardiac output remained same, heart rate was less, and stroke volume was greater than values obtained at high altitude, both at rest and in exercise. Authors discuss role of cardiovascular system in acclimatization to altitude changes.

2214. _____ and others. Cardiac output during exercise in sea-level residents at sea level and high altitude (Journal of Applied Physiology [American Physiological Association, Washington] 36:2, Feb. 1974, p. 169-172, bibl.)

Cardiovascular responses to altitude changes monitored in four Peruvian subjects native to sea level who underwent exercise at sea level and altitude of 4,350 meters. Cardiac output and maximal oxygen uptake decreased during initial high altitude exposure, and reductions were sustained after prolonged sojourns. Peripheral vascular resistance increased progressively at high altitude.

BIOMEDICAL STUDIES

2215. Arnt, Nilton and L. Morris. Smallpox outbreaks in two Brazilian villages: epidemiologic characteristics (JHU/AJE, 95:4, April 1972, p. 363-370, bibl.)

Epidemiological aspects of smallpox investigated in 134 cases occurring during recent outbreak in two villages from state of Minas Gerais, Bra. In each village infected households were not noticeably clustered together, but rather distributed throughout the locality. Inverse relationship found between age and susceptibility to the disease during the epidemics.

2216. Black, Francis L. and others. Evidence for persistence of infectious agents in isolated human populations (JHU/AJE, 100:3, Sept. 1974, p. 230-250, bibl., map, tables)

Study to determine which infectious disease agents are able to persist in small, isolated human populations. Immunity to various viral, bacterial, and protozoal infections investigated in 939 members of three Carib and four Cayapó Indian tribes from near the Amazon Basin in Brazil. Age of acquisition of immunity was relatively early. While some common antibodies exist at very high levels among these groups, others are rare or absent. Disease-producing organisms displayed variability with respect to stability of relationship with host communities.

2217. Boletín de Higiene y Epidemiología. Centro Nacional de Información de Ciencias Médicas. Año 9, Nos. 2/3, mayo/dic. 1971- . La Habana.

Series of reports on current aspects of health and disease in Cuba including clinical descriptions and epidemiological data on influenza, gastro-intestinal parasites, viral infections, and rabies. Also contains paper concerning the improvement of health conditions in Cuba.

2218. Cañedo, Luis. Rural health care in Mexico (AAAS/S, 185:4157, Sept. 1974, p. 1131-1137, bibl., map, tables)

Author points out that over 40 percent of Mexico's population currently lives in rural communities smaller than 2,500, most of which have limited or no access to medical facilities, doctors, health professionals, or other public health resources. Past attempts to improve the situation are reviewed, as are extant training programs in community medicine and public health. Information storage and retrieval plan is suggested.

2219. Dobkin de Ríos, Marlene. Curanderismo con la soga alucinogénica—ayahusca—en la selva peruana (III/AI, 31:3, julio 1971, p. 575-591, bibl.)

Use of the hallucinogenic vine ayahuasca for curing magical illnesses in the Peruvian jungles is examined. Both therapist and patient employ visual hallucinations during a healing session in order to isolate the cause of the particular affliction. Author believes drug relieves interpersonal anxieties and tensions. In this way, the ritualized use of the substance helps to promote curing and recovery. For ethnologist's comments, see *HLAS 35:1249-1252*.

2220. _____. Curing with *ayahuasca* in an urban slum (*in* Harner, Michael J. ed. Hallucinogens and shamanism. N.Y., Oxford Univ. Press, 1973, p. 67-85, bibl.)

Use of hallucinogenic drug *ayahuasca* for healing purposes explored in urban Peruvian population situated on Amazon River. *Ayahuasca* found to be most effective in curing diseases and illnesses believed to be magical in origin. Visual hallucinations interpreted by healer to determine cause of malady and to neutralize evil magic.

2221. ———. The influence of psychotropic flora and fauna on Maya religion (UC/CA, 15:2, June 1974, p. 147-164, bibl.)

Study of influence of drugs modifying mental activity upon Maya art and religion. Following a survey of mind-altering substances from Maya regions and a discussion of their psychological and physiological effects, three examples are given of psychotropic materials represented in motifs of ancient Maya art and religion. It is suggested that the properties of these substances were probably well known by the Maya shaman, priest, and artist.

2222. ———. The non-Western use of hallucinogenic agents (*in* United States National Commission on Marihuana and Drug Abuse. Drug use in America: problems in perspective; Appendix, the technical papers of the second report of the U.S. National Commission on Marihuana and Drug Abuse. Washington, GPO, 1973, p. 1179-1235)

Multifaceted and praiseworthy review article on subject of drug use in various cultures including five past and present Latin American societies. Social and biological components of usage patterns are identified and discussed. Especially useful are the several in-depth ethnographic case studies and the author's compilation of hallucinogenic substances and associated cultural practices in a number of world areas.

2223. Figueroa, Rolando B. and others. Intestinal lactase deficiency in an apparently normal Peruvian population (American Journal of Digestive Diseases [N.Y.] 16:10, Oct. 1971, p. 881-889, bibl.)

Comparison of prevalence of milk and lactose tolerance and intestinal lactase level in tolerant and intolerant individuals from Peru. Symptoms and reactions to milk ingestion described. Intolerants able to drink small amounts of milk without problem. Environmental and genetic factors discussed.

2224. Galbis, Ricardo. Métodos de curación entre los cuná y los otomí: estudio comparativo (III/AI, 34:4, oct./dic. 1974, p. 939-947, bibl.)

Comparative study of curing practices and healing methods in the Cuná Indians of Panama and the Otomí of Mexico. The development and transmission of medical thought in each of these cultures are described.

2225. García-Palieri, Mario R. Precursors of coronary artery disease in Puerto Rico (ASCN/J, 26:10, Oct. 1973, p. 1133-1137, bibl.)

Recent increase in coronary disease in Puerto Rico prompted examination of 9,814 men aged 45-64 in order to learn possible antecedent factors. Rural-urban differences found in various "risk factors:" relative weight, physical activity, intensity of smoking, blood pressure, vital capacity, heart rate, nutrition, prevalence of diabetes, and level of glucose and cholesterol in the blood.

2226. ———. and others. Interrelationship of serum lipids with relative weight, blood glucose, and physical activity (Circulation [American Heart Association, N.Y.] 45:4, April 1972, p. 829-836, bibl.)

Blood tests run on 5,800 adult Puerto Rican males indicated that serum cholesterol and blood glucose levels were significantly higher in urban, as compared to rural, subjects. Average body weight also greater in urban subjects. Authors believe findings demonstrate importance of weight control in reduction of serum lipids.

2227. Golubjatnikov, Rjurik; T. Paskey; and S.L. Inhorn. Serum cholesterol levels of Mexican and Wisconsin children (JHU/AJE, 96:1, July 1972, p. 36-40)

Cholesterol levels determined in serum for random sample of 209 Mexican and 328 Wisconsin children aged five-14. Mean cholesterol level was about twice as high in the US subjects. Within each study population, no significant difference in mean levels when five-nine year-olds and 10-14 year-olds were compared. Results may be important for assessing national differences in susceptibility to coronary diseases and the dietary factors influencing them.

2228. *Guatemala Indígena.* Instituto Indigenista Nacional. Vol. 6, No. 1, marzo 1971- . Guatemala.

Special issue devoted to popular and folk medicine practiced in Guatemala based on survey conducted by a national agency in 1969. Organized by area of country and specific diseases, the study explores methods and materials utilized by curanderos, brujos, zajorines, compenhuesos, and parteras empiricas. This compilation would be particularly useful for physical, medical, and cultural anthropologists.

2229. Harwood, Alan. The hot-cold theory of disease (Journal of the American Medical Association [Chicago, Ill.] 216:7, May 1971, p. 1153-1158, bibl.)

Traditional Puerto Rican perception of illness and medicine historically derive from the "humoral" theory of Hippocrates. In this system, a proper balance of "hot" and "cold" foods and medications are necessary to maintain good health. Adherence to the system influences attitudinal and biological responses of many Puerto Ricans to modern therapeutic regimens and public health programs which have recently been introduced to the population.

2230. Janiger, Oscar and **Marlene Dobkin de Ríos.** Suggestive hallucinogenic properties of tobacco

(Medical Anthropology Newsletter, 4:4, Aug. 1973, p. 6-11)

Use of tobacco in prehistoric and recent New World populations for religious and ceremonial purposes suggests possible hallucinogenic properties of the plant. Review of ethnographic literature on aboriginal usage of New World tobacco indicates it has often been ingested to induce trance or provoke visions, to facilitate divination, and to aid in curing practices.

2231. Kensinger, Kenneth M. *Banisteriopsis* usage among the Peruvian Cashinahua (*in* Harner, Michael J. *ed.* Hallucinogens and shamanism. N.Y., Oxford Univ. Press, 1973, p. 9-14, bibl.)

Ayahuasca, an hallucinogenic drink brewed from two different physchotropic plants, is commonly imbibed by the Cashinahua of Peru for ritual and medicinal purposes. Aspects of preparation, usage, and effects of the substance are described. While consumption patterns vary widely, certain hallucinations are seen to recur with regularity. Shamans typically employ the preparation as a supplement to normal healing paraphenalia.

2232. *Los Libros.* Para una crítica política de la cultura. No. 34, marzo/abril 1974- . B.A.

Issue devoted to mental health in Argentina. Selections include:
E. Pichon-Rivière and others, "Instituciones de Salud Mental en la Argentina" p. 4-15
F. Ulloa, "Salud Mental en la Argentina: Atención y Condiciones de Trabajo" p. 16-24
O. Bonnano, "Coyuntura Actual de la Salud Mental" p. 25-29
B.L. Perosio, "Salud Pública y Dependencia" p. 30-34.

2233. Likosky, William H. An epidemiological study of dengue type 2 in Puerto Rico, 1969 (JHU/AJE, 97:4, April 1973, p. 264-275, bibl.)

Review of historical reports of dengue occurrence in Caribbean followed by micro-analysis of 1969 Puerto Rico epidemic. Outbreak was primarily confined to northern part of island. Infection rates in affected regions ranged from eight percent to 79 percent, with an average of about 25 percent. Contraction of disease was not significantly influenced by age, sex, or previous exposure.

2234. Llopis, Alvaro. The problem of venereal diseases in the Americas (OSP/B, 6:1, 1972, p. 62-92, bibl., tables)

Incidence of syphilis and gonorrhea has increased in several Latin American countries since 1950. Scope of resulting morbidity and mortality changes is discussed for various nations. Recent rise in venereal diseases is partly attributable to increases in population size, youthful sex, population mobility, and sexual promiscuity. Programs designed to curb the venereal disease problem in Latin America are mentioned. Good deal of useful statistical data is drawn together in the article.

2235. Lobb, C. Gary. El uso de la coca como manifestación de cultura indígena en las montañas occidentales de Sudamérica (III/AI, 34:4, oct./dic. 1974, p. 919-938, bibl., maps, tables)

Coca leaf chewing among Quechua and Aymara Indians of South America is much more common than in nearby Mestizo and Caucasian groups, indicating a cultural component in usage patterns. Economic and socio-religious motivations for coca use are also discussed.

Logan, Michael H. Digestive disorders and plant medicinals in highland Guatemala. See item 1156.

2236. _____. Humoral medicine in Guatemala and peasant acceptance of modern medicine (SAA/HO, 32:4, Winter 1973, p. 385-395, bibl.)

Indian and Ladino peasants of highland Guatemala classify medicinal plants, illnesses, and modern medicines according to a cultural system stressing the opposing qualities of "hot" and "cold." This study reviews the history and structure of folk medical practices in the area and the reactions of the people to modern medical treatments.

2237. Lopes, Oscar Souza and **Lia de Abreu Sacohetta.** Epidemiology of Boraceia virus in forested area in São Paulo, Brazil (JHU/AJE, 100:5, Nov. 1974, p. 410-413, bibl.)

Boraceia virus, one of the Anopheles B group of arboviruses, infected a region near São Paulo. Antibody levels reported. Disease also affected other animals.

2238. López, F. and others. An outbreak of acute polyradiculo-neuropathy in Colombia in 1968 (JHU/AJE, 98:3, Sept. 1973, p. 226-230, bibl.)

Presentation of virologic, clinical, epidemiological, and immunological aspects of acute polyradiculoneuropathy outbreak in Itagui, Colo. Appearance of disease preceded by widespread respiratory and gastrointestinal disturbances in population.

2239. Lord, Rexford D. History and geographic distribution of Venezuelan equine encephalitis (PAHO/B, 8:2, 1974, p. 100-110, bibl., maps, tables)

Historical-epidemiological analysis of Venezuelan Equine encephalitis in Central and South America. Various outbreaks occurring since 1938 and their effects upon humans and animals are described. Areas of origination and geographic patterns of communication are outlined. Several related virus strains shown to precipitate the disease, which not only infects humans, but also poses an economic threat in many regions because of the heavy toll on horses, burros, cattle, and other important animals.

2240. Morales, Alberto and others. Recovery of dengue-2 virus from *Aedes* *aegypti* in Colombia (ASTMH/J, 22:6, Nov. 1973, p. 785-787, bibl.)

Dengue, viral disease transmitted by *Aedes* mosquito, studied during recent epidemic in Colombia. Nine strains of virus, recovered from two localities in Colombia where dengue was prevalent, are reported. Cause of epidemic traced to dengue-2 strains.

2241. Morase, Mario A.P. and G.M. Chaves. Onchoceriasis in Brazil: new findings among the Yanomama (PAHO/B, 8:2, 1974, p. 95-99, bibl., maps, tables)

Onchocera, tropical parasitic worm found in Africa and Central America, discovered among Yanomama of Brazil. Parasite has a predilection for the eyes and can cause blindness ("river blindness"). 27 of 57 Yanomama subjects (47.3 percent) found to be harboring the parasite, and condition was most common among older individuals. Results may indicate that Onchoceriasis is endemic among the Yanomama.

2242. Naranjo, Plutarco. El cocaísmo entre los aborígenes de Sud América (III/AI, 34:3, julio/sept. 1974, p. 605-628, bibl., plates, tables)

Cocaine ingestion through chewing coca leaves studied in South American Indians. Origin and diffusion traced through archaeological and historical evidence. Medical, magical, and religious uses of the drug are analyzed.

2243. Neel, James V. Control of disease among Amerindians in cultural transition (PAHO/B, 8:3, 1974, p. 205-211, bibl., plates)

Discusses health and disease patterns in native South American populations undergoing culture contact and acculturation. Many diseases found to be endemic, especially enteric viruses and other gastrointestinal parasites. Newborn children have relatively high passive immunity to local diseases and elevated antibody (e.g. Gamma globulin) production. Past and present relationships of populations and diseases are analyzed. Recommendations offered to supplement standard immunization and disease control programs already established. Author's references to these people as "primitive" are unfortunate.

2244. Noble, John and others. Hemorrhagic exanthem of Bolivia: studies of an unusual hemorrhagic disease in high-altitude dwellers at sea level (JHU/AJE, 99:2, Feb. 1974, p. 123-131, bibl., plate, tables)

Clinical, epidemiological, and laboratory investigations of epidemic of Hemorrhagic Exanthem in Riberalta, Bol. Disease characterized by severe cutaneous and systemic hemorrhaging, yet it produced few deaths and little fever. Etiology and mode of transmission of disease remain unknown.

2245. Pan American Health Organization (PAHO), Washington. Health conditions in the Americas: 1969-1972. Washington, World Health Organization (WHO), 1974. 226 p., bibl., maps, tables (Scientific publication, 287)

Useful statistical catalogue of current demographic and epidemiological trends in Latin America. Extensive data and commentary on population structure and demographic dynamics, prevalence and distribution of communicable diseases, available public health and hospital services, and environmental health programs and facilities. Important synthesis of diverse materials, especially morbidity and mortality patterns.

2246. _____, _____. Health research in Latin America. Washington, World Health Organization (WHO), 1973. 73 p., tables (Scientific publication, 275)

Report on general state of medical and epidemiological research currently going on in Latin America. Public health measures in different countries, population growth studies, and medical research are discussed in context of financial, educational, and political aspects of the research programs which have been established.

2247. _____, _____. Unidades de cuidado intensivo para la América Latina: hacia la atención progresiva del paciente. Washington, World Health Organization (WHO), 1973. 67 p., bibl., illus (Scientific publication, 264)

General outline of current picture of health care structure, function, and organization in Latin American countries.

2248. Pennington, Campbell, W. Plantas medicinales utilizadas por el pima montañés de Chihuahua (III/AI, 33:1,1. trimestre 1973, p. 213-232, bibl.)

Study of use of medicinal plants for curing of common diseases among the mountain Pima Indians of Mexican state of Chihuahua. Species from at least 51 plant families are utilized by the Pima, and these are catalogued and described.

2249. Pérez Mera, Amiro. El control de las epidemias de poliomielitis mediante la inmunización masiva: la experiencia de la República Dominicana (Ciencia [Santo Domingo] 1:1, enero/junio 1972, p. 7-16, bibl., tables)

History of polio epidemics in Dominican Republic since 1898 presented, including information on three widespread epidemics occurring between 1959 and 1971. Frequency of cases in different time periods compared to other Latin American countries. Seasonal variations and distribution of disease by age groups are delineated. Effectiveness of large-scale vaccination programs is evaluated.

2250. Petana, W.B. A revision of Trypanosoma [*schizotrypanum*] *Cruzi* strains from British Honduras, and the importance of strain characteristics in experimental chemotherapy of Chaga's disease (RSTMH/T, 66:3, 1972, p. 463-470, illus.)

Chaga's Disease, a severe communicable infection transmitted by the barbeiro insect (*Triatoma dimidiata*), comprises a major health problem affecting millions in Latin America. The protozoan responsible for the disease, *Trypanosoma cruzi,* is analyzed in present paper from observations in British Honduras. Morphology, virulence, and patterns of growth and reproduction are discussed. Characteristics of ten strains of *Trypanosoma cruzi,* from British Honduras are reviewed.

2251. Peters, C.J. Hemorrhagic fever in Cochabamba, Bolivia, 1971 (JHU/AJE, 99:6, June 1974, p. 425-433, bibl., map, tables)

Epidemiological investigation of outbreak during first three months of 1971 of hemorrhagic fever in Bolivian town. Clinical manifestations of the disease are reported.

2252. _____ and others. Antigenic subtypes of hepatitis B antigen in Panama (JHU/AJE, 99:5, May 1974, p. 375-380, bibl.)

Occurrence of hepatitis B antigenic subtypes in hepatatic patients hospitalized in Panama City compared with frequencies of subtypes among representative Panamanian populations. Prevalence of different types studied in relation to inter-populational variation, different forms of hepatitis, and presence of other infections.

2253. _____ and others. Epidemiology of hepatitis B antigen in Panama (JHU/AJE, 98:4, Oct. 1973, p. 301-310, bibl.)

Electrophoretic survey for hepatitis B antigenemia in 925 hospitalized hepatitis patients and in stratified sample of 2,412 in general population of Panama. Frequency of antigen carriers in various ethnic groups calculated. Significant differences associated with demographic characteristics of samples. Regional differences also related to environmental factors such as nutrition, sanitation, and insect activity. Non-Amerindian groups generally had a low prevalence of antigenemia (under one percent).

2254. Pochintesta, Mario and **Juvenal Botto.** Política y salud: Uruguay hoy, una teoría para el desarrollo concreto de la salud. Montevideo, Editorial Don Orione, 1972. 142 p., bibl., map, tables.

Synthesis of current public health situation in Uruguay, problems facing the country in improving health care, and some of the social, political, economic, and administrative factors involved. Authors offer what they feel are concrete solutions and beneficial changes in existing structure of health care.

2255. *Revista Venezolana de Sanidad y Asistencia Social.* Ministerio de Sanidad y Asistencia Social. Vol. 36, Nos. 3/4, sept./dic. 1971- . Caracas.

Report by Venezuelan government agency on national public health programs. Discussion of the following topics: recent medical-demographic studies, materials and practices of preventive medicine, occupational hygiene and medical services for workers, community psychiatry services, radiation and pollution control programs, and the activities and research of professional organizations and societies.

2256. Rosselot, Jorge. Maternal and child health in Latin America (OSP/B, 6:1, 1972, p. 21-32, bibl.)

Poor maternal and childhood care services are typical of the many economically underdeveloped regions of Latin America. A comprehensive program of protective health measures is proposed in order to help reduce the morbidity and mortality that is especially pervasive among children. Many of the causes of disease and early death in Latin America, such as contaminated water supplies and dietary deficiencies, are largely preventable.

2257. Schantz, P.M.; J.F. Williams; and **C. Riva Posse.** Epidemiology of hydatid disease in southern Argentina: comparison of morbidity indices, evaluation of immunodiagnostic tests, and factors affecting transmission in southern Río Negro province (ASTMH/J, 22:5, Sept. 1973, p. 629-641, bibl., map, tables)

Report on prevalence of infection by *Echinococcus,* a parasite transmitted by tapeworms, in southern Argentina province. Estimated rate of hospital diagnoses was 143 per 100,000 inhabitants, perhaps the highest regional concentration in the world. Many animals slaughtered for food were observed to be harboring the parasites. Analysis of methodological techniques is included.

2258. Sharrett, A. Richey and others. The control of streptococcal skin infections in South Trinidad (JHU/AJE, 99:6, June 1974, p. 408-413, bibl.)

Results of 40-week study of skin infection and associated nephritis in South Trinidad. Various treatments described.

2259. Shenkman, L. and others. Evidence of hypothyroidism in endemic cretinism in Brazil (LANCET, 2:7820, 1973, p. 67-70, bibl.)

Twelve cases of cretinism described from Goiaz, Bra. Patients characterized by mental retardation, short stature, motor defects, deaf-mutism, and nodular goiter. Individual pathologies also noted. Evidence indicates that subjects were hypothyroid during fetal life, and that it resulted in permanent neurological damage.

2260. Shiffer, Jeanette. The right to health: the Pan American Health Organization (OAS/AM, 25:5 [Special

Supplement] May 1973, p. 1-16, illus., plates)

Historical account of development of PAHO, present activities and projects, and future goals. Major accomplishment aided by Organization has been eradication and substantial reduction of various infectious diseases in Western Hemisphere such as smallpox, malaria, and yellow fever. PAHO has also worked to better health conditions in Latin America by improving water supplies, pollution problems, housing, nutrition, and public health programs. Structure and function of various health care organizations are discussed.

2261. Simpósio e Mesa Redonda de Plantas Medicinais do Brasil, *IV, Rio, 1973.* Plantas medicinais do Brasil: pts. 2/3 (SBPC/CC, 25:7, julho 1973, p. 627-659, tables; 25:8, agôsto 1973, p. 738-766, tables)

Proceedings of symposium on various biological aspects of medicinal plants native to Brazil and patterns of drug use in the country. 20 papers deal with following topics: geography and ecology of plant distribution, pharmacological features of natural and synthetic drugs, physiological and psychological effects, and evidence of drug dependence. Special emphasis on *Cannabis* derivatives. Although rather technical, collection should be of interest to medical and physical anthropologists. Notable contributions include the following:
Edith B. Lopes Bório; C. Cecy; and Y. Yassumoto "Contribuicão ao Estudo Farmacognóstico da Casca do Cuale da Aroeira *Schinus terebinthifolius* Raddi—Anacardiaceae" p. 631-634
F. Korte and D. Bieniek "Chemical and Biological Attempts to Elucidate Physiological Action of *Cannabis*" p. 634-643
A. Cesario de Melo; E.A. Carlini; and J.P. Green "Cross-tolerance Studies Among Nutmeg Compounds, Trans-Tetrahydrocannabinol and Mescaline" p. 644-647
E.A. Carlini and others "Propriedades Farmacológicas do Extratos Brutos de *Nectandra megabotamica* (Spreng) Chodat et Hassler, *Eupatorium maximiliani* Schrad, *Alpinia magnifica* Hoscoe, *Enterolobium timbouva* Mart. *Zeyheria digitalis* (Vell.) Hoene et Kulmann, *Jacaranda caroba* (Vell.) DC *Pachystroma ilicifolium* Meull. Arg." p. 653-659
Raphael Mechoulam "Chemistry and *Cannabis* Activity" p. 742-747
Claudio N. Albes and E.A. Carlini "Efeitos de Extratos de *Cannabis sativa* Sobre o Comportamento Muricida de Ratos" p. 755-758
Harris Isbell "Drug Dependence of the LSD (Hallucinogen) and *Cannabis* (Marihuana) Types" p. 758-764.

2262. Suárez, María M. Etiology, hunger, and folk diseases in the Venezuelan Andes (UNM/JAR, 30:1, Spring 1974, p. 41-54, bibl., map, tables)

Concepts of etiology and treatment of 184 cases of folk diseases examined in interviews with 69 adults from a Venezuelan municipality. Data also collected from midwives, medical herbalists, and sorcerers.

2263. Villarejos, Víctor M.; A. Gutiérrez; and W. Pelon. Identification of a type B hepatitis epidemic in Costa Rica: analysis of two outbreaks of viral hepatitis (JHU/AJE, 96:5, Nov. 1972, p. 372-378, bibl.)

Hepatitis B (Australia) antigen was discovered in high frequencies (67 percent) in 700 serum samples from individuals residing in Costa Rican zones affected by recent hepatitis epidemics. Findings from two separate epidemics occurring since 1963 are compared. Disease incidence was concentrated in children under ten years of age.

2264. _____. and others. Hepatitis epidemic in a Hyperendemic zone of Costa Rica: report of a second outbreak within four years (JHU/AJE, 96:5, Nov. 1972, p. 361-371, bibl.)

Two epidemics of viral hepatitis struck in two counties of Costa Rica within a four year period. The second epidemic was larger and longer in duration, reaching attack rates of five percent in certain districts. Over 36 percent of the 771 diagnosed cases were children under five years of age, and 92 percent were less than 15 years old. Person-to-person contact was the most likely vehicle of communicability. Clinical and epidemiological details are discussed.

JOURNAL ABBREVIATIONS

AAA/AA	American Anthropologist. American Anthropological Association. Washington.
AAA/AE	American Ethnologist. American Anthropological Association. Washington.
AAAS/D	Daedalus. Journal of the American Academy of Arts and Sciences. Harvard Univ. Cambridge, Mass.
AAAS/S	Science. American Association for the Advancement of Science. Washington.

AAC/AJ	Anthropological Journal of Canada. Quarterly Bulletin of the Anthropological Association of Canada. Quebec, Canada.
AFS/JAF	Journal of American Folklore. American Folklore Society. Austin, Tex.
AHIJH	Acta Haematologica. International Journal of Haematology. S. Karger. Basel, Switzerland.
AI/A	Anthropos. International review of ethnology and linguistics. Anthropos-Institut. Posieux, Switzerland.
AIA/A	Archaeological Institute of America. N.Y.
AINA/C	Cuadernos del Instituto Nacional de Antropología. Secretaría de Estado de Cultura y Educación, Dirección General de Institutos de Investigación. B.A.
AJPA	American Journal of Physical Anthropology. The official organ of the American Association of Physical Anthropologists [and] The Wistar Institute of Anatomy and Biology. Philadelphia, Pa.
ANC/B	Boletín de la Academia Nacional de Ciencias. Córdoba, Arg.
APS/P	Proceedings of the American Philosophical Society. Philadelphia, Pa.
ARCHEO	Archeologia. L'archeologie dans le monde et tout ce qui concerne les recherches historiques, artistiques et scientifiques sur terre et dans les mers. Paris.
ARMEX	Artes de México. México.
ASCN/J	American Journal of Clinical Nutrition. American Society for Clinical Nutrition. N.Y.
ASHG/J	American Journal of Human Genetics. The American Society of Human Genetics. Baltimore, Md.
ASTMH/J	American Journal of Tropical Medicine and Hygiene. American Society of Tropical Medicine and Hygiene. [Waverly Press]. Baltimore, Md.
AT/A	Antiquity. A quarterly review of archaeology. The Antiquity Trust. Cambridge, England.
ATS/ARRD	The American Review of Respiratory Diseases. Official Journal of the American Thoracic Society, Medical Section of the National Tuberculosis Association. N.Y.
AVAC/ACV	Acta Científica Venezolana. Asociación Venezolana para el Avance de la Ciencia. Caracas.
BBAA	Boletín Bibliográfico de Antropología Americana. Instituto Panamericano de Geografía e Historia, Comisión de Historia. México.
BGAEU/M	Mitteilungen der Berliner Gesellschaft für Anthropologie, Ethnologie and Urgeschichte. Berlin, FRG.
BJS	British Journal of Sociology. Published quarterly for the London School of Economics and Political Science. London.
BMA/J	British Medical Journal. British Medical Association. London.
BMHS/J	Journal of the Barbados Museum and Historical Society. Barbados, W.I.
CA	Critica d'Arte. Studio Italiano de Storia dell'Arte. Vallecchi Editore. Firenze, Italy.
CAEP/AP	Acta Prehistorica. Centro Argentino de Estudios Prehistoricos. B.A.
CAM	Cuadernos Americanos. México.
CCE/CHA	Cuadernos de Historia y Arqueología. Casa de la Cultura Ecuatoriana, Núcleo del Guayas. Guayaquil, Ecua.
CCE/RA	Revista de Antropología. Casa de la Cultura Ecuatoriana, Núcleo del Azuay. Cuenca, Ecua.
CIDG/O	Orbis. Bulletin international de documentation linguistique. Centre International de Dialectologie Générale. Louvain, Belgium.
CMS/IMR	The International Migration Review. Center for Migration Studies. N.Y.
CSSH	Comparative Studies in Society and History. Society for the Comparative Study of Society and History. The Hague.
CUA/AQ	Anthropological Quarterly. Catholic Univ. of America, Catholic Anthropological Conference. Washington.
CUH	Current History. A monthly magazine of world affairs. Philadelphia, Pa.
DGV/ZE	Zeitschrift für Ethnologie. Deutschen Gesellschaft für Völkerkunde. Braunschweig, FRG.
EANH/B	Boletín de la Academia Nacional de Historia. Quito.

EJ	Explorers Journal. N.Y.
EM/A	Årstryck. Ethnografiska Museum. Göteborg, Sweden.
EPHE/H	L'Homme. Revue française d'anthropologie. La Sorbonne, L'École Pratique des Hautes Études. Paris.
ESP	Espiral. Revista mensual de artes y letras. Editorial Iqueima. Bogotá.
FERES/SC	Social Compass. International review of socio-religious studies (Revue internationale des études socio-religieuses). International Federation of Institutes for Social and Socio-Religious Research (Fédération Internationale des Instituts de Recherches Sociales et Socio-Religieuses (FERES). The Hague.
FSCN/A	Antropológica. Fundación La Salle de Ciencias Naturales, Instituto Caribe de Antropología y Sociología. Caracas.
GIIN/GI	Guatemala Indígena. Instituto Indigenista Nacional. Guatemala.
HH	Human Heredity. Helbing and Lichtenhahn. Basel, Switzerland.
IAMEA	Inter-American Economic Affairs. Washington.
IBEAS/EA	Estudios Andinos. Instituto Boliviano de Estudio y Acción Social. La Paz.
ICA/RCA	Revista Colombiana de Antropología. Ministerio de Educación Nacional, Instituto Colombiano de Antropología. Bogotá.
ICACH	Icach. Organo de divulgación cultural del Instituto de Ciencias y Artes de Chiapas. Tuxtla Gutiérrez, Mex.
ICS/CJS	Caribbean Journal of Science. Univ. of Puerto Rico, Institute of Caribbean Science. Mayagüez, P.R.
IFEA/B	Bulletin de l'Institut Français d'Etudes Andines. Lima.
IGFO/RI	Revista de Indias. Consejo Superior de Investigaciones Científicas, Instituto Gonzalo Fernández de Oviedo. Madrid.
IGM/AGMG	Acta Geneticae Medicae et Gemellologiae. Instituto Gregorio Mendel. Roma.
IGM/U	L'Universo. Rivista bimestrale dell'Instituto Geografico Militare. Firenze, Italy.
III/A	Anuario Indigenista. Instituto Indigenista Interamericano. México.
III/AI	América Indígena. Instituto Indigenista Interamericano. México.
IJSP	International Journal of Social Psychiatry. London.
ILN	Illustrated London News. London.
INAH/A	Anales del Instituto Nacional de Antropología e Historia. Secretaría de Educación Pública. México.
INAH/B	Boletín del Instituto Nacional de Antropología e Historia. Secretaría de Educación Pública. México.
IPA/AP	Allpanchis Phuturinqa. Univ. de San Antonio de Abad, Seminario de Antropología, Instituto de Pastoral Andina. Cuzco, Peru.
IRR/R	Race. The Journal of the Institute of Race Relations. London.
IU/AL	Anthropological Linguistics. A publication of the Archives of the Languages of the World. Indiana Univ., Anthropology Dept. Bloomington, Ind.
IU/IJAL	International Journal of American Linguistics. Published by Indiana Univ. under the auspices of Linguistic Society of America, American Anthropological Association, with the cooperation of the Joint Committee on American Native Languages. Waverly Press Baltimore, Md.
JDA	The Journal of Developing Areas. Western Illinois Univ. Press. Macomb, Ill.
JGSWGL	Jahrbuch für Geschichte von Staat, Wirtschaft und Gesellschaft Lateinamerickas. Köln, FRG.
JHU/AJE	American Journal of Epidemiology. Johns Hopkins Univ., School of Hygiene. Baltimore, Md.
JSP	Journal of Social Psychology. The Journal Press. Provincetown, Mass.
KAS/P	Kroeber Anthropological Society Papers. Univ. of California. Berkeley, Calif.
KITLV/B	Bijdragen tot de Taal-, Land- en Volkenkunde. Koninklijk Instituut voor Taal-, Land- en Volkenkunde. Leiden, The Netherlands.
KMGMG/GM	Geologie en Mijnbouw. Koninklijk Nederlands Geologisch Minjnbouwkundig Genootschap. The Hague.

KU/IJCS	International Journal of Comparative Sociology. Karnatak Univ., Dept. of Social Anthropology. Dharwar, India.
LANCET	Lancet. London.
LING	Linguistics. An international review. Mouton. The Hague.
LNB/L	Lotería. Lotería Nacional de Beneficencia. Panamá.
LSE/PS	Population Studies. A journal of demography. London School of Economics, The Population Investigation Committee. London.
MEMDA/E	Etnía. Museo Etnográfico Municipal Dámaso Arce. Municipalidad de Olavarría, Provincia de Buenos Aires, Arg.
MH/OM	Objets et Mondes. Revue trimestrielle. Musée de l'Homme. Paris.
MLV/T	Tribus. Veröfferntlichungen des Linden-Museums. Museum für Länder- und Völkerkunde. Stuttgart, FRG.
MMFQ	Milbank Memorial Fund Quaterly. N.Y.
MNDJG/A	Anales del Museo Nacional David J. Guzmán. San Salvador.
MP/A	Arquivos do Museu Paranaense. Curitiba, Bra.
MP/R	Revista do Museu Paulista. São Paulo, Bra.
MPEG/B	Boletim do Museu Paraense Emílio Goeldi. Conselho Nacional de Pesquisas, Instituto Nacional de Pesquisas da Amazônia. Belém, Bra.
MPEG/PA	Publicações Avulsas. Museu Paraense Emílio Goeldi. Belém, Bra.
MV/BA	Baessler-Archiv. Beiträge zur Völkerkunde. Museums für Völkerkunde. Berlin, FRG.
MVL/J	Jahrbuch des Museums für Volkerkunde zu Leipzig. Berlin, FRG.
MVW/AV	Archiv für Völkerkunde. Museum für Völkerkunde in Wien und von Verein Freunde der Völkerkunde. Wien.
NAS/P	Proceedings of the National Academy of Sciences. Washington.
NWIG	Nieuwe West-Indische Gids. Martins Nijhoff. The Hague.
NWJS	Nature. A weekly journal of science. Macmillan & Co. London.
NYAS/A	Annals of the New York Academy of Sciences. N.Y.
OAS/AM	Américas. Organization of American States. Washington.
OAS/CI	Ciencia Interamericana. Organization of American States, Department of Scientific Affairs. Washington.
OAS/CI	Ciencia Interamericana. Organization of American States, Department of Scientific Affairs. Washington.
OSP/B	Boletín de la Oficina Sanitaria Panamericana. Washington.
PAA/D	Demography. Population Association of America. Chicago, Ill.
PAHO/B	Bulletin of the Pan American Health Organization. Washington
PEMN/R	Revista del Museo Nacional. Casa de la Cultura del Perú, Museo Nacional de la Cultura Peruana. Lima.
PUCIRA/BSA	Boletín del Seminario de Arqueología. Pontificia Univ. Católica del Perú, Instituto Riva Agüero. Lima.
RAI/M	Man. A monthly record of anthropological science. The Royal Anthropological institute. London.
RSTMH/T	Transactions of the Royal Society of Tropical Medicine and Hygiene. London.
SA/J	Journal de la Société des Américanistes. Paris.
SAA/AA	American Antiquity. The Society for American Archaeology. Menasha, Wis.
SAA/HO	Human Organization. Society for Applied Anthropology. N.Y.
SAA/R	Relaciones de la Sociedad Argentina de Antropología. B.A.
SAP/BM	Bulletins et Mémoires de la Société d'Anthropologie de Paris. Paris.
SBPC/CC	Ciência e Cultura. Sociedade Brasileira para o Progresso da Ciência. São Paulo.
SCNLS/A	Antropológica. Sociedad de Ciencias Naturales La Salle. Caracas.
SEB/EB	Economic Botany. Devoted to applied botany and plant utilization. Publication of The Society for Economic Botany. *Published for the Society by the* New York Botanical Garden. N.Y.
SEM/E	Ethnos. Statens Etnografiska Museu. Stockholm.
SHG/B	Bulletin de la Société d'histoire de la Guadeloupe. Point-á-Pitre.
SITS/VS	Vox Sanguinis. La Société Internationale de Transfusion Sanguine. Basel, Switzerland.

SL	Studia Linguistica. Revue de linguistique générale et comparée. C.W.K. Gleerup. Lund, Sweden.
SLN/ALN	Archivos Latinoamericanos de Nutrición. Órgano oficial de la Sociedad Latinoamericana de Nutrición. Caracas.
SM/M	The Masterkey. Southwest Museum. Los Angeles, Calif.
SMS/RMC	Revista Médica de Chile. Sociedad Médica de Santiago. Santiago.
SOCIOL	Sociologus. Zeitschrift für empirische Soziologie, sozialpsychologische und ethnologische Forschung (A journal for empirical sociology, social psychology and ethnic research) Berlin, FRG.
SSA/B	Bulletin. Sociéte Suisse des Américanistes. Geneva.
SSC/K	Katunob. Southern State College. Magnolia, Ark.
TAS/B	Bulletin of the Texas Archeological Society. Austin, Tex.
TGM	Tropical and Geographical Medicine. Foundation Documenta de Medicina Geographica et Tropica. Haarlem, The Netherlands.
TMR	The Massachusetts Review. A quarterly of literature, the arts and public affairs. Published independently with the support and cooperation of Amherst College, Mount Holyoke College, Smith College, and the Univ. of Massachusetts. Amherst, Mass.
TUMARI/P	Middle American Research Institute Publication. Tulane Univ. New Orleans, La.
UA/U	Universidad. Univ. de Antioquia. Medellín, Colo.
UASD/R	Revista Dominicana de Arqueología y Antropología. Univ. Autónoma de Santo Domingo, Facultad de Humanidades, Depto. de Historia y Antropología, Instituto de Investigaciones Antropológicas. Santo Domingo.
UBAIA/R	Runa. Archivo para las Ciencias del Hombre. Univ. de Buenos Aires, Facultad de Filosofía y Letras, Instituto de Antropologia. B.A.
UC/BPC	Boletín de Prehistoria de Chile. Univ. de Chile, Facultad de Filosofía y Educación, Depto. de Historia. Santiago.
UC/CA	Current Anthropology. Univ. of Chicago. Chicago, Ill.
UC/EDCC	Economic Development and Cultural Change. Univ. of Chicago, Research Center in Economic Development and Cultural Change. Chicago, Ill.
UCAB/M	Montalbán. Univ. Católica Andrés Bello, Facultad de Humanidades y Educación, Institutos Humanísticos de Investigación. Caracas.
UCARF/C	Contributions of the University of California Archaeological Research Facility. Berkeley, Calif.
UCEIA/H	Humanitas. Boletín ecuatoriano de antropología. Univ. Central del Ecuador, Instituto de Antropología. Quito.
UCGL/AHG	Annals of Human Genetics (Annals of Eugenics). University College, Galton Laboratory. London.
UCIA/R	Rehue. Univ. de Concepción, Instituto de Antropología. Concepción, Chile.
UCLV/I	Islas. Revista de la Univ. Central de las Villas. Santa Clara, Cuba.
UM/JIAS	Journal of Inter-American Studies and World Affairs. Univ. of Miami Press for the Center for Advanced International Studies. Coral Gables, Fla.
UM/REAA	Revista Española de Antropología Americana [Trabajos y Conferencias]. Univ. de Madrid, Facultad de Filosofía y Letras, Depto. de Antropología y Etnología de América. Madrid.
UMUP/E	Expedition. The bulletin of the University Museum of the Univ. of Pennsylvania. Philadelphia, Pa.
UNAM/AA	Anales de Antropología. Univ. Nacional Autónoma de México, Instituto de Investigaciones Históricas. México.
UNAM/RMS	Revista Mexicana de Sociología. Univ. Nacional Autónoma de México, Instituto de Investigaciones Sociales. México.
UNC/AAE	Anales de Arqueología y Etnología. Univ. Nacional de Cuyo, Facultad de Filosofía y Letras. Mendoza, Arg.
UNC/AIL	Anales del Instituto de Lingüística. Univ. Nacional de Cuyo, Facultad de Filosofía y Letras. Mendoza, Arg.
UNCIA/HC	Hombre y Cultura. Revista del Centro de Investigaciones Antropológicas de la Univ. Nacional. Panamá.

UNCP/AC	Anales Científicos de la Universidad del Centro del Perú. Univ. Nacional del Centro del Perú. Huancayo, Perú.
UNLPM/R	Revista del Museo de La Plata. Univ. Nacional de La Plata, Facultad de Ciencias Naturales y Museo. La Plata, Arg.
UNM/JAR	Journal of Anthropological Research. Univ. of New Mexico, Laboratory of Anthropology, Santa Fe. Albuquerque, N. Mex.
UNM/SWJA	Southwestern Journal of Anthropology. Univ. of New Mexico. Albuquerque, N. Mex.
UNMSM/L	Letras. Univ. Nacional Mayor de San Marcos. Lima.
UP/E	Ethnology. An international journal of cultural and social anthropology. Univ. of Pittsburgh. Pittsburgh, Pa.
UPR/CS	Caribbean Studies. Univ. of Puerto Rico, Institute of Caribbean Studies. Río Piedras, P.R.
USCG/ES	Estudios. Univ. de San Carlos de Guatemala, Facultad de Humanidades, Depto. de Historia. Guatemala.
USP/RA	Revista de Antropologia. Univ. de São Paulo, Faculdade de Filosofia, Ciências e Letras. São Paulo.
USPMAE/D	Dédalo. Revista de arqueologia e etnologia. Univ. de São Paulo, Museu de Arqueologia e Etnologia. São Paulo.
UT/G	Genetics. Genetics, Inc. Univ. of Texas. Austin, Tex.
UWI/SES	Social and Economic Studies. Univ. of the West Indies, Institute of Social and Economic Research. Mona, Jam.
UY/R	Revista de la Universidad de Yucatán. Mérida, Mex.
VOZES	Vozes. Revista de cultura. Editôra Vozes. Petrópolis, Bra.
WHO/B	Bulletin. World Health Organization. Geneva.
WRU/JMF	Journal of Marriage and the Family. Western Reserve Univ. Cleveland, Ohio.
WSU/HB	Human Biology. Official publication of the Human Biology Council. Wayne State Univ., School of Medicine. Detroit, Mich.
YU/IJCS	International Journal of Comparative Sociology. York Univ., Dept. of Sociology and Anthropology. Toronto, Canada.
ZMR	Zeitschrift für Missionswissenschaft und Religionswissenschaft. Lucerne, Switzerland.

Economics

GENERAL

JOHN M. HUNTER
Director
Latin American Studies Center
Michigan State University

PERHAPS THE OUTSTANDING FEATURE of the general economics literature regarding Latin America in the last few years is its quantity. New journals have appeared; there are more books, more publishers.

This change is not only quantitative but also qualitative in two forms at least. First, there is a great deal more Latin American content. A few years ago, even the leading journals were filled with translation from foreign journals that lagged two to four years. Books were mostly anthologies of articles encompassing various time periods, topics, and nationalities—and occasionally strung together with perceptive domestic contributions. It could be argued that more Latin American content is *per se* no measure of quality; and, as a matter of principle, one would have to agree. I will return to this point after noting that as quantity has increased, quality has improved. The few giants whose names have become so well known over the past decades have been joined by others working *con seriedad* in various countries and positions. Impressionistic, gut-feeling, pamphleteering, taxonomic economics is replaced by (or "complemented with") argument and even empirical research.

The increasing Latin American content is not necessarily a measure of improved quality; but consideration of all the contributing factors suggests a most commendable trend. It represents the coming-of-age of the profession of economics—the profession of "economics" as opposed to "ciencias económicas." The elements which contribute to this maturation are advanced training and the societal allocation of resources to investigating the kinds of problems economics deals with. This has permitted economists to devote their energies to the study of national and regional problems and implies research centers and support for research, the possibilities of full-time dedication to the tasks, readers and publishers. The process has been considerably more complex than a sentence or two can even suggest.

Some may say that my pronouncement is at least a decade too late; others may suggest that it is premature. Fortunately, we don't have to determine a precise date for the passing of the profession from infancy to adolescence or, more appropriately, from adolescence into maturity. But it is important to note that the process is occurring at a considerable pace.

There is another general observation—and I am equally uncertain about the appropriateness of its timing. As I reviewed the literature this biennium, it struck me that the institutional literature has matured a great deal. ECLA is joined by the IDB, INTAL, LAFTA, and the OAS in the production of solid, in-house research and publication. These seem to be part of a cohesive attack on the collectivity of problems rather than the occasional excellent but isolated studies which have appeared in the past.

To conclude, one must welcome the emergence of economic history as a serious discipline in Latin America. Since much of what appears on the economies of countries and regions stems from the authors' explicit or implicit interpretations or misinterpretations of history, there is a need to pay serious attention and systematically explore the root causes in the past. Joseph Schumpeter used to aver that an economist should also be a mathematician or historian; Latin American economics has been deficient in the latter. See especially, S.J. Stein and S.J. Hunt "Principal Currents in the Economic Historiography of Latin America" *(HLAS 34:1300)*, Raymond W. Goldsmith, "A Century of Financial Development in Latin America" (see item 4095) and "La Historia Económica en América Latina" (see item 4108).

4000. Abad Arango, Darío. Tecnología y dependencia (FCE/TE, 40[2]:158, abril/junio 1973, p. 371-392, bibl., tables)

A descriptive, speculative view of technological dependence—one of several co-existent dependencies. Little new in analysis or policy conclusion. Many of references are to Colombia.

4001. Adamczyk, Ricardo Calderón. Acuerdo Latino Americano de Libre Comercio y Mercado Común. Potosí, Bol., Univ. Mayor y Autonoma Tomás Frías, Depto. de Cultura, 1969. 21 p.

A superficial, legalistic analysis of LAFTA and the Andean Group Accord from a Bolivian point of view.

4002. Aguilar Monteverde, Alonso. Problemas estructurales del subdesarrollo. México, UNAM, Instituto de Investigaciones Económicas, 1971. 327 p., tables.

A series of more or less independent essays by the author. Pt. 1 touches on themes generally related to Latin America: the meaning of development, capital accumulation, the Alliance for Progress, population, etc. Pt. 2 consists of three essays dealing with Mexican problems: capital markets, land-ownership concentration, structural change.

4003. Ahmad, J. Trade liberalization and structural changes in Latin America (JCMS, 11:1, Sept. 1972, p. 1-17, tables)

Examines 1960-70 trade behavior for LAFTA and CACM countries on a relative basis and then again on basis of relative changes in national sectoral behavior because the aforementioned organizations are threatened by national insistence on reciprocal benefits particularly in industrial growth. Finds procedure better represents distribution of benefits than earlier procedures.

4004. Alamo Esclusa, Víctor. Indices de gestión empresarial. t. 1, Informe del Coordinador Técnico; t. 2, Estudio sobre índices de gestión empresarial; t. 3, Estudio sobre salarios básicos y renumeración total de trajadores que desempeñan cargos típicos en la industria eléctrica; t. 4, Estudio sobre composición del costo de la energía. Caracas, Comisión de Integración Eléctrica Regional, Subcomité de la Gestión Empresarial, 1970. 4 v. in 2 (Various pagings) maps, tables.

The Commission which published the study is restricted to South America. Vol. 1/2 consist of background for the studies which make up this report. Includes some comments on the substantive portions of the report. Vol. 3, is of considerable interest and consists of the careful study of renumeration and various fringes for different levels of employees. There were 29 companies who participated. Vol. 4 discusses the objectives which are largely company-oriented and which permits firms to compare their operations with others (31 firms participated). Variation is so great averages were not struck. The appendix to this volume includes the statistical results.

4005. Algunos aspectos básicos de la integración de la Cuenca del Plata. B.A., Instituto de Estudios e Investigaciones, 1967.

An anthology of essays covering historical antecedents, water availability, energy resources, the river network, transport coordination, dynamic regional economic structures, changing nature of frontiers. Some chapters contain some technical data.

4006. Almada, Carlos G. Compendio teórico-práctico de la ALALC. 5. ed. B.A., Organización Zona, 1973. 1 v. (Various pagings) illus.

A loose-leaf volume to serve as a LAFTA handy reference. Sec. 1 concerns LAFTA and has chapters on legal instruments, tariff legislation of member countries, complementation agreements, nomenclature. Sec. 2 has a few pages on the Andean Pact. Sec. 3 is a consolidated list of concessions.

4007. Angelopoulos, Angelos. The Third World and the rich countries: prospects for the year 2000. Translated by N. Constantinidis [and] C. R. Corner. Foreword by Josué de Castro. N.Y., Praeger Publishers, 1972. 248 p., tables (Praeger special studies in international economics and development)

Explanation of the increasing gap between the "haves" and "have nots" with some policy suggestions on amounts and conditions of aid, use of gold revaluation. Some will find particularly interesting his income projections, including the socialist world, to the year 2000.

4008. Annable, James E., Jr. Internal migration and urban unemployment in low-income countries: a problem in simultaneous equations (OUP/OEP, 24:3, Nov. 1972, p. 399-412, tables)

Examination of data from large number of LDC's testing hypothesis that rural-urban migration may be subject to equilibrium analyses with rural-push, modern sector pull, and traditional urban malemployment repulsion being major forces. Results consistent with hypothesis.

4009. Arnaudo, Aldo A. Economía monetaria. México, Centro de Estudios Monetarios Latinoamericanos, 1972. 296 p., tables.

The first work awarded the "Premio Rodrigo Gómez." A systematic study of the monetary economy between the level of total abstraction and the loss of generality through masses of description. Most data and references are to Argentina, but the level of generality far exceeds one country. Chapters on inflation and on external transmission agencies will be of particular interest.

4010. Asociación Latinoamericana de Libre Comercio. La industria del aluminio en los países de la ALALC. v. 1/2. Montevideo, Secretaría, 1971. 2 v. (482 p.) (Continuous pagination) tables.

A very careful study of the growing aluminum industry. Separate chapters consider conclusions and recommendations, technical changes and raw material supply, country reviews, factor supply, productivity of firms, regional trade and prospects. Vol. 2 contains four appendixes expanding on earlier themes and the statistical tables on which the study is based.

4011. _____. La industria naval en la ALALC. B.A., Banco Interamericano de Desarrollo, Instituto para la Integración de América Latina, 1971. 635 p., tables.

A broad study of a complex industry including such topics as potential, present state, demand, needs of various segments of the market, state policies, institutional and technico-economic aspects. Considerable reporting by country.

4012. Assadourian, Carlos Sempat. Modos de producción, capitalismo y subdesarrollo en América Latina. B.A., Ediciones Nueva Visión, 1973. 65 p., tables (Col. Fichas, 23)

A systematic criticism of André Gunder Frank, *Capitalism and Underdevelopment in Latin America*. By no means entirely unsympathetic.

4013. Aubey, Robert. Capital mobilization in Latin America (ISSQ, 22:1, Spring 1969, p. 56-67)

One reason "stage theory" faltered is the little attention to sub-phenomenon. Examines capital mobilization in three stages: family; investment groups; and integrated, diversified capital markets.

4014. Avery, William P. and James D. Cochrane. Subregional integration in Latin America: the Andean Common Market (JCMS, 11:2, Dec. 1972, p. 85-102)

A review of the development of the Andean Common Market. Some analysis of possible US domination and gain and the sorts of decisions necessary to avoid this.

Aznar, Luis. Dependencia, crecimiento económico y conflicto sociopolítico en América Latina: 1955-1965. See item 9605.

Baer, Werner. Import substitution and industrialization in Latin America: experiences and interpretations. See *HLAS 36:1682*.

4015. Balassa, Bela. Regional integration and trade liberalization in Latin America (JCMS, 10:1, Sept. 1971, p. 58-77, tables)

A thoughtful piece which concludes that trade liberalization *and* integration would benefit Latin America. The latter, however, requires coordination of many related policies, especially that of exchange rates.

4016. Baltra Cortés, Alberto. El Pacto Andino y el capital extranjero (UNAM/PDD, 2:5, oct./dic. 1970, p. 69-86)

The Andean group seen as result of crisis in LAFTA. Also insists that joint control over investments is necessary loss of sovereignty and especially applicable to foreign investments.

Bank of London and South America Review. See item 8009.

4017. Barnet, Richard and Ronald Müller. Global reach: pts, 1/2 (The New Yorker, 2 Dec. 1974, p. 53-128; 9 Dec. 1974, p. 100-159)

This two-part article covers enormous ground. Ostensibly it analyzes the roles, sins, and effects of the multinational corporations. The first generally analyzes their effects abroad, mostly in the Third World. The second part concentrates on domestic effects in the US and then on a set of policy conclusions. Those already convinced will be delighted with the new and influential outlet for the point of view. Some others will be infuriated anew. The work is critically lacking in argument; too much depends on assertion, unstated values, and spurious correlations. Careful scholarship it is not; well-done polemic it is. These articles preceded the publication of the author's book: *Global reach: the power of the multinational corporations* (N.Y., Simon and Schuster, 1974).

4018. Basch, Antonín and Milic Kybal. Recursos nacionales de inversión en América Latina. Con la colaboración de Luis Sánchez Masi. México, Centro de Estudios Monetarios Latinoamericanos, 1971. 259 p., bibl., tables.

An extension and revision of CEMLA's earlier *Análisis de mercados latinoamericanos de capitales.* Pt. 1 is general and discusses financing investment, financial institutions and capital markets, stock markets, and the prospect for regional integration of capital markets. Pt. 2 summarizes country studies: Venezuela, Peru, Mexico, Colombia, Brazil, Argentina, extensive bibliography.

4019. Baster, Nancy and Wolf Scott. Levels of living and economic growth: a comparative study of six countries, 1950-1965. Geneva, United Nations Research Institute for Social Development (UNRISD), 1969. 153 p., tables.

A study of the effect levels of living (measured by education, health) on economic growth, 1950-65 in Chile, Mexico, Jamaica, Morocco, Western Malaysia, Ceylon. An interesting topic well handled as a first step.

Bedregal, Guillermo. Integración defensiva de América Latina: algunos aspectos. See item 8708.

Behrman, Jack N. Conflicting constraints on the multinational enterprise: potential for resolution. See item 8709.

4020. _____. Foreign vs. local ownership (*Worldview* [Church Peace Union, N.Y.] 17:9, Sept. 1974, pp. 39-46)

Examines the myths and realities of various ownership patterns, in particular noting that requiring local joint ownership is not a guaranteed panacea.

4021. _____. Taxation of extractive industries in Latin America and the impact on foreign investors (*in* Mikesell, Raymond Frech and others. Foreign investment in the petroleum and mineral industries: case studies of investor-host country relations. Baltimore, Md., The Johns Hopkins Press *for* Resources for the Future, Inc., 1971, p. 56-80)

Includes country reviews of taxation in Colombia, Mexico, Peru, Venezuela; discussion of host country objectives; US tax policy.

4022. Benoit, Emile. Growth effects of defense in developing countries (SID/IDR, 14:1, 1972, p. 2-15, tables)

With following comment by R. Dorfman, a rejoinder by Benoit, conclusion by E. Hagen. Data show defense expenditures associated with growth. Issue is related to causality in short- and long-term.

4023. Bird, Richard M. Taxing agricultural land in developing countries. Cambridge, Mass., Harvard Univ. Press, 1974. 361 p., bibl., tables (Harvard Law School international tax program)

Land taxation is often urged upon Latin American governments by reform-mongers. Ch. 5 of this work surveys such proposals and their results, through about 1970, in Bolivia, Brazil, Chile, Panama and Uruguay, with passing notes on Colombia, Guatemala and Paraguay. Useful reference, since many of the sources are unpublished or out of print. [J. Strasma]

4024. Birou, Alain. Forces paysannes et politiques agraires en Amèrique Latine. Paris, Editions Economie et Humanisme [and] Les Editiones Ouvrières, 1970. 295 p., map, tables (Col. Développement et civilisations)

A middle level treatment with major divisions: historical survey, structures and tenure forms, economic problems (resources and production; technology; population, employment and nutrition; trade; etc.), organization and peasant movements, agrarian reform, role of the state. Descriptive rather than statistical.

4025. Bologna, Alfredo Bruno. Causas estructurales del estancamiento de América Latina. Santa Fe, Arg., Ediciones Colmegna, 1970. 56 p., bibl.

A small, superficial pamphlet which does little more than list "causes" gleaned from a number of sources without any sort of analysis.

4026. Bordaz, Robert. Après la Conférence de Santiago (Revue des Deux Mondes [Paris] 7, juillet 1972, p. 133-137)

A summary of the 1972 UNCTAD meeting includes indicating its general lack of progress. Reports particularly on aid to the very poor and on the demographic debate and possibilities.

4027. Brcich, Juan M. Programación financiera de corto plazo en países latinoamericanos. México, Centro de Estudios Monetarios Latinoamericanos (CEMLA), 1972. 74 p. (CEMLA, 30)

Also appeared in the *Boletín of CEMLA*, Feb./March, 1972. A fairly technical piece which defines and demonstrates country differences in various monetary indicators—i.e., the quantity of money, changes in same, liquidity, etc. Particular attention is paid to Argentina, Guatemala, Uruguay, Brazil, Venezuela, and Mexico.

4028. Brice, Max. Problemas metodológicos en el estudio cuantitativo del cambio tecnológico en la empresa latinoamericana (FCE/TE, 37:147, julio/sept. 1970, p. 575-600, bibl., tables)

Surveys usual models for measuring technical change in enterprises. Discards them and proposes a simpler one: fitting a curve between real expenditures for technology through time and the productivity of labor. The parameters represent technological progress.

4029. Brown, Harrison and **Edward Hutchings** eds. Cupo limitado: cambios tecnológicos y crecimiento de la población. México, Editorial Pax-México, 1972. 1 v. (Unpaged)

Translation of *Are our descendants doomed* (N.Y., Viking, 1972). The approach is global but considerable attention is given to Latin America. Consists of 12 papers by well-known scholars including systematic discussions.

4030. Bueno, Gerardo M. Los posibles efectos da la integración sobre el comercio de los países latino-americanos en la década de los años setenta (FCE/TE, 39:153, enero/marzo 1972, p. 37-58, tables)

Considers "gap" analysis and product-by-product approaches unsatisfactory. Examines falling share of Latin America in world exports and concludes the causes were mostly internal—and not deteriorating terms of trade. Import substitution was a major culprit and is in the slow evolution of integration. Concludes with general policy recommendations.

4031. Campos, Roberto de Oliveira. Desenvolvimento econômico e político da América Latina: uma difícil opção (IBE/RBE, 26:4, out./dez. 1972, p. 45-56)

Essentially an essay on the recognition of multiple and frequently conflicting objectives. "Latin American governments want capitalism without profits, socialism without discipline, and investments without foreign investors."

4032. Cardoso, Fernando Henrique. Impedimentos estructurales e institucionales para el desarrollo (UNAM/RMS, 32:6, nov./dic. 1970, p. 1461-1482, tables)

Seeks alternative explanations to "bottlenecks" and "failure of leading sectors" for poor performance in Latin America. The process of industrialization, started long ago with the development of internal markets, has resulted in a new dualism—with rural and urban dynamic and static segments.

4033. _____. Industrialización, dependencia y poder en América Latina (CPES/RPS, 7:19, set./dic. 1970, p. 104-116)

Translated from the French. An alternative sociological explanation to more traditional views (agrarian, oligarchies, domestic and foreign imperialism) of the current state of economic affairs.

4034. Carretero, Jimena and **Leopoldo Solís M.** Hacia una mayor eficiencia en la asignación de las inversiones en los países subdesarrollados (FCE/TE, 39:155, julio/sept. 1972, p. 461-490, tables)

Reviews much of the work on both employment and income distribution and suggests alternative measures to per-capita income for measurement of development. Considers the argument for inequality as a source of saving. Concludes with a useful comparison of the efficacy of investment in human capital compared with alternatives.

4035. Carrillo Flores, Antonio. Reflexiones sobre el comercio y las inversiones en Latinoamérica (FCE/TE, 39:153, enero/marzo 1972, p. 3-11)

A chatty piece touching on some of the issues of trade and investment. Pays particular attention to Mexico and its relations with the US.

4036. Casas González, Antonio. Industrialización e integración: seminario sobre la industrialización latinoamericana (BCV/REL, 9:35, 1973, p. 41-54)

Reviews various development policies in Latin America, stressing their weakness. Concludes attempts at integration have not succeeded and urges further attempts at cooperative planning, Latin American multinational companies, etc.

4037. Casillas, Luis R. La doble tributación y la inversión extranjera: una política sobre el movimiento de capitales en la América Latina (FCE/TE, 51[1]:161, enero/marzo 1974, p. 27-79, bibl., tables)

Considerably broader than title suggests. After initial background material, discusses US policy and then contemplated changes in same—particularly as these changes would be less liberal and especially regarding reinvested earnings. Insists this is an international problem to be resolved multilaterally and suggests some principles to be followed.

4038. _____. Empleo, inversión y equilibrio externo: un análisis sobre el impuesto al valor agregado (FCE/TE, 40[2]:158, abril/junio 1973, p. 325-369, bibl., tables)

A thoughtful piece analyzing the probable effects on a number of Latin American problems of substitution of the value-added tax. Concludes reporting two econometrics studies (of the US and Mexico) in which the simulations produce good results on variables such as growth, employment, balance of payment. Appendix and extensive bibliography.

4039. Castellanos, Diego Luis. América Latina y el financiamiento complementario (BCV/REL, 8/28, 1969, p. 61-88)

A review of a number of studies and conferences regarding compensatory financing by the developed countries for falling raw-materials prices as a short-to-medium run measure. Note date.

4040. Castro, Fernando Saboya de and **Wilson Vieira Passos.** Guia prático de ALALC. Rio, Federação das Indústrias do Estado da Guanabara, Centro Industrial do Rio de Janeiro, 1971. 90 p., tables (Cadernos econômicos, 9)

A very much "how-to-do-it" guide with chapters "instruments," "how to identify a traded product and tariff advantages," "procedures for the Brazilian exporter," etc. Probably very useful for specialized public.

4041. Castro Rodríquez, Leandro. Situación, presente y perspectivas de los mercados mayoristas en América Latina (IEAS/R, 21:79, abril/junio 1972, p. 87-100, tables)

On the basis of population projections, Latin America is fast becoming an urban region. The old and even the newer techniques of wholesale food marketing will no longer do.

4042. Chaparro-Alfonso, Julio. La calificación de origen en la ALALC (BCV/REL, 8:29, 1970, p. 103-241, bibl., tables)

A detailed and probably definitive study of the technical and important notion of origin in any sort of international economic integration.

4043. Chenery, Hollis B. and **Helen Hughes.** La división internacional de la fuerza de trabajo: el ejemplo en la industria (FCE/TE, 39:155, julio/sept. 1972, p. 415-460, bibl., tables)

Examines expanding manufactured exports as sort of evolutionary stage beyond export of raw materials, import substitution. Looks at various models and experiences with conditions appropriate for each. Concludes with policy implications for less and more developed nations and perspectives for 1970s. Successes will meet increasing resistance among the developed.

4044. Ciafardini, Horacio. Sur la question du mode de production en Amérique Latine (SEPHE/ER, 47, juillet/sept. 1972, p. 148-162, bibl.)

A comprehensive survey of the evolution of agricultural production in Latin America, with particular attention to the Marxian viewpoint.

Cockcroft, James D.; André Gunder Frank; and **Dale L. Johnson.** Dependence and underdevelopment: Latin America's political economy. See *HLAS 36:1465.*

4045. Commission on United States-Latin American Relations, N.Y. The Americas in a changing world. N.Y., Center for Inter-American Relations, 1974. p. 54.

A report of a multinational conference with recommendations particularly for a new US posture vis-à-vis Latin America. This report and some discussion papers are to be published in 1975 by Quadrangle Books.

4046. Common treatment of foreign capital, trademarks, patents, licensing agreements and royalties in the Andean Common Market (JCMS, 10:4, June 1972, p. 339-359)

An unofficial translation of the Andean Common Market document on the matters referred to in the title as amended through June 1971 and effective thereafter.

4047. Conferencia Especializada sobre la Aplicación de la Ciencia y la Tecnología al Desarrollo de América Latina, *Brasília, 1972.* Informe final. Washington, Organización de los Estados Americanos, Secretaría General, 1972. 180 p., bibl. (OEA/Ser. C/VI, 22, 1)

A full report of the conference including resolutions, delegations, considerable bibliography.

4048. Congreso Interamericano de Planificación, *VII, Lima, 1968.* América en el año 2000. v. 3, Simposio III: La integración y el desarrollo. Edición a cargo del Instituto Peruano de Estudios del Desarrollo. Lima, Sociedad Interamericana de Planificación, 1969? 266 p., tables.

Apparently essays discussed at the planning congress. Some are major pieces: Marcos Kaplan "The Public Multinational Corporation;" Ricardo Jordán Squella "Research and Teaching on Integration and Urban-Regional Development;" Claudio Veliz "Centralism, Nationalism, Integration;" Hélio Jaguaribe "Dependency and Autonomy;" Akio Hosono "Japan and Latin America;" Alejandro B. Rofman "Integration and Localization;" and Osvaldo Sunkel "Politics and Theory for the Planner."

4049. Conroy, Michael E. Rejection of growth center strategy in Latin America regional development planning (UW/LE, 49:4, Nov. 1973, p. 371-380)

Abandonment of "growth-center" strategies in Peru and Chile leads to investigation of dissatisfaction with them and assessment of alternatives. Dissatisfactions are grouped: "ideological," "theoretical," "political," and "practical."

4050. Cooper, Richard N. and Edwin M. Truman. An analysis of the role of international capital markets in providing funds to developing countries (CAUK/WA, 106:2, 1971, p. 11-183, tables)

An historical review of the international bond market as a source of funds for less developed countries. Reviews also current impediments to access to these markets (e.g., balance of payments restrictions by potential lenders). Considers the requisite internal characteristics for borrowing nations.

4051. Copello Faccini, Antonio. El problema económico de la empresa pública en los países subdesarrollados (PUJ/U, 41, 1971, p. 188-199)

Discusses, but superficially, means of evaluating public enterprises.

4052. Coppens, Huub. Vooruitzichten voor UNCTAD (NGIZ/IS, 26:5, 8 maart 1972, p. 443-460)

Applies a conflict approach rather than the underlying harmonious approach of rich and poor countries in seeking to evaluate the future of UNCTAD.

4053. Correa, Héctor. Sources of economic growth in Latin America (Southern Economic Journal [Chapel Hill, N.C.] 27:1, July 1970, p. 17-31, tables)

Uses "neo-classical" model to estimate contributions of several variables to growth, 1950-62, in Argentina, Brazil, Chile, Colombia, Ecuador, Honduras, Mexico, Peru, and Venezuela. International assets are found to contribute negatively; social investments in dwellings, nutrition and education have contributed significantly and positively.

4054. Cuadra, Héctor. En torno a la integración económica de América Latina y al derecho de la integración (Difusión Económica [Guayaquil, Ecua.] 10:2, agosto 1972, p. 21-61, tables)

Also appears in *Boletín Mexicano de Derecho Comparado* (3:9, 1970). Pt. 1 treats economic issues in a rather unorthodox manner. The bulk of the essay, though, deals with legal-organizational issues.

4055. Currie, Lauchlin. The "leading sector" model of growth in developing countries (Journal of Economic Studies [Oxford Univ., England] 1:1, May 1974, p. 1-6)

Examines the implications of the hypothesis that significant barriers to development are demand (rather than supply) shortages. Release of latent demands in carefully chosen sectors (e.g., exports, housing) can have large intersectional effects.

4056. Dajer Chadid, Gustavo. La crisis monetaria internacional. Bogotá, Editorial Temis, 1973. 325 p., bibl., tables.

A general treatment of the monetary crisis with special emphasis in Latin America (Chap. 4). Tends to be reportorial rather than synthesizing and analytic.

4057. Dean, Warren. Latin American golpes and economic fluctuations, 1823-1966. Austin, Univ. of Texas, Institute of Latin American Studies, 1970. 1 v. (p. 70-80) tables (Offprint series, 104)

Statistical study finds close relationship between the frequency of *golpes* and international trade cycles along with the development of world trade and financial markets.

4058. El desarrollo de América Latina y la Alianza para el Progreso. Prefacio [por] Walter J. Sedwitz. Washington, Organización de los Estados Americanos, Secretaría General, Consejo Interamericano Económico y Social, 1973. 514 p., maps, tables (OEA/Ser.

An important reference work. Pt. 1 deals with economic and social progress in the 1960s: the decade of development, internal efforts, external contributions, institutional aspects. Pt. 2 analyzes performance with respect to 93 objectives separately. Pt. 3 (over 200 p.) is statistical, graphic, and cartographic even though the text also includes considerable tabular material. The richness of the data does not suggest, however, that the considerable text be ignored; it is valuable for its analysis and synthesis.

4059. Di Tella, Guido. La manipulación de la demanda: el problema de las marcas (INTAL/RI,11, nov. 1972, p. 133-158, table)

An analysis of trade marks and (consequently) advertising in the general setting of value theory then extended to the international settings of less developed countries.

4060. Documentos: el Tercer Mundo ante la Conferencia de las Naciones Unidas sobre Comercio y Desarrollo— UNCTAD (BCV/REL, 9:33, 1972, p. 145-260)

A comprehensive set of documents prepared prior to the 1972 UNCTAD meetings in Santiago. The "Group of 77" met in Lima Oct.-Nov. 1971, in preparation. Covers wide variety of topics.

4061. Dull, John E. Transfer of technology to Latin America: a U.S. Corporate view (*in* Driscoll, Robert E. and Harvey W. Wallender *eds*. Technology transfer and development: an historic and geographic perspective. N.Y., Fund for Multinational Management Education *in cooperation with the Council of the Americas,* 1974, p. 261-275)

A superficial discussion of various practices in Latin America which reduce the inducement for US firms to participate in industrial technology transfer.

4062. Durán T., Marco Antonio. Antagonismos en torno a las reformas agrarias (FCE/TE, 39:153, enero/marzo 1972, p. 59-72)

A biting discussion of conventional views of agrarian reform. He defines such reform as the suppression of forms of land ownership which frustrate the progressive evolution of agricultural activities. The means to accomplish this is the massive, permanent, rapid political organization of the peasants. Beyond that, there is no positive program.

4063. *Economía y Administración.* Univ. de Concepción, Escuela de Economía y Administración. No. 16, 3. cuatrimestre 1970- . Concepción, Chile.

This number is in memory of Michal Kalecki and consists of eight of his articles dealing with "developed capitalism" and "underdevelopment." One has direct reference to Latin America (Boliva) and all but one (the same) have appeared elsewhere.

4064. *Ensayos ECIEL.* Programa de estudios conjuntos sobre integración económica latinoamericana. The Brookings Institution. No. 1, Nov. 1974- . Washington.

Ensayos, a new biannual journal is designed to disseminate work in progress, preliminary or partial results, and special studies under the ECIEL program. Articles may be in English, Spanish, or Portuguese, with abstracts in all three. This first issue treats comparative manufacturing efficiency, microeconomic data, income distribution, comparative labor productivity, comparative consumption standards. US address: Philip Musgrave *ed.,* The Brookings Institution, 1775 Massachusetts Avenue, Washington, D.C. Latin American address: Caixa Postal 740, Rio de Janeiro, Brazil.

4065. Ensayos sobre administración política y derecho tributarios. B.A., Ediciones Macchi, 1970. 700 p. (Col. Ciencias económicas. Temas de derecho tributario)

Much of this previously appeared in *Fiscal policy for economic growth in Latin America* (Baltimore, Md., The Johns Hopkins Univ. Press, 1965) as a report of the Santiago Conference on fiscal policy, 1962. There are a few substitutions (e.g., articles of Richard Goode, Dino Javach), and some new works are added. (e.g., Due) Some valuable pieces were omitted (e.g., Kaldor, Adler), but the collection is nonetheless solid.

4066. Escobar C., Luis. El financiamiento externo de América Latina: comentarios al artículo de Felipe Pazos (FCE/TE, 38:151, julio/sept. 1971, p. 755-765)

Critical of an article by Felipe Pazos in *El Trimestre Económico* (150, abril/junio 1971) who urges Latin America to learn to get along with less external financing. Escobar doubts Pazos' various theses that private foreign investment will be reduced and that it was counter-productive anyway.

4067. ———. El futuro de las empresas multinacionales en la América Latina (FCE/TE, 40:157, enero/marzo 1973, p. 105-110)

Discusses very generally the problems of private foreign investment and urges its greatest contribution is in technical transfer. Also suggests that the flow ought to involve governmental approval of the exporter as well as of the importer of investment.

4068. Espinosa, Juan Guillermo. Los trabajadores, la participación y la propiedad sobre los medios de producción (FCE/TE, 40[2]: 158, abril/junio 1973, p. 393-409)

Considers various aspects of operation in his preferred form of business organization—socialized property with financing external to the firm.

4069. Espinosa García, Manuel. La política económica de los Estados Unidos hacia América Latina entre 1945 y 1961. La Habana, Casa de las Américas, 1971. 194 p., bibl., tables.

The general theme of condemnation of the US is hardly surprising for the publisher's 1971 prize. One feature is the author's attempt to use only official US material or other impeccable sources. A good deal more literate than some others of this genre.

4070. Exportações latinoamericanas; evolução e estrutura (FGV/CE, 26:10, out. 1972, p. 50-56, tables)

A straight-forward statistical analysis of the trends in Latin American exports, particularly of seven principal countries, 1958-70. A good review—no surprises.

4071. Fabbrica Italiana Automobili Torino (FIAT), *Buenos Aires.* Oficina de Estudios para la Colaboración Económica Internacional, Mercado ALALC: fundamentos macroeconómicos para su evaluación. B.A., 1971. 367 p., tables.

Brings together data for the LAFTA area as a whole and also reports in the second section many relevant data for each of the member countries.

Fajnzyller, Fernando and others. Corporaciones multinacionales en América Latina. See item 8729.

4072. Farley, Rawle. The economics of Latin America: development problems in perspective. N.Y., Harper & Row, 1972. 400 p., bibl., illus., tables.

A text book with 300 p. of text and nearly 100 of tables, bibliography, etc. The coverage is general if somewhat uneven both with respect to geographic areas and topics. It seeks to serve a broad range of students.

4073. Fernandes, Florestan. Muster der externen Beherrschung in Lateinamerika. Ubersetzt von Heinz Mayer (*in* Gräbener, Jürgen *comp.* Kassengesellschaft und Rassismus [see *HLAS 35:8268*] p. 295-311, tables)

Traces stages of imperialism from colonial days. The last ("total") is symptom of the battle of capitalism to survive in the face of successful and expanding socialism. Success will require a powerful revolutionary rationalism—a new type of state capitalism.

4074. ———. Las pautas de la dominación externa en América Latina (CPES/RPS, 7:19, set./dic. 1970, p. 89-103, tables)

Traces forms of imperialistic domination historically to include the most recent, that of the giant foreign corporation. Socialism offers a means toward freedom and independence.

4075. Ffrench Davis, Ricardo. La inversión extranjera en la América Latina: tendencias recientes y perspectivas (FCE/TE, 40:157, enero/marzo 1973, p. 173-194, bibl., tables)

Discusses various aspects of the neglected effects of foreign investment. Demonstrates more of the problem and also indicates it is so small in total and not likely to be decisive. Very extensive bibliography.

4076. Figueroa, Emilio de. L' "inflation structurelle" et l'expérience latino-américaine (UP/TM, 10:39, juillet/sept. 1969, p. 533-552, tables)

Defines structural inflation and then uses a simple Keynesian model to demonstrate how it occurs and why orthodox policies were not successful in combating it.

4077. El financiamiento externo oficial en la estrategia del desarrollo de América Latina: implicaciones para los setenta. Prefacio [por] Walter J. Sedwitz. Washington, Organización de los Estados Americanos, Secretaría General, Consejo Interamericano Económico y Social, 1972. 119 p., tables (OEA/Ser. H/X.21; CIES/1856)

One of a series of policy studies for the 1970s. Reviews official lending of the past and reviews major issues for lenders, borrower, and intermediary institutions. To recommend on the basis of careful balance may "damn with faint praise," but it is a careful study recognizing the need to examine from a variety of points of view.

4077a. Foxley, Alejandro *ed.* Distribución del ingreso. México, Fondo de Cultura Económica, 1974. 523 p. (Lecturas, 7)

Complements item 4602, repeating only the essays by Foxley and Muñoz on Chile, and by Ffrench-Davis on the instruments of income redistribution. Other essays analyze income distribution and relevant policies in Latin America, the socialist countries, and even Puerto Rico. Although called "Readings", most of these monographs are not readily available elsewhere and are of excellent scholarship. [J. Strasma]

4078. *France-Amérique Latine.* Revue de la Chambre de Commerce. No. 5, nov. 1971- . Paris.

Not untypical of Chamber of Commerce publications—glossy, heavy with advertising. This issue dealt very largely with transportation in its articles from locomotives to bicycles. Some technical data. Mostly in Spanish and Portuguese.

4079. Frank, André Gunder. La dépendance est morte, vive la dépendance et la lutte des classes: une réponse aux critiques (Partisans [Paris] 68, nov./déc. 1972, p. 52-70)

An encyclopedic response of Frank to his critics of the "new dependence" found especially in *Lumpenbourgeoisie and Lumpen-development* including an extensive bibliography of the "debate." Critics are classified into groups and then further divided before being dealt with. Frank evidently has to be reckoned with.

4080. Freyssinet, Jacques. Técnicas de planificación del empleo. [and] Julio C. Neffa. Mercado de trabajo en Latinoamérica. B.A., Editorial El Coloquio, 1973. 177 p., bibl., tables (Temas de economía laboral)

The principal essay (Freyssinet) is the translation of a seminar presented at the Argentine National Univ. of La Plata. It is built around the conditions necessary to meet various kinds of equilibria e.g., quantity, qualification, spatial. The second essay (Neffa, p. 151-177) describes the labor force in Latin America in some of its statistical characteristics.

4081. Fucaraccio, Angel. El control de la natalidad y el argumento del ahorro y la inversión (UES/U, 95:5/6, sept./dic. 1970, p. 87-99, tables)

Disputes usual argument that falling birth rates benefit development because they lead to greater savings and investment.

4082. Fukuchi, Takao and **Akio Hosono.** Size of economy and aggregate production function: the case of Latin America (IAEA/DE, 10:2, June 1972, p. 185-195, bibl., tables)

A complex study of aggregate production functions for manufacturing in Brazil, Mexico, Peru, Colombia, Costa Rica. The size of firm is demonstrated to vary with the size of the economy; attempts are made then to incorporate effects of economies of scale and changing elasticities of substitution.

4083. Furtado, Celso. Dependencia externa y teoría económica (FCE/TE, 38[2]:150, abril/junio 1971, p. 335-349)

Seeks middle ground between neo-classical theorists and structuralists whose interchanges he describes as having been conversations between the deaf. Proposes sets of subsystems whose interrelationships are of cultural importance.

4084. _____. A hegemonia dos Estados Unidos e o subdesenvolvimento da América Latina. Rio, Civilização Brasileira, 1973. 192 p. (Col. Perspectivas do homem, 197. Série economia)

A new—little modified—edition of the same work published first in Portuguese then in English, French (1970), Italian (1971), Japanese (1972). Modifications in the new Portuguese version are essentially formal, eliminating and clarifying obscurities and ambiguities in the original version.

4085. Gallez, Paul. Analyse d'un cercle vicieux microéconomique de la misère (L'Actualité Economique [Montréal, Canada] oct./déc. 1970, p. 435-465)

The "vicious circle of misery" is examined—undernourishment, weakness, low productivity, and low earnings—as well as means of breaking the circle.

4086. Galtung, Johan. Diachronic analysis of relationships between human resources components and the rate of economic growth in selected countries (*in* Gostkowski, Zygmunt ed. Toward a system of human resources indicators for less developed countries. Warszawa, The Polish Academy of Sciences, Institute of Philosophy and Sociology *for* UNESCO 1972, p. 185-215, tables)

Time-series analysis of disaggregated human resource data gives some strange and unexpected (certainly not simple) results, e.g., what happens to lawyers through the course of development.

4087. Garbacz, Christopher. Industrial polarization under economic integration in Latin America. Austin, Univ. of Texas at Austin, Bureau of Business Research, Graduate School of Business, 1971. 101 p., bibl., maps, tables (Studies in Latin American business, 11)

Considers the tendency of development to occur around growth poles and the tendency for international integration to accelerate that tendency resulting in further inequalities between the less and more developed partners. Studies this as a problem for various Latin American integration efforts.

4088. García, Antonio. Dinámica de las reformas agrarias en América Latina. 4. ed. Bogotá, Editorial La Oveja Negra, 1972. 142 p. (Col. Tierra y revolución, 3)

Analysis of land reforms: "structural;" "conventional" or "establishment;" and "marginal." Each type is characterized with Latin American reforms then analyzed by the criteria discussed. Of primary interest are the causes and processes of revolutionary change.

4089. _____. Industrialización y dependencia en la América Latina (FCE/TE, 38:151, julio/sept. 1971, p. 731-754, tables)

Traces Latin America through four stages: preindustrialization, emergency industrialization of the 1930s, industrialization forced by total war, and postwar satellite industrialization. The final section deals with a new concept "technological colonialization" differentiated from the "industrial revolution."

4090. _____. ¿Reforma agraria o modernización tecnológica? La crisis del modelo tecnocrático de cambio (FCE/TE, oct./dic. 1972, p. 771-782, tables)

Sees little in current agricultural "modernization" models which can bring about agrarian reform and structural change. Nor is the pattern of "dependent industrialization" likely to help the rural situation.

4091. García, Norberto. El balance de pagos. B.A., Ediciones Macchi, 1972. 141 p.

A straightforward explanation of the balance of payments *as a document* and tool in international economic analysis. References are to the Argentine balance of payments as prepared by the Banco Central.

4092. Garza Quirós, Fernando. Algunos consideraciones sobre las técnicas de participación entre el personal de línea que labora en empresas industriales y la alta gerencia de las mismas (UNL/H, 11, 1970, p. 717-730)

An essentially philosophical approach to some personnel problems. No surprises in urging finally that widespread *participation* is productive.

4093. Gasparian, Fernando. Capital estrangeiro e desenvolvimento da América Latina: o mito e os fatos. Rio,

Civilização Brasileira, 1973. 196 p., tables (Col. Perspectivas do homem, 96. Série economia)

A scholarly work examines the effects of capital in development. Concludes the costs are too high for freely flowing capital but that the other extreme of denying capital from abroad is also too costly. The final chapter seeks to spell out a workable compromise.

4094. Gilbert, Gary G. Investment planning for Latin American economic integration (JCMS, 11:4, June 1973, p. 314-325)

Presents an approach for multi-country investment planning for an integrating Latin America. Such planning is necessary to avoid ad hoc investment decisions. Several techniques are compared.

4095. Goldsmith, Raymond W. A century of financial development in Latin America. New Haven, Conn., Yale Univ., Economic Growth Center, 1973. 107 p., tables (Center paper, 196)

Describes state of economic history regarding Latin America indicating sub-field of financial history even worse. Restricts discussion to Argentina, Brazil, Chile, Colombia, Mexico, Peru, Venezuela. Attention is given to infrastructure development (16 tables) and components of the financial structure (19 tables). Reaches conclusions and suggested policies for their future.

4096. Graciarena, Jorge. La dinámica del capitalismo subdesarrollado en América Latina (CM/FI, 13[52]:4, abril/junio 1973, p. 427-441)

Although some economic indicators showed improvement in Latin American performance after 1965, Graciarena views this as less than a healthy indication of the future. Latin America's dependence, role in a capitalist world, and the activities of its own elite are suggestive of continual failure to develop rapidly. The analysis of the educational "inflation" is particularly interesting.

4097. Gregory, Peter. Wage structures in Latin America (JDA, 8:4, July 1974, p. 557-579, tables)

Explains the role of a wage structure and components of the wage bill with considerable research reported on the relationship of payroll taxes and fringes to basic wages. Further, attention is given to occupation wage differences and inter-industry differences. Little is really known about effects and author urges caution in regulating price of labor by governmental fiat.

4098. Grieb, Kenneth J. Concentration of political power and levels of economic development in Latin American countries: a comment and a research proposal (JDA, 8:4, July 1974, p. 513-518, table)

Methodological criticisms of James F. Torres' article "Concentration of Political Power..." (see *Journal of Developing Areas*, 7/8:3, April 1973).

4099. Grunwald, Joseph; Miguel S. Wionczek; and **Martin Carnoy.** La integración económica latinoamericana y la política de Estados Unidos. México, Centro de Estudios Monetarios Latinoamericanos, 1973. 248 p., bibl., tables.

Translation of *HLAS 35:1821*.

4100. Gualco, Jorge Nelson. Cono Sur: elección de un destino. B.A., Compañía General Fabril Editora, 1972. 300 p., bibl., maps, tables.

At the outset, there are definitional problems: the "cono" is defined as the "cuenca del Plata" but less Brazil—for ideological (?) reasons—and adding Chile and Peru. The author has clear interests in hydrographic regionalism—as clearly frustrated by the imperialism of Brazil. About one-third appendixes with considerable attention to hydraulic projects.

4101. Guignabaudet, Philippe. Hacia una economía específica del Tercer Mundo: financiamieto [sic] de la producción en las naciones en proceso de desarrollo económico. Quito, Editorial Casa de la Cultura Ecuatoriana, 1971. 387 p.

Reference to the final chapter of synthesis reveals seven basic equilibria indicative of the sort of system developed: evolutionary equilibrium of human collectives; human labor equilibrium; physical equilibrium of production as opposed to monetary equilibrium of production; equilibrium between wages, production, and money; social equilibrium of consumption; and the equilibrium of modern financing.

4102. Harbison, Frederic H.; Joan Maruhnic; and **Jane R. Resnick.** Availability and conceptual validity of statistical data for a system of human resources development indicators in Africa and Latin America (*in* Gostkowski, Zygmunt ed. Towards a system of human resources indicators for less developed countries. Warszawa, The Polish Academy of Sciences, Institute of Philosophy and Sociology *for* UNESCO, 1972, p. 39-62)

Discussion of the availability and reliability of a very large number of possible indicators of the status of human resource development.

4103. Hassan, M.F. Unemployment in Latin America: causes and remedies (AJES, 32:2, April 1973, p. 179-190, bibl., tables)

A succinct and well documented exposition of causes of unemployment estimated to be up to 27 percent. Remedial efforts should be direct rather than seeking remedies through growth alone.

4104. Helfgott, Roy B. Multinational corporations and manpower utilization in developing nations (JDA, 7:2, Jan. 1973, p. 235-246, tables)

A study of eight US firms with overseas operations. A variety of personnel problems were surveyed with US-based personnel and some conclusions established, one of which is that multinational corporations are particularly suited to solution of these problems.

4105. Helleiner, G.K. Manufactured exports from less-developed countries and multinational firms (RES/EJ, 83:329, March 1972, p. 21-47, tables)

An important article which surveys trade possibilities for less developed countries. Particular attention is paid to the "next step," i.e. export of manufactures in which multinational firms can be expected to play a large role and in which labor-intensively produced components will be large.

4106. Herschel, Federico J. Problemas de política tributaria en América Latina: análisis crítico de la Tercera Conferencia Interamericana sobre tributación (IDES/DE, 13:49, abril/junio 1973, p. 135-167, tables)

A comprehensive critical review of the 1972 Inter-American Conference on Taxation with particular discussion of underlying values. Considerable of the differences depends on political possibility.

Hirschman, Albert O. A bias for hope: essays on development in Latin America. See *HLAS 36:1700*.

4107. ———. Cómo y por qué desinvertir en la América Latina (FCE/TE, 37:147, julio/sept. 1970, p. 489-514)

A translation of the seminal *How to divest in Latin America and Why* (Princeton, N.J., Princeton Univ. Press, International Finance Section, 1969).

4108. La historia económica en América Latina. v. 1, Situación y métodos. v. 2, Desarrollo, perspectivas y bibliografía. México, Secretaría de Educación Pública, 1972. 2 v. (266, 309 p.) (SepSetentas, 37, 47)

Vol. 1 surveys the status of the study of economic history (a "young and vigorous" discipline) in Latin America and concludes with two methodological essays. Vol. 2 follows with essays on specific aspects of economic history: the colonial period, what's needed in demographic study, etc. More than half the volume reprints six bibliographies. When so much current thought stands on the base of history, it is commendable to see serious attention being given the quality of the base.

4109. Hunt, Shane J. Evaluating direct foreign investment in Latin America (*in* Einaudi, Luigi R. ed. Beyond Cuba: Latin America takes charge of its future. N.Y., Crane, Russak, 1974, p. 145-161, tables)

A particularly perceptive discussion on what is involved in evaluating foreign investment.

4110. Hunter, John M. and **James W. Foley.** Economic problems of Latin America. Boston, Mass., Houghton Mifflin, 1975. 390 p., bibl.

An introductory university text concentrating on economic aspects of problems. Bibliography.

4111. Impérialistes, socialistes, sub-impérialistes pris dans le mécanisme de la crise: une analyse de André Gunder Frank (Partisans [Paris] 68, nov./déc. 1972, p. 48-51)

A summary, mildly critical of André Gunder Frank, see item 4079.

4112. Instituto Colombiano de Comercio Exterior, *Bogotá.* Bases para una política de cooperación entre el grupo subregional andino y la comunidad económica europea. Bogotá, Sub-Dirección de Integración e Intercambio Comercial, 1970. 1 v. (Various pagings)

Examines the historic base for Andean group relations with the European community and studies means of expanding these relations in trade, finance, technology.

4113. Inter-American Development Bank. Economic and social progress in Latin America: 1973 annual report. Washington, 1974? 374 p., tables.

A useful annual reference published in both Spanish and English editions. General articles cover regional trends, development finance, the external sector, and social development trends. A country-by-country summary follows. There are, furthermore, useful statistical appendixes.

4114. ———. A mobilização de recursos financeiros internos na América Latina. Rio, 1971. 208 p.

Consists of three major papers—and ensuing discussion—originally delivered at a round table of the XII Meeting of the IDB's Board of Governors held in Lima, 1971: Raymond W. Goldsmith "Mobilização dos Recursos Internos paro o Crescimento Econômico Através do Sistema Financeiro" p. 3-44; Claudio Sergré "Os Mercados de Capital Nos Países em Desenvolvimento: Problemas Institucionais e Perspectivas de

Crescimento" p. 45-78; Herculano Borges da Fonseca "As Institucões Financeiras do Brasil e da América Latina" p. 79-127.

4115. _____. Statement of Loans, 1973. Washington, 1974. 190 p.

A detailed accounting as of 31 Dec. 1973 for each loan in the several fund categories listed by countries. A highly specialized publication but extremely useful for its planning purposes.

4116. _____. **Instituto para la Integración de América Latina** (INTAL). La empresa industrial en la integración de América Latina: un estudio empírico. B.A., 1971. 222 p., tables (Estudios, 6)

This survey has two basic objectives: identification of industrial firms which participate in Latin American trade of manufactures and study of the characteristics of those firms which so participate. Period considered is 1966-69. Ten countries are included with a total of 534 firms.

4117. _____. _____. Exportaciones de manufacturas a América Latina, 1966-1967; análisis de la composición de las exportaciones de productos manufacturados seleccionados a la región y al resto del mundo, identificación de los principales productos exportados a los países de América Latina: Argentina; Brasil; Costa Rica, El Salvador, Guatemala, Honduras, Nicaragua, Panama; Haiti, Jamaica, República Dominicana, Trinidad y Tobago; Uruguay; Venezuela. B.A., 1969. 6 v. (82, 81, 256, 78, 45, 46 l.) tables (Serie Estudios, 1)

Six vols. of a larger (?) study on multinational firms. It is not clear whether the results were published for all countries or only for those listed above and excluding Chile, Paraguay, Bolivia, Perú, Ecuador, Colombia, and Mexico. Also it is not clear whether the series was continued beyond the initial period 1966-67. Contains methodological information as well as numerous statistical data.

4118. _____. _____. El proceso de integración de América Latina en 1972. B.A., 1973. 315 p., tables.

Presumably the first of what has become an annual publication following INTAL's *La integración económica de América Latina* covering pre-1968 developments and *El proceso de integración en América Latina* 1968-1971. Chapters cover commerce, fiscal aspects, money and finance, industry, agriculture, infrastructure, social participation, institutional and legal considerations, Latin American activities in the global context, convergence of regional and subregional activities.

4119. _____. _____. El proceso de integración en América Latina: 1968-1971. B.A., 1972. 296 p.

Continuation (covering 1968-71) of INTAL's initial 1968 report *La integración económica de América Latina*. Background; commercial aspects; integration by sectors; monetary, tax, financial aspects. The second part (roughly half) reports on individual integration efforts (CARIFTA, CACM, etc.) one by one.

4120. Jaber, Tayseer A. The relevance of traditional integration theory to less developed countries (JCMS, 9:3, March 1971, p. 254-267)

A very careful survey of the literature related to integration and LDC's. There is found to be general agreement that little can be said about the production effects of traditional theory: dynamic production effects *may* be welfare-favorable. The conventional generalizations of conditions favoring welfare gains are also found wanting when applied to LDC's. Dynamic effects and developmental effects are too little understood.

Jaffe, A.J. Notes on family income distribution in developing countries in relation to population and economic changes. See item 9647.

4121. Jaguaribe, Helio. Causas del subdesarrollo latinoamericano (CPES/RPS, 7:19, set./dic. 1970, p. 54-66)

Seeks to explain Latin American underdevelopment by developing two hypothesis: 1) dualism to 1930 and the conflicting interests of elites and masses prevented concerted action, and 2) the heritage of dualism in too small markets and overlarge masses. Based on wide historical examples.

4122. Jimenes-Grullón, Juan Isidro. La América Latina y la Revolución Socialista: análisis de la tesis dictadura con respaldo popular y sus ampliaciones, de Juan Bosch. t. 1. Santo Domingo, Editora Cultural Dominicana, 1971. 377 p.

A Marxist attack on the proposal of Juan Bosch for "dictatorship with popular support" as a viable means of governing in Latin America. It tends to be, too, an attack on Bosch. Vol. 2 apparently proceeds from this to other related themes.

Journal of Inter-American Studies and World Affairs. See *HLAS 36:1494*.

4123. Kaplan, Marcos. Aspectos políticos de la planificación en América Latina (UNAM/PDD, 2:6, enero/marzo 1971, p. 19-40)

Much more a comprehensive survey of the nature and problems of planning than of political problems related to planning.

4124. Kaynor, Richard S. and Konrad F. Schultz. Industrial development; a practical handbook for planning and implementing development programs.

N.Y., Praeger, 1973. 185 p., illus. (Praeger special studies in international economics and development)

A how-to-do-it manual for industrial development with chapters on such as: "providing equity and loan financing," "providing investment incentives (fiscal stimuli)." Useful as a sort of general guide drawn from rich case material; at the same time it necessarily lacks specificity for particular industries and countries.

4125. Kinsgston, Jerry L. Export instability in Latin America: the postwar statistical record (JDA, 7:3, April 1973, p. 381-395, tables)

Computes measures of export instability 1948-65 as portion of Latin American trade, by commodity, by destination. Finds little unusual instability, that primary exports do not account for disproportionate amounts of the instability, the US markets are not unduly responsible.

4126. Kula, Marcin. Capitalismo y atraso de América Latina según A.G. Frank (Estudios Latinoamericanos [Wroclaw, Poland] 1972, p. 317-321)

A severely critical review of André Gunder Frank's *Capitalism and underdevelopment in Latin America: historical studies of Chile and Brazil* (N.Y., Monthly Review Press, 1967, 298 p., bibl.), see HLAS 29:3057.

4127. Lago, Armando V. Aspectos sicológicos en la teoría del consumidor. B.A., Ediciones Macchi, 1971. 48 p., illus.

These notes and reflections concerning microeconomic theory (consumption curves) from the psychological point of view open up an interesting set of new variables (and corresponding modifications of price curves) which could inspire further studies. [Pedro F. Hernández]

4128. Lagunilla Iñárritu, Alfredo. Los mercados latinoamericanos de capitales: carteras cautivas y mercados marginales (CEML/TF, 10:5, mayo/junio 1971, p. 545-559)

Stresses the importance of saving and investment and points out that most conditions favor short-term debt instruments. Urges the development of equity share markets through a variety of devices to make such instruments relatively more attractive.

4129. Lanus, Juan Archibaldo. Sobre la integración económica en América Latina: el caso de la ALALC. B.A., Ministerio de Relaciones Exteriores y Culto, Instituto del Servicio Exterior de la Nación, 1970. 212 p., tables.

A sympathetic and carefully documented review of the theoretical and historical bases of LAFTA and of its performance in the 1960s. Views problems and prospects realistically.

4130. Lasuen, José Ramón. Tecnología y desarrollo: reflexiones sobre el caso de América Latina (*in* Funes, Julio César ed. La ciudad y la región para el desarrollo. Caracas, Comisión de Administración Pública de Venezuela, 1972, p. 2-66)

A careful, historical, descriptive analysis of the relationships between technology and development. Particular attention is paid to the need for indigenous technology and the reasons for its failure to develop. For panel discussion, reply, and apparently questions for the floor, see p. 46-66.

4131. *Latin American Perspectives.* Vol. 1, No. 1, Spring 1974- Riverside, Calif.

A new journal to be published tri-annually with each issue to be devoted to a single topic. The first is "Dependency Theory: a Reassessment" with eight articles (not all original) and two reviews. It is a "theoretical journal for the discussion and debate of urgent subjects." It declares "that nothing academic can ever be neutral and that all scholarship has a political function." For political scientist's comment, see item 8067.

4132. Lineamientos para alcanzar el mayor empleo y crecimiento en América Latina. Prefacio [por] Walter J. Sedwitz. Washington, Organización de los Estados Americanos, Secretaría General, Consejo Interamericano Económico y Social, 1973. 254 p., tables (OEA/Ser. H/X.21; CIES/1862)

An important study seeking to identify medium-term policies designed to reduce unemployment in a context, too, of increasing income and redistributing for greater equality. The study outlines sets of policies which can be employed in different combinations according to predilections and requirements of different countries. The product of considerable inputs. The final chapter is Rosenstein-Rodan's on short-run measures.

4133. Llorente, Rodrigo. L'Amérique Latine et la décennie du développement (UP/TM, 10:39, juillet/sept. 1969, p. 553-593)

An early and fairly comprehensive review of the "decade of development" in Latin America. Major attention is given to integration experience. Projections to the year 2000 are not favorable; European assistance could be helpful.

4134. Luisi, Héctor. Integración económica en América Latina (Revista del Colegio Interamericano de Defensa [Washington] 1:2, agosto 1972, p. 1-4)

A popular, short review of the highlights of integration.

4135. Manrique C., María Irma. La política monetaria en América Latina (UNAM/PDD 3:10, feb./abril 1972, p. 57-72)

Less a review of monetary policy in the 1960s (as it purports to be) than a general review of the decade of the 1950s, some results of the Alliance for Progress, and finally a discussion of the effects in Latin America of the dollar devaluation.

4136. Martínez Terrero, José. Futuro del turismo en América Latina (BCV/REL, 9:33, 1972, p. 121-141, tables)

Considerable emphasis on Venezuela and a rather superficial analysis of possibilities and requirements. Generally optimistic for return on investment.

Mayer, Robert. The origins of the American banking empire in Latin America: Frank A. Vanderlip and the National City Bank. See *HLAS 36:1708.*

4137. Mazz, Addy. Impuesto al valor agregado, impuesto nacional, características y comparación con el impuesto del M.C.E. (Mercado Común Europeo) Incentivos fiscales en los países en desarrollo. Montevideo, Fundación de Cultura Universitaria, 1971. 56 p., bibl.

Two essays. The first examines the value added tax particularly compared to other sales taxes in developmental contexts. The second essay examines the efficacy of various tax incentives. Both tend to be elementary with considerable attention to definitions.

4138. Meeting of the Board of Governors of the Inter-American Development Bank, *XIV, Kingston, 1973.* Proceedings. Washington, Inter-American Development Bank, 1973. 249 p.

Largely statements of individual governors. Adopted resolutions were routine.

4139. Melazzi, Gustavo *comp.* Industrialización y dependencia en América Latina: textos de CEPAL, Jaléc, Romanova, Frank, Guevara, Franco y Testa. B.A.? Editorial Cimarrón, 1974. 133 p., tables.

A reader. More than half consists of extracts from CEPAL's "Problemas y Perspectivas del Desarrollo Industrial Latinoamericano" (1963) and "El Proceso de Industrialización de América Latina" (1965).

4140. Mikesell, Raymond F. Conflict resolution in extractive industries (*in* Driscoll, Robert E. and Harvey W. Wallender *eds.* Technology transfer and development: an historic and geographic perspective. N.Y., Fund for Multinational Management Education *in cooperation with the* Council of the Americas, 1974, p. 276-293)

An account of most often met issues between LDC's and mining firms and what those firms can do to minimize the conflicts.

Milenky, Edward S. The politics of regional organization in Latin America: the Latin American Free Trade Association. See *HLAS 36:1709.*

4141. Molina Cabrera, Orlando. Participación, desarrollo y planificación. Mendoza, Arg., Instituto de Estudios Políticos para América Latina (IEPAL), 1970. 84 p., tables (Cursos y documentos)

Development plans have failed for a variety of reasons: inappropriate economics, failure of economics to recognize non-economic variables, the failure of planners to include the citizenry in the plans (participation), and some logical inconsistencies between liberal ideals and state intervention. Examines planning in this light.

4142. Montenegro, Abelardo F. Da Aliança para o Progresso à Ação para o Progresso. Fortaleza, Bra., Editôra Henriqueta Galeno, 1971. 169 p.

A fascinating little book which tries to interpret the transformation of Kennedy's Alliance for Progress to the Nixon Administration's policies vis-à-vis Latin America.

4143. Moore, Russell Martin. Imperialism and dependency in Latin America: a view of the new reality of multinational investment (UM/JIAS, 15:1, Feb. 1973, p. 21-35, bibl., table)

Urges a more sympathetic view of the multinational corporation than it is frequently accorded. In particular, its abuses should be controlled by intergovernmental policy rather than by reversion to an archaic nationalism. Multinational corporations more nearly resemble international organizations than extensions of the economies of the "home" country.

4144. Musto, Stefan A. Evaluierung sozialer Entwicklungsprojekte. Berlin, FRG, Hessling Verlag, 1972. 164 p., tables (Schriften des DIE, 9)

Important, comprehensive analysis of several methods used to evaluate the impact of social developmental projects in developing nations. The author analyses specific evaluation approaches and makes recommendations as to their applicability. [H.J. Hoyer]

4145. Naranjo, John and **Richard C. Porter.** Comment: the impact of the Commonwealth preference system on the exports of Latin America to the United Kingdom (JDS, 9:4, July 1973,

p. 581-597, bibl., tables)

Employing different techniques, disputes Wall's conclusion (see *The Journal of Development Studies*, 7:2, 1971) that Commonwealth preference particularly discriminated against Latin American export of manufactures to the UK and thus not only damaged total trade but also distorted it.

4146. Nelson, Michael. The development of tropical lands: policy issues in Latin America. Baltimore, Md., The Johns Hopkins Press *published for* Resources for the Future, 1973. 306 p.

An excellent analysis based on 24 field studies. Carefully evaluates projects by expectations and results and synthesizes experiences into general conclusions. A first-rate volume.

4147. Nickel, Herbert J. Marginalität als theoretischer Ansatz zur Erklärung von Unterentwicklung (SOCIOL, 21:1, 1971, p. 33-58)

The concept of "marginality" is examined and found to be more descriptive than analytic. Furthermore, there is no distinguishable difference in kind between marginality in developed and less developed societies.

4148. Noriega, Carlos. Estado actual de las cuentas nacionales en América Latina (IDES/DE, 14:53, abril/junio 1974, p. 131-150)

An excellent survey concluding with a statement of weaknesses and what can be done about them. General discussion without country specificity.

4149. North American Congress on Latin America (NACLA), *N.Y.* Yanqui dollar: the contribution of U.S. private investment to underdevelopment in Latin America. N.Y., 1971. 64 p., illus., tables.

A systematic summary of most of the critiques of US investment in Latin America.

4150. Odell, Peter R. and **David A. Preston.** Economies and societies in Latin America: a geographical interpretation. London, John Wiley, 1973. 265 p., illus., map (A Wiley-Interscience publication)

A regional socio-economic geography, not a treatise on individual countries. It concerns three particular issues: the large masses of only partly occupied areas, the patterns of urbanization, general aspects of the spatial structure on a continental scale. Appears to be innovative and of interest to others as well as geographers.

4151. Organization of American States. Centro Interamericano de Promoción de Exportaciones (CIPE). El comercio de América Latina con Estados Unidos, 1967-1970: selección estadística de 101 productos con posibilidades de exportación. Bogotá, 1972. 120 p., tables.

Pt. 1 treats exhaustively the statistical characteristics of US imports 1967-70 with particular attention to Latin American origins. Pt. 2 then describes US imports of 101 items in which Latin American trade might be expanded. Products are discriminated by Tariff Schedules Annotated of the United States.

4152. _____. Secretaría General. Comité Interamericano de la Alianza para el Progreso (CIAP). América Latina y la reforma del sistema monetario internacional; resultados y deliberaciones de una reunión convocada por el Presidente del CIAP y la Secretaría Ejecutiva, enero de 1972. Washington, 1972. 115 p. (OEA/Ser. H/14. CIAP 573)

Documents related to a small seminar of experts in 1972. Pt. 1 presents principal conclusions of the group and a summary of the discussions. Pt. 2 is a study presented by the Secretariat General "La Reforma del Sistema Monetario Internacional: Evaluación Sugerencias." A valuable publication.

4153. Ozawa, Terutomo. Transfer of technology from Japan to developing countries. N.Y., United Nations Institute for Training and Research, 1971. 50 p., tables (UNITAR Research reports, 7)

An interesting study but with little reference to Latin America, of 526 technology transfers (1964-69), 44 percent were to advanced countries and 26 percent were to North and Central (22 percent) and South (four percent) America.

4154. Paquien, Jorge Luis. La industria automotriz en la ALALC. B.A., Banco Interamericano de Desarrollo, Instituto para la Integración de América Latina, 1969. 252 p., tables.

The automotive industry is one of the dynamic sectors in industrialization in Latin America. Mexico, Brazil, and Argentina produced about 90 percent of the vehicles (1967—incidently, note date of publication) but Colombia, Chile, Peru, Uruguay, and Venezuela are also given attention. Much of the volume is devoted to reporting (production, exports, imports, legislation, etc.) on individual countries.

Patman, C.R. Probing potential in developing nations. See item 6539.

4155. Paz, Pedro F. Dependencia financiera y desnacionalización de la industria interna (FCE/TE, 37:146, abril/junio 1970, p. 297-329, tables)

Reviews the nature of dependency and argues that foreign investment replaces national industrial investment and reduces the possibilities of export expansion in manufactures. Suggests that the two-gap sort of model is far from useful in assessing the effects of foreign investment.

4156. _____. El método histórico en la economía (FCE/TE, 39:153, enero/marzo 1972, p. 73-89)

History is to economics as water is to navigation, but there are too many navigators who ignore this basic fact. Today's dependence can only be understood by understanding the evolution of dependence. Some of the economic theory attacked is in the nature of a straw man.

4157. Pazos, Felipe. Chronic inflation in Latin America. Translated by Ernesto Cuesta. N.Y., Praeger Publishers, 1972. 186 p., tables (Praeger special studies in international economics and development)

A first-class study of the causes, effects, and cures for "intermediate" (as opposed to "creeping" and "hyper") inflation in Brazil, Argentina, Uruguay, and Chile. This is an innovative study which concentrates on intermediate, chronic inflation as an independent phenomenon.

4158. _____. El financiamiento externo de la América Latina: ¿aumento progresivo o disminución gradual? (FCE/TE, 38[2]:150, abril/junio 1971, p. 455-476, tables)

Examines the question in the title by reviewing the Pearson, Peterson, Rockefeller, and Prebisch reports as well as two other by the OAS. Although all suggest greater finance on better terms, Pazos is not in agreement. Countries should reduce dependence on external finance because: 1) they may not get it, 2) there are good reasons to believe that they should not get it without substantial increase in exports, 3) which if it occurs, they won't need anyway, and 4) it does not seem politically wise to go on for long this way.

4159. Peña, Sergio da la. El antidesarrollo de América Latina. México, Siglo XXI Editores, 1971. 205 p., bibl., tables.

An elaborate and literate socio-economic discussion of development is followed by an interpretation of history in Latin America along these lines. Undesirable development occurs as capital-intensive means of production are imported by foreign investors.

4160. Pérez A., Jorge. Un ejemplo de financiamiento externo: la acción de los bancos internacionales de desarrollo en América Latina. Bogotá, Asociación Latinoamericana de Instituciones Financieras de Desarrollo, (ALIDE), 1973. 165 p., illus., tables.

A study of the IBRD and IDB with a view to demonstrating that their activities are a form of intervention with potentially important consequences on the economy and on the nations' priorities. A careful and not unsympathetic analysis.

4161. Pérez Brignoli, Héctor. En torno a un reciente debate: el intercambio desigual (Estudios Sociales Centroamericanos [San José] 1:1, enero/abril 1972, p. 117-154, tables)

A review of the terms of trade arguments through the history of thought with a Marxianization of the phenomenon largely through an interpretation of A. Emmanuel *L'Echange inégal* (Paris, François Máspero, 1969).

4162. Petras, James and **Robert La Porte.** Temas y problemas del desarrollo latinoamericano vistos por funcionarios estadounidenses: la década del setenta (IDES/DE, 10:38, julio/sept. 1970, p. 247-262)

Concentrates on the role of agriculture. A series of quotations from a series of interviews which then purport to represent AID. A severe indictment if, as one is expected to believe, these notions were either representative or governing.

Pike, Frederick B. Capitalism and consumerism in Spain of the 1960's: what lessons for Latin American development? See *HLAS 36:1713.*

4163. Pincemin, Roberto. La paz y el dinero: hacia la reforma de la propiedad capitalista. B.A., Forum Empresario-Gremila, 1972. 84 p.

A visionary pamphlet which seeks cures to national economic ailments through a fundamental revision of private property rights which primarily both permit continued capital accumulation and worker participation in its ownership.

4164. Pinho, Carlos Marques. Economia da educação e desenvolvimento econômico. São Paulo, Livraria Pioneira Editôra, 1971. 103 p., bibl., tables (Biblioteca Pioneira de Ciências Sociais. Educação)

A competent resumé and synthesis of the topic although there is little new. A useful bibliography.

4165. Pinto, Aníbal. El model de desarrollo reciente de la América Latina (FCE/TE, 38[2]: 150, abril/junio 1971, p. 477-498, tables)

Examines the implications of internal manufacturing growth without any appreciable external growth.

4166. _____. Notas sobre desarrollo, subdesarrollo, y dependencias (FCE/TE, 39[2]:154, abril/junio 1972, p. 243-264)

An examination of the different kinds of economies and of the different sorts of dependency relations they have. Seeks to develop indicators of dependence.

4167. ———— **and Jan Kñakal.** América Latina y el cambio en la economía mundial. Lima, Instituto de Estudios Peruanos, 1973. 191 p., bibl., tables (Col. América problems, 8)

The essays of Pinto "Marginalización y Dependencia de América Latina: el Sistema Centro-Periferia 20 Años Depués" (p. 19-142) and Kñakal ."Nexos Estratégicos entre América Latin y Estados Unidos: las Relaciones Económicas en los Años 1960" (p. 143-189) are essentially independent efforts Of the former, perhaps the chapter on the socialist countries as new "centers" and his concluding one on "options" are the most interesting. Kñakal concentrates on the increasing marginalization of Latin America (vis-à-vis the US) and suggests at least greater collective action to overcome that.

4168. Pons Lezica, Cipriano Ambrosio Patricio. Caminos de Barbarie. B.A., Distribuciones Guadalupe, 1971. 116 p., illus., table.

A series of popularly written essays on problems seen by the author as major threats to mankind—population, hunger, ignorance, etc.

4169. Prebisch, Raúl. Más allá del sistema económico (FCE/TE, 38[2]:150, abril/junio 1971, p. 499-513)

Touches on a number of diverse points—youthful exuberance, the ambivalence of technology, values, power, the need of self-identification in and of Latin America.

4170. ————. Panorama del desarrollo económico social de América Latina (BCV/REL, 8:30, 1971, p. 109-129)

Reviews major aspects of his IDB report—lack of dynamism, underemployment, aspects of foreign capital, population, etc.

4171. Randall, Laura. Inflation and economic development in Latin America: some new evidence (JDS, 9:2, Jan. 1973, p. 317-322, tables)

Seeks more refined data for examination of causes of sectoral shifts. Lets the difference between sectoral wholesale price indexes and retail price indexes represent sectoral profitability. This variable correlates better with sectoral changes than others previously tried.

4172. Reunión de Bolsas y Mercados de Valores de América, *III, Rio, 1968.* Resoluciones y recomendaciones finales aprobadas. Rio, 1969. 1 v. (Unpaged)

Recommendations and resolutions of the conference.

4173. *Revista de la Integración.* Banco Interamericano de Desarrollo, Instituto para la Integración de América Latina (INTAL). No. 9, nov. 1971- . B.A.

A highly specialized bimonthly journal surely of interest to those working in integration. There seem to be three major departments: 1) research reports (170 p.). This issue has four pieces—Jorge Marshall on exchange rate fluctuations, Angel Monti on the role of LAFTA in technology and industrialization, Raúl Hess on compensation for asymetrical fiscal effects of integration, and Tayseer Jaber on the value of traditional theory in understanding integration; 2) the bibliography section reviews four books on integration (10 p.) agricultural sector in the CACM (55 p.).

4174. Reynolds, Clark W. Interacción social y política en el desarrollo económico de un sistema en desequilibrio: algunos ejemplos latinoamericanos (INTAL/RI, 11, nov. 1972, p. 101-132)

A plea for and examination of a broad expansion of economic development theory to incorporate social and political variables and interactions as well. Suggests some first steps as to how this may be done. An important contribution.

4175. Robertson, O. Zeller, Jr. Education and economic development in Latin America: a causal analysis (IAMEA, 28:1, Summer 1974, p. 63-71)

An interesting statistical analysis seeking to measure the causal effects of school, higher education, and urbanization on per capita income and on growth. Education, particularly primary and secondary, seem more to be effects rather than causes.

4176. Robichek, E. Walter and Carlos E. Sansón. The balance of payments performance of Latin America and the Caribbean, 1966-70 (IMF/SP, 19:2, July 1972, p. 286-343, tables)

A five-year review attempting to assess the importance of 1) governmental policies, and 2) exogenous factors on balance of payments performance. There are six sections: 1) performance of 23 countries and the region, 2) compatibility between balance of payments and growth objectives?, 3) exogenous factor influence, 4) policy influence, 5) short-term capital movements, and 6) significance to Latin America of the first allocation of SDR's. A wealth of data in the statistical appendix.

4177. Robson, P. Planning and integration in Latin America (JLAS, 3:2, Nov. 1971, p. 191-201)

A review article touching on the issues and findings of a market-basket of seven widely different books particularly concerning integration. There is less on planning. Covers Hilton; Krause and Mathis; Little, Scitovsky, and Scott; Griffin and Enos; ECLA; Hildebrand.

4178. Rodríguez, Jorge G. ¿Va Latinoamérica hacia la opulencia de estado industrial? (Comunidad [Univ. Iberoamericana, México] 8:45, oct. 1973, p. 509-525, plate)

With Galbraith as text, argues that Latin America should not blindly follow the development path to the greater productivity which begets the need for greater consumption through advertising, etc.

4179. Rofman, Alejandro B. Efectos de la integración latinoamericana en el esquema de localización industrial (IDES/DE, 10:38, julio/sept. 1970, p. 215-246)

A careful review of localization theory, followed by careful attention to industrialization efforts in Latin America. Concludes with implications of localization consideration to integrated industrialization.

Santos, Milton. Las ciudades incompletas de los países subdesarrollados. See item 6543.

——. Los dos circuitos de la economía urbana en los países subdesarrollados. See item 6544.

Santos de Morais, Clodomir. Diccionario de reforma agraria latinoamericana. See item 6545.

4180. Sanz de Santamaría, Carlos. Algunos comentarios sobre el comercio exterior de la América Latina (FCE/TE, 38[2]:150, abril/junio 1971, p. 553-570, tables)

Much of the battle for the Alliance for Progress was over the issue of better trading conditions for Latin American products in the US. Coffee is good case in point and is compared to cost-of-living in US and also to price changes in other breakfast foods.

4181. Schydlowsky, Daniel M. Industrialization and growth (*in* Einaudi, Luigi R. *ed.* Beyond Cuba: Latin America takes charge of its future. N.Y., Crane, Russak, 1974, p. 129-143)

Latin American development is in trouble because industrialization is import-using and thus restricted in growth capacity by slowly growing exports. Since import using is largely policy induced, policies can be devised to improve the situation.

4182. Scioville-Samper, Henri. El BID y la vivienda (Revista del Colegio Interamericano de Defensa [Washington] 1:2, agosto 1972, p. 58-72)

Much broader in scope than a report of housing activities of the IDB. After assessing the problem, discusses the changing nature of urbanization, its relation to development. Concludes with policy recommendations for domestic action and for international agencies.

4183. Secchi, C. Internationale financiële en monetaire problemen van Ontwikkelingslanden (NGIZ/IS, 26:5, 8 maart 1972, p. 405-420)

Summary of a symposium whose participants were: Harry Johnson, Sidney Dell, K.B. Asante, and Edwin M. Martin.

4184. El sector externo y el desarrollo económico de América Latina (Economía y Desarrollo [Univ. de La Habana, Instituto de Economía, La Habana] 5, enero/marzo 1971, p. 3-59, tables)

A most interesting article especially because of its source. There is not much in the way of surprises. The theme is that development is minimal because of the foreign exchange gap which exists primarily because of exploitation by investors (Yankee firms extract seven dollars for each new dollar of investment) and because of the treatment given Latin American exports. (Among other things, the US turned to internal sources for wheat and corn which we had imported from Latin America in 1960!)

4185. Seidel, Robert N. American reformers abroad: the Kemmerer missions in South America, 1923-1931 (EHA/J, 32:2, June 1972, p. 520-545)

Concentrates on political aspects of US financial expertise moving into the new post-World War I World. At the heart of Kemmerer recommendations were the gold standard and central banking recommended to and adopted in a number of countries. Some of the issues of early foreign assistance are treated.

4186. Selowsky, Marcelo. La medición de la contribución de la educación al crecimiento económico (UCC/CE, 8:25; dic. 1971, p. 36-49, tables)

Seeks to quantify the contribution of education in growth particularly using Mexican and Chilean data. Originally published in English in the *Quarterly Journal of Economics* (Aug. 1969)

4187. Seminario Aspectos Económicos y Técnicos de la Planificación en el Sector de la Energía, Berlin, FRG, 1969. Seminario aspectos económicos y técnicos de la planificación en el sector de la energía del 9 de abril al 1º de mayo de 1969. v. 1, Documentación; v. 2, Informes de los delegados. Berlin-Tegel, FRG, Reiherwerder, Fundación Alemana para los Países en Vías de Desarrollo, Centro de Seminarios Internacionales, 1969? 2 v. (146, 383 p.) illus., maps, plate, tables (DOK 454 A/c. S 5/69. DOK 454 C. S5/69)

Vol. 1 describes the seminar and presents the papers given before it by the German hosts. Vol. 2 is a series of 14 reports given by participants regarding their own Latin American countries.

4188. Seminario de América Latina y España, *Instituto de Cultura Hispánica, Madrid, 1969.* Bases comunes para el incremento de las relaciones comerciales, financieras y de cooperación técnica: informe final; documentos, intervenciones, sugerencias, communicaciones, anejos, discursos. Madrid, Ediciones Mundo Hispánico, 1970. 711 p., tables.

A complete account of a large seminar held in Madrid in 1969. Reports major topics and discussion of them: theoretical base for relations between Spain and Latin America; commerce, finance, technical cooperation, and documents of IDB and OAS.

4189. Seminario Nacional sobre Ciencia y Tecnología para el Desarrollo, *II, Paipa, Colo., 1972.* Ciencia y tecnología para el desarrollo: segundo seminario nacional, Hotel Sochagota, Paipa, enero 17-21, 1972. Bogotá, Colciencias, 1972. 2 v. (118 1.) (Serie: Informes y referencias, 7)

Vol. 1 contains the background and recommendations of the seminar. Besides the usual housekeeping details (participants, opening and closing speeches). Vol. 2 contains a substantial background document by CACTAL with a series of propositions and policies leading to opportunity for international cooperation between Latin American countries in the area of science and technology.

4190. Seminario Planificación Integrada de Proyectos de Irrigación, *Berlin, FRG, 1970.* Documentación. Berlin-Tegel, FRG, Reinherwerder. Fundación Alemana para los Países en Vías de Desarrollo, Centro de Seminarios Internacionales, 1970. 226 p., illus., map, plate, tables (DOK 509 A/c. III-S 6/70)

A description of the seminar and formal papers presented. There are also recommendations from work groups.

4191. Seminario Utilización de Bosques Tropicales en Latino-américa, *Bogotá, 1969.* Informes de los delegados. Berlin, FRG, Fundación Alemana para los Países en Vías de Desarrollo, Centro de Seminarios Internacionales, 1969? 256 p., map, tables (DOK 440 A/c. S1/69)

Not certain this is complete report of the seminar. This volume has only reports of delegates from 16 countries which describe forests, discusses legislation regarding their use, etc. No integrating material.

4192. Shaw, R. Paul. Land tenure and the rural exodus in Latin America (UC/EDCC, 23:1, Oct. 1974, p. 123-132, tables)

An empirical test of some hypotheses concerning tenure patterns and migration in Chile, Costa Rica, Peru. Correlations between latifundismo and migration suggest policy implications.

4193. Sideri, S. Analysis and overall evaluation of Latin American trade policies. The Hague, Institute of Social Studies, 1973. 21 p. (Occasional paper, 42)

A terse, critical review of trade and exchange rate policies concluding they have led to further dependence on the US without much benefit.

Sito, Nilda. Estructura ocupacional: desarrollo y sindicalismo en los países latinoamericanos. See item 9685.

4194. Slighton, Robert L. A note on income redistribution (*in* Einaudi, Luigi R. ed. Beyond Cuba: Latin America takes charge of its future. N.Y., Crane, Russak, 1974, p. 163-169)

With recognition that unemployment is a growing problem, more attention will be paid to income redistribution in the future. Policies will require planning and comprehensive direct controls, inflation, and will in general bring disappointing results.

4195. Sloan, John W. LAFTA in the 1960's: obstacles to progress (SID/IDR, 14:1, 1972, p. 16-25, tables)

A more optimistic view than usual. Summarizes accomplishments, failures; reviews obstacles; outlines reasons to think LAFTA is "the most viable strategy of development available . . ."

4196. Sternberg, Marvin J. The latifundista: the impact of his income and expenditure patterns on investment and consumption (RU/SCID, 7:1, Spring 1972, p. 1-18, tables)

Tests hypotheses: That land-owner incomes are large, that consumption patterns of latifundistas are development-inhibiting, and that redirection of the use of this income could increase domestic investment and ease balance of payments difficulties significantly. Data are developed *on an area-wide basis* and hypotheses are found to be not inconsistent with the data.

4197. Streeter, Lanny E. and Ramón Pablo Guerrero Ortiz. The demand for international reserves: a cross-sectional study of a group of Latin American countries (UM/JIAS, 15:4, Nov. 1973, p. 432-453, bibl., table)

Four factors are thought to determine the amounts of

international reserves held: expected deficit size, variability of deficit, cost of holding reserves, cost of being short of reserves. Regression for 20 Latin American countries over nine years verified hypothesis. Implications are examined.

4198. Sunkel, Osvaldo. Capitalismo transnacional y desintegración nacional en la América Latina (FCE/TE, 38[2]: 150, abril/junio 1971, p. 571-628, illus., tables)

Seeks to put development, underdevelopment, dependency, marginalization, and spatial inequalities—the reality of Latin America—into a perspective from which will emerge a comprehensive, interdisciplinary, integrated interpretation. Development is a matter of process, structure, system. Polarization becomes major force.

4199. _____ ; G. Maynard; D. Seers; and J. H. G. Olivera. Inflación y estructura económica. B.A., Editorial Paidós, 1973. 139 p., tables (Biblioteca América Latina. Serie menor, 3)

Four essays all of which have appeared elsewhere (Maynard is possible exception) from 1958-64. In general, each deals with structuralism. Their juxtaposition may be convenient for some.

4200. Tamames Gómez, Ramón. La integración económica latinoamericana (IEAS/R, 21/79, abril/junio 1972, p. 155-167)

A straightforward account of the development of LAFTA from its beginning and including its period of "hibernation," 1968-69.

4201. _____. La integración económica y los paises de menor desarrollo relativo: la experiencia de Austria y Portugal en la EFTA. B.A., Banco Interamericano de Desarrollo, Instituto para la Integración de América Latina, 1972. 120 p., maps, tables.

An attempt to assess the affects of integration on Uruguay led to an assessment of the effects of the European Free Trade Association and then, specifically, experiences of Austria and Portugal in it. He finds "not a little" of interest in the European experience for the Latin American countries.

4202. Technical Seminar on Automated Data Processing in Tax Administration, *IV, Lima, 1971.* Report. English version revised by Maria Carolina Bellagamba. Panama, Inter-American Center for Tax Administration (CIAT), 1974. 314 p. (mimeo)

A series of papers organized around topics directed at tax agency use of data processing. Technical, but useful for those concerned with the problems.

4203. Teitel, Simón and Victor Tokman. Acerca del Informe Prebisch: *Transformación y desarrollo* (FCE/TE, 38:151, julio/sept. 1971, p. 767-792)

Sympathetically critical of Prebisch in finding some parts inconsistent (more foreign aid and less dependency), others too optimistic (amounts of future aid to be available), innovative in emphasis on employment as a goal, lacking in policy specificity.

4204. Terhal, P. UNCTAD: het gevecht tegen de bierkaai? (NGIZ/IS, 26:5, 8 maart 1972, p. 434-442)

Analysis of papers by Gosovic, Waldron-Ramsy, Tingergew, evaluating UNCTAD.

4205. Terrero, José Martinez. Futuro del turismo en América Latina (BCV/REL, 9:33, 1972, p. 123-141)

Brief, superficial. Notes demand for first-class tourist accomodation is increasing and urges that governments do something about it.

4206. Testa, Victor *ed.* and *comp.* Empresas multinacionales e imperialismo. B.A., Siglo XXI Argentina Editores, 1973. 210 p., tables (Historia inmediata)

A "reader" of the behavior of multinational firms with essays from a variety of non-Latin American authors and a variety of publications. The compiler provides considerable material himself in the form of an introduction.

4207. Tilbery, Henry. Tributação e integração da América Latina. Prefácio de Ruy Barbosa Nogueira. São Paulo, José Bushatshky, 1971. 180 p., bibl., tables.

A careful and very bibliographic survey of tax policy and economic integration. It is legalistic in nature rather than economic. Concludes with a call for much expanded academic research.

4208. Torales, Ponciano. Aporte al conocimiento integrado del desarrollo (UNAM/RMS, 32:6, nov./dic. 1970, p. 1483-1496)

A descriptive explanation of the facets involved in an integrated (interdisciplinary) view of "development."

4209. Torres, James F. Concentration of political power and levels of economic development in Latin American countries (JDA, 7:3, April 1973, p. 397-409, tables)

Examines relationships and causes thereof between political power concentration and development. Where power has been concentrated and wielded to maintain the status quo, development has been impeded.

4210. _____. Concentration of political power and levels of economic development in Latin American countries: a reply (JDA, 8:4, July 1974, p. 519-524, table)

Response to criticism by Zuvekas and by Grieb to his article, "Concentration of Political Power . . ." in the *Journal of Developing Areas* (April 1973). For political scientists's comment, see 8117.

_____. A new—and partial—approach to measurement of political power in Latin American countries. See item 8118.

4211. Trejo Reyes, Saúl. Un modelo de política económica: promoción de exportaciones y crecimiento óptimo de la economía (FCE/TE, 38:152, oct./dic. 1971, p. 1041-1067, bibl., tables)

A complex linear model which examines the developmental interrelated effects of the export sector and the disaggregated production sectors. Studies effects throughout of seeking to maximize exchange earnings.

4212. Trías, Vivian. La crisis del imperio. Montevideo, Ediciones de la Banda Oriental, 1970. 284 p., tables (Col. Reconquista, 38)

Another Marxist popular history of the 20th century pointed ultimately at the imperialistic causes of Latin American and Third World problems. As usual, the US is accorded a central role.

4213. Tyler, William G. and J. Peter Wogart. Economic dependence and marginalization: some empirical evidence (UM/JIAS, 15:1, Feb. 1972, p. 36-45, bibl., tables)

An empirical test of the dependency hypothesis in which correlation is computed between dependency variables and income distribution inequality (one of the hypothesized effects of dependency). R^2's are low but not sufficiently so to reject the hypothesis.

4214. United Nations. Comisión Económica para América Latina (CEPAL). Algunos problemas regionales del desarrollo de América Latina vinculados con la metropolización (UNECLA/B, 16:2, 2. semestre 1971, p. 199-229, tables)

Has strong statistical base including some income distribution estimations. Distinguishes problems for different sorts of regional—capital city—population patterns.

4215. _____. _____. Las empresas públicas: su significación actual y potencial en el proceso de desarrollo (UNECLA/B, 16:1, 1. semestre 1971, p. 1-62, tables)

A broad, descriptive study of rather arbitrarily defined activities: 1) activities by organizations as "firms," rather than by usual governmental organs; 2) in which all capital is governmentally provided—eliminating "mixed" companies. Because of data problems, most are at the national level, i.e. state and municipio enterprises are unintentionally excluded. Seeks to assess roles in development policy and to measure the relative significance of this form of enterprise in each subsector.

4216. _____. _____. Estudio económico de América Latina: 1971. N.Y., 1972, 252 p., tables (E/CN.12/935/Rev.1)

Pt. 1 examines Latin America in the world economy, looking forward to the decade of the 1970s and examining the principal tendencies of the 1950s and 1960s. Pt. 2 concentrates on Latin America in 1971 on both a regional basis and by individual countries.

4217. _____. _____. Estudio sobre la clasificación económica y social de los países de América Latina (UNECLA/B, 17:2, 2. semestre 1972, p. 155-218, tables)

An interesting exercise using a variety of indicators suggestive of welfare for purposes of inter-American comparisons. The results are informative, and the data are useful by themselves. Comparisons are made with other similar studies.

4218. _____. _____. La intermediación financiera en América Latina (UNECLA/B, 16:2, 2. semestre 1971, p. 145-198, tables)

A continuation of exploration of financial development, for pt. 1, see *Economic Bulletin for Latin America*, (15:2, 2. semester 1970). Concentrates on nature and functions, relationship of development and finance, the role of intermediary finance in various stages in Latin America, evolution in the 1960s. In spite of considerable progress in the decade, there are a number of weaknesses and courses of action for improvement. An appendix reports specifically on Colombia, Chile, Ecuador, and Peru.

4219. _____. **Departamento de Asuntos Económicos y Sociales.** Estudio económico mundial, 1969-1970: los países en desarrollo en el decenio de 1960; el problema de la evaluación de los progresos realizados. N.Y., 1971. 277 p., tables.

This particular volume does not fit the usual pattern of annual statistical reports on the world economy the title suggests. On the contrary, it is devoted entirely to the measurement of the process and outcome of development and the problems attendant thereto. Chapters cover production and supply, levels of living, productive capacity, equilibria, the external environment.

4220. _____. **Economic Commission for Latin America** (ECLA). Annual report. N.Y., 1972. 53 p. (Official records of the Economic and Social Council. Session, 53. Supplement, 6) (E/5135, E/CN.12/1931)

A detailed report of the activities of the ECLA, its various offices, subdivision, subsidiaries for the period. Reports on meetings, technical assistance seminars, publications, etc. Covers period 9 May 1971 to 30 April 1972. Useful to show great range of ECLA activities.

4221. _____. _____. Annual report. v. 1/2. N.Y., 1971. 2 v. (122, 122 p.) tables (Official records of the Economic and Social Council. Session, 51. Supplements, 4/4a) (EC/CN.12/867/Rev. 2, E/5027)

Same as item 4220, but for 8 May 1970 to 8 May 1971.

4222. _____. _____. Commodity problems and policies (UNECLA/B, 17:1, 1. half 9172, p. 1-40)

Latin American trends are matched against world trends in aggregate and specific commodity terms. Discusses problems of access and price instability.

4223. _____., _____. Financial resources for development (UNECLA/B, 17; 1, 1. half, 1972, p. 100-123)

Covers sources, conditions, destinations of capital flows. Attempts, further, to compare debt service burdens. The scope is worldwide with a special emphasis on Latin America's comparative position.

4224. _____. _____. Impact of economic groupings of developed countries (UNECLA/B, 17; 1, 1, half 1972, p. 65-99)

Considers evolving relations of Latin America with the European Economic Community, with the US, and with Japan. Considers more than just trade relations.

4225. _____. _____., Income distribution in Latin America. N.Y., 1971. 148 p., tables.

The definitive study until now of the topic. Pt. 1 covers general aspects (measures related to national averages, causes, aggregate distribution for the area). Pt. 2 examines variation within the region—Argentina, Venezuela, Mexico, Brazil, El Salvador. Pt. 3 examines specific aspects—functional distribution, urban-rural, regional distribution, sectoral distribution.

4226. _____. _____., Secretariat. [pt. a] The metal working industries in Latin America; [pt. b] Criteria and background information for programming the machine-tool industry; [pt. c] Methodological and operational aspects of machine-tool studies in developing countries (*in* Interregional Symposium on the Development of Metalworking Industries in Developing Countries, *Moscow, 1966.* Reports presented at the United Nations . . . . Wien, United Nations Industrial Development Organization, 1969, p. 51-56; 127-146; 203-214, tables)

Pt. a is a survey concentrating on heterogeneity between countries, sub-sectors, importance, policy, contribution to integration. Pt. b is a very technical piece which provides first steps in analysis of the feasibility of expansion of the machine tool industry as a part of capital goods production in developing economies. Pt. c is a preliminary report on methodological considerations in determining the demand for machine tools. Other articles (e.g., Leontief and Carter on input-output structural relationships and others on specific countries) will also be of interest to specialists.

4227. _____. _____. Trade in manufactures and semi-manufactures (UNECLA/B, 17; 1, 1. half 1972, p. 41-64)

A standard statistical analysis reporting trade by Latin America and comparing it to the world situation. An appendix table (p. 57-64) may be of special interest. It lists products by the Brussels Tariff nomenclature for which Latin American countries had asked for preferential treatment. The columns indicate which countries had acceded to these requests for each product.

4228. United Nations Conference on Transport and Development, *Geneva, 1970.* Current problems of economic integration; agricultural and industrial cooperation among developing countries. N.Y., United Nations, 1971 [i.e. 1972] 126 p., bibl (TD/B/375)

Two reports prepared for UNCTAD: 1) J. Mario Ponce "Expansion of Agricultural Trade among Clusters of Developing Countries," and 2) Havelock Brewster. "Systems of Industrial Integration."

4229. Urquidi, Víctor L. Technology, planning and Latin American development (SID/IDR, 13:1, 1971, p. 8-12)

Technology must be included as a dynamic variable in development planning including help to institutions which can contribute to indigenous technical needs.

4230. _____ and **Rosemary Thorp** eds. Latin America in the international economy. N.Y., John Wiley, 1973. 430 p.

An important book with a number of original contributions by scholars such as Alfred Maizels, Sven W. Arndt, Jorge M. Katz, Clark W. Reynolds. The level is somewhat uneven but generally superior to that found in anthologies of this sort. Of particular interest is the faithful if condensed reporting of the discussions of each paper, all of them delivered at a conference held by the International Economics Assn. in 1971, Mexico City.

4231. Valenzuela Feijóo, José. Capitalismo, subdesarrollo y cambio (UNAM/RMS, 33:4, oct./dic. 1971, p. 763-801, tables)

The principal inconsistency today is that which exists between socialism and capitalism, but it takes the particular form of a basic inconsistency between the revolutionary peoples of Asia, Africa, and Latin America and capitalistic imperialism led by the US.

4232. Varsavsky, Oscar. Largo plazo; ¿un solo estilo? (FCE/TE, 38:152, oct./dic. 1971, p. 1011-1040)

A preliminary consideration of planning with long-range goals in mind, considering problems of their definition. A number of variables for the model are given with suggestions as to their difficulty and how they might be handled. Concerned with various feasibilities - residually that of political feasibility.

4233. _____ and Alfredo Eric Calcagno *comps.* América Latina: modelos matemáticos, ensayos de aplicación de modelos de experimentación numérica a la política económica y las ciencias sociales. Santiago, Editorial Universitaria, 1971. 270 p., tables (Col. Tiempo latinoamericano)

Of considerable interest because it traces the various national and international elements of simulation modeling in Latin America since the early 1960s bringing under one cover a number of efforts concerning individual nations (e.g., Chile, Bolivia) and more general models.

4234. Vela, Carlos. Desarrollo e integración de América Latina. Madrid, Selecciones Gráficas, 1968. 446 p.

A broad treatment of the subject matter but severely limited by its publication date. Of particular interest is the emphasis given by the Jesuit author to the role and views of the Church. Integration is somewhat slighted with little attention to sub-regional plans. Economics finds little place in the matter of integration although considerably more on problems of development.

4235. Véliz, Claudio *comp.* Obstáculos para la transformación de América Latina. México, Fondo de Cultura Económica, 1969. 262 p. (Sección de obras de economía)

Published originally in 1965 as *Obstacles to change in Latin America* (see *HLAS 29:3212*) as a series of papers presented in a conference organized around that theme in London, 1965, by the Royal Institute of International Affairs. Papers are by such luminaries as: Chonchol, Fals Borda, Furtado, Gonzáles A. Pinto, Sunkel, T. Di Tella, Urquidi.

4236. Villagrán Kramer, Francisco. Teoría general del derecho de integración económica: ensayo de sistematización. San Juan, Editorial Universitaria Centroamericana, 1969. 559 p. (Col. Integración)

The first part is background material covering means and objectives. The major part is a careful, detailed statement regarding legal devices and processes for use in integration. Primarily a book concerning the law.

4237. Villate Bonilla, Eduardo and Antonio Copello Faccini. Aspectos generales de los sistemas de ahorro y préstamo en Chile, Brasil y Venezuela (PUJ/U, 43, Nov. 1972, p. 235-258)

Rather detailed accounts of the systems of "monetary correction" in the countries named with specific attention to presumed effects on savings and lending for low-cost housing.

4238. Vogel, R.C. The dynamic of inflation in Latin America, 1950-1969 (AEA/AER, 64:1, March 1974, p. 102-114, bibl.)

Extends the Harberger methodology (Chilean inflation) to 16 Latin American countries 1950-1969. Concludes that changes in money are highly correlated with (lagged) rates of price change very generally throughout Latin America despite its apparent diversity. Nonetheless "monetarist" policy conclusions do not necessarily follow.

4239. Wahab, I. Uitbreiding van de handel (NGIZ/IS, 26:5, 8 maart 1972, p. 421-433)

Summary of a symposium related to expansion of trade with the LDC's within the context of the EEC, especially as related to agricultural commodities.

Walton, John. Political development and economic development: a regional assessment of contemporary theories. See item 8126.

4240. Weisskoff, Richard. Distribución del ingreso y crecimiento económico en Puerto Rico, Argentina y México (*in* Foxley, Alejandro *ed.* Distribución del ingreso. México, Fondo de Cultura Económica, 1974, p. 111-147)

Modest effort, comparing the distribution at a global level between the agricultural and urban sectors in three countries, and also with the US. [J. Strasma]

4241. Williamson, Robert B.; William P. Glade; and Karl M. Schmitt *eds.* Latin American-U.S. economic interactions. Washington, American Enterprise Institute for Public Policy Research, 1974. 380 p.

Proceeds of a 1973 conference jointly sponsored by the AEI (its publisher), the Graduate School of Business and the Institute of Latin American Studies at the Univ. of Texas, Austin. A very high-powered, multinational group considers trade, investment, multinational lending, conflict and congruence, alternative forms of investment. A very useful volume.

4242. Wionczek, Miguel S. Estado actual y perspectivas de los movimientos de integración económica de los países en desarrollo (Boletín del Instituto Centroamericano de Derecho Comparado [Tegucigalpa] 9, 1968/69, p. 23-51)

Poses the problem of a world of 30 advanced countries and a 100 plus in all stages of underdevelopment. Only very few of the latter have any possibility of changing their statuses. Economic integration offers one of a few non-conventional approaches to alleviate the situation. A descriptive approach—Latin American, Africa, Asia are touched upon.

4243. _____. Hacia el establecimiento de un trato común para la inversión extranjera en la Mercado Común Andino (FCE/TE, 38[2]:150, abril/junio 1971, p. 659-702)

Analysis of various policies to deal with foreign investment. Includes detailed account of transnational firms in Colombia, Peru, Chile.

4244. _____. The Pacific market for capital, technology and information and its possible opening for Latin America (JCMS, 10:1, Sept. 1971, p. 78-95)

Discusses dynamic changes in Canada, Japan, Australia and comments on their ability to adjust to and to control foreign capital. Analyzes trade, aid projects, technology transfer, and investment possibilities.

4245. _____. Los problemas de la investigación sobre el desarrollo económico-social de América Latina (IDES/DE, 10:37, abril/junio 1970, p. 127-153)

A caustic survey of problems of social research in Latin America ranging from the nature of theory, the lack of data, the training of researchers to the effect of Camelot, the future of integration, and the mistaken efforts of much planning. Urges realism, feasibility and political sense in research.

Wolfe, Marshall. Development: images, conceptions, criteria, agents, choices. See item 8131.

4246. Woodhouse, Edward J. Re-visioning the future of the Third World: an ecological perspective on development (PUCIS/WP, 25:1, Oct. 1972, p. 1-33, tables)

The growth of GNP as a goal of development is misleading and in error. The ecological costs of affluence, the dwindling supplies of resources, population pressures make continued affluence for the rich unlikely and its achievement for the poor nations impossible. An international restructuring of goals is required.

4247. Wyndham-White, Eric and others. La integración latinoamericana en una etapa de decisiones. Introducción por Julio Lacarte Muró. B.A., Instituto para la Integración de América Latina (INTAL), 1973. 193 p., tables.

The general papers of a symposium on "Processes of Development" held in Montevideo, Sept. 1972. Contributors Wyndham-White, Bela Balassa, Prebisch, Enrique Iglesias, and Carlos Lleras Restrepo discuss "Economic, Social, and Political Integration." Others examine LAFTA and the Andino group and the European experience is considered in a final section.

4248. Zegers de Landa, Gerardo. El Pacto Andino y la industria subregional de artefactos de la línea blanca (UCC/CE, 8:25, dic. 1971, p. 111-147, tables)

An empirical attempt to measure the causes and effects of inter-group trade of refrigerators and stoves. Examines cost and price differences.

4249. *Zeitschrift für Geschichtswissenschaft.* Heft 6/8, Jahrgang 20, 1972- . Berlin.

Issue which includes a short interpretative essay examining Latin American economic development. [Hans J. Hoyer]

4250. Zéndegui, Guillermo de *comp.* Science, technology, and development: the consensus of Brasília (OAS/AM, 24:10, Oct. 1972, p. S1-S16, plates)

A popular and excerpted version of the final report of the Specialized Conference on the Application of Science and Technology in Latin America (CACTAL) held in Brasília, 12-19 May 1972. This version gives major highlights only.

4251. Zuvekas, Clarence, Jr. Concentration of political power and levels of economic development in Latin American countries: a comment (JDA, 8:4, July 1974, p. 507-512)

Methodological criticisms of James F. Torres' article "Concentration of Political Power . . ." in the *Journal of Developing Areas* (April 1973).

MEXICO

ROBERT L. BENNETT
Associate Professor of Economics
University of Maryland

THE MOST IMPRESSIVE ASPECT of the economic literature on Mexico in the current period is the relatively large number of excellent econometric studies. At the top of the list is the World Bank's multi-level planning study (item 4280). Several studies pertain to particular industries such as construction (items 4254 and 4263) energy production (item 4268), agriculture (items 4264 and 4290) and iron and steel (item 4303). An extremely important study of the effectiveness of monetary policy is the work by Nassef (item 4305). Some more specialized topics are covered in Barraza (item 4261) and Ladenson (item 4289), while the study by Huyser (item 4282) derives income elasticities of demand for a large number of commodity categories.

Agriculture continues to receive a great deal of attention, particularly since it is the sector in which Mexico's primary poverty problem is found. The major bibliographical work by Ríos (item 4312) will be of great assistance to the profession. The work by Fernández y Fernández (item 4275) is very helpful in understanding the minifundia problem. Other works which emphasize the minifundia and income distribution problem are Barkin (item 4259), Durán (item 4270), Paz Sánchez (item 4308), Puente Leyva (item 4310), Rivera Marín (item 4313), and Tello (item 4319). Additional works on agriculture which are worth noting include those by Cano and Winkelman (item 4264), Ciafardini (item 4267), Fernández y Fernández (item 4274), Fundación Alemana (item 4277), Ladman (item 4290), Martínez Escamilla and others (item 4298), Mendieta y Núñez (item 4299), and Noriega (item 4306).

Foreign trade and commercial policy is an area to which several good studies are devoted. Wionczek's and Leal's article (item 4323) is a masterpiece of policy recommendations concerning technology transfer. A major study of multinational corporations is the book by Sepúlveda and Chumacero (item 4314). The works by Aguilar (item 4252) and Zapata (item 4325) also concern the multinationals. König's study of Mexico's relations with the various efforts at economic integration in Latin America is a major aid in understanding the restrictions on such efforts and their likely success in the future. One should note also the article on tourism by Jud (item 4284) and the article on the foreign exchange liquidity trap by Ladenson (item 4289).

Three regional studies are included in the current period. The most comprehensive and interesting is the massive study of the Northwest by Bassols (item 4262). Cano and Winkelman's study is of the Puebla project and a case study of the Lerma-Santiago project is found in the book by the Fundación Alemana (item 4277).

In a class by itself is the important work on precolumbian economic relations in Mexico by Castillo Farreras (item 4265). The methodology of this work gives one greater confidence in the accuracy of its descriptions than in that of most earlier works.

In this section the reviewer has not included separately several recurring publications which may be of great interest to the researcher. Statistical data are available in the current editions of Banco de México's annual *Asamblea General de Accionistas;* Nacional Financiera's annual *Informe Anual* and bi-weekly *El Mercado de Valores;* Banco Nacional de Comercio Exterior's annual *Comercio Exterior de México* and monthly *Comercio Exterior;* Secretaría de Industria y Comercio's *Anuario de Estadística;* and Banco Nacional de México's quarterly *Review of the Economic Situation of Mexico.* The most comprehensive bibliographical information is found in Banco de México's annual *Bibliografía Económica de México* and bi-monthly *Boletín Bibliográfico.*

4252. Aguilar, Enrique. Criteria for measuring cost-benefits for foreign technology (*in* Driscoll, Robert E. and Harvey W. Wallender *eds.* Technology transfer and development: an historic and geographic perspective. N.Y., Fund for Multinational Management Education *in cooperation with* the Council of the Americas, 1974, p. 146-194)

The author explains some of the provisions and application of the new Mexican Law of Technology as they apply to multinational corporations.

Alisky, Marvin. CONASUPO: a Mexican agency which makes low-income workers feel their government cares. See item 8134.

———. Mexico versus Malthus: national trends. See item 8135.

4253. Alonso González, Francisco. Historia y petróleo: México en su lucha por la independencia económica, el problema del petróleo. México, Ediciones El Caballito, 1972. 322 p.

The author presents a history of the Mexican petroleum industry and advances the thesis that the expropriation of 1938 was the major step toward self-respect and self-reliance in Mexico's economic development. There is an introduction by E. Portes Gil, former President of Mexico.

4254. Araud, Christian. Generación de empleo en la construcción: el caso de una vivienda mínima en México (CM/DE, 7:2, 1973, p. 175-188, tables)

Ingenious use of input-output information for Mexico to estimate the direct and indirect employment of three classes of workers generated by the construction of a house. Extremely useful for estimating the employment generated in specific projects.

4255. Aubey, R.T. In the private sector: regional credit and the Mexican financial system (Growth and Change [Univ. of Kentucky, College of Business and Economics, Lexington] 2:4, Oct. 1971, p. 25-33)

4256. Ballance, R.H. Mexican agricultural policies and subsistence farming (AJES, 31:3, July 1972, p. 295-306)

4257. Banco Nacional de Comercio Exterior, *México.* México: la política económica para 1972. México, 1972. 353 p., tables.

Excellent source of 1971-72 policy statements by major government and quasi-government figures plus the texts of major new economic laws and regulations. The introductory chapters express the intentions of the current government to improve interpersonal and interregional income disparities.

4258. Barceló R., Víctor Manuel. Panorama económico del México moderno (Revista de Ciencias Económicas [B.A.] 5:8, julio/sept. 1970, p. 199-241, tables)

A quick history of modern Mexico with a largely admiring flavor.

Barkin, David. The demographic impact of regional development: a Mexican case study. See item 6656.

4259. ———. La persistencia de la pobreza en México: un analisis económico estructural (IDES/DE, 10:38, julio/sept. 1970, p. 263-284)

Argues against current Mexican development policies which result in high, rising incomes for the few and high rates of increase in GNP. Argues for direct government projects aimed at raising the real incomes of the majority of Mexican workers.

4260. Barona de la O., Miguel. Hacia una política de recursos humanos y pleno empleo (MSTPS/R, 2:1 [7. época] enero/marzo 1972, p. 15-21)

Cogently argues the case for economic planning which gives major attention to intelligent use and development of Mexico's human resources.

4261. Barraza, Luciano. The relevance of the theory of sectoral clashes to the Mexican economy (LARR, 4:3, 1969, p. 73-87, bibl., illus., tables)

Econometric study which finds little support for the hypothesis that the theory of sectoral clashes, developed some years ago to explain Chilean development, is relevant in Mexico.

4262. Bassols Batalla, Angel. El noroeste de México: un estudio geográfico-económico. México, UNAM, Instituto de Investigaciones Económicos, 1972. 622 p., bibl., tables.

A wide-ranging, erudite, multi-disciplinary study of the Mexican Northwest, which includes the states of Nayarit, Sinaloa, Sonora and Baja California together with Baja California Sur. Obviously a work of love based on the author's three decades of intimate experience with the region's economic and social development. Bassols shows how the region should and could develop with integrated planning for the 17 separate geographic-economic sub-regions. This planning should emphasize a decreasing reliance on the US market and a major reduction in *neo-latifundismo* and social exploitation.

4263. Boon, Gerard K. Empleo y vivienda en México: un estudio cuantitativo (CM/DE, 7:2, 1973, p. 189-202, tables)

Uses inout-output information to estimate the relative employment generated by the construction of a given value of different qualities of housing.

4264. Cano, Jairo and **Don Winkelmann.** Plan Puebla: un análisis de beneficios y costos (FCE/TE, oct./dic. 1972, p. 783-796, bibl., tables)

An excellent benefit-cost analysis of a plan which was effectuated in Puebla to improve yields in corn production. The plan is shown to have had a very high payoff.

4265. Castillo Farreras, Víctor M. Estructura económica de la sociedad mexicana según las fuentes documentales. Prólogo de Miguel León-Portilla. México, UNAM, Instituto de Investigaciones Históricas, 1972. 196 p., bibl., illus. (Serie de Cultura Náhuatl, monografías, 13)

An extremely important history of the economic structure of the Mexican society in the century before Cortez. The work's importance derives largely from the fact that almost the only sources are the codices and náhuatl texts, thus the "Europeanization" of the descriptions is largely avoided.

4266. Centro de Estudios Económicos del Sector Privado, *México*. Mecanismos de promoción a las exportaciones en México y otros países. México, 1972. 337 p.

The book lists methods of export promotion used in some 60 countries including Mexico and concludes that there are some methods which are used somewhere in the world but not at all or not sufficiently in Mexico. Naturally it is recommended that the Mexican government consider using these as well.

4267. Ciafardini, Horacio. México: la reforma agraria y los datos de 1960 (IDES/DE, 12:45, abril/junio 1972, p. 81-103, tables)

Data from the 1960s are used to show that the development of Mexican agriculture has been much more along capitalist than along socialist lines.

4268. Dagum, Camilo. Un modelo econométrico de la oferta y la demanda de energéticos: estudio de un caso, México (FCE/TE, 38[2]: 150, abril/junio 1971, p. 275-300, tables)

A distributed lag model is used to derive demand and supply equations for the different energy sources in Mexico. Separate equations are developed for petroleum and its derivatives, natural gas, all hydrocarbons, electricity, coal, and all sources.

4269. Dobner E., Horst K. Sistema y procedimientos de la tasación aplicados al planeamiento de nuevos sistemas catastrales. Toluca, Mex., Ediciones Gobierno del Estado de México, Dirección General de Hacienda, 1972. 77 p., bibl.

A discussion of definitions and practices that are important in assessing and taxing real estate—particularly in the state of México.

4270. Durán T., Marco Antonio. Apuntes acerca de la política agrícola mexicana (FCE/TE, 37:147, julio/sept. 1970, p. 525-536)

Many recommendations for improving the performance of the subsistence agriculture sector. Most of the recommendations are for improved planning and execution of current agrarian policies rather than for fundamental changes in the program.

Escamilla, Mercedes. Investigación socioeconómica directa de los ejidos de Aguascalientes. See item 6668.

4271. España Krauss, Emilio. Como exportar más. . . .pero mucho más a los E.U.A. México, n.p., 1969. 209 l.

For the first 50 p. the author argues that Mexico should export more to the US. The remainder of the book consists of US Dept. of Commerce figures for US imports from Mexico and all imports in 1967 and 1968.

4272. Evans, John S. Mexican border development and its impact upon the United States (South Eastern Latin Americanist [Florida State Univ., Tallahassee] 16:1, June 1972, p. 4-10)

A short history of border trade between Mexico and the US, emphasizing the recent Border Industrialization Program.

4273. Fernández, R.A. The Border Industrial Program on the United States-Mexican border (Review of Radical Political Economics [Union of Radical Political Economists, Ann Arbor Mich.] 5:1, Spring 1973, p. 37-52)

4274. Fernández y Fernández, Ramón. Cooperación agrícola y organización económica del ejido. México, Secretaría de Educación Pública, 1973. 175 p., bibl.

An introductory section consists of a general discussion of cooperatives, largely from European theory and practice. The bulk of the book is a good description of the economic organization (mostly the credit system) of the *ejido*.

4275. ———. Relaciones de la estructura de tenencia de la tierra con el crédito y el desarrollo agrícola (BNCE/CE, 22:5, mayo 1972, p. 428-437)

A reasonably thorough and careful evaluation of the problem of tiny land-holdings, both private and *ejidal*, and an assessment of the requirements for solutions.

4276. Franco diálogo entre gobierno y empresarios. México, Confederación Patronal de la República Mexicana, 1971. 98 p.

A pamphlet of press releases, interviews, etc. setting forth the views of COMPARMEX vis-à-vis Mexican governmental policy 1970-71. [J.M.Hunter]

4277. Fundación Alemana para los Países en Vías de Desarrollo, Berlin, FRG. Centro de Seminarios Internacionales. Seminario [de] planificación integrada de proyectos de irrigación: casos de estudio, 1970. Berlin, FRG, 1970. 160 l., maps.

Uses the Mexican plan for development of the Lerma-Santiago valley as one of three case studies for a seminar in integrated planning of irrigation projects.

4278. Germidis, Dimitrios A. The construction industry in Mexico. Paris, Organization for Economic Co-operation and Development, 1972. 91 p., bibl., tables.

This booklet contains a wealth of useful description of some aspects of Mexico's construction industry. Construction production and employment are related to several macro-economic variables in Ch. 1. Ch. 2 discusses low-cost housing production, needs, financing and plans. The final two chapters discuss unions and wages in the industry.

4279. Gilmore, Betty and **Don Gilmore.** Making money in Mexico and carefree retirement. Guadalajara, Mex., Lege-Quaeso Editores, 1972. 191 p., tables.

A cursory examination of Mexico for the potential private investor or retiree from the US.

4280. Goreux, Louis M. and **Alan S. Manne** eds. Multilevel planning: case studies in Mexico. Foreword by Hollis B. Chenery. Amsterdam, North-Holland and American Elsevier [N.Y.], 1973. 556 p., map, tables.

Easily the most important economics book on Mexico to appear recently. Pushes outward the frontiers of our knowledge of large scale, detailed mathematical programming techniques, especially the coordination of models at different levels of decision making. Since this is done with Mexican plans and statistics and with substantial participation of Mexican authors, it provides an excellent view of the potential effectiveness and possibilities of Mexican planning.

4281. Gutiérrez Santos, Luis E. Análisis de la eficiencia de la industria nacional de electricidad (BNCE/CE, 22:7, julio 1972, p. 610-614, bibl., tables)

Some factual material concerning the Mexican electricity industry, but primarily a case is made for using cost-benefit analysis in the industry's future decision making.

4282. Huyser, A.P. and **W.H. Somermeyer.** Elasticidades ingresos y cualitativas en México: una aplicación del modelo de asignación del gasto (CM/DE, 7:2, 1973, p. 203-237, tables)

A sophisticated econometric study using modern consumer theory to estimate income elasticities of demand for specific goods and services from the 1967 Mexican survey of household consumer expenditures.

4283. Ishii, Akira. Ejidos in Mexico: actual situation and problems (IAEA/DE, 11:3, Sept. 1973, p. 297-312, bibl., illus., tables)

Rather a cursory description of three ejidos in different parts of Mexico.

4284. Jud, G. Donald. Tourism and economic growth in Mexico since 1950 (IAMEA, 28:1, Summer 1974, p. 19-43, bibl., tables)

The paper emphasizes two major benefits of Mexico's sizeable and rapidly growing tourist industry: 1) employment for surplus agricultural labor, and 2) relaxation of the foreign-exchange constraint. Some attention is given to more indirect benefits and costs of tourism in Mexico.

4285. Kane, N.S. Bankers and diplomats: the diplomacy of the dollar in Mexico, 1921-1924 (HU/BHR, 47:3, Autumn 1973, p. 335-352)

4286. Katz, Bernard S. Mexican fiscal and subsidy incentives for industrial development (AJES, 31:4, Oct. 1972, p. 353-360, tables)

Elementary description of some Mexican "incentives" for industrialization.

4287. König, Wolfgang. México y la integración económica de América Latina. B.A., Instituto para la Integración de América Latina (INTAL), 1973. 313 p., tables.

One of the best works on the history and problems of liberalization of trade between Mexico and the rest of Latin America. The history of the past dozen years is emphasized and the author concludes that Mexico tends to sacrifice long-run developmental participation in the Latin American Free Trade Association for short-term commercial gains.

4288. Labastida, Horacio. Banco de datos censales para el desarrollo social. México, UNAM, Facultad de Ciencias Políticas y Sociales, 1972. 71 p.

After a plea for a national data bank for social statistics, the book reproduces a listing of social statistical series that were available in Mexico in 1966.

4289. Ladenson, Mark L. A foreign exchange liquidity trap for Mexico? East Lansing, Michigan State Univ., 1973. 10 p. (Workshop paper, 7209)

An excellent econometric test for the existence of the foreign exchange liquidity trap which Dwight Brothers and Leopolda Solís postulated for Mexico in 1966.

4290. Ladman, Jerry R. A model of credit applied to the allocation of resources in a case study of a sample of Mexican farms (UC/EDCC, 22:2, Jan. 1974, p. 279-301, illus., tables)

A very good economic analysis of the policy implications of insufficient ejidal credit to permit the ejidatario efficiently to allocate his resources.

4291. Laris Casillas, Jorge; José Merino Mañón; and **Jorge López Ochoa.** Sobre el impuesto predial. Toluca, Mex., Ediciones Gobierno del Estado de México, Dirección General de Hacienda, 1972. 172 p., illus., tables.

Three papers presented by officials of the Finance Ministry of the State of México at a conference of tax administrators in Panamá in 1971. Various aspects of property taxation in that state are discussed.

4292. Leal de Araujo, L. Extension of social security to rural workers in Mexico (ILO/R, 108:4, Oct. 1973, p. 295-312)

4293. López Rosado, Diego G. Curso de historia económica de México. México, UNAM, Instituto de Investigaciones Económicas, 1973. 529 p., bibl., tables.

This is the 3d. ed. of an excellent under-graduate Mexican economic history textbook which appeared first in 1954. Coverage ends in 1925—when the author feels the new Revolutionary government really began to govern effectively, thus ending the prior era.

4294. _____. Historia y pensamiento económico de México: finanzas públicas, obras públicas, v. 5. México, UNAM, Instituto de Investigaciones Economómicos, 1972. 435 p., bibl., maps, tables.

This volume on public finance and public works is the fifth in the series of textbooks (see *HLAS 34:1759* and *HLAS:35:1936*) by this distinguished author on the economic history and history of economic thought of Mexico prior to 1925. As is the case with the other volumes, this book provides indispensable background material for understanding Mexico's economic experience.

4295. Martínez Domínguez, Guillermo. Descentralización con desarrollo estatal y regional. México, n.p. 1972. 25 p.

Text of an interview of Guillermo Martínez Domínguez, Director of Nacional Financiera by Leopoldo Mendivil of *El Heraldo de Mexico*, 23 Nov. 1971.

4296. _____. Integración y desarrollo de la industria eléctrica de México: la obra 1965-1970 (FCE/TE, 38[2]:150, abril/junio 1971, p. 433-454, tables)

The author recounts the enormous developmental successes of the Mexican electricity industry during his years as Director General of the federal Electricity Commission.

4297. _____. Nacional Financiera promueve el desarrollo ecónomico de México. México, Nacional Financiera, 26 p.

A recounting by Nacional Financiera's director general of the many ways in which that institution has promoted the development of Mexico. Paper presented at the Seminario Internacional sobre el Papel de los Sectores Público y Privado en el Desarrollo Socioeconómico, 15-19 Nov. 1971, México.

4298. Martínez Escamilla, Ramón; Silvia Millan; Gloria González Salazar; and **Arturo Bonilla.** En torno al problema argícola de México (UNAM/PDD, 2:9, oct./dic. 1971, p. 25-96)

Four critiques of the three-vol. *Estructura agraria y desarrollo agrícola en México* by the Center for Agrarian Studies. The authors are criticized severely for their apparent subservience to the *status quo*.

4299. Mendieta y Núñez, Lucio. Las desviaciones de la reforma agraria. México, Asociación Nacional de Abogados, Academia de Derecho Agrario, 1972. 45 p. (Monografías agrarias, 8)

An extraordinarily well-informed and dispassionate discussion of reasons for the shortcomings of the agrarian reform.

4300. Merino Mañón, José. La fiscalidad del suelo y el desarrollo urbano. Toluca, Mex., Ediciones Gobierno del Estado de Mexico, Dirección General de Hacienda, 1972. 106 p. (Col. Estudios fiscales, 4)

An up-to-date, thorough description of the property taxation system in the State of México, which system is newly revised and apparently becoming quite advanced.

4301. Meyer L., Consuelo. Observaciones acerca de la actividad comercial en México (*in* Extremos de México: homenaje a don Daniel Cossío Villegas. México,

El Colegio de México, Centro de Estudios Históricos, 1971, p. 191-224, tables)

A thorough, reasoned discussion of the reasons for an importance of Mexico's having one of the world's highest ratios of commercial activities to total product.

4302. Nacional Financiera, *México.* La economía mexicana en cifras, 1970. Mèxico, 1972. 353 p., tables.

The most complete statistical source on the Mexican economy. This 1970 ed. brings most series up through 1969, but many extend through 1970.

4303. _____, _____. La industria siderúrgica nacional y el Proyecto Siderúrgico Lázaro Cárdenas: Las Truchas. México, 1972. 241 p., maps, tables.

Primarily a benefit-cost analysis of the Lázaro Cárdenas - Las Truchas steel project, but a good study of the Mexican steel industry is included.

4304. _____, _____. Morelos. México, 1972. 1 v. (Unpaged) illus., maps, plates, tables (Cuaderno, 15)

This is one of a series of information booklets on each of the Mexican states and which are designed to advertise the desirability of the state as a location for industry.

4305. Nassef, El Sayed. Monetary policy in developing countries: the Mexican case, an econometric study. Rotterdam, The Netherlands, Rotterdam Univ. Press, 1972. 250 p. bibl., tables.

Excellent econometric study of the effectiveness of monetary policy in promoting economic development, using Mexico as a case study. Anyone interested in the Mexican financial system and in monetary policy should read it carefully.

4306. Noriega, José Sotero. Desconcertantes panoramas de México: problemas de México vistos por un viejo. México, Tesis Rendiz, 1974. 803 p., maps, tables.

Approximately half of this book is a reprint of a 1931 work on Mexican Agrarian Reform by the author. Another 150 p. brings that subject up to 1966. Relatively minor parts of the book discuss the Tehuantepec Canal project favorably and Mexico's population, climate and resources. Noriega's position on the agrarian reform is strongly antagonistic, particularly in the matter of *ejidos*.

4307. Pacheco, Bernardo. México y la sociedad de consumo (ISTMO, 74, mayo/junio 1971, p. 39-43, plates)

Questions the desirability of Mexico's trying to become a consumption-oriented society in which goods rather than people are most important.

4308. Paz Sánchez, Fernando. Mexico: agricultura y subdesarrollo (UNAM/PDD, 1:2, enero/marzo 1970, p. 17-42, tables)

Brief discussion of several authors' points of view on the problem of low agricultural labor productivity in Mexico.

4309. Perrakis, S. The labor surplus model and wage behaviour in Mexico (Industrial Relations [Univ. of California, Institute of Industrial Relations, Berkeley] 11:1, Feb. 1972. p. 80-95)

4310. Puente Leyva. Recursos y crecimiento del sector agropecuario en México: 1930-1967 (FCE/TE, 38 [2]: 150, abril/junio 1971, p. 515-552, tables)

Traces the history of the agricultural sector since 1930 and finds in the last decade a slowing of growth in output, productivity, and capital accumulation in the sector. Suggests provision of capital such as irrigation to small farmers.

4311. Reyes Heroles, Jesús. México y su petróleo (CAM, 170:, mayo/junio 1970, p. 7-28, illus.)

A presentation by the Director of Petróleos Mexicanos at the 32nd anniversary of the expropriation of the petroleum companies. A recent history of the industry is presented.

4312. Ríos, Jorge Martínez. Tenencia de la tierra y desarrollo agrario en México: bibliografía selectiva y comentada; 1522-1968. México, UNAM, Instituto de Investigaciones Sociales, 1970. 305 p., bibl.

Annotated bibliography of 1553 works on Mexican agriculture which appeared between 1522 and 1968, with approximately 50 p. of introduction and overview. Should be consulted immediately by anyone planning to write on agrarian problems from an historical perspective.

4313. Rivera Marín, Guadalupe. Los mercados internos: uno de los grandes problemas del desarrollo econômoco de México (FCE/TE, 39:153, enero/marzo 1972, p. 111-124, tables)

The author argues that currently the primary restraint on further development of the production of non-luxury consumer goods in Mexico is inadequate internal markets. Shows that this inadequacy is the result of regional and occupational disparities in income.

4314. Sepúlveda, Bernardo and **Antonio Chumacero.** La inversión extranjera en

México. México, Fondo de Cultura Económica, 1973. 262 p., tables.

The book is especially useful as the best collection of statistics on foreign investment in Mexico in recent years. Particular attention is given to the harmful effects on Mexico of the large US multinational corporations.

4315. Shafer, Robert Jones. Mexican business organizations: history and analysis. Syracuse, N.Y., Syracuse Univ. Press, 1973. 397 p., bibl., tables.

An extraordinarily thorough description, history and analysis of the Mexican organizations of private businesses—national and local chambers of commerce and industry, etc. For historian's comment see *HLAS 36:2151*.

4316. Solís M., Leopoldo. Controversias sobre el crecimiento y la distribución: las opiniones de economistas mexicanas acerca de la política económica. México, Fondo de Cultura Económica, 1972. 230 p., bibl.

Three essays by this distinguished Mexican author. The first is an extension of his previous work in English on Mexican economists and their thought (see *HLAS 33:2729*). The second is a short essay on Mexican nationalism and political economy; the third argues for a reorientation of political economy toward emphasis on investment in human capital.

4317. ———. México en la posguerra: los economistas y la política económica. Bogotá, Fundación para la Educación Superior y el Desarrollo, 1973. 85 p.

Spanish version of *HLAS 35:2729*.

4318. Syrquin, M. Efficient input frontiers for the manufacturing sector in Mexico 1965-1980 (International Economic Review [Kansai Keizai Rengokai, Osaka, Japan] 14:3, Oct. 1973, p. 657-675)

4319. Tello, Carlos. Notas para el análisis de la distribución personal del ingreso en México (FCE/TE, 38[2]:150, abril/junio 1971, p. 629-657, tables)

Mexico's very unequal personal distribution of income is attributed to concentration of ownership of means of production, increased proletarianization, reduced relative unionization, insufficient education, and insufficient mobility of workers.

4320. Velasco, Gustavo R. El camino de la abundancia: una política social y económica para México. México, Editorial Humanidades, 1973. 336 p.

A collection of speeches, papers, interviews, etc., by the author which occurred roughly in the period since 1958. The recurrent theme is the von Mises, von Hayek style of "liberal" economic doctrine set in a Mexican context.

4321. Viscaya Canales, Isidro. Internal and external factors in the development of Monterrey as an industrial center (South Eastern Latin Americanist [Florida State Univ., Tallahassee] 16:1, June 1972, p. 1-4)

A very short business history of Monterrey.

4322. Watanabe, S. Constraints on labor-intensive export industries in Mexico (ILO/R, 109:1, Jan. 1974, p. 23-45)

4323. Wionczek, Miguel S. and **Luisa María Leal.** Toward rationalization of the transfer of technology to Mexico (BNCE/CE, 18:7, July 1972, p. 10-16)

An excellent article containing a wealth of practical recommendations which, if followed, would vastly improve the relative bargaining effectiveness of Mexico in obtaining foreign technology.

4324. Yarza C., Alberto J. El futuro del proceso de industrialización en México (FCE/TE, 38/151, julio/sept. 1971, p. 793-816, tables)

Argues for improved performance and efficiency of Mexican industry in the future through better planning at a macroeconomic level, better performance of interested government agencies, and, particularly, greater reliance on foreign competition to force efficiency.

4325. Zapata, Fausto. México: notas sobre el sistema político y la inversión extranjera. Washington, The Johns Hopkins Univ., School of Advanced International Studies, 1974. 64 p.

The author recounts post-revolutionary Mexican history, particularly as it relates to private foreign investment. He discusses the recent Law Promoting Domestic Investment and Regulating Foreign Investment as being far from anti-foreign. The law is reproduced in an appendix.

THE WEST INDIES AND CENTRAL AMERICA

(Except Puerto Rico and Cuba)

MARION HAMILTON GILLIM
Distinguished Professor of Economics
Eastern Kentucky University

TOPICS OF WIDESPREAD CURRENT INTEREST begin to appear in books and journal articles with a lag of one or more years. Thus unlike the columns of the daily press, the writings noted here have not yet taken up the pressing world problems of inflation, recession, and energy shortages. Unemployment is discussed in a number of the works below, but more as the problem of surplus population in underdeveloped countries than as a feature of an economic cycle. The chief economic topics of this region of Latin America continue to be development and integration, but some changes in emphasis over the previous two years can be noted.

Increasing attention appears to be directed toward the role of agriculture in development. For some time, although agriculture is the most important industry, the tendency has been to regard it as a symbol of a lack of development and to see manufacturing as the more worthwhile sector of the economy. Now agriculture is being examined for its capacity to offer employment, to supply food and fiber at home and save spending for foreign agricultural products, and to provide a source of foreign exchange through farm exports, with a new emphasis on tropical fruits and vegetables. Agriculture is also coming to be recognized as a potential source of tax revenue as yet hardly tapped.

The types of questions asked suggest some dissatisfaction with the kind of development that has occured and its results. Such questions include the following: Are the proffered incentives encouraging the most desirable kinds of investment? Is foreign investment and the multinational corporation leading to a general and healthy development of the economy? When economic growth takes place, do only a few enjoy its benefits? Is investment so capital intensive that it does little to employ the surplus labor force? How can the universities sponsor programs to help reduce a nation's dependency?

The Central American Common Market is still one of the main topics in this part of Latin America, but for some writers the tone has changed from one of almost unlimited optimism to one of doubt and pessimism as to the capacity of the organization to reach its goals. An increased number of articles on CARIFTA and the newer CARICOM have appeared. Several authors now write about the entire Caribbean region which encompasses: the Caribbean islands, Central America and the South American countries that border on the Caribbean Sea. It is tempting to suggest that the perception of this entire area as a unit is an outgrowth of the several movements towards economic integration.

It is encouraging to note the continued development of the use of statistics including the interpretation of census materials, the making of sample surveys, and the development of a new consumer price index for Santo Domingo.

Special attention is called to the collection and review by F. Andic and S. Andic of two decades of research and writing on the public sector of the Greater Caribbean. It is important in the field of public finance as a bibliography with an interpretative introduction. In addition, it is important in setting forth clearly the scope and growth of this literature for the Greater Caribbean Area. An increased interest in public finance and a greater role for government has accompanied both the planning, programming, and arranging incentives for economic development and the increased need for fiscal harmonization as a part of the moves toward economic integration.

WEST INDIES
(except Puerto Rico and Cuba)

4326. Andic, Fuat M. and Suphan Andic. The role of the public sector in the economic development of the greater Caribbean: a survey and commentary (LARR, 8:1, Spring 1973, p. 97-134, bibl.)

An important bibliography with significant comments on research and publication in the field of public finances and their role in furthering economic development in the Caribbean, and also in Central America, the three Guianas, Venezuela, and Colombia. A valuable aid for further research.

4327. Ascuasiati, Carlos. Diez años de economía dominicana. Santo Domingo, Ediciones de Taller, 1971. 43 p., tables (Col. Debate, 1)

The third ed. of this study comparing economic growth in the years 1950-64 with that in 1966-70.

4328. _____ . Diez años de economía dominicana (Revista de Ciencias Económicas [Univ. Autónoma de Santo Domingo] 1[1], marzo/junio 1972, p. 64-106, tables)

See preceding item 4327.

4329. _____ ; Bolívar Batista; and Ramón Flores. Una metodología de investigación económica para Latinoamérica y su aplicación a la República Dominicana (Ciencia [Santo Domingo] 1:1, mayo/junio 1972, p. 77-110, bibl., tables)

A mathematical model of an open economy designed to be applicable to underdeveloped countries and especially to problems of the Dominican Republic.

4330. Asociación de Libre Comercio del Caribe: CARIFTA (*in* Comunidad del Caribe—CARICOM. B.A., Banco Interamericano del Desarrollo, Instituto para la Integración de América Latina-INTAL, 1974, p. 211-244 [Sección, 5])

Concise and authoritative description of this new common market.

4331. Banco Central de Venezuela. Sección Integración. La Associación de Libre Comercio del Caribe—CARIFTA (Revista del Banco Central de Venezuela [Caracas] 32:323/325, enero/marzo 1972, p. 11-40, bibl., tables)

A useful description of the organization and its development bank with an appropriate examination of Venezuela's trade with its newly integrated neighbors.

4332. Baum, Daniel Jay. The banks of Canada in the Commonwealth Caribbean: economic nationalism and multinational enterprises of a medium power. N.Y., Praeger, 1974. 158 p., tables (Praeger special studies in international economics and development)

A comprehensive examination of the problems from both the Canadian and Caribbean sides.

4333. Budhoo, Davison L. The integrated theory of development theory: an initial statement. Mona, Jam., Univ. of the West Indies, Institute of Social and Economic Research, 1973. 79 p., bibl., table.

The author addresses this paper to the providers of aid. He examines critically some existing theories comparing project and programme-aid and offers an approach to the disbursement of aid designed to generate the most economic development.

4334. Corten, André. Sous-emploi et unites budgetaires familiales dans l'economie sucrière des Antilles (UPR/CS, 12:1, April 1972, p. 15-31, bibl., tables)

Discusses some possible effects on family life and patterns of expenditure of the seasonal nature of the sugar crop.

4335. Costa Rica. Programa Integral de Mercadero Agropecuario (PIMA). Como fomentar mejoras en el sistema de mercadeo de productos alimenticios en Costa Rica. 2. ed. San José. Instituto de Fomento y Asesoría Municipal, 1973. 82 p., bibl., maps, tables (Serie: Investigaciones, 201)

Recommendations for modernization designed to benefit buyers and sellers of farm products, prepared by employees of both the national government and the municipality of San José with consultants from Michigan State Univ.

4336. Demas, William G. The political economy of the English speaking Caribbean: a summary view. Bridgetown, Barbados, Caribbean Ecumenical Consultation for Development, 1972? 35 p., plates (Study paper, 4)

A background paper prepared by an economist from Trinidad and Tobago for a Conference of Churches. Offers some interdisciplinary proposals for change and growth.

Desruisseaux, Jacques. La structure foncière de la Martinique. See item 1227.

4337. Día de la Estadística Nacional: reseña histórica de la Cuarta Conmemoración, 1970. Santo Domingo, Oficina Nacional de Estadística, 1971. 87 p., illus.

The fourth annual celebration since its establishment in 1967. Publication contains some statements of statistical achievements in the country and of the value placed on them.

4338. Dominican Republic. Banco Central de la República Dominicana.

Oficina Nacional de Estadística. Estudio sobre presupuestos familiares. v. 1, Ingresos y gastos de las familias en la Ciudad de Santo Domingo, 1969. v. 2, Distribución del gasto de las familias en la Ciudad de Santo Domingo, 1969. v. 3, Metodología para el cálculo del indice de precios al consumidos en la Ciudad de Santo Domingo, 1969. v. 4, Indice de precios al consumidor en la Ciudad de Santo Domingo, 1960-1970. Santo Domingo, Agencia Internacional para el Desarrollo (USAID), 1971/1972. 4 v. (133, 145, 422, 158 p.) maps, tables.

A valuable and detailed presentation of the planning, execution, and results of a survey of the incomes and expenditures of 552 households in the capital city and the calculation of the consumer price index with weights drawn from the survey. The volumes include: I. The sample, the interviews, the results. II. Items purchased classified by family income. III. The prices obtained, the choice of a formula for the index. IV. The index, 1960-70.

4339. Economie antillaise. Paris, Editions Desormeaux, 1973. 416 p., illus., maps, plates, tables (Encyclopédie antilaise, 4)

Excellent reference source on the French Antilles covers geography, demography, history, social structure, future prospects and three case studies:
Louis Suivant "Présentation Géographique" p. 13-50
Francis Rifaux "Situation Démographique" p. 51-140
René Achéen "Fondements Historiques" p. 141-204
Alain Buffon "Structure Actuelles" p. 205-336
Jean Crusol "Trois Modèles Caribéens: le Barbade, Trinidad and Tobago, and Porto-Rico: Mythe ou Miracle?" p. 353-414. [Asst. Ed.]

Ehrlich, Allen S. Ecological perception and economic adaptation in Jamaica. See item 1229.

4340. Fletcher, L.P. The decline of friendly societies in Grenada: some economic aspects (UPR/CS, 12:2, July 1972, p. 99-111, tables)

This movement in Grenada through which members join to help each other in financing illness and funerals has declined under inflation, improved wages, and government neglect.

4341. Floyd, Barry. This changing world: agriculture in Jamaica (GA/G, 57:254, Jan. 1972, p. 32-36, illus., table)

Brief analysis of the Census of Agriculture of 1968-69 revealing disappointing data on the size of land holdings, the area under cultivation, and the number of farm workers.

4342. Girvan, Norman. Foreign capital and economic underdevelopment in Jamaica. Mona, Jam., Univ. of the West Indies, Institute of Social and Economic Research, 1971. 282 p., bibl., maps, tables.

A Jamaican economist offers suggestions to his government for improving the current situation in which he finds that foreign investment has produced economic growth without reducing poverty and dependency. Includes charts.

4343. _____. Teorías de dependencia económica en el Caribe y la América Latina: un estudio comparativo (FCE/TE, 40[4]: 160, oct./dic. 1973, p. 855-892, tables)

An analytical comparison of the thinking evolved independently under Raul Prebisch in Latin America and under W. Arthur Lewis and others in the English-speaking Caribbean.

4344. Gómez, Luis. La cuestión de las relaciones de producción en la sociedad dominicana (Ciencia [Santo Domingo] 1:1, mayo/junio 1972, p. 49-76, tables)

The first two sections on industrial production and agricultural production of a three-section essay adapting Marxist analysis to the Dominican situation.

4345. Haiti. Priorités de la planification et projections quinquennales. v. 1. Port-au-Prince, Presses Nationales d'Haiti, 1972. 31 p., plate, tables.

Recent growth, government priorities, investments, and expenditures with budget projections to 1976.

4346. _____. **Conseil National de Développement et de Planification (CONADEP). Bureau de Développement Régional.** Haiti: mission d'assistance technique intégrée. Washington, Organization of American States, General Secretariat, 1972. 3 v. in 1 (656 p.) maps, plates, tables.

The country's needs and resources with specific recommendations for economic development. This comprehensive report contains within its covers three volumes: 1) *Institutional development;* 2) *Sectoral development;* and 3) *Natural resources.* A useful set of maps on transport, population, soil, water use, geology, and education is provided under separate cover. An English summary precedes the French text.

Harewood, J. Changes in the demand for the supply of labour in the Commonwealth Caribbean: 1946-1960. See item 6565.

4347. Jamaica. Bank of Jamaica. Research Department. Balance of payments of Jamaica: 1972. Kingston, 1972. 37 p., tables.

Especially interesting because of the separate presentation of statistics on trade with CARIFTA.

4348. _____. **Department of Statistics.** Electricity and water supply. Kingston, 1973, 13 p., tables (Facts on Jamaica)

One of a series (see items 4349-4353) of useful government reports giving social and economic information scheduled to be published later in a yearbook form. This report describes the institutions responsible for electricity and water and presents statistics on their consumption.

4349. _____. _____. The labour force: 1968, 1969. Kingston, 1971. 61 p., tables (Facts on Jamaica)

The first published sample survey of Jamaica's labor force. Plans call for a continuous series based on periodic surveys.

4350. _____. _____. Mineral production. Kingston, 1973. 16 p., tables (Facts on Jamaica)

Like item 4348, this report includes information on bauxite and alumina companies and statistics on the reproduction and marketing of minerals.

4351. _____. _____. Physiography. Kingston, 1973. 35 p., tables (Facts on Jamaica)

Like item 4348, it consists of a detailed geographic description, including geology, and climate, sections on caves and mineral springs.

4352. _____. _____. Tourism. Kingston, 1973. 13 p., tables (Facts on Jamaica)

Like item 4348, this report contains statistics on number of tourists, their origin and length of stay.

4353. _____. _____. Trade and price indexes. Kingston, 1973. 28 p., tables (Facts on Jamaica)

Like item 4348, this report includes indices of price, volume and value of trade; consumer prices; and retail prices. Also provides the formulas for their construction.

4354. _____. **Ministry of Finance and Planning.** Town Planning Department. A national physical plan for Jamaica: 1970-1990. Kingston, 1971. 116 p., maps, plates, tables.

A 20-year program for both urban and rural land use in manufacturing, mining, tourism, and transportation with consideration of the needs of the population for housing, education, health, recreation, and employment. This study was financed by the UN Fund Project "Assistance in Physical Development Planning".

4355. Lockward Artiles, Andrés. Economía y cooperativismo: incidencia del cooperativismo en la economía dominicana. Santo Domingo, Editora del Caribe, 1971. 179 p., tables.

Present and potential advantages of the cooperative movement for the people of the Dominican Republic; its current status there; and recommendations for its future use.

4356. McIntyre, Alister. Current problems of economic integration: the effect of reverse preference on trade among developing countries. Geneva, United Nations Conference on Trade and Development (UNCTAD), 1974. 105 p., tables (United Nations publication, TD/B/435)

In Ch. 4 "Reverse Preferences in the Commonwealth Caribbean," (p. 39-60) the author, an economist of the region, states that it " . . . can be said to have the largest stake in the system of Commonwealth preferences."

4357. Manzano, Alfredo and **Marcelo Jorge.** La investigación tecnológica y el desarrollo racional dominicano (Ciencia [Santo Domingo] 1:1, mayo/junio 1972, p. 33-42, bibl.)

A proposed program of studies for the Autonomous Univ. of Santo Domingo to help the country counteract its dependent role as a supplier of raw materials.

4358. Messina Matos, Milton. La integración económica del Caribe. Santo Domingo, La Editora Cultural Dominicana, 1972. 358 p., bibl., tables.

A useful compilation of documents and statistics on CARIFTA and a description of its institutions and achievements in intraregional trade prepared for the Dominican office of export promotion.

4359. Mulchansingh, Vernon C. The bauxite/alumina industry of Jamaica (USM/JTG, 33, Dec. 1971, p. 20-30, maps, tables)

Compares the Jamaican bauxite industry with world production and consumption of aluminum. Because the industry in Jamaica consists largely of mining bauxite without further processing, the impact on the Jamaican economy is disappointing.

4360. Munroe, Trevor. The politics of constitutional decolonization: Jamaica, 1944-62. Mona, Jam., Univ. of the West Indies, Institute of Social and Economic Research, 1972. 239 p., bibl., tables.

A straight forward descriptive account of the process of Jamaican independence. Of particular interest is the epilog which describes the political economy in the years 1962-70. [J.M. Hunter]

4361. Nunes, Fred. Social structure, values and business policy in the Caribbean (UWI/CQ, 19:3, Sept. 1973, p. 62-76)

As an aid to business enterprise suggests possible changes in a social environment still somewhat stratified by color and classes of immigration. Suggested directions of change include radio programs, indigenous industries and their location.

4362. Odle, Maurice. A note on the share of wages and choice of labour subsidy in labour surplus economies (UPR/CS, 12:1, April 1972, p. 89-98, tables)

Proposals for subsidies to the hiring of workers in developing countries suffering from unemployment instead of incentives to capital-intensive production.

Oxaal, Ivar. The dependency economist as grassroots politician in the Caribbean. See item 1279.

4363. Pierre-Charles, Gérard. Dependencia e industrialización en las Antillas y en América Central (UNAM/RMS, 35:4, oct./dic. 1973, p. 783-799, bibl.)

Classification and illustrations of types and stages of dependency in the Greater Caribbean region.

4364. Ramsaran, Ramesh. Commonwealth Caribbean integration: progress, problems and prospects (IAMEA, 28:2, Autumn 1974, p. 39-50, tables)

A pessimistic appraisal of the future of the area's development through economic integration unless economic, regional, long-term goals come to transcend the political, national, short-term ones.

4365. Statement of Jamacanisation. Kingston, Farquharson Institute of Public Affairs, 1971. 3 p. (mimeo)

Proposes giving consideration of the use of subsidiary companies in the fields of banking and insurance because Jamaican purchase could give rise to problems in raising and exporting capital.

4366. Trinidad and Tobago. Ministry of Finance. Estimates of the revenues and expenditure of the Statutory Boards and similar bodies: 1969-1970. 5 v. (315, 30, 184, 30, 314 p.) tables.

Parts of a series on government expenditures, published annually by the government. An important source of information for anyone interested in Trinidad and Tobago.

4367. Vega, Bernardo. Evaluación de la política de industrialización de la Republica Dominicana. Santo Domingo, n.p., 1973. 221 p., bibl., tables.

On the assumption that some industries do more harm than good, this evaluation seeks to learn whether the laws providing incentives and benefits to investment aid those industries yielding a net benefit.

4368. Vilas, Carlos María. Aspectos estructurales de la dominación social en la República Dominicana (IDES/DE, 14:53, abril/junio 1974, p. 93-130, tables)

Class structure of Dominican society under Trujillo and afterwards through the 1960s.

Williams, R.L. Jamaican coffee supply, 1953-1968: an exploratory study. See item 6599.

CENTRAL AMERICA

4369. Aguilar Bulgarelli, Oscar; Carlos Araya Pochet; and Niní de Mora. El desarrollo nacional en 150 años de vida independiente. Ciudad Universitaria Rodrigo Facio, Univ. de Costa Rica [and] Comisión Nacional del Sesquicentenario de la Independencia de Centro América, 1971. 401 p., bibl., plates (Serie historia y geografía, 12)

Among sections on political institutions, education, the arts, and the press are two concentrated, informative chapters on Costa Rican industrial and banking development.

4370. Aitken, Norman D. and William R. Lowry. A cross-sectional study of the effects of LAFTA and CACM on Latin American trade (JCMS, 11:4, June 1973, p. 326-336, tables)

A statistical study using UN and SIECA data through 1967 in a regression analysis.

4371. Arias Sánchez, Oscar. Barriers to development in Costa Rica (SID/IDR, 15:2, 1973, p. 5-9)

An address by the Minister of Planning recognizing his country's progress towards economic development and analyzing the difficulties in the way of achieving an equitable distribution among all the people of the benefits of that growth.

4372. Asociación Salvadoreña de Industriales. San Salvador, 1973. 1 v. (Unpaged)

A directory and classification by industry and product, compiled from information supplied by the members.

4373. Baer, Donald E. Income and export taxation of agriculture in Costa Rica and Honduras (JDA, 8:1, Oct. 1973, p. 39-53, tables)

Reviews the two taxes in both countries. Shows that except for coffee and banana production, agriculture— the dominant industry—provides proportionately little government revenue.

4374. Browning, David. The rise and fall of the Central American Common Market (JLAS, 6:1, May 1974, p. 161-168)

An article reviewing three books: D.H. McClelland *The Central American Common Market* (see HLAS 35:1972); I.C. Orantes, *Regional integration in Central America;* and G.W. Wynia, *Politics and planners.* The first book is by an economist and the other two by political scientists.

4375. *Carta Económica Mensual.* Banco Nacional de Panamá, División de Planificación y Asesoria Económica, No. 16/18, oct./feb. 1972/1973- Panamá.

Each issue presents 20 to 30 p. of useful current information on money and banking, public finance, agriculture, business and commerce, construction, education, and health with an annex giving statistics in varied fields.

4376. Carvajal, Manuel J. and **David T. Geithman.** An economic analysis of migration in Costa Rica (UC/EDCC, 23:1, Oct. 1974, p. 105-122, tables)

Data from the 1963 Population and Housing Census, a sample drawn from it, and a model are used to study which groups migrate, why, the direction and distance migrated, and the effects on income.

4377. Censos nacionales de 1970: III censo agropecuario, 16 de mayo de 1971; cifras preliminares. Panamá, Dirección de Estadística y Censo, 1971. 26 p., tables.

Preliminary results obtained by sampling the data.

Cervantes Acuña, Carlos F. and **Roy McDonald Bourne.** Consumo industrial de frutas y hortalizas en Costa Rica durante 1972. See item 6614.

4378. Christou, G. and **W.T. Wilford.** Trade intensification in the Central American Common Market (UM/JIAS, 15:2, May 1973, p. 249-264, bibl., tables)

A theoretical paper finding that trade did indeed intensify in the CACM. It uses a model of trade flows to test for changes in trade within the market and with selected outside partners, during the period from 1960 (before CACM) and 1968 (before hostilities between Honduras and El Salvador).

4379. Cochrane, James D. and **John W. Sloan.** LAFTA and the CACM: a comparative analysis of integration in Latin America (JDA, 8:1, Oct. 1973, p. 13-37, tables)

A non-technical comparison of the origins, successes and failures, and continuing problems of these two major attempts at economic integration. Addressed especially to policy makers.

Coyner, Mary S. Agriculture and trade of El Salvador. See item 6622.

Elbow, Gary S. The impact of industrial development in Guatemala: a case study. See item 6628.

4380. Estudio de la industria de comercio. Tegucigalpa, Ministerio de Trabajo y Previsión Social, Depto. Nacional de Salarios, 1970. 178 p., tables.

A sample study with the results classified by three zones of the country and by the line of goods sold. The data are for 1964 and 1965 and include the number of employees, hours worked, and salaries earned; and the income and expenditures of the enterprises.

4381. Fabbrica Italiana Automobili Torino (FIAT), *Buenos Aires.* Oficina de Estudios para la Colaboración Económica Internacional. Mercado Común Centroamericano. B.A., 1968. 326 p., illus., maps, plates, tables (Síntesis económica y financiera, 2)

Economic, social, and geographic information on each of the five countries and on the CACM as a whole. The time series are still useful for observing changes in the common market during its first eight years.

4382. Facio B., Rodrigo. Obras. v. 1, Estudio sobre economía costarricense. San José, Editorial Costa Rica, 1972. 415 p., bibl., tables.

The first of a projected series of five volumes of the works of this distinguished Costa Rican economist. The selections in this volume include his valued thesis on the Costa Rican economy.

4383. Fuentes Mohr, Alberto. La creación de un Mercado Común: apuntes históricos sobre la experiencia de Centroamérica. B.A., Banco Interamericano de Desarrollo, Instituto para la Integración deAmérica Latina (INTAL) 1973. 270 p.

The background period, 1823-1950, followed by a documented history of the decade, 1951-62, written by an important participant in the events.

Galindo Pohl, Reynaldo. Condicionamiento sociopolítico de la integración. See item 8182.

4384. Gollás, Manuel. Mano de obra excedente y eficiencia económica en el sector tradicional de una economía dual: el caso de Guatemala (FCE/TE, 40[3]:159, julio/sept. 1973, p. 569-585, bibl., tables)

Spanish version of item 4385.

4385. ———. Surplus labour and economic efficiency in the traditional sector of a dual economy: the Guatemalan case (JDS, 8:4, July 1972, p. 411-423, bibl., tables¡

A statistical study using a sample survey of 348 highland farms to study an important issue of development economics, whether labor is redundant and resources inefficiently used in the traditional sector.

4386. Heath, Dwight B. Central America: un-common market (CUH, 64:378, Feb. 1973, p. 72-76, 85, 88)

A non-technical and pessimistic comment with a report of recent events in each Central American country including British Honduras and Panama as well as the CACM.

4387. Honduras. Instituto Nacional Agrario. 3 [i.e. Tres] años de labor: 1968, 1969, 1970. Tegucigalpa, 1971. 1 v. (Unpaged) illus., maps. plates.

The achievements and plans resulting from the activation of the 1962 Law of Agrarian Reform including sections on technical assistance, financing, acquisition of land, cooperatives and education.

4388. Hooker Cabrera, Herman. El Banco Centroamericano de Integración Económica (CM/FI, 13[52]:4, abril/junio 1973, p. 469-489, tables)

A challenging examination of the disproportionate distribution of the benefits of the CACM among its members and the difficulties posed for the Central American Bank for Economic Integration.

4389. Huezo Selva, Rafael. El espacio económico más singular del continente americano. San Salvador, The Author, 1972. 201 p., maps, tables.

A popular description of the economy of El Salvador with heavy emphasis on agriculture. Considerable comparison (e.g., gross product per square mile, cement production per square mile) with other Latin American countries. [J.M. Hunter]

4390. Informe al Gobierno de la República de Honduras sobre las cooperativas sindicales. Geneva, Oficina Internacional del Trabajo, Programa Regular de Asistencia Técnica, 1970. 37 p.

ILO expert, Frank C. Helm, following his mission in 1969-70 presents this report on the situation of workers' cooperatives in Honduras and his recommendations for improving them.

Jerez, César. La United Fruit Company en Guatemala. See item 6629.

4391. Kalnins, Arvids. Tributos municipales costarricenses: análisis crítico y perspectivas. San José, Instituto de Fomento y Asesoria Municipal, 1972. 193 p., tables (Serie documentos municipales, 1)

Description of taxes and a much needed compilation and analysis of the laws. Prepared by a UN consultant and published as the first of a projected series on the neglected subject of local government activities.

Lewis, A.B. Santa Ana Mixtan: a bench mark study on Guatemalan agriculture. See item 6630.

4392. El Mercado Común Centroamericano (*in* Inter-American Development Bank. Instituto para la Integración de América Latina. El proceso de integración en América Latina. B.A., 1974, p. 203-209)

Records and evaluates the progress of the CACM in recent years with statistics through 1973.

4393. Merrill, William C.; Lehman B. Fletcher; Randall A. Hoffmann; and Michael J. Applegate. Panama's economic development: the role of agriculture. Ames, The Iowa State Univ. Press, 1975. 219 p., bibl., map, plates, tables.

A summary of working papers prepared for Panama's agriculture study of 1970-73; relates their recommendations to the actual situation.

4394. Monteforte Toledo, Mario; Gérard Pierre-Charles; Catalina Gougain de Contreras; and Rolando Collado. Centroamerica: subdesarrollo y dependencia. México, UNAM, Instituto de Investigaciones Sociales, 1972. 438 p., maps, tables.

A sociological and political reference work also treating related economic factors throughout and especially in the sections on agriculture, industry, and economic integration. Includes Panama.

4395. Morrissy, J. David. Agricultural modernization through production contracting: the role of the fruit and vegetable processor in Mexico and Central America. N.Y., Praeger, 1974. 148 p., bibl., tables (Praeger special studies in international economics and development)

Systems analysis of processors of fruit and vegetables in five CACM countries and Mexico. Effects of precessors' methods on farm practices and marketing.

4396. Murillo, Miguel A. El núcleo de contradicciones del proceso integracionista centroamericano (Estudios Sociales Centroamericanos [San José] 1:1, enero/abril 1972, p. 73-84)

A Costa Rican engineer criticizes negatively the motives of US and Central American Support of the CACM.

4397. Panamá. Banco Nacional de Panamá. Invierta en Panamá. 1973. 74 p., tables (Cuadernos, 7)

Information for both Panamanian and foreign investors on resources, existing industries, infrastructure, public finances, fiscal incentives, banking, labor force and laws relating to investment. Also available in English as *Investment Opportunities in Panama.*

4398. Paz Barnica, Edgardo. Reestructuración institucional de la integración centroamericana. Tegucigalpa, Editorial Nuevo Continente, 1972. 534 p., bibl., illus. (Col. Ciencias jurídicas y sociales)

Examines in detail attitudes toward proposed revisions in the CACM and the meetings and accords aimed in this direction during the period from the start of hostilities between Honduras and El Salvador in July 1969 through 1971.

4399. Peterwerth, Reinhard. Das Vertragswerk des Zentralamerikanischen Gemeinsamen Marktes. Berlin, FRG, Colloquim Verlag, 1973. 134 p. (Biblioteca Ibero-Americana, 18)

A study of the legal framework of the Central American Common Market. The author cautions that increasing industralization and the elimination of tariff barriers among the five nations are not sufficient to alleviate the poverty of the great majority of Central Americans. He warns that revolution is inevitable unless the general standard of living of the population is improved. [H.J. Hoyer]

4400. La planificación en Guatemala: planes y proyectos agrícolas. Guatemala, Consejo Nacional de Planificación Económica, 1971. 563 p., maps, tables.

Includes the National Plan for Rural Development, 1968-70, and a number of more specialized projects related to an agricultural extension program and to the growing of specific fruits, vegetables, and flowers.

4401. Quirós, Félix Armando. Desarrollo económico: nuevas perspectivas (LNB/L, 201, agosto 1972, p. 1-7)

An outline of varied definitions of development.

4402. Rosenblum, Jack J. El interés norteamericano en la integración económica centroamericana (CM/FI, 13:1, julio/sept. 1972, 27-44, tables)

A lawyer discusses the effects on US investments and the social costs to Central Americans of the establishment of a common market.

Sandoval V., Leopoldo R. and Fernando Cruz. Cambios en la estructura agraria de Guatemala y metas de reforma. See item 6631.

Schmitter, Philippe C. Autonomy or dependence as regional integration outcomes: Central America. See item 8183.

4403. Seligson, Mitchel A. Transactions and community formation: fifteen years of growth and stagnation in Central America (JCMS, 11:3, March 1973, p. 173-190, bibl., tables)

A political scientist measures the strength of integration with two indicators, namely, the growth of intraregional trade relative to total trade and the sense of community as revealed by sampling the news in the daily press.

4404. *Tareas.* No. 27, dic. 1973/mayo 1974- . Panama.

Contains three articles critical of the role of foreign investment in Panama:
Jorge Arosemena R. "La United Fruit Co.: Enclave Colonial Panameña" p. 3-22
Marco A. Gandasequi, hijo "Industrialización e Inversiones Extranjeras" p. 23-69
Carlos J. Núñez L. "Exportación de Capital en la Fase Premonopolista: El Contrato del Ferrocarril de Panamá de 1850" p. 71-82.

4405. Villacorta Escobar, Manuel. Apuntes de economía agrícola. Guatemala, Editorial Universitaria, 1973. 146 p. bibl., tables.

This survey of Guatemalan agriculture emphasizes the importance to continuing development of the coordination of agricultural improvement with that in other sectors and of more attention to the level of living of the rural majority of the population.

Wheeler, James O. and Robert N. Thomas. Urban transportation in developing economies: work trips in Tegucigalpa, Honduras. See item 6636.

CUBA*

*Compiled by *HLAS* editorial staff.

4409. Adler-Karlsson, Gunnar. Kuba—seger eller nederlag? Stockholm, Prisma, 1971. 143 p., bibl., tables.

Swedish journalist's views on Cuba's social revolution. Though sympathetic, he recognizes that Castro has not succeeded in performing an economic miracle, but admires the accomplishments in education and health care. Contends that the only way to improve life in the Third World is to introduce the socialist world ideal embodied in the "New Man." [R.V. Shaw]

4410. Alphandery, Jean-Jacques. Cuba: l'autre révolution, douze ans d'économie socialiste. Paris, Editions Sociales, 1972. 285 p., tables (Socialisme)

Historical account of economic policies of the Cuban Revolution. According to the author the strategy of development in Cuba is based on the *tremplin* (springboard) principle which he defines as the "attachment of political significance to a purely economic objective which when attained triggers enthusiasm that spurs the population to further effort." Topics covered are: the effects of American imperialism, agrarian reform, the growth of bureaucracy and efforts to contain it, dominance of agriculture and efforts to industrialize, technological backwardness and future prospects. Comprehensive study heavily footnoted but lacking a bibliography. [Asst. Ed.]

4411. Barkin, David P. and **Nita R. Manitzas** eds. Cuba: the logic of the revolution. Andover, Mass., Warner Modular Publications, 1973. 192 p.

A compilation of nine essays, four reprinted and five new, on Cuba: antecedents and social class-egalitarianism (N. Manitzas); strategy of economic development and redistribution of consumption (D. Barkin); the controversy on economic organization and incentives (Bertram Silverman); new developments in education (Marvin Leiner); regional and urban policies (Jorge Hardoy); continuity in a group of political traits (Richard Fagen); Cuba as a lesson or symbol for Latin America (Fernando Cardoso). [Cuban Studies]

4412. Bonachea, Rolando E. and **Nelson P. Valdés** eds. Cuba in revolution. Garden City, N.Y., Doubleday, 1972. 544 p., tables.

This book is a collection of reprints of significant articles, chapters in books, documents, speeches and reports representing diverse viewpoints, together with three original papers on the Cuban Revolution. Topics covered are the origins, goals, and methods of the Revolution and its political, economic, labor, social-service, cultural, and ideological facets. The collection of reprints includes: C. Blasier's bibliographical essay on the origins of the revolution; G.C. Alroy on the peasant component of the revolutionary forces; J. O'Connor's Marxist interpretation of the causes of the revolution; G.W. Merkz and N.P. Valdés' study of consciousness and class; L. Aguilar's views on revolution and counter-revolution; R. Fagen's analysis of Castro's charismatic leadership and mass mobilization; M. Gutelman's writings on socialization of the means of production and agriculture; C. Mesa-Lago's evaluation of the economic significance of unpaid labor; M. Benedetti's review of cultural progress; and C.I. Lumsden's essay on ideology. Documents reproduced are the 26th of July Program, four speeches of F. Castro, a PCC's report on bureaucracy, the 1969 workers' dossier law, and a poem of H. Padilla. Two original papers by N.P. Valdés on education and public health and the introduction to the section on labor by both editors are significant contributions to this collection. [Cuban Studies]

4413. Breuer, Wilhelm M. Sozialismus in Kuba zur politschen Ökonomie. Cologne, FRG, Pahl-Rugenstein Verlag, 1973. 292 p. (Sammlung Junge Wissenschaft)

Based on Cuban sources such as Fidel Castro's speeches, government statistics, reports to the FAO, and other official sources as well as secondary works, this is a thorough examination of economic development in socialist Cuba up to the end of 1971. Also contains a final chapter on economic perspectives in the 1970s. Of interest to the specialist and all those studying contemporary Cuba. [G.M. Dorn]

4414. Cuba. Bogotá, Editores y Productores (EDYPROL), 1972. 124 p.

Complete texts of the Ley de Reforma Agraria, Ley de Reforma Urbana, Primera y II Declaración de La Habana. [Ed.]

4415. Cuba. Roma, Instituto Italo-Latino Americano, Vice Segreteria Economico-Sociale, 1971. 107 p., bibl., tables (Quaderni, 9)

Work divided into ten chapters each covering specific aspects of economic development including agriculture, industry, commercial structure, transportation, etc. [Ed.]

4416. Dumont, René. Is Cuba socialist? Translated by Stanley Hochman. London, André Deutsch, 1973. 159 p.

Study divided into four sections: 1) summary of the first two periods of Cuban socialism—a) guerrilla phase and b) the "rebellion"; 2) era of centralized and bureaucratic planning; 3) period of hard reality; and 4) construction of communism period. [Ed.]

4417. Ehrenpreis, Dag. Cuba. Uppsala, Sweden, Styrelsen fur Internationell Utveckling [Swedish International Development Authority] (SIDA), 1974. 137 p., bibl., tables (Landanalyser, 7)

Author attempts to present an unbiased statistical overview of the political, social, and economic reality of today's Cuba [R.V. Shaw]

4418. Estudios y documentos sobre Cuba. Estocolmo, Instituto de Estudios Ibero-

Americanos, 1971. 87 p., bibl., tables (Publicaciones serie B. Informes, 2)

Includes several articles on economic aspects of Cuba. Dated but of interest. [Ed.]

4419. Hagelberg, G.B. The Caribbean sugar industries: constraints and opportunities. New Haven, Conn., Yale Univ., Antilles Research Program, 1974. 173 p., bibl., tables (Occasional papers, 3)

4420. Le Riverend, Julio. Historia económica de Cuba. Barcelona, Ediciones Ariel, 1972. 277 p.

Divided into five major sections: 1) discovery and conquest; 2) colonial economy (1510-1659); 3) rise and fall of slavery (1659-1886); 4) imperialist phase (1886-1958); and 5) the Revolution. [Ed.]

4421. Marrero Artiles, Levi. Cuba: economía y sociedad, v. 1. Río Piedras, P.R., Editorial San Juan, 1972. 258 p.

The author, one of the top Cuban geographers of all times, is now a professor at the University of Puerto Rico. His classic work, *Geografía de Cuba* has been translated into several languages including Russian. First of an eight-volume treatise on the economic history of Cuba: 1) Antecedents and Sixteenth Century: The European Presence; 2) *Ibid.*: The Economy appeared in February of 1974); 3) Seventeenth Century; 4) From Monopoly to Free Trade. 1701-1762; 5) Sugar, Slavery and Conscience: 1763-1868; 6) The Price of Liberty: 1868-1898; 7) The New Sugar Economy: 1899-1925; 8) From Economic Nationalism to Socialism: 1926-1958. This book includes an overall description of Cuban geography, summaries of the societies and economies of both pre-Columbian Indian cultures in Cuba and in Spain at the time of the colonization, a review of Spanish exploratory voyages and first settlements on the island, and a detailed study and analysis of the population and depopulation of Cuba during the first half of the sixteenth century. The volume contains hundreds of maps, photographs, ancient drawings, graphs, and statistical tables; it is supported by numerous footnotes and enriched with a bibliography and an index. A basic work for economists, geographers, historians, sociologists, and students of Cuba. [Cuban Studies]

4422. Mesa-Lago, Carmelo. A continuum model to compare socialist systems globally (UC/EDCC, 21:4, July 1973, p. 573-590, tables)

A systematic attempt to rank five socialist countries (only Cuba from Latin America) on the basis of 17 differentiating variables. Combined scores suggest the aggregate "type" of socialism implied and may be used to foresee evolutionary changes. The author suggests the tentative nature of the model. [J.M. Hunter]

4422a. _____. Cuba in the 1970s: pragmatism and institutionalization. Albuquerque, Univ. of New Mexico Press, 1974. 179 p.

... Summarizes the policies of Cuba in the 1960s, describes in detail and analyzes the significant changes that have taken place in that country in the first half of the 1970s, and forecasts the probable direction of events for the rest of the decade. Divided into five chapters: 1) provides the background for the book by selecting twelve relevant features of the Cuban Revolution and systematically comparing them in four different stages between 1959 and 1970. Argues that there is a new stage, which began in 1970 and is still evolving, characterized by pragmatism and institutionalization . . . . documents the rising Soviet influence and its impact on the increasing Cuban ideological moderation. 2) On the economic front: strengthening of planning, improvement of capital efficiency and labor productivity, reduction of "socialist inflation," expansion of material incentives, and decline in the emphasis on sugar. The impact of these changes in production and economic perspectives are also discussed. In the socio-political arena: separation of government functions, democratization of the labor movement, union participation in decision making, organization of "popular power," restructuring of small farmers' and youth organizations, and the conflict with intellectuals. 4) On the foreign-affairs front: the Cuban new realpolitik with Latin America, conflict with *Fidelista* movements in that region, changes in the Latin American stand vis-a-vis Cuba, and conditions and possibilities for a Cuban-U.S. detente. 5) The final chapter reduces all the changes previously described into a set of sixteen variables which are integrated into a systematic model . . . [Cuban Studies]

4423. _____. The labor force, employment, unemployment and underemployment in Cuba: 1899-1970. Beverly Hills, Calif., Sage Publications, 1972. 72 p. (Sage professional papers in international studies series, 02-009)

Analytical history of the changes that have taken place in Cuba's labor force, employment, unemployment, and underemployment since the beginning of the Republic until today. Divided into three periods: 1) from 1899 to the end of the sugar boom of the 1920s (with apparent full employment); 2) from the Great Depression to the eve of the Revolution (with heavy unemployment and underemployment); 3) the first twelve years of the Revolution (with eradication of unemployment but increase of underemployment). For each period there is a discussion of all the available statistics (censuses, surveys, estimates) followed by an analysis of the changes that occurred, their causes, and policies to cope with unemployment. Some of the variables taken into account are occupation, location (urban vs. rural region), seasons, sex, race, and nationality. The final section evaluates the efficiency of the revolutionary policies and their positive and negative results. The study compresses all statistics generated between 1899 and 1970 into nineteen tables, which are supplemented by official reports, sociological surveys, leaders' speeches, laws, radio transmissions, and direct observations by scholars. Extensive bibliography. No index, [Cuban Studies]

4424. Millette, James. Cuba since 1959: a commonsense view of economic development. Port-of-Spain, United National Independence Party, 1973. 43 p. (A UNIP pamphlet)

Highly favorable analysis of the economic achievements of the Cuban revolution as the example for the rest of the Caribbean to follow. Author is the General Secretary of the United National Independence Party of Trinidad and Tobago. [Ed.]

4425. Morawski, Waclaw. Tworzenie podstaw ustrojowych Republiki Kuby [Creación de las bases del régimen de la República de Cuba] Lublin, Poland, Wydawnictwo Lubelskie, 1972. 172 p.

Deals with the formation of basic organizational structure of Cuba between 1959 and 1970. It is written for the Polish reader. Discusses socio-economic development and structure, governmental structure, provides information on party structure, and political, social, and professional organizations, and finally the activities of Cuban counter revolutionary movement and the measures taken by the government against it. Compares Cuba to a large laboratory. Although Cuba is building "socialism", its governmental structure differs from the rest of the socialist republics. [J.W. Hoskins]

4426. Olshany, Anatoli. A.D. Bekarévich and N.M. Kújarev. La Unión Soviética y Cuba: colaboración económica (URSS/AL, 1, 1975, p. 179-182)

4427. Petushkov, Iván. Desarrollo integral de la industria azucarera de Cuba (URSS/AL, 1, 1975, p. 29-44)

4428. Ritter, Archibald R.M. The economic development of revolutionary Cuba: strategy and performance. N.Y., Praeger, 1974. 372 p., bibl., tables (Praeger special studies in international economics and development)

"... Provides a preliminary evaluation of the wisdom of economic policy and of the performance of the economy of revolutionary Cuba from 1959 to mid-1972. Four dimensions of economic performance are considered: income distribution, employment, economic growth, and the reduction of economic dependence." [Ed.]

Rivière d'Arc, Hélène. Aménagement rural a Cuba: le plan Ceiba. See item 8240.

4429. Saínz Mont, Ramón. Cuba en llamas. N.Y., The Author, 1972. 513 p.

Anti-Castro discussion of the Cuban revolution with a chapter on agrarian reform, job market, etc. Strongly partisan. [Ed.]

Salinas, Fernando and others. La Habana metropolitana: un instrumento para el desarrollo socialista. See *HLAS 36:449*.

Silverman, Bertram. Labor and revolution in Cuba. See item 8243.

4430. Tondini, Angelo. Cuba: fine di un mito; ideologia e formazione del castrismo. Prefazione di Arrigo Levi. Milano, Italy, Centro Studi e Ricerche su Problemi Economico Sociali (CESES), 1972. 198 p., tables (Esplorazioni culturali, 6)

Italian political scientist who visited Cuba in 1970 analyzes the ideological evolution of "Castrism," beginning with its inception at Moncada and culminating with the adoption of Marxism-Leninism. Topics discussed are: evolution of political tactics; Castro's pragmatism, orthodoxy and improvisation in formulation of policies; the Cuban Communist Party; the campaign against bureaucratization; and Che Guevara's concept of the "new man." Chap. IV includes a section devoted to the Cuban economy (p. 113-134) with ten tables. Volume is footnoted but lacks a bibliography. [Asst. Ed.]

4431. Valey, E[mil'] B[orisovich]. Ekonomicheskaia geografiia Kuby [Economic geography of Cuba]. Edited by I. M. Maergoiz. Moskva, Izdatel'stvo Moskovskogo universiteta [Moscow University Press], 1972. 42 p., maps, tables.

Textbook for the course "Economic Geography of Foreign Socialist Countries," intended for geography departments of state universities. Sections on: General Survey (physical geography, natural resources, population), Economy, and Regional Survey. An introduction anticipated Cuba's entry in 1972 into the Council for Mutual Economic Assistance. [A. Navon]

4432. Yajuar, Rumi. Cuba: 12 years after. Sydney, Australia, Labour Press, 1970. 9 p. (A Labour press pamphlet)

Australian Trotskyist publication which bases its analysis on economic and social factors. [Ed.]

COLOMBIA, ECUADOR AND THE GUIANAS

R. ALBERT BERRY
Professor of Economics
University of Toronto

THE FLOW OF USEFUL STUDIES ON THE COLOMBIAN ECONOMY has increased rapidly over the last decade, to the point where it is difficult to keep up with it. As reflected in the studies annotated here, important foci of attention now are income distribution, employment, the foreign sector (trade and foreign investment), urbanization and overall development strategy. The Four Strategies Development Plan of the Pastrana Administration generated much controversy and writing, both in support and in criticism; its marked variance from earlier plans and general development orthodoxy was responsible for this (see excerpts of the Plan itself, item 4501, the Symposium organized by CORP, item 4509, and the ideological attack by García, item 4475). It may be anticipated that the next few years will see useful studies analyzing its results, not possible thus far except quite partially due to the lag in statistics and information and the further lag while they are analyzed.

Noteworthy studies of the foreign sector have emerged recently. Díaz-Alejandro's excellent work on Colombia's foreign trade in the post-war period (chapters of which is item 4471) provides the first broad description *cum* appraisal of foreign-trade policy to date. The minor export boom, an important event in Colombia's recent economic history, is fortunately receiving considerable attention, especially from FEDESARROLLO, as witness items 4460-4462. Melo's study of the foreign dominated gold industry (item 4491) complements Viatsos' earlier work on the impact of foreign investment in Colombia (item 4507).

The continuing attention to the urbanization process is partly a concomitant of the key role given to urban building in the Four Strategies Development Plan and partly a reflection of prior interest. The views of the Depto. de Planeación are reflected in item 4503; item 4504 reviews some aspects of the process as well as competing policy propositions; item 4474 focusses on the special problems of intermediate cities; and item 4479 looks at the "inquilinato" phenomenon.

Income distribution remains a popular area. Urrutia's study (item 4515) is one of a number he has published in recent years; García's critical review (item 4494) exemplifies the sort of reaction which helps to keep the discussion at a serious technical level. Although most of the necessary studies remain to be done in this area, it has nevertheless advanced faster perhaps than any other in recent years.

Noteworthy by their absence in the studies reviewed are analyses of the inflation which has plagued Colombia since 1970. Hopefully this serious gap will be remedied in the near future.

Although the literature on the Guianas is limited, Mandle's study of Guyana (item 4527) is an important addition, and serves the very valuable function of providing a frame work against which many aspects of that country's evolution can be interpreted.

Because of my late appointment as Contributing Editor to *HLAS*, I did not have time to review or access to works on Ecuador for the last two years. Therefore, in *HLAS 39* I intend to cover the economic literature for that country corresponding to 1973-77.

COLOMBIA

Abad Arango, Darío. Tecnología y dependencia. See item 4000.

4456. Arango R., Mariano and **Francisco Javier Gómez.** La estructura económica del Departamento de Antioquia. Medellín, Colo., Univ. de Antioquia, Facultad de Ciencias Económicas, Centro de Investigaciones Económicas [and] Gobernación de Antioquia, Depto. Administrativo de Planeación, 1973. 231 p., tables.

One of the first in-depth studies of the economy of a Colombian region: Antioquia dept. Presents and uses the regional income accounts for Antioquia, estimated by CIE. Separate chapters focus on the development of industry, agriculture and forestry, other problems and characteristics.

Arizmendi Posada, Octavio. Políticas contra el desempleo. See item 8300a.

4457. Armendariz, Amadeo. Monopolios y miseria en Colombia: el saqueo de América Latina. Bogotá, Ediciones Los Comuneros, 1974. 79 p., tables.

Marxist interpretation of the growth of and exploitation by foreign monopoly capital in Colombia.

4458. Bejarano, Jesús A. El capital monopolista y las inversiones privadas norteamericanas en Colombia. Bogotá, Círculo Rojo Editores, 1972. 116 p., tables.

A study of events in Colombia around the following hypothesis: 1) a shift of imperialist investment for production of raw materials to the production of manufactured goods for local consumption, 2) the tendency of foreign investment to gravitate toward areas with large monopoly elements and the most dynamic sector, 3) foreign investment seeks and earns greater rates of return than at home and greater rates of return than domestic industry, 4) monopolistic conditions in the control of technology when foreign firms predominate prevents Colombian growth in these sub-sectors. Further, the local national bourgeoisie develops ties to this foreign investment. [J.M. Hunter]

4459. Bernal C., Fernando and others. Estudio socioeconómico del oriente antioqueño. Bogotá, Instituto Colombiano Agropecuario (ICA), Depto. de Ciencias Sociales, Programa Nacional de Sociología Rural, 1972. 194 p., tables.

A broad survey of the physical, economic and social characteristics of eastern Antioquia. Undertaken to provide a benchmark study prior to the initiation of the East Antioquia Development Project.

4460. Bernhart, Michael and **Manuel Martínez.** Canales de información para los exportadores colombianos. Bogotá, Fundación para la Educación Superior y el Desarrollo (FEDESARROLLO), 1973. 73 p., tables.

Another useful FEDESARROLLO study of the mechanisms of the exportation of non-traditional (i.e. not coffee, petroleum, or bananas) exports from Colombia. Based on a sample of exporters, the authors analyse the process of entrance into the world market. The resulting benefits (profits and other less monetary ones), channels of information about potential buyers, and determinants of success. A trip to make contact with potential buyers is a usual step, and brings advantages. Intermediaries do not seem to be a readily accepted part of the mechanism at present.

4461. Calvo S., Haroldo and **José Francisco Escandón.** La exportaciones colombianas de manufacturas: 1963-1971. Bogotá, Fundación para la Educación Superior y el Desarrollo (FEDESARROLLO), 1973. 10 p., tables.

Valuable compilation of Colombian manufacturing exports (1963-71) by two and three-digit industrial sectors, based on data from INCOMEX (Instituto Colombiano de Comercio Exterior). A brief review of interpretations of the rapid growth of these exports over the period in question.

4462. _____ and **Manuel Martínez.** La ventaja comparativa de la industria manufacturera colombiana. Bogotá, Fundación para la Educación Superior y el Desarrollo (FEDESARROLLO), 1973. 39 p.

An attempt to identify those manufactured goods in which Colombia has a comparative advantage vis-à-vis the developed countries, and therefore the potential to export to them. Focuses on the output/labor and output/capital ratios as determinants of comparative advantage.

4463. Cardona G., Ramiro. Mejoramiento de turgurios y asentamientos no controlados: los aspectos sociales (DNP/RPD, 4:1, enero/marzo 1972, p. 3-21, illus., tables)

Describes existing policies towards the urbanization process in general and spontaneous (i.e. illegal) settlement in particular. Concludes these are for the most part based on a distorted perception of the urbanization process. The effective aids to integration of rural-urban migrants in the city are mostly informal, undertaken by the people themselves. The public sector should try to compliment these.

4464. Chaves, Milcíades. Aproximación al estudio del sistema científico y tecnológico de Colombia. t. 1, Informe de avance sobre los datos de las primeras 22 entidades de la encuesta. Bogotá, Fondo Colombiano de Investigaciones Científicas y Proyectos Especiales Francisco José de Caldas (COLCIENCIAS), 1972. 102 p., tables (Serie estudios, 17)

Very broad gauged review of the socio-economic evolution of Colombia from the colonial period on. Despite the title, the focus on science and technology is limited. An interesting introduction to some aspects of Colombian history.

4465. Chudnovsky, Daniel. La rentibilidad de las empresas multinacionales (IDES/DE, 13:52, julio/sept. 1974, p. 649-671, tables)

A scholarly study of returns to international investments—general practices, special circumstances related to investment in Colombia, results of efforts to compute "real" rates of return for 53 multinationals operating in Colombia. [J.M. Hunter]

Colombia. Departamento Administrativo Nacional de Estadística. Subempleo en las 7 principales ciudades del país, según el censo de 1964. See item 6879.

4466. ———. **Departamento Nacional de Planeción.** El plan de desarrollo colombiano en marcha. Bogotá, Ediciones Tercer Mundo, 1974. 271 p.

Series of essays, mostly by members of the Pastrana administration, dealing with various aspects and effects of the "Four Strategies" Development Plan, (1971-74). Useful discussions of savings, exports, urban policy, income distribution, etc.

4467. ———. ———. Plan de desarrollo económico y social 1970-1973. t. 1., Capítulos del I-VIII. t. 2, Capítulos del IX-XI. Bogotá, 1970. 2 v. (Various pagings) bibl., illus., fold. maps, tables.

The last Development Plan before the "Four Strategies" Plan. Discussions and projections for several of the sectors are of particular interest. A reasonably good source of information on the government's economic policy.

4468. ———. **Instituto Colombiano Agropecuario (ICA). Instituto Colombiano de Reforma Agraria (INCORA). Fondo Financiero Agrario.** Los insumos agropecuarios en Colombia: generalidades, maquinaria, fertilizates, plaguicidas, semillas, pecuarios, aspectos institucionales y legales, costos de los insumos y créditos agropecuarios, conclusiones. Bogotá, Sociedad de Agricultores de Colombia (SAC), 1973. 2 v. (521 p.) (Continuous pagination) illus., tables.

A detailed review of the inputs used in Colombian agriculture, their sources, prices, commercialization, etc. Includes figures on cost of production and credit. Good reference work.

4469. ———. **Ministerio de Agricultura.** Programas agrícolas: evaluación 1973, programación 1974, proyecciones 1975. Bogotá, 1973. 299 p., tables.

Useful as a reference work on details of what is produced in Colombian agriculture (over recent years), inputs used, etc. Also contains a brief exposition of the government's agricultural policies and programs.

Comité Interamericano de la Alianza para el Progreso (CIAP), *Washington.* La economía agrícola colombiana. See item 6892.

4470. Currie, Lauchlin. La limitación de las divisas al desarrollo: una solución parcial al problema (DNP/RPD, 3:3, oct. 1971, p. 3-24)

Describes the basic problem of development as being able simultaneously to take advantage of modern capital intensive technologies and to create jobs for the large supply of labor. Proposes as a solution the deliberate manipulation of the pattern of demand towards goods whose production is labor intensive and which require few imports, especially towards urban construction.

4471. Díaz Alejandro, Carlos Federico. Algunos aspectos cuantificables de las importaciones colombianas y del control de las importaciones [and] La luberación de importaciones en Colombia: 1965-1966. Bogotá, Fundación para la Educación Superior y el Desarrollo (FEDESARROLLO), 1974. 2 v. (15, 27 p.) tables.

Chapters of a book on the Colombian foreign sector being prepared by Diaz Alejandro as part of a series published by the National Bureau of Economic Research. Highlights of the first are the concentration of imports in a relatively small number of large firms and the apparent reinforcement of it by control mechanisms applied in the import sector. Preferential treatment is less potent, however, than access to credit and/or to foreign investment in biasing the operation of import controls in favor of larger firms. As to the import liberalization of 1965-66, Díaz notes that the step is neither a necessary nor a sufficient condition for a rapid increase of imports and not a sufficient condition for rapid growth of output and exports.

4472. Dos estudios sobre población en Colombia (DNP/RPD, 4:1, enero/marzo 1972, p. 37-111, maps, tables)

Two useful demographic studies, one predicting population by department in 1972, the other analyzing interdepartmental migration over 1951-64.

4473. Fadul, Maité and Jorge García Mujica. El desempleo disfrazado en Colombia: los efectos del trabajador adicional y desalentado. Bogotá, Univ. de los Andes, Facultad de Economía, Centro de Estudios sobre Desarrollo Económico (CEDE), 1974. 65 l., bibl. (Documento CEDE, 011)

A review and critique of the two main prior studies of disguised unemployment in Colombia, those of Urrutia and Salazar. Presents some theory which casts doubts on the methodology of those previous studies. Concludes that there is no serious evidence of the "discouraged worker" phenomenon in Colombia (i.e. people who do not look for jobs because the existence of unemployment discourages them). The conclusion is based on the use of age specific regressions relating participation to unemployment.

4474. Financiamiento del desarrollo urbano. Bogotá, Ediciones Tercer Mundo, 1974. 85 p., tables.

Studies the problems of intermediate cities in achieving adequate infrastructures. Cites the lack of an urban credit policy in Colombia, and the over importance of knowing people and the system if such a town or city is to get help. An interesting commentary.

4475. García, Bernardo. Anticurrie: crítica a las teorías de desarrollo capitalista en Colombia. Bogotá, Libros de Bolsillo de la Carreta, 1973. 210 p., tables.

Sweeping criticism of the Four Strategies Development Plan, of L. Currie's ideas, and of neo-classical economics as habitually applied in developing countries. Focuses on the alleged scientific or neutral character of such economics and argues that it is inextricably tied to class interests and conflict. Contrasts the positions of Baran and Currie with selected excerpts from each.

4475a. García Mujica, Jorge. Notas críticas y sugerencias en estudios de concentración en la distribución de ingresos. Bogotá, Univ. de los Andes, Facultad de Economía, Centro de Estudios sobre Desarrollo Económico, 1973. 66 p., bibl.

A useful critique of several studies of income-distribution in Colombia, in particular those of Urrutia-Villalba and Córdoba, focusing on the problems associated with the use of personal rather than family income, current rather than permanent income, etc. when the objective is to analyze welfare issues. Argues that with more relevant variables the inequality of distribution may be much less than indicated by the cited studies.

4476. Gaviria G., Juan F.; Francisco Javier Gómez; and **Hugo López C.** Contribución al estudio del desempleo en Colombia. Bogotá, Univ. Nacional de Antioquia, Centro de Investigaciones Económicas (CIE) [and] Depto. Administrativo Nacional de Estadística (DANE) 1971. 172 p., tables.

An attempt to explain the causes of unemployment in Colombia. Takes a broad look at the structure of industry and agriculture, and focuses especially on the question of labor-capital substitution, concluding that the production function is not a promising tool in its analysis.

4477. Gómez Campo, Fabio Hernán. Concentración del poder económico en Colombia. Bogotá, Centro de Investigación y Acción Social, 1974. 76 p., bibl., tables (Col. CIAS)

A study of the concentration of power in Colombia by looking at the occupants of selected positions. Concludes such power is highly concentrated, almost all in the hands of members of the traditional Liberal and Conservative parties, and is tightly related to family and social class.

Gómez Hurtado, Alvaro and **Alfonso López Michelsen.** El problema agrario en Colombia. See item 6895.

4478. Gómez Otálora, Hernando. La experiencia de los fondos financieros en Colombia (BCV/REL, 9:34, 1972, p. 201-232, tables)

Explains the functions of three Central Bank "funds" created in recent years in Colombia and directed to agricultural, industrial and urban development. Argues that they are useful tools of overall development.

4479. _____ and **Eduardo Wiesner Durán** eds. Lecturas sobre desarrollo económico colombiano. Bogotá, Fundación para la Educación Superior y el Desarrollo, 1974. 624 p., tables.

A very useful series of invited essays designed to summarize the results of research to date on the Colombian economy, by sectors and issues. Probably the best single reference work on the Colombian economy; valuable for teaching purposes.

4480. Hernández de Caldas, Angela. Documentos sobre transferencia de la tecnología. Bogotá, Cámara de Comercio de Bogotá, Centro de Informática Económica, 1973. 30 p. (Revista de la Cámara de Comercio de Bogotá, 13)

Useful bibliography of studies dealing with the international transfer of technology, with special emphasis on Latin America. [A. Berry]

4481. Ibiza de Restrepo, Ghislaine. La industrialización del oriente antioqueño. Medellín, Colo., Univ. de Antioquia, Facultad de Ciencias Económicas, Centro de Investigaciones Económicas (CIE), 1972. 116 p., bibl. (Documento de trabajo, 7)

Studies the industrialization process in eastern Antioquia, assumed to be a decentralization of industry away from the Medellín valley. Considers the motives of firms which have moved, the characteristics of the industrial development and its impact on the region.

4482. Junguito, Roberto. Objetivos de la política cafetera colombiana. Bogotá, Fundación para la Educación Superior y el Desarrollo (FEDESARROLLO), 1974. 23 p.

Describes the goals of Colombia's coffee policy (maximization of foreign-exchange receipts, long-run equilibrium between demand and supply, income maintainance for producers, export-price stabilization) and considers the extent to which they are consistent one with another.

4483. _____; Alvaro López; Alvaro Reyes; and **Diego Salazar.** Análisis de la estructura y evolución de la fuerza de trabajo colombiana: 1938, 1951 y 1964; proyecciones de la población económicamente activa: 1965-1985. Bogotá, Univ. de los Andes, Facultad de Economía, Centro de Estudios sobre Desarrollo Económico (CEDE), 1970. 177 p., fold. tables.

A compilation of demographic and labor force statistics, mainly from the population censuses of 1938, 1951 and 1964, accompanied by projections. An important reference work for persons working in those areas. Discussion of trends and their causes is interesting and informed, e.g. of participation rates and life expectancy.

4484. Levy de Nessim, Sary. Costos de la ayuda externa atada. Bogotá, Univ. de los Andes, Facultad de Economía, Centro de Estudios sobre Desarrollo Económico, 1973. 26 p., tables. (Documentos de trabajo, 007)

Analysis of four cases of purchases under tied-aid arrangements in three of which the price differential is quite large, e.g. 25 percent or higher. Concludes the issue warrants more detailed attention.

4485. López C., Hugo. Estudio sobre la inflación en Colombia: el período de los años 20. Medellín, Colo., Univ. de Antioquia, Facultad de Ciencias Económicas, Centro de Investigaciones Económicas (CIE), 1973. 185 p., tables (Documentos para investigaciones, 10)

Much broader than its title indicates; reviews Colombia economic development before World War I and in the 1920s before addressing the question of the causes of the inflation of the 1920s. Concludes that said inflation was not due to expansion of the money supply in the sense that such an increase could have been avoided by deliberate decision, and that it is more meaningful to explain it in terms of the inelasticity of supply in agriculture.

Lopez Michelsen, Alfonso; Alvaro Gómez Hurtado; María Eugenia Rojas; and **Hernando Echeverry Mejía.** Plataformas económicas de los candidatos presidenciales: 1974-1978. See item 8326a.

4486. Losada Lora, Rodrigo. Los institutos descentralizados de carácter financiero: aspectos políticos del caso colombiano. Bogotá, Fundación para la Educación Superior y el Desarrollo (FEDESARROLLO), 1973. 25 p.

Explains the factors which have contributed to the rapid growth of decentralized agencies and their relationships to the public sector (Congress, Ministry of Finance, etc.) including the political influences to which they are subject. The first such brief general survey for Colombia.

4487. McCallum, J. Douglas. Land values in Bogotá, Colombia (UW/LE, 50:3, August 1974, p. 312-317, maps)

Reports on several studies of land values in Bogotá. Concludes that in 1960-72 those values rose only about the same rate as per capita incomes which together with their spatial structure suggests that the land market functions fairly much like those of cities in developed countries.

Maher, Patric. Rural regeneration in Colombia: the possibilities of a labor-intensive strategy. See item 6901.

4488. Mantilla Suárez, Sergio. Las Cámaras de Comercio en Colombia. Bogotá, Pontificia Univ. Javeriana, Facultad de Ciencias Jurídicas y Socioeconómicas, 1972. 361 p.

A Javeriana Univ. thesis examines chambers of commerce, in the world at large and in Colombia. Includes relevant legislation, administrative structure, etc.

4489. Martínez Cárdenas, Jaime. Desempleo y estructura industrial. Bogotá, Centro de Investigación Acción Social, 1971. 30 p. (Documento de trabajo, 1)

A conceptual review of factors affecting the demand for labor in the industrial sector. Limited reference to Colombia data.

4490. Martínez Robá, Manuel. Obstáculos al desarrollo de exportaciones manufacturadas. Bogotá, Fundación para la Educación Superior y el Desarrollo (FEDESARROLLO), 1973. 24 p., tables.

A useful exposition of problems facing exporters of manufactured goods, based on PROEXPO sample of exporters and the author's own interviews. Important problems were: lack of working capital, quality and/or availability of national raw materials, marketing and promotion abroad.

4491. Melo, Héctor. El mercado internacional del oro y la explotación del oro en Colombia. Ciudad Universitaria?, Colo., Univ. Nacional de Colombia, Centro de Investigaciones para el Desarrollo (CID), 1974. 46., tables

A brief review of the world gold market, followed by a detailed study of gold mining in Colombia. Follows the development of this activity from its beginnings to the present, focusing on the major (foreign) companies involved. Concludes that the benefits from production have gone in striking degree to these foreign firms. We believe this is the most detailed study of the industry to date.

4492. Mohr, Hermann J. Economía colombiana: una estructura en crisis, análisis del proceso reciente y perspectivas. Bogotá, Ediciones Tercer Mundo [and] Centro de Investigación y Acción Social (CIAS), 1972. 315 p., tables (Col. Aventura del desarrollo, 12)

A text book on the Colombian economy by a well-read author. The approach is a systematic sector-by-sector one. Weaknesses of the book reflect the weaknesses of the literature on which it is built, but by and large it is one of the most useful overall reviews of the Colombian economy.

4493. Montes Llamas, Gabriel. Economía de la investigación agrícola en Colombia. Bogotá, Univ. de los Andes, Facultad de Economía, Centro de Estudios sobre Desarrollo Económico, 1974. 26 p., bibl., tables (CEDE, 017)

Reports that the social returns from the state's investment in research on soybeans, rice and cotton for 1971 were very high.

4494. See item 4475a.

4495. Organization of American States. Departamento de Asuntos Económicos. La economía agrícola colombiana. Washington, 1971. 131 p., bibl., map, tables.

Systematic review of the agricultural sector in Colombia, with emphasis on individual products and on some of the institutions which deal with agriculture. Descriptive rather than analytical.

4496. Owen, Wilfred. Urbanización planeadaÑ fin a la ciudad accidental (DNP/RPD, 4:1, enero/marzo 1972, p. 23-36, table)

Argues that the solution to some of the most important urban problems is careful planning of housing, economic activity and community services—not increases in the supply of transportation facilities. Also feels that the costs of significant improvements of the sort indicated are not prohibitive, even for developing countries.

4497. Palacios Mejía, Hugo. Antecedentes del estatuto normativo del Presupuesto General de la Nación. Bogotá, Talleres Gráficos del Banco de la República, 1973. 337 p.

In 1973 a new statute governing the presentation of the national budget was instituted, moving the systems towards the concept of financial flows and away from the generally less useful concept of the creation of debts and credits. This volume includes a discussion of the statute, background papers and speeches and letters related to it.

4498. Pantoja Revelo, Carlos. Saqueo, atraso y dependencia: de la piratería del siglo XVI al vampirismo del siglo XX. Bogotá, Ediciones Tercer Munco, 1974. 117 p., plates.

Broad ranging attack on the exploitation of Colombia by foreign interests, criticizing foreign involvement in petroleum, sale of blood plasma abroad, etc. Special focus on Nariño dept.

4499. Pérez Arbeláez, Jorge and Guillermo Perry Rubio. Economía y petróleo: aspectos internacionales y problemas colombianos. Bogotá, Funcación para la Educación Superior y el Desarrollo (FEDESARROLLO), 1974. 1 v. (Various pagings) illus.

Reports recent events in the International oil market and costs, production, and pricing of oil and its derivatives in Colombia. Concludes that in the light of high world prices the current pricing policy is inadequate (internal prices should be raised) if Colombia is to maximize its benefits from the industry.

4500. Ramírez Vargas, María Teresa and Susan Casement. La Cámara de Comercio de Bogotá y sus publicationes. Bogotá, Red Colombiana de Información y Documentación Económica, 1973? 115 p.

Mainly a list of bibliographies and studies prepared by the Bogotá Chamber of Commerce, mostly on economic topics. A useful research tool.

4501. *Revista de Planeación y Desarrollo.* Depto. Nacional de Planeación. Vol. 3, No. 4, dic. 1971- . Bogotá.

Excerpts from the Pastrana Administration's "Four Strategies" Plan wherein are explained the general criteria on which it was based and the philosophy underlying it. Includes discussions of savings, underemployment and foreign assistance.

4502. ———. ———. Vol. 5, No. 2, abril/junio 1973- . Bogotá.

A set of four essays on district aspects of monetary economics and monetary policy, in particular the objectives and instruments of monetary policy, the effects of monetary expansion on the price level, rediscount policy, the origin of the monetary base and the interrelations among money, the foreign sector, fiscal policy and central bank credit. By a highly competent group of authors: Luis Eduardo Rosas "La Política Monetaria" p. 8-19
Lauchlin Currie "La Política Monetaria y el Nivel de Precios" p. 20-45
Antonio Hernández Gamarra "Política de Redescuento 1950-1970" p. 46-67
Robert J. Barro "El Dinero y la Base Monetaria en Colombia 1967-1972" p. 68-80.

4503. _____. _____. Vol. 5, No. 3, julio/dic. 1973- . Bogotá.

Selected parts of a Planeación Nacional document on the role of urban policy in the National Plan. Focuses on how to orient urban growth in such a way as to permit cities the advantages of smaller size along with economies of scale, how to reduce transport costs, provision of appropriate housing, avoiding the segregation of different social groups.

4504. Robin, John P. and **Frederick C. Terzo.** Urbanization in Colombia. N.Y., Ford Foundation, International Urbanization Survey, 1973? 100 p., illus., maps.

A review of some aspects of urbanization and urban life in Colombia, with emphasis on the administrative, planning and legal side. Discusses also the development of regional planning and the major urbanization strategies put forward in Colombia, e.g. The Currie Plan and the Strategy implicit in Seer's ILO Report.

4505. Rodríguez, Cecilia de. La costa atlántica: algunos aspectos socioeconómicos de su desarrollo. Bogotá, Fundación para la Educación Superior y el Desarrollo (FEDESARROLLO), 1974? 176 p., tables.

Very useful survey of the economy of the North Coast departments, including demographic, educational and health aspects. Notes especially the differences in progress and living standard between the main coastal cities and the interior, the relatively low-level of services (education, health, etc.) and the expansion of exports from the area in recent years.

4506. Rodríquez Salazar, Oscar. Efectos de la Gran Depresión sobre la industria colombiana. Bogotá, Ediciones El Tigre de Papel, 1973. 118 p., tables.

Explains the role of the Great Depression and earlier events of the 1920s, including the inflow of foreign capital and the installation of a modern banking structure, in the flowering of industrial capitalism in Colombia from 1928. Tariff protection and the needs of the US to export capital goods to a consumer-good oriented industrial sector are highlighted.

4507. Rosas, Luis Eduardo. Demanda por dinero, intermediarios financieros y desarrollo económico (DNP/RPD, 3:2, julio 1971, p. 3-34)

An analysis with Colombian, Venezuelan and Mexican data of the income elasticity of demand for money. Concludes that the high elasticity usually recorded is due to the exclusion of a variable to reflect the level of monetization of the economy, which rises rapidly during development and cannot rise much farther in a growing developed country.

4508. _____. Temas sobre el desarrollo en Colombia. Bogotá, Depto. Nacional de Planeación, 1974. 150 p.

A collection of the articles and speeches of Luis E. Rosas during 1971-74, when he was Secretary General and then head of Planeación Nacional. Deals mostly with aspects of the Four Strategies Plan.

4509. _____ and others. Controversia sobre el Plan de Desarrollo. Bogotá, Corporación para el Fomento de Investigaciones Económicas (CORP), 1972. 280 p., tables.

Papers presented at a Simposium organized in 1971 by CORP to discuss and debate key aspects of the Pastrana Administration's Four Strategies Development Plan. Highlights are the critical review of the plan by Professor Gustav Ranis of Yale and its defense by Lauchlin Currie, and a review of possible problems in the Plan's implementation by Miguel Urrutia.

4510. Sandilands, Roger J. La modernización del sector agropecuario y la migración rural-urbana en Colombia (DNP/RPD, 3:3, oct. 1971, p. 25-57, bibl., tables)

Describes the dilemma of agricultural policy in Colombia as involving the conflict between modernization which raises output but increases the pressure on small subsistence farmers. Concludes that the best solution is an urbanization program which would put underutilized labor and capital to work and at the same time increase the demand for agricultural products.

4511. Seminario sobre Problemas y Objetivos de una Política de Transporte, *Popayán, Colo., 1973.* El desarrollo del transporte de carga, una necesidad nacional. Bogotá, Univ. Nacional de Colombia, Centro de Investigaciones para el Desarrollo (CID), 1973. 221 p.

A series of essays presented at a Seminar in Popayán, 1973. Discussions of the role of transport, development of the automotive industry, the new central wholesale market in Bogotá, and other themes. Primarily descriptive.

4512. Sloan, John W. Colombia's, new development plan: an example of post-ECLA thinking (IAMEA, 27:2, Autumn 1973, p. 49-66)

A good discussion of the Pastrana Administrations Four Strategies Development Plan. Highlights the pivotal role of Professor Launchlin Currie in the formulation of the Plan and its acceptance by the government. Reviews the major components of the plan and the key criticisms directed at it.

Solaún, Mauricio and **Fernando Cepeda.** Political and legal challenges to foreign direct private investment in Colombia. See item 8353.

4513. Temas colombianos: aspectos y problemas de una política de desarrollo. Bogotá, Centro de Investigaciones para el Desarrollo (CID), 1973. 419 p., tables.

A series of essays by authors of various ideological persuasions dealing with a range of issues from agricultural policy to cooperatives, the development of individual departments, and the future of political parties. Of particular interest is the essay by now President Alfonso López "Where is Colombia Headed?"

4514. Tobón, Alonso. La tierra y la reforma agraria en Colombia. Bogotá, La Oveja Negra, 1972. 162 p., tables.

Argues that the objective of land reform in Colombia is simply to break up those large latifundia demonstrably incapable of transforming themselves into capitalist enterprises; since these are relatively few, not much land has been transferred. The structure of rural property has remained essentially unchanged.

4515. Urrutia Montoya, Miguel. Variación histórica de la distribucion del ingreso en Colombia (BCV/REL, 9:36, 1973, p. 99-135, tables)

The author utilizes a range of information including wage rates, sectoral labor productivity and tax returns to reach conclusions about trends over time in Colombia's income distribution. Concludes that there was a period of deterioration (1923-53) followed by one of stability or slight improvement (1953-64), and notes the consistency of this with Kuznet's suggestion of a U-shaped relation between level of development and degree of income equality.

4516. _____ and Clara Elsa de Sandoval. Política fiscal y distribución del ingreso en Colombia (*in* Foxley, Alejandro *ed.* Distribución del ingreso. México, Fondo de Cultura Económica, 1974, p. 478-510)

Analysis of taxation and expenditure policy by the government; major tax reforms were implemented soon after this publication. [J. Strasma]

4517. Vaitsos, Constantine V. Transferencia de recursos y preservación de rentas monopolísticas (DNP/RPD, 3:2, julio 1971, p. 35-72, tables)

An analysis of the real rate of return on foreign capital in several Colombian industries (pharmaceuticals, chemicals, rubber, and electronics). Concludes that said rate is (as of the late 1960s) quite high but that a substantial portion (often a majority) of the profits is disguised by overinvoicing of imported imputs. Discusses the ways in which monopoly profits are preserved as foreign capital and technology are passed to the host country.

4518. Vallejo A., Joaquín. El estatuto de Lima y la integración latinoamericana (PUJ/Ú, 41, junio 1971, p. 201-222, tables)

A superficial treatment of the question of foreign investment and the Andean group's attitude toward it — especially from the Colombian point of view. [J. M. Hunter]

4519. Varela, Teodosio. Colombia: los monopolios y la penetración imperialista. Medellín, Colo., Ediciones Nueva Crítica, 1974. 93 p. (Col. Colombia: estudios históricos, 2)

A Marxist tract on the influence of imperialism (primarily US) in Colombia; and the predicted evolution of future events.

Villegas Moreno, Luis Alberto. Aspectos de la política social y económica de los tugurios y asentamientos no controlados. See item 6915.

_____. Vivienda y desarrollo urbano en Colombia. See item 6916.

4520. Young, Roger and Jean Currie. Dos temas sobre comercio exterior: las zonas francas y la promoción de exportaciones y la exportación de productos colombianos seleccionados. Bogotá, Fundación para la Educación Superior y el Desarrollo (FEDESARROLLO), 1974. 43 p., tables.

Young's study brings to bear general economic considerations and a limited amount of information to judge the probable results of Free Zones like that in Barranquilla. He concludes that the employment creating feature of the labor intensive processes generated by international firms must be weighted against the high level of implicit dependence. Currie analyses the development of specific minor export lines; she concludes that the benefits are large. The government support has been substantial but, she feels, necessary.

4521. Zorro Sánchez, Carlos and Edgar Reveiz Roldán. Primera etapa del estudio sobre los inquilinatos: vivienda compartida en arrendamiento en Bogotá. Bogotá, Univ. de los Andes, Facultad de Economía, Centro de Estudios sobre Desarrollo Económico (CEDE), 1974. 138 l., tables (Documento CEDE, 010)

Considers the "inquilinato" phenomenon in Bogotá. Discusses the presumed determinants of the demand in this housing type and summarizes various earlier estimates of its magnitude in Bogotá.

ECUADOR

4522. Comité de Información y Contacto Externo (CICE), *Quito.* Ecuador: población y crisis. Quito, 1973? 77 p. (Biblioteca CICE, 1)

Four essays on Ecuador's explosive population growth and implications for the future. CICE is an organization established to facilitate information for potential foreign investors; it has public and private sector members on its board, but increasingly serves as a forum for domestic business interests. [J. Strasma]

4523. _____ _____. Hacia una economía de superavit. Quito, 1974? 128 p. (Biblioteca CICE, 2)

Eleven essays, most by businessmen, on how Ecuador should change its economic policies as a result of the prospective enormous foreign exchange earnings from high oil prices. [J. Strasma]

4524. Sevilla, Santiago. Desierto verde. Quito, Editorial La Unión, 1975. 64 p.

Trenchant essays by a young economist and sometime bank manager, attacking fixed exchange rates, public sector dominance in the incipient capital market, and control of the universities by one sect (Marxists). [J. Strasma]

THE GUIANAS

Grant, C. H. Political sequence to ALCAN nationalization in Guyana: the international aspects. See item 8287.

Hanley, Eric R. Rice, politics and development in Guyana. See item 1241.

Hope, Kempe R. The role of government expenditure in the economic development in Guyana: 1960-1970. See item 8290.

4525. _____ and **Wilfred L. David.** Planning for development in Guyana: the experience from 1945 to 1973 (IAMEA, 27:4, Spring 1972, p. 27-46, tables)

A critical review of development planning in Guyana in the post World War II period. Concludes that it has had little impact on the economy, largely because the analysis underlying the plans was too academic in nature and done by persons not familiar with the intricacies of the society. Argues that rural development and savings deserve much more attention than they have received.

4526. King, K.F.S. A great future together: the development and employment plan. La Penitence, Guyana, Design & Graphics, 1973. 28 p., plates.

An outline of Guyana's II Development Plan (for 1972-76) with brief expositions on the government's plans for various sectors. King is the Minister of Economic Development, and this was his speech at the XVI People's National Congress, Queen's College, Georgetown, 8 May 1973.

4527. Mandle, Jay R. The plantation economy: population and economic change in Guyana 1838-1960. Philadelphia, Pa., Temple Univ. Press, 1973. 170 p., bibl., map, tables.

An effort to understand Guyana's failure to develop over the period considered. Mandle emphasizes the dominance of the plantation sector in the economy and in the government's attention as the major factor stifling development. As that sector opted for mechanization in the 1940s and subsequently, and the population explosion came to Guyana, a major problem of labor absorption emerged. Release of the Indian work force from the estates and their movement to the urban areas incited the terrible racial strife of 1962-64 as they became open competitors with the already urban blacks. He concludes that with the country's best resources still tied up in estate sugar, Guyana's future development will be difficult.

Molen, G. van der. De rol van de mijnbouw en bosbouw in de Surinaamse ontwikkeling. See item 1269.

4528 Reid, P. A. Budget speech; 1969. Georgetown, Ministry of Finance, 1969. 49 p.

A review of the government's policies and the economy's evolution over 1965-69.

Veen, L. J. van der. De funkties van banken en verzekeringsmaatschappijen voor de ontwikkeling van Suriname. See item 1298.

VENEZUELA

JORGE SALAZAR-CARRILLO
*Special Advisor and Technical Coordinator
Programa de Estudios Conjuntos
sobre Integración Económica Latinoamericana (ECIEL)
The Brookings Institution*

DURING THE PERIOD COVERED BY THIS EDITION of the *Handbook*, there has been a notable increase in the volume and a marked improvement in the quality of economic research on Venezuela. Moreover, the reduction in important contributions from foreigners attests to the scholarship of Venezuelans themselves.

As was noted in the *HLAS 35,* a few institutions continue to issue most books and articles on the country's economics: The Central Bank of Venezuela, the Planning Office (CORDIPLAN) and the Univ. Central de Venezuela, all of them in Caracas. One should note the quality of Central Bank publications in particular, e.g. studies like those of Hassan (item 4549), Peltzer (item 4563) and the three-decade review of the Venezuelan economy by the bank's staff (item 4532) all a credit to the institution's efforts on behalf of economic research in Venezuela.

As to subjects most frequently covered, Venezuelan economists seem to be chiefly concerned with oil and agriculture, the most and least successful sectors of the economy. There have also been a number of macroeconomic studies on industrialization, unemployment, and development in general, as well as on urban and regional studies.

A debt of gratitude is owed to Roberto Correia Lima, João Gonçalves de Souza Jr., and María Cristina Iriarte de Uricochea for their contribution in the form of annotations which bear their initials.

4529. Araujo, Orlando. La política de sustitución de importaciones en Venezuela (BCV/REL, 9:35, 1973, p. 55-84, tables)

The author analyzes the Venezuelan imports substitution policy of the last 20 years. Based on the study of industrial production and employment, he concludes that the policy adopted failed as it increased Venezuela's external dependence and as labor absorption in the industrial sector failed to be as high as had been expected. [R.C.L.]

4530. Balestrini C., César. Los precios del petróleo y la participación fiscal de Venezuela. Caracas, Univ. Central de Venezuela, Facultad de Ciencias Económicas y Sociales, División de Publicaciones, 1974. 130 p., bibl., tables.

Essay on the prices of oil in the recent decades, and how they have been used by the Venezuelan government to determine oil taxes. Generally the various Venezuelan administrations have based oil taxes on reference. Prices which differ from those declared by the companies' various regimes are compared.

4531. Baloyra, Enrique A. Oil policies and budgets in Venezuela: 1938-1968 (LARR, 9:2, Summer 1974, p. 28-72, tables)

An analysis of federal expenditures in Venezuela for the time period mentioned. The methodology used by Wilkie in his well known study of Mexico is utilized. However, the author introduces some changes which make it more useful, and restrict the inferences implied. A well done piece of research which illuminates the policies and overall impact of various Venezuelan regimes.

4532. Banco Central de Venezuela, *Caracas.* La economía venezolana en los últimos treinta años. Caracas, 1971. 318 p., tables.

A collection of the most important Venezuelan statistics on economic activity covering the 1940-70 period. These data are briefly analyzed in an introductory essay. An invaluable compendium.

4533. ———, ———. Memoria. Caracas, 1973. 83 p., tables.

Yearly report of the activities of the Central Bank of Venezuela. It includes financial statements and a synopsis of the evolution of the Venezuelan economy in 1973.

4534. Barreto, Irma. El dólar en caos: Venezuela dentro de la crisis. Caracas, Ediciones Lo de Hoy, 1973. 64 p., bibl., illus. (Información, 1)

A marxist analysis of the internacional monetary crisis and it's implications in the economy of Venezuela and other peripheric countries.

4535. *Boletín de la Cámara de Comercio*

de Caracas. Año 79, No. 717, agosto 1973- . Caracas.

A Venezuelan business periodical.

Burelli, Miguel Angel. Afirmación de Venezuela: itinerario de una inquietud. See item 8514a.

4536. *Business Venezuela*. American Chamber of Commerce of Venezuela. No. 12, Oct. 1970- . Caracas.

Special issue devoted to the Chamber's 20th anniversary, with information on its history.

4537. Carrillo Batalla, Tomás Enrique. Implicaciones económicas del desempleo en Venezuela (BCV/REL, 9:36, 1973, p. 43-98, tables)

The author, who has been Secretary of Treasury in his country, discusses in this paper: a) the notion of unemployment and the ambiguities that it involves; b) a typology of unemployment; c) the kind of unemployment generated in Venezuela, and d) a policy of unemployment. The paper is a good blend of theory, data and analysis. [M.C.U.]

4538. Casas González, Antonio. La energía eléctrica y el desarrollo económico. Caracas, Presidencia de la República, Oficina Central de Coordinación y Planificación [and] Editorial Sucre, 1973. 10 p.

Author's speech during inauguration ceremonies of the "Primeras Jornadas Nacionales de Potencia," at Ciudad Guayana, 21 Feb. 1973. Gives much insight, in an abbreviated form, on the energy (electrical power) sector of the economy, its problems, goals and future government plans. [J.G.S.J.]

4539. _____. Industrialización e integración. Caracas, Presidencia de la República, Oficina Central de Coordinación y Planificación [and] Editorial Sucre, 1972. 15 p.

Author's speech during the Seminar on Industrialization in Latin America, held on 19 June 1975, in Mexico City. Its main theme is that Latin America should strengthen its economic, political and social ties, so that, in the future, integrated economies could exist, in order to improve man's welfare and a more equitable international social justice. [J.G.S.J.]

4540. _____. Venezuela: el hombre como objetivo fundamental del desarrollo. Caracas, Editorial Sucre, 1973? 38 p.

The last presentation of the Planning Minister of Venezuela, at the end of the Caldera period, to the CIAP (Inter-American Committee of the Alliance for Progress). He reviews the accomplishments of the Caldera administration in fostering the economic development of Venezuela, and particularly in stressing the importance of the human factor in development.

4541. Chaves Vargas, Luis Fernando. Estructura funcional de las ciudades venezolanas. Mérida, Ven., Univ. de los Andes, Facultad de Ciencias Forestales, Instituto de Geografía y Conservación de Recursos Naturales, 1973. 157 p., bibl., tables.

A good attempt at classifying Venezuelan cities mainly using criteria developed in the fields of regional economics and urban planning. The various models used are discussed first, and integrated according to their applicability to the Venezuelan case. With a data base developed by CENDES, of the Univ. Central de Venezuela, from the 1961 Population Census, the theoretical framework is used to classify and analyze the economic structure of Venezuelan cities.

4542. Conde Regardiz, Pedro. Estimación de la influencia del progreso tecnológico en la economía nacional (BCV/REL, 9:33, 1972, p. 63-109, bibl., tables)

An attempt to measure the effect of technical progress on overall economic growth in Venezuela. The regional production function approach to the measurement of technical progress is utilized to estimate this impact. Sectoral estimates are also provided. A still simple study of technical progress in Venezuela, but a good first step in the analysis of this important aspect of development.

4543. *Cuadernos de la Sociedad Venezolana de Planificación*. Sociedad Venezolana de Planificación. Nos. 108/110, enero/marzo 1973- Caracas.

This issue includes four essays on income distribution: 1-2) The first two by Hector Valecillos, one on Venezuela's income distribution and its recent changes, the other on the effectiveness of traditional institutional mechanisms adopted in Venezuela for purpose of income redistribution, especially the bargaining power of workers' unions (syndicates); 3) Victor Tokman's is a study of income distribution, technology and employment in the Venezuelan industrial sector; and 4) Eleonora Medina's is a critical review of the different theories concerning income distribution. [R.C.L.]

4544. Executive compensation service: reports on international compensation, Venezuela. N.Y., American Management Associations (AMACOM), 1973. 62 p., tables.

Annual report on compensation paid by local and US companies in Venezuela. This report corresponds to the year 1973. Includes information on compensation policies and practices of such firms. Covers primarily the management positions and is limited to the industrial sector. Data presented are useful for international comparisons and time series, given that they are gathered on a yearly basis, and that similar surveys are conducted in other Latin American countries and Europe. However very little explanation is given of

4545. Falcón Urbano, Miguel A. Desarrollo e industrialización de Venezuela: un enfoque metodológico. Prólogo de D.F. Maza Zavala. Caracas, Univ. Central de Venezuela, Facultad de Ciencias Económicas y Sociales, 1969. 245 p., bibl., tables.

An analysis of the economic development of Venezuela from 1950 to 1965 using the tools proposed and followed by the Economic Commission for Latin America for the study of growth in these economies. Special emphasis is given to the industrial sector, which is considered basic to growth. The book is interesting both as an illustration of the ECLA method, and as a complete examination of Venezuelan growth based on a large number of tables and graphs. The author derives policy conclusions at the end of the book, which are based on a solid consideration of alternatives.

4546. Gilhodes, Pierre. L'Amérique Latine face aux nouveaux aspects du problème pétrolier (FNSP/RFSP, 22:6, déc. 1972, p. 1308-1328, tables)

A factual account of the development of petroleum policy in Venezuela and the external factors impinging on it. Some attention given to the rest of Latin America. [J.M. Hunter]

4547. Gómez Tamayo, Eduardo. Desarrollo y perspectiva de la industria azucarera (CVF/C, 1, 1973, p. 7-13, plates)

A brief description of the evolution of the sugar industry in the country and a consideration of its future development. Considers the role of the Corporación Venezolana de Fomento in helping to fulfill the industry's need for capital.

4548. Hanson, James A. Cycles of economic growth and structural change in Venezuela: 1950-1974. Santiago, Instituto Latinoamericano de Planificación Económica y Social (ILPES), n.d. 52 p., bibl., tables (mimeo)

Good summary of recent economic history of Venezuela, presented at the LASA Association Meetings, and shortly to appear in a book on Venezuela. It provides invaluable statistical series and references for the period examined.

4549. Hassan, Mostafa Fathy. Economic growth and employment problems in Venezuela: an analysis of an oil based economy. N.Y., Praeger Publishers, 1975. 185 p., bibl., tables (Praeger special studies in international economics and development)

One of the most comprehensive studies of the Venezuelan economy to appear in recent years. It covers the impact of oil on the economy from the 1950s on. Also examines the characteristics of Venezuelan growth, based on stability of prices, external transactions, etc., during these years. Contrasts all this with the increasing danger of unemployment and underemployment, considering the reasons why fast growth could only alleviate this problem, but not eliminate it. His analysis of this problem leads him into a consideration of the factors determining the rapid expansion of the labor supply, and an insufficient growth of labor demand in key sectors. At the end of the planning mechanism in Venezuela is examined and found deficient, and some policy conclusions are derived. This study is also available in a Spanish translation: *Crecimiento económico y problemas de empleo en Venezuela* (Traducción de Luis Cabana, Caracas, Banco Central de Venezuela, 1973, 205 p., bibl., tables [Col. de estudios económicos, 1]).

4550. Heaton, Louis E. The agricultural development of Venezuela. N.Y., Praeger Publishers, 1969. 320 p., tables (Praeger special studies in international economics and development)

A benchmark study of Venezuelan agriculture, in the style of those sponsored by the Ford Foundation in Latin America in the second half of the 1960s. The study examines the characteristics of the agricultural sector in Venezuela, considering its recent growth record with emphasis on the 1960-65 period, and its technical and institutional progress. Based on such factors, and on the expected growth of the economy as a whole, the development of agriculture in Venezuela is forecast to 1975. The book ends with suggestions and policy recommendations which would help accelerate the sector's growth. The study is an important contribution to research on Venezuelan agriculture.

4551. Herrera Navarro, Ramón. OPEP: precios del petróleo y crisis energética. Caracas, Univ. Central de Venezuela, Facultad de Ciencias Económicas y Sociales, División de Publicaciones, 1974. 97 p., bibl., tables.

A description of the origins, functioning and objectives of OPEC. An examination of the issues affecting the organization nowadays, and on their possible impact on the industrialized and developing nations, depending on OPEC action.

4552. Instituto Iberoamericano de Derecho Agrario y Reforma Agraria. Mérida, Ven., Talleres Gráficos Universitarios, 1973. 85 p., plates.

Most important aspects of the creation of this institute. Only of informative value.

4553. Izard, Miguel. La agricultura venezolana en una época de transición (FJB/BH, 28, enero 1972, p. 1-67, tables)

Historical analysis of the Venezuelan agriculture from 1777 to 1830 of interest to economists as well as sociologists. The author describes the process of rationalization of agriculture under the Bourbon dynasty and its further developments during the pre- and post-independence period. Interesting and useful for the historical data on crops, exports, prices, etc. [M.C.U.]

4554. Krivoy, Ruth O. de. El mercado monetario en Venezuela (ACPS/B, 33:52/53, enero/junio 1973, p. 101-127)

A good and clear review of the problems faced by the financial sectors (including of course the banking system) in Venezuela. Some proposals are made for an improvement of the situation, which stresses their contribution to stronger monetary policy. The author is one of the top economists at the Central Bank.

4555. Lasuen, José Ramón. Venezuela: un análisis de los cambios geográficos en la participación industrial (*in* Funes, Julio César ed. La ciudad y la región para el desarrollo. Caracas, Comisión de Administración Pública de Venezuela, 1972, p. 502-567, maps, tables)

The article is concerned with the geographical patterns of the economy. It refers specifically to changes in the industrial participation of the diverse Venezuelan regions from 1941-61. Lasuen concludes that the pattern of industrial concentration has not been reversed during this period, in spite of serious and otherwise successful government efforts towards creating a complex of highways and transport infrastructure. He suggests that the change will come only as a result of a specific governmental policy of a more balanced industrial participation of the different regions. The analysis was made on the basis of census data. [M.C.U.]

4556. López Acosta, Antonio. CORDIPLAN informa. Caracas, Oficina Central de Coordinación y Planificación, 1973. 126 p.

Varied short presentations on different economic matters by the previous undersecretary of planning of Venezuela. Prepared for public TV, they are simple in language and have only informative value. CORDIPLAN stands for Oficina Central de Coordinación y Planificación (Caracas).

4557. Losada Aldana, Ramón. Fetichismo del petróleo: aproximaciones a una sociología de la explotación petrolera en Venezuela (Ruedo Ibérico [Paris] 22/24, dic. 1968/mayo 1969, p. 155-175, bibl., table)

An interpretation of the impact of petroleum on Venezuelan society, based on the writings of marxists and neo-leftists both in Venezuela and abroad. Nothing new, but a good synthesis of the points of view prevalent at the Univ. Central de Venezuela.

4558. Lucena, Héctor R. La participación de los trabajadores en la gestión empresarial en Venezuela. Carabobo, Ven., Univ. de Carabobo, Facultad de Ciencias Económicas y Sociales, Escuela de Relaciones Industriales, 1973. 77 p., bibl., illus., tables.

An essay gathering the available information on the sharing of employers' profits and decision making with workers. It surveys Venezuelan labor legislation and union-labor contracts for such evidence, and finds that such participation in decision making has made only modest strides in Venezuela.

4559. Malavé Mata, Héctor. Aproximación al análisis estructural de la inflación en Venezuela (Ruedo Ibérico [Paris] 22/24, dic. 1968/mayo 1969, p. 179-211, tables)

The author, a well known economist from the Univ. Central de Venezuela, argues against a monetarist interpretation of inflation in his country. He submits a dialectical approach to the analysis of that phenomenon in Venezuela, which is a sort of modified structuralism. In such fashion he explains the existence of submerged inflation in this country.

4560. Maza Zavala, D.F. Consideraciones sobre la economía venezolana (UNAM/PDD, 2:6, enero/marzo 1971, p. 73-86)

An analysis written in 1971 of the Venezuelan economy and its place in that of the world economy. The author forsees a very gloomy future for the Venezuelan economy. [R.C.L.]

Mikdashi, Zunayr. The community of oil exporting countries: a study of governmental cooperation. See item 8528.

Monroe, Elizabeth and Robert Mabro eds. Oil producers and consumers: conflict or cooperation. See item 8078.

4561. Orta, Celio S. Impacto de los ingresos petroleros sobre el crecimiento del sector agrícola. Caracas, Univ. Central de Venezuela, Facultad de Ciencias Económicas y Sociales, División de Publicaciones, 1974. 66 p., bibl., tables. (Col. Esquema)

A short and superficial essay on the impact of oil-derived public revenues on the agricultural sector. Lack of data hampers the effort, which is concentrated on the late 1950s and the 1960s, including only a few years of the present decade. An introductory effort.

4562. Panorama de la economía venezolana durante el período enero-junio del año 1968; enero-junio del año 1969; segundo semestre del año 1971; tercer trimestre del año 1972; cuarto trimestre del año 1972 (BCV/REL, 7:25/26, 1969, p. 7-40, tables; 8:28, 1969, p. 7-41, tables; 9:33, 1972, p. 7-43, tables; 9:35, 1973, p. 7-40, tables; 9:36, 1973, p. 7-42, tables)

Bi-annual and quarterly analysis of the performance of the Venezuelan economy. Mostly based on the short-run evolution of monetary, fiscal and foreign-trade variables. Brief and not very deep, but well grounded in appended statistics. A good source of data on the short-run behavior of the country's economy which appears regularly in *Revista de Economía Latinoamericana* published in Venezuela's Central Bank.

4563. Peltzer, Ernesto. Ensayos sobre economía. Caracas, Banco Central de Venezuela, 1965. 457 p., tables.

A collction of articles, essays and documents, some of which have been published elsewhere, encompassing the intellectual production of one of Venezuela's Central Bank's chief advisors over a period of 15 years. Most of this first rate essay has to do with monetary matters, whether of an internal or external nature.

4564. Plaza, Salvador de la. Estructura agraria (Ruedo Ibérico [Paris] 22/24, dic. 1968/mayo 1969, p. 213-237, tables)

Interesting analysis of the evolution of the Venezuelan agrarian structure since independence, by a leftist professor of the Univ. Central de Venezuela. Includes useful statistics and emphasizes the more recent period.

4565. ———. El problema de la tierra. Caracas, Univ. Central de Venezuela, Facultad de Ciencias Económicas y Sociales, División de Publicaciones, 1973. 122 p., illus.

Series of four lectures given by the author from 1944 to 1959 stressing the urgent need for agrarian reform as a tool for economic development in Venezuela. From a marxist perspective, the author analyzes the ways in which the tenancy system inherited from colonial times accounts for the actual shortage of food and the need to import it. Thus, the "latifundio" indirectly impinges on problems in the balance-of-payments. [M.C.U.]

4566. Ramírez S., Thaís and Nelson Vigas D. La Corporación Venezolana de Fomento y el desarrollo económico de Venezuela. Caracas, Corporación Venezolana de Fomento, Sub-Gerencia de Servicios Técnicos, Depto. Unidad de Estudios, División de Estadística, 1972. 141 p., bibl., tables.

Gives an overall view of the "Corporación Venezolana de Fomento, its background, characteristics, objectives, functions, organogram, and its financial and economic activities during the period 1946-71. Contains also pertinent information on national planning schemes and state financial contributions. [J.G.S.J.]

Ravell, Carola. Le programme d'action communautaire rattaché à la Présidence de la République du Vénézuela. See item 8536.

4567. Reunión de Técnicos de Bancos Centrales del Continente Americano, X, Caracas, 1972. Memoria. Caracas, 1972. 3 v. (Various pagings) tables.

Proceedings of a meeting of Central Bank Technicians from the hemisphere. The Venezuelan Central Bank hosted the meeting and prepared the final volumes, consisting mainly of the numerous papers presented by invited authors. The papers are both in Spanish and English, and cover the whole breadth of monetary economics. Most anybody would be able to find something of interest in the volumes.

4568. *Revista del Banco Central de Venezuela,* Año 32, Nos. 323-325, enero/marzo 1972- . Caracas.

This issue (103 p., tables) contains: summary of economic activities; an article on the Caribbean Free Trade Association; main legislative measures of economic nature adopted during the first quarter of 1972; main legislative measures affecting the Central Bank of Venezuela as well as general studies made by the bank; and a statistical appendix. [J.G.S.J.]

4569. Robin, John P.; Frederick C. Terzo and Jaime Valenzuela. Urbanization in Venezuela. N.Y., Ford Foundation, International Urbanization Survey, 1973? 51 p., map, tables.

Survey of the country's current situation with regard to urbanization, along with a description of government efforts to invest heavily in the diversification of the sectoral and spatial base of its economy, presenting the case of Ciudad Guyana with considerable detail as an "experiment" in planning for those objectives. [M.C.U.]

4570. Roche, Eduardo; Oswaldo Armitano; and Pedro Burguillos. Programa de industrialización de la región del Alto Llano Occidental (*in* Funes, Julio César ed. La ciudad y la región para el desarrollo. Caracas, Comisión de Administración Pública de Venezuela, 1972, p. 432-500, tables)

A worthwhile piece of research examining the use of linear programming in planning the development of a backward and sparsely populated region near the Venezuelan Andes. Stresses industrial planning and assumes the convenience of decentralizing industrialization in order to create effective regional poles.

Rouhani, Fuad. A history of O.P.E.C. See item 8538.

4571. Sader Pérez, Rubén. Petróleo polémico y otros temas. Caracas, Síntesis Dosmil, 1973. 233 p. (Col. Libros para el desarrollo)

A collection of articles for the press, mostly on petroleum.

4572. Sardón José. La política petrolífera

internacional (ARBOR, 82:321/322, Sept./Oct. 1972, p. 79-90, tables)

A commentary on the relatively recent international petroleum scene.

4573. Soto, Oscar David. La empresa y la reforma agraria en la agricultura venezolana. Prólogo por José María Franco García. Mérida, Ven., Univ. de Los Andes, Facultad de Derecho, Instituto Iberoamericano de Derecho Agrario y Reforma Agraria [and] Fundación para la Cultura Campesina, Federación Campesina de Venezuela, 1973. 307 p., bibl., facsims., tables (Serie Investigaciones, 1)

A thorough and extensive historical survey of agriculture from colonial times down to our days. The author looks upon agrarian reform as an avenue in the transformation of the Venezuelan agriculture and calls for different production formulas as healthy way of coping with agrarian problems. [M.C.U.]

4574. Tokman, Víctor. Distribución del ingreso, tecnología y empleo en el sector industrial de Venezuela (*in* Foxley, Alejandro *ed.* Distribución del ingreso. México, Fondo de Cultura Económica, 1974, p. 415-477)

A careful look at the role of the technology used, in employment and income distribution. [J. Strasma]

Universidad de los Andes, *Mérida, Ven.* **Facultad de Economía. Instituto de Investigaciones Económicas.** Estudio de cuentas regionales para los Estados de Barinas, Mérida, Táchira y Trujillo: 1960-1966. See item 7039.

4575. Vallenilla, Luis. Auge, declinación y porvenir del petróleo venezolano. Caracas, Editorial Tiempo Nuevo, 1973. 757 p., fold. map, tables.

A careful and detailed examination of the evolution of the oil industry in Venezuela, mostly focusing on the relations between the industry and the Venezuelan government. This is mostly accomplished by an examination of the laws, regulations, decrees, etc., through which the changing oil policies of the government were implemented.

4576. Venezuela. Ministerio de Fomento. Dirección General de Estadísticas y Censos Nacionales. Estadísticas industriales: 1971. Caracas, 1973. 6 v. (Various pagings) tables.

Six volumes of data on the manufacturing sector based on monthly surveys during the year 1971. It presents data, classified according to the U.N. Industrial Classification, on value of production, sales, labor aspects, electricity, etc., sometimes on a monthly basis. Disaggregation varies according to type of data.

4577. ———. Ministerio de Minas e Hidrocarburos. Dirección General. Oficina de Economía Petrolera. Petróleo y otros datos estadísticos. 16 ed. Caracas, 1973. 239 p., illus., tables.

Its objective is to maintain the interested individual well informed of the changes that have occurred in the petroleum industry, nationally and worldwide. Numerous tables and illustrations clarify the text. [J.G.S.J.]

4578. ———. Presidencia. Oficina Central de Coordinación y Planificación (CORDIPLÁN). La planificación en la América Latina: legislación básica. Introducción por Tomás Polanco Alcantara. Caracas, Editorial Miguel Angel García, 1973. 389 p.

Brings together a collection of national laws and basic legislations pertinent to 20 nations (Argentina, Bolivia, Chile, Colombia, Costa Rica, Cuba, Dominican Republic, Ecuador, El Salvador, Guatemala, Haiti, Honduras, Jamaica, Mexico, Nicaragua, Panama, Paraguay, Peru, Urug̱ay and Venezuela) for those who wish to study juridical aspects of Latin American and Caribbean national planning. [J.G.S.J.]

4579. ———. ———. ———. Posibilidades de exportación de la industria venezolana. Prefacio por Meir Merhav. Caracas, Editorial Arte, 1973. 165 p., tables.

An analysis of Venezuela's export possibilities vis-à-vis the Fourth National Plan's export goals. Consists of five chapters: a synopsis of the traditional export structure with respect to the industrialization process, an analysis of the manufacturing industry's growth and future perspectives, contributions to the industrialization policy for export promotion, and evaluation of existing export financing policies and of the administrative bureaucracy engaged in export related acti̱ ities, and, finally, a few overall recommendations. [J.G.S.J.]

Yager, Joseph A. and others. Energy and U.S. foreign policy: a report to the Energy Policy Project of the Ford Foundation. See item 8133.

4580. Zavala, D.F. and others. Venezuela: crecimiento sin desarrollo. Caracas, Univ. Central de Venezuela [and] Editorial Nuestro Tiempo, 1974. 441 p., tables (Col. Latinoamerica hoy)

Consists of seven essays by Univ. Central scholars on Venezuela's economics and politics: 1) Maza Zavala shows Venezuela's position as a Third World, Latin American country, within the present global conjuncture; 2) Héctor Mata's is a brief summary of Venezuela's economic history; 3) Celio Horta analyzes the obstacles to the development of Venezuelan agriculture; 4) Orlando Araujo's is about the industrialization process in Venezuela; and 5) Maza Zavala, examines Venezuela's present economic situation and its future prospects. The sixth essay, by Bolívar Challet, discusses demographic behaviour in underdeveloped areas, specifically in Venezuela. The seventh essay, by Alfredo Chacon, analyzes the trajectory of leftist thought in Venezuela during the period 1958-1973. [R.C.L.]

BOLIVIA, CHILE, PARAGUAY, PERU AND URUGUAY

JOHN D. STRASMA
Professor of Economics and Agricultural Economics
University of Wisconsin, Madison

BRUCE H. HERRICK
Associate Professor of Economics
University of California, Los Angeles

THE VOLUME OF PUBLICATIONS DEALING WITH the countries covered continues unabated. The shifts to which we have called attention in the past—in particular, toward Latin American authorship—also rose during the biennium under review. Reflecting trends in the literature on economic development as a whole, the emphasis on employment, income distribution, and agricultural development has eclipsed the previous weight given to industrial economics and topics in applied monetary theory.

The Chilean situation continued to claim attention. The universities have been heavily restructured and at this writing, the national university [Univ. de Chile] continues under the direction of a military interventor with power of veto over the academic activities proposed by the rector and his council. Social sciences have not flourished and in some instances have been actively repressed under the military government. We see the results of these changes in the bibliography, and we expect it to be reflected in the next edition dedicated to the social sciences (*HLAS 39*) as well.

The Peruvian situation reflects that country's social experimentation under another group of generals, whose political and economic tendencies are considerably more heterodox. Perhaps the most noteworthy digression from conventional economic policy in Peru are the attempts at worker management of enterprises. These movements, while documented in some of the bibliographic items noted below, have not been adequately studied in their Peruvian variants. The comparisons between them and similar forays into new forms of economic organization in Yugoslavia, Israel, and China deserve more systematic attention than they have previously received.

Bolivia, Paraguay, and Uruguay continue the seeming absence of a research tradition. The only exception is the field of Bolivian agrarian reform, which has been the target of concentrated attention.

BOLIVIA

4581. La agricultura en Potosí: desarrollo y economía, año agrícola 1973/74. Potosí, Bol., Univ. Boliviana Mayor Tomás Frías, División de Extensión Universitaria, 1973. 55 p.

Speeches given at a meeting urging that more attention be paid to agriculture in a region whose economy is usually regarded as based on mining. Only one paper has any data, and that is on national wheat output. For a more complete study of this subject, see item 4593.

4582. Alurralde Anaya, Antonio. Cooperativas mineras. La Paz, Talleres Escuela Don Bosco, 1973. 369 p., bibl., plates.

Essentially a detailed tract, reviewing the mining cooperative movement and arguing for its extension. Notable photographs remind the reader of the labor-intensiveness of small mines.

4583. Bolivia. Instituto Nacional de Estadística. Clasificación de actividades económicas de Bolivia. La Paz, 1974. 60 l.

Provides the UN Uniform International Industrial Classification at the six-digit level. No information about output or industrial organization of any of these activities is given.

4584. Burke, Melvin. Estudios críticos sobre la economía boliviana. La Paz, Editorial Los Amigos del Libro, 1973. 271 p., tables.

The author, a North American professor of economics, reprints here in Spanish five of his articles that appeared elsewhere. Included are works on land reform, foreign aid, and capital formation.

4585. ———. Land reform in the Lake Titicaca region (in Malloy, James M. and Richard S. Thorn eds. Beyond the Revolution: Bolivia since 1952. Pittsburgh, Pa., Univ. of Pittsburgh Press, 1971, p. 301-339, tables)

Author fails to find significant differences between Peruvian agricultural properties and those across the Bolivian border affected by the post-1952 Bolivian land reform. This unexpected conclusion merits careful study. For Spanish translation see item 4584. An earlier version appeared in *Economic Development and Cultural Change* (18:3, April 1970, p. 410-450)

4586. Candia Navarro, René. Bolivia y la subregión andina (KO, 73, julio/sept. 1970, p. 7-20, tables)

Brief review of the Andean pact, with even briefer reference to implications for Bolivian development. Worthy of scholarly neglect.

4587. Clark, Ronald James. Land-holding structure and land conflicts in Bolivia's lowland cattle regions (IAMEA, 28:2, Autumn 1974, p. 15-38, tables)

Interview-based study of a hitherto neglected agricultural region in Bolivia. Foresees continued concentration in land holdings for cattle, but deals with the phenomenon on institutional grounds, rather than citing, e.g., economies of scale.

4588. Cuenca, Humberto. Memorias de un banquero. La Paz, Imprenta y Librería Renovación, 1972. 150 p.

Personalized and self-congratulatory reminiscences of the octogenarian ex-President of the Bolivian Central Bank.

4589. Heyduk, Daniel. The hacienda system and agrarian reform in highland Bolivia: a re-evaluation (UP/E, 13:1, Jan. 1974, p. 1-11)

A study of differential regional success in agrarian reform finds, not surprisingly, that regions of greater success were those where "the pre-existing hacienda system included patterns which foreshadowed reform objectives." For ethnologist's comment, see item 1489.

4590. Quiroga Santa Cruz, Marcelo. El saqueo de Bolivia. 2. ed. B.A., Ediciones de Crisis, 1973. 155 p. (Col. Política)

An official of the Bolivian Socialist Party (PSB) reviews the institutional links between foreign investment, national elites, international organizations, and Bolivian state corporations and banks, concentrating on 1971-72. Polemical in tone, but a detailed account.

4591. Romero Loza, José. Bolivia: nación en desarrollo. La Paz, Editorial Los Amigos del Libro, 1974. 457 p., bibl., tables.

Historical, polemical essays on national development and policies by a professional who in addition to having served as Finance Minister on four occasions and as a diplomat abroad, originally founded the Industrial Bank of Bolivia. He now resides in Santa Cruz as a farm operator.

4592. Seminario de Ideas y Proyectos Específicos (SIPE), *Santa Cruz, Bol., 1972.* Santa Cruz y el desarrollo. Santa Cruz, Bol., Corporación Regional de Desarrollo, Comité de Obras Públicas, 1972. 698 p., fold. map, illus., plates, tables.

Proceedings volume of a week-long meeting organized to inform the public and potential investors of possible development projects, and to pressure public officials to take the policy measures (and provide funds) needed to make them viable. Uneven, but an excellent view of the vision and present state of this dynamic region.

4593. Wennergren, E. Boyd and **Morris D. Whitaker.** The status of Bolivian agriculture. Foreword by G. Edward Schuh. N.Y., Praeger Publishers, 1975. 308 p., bibl., maps, tables (Praeger special studies in international economics and development)

Another in a series of Ford Foundation financed 'benchmark studies' of agriculture in Latin America, with both field work and an exhaustive combing of secondary sources, many unpublished, in 1971-73. The authors believe that low productivity in the countryside can and should be raised in ways which also reduce prevailing poverty; output and equity are complements, not trade-offs, in their views.

Whitehead, Laurence. El impacto de la gran depresión en Bolivia. See *HLAS 36:2966.*

CHILE

4594. Arellano M., José Pablo. El gasto público en salud y la distribución del ingreso. Santiago, Centro de Estudios de Planificación Nacional (CEPLAN), 1974. 60 p.

Study of clients and kinds of visits and outlays therefore, in cooperation with the Ministry of Health.

Related to the Income Distribution workshop, but not completed in time for that publication (see item 4602) and so published separately. Ceplan's address: Casilla 16496, Correo 9, Santiago, Chile.

Baklanoff, Eric N. The expropriation of Anaconda in Chile: a perspective on an export "enclave." See item 8427.

4595. Baltra Cortes, Alberto. Gestión económica del gobierno de la Unidad Popular. Santiago, Editorial ORBE, 1973. 143 p. (Col. Encuentro)

Critical review of Allende's economy, published in Dec. 1973. Data mostly drawn from *HLAS 35:2550* and item 4617. Skillful contrast of policies enunciated and actual government action, well-informed because the author was a Senator and senior economist of Allende's coalition until his part of the Radical Party (PIR) joined the Opposition in 1972.

4596. Barraclough, Solon. La reforma agraria en Chile (FCE/TE, 38[2]:150, abril/junio 1971, p. 223-257)

Coherent explanation of the agrarian problem as perceived by Allende's government and of the strategy which the Popular Unity reform intended to apply. The author is a scholar and FAO expert who was closely involved in research and staff training during both the Frei and the Allende reforms.

4597. Behrman, Jere R. Determinantes de las tasas anuales de cambio de los salarios sectoriales en una economía en desarrollo (UCC/CE, 9:27, agosto 1972, p. 102-119, tables)

Based on salary changes from 1945 through 1965, the study relates changes with output, public credit, capacity utilization, wage rates, profitability of the subsector, expectations as to coming inflation, and errors in those predictions. Concludes that wages are determined largely by laws, not by economic factors.

4598. _____ Elasticidades de sustitución sectoriales entre capital y trabajo en una economía en vías de desarrollo: análisis de series de tiempo para el período de postguerra en Chile (UCC/CE, 9:26, abril 1972, p. 70-88, tables)

Sophisticated study of the possible substitution of capital and labor in Chile, based on data from mid-1940s. For English version which appeared in *Econometrica* (40:2, March 1972, p. 311-326) see *HLAS 35:2190*.

4599. Bitar, Sergio. La presencia de la empresa extranjera en la industria chilena (IDES/DE, 13:50, julio/sept. 1973, p. 244-284, tables)

Based on studies at CORFO in 1969-70, analyzes the extent of foreign shareholdings in Chilean industry, and the evolution of foreign investment by subsectors between 1967 and 1969. Analyzes 81 specific investments to determine extent to which the resulting firms were monopolies, shared in oligopolies, or competed with many other firms. Analyzes patents, royalties, and influence of owner nationality on source of inputs; finds evidence of overpricing of imported inputs.

4600. _____ and **Hugo Trivelli O.** Cálculo de rentabilidades financieras y económicas de empresas industriales chilenas (UCC/CE, 6:19, dic. 1969, p. 42-66)

Analysis of 117 Chilean firms with assets over $125,000 and in business for at least three years, based on annual reports to the Superintendent of Corporations. The data refer to 1960 through 1965, and appear by firm in an appendix. Concludes with policy suggestions regarding sharper bargaining on the purchase of technology.

4601. Brown, Marion; David Stanfield; and Stephen Smith. Some consequences for production and factor use of Chilean agrarian reform (Newsletter of the Land Tenure Center [Univ. of Wisconsin, Madison] 46, Oct./Dec. 1974, p. 6-18)

Summary report on the changes in farming practices, production and resource allocation resulting from the agrarian reform carried out by President Frei (p. 64-70). Based on a before-and-after field survey of a large random sample of farms eligible in 1965 for reform action; results of output and change in output per hectare are analyzed for reform units and farms and parts of farms not expropriated. Basic source for work on the impact of land reform on production.

Carmagnani, Marcello. Banques étrangeres et banques nationales au Chili: 1900-1920. See *HLAS 36:2972*.

4602. Chile. Centro de Estudios de Planificación Nacional (CEPLAN). Bienestar y pobreza. Santiago, Univ. Católica de Chile, 1974. 315 p. (Ediciones Nueva Universidad)

Excellent set of essays, most prepared originally for an International Workshop on Income Distribution and Development organized by CEPLAN in March 1973. The first essay, by Heskia, presents data on income distribution in Chile in 1967 by deciles and by sectors; some data go to 1969. Eight other essays then analyze the theme from policy, social structure, health, employment and similar viewpoints, concluding with estimates of the consumption function by income groups. Valuable for research libraries or serious scholars in this field.

4603. _____ Instituto Nacional de Estadísticas. Cuarto censo nacional de manufactureras: antecedentes generales, resultados según ubicación geográfica, tamaño y ramo de actividad de los establecimientos de cinco y más personas ocupadas. t. 3. Santiago, 1971. 390 p.

The census was conducted in 1968 and refers to data for 1967.

4604. Chile: el desafío (the challenge). Santiago, Dinex, 1974? 80 p. (ODEPLAN document. Serie auriga)

Bilingual, slick-paper brochure of excellent quality, designed to attract foreign investors and to persuade the reader that the Government has well-conceived plans to restore Chile's previous stature as a sophisticated, pleasant country well on the way toward modern industrialization. A minimum of polemics, with only passing references to the period 1970-73.

4605. Contreras, Víctor Nazar. El proceso de formación de la clase obrera (UNAM/RMS, 36:1, enero/marzo 1974, p. 77-109, tables)

Based on interviews of 920 workers in 68 Chilean industries; part of a much larger study on political socialization in three countries. Interviews were conducted in 1967.

4606. Corbo, Vittorio. Precios y salarios industriales e inflación en Chile: un modelo trimestral (UCC/CE, 9:26, abril 1972, p. 11-69, tables)

Part of the author's PhD thesis on Chilean inflation, presented at MIT in 1971. With his quarterly model, concludes that the "structuralists" actually understate Chile's problems. Even if Chile had no "structural" problems in agriculture and foreign trade, he estimates that it would take over 12 percent unemployment to slow inflation significantly.

4607. De Kadt, Emanuel. Distribución de la salud en Chile. Santiago, Centro de Estudios de Planificación (CEPLAN), 1973. 80 p. (Documento, 29)

Preliminary, more complete version of the study which appears in brief form as a chapter in item 4602.

4608. Domínguez, Oscar and Cristina Osorio. Recursos humanos clasificados: sector público agrícola. Santiago, Instituto de Capacitación e Investigación en Reforma Agraria (ICIRA), Oficina de Planificación Agrícola (ODEPA), 1971. 153 p., tables.

Analysis of the staff of public sector agencies concerned with agriculture, based on office tabulations and field interviews. Useful background for scholars interested in the successes and failures of Chilean agriculture and land reform in the period 1970-73. Probably still available at ODEPA.

4609. Ffrench-Davis, Ricardo. La importancia del cobre en Chile: antecedentes históricos, la integración de la gran minería del cobre a la economía nacional: el rol de las políticas económicas. Santiago, Centro de Estudios de Planificación (CEPLAN), 1974. 1 v. (Unpaged) (Documentos, 34/37)

Useful references for study of copper in Chile to and through the Allende period.

4610. _____. Mecanismos y objetivos de la redistribución del ingreso. Santiago, Centro de Estudios de Planificación (CEPLAN), 1973. 1 v. (Unpaged) (Documento, 28)

Analysis of the many instruments with which Chilean governments can and have attempted to change income distribution. Basic paper for the International Workshop whose principal papers appear in item 4602.

4611. _____ El Pacto Andino: un modelo original de integración. Santiago, Centro de Estudios de Planificación (CEPLAN), 1974. 32 p. (Documento, 42)

Describes the current state and functioning of the Andean Common Market, and then offers suggestions for policies oriented at exporting both to that market and also to the rest of the world.

4612. Foxley, Alejandro. Alternativas de organización en el proceso de transformación de la economía chilena (IDES/DE, 12:48, enero/marzo 1973, p. 659-686, tables)

Analyzes the merits and problems of various forms of decentralization under socialistic economic models.

4613. _____. Opciones de desarrollo bajo condiciones de reducción en la dependencia externa: un análisis cuantatativo (FCE/TE, 39:154, abril/junio 1972, p. 203-242)

An econometric study seeking to quantify effects of four options for Chile, 1970-75. The options are: standard development; internal saving, import substitution, full employment; growth with external dependence; full employment with an open economy but reduced dependence. The latter involves a section of interest on the appropriate diversification of exports. [J.M. Hunter]

4614. _____ and Oscar Muñoz. Redistribucion del ingreso crecimiento económico y estructura social: el caso chileno. Santiago, Univ. Católica de Chile [and] Centro de Estudios de Planificación Nacional (CEPLAN), 1973. 46 1., tables (Estudios de planificación. Documento, 27)

Valuable effort to analyze changes in the income of the poorest and the next-to-poorest groups, especially in the cities. Illuminates some of the fears and forces at work during the Allende period (1970-73).

Gall, Norman. Copper is the wage of Chile. See item 8455.

4615. García, Antonio. Las cooperativas agrarias y el desarrollo de Chile

(FCE/TE, 40 [3]:159, julio/sept. 1973, p. 627-646, tables)

History of farm cooperatives in the context of Chilean politics from the 1930s through 1970. While the author is highly critical of land reform cooperatives in the Frei period (1964-70), there is almost nothing of substance on those developed in the Allende period.

4616. Gómez, Alejandro and Daniel Olden. Las causas económicas del crecimiento de ciudades in Chile (UCC/CE, 9:27, agosto 1972, p. 1-57, tables)

Stepwise multiple regression techniques were applied to 30 cities over 20,000, exploring the relative importance of industry, port activity, and the agricultural hinterland, etc. Port activity and previous rate of population growth turned out to be the most relevant.

4617. Gotuzzo, Lorenzo. Exposición sobre el estado de la hacienda pública, presentada por el Ministro de Hacienda Almirante . . . Santiago, Ministerio de Hacienda, 1973. 1 v. (Unpaged)

Basic source for the new government's version of fiscal affairs during the Popular Unity period, and explanation of the need for severe austerity measures.

4618. Instituto de Ingenieros de Minas, Santiago. La minería en Chile. Santiago, 1973. 1 v. (Unpaged) plates.

Attractive, well-written description of all of the major mines in Chile, both copper and others such as nitrates, coal and cement plants and oil fields. Excellent photography, and free of polemics.

4619. Jeftanovic P., Pedro. Estudio sobre el ahorro familiar en el gran Santiago (UCC/CE, 8:24, agosto 1971, p. 73-104, tables)

Personal savings estimated at 11 percent or 8.6 percent after allowing for depreciation of housing. Income a decisive variable; supports the permanent income hypothesis. Based on a survey of family budgets in 1968/69, the study refutes the long-held assumption among Chilean planners that personal savings are negative much of the error came from overlooking construction of improvements without building permits being issued or sought.

4620. LeGates, Richard T. A decade of struggle for housing in Chile (IAMEA, 28:2, Autumn 1974, p. 51-75, bibl.)

Based on research while a visiting professor at the Univ. of Chile, on the self-help housing schemes and other policy experiments under Frei and Allende. Notes the adverse impact of nationalization on steel and cement production.

4621. Lehmann, David. Agrarian reform in Chile, 1965-1972: an essay in contradictions (*in* Lehman, David *ed.* Peasants, landlords and governments: agrarian reform in the Third World. N.Y., Holmes & Meier Publishers, 1974, p. 70-149, bibl.)

Good survey of the rural situation in early 1972; despite the title, quite superficial on the Frei period. Good bibliography and glossary.

4622. Machicado S., Flavio. The redistribution of income in Chile and its impact on the pattern of consumption of essential foods: 1970-1971. Madison, Univ. of Wisconsin, Land Tenure Center, 1974. 58 p. (LTC paper, 62)

Cross-sectional studies of food consumption by income class, done in Greater Santiago in 1968-69, are used to project consumption in 1971 under the income redistribution that occurred following the election of Allende. Since no new surveys were conducted to confirm the results of the projections, they show potential effects for nutritional improvement rather than actual ones.

4623. Monckeberg, Fernando. Jaque al subdesarrollo. Santiago, Editora Nacional Gabriela Mistral, 1974. 209 p. (Col. Pensamiento contemporáneo)

Well-written protest that Chile falls far short of economic potential. The author stresses the need for research, investment in export products, and suggests ending payment for the use of foreign patents. Best is Dr. Monckeberg's own famed research on nutrition and the link between malnutrition and underdevelopment.

4624. Morales, Marcelo and Leonardo Díaz. Evolución de las reformas financieras en Chile. Santiago, Banco del Estado del Chile, Depto. de Política Financiera y Económica, 1971. 16 p. (POLFINEC, 1)

Excellent short history of banking and monetary policies from Independence to 1967, prepared by researchers at the Banco del Estado with the hope that it would help prepare fellow bank employees in the private sector to share their enthusiasm for nationalization of all banks.

Moran, Theodore H. Multinational corporations and the politics of dependence: copper in Chile. See item 8482.

4625. Musalem, José. Crónica de un fracaso: frustración de un pueblo. Santiago, Editorial del Pacífico, Instituto de Estudios Políticos, 1973. 399 p.

Selection of speeches, on and off the Senate floor, by one of the leading politicians and economists of the Christian Democratic Party. Along with the polemics, numerous useful tables on price levels, policies and proposed policies, and attacks on specific programs of the Popular Unity Government.

4626. Petras, James F. La reforma agraria en Chile (UNAM/PDD, 2:6, enero/marzo 1971, p. 87-102, tables)

Spanish version of an earlier essay critizing Frei's land reform; the most useful part concerns the details of peasant organization efforts.

4627. Porteous, J. Douglas. The company state: a Chilean case-study (CAG/CG, 12:2, Summer 1973, p. 113-126, bibl., illus., maps)

Study of the Chuquicamata and El Salvador mines, and the nearby towns dependent on business from the mines and company towns. Analyzes new worker reluctance to forgo new company housing and accept living in the comparatively run-down, depressed nearby cities such as Calama.

4628. Sáenz, Orlando. Un país en quiebra: 33 preguntas a ... Santiago, Ediciones Portado, 1973. 107 p.

Extracts from public speeches criticizing Allende's government, by the President of Chile's National Assn. of Manufacturers (Sociedad de Fomento Fabril).

4629. Scott, C.D. Some problems of marketing among small-scale proprietors in Chile (Boletín de Estudios Latinoamericanos [Univ. of Amsterdam, Centro de Estudios y Documentación, Amsterdam] 13, dic. 1972, p. 21-32)

Case studies carried out in 1968-69 lead the author to advocate greater vertical integration for co-operative organizations of small-scale farmers. This article also available from Univ. of Wisconsin, Madison, Land Tenure Center, LTC reprint 115, June 1974.

4630. Selowsky, Marcelo. El costo de desacelerar la inflación: problemas conceptuales y órdenes de magnitud para Chile (UCC/CE, 7:20, abril 1970, p. 29-52)

Attempts to determine which policies might slow inflation, and the quantitative extent to which such policies would have to be applied to achieve results, as well as the consequent slowing of economic growth.

4631. Tampeau, Valerie. Données pour éclairer la situation chiliènne (EP, 234, jan. 1974, p. 69-94, table)

A serious effort to explain Allende's economic problems to foreign sympathizers, based largely on quotes from *L'Humanité* (French Communist Party newspaper). The author believes Allende was gaining on these problems in mid-1973, causing the conspirators to strike at that time lest he succeed in building a socialist economy without bloodshed.

4632. Tironi, Ernesto. La mediana y pequeña minería del cobre en Chile. Santiago, Centro de Estudios de Planificación (CEPLAN), 1974. 1 v. (Unpaged) (Documento, 36)

Data on the history, operations and organization of the rest of the copper mining sector, generally overlooked in studies dwelling on the large foreign-owned mines.

4633. Verduga Vélez, César. Economía chilena: dos años de prueba (Difusión Económica [Guayaquil, Ecua.] 11:2, agosto 1973, p. 75-84)

Popular, uncritical survey of Allende's economy in 1971 and 1972.

4634. Winn, Peter and **Cristóbal Kay.** Agrarian reform and rural revolution in Allende's Chile (JLAS, 6:1, May 1974, p. 135-159)

Comprehensive review of the objectives and methods used in agrarian reform during the first two years of the Allende government. Best source to date on the internal struggle in the coalition as to how to reorganize agriculture, and peasant reactions to these efforts.

PARAGUAY

4635. *Comercio.* Cámara y Bolsa de Comercio y del Centro de Importadores. Año 1, No. 1, enero 1968 [through] Año 2, No. 14, febrero 1969- . Asunción.

Conservative economic review of national problems and policies. Valuable as expression of views by this segment of the society.

4636. Mareski, Sofía and **Oscar Humberto Ferraro** comps. Bibliografía sobre datos y estudios económicos en el Paraguay. Asunción, Centro Paraguayo de Estudios Sociológicos, Centro Paraguayo de Documentación Social, 1972. 82 l. (mimeo)

Unannotated bibliography, classified by principal topic. Complements *HLAS* listings.

PERU

4637. Banco Minero del Perú, Lima. Exportaciones mineras del Perú, 1970; 1971. Lima, 1970-1971. 2 v. (88, 89 p.) tables

Two voluminous statistical reports (1970-71) showing production by individual mines both large and small, as well as details such as the intermediary firms shipping the output of each mine, countries of destination, degree and place of refining, etc. Valuable source for scholars of Peruvian industrial structure and for those interested in trade and development as well as a rich source for analysts of multinational companies—as their relationships can be traced right down to amounts charged the Peruvian mines for refining abroad.

Bobbio Centurión, Carlos. Contratos de petróleo: modelo peruano. See item 8365.

4638. _____. La fuerza armada, la industrialización y el mercado interno en el Perú (IAEERI/E, 3:15, marzo/abril 1972, p. 61-68)

A Peruvian colonel urges an economic strategy based on satisfying internal demand, and details the steps the army should take to implement such a strategy effectively.

4639. Bonilla, Heraclio. El minero de los Andes. Lima, Instituto de Estudios Peruanos, 1974. 89 p.

First analysis of the labor force and personnel practices of the Cerro de Pasco copper mine, based on records dating back to the opening of the mine, recently purchased by the Peruvian Government.

4640. Brundenius, Claes. The anatomy of imperialism: the case of the multi-national mining corporations in Peru (JPR, 3, 1972, p. 189-207, tables)

Neo-Marxist economic history of Peruvian mining. Well documented.

4641. Capuñay Mimbela, Carlos; José Uchuya Capcha; and Nelson Vera Segura. La devaluación y el proceso de inflación en el Perú (USM/RCEC, 76, enero/junio 1968, p. 131-192, tables)

A structuralist study of Peruvian inflation accompanied by devaluation, emphasizing the period 1960-66. Views devaluation as harmful to the economy; urges policies to avoid it in the future. Detailed empirical tables.

4642. Conferencia Anual de Ejecutivos (CADE), *XII, Paracas, Peru, 1973.* Actualidad y perspectivas de la integración andina: anales. Lima, Instituto Peruano de Administración de Empresas (IPAE), 1973. 328 p., plates, tables.

4643. Figueroa, Adolfo. El impacto de las reformas actuales sobre la distribución de ingresos (*in* Foxley, Alejandro *ed.* Distribución del ingreso. México, Fondo de Cultura Económica, 1974, p. 392-414)

Analysis of the possible impact of land reform, creation of the worker-community participation schemes, and other recent changes in the distribution of incomes.

4644. Flores, Edmundo. La reforma agraria del Perú (FCE/TE, 37:147, julio/sept. 1970, p. 515-523)

Rambling and tentative review of the early stages of Peruvian agrarian reform following the 1968 take-over by the military.

4645. Frankman, Myron J. Sectoral policy preferences of the Peruvian government, 1946-1968 (JLAS, 6:2, Nov. 1974, p. 289-300, tables)

Traces Peruvian economic growth before the military takeover in 1968 to export-led development. Considers the public policy measures that led to these results.

4646. Garrido-Lecca, Guillermo and **Gerald T. O'Mara.** The urban informal credit market in a developing country under financial repression: the Peruvian case. Austin, Univ. of Texas, Institute of Latin American Studies, 1974. 64 p., bibl., tables (Special publication)

The financial repression of the title is simply a high differential between costs in the formal and informal money markets. Reviews urban credit markets in Lima and Callao and measures the differential. Solid microeconomic analysis.

4647. Gussoni, Enrique Oscar. Apertura económica peruana: el contrato "Cuajone" (IAEERI/E, 1:5, enero/feb. 1970, p. 10-18, tables)

Reviews the military government's mining policies with respect to the treatment of foreign capital. No substantial economic analysis.

4648. Horton, Susan Ramírez. The sugar estates of the Lambayeque Valley, 1670-1800: a contribution to Peruvian agrarian history. Madison, Univ. of Wisconsin, Land Tenure Center, 1974. 63 p., illus. (LTC research paper, 58)

Abbreviated version of author's MA thesis of the same title (1973).

4649. Johnson G. C., Charles W. Perú: los militares como un agente de cambio económico (UNAM/RMS, 34:2, abril/junio 1972, p. 293-315)

Describes and analyzes changes in Peru after 1968. Concludes that the military may succeed as a force to refocus relationships but it is not expected to bring about a change of *systems*. [J. M. Hunter]

4650. Lewis, Robert Alden. Employment, income, and the growth of the barriadas in Lima, Peru. Ithaca, N.Y., Cornell Univ., Latin American Studies Program, 1973. 358 p., bibl., tables (Dissertation series, 46)

Surveys the degree of integration of the barriada economy in the general metropolitan economy, on the basis of sample surveys and the construction of an input-output table. Good descriptive statistics. Complements Mangin's earlier work, see *HLAS 35:1435.*

4651. Mesa Lago, Carmelo. La

estratificación de la seguridad social y el efecto de desigualdad en América Latina: el caso peruano (IBEAS/EA, 3:2, 1973, p. 17-48)

As part of research done for a forthcoming book, the author analyzes the Peruvian social security system as the response to political, economic, and union pressures. Although some improvement is noted over time, the stratified nature of the system is revealed by his careful measurements to result in unequal benefits for the country's various social groups.

4652. *Monthly Bulletin.* Adela Investment Co. Feb/April 1975- . Lima.

This "house organ" for a major, multilateral, private enterprise is an effort to help stimulate economic development through investment in Latin America and regularly carries economic news on individual countries. For instance, this issue surveys the six Andean economies and the Andean Common Market more thoroughly than most other available sources, particularly for the countries with military governments and a controlled press. To subscribe write to: Adela Investment Company, Apartado 207, Lima, Peru.

4653. Moreira, Neiva. Modelo peruano. B.A., Editorial La Línea, 1974. 346 p.

Readable book by a foreign journalist with a clear grasp of the Peruvian process since 1968. Based mainly on interviews, the book includes details of the preparation of the 1968 coup, as well as some analysis of the agrarian reform, worker communities and social property laws. Two final chapters by colleagues touch on educational reform and the Peruvian Amazon.

4654. Pasará, Luis; Jorge Santistevan; Diego García-Sazón; and Alberto Bustamante. Dinámica de la comunidad industrial. Lima, Centro de Estudios y Promoción del Desarrollo (DESCO), 1974. 274 p.

Anthology of essays on the law, ideology, functioning and outlook for the 1970 Law of the Industrial Community, including full coverage of the organization and recent Congress of Industrial Communities. Best single source on this experiment in worker *co-gestión*.

4655. Peru. Sistema de Asesoramiento y Fiscalización de las Cooperativas Agrarias de Producción. Azúcar peruana: historia de un cambio. Lima?, Difusión ONAMS, 1973. 78 p., bibl., illus., plates.

Popularized treatment praises the progress of Peruvian agrarian reform on the sugar plantations under the post-1968 military government.

4656. Perú, 1968-1973: cronología política. Lima, Centro de Estudios y Promoción del Desarrollo (DESCO), 1974. 2 v. (749 p.) (Continuous pagination)

Invaluable source for scholars trying to place policies of the Revolutionary Military Government in the context of other policies, events or pronouncements. Excellent compilation, with summaries and quotations in chronological order as well as complete indexes.

4657. *Peruvian Times.* Andean Air Mail and Peruvian Times, Vol. 32, No. 1631, 14 April 1972. Lima.

For businessmen's mining finance and marketing survey, see p. 7-50, including map and tables.

4658. Pinedo del Aguila, Víctor M. Evaluación económica de los recursos forestales de la Amazonía peruana (USM/RCEC, 76, enero/junio 1968, p. 5-130, tables)

A detailed description of the economic flora of Amazonian Peru is accompanied by the author's analysis of its present lack of development.

4659. Pont, Guillermo Marco del. Perú: hacia la revisión de las políticas de asistencia al exterior (BNCE/CE, 22:7, julio 1972, p. 597-602)

Largely self-serving and uncritical presentation before the CIAP of the economic events and prospects of 1971-72.

4660. Roel Pineda, Virgilio. Estructuras económicas y sociales. Lima, Editorial Gráfica Labor, 1975. 185 p.

Textbook, moving from generalities on economics as a science to exposition of demographic, inout-output and national accounting techniques. Few actual statistics, and those generally for 1970. The author is a prolific writer and professor at Lima's Univ. of San Marcos; he was also a government advisor on planning several times during the last decade.

4661. ———. El imperialismo de las corporaciones transnacionales. Lima, Editorial Gráfica Labor, 1974. 68 p., tables.

Two lectures given in 1973. The first, based largely on Baran, Sweezy and Galbraith, concludes that multinational corporations no longer export capital but rather bring it back, ripping off the Third World. The second describes the provisions of the 1970 General Law on Industries, for foreign investment.

4663. Samamé Boggio, Mario. Minería peruana: biografía y estrategia de una actividad decisiva. 2. ed. Lima, Editorial Gráfica Labor, 1974. 712 p., illus., plates, tables.

Massive study, in general institutionally oriented, of Peruvian mining. Potentially valuable for its wealth of details.

4664. Torres y Torres Lara, Carlos. Propiedad y cooperativismo en el Perú. Lima, Ediciones de Divulgación Cooperativa, 1973. 90 p.

Reviews the Peruvian cooperative movement, including the steps taken toward worker-managed firms. Although the tone is one of advocacy, the work has interest from a comparative management point of view.

4665. Webb, Richard. La distribución del ingreso en el Perú (*in* Foxley, Alejandro *ed.* Distribución del ingreso. México, Fondo de Cultura Económica, 1974, p. 73-89)

Thorough analysis of income distribution among regions of Peru, as well as between rural and urban areas, and rich and poor, in relation to the policies pursued by successive governments, and the actual results of these policies as well as of other economic forces and events.

4666. Witte, Ann Dryden. Employment in the manufacturing sector of developing economies: a study of Mexico and Peru (JDS, 10:1, Oct. 1973, p. 33-49, tables)

High elasticity of factor substitution together with changes in relative factor prices led to slow growth of employment in manufacturing in Mexico and Peru, although output was expanding rapidly. Author uses multiple regression analysis on post-World War II data.

4667. Zaldívar, Ramón. Agrarian reform and military reformism in Peru (*in* Lehman, David *ed.* Peasants, landlords and governments: agrarian reform in the Third World. N.Y., Homes & Meier Publishers, 1974, p. 25-69)

Good source on current law, production, implementation of the law through various kinds of organizations, etc. Includes cases not previously published, as well as description of forms of resistance to the law not generally known.

URUGUAY

4668. Bustelo, Ana Margarita *comp.* Monografías y tesis universitarias sobre industrialización en el Uruguay: 1937-1972. Monteviedo, Univ. de la República, Facultad de Ciencias Económicas y Administrativas, Secretaría Técnica, 1973. 40 p.

Unannotated list of Univ. de la República's theses and monographs for the years 1937-72, classified according to major topics.

4669. Campiglia, Néstor. Montevideo: población y trabajo. Montevideo, Editorial Nuestra Tierra, 1971. 60 p., bibl., maps, plates, tables (Serie Montevideo, 7)

Valuable description of labor market variables at work in Montevideo, including labor force participation, unemployment, educational attainment, occupational distribution, and migration. Uses data from censuses and surveys of mid- and late-1960s.

4670. Collin-Delavaud, Anne. Paysandú, ville industrielle d'Uruguay (CDAL, 7, 1973, p. 191-194)

Brief sketch of economic activity in Uruguay's third most populous (60,000) city.

4671. Fierro Vignoli, Pablo. Información sobre la industria en el Uruguay (UR/RUG, 1 [2. serie] 1971, p. 1-31, bibl., plates, tables)

Uses secondary data to outline the dimensions of Uruguayan manufacturing during the 1960s, including rudimentary considerations of industrial location.

4672. Lázaro, Roberto Carballo; Washington Baliero Silva; and **Haydée Rodríguez Melitón.** Realidad y perspectivas de los procesos de integración económica. Prólogo por Rodolfo Sagrada. Montevideo, Ediciones Jurídicas Amalio M. Fernández, 173 p., tables.

Law professors survey economic integration throughout the world, for the general public.

4673. Massera, José Luis. Quien vacía el sobre de la quincena. Montevideo, Ediciones Pueblos Unidos, 1973. 155 p., bibl., illus.

Popular, slangy tract denouncing rich people and current government policy from a Marxist viewpoint.

4674. Melgar, Alicia; Edda Peguero; and **César Lavagnino.** El comercio exportador del Uruguay: 1962-1968. t. 1/2. Montevideo, Univ. de la República, Instituto de Economía, Depto. de Publicaciones, 1972. 2 v. (156, 153 p.) bibl., tables (Col. Nuestra Realidad, 14).

In their joint university thesis, the authors analyze monopoly foreign ownership, and market structure in a series of Uruguayan export commodities, comparing 1956 with the period 1962-1968. A detailed empirical study.

4675. Monzalvo, Carlos Andrés. Barcos y pueblos. Montevideo, Ucomar, 1972. 122 p.

A modest survey of the Uruguayan merchant marine emphasizing petroleum transport. Of interest only to specialists.

4676. Seminario Nacional de Estadística, *I, Montevideo, 1970.* Recomendaciones finales. Montevideo, Ministerio de Economía y Finanzas, Dirección General de Estadística y Censos, 1970. 157 p., tables.

4677. Uruguay. Ministerio de Economía y Finanzas. Dirección General de Estadística y Censos. Censo económico nacional: 1968, industria manufacturera A. Montevideo, 1971. 39 l., tables (mimeo)

Valuable primary data source.

4678. _____. _____. _____. Demografía. Montevideo, 1971. 49 p., tables (Anuario estadístico. Fascículo, 2)

Census data from 1963, together with vital statistics for the period 1964-68.

4679. _____. _____. _____. Encuesta de hogares: Montevideo. t. 5, Vivienda; t. 6, Ocupación y desocupación. Montevideo, 1970-1971. 2 v. (30, 28 p.) tables (mimeo)

The official record of the seminar's recommendations. Of limited technical interest only.

Results of periodic household survey of the city, a valuable primary data source.

4680. _____. _____. _____. Ganadería y agricultura: Anuario estadístico. Montevideo, 1971. 45 p., tables (Fascículo, 3)

Primary data from the late-1960s for Uruguay's most basic economic activity.

4681. _____. _____. _____. Indice de los precios del consumo: de julio a diciembre 1971. Montevideo, 1971. 2 v. (Unpaged) tables (mimeo)

Documents the country's consumer price levels, by item.

4682. _____. _____. _____. Territorio y clima. Montevideo, 1971. 23 p. tables (Anuario estadístico 1967/69. Fascículo, 1)

Almost entirely devoted to physical geography.

ARGENTINA

LOVELL S. JARVIS
Assistant Professor
University of California, Berkeley

ARGENTINA'S ECONOMICS PROFESSION HAS CONTINUED to gain in maturity and productivity during recent years. There has been a marked increase in the theoretical sophistication of published work, in the number of authors contributing to this literature—see, for example, the papers included in the two *Jornadas de Economía* (items 4730 and 4731) and the Reunión de Centros de Investigación Económica (item 4748)—and, at least as important in my opinion, greater concentration on topical problems of national interest. Among the themes receiving special attention are: income distribution, employment, stabilization policies, agriculture, foreign investment, technological development, and the relationship between economic and political development.

Growth of the economics profession has occurred despite periodic upheavals, caused by political issues, in the principal university departments, and staff reductions, caused by financial difficulties, at both the Instituto Torcuato Di Tella and the Fundación de Ivestigaciones Económicas (FIEL). These problems have inhibited the development of graduate teaching programs, limiting the number of young professionals, and student theses, which should otherwise have been forthcoming.

The future course of economic events, and of the economic literature, is difficult to foresee. The Argentine Revolution, which began with the military coup of July-1966, ended in May 1973 with the election of Héctor Cámpora as President. The subsequent re-election of Juan Perón, after 18 years exile, and after his death, the succession to power of his wife, Isabel Perón, previously Vice-President, have caused considerable economic and political turmoil. It is noteworthy that much of the economic literature appearing during this period is free of polemics and demogogery and demonstrates instead an openness, analytical clarity, and sensitivity to politically disruptive themes which is relatively new to Argentina. It is not clear that this tendency will endure. Argentine economists are wary of certain themes (for example, objective interpretations of the past three decades have only begun to appear), and more political persecution would doubtlessly increase this wariness.

The publications cited in this selection are not exhaustive of the literature, representing only those items which have come to the attention of the reviewer. Among those cited, four publications seem to be particularly significant. In the first (item 4740), Guillermo O'Donnell, a political scientists at the Instituto Torcuato Di Tella, combines his own discipline with astute economic observations to explain the breakdown in democratic government in Argentina, and the rise of "bureaucratic authoritarianism." The book is especially valuable in having initiated a discussion among Argentine social scientists of various disciplines to explain the post-World War II phenomenon of political instability, stop-go business cycles, inflation, and sub-optimal economic growth. A useful comment on O'Donnell's work is given by Brodersohn (item 4700). A second major publication, at this moment only half complete, is that by Juan Carlos de Pablo, a senior economists at FIEL. He has embarked on four essays treating subjects of considerable importance to the Argentine economy: income distribution, inflation, public enterprises, and the foreign sector. The first two essays (items 4741 and 4742) have been published and are notable for the innovativeness with which new and provocative light is thrown on old, often drab themes. A third notable project has been undertaken by Adolfo Canitrot, an economist at the Torcuato Di Tella Institute, who has carried out a detailed study of industrial employment under a grant from the ILO. One major publication has resulted (item 4703) and other papers on employment, productivity, and technological change in three specific industries (cotton spinning, metal structures, and meat packing plants) are forthcoming. The fourth principal study is the critical analysis of the National Institute of Agricultural Technology (INTA), by a team of scholars specialized in political science and public administration at the Instituto Torcuato Di Tella. Undertaken on request by INTA itself, the work (item 4726) provides an excellent perspective on the principal government institution empowered to generate and diffuse new technology to the agricultural sector. The economic implications in the work are numerous, important, and well spelled out.

Other empirical studies on the agricultural sector have appeared recently. A major proportion of these resulted from the PPEA Program (Proyecto Pro-Economía Agraria) initiated by The Ford Foundation in 1963. This program financed the graduate study abroad of 41 Argentines specializing in agricultural economics. Long one of the more neglected areas of economic research, the agricultural sector is now much better understood. The Ph.D. dissertations completed under this program to date are listed separately in this section, without annotation. They are usually available from University Microfilms. Among the most interesting are those by Aguirre, Barandiarán, Kaminsky, Mulleady, Nores, and Tandeciarz.

Other significant work on agriculture is the paper by Obschatko and de Janvry on technological adoption in the cattle industry (item 4738), Teubal's work on savings, investments and financial flows (item 4755), and Sturzenegger's paper on agricultural policy formulation (item 4753).

In addition to de Pablo's monograph, Diéguez and Petrecolla's research on the social security system and changes in the wage share (item 4711), and Tokman's innovative analysis of the concentration of economic power (item 4756), are important contributions to the discussion of income distribution.

Fodor and O'Connell's work on Argentina's Atlantic trade in the early 20th century is the most notable historical study (item 4718), but the piece by Cortés Conde (item 4705) is also worthy of attention.

Four papers on stabilization policy merit special attention. These are works by Brodersohn (item 4700), Maynard and van Rijckeghem (item 4734), Arnaudo (item 4692), and, in addition to the previously mentioned monograph, a nonduplicative piece by de Pablo (item 4743).

In public finance, the papers by Berlinski (item 4699) and by Núñez Miñana (item 4737) on fiscal federalism, by Nuñez Miñana (item 4736) on simplifying the federal tax structure, and by Guadagni (item 4725) on the operation of the national portable water supply system are also useful additions to the literature.

Several papers on international trade provide data series which should be useful for further empirical analysis. These include the papers by Givogri (item 4724), García (item 4721), Bartolomei (item 4698), and Diéguez (item 4710).

On the industrial sector, the most provocative analyses are those by Sercovitch (item 4751), discussing the advantages occurring to users of foreign technologies, and by Montuschi (item 4731), discussing the relationship between industrial concentration, foreign ownership, and wage inequality. Petrei (item 4745) provides estimates of the rates of return to capital.Remes Lenicov (item 4730) discusses government policy and the growth of the automobile industry, and Villanueva and Geretto (item 4730), the relationship between employment and productivity in the short run. Jorge Katz has continued his work, discussed in detail in *HLAS 35,* and additional publications from his research are expected in the future.

Among the special publications from the public sector, a report on investments by the public sector (item 4691), a study of the machine tool industry (item 4690), and a bibliographical reference on economic and planning studies (item 4707) should be the most useful to scholars.

DOCTORAL DISSERTATIONS
BY PPEA FELLOWS

Aguirre, Antonio. Welfare cost of protection: the fertilizer in Argentina. Univ. of California, Berkley, 1972.

Auerheimer, Leonardo. Essays on inflation. Univ. of Chicago, 1972.

Barandiarán, Edgardo. The control of money and bank credit in Argentina. Univ. of Minnesota, 1973.

Biondolillo, Aldo L. Social cost of production instability in the grape-wine industry: Argentina. Univ. of Minnesota, 1972.

Fiorentino, Raul. Public investment allocation in a backward region: the case of Misiones, Argentina. Univ. of California, Davis, 1973.

Frigerio, Norberto. Alternative wholesaling facility arrangements for fresh fruits and vegetables in the Buenos Aires metropolitan area. Michigan State Univ., 1973.

Giménez Dixon, Jorge J. An economic analysis of range improvement in the cattle breeding area of Buenos Aires province. Michigan State Univ., 1969.

Kimansky, Mario. The structure of production of multiple-output dairy farms in the Centro Santafecino region of Argentina; a multivariate analysis. Univ. of Wisconsin, 1971.

Kohout, José C. A price and allocation decision model for the beef economy in Argentina. Univ. of Illinois, 1969.

Liboreiro, Ernesto S. Effects of the European economic community agricultural policies on Argentine exports of beef. Michigan State Univ., 1970.

Martínez, J. C. On the economics of technological change: induced innovations in Argentine agriculture. Iowa State Univ., 1972.

Mulleady, Tomás. Technological change: the case of corn production in the Argentine Pampas. Iowa State Univ., 1972.

Nores, Gustavo A. Quarterly structure of the Argentine beef cattle economy: a short-run model, 1960-1970. Purdue Univ., 1972.

Reca, Lucio G. The price and production duality within Argentine agriculture 1923-1965. Univ. of Chicago, 1967.

Tandeciarz, Ignacio C. The measurement of productive efficienty: a case study in the agricultural sector. Univ. of California, 1971.

Trigo, Eduardo J. Structural changes in the food retailing market in the Buenos Aires metropolitan region of Argentina during the 1960-1970 decade. Univ. of Wisconsin, 1972.

Vergelín, César F. Water erosion in the Carcarañá watershed: an economic study, Univ. of Wisconsin, 1971.

Zapata, Juan Antonio. The economics of pump irrigation: the case of Mendoza, Argentina. Univ. of Chicago, 1969.

Zulberti, Carlos A. The economic evaluation of fattening beef cattale in Argentina. Cornell Univ.

4683. Abril, Juan Carlos. Estimaciones estacionales en series monetarias argentinas: primer informe. Tucumán, Arg., Univ. Nacional de Tucumán, Facultad de Ciencias Económicas, Instituto de Investigaciones Estadísticas, 1973. 40 l., tables (Cuaderno, 4)

Provides seasonally adjusted estimates of six basic money supply series in Argentina using data from 1941 through 1971.

4684. Agüero, Alicia; José A. Bartolomei; and Fernando H. Sonnet. Exportaciones e importaciones mensuales según la clasificación por uso económico de los bienes en el período 1959-65. Córdoba, Arg., Univ. Nacional de Córdoba, Facultad de Ciencias Económicas, 1974. 11 p., tables (Serie material de trabajo, 13)

Reclassifies Argentine exports according to potential use as intermediate, capital or consumer good, and within consumer goods as durables or nondurables. Provides conversion factors between traded goods classified by conventional nomenclature and by classification employed here. Data presented on a monthly basis.

4685. _____; _____; and _____. Exportaciones e importaciones mensuales según la clasificación por uso económico de los bienes en el período 1966-1971. Córdoba, Arg., Univ. Nacional de Córdoba, Facultad de Ciencias Económicas, 1973. 3 p., tables (Serie material de trabajo, 11)

Same as item 4684, but provides data for 1966-71.

4686. Altimir, Oscar. La contabilidad social regional: el caso de la provincia del Chubut (IDES/DE, 14:56, enero/marzo 1975, p. 719-748, tables)

Extends a previously published economic study of this province (see HLAS 35:2337) to include estimates of population, of labor force, redistributive effects of fiscal transfers, and a matrix of intersectoral transactions.

4687. Aráoz, Alberto and Carlos Martínez Vidal. Ciencia e industria: un caso argentino. Washington, Organization of American States, General Secretariat, Dept. of Scientific Affairs, Regional Program of Scientific Development and Technology, 1974. 108 p., tables (Estudios sobre el desarrollo científico y tecnológico, 19)

Examines the relationship between scientific activity and industrial development in Argentina, utilizing the Technical Assistance Service to Industry, Metallurgical Laboratory of the National Atomic Energy Commission (SATI) as a case study. Contains useful empirical information regarding development and the allocation of resources in SATI. Less complete in measuring the impact of its efforts, through suggestive of the problems encountered and needed changes in orientation.

4688. Archetti, Eduardo P. and Kristianne Stölen. Tipos de economía, obstáculos al desarrollo capitalista y orientaciones generales de los colonos del norte de Santa Fe (IDES/DE, 14:53, abril/junio 1974, p. 151-179, tables)

Interesting discussion of agrarian structure and economic problems among small producers in Santa Fe prov.

4689. Argentina. Consejo Nacional de Desarrollo [and] Consejo Nacional de Seguridad. Plan nacional de desarrollo y seguridad: 1971-1975. B.A., 1971. 267 p., tables.

Comprehensive plan for economic and social development. It is the culmination of the efforts of the military governments which came to power in 1966 to provide a technocratic policy outline. Contains some useful empirical information, but most interesting for impression it gives of the national priorities as seen by military government, and respective roles planned for the public and private sectors.

4690. _____. Dirección Nacional de Promoción Industrial. Departamento Sectoral. La industria de las máquinas herramienta de la República Argentina: situación actual y perspectivas futuras. B.A., 1971. 132 p., bibl., tables.

Highly useful document containing much empirical data on development of machine tool industry during the 1960s. Includes information on production, foreign trade, labor force, productive capacity, current technology, taxes, input prices, and financing of sales of product.

4691. _____. Ministerio de Hacienda y Finanzas. Dirección Nacional de Programación e Investigación. Inversión del sector público argentino por regiones: años 1968/1971. B.A., 1972. 100 l., tables.

Very useful reference containing data not elsewhere available. Investments of public sector given in current and deflated prices, by region, entity (federal and provincial governments, municipality of Buenos Aires and other municipalities, and publically owned enterprises), and by destination according to function, including special sections on public health, education and highways.

4692. Arnaudo, Aldo A. Comportamiento coyuntural de la economía argentina, 1950-69. Córdoba, Arg., Univ. Nacional de Córdoba, Facultad de Ciencias Económicas, Instituto de Economía y Finanzas, 1973. 33 p., bibl., tables (Serie de investigaciones, 17)

Develops and estimates simple econometric model to study effects of possible changes in government policy on rate of inflation. Concludes that unpredictable alternations in rate of inflation make government stabilization actions nearly impossible.

———. Economía monetaria. See item 4009.

4693. ———. El efecto escala en la demanda de dinero en las empresas. Córdoba, Arg., Univ. Nacional de Córdoba, Facultad de Ciencias Económicas, Instituto de Economía y Finanzas, 1973. 17 p., bibl., tables (Serie de investigaciones, 16)

Argues that there is evidence of economies of scale in transactions demand for money among Argentine firms and that accordingly the conventional bank policy of reducing bank credit proportionately for all firms in times of monetary tightness discriminates most severely against smaller firms.

4694. ———. Estimación trimestral de monto y servicios de la deuda externa privada con proveedores y contratistas, 1966-1972. Córdoba, Arg., Univ. Nacional de Córdoba, Facultad de Ciencias Económicas, Instituto de Economía y Finanzas, 1974. 12 l., tables (Serie material de trabajo, 12)

Provides estimates of private sector foreign debt, amortization of debt and interest payments, on a quarterly basis.

4695. ———. La nacionalización de los depósitos en 1946 y 1973. Córdoba, Arg., Univ. Nacional de Córdoba, Facultad de Ciencias Económicas, Instituto de Economía y Finanzas, 1974. 16 p. (Serie discusión, 2)

Brief review of differences in systems established by nationalization of bank deposits in 1946 and 1973.

4696. ———. and others. Proyecto económico argentino para la década. Córdoba, Arg., Univ. Nacional de Córdoba, Facultad de Ciencias Económicas, Instituto de Economía y Finanzas, 1974. 52 p. (Serie discusión, 2)

Summary of seminar on same topic. Written by five senior economists at a provincial university, paper is indicative of dramatic increase in concern among many academic economists for reform of economic system. Argues strongly that capitalism is incapable of satisfying Argentina's needs and calls for drastic income redistribution and sharply increased role of State. Specific policy recommendations include efforts to decentralize economic and political power regionally.

4697. Bacic, Uros. El comportamiento de los salarios nominales y reales en el sector educativo argentino, 1913-1968 (UNS/EE, 8:15/16, enero/dic. 1970, p. 159-180, tables)

4698. Bartolomei, José A. El mercado cambiario argentino, 1959-1971. Córdoba, Arg., Univ. Nacional de Córdoba, Facultad de Ciencias Económicas, Instituto de Economía y Finanzas, 1973. 40 p., tables (Serie material de trabajo, 8)

Discussion of Argentina's attempts to return to convertibility following entrance to International Monetary Fund. Contains information on international agreements and exchange crises, and monthly data from 1959 through 1971 on international reserves and on foreign exchange quotations in both official and "parallel" markets.

Beare, Adolfo and José Gabriel. Empresa multinacional y dependencia tecnológica: el imperialismo en América Latina hoy. See item 8872.

4699. Berlinski, Julio. El proceso de ajuste de las finanzas provinciales en la Argentina (IDES/DE, 13:51, oct./dic. 1973, p. 517-531, bibl., tables)

Econometric analysis of effect of cyclical variation in federal revenue-sharing on spending decisions by Argentine provincial governments.

4700. Brodersohn, Mario S. Sobre *modernización y autoritarismo* y el estancamiento inflacionario argentino (IDES/DE, 13:51, oct./dic. 1973, p. 591-605, tables)

Comment on O'Donnell's book (see item 4740). Brodersohn points out that improved data recently published by Central Bank indicates no prolonged period in recent Argentine history of economic stagnation, nor even markedly slower growth. Accordingly, economic stagnation per se, as argued by O'Donnell, is not an acceptable casual explanation for the development and continuation of "mass pretorianism" in Argentina. Comment contains a number of insights into relationship between policies and economics in Argentina. Does not diminish overall merit of O'Donnell's work, for whose response, see item 4739.

4701. Cabrera, Orlando Molina. Tipología de empresarios industriales del Gran Mendoza. Mendoza, Arg., Univ. Nacional de Cuyo, Facultad de Ciencias Políticas y Sociales, Centro de Investigaciones, Instituto de Estudios del Desarrollo, 1972. 135 p., bibl., tables.

4702. Canitrot, Adolfo and Juan Sommer. Productividad y ocupación en la producción de azúcar en Tucumán (UNLP/E, 18:3, set./dic. 1972, p. 251-278, tables)

A good analysis of changes in employment and poverty in Tucumán prov. as a result of changes in the supply and demand for sugar. Slow secular growth in the (sheltered) national demand for sugar, coupled with increases in sugar-cane yields and in mill productivity, and in relative technological backwardness in sugar production in Tucuman prov. has led to a secular decline in employment and income, a high local employment rate, and a strong outflow of labor. Contains considerable data on the sugar industry.

4703. _____ and **Pedro Sebess.** Algunos características del comportamiento del empleo en la Argentina entre 1950 y 1970 (IDES/DE, 14:53, abril/junio 1974, p. 69-91, tables)

Summary analysis of study conducted for International Labor Organization, is best review of employment generation in modern Argentina. Growth of industrial output exceeds growth in industrial employment during most of the period 1950-70 due to increases in labor productivity in the most rapidly growing industries, and slow growth in the traditional, more labor intensive industries. The rate of increase in labor employment grew markedly from 1965-70 because of increase in growth in total output, exports, and expansion of domestic consumption, and in particular because of the resurgence of traditional industries like foodstuffs, meatpacking, shoes and clothing. Concludes that 1965-70 period is anormal and that future growth in employment will be slower.

4704. Cimillo, Elsa and others. Acumulación y centralización del capital en la industria argentina. B.A., Editorial Tiempo Contemporáneo, 1973. 191 p., tables (Col. Economía y sociedad)

Thoughtful polemic utilizing "Marxist" approach and terminology. Much emphasis devoted to analysis of impact of foreign capital and alleged inability of local bourgeoisie to respond positively to growing foreign penetration.

4705. Cortés Conde, Roberto. El mercado de tierras. B.A., Instituto Torcuato Di Tella, Centro de Investigaciones Económicas, 1972. 61 l., tables.

Interesting study of relationship between immigration, productivity of land, prices of agricultural products, and prices and turnover of land in pampas between 1855-1914. Empirical data not available elsewhere.

Deheza, José A. Argentina: ¿país sin destino nacional? See item 8641.

4706. Delfino, José A. and **Carlos A. Givogri.** Una metodología para la programación del sector energético argentino. Córdoba, Arg., Univ. Nacional de Córdoba, Facultad de Ciencias Económicas, Instituto de Economía y Finanzas, 1973. 47 p., bibl., tables (Serie material de trabajo, 10)

Develops simple linear programming model of energy sector. Most interesting for perspective it provides on sources and magnitudes of different fuels used. Solution indicates domestic production of coal, petroleum and hydroelectric power should be increased, imports of gas oil reduced and imports of petroleum eliminated.

4707. Desarrollo económico y planificación en la República Argentina: selección bibliográfica, 1930-1972. B.A., Consejo Federal de Inversiones, 1972. 394 p. (Serie técnica, 13)

Very important reference. Contains index of principal economic studies undertaken in Argentina. Broad coverage by topic and type of publication. Includes works from both public and private sector, some academic theses, and material published abroad in English. Material is classified chronologically by year from 1930 to 1972, and within each year alphabetically by author. A separate list is given for the publications of several federal agencies: the National Investment Council (CFI), the National Secretariat of Planning and Governmental Action (ex-CONADE), the Subsecretary of Science and Technology (ex-CONACYT), and a selection is provided for the periodic publications, such as annual reports, of government, industry, and national associations. Includes an additional alphabetical index by author of all material in volume, but unfortunately no index by subject matter is given.

4708. Di Marco, Luis E. Buenos Aires y el Interio: un estudio de la relación de precios. Córdoba, Arg., Univ. Nacional de Córdoba, Dirección General de Publicaciones, 1973. 88 p., bibl., tables.

4709. Di Tella, Guido and **Manuel Zymelman.** Los ciclos económicos argentinos. With the collaboration of Alberto Petrecolla. B.A., Editorial Paidós, 1973. 365 p., tables (Biblioteca textos universitarios. Serie economía, 2)

Economic history. Revised version of second half of work published earlier under title *Las etapas del desarrollo económico argentino* (see *HLAS 31:3892*). This volume provides analysis of economic cycles in Argentina from 1876 to 1952. Much useful data. For historian's comment see *HLAS 36:3107*.

4710. Diéguez, Héctor L. Crecimiento e inestabilidad del valor y el volumen físico de las exportaciones argentinas en el período 1864-1963 (IDES/DE, 12:46, julio/sept. 1972, p. 332-349, bibl., tables)

Valuable economic data, but does not relate growth or instability of Argentine exports to other economic variables. For historian's comment see *HLAS 36:3106*.

4711. _____ and **Alberto Petrecolla.** La distribución funcional del ingreso y el sistema previsional en la Argentina, 1950-1972 (IDES/DE, 14:55, oct./dic. 1974, p. 423-440, tables)

Interesting analysis of impact of social security system

on labor force participation and distribution of income. Points out that social security system payments to retired are greater than payments to the system by wage earners so that total wage payments to active and retired workers compose larger share of GNP than is shown by wages to active workers alone.

4712. Drosdoff, Daniel. El gobierno de las vacas: 1933-1956, Tratado Roca-Runciman. B.A., Ediciones La Bastilla, 1972. 222 p., bibl., tables (Serie Borrón y cuenta nueva)

Originally presented as a doctoral thesis at the National Univ. of La Plata, this book dispassionately describes the elements of the famous Roca-Runciman treaty and analyzes its economic and political impact. Useful reading for the economic historian, historian, or political scientist interested in this period. For historian's comment see *HLAS 36:3109.*

4713. Elías, Víctor J. La formación de expectativas sobre inflación: el caso de las sociedades anónimas en la Argentina. Tucumán, Arg., Univ. Nacional de Tucumán, Facultad de Ciencias Económicas, Instituto de Investigaciones Económicas, 1972. 12 p., tables (Cuaderno, 72-2)

Preliminary study attempting to estimate the expected rate of inflation in Argentina during 1945-57 using data on corporation case and stock dividends.

4714. ———. Fuentes del crecimiento económico argentino y perspectivas futuras. Tucumán, Arg., Univ. Nacional de Tucumán [and] Harvard Univ., Cambridge, Mass., 1974. 43 p., bibl., tables (mimeo)

An effort to use growth accounting methodology to explain Argentine economic growth during 1935-72. Careful work, using best available data series on output and factor inputs, including education of labor force, provides a good overall perspective, but is unable to fully explain variation in residual.

4715. Ferrer, Aldo. Auslandsunternehmen: Bemerkungen zu den Erfahrungen in Argentinien (Vierteljahresberichte [Bonn] 49, Sept. 1972, p. 273-283)

Strong criticism of foreign investment in Argentina. Author argues that foreign investments do not benefit the economy as a whole, do not improve the unemployment situation, and fail to stimulate the nation's general rate of economic growth. Author calls for increasing the importation of technological and financial contribution to the development of industry while transferring the process of decision-making away from foreigners to domestic control. [H. J. Hayes]

4716. ———. La economía argentina: las etapas de su desarrollo y problemas actuales. 8. ed. rev. B.A., Fondo de Cultura Económica, 1970. 284 p.

Revised version of a book first published in 1963 (see *HLAS 27:2141*). Contains about one-third new text, most of which is devoted to discussion of the post-1930 period. A standard reference on Argentine economic history, the book is uncomfortably vague. The analysis is descriptive, few other studies are cited, no graphs or tables are given, and no statistical analysis is undertaken. Most valuable for impression it gives of an important ideological and political position in Argentina. The author, a conservative nationalist, was Minister of Economics for seven months in 1970-71.

4717. Fidel, Julio. Antecedentes y perspectivas de la inversión extranjera y la comercialización de tecnología: el caso argentino (IDES/DE, 13:50, julio/sept. 1973, p. 285-314, bibl., tables)

Interesting descriptive analysis of foreign direct investment during last two decades: historical evolution, legal environment, influence on balance of payments, technological effects. Contains policy recommendations.

4718. Fodor, Jorge G. and Arturo A. O'Connell. La Argentina y la economía atlántica en la primera mitad del siglo XX (IDES/DE, 13:49, abril/junio 1973, p. 3-65)

Stimulating analysis of the economic and political links between Argentina, Great Britain and the US from 1900 to 1950. Emphasizes the early triangular relationship between trade and capital flows, and the particular importance of the beef trade in determining policies in both Great Britain and Argentina during the early years of this century. For historian's view, see *HLAS 36:3134.*

4719. Frederick, Kenneth D. Agricultural development and water use in the Cuyo region of Argentina. Washington, Resources for the Future, 1973. 1 v. (Various pagings) tables.

Contains much useful data and considerable institutional detail. Evaluates impact of market forces and alternative government policies on the rate and efficiency of agricultural development and water use in one of Argentina's most important non-pampas agricultural areas. Concludes that water use efficiency would best be improved by increasing the marketability of water. Preliminary version of study.

4720. Gaignard, Romain. L'economie de l'Argentine: déséquilibres et retards de la croissance industrielle (FDD/NED, 28:4006/4007, 17 juillet 1973, p. 49-63, map, table)

Descriptive review of industrial policies and their impact on different sectors during the 1960s.

4721. García, Norberto. El balance de pagos de la República Argentina: una presentación uniforme de los datos del período 1951-1972. Córdoba, Arg., Univ. Nacional de Córdoba, Facultad de Ciencias Económicas, Instituto de

Economía y Finanzas, 1974. 9 l., bibl., tables (Serie material de trabajo, 14)

Useful data on balance of payments. For author's book on the subject, see item 4091.

4722. García Valeriano, F. A critical inquiry into Argentine economic history. Tucumán, Arg., Univ. Nacional de Tucumán, Facultad de Ciencias Económicas, Instituto de Investigaciones Económicas, 1973. 96 p., bibl., tables (Cuaderno, 73-3)

Reissue of author's PhD dissertation at Chicago. Argues that bank credit has a strategic role in determining changes in output, and that supply of bank credit to the private sector has been sporadic due to government error.

4723. Geller, Lucio. Politica cambiaria argentina: 1899 y 1914. Santiago, Univ. de Chile, Facultad de Economia Política, Instituto de Economía y Planificación, 1973. 72 p., tables (Publicación, 150)

Analysis of Argentina's return to gold standard in 1899 and abandonment of same in 1914. Challenges traditional view that changes reflected interests of landed oligarchy struggling to improve their income and power, arguing instead that 1899 decision was motivated by Argentina's entry into international economy and simply permitted exploitation of comparative advantage in agriculture. 1914 change reflected cautious passivity of monetary authorities, who resumed convertibility after uncertainty and international monetary turmoil associated with World War I had ended.

4724. Givogri, Carlos A. La exportación de productos no tradicionales y la independencia de la economía argentina: informe preliminar. Córdoba, Arg., Univ. Nacional de Córdoba, Facultad de Ciencias Económicas, Instituto de Economía y Finanzas, 1974, 38 p., bibl., tables (Serie de investigaciones, 19)

4725. Guadagni, Alieto Aldo. Aspectos económicos del saneamiento urbano en la Argentina (IDES/DE, 13:52, julio/set. 1974, p. 673-707, bibl., tables)

Analysis of urban water supply system in Argentina, showing global scarcity of water, and criticizing investment and pricing policy of the National Sanitary Dept. for its non-economic orientation.

4726. Instituto Torcuato Di Tella, *Buenos Aires.* **Centro de Investigaciones en Administración Pública.** Determinación de objetivos y asignación de recursos en el Instituto Nacional de Tecnología Agropecuaria: un análisis crítico. B.A., 1971. 205 p., tables.

Excellent, in-depth analysis undertaken at request of INTA. Team of researchers include Oscar Oszlak, Jorge Federico Sábato and Jorge Esteban Roulet who provide thoughtful criticism of organizational structure of INTA and its lack of connection with other policy-making institutions in agricultural sector. Report contains considerable data on allocation of resources within INTA, and this allocation is compared with stated goals of institution's and country's needs. Authors point out that efforts to isolate INTA from political influence have led to its concentrating on scientific instead of applied research, with less impact of agricultural sector. Written by political scientists, the study has great interest for economists concerned with agricultural sector.

Irazusta, Julio. Balance de siglo y medio. See *HLAS 36:3188.*

4727. Janvry, Alain de. A socioeconomic model of induced innovations for Argentine agricultural development (Quarterly Journal of Economics [Harvard Univ., Cambridge, Mass.] 87:3, Aug. 1973, p. 410-435, tables)

Building on theoretical model developed by Hayami and Ruttan, article considers the processes underlying the generation of agricultural innovations by the public sector in Argentina and the adoption of new technologies by individual entrepreneurs. Suggests large producers use influence to bias research efforts of national agricultural experimental stations away from actual needs of smaller producers. Provocative and insightful, but thrust of paper is at variance with analysis of INTA given in Di Tella study, see item 4726.

4728. Jarvis, Lovell S. Cattle as capital goods and ranchers as portfolio managers: an application to the Argentine cattle sector (JPE, 82:5, May/June 1974, p. 489-520, tables)

Develops microeconomic theory treating cattle as capital goods and applies this in estimation of econometric model of Argentine cattle sector. The results indicates strong producer price response, with slaughter declining in the short run, and rising only in the long run. This fact, given the importance of beef in Argentine exports, makes devaluation an ineffective approach to achieving short-run equilibrium in the balance of payments. Revision of chap. 2 and 8 of *HLAS 33:3017.*

4729. ———. Un ejemplo del uso de modelos económicos para la construcción de datos no disponibles: la estimación de la existencia del vacuno desagregado en Argentina, 1937-1967 (UNLP/E, 19:1, enero/abril 1973, p. 71-117, bibl., tables)

Constructs estimates of Argentine cattle herd from 1937-67, disaggregated by age and sex. These estimates differ significantly from official estimates during the 1950s and early 1960s. Reasons are suggested for the discrepancy. Technical change in the cattle industry, including changes in calving rates, is also investigated. Spanish revision of Chap. 4 of *HLAS 33:3017.*

4730. Jornadas de Economía. 1- . La Plata, Arg., Consejo Profesional de Ciencias Económicas de la Provincia de Buenos Aires, Univ. de La Plata, Facultad de Ciencias Económicas, 1973-

A number of fine papers in a new series sponsored by Univ. de La Plata. Among those not published elsewhere are: Mario Brodersohn "Política Económica de Corto Plazo: Crecimiento e Inflación en la Argentina 1950-1972;" Jorge L. Remes Lenicov "Algunos Resultados de la Política Desarrollista, 1958-64: el Caso de la Industria Automotriz; Horacio Nuñez Miñana "Desequilibrios de las Finanzas Públicas Provinciales en la Argentina;" and Javier Villanueva and Armando Geretto "Observaciones sobre el Empleo y la Productividad en el Corto Plazo."

4731. Jornadas de Economía, IX, Cordoba, Arg., 1974. Trabajos presentados en las . . . Córdoba, Arg., Univ. Nacional de Córdoba, Facultad de Ciencias Económicas, Depto. de Impresiones, 1974. 2 v. (721 p.) (Continous pagination) bibl., tables.

Conference organized by the Asociación Argentina de Economía Política under the auspices of the Univ. of Córdoba. Consists of 24 papers, roughly equally divided between empirical and theoretical topics. A number of the better papers have since been published and are annotated separately in *HLAS*. Other empirical papers of special interest are Aldo A. Dadone and Domingo F. Cavallo "Políticas Monetarias Selectivas en Argentina: 1935-1974," and Luisa Montuschi "Concentración y Trabajo Asalariado en la Industria Manufacturera Argentina: 1953-1963."

4732. Kaplan, Marcos. La primera fase de la política petrolera argentina: 1907-1916 (IDES/DE, 13:52, enero/marzo 1974, p. 775-810, tables)

Somewhat disjointed historical analysis of Argentina's petroleum policies in early 20th century is interesting because lack of fuels was important constraint on subsequent Argentine industrial development. Argues that imperialist approach of foreign oil companies was injurious. Little economic analysis, but useful facts. For historian's comments see *HLAS 36:3196-3197*.

4733. Liboreiro, Ernesto S. Efectos de la politíca del Mercado Común sobre las exportaciones argentinas de carne vacuna (UNS/EE, 8:15/16, enero/dic. 1970, p. 109-158, tables)

Analysis of world demand for beef through the year 1975, with an emphasis on the impact on Argentina of different agricultural policies which could be implemented by the EEC. Recommends policies for Argentina.

4734. Maynard, G. and W. van Rijckeghem. Argentina 1967-70: a stabilization attempt that failed (BNL/QR, 103, Dec. 1972, p. 396-412, tables)

Argues that attempt to stabilize Argentine economy after 1967 failed basically because increase in price of beef made it impossible to continue policy of progressive reductions in the rate of increase of money wages. Explains increase in price of beef as result of domestic policies, principally devaluation. Attention to changes in international price of beef during this period would also be useful. See article by de Pablo, item 4743.

Morris, Arthur S. The regional problem in Argentine economic development. See *HLAS 36:3241*.

4735. Nores, Gustavo A. Causas y efectos de los ciclos ganaderos: el rol de la información en la toma de decisiones. Castelar, Arg., Instituto Nacional de Tecnología Agropecuaria (INTA), Depto. de Economía, Escuela para Graduados en Ciencias Agropecurias, 1973. 14 p., bibl., tables (Serie Divulgación, 3)

One of few papers to deal effectively with relationship between cattle cycle and general economic cycles in Argentina.

4736. Núñez Miñana, Horacio. Algunos aspectos de la simplificación del sistema tributario argentino. La Plata, Arg., Univ. Nacional de La Plata, Facultad de Ciencias Económicas, Instituto de Investigaciones Económicas, 1974. 16 p., tables (Documento interno, 15)

Suggests that increasing complexity of tax-system between 1955-70 was due to imposition of numerous emergency taxes of relatively low yield, and that tax simplification would probably be economically beneficial.

4737. ———. El nivel de gobierno municipal dentro del sector público en la Argentina: algunos características cuantitativas. La Plata, Arg., Univ. Nacional de La Plata, Facultad de Ciencias Económicas, Instituto de Investigaciones Económicas, 1974. 28 l., tables (Documento interno, 16)

Useful discussion of municipal government expenditures in Argentina and their variation across cities and over time.

4738. Obschatko, Edith S. de and Alain de Janvry. Factores limitantes al cambio tecnológico en el sector agropecuario (IDES/DE, 11:42/44, julio 1971/marzo 1972, p. 263-285, tables)

Analyzes factors affecting rate of adoption of eight new technologies in cattle breeding. Argues that absentee ownership is major problem. Adoption of technologies without owner residence leads to actual decline in rate of return on investment, and adoption with owner residence is only marginally more profitable than traditional extensive exploitation.

4739. O'Donnell, Guillermo A. Comentario a la nota de M. Brodersohn (IDES/DE, 13:51, oct./dic. 1973, p. 606-612, tables)

O'Donnell responds to Brodersohn's critique, see item 4700.

4740. ———. Modernization and bureaucratic-authoritarianism: studies in South American politics. Berkeley, Univ. of California, Institute of International Studies, 1973? 219 p., bibl., tables (Politics of modernization series, 9)

An outstanding and pathbreaking analysis of the relationship between economic growth and the breakdown in liberal democracy in Latin American nations, taken from the Argentine and Brazilian cases. Essentially a political study, the book goes far to unifying politics and economics in explaining recent development trends among the more advanced Latin American countries. For critique and author's response, see items 4700 and 4739.

4741. Pablo, Juan Carlos de. Cuatro ensayos sobre la economía argentina. pt. 1, Distribución del ingreso. B.A., Fundación de Investigaciones Económicas Latinoamericanas (FIEL), 1974. 146 l., bibl., tables.

Preliminary version of the first of four essays treating income distribution, inflation (see item 4742), public enterprises and the foreign sector. This one on Argentine income distribution is one of the best available works on the subject. Discusses the available data; provides estimates of the size, sectoral and regional income distributions and their changes over time; analyzes the economic constraints on redistribution; and considers usefulness of different economic instruments for achieving redistribution.

4742. ———. Cuatro ensayos sobre la economía argentina. pt. 2, Inflación. B.A., Fundación de Investigaciones Económicas Latinoamericanas (FIEL), 1974. 1 v. (Various pagings) bibl., tables.

Provocative and thoughtful review of inflation in Argentina (a preliminary version of the second essay, see item 4741). Particularly good for giving an overall perspective. Reviews empirical data on general price increases and on associated relative price changes, considers the influence of foreign inflation, discusses the real impact of inflation on the public and private sector, analyzes the applicability of different causal theories of inflation to Argentina, and analyzes past stabilization programs. Argues that Argentina must either adopt improved programs to terminate inflation, which has not previously been accomplished, or accept inflation as a fact and adopt comprehensive indexing systems to ensure that the distortionary impact of inflation on income distribution, and on investments is kept to a minimum. See also *HLAS 35:2385*.

4743. ———. Precios relativos, distribución del ingreso y planes de estabilización: la experiencia de la Argentina durante 1967-70. B.A., Fundación de Investigaciones Económicas Latinoamericanas (FIEL), 1974. 38 p., bibl., tables.

An insightful analysis of the reasons for the failure of the stabilization policies initiated by the military governments during the Argentine Revolution from July 1966 to May 1973. Argues that the increase in international beef prices was transmitted to domestic beef prices in 1970, with consequent pressure on the cost of living, resulting in new wage demands. Also contains good analysis of particular strategy followed by Krieger Vasena while Minister of Economy from 1967 to 1969.

4744. Petras, James F. and **Thomas C. Cook.** Argentina: dependencia y burguesía industrial; actitudes de los directivos de empresas industriales hacia la inversión extranjera y la política de los EUA (UNAM/PDD, 3:10, feb./abril 1971, p. 19-56, tables)

On the basis of interviews with top level management in 92 large firms, authors conclude, contrary to their prior hypothesis, that there is widespread support for foreign participation in the economy. Authors argue there is no substantial group of "national capitalists" and that an independent political economy will have to be based on other social forces.

——— ———. Componentes de la acción política: el ejecutivo industrial argentino. See item 8675.

4745. Petrei, Amalio Humberto. Rates of return to physical capital in manufacturing industries in Argentina (OUP/OEP, 25:3, Nov. 1973, p. 378-404, bibl., tables)

Careful study using Harberger's methodology. Concludes private rate of return averages 11 percent and social rate of return 17 to 20 percent between 1961-67. Results also suggest investment moved toward areas where rates of return were highest. Summary of dissertation at Univ. of Chicago.

4746. Problemática del desarrollo patagónico (IAEERI/E, 1:3, sept./oct. 1969, p. 8-54, maps, tables)

Nontechnical, but interesting discussion of development potential of Patagonia and institutional means by which its growth and integration with rest of Argentina could be increased.

4747. Reca, Lucio G. and **Ernesto Gaba.** Poder adquisitivo, veda y sustitutos: un reexamen de la demanda interna de carne vacuna en la Argentina, 1950-1972 (IDES/DE, 50:13, julio/sept. 1973, p. 333-346, tables)

Article summarizes the existing literature on internal beef demand in Argentina and notes that the development of a modern food industry which could offer consumption substitutes for beef is an important factor in obtaining a reduction in internal beef consumption and consequent greater exportable surpluses.

4748. Reunión de Centros de Investigación Económica, VIII, Buenos Aires, 1972. Trabajos de investigación. B.A., Univ. Nacional de Buenos Aires, Facultad de Ciencias Económicas, Depto. de Imprenta, 1972. 3 v. (298, 352, 445 p.) bibl., tables.

Conference sponsored by the Asociación Argentina de Economía Política consists of 38 papers, most of which treat theoretical topics. The empirical paper of most interest is: Tulio Ceconi "Algunos Consideraciones sobre el Producto Bruto Interno Argentino Durante el Período 1945-70." Also of interest is Juan Carlos de Pablo "Impresiones sobre el Estado Actual de Nuestra Profesión en la Argentina."

Rocchetti, Tito L. El convenio multilateral en el sistema tributario argentino. See item 8684.

4749. Rofman, Alejandro B. and Luis A. Romero. Sistema socioeconómico y estructura regional en la Argentina. B.A., Amorrortu Editores, 1973. 227 p., maps, tables (Serie América Latina)

Attempts to explain unequal pattern of regional growth in Argentina as a result of policies implemented by favored economic sectors and political classes seeking improvement of their relative position. Explains the origin and nature of specific policies, and analyzes the regional impact of their implementation. Contains much empirical information. Interesting for the economist, historian, sociologists and regional planner.

Sampay, Arturo Enrique and others. Empresas multinacionales. See item 8786.

4750. Sánchez, Carlos E. Requerimientos futuros de mano de obra universitaria en la provincia de Córdoba, 1972-1982. Córdoba, Arg., Univ. Nacional de Córdoba, Facultad de Ciencias Económicas, Instituto de Economía y Finanzas, 1974. 105 p., tables.

Empirical study of demand and supply of university graduates. Analysis, which focuses on engineers and accountants, involved a detailed survey both of establishments to determine their use of professional and of past graduates to determine their occupational histories. This information is used to project future demand and supply, and to analyze professional suitability of current graduates. Article contains useful data.

Schwartzman, Simon. Empresarios y política en el proceso de industrialización: Argentina, Brasil, Australia. See *HLAS 36:3307*.

4751. Sercovich, Francisco C. Dependencia tecnológica en la industria argentina (IDES/DE, 14:53, abril/junio 1974, p. 33-67, bibl., tables)

Provocative analysis of the competitive advantages residing in the licensing of foreign technology among Argentine manufacturing firms. Econometric analysis utilizes qualitative variables. Results somewhat difficult to interpret. Summary of dissertation, Sussex Univ., England.

4752. Sigaut, Lorenzo Juan. Acerca de la distribución y niveles de ingreso en la Argentina: 1950-1972. B.A., Ediciones Macchi, 1972. 78 p., tables.

Useful elementary discussion of the distribution of income in Argentina. Contains some data not easily available elsewhere.

4753. Sturzenegger, Adolfo C. Aspectos de la política económica agropecuaria argentina. La Plata, Arg., Univ. Nacional de La Plata, Facultad de Ciencias Económicas, Instituto de Investigaciones Económicas, 1974. 26 p., tables (Serie Cuadernos, 16)

Points out that Argentine agricultural sector suffers from substantial negative effective protection. Develops simple theoretical model of agricultural sector which is used to evaluate the policies which have led to current situation.

4754. ———. Intento de diseño y cómputo de un modelo multisectorial para la economía argentina: aspectos analíticos. La Plata, Arg., Univ. Nacional de La Plata, Facultad de Ciencias Económicas, Instituto de Investigaciones Económicas, 1974. 37 1. (Documento interno, 18)

Presents and analyzes a multisectorial model of the Argentine economy designed to permit the study of structural changes in production and trade resulting from "exogenously" introduced changes in relative prices, such as might occur from shifts in government policies or via the foreign sector, but without necessarily implying aggregate growth.

4755. Teubal, Miguel. Estimaciones del "excedente financiero" del sector agropecuario argentino (IDES/DE, 14:56, enero/marzo 1975, p. 677-697)

Provides estimate of level of agricultural savings, investments, and financial "surplus" during the period 1950-67. Suggests that the level of savings is 30 to 40 percent of gross agricultural product, and relatively constant through time. Agricultural investment varies between 17 and 34 percent of gross agricultural product. Although this level of investment appears extremely high, it is lower than savings, permitting the transfer of a financial surplus of other sectors. Author is concerned that this financial surplus may not be socially well utilized and calls for higher agricultural taxation to appropriate it.

4756. Tokman, Victor E. Concentration of economic power in Argentina (World Development [Oxford, England] 1:10, Oct. 1973, p. 33-41, tables)

Penetrating, original analysis of economic interrelationships among families in Argentina. Shows that private national capital is highly concentrated, and that landowners' economic power extends beyond agriculture to industry, finance, and services. Author suggests that conventional analysis suggesting natural clash between interests of agricultural exporters and industrial producers is oversimplified.

4757. United States. Department of Agriculture. Economic Research Service. Argentina: growth potential of the grain and livestock sectors. Washington, 1972. 123 p., bibl., maps, tables (Foreign agricultural economic report, 78)

Useful English language reference containing much data and incorporating results of many recent academic studies on agricultural sector. Descriptive, not analytical.

4758. Winsberg, Morton D. Modern cattle breeds in Argentina: origins, diffusion and change. Lawrence, Univ. of Kansas, Center of Latin American Studies, 1968. 59 p., bibl., maps, tables (Occasional publications, 13)

Written by an economic geographer, this small study provides a succinct, enjoyable, and insightful history and analysis of one important type of technical change in the cattle industry. Essential reading for those interest in Argentine cattle sector. See also *HLAS 34:2824a.*

4759. Zemborain, Saturnino M. La verdad sobre la propiedad de la tierra en la Argentina: los orígenes de la propiedad, la movilidad social y el proceso de subdivisión de la tierra. B.A., Sociedad Rural Argentina, Institute de Estudios Económicos, 1973. 65 p., bibl., maps, tables.

Argues that ownership of agricultural land in Argentina is not highly concentrated. Attempts to show that there has been an active market in land historically, and considerably subdivision due to inheritance. Concludes that agrarian structure operates efficiently and that agricultural reform would be harmful. An increase in prices would lead to increase in production. Partisan position expected from association of largest landowners, the document nonetheless contains some interesting information on land ownership not easily accessible elsewhere, and a good bibliography on the subject.

BRAZIL

FRED D. LEVY, JR.
Economist
International Bank for Reconstruction and Development

JAN PETER WOGART
Institut für Weltwirtschaft
Universität Kiel

THE RAPID QUANTITATIVE AND QUALITATIVE growth of Brazilian economic literature, reported in the last edition, has continued unabated, and Brazilian scholars are increasingly dominating the scene. In addition to the already well-known research institutions in Rio 9IPEA, FGV) and São Paulo (IPE, CEBRAP, FGV), valuable contributions are now coming from the Center for Regional Economic Research (CEDEPLAR) in Belo Horizonte and the Univ. of Brasília, as well as the Center for Graduate Studies at the northeastern universities of Ceará, Pernambuco and Bahia, and the universities of Paraná and Rio Grande do Sul.

The range of topics covered has also broadened and become more balanced, with increasing attention being given to regional and urban planning, human resource development, foreign trade policies, and the development of the financial sector. At the same time, there is continued debate on the issue of income distribution, the plight of the Northeast, and the development of agriculture. Although there is still a tendency among economic historians to take the grand sweep, there is a marked increase in the number of historical monographs and in the skilled application of quantitative techniques. This development, along with the slowdown of growth engendered by changing conditions in the international economy, has placed the "Brazilian miracle" of 1968-73 in a longer-term perspective, the fruits of which should be apparent in future editions of the Handbook.

In sum, both the depth and diversity of Brazilian economic literature shows increased insight into the past, valuable criticism of current developments, and useful guidelines for future policy. Although far from being complete, it is hoped that the rather extensive bibliography presented here will provide some insight into the discussion of problems and processes of the Brazilian economy for the social scientist already familiar with this country, as well as serve as a starting point for those investigating specific topics and issues of Brazilian economic development. Finally, the rising importance of Brazil in the world economy, and of Brazilian economists in the literature, forecasts a bright future for teachers of Portuguese.

4760. Abreu, Marcello de Paiva. A Missão Niehmeyer (FGV/RAE, 14:4, julio/agôsto 1974, p. 7-28)

Study examines the origins, actions, and recommendations of the financial mission of Sir Otto Niehmayer to Brazil in 1931. Based on the increasing output of solid historical research in Brazil and documents from the British Foreign Office, the evidence suggests that here is another example of unused advice, which may have contributed partly to Brazil's ability to overcome the shock of the World Depression rather quickly.

4761. Aguiar, Neuma. Ideologias competetivas e um projeto de industrialização do Nordeste (IUP/D, 9, 1972, p. 21-52)

Evaluation of the Asimov project in Brazil's Northeast, the problems it faced and the transformation of the various small and medium sized industries, which were set up in the early 1960s, into larger enterprises, either heavily subsidized by the State or taken over by firms from the Center-South. Points out the lessons to be learned from installing small-scale industry in a poor region with seemingly little entrepreneurial talent.

4762. _____. Urbanização, industrialização e mobilização social no Brasil (IUP/D, 11, 1973, p. 146-172)

Analysis of the relationship between urbanization and industrialization on the one side and working-class mobilization into unions on the other. Quantitative analysis between 1940 and 1960 finds that rapid migration and urbanization without sufficient absorption into modern industry is responsible for increasing union membership and labor grievances taken to court.

4763. Ajace, Rodrigo. Contribuição dos pôrtos para o desenvolvimento. Rio, Companhia Brasileira de Artes Gráficas, 1972. 52 p., tables.

Due to Brazil's rapid expansion of exports and imports, the enlargement and modernization of ports has become a priority in the development drive. This essay is a brief introductory treatment of the subject.

4764. Almeida, José. A implantação da indústria automobilística no Brasil. Rio, Fundação Getúlio Vargas, Instituto de Documentação, Serviço de Publicações, 1972. 90 p., bibl., tables.

A brief but very useful study on the role of the automobile industry in Brazil, realizing its substantial contribution to development. Critical about the protectionist import substitution policies which have delayed adjustment to international competition.

4765. _____. Industrialização e emprêgo no Brasil. Rio, Instituto de Planejamento Econômico e Social, Instituto de Pesquisas (IPEA/INPES), 1974. 139 p., tables (Relatório de pesquisa, 24)

Analysis of the absorption of Brazilian manpower into modern industry; blames the relatively slow increase on the low quality of Brazil's labor force, which itself is a function of Brazil's poor educational system. Author is critical about the recent educational campaigns in Brazil, which tend to stress quantity rather than quality.

4766. Almeida, Wanderly J. Mauro de. Serviços de desenvolvimento econômico no Brasil: aspectos sectoriais e suas implicações. Rio, Instituto de Planejamento Econômico e Social, Instituto de Pesquisas (IPEA/IPNES), 1974. 125 p., tables (Relatório de pesquisa, 23)

Further study of the structure of Brazil's service sector with emphasis on its capacity to absorb labor. The problem of underutilization and low remuneration are seen to be a function of the low qualification of the labor force being employed in the traditional services. Policy proposals consequently stress the need for education and training to create more gainful employment in that sector.

4767. Alvargonzález Cruz, Rafael. Problemas del desarrollo económico en la zona nordestina brasileña (IEAS/R, 21:79, abril/junio 1972, p. 101-150, tables)

Author sees the modernization of agriculture as the sine qua non of development of the Northeast. Among the sources of its backwardness are poor soil and climatic conditions, unprofitable terms of trade, inadequate marketing facilities, and narrow market. Unless a comprehensive, heavily financed program is mounted—along the lines offered by Alvargonzález—the outlook is for steady exhaustion of the soil and further impoverishment.

4768. Andrade, Manuel Correia de. A dinâmica do desenvolvimiento do Nordeste (Symposium [Recife, Bra.] 12:2, 1970, p. 139-154, tables)

A brief and simplistic historical review of the underdevelopment of the Northeast and the Government's efforts to cope with it. Concludes that success hinges on the creation within the Northeast of a consuming market for the products of its industries.

4769. Andrade, Thompson Almeida. Regional inequality in Brazil. Belo Horizonte, Bra., Univ. Federal de Minas Gerais, Centro de Desenvolvimento e Planejamento Regional (CEDEPLAR), 1971. 24 l.

Paper presented during the Colloquium on Regional Inequalities of Development held in Vitória, Bra., 12-15 April 1974. Analyzes regional income distribution. With the help of quantitative methods it concludes that there has been a convergence of regional income data between 1939 and 1966. The major factors to be held responsible for the convergence are internal migration, favorable export markets for the lagging regions, and the increasing availability of short term capital in more recent times.

4770. Appy, Robert. O sistema bancário brasileiro (ITA/H, 4, 1968, p. 41-64, tables)

Although slightly outdated, article provides a useful summary outline of Brazilian monetary institutions as established by the reform instituted in 1964. Particular attention is given to the functions and interrelationships of the National Monetary Council, the Central Bank, and the Bank of Brazil. Author asserts that the necessary reforms could only have been promulgated by a strong government able to suppress the various pressure groups that had been benefiting from the previous system of uncontrolled monetary expansion.

4771. Aranjo, José Tavares de, Júnior and Vera Maria Dick. Govêrno, empresas multinacionais e empresas nacionais: o caso de indústria petrochémica (IPEA/PP, 4:3, dez. 1974, p. 629-654)

First part of a larger research project, which concentrates on the relationship between the private and the public sector and the technological policies of state enterprises. Authors argue that the various combinations of state and private participation in the petrochemical sector may also be useful in other key industries of the Brazilian economy.

4772. Aspectos de industrialização brasileira: conferências pronunciadas durante as comemorações do 40. °aniversário c ꓫIESP. São Paulo, Instituto Roberto Simonsen, 1969? 147 p.

Lectures on industrialization in Brazil offered in 1968 by four prominent students and participants in the process-Gilberto Paim, Roberto do Oliveira Campos, Clóvis de Oliveira, and Mader Gonçalves—on the occasion of the 40th anniversary of the Industrial Center of São Paulo (CIESP).

4773. Asplan S.A. (firm), *Brazil.* Plano agropecuário de desenvolvimento. v. d 1/5, Diagnósticos; v. e 1/2, Estudos; v. A, Anexos metodológicos. Rio, Secretaria de Agricultura e Abastecimento, 1970. 7 v. (643, 405, 117, 211, 181, 419, 126) illus., maps, plates, tables.

Voluminous study and plan of the agricultural sector in the state of Rio de Janeiro. Includes analysis of output and distribution of agricultural products as well as role of agriculture in over-all economy of the state.

4774. _____, _____. Plano de Govêrno do Estado do Ceará: PLAGEC 1971/1974; novas perspectivas do desenvolvimento econômico e social do estado. Fortaleza, Bra., 1971. 2 v. (645, 743 p.) illus., maps, tables.

Development plan of Ceará for the early 1970s. This document covers a lot of ground not usually found in purely economic development plans, such as public services, their organization and institutional setup.

4775. Associação dos Municípios da Zona Sul do Estado do Rio Grande do Sul, *Brazil.* Estudo preliminar ao Plano de Desenvolvimento Integrado dos Municípios da Zona Sul. Pelotas, Bra., Univ. Católica de Pelotas, Instituto Técnica de Pesquisas Assessorias (ITEPA), 1973. 2 v. (Unpaged) maps, tables.

Subregional plan of some of the most southern municipalities of Brazil. Surveys not only primary and secondary production but also services such as tourism.

4776. Auberger, Phillippe. Le modèle brésilien de lutte contre l'inflation: 1964-73 (FDD/NED [Problèmes d'Amérique Latine, 30] 4049/4050, Déc. 1973, p. 1-86)

Study commissioned by the French government of Brazil's inflation and its stabilization program, 1964-67. The last chapter treats a timely topic, the Brazilian way of adjusting to trotting inflation through indexing.

4777. Azevedo, Oswaldo Benjamín de. Agropecuária, alimentação e salários regionais (Carta Mensal [Rio] 16:203, fev. 1972, p. 15-33, tables)

Provides data on food prices and income levels in the

4778. **Bacha, Edmar Lisboa.** Hierarquia e renumeração gerencial (IPE/EE, 4:1, jan./março 1974, p. 143-161)

Essay discusses the nature of the growing gap between Brazil's top private and public managers and the rest of the working population, presenting empirical evidence from the largest enterprises and the salaries they paid between 1964 and 1972.

4779. _____. **Milton da Mata;** and **Rui Lyrio Modenesi.** Encargos trabalhistas e absorção de mão-de-obra: uma interpretação do problema e seu debate. Rio, Instituto de Planejamento Econômico e Social, Instituto de Pesquisas (IPEA/INPES), 1972. 257 p., illus., tables (Col. Relatórios de pesquisa, 12)

Analyzes the labor absorption problem of Brazil's industry in light of the rather heavy social security and other contributions the industrial firm has to pay for each worker. This much needed study concludes that these fees, which amount to 35 percent of total wages, contributed substantially to the capital intensity of Brazil's industry and should be replaced by increasing sales taxes. Text is followed by criticism and discussion by the IPEA staff.

4780. **Baer, Werner; Isaac Kerstenetsky;** and **Annibal Villela.** As modificações no papel do estado na economia brasileira (IPEA/PP, 3:3, dez. 1973, p. 883-912)

Essay presented at the conference of the BNDE (National Development Bank of Brazil) on the participation of state enterprise in Brazil's economy. Study looks into the origin, structure, and implications of state enterprise and participation for the process of economic planning and economic policy making. Final section speculates about possible future developments of public and private ownership in the Brazilian economy.

4781. **Baeta, Nilton.** A indústria siderúrgica em Minas Gerais. Belo Horizonte, Bra., Fundação João Pinheiro (FJP), 1973. 309 p., bibl., tables.

Historical and rather descriptive study of the most important industrial activity in Minas Gerais.

4782. **Bahia** (state), *Bra.* **Secretaria da Indústria e Comércio.** Industrial Center of Aratu (Centro Industrial de Aratu). Salvador, Bra., 1970. 31 l., tables.

Brief survey of Bahia's newest industrial center, which, due to special fiscal incentives of the central government and the help of SUDENE and the state governments, has become the fastest growing industrial region in Brazil's Northeast.

4783. _____, _____. **Secretaria do Trabalho e Bem Estar Social. Departamento de Mão de Obra. Divisão de Estudos e Pesquisas.** Alguns aspectos do mercado de trabalho, CIA: empresas em implantação. Salvador, Bra., 1973. 1 v. (Unpaged) tables.

Statistics on employment, qualification, recruitment and hiring of labor of the Industrial Center of Aratu, adjacent to Salvador, Bahia's capital.

4784. **Banco do Desenvolvimento do Espírito Santo,** *Vitória, Bra.* Aspectos fundamentais da política econômica do Espírito Santo. Vitória, Bra., 1971. 87 l., tables.

Regional development plan of Espirito Santo, a state and region which has been neglected by the rapid industrialization of Brazil's Southeast and the many subsidies granted to the Northeast. After a brief survey of the development between 1962 and 1968, forecasts are projected for the 1970s, and strategies and policies are evaluated to achieve more rapid growth.

4785. **Banco do Nordeste do Brasil** (BNB), *Fortaleza, Bra.* Perspectivas do desenvolvimento do Nordeste até 1980: síntese. Fortaleza, Bra., 1972? 109 p., tables.

Summary of a rather detailed analysis and forecast of the Northeast economy up to and including 1980 by economists of the Banco do Nordeste do Brasil. It is the aim of the Northeast not only to grow faster and reduce unemployment, but also to close the income-gap with the rich South. Economists interested in the Northeast will want to study the individual documents mentioned.

4786. _____, _____. I [i.e. Primeiro] Plan Quinquenal do BNB. Fortaleza, Bra., 1974. 222 p., tables.

Describes the past activities of the Bank of the Northeast and lays out its five-year plan for assisting the development of the Northeast. Programs are detailed by sector.

4787. _____, _____. **Departamento de Estudos Econômicos do Nordeste** (ETENE). A agro-indústria do caju no Nordeste: situação atual e perspectivas. Fortaleza, Bra., 1973. 220 p., maps, tables.

Empirical study on one of the most important crops of Brazil's Northeast. Estimates on external and internal demand lead to the conclusion that production should be stimulated. This is particularly important for the processing industries where substantial excess capacity exists.

4788. **Banco Nacional da Habitação** (BNH), *Rio.* Assessoria de Planejamento e Coordenação. BNH: avaliação e perspectivas. Rio, 1974. 117 p., tables.

Brief survey of the development and objectives of Brazil's Housing Bank and the policies it has followed since its creation in 1964.

4789. Banco Nacional do Desenvolvimento Econômico, *Rio.* FIPEME [Fundo de Financiamento da Pequena e Média Emprêsa]: apoio do BNDE às pequenas e médias indústrias no Brasil. Rio, 1973. 59 l., bibl., tables.

Conference paper of Brazil's National Development Bank on structure and financing of small and medium-sized industry in Brazil. The analysis does not show to what extent this policy helped to decrease the dualism of Brazil's industrial structure.

4790. _____, _____. Paneis internacionais sobre desenvolvimento econômico. Rio, APEC Editôra, 1974. 376 p.

Conference organized by Brazil's National Development Bank which brought together outstanding Brazilian economists and foreign scholars who had worked on the Brazilian economy. Topics ranged from discussion of alternative development strategies and the possibility of using the "model" of Brazilian "corrective" inflation in other countries to employment problems in a dual economy and other social problems which have to be tackled in Brazil.

Baracho, José Alfredo de Oliveira. Participação nos lucros e integração social: PIS. See item 9929.

4791. Barat, Josef. Notas sobre planejamento urbano no Brasil (IBE/RBE, 28:4, out./dez. 1974, p. 46-108)

These rather extensive notes analyze economic and administrative aspects of Brazil's urbanization process during the last 25 years. Author concludes that the market economy cannot be trusted to lead to an optimum urbanization pattern and he proposes the creation of federal institutions to direct and guide future urban development.

4792. _____. Política de transporte, avaliação e perspectivas face ao atual estágio de desenvolvimento do pais (IBE/RBE, 27:4, out./dez. 1973, p. 51-84)

Study emphasizes the necessity to plan for better and faster means of transportation in order to support rapid growth in output of goods. Includes detailed discussion of transportation problems of basic industrial, mineral, and agricultural commodities. Also notes problems entailed in integrating Brazil's transportaion network.

4793. Barros, Frederico José O. Robalinho de and Rui Lyrio Modenesi. Pequenas e médias indústrias: análise dos problemas, incentivos e sua contribuição ao desenvolvimento. Rio, Instituto de Planejamento Econômico e Social, Instituto de Pesquisas (IPEA/INPES), 1973. 192 p., bibl., tables (Col. Relatórios de pesquisas, 17)

Thorough analysis of Brazil's medium and small-scale industries, their structure and financing and the wide-ranging differences in various regions. Major internal and external problems are identified and policies for their solution are proposed.

4794. Barros, José Roberto Mendoça de. Exportações agrícolas não-tradicionais e o custo doméstico das divisas (IPE/EE, 5:3, agôsto 1973, p. 7-30)

Examines the exports of non-traditional agricultural goods such as cotton, sugar, soya-beans, manioc-flour, rice and peanuts and finds that, since the domestic resource costs are below the rate of exchange, Brazil has been able to use its comparative advantage to an increasing degree during the last seven years.

4795. Biato, Francisco Almeida; Eduardo Augusto A. Guimarães; and **Maria Helena Poppe de Figueiredo.** A transferência de tecnologia no Brasil. Rio, Instituto de Planejamento Econômico e Social, Instituto de Planejamento (IPEA/IPLAN), Setor de Indústrias, 1973. 220 p., tables (Série estudos para o planejamento, 4)

Empirical study of the transfer of technology in Brazil's industrial sector, which analyzes the technical services of foreign firms and their remuneration. It concludes that highest payments are not in the most complex industries, but in those where markets are dominated by foreign investment.

4796. Boisier, Sergio; Martin O. Smolka; and **Aluízio A. de Barros.** Desenvolvimento regional e urbano: diferenciais de produtividade e salários industriais. Rio, Instituto de Planejamento Econômico e Social, Instituto de Pesquisas (IPEA/INPES), 1973. 151 p., tables (Col. Relatório de pesquisa, 15)

Cross-sectional study on regional differences in productivity and salaries. Although productivity differentials seem to be mainly a function of the use of technology, wage differentials show a higher correlation with geographic factors.

4797. Bonelli, Regis. Produção industrial: sugestão metodológica para elaboração de índices e aplicações (IPEA/PPE, 3:2, junho 1973, p. 406-427, tables)

Statistical study which attempts to construct new and better indices for Brazil's industrial production, testing it with data available for 1966-69.

4798. Braile, Pedro Márico. Despejos industriais. Rio, Livraria Freitas Bastos, 1971. 254 p., bibl., illus., tables.

Studies industrial pollution in Brazil in general and water pollution especially. In spite of substantial computational work and discussion of anti-pollution laws there is little discussion of costs and benefits in order to analyze the problem from an economic point of view.

4799. Brandt, Sérgio Alberto and **Francisco Tarcízio Goes de Oliviera.** O planejamento da nova empresa rural brasileira. Rio, APEC Editora, 1973. 260 p., illus.

Study criticizes the accounting and planning practices of rural farms in Brazil and emphasizes the importance of reorientation, particularly for the now emerging agroindustries. This book is also designed for a course in business administration in agriculture.

4800. Brasil: operação sul (Brazil: operation south). São Paulo, O. R. Blenner, 1973? 400 p., maps, plates, tables.

Bi-lingual guide to economic and other aspects of the three southern states of Brazil: Paraná, Santa Catarina and Rio Grande do Sul.

4801. Brazil. Congresso Federal. Comissão Parlamentar do Inquérito. O Congresso Federal e a Carta de Brasília: projeto de Resolução No. 164 de 1966 aprova as conclusões da Comissão Parlamentar de Inquérito a fin de apurar a realidade brasileira quanto à pecuária e verificar os fatôres que obstam o seu desenvolvimento. Rio, Ministério da Agricultura, Serviço de Informação Agrícola, 1967. 128 p. (Série Documentária, 27) tables.

A report by an investigating committee of the Chamber of Deputies on needs and measures of the ranching industry, together with recommendations for national policy. [P. B. Taylor, Jr.]

4802. _____. Conselho de Desenvolvimento de Extremo Sul (CODESUL). A indústria textil catarinense. Florianópolis, Bra., 1970. 67 p., bibl., tables.

Industry study of textiles in Santa Catarina. Concludes that in spite of disadvantage relative to competition in major industrial areas of Brazil, the textile industry of Santa Catarina has been able to keep or even to increase in its share of the total market.

_____. Escritório de Análise Econômica e Política Agrícola. Aspectos sócioeconômicos da cultura de algodão arbóreo: primeiro relatório. See item 9935.

_____. Serviço Nacional de Aprendizagem Comercial (SENAC). Departamento Regional de Pernambuco. Divisão de Formação Profissional. Setor de Pesquisas. Levantamento ocupacional dos menores no comérico do Recife. See item 9937.

_____. Serviço Nacional de Aprendizagem Industrial (SENAI). Departamento Regional de Minas Gerais. Pesquisa de mercado de trabalho e necessidades de treinamento em Belo Horizonte e Cidade Industrial de Contagem. See item 9940.

4803. _____. Superintendência do Desenvolvimento do Nordeste (SUDENE). Departamento de Agricultura e Abastecimento. Divisão de Abastecimento e Financiamento da Produção. Perdas na comercialização de produtos horti-fruti-granjeiros no mercados de Teresina. Teresina, Bra., 1972. 1 v. (Unpaged) tables.

Another careful SUDENE study on the problem of distributing and marketing agricultural products in one city of Brazil's Northeast. Major losses, which amount to nearly 10 percent of production, are attributed to: poor quality, lack of storage facilities, and excessive time lag between the purchase and sale of farm produce.

4804. _____. _____. Departamento de Industrialização. Diagnóstico e programa de industrialização: subsídios para el elaboração do plano de desenvolvimento regional. Recife, Bra., 1972. 147 p., tables.

Triannual industrial plan of SUDENE, for 1972-74. Study analyzes industrial development of the Northeast in the 1960s. Looks at possible comparative advantages and proposed policies for continuous industrialization in that region.

4805. Brito, Fausto Alves de and **Thomas Merrick.** Migração, absorção de mão-de-obra e distribuição da renda (IPE/EE, 4:1, 1974, p. 75-11)

Study by two members of CEDEPLAR (Centro de Desenvolvimento e Planejamento Regional, Belo Horizonte, Bra.) which examines the interrelationship between urbanization, migration, unemployment and income inequality. Major findings are that the traditional low-productivity urban service and handicraft sector is equally used by migrants and inhabitants rather than by migrants only, and that the most important variables determining salaries and wages are occupational status and position, which do not always coincide with more education.

4806. Buescu, Mircea. 300 [i.e. Trezentos] anos de inflação. Prefácio de Mário Henrique Simonsen. Rio, APEC Editôra, 1973. 232 p., tables.

Buescu combs plantation account books, church records, and other scraps of information to derive price indices dating from 1570 to the founding of the Republic in 1889. Although heavily caveated because of the paucity of data, the author provides a fascinating history of 300 years of Brazilian inflation.

4807. Bulhões, Octavio Gouvêa de. O Brasil e a política monetária internacional (IBE/RBE, 26:4, out./dez. 1972, p. 31-44)

Short history of Brazil's international financial policies from its role in the 1943 discussions that culminated in Bretten Woods, through the period of overvalued exchange rates and diminished creditworthiness, to the recent period of large capital inflows. Provides a vehicle for the author's views on national economic policies and the direction of the international monetary reform.

4808. *Cadernos de Estudos Brasileiros.* Univ. Federal do Rio de Janeiro, Forum de Ciência e Cultura. No. 1, 1972- . Rio.

Issue consists of two essays in the series of lectures given at the National Univ. of Rio de Janeiro (83 p., illus., tables). Ernesto Geisel's discussion of the petroleum issue is still of interest in spite of what has happened since 1972-73. The second essay on the Amazon is more of an introductory survey to the region.

4809. Campos, Reginaldo Z. de. Saúde e desenvolvimento na Bahia: contribução de enfermagem. Salvador, Bra., Univ. Federal de Bahia, Depto. Cultural [and] Escola da Enfermagen, 1969. 167 p., tables.

Discusses the contribution of nursing to the state of health in Bahia. After comparing economic and health statistics of the South and Northeast only up to 1960, the book analyzes the structure and training of nursing schools and ends with several recommendations that would increase and improve the current personnel and facilities.

4810. Canambra Engineering Consultants (firm), *Nassau, Bahamas.* Power study of south Brazil. v. 1, Summary; v. 2, Comprehensive report. Nassau, Bahamas, 1969. 2 v. (Various pagings) bibl., illus., maps.

Comprehensive study of demand and supply of electrical power in southern Brazil sponsored by the Brazil-UN Development Program. Includes survey of the economy and analysis of various alternatives of power generation in that region. Appendices have some information on costs and rates of return for production and distribution of electrical power.

Cardoso, Fernando Henrique. Associated-dependent development: theoretical and practical implications. See item 9943.

4811. Carnoy, Martin. Distribução da renda e desenvolvimento: um comentário (FGV/RAE, 14:4, julho/agôsto 1974, p. 87-93)

A recent contribution to Brazil's income distribution debate. Criticizes the Langoni interpretation by stating that the growing concentration was mainly caused by government policies in the mid-1960s. Warns that continued spending of government resources on higher rather than primary education will widen the gap.

4812. Carvalho Filho, José Julianão de. Análise dos instrumentos da política caffeira do Brasil: 1961/1971 (IPE/EE, 5:3, agôsto 1973, p. 31-84)

Study discusses aims and implementation of Brazil's coffee policy and its interrelationship with the rest of the economy during the last decade.

4813. Castro, Antônio Barros de. La agricultura y el desarrollo en el Brasil (FCE/TE, 38:149, enero/marzo 1971, p. 55-105, tables)

Castro argues that agriculture has effectively played the role of a leading sector in Brazilian economic development, and he disputes the applicability of dualistic theories. Unfortunately, few data are presented in support of his case. [T. Villamil]

4814. _____. 7 [i.e. Sete] ensaios sôbre a economia brasileira. v. 2. Rio, Editôra Forense, 1971. 283 p., tables.

Essays on the regional aspects of the Brazilian economy, noting that there has been a strong preoccupation with internationalization of development by nearly all regions or states. One essay is on recent development of the Northeast.

4815. Castro, Claudio de Moura and **Alberto de Mello Souza.** Mão-de-obra industrial no Brasil: mobilidade, treinamento e produtividade. Rio, Instituto de Planejamento Econômico e Social, Instituto de Pesquisas (IPEA/INPES), 1974. 424 p., tables.

Socio-economic study of various aspects of the formation of Brazil's labor force, such as: the relation between special schooling and mobility, rates of return from higher education, informal education and traditional values. One interesting chapter analyzes the surprising adaptability of the skilled labor force to new and different tasks.

_____; **Milton Pereira de Assis;** and **Sandra Furtado Oliveira.** Ensino técnico: desempenho e custos. See item 6240.

4816. Cavalcante, Raimundo Nonato de Fátima; Mário Helder de Oliveira Carvalho; and **Francisco Monte.** Evolução e perspectiva da indústria do Nordeste (BNB/REN, 5:19, jan./março 1974, p. 5-62, bibl., tables)

Extensive essay on the industrial development of the Northeast, its past, present, and future patterns of income and employment and its relation to other sectors of the Northeastern economy. One section treats the impact of tax incentives on investment and the structural change it will bring to the traditional pattern of industrial output.

4817. Cavalcanti, Clóvis de Vasconcelos. Mercados para a pesca em Aracajú. Recife, Bra., Superintendência de Desenvolvimento de Nordeste (SUDENE), 1971. 119 p., tables.

Sponsored by SUDENE, this demand-and-supply analysis of fishing and its consumption in the city of Aracajú, Brazilian Northeast, is a good example of high quality research on microeconomic problems, which bear directly on economic development and improvement of living standards.

4818. Centro das Indústrias do Estado de São Paulo, *São Paulo.* O setor externo da economia brasileira. São Paulo, Serviço de Publicações FIESP-CIESP, 1973. 37 p., tables (Cadernos econômicos, 18)

A useful brief review of the changing volume and structure of Brazil's imports, exports, and balance of payments, and her evolving trade policies over the period 1950-70.

4819. Cibantos, Jubert S. and **Donald W. Larsen.** A demanda para fertilizantes em um pais em desenvolvimento: o caso de São Paulo, Brasil, 1948-71 (FGV/RAE, 14:4, set./out. 1974, p. 46-53)

Econometric study, emphasizing the importance of price changes for the use of fertilizers in Brazil. Demand was found to be inelastic in the short run but elastic in the long run, with substantially higher coefficients for the last ten to 12 years.

4820. Clan S. A. (firm), *Brazil.* Desenvolvimento da indústria petroquímica no Estado da Bahia: resumo. Salvador, Bra., Fundação de Planejamento (CPE), Conselho de Desenvolvimento do Recôncavo (CINDER) 1970? 106 p., illus., tables.

Analysis and plan of Bahia's petrochemical industry looking into supply problems and possible markets both within Brazil and in other Latin American countries. Portuguese translation of *HLAS 35:2427.*

4821. Coêlho, Jorge. Manual de colonização. pt. 1, Da colonização e do cooperativismo; pt. 2, Caracterização da área e do empreendimento: legislação sôbre colonização. 2. ed. Recife, Bra., Superintendência de Desenvolvimento do Nordeste (SUDENE), Depto. de Agricultura e Abastecimento, Divisão de Organização Agrária, Seção de Colonização, 1972, 335 p., tables.

Handbook with description and laws of colonization, agricultural cooperatives and land reform. Can be used as background material for study of colonization in the Amazon region.

4822. Cohen, Youssef. Crescimento demográfico, industrialização e urbanização no Brasil (FGV/RAE, 14:2, março/avril 1974, p. 107-113, tables)

Contests the thesis that the "superurbanization" in many LDCs today is due to people being "pushed" out of backward and poor rural areas, but maintains that "pull" factors of higher-income and better education opportunities play the decisive role in the migration process.

4823. Cohn, Gabriel. La industrialización en Brasil: proceso y perspectivas (UNAM/RMS, 33:3, julio/sept. 1971, p. 489-516)

Historical description of the socio-economic underpinning of the development of Brazilian-style capitalism. More sweeping than analytical. [T. Villamil]

4824. Conferência de Desenvolvimento Econômico do Rio Grande do Sul, *Pôrto Alegre, Bra., 1969.* Problemas e perspectivas para a industrialização do Rio Grande do Sul. Pôrto Alegre, Bra., 1972. 85 p., plates, tables.

Papers presented at a conference of industrial development in Brazil's southernmost state. Some of the contributions are useful as a basis for further study of industrialization in that region.

4825. Cônjuntura Econômica. Fundação Getúlio Vargas. Vol. 27, No. 12, dez. 1973- . Rio.

Various essays on Brazil's "coffee" sector, introduced by a survey on coffee policy from 1850 to 1972. Two essays treat policy questions, both domestic and international; one looks into the supply and demand of ground coffee and another attempts to present the decision-making process of coffee growers and sellers in a simplified model. Subject coverage is completed by a final ABC of the most important coffee terms.

4826. Contador, Claudio Roberto. Inflação e o mercado de ações no Brasil: teste de algumas hipóteses (IPEA/PP, 3:4, dez. 1973, p. 913-936)

Tests various theories of stock-market behavior with Brazilian data.

4827. _____. Tecnologia e rentabilidade na agricultura brasileira. Rio, Instituto de Planejamento Econômico e Social, Instituto de Pesquisas (IPEA/INPES), 1974. 257 p., illus. (Relatório de pesquisas, 28)

Studies rates of return to agricultural products in seven Brazilian states and concludes that substantial differences are directly related to "entrepreneurial capacity" of various farms. The latter variable is measured by the farmer's educational level and risktaking. Emphasizes role of technological change in agriculture.

4828. Costa, Ronaldo F.N. and **Alzira L.N. Coelho.** Hierarquia e participação regional da pequena, média e grande indústria no Brasil. Belo Horizonte, Bra., Federação das Indústrias do Estado de Minas Gerais (FIEMG) [and] Centro das Indústrias do Estado de Minas Gerais (CIEMG), 1974? 1 v. (Unpaged) tables.

Comparative analysis of small, medium, and large-scale industry in major industrial centers of Brazil with recommendations to increase the small and medium-sized establishments particularly in Minas Gerais.

4829. Costa, Rubens Vaz da. Desenvolvimento regional: balanço de uma década (BNB/REN, 5:19, jan./março 1974, p. 63-78, tables)

Survey of major development trends in the Northeast by former president of region's development bank (BNB). In spite of unprecedented growth in real income and employment, the relative position of that region to the rest of the nation worsened between 1960 and 1970 due to the predominantly rural and low-productivity activities of the Northeast.

————. Notas sôbre a formulação de uma política eficiente de emprego. See item 9962.

4830. ————. O primeiro passo; um testemunho sobre o Nordeste brasileiro. Rio, APEC Editôra, 1973. 405 p., tables.

The former President of the Bank of the Northeast discusses the development of the Northeast and the impact of fiscal incentives as well as credit granted by the Banco do Nordeste do Brasil. After looking into technological aspects and the importance of agricultural development, the book concludes with two chapters on the role of the Church in development and the population question. Recommended reading for students of Brazil's Northeast.

4831. ————; **José Eduardo de Oliveira Penna;** and **Harry James Cole.** Considerações sobre crescimento urbano. Rio, Banco Nacional da Habitação, Secretaria de Divulgação, 1974? 83 p., tables.

Three essays by officials of Brazil's National Housing Bank on urban growth and development, urban planning, and the financing of urban housing. Useful as an introduction to Brazil's urban problems.

4832. Distrito Federal, *Bra.* **Companhia do Desenvolvimento do Planalto Central (CODEPLAN).** Estudo dos orçamentos das unidades familiares do Distrito Federal. Brasília, 1971. 284 p., tables.

Interesting consumer survey of households in Brazil's capital. Useful for comparison with other household surveys done by the Getúlio Vargas Foundation in the early 1960s and the Planning Ministry in the late 1960s.

4833. ———— ———— ————. Estudos setoriais; aspectos urbanísticos, saneamento, comunicações financeiras, serviços diversos. Brasília, 1971. 283 p., fold. maps.

Several studies on sectoral aspects of Brasília between 1968 and 1970. The major economic activities of Brazil's capital such as commerce, finance, tourism as well as water, sewage and communication are analyzed, both from the demand and supply side. The first essay gives a rather superficial introduction into general urban problems in Brasília.

4834. Doellinger, Carlos von; Hugo Barros de Castro Faria; and **Leonardo Caseita Cavalcanti.** A política brasileira de comercio exterior e sus efeitos: 1967-1973. Rio, Instituto de Planejamento Econômico e Social, Instituto de Pesquisas (IPEA/INPES), 1974. 168 p., tables.

Good (summary) survey of recent Brazilian foreign trade policies and the structure of exports and imports between 1967-73. The following problems are pointed out: 1) conflicts between exports and the domestic market, which can only be solved by raising productivity in agricultural sector; 2) how import liberalization hampers further development of the capital goods industry; and 3) how influx of foreign capital substitutes for domestic resources which must increase to maintain the growth process.

4835. ————; ————; **Raimundo Nonato Mendonça Ramos;** and **Leonardo Caseita Cavalcanti.** Transformação de estructura das exportações brasileiras: 1964/70. Rio, Instituto de Planejamento Econômico e Social, Instituto de Pesquisas (IPEA/INPES), 1973. 268 p., bibl., tables (Col. Relatórios de pesquisa, 14)

Reviews the results of the Brazilian export promotion effort since 1964. The authors describe in considerable detail the changes that occurred in the volume and composition of exports through 1970, and attempt to explain them in terms of Brazilian policies, resource costs, and world demand. The characteristics of exporting firms are also studied. Although much has changed since 1970, this book is important reading on a key element of Brazilian economic policy.

4836. Engler, Joaquim J. de Camargo and **Richard L. Meyer.** Trigo: produção, preços e produtividade (IPEA/PPE, 3:2, junho 1973, p. 341-368, tables)

Essays on the economics of wheat production in Brazil focusing on import substitution policies which began in 1962-63 and their impact on the agricultural sector and its diversification during the 1960s and early 1970s. Final section analyzes alternative policies for the future.

4837. Ernst & Ernst (firm), *Rio.* Brazil:

characteristics of business entities. Rio, 1972. 47 p.

A useful handbook on forms of business organization in Brazil, intended as a guide to potential foreign investors.

Evans, Peter B. The military, the multinationals and the "miracle:" the political economy of the "Brazilian model" of development. See item 8561b.

4838. Faissol, Speridião. As regiões de desenvolvimento retardado (IBGE/B, 32:232, jan./feb. 1973, p. 7-18)

The Northeast is described as a dual economy within a dual economy within a dual economy; the three center-periphery pairs being composed of Northeast-urban/Northeast-rural; Southern-Brazil/Northeastern-Brazil; and industrial-countries/Brazil. The solution is in the internal integration of Brazil. Glad that problem is solved.

4839. Ferreira, Edésio Fernandes. A administração da politica monetário no Brasil (Revista Bancária Brasileira [Rio] 42:498, 30 junho 1974, p. 35-41, tables)

Reviews evolution of Brazilian monetary institutions and the theory and tools of Brazilian monetary policy.

4840. _____. O desenvolvimento do mercado do títulos públicos federais no Brasil (Revista Bancária Brasileira [Rio] 42:495, 30 março 1974, p. 35-40, tables)

Brief history of the internal market for federal debt issues, with particular emphasis on the importance of monetary correction, instituted in 1964. As a consequence, the public debt outstanding relative to all financial assets rose from just over one percent in 1964, to almost 18 percent by the end of 1973. The only alternative for financing the public debt previously had been the printing press. Moreover, the expanded market for government bonds by 1972 made possible open market operations as an effective tool of monetary policy.

4841. _____. As operações de mercado aberto e o desenvolvimento de mercado monetário (Revista Bancária Brasileira [Rio] 42:496, 30 abril 1974, p. 39-43, tables)

Continuing from previous article (item 4840) author describes the theory, development, and institutions of open market operations as a tool of Brazilian monetary policy.

4842. _____. A política monetária e a iniciativa privada (Revista Bancária Brasileira [Rio] 43:502, 30 out. 1974, p. 61-68, tables)

Useful description of the role and methodology of the Annual Monetary Budget, the basic planning and control mechanism of Brazilian monetary policy.

4843. _____; A. Sergio Carneiro Leão; and Elcio Giestas. Programaçao monetária, financeira e de renda a curto prazo no Brasil (IBE/RBE, 27:2, abril/junho 1973, p. 3-80, tables)

In the first part, Ferreira lays out the financial sector model used by Brazilian monetary authorities for short-term programming purposes in the elaboration of the Annual Monetary Budget. Leão and Giestas then attempt a more elaborate model wedding the financial sector to the national income accounts. Interesting primarily for its methodology.

4844. Fishlow, Albert. Distribuição da renda no Brasil: um novo exame (IUP/D, 11, 1973, p. 10-80)

Extension of previous work on Brazil's inequality problem focusing on the measurement of physical and human capital and their contribution to different levels of income as well as on the impact of income concentration on the demand for durable consumer goods in the late 1960s and the early 1970s. Concludes that income inequality is neither a natural outcome of the current stage of Brazil's development nor a requirement for future growth and recommends policies which will tackle the poverty problem directly. This study is also available in Spanish, see Alejandro Foxley ed. *Distribución del ingreso* (México, Fondo de Cultura Económica, 1974, p. 90-110).

4845. _____. Indexing Brazilian style: inflation without tears? (Brookings Papers on Economic Activity [The Brookings Institution, Washington] 1, 1974, p. 261-282, tables)

Analyzes the impact of Brazil's system of monetary correction on inflation, resource allocation, and income distribution, and explores its applicability to the US economy. Fishlow emphasizes that indexing Brazilian style has not been merely a passive adjustment to monetary depreciation in order to protect real values, but was rather a major tool of macroeconomic policy in which the correction factors were manipulated to achieve particular objectives. A primary underlying purpose was restoration of the allocative role of the market. Fishlow finds that monetary correction had nothing to do with the dampening of inflation through 1973, that it did contribute to sustained growth once an upturn had already been achieved in 1967, did contribute importantly (the crawling peg) to export growth, and also altered the functional distribution of income in favor of capital as opposed to wage earners. Although the US might benefit from the introduction of indexed securities and other limited adaptations of monetary correction, Fishlow concludes that the US and Brazilian contexts are too different for the experience of the latter to offer guidance to the former. The article is followed by a brief summary of comments from the Brookings staff.

4846. _____. Origens e consequencias da substitução de importacões no Brasil (IPE/EE, 2:6, dez. 1972, p. 7-76)

Attempt to reinterpret the origins of Brazil's industrialization from the beginning of the Republic, with special emphasis on the expansion of the textile industry and the impact of World War I as a booster of growth. Article also discusses the more recent post-World War II industrialization policies and their impact on Brazil's economic growth rate.

4847. Fundação Educacional do Sul de Santa Catarina (FESSC), *Tubarão, Bra.* **Departamento de Pesquisas e Desenvolvimento.** Carvão: representatividade econômica e social no Sul de Santa Catarina. Tubarão, Bra., 1973. 59 l., tables.

Regional study of Santa Catarina's southern region, evaluating the possibility of creating new employment opportunities to offset the gradual decline of labor absorption into coal mining.

4848. Fundação Getúlio Vargas, *Rio.* **Brazilian Institute of Economics. Center for Statistics and Econometric Studies.** Food consumption in Brazil: family budget surveys in the early 1960's. Jerusalem, Israel, Israel Program for Scientific Translations *for* the U.S. Dept. of Agriculture, Economic Research Service, 1970. 283 p., tables.

Study by the Getúlio Vargas Foundation analyzes food consumption patterns of Brazilian households. Study concludes that over 25 percent of the population is suffering from nutritional deficiencies, be it in the form of insufficient calories, protein, or fat. Although concentrated in the poorest regions these deficiencies are also quite numerous in the prosperous South. This report supplements the study entitled "Projections of Supply and Demand for Agricultural Products of Brazil through 1975," published by Getúlio Vargas Foundation in July 1968.

4849. Fundação IBGE [Instituto Brasileiro de Geografia e Estatística] *Rio.* **Instituto Brasileiro de Estatistica. Departamento de Censos.** Dados preliminares gerais do censo agropecuário: VIII recenseamento geral, 1970. Rio, 1970. 5 v. (38, 52, 115, 47, 85 p.), fold. maps, illus., maps, plates, tables.

Five IBGE monographs providing: data from the 1970 Agricultural Census, by state and municipality, on number of establishments, persons employed, number of tractors in use, cattle, hogs, and chickens. Comparable data are shown for the censuses of 1920, 1940, 1950, and 1960.

4850. Fundação João Pinheiro, *Belo Horizonte, Bra.* Minas Gerais: 1971-1975, perspectivas: directrizes de desenvolvimento econômico e social para o quinquênio. Belo Horizonte, Bra., 1971/72. 3 v. (149, 126, 101 l.) tables.

Extensive development plan of Minas Gerais, a state which in spite of its large iron-ore resources and growing industrialization, has large underdeveloped areas with extreme poverty. Plan stresses population growth and problems of labor absorption.

4851. _____, _____. Zona de Mata: programa de diversificação econômica; informe preliminar. Belo Horizonte, Bra., Banco de Desenvolvimento de Minas Gerais (BDMG), 1971. 320 l., maps, tables.

Plan to develop agricultural production in the southeastern part of Minas Gerais. Study analyzes costs and benefits of various agricultural activities and includes survey of infrastructure necessary to increase production and productivity in that region.

4852. Furtado, Celso. Formação econômica do Brasil. 21. ed. rev. São Paulo, Companhia Editôra Nacional, 1971. 248 p., tables.

Intended as an introductory textbook, now in its 11th ed., Furtado has written an eminently readable, broad-brush outline of Brazilian economic history from colonial times through the 1930s. Little space is given over to pure description, anecdote, or idle data; instead Furtado's purpose is to provide a tight analytical framework for understanding the cause-and-effect relationships among the various elements, foreign and domestic, that have shaped the Brazilian economy.

4853. _____. El modelo brasileño (FCE/TE, 40[3]:159, julio/sept. 1973, p. 587-599)

Describes Brazil as an example of how far an industrialization process can progress without changing the principal characteristics of underdevelopment: urban-rural dichotomy, mass poverty, rising urban underemployment, etc. Furtado finds that cause lies in the essential duality of capitalism as it impacts upon a developing country. Because of the ever increasing concentration of incomes, the narrow Brazilian market for consumer durables, dominated by multinational corporations, would bring growth to a halt if not supported by a variety of government subsidies, fiscal incentives, spending programs, and policies to redistribute income toward the rich. In no other country, according to Furtado, has capitalism depended so heavily on the State to assure the matching of supply and demand. As a consequence, the most notable characteristic of the Brazilian model is its inherent tendency to exclude the masses from the benefits of technical progress and capital accumulation. For English version of this article, see *Social and Economic Studies* (Univ. of the West Indies, Mona, 22:1, March 1973, p. 122-131).

4854. _____. O mito do desenvolvimento econômico. Rio, Paz e Terra, 1974. 117 p.

Analysis of Brazil's post-war development and its relation to the industrialized countries within the center-periphery framework of the dependency theory.

4855. Galvêas, Ernane. Brasil: fronteira

do desenvolvimento. Rio, APEC Editôra, 1974. 235 p.

Analysis of Brazil's post-war development and the obstacles which it faced and overcame. Author maintains that the recent success of Brazil's accelerated growth is linked to the increasing rationality introduced both into the public and private sector since 1964.

4856. Gau, Enno B.H.S. Os pôrtos como fator do desenvolvimento nacional: concurso de monografias do Ministério da Marinha. São Paulo, Ministério da Marinha, 1972. 34 p.

Short essay on the importance of ports in the development process.

4857. Geiger, Pedro Pinchas. O espaço mais desenvolvido do Brazil (IBGE/B, 31:231, nov./dez. 1972, p. 109-124, table)

Rambling article discussing, inter alia, the history of geography as a discipline in Brazil, the location of industrial activities in São Paulo and Rio, the difficulties of metropolitan government, the economic evolution of the Rio and São Paulo metropolitan areas, and the need for land-use planning in Brazil. For geographer's comment, see item 7114.

4858. Gelb, Alan H. Coffee prices and the Brazilian exchange rate (OUP/OEP, 26:1, March 1974, p. 104-119, bibl., tables)

Study measures response of the Brazilian exchange rate to changes in world coffee prices and concludes that the "rather large rate response implies the existence of enormous stabilizing influences on the world coffee production-consumption system."

4859. Goiás (state), *Bra.* **Companhia de Desenvolvimento do Estado do Goiás (CODEG). A economia goiana no PRODOESTE.** Goiânia, Bra., 1972. 253 p., fold. maps, tables.

Up-to-date survey of the economy of the state of Goiás with many tables and charts sponsored by the state government. Although population has been and is growing rapidly (over four percent per year) the employment structure has hardly changed since 1948 with agriculture still employing over 55 percent and services nearly 40 percent of the economically active population.

———, ———. **Departamento do Comércio.** Considerações gerais sobre o abastecimento de Goiânia. See item 7117.

4860. ———, ———. **Governo.** Levantamento histórico e econômico dos municípios goianos. Goiânia, Bra., 1971. 164 p., maps, tables (Série D, 1/6)

Basic demographic and economic statistics of the microregions of the State of Goiás for 1960-1970. Useful data for regional studies and comparisons.

4861. Goodman, David E. and **Roberto Cavalcanti de Albuquerque.** Incentivos a industrialização e desenvolvimento do Nordeste. Rio, Instituto de Planejamento Econômico e Social, Instituto de Pesquisas (IPEA/INPES), 1974. 394 p., tables.

This analysis of the effectiveness of major fiscal incentives to stimulate industrialization in the Northeast consists of a macro survey, already published earlier, and an analysis of 580 projects which have been approved by SUDENE between 1962 and 1970. Criticism is levied as to the missing linkage effects, the capital intensity and the local concentration of the new industrialization drive.

Graham, Douglas and **Sergio Buarque de Hollanda Filho.** Migration, regional and urban growth and development in Brazil: a selective analysis of the historical record, 1872-1970. See *HLAS 36:3587.*

4862. Haddad, Paulo Roberto and **Jacques Schwartzman.** Teoria dos pólos de desenvolvimento: um estudo de caso. Belo Horizonte, Bra., Univ. Federal de Minas Gerais, Centro de Desenvolvimento e Planejamento Regional, 1972. 73 l., tables (Monografia, 7)

Impact study of steel and textile industry on the economy of Itabirito, Minas Gerais, computing direct and indirect effects with the help of input-output analysis.

4863. ——— and **Thompson Almeida Andrade.** Política fiscal e desequilibrios regionais (USP/EE, 4:1, jan./março 1974, p. 9-54)

Study examines the historical development of regional income differences and analyzes the impact of current fiscal policy on future distribution patterns. With the help of two different models shows that the value added tax attracts industries indiscriminately to states where they achieve a high vertical integration within each region.

4864. Hexsel, Astor Eugênio. Govêrno municipal e desenvolvimento industrial. Pôrto Alegre, Bra., Univ. Federal do Rio Grande do Sul, 1971. 84 p., tables.

Study criticizes the passive role of the municipal government in attracting industry to Pôrto Alegre, the capital of Rio Grande do Sul, and suggests the establishment of an industrial center in that city which is well supplied with basic municipal services.

4865. Hiersemenzel, Uwe-Ludwig. Die Rolle der Exporte in der wirtschaftliche Entwicklung Brasiliens. Göttingen, FRG, Otto Schwartz Verlag, 1974. 121

p., illus., map (Arbeitsberichte des Ibero-Amerika-Instituts für Wirtschaftsforchung an der Univ. Göttingen, 14)

Using the vent-for-surplus theory as a basic framework, the author analyzes the impact of Brazil's exports on its economic development between 1889 and 1964. Originally a dissertation in economics at the Univ. of Göttingen.

Hilton, Stanley E. Military influence on Brazilian economic policy, 1930-1945: a different view. See item 8570.

4866. Huddle, Donald L. Disequilibrium foreign exchange systems and the generation of industrialization and inflation in Brazil (IEI/EI, 25:3, agosto 1972, p. 497-521, tables)

Describes the multiple exchange rate auction system introduced in 1953, and evaluates its effects on prices and output. Despite the large devaluation involved in adopting the new system, Huddle finds it had a deflationary impact on domestic prices. The reason: under the previous fixed-rate system, corrupt officials and favored importers shared the subsidies implied in the overvalued exchange rate, selling imported goods to the local market at their actual scarcity values. The new system engendered a shift of real income from these high-consumption individuals to the government and other high propensity savers. He concludes further that the multiple rate structure provided a major incentive for industrial growth in general conformity with efficient resource allocation, although excessively capital intensive. For a Portuguese translation of this article: "O Sistema Brasileiro de Taxas Cambiais Flutuantes: sua Equidade Distributiva, suas Relações com a Inflação e sua Eficiência," see *Revista Brasileira de Economia* (Fundação Getúlio Vargas, Rio, 26:4, out./dez. 1973, p. 149-168).

Hugon, Paul. Demografia brasileira: ensaio de demo-economia brasileira. See item 2042.

4867. Instituto de Planejamento Econômico e Social (IPEA), *Rio.* **Instituto de Planejamento** (IPLAN). Variações climáticas e flutuações da oferta agrícola no centro-sul do Brasil. v. 1, Relatório da pesquisa. Brasília, 1972. 419 p., bibl., maps, tables (Série estudos para o planejamento, 1)

Econometric analysis of the importance of climatic conditions on agricultural output. There is no significant relation for agricultural output as a whole, but the correlations are high and significant for cotton, rice, coffee, soy beans, wheat and peanuts in Brazil's most important agricultural regions of São Paulo, Paraná, Rio Grande do Sul, Minas Gerais and Goiás.

4868. Instituto Euvaldo Lodi *Florianópolis, Bra.* **Núcleo Regional de Santa Catarina.** Demanda e oferta de profissionais de nível superior na indústria catarinense. Florianópolis, Bra., 1974. 197 p., bibl., tables.

Empirical study of the supply of and demand for professionals in Santa Catarina which finds that there was an excess demand for qualified personnel in 1973-75. Concludes with wide ranging proposals regarding the need for qualitative changes in the educational system.

4869. Investimentos e reinvestimentos de capitais estrangeiros. Brasília, Banco Central do Brasil, 1974. 391 p., tables (Anexo especial do *Boletim do Banco Central do Brasil,* 2)

This study (a special addendum issue of the Brazilian Central Bank monthly bulletin) details foreign investment activities in Brazil from 1900 to 1973, based upon the Bank's registrations. Data are broken down by home country of investor, and sector. Book value is calculated showing original investment, reinvestments, and depreciation of original investment, reinvestments, and depreciation of the reinvestment.

4870. Katzman, Martin T. Urbanização e concentração industrial: 1940-1970 (IPEA/PPE, 4:3, dez. 1974, p. 475-532)

Author tests various industrial-location theories with data from São Paulo state. Finds that the availability of trained manpower as well as the services of already established medium and small industries were more important for industrial growth of that region than the linkage effects created by the new industries and the availability of social overhead capital. A further positive factor appears to be the immobility of capital markets and the availability of savings.

4871. Kingston, Jorge and **Lucia Silva Kingston.** A distribuição da renda no Brasil (IBE/RBE, 26:4, out./dez. 1973, p. 241-256, tables)

Yet another statistical examination of income distribution data from the 1960 and 1970 censuses. Authors find less income inequality among taxpayers than among those whose incomes are below taxpaying levels. They argue, along with Pareto, that little can be done to change income distribution unless the average income is growing, and they further support government policies of recent years by noting that the elimination of absolute poverty is more important than the equalizing of income shares.

4872. Kleinpenning, J. M. G. Objectives and results of the development policy in Northeast Brazil (TESG, 62:5, 1971, p. 271-284, bibl., map)

Rather dry description of Northeast development policies since the 1870s, with detailing of accomplishments—miles of road laid, teachers trained, etc.—in the period 1959-69. In general, the author gives policy makers good grades for effort but finds the results disappointing. Population growth is identified as one of the primary villains.

4873. Knight, Peter T. Substituição de importações na agricultura brasileira: a produção de trigo no Rio Grande do Sul (IBE/RBE, 26:2, avril/junho 1972, p. 3-31, illus., tables)

Sets out to "analyze one of the rare positive agricultural policies carried out by successive Brazilian governments over a period of two decades." Actually, Knight finds the first evidence of an official policy to stimulate wheat production in Brazil in 1534, but his analysis is confined to the period 1947-1967. Alas, he is forced to conclude that the policy has all these years been misguided, as well as perversely implemented, and that the resources would better be allocated to other crops.

4874. Krieger, Ronald A. Inflation and the "Brazilian Solution" (Challenge [New York Univ., Institute of Economic Affairs, N.Y.C.] 17:4, Sept./Oct. 1974, p. 43-52, tables)

Evaluation of Brazilian indexing closely paralleling Fishlow article. Krieger concludes that the system as applied in Brazil deserves high marks for raising the efficiency of resource allocation and for achieving some measure of equity, at least since 1967. However, inflation was dampened in the 1964-67 period by conventional monetary and fiscal policies, not indexing, and since 1967 indexing has probably contributed to the resurgency of inflation. Krieger concludes that the consideration of indexing in the US is premature but implies that it might become an appropriate step should rapid inflation become a permanent feature of the economy.

4875. Lacerda Filho, Murillo Carneiro de. Alguns aspectos de mercado de capital no Brasil (IBE/RBE, 25:2, abril/junho 1971, p. 113-158, tables)

Reviews evolution of the financial system from 1951 to 1967, with particular concern for the difficulty of the private sector to finance new investment in step with the expanding public sector. Inflation and the legal ceiling on interest rates largely eliminated the commercial banks from this process and stimulated the creation of parallel financial institutions and instruments. A good institutional backgrounder.

4876. Lambert, Denis-Clair. La croissance économique au Brésil, 1920-1970: atténuations et mutations de la dualité de structures (FDD/NED [Problèmes d'Amérique Latine, 27] 3937/3974, mars 1973, p. 67-96)

Extensive study of Brazil's rapid but unstable economic growth and the continuation of regional and sectoral imbalances between 1920 and 1970, using as a framework the "dualistic" analysis the author has developed in previous studies of Brazil.

4877. Langoni, Carlos Geraldo. As causas do crescimento econômico do Brasil. Rio, APEC Editôra, 1974. 120 p., bibl., tables.

The book, a translation of Langoni's doctoral dissertation, attempts to measure the relative contributions of investments in physical and human capital to Brazilian growth since 1950. Also provides estimates of the rates of return to education by levels and to physical capital by industry. Finds that a significant increase in Brazil's six percent average growth rate could be achieved by shifting investment at the margin in the direction of human capital, as well as by reallocations within the physical and human capital categories.

4878. _____. Distribuição da renda: resumo da evidencia (IUP/D, 11, 1973, p. 81-129)

This essay, written in answer to Fishlow's second look at Brazilian income inequality, reiterates the author's position based on previous findings. Langoni maintains that the ownership of fixed assets cannot explain the increasing inequality and that views on wage policy should take into account the regressive effects of the accelerated inflation before 1963. Argues that the current concentration of income is a function of imbalances in the labor market, which itself reflects the imbalances of Brazil's regional and sectoral growth process.

4879. Leff, Nathaniel H. El desarrollo económico del Brasil a largo plazo (FCE/TE, 37:147, julio/sept. 1970, p. 551-573, tables)

Makes use of recently developed data to demonstrate that, contrary to much conventional wisdom, Brazil's rapid growth and substantial industrialization started well before World War I, was positively correlated with export growth and the availability of imports, and involved considerable government intervention and protection at least since the mid-19th century. The fact that per-capita income was still low by the 1970s is largely attributable to rapid population growth and the stagnation of exports from the populous Northeast.

_____. Economic development and regional inequality: origins of the Brazilian case. See *HLAS 36:3600*.

4880. _____. Estimativa da renda provável no Brasil no século XIX com base nos dados sobre a moeda (IBE/RBE, 26:2, abril/junho 1972, p. 45-61, tables)

By applying a model based on the demand for real cash balances to the limited available data on money supply and price levels, Leff estimates that Brazil's per-capita income grew only around 0.1 percent per year between 1822 and 1913. These results contrast sharply with the picture of rather vigorous 19th century growth painted by Furtado and others.

4881. Lemgruber, Antônio Carlos. A inflação brasileira e a controvérsia sobre a aceleração inflacionária (IBE/RBE, 27:4, out./dez. 1973, p. 31-50, bibl., tables)

Finds econometric support for the validity in Brazil of Friedman's argument that there is a "natural" level of unemployment, institutionally determined, the modification of which is not amenable to demand management policies. The use of monetary measures to expand demand will generate inflation and a temporary reduction of unemployment, but, unless inflation is continually accelerated, the unemployment will reappear. The model is run on annual data for the period 1954-71, and on quarterly data for 1958I to 1972II.

4882. Lima, Fernando Cunha. Agricultura em descompasso. Brasília, Instituto de Pesquisas, Estudos e Assessoria do Congresso (IPEAC), 1973. 60 l. (Seminário sobre problemas brasileiros)

One of the technical reports to the Brazilian Congress focusing on the food problem, distortions in Brazilian agriculture, priorities for agricultural planning, and means to make the rural sector more dynamic.

4883. Lôbo, Eulalia Maria Lahmeyer and others. Evolução dos preços e do padrão de vida no Rio de Janeiro: 1820-1930, resultados preliminares (IBE/RBE, 25:4, out./dez. 1971, p. 235-265, tables)

By reconstructing the price movements of some 13 commodities, plus factory wages, rents, and the price of slaves, authors attempt to trace the changing structure of the Brazilian economy and the living standards of urban workers.

4884. Lodder, Celsius Antônio. Padrões locacionais de desenvolvimento regional (IBE/RBE, 28:1, jan./março 1974, p. 3-128)

Exhaustive study on regional and local development patterns in Brazil and their effects on employment and income.

4885. Magalhães, João Paulo de Almeida. A controvérsia brasileira sôbre o desenvolvimento econômico: uma reformulação. Rio, Gráfica Récord Editôra, 1966. 240 p.

In this book, now 10 years old, Magalhães reviews and actively participates in the debate on economic doctrine and policy that occupied Brazilian economists after World War II. Among the issues in dispute, as elsewhere, were the need for economic planning, the ability of government to accelerate growth, the causes of inflation, protection of domestic industry, and the desirability of foreign investment. The discussion is largely theoretical, and no impression is given of the heat these issues were generating in the political arena.

4886. Malan, Pedro and **José Eduardo de Carvalho Pereira.** A propósito de uma re-interpretação do desenvolvimento brasileiro desde os anos 30 (IUP/D, 10, 1973, p. 126-145)

Review essay of Oliveira's book *A economia brasileira: crítica a razão dualista,* which stresses the importance of historical research in general and the "long-run" view in the current policy debate about the Brazilian model specifically.

4887. Mata, Milton da. Custo social da mão-de-ôbra: Centro-Sul e Nordeste do Brasil (FGV/RBE, 27:4, out./dez. 1973, p. 85-127)

Examines the social costs of labor of the major regions in Brazil and finds that the shadow prices are between 50 and 72 percent of the actual labor costs in both regions. Proposes to subsidize labor, which should improve allocation of factors and increase employment.

4888. _____ and Edmar L. Bacha. Emprêgo e salário na industria de transformação, 1949-69 (IPEA/PPE, 3:2, junho 1973, p. 303-340)

Exploratory investigation of the development of employment, wages, and productivity of Brazil's industrial labor force in the 1950s and 1960s, which shows that no theories—classical, neo-classical or structuralist—can explain the complex and often contradictory development of Brazil's labor market.

4889. Matos, Odilon Nogueira de. Café e ferrovias: a evolução ferroviária de São Paulo e o desenvolvimento da cultura cafeeira. São Paulo, Editôra Alfa-Omega, 1974. 135 p., illus. (Biblioteca Alfa-Omega de ciências sociais. Série 2:1a. Col. Clio)

Contrary to the work by Richard Graham, which stressed the importance of British capital and technology in building an efficient railroad network in São Paulo state (see *HLAS 32:2927*) author believes that fiscal incentives and the capital of the cafeteiros played a major role in railway development and thus in the economic prosperity of the whole region. The author also discusses the migration and dislocation of people, which followed railroad building and suggests a number of interesting hypotheses for future investigations.

4890. Mattos, Fernando Marcondes de. Santa Catarina: nova dimensão. Prefácio de Colombo Machado Salles. Florianópolis, Bra., Univ. Federal de Santa Catarina, 1973. 446 p., bibl., tables.

Useful survey of the economic development in Santa Catarina, the smallest of the three southern states of Brazil. Although the enthusiastic evaluation may be misleading, the rich statistical material should help the reader to assess the structure and growth of that region in comparison with Brazil's development in the last two decades.

4891. Meirelles, Antônio Chagas. Economias de escala e a estructura do sistema financeiro: o caso brasileiro. Rio, Sindicato dos Bancos do Estado da Guanabara, 1974. 135 p., tables (Publicação, 2:2)

Describes the Brazilian Government's policy since 1968 to encourage the merging of banks and other financial intermediaries as an attempt to take advantage of the available economies and thus lower the costs of financial services and interest rates to the borrower. After examining the data from a variety of angles, Meirelles concludes that the evidence strongly supports the assumption that such scale economies exist.

4892. Mello, José Carlos. Transporte no Nordeste: análise econométrica de sua demand a (IBE/RBE, 28:2, avril/junho 1974, p. 47-74)

Regression analysis of the demand for transportation in Brazil's Northeast, with regional income, demand for cement, and availability of already paved roads being the major variables explaining the change and fluctuations of transportation in that region.

4893. Melo, Marlos Jacob de. As pequenas emprêsas no desenvolvimento industrial do Nordeste. Recife, Bra., Secretaria de Industria de Comércio (SIC), Nucleo de Assistência Industrial (NAI), 1971. 55 p., tables.

Briefly surveys the importance of small business in development, after a comparison with small business in India, Holland and the US, the study discusses the establishment of small business in the Northeast.

4894. Mont'Alegre, Omer. Capital e capitalismo no Brasil. Rio, Editôra Expressão e Cultura, 1972. 437 p., tables (Economia e administração)

In an interesting, almost anecdotal style, the author traces the evolution of the Brazilian financial system and industry, and the people who moved them, from colonial times to the immediate post-World War II period.

4895. Monteiro, Jorge Vianna and **Luiz Roberto Azevedo Cunha.** Alguns aspectos da evolução do Planejamento econômico no Brasil: 1934-1963 (IPEA/PPE, 4:1, fev. 1974, p. 1-24)

Brief analysis of major attempts by various Brazilian governments between 1934 and 1963 to introduce planning into the Brazilian economy.

4896. Morley, Samuel A. and **Jeffrey G. Williamson.** Demand, distribution, and employment: the case of Brazil (UC/EDCC, 23:1, Oct. 1974, p. 33-60, tables)

Authors utilize a dynamic linear input-output model to simulate alternative growth strategies for Brazil. The purpose is to study the impact different demand patterns might have had on labor absorption and income distribution in the period 1949-62. The link between demand patterns and the distribution of earnings is the differential pattern of derived demand for heterogeneous labor skills, including the indirect labor demand in the capital goods industry. Overall unemployment rates fell over the period with a progressive effect on income distribution. However, the growth of demand was particularly rapid in these sectors having the highest skill intensity, and this was a major explanation of the rising Gini coefficient. The latter is more sensitive to the rate of growth, however, and slow growth is generally more regressive than rapid growth. The authors conclude that increasing relative inequality of income distribution is, at least in direction, insensitive to alternative growth policies in a country at Brazil's level of development in the 1950s. Includes graphs.

4897. Mueller, Charles C. Análise das diferenças de produtividade da pecuária de corte em área do Brasil Central (IPEA/PPE, 4:2, junho 1974, p. 285-324)

Econometric study on the production of hides in three different regions in Goiás and Minas Gerais. Author concludes that the differences in productivity can be explained by differences in "X-efficiency" of entrepreneurs, credit granting, and technical aid.

4898. Naylor, Thomas H.; Martin Shubik; and **Ralph Zerkowski.** Modelos econométricos da economia brasileira: um sumário crítico (IBE/RBE, 25:1, jan./março 1971, p. 65-91, tables)

Briefly summarizes and evaluates several previous attempts to simulate the Brazilian economy by the Planning Ministry (10-year plan), Gerhard Tintner, the World Bank, ECLA, and others. Authors urge future econometricians against being unduly cautious because of data limitations. In English and Portuguese.

4899 ———— . and others. Um modêlo de simulação da economia do Brasil (IBE/RBE, 25:1, jan./março 1971, p. 39-63, tables)

Reports a preliminary version of a 16-equation simulation model of the Brazilian economy developed by the Getulio Vargas Foundation on the basis of data for the period 1947-68. The results of the model are compared favorably with that of the World Bank. Authors conclude with their plans for further development of the model. Article is presented in English and Portuguese.

4900. Ness, Walter L., Jr. Financial markets innovation as a development strategy: initial results from the Brazilian experience (UC/EDCC, 22:3, April 1974, p. 453-472, tables)

Describes Brazil's recent development strategy as keyed to the development of a modern financial system. Ness describes financial market innovations since 1964 and concludes that the comprehensive reforms succeeded in raising the rate of investment, lowering the capital-output ratio, and reducing at least potentially Brazil's dependence on foreign capital. He asserts, however, that the success of this strategy depended heavily on the stifling of the political process, and he has some misgivings about the strategy's impact on income distribution.

O'Donnell, Guillermo A. Modernization and bureaucratic-authoritarianism:

studies in South American politics. See item 4740.

4901. Oliveira, Francisco. La economía brasileña: crítica a la razón dualista (FCE/TE, 40[2]:158, abril/junio 1973, p. 411-484, tables)

Argues at some length that Western economic theory and concepts, including the notion of the dual economy, have no analytic utility for Brazil. Instead the economic system must be analyzed as an organic whole, in which industrialization has been built upon the exploitation of the working class. However, the contradictions inherent in Brazilian capitalism are over increasing, and the explosion cannot be far away. [T.Villamil]

4902. Oliveira, Francisco Tarcízio Góes de and Sérgio Alberto Brandt. O novo modelo brasileiro de desenvolvimento agricola. Rio, APEC Editôra, 1975. 156 p., bibl., illus.

Analysis of the agricultural firm within the new Brazilian development model. Whereas pt. 1 takes up the macro-performance of Brazil's agricultural sector, pt. 2 analyzes the economics of the micro-unit and its option to mix inputs and outputs in such a fashion as to maximize profits. Study concludes with a number of project evaluations.

4903. Paiva, Ruy Miller. Elementos básicos de uma política em favor da agricultura brasileira (IPEA/PPE, 4:2, junho 1974, p. 209-244.)

Macroeconomic investigation into Brazil's agricultural sector, focusing on factors which hinder and further development. Included is a section with policy proposals to improve the efficiency of that sector.

4904. Pandolfo, Clara. A Amazônia: seu grande potencial de recursos naturais e oportunidades de industrialização, Belém, Bra., Superintêndencia do Desenvolvimento da Amazônia (SUDAM), 1969. 113 p., bibl., tables.

This prize-winning essay on the natural resources of the Amazon discusses the advantage of developing the large forest reserves of that region. The analysis includes short surveys of world demand and supply of wood as well as various fiscal incentives which would stimulate a lumber industry in the Amazon area.

4905. Pará (state), *Bra*. **Associação de Crédito e Assistência Rural do Estado do Pará (ACARPA).** Investigação sobre os fluxos das interrelações urbano-rurais no Estado do Pará: termo de referência. v. 1/2, Contribuição a operacionalização do Plano Nacional de Desenvolvimento Norte (PNDN). Belém, Bra., 1973. 2 v. (349 p.) (Continuous pagination) bibl., illus., tables.

Extensive regional plan covering all major economic activities in Pará state until 1972. No forecasting is attempted.

4906. _____, _____. Instituto do Desenvolvimento Econômico-Social do Pará (IDESP). Laticínios em Marajó. Belém, Bra., 1971. 55 p., tables (Estudos paraenses, 36)

One of the many microstudies which are currently undertaken in Belém by the Institute of Economic and Social Studies. Analyzes production (inputs and outputs) of condensed milk, in and around a town in Pará.

4907. Paraná (state), *Bra.* **Coordenação de Planejamento Estadual.** Avaliação socio-ecônomica: por zona eléctrica do Paraná; por estado da região sul. Curitiba, Bra., 1972. 1 v. (Unpaged) tables.

Socio-economic analysis of Brazil's South (Paraná, Santa Catarina, Rio Grande do Sul) according to electrical regions.

4908. Paranhos, Oscar Torres; Reynaldo Botrel Alvarenga; Carlos Miguel Hecker de Abreu; and Claude Guibert. Conjuntura do arroz. Goiânia, Bra., Ministério de Agricultura, Superintendência Nacional do Abastecimento (SUNAB), 1969. 50 p., tables.

First part of a fairly competent study on the supply of rice in Brazil by the Ministry of Agriculture. The authors investigate the rather wide fluctuations of price, quantity and compare regional production and income data. They conclude that the low rate of return is partly to blame for the unsatisfactory supply of this important staple.

4909. Parizzi, Marcelo; Paulo Roberto Haddad; and Márcio Olympio Guimarães Henriques. Relações interindustriais em Minas Gerais. Belo Horizonte, Bra., Univ. Federal de Minas Gerais, Centro de Desenvolvimento e Planejamento Regional (CEDEPLAR), 1972. 33 p., tables (Monografia, 5)

One of the monographs produced by the Regional Development Center at the Univ. of Minas Gerais, constructing an input-output table for Belo Horizonte in 1959.

4910. Passos, Carlos de Faro. Estrutura financeira e desenvolvimento; o caso do Brasil. São Paulo, Editôra Atlas, 1973. 209 p., bibl., tables.

Describes and evaluates the evolution of the Brazilian financial system in two periods: 1945-65; and 1965-72. The first period is marked by the lack of effective controls on monetary expansion, high costs of intermediation, and the shortage of long-term financing for capital growth. All this was put on the road to rectification by the banking and capital market reforms implemented since 1965. Passos provides a useful institutional backgrounder for the newcomer to Brazilian finance.

4911. Pastore, Affonso Celso. Aspectos da política monetária recente no Brasil (USP/EE, 3:3, set./dez. 1973, p. 7-58)

Explanation of Brazil's inflation through regression analysis with changes in the money supply, wages, and exchange rates being the most important independent variables. The study examines also the efficiency of monetary policy in limiting money supply by analyzing the behavior of commercial banks during inflation.

4912. _____. A reposta da produção agrícola aos preços no Brasil. São Paulo, APEC Editôra, 1973. 170 p.

Econometric study of Brazil's agricultural sector, measuring the suppliers' responses to price changes. Author maintains that Brazilian entrepreneurs of the primary sector are reacting rationally, i.e. the supply of agricultural output correlates positively and significantly with changes in prices not only in the developed Center-South but also in the backward Northeast. In addition there is ample evidence that producers try to minimize costs and maximize profits by adjusting output correctly to changing prices.

4913. Pastore, José. Profissionais especializados no mercado de trabalho. São Paulo, Instituto de Pesquisas Econômicas (IPE), 1973. 146 p., tables.

A study of high and medium-level manpower in the State of São Paulo, based on primary statistics from 700 firms and 25,000 professionals. After investigating the supply and demand situation of that special market, the study discusses various characteristics, such as distribution by industry and age, and concludes that rates of return and their differences can be explained within the framework of neo-classical theory.

4914. _____ and **Anna Maria F. Bianchi.** Determinação de salários: uso de um modelo causal (USP/EE, 4:2, 1974, p. 7-26, bibl., illus., tables)

Examines the variables which determine the differences and fluctuations of salaries of various skill groups. Study concludes that the technological progress of the individual industry is especially important in explaining salary differentials.

4915. Patrick, George F. Desenvolvimento agrícola do Nordeste. Rio, Instituto de Planejamento Econômico e Social, Instituto de Pesquisas (IPEA/INPES), 1972. 319 p., bibl., tables (Col. Relatórios de Pesquisa, 11)

A comprehensive macroeconomic survey of Northeast agriculture in the period 1948-69. Separate chapters are devoted to the use and productivities of the inputs land, labor, and capital. Other chapters examine specific products, government policies, and the role of agriculture in the larger Northeast economy. Patrick finds that agricultural output in the region grew at an annual rate of 4.7 percent, higher than the national average over the period studied. The growth was attributable almost entirely to the expansion of land under cultivation rather than any improvements in inputs or technology.

4916. _____. Efeitos de programas alternativas do governo sobre a agricultura do Nordeste (IPEA/PPE, 4:1, fev. 1974, p. 49-82)

Author tests with the help of linear programming the impact of alternative agricultural policies in three microregions in Brazil's Northeast. Besides the very restrictive assumptions prognosis is rendered difficult by rather wide fluctuations of the key variables (interest and fertilizer prices) in order to make an accurate forecast of production in these regions.

4917. Peláez, Carlos Manuel. Historia de industrialização brasileira: crítica a teoria estruturalista no Brazil. Rio, APEC Editôra, 1972. 241 p., bibl., illus.

Collection of previous published essays (*Revista Brasileira de Economia*), which center around the role of exogenous shocks influencing industrialization policies and patterns, especially the Great Depression. In spite of an impressive array of statistics, the "furious" attack on the "structuralist" interpretation of the industrialization process would have been more convincing had it been repeated less often.

4918. _____. Mario Henrique Simonsen e o passado recente e o futuro do Brasil: políticas para o crescimento equilibrado (IBE/RBE, 26:2, abril/junho 1972, p. 33-44, bibl.)

One cannot fully understand Brazil's extraordinary economic progress of recent years without understanding Brazil's extraordinary economists. Peláez devotes this short article to the thoughts of the latest in a distinguished line of scholar-finance ministers. But, alas, Simonsen deserves a more thoughtful treatment than this, and the reader is advised to go directly to the master's work.

4919. Pereira, José Carlos. Estrutura e expansão da indústria em São Paulo. São Paulo, Univ. de São Paulo, 1967. 201 p., tables (Biblioteca universitária. Série 2: ciências sociais, 9)

Socio-economic study of the industrialization process in São Paulo with critical emphasis on market concentration and unused capacity from the late 1950s until 1965-66.

4920. Pereira, José Eduardo Carvalho. Financiamento externo e crescimento econômico no Brasil: 1966-73. Rio, Instituto de Planejamento Econômico e Social (IPEA), 1974. 273 p., tables.

Study first analyzes the interaction between the influx of foreign short-and medium-term capital and the development of Brazil's financial markets and industrial structure. Then, it criticizes the government's "debt-cum-growth" policy on the grounds that it did not generate new sources of foreign exchange, but mainly served to strengthen the working capital of multinational and some large national firms.

4921. Pernambuco (state), *Bra.* **Conselho de Desenvolvimento.** Programa de Ação Coordenada 1972/75. v. 1, Ação de govêrno e desenvolvimento. v. 3, Os orçamentos geral do estado, 1972 e plurianual de investimentos: 1972-1974. Recife, Bra., 1971? 2 v. (220, 584 p.) plates.

Development plan of Pernambuco, the central state of Brazil's Northeast. Besides analyzing possibilities and prospects of various sectors to expand their production this study emphasizes the employment aspect of that region which suffers from rates of unemployment and underemployment of over 20 per cent.

4922. Pinheiro Neto, J. M. Os investimentos estrangeiros no Brasil (Finanças Públicas [Ministério da Fazenda, Subsecretaria de Economia e Finanças, Brasília] 34:319, julho/set. 1974, p. 37-47)

Describes the process and rationale for the registration and regulation of foreign investments, direct and financial, and contracts for the transfer of technology in Brazil. As a consequence of these controls, the author asserts that the danger of foreign domination of any sector of economic activity has almost totally disappeared.

Pinto, Rogerio Feital. La ecología política del Banco Nacional de Desarrollo Económico del Brasil (BNDE): una tesis presentada al Departamento de Ciencias Políticas de la Universidad de Carolina del Norte. See item 8584.

4923. Prado, Lafayette. Panorama futuro dos transportes. Brasília, Instituto de Pesquisas, Estudos e Assessoria do Congresso (IPEAC), 1973. 197 l., tables (Seminário sobre problemas brasileiros)

Analysis of future demand for transportation and Brazil's capacity to meet this demand. Paper delivered to Brazilian Congress includes extensive discussion and contributions by Congressmen.

4924. Queiroz, José Maria Vilar de. Brasil: exportação e importação (Brazil: export and import. Brésil: exportation et importation). Rio, Crown Editores Internacionais, 1972? 1 v. (Various pagings) illus.

Descriptive analysis of Brazil's foreign trade policy and the performance of the foreign sector, which benefited from an expanding world economy in the 1960s and early 1970s.

4925. Rask, Norman; Richard L. Meyer; and **Fernando C. Peres.** Crédito agrícola e subsídios à produção como instrumentos para o desenvolvimento da agricultura brasileira (IBE/RBE, 28: 1, jan./mar. 1974, p. 151-172, bibl.)

Reports the preliminary results of an Ohio State Univ. research project. The considerable expansion of agricultural credit over the 1960s made possible the adoption of modern inputs, particularly by medium and large farms, in the South, but had little impact on production in the Northeast. Knowledge is the major limiting factor on productivity increases in both places, and the authors conclude that agricultural research must be given top priority for continued growth in the sector.

4926. Rattner, Heinrich *ed.* Tecnologia (FGV/RAE, 14:3, junho 1974, p. 145-152)

This issue reports on a conference at the Getúlio Vargas Business School in São Paulo on organization, principles, and problems of technology transfer and its impact on Brazilian economic and social development. Two contributions analyze the possibilities of developing a viable intermediate technology in Brazil.

4927. Resende, Eliseu. Highways and Brazil's development. Rio, n.p., 1973. 127 p., maps, tables.

Paper presented at the VII World Meeting of the International Road Federation in Munich describing and evaluating the ambitious highway program of Brazil. Contains useful maps and technical appendices.

4928. *Revista da Administração de Empresas.* Fundação Getúlio Vargas, Instituto de Documentação. Vol. 14, No. 1, jan./fev. 1974- . São Paulo.

Issue consists of a series of essays on Brazil's financial sector and its importance in the process of economic development. Of particular interest are the contributions on expansion and modernization of the financial system for small and medium-size industries and the effects of the mini-devaluation on the movement of foreign capital.

4929. Ribeiro, Sylvio Wanick. Desempenho do setor agrícola: década 1960/70. Rio, Instituto de Planejamento Econômico e Social (IPEA), 1973. 176 p., tables (Série estudos para o planejamento, 6)

Very useful survey of Brazil's agricultural development between 1969-70, which includes statistics on agricultural exports and imports as well as estimates for the income elasticity of demand and the production of individual food items.

4930. Rio (state), *Bra.* **Companhia de Desenvolvimento Econômico do Estado do Rio de Janeiro (CODERJ). Departamento Estudos e Projetos.** Diagnóstico do Estado do Rio de

Janeiro. Niterói, Bra., 1969. 414 p., illus., tables.

Economic survey of the coastal state of Rio de Janeiro which includes primary and secondary production, infrastructure, public and private services as well as two chapters on income and demographic characteristics of the population.

4931. Rio Grande do Sul (state), *Bra.* Programa de Acão: 1973-1975. Pôrto Alegre, Bra., 1974? 1 v. (Unpaged) illus., plates, tables.

A two-year program of Rio Grande do Sul containing mostly expenditures breakdown of various government activities.

Rodrigues, Eduardo Celestino. Problemas do Brasil potência. See item 8923.

4932. Rodrigues, Maria Magdalena E. Mischan. A velha e a nova industrialização (FGV/RAE, 12:3, julho/sept. 1972, p. 107-113, tables)

Reiteration of the structuralist, dependency model of Latin American development. Criticizes current Brazilian policy as failing to overcome the two central problems of a primary goods exporter: technological dualism and poor income distribution.

Rotstein, Jaime. Ciência e tecnologia. See item 6349.

4933. Sá, Jayme Magrassi de. Aspectos da economia brasileira. Rio, Editôra Alba, 1970. 198 p., tables.

A collection of 27 of the author's articles taken from magazines and newspapers. The topics range from birth control to the development of Brasilia and development of the financial system.

4934. Sahota, G. S. Causas e efeitos da inflação no Brasil (IBE/RBE, 26:4, out./dez. 1972, p. 257-294, tables)

Presents a four-sector, 52-equation econometric model of the Brazilian economy in an effort to identify the causes of inflation from 1951 to 1968. The result is strong support for the monetarists.

4935. _____. Proteção e industrialização (IBE/RBE, 26:2, abril/junho, 1972, p. 80-111, bibl., illus., tables)

In the face of substantial problems of data and definitions, Sahota sets out to compare the levels of protection in Brazil and India. Finds on average that protection in Brazil in the mid-1960s was considerably higher than in India, with evidence of protection-engendered resource misallocations in both. In both countries, the highest levels of protection went to the older industries, such as textiles, rather than in infant industries that offered economies of scale or the prospect of dynamic growth.

4936. Salm, Claudio. Evolução do mercado do trabalho, 1969-72 (Estudos CEBRAP [Centro Brasileiro de Análise e Planejamento, São Paulo] 8, avril/janho 1974, p. 103-119)

Brief analysis of changes in the Brazilian employment structure between 1968 and 1972 based on the national household surveys by the Instituto Brasileiro de Geografia e Estatística (IBGE). Major conclusions are: 1) migration to the cities continues to grow and with it "marginalization;" 2) a major increase in employment is occurring in the modern factory sector; and 3) inspite of increased labor absorption, supply continues to exceed demand except for some skilled jobs in the South.

4937. Santos, M. Coutinho dos. Crédito, investimentos e financiamentos rurais. Rio, Livraria Freitas Bastos, 1972. 425 p., bibl., tables.

An elementary textbook on rural credit in Brazil. Readers whose knowledge goes beyond the need for basic definitions may still find it a useful handbook on the Brazilian legal and institutional context.

4938. Santos, Roberto. Leis sociais e custo da mão-de-obra no Brasil. São Paulo, Univ. de São Paulo [and] LTR Editôra, 1973. 393 p., bibl., tables.

Detailed analysis of social, legal and economic influences on labor costs in Brazil, covering wages in urban and rural areas, minimum wage and social security policies and an international comparison of labor costs.

4939. Santos, Theóphilo de Azeredo. Empresas internacionais e multinacionais. Brasília, Instituto de Pesquisas, Estudos e Assessoria do Congresso (IPEAC), 1973. 85 l., tables.

One of four papers delivered to the Brazilian Congress during the Seminário sobre Problemas Brasileiros held 27 Sept. 1973. More data from Latin America in general than from Brazil. Some interesting questioning by Congressmen reflects part of the public attitude vis-à-vis foreign investment.

4940. _____. Sistema bancário: alterações e atualizações no funcionamento (Revista Bancária Brasileira [Rio] 42:497, 30 maio 1974, p. 37-40, tables)

Describes recent institutional evolution of the Brazilian banking system and presents data on foreign capital in the banking sector. Interesting to note that as of March 1973, foreign banks and domestic banks under foreign control combined accounted for less than two percent of banking offices, less than four percent of loans, and slightly more than four percent of total deposits.

4941. São Paulo (state), *Bra.* **Governo. Secretaria de Economia e Planejamento.** Interiorização do desenvolvimento paulista. São Paulo, 1972. 40 p., illus., maps, plates.

Reprints of speeches and articles of São Paulo top administration and economists, with emphasis on the development of the interior of São Paulo, i.e. decentralization.

4942. _____, _____. _____. _____. **Coordenadoria de Ação Regional.** Terceira/décima primeira região administrativa: diagnóstico. São Paulo, 1972. 9 v. (Various pagings) illus., maps, tables.

Economic and social surveys of economic subregions of the state of São Paulo with simple statistics on population, education health and economic activities. Useful as a base for comparative studies with other regions in Brazil.

4943. _____, _____. **Secretaria da Agricultura.** Desenvolvimento agrícola: um grande desafio. São Paulo, 1972. 139 p., illus., maps, tables.

Agricultural plan of São Paulo state with special emphasis on technical and research aid to farmers in Brazil's most prosperous region.

Schwartzman, Simon. Empresarios y política en el proceso de industrialización: Argentina, Brasil, Australia. See item 8593.

4944. Seabra, Manoel. Vargem grande: organização e transformações de um setor do cinturão-verde paulistano. São Paulo, Univ. de São Paulo, Instituto de Geografia, 1971. 229 p., bibl., illus., maps, tables (Série teses e monografias, 4)

Thesis of the State Univ. of São Paulo investigating the production of green beans in São Paulo in a historical context, stressing the importance of Japanese skills and initiative.

4945. Serra, José. El milagro económico brasileño: ¿realidad o mito? (UNAM/RMS, 34:2, abril/junio 1972, p. 245-292, tables)

Serra argues that from the point of view of the working class the Brazilian economic miracle has been largely a myth. According to his analysis, the relative income distribution has worsened since 1960, and real wages have not kept up with the gains in worker productivity. No distinction is made between wage rates and the actual take-home earnings. [T. Villamil]

4946. Silva, Edmundo de Macedo Soares e. As instituições de industria e comérico do Brasil (Industrial and Commercial Institutions in Brazil). Rio, Crown Editores Internacionais, 1972. 799 p.

The book, with complete texts in both Portuguese and English, begins with a brief history of entrepreneurship, corporate management, and business-government relations in Brazil. The remainder of the substantive chapters are devoted to detailed sectoral discussions, including, inter alia, energy, nonferrous metals, rubber, steel, and chemicals. Although sometimes rambling too far afield into a discussion of historical and international data, the book is a valuable reference source for the details of Brazilian industrial development. The volume ends with a series of short monographs on major Brazilian corporations and trade associations.

4947. Silva, Fernando Antônio Rezende da. Avaliação de setor público na economia brasileira: estrutura funcional da despesa. Rio, Instituto de Planejameto Econômico e Social, Instituto de Pesquisas (IPEA/INPES), 1972. 252 p., bibl., tables (Col. Relatórios de pesquisa, 13)

Explores the growth of public sector expenditures from 1947 to 1969, when total government spending in Brazil rose five times in real terms, to reach 30 percent of the gross domestic product and half of all investment. Concentrating on the years since 1964, Silva finds the large extent to which specific expenditures are tied to specific revenues greatly reduces the discretionary authority of the government to allocate resources in accordance with shifting priorities. State and federal budgets are examined separately, and the consolidated public sector spending pattern is compared with international norms. The institutional problems that inhibit effective planning and programming are discussed.

4948. _____ and **Dennis Mahar.** Saúde e previdência social: uma análise econômica. Rio, Instituto de Planejamento Econômico e Social, Instituto de Pesquisas (IPEA/INPES), 1974. 222 p., tables.

Discussion of the development and financial structure of the Brazilian social security system as well as its efficiency to improve the health of the population and mobilize savings for the capital market. Policy proposals contain the redistribution of expenditures from private to public health measures and the transfer of certain activities from the social security administration to the Ministry of Health.

4949. Silva Filho, Amilcar Pereira da; Maurício Jorge Cardoso Pinto; Antônio Carlos da Motta Ribeiro; and **Antônio Carlos de Araujo Lago.** Mercado brasileiro de productos petroquímicos. Brasília, Instituto de Planejamento Econômico e Social, Instituto de Planejamento (IPEA/IPLAN), 1973. 171 p., tables (Série estudos para o planejamento, 3)

Technical studies on the supply of and demand for synthetic fibers and plastic. This industry survey is part of the national development plan 1972-74.

4950. Silvers, Arthur L. and **Moran de Mello Moreira.** A absorção da força de trabalho não qualificada em Minas Gerais: evidencia em favor da hipótese de Todaro? (USP/EE, 4:1, jan./maio 1974, p. 55-74)

Empirical study examines migration flows and income differentials in small (17-40,000 inhabitants) and medium sized towns (41-70,000 inhabitants). Authors find that the step-wise migration from small to medium-sized cities is not justified by wage differentials, which leads to a critical evaluation of the Todaro thesis.

4951. Simonsen, Mário Henrique. Brasil 2002. Rio, Biblioteca do Exército [and] APEC e Bloch Editôras, 1973. 180 p., tables (Col. General Benício, 108:431)

Brazil's current Finance Minister talks of the future, complete with econometric models and diagrams. [P. B. Taylor, Jr.]

4952. _____. The Brazilian miracle: the next phase (IAMEA, 28:1, Summer 1974, p. 51-61, table)

Policy statement by Brazil's current Finance Minister, a technical advisor to the Brazilian government since 1964. Discusses both short-run problems arising from the sudden hike in oil prices and long-run issues of income inequalities and underemployment. Proposes continuation of growth policies which will permit the freeing of more resources for social projects.

4953. _____. A força de trabalho no Brasil (IBE/RBE, 28:4, out./dez. 1974, p. 29-45, tables)

Reviews changes in the labor force and income distribution reflected in the 1960 and 1970 censuses, and argues that the primary cause of increasing inequality of income distribution over the period was the short supply, relative to demand, of skilled labor. The military government's wage policy, moreover, had little effect on income distribution. Furthermore, it is wrong to deprecate the Brazilian "miracle" on distributional grounds inasmuch as data are not yet available to evaluate the impact of the rapid growth that began in 1968. Simonsen lauds the Government's educational programs as the primary solution to the distributional problem. Among the programs described is Mobral, the adult literacy campaign, which the author himself headed before being named Minister of Finance.

4954. _____. O model de realimentação inflacionária e as experiências de estabilização (IBE/RBE, 26:4, out./dez. 1972, p. 227-239, tables)

Brief discourse on inflation theory, its implications for stabilization policy, and the experience of the real world. The author outlines a "feedback" model in which economic groups attempt to regain the real incomes lost to past inflation. Such expectations are eliminated by traditional policies only at the cost of a period of high unemployment and lost output. The model is used to explain Brazil's gradualist stabilization policy after 1964.

4955. _____ and Roberto de Oliveira Campos. A nova economia brasileira (The new Brazilian economy). Rio, Crown Editôra Internacionais, 1974. 631 p., plates, tables.

The first 190 (oversized) p. consist of a series of essays by Simonsen and Campos on general development topics as well as, inter alia, the Brazilian development model, the impact on development of Brazilian social and political attitudes, the Brazilian planning experience, investments in education and Brazil's future political options. Then follows 436 p. of Standard and Peer-type data sheets on Brazil's major industrial, commercial, and financial enterprises. This elegantly bound book, with complete texts in both Portuguese and English, is must reading for the student of Brazilian economic growth and the thinking that guides its technocratic elite.

4956. Singer, Paul Israel. Economia política da urbanização. São Paulo, Editôra Brasilense [and] Centro Brasileiro de Análise e Planejamento (CEBRAP), 1973. 152 p.

Study on urbanization and related issues such as migration and marginalization. Theoretical framework is applied to urbanization and the problem of urban planning in São Paulo.

4957. _____. Fôrça de trabalho e emprêgo no Brasil: 1920-1969. São Paulo, Centro Brasileiro de Análise e Planejamento, 1971. 106 p., tables (Cadernos CEBRAP, 3)

Excellent study on the growth of Brazil's labor force and the change of the employment structure between 1920 and 1969. The attempt is made to measure productivity in various sectors of the economy. Author concludes that there is little evidence of tertianization in Brazil.

4958. _____. El milagro brasileño: causas y consecuencias (FCE/TE, 40[4]:160, oct./dic. 1973, p. 753-819, bibl., tables)

After a lengthy historical comparison of West Germany, Japan, and Brazil, Singer concludes that rapid, noninflationary growth is possible in capitalist economies over extended periods only if the growth of wages is kept below the growth of productivity. Real wages have been held down for unskilled workers in Brazil by the essentially "unlimited" supply. For a longer version of this article see the Portuguese original: *O milagre brasileiro: causas e consequências* (São Paulo, Centro Brasileiro de Análise e Planejamento [CEBRAP], 1972, 81 p., tables [Cadernos CEBRAP, 6]). [T. Villamil]

4959. Smolka, Martin O. and Celsius A. Lodder. Concentração, tamanho urbano e estrutura industrial (IPEA/PPE, 3:2, junho 1973, p. 447-468, tables)

Study of the relationship between size of urban areas and type of industry established therein. Although there is no systematic relation between size of city and size of firm, the majority of large and modern industries are located in or near the largest cities of one million or more inhabitants. On the other hand, the smallest urban centers are often dominated by one resource based industry.

4960. Solanet, Manuel A. Análisis económico de la sustitución de ramales ferroviarios por caminos. Rio, Instituto de Pesquisas Rodoviárias, 1972. 40 p. (Publicação, 572)

Brief technical study comparing transport costs of road vs. rail traffic, establishing minimum distance and load factor for the operation of each transport means, and the critical area where a shift from one to the other becomes mandatory.

4961. Solar, Franz. Contribución austríaca al programa de desarrollo del Brasil meridional (ZPKW/A, 7:7, [1. semestre] 1971, p. 22-41, table)

Description and evaluation of the technical assistance provided by Austria for agricultural development in Rio Grande do Sul. Of little interest to the general reader. [T. Villamil]

4962. Souza, Eli de Moraes and others. Formação de capital e mudanças tecnológicas ao nível de emprêsas rurais: Lajeado, Caràzinho e Não-Me-Toque, relatório descritivo. Pôrto Alegre, Bra., Univ. Federal do Rio Grande do Sul, Faculdade de Ciências Econômicas, Centro de Estudos e Pesquisas Econômicas (IEPE), 1971. 95., tables (Estudos e trabalhos mimeografados, 11)

Study based on empirical survey of three communities. Analyzes the use of capital and labor in agricultural enterprises of Rio Grande do Sul. Although no theoretical framework is provided, statistical compilation is useful basis for further study.

4963. Suplicy, Eduardo M. Alguns aspectos da política salarial (FGV/RAE, 14:5, set./out. 1974, p. 32-45)

Study traces the fall of the "real" minimum wage since the early 1960s and argues that the average real wages in the major sectors—although increasing in absolute terms—have not kept pace with increases in productivity. The author indicates that not only is the redistribution of income a consequence of the stringent wage policy of the government, but that there may also be a connection between the wage variable and the higher infant mortality, which occurred in São Paulo during the last ten years.

4964. Suzigan, Wilson; José Eduardo de Carvalho Pereira; and **Ruy Affonso Guimarães de Almeida.** Financiamento de projetos industriais no Brasil. Rio, Instituto de Planejamento Econômico y Social, Instituto de Pesquisas (IPEA/INPES), 1972. 420 p., bibl., tables (Col. Relatórios de pesquisa, 9)

Describes the recent evolution of Brazil's financial system as it has affected the process of industrialization, and describes in detail the major industrial credit institutions and mechanisms extant in 1972. On the basis of flow of funds data, authors attempt to analyze dependence of Brazilian industry—by sector, size of firm, and use of product—on financial sector for its capital. They conclude, interalia, that financial reforms since 1964 have made substantial new short- and medium-term funds available from private domestic and foreign financial intermediaries, but that industry continued to rely almost entirely on public sector intermediaries for long-term funds.

4965. _____. and others. Crescimento industrial no Brasil: incentivos e desempenho recente. Rio, Instituto de Planejamento Econômico e Social (IPEA), 1974. 281 p., bibl., tables.

After a discussion of industrial policies and their impact on industrial growth during the last 15 years, the authors analyze major phases of the recent boom and its relation to the middle-1960s recuperation period. Although they stress the importance of the domestic market, they believe that future development will depend largely on further diversification and expansion of industrial exports as well as on continuous import substitution of more sophisticated capital goods.

4966. Syvrud, Donald E. Foundations of Brazilian economic growth. Stanford, Calif., Stanford Univ., Hoover Institution Press [and] American Enterprise Institute for Public Policy Research, Washington, 1974. 295 p., bibl., tables (AEI-Hoover research publications, 1)

A most welcome addition to the literature, providing a comprehensive survey and evaluation of Brazilian postwar economic policies, concentrating particularly on the period 1964-1972. This is must reading for anyone wishing to understand the mechanisms of macroeconomic policy in Brazil. Not everyone will accept all of Syvrud's argument, such as the responsibility of pre-Revolution policies for the deterioration of income distribution and growing foreign presence in industry, and the dedication of the governments since 1964 to the reversal of these trends. Nevertheless, he makes a persuasive case that the proper explanation of the ups and downs of Brazilian economic fortunes over the past 30 years lies not in the stars but in the quality of government policymaking. For political scientist's comment, see item 8597a.

4967. Tavares, Maria de Conceição. Da substituição de importações ao capitalismo financeiro: ensaios sobre economia brasileira. Rio, Zahar Editóra, 1972. 263 p. (Biblioteca de ciências sociais)

Pt. 2 of structuralist analysis of Brazil's industrialization process. Pt. 1 was published in ECLA's *Economic Bulletin for Latin America*. This section is mainly concerned with aspects of concentration in industry and finance and its consequences for the distribution of income.

4968. _____. and José Serra. Más allá

del estancamiento: una discusión sobre el estilo de desarrollo reciente (FCE/TE, 38:152, oct./dic. 1971, p. 905-950, tables)

Examines Brazilian economic experience after 1964 in the light of Celso Furtado's stagnation thesis. They find an apparent, but not necessary, contradiction between performance and expectations from the thesis. They see nothing in the Brazilian experience which requires that it be self-limiting. [J. M. Hunter]

4969. Tavares, Vania Porto; Cláudio Monteiro Considera; and Maria Thereza L.L. de Castro e Silva. Colonização dirigida no Brasil: suas possibilidades na região amazônica. Rio, Instituto de Planejamento Econômico e Social, Instituto de Pesquisas (IPEA/INPES), 1972. 201 p., bibl., illus., tables (Col. Relatório de pesquisa, 8)

Discusses the role of agriculture in the colonization process of the Amazon. After comparing various colonization schemes in Brazil and abroad, the authors examine various projects for the Transamazônica and conclude that the colonization process will finance itself in the long run.

4970. Teixeira Filho, A. L.; Bruce W. Cone; and L.M. Eisgruber. Comparação de duas alternativas para o aumento de produção agricola, fertilização e incorporação de cerrado (FGV/RBE, 28:1, jan./março 1974, p. 129-149)

Econometric study about the possibilities of more intensive land use in the "Triángulo Mineiro." In conclusive as to whether or not a more intensive use based on fertilizer would be more profitable than the current practice of extensive use in the potentially rich lands south of Minas Gerais.

4971. Tolipan, Ricardo and Arthur Carlos Tinelli eds. A controversia sobre distribuição de renda e desenvolvimento. Rio, Zahar Editôres, 1975. 319 p., tables.

Collection of essays, which re-examine the income distribution issue and its possible causes and consequences in Brazil.

4972. Tolosa, Hamilton C. Diferenciais de produtividade industrial e estrutura urbana (IPEA/PPE, 4:2, junho 1974, p. 325-352)

Article empirically defines and tests major factors in the location of industry and compares them with indices such as size of cities, interdependence, and access to major consumer markets.

4973. Torloni, Hilário. Estudo de problemas brasileiros: de acôrdo com as normas e diretrizes oficiais. São Paulo, Livraria Pioneira Editôra, 1972. 357 p., tables (Pioneira. Manuais de estudo)

Intended as a handbook for a "great issues" survey course. Chapters are devoted to such topics as economic development, population explosion, pollution, drug addiction, energy policy, and capital markets. The level of discussion is elementary.

4974. Tôrres, Antônio Francisco and Orêncio Longino de Arruda. Produção industrial do Estado do Rio de Janeiro. Niterói, Bra., Companhia de Desenvolvimento Econômico do Estado de Rio de Janeiro (CODERJ), Depto. de Estudos de Projetos, 1967. 86 p. (Publicações da CODERJ, 3)

Statistical survey of industrial establishments, their employment and sales, broken down by municipalities in the State of Rio de Janeiro. The brief text proposes further industrialization for processing of agricultural products.

4975. Tyler, William G. O emprego e a expansão da exportação de manufaturados numa economia em desenvolvimento: o caso brasileiro (IBE/RBE, 27:4, out./dez. 1973, p. 3-18, tables)

Tyler examines, by means of a 1959 input-output table for Brazil, the efficacy of export promotion as a means for substantially reducing unemployment in developing countries. He emphasizes the importance of indirect effects—i.e., interindustry linkages—that can reduce (or raise) significantly the apparent labor intensity, and hence job-creating potential of a given final export good. Often capital-intensive export industries, because of their high backward linkages, offer the greatest employment creation potential highly integrated developing countries such as Brazil. Estimates are provided of job creation by industrial exports in 1964 and 1969. The totals are small relative to the growth of the labor force because of the small fraction of the total economy represented by the export sector. Tyler thus concludes that exports, despite their recent rapid growth in Brazil, cannot provide the solution to the employment problem in the near term but will become increasingly important over time.

4976. ———. Manufactured export promotion in a semi-industrialized economy: the Brazilian case (JDS, 10:1, Oct. 1973, p. 3-15, bibl., tables)

Attempt to analyze the behavior of manufactured exports with the help of a regression model. The most important variables determining rapid development of these exports are changes in the exchange rate, fiscal incentives, the emergence of LAFTA, and the fluctuations in domestic industrial production.

4977. ———. A substituições de importações e expansão de exportações como as "fontes" do crescimento industrial no Brasil (USP/EE, 5:3, agôsto 1973, p. 85-100)

Quantitative "ex-post" analysis of the importance of import substitution and export diversification in Brazil's economic development. Whereas the strategy of import substitution contributed significantly to economic growth between 1949 and 1964, the export drive, as of 1964, has not. However, it is possible that as more reliable data (after 1969) becomes available one will be able to assess more accurately the effects of the export drive on the Brazilian economy.

4978. ———. Trade in manufactures and labor skill content: the Brazilian case (IEI/EI, 25:2, maggio 1972, p. 314-334, tables)

English version of article reviewed in HLAS 35:2473.

4979. United States. Department of Commerce. Brazil: survey of U.S. export opportunities. Washington, GPO, 1974. 241 p., bibl., tables.

Comprehensive survey of Brazilian industry intended as a guide to US exporters of capital goods. Most data are for the years 1971-73.

4980. Universidade Federal de Minas Gerais, Belo Horizonte, Bra. **Centro de Desenvolvimento e Planejamento Regional** (CEDEPLAR). Migrações internas e desenvolvimento regional. v. 1/2. Belo Horizonte, Bra., 1973. 2 v. (230, 193 p.) tables.

Compilation of contributions presented at the I Symposium of Economic and Social Aspects of Internal Migration and Regional Development, Belo Horizonte, 1973. Vol. 1 concentrates on social issues related to migration, adjustment problems, and marginality; and Vol. 2 looks into economic aspects of regional migration, analyzes its possible causes and consequences on such variables as income and urbanization.

4981. Universidade para o Desenvolvimento do Estado de Santa Catarina, Florianópolis, Bra. **Instituto Técnico de Administração e Gerência.** Implantação de um distrito industrial em Imbituba: estudo de viabilidade. Florianópolis, Bra., 1971? 1 v. (Unpaged) fold. map, tables.

Urban and industrial plan for development of a small town on the coast of Santa Catarina. Study emphasizes the importance of chemical industry based on coal and necessary investments in infrastructure to facilitate transport in that relatively little developed region.

4982. Utumi, Américo and others. A problemática cooperativista no desenvolvimento econômico. São Paulo, Fundação Friedrich Naumann, Bonn, FRG, 1973. 359 p., tables.

Collection of essays covering economic as well as legal issues concerning cooperatives, both for producers and consumers, with special emphasis on the recent importance of such associations in the economic development of Brazil.

Valente, Murillo Gurgel. A política de transportes marítimos no Brasil: crônica de uma batalha. See item 8603.

4983. Vasconcelos, Jarbas. Uma análise da economia canavieira de Pernambuco. Recife, Bra., Tipografia Marista, 1973. 92 p., bibl., plates.

Brief evaluation of the sugar economy in the state of Pernambuco and critique of the various public policies which were designed to improve the economic and social situation in this sector.

4984. Velloso, Diderot M. A economia do Rio Grande do Sul na década de 60. Pôrto Alegre, Bra., Pontifícia Univ. Católica do Rio Grande do Sul (PUCRGS), Instituto de Estudos Sociais, Políticos e Econômicos, 1973. 127 p., tables (Série ensaios e pesquisas, 7)

Economic study of production of goods and services in Brazil's southernmost state between 1960 and 1968/69. Most data are taken from the publications of the Getúlio Vargas Foundation or the Instituto Brasileiro de Geografia Estatística (IBGE).

4985. Velloso, Tânia Pütten; Dorivaldo Poletto; Naira Lapis Ferrari; and **Gricelda A. Arrieta.** O empresário industrial do Rio Grande do Sul e a inovação tecnológica. Pôrto Alegre, Bra., Pontifícia Univ. Católica do Rio Grande do Sul (PUCRGS), Instituto de Estudos Sociais, Políticos e Econômicos (IESPE), 1973. 187 p., bibl., tables.

Entreprenurial survey of Brazil's southernmost state based on interviews. Concludes that the drive for innovation and improvement is apparent in both the rapid industrialization throughout Brazil and Latin America as well as in local government attempts to attract the latest industrial plants to its region.

4986. Villela, Annibal and **Wilson Suzigan.** Política do governo e crescimento da economia brasileira: 1889-1945. Rio, Instituto de Planejamento Econômico e Social (IPEA), 1973. 468 p., bibl., tables.

Large and well documented historical analysis which traces Brazil's industrialization effort back to the end of the 19th century. Valuable document which should become a classic in the field of Brazilian economic history.

4987. Vital, Sebastião Marcos. Economias de escala em bancos comerciais brasileiros (IBE/RBE, 27:1, jan./março 1973, p. 5-41 bibl., tables)

Examining both cost functions and production functions (1970 data), author finds that economies of scale do exist for banks with deposits above 200 million cruzeiros. See item 4891 for further exploration of this topic.

4988. _____ **and Walter L. Ness, Jr.** O progresso do mercado brasileiro de capitais: uma avaliação crítica **(FGV/RAE, 13:1, jan./março 1973, p. 7-17)**

This study compares the behavior and structure of Brazil's capital markets with those of more developed countries. In spite of intensification of activities there are various fundamental and structural differences. Financial markets in Brazil are less equilibrated and more susceptible to economic fluctuations and noneconomic factors, which have damaged individual investors as well as overall capital formation in recent times.

4989. Wogart, Jan Peter. A contenção das expectativas inflacionárias: um modêlo de política e um caso exemplificativo **(IBE/RBE, 25:4, out./dez. 1971, p. 223-234, tables)**

With the support of an econometric model of Brazil in the 1960s, Wogart argues that fiscal policy will be an ineffective device for combating inflation in the face of competition for income shares spurred by inflationary expectations. Given, in addition, reluctance to apply monetary restraints vigorously, the only alternative may be wage and price controls.

4990. _____. Stabilisierungs- und Wachstumspolitik in Brasilien: Die Bekämpfung der Inflation nach 1964. **Stuttgart, FRG, Ernst Klett Verlag, 1974. 129 p., bibl., tables.**

Analysis of the short-run and long-run implications of Brazil's stabilization and development program in the mid-1960s, based on the authors dissertation on "Demand-Pull, Corrective, and Cost-Push Inflation: The Case of Brazil, 1964-1966."

JOURNAL ABBREVIATIONS

ACPS/B	Boletín de la Academia de Ciencias Políticas y Sociales. Caracas.
AEA/AER	American Economic Review. Journal of the American Economic Association. Evanston, Ill.
AJES	The American Journal of Economics and Sociology. Published quarterly under grants from the Francis Neilson Fund and the Robert Schalkenbach Foundation. N.Y.
ARBOR	Arbor. Revista General de Investigación y Cultura. Madrid.
BCV/REL	Revista de Economía Latinoamericana. Banco Central de Venezuela. Caracas.
BNB/REN	Revista Econômica do Nordeste (REN). Banco do Nordeste do Brasil Depto.de Estudos Econômicos do Nordeste (ETENE). Fortaleza, Bra.
BNCE/CE	Comercio Exterior. Banco Nacional de Comercio Exterior. México.
BNL/QR	Quarterly Review. Banca Nazionale del Lavoro. Rome.
CAG/CG	Canadian Geographer. Le Géographe Canadien. Canadian Association of Geographers. Toronto, Canada.
CAM	Cuadernos Americanos. México.
CAUK/WA	Weltwirschaftliches Archiv. Zeitschrift des Instituts für Weltwirtschaft an der Christians-Albrechts-Univ. Kiel. Kiel, FRG.
CDAL	Cahiers des Amériques Latines. Paris.
CEML/TF	Técnicas Financieras. Centro de Estudios Monetarios Latinoamericanos. México.
CM/DE	Demografía y Economía. El Colegio de México. México.
CM/FI	Foro Internacional. El Colegio de México. México.
CPES/RPS	Revista Paraguaya de Sociología. Centro Paraguayo de Estudios Sociológicos. Asunción.
CUH	Current History. A monthly magazine of world affairs. Philadelphia, Pa.
CVF/C	Cuadernos de la C[orporación] V[enezolana] [de] F[omento]. Caracas.
DNP/RPD	Revista de Planeación y Desarrollo. Depto. Nacional de Planeación. Bogotá.
EHA/J	Journal of Economic History. New York Univ., Graduate School of Business Administration *for* The Economic History Association. Rensselaer, N.Y.
EP	Economie et Politique. Revue marxiste d'economie. Paris.
FCE/TE	El Trimestre Económico. Fondo de Cultura Económica. México.
FDD/NED	Notes et Études Documentaires. France, Direction de la Documentation. Paris.

FGV/CE	Conjuntura Econômica. Fundação Getúlio Vargas, Instituto Brasileiro de Economia. Rio.
FGV/RAE	Revista de Administração de Empresas. Fundação Getúlio Vargas, Instituto de Documentação. São Paulo.
FJB/BH	Boletín Histórico. Fundación John Boulton. Caracas.
FNSP/RFSP	Revue Française de Science Politique. Fondation Nationale des Sciences Politiques, l'Association Française de Science Politique, avec le concours du Centre National de la Recherche Scientifique. Paris.
GA/G	Geography. Journal of the Geographical Association. London.
HU/BHR	Business History Review. Harvard Univ. Graduate School of Business Administration. Boston, Mass.
IAEA/DE	The Developing Economics. The journal of the Institute of Asian Economic Affairs. Tokyo.
IAEERI/E	Estrategia. Instituto Argentino de Estudios Estratégicos y de las Relaciones Internacionales. B.A.
IAMEA	Inter-American Economic Affairs. Washington.
IBE/RBE	Revista Brasileira de Economia. Fundação Getúlio Vargas, Instituto Brasileiro de Economia. Rio.
IBEAS/EA	Estudios Andinos. Instituto Boliviano de Estudio y Acción Social. La Paz.
IBGE/B	Boletim Geográfico. Conselho Nacional de Geografia. Instituto Brasileiro de Geografia e Estatística. Rio.
IDES/DE	Desarrollo Económico. Instituto de Desarrollo Económico y Social. B.A.
IEAS/R	Revista de Estudios Agro-Sociales. Instituto de Estudios Agro-Sociales. Madrid.
IEI/EI	Economia Internazionale. Rivista dell'Istituto di Economia Internazionale. Genova, Italy.
ILO/R	International Labour Review. International Labour Office. Geneva.
IMF/SP	Staff Papers. International Monetary Fund. Washington.
INTAL/RI	Revista de la Integración. Economía, Política, Sociología. Banco Interamericano de Desarrollo, Instituto para la Integración de América Latina. B.A.
IPE/EE	Estudios Econômicos. Univ. de São Paulo, Instituto de Pesquisas Econômicas. São Paulo.
IPEA/PP	Pesquisa e Planejamento. Instituto de Planejamento Econômico e Social. Rio.
IPEA/PPE	Pesquisa e Planejamento Econômico. Instituto de Planejamento Econômico e Social. Rio.
ISSQ	The Indiana Social Studies Quarterly. Indiana Council for Social Studies. Ball State Univ. Muncie, Ind.
ISTMO	Istmo. Revista del Centro de América. México.
ITA/H	ITA-Humanidades. Ministério de Aeronáutica, Instituto Tecnológico de Aeronáutica. São José dos Campos, Bra.
IUP/D	Dados. Publicação semestral do Instituto Universitário de Pesquisas do Rio de Janeiro. Rio.
JCMS	Journal of Common Market Studies. Oxford, England.
JDA	The Journal of Developing Areas. Western Illinois Univ. Press. Macomb, Ill.
JDS	The Journal of Development Studies. A quarterly journal devoted to economics, politics, and social development. London.
JLAS	Journal of Latin American Studies. Center or institutes of Latin American studies at the universities of Cambridge, Glasgow, Liverpool, London and Oxford. Cambridge Univ. Press. London.
JPE	Journal of Political Economy. Univ. of Chicago, Chicago, Ill.
JPR	Journal of Peace Research. Edited at the International Peace Research Institute. Universitetforlaget. Oslo.
KO	Kollasuyo. Revista de estudios bolivianos. La Paz.
LARR	Latin American Research Review. Latin American Studies Association. Univ. of Texas Press. Austin, Tex.
LNB/L	Lotería. Lotería Nacional de Beneficencia. Panamá.
MSTPS/R	Revista Mexicana del Trabajo. Secretaría del Trabajo y Previsión Social. Publicación bimestral. México.

NGIZ/IS	Internationale Spectator. Tijdschrift voor internationale politiek. Het Nederlandsch Genootschap voor Internationale Zaken. The Hague.
OAS/AM	Américas. Organization of American States. Washington.
OUP/OEP	Oxford Economic Papers. Oxford Univ. Press. London.
PUCIS/WP	World Politics. A quarterly journal of international relations. Princeton Univ., Center of International Studies. Princeton, N.J.
PUJ/U	Universitas. Ciencias jurídicas y socioeconómicas. Pontificia Univ. Javeriana, Facultad de Derecho y Ciencias Socioeconómicas. Bogotá.
RES/EJ	Economic Journal. Quarterly journal of the Royal Economic Society. London.
RU/SCID	Studies in Comparative International Development. Rutgers Univ. New Brunswick, N.J.
SEPHE/ER	Etudes Rurales. Revue trimestrielle publiée par l'Ecole Pratique des Hautes Etudes, Sorbonne, Sixième Section: Sciences économiques et sociales, *avec le concours du* Centre Nationale de la Recherche Scientifique. The Hague.
SID/IDR	International Development Review. The Society for International Development. Washington.
SOCIOL	Sociologus. Zeitschrift für empirische Soziologie, sozialpsychologische und ethnologische Forschung (A journal for empirical sociology, social psychology and ethnic research) Berlin.
TESG	Tijdschrift voor Economische on Sociale Geographie. Netherlands Journal of Economic and Social Geography. Rotterdam, The Netherlands.
UC/EDCC	Economic Development and Cultural Change. Univ. of Chicago, Research Center in Economic Development and Cultural Change. Chicago, Ill.
UCC/CE	Cuadernos de Economía. Univ. Católica de Chile. Santiago.
UES/U	La Universidad. Univ. de El Salvador. San Salvador.
UM/JIAS	Journal of Inter-American Studies and World Affairs. Univ. of Miami Press *for the* Center for Advanced International Studies. Coral Gables, Fla.
UNAM/PDD	Problemas del Desarrollo. Revista latinoamericana de economía. Univ. Nacional Autónoma de México, Instituto de Investigaciones Económicas. México.
UNAM/RMS	Revista Mexicana de Sociología. Univ. Nacional Autónoma de México, Instituto de Investigaciones Sociales. México.
UNECLA/B	Economic Bulletin for Latin America. United Nations, Economic Commission for Latin America. N.Y.
UNL/H	Humanitas. Anuario del Centro de Estudios Humanísticos. Univ. de Nuevo León. Monterrey, Mex.
UNS/EE	Estudios Económicos. Univ. Nacional del Sur, Instituto de Economía. Bahía Blanca, Arg.
UP/E	Ethnology. An international journal of cultural and social anthropology. Univ. of Pittsburgh. Pittsburgh, Pa.
UP/TM	Tiers Monde. Problémes des pays sous-développés. Univ. de Paris, Institut d'Etude du Développement Economique et Social. Paris.
UPR/CS	Caribbean Studies. Univ. of Puerto Rico, Institute of Caribbean Studies. Río Piedras, P.R.
UR/RUG	Revista Uruguaya de Geografía. Univ. de la República, Facultad de Humanidades y Ciencias, Depto. de Geografía. Montevideo.
USM/JTG	The Journal of Tropical Geography. Univ. Singapore and Univ. of Malaya. Departments of Geography. Singapore.
USM/RCEC	Revista de la Facultad de Ciencias Económicas y Comerciales. Univ. Nacional Mayor de San Marcos. Lima.
USP/EE	Estudos Econômicos. Univ. de São Paulo, Instituto de Pesquisas Econômicas. São Paulo.
UW/LE	Land Economics. A quarterly journal of planning, housing and public utilities. Univ. of Wisconsin. Madison, Wis.
UWI/CQ	Caribbean Quarterly. Univ. of the West Indies. Mona, Jam.
ZPKW/A	Aconcagua. Iberoamérica-Europa. Zeitschrift für Politik, Kultur and Wirtschaft für die Länder iberisher und deutscher Sprache. Vaduz, Lichtenstein.

Education

Latin America

(Except Brazil)

GORDON C. RUSCOE
Professor
School of Education
University of Louisville

WRITINGS ON UNIVERSITIES CONTINUE to dominate the materials on Latin American education. Of the approximately 200 citations included in this year's annotations, some 40 percent deal with various themes associated with universities, and of these about one-half might best be described as argumentative or polemic in nature. Unlike previous years, however, there are few institutional histories and a fairly large number of research analyses.

Looking first at the fairly standard works on universities, Febres-Cordero's history of the Univ. Central de Venezuela's dentistry faculty contains some interesting historical documents on university reform and student politics (see item 6188). Apmann's (item 6166) examination of engineering education in Paraguay and the National Univ. of Cuyo's (item 6096) general report on university reform are sound works. And the most recent university census prepared by the Union of Latin American Universities (item 6004) is always a welcomed addition to the basic information on university structure.

Research studies on university students are represented by several solid reports. Liebman, Walker and Glazer's (item 6039) six-nation study of university students is by far the most ambitious and satisfying of these studies. It is a careful analysis and interpretation of data from Colombia, Mexico, Panama, Paraguay, Puerto Rico and Uruguay. Research on Puerto Rican students' reactions to the 1971 strike and related problems (item 6205) and Venezuelan students' reports on how positions are obtained (item 6197) are also worth examining, although the former presents some methodological problems and the latter is based on a very limited sample of students. Sample size also limits the usefulness of the Cirigliano and others' study (item 6082) of Argentine students' use of and knowledge about libraries and research. Nonetheless, the authors' comments on university training are worth considering.

In some respects the most interesting of the research studies is that of Cañibe (item 6152), who surveyed public opinion following the 1968 student disturbances in Mexico. He reports that working-class and lower-middle-class respondents did not identify with or support student actions, favoring instead a law-and-order government. The respondents did, however, voice support for student activities which would provide concrete benefits to the people themselves.

Of the many, many general pieces dealing with universities, their reforms, problems and roles, three stand out as deserving mention. Joworski's (item 6171) explication of Peru's new university law raises some substantive questions about the ways in which universities can respond to national needs. Batista and Solano's (item 6200) call for increased efforts in university-based research, while attempting to be unrealistically apolitical, also examines the universities' relationships to national needs. And Germani's (item 6022) discussion of the tensions created in universities by the changes occurring in the role of the professors is a model of careful analysis of a complex subject.

The more polemic writings on universities are represented by a number of forceful essays, some quite conservative, some much more radical. Franco (item 6170) is perhaps unduly harsh in criticizing students for the paradoxes and inconsistencies of their positions, but he is careful to delineate the bases of his criticism. Linares (item 6040), too, takes care to support his argument that universities fail to promote intellectual rigor among students because of the excessive preoccupation with professional training.

In another vein, Arroyo (item 6001) criticizes what he considers both sterile leftism and regressive rightism and advocates a university which is socialistic in outlook and in action. Similarly, Stavenhagen (item 6062) calls for a more radical approach to the social sciences. Two other essays (items 6125 and 6161), however, raise serious questions about the extent to which universities can spearhead social change.

The possible role of education in general in promoting reform and social change provokes as diverse a body of opinion as does the role of universities. The contrasts here, however, are perhaps even sharper and more clearly drawn. At one extreme, materials on educational planning and related subjects continue to be plentiful. These materials are not necessarily wrong (although they may be "wrong-headed"), but they are based on certain assumptions about the nature of education and social change which can best be described as the belief in greater efficiency as the solution to educational—and, by implication, social—problems. For example, UNESCO's (item 6138) models for analyzing wastage rates and several documents from Argentina (items 6072 and 6074-6075), as well as many other less important pieces, are based on what now appears to be the very questionable belief that what is wrong with schools can be corrected through more intensive application of techniques. A similar viewpoint seems to underlie many of the materials which deal with school practices and curricula. Even works which deal with "innovations" (for example, item 6009) or with bureaucratic problems (for example, item 6086) largely center on problems of efficiency.

In contrast, both at the country level and more generally, serious discussion is occurring about the purposes of education and about the ways in which schools may actually retard rather than promote social change. Baptista's (items 6099 and 6100) discussions of Bolivian education, worth reading in their own right, attain greater significance when read with materials dealing with rural education (items 6102-6103, and 6105) and with the Bolivian Catholic position on education (item 6101). Taken together, these materials reflect both the hopes for and the almost insurmountable problems of reforming education.

Debate over the purposes of education is perhaps most clearly drawn in Mexico, where Avilés (item 6150) calls for teachers to assume a militant socialist stance, while Zea (item 6165) calls for the production of more technicians. In Allende's Chile educational reform to match changes in the purposes of education was beginning to take form (items 6118 and 6120 are good illustrations), while in Cuba the purposes of education seem to be becoming even more precisely defined and interpreted (items 6140a-6142 and 6145-6146).

The Illich-Freire approaches to analyzing schooling continue to appear, but not, apparently, in the quantity we earlier anticipated. Illich's writings (items 6026-6028) continue, and Illich and Freire are represented in current journal literature (for example, item 6008).

Analyses of schooling have also been done by Carnoy (item 6167), Cirigliano (item 6080), and Labarca (item 6037), and Moreno (item 6042), each of whom raises important questions about the purposes and potentials of the educational system. In similar fashion, Arnove (item 6000) and Egginton and Ruhl (item 6127) examine problems of education in rural areas, and McGinn (item 6041) examines problems of education in urban areas.

Despite the growing scepticism about the role of schools in promoting social change, the few studies which examine the opinions of students concerning education and society in general document continued optimism about education and society in general. Thus, Castro (item 6241), LaBelle (item 6192), and Sosnowsky (item 6195) all report, in varying forms, the general optimism of students and youths in general as regards the role of education in promoting social betterment, at least—and this might be the important catch—at the individual level.

As usual, one cannot conclude a review of current literature in any field without pointing out worthwhile publications which do not easily fit into any category. This year, three quite different works merit special attention. First, the Regional Office of UNESCO (item 6047) has produced a most useful listing of periodicals from Latin America concerned with education. Those who wish to pursue topics in Latin American education may find this a valuable reference. Second, Myers (item 6172) has given us a report on a longitudinal study of Peruvians trained in the US in which he argues that, despite fears of a braindrain, such training has benefits for Peru. And, finally, Herrera (item 6024) presents a most provocative essay on science policy in which he argues that the political determinants of research are not to be ignored.

All in all, this year's batch of materials is neither better nor worse than those of preceding years. On the one hand, we continue to know little about the internal functioning of schools or about the specific problems of educational change. On the other hand, serious questions about schooling and its purposes in the context of Latin American society are being asked with increased insistence.

GENERAL

6000. Arnove, Robert F. Education and political participation in rural areas of Latin America (CES/CER, 17:2, June 1973, p. 198-215)

Wide-ranging discussion of education and political participation, including assessment of effects of current rural schooling and speculation on alternatives. Good review of appropriate literature.

6001. Arroyo Lasa, Jesús. Hacia una universidad latinoamericana de compromiso socialista (PUJ/U, 42, junio 1972, p. 18-37)

Careful analysis of current university situation which, author contends, is usually sterile leftism or regressive rightism. Arroyo, a Jesuit, calls for a university which is a political community dedicated both to studying *and* taking action on problems, a university which itself is socialistic in outlook and in distribution of power. Well worth reading.

6002. Basave Fernández del Valle, Agustín. Ser y quehacer de la universidad: estructura y misión de la universidad nacional. Prólogo de Fritz J. von Rintelen. México, Univ. Autónoma de Nuevo León, Centro de Estudios Humanísticos, 1971. 496 p.

Arguing that by nature the university must respond to human needs and vocations rather than merely to training professionals, author examines historical and contemporary university patterns in Latin America and elsewhere. Concludes that humanism and intellectuality must be the ultimate goals of university life.

6003. Cambre Mariño, Jesús. La planificación educativa en América Latina (UNAM/PDD, 2:7, abril/junio 1971, p. 47-70, tables)

Fairly conventional review of the problems of educational planning, including summaries of different approaches to planning.

6004. Censo universitario latinoamericano, 1970. México, Unión de Universidades de América Latina, Secretaría General, 1973. 735 p., tables.

Valuable general reference listing Latin American universities, by country, and including data on staff, enrollments, budgets, and schedules.

6005. La ciencia y la tecnología al servicio de los pueblos de América: programa regional de desarrollo científico y tecnológico de la OEA (OAS/CI, 14:1/2, enero/abril 1973, p. 22-33, tables)

Information on current OAS-sponsored regional programs by country and by type of activity.

6006. La ciencia y la tecnología en América Latina (OAS/CI, 13:5/6, sept/dic. 1972, p. 25-36, plate, table)

Information on current programs sponsored by individual countries.

6007. Conferencia Internacional sobre la Contribución de la Investigación Científica Educacional para la Reforma Escolar en los Países Andinos, *Lima, 1971.* La contribución de la investigación científica educacional a la reforma escolar en los países andinos. Lima, Fundación Alemana para los Países en Vías de Desarrollo, Subdivisión Educación y Ciencia, 1971. 224 p., tables (DOK 626 A/c. IIA-IT 16/71 [ex])

Report of 1971 conference, including recommendations for founding of Andean Regional Center of Education.

6008. *Cristianismo y Sociedad.* Junta Latino Americana de Iglesia y

Sociedad. Año 10, Nos. 29/30, 1972- . Montevideo.

Liberal journal devoted to articles on popular education and reform. Current number contains article by Illich and interview with Freire.

6009. Cummings, Richard L. and Donald A. Lemke. Educational innovations in Latin America. Metuchen, N.J., The Scarecrow Press, 1973. 357 p., tables.

An uneven but useful collection of articles, by both North and Latin Americans, on education, including general papers and specific topics such as TV instruction in El Salvador and rural education in Guatemala. The "innovations" theme is not always explicit.

6009a. Cunha, Maria Auxiliadora Versiani. Didática fundamentada na teoria de Piaget. 2. ed. Rio, Editôra Forense, 1973. 88 p., bibl., illus., plates.

A succinct and faithful summary of Piaget's theories and the educational style or philosophy that has emerged in England and the US as a result. The author also includes chapters on Glasser, on team-learning, and on the needed changes in teacher training if Piagetian education is to receive support in the classroom. Style is very simple and direct, there is a list of supplementary references, and photographs of children engaged in classroom tasks accompany the text. [A.E. Toward]

6010. Dáhbar, Juan. Universidad y violencia. B.A., Ediciones LH, 1972. 63 p.

Generally unclear examination of student movements and their relationship to violence.

6011. Duarte de Acquaviva, Edelmira. Orientación y educación. Maracaibo, Ven., Univ. del Zulia, Facultad de Humanidades y Educación, 1972. 237 p., bibl.

General explication of guidance procedures, with little direct reference to Latin America.

6012. La Educación. Organización de los Estados Americanos, Departamento de Asuntos Educativos. Año 14, Nos. 53/55, enero/dic. 1969- . Washington.

Devoted largely to reprinting the resolutions of the Inter-American Council on Education, Science and Culture from 1943 to 1969. Includes detailed examination of 1967-69 period.

6013. La Educación. Organización de los Estados Americanos, Departamento de Asuntos Educativos. Año 15, Nos. 56/58, enero/dic. 1970- . Washington.

Review of educational research, including both theoretical articles and reports on specific research activities.

6014. La Educación. Organización de los Estados Americanos, Departamento de Asuntos Educativos. Año 16, No. 59, enero/abril 1971- . Washington.

General index to all issues of La Educación from 1956 (No. 1) through 1970 (No. 58).

6015. La Educación. Organización de los Estados Americanos, Departamento de Asuntos Educativos. Año 17, Nos. 62/64, enero/dic. 1972- . Washington.

In addition to country reports, articles on the Brazilian "salário-educação" system for financing fundamental education, analysis of primary education problems and educational supervision.

6016. La Educación. Organización de los Estados Americanos, Secretaría General. Año 18, No. 65, enero/abril 1973- . Washington.

Country reports and articles on open university reforms in England, the US and Mexico.

6017. La Educación. Organización de los Estados Americanos, Secretaría General. Año 18, Nos. 66/67, mayo/dic. 1973- . Washington.

Articles on university budgeting, university education in Colombia, education and social change, and primary education.

6017a. Figueiredo, J.C. Fundamentos históricos e filosóficos da educação. Belo Horizonte, Bra., Edições Júpiter, 1973. 189 p.

A textbook for students, based on other texts, such as Dewey's *Democracy and education*. While arguing that philosophy cannot be studied without attention to the historical context, the author warns the reader that she is beginning with the contemporary period in order to emphasize the importance of considering the forces that have shaped and determined the present. Units examine the following: What is Philosophy?, Philosophical Premises, Avenues to Knowledge and Understanding, Education in Western Society, and Our Contemporary Situation. [A.E. Toward]

6018. Flores Olea, Víctor; Ernest Mandel; Robin Blackburn; and **Franz Marek.** La rebelión estudiantil y la sociedad contemporánea. México, UNAM, Facultad de Ciencias Políticas y Sociales, 1973. 133 p. (Serie: Estudios, 33)

Of particular interest in Flores' essay on Mexico, but all merit reading as a collection which seeks to understand the worldwide student movement.

6019. Ford, Donald F. University

autonomy (Revista del Colegio Interamericano de Defensa [Washington] 1:2, agosto 1972, p. 32-45)

Extensive review of literature on university autonomy which appeared between 1960 and 1970 and some forecasts of future developments. Uneven quality and marred by numerous typographical errors.

6020. Galiana, G.R. Juan Francisco Yela Utrilla: filosofía de la educación (UC/A, 29:1/2, enero/junio 1973, p. 168-194)

Account of the life and philosophy of Yela Utrilla, a professor of philosophy at the Univ. of Madrid until his death in 1950. Little direct reference to Latin America.

6021. García, Juan César. La educación médica en la América Latina. Washington, Organización Panamericana de la Salud, Oficina Sanitaria Panamericana, Oficina Regional de la Organización Mundial de la Salud, 1972. 413 p., tables (Publicación científica, 255)

Extensive study of medical education, including comparisons of curricula, students and professors, with stress on developments in the teaching of preventive medicine. Insightful epilogue on social aspects of medicine.

6022. Germani, Gino. O professor e a cátedra (CLAPCS/AL, 13:1, jan./março 1970, p. 83-101)

Careful consideration of changes in role of the Latin American professor and tensions which these changes have produced in the universities.

6023. Herrera, Amílcar O. Los determinantes sociales de la política científica en América Latina: política científica explícita y política científica implícita (IDES/DE, 13:49, abril/junio 1973, p. 113-134)

Spanish version of item 6024.

6024. _____ . Social determinants of science policy in Latin America: explicit science policy and implicit science policy (JDS, 9:1, Oct. 1972, p. 19-37, bibl.)

Intriguing analysis of science policy in which author argues that implicit policy has been to deter R and D in order to maintain status quo, despite outward appearance of welcoming research. The conventional lamenting over structural and historical constraints which make research largely inoperable is, the author contends, neither useful nor realistic. For Spanish version, see item 6023.

6025. Hines, Paul. Education for the future: the dilemma of Latin America (ISSQ, 22:1, Spring 1969, p. 32-43)

Cursory examination of Latin American educational problems, with some special attention to Mexico.

6026. Illich, Ivan. Convivial tools (Saturday Review of Education [San Francisco, Calif.] 1:4, April 1973, p. 63-64, 67).

From book of same name, Illich warns that schools and other institutions have so monopolized tools (e.g., books) that they are no longer available to all, a condition which leads to a manipulative rather than a convivial society.

6027. _____ . Desenmascarando los países *desarrollados* (Difusión Económica [Guayaquil, Ecua.] 10:3, dic. 1972, p. 67-79).

In this "unmasking" of the developed countries, Illich continues his critique of modern, packaged solutions to the problems of underdevelopment which, he feels, are likely to cause more problems than they solve. Schools, as usual, come under attack as too expensive and too irrelevant to developing countries' needs.

6028. _____. En América Latina ¿para qué sirve la escuela? B.A., Ediciones Búsqueda, 1973. 80 p.

Essentially a partially updated Spanish version of Illich's thoughts on demystifying schooling and deschooling society and on the need for a cultural revolution.

6029. Inter-American Council for Education, Science, and Culture, *II, Lima, 1971.* Final report. Washington, Organization of American States, General Secretariat, 1971? 211 p., tables (OEA/Ser.C/V.11)

Devoted largely to summarizing resolutions passed at 1971 meeting.

6030. _____, _____, _____, *IV, Mar del Plata, Arg., 1972.* Final report. Washington, Organization of American States, General Secretariat, 1973. 150 p., tables.

Resolutions of 1972 meeting.

6031. Inter-American Rural Youth Leaders' Conference, *Rio and Belo Horizonte, Bra., 1966.* Make the best better: proceedings of the . . . San José, Inter-American Rural Youth Program, 1966. 189 p., plates, tables.

The 1966 conference, devoted to evaluation of success of rural youth (4-H) clubs, stresses need for continued expansion of such clubs and greater efforts to promote extension and information work. See also item 6034.

6032. _____, *San Salvador, 1968.* Youth leadership in rural development; summary report of the . . . San José, Inter-American Rural Youth Program, 1969. 136 p., plates, tables.

The 1968 conference devoted to role of youth in rural development.

6033. _____, *Mar del Plata and B.A., Arg., 1970.* Movilizar a la juventud rural para el desarrollo: informe resumido de la Conferencia Interamericana de Líderes de Juventudes Rurales, 1970. B.A., Programa Interamericano para la Juventud Rural (PIJR) *en colaboración con el* Instituto Nacional de Tecnología Agropecuaria (INTA), 1970. 176 l., plates.

The 1970 conference examines ways to mobilize rural youth to promote national development.

6034. _____, *San Juan, 1972.* Activando el potencial de la juventud rural: informe de la Conferencia Interamericana de Líderes de Juventudes Rurales, 10 al 15 de diciembre de 1972, San Juan, Puerto Rico. San José, Programa Interamericano para la Juventud Rural *en cooperación con la* Univ. de Puerto Rico, Recinto de Mayaqüez, Servicio de Extensión Agrícola, 1972? 198 l., plates.

The 1972 conference examined role of rural youth and rural education in national development. See also item 6031.

6035. Jimenes Grullón, Juan Isidro. La problemática universitaria latinoamericana: raíces, rasgos actuales y soluciones revolucionarias; dos ensayos. Santo Domingo, Univ. Autónoma de Santo Domingo, 1970. 113 p., bibl. (Publicaciones de la UASD, 142)

In two essays, author calls for university reform, particularly stress on applied science and technology, and critically reviews Risieri Frondizi's recent writings.

6036. Kleiner, Bernardo. Revolución científico-técnica y liberación. B.A., Ediciones Centro de Estudios, 1973. 196 p.

Fearing the scientific-technical revolution is transforming the Latin American university into another capitalistic business enterprise, Kleiner issues the familiar call to reform the university by "reestablishing" its independent, political reformist position.

6037. Labarca, Guillermo. El sistema educacional: ideología y superestructura (UNAM/RMS, 35:3, julio/sept. 1973, p. 569-584).

Careful criticism of the role of the school in promoting democratization of society, in which author contrasts the claims made for schooling with the actual facts of schooling.

6038. Lechín, Fuad and **Bertha van der Dijs.** Situación actual de la investigación científica en Latinoamérica con especial referencia al campo de la medicina y ciencias afines (AVAC/ACV, 24:6, 1973, p. 195-197, bibl., tables)

Fascinating study of 1970 Index Medicus to determine representation of Latin American publications in medical sciences. Among other things, authors discover that only 30 percent of Latin American medical-science journals are indexed internationally and that only 42 percent of regional medical-science journals in Latin America carry original articles.

6039. Liebman, Arthur; Kenneth N. Walker; and **Myron Glazer.** Latin American university students: a six nation study. Cambridge, Mass., Harvard Univ. Press, Center for International Affairs, 1972. 296 p., bibl., tables.

Very good comparative study of students in Colombia, Mexico, Panama, Paraguay, Puerto Rico and Uruguay (based largely on 1964-65 questionnaire data), and including discussion of historical and contemporary role of students in university and national politics.

6040. Linares, Julio, h. Universidad, estructura intelectual y desarrollo social (Encuentro [Univ. Centroamericana, Managua] 3:11, 1970, p. 1-12)

Argues that universities fail to develop intellectual rigor in students, largely because they devote too much time and energy to narrow professional training.

6041. McGinn, Noel F. Problems of human development in urban Latin America. Boston, Mass., Harvard Univ., Graduate School of Education, Center for Studies in Education and Development, 1971. 72 p. (Occasional papers in education and development, 6)

Following insightful review of several competing views of urban problems and their causes, author argues that urban education stressing urban competence is needed.

6042. Moreno Avendaño, José. Cooperativas de educación: colegios cooperativos; una nueva dimensión educativa para el cambio en los países del tercer mundo, planeación, organización, operación, control. Bogotá, Ediciones Tercer Mundo, 1973. 254 p., illus., tables.

Attempt to apply the methods and organization of cooperatives to schools. To do so, author argues, is necessary to promote social change and community well-being and to diminish harmful competition and individualism.

6043. Ocampo Londoño, Alfonso. Higher education in Latin America: current and future. N.Y., International Council for Educational Development, 1973. 52 p., tables (Occasional paper, 7)

Essentially optimistic but frank appraisal of university problems of administration, finance and growth. Little comment on the goals of university education.

6043a. Organization of American States. Centro Interamericano para la Producción de Material Educativo y Científico para la Prensa. En lucha contra el hambre. Bogotá, Ministerio de Educación Nacional, Instituto Colombiano de Pedagogía, 1972. 104 p., plates (Biblioteca colombiana de Cultura. Col. Popular)

CIMPEC is an OAS organization with headquarters in Bogotá and a mandate to produce scientific, educational, and cultural information for dissemination to the media in Latin America. The material produced by CIMPEC is published in 200 daily newspapers and is designed to be of interest to secondary level students and the general public. One of the articles in this small paperback describes a severe smog condition in Los Angeles in 1969, quotes Paul Erlich, and uses this example to illustrate how man destroys the environment. Other topics include chemical warfare, food supply, the oceans, and nutrition. [A.E. Toward]

6044. Plana. Oficina de Educación Iberoamericana. Nos. 143/164, mayo 1970/agosto 1972-   . Madrid.

6045. Polišenský, Josef and Lubomír Vebr. La Iberoamericanística en la Europa Occidental, la Unión Soviética y los países socialistas: 1964-1967 (UCP/IAP, 2, 168, p. 229-233)

Brief bibliographic essay (part in Spanish, part in English) on recent interest in Ibero-America on the part of Western Europe (in which authors include US), USSR and other communist-bloc countries.

6046. Prede Actualidades. Organización de los Estados Americanos, Secretaría General, Depto. de Asuntos Educativos. enero/feb. 1973-   . Washington.

Review of educational activities of OAS and member states.

6047. Repertorio de publicaciones periódicas de educación de América Latina y el Caribe. Santiago, UNESCO, Oficina Regional de Educación para América Latina y el Caribe, 1972. 103 p.

Lists, by country, well over 500 publications which deal with education.

6048. Robertson, O. Zeller, Jr. Education and economic development in Latin America: a causal analysis (IAMEA, 28:1, Summer 1974, p. 63-71, illus., tables)

Examination of relationship among educational, economic and urbanization factors, from which author concludes that role of education in development should be reevaluated. Unfortunately, limited data and statistical analysis make the conclusions, however welcomed, most tenuous.

6049. Sanguineti de Rey, Margarita and **María Eugenia Norton de Stöcker.** El control de gestión de educación. B.A., Centro Nacional de Documentación e Información Educativa, 1972. 120 l., tables (Nueva serie divulgación, 3)

Examination of management and decision-making concepts and models in relation to education and some prescriptions for improvement of administration.

6050. Schipani, Daniel S. and Daniel E. Tinao. Educación y comunidad. B.A., El Ateneo, 1973. 62 p., bibl.

Two short essays which seek to describe the relationship between school and community and the role of group situations in teaching.

6051. Simpson, Miles. Authoritarianism and education: a comparative approach (ASA/S, 35:2, 1972, p. 223-234, tables)

In a study of US, Finland, Mexico and Costa Rica; Simpson reports that increased education does not necessarily reduce authoritarianism, as is conventionally assumed, except when education stresses cognitive (US) rather than rote learning (Mexico and Costa Rica) or is staffed by non-authoritarian teachers.

Smith, David Horton. Latin American student activism: participation in formal volunteer organizations by university students in six Latin cultures. See item 8107.

Thomas, Dani B. and Richard B. Craig. Student dissent in Latin America: toward a comparative analysis. See item 8115.

Troncoso, Oscar. La rebelión estudiantil en la sociedad de posguerra. See item 8119.

6052. UNESCO en Chile. Boletín de la Comisión Nacional. No. 42, mayo 1973-   . Santiago.

Pre-coup bulletin contains business-as-usual reports on worldwide education.

6053. Universidades. Unión de Universidades de América Latina. Año 10, No.

41, 2. serie, julio/sept. 1970- . México.

Articles on Catholic universities, on university reform and on cultural integration in Latin America.

6054. Universidades. Unión de Universidades de América Latina. Año 10, No. 42, 2. serie, oct./dic. 1970- . México.

In addition to articles on current university concerns, Diaz de Cossio speculates on the future of Mexican universities.

6055. Universidades. Unión de Universidades de América Latina. Año 11, No. 43, 2. serie, enero/marzo 1971- . México.

Articles on neocolonialism and universities and on Chilean university reform, and reprint of material on Peruvian educational reform.

6056. Universidades. Unión de Universidades de América Latina. Año 11, No. 44, abril/junio 1971- . México.

Articles and reports by Darcy Ribeiro and others on universities and university teaching.

6057. Universidades. Unión de Universidades de América Latina. Año 11, No. 45, julio/sept. 1971- . México.

Devoted largely to papers given at II Latin American Conference on Cultural Diffusion and University Extension.

6058. Universidades. Unión de Universidades de América Latina. Año 11, No. 46, 2. serie, oct./dic. 1971- . México.

Articles on Peru and Mexico and papers by Zea and Miro Quezada to cultural diffusion conference, see item 6057.

6059. Universidades. Unión de Universidades de América Latina. Año 12, No. 47, enero/marzo 1972- . México.

Article on underdevelopment and human rights, working document from National Univ. of Rosario and other pieces.

6060. Universidades. Unión de Universidades de América Latina. Año 12, No. 49, 2. serie, julio/sept. 1972- . México.

Lead articles on the "open university" of UNAM and on German universities.

6061. Universidades. Unión de Universidades de América Latina. Año 13, No. 51, 2. serie, enero/marzo 1973- . México.

Variety of articles on Latin American higher education.

6062. Universidades. Unión de Universidades de América Latina. Año 13, No. 53, 2. serie, julio/sept. 1973- . México.

Salazar Bondy's article on Peruvian school reform and Stavenhagen's call for radical social sciences highlight this issue.

6063. Velasco Fernández, Hugo Mauricio. Una nueva escuela. México, B. Costa-Amic Editor, 1973. 287 p., tables.

Wide-ranging exposition of author's views of schooling, presumably derived from study of psychology and education. Filled with advice to parents and teachers.

6064. Venezuela. Ministerio de Educación. Enseñanza media estructura social y desarrollo en América Latina. Caracas, Dirección de Planeamiento, Depto. de Documentación e Información Pedagógica, 1972. 61 1., tables.

Very good examination of educational growth, both general and secondary, throughout Latin America (with reference to European development patterns) and the likely effects continued growth will have on economic and political conditions.

6065. Waggoner, George R. National planning, university autonomy, and the coordination of higher education: Latin American points of view (UM/JIAS, 16:3, Aug. 1974, p. 372-378, bibl.)

All too brief examination of Latin American views (based on questionnaire study of 37 respondents) of relationship between need for national planning and need for university autonomy. Enticing but incomplete argument.

Ward, Douglas S. Needed: effective educational assistance to Latin America. See item 8127.

6066. Zéndegui, Guillermo de comp. Education and science development: three years of inter-American cooperation. (OAS/AM, 24:4 [Supplement] April 1972, p. S1-S48, illus., maps, plates)

Covering period from 1968 to 1971, examines OAS Regional Programs in Education, Science and Technology. Contains information on program organization and implementation, official pronouncements, budgets, and personnel. No concrete evaluations are included, however.

ARGENTINA

6067. Abihaggle, Carlos E. and Coloma Ferrá. Educación y análisis regional: la deserción en el nivel primario en la República Argentina. Mendoza, Arg., Univ. Nacional de Cuyo, Facultad de Ciencias Económicas, 1970. 13 1., maps, tables (Serie Cuadernos. Sección economía, 87).

Regional analysis of desertion rates reveals relationship between low rates and regional economic well-being. In addition, high desertion rates seem to be attributable to large rural populations and to low parent literacy rates.

6068. Argentina. Ministerio de Cultura y Educación. Centro Nacional de Documentación e Información Educativa. Bases para el curriculum de las escuelas de nivel elemental. B.A., 1971. 379 p., bibl., illus., tables.

Presentation of curriculum outline for grades one through three, including some comments on how and why curriculum was developed in this fashion. See also item 6070.

6069. _____. _____. _____. Institutos superiores de formación docente [and] Profesorado de nivel elemental. B.A., 1970. 62 p. (Serie La reforma educativa, 6)

Part of an educational reform that has removed teacher training from normal schools, transferring it to the university level, this publication presents the Resolution No. 2321 of 1970 instituting the change, the agreements pursuant to its implementation, and a speech by the Subsecretary of Education in which he describes the new program. [A.E. Toward]

6070. _____. _____. _____. Lineamientos curriculares de 1° a 7° grados. B.A., 1972. 512 p., tables.

Typically detailed syllabi for primary grades. Some attention given to how to evaluate student performance.

6071. _____. _____. **Departamento de Estadística Educativa.** Argentina: la educación en cifras; 1961-1970. B.A., 1971. 297 p., maps, tables.

Detailed data on growth of education at all levels. No analysis or interpretation, however.

6072. _____. _____. **Dirección General de Administración.** Contabilidad pública y rendición de cuentas. B.A., 1970. 21 p., tables (Serie Cuadernos de administración educativa, 3)

Examination of current accounting procedures and their deficiencies as adequate indicators of educational expenditures and accomplishments.

6073. _____. _____. _____. Las inversiones en educación durante la década 1961-1970. B.A., 1972. 85 1., tables (Serie Presupuestos educativos, 10)

Extensive presentation of data on enrollments and budgets for the decade. Useful reference despite lack of interpretive analysis.

6074. _____. _____. _____. Presupuestos por programa. B.A., 1970. 1 v. (Unpaged) tables (Serie Cuadernos de administración educativa, 1)

Attempt to explicate program budgeting in the context of Argentine education.

6075. _____. _____. _____. Las remuneraciones del personal docente. B.A., 1970. 24 1., tables (Serie Cuadernos de administración educativa, 2)

Analysis of legal and financial bases for teachers' salaries, including some comments on problems inherent in the current system.

6076. Avila, Héctor F. and Raúl P. Mentz. Economía y estadística en las decisiones sobre la educación universitaria. Tucumán, Arg., Univ. Nacional de Tucumán, Facultad de Ciencias Económicas, Instituto de Investigaciones Económicas, 1969. 15 p. (Nota, 68-4)

Actually reprints of two papers prepared for 1968 conference on university statistics. In first, Avila reviews techniques of estimating relationship between education and development; in second, Mentz suggests types of statistical studies useful to understanding university students' careers and problems.

6077. Bravo, Héctor Félix. Las erogaciones en educación: un análisis del caso argentino, fundado en el presupuesto nacional. B.A., Centro de Investigaciones en Ciencias de la Educación, 1972. 107 p., tables (Documento de trabajo, 5)

Using data from 1964 to 1968, author first details the making and structure of national budget, then examines educational expenses. Argues that allocations to education are low and that too little is spent on capital and on secondary education, too much on administration. Useful reading.

6078. Cantini, José Luis. Las provincias y la reforma educativa. B.A., Ministerio de Cultura y Educación, Servicio de Difusión, 1970. 18 p. (Serie: Discurso)

Speech by Minister of Education in province of Corrientes, praising provincial efforts in education and explaining decentralization plans and their importance.

6079. Castex, Mariano N. La ciencia en la Argentina, hoy (*in* Ara, Guillermo and others. ¿Qué es la Argentina? Prólogo de Jorge Luis Borges. B.A., Editorial Columba, 1970. p. 134-143, plate)

Congratulatory description of current Argentine achievements in science, in which this Jesuit author maintains that Argentine science and scientists now have an international reputation.

6080. Cirigliano, Gustavo F. J. La educación en la Argentina, hoy (*in* Ara, Guillermo and others. ¿Qúe es la Argentina? Prólogo de Jorge Luis Borges. B.A., Editorial Columba, 1970, p. 146-207)

Cirigliano, in his usual carefully developed approach, examines Argentine education and raises serious questions about its contradictions and difficulties, particularly for future developments of the country.

6081 _____. Filosofía de la educación. B.A., Humanitas (EH), 1973. 286 p. (Col. Guidance, 9)

Reprint of "Análisis Fenomenológico de la Educación" (1962) and a collection of other, previously published pieces on such topics as discipline, audiovisual methods and propaganda. A good sampling of Cirigliano's thought.

6082 _____; **Horacio H. Hernández; Roberto D. Juarroz;** and **Estela Minervini.** La conducta informativa en universitarios argentinos: investigación sobre la habilidad y capacidad de los jóvenes graduados universitarios para manejar y utilizar las fuentes de información bibliográfica. B.A., Univ. de Buenos Aires, Facultad de Filosofía y Letras, Centro de Investigaciones Bibliotecológicas, 1971. 97 p., tables (Investigaciones, 1)

In questionnaire study of 87 Argentine university students, found that knowledge and use of information and library resources was generally inadequate and, where adequate, not attributable to formal training.

6083. Corrientes (province), *Arg.* Ministerio de Bienestar Social. Subsecretaría de Educación y Cultura. Dirección General de Planificación e Investigación Educativa. Apuntes de discusión sobre estudio y análisis de la situación educativa provincial. v. 1/2. Corrientes, Arg., 1970? 2 v. (49, 106 l.) maps, tables.

Wide-ranging analysis of education in Corrientes, including consideration of problems of articulación, desertion and coordination of educational efforts.

6084. Estructura financiera de las universidades nacionales. B.A., Consejo de Rectores de Universidades Nacionales (CRUN), Secretaría de Evaluación, 1972. 21 p., tables.

Analysis of budget date, 1965-71, reveals worsening financial status for universities and inconsistencies and uncertainties in funding procedures and policies.

6085. *Hoja Informativa.* Centro de Documentación e Información Educativas. Año 1, No. 2, junio/julio 1970 [through] Año 2, Nos. 1/2, enero/junio 1971- . Villa María, Arg.

General news and reviews of education, especially in Villa María and Córdoba in general.

6086. Ivanissevich de D'Angelo Rodríguez, Magda. Descenso a los infiernos de la burocracia en la enseñanza secundaria: memorias de un inspector de zona. Prólogo de Leonardo Castellani. B.A., Libro de Edición Argentina, 1970. 95 p.

Strong attack on Argentine education bureaucracy by a former school inspector. Unfortunately, too much generalization from too little evidence.

6087. *Los Libros.* No. 31, agosto/set. 1973- . B.A.

Issue entitled "Para una Crítica Política de la Cultura" devoted largely to four articles critical of official positions in education in Argentina.

6088. *Limen.* Revista de orientación didáctica. Kapelusz Revistas. Año 10, Trimestre 3, 1972- . B.A.

6089. Mallmann, C.A. Futuro de la investigación científica y tecnológica en la Argentina. San Carlos de Bariloche, Arg., Fundación Bariloche, 1969. 24 l.

Examining research as a creative process, author concludes that Argentina's ability to promote research is largely a matter of money.

6090. Profesorado de tiempo completo. B.A., Ministerio de Cultura y Educación, Servicio de Difusión, 1970. 84 p., tables (Serie: La reforma educativa, 2)

Review of one-year experiment in which 44 secondary schools were staffed only by full-time teachers. Unfortunately, no evaluation of the project is included.

6091. *Revista del Centro de Investigación y Acción Social.* Univ. de la Patria Nueva. Año 22, No. 228, nov. 1973- . B.A.

Devoted to article by Rector of Catholic Univ. of Córdoba which argues for legal protection for private education.

Solari, Manuel H. Historia de la educación argentina. See *HLAS 36:3321.*

6092. Universidad de La Pampa, *Santa Rosa de Toay, Arg.* Diagnóstico y proyección. La Pampa, Arg., 1970? 1 v. (Unpaged) illus., maps, tables.

Analysis of first 10 years of activity, including comparisons to older established universities, and forecasts of growth and role of the institution to 1980.

6093. Universidad Nacional de Córdoba, Arg. Dirección de Planeamiento. Edad de los graduados y duración real de las carreras. Córdoba, Arg., 1972. 48 p., tables.

Study reveals that only 44 percent of students complete their degrees in normal amount of time. Unfortunately, data not available to explore fully why this is the case.

6094. _____, _____. _____. Los graduados de la Universidad Nacional de Córdoba: informe preliminar. Córdoba, Arg., 1971. 127 p., tables.

Study of Córdoba graduates from 1960 to 1969 and forecasts to 1980. Indicates that increasingly graduates will come from science, technology and economics.

6095. _____, _____. **Secretaría Técnica de Planeamiento.** Costos por alumno y egresado en la Universidad Nacional de Córdoba. Córdoba, Arg., 1969. 85 p., tables (Serie Estudios, 2)

Exploring costs in Córdoba, author finds that costs are rather high. Long on tables and short on interpretation.

6096. Universidad Nacional de Cuyo, Mendoza, Arg. Rectorado. Reforma educativa: estudio de comisión; primer informe. Mendoza, Arg., 1971. 1 v. (Various pagings)

Reports of two commissions established to examine role of university in promoting educational reform. Includes critical analysis of elementary teaching staffs and calls for university involvement in elementary teacher training.

6097. Universidad Nacional de Tucumán, Arg. Programa de Estadísticas Universitarias. Censo universitario, 1969. Tucumán, Arg., 1969. 223 p., tables (Publicación, 1047)

Detailed report on students, their background and academic careers. In part based on questionnaire data.

6098. Wiñar, David L. Poder político y educación: el peronismo y la Comisión Nacional de Aprendizaje y Orientación Profesional. B.A., Instituto Torcuato Di Tella, Centro de Investigaciones en Ciencias de la Educación, 1970. 61 p., tables (Documento de trabajo, 3)

Examining secondary technical education and the National Commission between 1944-1955, author argues that peronism did not really enlarge the role of the working class in education or in politics but merely extended traditional structures to incorporate more people.

Zanotti, Luis Jorge. Etapas históricas de la política educativa. See *HLAS* 36:3349.

BOLIVIA

6099. Baptista-Gumucio, Mariano. Alfabetización: un programa para Bolivia. La Paz, Editorial Los Amigos del Libro, 1973. 243 p., illus., plates, tables.

Collection of documents relative to Baptista-Gumucio's attempts as Minister of Education to initiate adult literacy campaigns. Most fascinating is the introduction, in which author recounts reactions to the proposed literacy program.

6100. _____. La educación como forma de suicidio nacional. La Paz, Ediciones Camarlinghi, 1973. 215 p. (Col. Popular. Serie 14:40)

Sometimes impassioned, sometimes disjointed collection of thoughts on Bolivian education, its problems and possible solutions.

6101. Conferencia Episcopal de Bolivia, La Paz, 1971. Carta pastoral sobre educación. La Paz, 1971. 68 p.

Explication of Catholic position as regards Bolivian education and call to do more, particularly in rural areas, to promote education.

6102. *Educación Popular para el Desarrollo.* Instituto de Investigación Cultural para Educación Popular. Año 1, No. 3, junio 1970- . Oruro, Bol.

Fascinating journal which reacts to Bolivian education from a distinctly rural and Indian viewpoint. Present number includes editorial on dangers of literacy training which destroys cultural heritage.

6103. _____. _____. Año 1, No. 4, oct. 1970- . Oruro, Bol.

Devoted to articles, many by the Institute staff, about the aims of and methods for promoting popular education in Bolivia.

6104. Fortún, Julia Elena. Educación y desarrollo rural. México, Instituto Indigenista Interamericano, 1973. 105 p., bibl., plates (Serie: Antropología social, 13)

Careful analysis of rural education, with reference to Bolivia, and reasonable proposals for its improvement.

6105. Payne O., Ruth and **Maritza Balderrama C.** Contenido y métodos de la enseñanza en Bolivia. La Paz, Comisión Episcopal de Educación, Secretariado Nacional, 1972. 488 p., bibl., tables (Estudios educacionales, 1)

Extensive study of plans, programs, textbooks and classroom teaching practices in a sample of 300 Bolivian secondary schools, both public and private, urban and rural. Authors conclude that traditional education and its many problems reflects a cultural crisis which, á-la-Freire, produces "educación alienante" rather than "formación integral." Excellent source of data, including classroom observations.

6106. Programa nacional de alfabetización y educación de adultos: 1970-1975. La Paz, Ministerio de Educación y Cultura, 1970. 56 p., plates (Col. Documentos fundamentales, 2)

Reprint of 1970 decree establishing national adult education program, its aims and methods. Also includes two official speeches inaugurating the decree.

6107. Reyeros, Rafael A. La educación pública en Bolivia (Kollasuyo [Univ. Mayor de San Andrés, La Paz] 73, julio/sept. 1970, p. 54-100)

Rambling and disgruntled account of attempts at educational reform in Bolivia. Author argues that in part the problem arises because each government has itself failed to establish models appropriate to the "estado docente."

6108. Soria Galvarro R., Jorge. Objetivos de la reforma universitaria: la universidad necesaria que exige el desarrollo económico-social. Cochabamba, Bol., Editorial Universitaria, 1972. 24 p.

Fairly conventional cataloguing of problems facing Latin American universities and of suggestions for reform, presumably in the Bolivian context.

CENTRAL AMERICA

6109. Ashcraft, Norman. Educational planning in a developing society: the case of British Honduras (UWI/CQ, 18:3, Sept. 1972, p. 23-33)

Unclear argument that a mix of humanistic and technical education best serves the needs of developing countries. Criticism of education-as-investment controversy, while welcomed, is not very convincing.

6110. Gutiérrez Carranza, Claudio. Análisis de información sobre rendimiento académico de estudiantes. Cuidad Universitaria Rodrigo Facio, C.R., Univ. de Costa Rica, Oficina de Planificación Universitaria, 1972. 67 p., tables.

A first presentation of data on nearly 13,000 students who entered university between 1965 and 1971. Little analysis, but important to note that the information is now contained in a data bank.

6111. Guzmán Bockler, Carlos. Colonialismo, violencia y universidad (CLAPCS/AL, 13:1, jan./março 1970, p. 3-17)

Using Univ. of San Carlos, Guatemala, as example,

author argues that universities can make few academic improvements because colonialized bourgeoisie sees university as source of social mobility rather than of knowledge.

Luján, Muñoz, Jorge. Situación actual de la enseñanza de la historia en la Facultad de Humanidades y recomendaciones para su mejoramiento. See *HLAS 36:2184.*

6112. *Noticias del CSUCA.* Consejo Superior Universitario Centroamericano, Secretaría Permanente. Año 1/8, No. 1/20, nov. 1964/marzo 1970- . San José.

6113. Ramazzini, Lucía; Susana J. Icaza; and Concha Barnoya de Asturias. Estudio de los recursos humanos en Centro-América y Panamá en relación con la educación alimentaria en la escuela (USC/U, 73/78, mayo/dic. 1968/enero/dic. 1969, p. 194-222, tables)

In questionnaire study of primary and secondary supervisors in Central America, authors discovered that few have training in nutrition, such training is limited and few use teaching materials, including those prepared by INCAP, in the area of nutrition.

6114. Torres Padilla, Oscar. Diagonóstico sobre la utilización de los recursos humanos y su relación con las necesidades educativas. San José, Instituto Nacional de Aprendizaje, Depto. de Recursos Humanos, 1971. 73 1., tables.

Attempt to document sources of possible imbalance between supply of and demand for trained manpower. Unfortunately, presentation is hard to follow.

CHILE

6115. *Boletín de la Universidad de Chile.* Nos. 98/90, nov./dic. 1968- . Santiago.

Current number largely devoted to short pieces on university reform, in Chile and elsewhere.

6116. *Cuadernos de Psicología.* Univ. de Chile, Depto. de Psicología. No. 1, 1972- . Santiago.

Reports of Univ. of Chile research in such areas as statistics and tutorial instruction.

6117. Goldfarb, Marsha. Algunas evidencias sobre relaciones educacionales en Chile (UCC/CE, 10:30/31, agosto/dic. 1973, p. 3-36, tables)

Extensive examination of data on desertion in private schools and on the relationship between schooling and workers' salaries. Author examines assumptions and conclusions of this and similar studies carefully and intelligently.

6118. Huneeus Madge, Carlos. La reforma en la Universidad de Chile. Santiago, Corporación de Promoción Universitaria, 1973. 493 p. (Serie Aportes universitarios, 7)

Now, unfortunately, more of historical interest. Author explicates reform envisioned under Allende government.

6119. *Revista de Educación.* Ministerio de Educación. Nos. 21/28 (nueva época) mayo 1968 [through] Nos. 32/33, mayo 1971- . Santiago.

Ministry of Education review of contemporary educational events in Chile and abroad. Includes detailed syllabi for reformed secondary programs and educational policy statements of the Allende government.

6120. Santelices C., Rómulo and others. La ENU ¿control de las conciencias o educación liberadora? Talca, Chile, Fundación Manuel Larraín E., 1973. 51 l.

Four articles which critically examine the proposed Escuela Nacional Unificada (1973), largely within the context of Catholicism. The criticism is mild, and the proclaimed theme of control vs. liberation is not fully examined.

6121. Yunis Ahues, Eugenio. Asignación de recursos y política de investigación para la ciencia y la tecnología: el caso de la Universidad de Chile. Santiago, Corporación de Promoción Universitaria, 1973. 108 p., tables (Serie Aportes universitarios, 9)

Proposals to strengthen research, especially in Univ. of Chile, within the Allende framework.

COLOMBIA

6122. Arizmendi Posada, Octavio. La transformación educativa nacional. Bogotá, Instituto Caro y Cuervo, 1969. 227 p., maps, plates, tables (Col. Transformación educativa nacional, 1)

Extended coverage of ministerial actions for the 1968-1969 school year, plus analysis of educational problems and data on the school system. Useful reference, especially in conjunction with item 6126.

6123. Asamblea Nacional Popular Femenina. Comité Educativo. Informe femenino sobre el paquete educativo preparado por el Comité Educativo Preparatorio de la primera Asamblea Nacional Popular Femenina: pt. 1. Bogotá? 1970? 31 l., tables.

Attack on seven proposed educational laws which, the committee argues, would do little to rectify Colombian educational problems. Significance of document lies in both arguments presented and nature of the committee.

6124. Castro, Julio. Tasas internas de retorno social y privado a la educación universitaria en Colombia (Uninorte [Barranquilla, Colo.] 2, oct./dic. 1971, p. 5-16, tables)

Castro questions the assumptions for and recommendations arising from a 1969 rate-of-return study which suggested that educational investment should be directed at primary and, to a lesser degree, secondary rather than higher education.

6125. Colmenares, Germán. ¿Es posible todavía la Universidad liberal? (Logos [Bogotá] 4/5, enero/marzo 1973, p. 149-157)

Wondering if the Colombian university can lead — or at least contribute to — a revolution, author is pessimistic, especially given the US-inspired changes which have already taken place in Colombian higher education.

Consuegra Higgins, José. Como se reprime la universidad en Colombia: informe a la comunidad de la Universidad del Atlántico. See item 8312.

6126. La educación ante el Congreso. Bogotá, Ministerio de Educación Nacional, 1972? 361 p., plates.

Collection of newspaper pieces, congressional records and ministerial documents relative to Minister of Education Galán's attempts in the early 1970s to reform Colombian education. Excellent source for examining legislative debate on educational matters. See also item 6122.

6127. Egginton, Everett and J. Mark Ruhl. Reacción de los campesinos a la Reforma Agraria (Revista Nacional de Agricultura [Sociedad de Agricultores de Colombia, Bogotá] 809, 30 julio 1974, p. 15-18)

Resume of study of INCORA and non-INCORA campesinos which, in part, documents failure of educational programs of land reform.

6128. Gilbert, Alan. Stagnant schooling in rural Colombia (GM, 65:1, Oct. 1972, p. 8-12, map, plates)

Journalistic account of urban-rural differences in opportunities for and quality of schooling in Colombia.

6129. Hanson, Mark. Reform and governance in the Ministry of Education: the case of Colombia (UNESCO/IRE, 22:2, 1974, p. 155-177, illus.)

Illuminating analysis of the development and successes of the Fondos Educativos Regionales (FER) by which the National Ministry of Education has sought to improve its control over state educational activities and thus improve Colombian education. Recommended reading for those who want to understand the administration of education in Colombia—and elsewhere.

6130. Hernández de Alba, Guillermo. Documentos para la historia de la educación en Colombia. t. 1, 1540-1653. Bogotá, Patronato Colombiano de Artes y Ciencias, Colegio Máximo de las Academias de Colombia, 1969. 225 p., facsims., plates.

6131. International Labor Organization, *Geneva.* Formación profesional en Colombia. Geneva, Programa de las Naciones Unidas para el Desarrollo [and] Organización Internacional del Trabajo, 1970. 127 p., plates, tables.

Review of SENA (Servicio Nacional de Aprendizaje) with special reference to its projects sponsored by UN Special Fund to train instructors.

6132. Lloreda, José Antonio. Colombia: ¿universidad popular o elitista? Bogotá, Centro de Investigaciones y Acción Social [and] Instituto de Doctrina y Estudios Sociales, 1971. 45 1., tables (Documento de trabajo, 3)

Earlier printing of article which appears in item 6136.

6133. Ochoa Isaza, Gabriel. El lenguaje docente y el ausentismo estudiantil (UA/U, 182, julio/sept. 1971, p. 423-428, bibl.)

Appeal to teachers to give greater attention to difficulty levels and uses of vocabulary in their teaching, regardless of subject matter. Lack of concern with appropriate levels of vocabulary is linked to widespread student failure and lack of achievement.

6134. Ortiz C., Elva L. La Universidad del Valle, 1945-1970. Cali, Colo., Univ. del Valle, División de Humanidades, 1971. 166 p., bibl. (Cuadernos del Valle, 7)

Slow-moving institutional history. Virtually no commentary on the significance of the events recounted in numbing detail.

6135. Rama, Germán W. Algunas hipótesis sobre investigación y modernización en la Universidad Nacional de Colombia (CLAPCS/AL, 13:1, jan./março 1970, p. 30-45)

Rama maintains that academic improvement and research, initiated from above, must ultimately rest on creating incentives for the development of "teacher-researchers."

6136. *La Sociedad y el Universitario.* Un análisis del conflicto estudiantil y de la educación superior en Colombia. Univ. Industrial de Santander. Vol. 1, 1971- . Bucaramanga, Colo.

Collection of essays which explore Colombian universities' failure to reform themselves and their society.

6137. Ta Ngoc Châu and Françoise Caillods. Colombia: a case study (in Ta Ngoc Châu *ed.* Population growth and costs of education in developing countries. Paris, UNESCO, International Institute for Educational Planning, 1972, p. 120-174, tables)

After extensive review of Colombian education, particularly primary and teacher training; authors attempt to relate population growth to educational costs. Using several growth assumptions, authors conclude that cost of primary and teacher education will be at least four times greater in 1989 than in 1966.

6138. United Nations Office of Educational, Scientific and Cultural Organization (UNESCO). Office of Statistics. A statistical study of wastage at school. Paris, UNESCO *for* International Bureau of Education, 1972. 121 p., tables (Studies and surveys in comparative education)

Exposition of UNESCO approach to analysis of wastage and case study of Colombia from 1960 to 1968. Useful for both approach and Colombian data.

6139. Universidad Nacional de Colombia, *Bogotá.* **División de Programación Económica.** Análisis del censo de graduados. Bogotá, 1970. 48 1., tables.

Analysis of 885 UN graduates of 1967 reveals that graduates largely came from affluent urban families, attended private secondary school, received classical bachilleratos, had some failures at university and gained employment through contacts of family and friends. Data presentation and analysis unfortunately sketchy.

6140. Vivas Dorado, Raúl. Diagnóstico de la educación privada. Introducción [de] P. Rodrigo Díaz. Bogotá, Confederación Nacional de Centros Docentes (CONACED), 1971. 94 p., tables.

An attempt to show that private education, at all levels, plays an important role in Colombia and that the government ought to aid private education more.

CUBA

6141. *Educación.* Ministerio de Educación. Año 1, No. 3, oct./dic. 1971- . La Habana.

Exceedingly useful journal containing feature articles on Cuban education, current educational legislation, book reviews, reports on education elsewhere in Latin America and in the Eastern Bloc. Present issue features articles on the *escuela al campo* program and on educational research.

6142. García Galló, Gaspar Jorge. La concepción marxista sobre la escuela y la educación (Santiago [Univ. de Oriente, Cuba] 10, 1973, p. 7-98, bibl.)

Analysis of writings of Marx and Engels to extract Marxist thoughts on education and comparison of these with other philosophies of the time. Ambitious but well-done, and provides background to current Cuban educational practices.

6143. González Carbajal, Ladislao. La reforma universitaria de los años 20 y la rebelión estudiantil de nuestros días (BNJM/R, 60, 11:3 [3. época] sept./dic. 1969, p. 51-97)

Marxist interpretation of the Córdoba reform movement and its specific development in Cuba during 1920s. Although author argues that the revolutionary left continues to promote university reform everywhere, he is strangely silent on current Cuban events.

6144. International Conference on Education, *XXXIV*, *Geneva*, *1973*. Cuba: organización de la educación, 1971-1973. La Habana, Ministerio de Educación (MINED), Dirección de Producción de Medios de Enseñanza, 1973? 212 p., tables.

Report to XXXIV International Conference on Education on educational development in Cuba. Published in Spanish, French, and English.

Paulston, Rolland G. La educación rural en Cuba: una estrategia para el desarrollo revolucionario. See item 8233.

6145. El Primer Congreso Nacional de Educación y Cultura (BNJM/R, 62:2, mayo/agosto 1971, p. 5-16)

Contains final portion of Declaration of this 1971 Cuban conference, in which cultural and educational activities are tied to revolutionary goals. Perhaps useful source to get very general understanding of the nature of the Cuban interpretation of education and society.

6145a. Roca, Blas. Lecturas. La Habana, Ministerio de Educación, Dirección Provincial de Planes Especiales, 1972. 175 p., illus., plates.

A book of readings for the Cuban elementary schools. [A. Suárez]

6146. Tavárez Justo, Emma. La educación en Cuba (Ahora [Santo Domingo] 12:505, July 1973, p. 24-29, illus.)

Interview with Univ. of Havana professor of pedagogy, including description of current growth of Cuban education, stress on work-study relationships at all levels, expansion of scholarship and boarding school programs. Important concluding comments on the "Padilla affair."

ECUADOR

6147. Galiana, G. R. Metodología de los seminarios de reforma universitaria (UC/A, 28:3/4, julio/dic. 1972, p. 159-183)

Disjointed attempt to suggest changes in UNESCO programs of research and technical assistance for university reform in Latin America in general and Ecuador in particular. Does raise some important questions about the role of "experts" and of the public in determining the nature of reform.

Murgueytio, Reinaldo. Bosquejo histórico de la escuela laica ecuatoriana, 1906-1966. See *HLAS 36:2874*.

6148. *Revista Ecuatoriana de Educación*. Casa de la Cultura Ecuatoriana. No. 66, 1972- . Quito.

MEXICO

6149. Alvarez Barret, Luis. Orígenes y evolución de las escuelas rurales en Yucatán (UY/R, 13:78, nov./dic. 1971, p. 26-51)

Examines development of rural schooling and argues that rural schools have been used for a variety of purposes in Mexico, ranging from the hacendados' early attempts to subjugate the campesino to current agrarian reform attempts to help him. Useful case study of how schooling purposes change.

6150. Avilés, René. Educación y revolución: manual del maestro mexicano. México, B. Costa-Amic Editor, 1971. 125 p.

A call for Mexican teachers to assume a more militant, socialistic stance in order to promote the true educational aims of the Revolution. Perhaps useful as illustration of a particular interpretation of teaching and schools.

6151. Bravo Ahuja, Víctor. La universidad no puede permanecer ajena a los requerimientos del México actual (UY/R, 13:78, nov./dic. 1971, p. 10-14)

Secretary of Public Education, arguing that education is crucial to realizing the goals of the Revolution, calls on universities to take a more direct role in solving national problems and pledges government financial support.

6152. Cañibe, Juan Manuel. El movimiento estudiantil y la opinión pública (CLAPCS/AL, 14:1/2, janeiro/junho 1971, p. 21-39)

In a study of public opinion in Mexico City following student disturbances of 1968, author finds that working-class and lower-middle-class respondents do not identify with student actions and generally favor a law-and-order government, but might support students whose demands seem feasible and of concrete benefit to the people themselves.

6153. Carmona, Fernando and others. Reforma educativa y apertura democrática. México, Editorial Nuestro Tiempo, 1972. 276 p. (Col.: Los grandes problemas nacionales)

Good collection of papers which interpret Mexican education as attempt by dominant class to depoliticize and domesticate the masses. Includes chapters on women, art and rural education.

6154. Chávez, Ezequiel A. Acerca del laicismo en las escuelas particulares y en las oficiales. México, Asociación Civil Ezequiel A. Chávez, 1968. 1 v. (Various pagings)

Reprint of author's 1931 work attacking Mexican approach to secularism in education as a divisive and false neutrality.

6155. Comité Administrador del Programa Federal de Construcción de Escuelas (CAPFCE), *México.* Obra realizada, 1965-1970. México, 1970. 1 v. (Unpaged) plates.

Incredibly beautiful collection of photographs of new schools built throughout Mexico between 1965 and 1970. Appropriate quotations about schooling and architecture scattered throughout.

6156. Díaz-Guerrero, Rogelio. La enseñanza de la investigación en psicología en Iberoamérica: un paradigma (Revista Latinoamericana de Psicología [Bogotá] 3:1, 1971, p. 5-36, bibl.)

After detailing both the nature of physological research and its present status, particularly in Mexico, author describes cross-cultural research program at UNAM, its goals and its importance in training researchers.

6157. *Docencia.* Univ. Autónoma de Guadalajara, Comunidad Académica. No. 1/3, agosto/dic. 1973 [and] No. 1, feb. 1974- . Guadalajara, Mex.

La Educación. Organización de los Estados Americanos, Depto. de Asuntos Educativos. Año 18, No. 65, enero/abril 1973- . Washington. See item 6016.

La Educación. Organización de los Estados Americanos, Depto. de Asuntos Educativos. Año 18, Nos. 66/67, mayo/dic. 1973- . Washington. See item 6017.

García Cantú, Gastón. Javier Barros Sierra 1968: conversaciones con Gastón García Cantú. See item 8152.

6158. Hasperué Becerra, Oscar. Universidad de América. Acapulco, Mex., Editorial Americana, 1970. 45 p. (Textos de cultura americana, 11)

Rationale and plans for establishing a Univ. of America at Acapulco, home of the Casa de Cultura Americana.

Hines, Paul. Education for the future: the dilemma of Latin America. See item 6025.

6159. Jiménez y Coria, Laureano. La evaluación del aprendizaje y del maestro. México, Editorial Porrúa, 1972. 178 p., bibl., illus.

Guide to testing and evaluating students, with special reference to Mexican students and tests.

6160. Mir, Adolfo. Orígenes socioeconómicos, status de la escuela y aspiraciones y expectativas educativas y ocupacionales de estudiantes de secundaria (UNAM/RMS, 34:2, abril/junio 1972, p. 169-192, bibl., tables)

In study of over 500 secondary students in Monterrey, author finds strong relationship between students' socioeconomic background and their occupational and educational expectations. Good discussion of meaning of these findings.

Modiano, Nancy. Indian education in the Chiapas Highlands. See item 1166.

6161. Ramírez Gómez, Ramón and **Alma Chapoy Bonifaz.** Estructura de la Universidad Nacional Autónoma de México: ensayo socioeconómico. México, Fondo de Cultura Popular, 1970. 105 p., tables.

Extensive review of UNAM in which authors attribute university problems to general malaise of Mexican society. Worth reading.

6162. Repetto Milán, Francisco. Reforma educativa a nivel universitario (UY/R, 13:73, enero/feb. 1971, p. 13-18.

Rector of Univ. of Yucatan reviews university reform but says little about its prospects or accomplishments.

6163. Sierra, Augusto Santiágo. Las misiones culturales: 1923-1973. México, Secretaría de Educación Pública, 1973. 188 p., bibl. (SepSetentas, 113)

Very short history of Mexican cultural missions and, perhaps more interesting, reprints of several documents pertaining to the founding and functioning of the missions.

6164. Wing, Juvencio and others. Los estudiantes, la educación y la política. México, Editorial Nuestro Tiempo, 1971. 175 p. (Encuestas y debates)

Collection of articles exploring, generally sympathetically, university student movements, particularly in Mexico. Includes articles on events outside the Federal District.

6165. Zea, Leopoldo. De la reforma educativa (*in* Extremos de México: homenaje a Don Daniel Cosío Villegas. México, El Colegio de México, Centro de Estudios Históricos, 1971, p. 577-589)

Argues that Mexican educational reform must concern itself with more than the expansion of schooling and the training of more technicians. Unfortunately, Zea does not make clear what this "more" is and how it is to be accomplished.

PARAGUAY

6166. Apmann, Robert P. Engineering education in Paraguay (JDA, 8:2, Jan. 1974, p. 257-270)

Excellent review of Paraguayan education, especially university-level engineering, and details on need for and potentials in expanded engineering programs.

PERU

6167. Carnoy, Martin. Education as cultural imperialism. N.Y., David McKay, 1974. 278 p., tables.

As part of larger theme, author (with Isaura Belloni Schmidt) explores role of schooling in Brazil and Peru in preserving traditional social order.

6168. Castro Harrison, Jorge. Prolegómenos. v. 1, Planeamiento integral y administración de la educación. v. 2, Notas o apuntes para el planeamiento integral y administración de la educación. Lima, El Siglo, 1971. 2 v. (649, 790 p.) tables.

Two lengthy volumes in which author attempts to cover entire issue of educational planning, including procedures, meetings and seminars, and problems. Second volume contains some useful data on Peruvian education.

6169. Céspedes Bedregal, J. Teófilo. Doctrina y sistema de una nueva educación peruana: proyección; perfil doctrinario, marco principista, estructura funcional, curriculum vital, dinámica operativa, nuclearización orbital. Lima, Editora Nueva Constitución, 1972. 215 p., illus.

Lengthy discussion of Peru's "new education" and how it can be implemented.

6170. Franco, Oscar. La última clase. Lima, Editorial Milla Batres, 1974. 77 p.

General attack on students, in which author examines paradoxes of student opinion and wonders at one point if universities are in fact producing delinquents.

6171. Joworski, Helam. La nueva ley universitaria: universidad y sociedad en el Perú (IESSC/C, 5:14, mayo/agosto 1970, p. 7-28)

Careful explication of the problems involved in the 1969 university law and a case for reformulation to allow the universities to respond to national needs while maintaining their independence.

6172. Meyers, Robert G. International education, emigration, and national policy; a longitudinal case study of Peruvians trained in the United States (CES/CER, 17:1, Feb. 1973, p. 71-90)

Useful analysis of data concerning status in 1970 of Peruvian students who were studying in the US in 1966. Author points out that, although there is a brain drain, it is not as great as usually described and that the costs of training abroad are in general outweighted by gains in providing needed personnel who do return to Peru.

6173. Paulston, Rolland G. La educación no-formal: la experiencia peruana (USIA/PI, 19:6, nov./dic. 1972, p. 11-22, plates, tables)

Arguing that deficiencies in the formal school must be alleviated by greater attention to informal education, author reviews programs of such agencies as SENATI and argues for greater resources for such programs.

6174. Peru. Ministerio de Educación. Perú: algunos aspectos de la reforma educativa (Boletín Técnico [Caracas] 6:16, 1972, p. 60-74, tables)

Extensive review of programs and goals of Basic Labor Education (EBL), designed to train adolescents and adults who have not had regular schooling opportunities. Includes both general and vocational education, as well as "citizen" training.

6175. Portocarrero, Felipe. Universidad y política: situación actual (Sociedad y Política [Lima] 1:2, oct. 1972, p. 34-38)

Traces Peruvian university reform movement from 1960 to 1972, particularly the problems and failures of the 1969 changes and their relationship to the 1972 revisions in university reform.

Tello Palomino, Moisés. Panorama de los estudios filosóficos en el Perú. See *HLAS 36:5074*

URUGUAY

6176. Cernuschi, Félix. Educación, ciencia, técnica y desarrollo. Montevideo, Univ. de la República, Depto. de Publicaciones, 1971. 124 p., bibl., tables (Col. Historia y cultura, 14)

Somewhat disorganized collection of arguments, the major premise of which is that development in Uruguay depends on expansion of science and technology. Even political problems, the author hints, will disappear once science and technology are firmly established.

6177. Graciarena, Jorge. La deserción y el retraso en los estudios universitarios en Uruguay (CLAPCS/AL, 13:1, jan/março 1970, p. 45-65)

Examining causes for low university retention rates in Uruguay, author hypothesized that major reason is that students become demoralized, because of lack of job opportunities.

6178. Irisity, Jorge and others. Respuesta educacional para la década del 70. Montevideo, Univ. de la República, Depto. de Publicaciones, 1971. 300 p., tables (Col. Historia y cultura, 19)

Collection of what were originally university lectures on education for the future. Not always clear is the extent to which the articles rest on anything more than personal predilection.

6179. Reyes, Reina. El derecho a educar y el derecho a la educación: ensayo. 5. ed. Montevideo, Editorial Alfa, 1972. 117 p. (Col. Tiempo y memoria)

This fifth edition of Reyes' essay reviews legal bases of Uruguayan education with special reference to problems of secularism.

6180. Sosa, Ademar L. Autonomía de los entes de enseñanza en el Uruguay. 2. ed., corregida y actualizada. Montevideo, Ediciones de la Banda Oriental, 1972. 62 p. (Temas de educación, 1)

Interesting analysis of historical and current status of relationship between government and education, including legal and financial limitations on autonomy.

6181. Universidad de la República, *Montevideo*. Escuela Nacional de Bellas Artes. Una experiencia educacional. Montevideo, 1970. 93 p., illus., plates.

Description of innovations in National School for Fine Arts which seek to integrate training with current national and cultural problems and concerns.

6182. Uruguay. Ministerio de Instrucción Pública y Previsión Social. Comisión Coordinadora de los Entes de Enseñanza. Síntesis de la evolución educativa del Uruguay entre 1956 y 1965 y su probable desarrollo. Montevideo, 1966. 38 p., tables.

General collection of data on enrollments and finances and several projections through 1974.

6182a. Vallarino, Yolanda and others. Programa escolar urbano: reestructuración de objetivos y contenidos. Montevideo, Ediciones Tauro, 1972. 111 p. (Estudios de Tauro, 2)

A small paperback written by a group of teachers as part of their effort to qualify as school inspectors in Uruguayan schools, the contents are quite specific and stress curricular and administrative concerns of urban schools. Sections are devoted to spelling, reading, mathematics, social sciences, natural sciences, and fine arts. [A.E. Toward]

VENEZUELA

6183. Albornoz, Orlando. La profesión de ingeniero en una sociedad en desarrollo (CLAPCS/AL, 13:1, jan./março 1970, p. 18-29)

Focusing on Venezuelan engineers, Albornoz argues that professionals have failed to develop a collective sense of responsibility to society.

Andrianza Alvarez, H. Presencia del pasado: homenaje del Centro Histórico a la Universidad del Zulia en los 75 años de su instalación y 20 de la reapertura. See *HLAS 36:2841.*

6184. *Boletín Técnico.* Instituto Nacional de Cooperación Educativa, Dirección de Programación y Servicios Técnicos. Año 7, No. 18, 1973- . Caracas.

Issue devoted to new methods and equipment in education, including audiovisual techniques, programmed instruction and correspondence education. Not all articles are devoted specifically to Venezuela.

6185. Castañeda, Eduardo; Margarita Dobles; and **Víctor Silva.** La educación en Venezuela: situación actual y perspectivas. Caracas, Ministerio de Educación, Dirección de Planeamiento, Depto. de Documentación Pedagógica, 1971. 40 l., tables.

Very general review of Venezuelan education and its problems.

6186. *EDUPLAN Informa.* Ministerio de Educación, Centro de Documentación e Información, Dirección de Planeamiento. Vol. 5, No. 2, abril 1972- . Caracas.

Reports and news items related to educational planning in Venezuela, including, in this issue, a report on the III Meeting of the Consejo Interamericano para la Educación, the 1971 ministerial statement on reading.

6187. Esaá Crespo, Cecilia. Aspiraciones educacionales. Valencia, Ven., Univ. de Carabobo, Facultad de Ciencias Económicas y Sociales, Centro de Planificación y Desarrollo Económico, 1968. 117 p., bibl., tables.

Questionnaire study of Ciudad Guayana residents reveals strong aspirations for careers without accompanying knowledge of steps necessary to reach these careers.

6188. Febres-Cordero, Foción. Historia de la Facultad de Odontología de la Universidad Central de Venezuela. t. 2, Documentos. Caracas, Univ. Central de Venezuela, Facultad de Odontología, 1967. 227 p.

Collection of documents dating back to 1852 which chronicles the establishment and development of the faculty and which includes interesting pieces on student strikes, curriculum reform and defense of the faculty's degrees.

6189. Ferrá, Coloma; Angel Ginestar; and María Elena Nieto de Negrette. Análisis metodológico para calcular costos de la educación universitaria en Venezuela y su aplicación en la programación presupuestaria. Caracas, Consejo Nacional de Universidades [and] Organización de los Estados Américanos, 1973. 460 p., bibl., tables.

Development of method to calculate cost per student and per graduate. Data reported as interesting as the method.

6190. Herranz M., Julián; Luis Suárez G.; and Gema Tata de Suárez. Estudio sobre la zona rental de la Universidad de Carabobo. 3. ed. Valencia, Ven., Univ. de Carabobo, Centro de Planificación y Desarrollo Económico, 1969. 99 p., tables.

Attempt to determine profitable uses of land owned by University and recommendation to build shopping center.

6191. Instituto Nacional de Cooperación Educativa. 10 [i.e. Diez] años del INCE. Caracas? n.d. 2 v. (81, 82 p.) plates, tables.

General review of the Instituto National de Cooperación Educativa, including its history, structure, programs and personnel. Laudatory rather than critical evaluation.

6192. La Belle, Thomas J. The new professional in Venezuelan secondary education. With the assistance of Jan R. Van Orman. Los Angeles, Univ. of California, Latin American Center, 1973. 195 p., bibl., tables.

Questionnaire study of 638 university and institute students majoring in secondary education reveals that the sample sees education as a major part of national development and a hope for future progress. Author raises questions about the appropriateness of these expectations.

6193. Peñalver, Luis Manuel. La ciencia y la tecnología en Venezuela (OAS/CI, 13:5/6, sept./dic. 1972, p. 2-11, map, tables)

Detailed summary of current state of science and technology, including data on personnel and funds by field of research, and description of role of CONICT (Consejo Nacional de Investigaciones Científicas y Tecnológicas), created in 1967 and staffed in 1969.

6194. Reunión Nacional de Educación Agrícola Superior, *Maracay, Ven., 1969.* Informe. Maracay, Ven., Univ. Central de Venezuela, Facultad de Agronomía [and] Instituto Interamericano de Ciencias Agrícolas de la OEA, Programa de Educación Superior-Zona Andina, 1969. 1 v. (Various pagings) plates.

Record of first national meeting of higher agricultural education, including resolutions and brief position papers on planning for agricultural education, research and accreditation. Includes resolution creating AVIEAS (Asociación Venezolana de Instituciones de Educación Agrícola Superior).

6195. Sosnowsky, Valentín. Expectativas y motivaciones de la juventud de Caracas. t. 3. Caracas, Tecnotrónica Internacional, 1973. 1 v. (Various pagings) tables (Proyecto juventud)

Report of study of Caracas youth which concludes that youth tend to feel negative toward adults and authorities, schools and teachers, and present society; but tend to feel positive toward themselves, their families (especially their mothers), and education for social mobility. Worth reading and analyzing.

6196. Testimonios sobre la formación para el trabajo: 1539-1970. Caracas, Instituto Nacional de Cooperación Educativa, 1972. 469 p.

In many ways an excellent collection of documents on work training, many of which would not be normally available. One wonders, however, why only three of the 78 documents reprinted date from 1958 on while 23 date from 1539 to 1799. Moreover, some attempt to tie together and synthesize the documents would have been useful.

6197. Zchock, Dieter K.; Aníbal Fernández; George W. Schuyler; and W. Raymond Duncan. The education-work transition of Venezuelan university students (UM/JIAS, 16:1, Feb. 1974, p. 96-118, bibl.)

Although based on small sample, compelling argument that Venezuelan employment practices reward merit as much as ascription and depend on *amistad* as much as *palanca*. Students in civil engineering and business administration at Univ. Central de Venezuela (UCV) and Univ. Católica Andrés Bello (UCAB) and members of elite included in sample.

WEST INDIES
(except Cuba)

6198. Avelino, Andrés, h. La educación superior y el desarrollo dominicano (Ciencia [Santo Domingo] 1:1, mayo/junio 1972, p. 17-32)

Fairly standard analysis of the Latin American university, with emphasis on role of university in transforming society through greater stress on revolutionary and socialist analysis and social change.

6199. Bahamas. Ministry of Education and Culture. Focus on the future: white paper on education. Nassau, 1972? 17 p.

Surprisingly, clear policy statement which in particular stresses the need for general secondary education, a Bahamian college and Bahamianization of teaching staffs. Specific programs and their financial consequences, however, are not detailed.

6200. Batista, Guarocuya and **Darío Solano.** Docencia universitaria e investigación de la realidad nacional (Ciencia [Santo Domingo] 1:1, mayo/junio 1972, p. 111-125, bibl., tables)

Well-reasoned argument to improve university research activities directed toward national needs, including incorporating students into such activities. Careful avoidance of political implications.

6201. Benítez, Jaime. La universidad como casa de estudios dentro de la libre comunidad hispánica de Puerto Rico (UPR/LT, 17:66, oct./dic/1969, p. 11-17)

Jumbled tribute to the Univ. of Puerto Rico.

6202. *El Búho.* Colegio Regional de Humacao. Vol. 6, No. 3, oct. 1971- . Humacao, P.R.

6203. Conference on Teacher Education in the Eastern Caribbean, *VI, Montserrat, Leeward Islands, 1970.* Cave Hill, Barbados, Univ. of the West Indies, Institute of Education, 1970? 182 1., tables.

Collection of summaries of sessions and papers exploring such topics as new curricula and training programs and programs of specific institutions. Good if necessarily abbreviated picture of teacher training in the area.

6204. Edwards, P.A. Education for development in the Caribbean. Bridgetown, Caribbean Ecumenical Consultation for Development, n.d. 15 p. (Study paper, 3)

Arguing that conflict between church and state has shaped Caribbean education, author concludes that church must reexamine its role in the face of a state school system which fails to provide moral training.

6205. García Esteve, Joel and **Gabriel Cirino Gerena.** Los problemas estudiantiles de la Universidad de Puerto Rico en 1971 (UPR/RCS, 16:3, sept. 1972, p. 419-430, tables)

In questionnaire study of stratified sample of Univ. of Puerto Rico students, authors report that students consider interruptions of studies caused by 1971 strike a most serious problem but that other academic and university problems also are of concern, especially poor teaching and poor registration and guidance procedures. Results interesting although study methodologically problematic.

6206. Hernández, Frank Marino. Recursos humanos de nivel superior en la República Dominicana. Santo Domingo, Ediciones Sargazo, 1972. 128 p., tables (Recursos humanos, 1)

In study of university-trained human resources, author concludes that major problem is lack of sufficient data to make more than rough estimate of supply and demand.

BRAZIL

AGNES E. TOWARD

Institute for Cultural Pluralism
San Diego State University

6207. Aguiar, Wilson A. TV didática. Brasília, Editôra de Brasil (EBRASA), 1972? 243 p., illus., maps, plates.

Aguiar cites examples from around the world in his discussion of instructional TV and its potential for Brazil. Instead of the more common rhetorical approach full of promises of future technological miracles for Brazil, he presents a very practical and matter-of-fact survey of television, from equipment to program formats. A generous supply of photographs accompanies the text.

6208. Albuquerque, Therezinha Lins de. Acompanhamento psicológico à professora: uma experiência. Petrópolis, Bra., Editôra Vozes, 1972. 102 p., bibl.

The author has impressive credentials to support her ideas — Chief of the Youth Guidance Center of the Ministry of Health, Accredited Supervisor for the Brazilian Association of Applied Psychology and Professor at the Catholic Univ. in Rio. Her work in this instance is a review of her experience with the guidance and counseling program at the Guatemala School in Rio, a school that served as a training center for counselors and psychologists. On the scene reminiscences and observations of a program that focussed on student-teacher relationship, from the expert who was there.

6209. Alfabetização de adultos: orientação nova da UNESCO. Tradução de Abgar Renault (Revista do Ministério da Educação e Cultura [Rio] 11:47, fev./nov. 1970, p. 28-30)

Functional literacy, as now defined, comprises more than just reading and writing; it presupposes the acquisition of certain kinds of knowledge, skill, and an awareness of its value to society. For literacy programs the recommendations are: constant revision of goals, schedule, location, methodology, and materials; exchange of experiences; and adequate training of teachers, including evaluation of projects and programs. [BBE]

6210. Amado, Gilson. Televisão educativa no Brasil: conferência pronunciada perante a Comissão da Educação e Cultura do Senado em 11 novembro de 1971 (Revista de Informação Legislativa [Senado Federal, Diretoria de Informação Legislativa, Rio] 8:32, out./dez. 1971, p. 37-50)

Television plays a major role in shaping Brazilian society, according to recent research which revealed that TV makes up about 70 percent of the communication media. The Ministry of Education, through the National Educational Research Center (INEP), will conduct a survey on educational TV to discover if programs for young children and adolescents are representative and appropriate. Amado describes educational TV in other nations but urges that Brazilian mores and models determine the format in Brazil. [BBE]

6211. Aragão, Jarbas Cavalcante de. Educação e desenvolvimento. Rio, Editôra Laudes, 1972? 2 v. (674 p.) (Continuous pagination)

An ambitious attempt to consider education from the time of the Greeks up to the current concerns of contemporary societies, including pollution, depletion of resources, and the impact of technology. The author, professor of Portuguese, philologist and member of the Institute of Geography and Military History, comments on so many topics (geography, industry, health, politics, semantics, public administration, and nutrition are a few) that the reader may have difficulty following his central theme. A northeasterner, he writes in detail of the social and economic problems of the Northeast. An encyclopedic and synoptic treatment in two volumes, with two indices but no bibliography.

6212. Arozo, Maria Amália. A reforma do ensino superior e sua adequação à Amazônia: o curso de serviço social. Niterói, Bra.? Cidade Universitária, Univ. Federal do Rio de Janeiro, Serviço Industrial Gráfico, 1971. 28 p., tables.

References to previous legislation governing higher education appear first in this paper presented at the Seminar on Brazilian and Amazonian Reality, held in Manaus in 1968. Emphasis here is on social service programs in the Amazon region.

6213. *Arquivos Brasileiros de Psicologia Aplicada.* Fundação Getúlio Vargas, Instituto de Seleção e Orientação Profissional. Vol. 23, No. 3, julho/set. 1971- . Rio.

In this issue (169 p.) dedicated to the memory of Professor Lourenço Filho, appear some of his articles on philosophy of education, experimental psychology, problems of counseling and training professionals, literacy problems, and essays on reform. The bibliography reveals his contributions to psychology and his personal convictions. [BBE]

6214. Atividades didáticas na educação de adultos. Belo Horizonte, Bra., Instituto de educação de Minas Gerais, n.d. 272 p., bibl., illus. (Revista AMAE Educando)

A basic textbook and guide for teachers of adult students, with chapters containing didactic material on mathematics and language. Illustrations accompany math problems; reading selections, and sample questions, while activities follow the language lessons.

6215. Azevedo, Fernando de. Figuras de meu convívio. 2. ed. rev. e aumentada. São Paulo, Editôra Duas Cidades, 1973. 244 p.

The subtitle of this work, *Family portraits and portraits of teachers and educators,* aptly describes the contents. Since Azevedo played an outstanding role in Brazilian education and various sectors of public life, he was acquainted with many of the best known and admired public figures, some of whom he writes about in these personal reminiscences. They span many years and describe many personalities active in the educational and cultural life of the times, such as Roger Bastide, Júlio de Mesquita Filho, Anisio Teixeira, Roquette-Pinto, and Monteiro Lobato. The selections include speeches, eulogies, articles, and reminiscences.

6216. Baiocchi, Josephina Desounet and **Nelson Braga Octaviano Ferreira.** Montagem de projetos de ação pedagógica. Brasília, Editôra de Brasil (EBRASA), 1972. 145 p., bibl., tables.

A handbook designed to serve as a reference for training programs in educational planning and project development. Many graphics illustrate various approaches to projects and to organizational structure.

6217. Bán, Alzira Dornelles and **Halina Brzezinska.** A nova escola: gerência científica. Pôrto Alegre, Bra., Livraria Sulina Editôra, 1973. 289 p., bibl., illus., tables (Col. Organização)

This work has a misleading title, in that it treats very specifically of the *"escola média"* rather than just any new school. After defining secondary school and identifying its principal goals, the authors state what such a school should *not* be, present a philosophy, and proceed to the heart of their effort—issues of organization and administration. Fresh from a master's degree in School Administration in the US, Alzira Dornelles Ban has been thorough in her treatment of administrative problems at the secondary level. Many illustrations, diagrams, graphs, and tables.

6218. Barata, Mário. Escola Politécnica do Largo de São Francisco: berço da engenharia brasileira. Rio, Associação dos Antigos Alunos da Politécnica, Clube de Engenharia, 1973. 112 p., plates.

A luxury edition of book commemorating the 150th anniversary of the National School of Engineering and its historical site in Rio. Published by the alumni association in cooperation with the Engineering Club, the book was edited by historian Mário Barata and has, as one of its purposes, the preservation of the building in which the School's long and admirable history has evolved. 24 pages of photographs and drawings complete the history, which begins in 1750.

6219. Barroso, Carmen Lúcia de Melo and **Lólio Lourenço de Oliveira.** O madureza em São Paulo. São Paulo, Fundação Carlos Chagas, 1971. 97 p., tables (Série Pesquisas educacionais, 4)

Equivalency examinations have been part of the Brazilian education system since at least 1890, according to the background information presented in this study of their role and impact now. Among questions raised were the following: Are these examinations fulfilling an educational function or simply "authorizing" the eligibility of individuals requiring a certificate or diploma? Is its predominant function that of preparing students for the university entrance examinations? Is it an avenue of social mobility? An ample supply of statistical data accompanies this study.

6220. Barroso, Manoel Antônio. Brasil: 50 anos de universidade (Revista do Ministério da Educação e Cultura [Rio] 11:47, fev./nov. 1970, p. 10-16)

Describes the historical evolution of Rio's Federal Univ. since 1920, its organization, administration, role as a legal standard for higher education and pioneer in the struggle for university reform. Today it has approximately 25,074 students, of which 5,537 are at various centers pursuing graduate studies. Also contains references to the development of the university city, research plans, resources, and scholarships, and leaders who have dedicated themselves to the university. [BBE]

6221. Bases da política educacional (Revista do Ministério da Educação e Cultura [Rio] 11:47, fev./nov. 1970, p. 54-61)

Inaugural speech of Minister Jarbás Passarinho at the Catholic Univ. of Minas Gerais, in 1970, in which he discusses problems of Brazilian education and the steps to handle them. He defends university reform, adequate salaries for professors, professionalization of educators and active roles for students in the educational process, including representation on university councils. He praises industrial, agricultural, commercial, and normal education programs, emphasizing the need to train for the job market. He also proposes that medical students be required to serve a training period in the interior of the country. [BBE]

6222. Beisiegel, Celso de Rui. Estado e educação popular: um estudo sobre a educação de adultos. São Paulo, Livraria Pioneira Editôra, 1974. 189 p., bibl., tables (Biblioteca pioneira de ciências sociais. Sociologia)

Although Beisiegel's experience with adult education began as a participant-observer in one of the first adult literacy campaigns using the Freire method, he prefers to take a historical, rather than an ideological, approach to his subject. As he explains in the preface, the early chapters present the origins, evolution, ideas, and documentation relevant to education of adults and illiterates, especially in São Paulo state. Placed in the context of "traditional pedagogy," Brazilian educational thought, and the connections between adult education and development, this study poses, rather than answers, questions.

6223. *Boletim de Intercâmbio.* Serviço Social do Comercio, Depto. Nacional. No. 14, dez. 1971- . Rio.

Various selections collected and published in order to provide a clear understanding of the work of the various agencies and departments within SESC (Serviço Social do Comercio). The evolution of SESC's educational policy, including a description of its administration and its training center, precedes articles on various topics in education.

6224. *Boletim UEG.* Univ. do Estado da Guanabara. No. 73, maio 1972- . Rio.

This university bulletin, issued monthly, provides an editorial (the topic this month is "Culture, Museums, and Tourism"), a record of official correspondence and administrative actions, news notes, biographies of educational leaders, and an annotated bibliography.

6225. Borges, Kléber. Ação educativa para a saúde escolar. 2. ed. Rio, Secretaria de Saúde e Saneamento, 1971. 87 p., bibl., tables.

A guidebook for school personnel responsible for health services and a healthy school environment. Information is based on agencies, organizations, etc., in the state of Rio where this publication was produced by the Secretariat of Health and Sanitation. Information and suggestions are provided on weight, general health, disease control, sanitation, family services, and health education.

6226. Boschi, Renato Raul. O estudo pós-graduado no exterior: características por ramo de especialização. Rio, Fundação Getúlio Vargas. Instituto Brasileiro de Relações Internacionais. Escola Brasileira de Administração Pública (EBAP), 1971. 15 l., tables (Projeto retorno. Doc., 3)

Preliminary analysis of data collected as part of Project Return, a national research project designed to examine the impact of higher education study abroad. It reveals that: Social Sciences and Pure Sciences are the areas with the greatest number of completed doctorates; the implication drawn from this is that these two areas require a longer study period abroad; funding for sciences and technical studies has come largely from Brazilian, or national, sources while funding for the humanities and social sciences was generally from abroad. A brief, but informative report.

6227. Brazil. Ministério da Educação e Cultura. Melhoria do rendimento. Rio, 1971. 71 p.

A research project of INEP (Instituto Nacional de Estudos Pedagógicos), designed to investigate the causes for the high rate of failure between the 1st and 2nd years of primary school in Brazil. Factors reviewed included: changes in methods and resources, teacher expectations, revision of theories about maturity, reading readiness, and reading. Later research will examine teacher preparation, psychological and physical problems of learners, and other issues. A large portion of the report is devoted to reading, since reading problems are considered critical at this level. A carefully performed, reported, and edited effort that also provides statistical data.

6228. _____. _____. Comissão Nacional de Moral e Civismo. Educação moral e cívica: Decreto-Lei no. 869, de 12 de setembro de 1969; estrutura dos currículos; programas basicos; indicação no. 8/70 do CFE; professôres, suas condições. Pôrto Alegre, Bra., Univ. Federal do Rio Grande do Sul, Comissão Central de Publicações, 1970. 63 p. (Col. Documentos, 2)

Legislation pertaining to civic and moral education, including general curricular guidelines and qualifications of teachers responsible for this area of education.

6229. _____, _____. Conselho Federal de Educação. Departamento. de Documentação e Divulgação. Currículos mínimos dos cursos de nível superior. Brasília, 1974. 315 p.

A compilation of all of the Federal Education Council opinions, interpretations, and guidelines regarding basic requirements for higher education courses, according to Law No. 4024 and Law No. 5540. Contents include all material applicable to minimum requirements in effect as of Dec. 1973. As a help in interpreting these guidelines, the actual text of each Council opinion establishing a minimum is provided.

6230. _____. _____. Departamento de Ensino Fundamental. Aspectos do ensino de 1º grau: 1970-1973. Brasília? 1974. 67 p., plates, tables.

Brilliantly colored graphics illustrate this Ministry report on the state-of-the-art in primary education. Evidence of change, expansion, and reform is presented throughout, including increases in enrollment, number of schools, qualifications of personnel, and federal services to the states. Plans for implementation of Law No. 5.692, emphasizing sequential strategies to be applied, are briefly described and the various departments responsible for fundamental education are identified.

6231. _____. _____. Secretaria Geral. Sector plan for Education and Culture: 1972-1974. Brasília, 1971. 250 p., tables.

A clear, straightforward presentation of plans and priorities in education as identified and developed by the Ministry of Education in accordance with Law No. 9 of December 11, 1970. Described in detail, including budget, are the following: Operation School, Upgrading and Improvement of Teachers for Fundamental and Normal Schools, National Literacy Program, Construction of University Campuses, Administrative Reform, and Intensive Labor Program. A total of 33 projects comprise the Plan.

6232. _____. _____. _____. Serviço de Documentação. Estabelecimentos de ensino médio no Brasil: comercial e industrial; atualizados até 31-12-1969. Rio, 1970. 190 p. (Col. Educação e cultura, 14)

Compilation of commercial and industrial secondary schools as of Dec. 1969 which lists the name, location, legislation, and status of these schools throughout Brazil. Any researcher seeking information regarding the number of such schools in a given area or state would have to count the listings, particularly if interested in making comparisons. No information is provided on size, cost, size of staff, course of study, date of founding, or facilities. The list is geographical rather than alphabetical, beginning with schools in the north, moving south, and concluding in the interior, with Brasília.

6233. _____. Presidência. PBDCT: Basic Plan for Scientific and Technological Development: 1973/74. Rio, 1974. 158 p., tables.

A comprehensive statement of development goals at the national level in the areas of oceanography, nuclear energy, communications, industry, agriculture, social development, basic and graduate research, and education. Projects in education include: SACI (an advanced system of interdisciplinary communications), nucleus for research and development of educational technology (development of new instructional materials), Lobate Project (models for evaluation of educator/pupil communication via television), João da Silva Project (first grade instruction via TV for adult literacy programs) and project for evaluation of an educational radio system. In all areas, projects are identified, responsible groups or participants are listed, and objectives are stated. A glossary of acronyms is provided. The plan, described here in English, was delivered to the Medici government in 1973.

6234. _____. Serviço Nacional de Aprendizagem Comercial (SENAC). Relatório das atividades desenvolvidas em 1971. Curitiba, Bra.? Depto. Regional do Paraná, 1971. 118 1., tables.

The annual report of SENAC activities in Parana state, presented to the Regional Council in Curitiba. Photographs illustrate SENAC events; budgets and enrollments accompany program reports. Data is very specific and local, including lists of personnel, numbers of students completing various courses of study, reports on facilities and transfers to new locations.

6235. Brazil Universitário. Editôra Anais Científicos. Año 25, Nos. 78/79, junho 1970- . São Paulo.

This publication might serve as an easy source to consult for researchers interested in higher education, since it is published in Portuguese and English, with summaries of each article in both languages. Several photographs accompany each article, showing new buildings, student activities, administrators, and special events. Articles in this issue: "The Brazilian University: an Institution in Transition;" "The Basic Cycle: its Nature and Organizational Problems;" "University Archives: a Report on the 10th Meeting of University Rectors." All higher education institutions are listed, by state, in the back section, with information about their enrollments, composition, and administration.

6236. Cadernos de Pesquisa. Fundação Carlos Chagas, Depto. de Pesquisas Educacionais. Vol. 4, 1972- . São Paulo.

This issue (103 p.) includes two articles: 1) Bernadette Angelina Gatti; Guiomar Namo de Mello; and Nara Maria Guazzelli Bernardes "Algumas Consideraçoes sobre Treinamento do Pessoal de Ensino" concerns professional development of educators, which in this instance refers to inservice rather than preservice training, and to preparation for change and was prepared by the Dept. of Educational Research of the Carlos Chagas Foundation. 2) Philip H. Coombs "¿Que é Planejamento Educacional?" discusses effective educational planning and was originally published by UNESCO.

6237. Carneiro, David. Educaçao, universidade e história da primeira universidade do Brasil. Curitiba, Bra.? Univ. Federal do Paraná, 1971. 204 p., plates, tables.

Many quotes from Anísio Teixeira are scattered throughout this text, which gets around to the topic of the first Brazilian university about two-thirds through its 204 pages, after chapters on the evolution of education in the middle ages, the great education systems of the world, universities in the Americas, and a global description of Brazilian education. It may surprise some readers to learn that the first university was the Univ. of Paraná, rather than one of the old *faculdades* such as Recife. Carneiro identifies 1912-13 as the first year of the University, and proceeds to give a detailed account of its development.

6238. Carvalho, Guido Ivan de. Ensino superior: legislação e jurisprudência. 3. ed. Rio, The Author, 1971. 758 p., tables.

Third edition of a compendium of legislation on higher education in Brazil, updated to include material for the period 1969-71 and featuring opinions and jurisprudence from the Federal Education Council, a new index, legislative summaries, and a reorganization of the contents into four sections: organization of the university; instructional staff; student population; and financing.

6239. Carvalho, Irene Mello. O processo didático. Rio, Fundação Getúlio Vargas, Instituto de Documentação, Serviço de Publicações, 1972. 389 p., bibl., tables.

A comprehensive treatment of questions related to the changes taking place in education, as the emphasis shifts from content-centered instruction to individualized programs that focus upon the learner and upon interpersonal relationships. The author, a long-term staff member of the Getúlio Vargas Foundation, writes primarily for teachers and other educators, expressing a concern for a curriculum and methodology that provide for a more humanistic approach to education and a more creative role for the teacher. The bibliography includes some rather obscure sources, e.g., V.T. Thayer *The passing of the recitation,* D.C. Heath, 1928.

6240. Castro, Cláudio de Moura; Milton Pereira de Assis; and **Sandra Furtado Oliveira.** Ensino técnico: desempenho e custos. Rio, Instituto de Planejamento Econômico e Social (IPEA) [and] Instituto de Pesquisas (INPES), 1972. 328 p., tables (Col. Relatórios de pesquisa,10)

An effort to examine the instructional cost-effectiveness of technical education programs. The authors visited various representative programs in the states of São Paulo and Guanabara and included a study of the relationship between the expectations and economic backgrounds of students and the various kinds of technical education programs. One outcome claimed by the investigators is the establishment of benchmarks for each identified cost factor, such as the average cost of supplies per student or the relationship between the purchase cost and the maintenance cost of equipment. A liberal supply of tables accompanies the text and samples of the questionnaires used in the investigation are provided.

6241. Castro, Ormindo Viveiros de. Juventude e esperança (PUC/V, 16:63/64, dez. 1971, p. 231-252, tables)

Questionnaire study of 449 private secondary and university students in Brazil prepared for the IV Congress of Organization of Latin American Catholic Universities. Author concludes that students do have hope for the future of humanity, believe that man can shape his future, and are fairly religious. [G.C. Ruscoe]

6242. Cavalcanti, Jayme. O Brasil face ao desenvolvimento científico e tecnológico mundial (SBPC/CC, 25:10, oct. 1973, p. 940-945)

The author, director of the Fundação de Amparo a Pesquisa do Estado de São Paulo, reviews various opinions on the current status of world problems and developmental research, particularly in the areas of pollution, hunger, and use of natural resources. He notes the lack of a definite policy for science and scientific research in Britain and the US, as well as in Brazil, cites several English language publications dealing with ecology, environmental concerns, and questions of technology, and proceeds to describe the situation in São Paulo, particularly in relation to the Foundation's goals and programs, which are in the process of reevaluation and assessment.

6243. Cesarino Júnior, A.F. Reforma universitária: curso de graduação. São Paulo, Edição Saraiva, 1971. 142 p., bibl.

A specific reference source dealing with the interpretation of legislation regulating undergraduate courses and focusing on the Univ. of São Paulo's Law, Economics, and Administration faculties. Intended as an exegesis of *Portaria GR No. 1 380 of 1971*, this work includes some historical background in the form of single paragraph summaries of previous laws and reforms and commentaries on credit, curricula, transfers, evaluation, schedules, and supervision. A limited bibliography; a very functional index.

6244. Charbonneau, Paul-Eugène. Educar diálogo de gerações. São Paulo, Editôra Pedagógica e Universitária (EPU), 1973. 229 p., bibl.

Author of several books on Christian marriage, morality, and related subjects, Charbonneau devotes the major portion of this work to a consideration of parenting, the relationships between parents and children, and the problems associated with adolescents. He makes use of many literary sources, citing Kafka, Proust, Hesse, and Solzhenitsyn.

6245. _____. A escola moderna, uma experiência brasileira: o Colégio Santa Cruz. São Paulo, Editôra Pedagógica e Universitária (EPU), 1973. 217 p., plates, tables.

The history of the development of *Colégio Santa Cruz* is summarized very neatly by its director in the preface to this book, which then devotes the first 50 p. to a general discussion of education, the school, instruction, the system, and respect for the individual before taking up the theme of the *Colegio*. Established by Canadian priests who arrived in São Paulo in the early 1950s, the Colegio now has an extensive, modern campus and offers a full course of study at both primary and secondary levels.

6246. Collier, Maria Elisa Dias. Notas sôbre Gilberto Freyre (CFC/RBC, 3:7, jan./março 1971, p. 77-83)

Biographical information about the professor, writer and sociologist, which focuses on his intellectual innovations in the area of tropicalism and the psychosocial field, as revealed by an analysis of his various works. [BBE]

6247. Coloda, Santos Carlos and **Itamar Navildo Vian.** Cinema e TV no ensino. Pôrto Alegre, Bra., Livraria Sulina Editôra, 1972. 141 p., bibl., illus., plates (Col. Didática Sulina. Nivel superior)

Designed as a textbook, with questions at the end of each chapter, this work is intended for film and media students, as well as professors teaching communications courses. There is more emphasis on film than on television. In the chapter on the history of movies there is some interesting material on Brazilian films and the contemporary film industry in Brazil. Scenes from films illustrate the chapters dealing with technique.

6248. *Comunicações e Artes.* Univ. de São Paulo, Escola de Comunicações e Artes. No. 1, 1970- . São Paulo.

A publication that first appeared in 1970 as "a specialized publication from the School of Arts and Communication, with the objective of disseminating information, whether theoretical or professional, in the area of the arts and science of communication." This magazine supplants an earlier one and represents the new importance and role of the School of Arts and Communication at the Univ. of São Paulo. The format has been altered to permit articles by authors not associated directly with the School. Articles in this first issue include: "Public Relations in the Government," "Use of Audio-visual Techniques in the Teaching of Languages," and "The Media and the Youth Revolution."

6249. Conferência de Educadores do Distrito Federal, *III*, Brasília, 1968. Anais. Brasília, Conselho de Educação do Distrito Federal, 1972. 93 p.

Opening with a speech from the Minister of Education, Tarso Dutra, the III Education Conference for the Federal District met for three days in Dec. 1968. Primary objectives of the Conference were: to disseminate information about the federal government's social and economic development program, to discuss guidelines for an education plan to be implemented in the Federal District and to examine questions related to the primary school. Major participants included representatives from INEP, MEC, IPEA and from the Education Council of the Federal District.

6250. Congresso Nacional de Educação, XII, Rio, 1967. Educação para o desenvolvimento científico e tecnológico. Rio, Associação Brasileira de Educação, 1968. 83 p., plates, tables.

Publication of the Brazilian Education Association, source of information on Association activities and of articles on educational questions and problems. This issue is devoted to the XIII National Education Congress, sponsored by the Association, so all articles are based on themes and topics discussed at the Congress, held in Guanabara in 1968.

6251. Conjuntura Econômica. Ciência e tecnologia. Fundação Getúlio Vargas. Vol. 28, No. 1, janeiro 1974-   . Rio.

In July, 1973, the Brazilian government approved a Basic Plan for Scientific and Technological Development. In this number of the Getúlio Vargas Foundation magazine dealing with economics, various analysts discuss the major aspects of the plan, contributing articles on: the Plan itself, investments in technology, research on mineral resources, energy resources, ecology and pollution, physics research, and many more. Apart from the articles devoted to the Plan, regular features such as economic indexes, book reviews, the editor's report and the rate of exchange also appear in this issue.

6252. Costa, Maria do Carmo. O Exército e sua contribuição no campo da educação. Ponta Grossa, Bra., Univ. Estadual de Ponta Grossa, 1973. 66 p., bibl. (Cadernos universitários, 3)

"Without security, there is no development" states Costa in the first chapter of this study of the role of the army in education. Control of the economy becomes more efficient and the growth rate accelerates in proportion to the degree of government control of order and development. In terms of education, the Army fulfills an important role by providing moral as well as military instruction for citizens. This work was awarded first prize in a literary contest to honor Army Week, in 1972. The army as an educational agency, its importance in moral, civic, and professional education, and its contribution to "national integration" are the major themes presented.

6253. Criança e Escola. Centro Regional de Pesquisas Educacionais João Pinheiro. No. 24, n.d. Belo Horizonte, Bra.

Publication of the Minas Gerais regional research center, concerned with primary and normal school education. This issue is devoted to civic education, including questions of patriotism and the artistic and historical patrimony of Brazil. Regular features include an "in the classroom" section, a question and answer section, and book reviews.

6254. _____. _____. No.29, agosto/set. 1971-   . Belo Horizonte, Bra.

Articles on dramatization in the classroom, petroleum (natural sciences), audiovisual aids for the teacher and an interview with a member of the State Education Council on educational reform appear in this issue of the magazine published by the regional educational research center in Minas Gerais. Lesson plans, an advice column, cartoons, poems, and photographs of school events and personnel also appear.

6255. _____. _____. No. 33, junho/julho 1972-   . Belo Horizonte, Bra.

A sesquicentennial issue featuring articles about Dom Pedro I, first emperor of Brazil, the long road to Independence, national symbols, and origins of the bureaucratic state. An article on "the classroom without walls" compares a Brazilian experience in open classroom education with the open classroom concepts in practice in the US.

6256. Cunha, Luiz Antônio Constant Rodrigues da. Política educacional no Brasil: a profissionalização no ensino médio. Rio, Eldorado, 1973? 157 p., bibl., tables (Col. Meta)

Attempt to analyze the hidden agendas and policy implications of recent education legislation, beginning with the Law of Directives and Guidelines (passed in 1961) and considering the Law of Primary and Secondary Guidelines (passed in 1971). The author explains in early chapters how he intends to examine the ideological aspects of educational legislation and organization through an analysis of the secondary industrial school and its program, especially its explicit and implicit functions within the system.

6257. Documentário. Conselho Estadual de Educação. No. 16, abril/junho 1971-   . Pôrto Alegre, Bra.

Opinions of the State Council of Education, Rio Grande do Sul, covering the period April to June, 1971.

6258. Duarte, Sérgio Guerra. A reforma do ensino: todos os esclarecimentos necessários à perfeita interpretação e aplicação da Lei 5 692. Rio, Editôra Expressão e Cultura, 1972. 251 p., tables.

An unusual treatment of legislative interpretation, organized in a manner both practical and effective for the professional or the layman. There have been many analyses of education laws and reforms which discuss, in considerable detail, the implications and interpretations of the legislation itself. In this case, an extensive survey was conducted to identify the most frequent or persistent questions asked about Law 5692, pertaining to primary and secondary education as of August, 1971. These questions have been grouped according to subject and presented in a question and answer format.

Full text of the law appears in an appendix. Although there is no index, this looks like it would be a very useful reference book for administrators involved in the implementation of the reform.

6259. Dutra, Dilza Délia. Teatro é educação o teatro na escola: 1.º e 2.º graus. Florianópolis, Bra., Edições a Nação, 1972. 182 p., bibl., illus., plates.

Varied collection of suggestions, sources, and guidelines for theatre arts programs in elementary and secondary schools. The author comments on examples of instruction in folklore, public speaking, entertainment, and special events in local schools and provides background on the history of the theatre, technical information for school performances, and suggestions for material and projects. Everything from exercises to an interview with a leading Brazilian actress is included in this "source" book.

6260. *Ebsa.* Documentário de Ensino. Editôra do Brasil. Ano 25, Nos. 292/293, julho/agosto 1972-   . São Paulo.

A highly informative monthly bulletin containing a report on recent legislation and administrative actions at the federal level, followed by summaries of recent events, news reports from some states (in this number, Goiás, Guanabara, São Paulo, and Santa Catarina) and selected excerpts or commentaries from newspapers. The masthead identifies *Ebsa* as a publication for secondary level educators, but the content is relevant to all levels of education.

6261. *Educação.* Ministério da Educação e Cultura, Depto. de Apoio, Diretoria de Documentação e Divulgação. Ano 1, No. 1, abril/junho 1971-   . Brasília.

The first issue of *Educação,* in 1971, coincided with the passage of Law No. 5692 which provided for reforms in primary and secondary education. Minister of Education, Jarbas Passarinho, states in his preface that this publication will concentrate resources and effort in a few quality publications. The appearance of *Educação* suggests that it has had the benefit of substantial funding and skilled production. Articles include: "Industrial Design: the Impasse of Methodology," "Basic Education and the Use of Space," and "The National Observatory and Astronomy Research in Brazil."

6262. _____. _____, _____, _____. Ano 1, No. 3, out./dez. 1971- Brasília.

Summaries in English, Spanish, and French are provided in the back of this magazine, which publishes articles, photographs, and other material representative of the best that is happening in Brazilian education. The format continues to be luxurious, with good quality paper, excellent photographs, and occasional articles written by prominent educators. Topics discussed in this issue are: Music and Communication; the Univ. of Brasília (its present stage of development, etc.); Teaching the Gifted; and the Fourth Year of Secondary Education (written by Clovis Salgado, a former Minister of Education).

6263. *Educação e Cultura.* Camara dos Deputados, Comissão de Educação e Cultura. Ano 1, No. 2, 1971-   . Brasília.

A trimester publication of the Education and Culture Commission of the Chamber of Deputies, edited and published in Brasilia, offering a very eclectic collection of articles, poems, speeches, etc. Apart from contributions of senators and deputies, material includes selections from "prominent Brazilians" and articles on political parties, health in the Northeast, and constitutional questions. Biographies of each author/contributor precede their article or item.

La Educación. See item 6015.

6264. Encontro de Reitores de Universidades Públicas e Diretores dos Estabelecimentos Públicos Isolados de Ensino Superior, *II, Brasília, 1973.* Avaliação da reforma universitária no ambito de uma universidade: a Universidade Federal do Ceará. Brasília, Ministério da Educaçao e Cultura, Secretaria Geral/CODEAP, 1973. 77 p., map, tables.

A two-volume presentation of the Univ. of Ceará at the II meeting of University Presidents, containing a detailed description of the reforms, both structural and physical, that have been implemented at the university in conjunction with the University Reform Movement in Brazil. V. 2 contains all of the documents pertinent to the changes. A luxury edition with handsome graphics throughout.

6265. Fernandes, Florestan *comp.* Comunidade e sociedade no Brasil: leituras básicas de introdução ao estudo macrosociológico do Brasil. São Paulo, 1972. 587 p. (Biblioteca universitária, série 2. Ciências sociais, 37)

The fourth volume of a series on community and society written by both Brazilian and foreign specialists and intended to serve as an introduction to a macrosociological study of Brazilian communities. In the first part, called "Community," the topics are: the tribal village, the small community, the traditional city and the modern city. In the second part appear works dealing with tribal society, caste and class, and national problems. [BBE]

6266. Fernandes, Francisca Nolasco. Menina feia e amarelinha. Natal, Bra., Univ. Federal do Rio Grande do Norte, 1973. 152 p., illus.

Reminiscences of a girl from a small town in the interior of Rio Grande do Norte who became a teacher, school director, and prominent leader of society in the capital, Natal.

6267. Ferreira, Luis Pinto. A idéia da universidade e a recente reforma universitária alemã. Recife, Bra., Univ. Federal de Pernambuco, 1971. 68 p.

Observations on the origin and role of the university in society, with references to universities throughout the world, followed by a review of university structures in Italy, England, Germany, the US, Russia, and China. Statistics pertaining to each of these systems are presented in tables and sources for them are identified in the text, although there is no bibliography. In his discussion of university reform the author argues that the infrastructure of the university must be changed, foreign models should not be slavishly followed, and reforms should address themselves to the university's mission in a developing nation. The title of this work is misleading in that it devotes very little space to consideration of German university reforms.

6268. Fontoura, Amaral. A reforma do ensino: lei no. 5.692-de 11 de agosto de 1971. Rio, Editôra Aurora, 1972. 302 p., tables (Biblioteca Didática Brasileira. Série 4, Legislação brasileira de educação)

Fontoura, who is the author of numerous books, including several others dealing with education laws, presents an introduction to the Reform Law No. 5692 of 1971 which includes commentary on the previous reform law of 1961, a synopsis of Brazilian history, and a summary of the new concepts in the Law of 1971. He then proceeds to the complete text of Law No. 5692, accompanying each article with commentaries, explanations, or interpretations. An alphabetical index helps the reader locate specific articles or subjects.

6269. Freire, Paulo. Conciencia critica y liberación: pedagogía del oprimido. Bogotá, Ediciones Camilo, 1971. 237 p.

Published in Santiago, Chile, after three years of exile, this work is described by Freire as "an introductory essay, based on observations, on concrete situations, involving reactions from workers, peasants, and the middle class." Chapter topics include: Freire's "banking" theory of education, education as freedom for self-realization, and the rationale for a pedagogy of the oppressed. While this essay deals with Freire's philosophy, rather than his method, the emphasis on "praxis" and the importance of self-discovery, awareness, and actualization through language continues as a dominant theme.

6270. Fundação Educacional do Estado do Paraná, *Curitiba, Bra.* O ensino normal do Paraná e os recursos humanos para o desenvolvimento. Curitiba, Bra., 1971. 88 p., tables.

The enrollments in normal schools, the secondary level institutions that train primary school teachers in Brazil, increased remarkably in the period 1950-61 with the addition of 121 new schools, followed by an additional increase of 47 schools by 1968 when the enrollments were the highest of all secondary level schools. Nevertheless, the critical need for teachers continues, since the increase in schools has not followed any rational criteria and many of the normal school students do not enter teaching. In this report normal school education is examined in relation to the need for human resource development and for improved primary school education throughout Brazil.

6271. ———, ———, ———.Grupo

Assessor de Planejamento. Sugestão para estrutura curricular adaptada para 5ª série em 1972. Curitiba, Bra., 1972. 64 p.

Preliminary recommendations for curricular plans under the new legislation (Law No. 5692), prepared by educational experts in Paraná and intended to serve as curricular models for schools developing their own programs. Eight regional centers throughout the state will serve as pilot centers for implementation of reform programs. These guidelines and recommendations will be offered as a contribution to that implementation. Discussion of the law is followed by sections devoted to methodology, assessment, and lesson plans.

6272. Fundação Getúlio Vargas, *Rio.* **Serviço de Publicações.** In memoriam de Anísio Teixeira. Rio, Fundação IBGE, Serviço Gráfico, 1971. 48 p., plate.

Seven reminiscences by educators, historians, and colleagues of Anísio Teixeira, in which they comment on his outstanding contributions to Brazilian education and recount their own views of his role as a reformer and educational leader.

6273. Gomes, Felipe Tiago. Escolas da comunidade. 4. ed. rev. e atualizada. Bonsucesso, Bra., CNEC-Escritório Central de Compras, 1973. 191 p.

Episodic recounting of the history of the National Community Schools Movement, begun as the Free Secondary Schools for Poor Students in 1943. Novelist Rachel de Queiroz contributes a preface and Felipe Tiago Gomes, one of the four students who began the free school campaign, narrates their adventures in Rio. He describes how they tried to obtain support and official approval for the venture, the early responses to their efforts, and subsequent successes. An exceptionally humanistic history of an educational movement, full of personalities, issues, and revealing first-person accounts.

6274. Gomes Neto, J. Mobral. S.C. a expressão de um trabalho positivo (Boletim do Centro de Estudos e Pesquisas Educacionais [Fundação Educacional de Santa Catarina, Florianópolis, Bra.] 6:35, set. 1971, p. 2-16)

A study of the Mobral (literacy campaign) program in Santa Catarina state during the year 1970. Examined were: the philosophy, strategy, goals, administration, instructional materials used, courses offered, and human and financial resources invested. [BBE]

6275. Goodman, David E.; Julio F. Ferreira Sena; and **Roberto Cavalcanti de Albuquerque.** Os incentivos financeiros, a industrialização do Nordeste e a escolha de tecnologias (IPEA/PPE, 1:2, dez. 1971, p. 329-365, table)

A study prepared by the senior staff of IPEA/INPES (Instituto de Pesquisa Econômico-Social Aplicada and

Instituto Nacional de Pesquisas Espaciais) within the technical assistance program of the Ford Foundation. The study consists of four parts: 1) an analysis of the incentive mechanisms for the stimulation of new industrial activities; 2) a discussion of industrial policy; 3) an econometric exercise based upon data from projects initiated between 1962 and 1970, and 4) an inquiry based on the implications of industrialization policies derived from current activities.

6276. Gouveia, Aparecida Joly. O emprego público e o diploma de curso superior. São Paulo, Fundação Carlos Chagas, 1972. 31 p., bibl., tables (Série Pesquisas educacionais, 5)

When a national competition for public-government jobs was announced for 1970, researchers interested in examining the quality and quantity of university graduates who become candidates in such public competitions saw it as an opportunity to conduct their research based on a national sample. Findings suggest that even though university graduates find government employment a less desirable option than self-employment or private employment, there is always a large pool of candidates for those jobs. The author then asks whether or not there is an imbalance between the graduates leaving the universities and the job market they hope to enter.

6277. ———. Professôras de amanhã: um estudo de escolha ocupacional. 2. ed. rev. São Paulo, Livraria Pioneira Editôra, 1970. 157 p., bibl., tables (Biblioteca pioneira de ciências sociais. Educação)

One of Brazil's social scientists looks at occupational choices of women in a rapidly industrializing society, examining the influences, at home and in school, which shape those choices and the socializing process which determines values relevant to those choices. Gouveia's hypothesis, that women who choose teaching as a career are likely to have more traditional values, lends itself to analysis from various approaches, as she reveals in her chapter summaries. She concludes with additional questions to be investigated, suggesting that some comparative studies need to be made.

6278. Gouveia Neto, Hermano. Anísio Teixeira: educador singular. São Paulo, Companhia Editôra Nacional, 1973. 150 p.

A *bahiano* writes about a revered Bahian educator — Anísio Teixeira. Gouveia, a specialist in educational administration who knew Anísio Teixeira when they both were active in Bahian education, has carefully studied Teixeira's work and all of his writings as preliminary to the preparation of this book. In his introduction he declares that his purpose here is to: "explore his (Teixeira's) ideas, understand his work, and examine the opinions of his contemporaries about it" so that this work will be a "contribution to the studies of Teixeira's work and life." Here, then, is the story of Teixeira's life and career, 70 years dedicated to education, as Secretary of Education for Bahia, Director of INEP, founder of the Escola Parque, Rector of the Univ. of Brasília, philosopher, reformer, administrator, and author.

6279. Guanabara (state), *Bra*. **Comissão Estadual de Currículo.** Subsídios para a elaboração dos currículos plenos dos estabelecimentos oficiais de ensino de 1° grau. Rio, Edições Bloch, 1973. 301 p., bibl., tables.

A document intended to be a basic orientation to primary schools introducing new curricula at the primary level. A very specific, pragmatic presentation of the various areas, including general objectives, organization of the curriculum for activities, reading and writing, social studies, Portuguese, art, physical education, and music. An extremely large group of educators contributed to each area (26 on communication and expression, for example) under the direction of a coordinator.

6280. Guimarães, Antônio Barreto. Nos caminhos da educação. Recife, Bra., Companhia Editôra de Pernambuco, 1973. 94 p., plate.

On the 25th anniversary of the founding of the Social Welfare Service of Olinda and its five local schools, Barreto Guimarães, Vice-Governor, Professor, and former director of GERAN (Grupo Especial para Racionalização da Agroindústria Canavieira do Nordeste, Recife), collected these lectures and speeches as a commemoration for the occasion. The first two date from 1967, the others are based on speeches delivered since 1971. The final selection (dated April, 1973, on the topic Concepts of Administration) contains some interesting information on community development, government projects, and industrialization in Pernambuco and the Northeast.

6281. Guimarães, Archimedes Pereira. Escola Politécnica da Bahia. n.p., n.p., 1972. 386 p.

A very detailed history of the Polytechnic School of Bahia, beginning with an account of its organization and founding, in 1897, and devoting a chapter to each year of its existence, up to 1947. There is a brief biography of the author, who has written many other histories and articles about chemistry, but who apparently specializes in writing about polytechnic schools.

6282. Hamburger, Ernest W. O exame vestibular e os desajustes do sistema de ensino (Educação Hoje [Brasiliense Sociedade, São Paulo] 13, jan./fev. 1971, p. 3-14)

Considering the purpose of the entrance exam (exame vestibular), the author calls attention to its limitations when it provokes a proliferation of preparatory courses which do not improve the level of secondary education. It results in the selection of candidates according to socioeconomic rather than academic qualifications and it develops a plan of study based on only the test results. [BBE]

6283. Hans, Nicholas. Educação comparada. Tradução de José Severo de Camargo Pereira. 2. ed. São Paulo,

Editôra Nacional, 1971. 478 p. (Atualidades pedogógicas, 79)

Contains two special chapters for the Brazilian edition, one written by the author on Latin American education; the other, by Anísio Teixeira, on education in Brazil. [BBE]

6284. Inforzato, Hélio. Fundamentos sociais da educação: sociologia geral; sociologia aplicada à educação; análise dos problemas brasileiros. São Paulo, Livraria Nobel, 1972. 208 p.

Brazilian problems, and the role of education in solving them, constitute the major theme of this textbook, intended for secondary students interested in a teaching career. The first section of the book presents an introduction to sociology and behavior; the second, the sociology of education and the role of education in a developing nation; and the third or final section, education in Brazil, where the imperatives of development and industrialization are calling attention to the anachronistic nature of the educational system.

6285. Lago, Benjamin do. Comunicação, educaçao e desenvolvimento. 2. ed. Rio, Edições Gernasa, 1971. 116 p.

A new edition of a work originally published in 1969, and titled *Radio and development,* in which the author presents his suggestions for future programs in media education. In his plan for a National Radio Center he includes a training campaign for media personnel, an industrial training campaign, and a campaign to educate the rural worker. The appendices include assorted newspaper articles and speeches, one of which, "Popular Education," presents a description of the Univ. of the Air, begun in 1947 in São Paulo. There is a chronological list of all legislation pertaining to radio.

6286. Lapassade, Georges. Um ensaio de análise da linguagem institucional (VOZES, 65:5, junho/julho 1971, p. 357-365)

Pragmatic, succinct explanation of the "institutional balance" method of analysis applied to an educational institution. Lapassade uses his experience as an analyst and consultant to the Univ. of Quebec (over a three-month period) as a case study to illustrate how stresses, priorities, and problems can be identified by his method. While he finds some differences between responses from Canadian and French settings, he makes his points clearly and effectively.

6287. Lima, João Franzen de. Sociedade Pestalozzi de Minas Gerais. Belo Horizonte, Bra., Imprensa Oficial, 1972. 29 p.

The Pestalozzi Society of Minas Gerais maintains the *Fazenda do Rosario* outside of the city of Belo Horizonte, for the care and education of exceptional or handicapped children. The author, as president of the Society, reports on the history, activities, budget, and future plans of the Society and the institution it supports.

6288. Lima, Lauro de Oliveira. Escola no futuro: orientação para os professores de prática de ensino. 2. ed. rev. e aumentada. Rio. Livraria José Olympio Editôra, 1974. 285 p.

A proponent of Piagetian thought as applied to learning, the author here presents material first disseminated over 15 years ago, before the national reform law of 1961, and now reissued as still pertinent to schools, learning, and the future of education. As the leader of a reform gróup in Ceará that offered workshops and study circles for teacher-educators interested in the psychogenetic approach and in new ideas, the author trained large numbers of teachers and established an extensive network of teacher trainers throughout Brazil in 1964. Advocating greater attention to the young child, he argues that the school of the future will be more complex, more systematic, more scientific, and more sophisticated.

6289. _____. Estórias da educação no Brazil: de Pombal a Passarinho. Brasília, Editôra Brasília, 1974. 273 p. (Col. Pedagogia)

An original work in which the author provides a panoramic view of what was, is, and has been planned for in Brazilian education, including analyses of the motivations, attitudes, cultural, political, and economic goals, and historical roots of current educational reforms, principally the Law No. 5692 of 1971 which he calls "perhaps the most radical and detailed educational reform ever attempted." In style, Oliveira Lima has permitted himself a freewheeling attack that is irreverent, audacious, thorough, and frank about his own biases and contradictions. Here are all of the projects, programs, reforms, issues, and personalities (from Pombal to Passarinho) on parade.

6290. Lôbo, Francisco Bruno. O ensino da medicina no Rio de Janeiro. v. 4. Riõ, Conselho Federal de Cultura, 1969. 331 p., tables.

Fourth in a series (for previous vols., see *HLAS 33:4808* and *HLAS 31:4374*), this study is dedicated to the preservation of ephemeral materials dealing with the history of the School of Medicine in Rio. Published with assistance from the Federal Council on Culture, this vol. covers the period 1858-61 and provides excellent examples of the detailed legislation characteristic of programs of instruction in Brazil. The careful reader will glean such information as the cost of a porter's salary, the rent, laboratory supplies, and incidental expenses in 1859 and a note stating that the Emperor attended all oral examinations in 1858.

6291. Lodi, Nilce Aparecida e Goes and **Ivoni dos Santos Goes.** O estudante de pedagogia (Boletim Sapere Aude [Faculdade de Filosofia, Ciências e Letras de São José do Rio Prêto, Depto. de Pedagogia, Bra.] 6, 1972, p. 1-21)

Research conducted Aug. 1970 at the Faculdade de Filosofia, Ciências e Letras in São José do Rio Prêto, based on a 56-item questionnaire (administered to 148 students) and 140 replies. Objective of the research was to study the general characteristics of education students, including their social and geographical background and the reasons they chose to study education. Conclusions: over 60 percent picked their course of study for personal reasons or in response to the pressure to get a college education. They do not enter the job market as teachers, however, but go on to postgraduate study. [BBE]

6292. _____ and Maria da Graça Nicoletti. A importância das profissões no julgamento de crianças de Bady Bassit (Revista do Curso de Pedagogia [Faculdade de Filosofia, Ciências e Letras, São José do Rio Prêto, Bra.] 6, 1970, p. 77-85)

A questionnaire about occupations was administered to 85 students between the ages of eight and 15 at the Bady Bassit School in São Paulo. Boys chose the professions of doctor, professor, administrator, engineer, or mechanic; girls favored teaching and administration. No social values were attributed to any of the occupations in this survey. [BBE]

6293. Lourenço Filho, M.B. Maturação e aprendizagem da leitura e da escrita (Arquivos Brasileiros da Psicologia Aplicada [Fundação Getúlio Vargas, Rio] 23:3, julho/set. 1971, p. 55-61)

Based on observation of the lack of correlation between chronological age and reading ability, the author presents the hypothesis that other factors may justify or explain the individual's failure to learn to read. He identifies these factors under the global term of "maturity" and attempts to diagnose the various levels and aspects vital to the learning of reading. Lourenço Filho develops the ABC test, which includes visual memorization, sensorimotor coordination, vocabulary, general comprehension, focus of attention, and resistance to fatigue. Test results verify early impressions and observations, and suggest the need for diversified groupings in classes. [BBE]

6294. _____. Orientação em un país latinoamericano em rápida industrialização: Brasil (Arquivos Brasileiros de Psicologia Aplicada [Fundação Getúlio Vargas, Rio] 23:3, julho/set. 1971. p. 63-78)

Industrial progress in Brazil during the decade of the 1950s motivated the population to search for social and economic progress, leading to new directions in education by the Church and the State, in psychology, and in the techniques of educational and vocational counselling. Because of the diversity of occupations and the need for better assessment of aptitudes leading to greater productivity and personal satisfaction, SENAI and SENAC initiated investigations of the development of skilled labor, including the educational aspects. The influence of technology in increasing the productivity of labor and of material goods has weakened the sense of continuity, requiring that the public's faith in the new counselling methods be reinforced. [BBE]

6295. _____. A psicologia no Brasil (Arquivos Brasileiros de Psicologia Aplicada [Fundação Getúlio Vargas, Rio] 23:3, julho/set. 1971, p. 113-142)

Panoramic historical overview of the contributions of outside specialists (e.g., doctors, educators, engineers, administrators, priests, and Catholic leaders) to educational psychology and its evolution in Brazil. According to recent publications in the field, there is much emphasis on research now.

6296. Maranhão (state), *Bra.* **Escola de Administração do Estado do Maranhão. Centro de Pesquisas.** Pesquisa sôbre ocupação nível de renda e nível de auto-identificação dos alunos da Escola de Administração, São Luís, Bra., 1973. 1 v. (Various pagings) tables (Caderno de pesquisa, 1)

The first research conducted and completed by the School of Administration of Maranhão, this monograph presents the results of an effort to identify the needs of students in the School, so that the program might be adjusted to provide better preparation for specialists in administration. As the only institution in Maranhão offering such training, the School is attempting to satisfy the demand throughout the state for trained specialists and has organized a research program to help define policy for the future. This study focuses on the occupation, income level, and image of administration majors.

6297. Martins, Joel. Objectivos e estrutura de um curso de pos-graduação para pesquisadores educacionais (SBPC/CC, 23:6, dez. 1971, p. 741-746)

Martins devotes two-thirds of his article to a discussion of what educational research should be, before finally getting around to his topic — how to prepare educational researchers. Includes sections on: problems in educational research; the current situation in educational research; educational research: possible models; practical research and theoretical research; methods of testing hypotheses; and educational research methods (he lists three). Last section discusses training researchers.

6298. Mejias, Nilce Pinheiro. Modificação de comportamento em situação escolar. São Paulo, Editôra Pedagógica e Universitária [and] Univ. de São Paulo, 1973. 163 p., bibl., tables.

The author, a school psychologist, presents examples of behavior modification in a Brazilian school and describes her role as a trainer of teachers in behavior modification techniques.

6299. *Mensagem Pedagógica.* Secretaria da Educação, Plano Nacional de Educação. Ano 5, No. 6, 1971- Florianópolis, Bra.

A publication of the Secretariat of Education in Santa Catarina with a glossy magazine format and a wide variety of topics related to all levels of instruction, including adult education, bilingual education, and media education. The complete text of Law No. 5692, revising primary and secondary education, appears in this issue.

6300. Micotti, Maria Cecília de Oliveira.

A escola primária e o problema de formação de professores (Educação Hoje [Brasiliense Sociedade, São Paulo] 13, jan./fev. 1971, p. 94-104)

According to research conducted in Paraíba, São Paulo, and Guanabara, common problems of recently-graduated primary school teachers in those states include: methodology, school-community relations, and evaluation of their own work. Results suggest that normal schools are in need of reorganization in order to meet the needs of teachers teaching today. [BBE]

6301. **Minicucci, Agostinho.** Dinámica de grupo escola. 2. ed. rev. Prefácio de Lourenço Filho. São Paulo, Edições Melhoramento, 1971. 238 p., illus., tables (Biblioteca de educação. Série iniciação e debate)

Beginning with discussion of the dynamics between teacher and students and examining classroom communication, the author then presents three chapters on sociograms and sociometric study techniques, followed by several chapters dealing with the practical application of these techniques in the classroom. Much of his concern emphasizes the importance of group dynamics in education at all levels. There is a generous supply of illustrations. Professor Lourenço Filho's preface on human relations in education dates from 1969.

6302. **Moser, Alvino.** Educação e manifestaçao do homem. São Paulo, Editôra Juriscrédi, 1972. 128 p., bibl.

Condensed versions of lectures presented at the Univ. da Associação de Ensino de Riberão Prêto, to students and faculty of the Education Faculty in 1971. A subjective group of selections, based not on comparison of philosophies of education, but on personal reflection of the author. Chapter topics are: the concept of education throughout history, values, man's destiny, aesthetic education, and the possibility or necessity of education.

6303. **Mosquera, Juan José Mouriño.** Educação: novas perspectivas. Pôrto Alegre, Bra., Livraria Sulina Editôra, 1974. 114 p., bibl. (Col. Universitária)

In a book dedicated to his students in Introductory Education classes, the author presents chapters on: education as scientific reality: models, structures, paradigms; educational planning and community needs; development, economics, and education; theories of education; cybernetics in education; schooling or deschooling; and education of adults. Bibliographies follow each chapter. Among sources cited are: Peter Drucker, Ivan Illich, Everett Reimer, Gordon Lippitt, Amitai Etzioni, and Talcott Parsons.

6304. _____. Psicologia social do ensino. Pôrto Alegre, Bra., Livraria Sulina Editôra, 1973. 169 p., bibl. (Col. Universitária)

Chapters on different topics (antecedents of juvenile delinquency, classroom interaction, the individual and the group, teaching from the perspective of Carl Rogers, operant conditioning, etc.) written by a group of professors who organized an Educational Psychology course for the X Seminar of Professors of Psychology in Rio Grande do Sul state, held in 1972. Authors are: Mosquera, Rovilio Costa, Sonia Azambuja Fonseca, Maria de Lourdes Regis Hailliot, Noeli Reck Maggi, Bruno Edgar Ries, Sonia Pereira dos Santos, Themis Drugg Eifler Ermida, and Fernando Becker. The editor states that their purpose was to review a series or cluster of problems that all teachers must take into consideration when teaching.

6305. _____. O que é um professor? Aspectos psicológicos da profissão (PUC/V, 16:63/64, dez. 1971, p. 215-223)

A rhetorical essay that rambles among the multiple generalities applied to the immense area of learning, teaching, and education and concludes that "it is not easy to arrive at specific points regarding professors (teachers) because one has to consider the entire range of thought and environment as basic elements in the dynamic process of teaching and learning." No bibliography.

6306. Le mouvement éducatif dans 75 pays: rapports nationaux (UNESCO/AIE, 31, 1969, p. 15-18; 54-55; 75-77; 112-113; 118; 161-163; 172-173)

This compilation of reports on education from many countries includes the one by Brazil's Minister of Education for 1970. It emphasizes the following: the importance of educational reforms, a focus on manpower and human resource development, substantive changes in secondary education (particularly with the establishment of *ginasios polyvalentes*), full time faculty for universities, and plans to modify the educational system so that it will be more responsive to national needs and interests.

6307. **Nérici, Imídeo Giuseppe.** Educação e maturidade. São Paulo, Editôra Atlas, 1973. 167 p., bibl.

Nérici has published a number of books in the area of counselling, family relationships, and instructional methods. He divides this one into four main topics: parent expectations, maturity and immaturity, causes of failure in school, and study habits. He concludes with a list of suggestions for the student. For another example of Nérici's work, see item 6309.

6308. _____. Ensino renovado e fundamental. 2. ed. São Paulo, Livraria Nobel, 1972. 188 p., tables.

Beginning with questions like: Why education? Nérici moves on to discuss why educational reforms are needed, devotes at least half of this book to a description of the philosophy and methodology of basic, revised education, and then undertakes a detailed description of primary education as modified by Law 5692 of 1971. Legislation pertaining to the reforms discussed appears in the appendix.

6309. _____. Lar, escola e educação. 3. ed. São Paulo, Editôra Atlas, 1972. 224 p., bibl.

This is the second Nérici book concerned with the importance of cooperation between home and school. The author is a psychologist who has taught extension courses at various universities. He favors an education that takes into consideration the moral and civic roles of citizens, that permits the full realization of each individual's potential, and that encourages involvement and participation. Chapter topics are: friendship and love, marriage, the home, education in the home and in the school. In the section on the home he discusses styles of parenting and the need for economic, social, moral, political, and sexual education. His views on guidelines for the latter are quite conservative by today's standards.

6310. Niskier, Arnaldo. Administração escolar para estudantes de faculdades de filosofia, ciências e letras, faculdades de educação, institutos de educação e escolas em geral. 4. ed. Pôrto Alegre, Edições Tabajara, 1972. 260 p., illus., plates (Col. Normalista, 3)

Fourth edition of a work first published in 1969, brought up-to-date with the addition of the text of the Reform Law of Primary and Secondary Education (passed in 1971) and legislation pertaining to Prontel (Programa Nacional de Teleducação) and Premen (Programa de Expansão e Melhoria do Ensino). Topics presented range from a description of PERT and the critical path method to the school of tomorrow.

6311. Nóbrega, Vandick L. da. Ensino planificado e educação comparada. Rio, Livraria Freitas Bastos, 1974. 398 p., bibl., tables.

Motivated by a desire to reinforce Brazilian patriotism and resistance to communism and to transmit to educators some of the information he gained on a study tour to Germany, Denmark, Sweden, and Spain, the author presents this work on the 10th anniversary of "A New Brazil," as a commemoration of the anniversary of the Revolution of 1964. Chapter topics are: education and the National Army; the ivory tower, schools are alive in Brazil: example, Mobral; and in the second half — university education in the Communist world, education in Denmark, and education in Spain.

6312. Novaes, Paulo. Tecnología e recursos humanos. Rio, Editôra Renes, 1972. 145 p., tables (Série problemas brasileiros)

Part of a series on Brazilian problems published by the Social Science Center at the Catholic Univ. in Rio (PUC) and written by a veteran educator, an engineer who has been chief of SENAI (Industrial Apprenticeship Programs) since 1942 and who participated in planning programs in Human Resources Development during the 1960s. Since the author alleges the impossibility of identifying the exact origin of the ideas he discusses and states that he has based this work on his own experience and study over the course of many years, there is no bibliography, and no footnotes are provided. After a chapter on What is Technology? ("a little history," "viability of technologies," other subheadings) the author explores questions of technology in relation to culture and society, the impact of technology on policy, and the relationship between technology and planning. Novaes writes from a general, rather than a Brazilian, point of view and therefore does not provide examples from his 43 years of experience with various Brazilian agencies and institutions.

6313. Oliven, Ruben George. Educação e sociedade moderna: funções da educação no contexto urbano. Pôrto Alegre, Bra., Edições URGS, Univ. Federal do Rio Grande do Sul, 1972. 72 p., bibl. (Lançamentos de 72)

As a specialist in urban planning, Oliven is interested in information systems, urban environments, and sociocultural integration. His style is forthright, his bibliography is interdisciplinary, and he provides two or three pages on the following topics: the city as an information system, apprenticeship and culture, rational and irrational conduct (behavior), motivation, the concept and role of education, information and education, and the functions of education in the urban environment. His view of the role of education in urban environments is that education, in modern cities, should enable citizens to adjust to constant change and to survive in an urban environment. He says: "more and more, education is provided by the city, rather than by the school," because the city bombards us constantly with a vast quantity of information. Much of his argument is the familiar one stressing the impact of television and urban pressures on modern life and the need to teach the individual to learn and absorb information, rather than to convey facts that are soon out-of-date or obsolete.

6314. O'Neil, Charles. Problems of innovation in higher education: the University of Brasília, 1961-1964 (UM/JIAS, 15:4, Nov. 1973, p. 415-431, bibl.)

A brief look at the background and personalities that contributed to the development and structure of the Univ. of Brasília. O'Neil begins by describing the preceding history of the INEP group of educational leaders and reformers, especially Anísio Teixeira. He then proceeds to summarize their complaints about the educational system and finally discusses the development, legal structure, and eventual collapse of the Univ.

6315. Otão, José. A ação da universidade no desenvolvimento de sua área geoeducacional (PUC/V, 16:62, junho 1971, p. 87-92)

A presentation of the Rector of the Catholic Univ. of Rio Grande do Sul state to the IV Meeting of GULERPE (Latin American University Group for the Study of Reforms and Improvement of Education). His conclusions: that a University that aspires to promote the development of its region must a) develop human resources, b) conduct research designed to identify and develop natural resources for that region, and c) create task forces capable of applying planning techniques to regional needs.

6316. Pacini, Dante. Estudo brasileiro de política e educação: filosofia e ciência; filosofia das ciências sociais e a importância da ciência política como estrutura-primeira neste contexto. Rio, Livraria São José, 1974. 165 p., bibl.

The author, a lawyer and criminologist, presents a book of criticism and "debate" on issues in which sociology, law, philosophy, economics, pedagogy and psychology are all interrelated. Citing everyone from Adler to Weber, his chapters refer to such topics as: the personal infrastructure of the government, problems of future society, classicism and humanism, the relationship between the social sciences and politics, and education as a political idea.

6317. Paiva, Vanilda Pereira. Educação popular e educação de adultos: contribuição à história da educação brasileira. São Paulo, Edições Loyola, 1973. 368 p., bibl. (Instituto Brasileiro de Desenvolvimento [IBRADES]. Temas brasileiros, 2)

A descriptive history of adult and mass education movements in Brazil, based on two hypotheses: 1) that the promotion of "popular" education movements has always been related to attempts to manipulate political power, and 2) that until World War II adult education was always viewed as a part of mass, popular education, after which it became an area of special concern because of its political implications. The author begins with the colonial period, but emphasizes events since 1930.

6318. Palermo, Alfredo. Estudo de problemas brasileiros: educação moral e cívica; nível superior e organização política e social. 2. ed. rev. e ampliada. São Paulo, LISA-Livros Irradiantes, 1972. 329 p., bibl.

When Law No. 869/69 established moral and civic education as a required course of study at all levels, the Federal Education Council presented a course of study called "Study of Brazilian Problems" to be given at the higher education level. This text, which preceded the official course of study, contains chapters on the political, economic, military, technical-scientific, and psychosocial aspects of modern Brazil. Some areas discussed: know-how for development, modern warfare, national resources, political parties, and health.

6319. Parahym, Orlando da Cunha. Escola, alimentação e saúde. Recife, Bra., Govêrno do Estado de Pernambuco, Secretaria de Estado de Educação e Cultura, Depto. de Cultura, 1969. 59 p., bibl., tables.

The author has been concerned with problems of nutrition, especially in the Northeast, since the 1930s. A long-time resident of the interior of Pernambuco, he writes from first-hand experience and observation. This essay therefore benefits from his wealth of information as a specialist in public health and nutrition for over 30 years. Chapters include: Nutrition and Mental Efficiency, Malnutrition and Military Service, and School, Nutrition Education, and Sanitation.

6320. Pastore, José. O ensino superior em São Paulo: aspectos quantitativos e qualitativos de sua expansão. São Paulo, Companhia Editôra Nacional, Instituto de Pesquisas Econômicas, 1972. 221 p., tables (Série IPE-USP, 3)

The first of two volumes, this study is based on research completed in 1968-69 and sponsored by the Economic Research Institute. Approximately 150 administrators and 7,300 students were contacted in 1969, and a sample of the questionnaire used and the statistical data gathered appear in appendices. The Federal and State Education Councils and the Secretariat of Education also supported the research. A rich and concentrated source of data for those interested in higher education, but not to be assumed representative of the situation in other areas of Brazil.

6321. Patto, Maria Helena Souza. Privação cultural e educação pré-primária. Rio, Livraria José Olympio Editôra, 1973. 110 p., bibl. (Col. Psicologia contemporânea)

Beginning with the basic propositions regarding predetermination and general discussion of the characteristics of the culturally deprived child, the author then presents examples of preschool programs such as Headstart, the Peabody Project (and Montessori as a suitable strategy) and compensatory programs. She is strongly influenced by models from the US and her own experience in the US. Readers interested in preschool programs and in some very basic statistics on Brazilian school programs will want to consult the introduction and the too-brief "Panorama da Educação Pre-Escolar Brasileira" (p. 89-90).

6322. Paula, Jardel Barcellos do and others. Diagnóstico do setor educação no Distrito Federal. Brasília, Govêrno do Distrito Federal, Secretaria do Govêrno, Companhia do Desenvolvimento do Planalto Central (CODEPLAN), 1970. 383 p., tables.

A detailed and thorough compilation of educational statistics prepared by a group of economists for CODEPLAN (Development Organization for the Central Planalto) and covering all aspects of the education system of the Federal District (Brasília). Information on buildings, services, personnel, enrollments, and funding for primary and secondary schools is presented in narrative and tabular formats. Potentially useful reference for those seeking specific information on the system's capacity, the present level of statistical analysis or a comparison with other systems or areas.

6323. Pereira, Maria Lúcia da Cruz and others. Condições de trabalho no campo da psicologia aplicada (Boletim do Centro de Psicologia Aplicada [Centro Educacional e de Pesquisa Aplicada, Rio] 3, set. 1971, p. 9-14)

A survey of 46 institutions including schools, industries, clinics, and others, offering counseling services. Administrators of these agencies and institutions were interviewed, using a questionnaire. Results include statistics on the number of professional employees, facilities, etc. [BBE]

6324. Pereira, Sylvia L. de Melo. O cinema na escola (Educação Hoje [Braziliense Sociedade, São Paulo] 13, jan./fev. 1971, p. 46-52)

Analysis of the film as a course of culture, artistic expression, and communication of social values, including its influence on the adolescent. Examines the role of the school in encouraging a media education, supporting film clubs, and developing personal judgment and sensibility of individual students. [BBE]

6325. Perracini, Aldo. A escola renovada: 10 anos de realizações na renovação do ensino. Pôrto Alegre, Bra., Edições Tabajara, 1972. 173 p.

Perracini attributes the experimental classes begun in Brazil to one source, the Centro Internacional de Estudos Pedagógicos of the Liceu de Sèvres, in France, because he established the first private *Ginásio Renovado* in São Paulo, based on the active learning approach of Sèvres. In this book he presents his entire program, including courses of study, integrated lesson plans, methods of evaluation, resources to be employed, and administrative options.

6326. Pinheiro, Lúcia Marques and Maria do Carmo Marques Pinheiro. Planejamento do Instituto de Educação de Vitória. Preparado para a Secretaria de Educação do Estado do Espírito Santo. Rio, n.p., 1970. 193 p. (mimeo)

Describes the organization of the Institute which is designed to facilitate the progress of normal and primary schools through the specialized training and staff development of teachers, counselors, librarians and administrators and through the maintenance of centers and experimental schools. [BBE]

6327. Pires, Nise. Educação especial em foco. Rio, Ministério da Educação e Cultura, Instituto Nacional de Estudos e Pesquisas Educacionais, Centro Brasileiro de Pesquisas Educacionais, 1974. 162 p., bibl., illus., tables.

Report of the Task Force charged with the responsibility for developing guidelines and strategies for the implementation of special education programs. One outcome of the Task Force's work during 1972-73 is the establishment of a National Center for Special Education, designed to improve the education of the handicapped, the exceptional, the gifted, and the deficient. A comprehensive report, this book provides chapters dealing with the needs of the various special groups, identifying priorities, suggesting strategies, and providing guidelines for projects. UNESCO and USAID experts have contributed monographs to this work.

6328. Pletsch, Protásio. Formação profissional do professores de ciências e de letras para a região da fronteira oeste do Rio Grande do Sul. Pôrto Alegre, Bra., Pontifícia Univ. Católica do Rio Grande do Sul, Faculdade de Filosofia, Ciências e Letras de Uruguaiana, 1973? 51 p., bibl., tables.

A modest survey, covering 37 secondary schools, based on a questionnaire that identified minimal information about the teaching staff (name, subject taught, level taught, education). Objective of the survey was to describe the actual situation in the western frontier area of Rio Grande do Sul in terms of the number of qualified secondary teachers available, their distribution among levels, locations, and subject, and the areas of greatest need.

6329. Pontifícia Universidade Católica do Rio Grande do Sul, *Pôrto Alegre, Bra.* 40 [i.e., Quarenta] anos a serviço da cultura: 1931-1971. Pôrto Alegre, Bra., 1971. 119 p., plates.

In 1971 the Catholic Univ. of Rio Grande do Sul completed 40 years of service, a record commemorated in this account of those years, which includes photographs of the founders and of previously used sites.

6330. ———— ————, ————. 25 [i.e., Vinte e cinco] anos de universidade: 1948-1973. Pôrto Alegre, Bra., 1973. 224 p., plates.

Following two years after a very similar publication, which commemorated 40 years of the University's life (see item 6329), this version, covering the period 1948-73 refers to the years after the University was formally organized as such, in 1948. Everything is reported in loving detail, including honorary degrees conferred, university publications, and descriptions of departments, activities, and institutes.

6331. Poppovic, Ana Maria. Alfabetização: um problema interdisciplinar (Cadernos de Pesquisa [Fundação Carlos Chagas, São Paulo] 2, 1971, p. 1-47)

Research objectives: establish a chronological age for the introduction of literacy; clarify which factor(s) is most important for the literacy process — intelligence or maturity. Methodology: two groups, an experimental and a control, were selected in a preschool course, after verification of level of intelligence by the INV test and level of maturity by the Metropolitan Readiness Test. These groups were divided into two classes each with three subgroups (based on intelligence) under the direction of trained teachers. Three tests were administered throughout the year. Conclusions: a) six-year-old children with sufficient maturity can be taught to read, and b) the selection should be made on the basis of the level of maturity in functions basic to literacy. Children should then be placed in classes according to their intelligence level. [BBE]

6332. O problema da educação no Estado do Rio Grande do Norte: proposta de sua adequação a fim de transformá-la em efetivo instrumento do desenvolvimento regional. Natal, Bra., Imprensa Universitária, 1972. 21 p., bibl.

A capsule picture of the major educational problems confronting a northeast state, but also representative of the kinds of problems still awaiting solution throughout Brazil, i.e., scarcity of space, funds, and resources, lack of professionally qualified teachers, high dropout rate, high percentage of students retained in each grade, and an extremely high percentage of the school-age population not enrolled in school. Statistics from 1969 forward on the educational level of teachers, the percentage of truancy or retention, the distribution of enrollments among municipal, state, federal, and private schools, and the use of space are revealing in relation to the problems identified.

6333. Proença Filho, Domício. Língua portuguesa, literatura nacional e a reforma do ensino. Rio, Editôra Liceu, 1973. 127 p., bibl.

Among the several reforms legislated since 1960, Law 5692 has prompted the renovation of curricula in many areas, including language. In this book the reader will find a discussion of language and literature as communication and expression, and an examination of linguistic standards, oral and written expression, and the selection of textbooks. The author teaches Portuguese and Brazilian Literature and served on the commission that drew up implementation plans for educational reforms in Guanabara state.

6334. Rabello, Ophelina. Um estudo sócio-econômico do estudante universitário. Campinas, Bra., Univ. Estadual de Campinas, Instituto Nacional de Estudos e Pesquisas Educacionais, 1974. 92 p., bibl., tables.

Social stratification, social status of the student, the student and work, student migration, student assistance, and free higher education are the chapter headings of this investigation of the university student in Brazil. Based on questionnaires and interviews administered to students of the universities of Amazonas, Maranhão, Mato Grosso, Juiz de Fora, Santa Maria, Paraná, Sergipe, and Campinas (3,567 students participated) and later extended to include 175 interviews with students from the federal universities of Rio, Fluminense, Pernambuco, Bahia, Minas Gerais, Rio Grande do Sul, Ceará, and Goiás, as well as the state universities of Guanabara and São Paulo. The investigation produced so much data that the results were reported in three volumes, of which this is the second. In this volume the primary goal was to delineate and describe the socioeconomic status of university students based on analysis of data concerning their family and class status, the degree of assistance they require, and any employment they accept while students.

6335. _____. Universidade e trabalho: perspectivas. Campinas, Bra., Univ. Estadual de Campinas, Instituto Nacional de Estudos e Pesquisas Educacionais, 1973. 118 p., bibl.

This is the first volume of a three-volume study of the university student and the job market. The original research plan called for only one book, based on a survey and interviews conducted at eight regional universities; however, the research was expanded to include ten additional universities located in urban centers, including Guanabara and São Paulo. In the first volume, data is presented on the present level of university students in the job market, followed by chapters on work-study or apprentice programs, the job market, socioeconomic aspects, and some recommendations for future programs.

6336. Rabello, Ricardo da Costa; Virgília Riberio Peixoto; and **Bernadete Figueiredo Coutinho.** O universitário nordestino. Recife, Bra., Instituto Joaquim Nabuco de Pesquisas Sociais, 1972. 205 p., bibl., map, plate, tables (Série estudos e pesquisas)

An investigation based on questionnaires distributed to university students in Salvador, Fortaleza, and Recife. The survey was conducted at seven universities, and the results reported in this summary are based on responses from 900 students in Salvador, 563 students in Fortaleza, and 900 students in Recife. Since the purpose of the investigation was to discover as much as possible about the circumstances under which rural students come to urban universities, participants were selected because they had migrated from rural areas. The investigation examined the following: economic, social, and psychological factors influencing rural youths to migrate to urban higher education centers; the adjustments students have to make to both the university and to the urban environment; the extent to which rural values are modified toward urban values; and the distribution of students from rural areas among the various fields of study. The structure of the questionnaire included some open-ended questions so that opinions and attitudes could be solicited. Results: the highest proportion of rural students was found to be at Fortaleza; students tended to migrate with their families, which led to later hardships; courses of study were selected on the basis of little or no information; students did not expect to remain in the capital on completion of their studies; and the majority did not work or hold jobs outside of the university. On attitudes: favorable to democracy; favorable to divorce and birth control, although the majority are Catholic. A sample questionnaire is provided, as well as a bibliography.

6337. Rafael, Georgina. Hereditariedade. Belo Horizonte, Bra., Centro Regional de Pesquisas Educacionais João Pinheiro, Divisão de Aperfeiçoamento do Professor, Serviço de Psicologia, 1970. 23 p., bibl., illus. (Cadernos de educação, 7)

Heredity, viewed from the perspectives of: biology and the environment, genetics, prenatal influences (diet, viruses, Rh factor, for example), individual development, and education. Apparently, this slim volume is intended as a mini-reference for teachers, although there is no identification of its purpose or its author's background.

6338. Réis, Arthur Cézar Ferreira. Manoel de Nóbrega e a pedagogia jesuítica (CFC/RBC, 3:7, jan./março 1971, p. 85-92)

Describes the colonizing activities of Nóbrega during the governments of Tomé de Sousa, Duarte de Costa and Mem de Sá, and his ideas in education. By creating centers for instruction, literacy schools, and professional schools and accepting the children of Indians and Portuguese colonists, he stimulated communication. He also tried to integrate them by using their experiences when teaching reading, writing, math, and music thereby furthering the development of theatre, painting, and ceramics. He used the languages most commonly spoken along the coast, creating dictionaries for them and developing texts or grammars in order to facilitate communication. [BBE]

6339. Reis, J. Educação é investimento. Prefácio de Tristão de Athyade. São Paulo, Instituição Brasileira de Difusão Cultural (IBRASA), 1968. 337 p., bibl. (Biblioteca psicologia e educação, 34)

Collection of essays based on speeches presented at various educational institutions throughout Brazil in the 1960s. The list of locations provided by the author includes Marília, Riberao Prêto, Sorocaba, Araraquara, Santos, and Piracicaba, as well as more urban areas, but specific selections are not identified with either dates or locations. In his preface Amoroso Lima (Tristão de Athayde) describes the author as a scientist who has succeeded in bringing together his scientific spirit and ideas in the form of journalistic essays in this collection. Since this book was published in 1968 there are references to political issues related to events after 1964, particularly with regard to university students and faculty. Topics include: Education for Development; Responsibility of the Universities; Students and Politics; Public Instruction — Paid or Free?; Health, Education, and Society; and Creativity and I.Q. Professor Reis founded Science Clubs and established Science Fairs throughout the state of São Paulo. In the final chapters he describes and discusses the organization and objectives of these activities. A bibliography is provided for each chapter; the majority of sources are in English.

6340. Relações de publicações de Lourenço Filho em psicologia (Arquivos Brasileiros de Psicologia Aplicada [Fundação Getúlio Vargas, Rio] 23:3, julho/set. 1971, p. 153-158)

Bibliography of 94 items, including books, translations, articles and essays published in national and foreign publications, as well as prefaces to Brazilian works. [BBE]

6341. *Revista da Faculdade de Educação da UFF.* Univ. Federal Fluminense, Centro de Estudos Sociais Aplicados. Ano 2, No. 2, maio 1972-   . Niterói, Bra.

A monthly publication of the School of Education, with articles by professional educators for professional educators. In contrast to many professional publications, there is no section of news notes or book reviews. Authors are not identified as to institutional affiliation or degrees, so may be students as well as faculty at the Univ. Topics in this issue include: What is the role of counseling vis-á-vis the expansion of primary and secondary education?, English language and communication, religious education, and reflections on the role of the teacher.

6342. Ribeiro, Clélia Monteiro and Luis Dias de Andrade. Estudo psicométrico de atitudes sociais de adolescentes (Jornal Brasileiro de Psiquiatria [Instituto de Psiquiatria, Rio] 19:3/4, julho/dez. 1970, p. 153-161)

A pilot study examining political attitudes of adolescents and based on a survey of 138 students in the second year of secondary school in São Paulo. [BBE]

6343. Ribeiro, Darcy. La universidad nueva: un proyecto. B.A., Editorial Ciencia Nueva, 1973. 158 p., illus.

Darcy Ribeiro, one of the architects of the plans for the Univ. of Brasília and an educational and political activist during the Goulart regime, is now in Peru organizing a Study Center for Popular (Public) Participation. He presents here his ideas for a revised approach to higher education, many of which require opening the university to non-traditional avenues of study. In his introduction he identifies his discontent with the Latin American university because of "its irresponsibility in the face of the problems of the population that maintains it" and because of "its connivance with the forces responsible for the dependency and backwardness of Latin America." He offers here a theoretical model to serve as a standard against which to measure the university now and in the future. In his conclusion he warns that any reform will fail if it is implemented by those presently involved in university administration, since their efforts will only succeed in modernizing and creating greater efficiency for the university's present role of maintaining the status quo. Ribeiro wants the university to become an agency of accelerated evolution for society, i.e., a source for societal change. As the essential prerequisite to establishing his theoretical model, Ribeiro calls for both student and faculty participation in the administration, in the form of *"cogobierno."*

6344. Rio de Janeiro (state), *Bra.* **Secretaria de Saúde e Assistencia. Serviço de Educação Sanitária.** Problemas de saúde na escola primária. 5. ed. Niterói, 1969. 97 p., illus. (Série: Higiene escolar)

A collection of short articles by practitioners in school health programs, on topics such as: communicable diseases during the preschool age, personal hygiene, the teacher as a health model, primary schools and sanitation, and mental health in the primary school. Published by the Secretariat of Health and Welfare, and intended as a help for public school teachers.

6345. Rio Grande do Sul (state), *Bra.* **Assembléia Legislativa. Comissão de Educação e Cultura.** Súmula dos encontros educacionais. Pôrto Alegre, Bra., 1973. 93 p., tables.

On behalf of more effective implementation of recent educational reform measures, the legislature joined forces with the State Education Council, the Ministry of Education, and the Secretariat of Education to hold a series of meetings designed to explore, discuss, and consider educational issues and problems. Summaries of the results, reported in this volume, deal in-

6346. Rio Grande do Sul (state), *Bra.* **Secretaria de Educação e Cultura.** Ensino de 1º grau no Rio Grande do Sul. v. 1, Caracterização de currículo. v. 2, Currículos das 1ª, 2ª e 3ª séries. v. 3, Currículos por área. v. 4, Area de iniciação à técnica. v. 5, Avaliação dos resultados do processo ensino-aprendizagem. Pôrto Alegre, Bra., 1973. 5 v. (50, 159, 94, 75, 84 p.), plates, tables.

A five-volume series outlining the organization, objectives, curriculum, philosophy, terminology, priorities, and methods for primary level education in Rio Grande do Sul. V. 1 serves as a general presentation and introduction; v. 2 consists entirely of sample lesson plans; v. 3 presents rationales and suggestions for different curricular areas (science, arts, physical education; v. 4 provides information on techniques, including the project method; and v. 5, evaluation procedures.

6347. _____, _____. _____. Sistema de planejamento da Secretaria de Educação e Cultura do Rio Grande do Sul: documento básico. Pôrto Alegre, Bra., 1972. 96 p., plates, tables.

The basic plan for an educational planning sector in Rio Grande do Sul, for the period 1971-74, as prepared and presented by the Secretariat of Education. Result of research and studies conducted at the Secretariat, this document is intended to serve as a guide to the establishment of a planning office and a planning methodology for the state.

6348. _____, _____. _____. **Departamento de Educação Média.** Ensino de 2º grau no Rio Grande do Sul. Pôrto Alegre? Bra., 1974. 52 l.

In order to assist local educators with the establishment and expansion of secondary schools in areas where they were not previously available, the Dept. of Secondary Education prepared this book of instructions. Samples of the documentation required for each kind of school are presented.

6349. Rotstein, Jaime. Ciência e tecnologia. Brasília, Câmara dos Deputados, Diretoria Legislativa, Divisão de Publicaçoes, 1973. 56 p.

A speech, delivered in Aug. 1971, before the Chamber of Deputies' Special Commission for the Encouragement of Scientific and Technological Research as part of the program of presentations dealing with Brazil's current situation and sponsored by the National Leadership of ARENA, the majority political party. Rotstein, former vice-president of the Engineers Club, author of several books, and president of Sondotechnica, S.A., presents an agenda for the future and some models for science and technology in Brazil. Six deputies debate his ideas and their comments follow the text of his speech.

6350. Saldanha, Louremi Ercolani. Ensino individualizado: modelo de organização do ensino com vistas à individualização. Pôrto Alegre, Bra., Univ. Federal do Rio Grande do Sul, Editôra da URGS [and] São Paulo, Editôra McGraw-Hill do Brasil, 1972. 131 p., bibl., illus.

How to organize and plan for individualized instruction is the theme of this book, written by a professor presently engaged in teaching methods at a major university. Early chapters dwell on the historical background from Socrates forward, then the author presents examples of individualized instruction plans, accompanied by statistics supporting the efficacy of individualizing as compared to other methods. The bibliography includes Taba, Piaget, Horney, Gagné, and Skinner.

6351. _____ and **Luzia Garcia de Mello.** Planos de ensino: sugestões de procedimento para sua elaboração. Pôrto Alegre, Bra., Univ. Federal do Rio Grande do Sul, 1972. 58 p., bibl., tables (Col. Documentos, 11)

Writing behavioral objectives, developing, organizing, and using lesson plans, programming and educational technology are the topics discussed by the authors, who supply examples from their own experiences.

6352. São Paulo (state), *Bra.* **Secretaria de Economia e Planejamento. Departamento de Estatística. Divisão de Estatísticas Físicas, Sociais e Culturais.** Ensino superior: 1968. São Paulo, 1969. 48 p., tables.

The state government report on higher education statistics gathered by the Dept. of Statistics of the Secretariat of Economics and Planning of São Paulo state in 1968. Part of a major effort to maintain and publish current, accurate statistical reports on education at all levels.

6353. Schrader, Achim; Manfredo Berger; and **Birgit Schrader.** Oferta e procura educacional: pesquisa realizada no interior do Rio Grande do Sul. Pôrto Alegre, Bra., Univ. Federal do Rio Grande do Sul, 1973. 270 p., bibl., tables.

Apart from the now familiar discovery that a very high proportion of school-age children are in the first year and that many of them repeat the first year and never complete even a primary education, this study of rural schools in Rio Grande do Sul produced some fresh information about the actual situation in primary education outside of the urban centers. Schrader finds that the ethnic and economic status of the family has a significant influence on the amount and quality of education obtained. Statistics and a bibliography accompany each chapter.

6354. Sergipe (state), *Bra.* **Secretaria de Educação e Cultura.** Plano estadual de educação e cultura: 1971-1974. Aracaju, Bra., 1970. 133 1., tables.

In this four-year plan for education and culture in the state of Sergipe, chapters are devoted to: reform of the Secretariat of Education; priorities, according to municipalities and regions; equipment and facilities; human resources; primary education; secondary education; adult education; higher education; culture and historical patrimony; and budget. All priorities and objectives are listed in the form of a time table covering the period 1971-74 and broken down into sequential stages of development.

6355. Silva, Hilberto Mascarenhas Alves da. Educação e treinamento em bancos e instituições de desenvolvimento. Fortaleza, Bra., 1972. 23 p.

The author, president of the Bank of the Northeast of Brazil, describes the training programs that the Bank has established to provide for staff development. He begins by describing the Bank's role and functions, then explains how the training programs began, identifies the major types of training, describes cooperative programs with universities, and other programs conducted by agencies other than the Bank. His comments were delivered to a meeting in B.A. of the Association of Latin American Development Banks, in 1972.

6356. Silva, Iná. Opinião dos professores sobre o trabalho em classes de recuperação: interior do Estado do Rio Grande do Sul, 1968. Pôrto Alegre? Bra., Centro de Pesquisas e Orientação Educacionais e de Educação Especializada, Divisão de Pesquisas, Serviço de Pesquisas, 1970. 27 p. (mimeo)

A total of 220 teachers from the interior of the state completed a questionnaire about their work and problems with classes in compensatory education. Respondents identified their greatest difficulty in the area of working with low achievers who combined a pattern of poor health, low intelligence, immaturity, and lack of family support. They asked for better training in child psychology and specific skills in adjusting to the performance levels of their students. [BBE]

6357. Silva, Luiz Carlos. Aspectos do sistema de treinamento no Brasil. Rio, Centro Nacional de Recursos Humanos, 1971. 24 1., tables (CNRH/Ser. Estudos TT. Doc. 140)

An examination of the various professional preparation programs and the relationship between regular education programs and professional training. The author points out that many technical or professional programs are regarded as separate from "formal education," and students who enroll in professional courses or apprenticeship programs cannot easily reenter the general education course sequence. Graduates of secondary level technical programs (in industrial, commercial, or agricultural sequences) are eligible to enroll in universities, however. This study focuses on SENAI and SENAC since they bear the major responsibility for technical education and on the correlation between the job market and professional preparation programs.

6358. Simpósio sobre a Reforma do Ensino de 1º e 2º Graus, *Pôrto Alegre, 1972.* Anais. Pôrto Alegre, Bra., Assembléia Legislativa do Rio Grande Do Sul, Comissão de Educação e Cultura, 1972. 188 p.

Dialogues, debates, and seminars constituting the Symposium on Educational Reform held in Rio Grande do Sul in 1972. The Symposium was sponsored by the legislature and included participation of legislators from other states. Later sections, and comments referring to Law 5692, a major reform law, are particularly informative for the careful reader.

6359. Simpósio sobre Planejamento da Educação, *São Paulo, 1972.* Simpósio sobre planejamento da educação organizado pela Fundação Carlos Chagas e realizado no XXIV Reunião Anual da Sociedade Brasileira para o Progresso da Ciência (SBPC) a 4 de julho de 1972 em São Paulo. São Paulo, 1972. 79 p., tables.

Papers first presented at the Symposium on Educational Planning organized and sponsored by the Carlos Chagas Foundation and held July 4, 1972 in São Paulo, in conjunction with the XXIV Annual Meeting of the Brazilian Society for the Advancement of Science. Topics include: planning and development; economic aspects of higher education planning; problems of administration; and educational statistics and planning.

6360. Souza, Heitor G. de; Darcy F. de Almeida, and **Carlos Costa Ribeiro.** Política científica. São Paulo, Editôra Perspectiva, 1972. 293 p., tables (Col. Debates, 65)

On the 25th anniversary of the Biophysics Institute at the Federal Univ. of Rio, a select group of social scientists and a limited number of participants were invited to a Symposium on Political Science. This volume contains the edited presentations made at that gathering by, among others, Yves de Hemptinne, Director of the Political Science Division of UNESCO; Arlindo Lopes Correa, Executive Secretary of the National Center for Human Resources; and Luiz Simões Lopes; President of the Getúlio Vargas Foundation. Topics include: new educational technologies, public administration and the quality of life, and priorities and goals of national development.

6361. Souza, Júlio César de Mello. Antologia do bom professor. Rio, Casa Editôra Vecchi, 1969. 180 p.

In these pages one finds quotes (Spencer, Dewey,

Kuan-Tzu) and selections (Hilton Rocha, Roberto de Oliveira Campos, Paulo Sá, Ruth Gouvéia, Fenelon, Lourenço Filho, and many others) on everything from Group Study to The Desire to Learn, from Weekend Professor to Sex Education. Lightweight material, but probably fun reading for a "weekend educator." The title page accurately proclaims—"hundreds of articles, notes, critical observations, commentaries, episodes, famous thought," etc.

6362. _____. Roteiro do bom professor. Rio, Casa Editôra Vecchi, 1969? 180 p.

With a bias toward the Catholic educator's point of view this volume is a companion to item 6361, a mixture of short pieces by well-known and not-so-well-known educators. Most selections are only one page long—light reading.

6363. Sperb, Dalilla C. Problemas gerais de currículo. 2. ed. Pôrto Alegre, Bra., Editôra Globo, 1972. 337 p.

A comparative study of curriculum development and educational planning, intended to serve as a text for normal-school students, postgraduate students, and students in schools of education. The author completed a master's degree in Education at Teachers College of Columbia Univ. then took a doctorate in Pedagogy at the Catholic Univ. of Rio Grande do Sul. Her approach to curriculum is student-centered, emphasizing self-actualization and adaptability to change.

6364. Sucupira, Newton. O ciclo básico: 1º ciclo geral de estudos. 2. ed. aumentada. Rio, Conselho de Reitores das Universidades Brasileiras, 1970. 71 p. (CR-14-PE-7)

Valnir Chagas (Rector of the Univ. of Brasília), Newton Sucupira (Director of the International Relations Division of the Ministry of Education), and Rubens Maciel (former member of the Federal Education Council) are the authors of the three position papers presented in this slim volume. Sucupira's topic is "O Ciclo Básico: Sua Natureza e Problemas de Sua Organizaçao;" Chagas writes on "A Seleção e o Vestibular na Reforma Universitária;" and Maciel contributes "Organização e Funcionamento do Ciclo Básico." All comments were originally delivered at two seminars sponsored by the Council of Rectors of Brazilian Universities and held in 1970.

6365. Superintendência do Desenvolvimento da Região Sul (SUDESUL), *Pôrto Alegre, Bra.* **Divisão de Documentação.** Bibliografia de educação e assuntos correlatos: material bibliográfico existente na Divisão de Documentação da SUDESUL. Pôrto Alegre, Bra., 1970. 1 v. (Unpaged)

A bibliography of 249 items on education and related topics comprising the library maintained by the Documentation Division of SUDESUL (Superintendency of Development for the Southern Region).

6366. Superintendência do Desenvolvimento do Nordeste, *Recife, Bra.* **Departamento de Recursos Humanos.**

Divisão de Educação. Cadastro de prédios escolares do Nordeste: detalhamento do plano de trabalho para 1971. Recife, Bra., 1971. 90 p. (mimeo)

Pictures and graphics illustrating construction and utilization of buildings in states within the SUDENE program, with budget items for municipalities and regions listed for 1971. [BBE]

6367. *Symposium.* Univ. Católica de Pernambuco. Vol. 14, No. 1, 1972- . Recife, Bra.

Articles on several subjects and news notes of events at the Catholic Univ. Topics in this issue include: colonization and population of Brazil, the new structure of the university, and isolation or cosmopolitanism? Of greatest interest, particularly to historians, is the article by Nilo Pereira detailing the history of the Palácio de Soledade, original site of the Archdiocese of Olinda and Recife, home and prison of Dom Vital, and now used by the Law faculty of the university.

6368. Tobias, José Antonio. Educação brasileira: temas e problemas. São Paulo, Editôra Juriscrédi, 1973? 284 p.

Early chapters of this book suggest that the author is primarily concerned with elementary education; however, he moves on to discuss materialistic psychology, leadership in higher education, statistics for elementary and secondary education, and other equally varied topics. One chapter, on new teaching methods, is an attack on the importation of educational ideas from abroad, principally from the US, finding such imported methods all too often contrary to Brazilian values and interests.

6369. Trabalho inédito de Anísio Teixeira sobre o brinquedo (Arte e Educação [Escolinha de Arte do Brasil, Rio] 1:7, julho 1971, p. 7)

Focuses on infancy as the period of greatest learning because of the sharp curiosity and exploratory capacity of the young child. The "toy" is viewed as the adult's equivalent for this stage of development, product of the child's imagination yet changed into a utilitarian object, thus deforming the magic nature of the child's invention, subjecting it to adult standards and uses. [BBE]

6370. Trindade, Maria Zélia Damásio. Ouro Prêto também para crianças. Ouro Prêto, Bra., Fundação de Arte de Ouro Prêto, 1972. 112 p., fold. map, illus.

Brazilian history in the form of a child's diary, written at a level appropriate for the upper elementary grades. A very attractive book with a brightly colored cover illustration and several other drawings plus a map accompanying the text. Although published by the Ouro Preto Art Foundation, there is no identification of any of the art. Information about Ouro Preto itself, the gold rush, the *bandeirantes,* and other aspects of history appear in every episode.

6371. Universidade Católica de Pelotas,

Bra. Universidade Católica de Pelotas. Pelotas, Bra, 1970? 189 p., plates.

A commemorative issue honoring the 10th anniversary of the founding of the Catholic Univ. of Pelotas, in Rio Grande do Sul. Photographs dispersed throughout convey a very personal impression of the university's development, showing the faculty and administrators who have worked for its success, the gradual installation and expansion of facilities, and the various activities and programs offered throughout the first ten years.

6372. Universidade de Brasília, *Bra.* Catálogo geral: 1974. Brasília, Fundação Univ. de Brasília, 1974. 187 p., plates.

Typical university catalogue providing information about: courses, requirements, general plan of education and organization of the university, credits, and departments. Since the Univ. of Brasília does not follow the traditional Brazilian university's organizational structure, this catalogue is quite similar to that of American universities.

6373. Universidade de São Paulo, *Bra.* **Museu de Arte Contemporânea.** A expressão plástica da criança excepcional. São Paulo, 1972. 1 v. (Unpaged) illus.

A collection of comments concerning exceptional children, their ability and capacity for self-expression in art, and their education. Result of collaboration among several schools with special education programs, professors at the Univ. of São Paulo, and the University Art Museum, this text accompanied an exposition of art work by mentally retarded children held in São Paulo 25 Aug.-10 Sept., 1972. Contributors include: Victor Lowenfeld, Erika Steinberger (of the Adams School in N.Y.) and Walter Zanini, Director of the Museum.

6374. Universidade Federal de Minas Gerais, *Belo Horizonte, Bra.* Ordenamentos básicos: plano de restruturação, estatuto, regimento geral. Belo Horizonte, Bra., 1972. 179 p. (Publicaçao, 550)

Legislation affecting the reorganization of the Federal Univ. of Minas Gerais, in compliance with higher education reform laws of 1966 and 1967.

6375. Universidade Federal do Rio Grande do Norte, *Natal, Bra.* Reforma administrativa: experiência da UFRN. Natal, Bra., 1973. 52 p., tables.

A description of the reorganization of the university's administration based on a systems analysis approach. Seminars for staff development, analysis of needs and structures, and development of policy preceded the implementation of reform measures. Task forces were organized, administrative tasks became staff rather than academic functions, and new departments were established. The report includes a generous supply of charts and illustrations.

6376. Universidade-Industria: uma integração que já e realidade (Guanabara Industrial [Federaçao das Indústrias do Estado da Guanabara, Rio] 8:91. fev. 1971, p. 4-7)

An agreement signed by the Development Institute of Guanabara with the Catholic Univ. is designed to develop an integrated program of university field work coordinated with industry. In this manner, it would provide professional training for university students but also benefit the productivity of industries in which they would be working. [BBE]

6377. Universidade para o Desenvolvimento do Estado de Santa Catarina, *Florianópolis, Bra.* **Faculdade de Educação. Centro de Estudos e Pesquisa Educacionais.** Dificuldades na iniciação da aprendizagem. Florianópolis, Bra., 1972. 91 p., bibl., tables.

A study, prompted by the reform of education according to the State Plan and based on public school students in Florianopolis, the capital, which was designed to examine the efficacy of the first year of instruction. Objectives listed in the research report were: to assess the intelligence of first-year children and correlate reading-and-writing instruction with the results; to verify results of the new program during the first year; to observe how administrators were implementing the new program; and to study the problems of students who were not succeeding. Findings indicate that problems arise due to lack of proper nutrition, opportunities for preschool education, and appreciation of other causes for school failure then lack of intelligence. Training of teachers needs to be changed, to provide for an awareness of different kinds of learning problems; student teaching experiences need to be improved and methods of retaining experienced teachers devised, so that the youngest and most inexperienced will not always teach first-year students.

6378. ———, ———. ———. ———. Evasão escolar e repetência nas comunidades pesqueiras de Santa Catarina: relatório de pesquisa. Florianópolis, Bra., 1968. 146 p., bibl., tables.

Although Santa Catarina is a state dominated by coastline, the coastal communities are stagnating and becoming more and more isolated, economically and socially, from the mainstream. This research focuses on the educational sector and examines questions related to schooling provided in the fishing communities. The research team concludes with two recommendations: that the government encourage a plan for integrated socioeconomic development in these communities and that the schools adapt their programs to local conditions.

6379. Vargas, Arete Saldanha. Plano intermediário: projeto (RGS/RE, 18:136, 1971, p. 5-7)

An analysis of the "project method," based on Dewey's ideas and Kilpatrick's evolution of them. Description of: interaction, preparation, execution, and appreciation stages of the plan which the student evolves with the collaboration of his teacher. [BBE]

Widmer, Ernst. O ensino da música nos conservatórios. See *HLAS 36:4565.*

6380. Witter, Geraldina Pôrto. A instrução programada e o ensino de excepcionais (UNZ/C, 21:3, 1969, p. 659-665, bibl., tables)

Witter argues that all of the reasons for adopting programmed instruction also apply to the instruction of exceptional students and proceeds to enumerate the reasons and relate them to programs for exceptional students. She warns against the indiscriminate use of programmed instruction, cautioning the reader that unless programs and tests are well-constructed, the educational and technological benefits will be lost. The bibliography is entirely in English.

6381. _____; Euza Maria de Rezende Bonamigo; and Maria Cecília Manzolli. Condicionamento verbal: pesquisa e ensino. São Paulo, Editôra Alfa-Omega, 1974. 187 p., bibl.

A joint effort of psychologists at three Brazilian universities in response to increased awareness of and interest in verbal conditioning, psycholinguistics, and sociolinguistics. Based on research conducted in Brazil, and consisting of excerpts from their several doctoral theses, this follow-up to several translations of works from foreign sources provides a bibliography after each chapter and supplementary tables as necessary. Techniques of Greenspoon and Taffel are discussed.

JOURNAL ABBREVIATIONS

ASA/S	Sociometry. American Sociological Association. N.Y.
AVAC/ACV	Acta Científica Venezolana. Asociación Venezolana para el Avance de la Ciencia. Caracas.
BNJM/R	Revista de la Biblioteca Nacional José Martí. La Habana.
CES/CER	Comparative Education Review. Comparative Education Society. N.Y.
CLAPCS/AL	América Latina. Centro Latino-Americano de Pesquisas em Ciências Sociais. Rio.
GM	The Geographical Magazine. London.
IAMEA	Inter-American Economic Affairs. Washington.
IDES/DE	Desarrollo Económico. Instituto de Desarrollo Económico y Social. B.A.
IESSC/C	Comunidades. Instituto de Estudios Sindicales, Sociales y Cooperativos, Centro de Prospección Social. Madrid.
ISSQ	The Indiana Social Studies Quarterly. Indiana Council for Social Studies. Ball State Univ. Muncie, Ind.
JDA	The Journal of Developing Areas. Western Illinois Univ. Press. Macomb, Ill.
JDS	The Journal of Development Studies. A quarterly journal devoted to economics, politics and social development. London.
OAS/AM	Américas. Organization of American States. Washington.
OAS/CI	Ciencia Interamericana. Organization of American States. Dept. of Scientific Affairs. Washington.
PUJ/U	Universitas. Ciencias jurídicas y socioeconómicas. Pontificia Univ. Javeriana, Facultad de Derecho y Ciencias Socioeconómicas. Bogotá.
UA/U	Universidad. Univ. de Antioquia. Medellín, Colo.
UC/A	Anales de la Univ. de Cuenca. Cuenca, Ecua.
UCC/CE	Cuadernos de Economía. Univ. Católica de Chile. Santiago.
UCP/IAP	Ibero-Americana Pragensia. Univ. Carolina de Praga, Centro de Estudios Ibero-Americanos. Praga.
UM/JIAS	Journal of Inter-American Studies and World Affairs. Univ. of Miami Press *for* Center for Advanced International Studies. Coral Gables, Fla.
UNAM/PDD	Problemas del Desarrollo. Revista latinoamericana de economía. Univ. Nacional Autónoma de México, Instituto de Investigaciones Económicas. México.
UNAM/RMS	Revista Mexicana de Sociología. Univ. Nacional Autónoma de México, Instituto de Investigaciones Sociales. México.
UNESCO/IRE	International Review of Education. United Nations, Educational, Scientific and Cultural Organization, Institute for Education. Hamburg, FRG.
UPR/LT	La Torre. Revista General de la Univ. de Puerto Rico. Río Piedras, P.R.
UPR/RCS	Revista de Ciencias Sociales. Univ. de Puerto Rico, Colegio de Ciencias Sociales. Río Piedras, P.R.

USC/U	Universidad de San Carlos de Guatemala. Guatemala.
USIA/PI	Problemas Internacionales. United States Information Agency. Washington.
UWI/CQ	Caribbean Quarterly. Univ. of the West Indies. Mona, Jam.
UY/R	Revista de la Universidad de Yucatán. Mérida, Mex.

Geography

GENERAL

CLINTON R. EDWARDS
Professor of Geography
University of Wisconsin-Milwaukee

AS EMPHASES ON ECONOMIC AND SOCIAL CHANGE, land tenure, agrarian reform, and the rural-urban migration with attendant slum problems continue, a theme related to all of these is receiving increased attention. This is the concern for adverse environmental consequences of change in these and other economic and social aspects of Latin American life. Scholarly interest in environmental problems of Latin America is of course not new. For example, in 1940 the Instituto Panamericano de Geografía e Historia published Wallace W. Atwood's *The protection of nature in the Americas* (IPGH publicación No. 50), an inventory of and extended comments on Latin America's national parks and other nature reserves. In this work the main concern was the preservation of nature in the older style—the administration of forests, game sanctuaries, avian refuge areas, and the like. Comparison with a modern inventory, item 0000, will be interesting. But the modern Latin American literature conforms quite identifiably to the change in emphasis that has characterized North American expressions of concern in the past few years; that is, the current stressing of environmental problems directly traceable to rapid technological change.

Although the burgeoning automobile population of several Latin American countries still lags behind that of the US, some local problems of air pollution from exhaust emissions seem every bit as bothersome as those in Los Angeles or Chicago. One result is a growing literature that includes discussions in symposia (item 6554) and instructive manuals on the role of the automobile in air pollution (item 6501).

The advocacy of economic development that had become so insistent in recent years is now being more and more tempered with commentary on possible adverse consequences, as in items 6503, 6513, and 6528. Also, sequels to the recent *mesas redondas* on natural resources (see *HLAS 35:6567*) now take the form of *mesas redondas* on "development and ecology" (item 6690).

The new bibliography on agrarian reform by the Univ. of Wisconsin-Madison's Land Tenure Center (item 6557) is an important addition to our inventory of reference tools. Study of agrarian reform is also aided significantly by the publication a year earlier of a useful dictionary of terminology and special usage in that field, treated topically (item 6545).

Many of the foregoing subjects are treated in a series of readings on problems of "modernization" in Latin America (item 6548), and in a more general way in the Rehovot Conference on urbanization and development in the less developed countries (item 6541).

Much of the older literature on development has advocated various types of reform and strategies for economic and social improvement. The more recent works tend toward retrospective evaluation of earlier suggestions, based on some backlog of experience with some of them. In this sifting of ideas, purely economic solutions are found wanting occasionally, and one perceives a stronger emphasis on social investigation, with some overtones of social engineering. The other important ingredient of re-evaluation is the aforementioned trend toward investigation of the proposition that not all economic development is compatible with rational approaches to environmental problems.

Although the preoccupation with development and other forms of change dominates the literature of interest to geographers, more traditional concerns in Latin American geography are not unrepresented. The spate of Humboldtiana engendered by the recent centenary continues with items 6504, 6523, and 6574. And the 16th-century politics of charting the seas still draws commentary (item 6533).

6500. Amérique. v. 2, Pays & continents: géographie, économie, politique, Paris, Editions Lidis, 1973. 403 p., bibl., maps, plates, tables.

Lexicon-atlas with many colored photos. Arrangement: l'Amérique Centrale; les Antilles; l'Amerique du Sud; Venezuela et pays andins; Argentine, Chili, Paraguay, Uruguay; and Brésil, Guyanes. Commentary emphasizes social, economic, and political questions and problems.

6501. Los automotores como fuentes contaminantes. B.A., Univ. de Buenos Aires, Facultad de Ingeniería, Instituto de Ingeniería Sanitaria, Centro de Investigación de Ingeniería Ambiental, 1971. 152 p., bibl., tables (Temas de contaminación atmosférica. Publicación, 10)

Derives from a course in the Instituto de Ingeniería Sanitaria of the Univ. de Buenos Aires. Contains chapters on all aspects of air pollution caused by automobile exhaust emissions, including material on combustion processes, contaminants emitted, incidence of pollution, methods of reducing pollution, and alternate sources of energy for automobile propulsion.

6502. Báez, Mauricio. La productividad por agricultor en los paises americanos. Caracas, Ministerio de Agricultura y Cria, 1971? 149 p., bibl., tables.

Emphasizes land use, land tenure and population as significant factors in agricultural productivity. Many comparisons of production, productivity, yields and other agricultural data are presented in tables. Recommendations for improvement in productivity include reducing *minifundismo;* improving means of economic assistance to individual farmers; and providing appropriate infra-structure in developing areas to assist in the transition from subsistence to commercially oriented agriculture. For economist's comment, see *HLAS 35:1781a.*

6503. Barrera Carrasquilla, Antonio. América Latina y el equilibrio ecológico mundial (IGAC/CG, 3:1, 1. semestre 1972, p. 75-99, bibl., tables)

Discusses a simulation model of population and economic growth in relation to food supply, natural resources, energy, and pollution.

6504. Bedoya M., Angel N. Federico Enrique Alejandro, Barón de Humboldt (UCEIA/H, 7:1, 1969-1970, p. 71-78)

Brief commentary on pre-Humboldt intellectual history, and capsule descriptions of ruins noted by Humboldt in the Ecuadorian highlands.

6505. Beltrão, Pedro Calderan. Demografia: ciência da população; análise e teoria. Pôrto Alegre, Bra., Livraria Sulina Editôra, 1972. 335 p., bibl., tables (Col. Universitária)

Text on demographic analysis and theory, with bibliographies on the theory of population optimum and the theory of the demographic transition.

6506. Brown, Lester. Rich countries and poor in a finite, interdependent world (AAAS/D, 102:4, Fall 1973, p. 153-164)

Global economy doubles every 16 to 18 years, increasing pressure on Earth's capacity to support economic activity and burgeoning population. Contains a few references to various Latin American countries in general commentary.

6507. Butland, Gilbert J. Latin America: a regional geography. 3. ed. London, Longman, 1972. 464 p., maps, plates, tables (Geographies: an intermediate series)

New concluding sections are added to each chapter, statistical matter is revised, and many new maps, diagrams, and statistical tables are included. See *HLAS 29:5006* for second ed.

6508. Cardona Gutiérrez, Ramiro. Apuntes sobre la llamada "crisis" de las grandes ciudades (Revista Cámara de Comerico de Bogotá, 3:12, sept. 1973, p. 129-143, bibl., tables)

Problems thought to be characteristic of cities are actually national or multinational in scope. Noise, traffic congestion, air pollution and other urban ills are not necessarily products of overpopulation of cities. Cities are the most important agencies of social change in Latin America.

6509. Cesarman, Fernando. Ecocidio: estudio psicoanalítico de la destrucción del medio ambiente. México, Editorial Joaquín Mortiz, 1972. 90 p.

Discussion of human attitudes toward environments and environmental problems, from the viewpoint of psychoanalyst.

6510. Clarke, John I. Fertile people in infertile lands (GM, 45:8, May 1973, p. 582-589, maps, plates, tables)

Commentary on man-land-resource relationships in an increasingly crowded world, emphasizing Third World problems with some reference to Latin American countries.

Conference of Latin Americanist Geographers, *II, Boston, Mass., 1971.* Population dynamics of Latin America: a review and bibliography. See item 2025.

6511. Conferencia Regional Latinoamericana de Población, *México, 1970.* Actas. México, Unión, Internacional para el Estudio Científico de la Población, Centro Latinoamericano de Demografía, Comisión Económica para América Latina [and] El Colegio de México, 1972. 2 v. (648, 519 p.) maps, tables.

The conference was divided into the following sessions, with many topical and regional contributions in each: v. 1, Mortality; Fertility; Migration, Urbanization and Regional Distribution; v. 2, Population and Economic and Social Development; Future Population Trends in Latin America; Population Policies; Research and Education in Latin American Demography.

6512. D'Antonio, William V. The problem of population growth in Latin America (ISSQ, 22:1, Spring 1969, p. 44-55, tables)

After presenting standard data on population growth, discusses the role of governments, the Roman Catholic Church, and the family. Notes various social changes and changes in government attitudes over the last two decades. Predicts wide acceptance of contraceptives and of the idea that family size must be limited.

6513. Dean, Warren. Economic development and environmental deterioration (RU/SCID, 7:3, Fall 1972, p. 278-287)

Poses the question, "is it possible for standards of consumption to rise and for population to continue to increase if the Earth's resources are finite and if the biosphere is incapable of sustaining further interventions by man?" Summarizes some possible ecological results of development in Latin America, and considers the possible course of development as ecological problems become more pressing.

6514. Dill, Hans-Otto. Natur und Gesellschaft in Lateinamerika (WZHUB, 20:3, 1971, p. 331-346)

Topics include man and nature in the social-historic reality of Latin America, nature and society in Latin American ideological history, and nature and society in Latin American literature.

6515. Eastman, Jorge Mario. América Latina: población y desarrollo (Revista Cámara de Comercio de Bogotá, 3:12, sept. 1973, p. 115-123)

In the face of population pressures in Latin America, recommends a flexible democratic-political stance combined with encouragement of social change conforming to needs for economic development.

6516. Escudero, Carlos J. Molestina. Suplemento: Instituto Interamericano de Ciencias Agrícolas (OAS/AM, 25:4, April 1973, p. s1-s16, illus., maps, plates, tables)

Interesting summary of Latin American agricultural history leads to discussion of agriculture's inadequate role in development. Self-sufficiency in food production is lacking, and agricultural unemployment figures are high. Significant changes have been made through agrarian reform, agricultural credit, and application of modern technology.

6517. Franco, Alberto. Regionalización de la reforma agraria (Desarrollo Rural en las Américas [Instituto Interamericano de Ciencias Agrícolas, Bogotá] 2:2, mayo/agosto 1970, p. 125-129)

Usually Latin American governments do not follow only one criterion for regionalization of agrarian reform. Political, social and economic objectives are strongly influential. Where campesinos are organized they can play a role in the process. [R. C. Eidt]

6518. Grigg, David. The rural revolution (GM, 45:10, July 1973, p. 734-739, map, plates, table)

A general article for public education on problems of Third World agriculture, with a few remarks on the Latin American tropics.

6519. Hall, Françoise. Population growth: U.S. and Latin American views (LSE/PS, 27:3, Nov. 1973, p. 415-429)

Summary of rate of population growth in Latin America, followed by commentary on how the US and Latin America have reacted, how Latin America has viewed the response by the US, and how US viewed the Latin American response. Presents some guidelines based on an admittedly personal interpretation.

6520. Hardoy, Jorge E. Potentials for urban absorption: the Latin American experience (*in* Poleman, Thomas T. and Donald K. Freebairn *eds.* Food, population, and employment: the impact of the Green Revolution. N.Y., Praeger Publishers *for the* Cornell Univ. Program on Science, Technology, and Society, 1973, p. 167-192, tables)

Classifies Latin American countries according to urban stability, or potential for urbanization. Just over half are "very unstable," while the rest have varying degrees of potential for development. Agrarian reform and the process of urbanization are interrelated, with land tenure a significant element in the decision to move to the city. Concludes that "it is doubtful that several Latin American countries can individually overcome their underdevelopment with the limited resources that exist within their borders."

6521. _____ and **Oscar Moreno.** Tendencias y alternativas de la reforma urbana (IDES/DE, 13:52, enero/marzo 1974, p. 627-647)

Describes the process of urban concentration leading to the creation of metropolitan areas, including the role of industrial development. Urban reform is influenced heavily by national as well as regional political considerations.

6522. International Atomic Energy Agency, *Wien.* Market survey for nuclear power in developing countries: general report. Wien, 1973. 1 v. (Various pagings) charts, illus., tables.

Objective was to "determine the size and timing of nuclear power plants that could, on economic grounds, justifiably be built in the countries studied and commissioned during the period 1980-1989." Latin American countries studied were Argentina, Chile, Jamaica, and Mexico.

6523. Jones, Calvin P. The Spanish-American works of Alexander von Humboldt as viewed by leading British periodicals, 1800-1830 (AAFH/TAM, 29:4, April 1973, p. 442-448)

Political, social, and economic overtones of British interest in Latin America, as whetted by reports and reviews of Humboldt's works.

6524. Kumar, Joginder. Population and land in world agriculture: recent trends and relationships. Berkeley, Univ. of Calif., Institute of International Studies, 1973. 318 p., bibl., tables (Population monograph series, 12)

A study of changes in the agricultural population of the world in relation to the world's agricultural resources, to accompany the two-volume work, *World Urbanization, 1950-1970,* published previously in the Population Monograph Series. Includes data from various Latin American countries and regions, and in an appendix there are notes on sources of basic data for Mexico and Paraguay.

6525. Loker, June. Defensa de la naturaleza (OAS/AM, 25:6/7, [Suplemento especial] junio/julio 1973, p. 1-16, plates)

OAS-oriented commentary on Latin American development and the environment, including topics of adequate use of natural resources, the natural resource program of the OAS, interamerican and international cooperation, education, and the role of special agencies of the OAS.

6526. Lorente Mourelle, Rafael. América Latina: urbanización y vivienda. Prólogo [de] Juan Pablo Terra. Montevideo, Editorial Tierra Nueva, 1973. 68 p., bibl., tables (Biblioteca Científica)

Urbanization in Latin America occurred in four stages: precolumbian, colonial, republican, and the current period of economic imperialism. Discussion of fundamental characteristics and causes of acceleration of urbanization leads to commentary on its consequences, with the emphasis on peripheral slums and policies for dealing with the various problems they present.

6527. Mabogunje, A.L. Role of the city in the modernization of developing countries (CAG/CG 17:1, Spring 1973, p. 67-75)

Commentary on papers read at the Symposium on the Role of the City in the Modernization of Developing Countries, Univ. of Toronto, 1/9 Aug. 1972, including Pedro Pinchas Geiger "Observations Regarding the Urbanization Process in Brazil," Erdmann Gormsen "Considerations on the Formation of Systems in Developing Countries," and "Villes d'Avant-Poste et Developpement de l'Interieur d'un pays: le Cas de Linden en Guyana."

6528. Maestre Alfonso, Juan. Condicionamientos ecológicos del desarrollo social y agrario en América Latina (Revista de Estudios Agro-Sociales [Instituto de Estudios Agro-Sociales, Madrid] 83, abril/junio 1973, p. 175-178)

Geographical factors in the tropics as they relate to social problems and agricultural development, emphasizing shifting field agriculture.

6529. Márquez Mayaudón, Enrique. El medio ambiente. México, Fondo de Cultura Económica, 1973. 100 p. (Archivo del fondo, 4)

Discusses various biological subjects such as the origins of life and the nature of ecosystems, leading to the themes of pollution in relation to population and urbanization.

6530. Mauro, Frédéric. El rol de las ciudades en el desarrollo regional en

América Latina: industrialización y urbanización: información resumida (UNAM/RMS, 34:1, enero/marzo 1972, p. 65-73)

Summary of studies of Cuzco, Medellín, and Guadalajara emphasizing historical, geographical, economic, and sociological aspects of their importance as regional centers.

6531. Miller, John and **Ralph A. Gakenheimer** eds. Latin American urban policies and the social sciences. Beverly Hills, Calif., Sage Publications, 1971. 398 p., bibl., illus., maps, tables.

Contents: John Miller, "The Urban Phase: Reason d'être for Policy;" John Miller, "The Rapprochement of Nations with Contiguous Regions;" Poul Ove Pedersen and Walter Stohr, "Economic Integration and the Spatial Development of South America;" John Miller, "Channeling National Urban Growth in Latin America;" John Friedmann, "The Role of Cities in National Development;" Richard M. Morse, "Planning, History, Politics: Reflections on John Friedmann's "The Role of Cities in National Development;" John Friedmann, "A Theory of Urbanization? Rejoinder to Richard M. Morse;" John Miller, "The Distribution of Political and Government Power in the Context of Urbanization;" Robert T. Daland, "Urbanization Policy and Political Development in Latin America;" Carlos Delgado, "Three Proposals Regarding Accelerated Urbanization Problems in Metropolitan Areas: The Lima Case;" John Miller, "The Contribution of the Social Sciences to Urban Policy Formulation in Latin America." An appendix contains a summary by Kalman H. Silvert of the Jahuel Seminar.

6532. Morse, Richard M.; Michael L. Conniff; and **John Wibel** eds. The urban development of Latin America: 1750-1920. Introductory and concluding chapters by Richard M. Morse and William P. McGreevey. Stanford, Calif., Stanford Univ., Center for Latin American Studies, 1971. 129 p., bibl., maps, tables.

A general article on 19th-century cities is followed by contributions on Argentina, Brazil, Chile, Colombia, Cuba, Mexico, Peru and Venezuela. The final article analyzes primacy and lognormality in size distribution.

6533. Mota, A. Teixeira da. Reflexos do Tratado de Tordesilhas na cartografia náutica do século XVI. Coi Portugal, Junta de Investigações de Ultramar, Agrupamento de Estudos de Cartografia Antiga, Secção de Lisboa, 1973. 15 p., maps (Série Separatas, 80)

Uses example of the Treaty of Tordesilhas to point out various reasons for inaccuracies on 16th-century nautical charts. Analysis must take into account the projection and errors ranging from casual to those inserted deliberately for political motives.

6534. Neira, Eduardo. La planificación regional y urbana en tela de juicio (*in* Funes, Julio César ed. La ciudad y la región para el desarrollo. Caracas, Comisión de Administración Pública de Venezuela, 1972, p. 569-600)

Questions about and analysis of strategies for urban and regional development.

6535. Núñez, Benjamín. Términos topográficos en la Argentina colonial: 1516-1810; un análisis lingüístico-cultural. Rio, Instituto Pan-Americano de Geografia e História, Comissão de Geografia, 1965. 351 p., bibl., maps (Publicación, 140)

Introductory material inclufconcise essays on geology, geography and human occupation as background for the linguistic and cultural analyses of the toponyms. Analyzes terms according to their correlations, e.g., those associated with water, the land, vegetation; according to origins, e.g., americanismos, indigenismos, castellanismos; and according to topographic features. Covers 472 terms, with 1,889 citations of usage.

Odell, Peter R. and **David A. Preston.** Economies and societies in Latin America: a geographical interpretation. See item 4150.

6536. Orejas Miranda, Braulio. Parques zoológicos: su función educativa y su aporte a la preservación de especies (OAS/CI, 14:1, enero/abril 1973, p. 12-21, bibl., map, tables)

Educative and scientific justification for establishment and maintenance of zoos in Latin America, with an interesting section on the history of collecting and keeping wild animals; the role of the veterinary activities in public health; and concern over reduction of habitat and numbers of wild species.

6537. Organization of American States. Department of Social Affairs. Datos básicos de población en América Latina: 1970. Washington, 1970. 115 p., tables.

General data on demography, education, public health facilities, dwellings and economy, followed by country-by-country entries with the same categories.

6538. Parsons, James J. Latin America (*in* Mikesell, Marvin W. *ed.* Geographers abroad: essays on the problems and prospects of research in foreign areas. Chicago, Ill., The Univ. of Chicago, Dept. of Geography, 1973, p. 16-46 [Research paper, 152])

Parsons is an extraordinary geographical evangelist and advocate for Latin America. In this review of recent geographical research on Latin America (updating one now ten years old), Parsons again demonstrates his grasp of historical, physical, ecological, human, agricultural, urban, political, and regional geography. He presents strong arguments for pursuing cultural and historical studies which investigate Latin America's unique cultural pluralism while noting that the much-heralded "new geography" directed toward theory construction and development has made little headway in the literature although its aims are advocated by many geographers and supported by such organizations as the new conference of Latin Americanist Georgraphers. For another view of geographical research in the Caribbean, see item 6570. [T.L. Martinson]

6539. Patman, C.R. Probing potential in developing nations (GM, 45:9, June 1973, p. 641-647, plates, tables)

Despite the large number of national development plans created for less developed countries, no adequate framework exists for the synthesis of economical and social factors in planning for the future. Economic theories have changed, and geographers have recently contributed perspective on unique character of countries and regions. Emphasis on capital investment and industry has not proved justified. Suggests that planners have not taken sufficiently into account, nor funded investigation of, the social component of development strategies.

6540. Peláez, César and **George Martine.** Las tendencias de la población en el decenio de 1960 y sus repercusiones sobre el desarrollo (UNECLA/B, 18:1/2, 1973, p. 88-116, tables)

Analizes demographic characteristics of the decade 1960-70, with commentary on growth and migration. Redistribution to reduce problems of urban concentration is difficult in the face of strong socio-cultural factors that are often more powerful than economic objectives.

6541. Rehovot Conference, *VI, Jerusalem and Rehovot, Israel, 1971.* Urbanization and development in developing countries. Edited by Raanan Weitz. N.Y., Praeger Publishers *in cooperation with the Continuation Committee of the Rehovot Conference,* 1973. 308 p. (Praeger special studies in international economics and development)

This is " . . . neither a report nor proceedings of the Conference but represents the subject matter presented in the form of papers or discussions as seen through the eyes of the editor." Pt. 1, "Reality," deals with descriptive and analytical material on descriptive relationships among urbanization, economic growth, and society. Pt. 2, "Challenge," has chapters on urbanization and production, development policies, and urbanization strategies. Pt. 3, "Methods and Means," discusses urban and regional planning, slum areas, and means of implementation of urban planning and development.

6542. Sachs, Ignacy. Población, tecnología, recursos naturales y medio ambiente: ecodesarrollo; uvrte a la definicíon de estilos de desarrollo para América Latina (UNECLA/B, 18:1/2, 1973, p. 117-129)

Suggests M.F. Strong's concept of "ecodesarrollo" as useful in Latin American development. The rational use of the environment and natural resources should be an integral part of, not a substitute for, socioeconomic development. "Ecodesarrollo" is potentially very useful in regional planning, especially in planning for the population of currently uninhabited or sparsely inhabited areas.

6543. Santos, Milton. Las ciudades incompletas de los países subdesarrollados (*in* Funes, Julio César *ed.* La ciudad y la región para el desarrollo. Caracas, Comisión de Administración Pública de Venezuela, 1972, p. 239-271, tables)

Incomplete cities are those that, although metropolitan in size, are incapable of all the functions appropriate to such urban agglomerations, such as production of capital or development of technologies adapted to the needs of the national economy or society.

6544. ———. Los dos circuitos de la economía urbana en los países subdesarrollados (*in* Funes, Julio César *ed.* La ciudad y la región para el desarrollo. Caracas, Comisión de Administración Pública de Venezuela, 1972, p. 67-99, tables)

The two *circuitos* are the modern and the traditional forms of production, distribution, and consumption, with many interrelationships. Traditional forms play important roles in the urban economy with respect to rural immigrants.

6545. Santos de Morais, Clodomir. Diccionario de reforma agraria latinoamerica. Prefacio de Josué de Castro. San José, Editorial Universitaria Centroamericana (EDUCA), 1973. 533 p., bibl.

Terms listed and defined under 12 headings: Agriculture, Economics, Legal, Social, Agricultural Labor, Rural Localisms, Organizations of Agricultural Workers, Latin American Weights and Measures, Soil and Water, Land Tenure, Types of Workers and of Agricultural Employment, and Vegetation and Forests. An appendix contains some terms from non-Latin American countries.

6546. Schleiffer, Hedwig *comp.* Sacred narcotic plants of the New World Indians: an anthology of texts from the sixteenth century to date. Introductory words by Richard Evans Schultes. N.Y., Macmillan, Hafner Press, 1973. 156 p., illus., plates.

Useful collection of descriptions and commentary concerning narcotic plants, arranged by botanical family and with indices of scientific and vernacular names.

The citations constitute a good bibliography for geographers interested in distributions of narcotic plants and associated practices.

6547. Schteingart, Martha and **Horacio Torres.** Procesos sociales y estructuración metropolitana en América Latina: estudio de casos (IDES/DE, 12:48, enero/marzo 1973, p. 725-760, illus., tables.)

Case studies include B.A., Santiago, and Lima, dealing with developmental processes related to economic, social and spatial factors.

6548. Scott, Robert E. *ed.* Latin American modernization problems: case studies in the crises of change. Foreword by Carl W. Deal. Urbana, Ill., Univ. of Illinois Press, 1973. 365 p.

Contents: Robert E. Scott, "Latin America and Modernization;" Robert Byars, "Culture, Politics, and the Urban Factory Worker in Brazil: the Case of Zé Maria;" Roger W. Findley, "Problems Faced by Colombia's Agrarian Reform Institute in Acquiring and Distributing Land;" René Vandendries, "Internal Migration and Economic Development in Peru;" Douglas Butterworth, "Squatters or Suburbanites? The Growth of ShantytownfiOaxaca, Mexico;" Joseph Love, "External Financing and Domestic Politics: The Case of São Paulo, Brazil, 1889-1937;" René Vandendries, "An Appraisal of the Reformist Development Strategy of Peru;" and Robert E. Scott, "National Integration Problems and Military Regimes in Latin America."

6549. Seminario Interamericano sobre la Definición de Regiones para la Planificación del Desarrollo, *I, Hamilton, Canada, 1968.* Documentación del . . . Rio, Instituto Panamericano de Geografía e Historia, Comisión de Geografía, 1969. 334 p., maps.

Seminar held at McMaster Univ., Hamilton, Canada.
Contents are:
Harold A. Wood "Palabras de Bienvenida al Seminario" p. 1-3
Harold A. Wood "First Inter-American Seminar on the Definition of Regions for Development Planning: Introduction to the Seminar" p. 4-11
Luis Vera "Perspectivas para la Planificación del Desarrollo Regional en América Latina" p. 12-36
Benjamin Higgins "The Scope and Objectives of Planning for Underdeveloped Regions" p. 37-62
Walter Stöhr "The Definition of Regions in Relation to National and Regional Development in Latin America" p. 63-82
Harold A. Wood "Ejemplo de Regionalización Nacional: La Regionalización de la República Dominicana" p. 83-91
Harold A. Wood "Ejemplo de Regionalización Nacional: El Caso del Perú" p. 92-101
Pedro Salazar Chambers "Planificación Regional en Panamá, Experiencia y Perspectiva" p. 102-122
Walter Stöhr "Ejemplo de Regionalización Nacional: El Caso de la República de Chile" p. 123-135
Pedro Pinchas Geiger "Regionalização do Brasil" p. 136-145
Luis Vera "Problemas Estructurales de la Regionalización: Análisis de Casos de Brasil y de Perú" p. 146-178
Manuel Achura L. "Organización y Funciones de la Planificación Regional en Chile" p. 179-194
Jorge Cañas "La Planificación Regional de Magallanes" p. 195-205
Robert L. Thomson "The Kurces Inventory and Evaluation Technique as a Basic Toll for Regional Planning" p. 215-224
Manuel Arreguín "Planificación Regional: el Ejemplo de la Cuenca Lerma—Santiago" p. 225-229
Tulio E. Ramírez S. "Problemas de Regionalización: Integración de las Zonas Fronterizas Colombo-Venezolanas" p. 230-244
Wilson Garcés "Resumen General de las Necesidades de Planificación en América Latina" p. 245-248.

6550. Seminario Internacional para Profesores de Suelos, *Maracay, Ven., 1969.* Informe. Caracas? Univ. Central de Venezuela, Facultad de Agronomía [and] Instituto Interamericano de Ciencias Agrícolas de la OEA, Programa de Educación Agrícola Superior-Zona Andina, 1969? 1 v. (Various pagings) plates, tables.

Distributed for a seminar held at Maracay, V/ 23-28 June 1969. Seminar objectives were to analyze programs of study in souvience existing in agricultural education curricula in Andean countries; to make recommendations for implementing programs and improving the teaching of soil science; to facilitate the interchange of ideas and experiences among soil science teachers; and to create a working document, comprising the report on the seminar and individual working sessions, for further analysis and discussion at conferences held in individual countries.

6551. Seminario sobre Evaluación de la Contaminación Ambiental, *I, Atlihuetzia, Mex., 1971.* Primer Seminario sobre Evaluación de la Contaminación Ambiental. México, Instituto Mexicano de Recursos Naturales Renovables, 1972. 161 p.

Contains presentations on air and water pollution, radioactive contamination, and a study of pollution in the lower Río Coatzacoalcos region. Seminar was held 21/24 Oct. 1971 at the Centro de Capacitación of the Comisión Federal de Electricidad in Atlihuetzia.

6552. Seminario sobre Regionalización de las Políticas de Desarrollo en América Latina, *II, Santiago, 1969.* Documentación del . . . Rio, Comisión de Geografía, Instituto Panamericano de Geografía e Historia, 1972. 465 p., maps, tables (Publicación, 330)

Papers presented list the contents, starting with "Metas de las Políticas Regionales . . .," by Kuklinski, and ending with "Informe de Venezuela," by Valderrama.

6553. Simpósio sôbre Desenvolvimento Urbano, *Rio, 1974.* Simpósio sobre desenvolvimento urbano. Rio, Banco Nacional da Habitação, Secretaria de Divulgação, 1974. 182 p., bibl., tables.

Contributions in international and theoretical contexts in fields of planning, transportation, land use, slum problems, and urban economics. Geographers' viewpoint is represented by Jean Gottman in his article on planning in large cities.

6554. Simpósio sôbre Poluição Ambiental, *I, Brasília, 1971.* Simpósio: documento—síntese. Brasília, Câmara dos Deputados, Comissão Especial sôbre Poluição Ambiental, 1971. 129 p.

Proceedings of the symposium, including recommendations of commissions on air, water and soil pollution. Recommendations by all participants included the establishment of federal legislation and national prevention agencies to combat pollution and administer the preventive measures.

6555. Stamper, B. Maxwell. Population policy in development planning: a study of seventy less developed countries. N.Y., Population Council, 1973. 30 p., bibl., tables (Reports on population/family planning, 13)

Survey of development plans and population policy. Includes data on Barbados, Colombia, Jamaica, Panama, and Trinidad and Tobago.

6556. Stenger, Carl. Reise durch Lateinamerika. Frankfurt am Main, FRG, Deutschen Postgewerkschaft, 1965. 83 p., map, plates.

Superficial travel descriptions of Latin America. Contains a few scenic pictures. [H.J. Hoyer]

6557. University of Wisconsin, *Madison.* **Land Tenure Center** *comp.* Agrarian reform in Latin America: an annotated bibliography. Madison, Wis., 1974. 2 v. (667 p.) (Continuous pagination)

Over 5,000 annotated entries relating to agrarian reform and land tenure in Latin America, with many items of use to geographers. Separate bibliographies for most countries; regional bibliographies for "Latin America" (All Spanish speaking South American countries, and Mexico), Central America (including Panama), and the Caribbean, with separate country bibliographies in the latter section for Cuba, the Dominican Republic, and Puerto Rico. Reference matter includes a list of topical bibliographies, appendices listing journal abbreviations and acronyms, and indexes of personal and corporate authors, and classified outline of subject. Many of the materials represented are in the Land Tenure Library at Madison.

6558. Vaughan, Denton R. *comp.* Urbanization in twentieth century Latin America: a working bibliography. Austin, The Univ. of Texas at Austin, Institute of Latin American Studies, Population Research Center, 1970. 122 p., bibl.

Periodical literature for the years 1965-69 was searched, with review of some of the more important periodicals back to 1960. Languages covered are English, Spanish, Portuguese, and French. About 90 percent of the entries are post World War II, reflecting the recency of Latin American urbanization.

6559. Walter, Heinrich. Ecology of tropical and subtropical vegetation. Translated by D. Mueller-Dombois. Edited by J.H. Burnett. N.Y., Van Nostrand Reinhold, 1971. 539 p., bibl., illus., maps, plates, tables.

This is the first volume of a projected series on the vegetation of the world, stemming from a request that Walter revise the fourth edition of A.F.W. Schimper's *Pflanzengeographie.* V. 2 will cover the temperate and arctic zones, to be followed by continental and regional monographs. "Tropical" and "subtropical" are used in the latitudinal rather than the climatic sense, and the world's arid regions are included. Matter concerning the humid tropics is arranged in a gradation from the "continuously wet tropical rain forest" to "natural savannahs," whereas deserts are treated individually by region, e.g., Sonoran, Sahara.

MIDDLE AMERICA

(Caribbean Islands, Central America, Mexico)

TOM L. MARTINSON
Professor of Geography
Ball State University

AN EMPHASIS ON POPULATION AND AGRICULTURE is apparent in the geographical literature on Middle America this year and travel books are even more abundant and varied than in last year's listings, but new works on transportation, ecology-conservation, and economic development are especially noteworthy. An excellent new survey of geographical research on the Caribbean by Lowenthal (item 6570) reports and reflects on these and many other recent trends.

The population studies range from historical works such as those by Vivo Escoto (item 6612) and García Palacios (item 6675) to analyses of modern urbanization (items 6658, 6662, 6667, 6687, and 6698) with works on migration and economic development by Brunn and Thomas (item 6632), Barkin (item 6656), Eyre (item 6595), and Teller (item 6635) most attractive.

Agricultural themes are varied, but studies of agricultural colonization (item 6702) and agricultural diversification and modernization by Seele (item 6709), Stouse (item 6712), Sandoval and Cruz (item 6631), Sander (item 6706), Helbig (item 6679), Wenzens (item 6717), Dickinson (item 6627), Winkelman (item 6719), and Williams (item 6718) especially noted. Several authors have stressed water use in agriculture, particularly with reference to Mexican agrarian problems (items 6661, 6666, 6674, 6680, 6703, and 6713).

The important new themes are presented by many works. General studies of transportation include those by Etcharren (item 6669) and Churchill and others (item 6609), while special studies of urban transportation (item 6636), the consequences of closing the Darien Gap (item 6645), and the human problems involved in constructing a new transisthmian canal (item 6650) are surveyed as well. The conservation-ecology-natural history movement is becoming stronger in Middle America, as exemplified by the continuing series of the Instituto Mexicano de Recursos Naturales Renovables (items 6660 and 6699) as well as notable individual efforts by Rees (item 6701), Villa (item 6643), and Méndez (item 6647). Geographical studies of industrial development in Middle America are especially welcome because they are rare. For good examples of these efforts, see Escamilla (item 6668), Mundingo (item 6634), and Elbow (item 6628).

CARIBBEAN ISLANDS
GENERAL

6560. American Automobile Association, *Washington.* Caribbean, Bahamas and Bermuda; travel guide: what to see, where to stay, where to dine—a catalog of complete travel information. Washington, 1971. 120 p., maps, tables.

Directs tourists to the most exclusive and expensive establishments in the Caribbean.

Antigua black: portrait of an island people. See *HLAS 36:437*.

6561. Aspinall, W.P.; Haraldur Sigurdsson; and **J.B. Shepherd.** Eruption of Soufrière volcano on St. Vincent Island: 1971-1972. (AAAS/S, 181:4095, July 1973, p. 117-124, bibl., maps, plates, tables)

One of the world's most destructive volcanoes is capable of two types of eruption: the traditional highly explosive type preceded by earthquakes, and the recent (1971-72) type, which is non-explosive and slow.

6562. Berney, Henri-Maurice and **Helmut Blume.** Antillen: Tropische Inseln im Karibischen Meer. Bern, Kümmerly & Frey Geographischer Verlag, 1972. 128 p., maps, plates, tables.

A brief but extremely colorful introduction to the Caribbean islands. One-third of book consists of beautiful photos. [H.J. Hoyer]

6563. Buck, Wilbur F. Agriculture and trade of the Caribbean region: Bermudas, The Bahamas, The Guianas, and British Honduras. Washington, U.S. Dept. of Agriculture, Economic Research Service, 1971. 102 p., maps, tables.

Author states that: "this study examines some of the factors affecting the Caribbean region's recent past and short-term future agricultural and industrial developments in this nearby area of increasing American influence. Special attention has been given to the extent and direction of Caribbean trade, particularly its relationship to U.S. agriculture and industry."

6564. Cross, Cliff. Yucatan peninsula: Mexico, British Honduras, Guatemala. North Palm Springs, Calif., n.p., 1971. 127 p., illus., maps, plates, tables.

Guide for travelers and campers contains many detailed sketch maps, photos, and historical vignettes on the peninsula.

6565. Harewood, J. Changes in the demand for the supply of labour in the Commonwealth Caribbean: 1946-1960 (UWI/SES, 21:1, March 1972, p. 44-60, bibl., tables)

Author measures the relative importance of labor demand and supply as contributing to the decline in economic activity participation from 1946 to 1960, concluding that the decline in the supply industries was less important than the decline in demand industries in explaining the decline in general worker rates in Trinidad, Tobago, and Barbados.

6566. Hunte, George. The West Indian islands. N.Y., The Viking Press, 1972. 246 p., bibl., maps, plates (A Studio book)

Although obviously a labor of love, this tourist guide is superficial and disorganized.

6567. Las islas del Caribe: Rep. Dominicana, Haití, Puerto Rico, Jamaica, Cuba. Barcelona, Editorial Mateu, 1970? 377 p., maps, plates (América en color, 6)

A commonplace review of basic information on the Caribbean islands, accentuating history and customs, with many color photos and several base maps, some marred by overzealous trimming during the binding process.

6568. Jesse, Charles. St. Lucia: the romance of its place names. Foreword by B.H. Easter. Preface by Monsieur le Duc de Castries. Castries, St. Lucia, St. Lucia Archaeological and Historical Society, 1966. 63 p., maps (St. Lucia miscellany, 1)

Properly a geographical dictionary which contains only 200 names drawn from 13 early French and English maps, plans, and books.

6569. Leitch, Adelaide. St. Lucia, island in transition (RCGS/CGJ, 85:6, Dec. 1972, p. 210-215, illus., plates)

Brief sketch of historical and contemporary life in St. Lucia, which became independent in 1967.

6570. Lowenthal, David. The Caribbean region (*in* Mikesell, Marvin W. *ed.* Geographers abroad: essays on the problems and prospects of research in foreign areas. Chicago, Ill., The Univ. of Chicago, Dept. of Geography, 1973, p. 47-69 [Research paper, 152])

Lowenthal traces the tradition of synthesis practiced by eclectic Caribbean geographers and predicts that future geographical work in the Caribbean will be more specialized, programmatic, group-oriented, and government-linked. Lowenthal's survey, as opposed to that by Parsons (see item 6538) indicates that the professionalization of geography is leading research away from broad, humanistic syntheses toward applied, service-oriented enterprises. Lowenthal believes the potential contributions of geography to Caribbean studies lie in three broad realms of inquiry: matters of scale and location, of environment and habitat, and of connections with the wider world.

6571. Peter, George. Geology and geophysics of the Venezuelan continental margin between Blanquilla and Orchilla Islands. Boulder, Colo., U.S. Dept. of Commerce, National Oceanic and Atmospheric Administration, 1972. 82 p., illus., tables (NOAA technical report ERL 226-AOML 6)

Dissertation research traces the nature of the junction between the Lesser Antilles island arc and the South American continent, concluding that the basins of the Caribbean Sea developed between the small continental fragments left behind as North America drifted away from South America in Early Mesozoic time.

6572. Rand, Abby. Abby Rand's guide to Puerto Rico and the U.S. Virgin Islands. N.Y., Charles Scribner's Sons, 1973. 276 p., maps, plates.

Informative guide to accommodations and entertainment, written in breezy journalese.

6573. Wilensky, Julius M. Yachtsman's guide to the Windward Islands. Edited by John R. Van Ost. Tenafly, N.J., Caribbean Sailing Yachts (CSY), 1973. 224 p., illus., plates.

Although written for sailors, volume is perhaps one of the best general guides to the Windwards because of its treasury of information on everything from navigation maps to vista points. Many maps and photos.

CUBA

Acosta, Maruja and **Jorge Enrique Hardoy.** Reforma urbana en Cuba revolucionaria. See *HLAS 36:443.*

6574. Bayo Cosgaya, Armando. Humboldt. La Habana, Instituto del Libro, Editorial de Ciencias Sociales, 1970. 239 p., bibl. (Historia)

Attempts to emphasize Humboldt's association with Cuba. [C. Edwards]

6575. _____ . Humboldt, segundo descubridor de Cuba (UH/U, 33:194, abril/junio 1969, p. 3-12, illus., map, table)

Grants a pivotal role to Humboldt as an analyst of the 19th-century Cuban physical and cultural situation.

6576. Blutstein, Howard I. and others. Area handbook for Cuba. Washington, The American Univ., Foreign Area Studies, 1971. 505 p., bibl., maps, tables (DA-PAM, 550-152)

Illustrative of increasing interest in Cuba, volume's appearance will be welcomed by the reader seeking general information on the country's social, political, and economic character as well as its national security system.

6577. Funtanella, Carlos. Humboldt en nuestra historia (UN/U, 33:194, abril/junio 1969, p. 13-25)

Humboldt's work constituted a scientific rediscovery of Cuba and, particularly because of his treatment of oppressed minorities, author indicates Humboldt may be considered a prophet of the modern Cuban experience.

6578. Furrazola-Bermúdez, Gustavo and others. Geología de Cuba. La Habana, Ministerio de Industrias, Instituto Cubano de Recursos Minerales, Depto. Científico de Geología [and] Editorial Nacional de Cuba, Editora del Consejo Nacional de Universidades, 1964. 2 v. (239 p.) (Continuous pagination) fold. maps, maps, plates.

Reputed to be the first compilation of information on Cuba's geology, text suffers from an encyclopedic approach to the subject. Well-executed maps in the accompanying map folio. V. 2 is an appendix of folded maps.

6579. García Báez, Carlos. Condiciones oceanográficas de la Bahía de Cienfuegos. La Habana, Univ. de la Habana, Centro de Información Científica y Técnica, 1972. 23 p., illus. (Ciencias. Serie 7: geografía, 2)

Consists primarily of maps of temperature, salinity, depth, water density, and currents in Cienfuegos Bay with some observations on these characteristics.

6580. Grelier, Joseph. Cuba, carrefour des Caraïbes. Paris, Société Continentale d'Editions Modernes Illustrées, 1970. 355 p., illus., maps, plates (Connaissance des îles)

A cultural history centering on the first phases of indo-European contact and the early role of sugar in the Cuban economy, with little mention of Castro-era agrarian reform.

6581. Larragoiti, Luis; Teresa López; and René Menéndez. Estudio climatológico del Valle Perú. La Habana, Univ. de la Habana, Escuela de Geografía, Sección de Meteorología y Climatología, 1972. 5 p., illus., tables (Ciencias. Serie 7: geografía, 4)

Basic rainfall data for a valley southeast of the city of Havana. Precipitation is 25 percent greater than for areas outside the valley but very uniform within the valley and unaffected by orography. [R.C. Eidt]

6582. Paulukat, Inge. Das sozialistische Kuba: Probleme seiner strukturellen und territorialen Wirtschaftsentwicklung (GDRMK/ZE, 23:2, 1971, p. 41-51, tables)

General review of Cuba's contemporary economic situation reveals some success in efforts toward diversification of industry.

6583. Perekhrest, Stephan Makarovich. Los pantanos de Cuba y su importancia para el aumento de la producción agrícola y fortalecimiento de la economía del país. Traducción de G.A. Lozhkin. La Habana, Instituto Nacional de Recursos Hidráulicos, 1964. 77 p., bibl., maps.

Author advocates effective use of "virgin" marshes for agricultural purposes, listing costs and benefits of specific projects.

6584. Ritter, Arch R.M. Growth strategy and economic performance in revolutionary Cuba: past, present, and prospective (UWI/SES, 21:3, Sept. 1972, p. 313-337, tables)

Analysis of the growth strategy in Cuba's "strategic master plan" (1970-75) concludes that it appears essentially sound although the take-off stage will extend beyond 1975 due to slow growth of exports and therefore of capital goods imports and capital accumulation.

Rivière d'Arc, Hélène. Aménagement rural a Cuba: le plan Ceiba. See item 8240.

Salinas, Fernando and others. La Habana metropolitana: un instrumento para el desarrollo socialista. See *HLAS 36:449.*

6585. Taylor, Duncan. Travel guide (GM, 45:8, May 1973, p. 562-567, illus.)

A Cuban vacation often consists of volunteer labor, but some resorts, parks, and museums are available and well-kept.

6586. Trusov, Ivan I. Las precipitaciones en la isla de Cuba. La Habana, Instituto Nacional de Recursos Hidráulicos, 1967. 61 p., illus., maps.

Reported to be the first compilation of its kind, this study is an investigation of the distribution of precipitation in Cuba, including rainfall probabilities at selected stations and an analysis of the distribution of precipitation resulting from the passage of Hurricane Flora (1963), with many appropriate maps.

DOMINICAN REPUBLIC

6587. Pérez Rancier, Juan Bautista Victoriano. Geografía y sociedad. Liminar de E. Rodríguez Demorizi. Santo Domingo, Editora del Caribe, 1972. 697 p., illus. (Publicación de la Sociedad Dominicana de Geografía, 3)

Third volume in this new series traces the life and contains some of the works of Dr. Juan Bautista Pérez (1883-1968), noted Dominican intellectual.

6588. Rodríguez, Héctor Luis. Producción agropecuaria para el año 2,000 (AULA, 1:2/3, julio/dic. 1972, p. 142-155)

Review of major crops in the Dominican Republic reveals major population/resource imbalances will occur by the year 2000 unless steps are taken now to introduce better seed and agricultural practices.

6589. Rodríguez Demorizi, Emilio. Relaciones geográficas de Santo Domingo. v. 1. Santo Domingo, Editora del Caribe, 1970. 455 p. (Publicación de la Sociedad Dominicana de Geografía, 1)

Welcome new publication, the first in a series, consists of a collection of essays ranging from colonial era letters on the geography of Santo Domingo to a 1936 geographical excursion to the central part of the island.

6590. Simposio sobre el Uso de los Datos de Población del Censo de 1970, Santo Domingo, 1972. Documentos, discusiones, conclusiones. Santo Domingo, Presidencia, Secretariado Técnico, Oficina Nacional de Estadística, 1972. 340 p., tables.

Results of a symposium on the use of the 1970 population census of the Dominican Republic, with sections on the historical antecedents of the census, sampling procedures used, and the composition of the population, with appendices on population distribution, migration, education, mortality, and related topics. The census is regarded as the first "modern" census of the country.

6591. United States. Department of the Interior. Board of Geographic Names. Defense Mapping Agency. Topographic Center. Dominican Republic: official standard of names. Washington, 1972. 477 p., tables.

HAITI

6592. Zéndegui, Guillermo de comp. Imagen de Haití (OAS/AM, 24:3 [Suplemento especial] marzo 1972, p. 1-24, illus., facsims., maps, plates)

A general introduction to the geography, history, economy, and culture of Haiti; part of an OAS series on the American republics.

JAMAICA

6593. Adams, Charles Dennis. The Blue Mahoe & other bush: an introduction to plant life in Jamaica. Kingston, Sangster's Bookstores *in association with* McGraw-Hill Far Eastern Publishers [Singapore], 1971. 159 p., plates.

Brief general descriptions of important or particularly interesting Jamaican plants and their habitats. Illustrated.

6594. Carey, Beverly. Portland and the Rio Grande Valley. Kingston, Public Relations Advisory Service, 1970. 39 p., illus., plates (A Jamaican series souvenir folk history guide)

Although the avowed purpose of this pamphlet is to promote tourism, it is largely concerned with the establishment and maintenance of the Maroon colonies in the island's interior.

Ehrlich, Allen S. Ecological perception and economic adaptation in Jamaica. See item 1229.

6595. Eyre, L. Alan. The shantytowns of Montego Bay, Jamaica (AGS/GR, 62:3, July 1972, p. 394-413, maps, plates)

Montego Bay's shantytowns reflect urban vigor rather than urban breakdown for they are populated by industrious, upwardly mobile families escaping from the city slums. This movement of the poor from city center to suburbs has not been recognized elsewhere.

6596. Hughes, I.G. and others *comps.* The mineral resources of Jamaica. Kingston, Ministry of Mining & Natural Resources, Geological Survey Dept., 1973. 87 p., maps, tables (Bulletin, 8)

A summary of the mineral resources of Jamaica, including a brief description of the island's economic geology (with maps) and its mining regulations.

6597. Jamaica. Department of Statistics. Commonwealth Caribbean population census 1970: Jamaica; population census 1970, preliminary report. Kingston, Division of Censuses and Surveys, 1970? 32 p., fold. map, illus., maps, plates, tables.

Preliminary estimates from the tenth census of population includes population by parish according to sex, age, and type of dwelling as well as population in selected towns.

6598. Rodríguez, D.W. Pimento: a short economic history. Kingston, Agricultural Information Service, 1969? 52 p., plates, tables.

Pimento trees and their berries, allspice, are native to Jamaica and are the country's fourth largest export commodity. Pamphlet describes the product's history, botany, cultivation, processing, and marketing.

6599. Williams, R.L. Jamaican coffee supply, 1953-1968: an exploratory study (UWI/SES, 21:1, March 1972, p. 90-103, tables)

Author attempts to explain the lag function of coffee supply in Jamaica in terms of a number of variables, especially price.

PUERTO RICO

6600. Calitri, Princine. Come along to Puerto Rico. Minneapolis, Minn., T.S. Denison, 1971. 212 p., plates.

Account of a visit among Puerto Rico's elite is a bit too ego-gratifying.

6601. Connors, Robert E. and **Donald R. Haener** *comps.* Puerto Rico: an island on the move. Cooperstown, N.Y., Discovery Enterprises, 1972. 159 p., illus., maps, plates, tables.

Book is only one part of a multi-media kit on Puerto Rico designed for use in the public schools. Innovations include bi-lingual photo captions, cartoons, and emphasis on such contemporary notables as baseball players and Miss Universe winners. Geography section overemphasizes physical facts at the expense of spatial distributions.

6602. Curnee, Russell H. Exploration of the Tanama (EJ, 51:3, Sept. 1972, p. 159-171, plates)

First exploration of the Puerto Rican river which drops 600 ft. and goes underground nine times in a ten-mile course.

6603. Dusart, Etienne R. TUSCA: Transportation and Urban Settlements Combined Action (ATI/E, 34:202, 1972, p. 211-216, maps)

The highly urban, industrial society of modern Puerto Rico has led to a deterioration of environment which TUSCA hopes to combat by implementing a comprehensive transportation-land-use-settlement system.

6604. Kimber, Clarissa T. Spatial patterning in the dooryard gardens of Puerto Rico (AGS/GR, 63:1, Jan. 1973, p. 6-26, plates, tables)

The *jíbaro* garden and the manor garden represent the extremes of dooryard gardens in Puerto Rico, but intermediate types are gaining popularity with cultural change. The investigation of dooryard gardens offers an insight into personal space attitudes.

6605. Salivia, Luis A. Historia de los temporales de Puerto Rico y las Antillas: 1492 a 1970. San Juan, P.R. Editorial Edil, 1972. 385 p., bibl., illus.

A listing and brief description of 101 *temporales* which have affected Puerto Rico from 1492 to 1970, without investigation of their meteorology.

6606. Wagenheim, Kal. Puerto Rico: a profile. Foreword by Piri Thomas. N.Y., Praeger Publishers, 1970. 286 p., bibl., maps, plates, table (Praeger country profile series)

Extensive and objective survey of Puerto Rican life suitable for supplementary reading in a college-level course. Especially valuable is its approach to the "independence" problem.

6607. Weeks, Morris, Jr. Hello, Puerto Rico. N.Y., Grosset & Dunlap, 1972. 170 p., plates.

Pop social survey asserts that Puerto Ricans suffer from an identity crisis.

CENTRAL AMERICA
GENERAL

6608. Bonasera, Ilda Finzi. I parchi nazionali del mondo: nel Canada, nel Messico e nell'America Centrale (IGM/U, 52:1, gen./feb. 1972, p. 137-172, maps, plates)

Profusely-illustrated guide does not include some new national parks in Central America.

6609. Churchill, Anthony; Klaus Huber; Elke Meldau; and **Alan Walters.** Road user charges in Central America. Washington, International Bank for Reconstruction and Development, 1972. 176 p., bibl., tables (World Bank staff occasional papers, 15)

An application of the principles of pricing of road user services which advocates the lowering of user charges in rural areas and raising them in urban areas. Very useful in its practical approach to "real" road problems and for the data used in its analyses.

6610. Haefkens, Jacobo. Viaje a Guatemala y Centroamérica. Traducción del holandés [by] Theodora J.M. van Lottum. Edición, revisión, notas e índice temático [by] Francis Gall. Prólogo [by] Luis Luján Muñoz. Guatemala, Editorial Universitaria, 1969. 321 p., facsims., fold. map, plate (Sociedad de Geografía e Historia de Guatemala: serie viajeros, 1)

First volume of an intended series of works by 19th-century visitors to Guatemala. Haefkens, Dutch consul to Central America 1826-1829, travelled widely and reported extensively on his visits, but his writings are little known whereas similar diaries produced by Gage and Stephens have reached a larger audience. His works are considered accurate pictures of early Central America even though they reflect a bias against local customs.

6611. Pichler, Hans and **Richard Weyl.** Petrochemical aspects of Central

American magmatism (GV/GR, 62:2, 1973, p. 357-396, maps, tables)

Authors use chemical bulk analyses to provide new information on Cretaceous-Cenozoic magmatic events in Central America. Revealed are the facts that a continental crust exists only in northern Central America, that the northern geologic formations are composed of andesitic magmas and ignimbrites, and the southern formations have resulted from submarine eruptions of basalt and intrusions of peridotite. In both parts of Central America Quaternary vulcanism produced andesites on one hand and rhyolites on the other.

6612. Vivó Escoto, Jorge A. El poblamiento náhuat en El Salvador y otros países de Centroamérica (UNAMCG/A, 10, 1970, p. 11-43, maps)

The migration of Nahuat people, believed to originate in Mexico, is traced by place name into Guatemala, El Salvador, Honduras, Nicaragua, and Costa Rica over several historical periods.

6613. Wilkes, H. Garrison. Maize and its wild relatives (AAAS/S, 177:4054, Sept. 1972, p. 1071-1077, bibl., map, plates)

The process by which modern maize has evolved is in danger of disappearing because *teosinte*, its hybridizing partner, is threatened with rapid extinction.

COSTA RICA

6614. Cervantes Acuña, Carlos F. and **Roy McDonald Bourne.** Consumo industrial de frutas y hortalizas en Costa Rica durante 1972. San José, Instituto de Fomento y Asesoría Municipal (IFAM) 1973. 70 l., tables.

A crop-by-crop appraisal of the purchases of fruits and vegetables by Costa Rican processors in 1972, with a list of 43 such industries.

6615. La ciudad de San José: 1871-1921. San José, Banco Nacional de Costa Rica, 1972. 1 v. (Unpaged) plates.

Issued on the sesquicentennial of the emancipation of Central America, volume documents in photos the physical changes in the city of San José from 1871 to 1921.

6616. Costa Rica. Dirección General de Estadística y Censos. Población total de la República de Costa Rica, por provincia, cantones y distritos: cálculo al 1 de enero de 1970. San José, 1971. 18 p., tables (Publicaciones, 19)

Population growth, including migration and natural increase, is reported down to the local level.

6617. _____. _____. Sección de Publicaciones. Censo de población: 1963. San José, 1966. 633 p., plates, tables.

6618. Nombres geográficos de Costa Rica. v. 2, Oronimia. San José, Ministerio de Obras Públicas y Transportes, Instituto Geográfico Nacional, Sección de División Territorial, 1972. 87 p., illus., maps.

A list of geographic names found on Costa Rica's 1:50,000 and 1:500,000 topographic map series, with the name's origin, altitude, geographic position, and location on the map.

6619. Sawicki, Sandra. Costa Rica in pictures. N.Y., Sterling, 1974. 64 p., illus., plates (Visual geography series)

Encyclopedic, descriptive volume illustrates the difficulty in presenting factual information without an analytical focus.

EL SALVADOR

6620. Argueta Cordón, Antonio. El problema demográfico en El Salvador: una perspectiva cultural y una hipótesis sobre desarrollo psicológico (UES/U, 95:5/6, sept./dic. 1970, p. 117-122)

Author probes the hypothesis that growth of the poorer classes leads to a greater number of psychologically as well as economically deprived people in El Salvador.

6621. Carpenter, Allan and **Eloise Baker.** El Salvador. Chicago, Ill., Children's Press, 1971. 95 p., map, plates (Enchantment of Central America)

As with the other volumes in this series (see *HLAS 35:6679, 6692,* and *6698*) an excellent introduction to El Salvador for secondary students.

6622. Coyner, Mary S. Agriculture and trade of El Salvador. Washington, U.S. Dept. of Agriculture, Economic Research Service, 1971. 27 p., map, tables.

Updates an out-of-print predecessor. Valuable for general background information on Salvadorean resources, economic trends, factors affecting agricultural production, crop and livestock distribution, and trade in agricultural products.

6623. El Salvador. Dirección General de Estadística y Censos. Cuarto censo nacional de población: 1971. San Salvador, 1971. 20 l., tables.

Preliminary report on the 1971 census contains data on the total population of the country, differentiated by departamento, municipio, urban/rural location, number of dwellings, and sex.

6624. Haverstock, Nathan A. and **John**

P. Hoover. El Salvador in pictures. N.Y., Sterling, 1974. 64 p., illus., plates (Visual geography series)

A thumbnail sketch and introduction to El Salvador which does not appear as successful as those produced by Children's Press (see item 6621).

6625. Imagen de El Savador. Washington, Organization of American States, General Secretariat, 1973. 24 p., illus., maps, plates.

A thumbnail sketch of El Salvador's history and customs, designed for the beginning reader.

White, Alastair. El Salvador. See *HLAS* 36:2203.

GUATEMALA

6626. Chickering, Carol Rogers. Flowers of Guatemala. Foreword by Julian A. Steyermark. Norman, Univ. of Oklahoma Press, 1973. 128 p., illus., maps, plates.

Author divides Guatemala into 12 botanical climate regions and then presents a visitor's view of the vegetation to be found in each belt. Included are 50 color plates, painted by the author, each illustrating a different common flowering plant of the area.

6627. Dickinson, Joshua C. Fisheries of Lake Izábal, Guatemala (AGS/GR, 64:3, July 1974, p. 385-409, illus., map, plates)

Modernization, mechanization, and increased efficiency are seemingly beneficial to the development of fisheries, but in this case they are detrimental for they reduce the aquatic resource base and consequently the quality of life in the area.

6628. Elbow, Gary S. The impact of industrial development in Guatemala: a case study (RMSSA/J, 10:2, April 1973, p. 17-26, illus., map, table)

The recently-constructed industrial plants serve the growing demand for internal consumer goods rather than export goods. The town chosen for study is Amatitlán.

6629. Jerez, César. La United Fruit Company en Guatemala (ECA, 26:269, 1971, p. 117-128, bibl.)

Author believes the impression left by United Fruit in Guatemala is one of oppression and economic imperialism, a view not obscured by the company's move from visible control of land and transportation to the invisible control of industry.

6630. Lewis, A.B. Santa Ana Mixtan: a bench mark study on Guatemalan agriculture. East Lansing, Michigan State Univ., Latin American Studies Center, 1973. 87., tables. (Monograph series, 11)

Results of a 1955 study of the agricultural economy of a small community in Esquintla, including such measures as size of farm, crop choice and yields, tenancy type, farm receipts and expenditures and population and labor trends. Valuable as an example of microscale study and as a benchmark for research on agricultural change.

6631. Sandoval V., Leopoldo R. and **Fernando Cruz.** Cambios en la estructura agraria de Guatemala y metas de reforma (USC/U, 73/78, mayo/dic. 1968/enero/dic. 1969, p. 109-127, bibl., tables)

There are now more *minifundistas* in Guatemala than in 1950, a condition which leads to agricultural and social disequilibrium. Author advocates a massive agrarian reform program.

HONDURAS

6632. Brunn, Stanley D. and **Robert N. Thomas.** Socio-economic environments and internal migration: the case of Tegucigalpa, Honduras (UWI/SES, 21:4, Dec. 1972, p. 463-473)

Almost half the variation in the place of last residence of migrants to Tegucigalpa can be accounted for by reference to traditional rural, dynamic urbanization, agricultural frontier, progressive peasantry, and accessibility factors.

6633. Martinson, Tom L. Economic rent and selected changes in agricultural production along the western highway of Honduras, 1952-1965 (PAIGH/G, 71, dez. 1969, p. 65-74, maps)

6634. Mundigo, Axel I. Elites, economic development and population in Honduras. Ithaca, N.Y., Cornell Univ., 1972. 310 p., bibl., tables (Latin American Studies Program dissertation series, 34)

Dissertation research reveals that Honduran elites are unable to reach consensus on development priorities in general. Population growth, although extremely rapid, is not viewed as a menace to development planning.

6635. Teller, Charles H. Internal migration, socio-economic status and health: access to medical care in a Honduran city. Ithaca, N.Y., Cornell Univ., 1972. 302 p., bibl., tables (Latin American Studies Program dissertation series, 41)

Exploration of the relationship between migration and medical care utilization among migrants to San Pedro Sula concludes that there is little difference between migrants and natives with regard to access to medical care; both groups were served poorly by the existing medical structure.

6636. Wheeler, James O. and **Robert N. Thomas.** Urban transportation in developing economies: work trips in Tegucigalpa, Honduras (AAG/PG, 25:2, May 1973, p. 113-120, bibl., map, tables)

Authors describe the dominant streams of work trips and measure their interactions as well as the functional distance among residential and workplace locations, concluding that work trips in Tegucigalpa reflect a high level of immobility.

NICARAGUA

6637. Carpenter, Allan and **Tom Balow.** Nicaragua. Chicago, Ill., Children's Press, 1971. 95 p., map, plates (Enchantment of Central America)

Competent thumbnail sketch of Nicaragua, as others in this series (see, for example, *HLAS 35:6679, 6692*, and *6698*). Completed before the recent disastrous Managua earthquake.

6638. Estrada Uribe, Gabriel. Managua antisísmica: su ruina y su reconstrucción. Bogotá, Univ. Nacional de Colombia [and] Fondo Colombiano de Investigaciones Científicas y Proyectos Especiales Francisco José de Caldas (COLCIENCIAS), 1973. 230 p., plates.

The most detailed and complete description in Spanish of the Managua earthquake produced thus far, containing appropriate diagrams, photos, and maps.

6639. Incer Barquero, Jaime. Geografía ilustrada de Nicaragua. Con un apéndice sobre el reciente terremoto de Nicaragua. Managua, Librería y Editorial Recalde, 1973. 255 p., illus., plates.

A new edition of the author's encyclopedic 1970 volume revamped as a secondary school text with additional information on the December 1972 earthquake. The only work of its kind on Nicaragua, and welcome.

6640. _____. Nueva geografía de Nicaragua: ensayo preliminar. Managua, Talleres de Editorial Recalde, 1970. 582 p., bibl., maps, plates, tables.

6641. Nietschmann, Bernard. Hunting and fishing focus among the Miskito Indians, Eastern Nicaragua (Human Ecology [Plenum Publishing Corp., N.Y.] 1:1, March 1972, p. 41-67, bibl., maps, plates, tables)

Subsistence agriculture is being disrupted and reduced by a shift of labor from traditional to commercial primary economic activities.

6642. Ponsol, Bernardo. Zonas biogeográficas de la flora y fauna nicaragüenses y factores ecológicos. Managua? Academia Nicaragüense de la Lengua, 1973? 113 p. (Publicación, 6)

Sketchy volume contains descriptions of vegetation associations found within broad ecological zones in Nicaragua.

6643. Villa, Jaime. Anfibios de Nicaragua: introducción a su sistemática, vida y costumbres. Managua, Instituto Geográfico Nacional [and] Banco Central de Nicaragua, 1972. 216 p., illus., maps, plates, tables (Col. Fauna nacional)

Detailed review of the amphibians of Nicaragua complete with drawings, photos, and distribution maps. First volume of a planned series on Nicaraguan biogeography.

PANAMA

6644. Hanbury-Tenison, A. Robin. Darien Indians in the shadow of progress (GM, 44:12, Sept. 1972, p. 831-837, plates)

The physical and cultural destruction which would occur as a consequence of constructing a road through Panama's Darien is enormous and should be avoided.

6645. _____ and **P. J. K. Burton.** Should the Darien gap be closed? (RGS/GJ, 139:1, Feb. 1973, p. 43-52, map, plates)

Bridging Panama's Darien Gap, last unfinished segment of the Pan-American Highway, would damage an unspoiled wilderness and drive Indians from their homes.

6646. Jones, David. Panama's non-transit attractions (GM, 44:1, Oct. 1971, p. 3-6, maps, plates)

Apparently mis-titled article deals with the potential agricultural and industrial uses of the Canal Zone if it were to revert to Panama upon completion of a new trans-isthmian canal.

6647. Méndez, Eustorgio. Los principales mamíferos silvestres de Panamá. Panamá, I. Bárcenas, 1970. 283 p., illus., tables.

A fine contribution to the natural history of Panama, containing not only brief descriptions of mammal species but also drawings and location maps.

6648. Panama. Dirección de Estadística y Censo. Censos nacionales de 1970: séptimo censo de población, tercer censo de vivienda, 10 de mayo de 1970. v.1, Lugares poblados de la República. Panama, 1970. 542 p., tables.

First in a continuing series of reports on the 1970 census of population in Panama, apparently one of the most detailed and complete in the hemisphere.

6649. Reseña histórica del Proyecto Tapón del Darién. 3. ed. Panamá, Organization of American States, Economic and Social Council, Inter-American Congress of Highways, Darien Subcommittee, 1965. 100 p., maps, plates.

Spanish version of *HLAS 33:5126*.

6650. Torres de Araúz, Reina. Human ecology of Route 17—Sasardi-Morti—region, Darien, Panama. Translated and edited by Felix Webster McBryde. Columbus, Ohio, U.S. Atomic Energy Commission, Columbus Laboratories, Battelle Memorial Institute, 1970. 172 p., illus., plates, tables (Bio-environmental and radiological-safety feasibility studies: Atlantic-Pacific inter-oceanic canal)

Report accentuates the general relationships between man and his physical environment, demography of the various cultural groups, and quantitative aspects of the diet of the inhabitants of the region which would be most directly affected by the construction of a sea-level canal using nuclear explosions. A rich data source which makes no judgments on the feasibility or advisability of the canal or moving any individual group of natives from the area.

MEXICO

6651. Almada, Francisco R. Diccionario de historia, geografía y biografía chihuahuenses. 2. ed. Chihuahua, Mex., Univ. de Chihuahua, Depto. de Investigaciones Sociales, Sección de Historia, 1968. 578 p., bibl.

Revision of a 1928 ed., work contains a variety of information ranging from the biographies of important persons to the names and locations of rivers. Useful for the rather detailed summaries of information on the *municipios* within Chihuahua.

6652. Almazán Cadena, Antonio. Síntesis geográfica del Estado de San Luis Potosí. San Luis Potosí, Mex., Ediciones del Ateneo Nacional de Investigaciones Geográficas, 1971. 223 p., bibl., maps, plates.

Encyclopedic survey of the state's physical and human resources, containing many maps which are poorly drawn and badly reproduced.

6653. Altamira G., Armando. Alpinismo mexicano. México, Editorial ECLAL, 1972. 207 p., bibl., illus., maps, plates.

Accounts of climbing several important Mexican mountains, illustrated with appropriate instructions, maps, and photographs as well as some archaeological finds.

6654. Aragón, Eliseo B. Toponimias en lengua náhuatl del estado de Morelos. México, Editorial Herrera, 1969. 102 p., illus., plates.

A dictionary of some place names based on an interpretation of Nahuatl hieroglyphics, many of which are reproduced in color.

6655. Ayala Echavarri, Rafael. San Juan del Río: geografía e historia. México, Editorial Luz, 1971. 209 p., maps, plates.

The natural history of Querétaro *municipio* accentuating its public works and notable sons.

6656. Barkin, David. The demographic impact of regional development: a Mexican case study (Growth and Change [Univ. of Kentucky, Lexington] 3:4, Oct. 1972, p. 15-22, tables)

Investigation of the migration effects of the Comisión del Tepalcatepec on the northern part of the state of Michoacán suggests that although population in this area has increased as a result of increased employment opportunities, this increase has not made a substantial contribution to solving the overall problem of rural-urban migration in Mexico.

6657. Bassols Batalla, Angel. Geografía para el México de hoy y de mañana. México, Editorial Nuestro Tiempo, 1971. 227 p., maps, tables (Col. La cultura al pueblo)

A fine example of a new development-oriented research geography now appearing in Mexico; written for a popular audience.

6658. Bataillon, Claude and Hélène Rivière D'Arc. La ciudad de México. Traducción de Carlos Montemayor y Josefina Anaya. México, Secretaría de Educación Pública, 1973. 183 p., maps., tables (SepSetentas, 99)

An extremely valuable, concise guide to Mexico City which concentrates on its population growth and urban functions. Contains a data appendix and small but readable maps.

6659. Beals, Carleton. Mexican maze. With illustrations by Diego Rivera. Westport, Conn., Greenwood Press, 1971. 369 p., illus.

Reprint of the 1931 ed. reasserts the author's view of the Mexican spirit as "beautiful, enduring, and proud." A classic because of its penetrating analysis of Mexican life and its vitality in the face of change.

6660. Beltrán, Enrique and others. Aspectos internacionales de los recursos renovables de México. México, Instituto Mexicano de Recursos Naturales Renovables, 1972. 118 p., bibl.

Contains the presentations of seven conservationists on the natural resources of Mexico, including its forestry, fauna, fisheries, and crocodiles as well as general themes such as conservation education, the control of the natural environment, and programs for protecting the country's renewable natural resources. Papers delivered at both the XXVI Annual Meeting of the National Wildlife Federation and the XXXVII American Wildlife and Natural Resources Conference.

6661. Benassini, Oscar. Aprovechamiento de los ríos internacionales mexicanos-guatemaltecos (Recursos Hidraúlicos [Mexico] 1:4, 1972, p. 415-425, map, plates, tables)

Commentary on the hydroelectric projects on the Grijalva-Usumacinta river systems. Contains a useful project map.

6662. Brown, Jane Cowan. Patterns of intra-urban settlement in Mexico City: an examination of the Turner theory. N.Y., Cornell Univ., 1972. 203 p., bibl., maps, tables (Latin American Studies Program dissertation series, 40)

New migrants to Mexico City find accomodations in the older squatter settlement ring (not the inner city slums) and then move to a more stable dwelling place in the new low-income subdivisions at the urban fringe.

6663. Burrus, Ernest. La obra cartográfica de la provincia mexicana de la Compañía de Jesús, 1567-1967. v. 2. Madrid, Ediciones J. Porrúa Turanzas, 1967. 1 v. (Unpaged) maps (Col. Chimalistac. Serie José Porrúa Turanzas, 2)

A collection of 46 reprints of Mexican maps drawn from 1567 to 1967. The maps range widely in scale, locale, intent, authorship, source, and quality or reproduction.

6664. Calderón Quijano, José Antonio. Nueva cartografía de los puertos de Acapulco, Campeche y Veracruz. Sevilla, Escuela de Estudios Hispanoamericanos, 1969. 49 p., facsims., maps, plates (Publicaciones, 184. Col. Anuario, 171)

Brief description of a series of maps, charts, and views of three Mexican ports drawn from 1614 to 1862. Illustrated with the maps themselves, which are, for the most part, well-reproduced.

6665. César, J.N. Tlacotalpan: noticias estadísticas sobre aquella municipalidad del Distrito de Veracruz. Prólogo de Leonardo Pasquel. México, Editorial Citlaltepetl, 1973. 163 p. (Col. Suma Veracruzana. Serie historiografía)

Reprint of an 1859 resumé of the *municipio's* history, physical geography, population, and economy.

6666. Cummings, Ronald G. Water resource management in northern Mexico. Washington, Resources for the Future, 1972. 68 p., bibl., tables.

Develops a methodology for the allocation of irrigation water to maximize the net value of agricultural production in arid northern Mexico, an area responsible for about half the country's agricultural production.

6667. Dillman, C. Daniel. Border town symbiosis along the lower Rio Grande as exemplified by the twin cities, Brownsville, Texas and Matamoros, Tamaulipas (PAIGH/G, 71, dez. 1969, p. 93-113, maps, plates)

Matamoros is distinctive among border towns in that it produces a foreign trade surplus, but this surplus is reduced by economic dependence on Brownsville.

6668. Escamilla, Mercedes. Investigación socioeconómica directa de los ejidos de Aguascalientes. México, Instituto Mexicano de Investigaciones Económicas, 1970. 159 p., bibl., tables.

Aguascalientes, one of the smallest and most homogeneous Mexican states, is analyzed in the light of its experience with the *ejido*, concluding that without technical assistance in its agriculture and without promotion of its industrial and commercial possibilities the state is likely to continue to be very poor.

6669. Etcharren, René. Manual de caminos vecinales. México, Asociación Mexicana de Caminos [and] Representaciones y Servicios de Ingeniería, 1969. 387 p., bibl., illus., tables.

Basically a highway engineer's handbook, volume also contains a short history of highway construction in Mexico.

6670. Fages, Eduardo. Noticias estadísticas del departamento de Tuxpán. Prólogo por Leonardo Pasquel. México, Editorial Citlaltepetl, 1973. 221 p., tables (Col. Suma veracruzana. Serie historiografía)

Reprint of an 1854 survey of the Mexican departamento includes general information on its history, physical geography, population, and economy.

6671. Fodor, Eugene *ed.* Fodor's Mexico, 1973. N.Y., David McKay, 1973. 772 p., fold. map, illus., maps, plates, tables.

Informative, well-illustrated, and free from most North American bias.

6672. Ford, Norman D. All of Mexico at low cost. Greenlawn, N.Y., Harian Publications, 1972. 188 p., illus.

The usual tourist information, but organized on several formats, including mile-by-mile logs of important highways, a shopper's and gourmet's guide, and a directory of Mexico's cities "from A to Z."

6673. Franz, Carl. People's guide to Mexico. Santa Fe, N. Mex., John Muir Publications, 1972. 380 p., illus.

Exactly the book to recommend to the freshman free spirit who insists on travelling to Mexico in a broken-down Volkswagen on 50 cents cash.

6674. Fuentes Aguilar, Luis. La productividad de los distritos de riego en la República Mexicana (UCIG/IG, 20, 1970, p. 69-92, bibl., illus., maps, plates, tables)

After summarizing aspects of the physical geography of Mexico which contribute to aridity, author outlines the history and significance of irrigation projects, concluding that they have improved crop yields and farmer profits.

6675. García Palacios, Emma. Los barrios antiguos de Puebla. Puebla, Mex., Centro de Estudios Históricos de Puebla, 1972? 235 p., bibl., facsim.

An encyclopedic history of the neighborhoods of Puebla, indicating the type and placement date of various community landmarks.

6676. Gilmore, Betty and **Don Gilmore.** A guide to living in Mexico. N.Y., G.P. Putnam's Sons, 1971. 233 p., bibl., map.

A guide to daily living directed to those who have never lived outside the US.

6677. Hargrave, Lyndon L. Mexican macaws: comparative osteology and survey of remains from the Southwest. Tucson, The Univ. of Arizona Press, 1970. 67 p., illus., maps, plates, tables (Anthropological papers of the Univ. of Arizona, 20)

Author's purpose is to differentiate between the skeletal remains of the Military macaw (Ara militaris) and the Scarlet macaw (Ara macao) as well as to review macaw remains recovered from archaeological sites in the southwestern US.

6678. Harris, David. Vagabundos del mar: fisherman of the Sea of Cortez (Oceans [San Diego, Calif.] 5:1, Jan./Feb. 1972, p. 61-72, map, plates)

Informal observations on shark fishing in the Gulf of California in early May.

6679. Helbig, Carlos. El soconusco y su zona cafetalera en Chiapas. Tuxtla Gutiérrez, Mex., Instituto de Ciencias y Artes de Chiapas, 1964. 133 p., maps, plates.

Fine survey, based on personal fieldwork, of the physical environment and human use of this famous Mexican coffee-producing area by a noted German geographer. German original published in Bremmen, FRG, Friedrich Trüjen Verlag, 1961.

6680. Hernández Terán, José. México y su política hidráulica. México, Gráficos de la Nación, 1967. 63 p., illus., plates, tables.

A summary of Mexican water policies from precolumbian times to the present, with particular emphasis on irrigation systems. Lists 54 important storage dams with their capacities.

6681. La investigación de los recursos marinos en México. México, Secretaría de Marina, Dirección General de Faros e Hidrografía, 1971. 16 p., maps, plates, tables.

A layman's introduction to the recent work by a new Mexican oceanographic vessel in the Gulf of Mexico.

6682. Jáuregui O., Ernesto. Mesomicroclima de la ciudad de México. México, UNAM, Instituto de Geografía, 1971. 87 p., bibl., maps, plates.

An investigation of the urban heat island produced over Mexico City, with maps showing the city's monthly minimum and maximum temperatures, rainfall intensity, electrical storms, cloudy days, precipitation, relative humidity, and atmospheric pollution, but no analysis of the interrelationships among these measures.

6683. Kenney, Nathaniel T. A new Riviera: Mexico's west coast (NGS/NGM, 144:5, Nov. 1973, p. 670-698, plates)

Mexico's West Coast suffers from mild schizophrenia while the old charm fades to be replaced by modern resorts with jet airports.

6684. Klunder y Díaz Morón, Juan. Las antiguas calles de Veracruz. Prólogo de Leonardo Pasquel. Mexico, Editorial Citlaltepetl, 1972. 96 p. (Col. Suma veracruzana. Serie historiografía)

A place name history of 56 city streets. No map.

6685. MacDonald Escobedo, Eugenio. Una aproximación al conocimiento turístico: bibliografía, su lectura y localización. México, UNAM, Facultad de Ciencias Políticas y Sociales, 1970. 149 p.

Primarily a bibliography of primary source materials on Mexican tourism and a listing of Mexican and foreign agencies offering tourist information.

6686. McDowell, Jack. Mexico. Menlo

Park, Calif., Lane Magazine and Book Co., 1973. 255 p., bibl., plates (A Sunset pictorial)

A picture book which could be appealing to Mexico-bound travelers because of its regional layout and excellent photos.

6687. Macgregor, María Teresa G. de. La ciudad de México: estudio de geografía urbana; 1325-1970 (UCIG/IG, 20, 1970, p. 171-184, illus., maps, tables)

Brief survey of the history of Mexico City, concentrating on its recent rapid demographic and physical growth.

6688. McMahan, Mike. There it is: Baja! Mexico's puzzling peninsula. Riverside, Calif., Manessier Publishing Co., 1973. 240 p., bibl., illus., maps, plates.

A backcountry travel/hunting/fishing guide interspersed with salty comments from a seasoned traveler.

6689. Méndez Nápoles, Oscar and others. Los recursos humanos y el desarrollo agrícola: siete ensayos. México, Ediciones Productividad, 1969. 186 p., tables (Col. Ciencia y tecnología)

First volume of a new series, book contains essays by seven scholars on how to mobilize the human resources portion of the Mexican agrarian reform movement. Most contributions emphasize rural and/or vocational education at several levels.

6690. Mesas Redondas sobre Desarrollo y Ecología, *México, 1973.* Mesas redondas sobre desarrollo y ecología. México, Instituto Mexicano de Recursos Naturales Renovables, 1974. 254 p., bibl., illus.

Seventeenth in the series of Mesas Redondas begun by the Instituto Mexicano de Recursos Naturales Renovables in 1955. Five sessions dealt with "Evolution of and Perspectives on Natural Resources in Mexico" (Juan Puig), "Exploitation and Reserves of Non-Renewable Resources" (Guillermo P. Salas), "The Use of Renewable Resources" (Oscar Brauer Herrera), "Availability and Use of Energy" (Francisco Guzmán Lazo), and "Conservation as an Instrument of Development" (Enrique Beltrán). [C. Edwards]

6691. Molina Molina, Flavio. Nombres indígenas de Sonora y su traducción al español. Hermosillo, Mex., The Author, 1972. 187 p.

A dictionary which contains a sketch map illustrating the idiomatic regions of Sonora based on its Indian geographic names.

6692. Monterrey en cifras: 1970. 5. ed. Monterrey, Mex., Cámara Nacional de Comercio de Monterrey, 1970. 1 v. (Unpaged)

A Chamber of Commerce promotion, slim volume presents Monterrey's attractions as a production, distribution, finance, cultural, and tourist center. Some data on city services.

6693. Nolen, Barbara *ed.* Mexico is people: land of three cultures. With an introduction by Concha Romero James. N.Y., Charles Scribner's Sons, 1973. 210 p., plates.

A collection of very short essays drawn from a wide variety of sources (ranging from the Popul Vuh to Oscar Lewis) in order to illustrate the variety of Mexican tradition.

6694. Ochoterena F., H. and A. Silva-Bárcenas. *Cuvieronius Arellanoi Sp. N.:* mastodonte del Pleistoceno del estado de Oaxaca. México, UNAM, Instituto de Geología, 1970. 22 p., plates (Paleontología mexicana, 33)

Presents and describes a new species of Upper Pleistocene Mastodon discovered in northwestern Oaxaca.

6695. Partido Revolucionario Institucional (PRI). Comisión Nacional Editorial, *México.* Datos básicos: exposición gráfica de la obra del Gobierno Federal. México, 1971. 31 v.

A 31-volume study, one for each Mexican state and territory, containing sections on recent history, physical and human resources, communications, electrification, irrigation, credit institutions, public finance, agriculture, land tenancy, cattle raising, forestry, mining, industry, commerce, and tourism, interspersed with color photos of President Luís Echeverría. Volumes are identical in format, and data is drawn primarily from the 1970 census of population, the 1966 industrial census, the 1960 census of agriculture, and the recent *Anuario Estadístico* issues. Titles of the 31 volumes are: v. 1, *Aguascalientes*; v. 2, *Estado de Baja California* (41 p., illus., maps, plates, tables); v. 3, *Territorio de Baja California* (31 p., illus., maps, plates, tables); v. 4, *Campeche* (44 p., illus., plates, tables); v. 5, *Coahuila* (46 p., illus., plates, tables); v. 6, *Colima* (29 p., illus., plates, tables); v. 7, *Chiapas* (44 p., illus., maps, plates, tables); v. 8, *Chihuahua* (43 p., illus., maps, plates, tables); v. 9, *Durango* (47 p., illus., maps, plates, tables); v. 10, *Guanajuato* (50 p., illus., maps, plates, tables); v. 11, *Guerrero* (44 p., illus., maps, plates, tables); v. 12, *Hidalgo* (41 p., illus., maps, plates, tables); v. 13, *Jalisco* (56 p., illus., maps, plates, tables); v. 14, *Estado de México* (48 p., illus., maps, plates, tables); v. 15, *Michoacán* (48 p., illus., maps, plates, tables); v. 16, *Morelos* (43 p., illus., maps, plates, tables); v. 17, *Nayarit*, (32 p., illus., maps, plates, tables); v. 18, *Nuevo León* (47 p., illus., maps, plates, tables); v. 19, *Oaxaca* (39 p., illus., maps, plates, tables); v. 20, *Puebla* (36 p., illus., maps, plates, tables); v. 21, *Querétaro* (38 p., illus., maps, plates, tables); v. 22, *Quintana Roo* (40 p., illus., maps, plates, tables); v. 23, *San Luís Potosí* (41 p., illus., maps, plates, tables); v. 24, *Sinaloa* (52 p., illus., maps, plates, tables); v. 25, *Sonora* (44 p., illus., maps, plates, tables); v. 26, *Tabasco* (37 p., illus., maps, plates, tables); v. 27, *Tamaulipas* (33 p., illus., maps, plates, tables); v. 28, *Tlaxcala* (46 p., illus., maps, plates, tables); v. 29, *Veracruz* (77 p., illus., maps, plates, tables); v. 30, *Yucatán* (42 p., illus., maps, plates, tables); and v. 31, *Zacatecas* (39 p., illus., maps, plates, tables).

6696. Pasquel, Leonardo. Aspectos de la navegación mexicana. t. 1. México, Editorial Citlaltepetl, 1970. 141 p., illus., maps, plates (Col. Suma veracruzana)

A general introduction to the history of the Mexican Gulf, beginning with the Creation and ending with navigation in the era of the Mexican Revolution. Many old maps, photos, and drawings.

6697. Pommeret, Xavier. Mexique. Paris, Editiones Seuil, 1972. 187 p., illus., maps, plates, tables (Col. Microcosme petite planète, 34)

One of a series on countries around the world, this small volume accentuates the cultural history of Mexico with emphasis on the contact between the country's surviving Indian heritage and modern Mestizo hustle.

6698. Price, John A. Tijuana: urbanization in a border culture. Notre Dame, Ind., Univ. of Notre Dame Press, 1973. 195 p., bibl., maps, tables.

One of the most detailed and perceptive sociological studies of this profound cultural barrier-border. Especially interesting is the sketch of life in Tijuana's prison.

6699. Los recursos naturales del estado de Puebla y su aprovechamiento. México, Ediciones del Instituto Mexicano de Recursos Naturales Renovables, 1972. 251 p. (Serie de mesas redondas, 16)

Contains presentations on the state's history and anthropology, agricultural and forest resources, art, industry, and economic development plans.

6700. Reddell, James R. and Robert W. Mitchell *eds.* Studies on the cavernicole fauna of Mexico. Austin, Tex., The Speleo Press, 1971. 239 p., bibl., illus., plates, tables (Bulletin of the Association for Mexican Cave Studies, 4)

A compilation of 14 papers on the newly-discovered cave fauna of Mexico, adding more than 200 species to those already known and described.

6701. Rees, John D. Paricutín revisited: a review of man's attempts to adapt to ecological changes resulting from volcanic catastrophe (Geoforum [Oxford, England] 4, 1970, p. 1-25, bibl., maps, plates)

The surrounding area has yet to recover from the 1943 Paricutín eruption. Land use on four ecological zones affected by volcanic activity is mapped and related to the advance of selected plants.

6702. Revel-Mouroz, Jean. Amenagement et colonisation du tropique humide mexicain le versant du golfe et des Caraïbes. Paris, Univ. de Paris, Institut des Hautes Etudes de l'Amérique Latine, 1972. 269 p., illus., maps, plates (Travauz & memoires, 3:27)

Massive and detailed study examines the demography, general characteristics of colonization (with examples from Veracruz, Tabasco, and Yucatan), types of colonization, and impact of colonization, concluding that more care should be given to developing adequate infrastructure to support colonization in the Mexican humid tropics.

6703. Reyna T., Teresa. Relaciones entre la sequia intraestival y algunos cultivos en México. México, UNAM, Instituto de Geografía, 1970. 78 p., bibl., fold. maps, tables (Serie Cuadernos)

Study of the effects of the mid-summer drought on the growing of corn and beans concludes that the seasonal water deficit lowers their yields and therefore either irrigation or drought-resistant plants be substituted in the part of the country most severely affected.

6704. Rivera Cambas, Manuel. Viaje a través del Estado de México: 1880-1883. Nota inicial de Gustavo G. Velázquez. México, Biblioteca Enciclopédica del Estado de México, 1972. 294 p., facsims. (Biblioteca Enciclopédica del Estado de México, 26)

Volume consists of several reprinted essays by the Mexican artist Manuel Rivera Cambas on his travels through the country.

6705. Romero, Héctor Manuel *ed.* Enciclopedia mexicana del turismo. México, Talleres Impresora MAPAR, 1970. 4 v. (309, 329, 292, 331 p.) bibl., illus., maps, tables.

Unique four-volume encyclopedia consists of two volumes of social, economic, and cultural themes and two volumes of geography and tourist information.

6706. Sander, H.J. Zum problem der sozialökonomischen Differenzierung kleinbäuerlicher Familien em zentralmexikanischen Hochland (GZ, 60:4, 1972, p. 375-389, bibl.)

The change from a rural-agricultural to an urban-industrial society in Mexico does not parallel the change observed earlier in West Germany.

6707. Schempp, Hermann. Colonia Guadalupe: eine ehemalige russische Sektensiedlund in Niederkalifornien (GR, 25:1, Jan. 1973, p. 17-21, illus.)

Guadeloupe, a Russian colony established in Baja California in 1905-06, has persisted in its Russian traditions for several generations but now is disintegrating with increasing accessibility to this area.

6708. Schlundt, Hayes C. The truth about living in Mexico. With a foreword by Philip H. Hersey. Beverly Hills, Calif., Woodbridge Press Publishing Co., 1973. 126 p., plates.

Aims to answer the basic questions on retirement in Mexico and does so in a refreshing and sympathetic manner.

6709. Seele, Enno. Modificación en el uso del suelo agrícola en la región de Puebla-Tlaxcala (UNAMCG/A, 10, 1970, p. 223-229, fold. maps)

Author maintains that contemporary land use in the Mexican highlands is the result of influences from the conquest, the independence movement, and the Revolution. Detailed agricultural land use maps of several Puebla *municipios* accompany the article.

Seminario sobre Evaluación de la Contaminación Ambiental, *I, Atlihuetzia, Mex., 1971.* Primer Seminario sobre Evaluación de la Contaminación Ambiental. See item 6551.

6710. Seminario sobre Exploración Geológico-Minera, *II, México, 1970.* Memoria de las mesas redondas de información sobre exploraciones y resultados obtenidos en el sexenio: 1965-1970. México, Consejo de Recursos Naturales No Renovables, 1970. 392 p., illus.

Evaluation of mining and mining districts in Mexico reveals that mineral exploration has become an increasingly important activity in recent years.

6711. Sierra, Carlos J. Historia de la administración hacendaria en México: 1821-1970. Mexico? Secretaría de Hacienda y Crédito Público, Dirección General de Publicaciones, 1970. 93 p., illus., plates.

Mistitled book is a brief history of the Mexican Treasury Dept. as seen through its first 100 secretaries, who served from 1821 to 1911.

6712. Stouse, Pierre A.D., Jr. El municipio de Huasca, Hidalgo: la tierra y la población (UNAMCG/A, 10, 1970, p. 45-168, bibl., illus., maps, plates, tables)

Author considers the effect of innovations on the land tenure system in Huasca, concluding that the future is likely to be similar to the present if outside influences are absent. Findings include a high positive correlation between agriculturally-productive private property and population density as well as the wide distribution of two types of tenancy among farmers, possession of small private lands and right to use *ejido* lands.

6713. Stringer, Hugh. Land, farmer and sugar cane in Morelos, Mexico (UW/LE, 48:3, Aug. 1972, p. 301-303)

Study of costs and revenues for farmers and refineries suggests that sugar cane is not the most profitable crop on the irrigated farmland of Morelos.

6714. Suárez Sarabia, Irene Alicia. Estudio preliminar sobre la tipología del ejido mexicano (UNAMCG/A, 10, 1970, p. 169-182, tables)

Brief descriptive survey of the growth and general character of the Mexican *ejido* using 1960 data.

6715. Téllez Girón Padilla, Marcio. Estudio agrícola ganadero de un área del Río Sonora (Recursos Hidráulicos [Mexico] 1:4, 1972, p. 405-413, plates, tables)

Encyclopedic, short survey of the agriculture of a portion of Sonora concludes that cattle raising and dairying are the most important activities but both could be strengthened by adopting new techniques.

6716. Trautmann, Wolfgang. Probleme der Kulturlandschaftsgeschichte im Zentralmexikanischen Hochland (GZ, 60:1, 1972, p. 40-52, map)

Unraveling the early cultural history of the Mexican highlands is a complex task but necessary to the understanding of contemporary patterns.

6717. Wenzens, Gerd. Wirtschaftliche Veränderungen in der Comarca Lagunera—Nordmexiko (GR, 25:1, Jan. 1973, p. 12-16, map, tables)

A former cotton-producing area is now diversifying in response to price fluctuations on the world market; Torreón and Gómez Palacio are becoming primary processing centers.

6718. Williams, Barbara J. Tepetate in the Valley of Mexico (AAG/A, 62:4, Dec. 1972, p. 618-626, plates)

A study in the Valley of Mexico indicates a relationship between population, cultural values, and cultivation of *tepetate* (pedologically, a chestnut soil). The exposure of this soil initial material at the surface reflects periodic land misuse or abandonment for as long as 2000 years.

6719. Winkelman, Don. The traditional farmer: maximization and mechanization. Paris, Development Centre of the Organisation for Economic Co-Operation and Development, 1972. 94 p., bibl., illus., tables (Development Centre studies. Employment series, 7)

Economic study uses Mexican examples in demonstrating that labor, leisure, and income are the most important variables in shaping the behavior of the traditional farmer and that the farmer prefers strategies favoring greater labor use and income over those yielding more leisure but less income.

6720. Zenkovich, Vselvolod Pavlovich. Mezh Dvukh Okeanov (Between the two oceans). Moskva, Izdatel'stvo Mysl, 1972. 294 p., illus., maps, plates, tables.

The account of an eminent Soviet geographer's expedition in Mexico. Concentrates on the geologic and geographic aspects of Mexico's Caribbean and Pacific coasts. [T.S. Cheston]

SOUTH AMERICA

(Except Brazil)

ROBERT C. EIDT
Professor of Geography
University of Wisconsin-Milwaukee

MARIO HIRAOKA
Assistant Professor of Geography
Millersville State College

OF THE SEVERAL HUNDRED CONTRIBUTIONS reviewed for this *Handbook*, the largest number came from the country of Colombia which is to be credited with 20 percent of the total. Selections were also topically more varied for Colombia than for any other nation. Perhaps the most surprising thing about these conclusions, which were determined only after summarizing the entire list of randomly selected research papers and monographs, is that Argentina has finally lost its lead position of some years standing—a possible reflection of increasingly serious political and economic difficulties in that country. Argentina was even displaced by Peru whose review items were almost as numerous as those from Colombia, and tied for third place with Chile. Both third place countries contributed about 12 percent of the total. Thus, items representing Colombia, Peru, Argentina, and Chile constituted well over half the total. The remainder was divided among Ecuador, Bolivia, Venezuela, Paraguay, Uruguay, and Guyana, in that order.

Topically, human geographical studies led all the rest with about half the final number. This was followed by regional items (26 percent), physical entries (23 percent), and cartography and methodology (one percent). In human geography, settlement investigations and economic reports shared high honors. These were followed by items dealing with travel and exploration, demography, and land reform. Regional research was generally broad in scope, but often dealt with economic problems to varying degrees, thus continuing a trend established some years ago in connection with reform projects. Physical geography was marked by items on geomorphology (including earthquake postmortems) natural vegetation, and climate.

A general, or multi-country section, has been included again this year, and was characterized by research on human geography, exploration and discovery, and physical geography, in that order of importance.

Foreign language items (i.e., non-Spanish) continue to be significant for South America and were primarily English-oriented. This contrasts with reports of previous years for this section when German research tended to dominate foreign entries. Peru, Chile, Argentina, and Ecuador received the greatest English coverage. For a change, numbers of entries in French and German were about equal and were surprisingly limited.

Each year certain materials analyzed for this section stand out above the others and seem to merit special mention. It is felt that work in Argentina on the diffusion of cultivation indices, begun in 1944 with the creation of the national Instituto de Suelos y Agrotecnia, has now reached that point. In a typically valuable report, in this case for the Province of Santiago del Estero (item 6764), Institute personnel have recognized 50 regions based on 18 cultivation indices, and have prepared 18 maps representing the diffusion of so-called indicator crops. Critical isotherms and isohyets, abundance of indicator plants, yields, and plant age are among factors utilized in assessing diffusion conditions. From these data six agroclimatic districts have been outlined for which ecological aptitudes are summarized and potential crop production is listed. The results are published in extremely useful booklets of existing farm settlers and for pioneers who still open considerable amounts of new land each year in Argentina. The entire system may be compared with US Soil Conservation Service *County soil survey manuals*, and serves a similar, although more restricted, purpose.

A second item of exceptional interest is one dealing with establishment of Manu National Park in southeastern Peru (item 7002). This is the largest national park in South America (15,328 km²). The principal individual behind creation of this park is Dr. Felipe Benavides, a Peruvian ecologist who won the J. Paul Getty International Wildlife Conservation Prize of $50,000 in 1975 for his work. He has also been responsible for establishing a sizeable vicuña reserve in Peru and for persuading the governments of Peru and Bolivia to ban killing this rare animal as well as exporting products from the vicuña. He has since convinced Argentina and Chile to join in a campaign to save the vicuña from extinction and has succeeded in having the US and Great Britain outlaw importation of vicuña skins. Dr. Benavides has, in effect, become the spearhead of a new South American interest and pride in ecology.

Of equal importance is the continued attention given to South America by geographers from communist countries, a topic first mentioned in this section of *Handbook 29*. Recent articles in a Colombian geographical journal deal with atlases from all Latin America (item 6918), and with conservation measures in Colombia (item 6903). Professors Zonn and Kugenev, who helped write the aforementioned articles were invited to attend the first *Semana del Suelo* ever held in Colombia.

Special attention should be given to the Group of the Year 2000, formed in 1970 in Colombia as an official agency for investigating man-land problems in South America. Cooperative research with UN agencies, and with other countries, is now under way. The first in what should be a series of articles from this organization appears as item 6894. From it we learn that research in the future will be focused on colonization and on economic development.

Outstanding among the general publications for this *Handbook* section is item 6755, a book written by J.W. Wilkie, which presents latest available land reform statistics for Latin America with emphasis on conditions in Bolivia and Venezuela. There is an interesting prediction that land reform will continue as unfinished business in South America, and will by the year 2000 have taken a pronounced turn toward creation of large-sized holdings out of shear necessity for increasing food production of a commercial type.

GENERAL

6721. Bigarella, João José. Continental drift and paleocurrent analysis (Boletim Paranaense de Geociências [Univ. Federal do Paraná, Instituto de Geociências, Curitiba, Bra.] 30, 1972, p. 73-97, bibl., maps, tables)

This article examines paleocurrent evidence for continental drift and concludes that data agree well with those from paleomagnetic and ice-flow patterns.

6722. Bowman, Isaiah. Desert trails of Atacama. N.Y., AMS Press, 1971. 362 p., illus., maps, plates, tables (American Geographical Society special publication, 5)

A well-written regional study of the desert and *puna* of Atacama, and portions of the Chaco in northwestern Argentina, and southern Bolivia. Originally published in 1924 by the American Geographical Society of N.Y.

6723. Branston, Brian. The last great journey on earth. London, Hodder and Stoughton, 1970. 256 p., maps, plates.

Popularized accounts of the British hovercraft expedition from Manaus, Bra., to Port-of-Spain, Trinidad, along the Negro and Orinoco rivers through the Casiquiare canal. The group, which included personnel from the *Geographical Magazine*, and the British Broadcasting Corporation (BBC), and three geographers, collected invaluable data about this little-known portion of northern Brazil and southern Venezuela.

6724. Burkart, Walter. Der Reiherjäger vom Gran Chaco: Als Jäger und Goldsucher vom Amazonas zum La Plata. Nachwort von Carl Seelig. Zürich, Switzerland, Schweizer Druck und Verlaghaus, 1962. 225 p.

Fascinating travel account of a journey through the Gran Chaco and the Amazonas. [H.J. Hoyer]

6725. Cabrera Ortiz, Wenceslao. La geografía, el campo geográfico, el profesional de geografía (SGC/B, 27:102, 1970, p. 105-110)

The integrative nature of the discipline of geography is discussed in this article.

6726. Carrizosa Umaña, Julio comp. Notas para una política de Amazonia y Orinoquia (IGAC/CG, 3:1, 1. semestre 1972, p. 43-51, plates)

In this article a series of proposals for cooperation among the countries of the Orinoco and Amazon basins is made for studies of soils, exploitation of resources, transportation, industrial development, agricultural development, and planning.

6727. Cei, José Miguel. Mesete e laghi basaltici della Patagonia extra-andina (IGM/U, 51:4, luglio/agosto 1971, p. 777-816, bibl., maps, plates)

Detailed descriptions of various mesetas and lakes in basaltic formations along the Chilean-Argentine border of Patagonia. Useful categorization of vegetation and wildlife types, as well as of geological origins of landforms.

6728. Cordani, Umberto G.; Gilberto Amaral; and Koji Kawashita. The precambrian evolution of South America (GV/GR, 62:2, 1973, p. 309-317, map)

Most of the Brazilian "shield" area was consolidated about 1800 million years ago. A large part of South America was also affected by the Brazilian orogenic cycle of late pre-Cambrian times (about 650 million years).

6729. Crist, Raymond E. and Charles M. Nissly. East from the Andes: pioneer settlements in the South American Heartland. Gainesville, Univ. of Florida Press, 1973. 166 p., bibl., maps, plates (Univ. of Florida social sciences monograph, 50)

An excellent summary of recent settlement activities along the eastern Andean foothills between Venezuela and Bolivia. The book provides a comprehensive view of new land development attempts in the Upper Amazon. In addition to the descriptions of contemporary conditions, the authors provide suggestions that are socially, economically, and environmentally sound.

6730. Deffontaines, Pierre. La vie pastorale dans les Andes du Nord et du Centre (SGB/COM, 26:101, jan./mars 1973, p. 5-38, illus., maps)

Pastoralism is discussed for the north and central Andes. In the humid North there are small flocks and trails for herding livestock from the Llanos to the Caribbean. The Central Andes are high and cold and used to be characterized by the llama as wool supplier and beast of burden. Trucking is displacing the llama and animal production is declining.

6731. De Schauensee, Rodolphe Meyer. A guide to the birds of South America. Illustrated by Earl L. Poole, John R. Quinn, and George M. Sutton. Wynnewood, Pa., Livingston Publishing Co. *for the* Academy of Natural Sciences of Philadelphia, 1970. 470 p., illus., maps, plates.

An illustrated guide to birds of South America prepared for the scientific traveler. The 2924 species of South America are described with notes on range and habitat.

6732. Díaz, José María. Patria de la miel: estampas del Río Uruguay. Santa Fe, Arg., Ediciones Colmegna, 1971. 108 p. (Col. Entre ríos, 4)

This small book is a well written series of short essays on modern life (emphasis on fishing) on the islands of the Río Uruguay.

6733. Díaz Montero, Aníbal. América del Sur: crónicas. San Juan, P.R. n.p., 1972. 130 p.

Chronicle of major South American capitals and tourist centers by a Puerto Rican. Descriptions are sketchy and often erroneous.

6734. Engel, Lyle Kenyon. A Simon & Schuster travel guide: South America. N.Y., Cornerstone Library, 1973. 192 p., plates.

A hastily written guide to South America. Excepting the numerous photographs, most of the information can be extracted from airline pamphlets.

6735. Escalante, Rodolfo. Aves marinas del Río de la Plata y aguas vecinas del Océano Atlántico. Ilustraciones por Víctor García Espiell. Montevideo, Editorial Barreiro y Ramos, 1970. 199 p., bibl., illus., plates.

A guide to the birds of the Río de la Plata and the adjoining areas along the Atlantic coast. Each species is given a short description for identification purposes. This is followed by information such as nesting and general habits, and geographical distribution.

6736. Ferreira Sobral, Eduardo *comp.* Soils bibliography. B.A., Instituto Nacional de Tecnología Agropecuaria (INTA), Estación Experimental Agropecuaria Pergamino, 1968. 2 v. (321, 323 p.) (Serie bibliográfica, 6)

These two volumes give a spotty representation of soils literature in the English and Spanish languages. Organized by methodological and topical subjects.

6737. Field, Julia Allen. Amazonia como um modelo mundial (IGAC/CG, 3:1, 1. semestre 1972, p. 53-62, plates)

Proposal by the Committee of the Year 2000 that the Amazon region be treated as a model for ecological studies with major human problems for resolution; that the UN support the notion. Concern over potential ruin of area if and when petroleum reserves are exploited, and over the potential of the region for supplying vital needs for man.

6738. Finzi-Bonasera, Ilda. I Parchi nazionali del mondo: nell'America Meridionale (IGM/U, 52:6, nov./dic. 1972, p. 1173-1216, bibl., maps, plates)

Listing and brief descriptions of national parks in South American countries—a useful inventory. [C. Edwards]

6739. Fodor, Eugene and Stephen

Birnbaum eds. Fodor's South America: 1974. N.Y., David McKay, 1974. 614 p., illus., plates.

A revised edition of the well-known travel guide to South America.

6740. González-Ferrán, Oscar and **Yoshio Katsui.** Estudio integral del volcanismo cenozoico superior de las islas Shetland del Sur, Antártica. Santiago, Univ. de Chile, Facultad de Ciencias Físicas y Matemáticas, Depto. de Geología, 1970. 174 p., bibl., illus., plates, tables (Serie apartados, 25)

Study of petrographic, distribution, and structural relations of late Cenozoic volcanic rocks in the South Shetland Islands. The volcanic rocks in the islands were probably formed by an aluminous basaltic magma rich in soda.

6741. Hardoy, Jorge E. Planeamiento del paisaje con referencia a las áreas urbanas: el caso de Sudamérica (Planificación [Mexico] 6, enero/abril 1970, p. 24-37, plates)

Urban pollution creates different problems in underdeveloped nations when compared with advanced ones. Poor people, for example, who now constitute the majority in Latin American cities, cannot escape to places without contamination for recuperation and recreation. Various urban models are presented along with a plea for more appropriate future planning.

6742. Harrington, Horacio Jaime. Desarrollo paleogeográfico de Sudamérica. Tucumán, Arg., Univ. Nacional de Tucumán, Fundación e Instituto Miguel Lillo, 1968. 74 p., bibl., maps (Miscelánea, 26)

Paleographic development of South America since Cambrian time is summarized according to five structural groups (cratons, inter-cratonic basins, pericratonic basins, nesocratons and geosynchlines). Numerous maps and lengthy bibliography.

6743. Heredia Cano, Fabio. Abundancia de nichos y diversidad de especies en los trópicos (UA/U, 182, julio/sept. 1971, p. 371-378, bibl.)

A poorly written article concerning the affluence of niches and the diversity of species in the tropics. To demonstrate the variety of flora and fauna in the low latitudes, the author chooses the frogs of Colombia as an example. Most of the data presented are from other sources.

6744. Loy, Jane M. Los llanos en la historia de Colombia y Venezuela: una región frontera tropical (ANH/B, 57:225, enero/marzo 1974, p. 109-113, bibl.)

Report of a proposed study of the llanos frontier in Colombia and Venezuela. Brief bibliography.

6745. Meggers, Betty J.; Edward S. Ayensu and **W. Donald Duckworth** eds. Tropical forest ecosystems in Africa and South America: a comparative review. Washington, Smithsonian Institution Press, 1973. 350 p., bibl., illus., maps, plates.

A collection of 25 informative and provocative essays on the forest ecosystems in Africa and South America. The past human record and the possible effects of future settlement and intervention of the tropical rainforest are explored in five articles, following the presentation of a number of comparative studies on the flora and fauna of both regions.

6746. Ortolani, Mario. A proposito delle più alte sedi nelle Ande centrali (SSG/RGI, 80:2, giugno 1973, p. 113-129, illus., maps, plates)

Human settlements are among the highest in the world in the Andes. Average upper limits of cultivation are at 4100 m. above sea level in Bolivia and Peru. 700 m. above that, grazing still occurs, and ore deposits are mined to 5,000 m.

6747. La Revue Française de l'Elite Européenne. No. 263, mai 1973- . Paris.

This special issue has various articles, all with excellent photographs, summarizing agricultural, industrial, general economic, and cultural progress. Articles to be noted are: Hernando Durán Dussan "Le Commerce Franco-Colombien;" Luis Prieto Ocampo "Analyse Générale de l'Èconomie;" and Germán Flórez Márquez "Agriculture et Élevage."

6748. Riccardi, Riccardo. L'America meridionale: lineamenti geografici. 4. ed. Roma, Cremonese, 1971. 223 p., bibl., maps.

The first chapter in the fourth ed. of this book deals with physical geography of the entire continent of South America. Ch. two is a resumé of discovery and exploration. The remaining ten chapters deal with the Guyanas, Brazil (four chapters), the Andes (two chapters), Chile, Argentina and Paraguay.

6749. Schreider, Helen and **Frank Schreider.** Exploring the Amazon. Washington, National Geographic Society, 1970. 207 p., illus., maps, plates.

Descriptions of the Amazon River from its sources in Mount Huagra, Peru, to its mouth in Belém, Bra. The authors who travelled and observed the entire length of the river in order to ascertain its source and length provide a vivid account of riverine life. The book is illustrated with excellent photographs.

6750. Sciences de la terre: pt. 2, Géologie appliquée (Bulletin Signalétique [Centre National de la Recherche Scientifique, Paris] 31:1 [Section 214] 1970, p. 1-48)

A bibliography of earth sciences which includes citations in applied geophysics, mining, and hydrology.

Seminario Internacional para Profesores de Suelos, Maracay, Ven., 1969. Informe. See item 6550.

6751. Snow, Sebastian. Half a dozen of the other. Foreword by Christian Bonington. London, Hodder and Stoughton, 1972. 222 p., plates.

Narratives of the author's six journeys into little known parts of the Andes, and the Amazon and Orinoco basins.

6752. Taylor, Alice. Focus on South America. N.Y., Praeger Publishers *in cooperation with* the American Geographical Society, 1973. 274 p., maps, plates, tables.

This book has been designed to provide up-to-date reports on the developing areas of South America. Pt. 1 is an overview, with articles on population problems, unemployment, development schemes, and case studies; and pt. 2 deals with each nation individually.

6753. Valdez y Palacios, José Manuel. Viaje del Cuzco a Belén en el Gran Pará: por los ríos Vilcamayo, Ucayali y Amazonas. Estudio preliminar por Estuardo Núñez. Lima, Biblioteca Nacional de Perú, 1971. 104 p. (Serie 3: viajeros)

Translation from the Portuguese of a detailed account of a journey made in 1843 from Cuzco to Belém by a Peruvian political refugee. The author is considered the first Peruvian writer to describe the *selva* in that country. His journey took him through the Santa Ana Valley near Machu-Picchu, to the Ucayali River, and down the Amazon.

6754. Van der Hammen, Thomas. Ensayo de un esquema en tiempo y espacio de la vegetación y el medio ambiente en el noroeste de Suramérica (ACCEFN/R, 13:52, 1970, p. 473-478)

Detailed survey of pollen diagrams for northwest South America tracing vegetation patterns from Cretaceous to Holocene. Special reference to the Sabana de Bogotá.

6755. Wilkie, James W. Measuring land reform. Los Angeles, Univ. of California, Latin American Center, 1974. 165 p., maps, plates, tables (*UCLA Statistical Abstract of Latin America: Supplement series, 5)*

By the end of the 1960s, Bolivia and Venezuela had carried out the most extensive programs of land-title redistribution in South America. Therefore the author has analyzed a span of data concerning land reform in these two counries from the 1950s to 1969 in five chapters: "Introduction," "Bolivia," "Venezuela," "Policy Dilemmas and Educational Problems," and "Conclusion." In a pessimistic note, the conclusion is reached that land reform data are inflated, that from such erroneous data policy decisions have been made, and that contentment of peasants with only subsistence-level plots of land will end by the end of this century so that Mexico's Díaz-type regime, based on large holdings, will be repeated in Bolivia and Venezuela. Thus, land reform will remain an unfinished business. Comparative analysis of land reform in Latin America, as well as in the two main countries stressed in the investigation, make this a valuable reference source.

6756. Yepes, J.M. La plataforma continental submarina (SGC/B, 27:102, 1970, p. 89-103)

Useful resumé and discussion of the problem of national off-shore limits in Latin America.

ARGENTINA

6757. Argentina. Dirección Nacional de Turismo. Antártida Argentina. B.A., 1971? 42 p., bibl., map.

Historical resumé of exploration and scientific work in the Antarctic, weather, optics, flora and fauna, Argentine armed forces in the Antarctic, and political considerations of Argentine sovereignty.

6758. ———. Junta de Investigaciones Científicas y Experimentales de las Fuerzas Armadas (JICEFA). Bases para la formulación de una política portuaria. B.A., Secretaría de Estado de Transporte, Administración General de Puertos, 1969. 1 v. (Various pagings) fold. maps, maps, tables.

Basic information about individual Argentine ports, cargo movement, and general port needs. Useful source of information for transportation investigations.

6759. ———. ———. Canal lateral del Apipé: antecedentes económicos para el estudio de su factibilidad. B.A., Secretaría de Estado de Obras Públicas, Dirección Nacional de Construcciones Portuarias y Vías Navegables, 1969. 1 v. (Various pagings) fold. maps, maps, tables.

The Paraná River is one of the main traffic arteries of South America. It serves the countries of Argentina, Paraguay, and Brazil and foreign countries which trade with these nations as well. Trade on the upper Paraná is hampered by rapids about 47 km. from the settlement of Ituzaingó in Corrientes prov. near Apipé Island (Par.). In order to bypass the rapids, an 18 km. canal has been proposed. The main benefits of the canal would be exploitation of the forests of Misiones prov. which cover 80 percent of that area, and improvements in the economies of adjacent areas of Paraguay.

6760. ———. Ministerio de Agricultura y Ganadería. Comisión Reguladora de la Producción y Comercio de la Yerba Mate. Comité de Propaganda del Consumo de la Yerba Mate. La yerba mate. B.A., 1971? 40 p., illus., tables.

Brief history of the rise of yerba mate to prominence in commercial agriculture and of methods of preparation and use. Well written and succinct.

6761. _____. _____. **Subsecretaría de Recursos Naturales Renovables. Servicio Nacional Forestal.** Argentina forestal. B.A., 1972. 41 p., illus., plates.

Argentina has the highest per capita consumption in Latin America of sawn wood and paper in spite of having the greatest deficit of forests. Sixty percent of its lumber comes from Brazil. Argentina produces the rest in about equal amounts from natural stands and plantations. Almost all the country's newsprint is imported, although nearly all other paper products are produced in the country. Types of plants are described as to use, and color plates illustrate forestry activities in this informative book which is one of a number of publications from the VII World Forestry Congress held in B.A. in 1972.

6762. Aspectos específicos de la problemática patagónica (IAEERI/E, 1:3, sept./oct. 1969, p. 131-159, tables)

Analysis of demographic characteristics in Patagonia and Comahue, Arg., and their role in the economic development of the two regions.

6763. Banco Ganadero Argentino, *Buenos Aires.* La producción rural argentina en 1970. B.A., 1971. 81 p., maps, tables.

A two-part presentation of Argentine agricultural production data for 1970. The first part consists of the analysis of production changes by commodities, and by regions. The second half is composed primarily of statistical tables.

6764. Barbalarga, Carlos L. Difusión geográfica de cultivos: índices en la provincia de Santiago del Estero y sus causas. 2. ed. B.A., Instituto Nacional de Tecnología Agropecuaria (INTA), Centro de Investigaciones de Recursos Naturales, 1974. 31 p., maps.

Represents a second, improved version of a publication that appeared in 1953, based on interpreting agroecological conditions from the presence of 18 cultivated plants. Abundance of the plants, yields, and state of maturity are ranked, along with natural and economic conditions which are published in tables.

6765. Beretta, Pier Luigi. La XXXIV [i.e. trenta quattresimo] settimana di geografia in Argentina: Buenos Aires, 30 settembre-11 ottobre 1972 (SGI/B, 10:2 [1/6] gennaio/giugno 1973, p. 169-180, plates)

Article summarizes events of the XXXIV Annual Geographical Week of Argentina held in B.A. in 1972. Papers on physical, human and regional geography were presented and field trips to the Paraná Delta and Neuquén and Río Negro provinces were undertaken.

6766. *Boletín de Estudios Geográficos.*
Univ. Nacional de Cuyo, Facultad de Filosofía y Letras, Instituto de Geografía. Vol. 14, Nos. 54/57, enero/dic. 1967- . Mendoza, Arg.

The present issue is devoted entirely to one topic, the climatology of Mendoza prov., Arg. In addition to the detailed climatic analysis of the area, the author provides information on local winds such as the *zonda* and their influences on man and his economic activities.

6767. _____. _____, _____, _____.
Vol. 16, No. 62, enero/marzo 1969- . Mendoza, Arg.

Pt. 1 is a landform investigation of the upper Mendoza Valley which presents hypotheses concerning development of moraines and landslides. Fluvio-glacial phenomena are also explained along with block diagrams. Pt. 2 is a paper on vineyard production and the role of Giol, a state industry, in establishing uniform standards.

6768. _____. _____, _____, _____.
Vol. 16, Nos. 64/65, julio/dic. 1969- . Mendoza, Arg.

The entire issue is devoted to the analysis of a nodal region around San Rafael, a central place along the foothills of the Andes, in Mendoza, Arg. Originally submitted as a thesis, this case study focuses on the historical evolution of an oasis community and its area of influence.

6769. Bruning, Donald F. The greater Rhea chick and egg delivery route (AMNH/NH, 82:3, March 1973, p. 68-75, plates)

Social habits of the two types of South American rhea are investigated. Reversal of the normal male-female role is associated with maximum hatching efficiency in a given landscape and is lucidly explained in this article.

6770. Buenos Aires (province), *Arg.* **Ministerio de Bienestar Social.** Area central pampeana. 1 v. (Unpaged) illus., maps.

Resumé of main socio-economic characteristics in the central pampa as depicted on maps and graphs.

6771. Casamiquela, Rodolfo. Sobre el significado de Choele Choel: novedades decisivas. Viedma, Arg., Ministerio de Asuntos Sociales, Centro de Investigaciones Científicas, Centro Provincial de Documentación e Información Educativa y Social, 1970. 111. (Serie Estudios y documentos, 1) (mimeo)

On the various meanings and difficulties of native etymology in Patagonia.

6772. Colonización de la cuña boscosa santafesina: reseña general. Rosario, Arg., Ministerio de Agricultura y

Ganadería de la Provincia de Santa Fe, 1971. 172 p., illus., fold. maps, plates, tables.

Description of provincial plans and accomplishments in colonizing some 300,000 hectares of fiscal lands in northern Santa Fe prov.

6773. Daus, Federico A. *ed.* and *comp.* República Argentina: guía turística e informativa; zona 6, Provincia de Buenos Aires. B.A., Automóvil Club Argentino, 1969. 231 p., illus., maps, plates, tables.

This tourist guide, produced under the editorship of geographer F.A. Daus, contains regional and subregional descriptions of Buenos Aires prov. in a fashion like that of AAA guides from the USA.

6774. Entre Ríos (province), *Arg.* **Secretaría del Consejo Provincial de Desarrollo. Dirección de Estadística y Censos.** Estadística agropecuaria, 1969. Paraná, Arg., 1970. 1 v. (Unpaged) tables.

Agricultural census data for Entre Ríos prov., Arg. The enumeration which took place in Sept. 1969, includes information on livestock, crops, and precipitation.

6775. La evolución de la ganadería vacuna en el período: 1972-1973 (SRA/A, 108:1/2, enero/feb. 1974, p. 8-16, plates, tables)

A forecast for 1974 of 54.77 million head of cattle for Argentina is somewhat lower than expected due to difficult physical and human geographical conditions (floods, heavy precipitation, high slaughter rate).

6776. Gioja, Rolando I. Región pampeana y planeamiento: el partido de Juárez y la región triángulo de crecimiento, provincia de Buenos Aires. Juarez, Arg., Municipalidad de Juárez, 1972. 54 p., illus., maps, tables.

6777. Girard, Daniel. Proyección de la población urbana y rural por sexo y grupos de edad: 1960-1985. Posadas, Arg., Dirección General de Estadística, 1970. 21 p., tables.

Population of Misiones prov. estimated at 597,516 for 1975 and 853,244 for 1985.

6778. Gómez Fuentealba, Raúl. Una provincia llamada Neuquén: geografía, turismo, reseña histórica y folklore de la provincia de Neuquén. B.A., Editorial Lito, 1972. 299 p., bibl., maps.

Tourist book on one of Argentina's remote but beautiful provinces.

6779. Guevara, Elena Ortiz de. Población de la región de Bahía Blanca: evolución y estructura (UNS/EE, 8:15/16, enero/dic. 1970, p. 181-212, tables)

Analysis of the demographic structure of Bahía Blanca is presented. Volume and evolution of the total population, age and sex structure, spatial distribution, and activity sectors were considered for analysis; 1960 census data employed.

6780. Guía turística de Misiones con suplemento de Corrientes. 5. ed. Posadas, Arg., Jorge Velázquez, 1971. 233 p., illus., maps, plates, tables.

Tourist guide to Northeast Argentina with numerous statistics. Population data useful, but given for whole departments, not for cities as seems to be the case.

6781. Harrington, Richard. Falkland Islands: Shetlands of the south (RCGS/CGJ, 87/3, Sept. 1973, p. 20-25, map, plates)

A short description of natural and human life in the Falkland Islands. Illustrated with vivid photographs.

6782. Hormann, Paul Karl; Hans Pichler; and **Werner Zeil.** New data on the young volcanism in the Puna of NW-Argentina (GV/GR, 62:2, 1973, p. 397-418, map, plates, tables)

The Puna of northwest Aregntina consists geologically of a basement complex and a sedimentary cover. The former was folded and faulted in Caledonian orogeny. The latter consists of red layers of Cretaceous and Tertiary sediments, covered by mid-Tertiary to Quaternary volcanics.

6783. Ibáñez, Francisco Maximiliano. Toponimia de Entre Rios: la tierra, el hombre y los hechos. Sante Fe, Arg., Ediciones Comlegna, 1971. 109 p. (Col. Entre Ríos, 8)

Annotated listing of major toponymies in Entre Ríos prov., Arg. Each toponym is followed by a short description containing location, physical features, and the sequence of human occupation.

6784. Igarzábal, Antonio P. Remoción en masa en la Quebrada del Toro, Salta. Tucumán, Arg., Univ. Nacional de Tucumán, Fundación e Instituto Miguel Lillo, 1971. 60 p., bibl., fold. maps, plates (Opera Lilloana, 21)

Study of mass wasting effects in a valley in Salta, Arg., with practical applications in route selection for road building.

6785. Kühnemann, Oscar. Vegetación marina de la ria de Puerto Deseado. Tucumán, Arg., Univ. Nacional de Tucumán, Fundación e Instituto Miguel

Lillo, 1969. 125 p., bibl., illus., maps, plates, tables (Opera Lilloana, 17)

This detailed analysis of marine vegetation along a section of the Patagonian coast includes ecologic zonation and is well illustrated.

6786. Martínez, Alvaro M. Buenos Aires: reina y Cenicienta. B.A., Ediciones Patria, 1972. 197 p.

Thought-provoking historical treatment of the founding and growth of B.A. including problems caused by position, political, and external events, all of which have a bearing on modern urban problems. Overconcentration of power in one urban center has always been a difficulty for the country and the idea of centralism is associated with tendencies toward dictatorial government.

6787. Mendoza (province), *Arg.* **Instituto de Investigaciones de las Zonas Aridas y Semiáridas.** Aportes al inventario de los recursos naturales renovables de la provincia de Mendoza. v. 1, La reserva forestal de Ñacuñán. Mendoza, Arg., 1971. 239 p., bibl., illus., plates, tables.

Plant inventory from a semi-arid area in Mendoza prov., western Arg. The volume is the first of a series intended to provide a comprehensive background about the arid and semi-arid environments of Mendoza.

6788. Milia, José L. Problemas del desarrollo del noreste argentino y sus soluciones (UH/U, 81, julio/dic. 1970, p. 113-144, tables)

Historical resumé of colonization in the northeast of Argentina, an area defined as east of the provinces of Salta and Santiago del Estero and North of 30° South. Extractive industries, hydroelectric potential, and agriculture are the sources of economic wealth which could, with better transportation, be improved.

6789. Molino, Domenico. Río Gallegos e la sua provincia (IGM/U, 52:3, maggio/giugno 1972, p. 627-642, bibl., maps, plates)

Popularized account of a flight from B.A. to Río Gallegos with data on Santa Cruz prov.

Morris, Arthur S. The regional problem in Argentine economic development. See *HLAS 36:3241.*

6790. Müller, María S. Bibliografía para el estudio de la población de la Argentina (IDES/DE, 12:48, enero/marzo 1973, p. 887-902)

A bibliography of interest to demographers with a focus on Argentina. Contains wide variety of sources, including foreign.

6791. Orlando, Héctor. Las flores fósiles de Antártida Occidental y sus relaciones estratigráficas. B.A., Ministerio de Defensa Nacional, Dirección General del Antártico, Instituto Antártico Argentino, 1971. 12 p., bibl. (Contribución del Instituto Antártico Argentino, 140)

Analysis of the Mesozoic and Cenozoic flora of the South Shetland Islands, the Antarctic Peninsula and the neighboring islands. A new Triassic fossil flora from the Livingstone Island is discussed, while some Cenozoic flora are compared to those of Patagonia, Chile, New Zealand, and Australia.

6792. Peña, Hugo A. Bibliografía geológica de Tucumán. Tucumán, Arg., Univ. Nacional de Tucumán, Fundación e Instituto Miguel Lillo, 1971. 35 p. (Miscelánea, 38)

Annotated geological bibliography for Tucumán prov., Arg. The present work should prove useful to physical geographers and geologists interested in northwest Argentina.

6793. Polanski, Jorge. Carbónico y pérmico de la Argentina. B.A., Editorial Universitaria de Buenos Aires (EUDEBA), 1970. 216 p., bibl., illus. (Manuales de EUDEBA. Geología)

A systhesis of over 400 papers on the Upper Paleozoic geology of Argentina which attempts to introduce a uniform terminology and provide a temporary interpretation of the general and regional problems of geologic description in that country. [T. L. Martinson]

6794. Ramlot, Michel Jean Paul. Hacia un porvenir de la región guyana. Mendoza, Arg., Univ. Nacional de Cuyo, Facultad de Ciencias Ploticas y Sociales, Centro de Investigaciones, Instituto de Estudios del Desarrollo, 1972. 261 p., illus., maps, tables.

In 1966 Argentina instituted its Sistema Nacional de Planeamiento y Acción para el Desarrollo and a year later divided the national territory into development regions. This book deals with one of the regions, that of Cuyo, encompassing the provinces of Mendoza and San Juan. Pt. 1 deals with hydrological problems, pt. 2 with the regional economy, and pt. 3 studies growth rates and the future. Consultant teams are recommended for planning.

6795. Reboratti, Carlos E. Santa Victoria: estudio de un caso de aislamiento geográfico (IDES/DE, 14:55, oct./dic. 1974, p. 481-506, maps)

Various types of settlement isolation such as physical, voluntary, or cultural exist in many parts of the world. The author of this interesting and well-written article deals with non-voluntary, cultural isolation, the ways of measuring such isolation, and with data from a specific example (Santa Victoria) from northern Argentina.

Recchini de Lattes, Zulma L. La población de Buenos Aires: componentes demográficos del crecimiento entre 1855 y 1960. See *HLAS 36:3275*.

_____. El proceso de urbanización en la Argentina: distribución, crecimiento y algunas características de la población urbana. See *HLAS 36:3276*.

Reina, Rubén. Paraná: social boundaries in an Argentine city. See *HLAS 36:3277*.

6796. Remusi, Carlos A. El cultivo de la soja en la Argentina (SRA/A, 105:10/11, oct./nov. 1971, p. 46-50, plates, tables)

Cultivation of soya beans has expanded greatly in Argentina. Methods of seed preparation, planting practices, and a map showing distribution of varieties throughout the country are briefly touched upon in this article.

6797. Revista de la Dirección Nacional de Geología y Minería. Año 7, No. 25, sept./dic. 1971- . B.A.

The Department of Geography of the DNGM is concerned primarily with mapping the country. In its 60 years of activity it has finished 900,000 km.² of area, almost all of which is in mountainous topography.

6798. Sábato, Mario. Buenos Aires. B.A., Arcograf Editores, 1971. 93 p., plates (Col. Argentina en color)

Colored photographs of B.A. from the series *Argentina en color*.

6799. Santamarina, Estela Barbieri de; Alicia I. García; and Hilda M. Díaz. Nueva bibliografía geográfica de Tucumán. Tucumán, Arg., Univ. Nacional de Tucumán, Facultad de Filosofía y Letras, Depto. de Geografía, 1972. 182 p., bibl., map (Serie monográfica, 20)

Updated version of a bibliography originally published in 1946. An impressive 1081 titles are listed in alphabetical order by authors. The bibliography would be of great assistance to those interested in northst Argentina.

6800. Santillán de Andrés, Selva E. and **Teodoro Ricardo Ricci.** La región de la Cuenca de Tapia-Trancas. Tucumán, Arg., Univ. Nacional de Tucumán, Facultad de Filosofía y Letras, Depto. de Geografía, 1966. 69 p., illus., maps, plates (Serie monográfica, 15)

Geographical interpretation of the Tapia-Trancas basin, a small watershed in northern Tucumán, Arg. The study concentrates primarily in explaining the revolutionary processes of the agrarian landscape since the colonial period. One major drawback of the monograph is the lack of a bibliography.

6801. _____; Estela Barbieri de Santamarina; and Teodoro Ricardo Ricci. La real distribución de la población de la provincia de Tucumán. Tucumán, Arg., Univ. Nacional de Tucumán, Facultad de Filosofía y Letras, Depto. de Geografía, 1966. 14 p., fold. map (Serie monográfica, 14)

Unequal population distribution in the Argentine prov. of Tucumán is explained by climatic-economic factors.

6802. _____; _____; _____; and Enrique José Würschmidt. La región de las sierras del nordeste de la provincia de Tucumán. Tucumán, Arg., Univ. Nacional de Tucumán, Facultad de Filosofía y Letras, Depto. de Geografía, 1967. 89 p., bibl., illus., maps, plates, tables (Serie Monográfica, 16)

A geographical interpretation of man and environment in an area of northeastern Tucumán, Arg. The authors provide a comprehensive description of the people and their relations to the land in the Sierra de Burruyacu and adjoining lowlands, located to the north and northeast of the city of Tucumán.

6803. _____. and others. La región del Valle de Lerma: provincia de Salta. Tucumán, Arg., Univ. Nacional de Tucumán, Facultad de Filosofía y Letras, Depto. de Geografía. 1968. 126 p., illus., maps, plates (Serie monográfica, 17)

Monograph on the Río Lerma Valley in Salta prov. is a detailed but conventional study of the physical and human geography of a large (5000 km.²₁) intermontane valley in northwest Argentina. The section on population and settlement is especially informative.

6804. Sargent, Charles S. The spatial evolution of Greater Buenos Aires, Argentina, 1870-1930. Preface by Richard M. Morse. Tempe, Arizona State Univ., Center for Latin American Studies, 1974. 164 p., bibl., maps, plates, tables.

The author describes and analyzes B.A.'s development from the foundations of modern urban growth (pre-1870) to the creation of Greater Buenos Aires by 1930. Settlement, transportation, and land sale expansion break the colonial framework of the city during the present century and interact to produce a polycentric urban area similar to that of other large cities.

6805. Setti, Enrique de Jesús. Aspectos geográficos del dique "El Cadillal" y su zona de influencia (UNT/H, 16:22, 1970, p. 135-152, bibl., illus., maps, plates, tables)

El Cadillal canal is located 22 km. north of Tucumán, northwest Arg., and supplies the city with water. The canal is discussed historically with reasons for its construction. Infrastructural works, planning for the future of the city's water supply, and problems of salinity are presented.

6806. Sociedad Rural Argentina, *Buenos Aires.* Memoria: período 1971-1972. B.A., 1972. 131 p., tables.

This issue contains useful statistics on export and internal consumption of beef, dairy products, etc., for 1971-72.

6807. Soler, Carlos Marcelino. Geografía económica mundiales y argentinos. B.A., Editorial El Coloquio, 1972. 163 p., maps, tables.

World economic geography is presented by topic in 77 chapters in this book. At the end of each chapter Argentine information is given for comparison.

6808. Strange, Ian J. The silent ordeal of a south Atlantic archipelago (AMNR/NH, 82:2, Feb. 1973, p. 30-39, plates)

Ecological problems in the Falkland Islands caused first by man's overuse of tussock grasses, then by penguin burrowing because of lack of nesting grass, loss of the seal population, and attitudes of farmers are discussed. In the last decade corrective action has begun to restore native bird and animal life, but it is doubted whether the Falkland Islands can survive another round of exploitation.

6809. Tomo, Aldo P. Aves y mamíferos antárticos: guía para su reconocimiento. B.A., Ministerio de Defensa Nacional, Dirección Nacional del Antártico, Instituto Antártico Argentino, 1971. 117 p., illus., maps (Dirección Nacional del Antártico. Divulgación, 1)

Description given of captured birds and mammals from the Antarctic made during field studies coupled with data from existing bibliographies. Maps of aerial distribution of species examined and color plates are presented.

6810. Vila, Fernando. Conocimiento actual de la plataforma continental argentina. B.A., Secretaría de Marina, Servicio de Hidrografía Naval, 1965. 25 p., bibl., maps, tables (Público, H-644)

This monograph describes the morphological and geological characteristics of the submerged plains and emerged coastal sectors of Argentina. Relations among structural characteristics and magnetic-gravimetric anomalies are presented, along with stratigraphic sequences.

6811. Virasoro, Rafael. La Forestal Argentina. B.A., Centro Editor de América Latina, 1971. 112 p., plates (La historia popular. Vida y milagros de nuestro pueblo, 75)

Rise and fall of the quebracho industry as seen through the fortunes of The Forestal Company in the Argentine Chaco. Includes discussion of tannin on the world market, and living conditions in lumber camps.

6812. Winsberg, Morton D. Una regionalización estadística de la agricultura en la pampa argentina (PAIGH/G, 72, junho 1970, p. 45-60, maps, tables)

Continuation of *HLAS 35:6840.* Discusses percentage of man-days in nine major agricultural activities on part of the Argentine pampa. Two dairy regions in Córdoba and Santa Fe and one transitional beef-dairy zone in southwest B.A. are newly identified by the method. Neither sheep nor oilseed production resulted as important enough to be included, as is sometimes suggested from normal field-work procedures.

6813. Zemborai, Saturnino. Como incrementar el rendimiento de la producción ganadera en la mesopotamia argentina (SRA/A, 105:1/2, enero/feb. 1971, p. 38-39, plates)

There are seven million head of cattle and six million sheep in Entre Ríos and Corrientes provinces, Arg. Problems with expansion of the herds are discussed, such as shortages of feed, and the need for legume planting in the area. Mechanization intensification is also recommended.

BOLIVIA

6814. Ahlfeld, Federico E. Geología de Bolivia. La Paz, Editorial Los Amigos del Libro, 1972. 189 p., bibl., facsims., illus., maps, tables.

An updated and summarized version of Ahlfeld's 1946 work about the geology of Bolivia. This is probably still the best synopsis of Bolivian geology. The book is illustrated with a number of original maps, and it also contains a good bibliography.

6815. *Américas.* Organization of American States, General Secretariat. Vol. 25, No. 10, Oct. 1973- . Washington.

The supplement section of this issue is devoted to Bolivia. The study serves to provide a general background of the country, such as, the physical environment, history, and cultural landscapes.

6816. Antezana E., Luis. El problema del minifundio en Bolivia. La Paz, n.p., 1971. 32 p.

The problem of minifundia in Bolivia originated as a result of agrarian decrees signed by president Melgarejo in 1864, and has been intensified following the 1953 agrarian reform. The problems resulting from the minifundia are analyzed for the three regions of Altiplano, Valles, and Oriente.

6817. Barja Berríos, Góver and **Armando Cardozo González.** Geografía agrícola de Bolivia. La Paz, Editorial

Los Amigos del Libro, 1971. 257 p., bibl., fold. maps, maps, tables.

Since Bolivia's last agricultural census in 1950, no comprehensive updating has been undertaken. Consequently, most of later data has been based on estimates of questionable character. The maps are likewise of little use because of poor cartographic presentation.

6818. Bejarano B., Gastón. El trópico boliviano (KO, 73, julio/sept. 1970 p. 41-53)

A very sketchy and poor description of Amazonia, and especially of the Bolivian tropics.

6819. Bolivia. Corporación Minera de Bolivia. Reservas mineralógicas de Bolivia. La Paz, 1967. 50 p., maps, tables.

Brief description of principal minerals and their reserves in Bolivia.

6820. ———. Ministerio de Agricultura. Departamento de Suelos. Informe de reconocimiento detallado de suelos area Yacuiba y Gran Chaco. La Paz, 1969. 82 p., bibl., maps, tables.

Soil survey of a portion of the Andean foothills and adjoining lowlands in southern Bolivia. A triangular area of approximately 300,000 hectares in southeastern Tarija dept. was investigated for development by agricultural colonization.

6821. Cárdenas, Martín. Por las selvas, las montañas y los valles de Bolivia: memorias de un naturalista. La Paz, Editorial Don Bosco, 1972. 442 p., plates.

Memoirs of an eminent Bolivian botanist. The book provides valuable information about plant distribution in both the highlands and lowlands of Bolivia. Detailed descriptions of rural settlements may be of use to geographers.

6822. Cardozo G., Armando; Julio Rea C.; and Irma A. de Viscarra. Bibliografía de la Quinua y la Cañahua. La Paz, Sociedad de Ingenieros Agrónomos de Bolivia, 1970. 1 v. (Various pagings) (Boletín bibliográfico, 13)

This bibliography on *quinua* and *cañahua* is the 13th of a series of agricultural bibliographies published by the Sociedad de Ingenieros Agrónomos de Bolivia, and it is based on the Ministry of Agriculture Library's holdings in La Paz.

6823. Costa de la Torre, Arturo. Panegírico: a la Ciudad de Nuestra Señora de La Paz. La Paz, n.p., 1970. 36 p.

Brief and sketchy description about the origin and development of La Paz.

6824. Dereims, A. La altiplanicie de Bolivia (KO, 72, abril/junio 1970, p. 119-133)

Spanish version of an article which originally appeared in *Annales de Géographie* (v. 16, 1907). A short account of the physical geography of the Bolivian altiplano.

6825. Díaz Arguedas, Julio. Expedicionarios y exploradores del suelo boliviano. t. 1. La Paz, Ediciones Camarlinghi, 1971. 198 p., bibl., maps (Col. Popular. Serie 11:31)

The author divides Bolivia into two regions: "North and Northeast," and "Oriental," and presents a chronological survey of scientists and their work such as Haenke, D'Orbigny, Rivero, and others.

Gade, Daniel W. Spatial development of Latin American seats of government: from Sucre to La Paz as the national capital of Bolivia. See *HLAS 36:2943*.

Guzmán, Augusto. Cochabamba: panorama geográfico, proceso histórico, vida institucional, instrucción pública, reseña cultural. See *HLAS 36:2946*.

6826. Hiraoka, Mario. Boribia ni okeru shokumin to keizai kaihatsu (The Human Geography [Assn. of Human Geographers, Kyoto, Japan] 23:5, 1971, p. 554-570, bibl., maps, tables)

A review of pioneering activities along the eastern foothills of Bolivian Andes. The major colonization areas of Alto Beni, Chapare-Chimoré, and Santa Cruz areas are analyzed and valuable suggestions are offered for further developments.

6827. ———. Boribia no nochi kaikaku to nettai teichi ishokumin (Ijyu Kenkyu [Kaigai Ijyu Jigyodan, Tokyo] 8, 1972, p. 23-38, maps, tables)

Despite valuable expenditures of human, economic, and environmental resources in opening the tropical lowlands east of the Andes, the Bolivian government has been able to attract only limited numbers of settlers to the region. Likewise, socioeconomic and political benefits to the country have been insignificant. The author advocates that some of the existing problems could be solved by thorough institutional changes.

6828. ———. Structural variations among dwellings in the Japanese colony of San Juan de Yapacaní, Bolivia (APCG/Y, 34, 1972, maps, plates)

A study of a Japanese pioneer settlement in eastern Bolivia. An analysis of structural forms reveals that pioneer homes go through a series of changes prior to the construction of permanent homes. It is believed that dwelling size, form, orientation, ground plan, and construction materials are dependent on a number of physical and cultural geofactors.

6829. Knoerich, Eckart. Die Yungas in Bolivien: Agrargeographische Betrachtung zur Lage und Entwicklung (GR, 24:12, Dez. 1972, p. 508-511, table)

The Yungas are defined as an east cordilleran region in Bolivia between 16°-17° south latitude and from 3200 m. to 2500 m. in elevation. The principal settlements, Chulumani, Coroico, and Caranavi, are discussed in relationship to their surroundings and their role in the national economy. Agricultural production is stressed along with possibilities for improvement.

6830. Kreisel, Werner and **Wolfgang Schoop.** Landnahme und Kolonisation im Französischen und schweizerischen Jura und im nnordöstlichen Andenabfall Boliviens: eine vergleichende Untersuchung zur Besiedlung sweier bewaldeter Gebirgsregionen (GH, 26:4, 1971, p. 181-186, illus.)

In this excellent article the authors have compared natural conditions, historical events, and resultant settlement structure between east Bolivian Andean and Swiss Jura colonies which demonstrated morphological convergence.

6831. Lester, Kip and **Jane McKeel.** Discover Bolivia: the first English guidebook of Bolivia. Assisted by Barbara Roose; Susan Schlotthauer; and Helga Welz. Illustrated by Carlos Rimassa. La Paz, Editorial Los Amigos del Libro, 1972. 330 p., illus., map, plates.

Travel guide with poor maps, interesting photographs.

6832. Muñoz Reyes, Jorge. Biografía de un lago: el Titicaca (KO, 71, 1970, p. 11-28, bibl.)

Following a general description of Lake Titicaca and the neighboring areas, an attempt is made to describe the sequence of human occupation along the lake shores from prehistoric to modern times. A list of major works about the Titicaca basin is appended at the end of the work in annotated form.

6833. Preston, David A. L'agriculture dans un désert d'altitude: l'Altiplano central de Bolivie (SGB/COM, 26:102, avril/juin 1973, p. 113-128, maps, plates)

The central part of the Bolivian altiplano is described first in its physical context and then as an area where agriculture meagerly supports a human population by food (potatoes and quinua) and animal (sheep and llamas) production. Irrigation would be possible but is not practiced. Significant migration of families occurs toward Chile and Argentina.

6834. Stearman, Allyn MacLean. San Rafael: Camba town. Gainesville, Univ. of Florida Press, 1973. 126 p., bibl., map, plates (Latin American monographs. 2. series, 12)

An accurate portrayal of rural life as seen and experienced by a Peace Corps volunteer in the community of San Rafael (pseudonym for San Carlos), located about 100 km. to the north of Santa Cruz, in the eastern lowlands of Bolivia. The description includes the interpretation of San Carlos, its institutions, its people, and an in-depth study of a peasant family.

6835. Valenzuela, Salomón Rivas. GEOBOL: Servicio Geológico de Bolivia. La Paz, Ediciones El Siglo, 1970. 51 p., bibl., maps, fold. map, plates, tables (Boletín, 12)

Geological interpretation of the highly mineralized Llallagua area in the Cordillera Oriental of Bolivia. The information should be of interest to geomorphologists. Includes a folding map in book's pocket.

CHILE

6836. Agnew of Lochnaw, C.H., yr. Mapmaking on the Patagonian ice-cap (GM, 46:12, Sept. 1974, p. 709-713, maps, plates)

A British Joint Services Expedition to map the northern ice cap of Chile (Hielo Patagonia del Norte) at about 47 degrees south latitude. Numerous illustrations.

6837. _____ and **C.S. Gobey.** The Joint Services Expedition to Chilean Patagonia: 1972-73 (RGS/GJ, 140:2, June 1974, p. 262-268, maps)

This paper is based on a lecture given at the Royal Geographical Society House on 29 Oct. 1973. It is a brief report of an expedition sponsored by the Royal Highland Fusiliers and the Coast Survey undertaken during five months in 1972-73 to survey hydrography, geology, glaciology, natural history, meteorology and geomorphology in Chilean Patagonia.

6838. Alaluf, David and others. Reforma agraria en Chile: seis ensayos de interpretación. Santiago, Instituto de Capacitación e Investigación en Reforma Agraria (ICIRA), 1970. 125 p., illus., tables (Publicaciones de ICIRA, 21)

Six essays on interpretation of agrarian reform in Chile are presented in this book. Objectives, politics, reversibility of program, expropriation, and reasons for reform are discussed.

6839. Alvarado, Luis. La vida rural en el altiplano chileno. Santiago, Instituto de Capacitación e Investigación en Reforma Agraria (ICIRA), 1970. 80 leaves, tables (ICIRA-Chile/UN/FAO, 38113)

A descriptive study of human settlement and land use in the Chilean altiplano and the adjoining sub-Andean foothills. The author believes that the marginal living conditions in the region are caused by the harsh environment and the marginal location of the region from the traditionally settled portions of the country.

6840. Aranda Baeza, Ximena. Algunas consideraciones sobre la trashumancia en el Norte Chico (UCIG/IG, 20, 1970, p. 141-169, bibl., maps, tables)

This study emphasizes time of stay in Andean pastures (*veranadas*) and economic traits generated by people engaged in transhumance in northern Chile. It concludes that numbers of livestock can be doubled when they are fed for five months in the veranadas.

6841. Araya Vergara, José. Contribución al estudio de los procesos estuariales en las desembocaduras de los ríos Rapel y Maipó (UCIG/IG, 20, 1970, p. 17-38, bibl.)

The Chilean Rapel and Maipó rivers drain coastal plain lands in different ways. The Maipó is turbid and lacks the stratification seen in the Rapel bottoms. The latter shows water types with a seaward moderate gradient and an upsteam salt wedge. The Maipó demonstrates homogeneity.

6842. Bianchi, Lois. Chile in pictures. N.Y., Sterling Publishing Co., 1971. 64 p., illus., maps, plates (visual geography series)

A short pictorial book of Chile. Photos in the book are outdated.

6843. Börgel Olivares, Reynaldo. Correlaciones fluviomarinas en la desembocadura del río Choapa (UCIG/IG, 20, 1970, p. 55-68, bibl., illus., maps, tables)

Study of Chilean coast terraces in which only those terraces below 100 m. msl are considered related to eustatic formative processes. A geological chronology for the terraces is proposed.

6844. _____. Mapa geomorfológico de Chile: descripción geomorfológica del territorio. Santiago, Univ. de Chile, Facultad de Filosofía y Educación, Instituto de Geografía, Sección Aplicada, 1965. 106 p., maps.

A general description of Chilean landforms. The country is divided into six physiographic regions and the characteristics for each of the regions are given. One notable drawback of the study is the lack of maps.

6845. Borsdorf, Axel. Chile: a sociogeographical survey (GR, 26:6, Juni 1974, p. 224-232, bibl.)

After a brief, but lucid introduction to Chile, the author discusses spatial economic changes which have taken place as the result of changes in political philosophy from colonization to capitalism to communism to a dictatorial form at present.

6846. Cecioni, Giovanni. Esquema de paleogeografía chilena. Santiago, Editorial Universitaria, 1970. 143 p., bibl., maps (Col. Recursos naturales)

An explanation of paleogeography of Chile which refutes the continental drift theory. The book includes a section where the author advances the idea that the Polynesians were probably the first inhabitants to arrive in South America between the Miocene and the Holocene, when numerous islands existed in the southern portion of the Pacific basin.

6847. Chile. Dirección de Estadística y Censos. Algunos resultados provinciales del II Censo de Vivienda obtenidos por muestreo: XIII Censo de Población y II de Vivienda levantados el 29 de noviembre de 1960. Santiago, 1963. 71 p., tables.

Description of the samples obtained during the national census of Chile (1960) with analysis of errors.

6848. Corvalán, Antonio comp. Antología chilena de la tierra. Santiago, Instituto de Capacitación e Investigación en Reforma Agraria (ICIRA), 1970. 184 p., illus., tables (Publicaciones de ICIRA, 23)

Collection of selected writings by Chilean authors reviewing the systems of labor and resource utilization. Topics such as agrarian structure in Chile, the *afuerinos* or seasonal laborers, and the sheep ranching in Magallanes prov. are described.

6849. Cunill Grau, Pedro. Factores en la destrucción del paisaje chileno: recolección, caza y tala coloniales (UCIG/IG, 20, 1970, p. 235-264, plates)

The author points to destructive exploitation of such items as minerals, water supplies, and fish during colonial times and to the long-term effects on the physical landscape.

Domeyko, Ignacio. Araucanía y sus habitantes. See *HLAS 36:2977.*

6850. Dos Passos, John. Easter Island: island of enigmas. Garden City, N.Y., Doubleday, 1971. 150 p., plates.

Popularized account of culture history of Easter Island mixed with personal travel notes.

6851. Fuller, Gary. On the spatial diffusion of fertility decline: the distance-to-clinic variable in a Chilean community (CU/EG, 50:4, Oct. 1974, p. 324-334, bibl.)

Analytical procedures are employed to determine the real role of distance to clinic in influencing acceptance of birth control measures. The distance variable emerges as the single most powerful discriminator between users of birth control and non users.

6852. García Gatica, Tomás and **Carlos Thayer Escalona.** Reforma agraria y pequeña propiedad: estudio del área Aconcagua-Putaendo (UCIG/IG, 20, 1970, p. 103-140, bibl., illus., maps, plates, tables)

Agrarian reform has affected both land tenure and use in Chile. Abrupt cessation of the usual relationships between latifundismo and minifundismo is noted in this article, but the question is asked whether the relationships persist on large holdings which have not been broken up but have been subjected to reform measures. The conclusions point to further aggravation of the problems of minifundismo under such conditions of agrarian reform.

6853. Hernandez, Silvia. Geografía de plantas y animales de Chile. Santiago, Editorial Universitaria, 1970. 212 p., bibl., illus., maps, plates, tables (Col. Manuales y monografías, 8)

Intended as an aid for secondary school teachers and aficionados, this well-balanced volume provides the basic information about the Chilean flora and fauna. The data are presented according to the three ecological regions: arid north, mediterranean zone, and humid south.

6854. *Informaciones Geográficas.* Univ. de Chile, Facultad de Filosofía y Educación, Depto. de Geografía. Año 15, 1965-Santiago.

Issue contains a summary article of contributions to geography and geology by Eusebio Flores, a useful article on owner-cultivators in Central Chile, and contributions on geomorphology of terraces along the Río Copiapó and fluvial morphology in the coast's ranges. Two sections present bibliographies for 1964 of articles on Chile by citizens of that country and by foreigners.

6855. _____. _____, _____, _____. Años 18/19, 1968/1969- . Santiago.

Special issue from the Dept. of Geography, Univ. of Chile, contains seven articles of general interest to Latin Americanists. One deals with hydrology in the Aconcagua Basin, one with ecological observations from the Juan Fernández archipelago, and the rest with various aspects of economic geography, primarily in Santiago. Topics include population changes, industrial development, and water supplies.

6856. Lizana V., María Victoria. Catálogo de informes inéditos. Santiago, Univ. de Chile, Facultad de Ciencias Físicas y Matemáticas, Depto. de Geología, 1972. 30 p., bibl. (Comunicacion, 17)

Over 300 geological studies made in the Andes by consultants are listed in this publication. All are now available to the public.

6857. MacPhail, Donald D. The geomorphology of the Río Teno Lahar, Central Chile (AGS/GR, 63:4, Oct. 1973, p. 517-532, plates, maps)

Presence of lahars (mudstreams) in the Valle Longitudinal of Chile is accounted for by postulating a sustained volcanic eruption, or (less likely) release of glacial lake water, or heavy rains.

6858. Manns, Patricio. Los terremotos chilenos. Santiago, Empresa Editora Nacional Quimantú, 1972. 2 v. (96, 95 p.), bibl., plates (Nosotros los chilenos, 15/16. Serie Hoy contamos)

These small volumes are historically oriented disaster reports with photographs of the results of earthquakes which have occurred in Chile.

6859. Martinic Beros, Mateo. Magallanes: síntesis de tierra y gentes. B.A., Editorial Francisco de Aguirre, 1972. 195 p., bibl., plates (Biblioteca Francisco de Aguirre, 33. Col. Cruz del sur, 8)

A geographical, historical, and economical synthesis of the southernmost Chilean prov. of Magallanes. A lengthy description of natural elements is followed by a section containing the economic and settlement history. One of the major drawbacks of the book is the complete absence of maps.

6860. _____. Reseña del descubrimiento y de la evolución cartográfica de la región magallánica. Punta Arenas, Chile, Instituto de la Patagonia, 1971. 1 v. (Unpaged) bibl.

Account of the history of discovery and the cartographic representation of the southern tip of South America between the 16th and the 18th centuries.

6861. Olivares, José. Programación del uso de la tierra en una zona de reforma agraria. Santiago, Univ. de Chile, 1968. 113 p., bibl., tables.

Attempt at using linear programming techniques in creating land use models. The Hacienda Choapas in Coquimbo prov., Chile, is taken as a sample area for testing the model. Despite some drawbacks, the author concludes that the technique could serve as a valuable tool for land use studies.

6862. Peebles L., Federico and **Erik Klohn H.** Geología de los yacimientos de manganeso de Corral, Quemado, Arrayán y Fragua, provincia de Coquimbo. Santiago, Instituto de Investigaciones Geológicas, 1970. 56 p., bibl., fold., maps, illus., maps, plates, tables (Boletín, 27)

Sedimentary deposits of manganese intercalated in lenticular form within a volcanic matrix are studied in an area at about 30° S on the west coast of South America.

6863. Phelan, Nancy. The Chilean way:

travels in Chile. London, MacMillan, 1973. 261 p., maps, plates.

Description of modern-day Chilean life as seen and interpreted by an Englishwoman.

6864. San Martín Ferrari, Hernán. Geografía humana de Chile. Santiago, Empresa Editora Nacional Quimantú, 1972. 96 p., illus. (Col. Nosotros los chilenos, 17. Serie Hoy contamos)

Well-illustrated account of types of people in Chile and their problems.

6865. _____. Nosotros los chilenos; tres ensayos antropológicos de interpretación. Santiago, Editora Austral, 1970. 288 p., bibl.

Prehistory, present-day inhabitants, and folklore of Chile presented in a journalistic style. Material is poorly organized.

6866. Schneider S., Hans. El aporte de Elías Almeyda Arroyo al estudio del clima de Chile (UCIG/IG, 20, 1970, p. 11-16, bibl.)

Brief resumé of contributions of Elías Almeyda Arroyo to climatological studies in Chile.

6867. Subercaseaux, Benjamin. Chile: a geographic extravaganza. Translated by Angel Flores. N.Y., Hafner Publishing, 1971. 255 p.

This facsimile of the 1943 ed. is a geographical interpretation of Chile. Instead of the traditional threefold division, the country is partitioned into six major regions: land of tranquil mornings, land of the interrupted path, land of the snow-capped wall, land of the trembling earth, land of the blue mirrors, and land of the twilight night.

6868. Thome, Joseph R. A brief survey of the Chilean agrarian reform program. Madison, Univ. of Wisconsin, Land Tenure Center, 1969. 19 p., tables (LTC, 28)

Under Eduardo Frei's government, two major agrarian reform laws were passed to relieve some of the social and economic problems arising from unequal distribution of land in Chile. By 31 May 1968, a total of 654 latifundia representing 1,248,647 ha. had been alienated from the large landholders and distributed in favor of the landless peasants.

6869. Ure, John. Cucumber sandwiches in the Andes. London, Constable, 1973. 165 p., bibl., map, plates.

Accounts of travel across the Andes of central Chile. The author's own experience combined with library research makes this work both entertaining and informative.

6870. Uribe Ortega, Graciela and Cris-

tiana Castillo Campano. Estrategia para un desarrollo planificado: la microregión de Chiloé Insular (UCIG/IG, 20, 1970, p. 185-234, maps, tables)

Report from part of a team which investigated development planning in the cities of Ancud and Castro during 1969. Regional economic reorganization, decentralization of activities, and changes in the urban transport system are discussed.

6871. Weischet, Wolfgang. Agrarreform und Nationalisierung des Bergbaus in Chile. Darmstadt, FRG, Wissenschaftliche Buchgesellschaft, 1974. 106 p., maps, tables (Zugleich eine Aktualisierung der Wissenschaftlichen Länderkunde, 2/3)

Pt. 1 of this book analyzes the system of agrarian reform applied in Chile following Law 15020 (1962), with special reference to colonization processes, and the force-methods and effects of the Allende administration on rural land takeover. The conclusion is that the Allende changes have had little success in altering the cultural landscape or in improving the lot of the peasant worker. Pt. 2 of the book is a brief analysis of the nationalization of the copper industry and the financial problems which characterize its operation.

6872. Yudelevich, Moisés and others. Inventario de las plantaciones forestales de la zona centro sur de Chile. Santiago, Instituto Forestal, 1966. 93 p., fold. maps, illus., maps, plates, tables (Informe técnico, 24)

Resource investigation of artificial forest stands in eight provinces between Maule and Cautín, central Chile. Some 77 percent of the 2.5 million hectares of reforestable land have been planted in *Pinus* sp., and eucalyptus, mainly. Between 1962-63 some 178 million feet of pine (33.5 percent of the nation's lumber) were cut.

COLOMBIA

6873. Alvarez Múnera, Guillermo. Urabá: ante el reto del desarrollo regional; informe especial de Gerencia sobre el Plan Integral de Desarrollo Regional (PID). Urabá, Colo., Corporación Regional de Desarrollo de Urabá (CORPOURABA), 1972? 29 l.

Noting the disorganized economic and social factors of development in a difficult physical landscape, the author of this planning scheme for Urabá, Colo., deplores the lack of official and private assistance, the restraining influence of usury, market exploitation and poor transportation. He suggests development by expanding colonization and use of new resources.

6874. Arévalo, Jorge. Ajuste del *Censo de Población de Colombia de 1964.*

Santiago, Centro Latinoamericano de Demografía, 1968. 30 p., tables.

Evaluation and adjustment of demographic data from the July 1964 Colombian census for use in population projection studies. Originally a document presented at the Conferencia Panamericana sobre Enseñanza de la Demografía en las Facultades de Medicina, held in Bogotá, 23-26 June 1968. Includes appendices.

6875. Avila Bernal, Alvaro. La población y el problema de la vivienda en Colombia (Revista Cámara de Comercio de Bogotá, 3:12, sept. 1973, p. 9-49, bibl., tables)

Article analyzes the population structure in Colombia, its growth characteristics, regional traits, and associations with housing types. Colombia managed to construct only 2.2 houses per 1,000 inhabitants in 1971—considerably below the 10 per 1,000 figure needed by developing nations. The deficit will produce a real crisis by 2,000 AD.

6876. *Boletín de la Sociedad Geográfica de Colombia.* Academia de Ciencias Geográficas. Vol. 26, No. 97, 1. trimestre 1968- . Bogotá.

One of a good reference series dealing with departments and territories of Colombia. Economic data, settlement maps, and information on natural resources presented in brief form.

6877. Brunnschweiler, Dieter. The llanos frontier of Colombia: environment and changing land use in Meta. East Lansing, Michigan State Univ., Latin American Studies Center, 1972. 71 p., maps, plates, tables (Monograph, 9)

The changes that are taking place in the tropical lowlands of the state of Meta are analyzed. The author believes that if the region is to provide significant contributions to the country, both the government and private concerns will have to participate more actively in the development of the region.

6878. Camargo, Hernando. Colono: fundación de un poblado (Revista de la Dirección de Divulgación Cultural [Bogotá] 10, marzo 1972, p. 139-170, illus., map)

Residents of the vereda El Alto Raudal, Meta dept., eastern Colo., founded a new group settlement in 1971 on the southwest edge of the Sierra de la Macarena. Students of the National Univ. (Bogotá) formulated an innovative plan for layout and growth of the community which is presented in this article.

6879. Colombia. Departamento Administrativo Nacional de Estadística. Sub-empleo en las 7 principales ciudades del país, según el censo de 1964. Bogotá, 1969. 166 p.

Underemployment (average number of months worked multiplied by 100 and divided by 12) is analyzed fo the seven principal cities of Colombia. Miners, construction workers and domestic servants have the highest percentage of underemployment.

6880. _____. Fondo de Promoción de Exportaciones (PROEXPO). Maderas colombianas. Bogotá, 1970? 117 p., bibl., plates, tables.

This unusual handbook presents excellent color plates illustrating the appearance of wood from nearly 200 tree types. Physical properties such as flexibility, compression, impact traits, etc., are listed along with information about distribution of the trees by region, and possible uses.

6881. _____. Instituto Colombiano de la Reforma Agraria (INCORA). Proyecto Bolívar. v. 1. Bogotá, 1969. 18 p.

Description of Proyecto Bolívar No. 1, just southeast of Cartagena, Colo. The project has as its goal the improvement by irrigation of 25,000 hectares. A large dam is being built by a Mexican firm, and International Land Development Consultants, N.V., of Arkem, Holland, are serving as advisors.

6882. _____. _____. Reforma agraria colombiana: organización, funciones, programas, realizaciones. Bogotá, 1970. 37 p., maps, plates, tables (Serie Divulgativa, 106)

Popularized review of the history of INCORA, and national laws 200 (1936), 100 (1944), and 135 (1961). Function and programs of INCORA described. Distribution of projects shown on highly generalized maps.

6883. _____. _____. Oficina de Planeación. Plan quinquenal: 1970-1974. v. 1, Programa, presupuesto. Bogotá, 1970. 51 l., tables.

Colombian Institute of Agrarian Reform and Colonization's (INCORA) plans for the period of 1970-74. The quantitative data in the text enable us to see INCORA's trend in matters relating to land tenure, title processing, colonization, and agricultural credit. The data also illustrate official attitudes toward agrarian reform.

6884. _____. Instituto Geográfico Agustín Codazzi. Diccionario geográfico de Colombia. t. 1, Letras A-L; t. 2, Letras M-Z. Bogotá, Banco de la República, 1971. 2 v. (1447 p.) (Continuous pagination) maps, plates, tables.

This volume is more than the title indicates. It not only lists place names in Colombia, but presents important statistics, including elevation, annual temperature, and human characteristics. Excellent color and black-and-white photographs make the publication a reference "must."

6885. _____. _____. Memoria sobre los trabajos ejecutados durante el primer semestre de 1971. Bogotá, 1971. 37 p., tables (mimeo)

Performance ratings are given in this report for the various tasks assigned to the Instituto Geográfico Agustín Codazzi in Bogotá for the first part of 1971.

6886. ———. ———. Problemas de la colonización del Putumayo. Botogá, 1973. 62 p., fold. maps, plates, tables.

Informative analysis of colonization in Puerto Asís, Colo., with physical and human geographical component sections. Puerto Asís, founded in 1912 by Capuchin missionaries, was converted to an army base of 1,000 men during the war with Peru in the 1930s. The subsequent discovery of oil has led to modern colonization, the effects of which are well depicted on a sequent occupance map for 1946, 1962, and 1967. Case studies and illustrations help make this a valuable book.

6887. ———. ———. Oficina de Estudios Geográficos. Monografía del departamento de Antioquia. Bogotá, 1969. 94 p., maps, plates, tables.

Geographical monograph of Antioquia. A valuable source of information, similar in character to the *Enciclopedia dos Municipios Brasileiros* published by the Instituto Brasileiro de Geografia e Estatística in the 1960s.

6888. ———. Ministerio de Agricultura. Corporación Nacional para el Desarrollo del Chocó. El terremoto de Bahía Solano del 26 de Septiembre de 1970: informes técnicos. Bogotá, 1971. 52 p., maps, tables (Instituto Geofísico de los Andes Colombianos. Publicación serie A. Sismología, 33)

Earthquakes are not new phenomena on the Pacific coast of South America. In 1970 three quakes in the Colombian settlement of Puerto Mutis (founded in 1935 and now called Puerto Solano), just west of the Río Atrato, destroyed over three-fourths of the dwellings. The settlement was founded on a sandy, alluvial fan, and it is recommended that six-meter support pilings be used in future construction, that only one-story buildings be erected, and that a local bridge be rebuilt.

6889. ———. ———. Instituto de Fomento Algodonero. La importancia de un cultivo: el algodón en Colombia, estadísticas. Bogotá. 1 v. (Unpaged)

Cotton cultivation in Colombia is presented by region with statistics from 1958-67. Although no maps are given, they could be constructed from information in this book.

6890. *Colombia Geográfica*. Revista del Instituto Geográfico Agustín Codazzi. Año 2, Vol. 2, No. 1, 1. semestre 1971- . Bogotá.

This issue contains a brief report on the economic geography of the Chocó, Colo., found in Germany among the manuscripts of A. von Humboldt in 1969 by Father Jesús Emilio Ramírez, S.J. The manuscript was presented by the governor of Chocó, Pedro Murgueytio, in 1823, to Vice-President Santander.

6891. Coloquio de Suelos, I, Medellín, Colo., 1970. Acidez y encalamiento en el trópico. Bogotá, Sociedad Colombiana de la Ciencia del Suelo, 1971. 309 p., bibl., illus., maps, tables (Suelos ecuatoriales, 3:1)

With the publication of this volume of articles dealing with problems of soil acidity in the tropics, the journal *Suelos Ecuatoriales* has been revived (Vol. 3, No. 7). Theories on soil acidity, determination of acidity, and correction of soil acidity are major themes.

6892. Comité Interamericano de la Alianza para el Progreso (CIAP), *Washington*. La economía agrícola colombiana. Washington, Organización de los Estados Americanos, Secretaría General, Depto.de Asuntos Económicos, Unidad de Estudios Sectoriales, 1971. 131 p., bibl., illus., tables.

Statistical indices of Colombian agricultural production growth and areas cultivated are presented. Comparative yields are not given, unfortunately, and text matter is brief. Some land tenure information is included in the text.

6893. Crist, Raymond E. Popayán (OAS/AM, 23:4, abril 1971, p. 25-32, plates)

A geographical appraisal of the southern Colombian city of Popayán, founded by Benalcázar in 1536. Historical and economic treatment with the author's informative case study approach.

6894. Franco Camacho, Guillermo. Tendencias recientes de la prospectiva en Colombia (IGAC/CG, 3:1, 1. semestre 1972, p. 11-22, illus.)

The *Group of the Year 2000* was formed in 1970 in Colombia as an official agency for investigating the most desirable solutions to man's greatest problems in a rational way. Imaginative ideas will be put to rigorous scientific analysis, and, hopefully, applied where they will do the most good to alleviate human suffering. Eleven committees have been created which will concern themselves with man and the biosphere, development of new lands, technology, transportation, cultural integration, social organization, regional development, energy, education, international cooperation, and public relations. Special attention has already been given to cooperative research with Brazil in Amazonia, and to coordination with UN organizations.

6895. Gómez Hurtado, Alvaro and **Alfonso López Michelsen.** El problema agrario en Colombia (PUJ/U, 43, Nov. 1972, p. 291-302)

Some 43 percent of the Colombian population still

lives in rural areas and produces 95 percent of the country's foodstuffs and over half the prime materials used by industry. In spite of this, public opinion remains indifferent to agriculture and has never demanded a national farm policy. Coffee still occupies too important a place and planning is insufficient in general.

6896. Greiff, Jorge Arias de. Algo mas sobre Caldas y Humboldt: el documento inédito de una lista de instrumentos (SGC/B, 27:101, 1970, p. 3-15, facsims.)

Physical geography of the Lago de La Cocha in the south of Colombia.

6897. Heredia Cano, Fabio. Un estudio ecológico para la protección de la selva húmeda tropical de Colombia (UA/U, 48:186, enero/marzo 1973, p. 27-34, bibl.)

Author presents structural and functional analysis of the ecosystem of the humid tropical selva and a statement about protection of natural resources.

6898. Herrman, Reimer. Las causas de la sequía climática en la región costera de Santa Marta, Colombia (ACCEFN/R, 13:52, 1970, p. 479-489)

Explanation of rapid vegetation changes within short distances on north coast of Colombia. Causes of the changes are mainly divergence of coast winds and associated subsidence of air, orographic descent of air, stress-differential induced divergence, and dry katabatic winds.

6899. Laverde Goubert, Luis. Fronteras terrestres. Bogotá, Instituto Geográfico Agustín Codazzi, 1969. 160 p., bibl., map, tables.

Historical treatment of Colombian frontiers, their development, problems, and changes. Useful reference data on specific border situations.

6900. McGreevey, William Paul. Urban growth in Colombia (UM/JIAS, 16:4, Nov. 1974, p. 387-408, bibl., tables)

With 30 cities larger than 50,000 in size, Colombia has a greater diversity of urban settlements than any other Latin American country. Although the country does not have the problem of a single, dominant capital city, the population of Bogotá has increased so fast in recent decades that the concept of balanced national urban growth is now challenged. This first-class contribution to knowledge about Colombian urbanism will be of interest to environmental specialists.

6901. Maher, Patric. Rural regeneration in Colombia: the possibilities of a labor-intensive strategy. Washington, Organization of American States, Dept. of Economic Affairs, Division of Institutional Development, Research Cooperation Program, Public Administration Unit, 1971. 63 p., bibl. (UP/G. 16/21)

It is suggested that, for the economic development of Colombia, a greater emphasis should be placed in the agricultural sector. To avoid rapid urban growth and consequent social and economic problems resulting from unchecked rural-urban migrations, the regional or local central places should be made into foci.

6902. Mantilla S., Guillermo and Luis A. León S. Estudios en suelos del Valle del Cauca con relación Ca:Mg invertida; el efecto de varias enmiendas en las propiedades químicas y físicas de un suelo de Guayabito (Revista ICA [Instituto Colombiano Agropecuarios, Bogotá] 6:1, marzo 1971, p. 57-72, bibl., illus., tables)

The optimum value of the Ca:Mg ratio for crops like sugar cane and rice is above one. Although studies of soils with a ratio less than one are rare, this article adds to the literature with its evaluation of a poorly drained, basic clay soil near the Laguna de Sonso (Galpón series). Chemical analysis and recommendations for improving such soils are presented.

6903. Molano Campuzano, Joaquín and P.V. Kugenev. Un tesoro del mundo: la Sierra de la Macarena [and] Otra vez acerca de la Sierra de la Macarena, tesoro del mundo (SGC/B, 27:103, 1971, p. 232-262, bibl., plates)

Critique of conservation measures applied to the Sierra de la Macarena in eastern Colombia.

6904. Molina Ossa, Camilo. La reforma agraria colombiana. Cali, Solo., Imprenta Departamental, 1970. 134 p., bibl., plates, tables.

Newspaper articles about failures of the program for agrarian reform in Colombia are presented for 1970. Some insight into problems may be gained by reading, but articles tend to be polemics.

6905. Morales V., Jesús María. Informe del reconocimiento detallado de los suelos de la Estación Experimental Agropecuria El Mira, municipio de Tumaco, Nariño. Bogotá, Ministerio de Agricultura, Instituto Colombiano Agropecuario (ICA), Subgerencia Técnica, División de Investigación, Depto. de Agronomía, 1972. 206 1., fold. maps, tables.

Lengthy report delimits series and types of soils on an experimental farm on the Pacific Coast south of Tumaco.

6906. Niveles de atención médica para un sistema de regionalización en Colombia. Bogotá, Ministerio de Salud Pública, Asociación Colombiana de

Facultades de Medicina (INEPS), 1970? 54 p., illus.

The principal characteristics of location of medical facilities are a pyramidal system with a wide base in rural zones surrounding a high-level urban facility or facilities, various levels of service and personnel throughout the regional system, and integration of personnel services and facilities.

6907. Olivares, Juan. Proyecciones de la población del distrito especial de Bogotá, 1965-1985. Prólogo [de] Enrique Pérez S. Bogotá, Ediciones Univ. de los Andes, 1970. 91 p., tables.

Published thesis from the Univ. of the Andes dealing with population by age and sex for the Federal District of Bogotá (1965-85).

6908. Pérez S., Enrique. Parámetros demográficos, 1951-1964 y proyecciones de población, 1965-1985. Bogotá, Univ. de los Andes, Centro de Estudios sobre Desarrollo Económico (CEDE), 1970. 280 p., tables (Col. CEDE sobre demografia, 8)

The demographic parameters, mortality, birth rate, and migration are analyzed statistically in this handbook on Colombian population characteristics. Projections to 1985 are given by department for male or female segments of the population, and for total amounts.

6909. Pineda, Aníbal. Historia de las telecomunicaciones en Colombia. Bogotá, Empresa Nacional de Telecomunicaciones de Colombia (TELECOM), 1970. 191 p., illus., facsims., maps, plates, tables.

Detailed history of various forms of communications in Colombia starting from pre-Spanish times. VHF and microwave installations, and manufacture of transmission equipment in Colombia are among items discussed.

6910. Ramírez, Jesús Emilio. Historia de la primera colección de minerales de Colombia. La de la expedición botánica (SGC/B, 26:100, 1968, p. 259-266)

Summary statement about the fate of the mineral and animal collection of the colonial *Expedición Botánica* in Colombia.

6911. Rodman, Selden. The Colombian traveler. N.Y., Hawthorn Books, 1971. 173 p., facsims., plates.

Perhaps this interesting book may be thought of as a companion to K. Romeli's *Colombia: gateway to South America*. Whereas Romeli's well-researched book gives a feeling for the land of Colombia, Rodman's gives more of a feeling for the people and politics. Contents include: pt. 1, "History;" pt. 2, "Colombia Illustrated," and pt. 3, "Colombia Travelogue."

6912. Samper Gnecco, Andrés. Cuando Bogotá tuvo tranvía. Bogotá, Instituto Colombiano de Cultura, 1973. 128 p. (Biblioteca colombiana de cultura. Col. Popular, 88)

Popularized account of a past transportation era in Bogotá, Colo., dealing with life in the city when streetcars were the main commercial form of public conveyance. Of possible interest to economic and historical geographers.

6913. Sole Sanroma, Nuria. Estudio esporo-polínico de la Formación Guadas: Maastrichtiense-Paleoceno en la sabana de Bogotá, Colombia. Barcelona, Univ. de Barcelona, Secretariado de Publicaciones, Intercambio Científico y Extensión Universitaria, 1970. 10 p., bibl.

The name Guaduas was introduced for a geological formation in Colombia's Cordillera de Bogotá by Alfred Hettner in 1892. Since then the formation's name has been extended far beyond the original area of description to places with quite different formations. E. Hubach has redefined the term Guaduas to describe a sandstone occurring between the Guadalupe and Bogotá formations. Paleontological investigations place the age of the redefined Guaduas as Paleocene in its uppermost portions.

6914. Toro Patiño, Alfonso. El Quindío: perfil histórico y socio económico. Prólogo de John Agudelo Ríos. Bogotá, Empresa Tipográfica Alvear, 1966. 90 p., illus., tables.

Description of the smallest dept. in Colombia which presents economic development data.

6915. Villega Moreno, Luis Alberto. Aspectos de la política social y económica de los tugurios y asentamientos no controlados. Medellín, Colo., n.p., 1970. 14 p.

The author presents problems associated with tugurios in Colombia. He criticizes economists for analyzing data without dealing in causes of slum generation or solutions. Formation of regional markets and of economic blocks believed to be an answer to difficulties.

6916. ———. Vivienda y desarrollo urbano en Colombia. Bogotá, Instituto de Crédito Territorial, 1970. 95 p., tables.

Urban problems in Colombia are probably typical for countries of South America, so this small volume of their economic, regional, and physical disequilibrium will be of interest to Latin Americanists.

6917. Zethelius, Sven. Una posible tecnología para la Amazonia (IGAC/CG, 3:1, 1. semestre 1972, p. 25-42, plates)

The ecological deterioration in the Colombian Amazonia resulting from man's stepped-up interventions is pointed out; then, alternative methods more compatible with the environment are presented.

6918. Zonn, S.V.; R.S. Narskih; and N.A. Timofeeva. *El atlas geográfico de Colombia* (SGC/B, 27:103, 1971, p. 263-272)

Thorough review of the second ed. of the *Atlas de Colombia* published in Bogotá in 1969. Although criticisms such as the lack of explanation of demographic growth, the presentation of six zones of population displacement without detailed analysis, lack of educational data, inaccurate placement of industrial symbols, and lack of information about agrarian reform, the *Atlas* is given much praise.

ECUADOR

6919. Acosta Solís, Misael. Glumifloras del Ecuador: catálogo fitogeográfico de las gramíneas, ciperáceas y juncáceas. Quito, Instituto Ecuatoriano de Ciencias Naturales, 1969. 192 p., illus., plates, tables.

A list of glumaceous plants of Ecuador collected primarily from the Andean highlands. According to the catalogue, there are 127 genera of *Graminea* composing 506 species, and varieties, and 18 genera of *Cyperaceae* comprising 80 species.

6920. ———. La lucha contra la sequía y la erosión en la mitad del mundo. Quito, Editorial Casa de la Cultura Ecuatoriana, 1971. 63 p., bibl., plates, tables.

Monograph of article annotated in *HLAS 35:6925* contains various comments of an ecological nature with special reference to erosion in Ecuador.

6921. ———. Naturalistas y viajeros científicos que han contribuído al conocimiento florístico y fitogeográfico del Ecuador. Quito, Casa de la Cultura Ecuatoriana, 1968. 138 p., bibl., illus.

A chronological list of explorers, naturalists, and botanists who have contributed to the knowledge of Ecuadorian flora from the early 18th century to the present.

6922. ———. La selva occidental del noroccidente ecuatoriano (ACCEFN/R, 13:52, 1970, p. 499-533)

A 10,000 km.² triangle between the Bahía de Ancón de Sardinas and the Boca del Santiago along the Ecuadorian coast and Lita in the interior is examined according to topography, edaphology, climate, vegetation, forest economy, and colonization possibilities.

6923. *El Año Ecuatoriano.* No. 18, 1970/1971- . Quito.

Yearbook of Ecuadorian affairs for 1970. Includes sections on political, social, cultural, and economic subjects.

6924. Arias Bazantes, Manuel. Análisis de la estructura agraria del Ecuador. Quito, Junta Nacional de Planificación y Coordinación, Sección Publicaciones, 1969. 156 p., tables.

Interpretation of the Ecuadorian rural structure based on the 1954 agrarian census data. Aspects such as holding size, tenurial patterns, and areal differences in agricultural productivity are discussed. Suggestions for improvements include changes in the outmoded agrarian institutions and promotion of colonization as part of general agrarian reform.

6925. Balázas, Dénes. Galápagos. Budapest, Gondolat, 1973. 216 p., illus., maps, plates.

A Hungarian naturalist describes rather thoroughly the fascinating world of the Galápagos Islands. Emphasis is placed on the history and on the perfect balance of nature which can be found in these islands. The author's own excellent photographs illustrate this interesting work. Aimed at the non-specialist. [G.M. Dorn]

Bedoya M., Angel N. Federico Enrique Alejandro, Barón de Humboldt. See item 6504.

6926. Bromley, Raymond J. The Llanganatis of Ecuador (EJ, 51:3, Sept. 1972, p. 141-149, map, plates)

Travel accounts of a British scientific expedition to the Llanganatis mountains of central Ecuador conducted between July-Sept. 1969.

6927. Dalmasso, E. and P. Fillon. Aspectos de la organización espacial del Ecuador (UNAM/RMS, 34:1, enero/marzo 1972, p. 75-94, tables)

Urban organization of Ecuador is a reflection of economic and general spatial organization in the country. Coastal cities are recent and oriented toward commerce. Cities of the sierra are older and represent administrative centers and a certain type of intellectual life. Cities as such do not exist yet in the Oriente. The effects of competition between Quito and Guayaquil are discussed.

6928. Dawson, E. Yale. A brief natural history of the Galápagos Islands for young people (Historia natural de las Islas Galápagos, breve relato para jóvenes). Traslation by Eva V. Chesneau, Washington, Organization of American States, General Secretariat [and] Charles Darwin Foundation for the Galápagos Islands, Ghent, Belgium [and] Smithsonian Institution, Washington, 1970. 55 p., illus., maps, plates.

A brief natural history of the Galápagos Islands for young people.

6929. Ecuador, Corporación Ecuatoriana de Turismo. En Loja y Zamora. Quito, 1971? 114 p., plates, tables.

A tourist guide to the provinces of Loja and Zamora in southern Ecuador. Contains a detailed description of history, people, and land.

6930. _____ . Junta Nacional de Planificación y Coordinación Económica. División de Estadística y Censos. División territorial de la República del Ecuador. Quito, 1964. 58 p.

Presents division of provinces by *cantones* and their respective *parroquias* by alphabetical listing. Numbers of urban and rural settlements are summarized for 1964.

6931. _____. _____. _____. Segundo censo de población y primer censo de vivienda. t. 1/2. Quito, 1964. 2 v. (285, 325 p.) tables.

Final Ecuadorian returns from the 25 Nov. 1962 demographic and dwelling census. The two-volume enumeration does not include interpretation of the data.

6932. _____ . Misión Andina del Ecuador. Oficina de Investigaciones Sociales. Area de Pimampiro. Quito, 1970. 101 p.

One of a series of investigations in Ecuador which deal with local regions: in this case, the area of Pimampiro in the Cordillera Oriental. National and human resources are discussed.

6933. _____. _____. _____. Pucayacu. Quito, 1970. 157 p., maps, tables.

Six *parroquias,* the highest, within the Cotopaxi prov., Ecua., are analyzed with reference to natural and human resources. Social structure of the population, commerce, and political-administrative traits of the region are given special attention. 1970 statistics employed throughout.

6934. International Labour Organization, *Geneva.* **Programa Regular de Asistencia Técnica.** Informe al gobierno del Ecuador sobre reforma agraria y colonización. Geneva, 1966. 82 p.

Review of agrarian reform and colonization projects in Ecuador since the establishment of the Instituto Ecuatoriano de Reforma Agraria y Colonización (IERAC) in 1964. Recommendations are made to place priority on spontaneous and semi-directed colonization being carried out in the coastal and Amazon lowlands, instead of agrarian reform projects in the highlands. In addition, suggestions are made for the reorganization of the IERAC and for the agrarian reform law implementation.

6935. Tinajero, Jorge R. Herbario del Padre Luis Sodiro (UCE/A, 96:351, junio 1968, p. 67-192)

A comprehensive list of Ecuadorian flora, accompanied with notes on local plant nomenclature and uses.

6936. Vargas, José María. Ecuador monumental y turístico. Quito, Editorial Santo Domingo, 1970? 123 p., plates.

Discussions of Humboldt's trips to the crater of Pichincha, Quito and its museums, and various points of interest throughout Ecuador are presented with illustrations and historical comments.

6937. Villacres Moscoso, Jorge W. Distribution of plant-life in a torrid zone: the vegetation of Ecuador. Guayaquil, Ecua., Tropical Geography Center, 1971. 13 l.

Description of natural vegetation in Ecuador is divided into six categories with plant types based on the following regional subdivisions: coast, Cordilleran slopes, inter-Andean tableland, *páramos,* Oriente, and Galápagos Islands.

6938. Vivanco, Jorge E. El puente Río Guayas: síntesis histórica de su construcción. Quito, n.p., 1969. 45 p., maps, plates.

A short historical sketch about the construction of a bridge across the Guayas River, Ecua.

6939. White, Jeanne. Galápagos: evolution's living laboratory (RCGS/CGJ, 89:6, Dec. 1974, p. 16-23, plates)

Brief statement of history of settlement and problems with protection of wildlife.

6940. Wiggins, Ira L. and Duncan M. Porter. Flora of the Galápagos. Stanford, Calif., Stanford Univ. Press, 1971. 998 p., bibl., illus., maps, plates, tables.

A comprehensive description of Galápagos' flora based on the 1964 Galápagos Islands Scientific Project. Plants are listed by genus and species, and they are accompanied by maps, sketches, and color photographs.

THE GUIANAS

6941. Cummings, Leslie P. *ed.* Essequibo Islands: land tenure and land use. Georgetown, Univ. of Guyana, Dept. of Geography, 1973. 92 p., maps, plates, tables (Occasional papers series, 2)

The developments of settlement, land tenure systems, and land use in the islands of Leguan and Wakenaam located along the Essequibo River are described and analyzed.

6942. Dupont-Gonin, Pierre. La Guyane Française: le pays, les hommes, ses problémes et son avenir. Geneva, Librairie Droz, 1970. 277 p., bibl., maps, tables.

Analysis of economic situation in French Guiana by a former customs administrator. The problems facing the development of the colony are analyzed, following a brief description of its land and history. The study is concluded by a series of realistic recommendations for the region's economic change. Includes index.

6943. Eden, M.J. Some aspects of weathering and landforms in Guyana, formerly British Guiana (ZG, 15:2, Juni 1971, p. 181-198, bibl., illus., maps, plates)

Study of planation surfaces on the Guiana highlands of South America. Following the investigation of the Shea-Aishalton area of southern Guyana, the author refutes previous theories that the present landforms have been the result of physical weathering processes. Instead, he proposes that the inselberg morphology has evolved through deep chemical weathering processes.

6944. Guyana handbook: industry, tourism, commerce. Georgetown, Guyana Manufacturers Association *in cooperation with the* Ministry of Information; the Guyana Development Corporation; and Guyana Graphic, 1970? 183 p., illus., plates, tables.

Popularized listing of facts about Guyana including history, transportation, physical geography, and other almanac style information.

6945. Kirke, Henry. Twenty-five years in British Guiana. Westport, Conn., Negro Universities Press, 1970. 364 p., plates.

A late 19th-century account of man and land in Guyana by a British district judge. The book, a re-impression of an 1898 ed., provides interesting insights about the people, customs, settlements, and economic activities in the former British colony.

6946. A new Guyana. Georgetown, Ministry of Information, Culture and Youth, 1973? 62 p., plates.

Black-and-white photographs interspersed with poetry by famous Caribbean writers in a very thin volume. [T.L. Martinson]

6947. Richardson, Bonham C. Distance regularities in Guyanese rice cultivation (JDA, 8:2, Jan. 1974, p. 235-255, illus., maps, tables)

Agricultural theory according to the von Thünen model and its variations need not yet be discarded as old fashioned. There are good reasons to illustrate conformality among peasant-oriented rice farm operations in Guyana. The author's findings also indicatee that modern application of von Thünen's ideas suggests that agricultural location theory accommodates single product operations which involve different techniques as is common in Guyana.

6948. Schomburgk, Robert H. A description of British Guiana geographical and statistical, exhibiting its resources and capabilities together with the present and future condition and prospects of the colony. London, Frank Cass, 1970. 155 p., fold. map, tables.

Reprint of the original published in 1840. For more on Schomburgk's travels in the Guianas, see *HLAS 33:5338.*

PARAGUAY

6949. Bareiro-Saguier, Rubén. Le Paraguay. Traduit de l'espagnol par Jean-Paul Duviols. Paris, Bordas, 1972. 128 p., bibl., map, plates (Col. Études, 201)

Popularized four-chapter work emphasizing historical, population, and economic bases of Paraguayan life.

6950. Fogel, Gerardo; Oscar Santacruz Galcano; Ramón Fogel; and Ruth de Vela. Paraguay: realidad y futuro, una aproximación al presente del país y sus perspectivas. Asunción, Instituto de Desarrollo Integral y Armónico (IDIA), 1970? 133 p., bibl., maps, tables.

A systesis of modern-day socioeconomic and geographic conditions of Paraguay. Contains chapters on physical geography, demography, history, transportation, economy, social aspects, and past attempts at development planning.

6951. Franco Viedma, Pablo. El Paraguay: su geografía general, ajustada al programa de estudio vigente del primer curso básico. Asunción, Talleres de Imprenta Comuneros, 1972. 119 p., bibl., fold. maps, illus., maps.

School book geography for secondary education in Paraguay.

6952. Gorham, J. Richard *ed.* Paraguay: ecological essays. Introduction by Jesse D. Perkinson. Miami, Fla., Academy of the Arts and Sciences of the Americas, 1973. 296 p., facsims., illus., maps, plates, tables.

A collection of 12 essays intended to provide basic information concerning man and land in Paraguay. Although the subjects are not well-balanced and the article qualities vary, they provide a fair background of Paraguayan environment.

6953. Halley Mora, Gerardo. Imágenes de un tiempo en fuga. Asunción, Editorial La Voz, 1971. 195 p.

This small book is a series of stories about folkloric beliefs of the people of Paraguay. Explanations of days of fiesta and other aspects of life create a "feeling" for aspects of the human geography of the area.

6954. McKerna, Mrs. James F. ed. Land of lace and legend: an informal guide to Paraguay. 4. ed., rev. Preface [by] Mrs. Harold Grover and Mrs. Howard Murray. Asunción, Las Amigas Norteamericanas del Paraguay, 1969. 208 p., illus., map, plates.

A guide to Paraguay intended for both tourists and new immigrants.

6955. Makoto, Simón. Manual turístico del Paraguay. Asunción, Dirección General de Turismo, 1972. 94 p., fold., maps, illus., maps, plates, tables.

This small volume contains the usual tourist information plus a small Guaraní grammar for beginners.

6956. Paraguay today: information handbook. London, Paraguayan Trade Centre, 1971? 50 p., illus., plates, tables.

A guidebook intended to introduce Paraguay to the layman.

6957. Pavetti Morián, Justo Manuel comp. Datos de la ciudad: nomenclatura, barrios, avenidas, calles, pasajes. Asunción, Municipalidad de Asunción, Dirección de Catastro, 1970. 142 p. (Libro, 3. Sección Catastro)

List of names of streets, avenues, and barrios of Asunción, their location, and a short description on the origin of names, along with ordinances that created them.

6958. Pitaud, Henri. El mar de palmas. Asunción, Editorial France-Paraguay, 1971. 292 p.

This translation of the French La mer des palmes is fictional literature about the eastern Paraguayan Chaco. The novel provides a good description of nature, history, and life in the Chaco of the early 1950s.

6959. Rivarola, Domingo M. ed. Estudios y datos sobre la población en el Paraguay. Asunción, Centro Paraguayo de Estudios Sociológicos, 1970. 27 p., bibl.

A short annotated bibliography of Paraguayan demographic studies. The hastily gathered material is far from being complete and contains numerous errors.

6960. Samaniego, Marcial. El plan quinquenal de los transportes nacionales como factor determinante en el proceso de desarrollo socio-económico de nuestro país. Asunción, Ministerio de Obras Públicas y Comunicaciones, 1970. 13 p., maps, tables.

Review of present situation of transportation systems in Paraguay and projections for the 1971-75 period. Valuable statistical data, maps, and graphs included.

PERU

6961. Amiran, David H.K. El Desierto de Sechura, Perú: problems of agricultural use of deserts (PAIGH/G, 72, junho 1970, p. 7-12, map)

Continuation of *HLAS 35:6946*. Agricultural development and management are discussed for the Piura area (Sechura desert) of north coastal Peru. Long-staple cotton still dominates in a relatively sound farm economy, which does not always practice good ecological constraints.

6962. Atherton, M.P. and P.J. Brenchley. A preliminary study of the structure, stratigraphy and metamorphism of some contact rocks of the Western Andes, near the Quebrada Venado Muerto, Peru (RGS/GJ, 8:1, 1972, p. 161-178, bibl., illus., map, plates, tables)

Geological interpretation and description of Quebrada Venado Muerto, Ancash, Peru. The author provides preliminary information about structural changes that occur when volcanic rocks are solidified around batholiths. Findings from the area are compared to those described for other locations.

6963. Barrón, Daniel. Notas sobre las fanerogamas de la zona de influencia del río Higueras-Mito-Huánuco (UNCP/AC, 2, 1973, p. 351-381, bibl.)

A cross-sectional description of natural elements along the Mito river, a tributary of the Huallaga, in eastern Peru. The vertical floral differentiation is extensively treated.

6964. *Boletin del Instituto del Mar del Perú*. Vol. 2, No. 9, 1973- . Chucuito, Perú.

Contributions to the study of population dynamics of the Peruvian anchovy with special reference to the years 1971-72 during which serious shortages were noted. Tagging experiments, egg production, yields and management strategy are discussed.

6965. Bowen, J. David. The land and people of Peru. Philadelphia, Pa., J.B. Lippincott, 1973. 158 p., plates (Portrait of the nation series)

An easy to read popular account of the land, society, economy, and people of Peru.

6966. Buse, Hermann. Los peruanos en Oceania: geografía y crónicas del

Pacífico. Lima, Talleres Gráficos P.L. Villanueva, 1967. 381 p., plates.

A poorly documented account of the exploration and discovery of the Pacific islands by people departing from the Peruvian coast. Pt. 1 is a description of the natural environment; pt. 2 is the author's chronicle about the crossing of the Pacific, and pt. 3 consists of a short history of the Peruvians in Oceania.

6967. Castro Bastos, Leónidas. Paisajes natural y cultural del Perú. Lima, Editorial Universo, 1971. 251 p., illus., plates.

Non-technical interpretation of physical and cultural landscapes of Peru.

6968. Collin-Delavaud, Claude. Les régions côtières du Pérou septentrional (IG, 36:1, jan./fév. 1972, p. 59-54)

Regional description and discussion of problems such as latifundismo in the depts. of La Libertad, Lambayeque, Piura, and Tumbes of northern Peru.

6969. Comité Peruano de Zonas Aridas, Lima. Informe nacional sobre las zonas áridas. Lima, 1963. 105 p., plates, tables.

The book provides basic information for understanding the environment and human occupation of the arid and semiarid region of coastal Peru. Although a little outdated (1963), the basic pattern still holds true. Study prepared for the Conferencia Latinoamericana sobre el Estudio de las Regiones Aridas.

6970. Córdova-Ríos, Manuel and F. Bruce Lamb. Wizard of the upper Amazon. N.Y., Atheneum, 1971. 87 p., bibl., maps.

This book is the case history of a Peruvian captured by Amahuaca Indians. It reveals a real grasp of conditions of Indian life in the selva, and should be of interest to environmentalists.

6971. Cortázar, Pedro Felipe. Imágen del Perú: un país distinto [Image of . . . Bildnis . . . L'Image . . . Immagine . . .] Lima, Ioppe Editores, 1971? 276 p., maps, plates.

Pictorial book about Peru with informative captions in five languages: Spanish, English, German, French, and Italian.

6972. Departamento de Puno. Lima, Ioppe Editores, 1970. 158 p., map, plates (Col. Documental del Perú, 21)

One of a series of 24 guide books which provides elementary social, historical, and cultural information on each of the Peruvian depts. The volume may be of interest to tourists with limited local knowledge.

6973. Doughty, Paul L. From disaster to development (OAS/AM, 23:5, May 1971, p. 232-235, plates)

The effects of the 31 May 1970 earthquake and the accompanying snow, rock, and mudslides in the Callejón de Huaylas, Peru, which caused extensive damages to lives and properties are assessed and future developments are discussed.

6974. Franklin, William L. Salvemos a la vicuña (OAS/AM, 25:4, April 1973, p. 2-10, plates)

At the end of 1960 it was estimated that only 5-10,000 vicuñas were left in Peru. They were placed on the endangered rare species list in 1968, and a reserve area of 60,000 hectares has been established on the Pampa Galeras in Ayacucho dept. Bolivia and Chile have followed suit.

6975. Gade, Daniel W. and Mario Escobar. Canyons of the Apurimac (EJ, 51:3, Sept. 1972, p. 135-140, map, plates)

General description of the Apurimac canyons. In addition to the physical environment, information about population, settlements, land use, and other economic activities in and around the gorges are presented.

6976. Hefley, James and Marti Hefley. Dawn over Amazonia: the story of Wycliffe Bible translators in Peru. Waco, Tex., Word Books, 1972. 193 p., illus., map, plates.

Historical description of development of the Summer Institute of Linguistics based at Yarinacocha, Peru. Geographers who have been guests at this eastern Peruvian base, as well as others, will enjoy this popularized story.

6977. Humm, Madeline. Mein peruanisches Tagebuch. Wien, Osterreichischer Bundesverlag, 1965? 189 p. (OBV-Taschenbücher, 63)

The daughter of writer R.J. Humm describes her experiences in Peru in colorful, vivid style in this worthwhile book. Details of everyday life among various social groups and deep observational insight into Peruvian personality traits make this valuable reading.

6978. Image of Peru. Washington, Organization of American States, General Secretariat, Dept. of Cultural Affairs, 1972? 24 p., map, illus., plates.

A booklet that attempts to present a kaleidoscopic view of Peru. Following a brief description about the land, the history, people, and economy of Peru are treated.

6979. Mangin, William. Autobiographical notes on a rural migrant to Lima, Peru (SOCIOL, 21:1, 1971, p. 58-76, bibl., plates)

A case study of a representative inhabitant of a Lima *barriada*. Living conditions in highland Peru, migration process, final settlement in Lima, and life in the squatter settlement are presented by selecting a woman emigré and recounting her life story.

6980. Masters, Robert V. Peru in pictures. N.Y., Sterling Publishing Co., 1971. 64 p., map, plates (Visual geography series)

A short pictorial book about Peru where the land, history, government, business, and people are briefly explained.

6981. Miró Quesada, Aurelio. Costa, sierra y montaña. Madrid, Editorial Revista de Occidente, 1969. 290 p., map.

A well-written dept-by-dept. description of contemporary Peru. The author's sound knowledge coupled with perceptive insights makes the book a valuable addition to the country's geography.

6982. Peñaherrera del Aguila, Carlos. Síntesis geográfica del Perú. Rio, Instituto Pan-Americano de Geografía e História, Comissão de Geografía, 1966. 119 p., bibl., map, tables.

As the title aptly describes, this handbook consists of a geographical summary of Peru.

6983. Perloff, Harbey S. and others. La nueva cultura. Lima, Ediciones de la Sociedad Interamericana de Planificación, 1969? 137 p., tables.

Simposio IV of the III Congreso Interamericano de Planificación held in Lima in 1968. For main entry see *HLAS 33:132a*.

6984. Peru. Amsterdam, Koninklijk Instituut voor de Tropen, 1969. 38 p., maps, plates, tables (Landendocumentatie, 125)

Economic and political report on Peru with emphasis on land use.

6985. Peru. Oficina de Desarrollo del Norte (ORDEN). Aguas subterráneas. Lima, 1969. 77 p., bibl., fold. maps, maps, tables (Análisis general de situación: región norte, 6)

Actual conditions and proposals for better use and conservation of underground water in northern Peru. Twenty-one valleys in the dept. of Ancash, La Libertad, Lambayeque, Piura, and Tumbes were investigated, where over 3,000 wells draw almost 900 million cubic m. of water per annum. It is believed that local aquifers offer potentials for more water if detailed hydrogeologic studies are made. Existing wells could yield water on a sustained basis if proper recharging mechanisms were understood.

6986. _____. Comunicaciones. Lima, 1969. 55 p., bibl., fold. maps, maps, tables (Análisis general de situación: región norte, 4)

Overview of communications system in northern Peru. It has been found that the postal, telegraph, and telephone services are poor. Similarly, the regional contribution in published materials is low in contrast to other parts of the country, especially Lima where 81 percent of the printed material originates. This has a negative influence on local population who are often attracted to Lima, based on propagandistic literature.

6987. _____. _____. Educación. Lima, 1969. 109 p., bibl., fold. maps, maps, tables (Análisis general de situación: región norte, 5)

The educational situation in northern Peru is analyzed for development planning purposes. In addition to the lack of qualified personnel, there is a general lack of coordination among various educational institutions and programs existing in the region. The result has been a higher illiteracy level in comparison with other parts of the country. The region is also plagued by the lack of adequate teaching equipment and facilities. There is no vocational orientation for graduates, and a high proportion of college students is majoring in education and humanities, and not in sciences.

6988. _____. _____. Energía. Lima, 1969. 117 p., bibl., fold. maps, maps, tables (Análisis de situación: región norte, 3)

A review of the energy situation in northern Peru (dept. of Tumbes, Piura, Lambayeque, Cajamarca, Amazonas, San Martín, La Libertad, and Ancash). Electric power development in the region has not accompanied population growth. Thus, over 500,000 inhabitants do not have access to electricity. Enormous potential exists in the region for power generation by tapping the rivers which flow either to the Pacific or Atlantic coasts. However, developments have been slowed by the lack of adequate data and antiquated energy laws. Production, consumption, and rates vary widely within the region.

6989. _____. _____. Industrias. Lima, 1969. 185 p., bibl., fold. maps, maps, tables (Análisis general de situación: región norte, 7)

Evaluation of the industrial sector of Northern Peru to 1967. Industry in the region is still insignificant, contributing only 3.8 percent of the domestic industrial production. Among the local manufacturers, consumer goods top the list. The majority of the industries located in Chimbote, Trujillo, Chiclayo, and Talara were characterized by old or obsolete machinery, high production costs, and low productivity. However, with incentives provided by recent development laws, large, modern plants have been built. Thus, in the near future the region's industries will become more diversified, and their contribution to the nation's industrial output will increase.

6990. _____. _____. Población. Lima, 1969. 115 p., bibl., fold. maps, maps, tables (Análisis general de situación: región norte, 1)

First of a series of seven volumes (see items 6985-6989 and 6991) intended to provide basic information for the social and economic development of northern Peru.

The demographic characteristics of the region are analyzed in the first volume. Data for the study are based on the 1940 and 1961 censuses.

6991. _____. _____. Recursos naturales. Lima, 1969. 187 p., bibl., fold. maps, maps, tables (Análisis general de situación: región norte, 8)

A pilot study on natural resources in the north of Peru which presents physical geography and resource potential in detail.

6992. _____. _____. Transportes. Lima, 1968. 175 p., bibl., fold. maps, maps, tables, (Análisis general de situación: región norte, 2)

Analysis of transportation systems in northern Peru. The region still depends overwhelmingly on road transport. Excepting the Carretera Marginal de la Selva and the penetration highways, there are no roads destined for regional development. Rail transport is losing its importance as a result of rapid developments in road transport. Air and water transport are mentioned and their importance in regional development is also analyzed.

6993. Peterson, Ulrich. Metalogenia del Perú en el marco continental (SGP/B, 41, 1971, p. 33-47, map, tables)

In this article the author outlines the distribution of some major mineral deposits on the continent of South America and makes interpretations of the competitive position of Peru. Continental maps and a geologic overlay are presented. Will be of much interest to geographers and others who want a small-scale view.

6994. Pulgar Vidal, Javier. Geografía del Perú: las ocho regiones naturales del Perú. Lima, Editorial Universo, 1973? 256 p., bibl., maps, plates, tables (Col. Textos universitarios)

Uses the local toponyms Chala, Yunga, Quechua, Suni, Puna, Janca, Ruparupa, and Omagua to identify the eight natural regions of Peru. Pulgar Vidal's classification, based on the natural and cultural geofactors, is corroborated by the ecological map elaborated by J.A. Tosi, Jr.

6995. Rho, Franco. Perú e fantasmi. Novara, Italy, Instituto Geográfico De Agostini, 1964. 217 p., plates.

An account of the Peruvian landscape between Lima and Chachapoyas as seen by the author who accompanied an archaeological expedition in 1961 headed by Duccio Bonavia.

6996. Robertson, F.J. Changing the coffee blend (GM, 46:12, Sept. 1974, p. 677-682, plates)

Since 1968 the *barriadas* of Lima have been more euphemistically called *pueblos jóvenes*. The creation of a network of 24 city parks has begun to make life somewhat more bearable in these places.

6997. Romero, Emilio. Biomas en la tierra y en el mar del Perú (SGL/B, 90, julio/dic. 1971, p. 33-59)

This article is a primer on flora and fauna from the Peruvian offshore area eastward to the eastern lowlands. Lists of common and Latin names for representative life forms are given.

6998. _____. Perú: una nueva geografía. Lima, Librería Studium, 1973? 2. v. (376, 329 p.) bibl., fold. maps, maps, plates.

Peruvian physical and human geography. V. 1 treats the environmental aspects, in addition to sections dealing with the country's borders. V. 2 includes the flora and fauna, population, settlements, and economy of Peru.

6999. Simposio sobre el Desarrollo de la Piscicultura en el Peru, *Lima, 1973.* El desarrollo de la piscicultura en el Perú. Lima, Univ. Nacional Agraria, Programa Academico de Pesquería, 1973. 164 p., illus.

This volume represents the proceedings of the conference on fishing held in March 1973 at Lima's Univ. Nacional Agraria. Cultivation of certain fish species, problems in the tropics, national fishing policies, and pollution are discussed.

7000. Smith, Clifford T. Inquiry into people: the promise of Eldorado (GM, 46:10, July 1974, p. 544-549)

High rates of population increase in cities of Peru have created massive problems, including overcrowding and a disparity in standards between Lima and the rest of the country and between urban and rural areas.

7001. Teves R., Néstor. Los sedimentos litorales en el sector comprendido entre La Punta y la Herradura: Lima, Perú (Revista Villarreal [Univ. Nacional Federico Villarreal, Lima] 1:1, 2. etapa, oct./dic. 1971, p. 85-96, bibl., tables)

In the Punta and Callao zones marine erosion is intense. It diminishes toward San Miguel and again intensifies in the Chira sector. Volcanics, andesites and breccias dominate the lithology along the shoreline.

7002. Tinker, Jon. National park in the Amazon rain forest (GM, 47:1, Oct. 1974, p. 33-39, plates)

Peru has established the Manu National Park along the Manu River, a tributary of the Madre de Dios. The park has an area of 15,328 km^2, but is threatened by the possibility of petroleum exploitation.

7003. Tord, Luis Enrique. Guía de Machu Picchu. Lima, DELFOS*ediciones,* 1973. 85 p., bibl., plates.

A concise guide to the archaeological site of Machu Picchu, Peru. The booklet, written by an anthropologist for the layman, provides useful information to visitors with little or no previous knowledge of the former Inca border settlement.

7004. Tovar, Oscar. Revisión de las especies peruanas del género *festuca, gramineae.* Lima, Univ. Nacional Mayor de San Marcos, Dirección Universitaria de Biblioteca y Publicaciones, 1972. 93 p., illus. (Memorias del Museo de Historia Natural Javier Prado, 16)

A taxonomic revision of the *Festuca* species (*Gramineae*) occurring in Peru. The study points out that 37 species of *Festuca* have been identified from varied regions of Peru, the majority occurring in the Andes, at elevations between 3,900 and 4,500 m.

7005. Uhlig, Ralf-Dieter and Horst Dickudt. Peru: mit Stadtführer Lima und Cuzco. 2. ed. rev. München, FRG, Volk und Heimat, 1972. 94 p., maps, plates (Mai's Weltführer, 6)

This second, updated miniature Baedeker covers the essentials about Peru's land and people in readable fashion.

7006. Veeh, H. Herbert; William C. Burnett; and Andrew Soutar. Contemporary phosphorites on the continental margin of Peru (AAAS/S, 181:4102, Aug. 1973, p. 844-845, map, table)

Phosphate in the form of apatite rich in flourine is found as a matrix in nodules off the coast of Peru. Uranium-series methods used to date the formation result in 300,000 years to recent. It appears that such nodules occur in a distribution pattern reflecting the interface of the oxygen minimum layer and the continental margin.

7007. Visite el Perú sus hoteles. Lima, Publicaciones, Perú, 1971. 224 p., maps, plates, tables.

A comprehensive tourist guide which serves to supplement the well-known annual publication: *South American handbook.*

7008. Zavaleta Figueroa, Isaías. El Callejón de Huaylas: antes y después del terremoto del 31 mayo de 1970. Caraz, Perú, Ediciones Paron, 1970. 49 p.

Collection of accounts about the earthquake and the accompanying mudslide which destroyed the settlement of Callejón de Juaylas, Peru, on 31 May 1970. Descriptions derived from interviews with survivors of the catastrophe, and newspaper articles.

7009. Zeballos Barrios, Carlos O. Arequipa: ciudad y contornos (The city and its countryside; la ville et ses alentours). Arequipa, Peru, Cuzzi, 1973. 103 p., map, plates.

A pictorial bilingual guidebook for the Peruvian city of Arequipa and its environs which offers an introduction to the colonial architecture and rural landscape of southern Peru.

URUGUAY

7010. Asociación Nacional de Profesores de Geografía, *Montevideo.* Hacia una geografía regional. Montevideo, Editorial Nuestra Tierra, 1969. 56 p., bibl., plates, tables (Nuestra tierra, 33)

The booklet attempts to demonstrate the role geographers could play in the economic development of Uruguay. Several regional development programs are described and geographical interpretations given.

7011. Collin-Delavaud, Anne. L'Uruguay: un exemple d'urbanisation originale en pays d'élevage (SGB/COM, 25:100, oct./déc. 1972, p. 361-389, maps, plates, tables)

Uruguay, the most urbanized country in Latin America, has problems in developing a normal settlement hierarchy. The overwhelming influence of the capital city does not enable country towns to function properly. A settlement classification is presented.

7012. Congreso Nacional de Profesores de Geografía, *III, Rivera, Uru., 1971.* Tercer Congreso Nacional de Profesores de Geografía. Rivera, Uru., Asociación Nacional de Profesores de Geografía, 1971. 2 v. (398 p.) (Continuous pagination) illus., maps, tables.

Interesting collection of ideas—including many from the Communist side—about how to teach and do research in geography. The conclusion is that geography alone is not enough—it must be applied.

7013. Franzini, Julio César. Nuestra política pesquera. Montevideo, Servicio Oceanográfico y de Pesca, 1972. 369 p., illus., maps, plates, tables.

This book deals with the development and activities of the Uruguayan Servicio Oceanográfico y de Pesca, founded in 1945. It presents arguments favoring the development of the fishing industry within the 200 mile offshore limit.

7014. Griffin, Ernst. Testing the Von Thünen theory in Uruguay (AGS/GR, 63:4, Oct. 1973, p. 500-516, maps, tables)

One of many field tests of the Von Thünen theory of land use. In this case field findings tend not to agree with theory, although reasons for disagreement are not analyzed.

7015. Lombardo, Atilio. Las plantas acuáticas y las plantas florales. Montevideo, Intendencia Municipal de Montevideo, Depto. de Arquitectura y

Urbanismo, Dirección de Paseos Públicos, 1970. 293 p., bibl., illus., plates.

Description of species, varieties, and forms of aquatic plants and flowering plants cultivated in the Jardín Botánico and other parts of the city of Montevideo.

7016. Marchesi, Enrique and others. El trigo en el Uruguay. Montevideo, Univ. de la República, Depto. de Publicaciones, 1971. 144 p., tables (Col. Nuestra realidad, 15)

Land management changes in Uruguayan wheat production affect soil composition in different ways. Previous cultivations, changes in humus content, rotation techniques, soil loss, and other factors such as fertilizers, seeds, and insects are considered. Production results are also presented in this practical study.

7017. Martínez Carril, Manuel. Turismo en el Uruguay. Montevideo, Editorial Nuestra Tierra, 1969. 76 p., plates, tables.

An analysis of tourism in Uruguay. The significance of tourism as a source of foreign exchange is emphasized. Factors responsible for the limited influx of tourists are diagnosed and recommendations for future developments are offered.

7018. Rosengurt, Bernardo; B.R. Arrillaga dè Maffei; and **P. Izaguirre de Artuccio.** Gramíneas uruguayas. Montevideo, Univ. de la República, Depto. de Publicaciones, 1970. 489 p., bibl., illus.

A comprehensive and well-documented handbook of Uruguayan *Graminea* written for the nonprofessional, as well as the serious student. Contains detailed diagrams, glossary, and bibliography.

7019. Uruguay. Administración de Ferrocarriles del Estado (AFE). Temas ferroviarios: situación actual del ente y medidas para recuperarlo. Montevideo, 1970. 123 p. (mimeo)

Conditions for cargo, personnel forecasts, and tasks are among topics discussed in this booklet on Uruguayan railroads.

7020. ———. Ministerio de Hacienda. Dirección General de Estadística y Censos. Mapas demográficos. Montevideo, 1969. 21 p., maps.

The set of maps under the heading of *Mapas demográficos* has no relation to the title. The maps consist of 18 poorly reproduced maps of Uruguayan departments, depicting highways, and central places.

VENEZUELA

7021. *El Agricultor Venezolano.* Ministerio de Agricultura y Cría. Año 34, No. 252, julio/agosto 1970- ———. Caracas.

This issue includes an article on "La Conservación de Pastos Aumenta la Productividad del Ganado" (p. 42-47) which established the types of storage silos (trench, lumber) needed in different kinds of terrain and soil types to overcome problems created by periodic forage shortages.

7022. Andressen, Rigoberto. Densidad de población en las áreas de ranchos de la ciudad de Caracas y su relación con el numero de viviendas, topografía y distancia al centro de la ciudad (ULA/RG, 11:24/25, enero/dic. 1970, p. 5-24)

A correlation analysis of demographic density and dwelling numbers, topography, and distance to central city. The study shows that little correlation exists for the variables chosen, and the author concludes that parameters other than those considered would explain the population density.

7023. *Anuario Estadístico de Venezuela: 1969.* Ministerio de Fomento, Dirección General de Estadísticas y Censos Nacionales. No. 22, 1972- ———. Caracas.

This yearly series begun in 1938 is an indispensable aid to investigations of a geographic, demographic, economic, or educational type. This issue consists of 733 p., tables.

7024. Asamblea General del Instituto Panamericano de Geografía e Historia, *VIII, Guatemala, 1965.* Informe nacional. Caracas, Instituto Panamericano de Geografía e Historia, Sección Nacional, Comisión de Cartografía, 1965. 44 p., fold. maps.

Cartographically presented report on progress in mapping the country of Venezuela.

7025. Bartra, Roger. La estructura de clases en el agro andino venezolano (UNAM/RMS, 33:4, oct./dic. 1971, p. 661-677, tables)

The author of this well-written article takes issue with the notion that Latin America can be explained in terms of the dichotomy: undeveloped-zones/developed-zones which form part of a continuum best classified as domestic colonialism. Technological status of farming, land tenure, effects of migration, and the class system are analyzed with their interwoven effects on economy.

7026. Best, Robin. Caracas develops upwards (GM, 45:7, April 1973, p. 501-505, maps, plates)

Over one-fourth of Caracas' residents are squatters who take up a fifth of the city's area. Government high rise dwelling units for the poor, and middle-class residential tower block structures are making this a vertically oriented urban settlement with respect to its residential quarters.

7027. El campo venezolano. Caracas, Fundación Eugenio Mendoza, 1972. 240 p., plates, tables.

This colorful book consists of four chapters: Ramón J. Velásquez "Aproximación de la Historia Rural de Venezuela;" Marco A. Vila "Las Áreas Fisiográficas;" Francisco Tamayo "Como es el Hombre de Campo;" and Alonso Caratrava "Trayectoria y Perspectivas de la Agricultura Venezolana."

7028. Dauxion Lavaysse, Jean Francois. Viaje a las islas de Trinidad, Tobago, Margartia y a diversas partes de Venezuela en la América meridional. Traducción de Angelina Lemmo e Hilda T. de Rodríguez. Caracas, Univ. Central de Venezuela, 1967. 400 p., bibl., facsims.

Late colonial chronicles of the Lesser Antilles and northern Venezuela by a French adventurer. The author provides detailed narratives of man and environment for the eastern Caribbean where he traveled between 1791 and 1807. The work covers the historical lacuna for the late colonial period, and thus should be of interest to historical geographers.

7029. Drenikoff, Ivan. Mapas antiguos de Venezuela grabados e impresos antes de 1800 con la reproducción del primer mapa impreso en Venezuela y de mapas antiguos. Caracas, Ediciones del Congreso de la República, 1971. 57 p., map.

A chronological listing of Venezuelan maps published between 1598 and 1795. A total of 81 maps classified by title, publisher, and size. Unfortunately the author does not provide information about where the maps can be located.

7030. López Pellón, Nivio. Guayana, la nueva Venezuela (MH, 320, nov. 1974, p. 46-51, plates)

A short, up-to-date essay on Ciudad Guayana, Ven., and the industrial and mineral developments occurring in the Guiana highlands of southern Venezuela.

7031. Lynch, Edward. Propositions for planning new towns in Venezuela (JDA, 7:4, July 1973, p. 549-570, illus., maps)

New town planning in Venezuela during the 1960s at Ciudad Guayana, Tuy and El Tablazo is discussed. Tuy, southeast of Caracas, and El Tablazo, on the eastern shore of Lake Maracaibo, are less well-known complexes which are destined for large areal expansion. Planning for poor families, use of consultant planners from abroad and within Venezuela, and speed and flexibility of planning are considered.

7032. Martínez, Francisco A. Diccionario geográfico del Estado Zulia. Mérida, Ven., Univ. de los Andes, 1968. 244 p., bibl., plates (Publicaciones del Rectorado)

A general regional study of the state of Zulia with lengthy historical summary (32 p.), chapters on physical geography (10 p.), ethnography (4 p.), agriculture (18 p.), and industry (17 p.). Useful listing of settlements includes municipios, distritos, and veredas and their inhabitants.

7033. Monasterio, Maximina. Ecología de las sabanas de América tropical II: caracterización ecológica del clima en los llanos de Calabozo, Venezuela (ULA/RG, 9:21, julio/dic. 1968, p. 5-38, bibl., map, tables)

Another in a series of over 40 contributions on the ecology of the region of the Llanos de Calabozo (Central Llanos) since active work began at the Biological Field Station near the city of Calabozo in the 1960s. Climatic study of the central Llanos near Calabozo, with emphasis on rainfall and temperature values. Relative humidity, radiation, and light are also investigated. The area has nearly four dry months, but if for two consecutive years the precipitation is below the average, six dry months may be anticipated. Only one dry month occurs if the average is exceeded for two years. These observations, coupled with information about the tropical temperature regime, are employed to explain the natural vegetation characteristics.

7034. Pagney, M.P. Reflexions sur les pluies au Venezuela (AGF/B, 49:400/-401, juin/oct. 1972, p. 299-313, bibl., maps)

Rainfall distribution analysis for Venezuela shows four principal regimes: 1) alternating wet (July peak)—dry seasons of the Llanos; 2) end of the year peak on the Lara-Falcon coast and Seaward islands; 3) a May-Oct. peak in Maracaibo; and 4) a mixed zone with characteristics of both 1) and 2) on the Caribbean coast north of the coast range. Explanations with maps presented.

7035. Pittier, Henri. Manual de las plantas usuales de Venezuela y su suplemento. Prólogo por Francisco Tamayo. Caracas, Fundación Eugenio Mendoza, 1970. 679 p., plates.

Republication of plant studies made by Swiss botanist after his arrival and settlement in Venezuela in 1919. Useful summary of scientific investigation in Venezuela from early times to the present century.

7036. Powell, John Duncan. The role of the Federación Campesina in the Venezuelan agrarian reform process. Madison, Univ. of Wisconsin, Land Tenure Center, 1967. 52 p., tables (LTC Research paper, 26)

In Venezuela, unlike Mexico, Bolivia, and Cuba where massive agrarian reform has occurred, several political parties have supported change. As a consequence, peasant *ligas* have been incorporated into political parties and play an important role in land distribution.

7037. Sarmiento, Guillermo and Maximina Monasterio. Ecología de las sabanas de América tropical: análisis macroecológico de los Llanos de Calabozo, Venezuela. Mérida, Ven., Univ. de los Andes, Facultad de Ciencias Forestales, Instituto de Geografía y Conservación de Recursos Haturales,

1971. 126 p., bibl., maps, plates, tables (Cuadernos geográficos, 4)

For this ecological investigation the term Llanos de Calabozo has been applied to the region of sabanas between the Tiznados and Orituco rivers, with the city of Calabozo about in the center. This sabana region is not typical for those of the Llanos Orientales in that the density and height of trees is greater and no long periods of major flooding occur. The authors previously (1968, 1969) established ecological regions and investigations in this area and here present at an intermediate scale of study of part of their research region. Bibliography and list of plant types are useful.

7038. Traveiso, Carmen Clemente. Anécdotas y leyendas de la vieja Caracas. Prólogo por Ernesto Silva Tellería. Caracas, Consejo Municipal del Distrito Federal, 1971. 246 p., bibl., illus., plates.

Historically oriented stories about Caracas including topics such as market center, business modes, transportation facilities, and population. Brief bibliography included.

7039. Universidad de los Andes, Mérida, Ven. Facultad de Economía. Instituto de Investigaciones Económicas. Estudio de cuentas regionales para los Estados de Barinas, Mérida, Táchira y Trujillo: 1960-1966. Mérida, Ven., 1971. 209 p., tables.

This practical study of the so-called Venezuelan "Región Andina" was first produced in 1966 in order to assess the economic potential of the area. The original statistical investigation has been amplified and some data come directly from field work. Several economists and their students have organized the data into sections on general production, agriculture, mining, petroleum, industry, commerce, transportation, and services. Data are presented primarily in tabular form.

7040. Venezuela. Comisión del Plan Nacional de Aprovechamiento de los Recursos Hidráulicos (COPLANARH). Inventario nacional de aguas superficiales. v. 2, Planos. Caracas, 1969. 1 v. (Various pagings) fold. maps.

Series of color maps of Venezuela at a scale of 20 km/cm presenting: regions, average annual rainfall, and average annual temperature, evapotranspiration, surface runoff, surface runoff for the Lake Maracaibo region, for the Costa Nor-Occidental, Llanos, Región Central (two maps), Región Central-Oriental, Guayana Occidental, Amazonas, and a profile of the Rio Orinoco.

7041. Venturini, Orlando. Aspectos geográficos de la colonización del Piedemonte noroccidental de los Andes venezolanos: zona de El Vigía (ULA/RG, 9:21, julio/dic. 1968, p. 73-95, bibl., map, tables)

Analysis of pioneer settlement along a section of the Pan American highway near Mérida, Ven. Invasion of the area known as Sur del Logo, began in 1953 and has been sustained by numerous Colombian pioneers. It is a zone of unstable, disorganized settlement although the population of El Vigía, a small town, has increased by eight times in the last 12 years. Yuca, tropical fruits, pasture, and much fallowed land characterize the area. There is a strong tendency to concentrate holdings in the hands of cattlemen, and the few new group settlements with central place functions along the Panamericana have a high incidence of crime and unemployment.

7042. Vila, Marco-Aurelio. Conceptos sobre geografía histórica de Venezuela. Caracas, Monte Avila Editores, 1971. 227 p., bibl., plates, tables (Col. Temas venezolanos)

An attempt to understand Venezuelan historical events by applying geographical concepts. The book is of limited use for those interested in the historical geography of Venezuela.

7043. ———. La integración humano-económica en Venezuela (Ruedo Ibérico [Paris] 22/24, dic. 1968/mayo 1969, p. 137-152)

A generalized geographical-historical account of the entire country of Venezuela, with good regional economic development for those desiring an up-dated, overall picture of national achievements.

BRAZIL
KEMPTON E. WEBB
Professor of Geography
Director, Institute of Latin American Studies
Chairman, Department of Geography, Columbia University

7044. Agrar- und Hydrotechnik GmbH (firm), *Essen, FRG.* Wasserwirtschaftliche Rahmenplanung und regionale entwicklungsstudie für das Einzugsgebiet des Rio Cai (Planejamento hidrológico e estudo de desenvolvimento regional da bacia do Rio Cai). v. 1, Zusammenfassung (resumo); v. 2, Dados naturais; v. 3, Estudo socio-economico; v. 4, Planejamento hidrológico; v. 5, Anlagen (anexos). Essen, FRG, Agrar- und Hydrotechnik GmbH *for* Govêrno do Estado do Rio Grande do Sul,

Secretaria das Obras Públicas, 1970/1971. 5 v. (Various pagings) illus., maps, plates, tables.

Unnecessarily oversized hydrologic and regional planning study of a small river basin near Pôrto Alegre, Bra.

7045. Albuquerque, Rubens José de Castro. Política para o setor agrícola brasileiro: síntese de conferência realizadas pelo Presidente da COBAL Brasília, Ministério da Agricultūra, Grupo Executivo de Modernização do Sistema de Abastecimento (GEMAB), Companhia Brasileira de Alimentos (COBAL), 1973. 1083 p., plates, tables.

Very significant policy statement in Portuguese, English, and Spanish which underlines the priorities to be given to the agricultural and food sectors.

7046. Amazonas (state) *Bra.* **Secretaria de Estado de Planejamento e Coordenaçao Geral (SEPLAN). Comissão de Desenvolvimento do Estado do Amazonas (CODEAMA).** Estudo de mercado, a nível internacional, para produtos agrícolas passíveis de cultivo e processamento no Estado do Amazonas. 2. ed. Manaus, Bra., 1973. 194 p., bibl. (Estudios específicos, 9:45)

Market feasibility study for export crops from Amazonas i.e., tropical fruits, industrial fibers, oils, cereals, and grains.

7047. Andrade, Manuel Correia de Oliveira. Cidade e campo no Brasil. São Paulo, Editôra Brasiliense, 1974. 223 p., tables.

A collection of essays written between 1969 and 1973 which document the modernization process and its manifestations in both urban and rural areas of Brazil. Author is most knowledgeable about Northeast Brazil.

7048. _____. A terra e o homem no Nordeste. 3. ed. rev. e atualizada. São Paulo, Editôra Brasiliense, 1973. 251 p., bibl., maps, plates.

New edition of authors 1965 work. One of the half dozen best books on Northeast Brazil. Counterpoint of land and labor fully explored.

_____. Paisagens e problemas do Brasil: aspectos da vida rural brasileira frente a industrialização e ao crescimento econômico. See item 8543a.

7049. Andreazza, Mário David. Os transportes no Brasil: planejamento e execução. Brasília, Ministério dos Transportes, 1973. 1 v. (Unpaged) illus., maps, plates.

Profusely illustrated document showing the very latest advances in highway, rail, port, and merchant marine activity. The geography of Brazil is being radically transformed.

7050. Angely, João. Flora analítica e fitogeográfica do Estado de São Paulo. v. 1. São Paulo, Univ. de São Paulo, Laboratório de Botânica, 1969. 240 p., illus., maps (Col. Amador Aguiar)

Small maps show geographic range of each plant type.

7051. Araújo, Acrísio Tôrres. Geografia de Sergipe. Aracajú, Bra., Livraria Regina, 1969. 135 p., maps, plates.

Popular, non-professional introduction to a long neglected state which is now extracting petroleum, and experiencing economic growth.

7052. Associação dos Geógrafos Brasileiros, *Presidente Prudente, Bra.* Guias de excursões. Presidente Prudente, Bra., 1972. 256 p., bibl., illus., fold. map, tables.

Excursion guidebook for a meeting of the Brazilian Association of Geographers, held at Presidente Prudente.

7053. Bahia (state), *Bra.* **Secretaria do Trabalho e Bem Estar Social.** Mão de obra no setor primário: cultura do dende. Bahia, Bra., 1972. 117 l., bibl., tables.

Government of Bahia is aware of need to solve employment problems in the primary sectors.

7054. Banco de Desenvolvimento do Paraná, *Curitiba, Bra.* Parana now. Curitiba, 1972. 1 v. (Unpaged) illus.

Vivid promotional document. Paraná will become another São Paulo but avoiding some of the pitfalls of unplanned growth.

7055. Banco do Nordeste do Brasil, *Fortaleza, Bra.* **Departamento de Estudos Econômicos do Nordeste (ETENE). Divisão de Agricultura.** A cultura do gergelim e suas possibilidades no Nordeste. Fortaleza, Bra., 1970. 69 p., tables.

Feasibility study for Northeast Brazil based upon success of *gergelim* (sesame) in Venezuela.

7056. _____. _____. Custo de produção do algodão arbóreo no seridó cearense. Fortaleza, Bra., 1971. 66l., tables.

Economics of arboreal cotton production in the driest area of Ceará state.

7057. _____. _____. Turismo no Nordeste: relatório da pesquisa de avaliação da I Campanha de Incentivo ao

Turismo no Nordeste. Fortaleza, Bra., 1972. 75 p., illus.

Tourism is being pushed in Northeast Brazil.

7058. _____. _____. A carnaubeira e seu papel como uma planta econômica. Fortaleza, Bra., 1972. 104 p., bibl., maps, plates, tables.

Excellent introduction to this economic mainstay of Ceará.

7059. _____. Setor de Investigações Agrícolas. Programa especial de créditor rural: documento elaborado pelo setor de investigações argícolas do DERUR [Departámento Rural]. Fortaleza, 1970. 184 p., map, tables.

Includes succinct description of agriculture in Northeast Brazil, as well as of rural credit programs.

7060. Barahuna, Epaminondas. Estórias amazônicas. Rio, Edições O Cruzeiro, 1974. 189 p.

Folktales and legends of the Amazon.

7061. Barbosa, José Maria de Azevedo. Amazônia! Meta de govêrno. Belém, Bra., Secretaria de Estado da Viação e Obras Públicas, 1970. 95 p., plates.

Unusual account of the menial tasks necessary in the remote areas of the Amazon when cargoes must be unloaded by lighters and by hand.

7062. Barboza, Mario Gibson. A cartografia política do Barão do Rio-Branco. Brasília, Ministério das Relações Exteriores, Seção de Publicações, 1970. 1 v. (Unpaged) facsims.

Tidbit of political-historical geography, originally a lecture delivered before the Brazilian Geographic Society.

7063. Barros, Henrique; Amândio Galvão; Carlos da Silva; and José M.V. Barrocas. Análise e planeamento da emprêsa agrícola. Viçosa, Bra., Univ. Federal de Viçosa, Escola Superior de Agricultura, Depto. de Economia Rural, 1972. 2 v. (599 p.) (Continuous pagination) tables.

Typical of the useful materials which come out of Viçosa.

7064. Becker, Bertha K. O norte do Espírito Santo: região periférica em transformação (IBGE/R, 35:3, julho/set. 1973, p. 107-132, maps, tables)

Good regional profile of this peripheral state.

7065. Bellomo, Harry Rodrigues and **José Celso Bortoluzzi da Silveira.** Estudos brasileiros: a terra, a economia. Pôrto Alegre, Bra.?, n.p. 1973. 128 p., maps, tables.

A low level school-text.

7066. Bernardes, Nilo ed. A case of regional inequality of development: Espírito Santo state, Brazil. Rio, International Geographical Union, Commission on Regional Aspects of Economic Development, 1971. 2 v. (Various pagings) illus., maps, plates, tables.

Document submitted to the Colloquium on Regional Inequalities of Development held in Vitória, Bra. 1971. Geographer's study of a neglected state.

7067. Biblioteca Nacional, *Rio.* Nordeste brasileiro: catálogo da exposição. Rio, 1970. 86 p., bibl., plates.

Valuable bibliography of 348 items on Northeast Brazil. Not comprehensive but useful for earlier periods.

7068. *Boletim Carioca de Geografia.* Associação dos Geógrafos Brasileiros, Secção Regional do Rio de Janeiro. Año 23, 1972- . Rio.

Articles contained in this issue are: Pedro P. Geiger; João Rua and Luiz; and Antônio Ribeiro "Notas sobre Aplicações do Modelo Probabilístico de Distribuição Poisson ao Sistema Urbano;" Maria do Socorro Diniz "A Rede de Localidades Centrias do Rio Grande Do Sul, Determinada a través da Teorio dos Grafos;" Ana Maria de Souza Mello Bicalho and others "Transformações na Periferia urbana do Rio de Janeiro: Crescimento e Diversificação da Pecuaria Leiteria;" Zilá Mesquita Mold "A Política de Desenvolvimento Urbano no Processo de Desenvolvimento Nacional;" Maria do Socorro Diniz "Um Aspecto da Urbanização no Estado do Espírito Santo;" Gilda Campos I. de San Martins "Contribuição ao Estudo da Estrutura Interna da Area Metropolitana do Rio de Janeiro: O Caso de Xerém (Duque Caxias);" Irio Barbosa da Costa "Contribuição para o Estudo da Pesca no Nordeste;" and Irio Barbosa da Costa "Comentário do Libro Didático Intitulado *Geografia Ativa.*"

7069. *Boletim Paranaense de Geociências.* Univ. Federal do Paraná, Conselho de Pesquisas, Instituto de Geologia. No. 28/29, 1970/1971- . Curitiba, Bra.

Several articles on dune formation and paleowind patterns.

7070. *Brasil Açucareiro.* Ministério da Indústria e do Comércio, Instituto do Açúcar e do Alcool. Ano 41, Vol. 82, No. 4, out. 1972- . Rio.

Special commemorative edition with several articles on the problems of productivity of sugar cane in Brazil.

7071. Brazil. Conselho de Desenvolvi-

mento do Extremo Sul (CODESUL). Diagnóstico da atividade pesqueira no Estado do Paraná: primeira aproximação. Florianópolis, Bra., 1970. 126 p., plates, tables.

Basic lineaments of the fisheries industry of Paraná state. A yet-to-be-developed resource.

7072. _____. Development Series/Série Desenvolvimento Brasileiro. 3- . São Paulo, Telepress Serviço de Imprensa, 1972- .

This monographic series is designed to provide information on the programs and achievements of government agencies in the field of regional and urban development. V. 1/2 were devoted to the "National Housing Plan." This issue (v. 3) discusses Amazonia, the Trans-Amazonian Highways, SUDAM, the Northeast, SUDENE, SUFRAMA, etc. Useful promotion document in English and Portuguese.

7073. _____. **Directoria de Hidrografia e Navegação.** XLVI [i.e. Quadragésimosexta] Comissão Oceanográfica: Operação Geomar II, costa norte/geologia marinha. Rio, 1972. 80 p., bibl., fold. maps.

Sedimentation characteristics beyond the Amazon River's mouth.

7074. _____. **Ministério da Agricultura. Instituto Nacional de Colonização e Reforma Agrária (INCRA). Comissão de Aliendção de Terras Públicas.** Marabá-Rondonia. Brasília, 1972. lv. (Unpaged) illus., maps, tables.

Sample colonization plan-document of INCRA for Marabá-Rondonia.

7075. _____. _____. _____. **Departamento de Desenvolvimento Rural. Divisão Cooperativismo e Sindicalismo.** Cooperativismo no Brasil. Brasília, 1973. 197 p., tables.

List of cooperatives in all Brazil.

7076. _____. **Ministério das Minas e Energia. Departamento Nacional da Produção Mineral.** Contribuição ao desenvolvimento geo-econômico de São Paulo e Paraná: documento básico. Rio, 1970. 111 p., bibl., tables.

Ten year plan for a mineral resources inventory of São Paulo and Paraná states. A first step for resource development.

7077. _____. **Ministério do Interior. Serviço Federal de Habitação e Urbanismo (SERFHAU).** Planejamento metropolitano: anais do II curso de planejamento urbano e local. Brasília, 1972. 2 v. (246, 152 p.), bibl.

Planning is the watchword.

7078. _____. _____. **Superintendência do Desenvolvimento da Amazônia (SUDAM). Departamento de Recursos Naturais.** Estudo de viabilidade da exploração industrial da Mata Amazônica na Região do Curuá—UNA. Belém, Bra., Assessoria de Programação e Coordenação, Divisão de Documentação, 1972. 134 p., illus., maps, tables.

Feasibility study of lumbering operation and cellulose production based upon pine reforestation. Plant planned 100 miles east of Santarém on the Amazon River.

7079. _____. _____. **Divisão de Documentações.** Amazônia modelo de integração (The Amazon region: a model of integration). Rio, 1973. 1 v. (Unpaged) illus., plates, tables.

Good photographic introduction to the Amazon region with up to date text.

7080. _____. _____. **Superintendência do Desenvolvimento do Nordeste (SUDENE). Departamento de Agricultura e Abastecimento. Divisão de Abastecimento e Financiamento da Produção.** Suprimento de gêneros alimentícios na cidade de Teresina. Teresina, Bra., 1972. 123 p., bibl., tables.

Another welcome urban food supply study but unfortunately it is aspatial.

7081. _____. _____. _____. **Departamento de Industrialização. Divisão de Pesquisas e Planejamento.** Resultados do programa de industrialização até 1968: relatório de pesquisa. Recife, Bra., 1972. 82 p., tables.

SUDENE approved 519 industrial projects of which the majority were in textiles, non metallic minerals and food-processing.

7082. _____. _____. _____. _____. Estudo sôbre mercado e comercialização de produtos hortigranjeiros: zona da mata Pernambuco e Alagoas, relatório 1972. Recife, Bra., 1972. 247 l., tables.

Important data source on market garden food supply in the humid zones of Pernambuco and Alagoas.

7083. _____. _____. _____ **Setor de Demografia.** Projeções da população do Nordeste brasileiro: 1975-1990. Recife, Bra., 1972. 149 p., tables.

Three percent increment in population projected 1975 through 1990. Total projected of 37 million in Northeast in 1975 to 58 million in 1990 but 10 million will have emigrated to other areas.

7084. _____. **Ministério do Planejamento e Coordenação Geral. Fundação Instituto Brasileiro de Geografia e Estatística (IBGE). Superintendência de Estatísticas Primárias. Departamento de Censos.** Censos demográfico: Brasil. Rio, 1973. 267 p., maps, tables.

First summary volume of the 1970 *Demographic census of Brazil.* Control groups and sampling procedures explained.

7085. _____. _____. **Instituto de Planejamento Econômico e Social. Instituto de Planejamento.** Aproveitamento atual e potencial dos cerrados. v. 1, Base física e potencialidades da região. Brasília, 1973. 197 p., bibl., fold. maps, maps, tables. (Série estudos para o planejamento, 2)

Specific recommendations to render the cerrado more productive, i.e. plant pastures and trees.

Carrizosa Umaña, Julio comp. Notas para una política de Amazonia y Orinoquia. See item 6726.

7086. Cascudo, Luís da Câmara. Nomes da terra: geografia, história e toponímia do Rio Grande do Norte. Rio, Fundação José Augusto, 1968. 321 p. (Col. Cultura)

Definitive toponomic study of Rio Grande do Norte by the leading historian of that northeastern state. The place names convey much geographic content of the region.

7087. Cavalcanti, Clóvis de Vasconcelos. O mercado de pescado em Maceió. Recife, Bra., Ministério do Interior, Superintendência do Desenvolvimento do Nordeste (SUDENE) [and] Ministério da Educação e Cultura, Instituto Joaquim Nabuco de Pesquisas Sociais (IJNPS), 1971. 98 l., maps, tables.

Complete food survey of fish-marketing potential for Maceió, Alagoas. Solid data.

7088. _____. Mercados para a pesca em Aracajú. Recife, Bra., Ministério do Interior, Superintendência do Desenvolvimento do Nordeste (SUDENE) [and] Ministério da Educaçao e Cultura, Instituto Joaquim Nabuco de Pesquisas Sociais (IJNPS), 1971. 119 p., tables.

Basic document for planning purposes adds to knowledge of food supply context of Northeast Brazil.

7089. Ceará (state), *Bra.* **Superintendência do Desenvolvimento (SUDEC). Serviço de Informações de Mercado (SIM).** Comercialização de alimentos na cidade de Fortaleza: dados estatísticos. Fortaleza, Bra., Univ. Federal do Ceará (FUC), 1972. 56 p., tables.

Basic data on prices and commodity movements.

7090. Ceron, Antonio Olivio. Alguns padrões de utilização da terra agrícola no planalto ocidental de São Paulo (AGB/BPG, 47, maio 1972, p. 3-29, bibl., maps)

Fairly detailed land-use map for northwestern São Paulo state.

7091. _____ and **José Alexandre Felizola Diniz.** Orientação da agricultura no Estado de São Paulo. São Paulo, Univ. de São Paulo, Instituto de Geografia, 1969. 23 p., bibl., map, tables (Geografia econômica, 7)

A short treatise on how the particular mix or combinations of agricultural activities may be presented and analyzed.

7092. Clan S.A. (firm), *Brazil.* Desenvolvimento da indústria petroquímica no Estado da Bahia. Salvador, Bra., 1970. 2 v. (475 p.) (Continuous pagination) bibl., maps, tables.

Sees petrochemical industry as a stimulus to regional development of Bahia state. Includes useful glossary of acronyms and bibliography (six p.). For English version, see *HLAS 35:2427.*

7093. _____. Plano de turismo do recôncavo: resumo. n.p. 1973? 1 v. (Various pagings) illus., fold. maps, tables.

Development may kill the charm of Bahia.

7094. Companhia do Desenvolvimento do Planalto Central (CODEPLAN), *Brasília.* Distrito industrial do Distrito Federal: estudo preliminar. Brasília, 1972. 222 p., maps, tables.

A preliminary planning document of Brazília's industrial park, with reference to comparable plans in other parts of Brazil and abroad.

7095. *Conjuntura Econômica.* Fundação Getúlio Vargas. Vol, 28, No. 5, maio 1974- . Rio.

First of several articles in this number which update the current developments in Brazilian transportation. Railroads are finally being doubled in trackage by 1978.

7096. Correia, Ronaldo Nunes. Doces e

sucos de frutas regionais: subsídios para a programação industrial. Recife, Bra., Ministério do Interior. Superintendência do Desenvolvimento do Nordeste (SUDENE), Depto. de Industrialização, Divisão de Pesquisa e Planejamento Industrial, 1972. 89 p., tables (Serie: Estudos setoriais)

Feasibility study.

7097. Corte, Judith de la. O tomate no abastecimento da cidade de São Paulo. São Paulo, Univ. de São Paulo, Instituto de Geografia, Setor de Pesquisas, 1966. 20 p., maps, tables (Geografia econômica, 3)

Another in the series of food-supply studies for São Paulo such as *HLAS 35:7160.*

7098. Costa, Rubens Vaz da. Crescimento demográfico e poluição do meio ambiente. Rio, Banco Nacional de Habitação, Secretaria de Divulgação, 1973. 63 p., tables.

A bold significant statement favoring a decrease of population growth and environmental conservation.

7099. Cunha, Alda das Mercês Moreira da; Maria Thereza Alves; Clara Maria Galvão; and Saphyra Farias Leitão *comps.* Geografia da Amazônia: bibliografia. Belém, Bra., Univ. Federal do Pará, Centro de Filosofia e Ciências Humanas, 1974. 85 l., bibl.

Excellent geographical bibliography of the Amazon region which includes a useful index. Originally presented at the III Congress of Brazilian Geographers, Belém do Pará, 1974.

7100. Cunha, Osvaldo Rodrigues da and Therezinha Xavier Bastos. A contribuição do Museu Paraense Emílio Goeldi à meteorologia na Amazônia. Belém, Bra., Conselho Nacional de Pesquisas, Museu Paraense Emílio Goeldi, Instituto Nacional de Pesquisas da Amazônia, 1973. 42 p., bibl., tables (Publicações avulsas, 23)

Importance of data kept (at the Museu Goeldi) from 1895-1922 for a climatological understanding of northern Brazil.

7101. D'Apote, Vincenzo and others. Bases para uma política de reforma agrária e colonização no Nordeste do Brasil: relatório preliminar. Recife, Bra., Ministério do Interior, Superintendência do Desenvolvimento do Nordeste (SUDENE), Depto. de Agricultura e Abastecimento, Divisão de Programação e Fiscalização, 1972. 124 p., tables.

A controversial preliminary plan for agrarian reform stressing numbers of peoples rather than processes.

7102. Diógenes, Luciano. Os 7 [i.e. Sete] pecados de capital: Fortaleza; passado, presente, futuro. Fortaleza, Bra., Prefeitura Municipal de Fortaleza, 1971. 37 p., facsim., maps.

Describes the most pressing urban services needed in Fortaleza.

7103. Duarte, José Bacchieri *ed.* Rio Grande do Sul. Pôrto Alegre, Bra., Sociedad Editôra de Veículos de·Comunicação Empresarial (SEVEM), 1973? 144 p., illus., plates, tables.

Visual portrait of Rio Grande do Sul.

7104. Elfes, Alberto. Campos Gerais: estudo da colonização. Curitiba, Bra., Ministério da Agricultura, Instituto Nacional de Colonização e Reforma Agrária (INCRA), Coordenadoria Regional no Paraná, 1973. 158 p.

7105. Espírito Santo, Antônio. O vale amazônico no futuro do mundo. 3. ed. São Paulo, n.p., 1974. 278 p.

Volume of no value compared to serious studies in existence.

7106. Estudo de problemas brasileiros. Recife, Bra., Univ. Federal de Pernambuco, 1974. 538 p., tables.

Collected essays on all aspects of Brazilian development by wide variety of specialists. No connections between the essays.

7107. Faissol, Speridião. Migrações internas no Brasil e suas repercussões no crescimento urbano e desenvolvimento econômico (IBGE/R, 35:2, abril/junho 1973, p. 3-102, tables)

Excellent detailed study of the different phases of movement in the migration processes. A majority of migrants are urban to urban. Loaded with data in interpretations applicable to several fields of social inquiry.

7108. ———. O processo de difusão no sistema urbano brasileiro: análise do padrão de distribuição espacial de centros urbanos e seu ajustamento a distribuições de probabilidades (IBGE/R, 35:3, julho/set. 1973, p. 3-106, bibl., maps, tables.)

Application of grid techniques and poisson probability models contrasts arrangement of cities in the Northeast and in the Center South. Conclusions confirm existing knowledge on urban hierarchies.

7109. Ferreira, Evaldo Osório. Carta tectônica do Brasil: notícia explicativa (Tectonic map of Brazil: explanatory note). Rio, Ministério das Minas e Energia, Depto. Nacional da Produção Mineral, 1971. 14 p., bibl. map, (Boletim, 1)

Strikingly beautiful and informative map at scale of 1:5,000,000 of tectonic activity in relation to the crystallin basement and sedimentary cap formations. In Portuguese and English.

7110. Ferreira, Ignez Costa Barbosa and **Aldo Paviani.** As correntes migratórias para o Distrito Federal (IBGE/R, 35:3, julho/set. 1973, p. 133-162, bibl., maps, tables)

Factor analysis and luster analysis applied to migration study of Brasília. No new insights.

7111. Fontenelle, L.F. Raposo. Rotina e fome em uma região cearense: estudo antropológico. Fortaleza, Bra., Imprensa Universitária do Ceará, 1969. 184 p., illus.

A commentary study of rural Ceará. Poverty exists in wet areas as well as dry ones.

7112. Fontes, Eduardo. O Lagamar que eu conheci. Fortaleza, Bra., n.p., 1974. 103 p., plates.

A tidal-level favela of Fortaleza presented by a writer in all of its squalor and hopelessness.

7113. Fyfe, W.S. and **O.H. Leonardos, Jr.** Ancient metamorphic-migmatite belts of the Brazilian African coasts (NWJS, 244:5417, Aug. 24, 1973, p. 501-502, map)

In context of current theories of continental drift, considers evidence from Africa and Brazil to explain why rifts on a continental scale occur where they do. [C. Edwards]

7114. Geiger, Pedro Pinchas. O espaço mais desenvolvido do Brasil (IBGE/B, 31:231, nov./dez. 1972, p. 109-124, table)

Analysis of anticipated growth patterns and processes of Brazil's urbanization.

7115. ——— and **R. Lobato Corrêa.** From Vitória to Belo Horizonte by the Rio Doce Valley. Rio, International Geographical Union, Commission on Regional Aspects of Economic Development, 1971. 86 p., maps, tables.

Excellent field-trip comments and analysis in English are in this guidebook to the study trip made on the occasion of the Colloquium on Regional Inequalities of Development held at Vitória, Espirito Santo, Bra., April 1971.

7116. Geobrás (firm) *Brazil*. Vale do Pajeú: recursos em água e solo. Recife, Bra., Ministério do Interior, Depto. Nacional de Obras contra as Sêcas, Directoria de Pesquisas Estudos e Projetos, 1968. 2 v. (Unpaged) tables.

Self-explanatory and complete.

7117. Goiás (state), *Bra.* **Departamento do Comérico.** Considerações gerais sobre o abastecimento de Goiânia. Goiânia, Bra., 1972. 43 l., illus., plates, tables (Caderno informativo série B, 4)

Economists did this food supply study but it does not measure up to the geographers high standards of other studies of the Northeast, São Paulo, etc. No spatial sense.

7118. ———. Secretaria da Indústria e Comércio. Departamento da Indústria. Goiás: um convite ao investimento. Goiâna, Bra., 1972. 1 v. (Unpaged) illus., maps, plates, tables.

A convincing promotional piece. Richly illustrated.

7119. ———. Secretaria do Planejamento e Coordenação. Companhia de Desenvolvimento do Estado de Goiás (CODEG). A economia goiana no PROTERRA. Goiânia, 1973. 176 p., illus., maps, tables.

The objectives and performance of PROTERRA (Program of Land Redistribution and Agroindustrial Stimuli of the North and Northeast) which was intended to facilitate ownership of land by small and middle-size farmer-enterpreneurs. Very preliminary document but useful.

7120. Goldstein, Léa and **Rosa Ester Rossini.** O bairro industrial do Jaguaré, São Paulo (AGB/BPG, 47, maio 1972, p. 30-72, bibl., tables)

Profile of the industrial growth of Jaguaré since 1930 and the accompanying increase of vehicular movement.

7121. Gomes, Raymundo Pimentel. Corografia dinâmica do Ceará. Fortaleza, Bra., Depto. de Imprensa Oficial do Ceará, 1971. 308 p., bibl., plates.

Rambling state portrait by non-geographer.

7122. Guanabara (state), *Bra.* **Secretaria de Planejamento e Coordenação Geral.** Plano de melhoria dos conjuntos habitacionais. Rio, 1973. 73 p., map, tables.

Recent inventory of housing projects and needs for Guanabara state.

7123. Guerra, Francisco das Chagas Uchôa. Colônias agroflorestais. 2. ed. rev. e aumentada. Belém, Bra., Ministério do Interior, Superintendência do Desenvolvimento da Amazônia (SUDAM), Assessoria de Programação e Coordenação, Divisão de Documentação, 1973. 17 p.

Summary of forest colonization scheme in Amazônia supported by SUDAM.

7124. Guerra, Phelippe and **Theophilo Guerra.** Seccas contra a secca: Rio Grande do Norte. 2. ed. Natal, Bra., Fundação José Augusto, 1974. 313 p. (Col. Mossoroense, 29)

Facsimile of 1909 ed. about the history of droughts in Northeast Brasil, reissued for the XXV Congresso Nacional de Botânica.

7125. Heinsdijk, Dammis. Forestry in southern Brazil. Rio, Instituto Brasileiro de Desenvolvimento Florestal [and] Ministry of Foreign Affairs, Directorate International Technical Assistence, The Hague, 1972. 72 p., plates, tables.

Admirable summary of the deforestation process in southern Brazil and of the significance of the 1968 law which requires that for every cubic meter of wood cut, four trees be planted in areas of at least five hectares. Prognosis is hopeful.

7126. International Seminar of Tropical Meteorology, *Campinas, Bra., 1969.* Proceedings. Brasília, Escritório de Meteorología, 1970. 334 p., maps, plates, tables.

Valuable recent findings applicable to much of Latin America.

7127. Irwin, Richard and **João Lyra Madeira.** Dedução de uma tábua de vida através de análise demográfica: Brasil, 1960/70 (IBGE/RBE, 33:132, out./dez. 1972, p. 697-771, tables)

Demographic life-tables summarized showing mortality rates higher in rural than urban areas, and proportionately more children in rural areas than urban.

7128. Jambeiro, Marusia de Brito. Engenhos de rapadura: racionalidade do tradicional numa sociedade em desenvolvimento. São Paulo, Univ. de São Paulo, Instituto de Estudos Brasileiros, 1973. 193 p., plates, tables.

Physical isolation protects these remnants of pre-industrial Brazil. A complete survey.

7129. Kaupmann, Kierulff & Saxild (firm), *Copenhagen.* Estudo de transportes do Brasil: relatório sôbre o estudo de organização rodoviária no Paraná, Santa Catarina e Rio Grande do Sul. v. X-A, Texto; v. X-B, Anexos e suplementos. Copenhagen, 1969. 2 v. (Various pagings) plates, tables.

Basic planning document of highway system for southern Brazil in two volumes.

7130. Lacaz, Carlos da Silva; Robert G. Baruzzi; and **Waldomiro Siqueira Júnior.** Introdução à geografia médica do Brasil. São Paulo, Univ. de São Paulo [and] Editôra Edgard Blücher, 1972. 568 p., bibl., plates, tables.

Monumental treatise on medical geography in Brazil profusely illustrated with maps, photos, and an extensive bibliography.

7131. Lambert, Levindo Furquim. Bibliografia de uma cidade mineira. Belo Horizonte, Bra., Imprensa Oficial, 1973. 301 p.

Old style sentimental town history; *not* a biogeographical study.

7132. Ligocki, Marcus. Projeto de subsistema regional de documentação e informação agrícola da Amazônia. Belém, Bra., Associação de Crédito e Assistência Rural do Estado do Pará (ACAR), 1973. 73 p., tables.

The development process is being supported by a rational information and documentation system. This study was prepared with the assistance of the Centro Interamericano de Documentação e Informação Agrícola (IICA/CIDIA).

7133. Lima, Miguel Alves de; Marília Velloso Galvão; and **Speridião Faissol.** As dimensões regionais do espaço brasileiro (IBGE/B, 31:230, set./out. 1972, p. 186-214, tables)

Interesting analysis of the spatial aspects of regional and urban growth. A rationale for urban planning intervention.

7134. Lindman, Carl Axel Magnus and **M.G. Ferri.** A vegetação no Rio Grande do Sul. São Paulo, Univ. de São Paulo [and] Itatiaia Editôra [Belo Horizonte], 1974. 377 p., bibl., illus.

Fascinating facsimile ed. of 1900 study by the Swiss botanist Lindman with more recent photos by Ferri. Several 1890s photos to compare with present landscapes.

7135. Lucena, Vinicius Guerreiro de. Fertilizantes: um polo de desenvolvimento, susídios e perspectivas. Recife, Bra., Companhia de Desenvolvimento Industrial de Pernambuco (DIPER), 1973? 102 l., tables.

The leverage potential of fertilizers is seen for Pernambucan agriculture.

7136. Macedo, Sérgio D. Teixeira de. Transamazônica: integração, redenção do Norte. Rio, Distribuidora Record, 1973? 93 p., plates.

Non-professional travels and impressions.

7137. Martins, Marseno Alvim. A Amazônia e nós. Rio, Biblioteca do Exército, 1971. 290 p., bibl., maps, plates (Publicação, 419. Col. General Benício, 94)

Narrative account of the army's role in opening up part of Amazonia. Man wins over nature.

7138. Matos, Odilon Nogueira de. Café e ferrovias: a evolução ferroviária de São Paulo e o desenvolvimento da cultura cafeeira. Prefácio [por] José Sebastião Witter. São Paulo, Editôra Alfa-Omega [and] Editôra Sociologia e Política, 1974. 135 p., bibl., maps (Biblioteca alfa-omega de ciências sociais. Série 1:2. Col. Clio)

Effective analysis of how the combination of coffee and access to markets via railroads guarantees sustained economic growth for São Paulo over the past 100 years. Historical geography.

7139. Melo, Acyr Alves Oliveira de and **Luiz Ferreira da Silva.** Solos da faixa litorânea Itacaré-Camamu, Bahia. Bahia, Bra., Comissão Executiva do Plano de Recuperação Econômico-Rural da Lavoura Cacaueira (CEPLAC), 1971. 31 p., maps (Boletim técnico, 14)

Brief analysis of the soils characteristics of the Bahian cacao region/and their relationship to actual land-use patterns. Air photos interpreted. Rubber and oil palm are urged in this area.

7140. Mendes, Armando D. Estradas para o desenvolvimento. Belém, Bra., Instituto do Desenvolvimento Econômico-Social do Pará (IDESP), 1971. 243 p., tables (Cadernos paraenses, 6).

Rationale for a highway plan for Pará state.

7141. _____. A invenção da Amazônia. Belém, Bra., Univ. Federal do Pará, 1974. 193 p., tables (Col. Amazônica. Série Tavares Bastos)

A preliminary planning prospectus for the entire Amazonas region.

7142. Mesquita, Alfredo. Brasil: viagem ao Norte e Nordeste, reportagem. São Paulo, Martins, 1974. 287 p., maps, plates.

A modern day travels and observations of Brazil. More and more Brazilians are touring and discovering their own homeland with considerable amazement and pride.

7143. Minas Gerais (state), *Bra.* **Conselho Estadual do Desenvolvimento. Instituto de Geo-Ciências Aplicadas. Esquema de Trabalho Integrado no Setor Mineral.** Pode existir lugar melhor para explorar minérios do que um estado chamado Minas Geraís? Belo Horizonte, Bra., 1973? 50 p., illus., maps.

A frank and open invitation to exploit the vast mineral storehouse comprising the state of General Mines (Minas Gerais).

7144. _____. Departamento de Estradas de Rodagem. Serviço de Planejamento Rodoviário. Estudio para a determinação de polos no Estado de Minas Gerais. Belo Horizonte, Bra., 1968? 238 p., tables.

Growth poles research results seen in relation to highway developments. Basic data.

7145. _____. Plano mineiro de desenvolvimento econômico e social: 1972-76. Belo Horizonte, Bra., Depto. Estadual de Imprensa, 1971. 292 p., tables.

The implementation of regional five-year plans such as this explains why Brazil's growth will continue uninterrupted.

7146. _____. Projeto do plano mineiro de desenvolvimento econômico e social: estratégia. Belo Horizonte, Bra., Depto Estadual de Imprensa, 1971. 310 p., tables.

Development strategy of a key state of Brazil. The mineiros take charge of their own destiny and also contribute to Brazil's national development. A well conceived statement.

7147. Moreira, Amélia Alba Nogueira. A cidade de Teresina (IBGE/B, 31:230, set./out 1972, p. 3-185, maps, tables)

Long functional urban analysis of Teresina, Piauí, a remote city experiencing rapid expansion and growth.

7148. _____. O espaço regional de Teresina (IBGE/B, 31:231, nov./dez. 1972, p. 3-98)

Comprehensive profile of Teresina and its regional context. The city lies in the path of Amazon development from the Northeast.

7149. Moreira, Júlio Estrella. Eleodoro ebano Pereira e a Fundação de Curitiba à luz de novos documentos. Curitiba, Bra., Univ. Federal do Paraná, 1972. 148 p., illus., fold. maps (Boletim do Instituto Histórico, Geográfico e Etnográfico Paranaense, 16)

Use of original documents, colonial maps, and air photos to reconstruct the founding of Curitiba City.

7150. Morris, Fred B. A geografia social no Rio de Janeiro: 1960 (IBGE/R, 35:1, jan./março 1973, p. 3-70, bibl., maps)

A masters essay applying factoral analysis to the social geography of Rio in 1960. Methodology is more profound than the insights into Brazil's urban structure, which has been more deeply analyzed by Brazilian geographers.

7151. Muller, Keith Derald. Pioneer settlement in south Brazil: the case of Toledo, Paraná. The Hague, Martinus Nijhoff, 1974. 75 p., maps, tables (Publications of the Research Group for European Migration Problems, 19)

This latest volume of a well-known series has seven chapters which deal with planned and spontaneous settlement in western Paraná, Bra. Analysis of recent migration, case studies of various representative pioneer farm types, analysis of settlement form, structure, size, and function are among topics treated in detail for the colony of Toledo founded in 1946. Favorable conclusions about progress are drawn which point to advantages of use of the long-lot settlement form, colonists with homogeneous backgrounds, and vertical integration of regional production. [R.C. Eidt]

7152. Nabuco, José Thomaz. Política demográfia para o Brasil. Belo Horizonte, Bra., Univ. Federal de Minas Gerais [and] Edições da *Revista Brasileira de Estudos Políticos,* 1973. 156 p., bibl., tables (Estudos sociais e políticos, 32)

Broad overview of population history and policy questions of Brazil by Joaquim Nabuco's son.

7153. Navarro, Newton. Natal. Fotos de Francisco Améndola. Versão para o inglês do Dalton Melo de Andrade. São Paulo, Gráficos Brunner, 1972. 58 p., illus., plates (Col. Mercator)

Beautiful color photos of Natal.

7154. Neto, Antônio Delorenzo. A reorganização das áreas metropolitanas: urbanização e descentralização. São Paulo, Livraria Pioneira Editôra, 1972. 137 p., bibl., fold. maps, tables

(Biblioteca pioneira de ciencias sociais. Sociologia)

This sociological work is methodologically and conceptually less sophisticated and less substantial than the geographers' writings on cities of Brazil.

7155. Neves, Marco Flavio. A viabilidade económica de projetos rodoviárias. Belo Horizonte, Bra., Gôverno do Estado de Minas Gerais, Depto. de Estradas de Rodagem, 1968? 33 p., bibl., tables.

Road building has been a major activity since 1956. Study, originally presented at the IV Simpósio de Pesquisas Rodoviárias.

7156. Novaes, Fernando C. Aves de uma vegetação secundária na foz do Amazonas. Belém, Bra., Conselho Nacional de Pesquisas, Instituto Nacional de Pesquisas da Amazônia, Museu Paraense Emílio Goeldi, 1973. 88 p., bibl., maps, plates, tables (Publicações avulsas, 21)

Biogeography of birds in the Amazon forests.

7157. Ortolani, Altino Aldo; Adolpho Carlos Camargo Viana; and **Roberto Gonçalves de Abreu.** *Hemileia vastatrix berk et br.:* estudos e observações em regiões da África e sugestões á cafeicultura do Brasil. Rio, Ministério da Indústria e do Comérico, Instituto Brasileiro do Café, 1971. 193 p., bibl., tables.

Interesting results of African trip during which coffee areas were visited to obtain ideas for combating rust in Brazilian coffee plantations.

7158. Pandolfo, Clara Martin. Seminário sobre a realidade amazônica para professores da disciplina "Estudos de Problemas Brasileiros;" Tema: Amazônia brasileira, o meio físico. Os recursos naturais. Brasília, Ministério do Interior, Superintendência do Desenvolvimento da Amazônia (SUDAM), 1973. 43 p., maps, tables.

A teacher's manual for seminar/course on the natural resources of the Amazon Basin.

7159. Paraíba (state), *Bra.* **Comissão Estadual de Planejamento Agrícola (CEPA).** O sisal na Paraíba: aspectos econômicos. João Pessoa, Bra., 1971. 62 p., bibl., maps, tables.

A boom cash crop in the 1960s before a decline. This is not a definitive study.

7160. Paz, Luiz Gonzaga da; Geraldo Afonso da Silva; and **Jurandir Bezerra**

de Siqueira. Considerações sobre o dimensionamento de projetos de pecuária bovina. Recife, Bra., Ministério do Interior, Superintendência do Desenvolvimento do Nordeste (SUDENE), 1971. 91 l., tables.

Climatic variables are seen in a deterministic role when recent Northeast history have seen reservoirs and *palma* cactus counteract the effects of aridity.

7161. Penteado, Antônio Rocha. Problemas de colonização e de uso da terra na região Bragantina do Estado do Pará. Belém, Bra., Univ. Federal do Pará, 1967. 2 v. (488 p.) (Continuous pagings) maps, plates, tables (Col. Amazônica. Série José Veríssimo)

A thorough treatment of colonization in this older zone of Pará.

7162. _____. O sistema portuário de Belém. Belém, Bra., Univ. Federal do Pará, 1973. 260 p., bibl., plates, tables (Col. Amazônica. Série José Veríssimo)

An Amazon specialist examines how the port of Belém functions, its relations to the larger region, and the changing functions of the gateway port city.

7163. Pereira, Odon. Fontenelle: depoimentos e documentos. São Paulo, Editôra Obelisco, 1967? 150 p., plates.

Fascinating account of the problems of urban traffic in São Paulo and of one man's stunning campaign to solve them. Fontenelle becomes a household word when he let air out of illegally parked cars in Rio and São Paulo.

7164. Pinto, Aloísio de Arruda and **Maria das Graças Moreira Ferreira.** Bibliografia de bibliografias agrícolas do Brasil. Viçosa, Bra., Univ. Federal de Viçosa, Biblioteca Central, Seção de Bibliografia e Documentação, 1974. 86 p., bibl. (Série Bibliografia especializada, 6)

A useful index. Cites 438 items.

7165. Plano diretor de Itapetinga. Bahia, Bra., Univ. Federal de Bahia, 1973. 2 v. (210, 110 p.) tables.

Datum base for a variety of community studies of this Bahian city.

7166. Pompeu Sobrinho, Thomaz. Sesmarias cearenses: distribuição geográfica. Fortaleza, Bra., Secretaria de Cultura do Ceará, 1970. 1 v. (Unpaged) illus., tables.

Comprehensive listing or original land grants by location, size, grantees, and special observations. Ready to map.

7167. Prado, Marcos. Trânsito louco. São Paulo, Editora F.T.D., 1973. 141 p., maps, plates.

Assertion that urban space should belong to human beings. Assails "crazy traffic" of Brazilian cities.

7168. *Problemas Brasileiros.* Revista mensal de cultura. Conselho Regional do Serviço Social do Comércio. Ano 11, No. 119, julho 1973- . São Paulo.

The planning of cargo terminals for São Paulo within the larger urban plan.

7169. Rattner, Henrique. Planejamento urbano e regional. São Paulo, Companhia Editôra Nacional, 1974. 161 p., bibl. (Biblioteca universitária. Ciências sociais, 50: Série, 2a)

Collection of six essays on urban and regional planning in Brazil. Useful bibliography.

7170. Recomendações das classes produtoras do Amazonas, submetidas à consideração do Exmo. Snr. Presidente da República. Manaus, Bra., Associação Comercial do Amazonas, Federação das Indústrias do Estado do Amazonas, Federação do Comércio, Federação da Agricultura do Amazonas, 1968. 1 v. (Unpaged)

Regional plan for the western part of the Amazon Basin.

7171. Recursos humanos do Rio Grande do Sul: população, mão-de-obra, educação. Pôrto Alegre, Bra., Univ. do Rio Grande do Sul (UFRGS), Superintendência do Desenvolvimento da Região Sul (SUDESUL) [and] Organização dos Estados Americanos (OEA), Centro Interamericano para o Desenvolvimento Social Integrado, 1973. 596 p., maps, tables.

Basic social indicators and other fundamental statistics of this principal southern state.

7172. Rio Grande do Norte (state), *Bra.* **Serviço de Informações de Mercado.** Avaliação do índice de perdas dos produtos horti-fruti-granjeiros na cidade do Natal. Natal, Bra., 1972. 59 l., tables.

Heightened awareness of food loss determinants within the entire food supply process.

7173. Rio Grande do Sul (state), *Bra.* **Assembléia Legislativa. Comissão Parlamentar para o Estudo da Poluição e Defesa do Meio Ambiente.** Anais da Comissão Parlamentar Especial que estudou os problemas da poluição e do meio ambiente. Pôrto Alegre, Bra., 1972. 562 p.

Lengthy statement supporting awareness and measures which combat environmental pollution. Focus on Rio Grande state.

7174. Rodrigues, Tarcísio Ewerton; Ivo Katuji Morikawa; Raimundo Sousa dos Reis; and Italo Claudio Falesi. Solos do distrito agropecuário da SUFRAMA: Convênio Levantamento Pedológico da Area do Distrito Agropecuário da SUFRAMA. Manaus, Bra., Ministério da Agricultura, Escritório de Pesquisas e Experimentação Agropecuárias do Norte (IPEAN), 1971. 99 p., bibl., fold. maps, maps, plates, tables (Série Solos, 1:1)

Soil characteristics of an area in Amazonas, and measures recommended to improve their productivity.

7175. Rosa, Carlos Nobre. Os animais de nossas praias. 2. ed. São Paulo, São Paulo Livraria Editôra (EDART), 1973. 187 p., bibl., illus., plates.

Contribution to biogeography of the Brazilian littoral.

7176. Rua, João. A organização urbana do Espírito Santo analisada através da circulação de onibus intermunicipais (IBGE/R, 35:2, abril/junho 1973, p. 103-123, tables)

Urban hierarchy of Espírito Santo state is related to the patterns of circulation and areas of urban influence. A little-studied state.

7177. Santos, José Wilson de O. Transporte & exportação. Rio, Banco do Brasil, Carteira de Comércio Exterior (CACEX), Centro de Promoção da Exportação, 1972. 99 p., bibl., map, tables.

Cargo handling practices and transport policy.

7178. São Paulo (state), *Bra.* **Departamento de Estatística.** Aspectos estatísticos cartográficos. São Paulo, 1973. 1 v. (Unpaged) illus., maps, tables.

Rudimentary atlas of São Paulo state. Level of cartographic sophistication not up to standards of the Brazilian geography profession.

7179. _____. Secretaria de Economia e Planejamento. Superintendência do Desenvolvimento do Litoral Paulista (SUDELPA). Area de atuação, caracterização física, econômica, social. São Paulo, 1973. 2 v. (Various pagings) maps, tables.

The Brazilian development process is filling in the emptier areas adjacent to the already settled areas. Next area: the coast of São Paulo state.

7180. _____. _____. Oportunidades de investimentos no Vale do Ribeira. São Paulo, 1973. 26 l., maps, plates.

Example of colorful promotional literature to attract investment to the southern coast region of São Paulo state.

7181. _____. Secretaria dos Serviços e Obras Públicas. Departamento de Águas e Energia Eléctrica. Serviço do Vale do Ribeira. Complexo Valo Grande, Mar Pequeno, Rio Ribeira de Iguape. São Paulo? Geobrás, 1966. 2 v. (Various pagings) illus., maps, plates, tables.

A regional development assessment of coastal area in economic stagnation in São Paulo state.

7182. Schultes, Richard Evans. Tropical American hallucinogens: where are we and where are we going? (SBPC/CC, 25:6, junho 1973, p. 543-561, bibl., plates)

These plants form an important part of the cultures of many native Americans. Their use forms part of the cultural geography of Latin America.

7183. Seligsohn, Otto E. Cacau da Bahia: história e problemática. Salvador, Bra., Univ. Católica de Salvador, Faculdade de Ciências Econômicas, Instituto de Pesquisas Econômicas, Sociais e Administrativas, 1973? 122 p., plates, tables.

Illustrated history, geography and industrialization of cacao, an historic economic mainstay of southern Bahia.

7184. Semana Social do Rio Grande do Sul, *V, Pôrto Alegre, Bra., 1971.* Desenvolvimento urbano do Rio Grande do Sul. Pôrto Alegre, Bra., 1971. 1 v. (Various pagings) tables.

Collection of essays.

7185. Seminário de Avaliação do Desenvolvimento Agropecuário do Nordeste, *I, João Pessoa, Bra., 1971.* João Pessoa, Bra., 1971. 48 p.

Concise evaluations of the needs and potential for agricultural development in the Northeast.

7186. Seminário de Tropicologia, *Recife, Bra., 1974.* Trópico & língua e literatura, instituição militar, energia solar, desporto, transportes, arquitetura, farmacopéia, música, tropicalidade, como um conceito ecológico-geográfico [por] Henrique Mindlin and others. Recife, Bra., Univ. Federal de Pernambuco, 1974. 2 v. (763 p.) (Continuous pagination)

Two volumes of proceedings of the Tropicology Seminar organized by Gilberto Freyre in Recife. A broad interdisciplinary look at the significance of the tropical regions and their effects upon everything from language and literature to sports to music to architecture to military institutions and transportation; causal relationships vs. coincidental relationships not always distinguished.

7187. Senna, Milton Câmara. Amazônia: política e estratégia de ocupação e desenvolvimento. Brasília, Ministério do Interior, Superintendência do Desenvolvimento da Amazônia (SUDAM), 1973. 25 l., maps.

Concise statement of development plans for Amazônia. Conservationists notwithstanding, Brazil shall occupy her national territory.

7188. Sergipe (state), *Bra.* **Conselho Estadual de Agricultura. Comissão Estadual de Planejamento Agrícola** (CEPA). Citricultura em Sergipe: abordagem conjuntural. Aracajú, Bra., CEPA-SE *em convênio com* SUDENE, CONDESE, SUDAP [and] ANCARSE, 1973. 111 p., bibl., tables.

Citrus production has important opportunities in both domestic and foreign markets.

7189. Silva, Paulo de Castro Moreira da. O desafio do mar. 2. ed. Rio, Editôra Sabia, 1972? 119 p., tables.

A superficial look at what potential uses the oceans have for Brazil by a career Naval officer.

7190. Simpósio Florestal na Bahia, *I, Salvador, Bra., 1973.* Anais. Salvador, Bra., Gôverno da Bahia, Secretaria da Agricultura, Instituto Brasileiro de Desenvolvimento Florestal (IBDE) [and] Comissão Executiva do Plano de Recuperação da Lavoura Cacaueira (CEPLAC), 1973. 231 p., maps, tables.

Basic inventory of forest resources and forest management agencies in Bahia state. Emphasis given to cacao possibilities.

7191. Simpósio International sobre Fauna Silvestre e Pesca Fluvial e Lacustre Amazônica, *Manaus, Bra., 1973.* Relatório. Manaus, Bra., Ministério da Agricultura, Instituto Brasileiro de Desenvolvimento Florestal (IBDF), Superintendência do Desenvolvimento da Pesca (SUDEPE) [and] Organização dos Estados Americanos, Instituto Interamericano de Ciências Agrícolas, Programa Cooperativo para o Desenvolvimento do Trópico Americano (IICA—TROPICOS), 1973. 2 v. (Unpaged) illus., tables.

Detailed accounts of how fauna and fish of the Amazon area are hunted and processed. Useful for biogeographers.

7192. Souza, Eli de Moraes and Humberto Vendelino Richter. Sistemas predominantes de exploração e capacidade produtiva em pecuária no Rio Grande do Sul. Pôrto Alegre, Bra., Univ. Federal do Rio Grande do Sul, Faculdade de Ciências Econômicas, Centro de Estudos e Pesquisas Econômicas (IEPE), 1971. 52 l., bibl., tables.

Cattle prospects in Rio Grande do Sul.

7193. Souza, Levy Xavier de. São Paulo project: a challenge in the worldly race for the social and economic development. São Paulo, Research and Documentation Brazilian Institute (IBRADOC), 1970. 99 p., maps, plates (Documents of nosso tempo)

An appalling translation into English of a promotional document on São Paulo city.

7193a. Sternberg, Hilgard O'Reilly. The Amazon River of Brazil. Wiesbaden, FRG, Franz Steiner Verlag GMBH, 1975. 74 p. (Geographische Zeitschrift)

Excellent brief monograph focusing upon the alluvial morphology of the great river and upon the processes of modernization and their impact in the region. Bulk of study is English version of 1950's thesis dealing with man and water on Careiro Island (in Portuguese—limited publication).

7194. Sturm, Alzemiro E. O efeito do isolamento na difusão das prácticas agrícolas em Santa Cruz do Sul, Brasil. Pôrto Alegre, Bra., Univ. Federal do Rio Grande do Sul, Faculdade de Ciências Econômicas, Instituto de Estudos e Pesquisas Econômicas, 1969. 71 l., maps, tables (Estudos e trabalhos mimeografados, 7)

M.S. thesis in rural sociology at Pennsylvania State Univ.

7195. Técnica Buck Ltda. (firm), *Brazil.* Plano diretor de desenvolvimento. v. 1. Toledo, Bra., 1972. 300 p., maps, tables.

Representative of a flood of urban master plans being drawn in Brazil.

7196. Tobelem, Alain. Josué de Castro e a descoberta da fome. Prefácio de Souza Barros. Rio, Editôra Leitura, 1974. 170 p.

Commentary and critical review of Josué de Castro's writings and ideas concerning the determinants of hunger.

7197. Universidade Federal da Bahia, *Salvador, Bra.* Laboratório de Geomorfologia e Estudos Regionais. Contribução ao estudo do recônvaco. v. 1, Alagoinhas. Salvador, Bra., 1968. 31 l., maps, tables.

Good regional study by a group of Bahian geographers, including students, of a second ranking city of Bahia.

Valente, Murillo Gurgel. A política de transportes marítimos no Brasil: crônica de uma batalha. See item 8603.

7198. Vasconcelos Sobrinho, J. As regiões naturais do Nordeste, o Meio e a civilização. Recife, Bra., Conselho do Desenvolvimento de Pernambuco, 1970. 441 p., maps, plates.

New expanded edition of a former study. Interesting illustrations.

7199. Velho, Otávio Guilherme. Frentes de espansão e estrutura agrária: estudo do processo de penetração numa área da transamazônica. Rio, Zahar Editôres, 1972. 178 p., bibl., maps, tables.

A study of settlement and development of an area around Maraba, in eastern Amazonia. The inter-relations among various settlement fronts in the region are traced historically in an attempt to explain the present agricultural landscape. Includes a chapter on the effects of the Transamazon highway in changing the regional settlement characteristics. [M. Hiraoka]

7200. Vilaça, Antônio. A sombra de dois pinheiros. Rio, Edições Arquímedes, 1973. 314 p., facsims., plates.

Sentimental history of the cooperative of Limoeiro, Pernambuco.

7201. Warming, Eugênio and Mário G. Ferri. Lagoa Santa e a vegetação de cerrados brasileiros. Belo Horizonte, Bra., Livraria Itatiaia Editôra [and] Editôra Univ. de São Paulo, 1973. 362 p., bibl., illus., plates, tables.

Another facsimile edition of the botanist Warming's volume on the vegetation of the Brazilian cerrados originally published in Danish in 1892.

7201a. Webb, Kempton E. The changing face of Northeast Brazil. N.Y., Columbia Univ. Press, 1974. 205 p., bibl., maps, plates.

Basic study in English on the geography of Northeast Brazil employing the methodology/concept of landscape evolution. Based upon extensive field research and use of archival materials. Epilog written in 1973 views directions of change over the past 20 years. Revolution of Brazilian food supply documented.

CARTOGRAPHY

JOHN R. HÉBERT

Latin American, Portuguese, and Spanish Division
Library of Congress

WE HAVE CONTINUED IN THE SAME MANNER IN this *Handbook* as was done in volume 35, providing information on current, available maps, atlases and cartographic reference works pertaining to the Latin American region and considered of interest to generalists and specialists alike. Noteworthy atlases that have been reviewed by this contributor during the past two years include the 2. ed. of the *Atlas of Mexico* (1975) prepared by Stanley Arbingast and his colleagues at the Univ. of Texas; Randle & Gurevitz's 1971 *Atlas de geografía histórica de la pampa anterior* which provides information on the development of the Pampa as an agricultural region; the Instituto Brasileiro de Geografia's important studies and publications, *Atlas do Ceará* (1973) and the 46-sheet *Carta internacional do mundo ao milionésimo* (1972); and two additional Brazilian publications, *Atlas geográfico da Guanabara* (1972) by the state Secretaria de Planejamento e Coordenação Geral and *Evolução administrativa do estado do Rio Grande do Sul* by the Instituto Gaúcho de Reforma Agraria, Pôrto Alegre, Bra., which provide useful and informative planning data of Guanabara administrative history and of the state of Rio Grande do Sul respectively.

As usual, unique single and series maps were reviewed in this volume, including the OAS's Bureau of Regional Development study of Haiti (1972) in which seven thematic maps accompanied an extensive text and new edition sheets for the British D.O.S. series 443 Anguilla (1973), 346 Tortola (1973), E803 St. Vincent (1973) and Guyana's new edition of series E491 (1972). The quality of many of the national maps remained high. As in our previous contribution, in volume 35, we have tried to offer a representative list of plans for the major Latin American cities. Some of the entries, undoubtedly, are simply more recent editions of previously mentioned city plans. Of interest are the detailed maps of minor cities prepared by the national mapping agencies of several countries including those of Costa Rica, Dominican Republic and Venezuela of which singular examples are listed. One city plan worthy of mention is the 1973 Nicaraguan Instituto Geográfico Nacional's photomap of Managua on which the fissures of the 1972 earthquake have been added.

As we indicated in volume 35, we want to include references to maps of historic quality that have been prepared in facsimile and that would appeal to further historic, sociological or historical geographic studies. In the past two years, several publications dealing with historical cartographic studies or simply reproductions of facsimiles have been produced. The 1973 publication *Cartografía colonial chilena* by the Sociedad de Promoción de Valores Nacionales and Nectario María's *Mapas y planos de Maracaibo y su región 1499-1820* (1973) are examples of facsimile publications of historical maps. From the historical geography and archaeological viewpoints, the impressive studies and maps of Teotihuacán by René Millon, Armando Cerda and others, and Javier Aguilera Rojas' *Urbanismo español en América* (1973) are welcome additions to the growing field of cartographic inquiry. Finally, a most impressive historical work is *Links with the past* (1973), a study of the history of Surinam cartography 1500-1971 prepared by F.C. Bubberman, C. Koeman, J.B. Wekker and others; this latter study is of interest not only for the information it provides on the mapping of Surinam but also on the variety of map makers, of many nationalities, engaged in its production.

No review of current cartographic materials would be complete without some information on how to acquire maps from Latin America. Peter Johnson's article "Sources and Methods to Latin American Flat Map Procurement" in the *Special Library Association Geography and Map Division Bulletin* (see item 7203) should be a useful how-to-do-it article for the neophyte and a good refresher for the seasoned professional.

It is hoped that the variety of the contents of this cartographic section will hold wide appeal for all of the users of the *Handbook,* as was our stated intent in volume 35.

ARTICLES AND CARTOBIBLIOGRAPHIES

7202. Aguilera Rojas, Javier comp. Urbanismo español en América. Selección de planes y textos: Javier Aguilera Rojas [and] Luis J. Moreno Rexach. Realización: Dirección General de Ordenación del Turismo. Madrid, Editora Nacional, 1973. 234 p., Colored plates. 25 x 35 cm.

City plans of colonial Spanish America contained in the collections of the Archivo General de Indias (Sevilla) and Archivo del Servicio Histórico Militar (Madrid). Various categories are given to describe the towns: date of foundation, conformity to a plan, defensive, location on coast or inland, function (commercial, mining, etc.), new initiative in region, and pattern of development. An important attempt on the development of the Spanish cities of the Americas. The plans are analyzed and reproduced in full color. This is an excellent work for historical cartographer, geographer and historian.

7203. Johnson, Peter T. Sources and methods to Latin American flat map procurement (Bulletin [Special Libraries Assn., Geography and Map Division, N.Y.] 95, March 1974, p. 40-47, 60)

An interesting and valuable article which discusses the methods to adopt in acquiring maps in Latin America. The names of book dealers in Latin America who will process map orders are also listed.

7204. Stephenson, Richard W. Atlases of the western hemisphere: a summary survey (AGS/GR, 62:1, Jan. 1972, p. 92-119)

Stephenson surveyed the various regional atlases of the Western Hemisphere that have appeared since Ena L. Yonge's "Regional Atlases: A Summary Survey", *Geographical Review* (Vol. 52, 1962) and *her* "World and Thematic Atlases: A Summary Survey", *(same issue).* While atlases pertaining to the Western Hemisphere as a unit were limited (only one paragraph in the article), many for Latin America and the individual countries were listed and described, see p. 110-119 in the article.

GENERAL

7205. Geographia Ltda. (firm), *London.* The *Daily Telegraph* map of South

America. London, 1973. Colored. 95 x 72 cm. Scale 1:10,000,000. Inset maps: Land utilization-economy; physical; Atlantic Ocean.

General political map of continent with transportation, major towns, and streams indicated. The map is a distinctive general map of the region.

7206. John Bartholomew and Son, Ltd. *(firm), Edinburgh, Scotland.* South America. Edinburgh, Scotland, 1974. Colored. 86 x 61 cm. Scale 1:10,000,000. Inset: Galápagos Islands.

General political and transportation map of South America with relief indicated by color tints and spots heights in meters. An attached cover contains information on various points of interest with their geographical coordinates. The map is part of Bartholomew's World Travel Series of maps.

7207. Kummerly and Frey (firm), *Berne.* South America. Berne, 1973. Colored. 114 x 75 cm. Scale 1:8,000,000.

General map of Latin America with legend, in English, French, German, Portuguese, Spanish and Italian.

7208. National Geographic Society, *Washington.* South America. Washington, 1973. Colored. 150 x 109 cm. Scale 1:5,540,000.

Large wall map of South America having international boundaries, roads, oil fields, airports, towns, and streams shown. Useful and colorful map for general use.

7209. Pan-American Institute of Geography and History (PAIGH), *Rio.* **Commission on Cartography. Committee on Special Maps.** América Latina: mapa general de transportes. Ottawa, Canada, Mapping and Charting Establishment *for* PAIGH, 1968. 2 colored maps, 77 x 112 cm. ea. Scale ca. 1:5,000,000.

Incomplete in two sheets; third sheet covering Central America, Mexico and the Caribbean not seen. Information given includes classes of roads, railroads, pipelines, ports, airports. A general land use is indicated by five color bands—cultivated, combined fields and pastures, savannas, desert and mountains, and forests. This colorful map provides useful information for the specialist.

ARGENTINA

7210. Argentina. Instituto Geográfico Militar. Atlas de la República Argentina. pt. 1, Política. B.A., 1972. 122 p. 31 cm.

New ed. of the 1965 Instituto Geográfico Militar atlas. Contains a general map of Argentina and maps for each province and for the major city in each province. A gazetteer with references to the page of the atlas on which a location can be found is provided. The gazetteer lists the train line servicing the particular towns. Each provincial map is accompanied by a population density chart divided into depts. The atlas is colorfully illustrated.

7211. _____. Servicio Nacional de Parques Nacionales. Cartas topohidrográficas del lago Nahuel Huapi, provincias de Río Negro y Neuquén. B.A., 1971. 12 l. 71 x 70 cm.

Charts one-ten are drawn to a scale of 1:25,000. Index map and separate chart of Puerto Blest, Pañuelos and Anchorena are included. Maps provide information on depths of the lake and land information such as roads, telecommunication lines, and altitude.

7212. Automóvil Club Argentino, *Buenos Aires.* **División Cartografía.** Córdoba: red caminera principal. B.A., 1972. Colored. 67 x 47 cm. verso and recto. Scale 1:1,000,000.

Road map on which variant grades of roads are shown. Central city plans of Córdoba and Río Cuarto and vicinity maps of the same appear on the verso. Index to cities also appears on the verso of the main map.

7213. _____, _____. _____. Corrientes: province. B.A., 1972. Colored. 39 x 41 cm. verso and recto. Scale 1:1,200,000.

Road map of the province with city plan and vicinity map of Corrientes included. General sites of interest in the city and the province are listed. Index to towns appears on the verso of the map.

7214. _____, _____. _____. Entre Ríos. B.A., 1973. Colored. 48 x 46 cm. verso and recto. Scale 1:1,200,000.

Road map of province with city and vicinity plans of Paraná, La Paz, Concordia, Concepción del Uruguay and Gualeguaychú. Index to cities appears on verso of map.

7215. _____, _____. _____. República Argentina: carta turística. B.A., 1970. 8 sheets, sizes vary. Scale 1:1,900,800.

Useful highway information for the nation is furnished on these appealing maps. The versos of each section contain city plans, vicinity maps and an index to communities found in the section map. Service stations, hotels, motels, and restaurants for the sections are listed.

7216. _____, _____. _____. Santa Fe. B.A., 1973. Colored. 69 x 42 cm. verso and recto. Scale 1:1,100,000.

Road map of province on one side with central city plans of Rosario and Santa Fe and vicinity maps of the two cities on the verso. Index to communities also appears on the verso.

7217. Campal, Esteban F. *ed.* Regionalización ganadera en la Cuenca del Río de la Plata. Montevideo, Instituto Interamericano de Ciencias Agrícolas, 1972. [Inserts] 7 maps showing livestock information on the La Plata Basin: I. Densidad de población ganadera en el territorio agrícola; II. Relación ovinos/bovinos (cabezas); III. Porcentaje de tierras de pastoreo; IV. Porcentaje de tierras en cultivos; V. Capacidad pastoril de las tierras de pastoreo; VI. Producción de lana en el territorio agrícola; VII. Producción anual de leche en el territorio agrícola, ea. map is 36 x 29 cm. Scale 1:5,200,000.

Maps provide detailed information down to secondary political divisions in the portions of Argentina, Paraguay, Uruguay and Brazil that border the La Plata River.

7218. Editorial Mapa (firm), *Buenos Aires*. Zona urbana del Gran Buenos Aires. 12. ed. B.A., 1973. Colored. 80 x 116 cm. Scale 1:40,000.

Detailed city plan of metropolitan Buenos Aires accompanied by index entitled Guía de Calles.

7219. Randle, Patricio H. and **Nélida Gurevitz.** Atlas geografía histórica de La Pampa Anterior. v. 1, Memoria descriptiva; v. 2, Láminas. B.A., EUDEBA, 1971. 2 v. (39 p., 38 maps)

Excellent work on the development of the pampas as an agricultural area. Using the same base and outline, the authors furnish comparative information on rural population for 1869, 1895, 1914, 1947, and 1960 as well as land distribution for the same period, density of cultivation since 1895; the base map also has applied to it cultural feature information from 1869-1960. A text accompanies the atlas.

7220. Ricci, Susana M. Provincia de Río Negro: mapa minero, 1971. B.A., Dirección Nacional de Promoción Minera, 1971. Colored. 69 x 109 cm. Scale 1:750,000.

Mines are indexed and located by cross grid. Mines, roads, streams, railroads, and departmental and provincial boundaries are given. This map complements the similar efforts by Ricci for the provinces of La Pampa, San Luis, and Neuquén reported in *HLAS 35:7233-7235.*

7221. Río Negro (province),*Arg*. **Ministerio de Gobierno.** Atlas básico de los municipios. Viedma, Arg., 1970. 137 p., illus., maps. 27 cm.

Atlas contains maps of 43 communities and various information, e.g. origin of names, date of origin, distance from capital, population in 1947-60-70, schools, churches, doctors, services, major production and tourist information in 54 communities. Statistical information in graphs and table format on population, agricultural production, petroleum and mining and a map of the transportation network in the province precedes the community maps. This work is a useful guide to the urban areas of the province and supplies detailed information on community facilities.

BOLIVIA

7222. Bolivia. Dirección General de Desarrollo Urbano. La Paz 73: plano oficial de la ciudad de La Paz. La Paz, La Papelera, 1972. Colored. 2 sheets, ea. 97 x 69 cm. Scale 1:11,000.

General plan of the city showing built up, areas, churches, plazas, forest, projected or under-construction areas, and principal buildings and schools. Excellent large scale plan for the city.

7223. _____. Instituto Geográfico Militar. Mapa de la República de Bolivia: carta preliminar. La Paz, 1973. Colored map series, complete in 9 sheets. ea. 63 x 51 cm. Scale 1:1,000,000. Inset map: situación geográfica de Bolivia en el continente.

General topographical map series of Bolivia on which roads, towns, streams, and administrative boundaries appear. Contour lines drawn at 100,250 and 500 m. intervals are provided. No index accompanies the series. Inset map shows the historic land claims of Bolivia.

7224. _____. Servicio Nacional de Caminos. Mapa vial de Bolivia. La Paz, 1972. Colored. 66 x 56 cm. Scale 1:2,500,000.

General road map of Bolivia on which road types, railroads, boundaries, towns and streams are shown. On the verso are 11 strip maps of portions of the road system in the country.

7225. Martínez, Claude; Pierre Tomasi; Tomás Zubieta; and **Rubén Botello.** Mapa tectónico de Bolivia. La Paz, Univ. Mayor de San Andrés [and] Servicio Geológico de Bolivia, 1973. Colored. On sheet 44 x 59 cm. Scale 1:5,000,000.

Map includes color codes for geologic, altitude and volcanic activity. The map is presented in Spanish and French; the French Office de la Recherche Scientifique et Technique Outre Mer (Paris) was involved in the project. The map differentiates three orogenic cycles: precambrian, hercynian and Andean. An explanatory booklet accompanies the map.

7226. Talleres-Escuela Don Bosco, *La Paz*. La ciudad de La Paz. La Paz, 1972. Colored. 50 x 87 cm.

General city plan which includes a location guide to streets and plazas. Not as detailed as the La Paz 73 elsewhere described.

BRAZIL

7227. Brazil. Fundação Instituto Brasileiro de Geografia e Estatística. República Federativa do Brasil. Rio, 1973. Colored. 94 x 114 cm. Scale 1:5,000,000.

Political map of the country with state boundaries, roads, towns, and streams indicated. Brazil's coastal claims, i.e. 200 mi. limit, is distinctively given.

7228. _____. _____. República Federativa do Brasil. Rio, 1973. Colored. In 4 parts, ea. 87 x 91 cm. Scale 1:2,500,000.

General political map of the country with roads, streams, towns, parks, ports and state boundaries clearly given. Altitude is indicated by contour lines. A fine wall-sized map which provides much general information.

7229. _____. Fundação Nacional de Material Escolar. Atlas das potencialidades brasileiras; Brasil grande e forte. Rio, 1974. 158 p. 36 x 25 cm.

General thematic atlas of Brazil providing colorful maps and graphs illustrating Brazilian education, agriculture, fisheries, petroleum, industry, financial organization, etc. Explanatory text provides much useful information.

7230. _____. Instituto Brasileiro de Geografia. Brasil: carta internacional do mundo ao milionésimo. Rio, 1972. 46 sheets of maps with index. ea. 64 x 77 cm. Scale 1:1,000,000.

English and Portuguese language atlas of 46 sheets providing current topographical information on Brazil. The atlas was published "commemorativa do sesquincentenário da independencia." This volume brings up to date the 1960 published "album da carta do Brasil ao milionésimo."

7231. _____. Ministério dos Transportes. Departamento Nacional de Estradas de Rodagem. Plano nacional de viação: sistema rodoviario federal. Rio, 1974. Colored. 47 x 50 cm. Scale 1:10,000,000.

Map shows conditions of roads (paved, under construction, planned) in the country. Five types of roads, divided into direction or localness of the route, are given with particular numbers shown on the map relating to the route given in the key, e.g. route 401 is shown to extend from Boa Vista, via Fronteira to Guiana, etc. A useful map of the development of the transportation system of the nation via their roadways.

7232. _____. Superintendência do Vale do São Francisco (SUVALE). Indice de levantamentos básicos da Bacia do São Francisco. Rio, 1970. 1 v. (Unpaged) illus. 39 cm.

Index to large scale map coverage of the São Francisco Valley. Separate index sheets list aeriphotographic, planimetric, geologic, hydrogeologic, geormorphologic, and soils maps.

7233. Edição Atualizada (firm), *Rio.* Brasil—didático—rodoviário—turístico. Rio, 1974. Colored. 91 x 85 cm. Scale ca. 1:5,000,000. Insets: Maps of ilhas oceanicas, centros of Salvador, Belém, Fortaleza, Recife, Curitiba, Pôrto Alegre, São Paulo, Belo Horizonte, Rio and Brasília.

Map shows main roads, streams, cities and boundaries of states. A distance chart and vital information on each state are included. This is a useful, colorful map of Brazil for the general public.

Ferreira, Evaldo Osório. Carta tectônica do Brasil: notícia explicativa (Tectonic map of Brazil: explanatory note). See item 7109.

7234. See item 7247a.

7235. Melém, Maria de Nazaré and J.B. Melém. Amazônia legal. Belém, Bra., Cartografia da Amazônia, 1974. Colored. 73 x 99 cm. Scale 1:3,500,000.

General map of area which includes Mato Grosso northward and east to Maranhao. Map indicates location of 35 minerals found in the region.

7236. See item 7250a.

7237. See item 7256a.

7238. Quatro Rodas (firm), *Rio?* Mapa Brasil: pt. 1, Nordeste-norte-noroeste; pt. 2, Sul-centro-este-oeste. Rio, 1973. Colored maps. ea. 78 x 98 cm verso and recto; Scale 1:1,700,000. Extreme northern Brazil, scale 1:3,000,000.

Colorful maps of Brazilian roads with city index. Roads, towns, streams, state boundaries and relief are shown. Maps prepared for Texaco.

7239. See item 7256b.

7240. Sociedade Comercial e Representações Gráficas Ltda. (firm), *Curitiba, Bra.* Esquema rodoviário do Sul do Brasil. Curitiba, Bra., 1973. Colored. 111 x 81 cm. Scale 1:1,250,000.

General road map with only major towns listed. No index and no relief appear.

7241. United States. Central Intelligence Agency. Brazil. Washington? 1973. Colored. 39 x 44 cm. Scale 1:11,800,000.

Another one of the fine maps of nations produced by the Central Intelligence Agency and sold by the US Government Printing Office for 70 cents (US). These maps furnish quick reference information and may be purchased for a nominal fee. The main map of Brazil shows transportation routes, streams, major cities, and spot elevations. Relief is indicated by shading. The inset maps furnish a wealth of general statistical information.

STATES AND REGIONS

7242. Alegria, Agnaldo. Mapa turístico rodoviário: Estado do Rio de Janeiro. Niterói, Bra.? 1974. Colored. 45 x 70 cm. Scale 1:608,250.

General map of the state with roads, towns, and streams indicated. On verso, tourist information of the state is included.

7243. Brazil. Instituto Brasileiro de Geografia. Atlas do Ceará. Rio, 1973. 78 p., 40 maps.

Includes maps with information about population, climate, land use, industry, education, and physical information. Population density by municipios is given. All of the maps are colorful and appear useful to the researcher.

7244. _____. Instituto Nacional de Colonização e Reforma Agrária. Geomorfologia: Rio Grande do Sul. Brasília, 1972. 102 x 107 cm. Scale 1:7,500,000.

Division of rock (sedimentary, metamorphic and efusive) as well as morphologic divisions (fluvial, limnico, eolic, tectonic and denuded) are given on this well researched and colorful map.

7245. Ceará (state), *Bra.* **Convénio Governo.** Mapa geológico preliminar do Estado do Ceará. Fortaleza, Bra., 1972. 129 x 97 cm. Scale 1:500,000.

Geologic map issued as part of the state's "projeto levantamento dos recursos mineras do Estado do Ceará."

7246. Editôra e Publicidade Ltda., *Rio.* Rio Grande do Sul: mapa didático, rodoviário e turístico. Rio, 1973. Colored. 66 x 104 cm. Scale 1:1,000,000.

Road map of the state with subdivisions from communities of over 200,000 to under 5,000 inhabitants. Also includes an inset map of the center of Pôrto Alegre showing an access route to Beira Rio Stadium. Index to communities appears on right side of the map.

7247. Editôra Presidente Ltda. (firm), *Rio.* Mapa Schaeffer: Estado de São Paulo. 6. ed. Rio, 1973. Colored. 64 x 94 cm. Scale 1:1,000,000.

Map of state includes classes of roads, towns, streams, rail lines and tourist conveniences. An accompanying booklet provides useful tourist information for hotels and restaurants in the major towns of the state.

7247a. Goiás (state), *Bra.* **Departamento de Industria.** Cartogramas socioeconômicos. 2. ed. melhorada. Goiánia, Bra., 1972. 52 maps. 32 cm.

This collection of maps appears as No. 6 in the Secretaria da Industria e Comércio Caderno Informativo Série A. Informative economic atlas of the state with comparative statistics of each micro region. The statistical information used is no earlier than 1968 with most of the information from 1970 on.

7248. Guanabara (state), *Bra.* **Departamento de Estradas de Rodagem.** Mapa rodoviário do Estado da Guanabara. Rio, 1973. Colored. 66 x 120 cm. Scale ca. 1:600,000.

Map shows roads (existing and under construction), towns, streams. Relief is shown by contour lines and spot heights. A legend on the left side of the map is included.

7249. _____, _____. Secretaria de Planejamento e Coordenação Geral. Atlas geográfico da Guanabara. Rio, 1972. 144 p. 44 x 55 cm.

Atlas provides thematic maps covering the broad areas of administrative divisions, natural conditions, population, economic activity, cultural, urban sections, urban equipage and foreign relations. Population distribution maps for each decade from 1920 to 1970 (less 1930), industrial areas, locations of schools, libraries, museums, religious units, locations of favelas, electrical systems, telephones, etc., are indicated in monochrome and two color base maps of the state.

7250. Instituto Gaúcho de Reforma Agraria, *Pôrto Alegre, Bra.* **Divisão de Geografia e Cartografia.** Evolução administrativa do Estado do Rio Grande do Sul. Pôrto Alegre, Bra., n.d. 92 p.

Fine atlas showing the administrative development of the state from 1809 to 1965.

7250a. Melo, Edna Luísa de and **Judite Ivanir Breda.** Carta arqueológica. Goiánia, Bra., Univ. Federal de Goiás, 1972. 101 p. 31 x 22 cm.

Maps include archaeological zones, geology and list of sites (diggings) in the state.

7251. Minas Gerais (state), *Bra.* **Instituto de Geo-Ciências Aplicadas.** Estado de Minas Gerais: cartograma. Belo Horizonte, Bra., 1973. Colored map. 47 x 58 cm. Scale 1:2,344,320.

Outline map of the state with municipios indicated; this serves as a useful base map of Minas Gerais.

7252. _____, _____. _____. Estado de Minas Gerais: micro regiões homogêneas. Belo Horizonte, Bra.,

1972. Colored map. 47 x 58 cm. Scale 1:2,344,320.

This map divides the state into 46 regions (named Micro Homogêneas) with municipios, streams and regions indicated.

7253. _____, _____. _____. Estado de Minas Gerais: zonas geográficas. Belo Horizonte, Bra., 1972. Colored map. 47 x 58 cm. Scale 1:2,344,320.

The state is shown divided into 15 geographic zones.

7254. Pará (state), *Bra.* **Departamento de Estradas de Rodagem do Pará.** Mapa rodoviário. Belém, Bra., 1973. Colored. 73 x 79 cm. Scale 1:2,000,000.

Physical map of the state with roads, towns, municipal limits, streams and other geographical features indicated. Inset map of Belém is useful although not detailed.

7255. Paulini, J. (firm), *Rio.* O Grande Rio: Guanabara & arredores. Rio, Edificio Christian Barnard, 1974. Colored. 72 x 109 cm. Scale 1:81,000.

Colorful map of Rio and vicinity giving municipal boundaries, various street categories and towns. Relief shown by contour lines in 100 m. intervals. An index to localities is included.

7256. _____, _____. Guanabara: indicador estácio de Sá. Rio, Edificio Christian Barnard, 1973. Colored map in 4 sections. ea. 70 x 98 cm. Scale 1:25,800.

Road map of Guanabara state which indicates the progress made in road construction. Map also includes railroad lines and stations, towns, streams. Streets and roads are named. A very detailed map of the state.

7256a. _____, _____. Map of Territôrio Federal de Rondônia. Produção de Paule Novais. Rio, 1974. Colored. 46 x 64 cm. Scale 1:1,500,000. Inset: Amazônia pequeno roteiro da região mais fascinante do brasil..

General highway map showing classes of highways, towns, streams and shaded relief.

7256b. Rio Grande do Sul (state), *Bra.* **Central de Comandos Mecanizados de Apôio a Agricultura.** Vegetação e uso da terra. Pôrto Alegre, Bra., 1972. Colored. 101 x 106 cm. Scale 1:750,000.

Distinctive map providing excellent thematic information in type of agricultural usage of land in Rio Grande do Sul.

7257. Sociedad Comercial e Representações Gráficas Ltda., *(firm), Curitiba, Bra.* Mapa do Estado da Guanabara.

Curitiba, Bra., 1973. Colored. 71 x 129 cm. Scale 1:58,925.

General reference map of the state with built up areas especially noted. All classes and states of roads are marked and a proposed new urban area "Futuro Centro Metropolitano" is indicated. Relief is indicated by contour lines. The map is not indexed.

7258. _____, _____, _____. Mapa do Estado de Santa Catarina. Curitiba, Bra., 1973. Colored. 79 x 113 cm. Scale 1:500,000.

General map with municipios and classes of roads indicated. The work contains no index.

7259. _____, _____, _____. Mapa do Estado do Pará. Curitiba, Bra., 1973. Colored. 103 x 99 cm. Scale 1:1,500,-000.

General reference map. Classes of roads, towns and boundaries are indicated. Relief is indicated by contour intervals of 100 meters. No index appears with the map.

7260. Universidade Federal da Bahia, *Salvador, Bra.* **Instituto de Geociências.** Projeto de regionalização administrativa para o Estado da Bahia. v. 2, Atlas. Rio, 1973. 24 p., 14 maps.

Atlas prepared by the Institute Geoscience at Bahia Federal Univ. for the Secretaria do Planejamento, Ciencia e Tecnologia (Bahia). Maps show administrative, geologic, transportation, population information. Map nine analyzes the urban nuclei and is quite interesting.

CITIES

7261. Bahia (state), *Bra.* **Prefeitura Municipal do Salvador.** Mapa da cidade do Salvador. Salvador, Bra., 1972. Colored, in 9 sheets, ea. 84 x 121 cm. Scale 1:5,000

Excellent detailed city plan with no index. Locations of developed areas are given.

7262. Belo Horizonte (city), *Bra.* **Conselho Municipal de Planejamento do Desenvolvimento.** Mapa do município de Belo Horizonte. Belo Horizonte, Bra., 1970. Colored. 105 x 73 cm. Scale 1:30,000.

City plan with streets named, barrios given and relief shown by contours and spot heights.

7263. Editôra Presidente Ltda. (firm), *Rio.* Guia Schaeffer, Rio: cidade do Rio de Janeiro, Estado da Guanabara. 3. ed. Rio, 1974. Colored. 86 x 123 cm. Scale 1:25,200.

Index to streets appear on the verso of the general city plan of Rio.

7264. _____, _____. Plano Schaeffer da cidade de Niterói, capital do Estado de Rio de Janeiro. 1. ed. Rio, 1973. Colored. 94 x 63 cm. Scale 1:10,000.

General city plan.

7265. Holdridge Propaganda (firm), *Belém, Bra.* Cidade de Belém. 8. ed. Belém, Bra., 1971. 36 x 47 cm. Scale 1:16,727. Inset: Plan of Bairro da Marambaia. Verso: Entrada do Pôrto de Belém.

General plan of the city with principal sites identified and located. Oriented with north at the upper right.

7266. Oliveira, Waldemir Bezerra. Mapa de cidade de Manaus: capital internacional da zona franca. Manaus, Bra.? Tipografia Torres, 1973. 45 x 45 cm. Scale 1:20,000. Inset: Zona comercial.

City plan of Manaus with 34 important sites located.

7267. Paulini, J. (firm), *Rio.* Baixada Fluminense: Duque de Caxias-Nilópolis-Nova Iguaçu—São João de Meriti. Rio, 1975. Colored, in 2 sheets, one is 83 x 124 cm and one is 83 x 63 cm. Scale 1:25,000

Map shows street pattern, roads, districts and boundaries. No index accompanies the map.

7268. Santa Catarina (state), *Bra.* **Departamento Estadual de Geografia e Cartografia.** Florianópolis. Florianópolis, Bra., 1972. 53 x 80 cm. Scale 1:9,884.

General street plan of the city with contour lines of 25-meter intervals included.

7269. Sociedade Comercial e Representações Gráficas Ltda. (firm), *Curitiba, Bra.* Planta da cidade de Brasília. Curitiba, Bra., 1973. Colored. 91 x 72 cm. Inset: Esplanada dos Ministérios.

City plan of Brasília with embassies, government offices, and tourist information provided.

7270. Thofehrn, Hans A. Carta topográfica da cidade de Pôrto Alegre. Apresentação gráfica por Edgar Klettner. Colaboração do Lydio Costa de Andrade e Dorival Rosa de Azevedo. Pôrto Alegre, Bra., Livraria do Globo, Seção de Cartografia, 1972. Colored. 105 x 78 cm. Scale 1:15,000. Inset: Planta do município de Pôrto Alegre, scale 1:150,000. Praias Balneárias entre o morro do Sabiá e a Ponto da Serraria.

Detailed city plan of Pôrto Alegre. No index included.

CHILE

7271. Sociedad de Promoción de Valores Nacionales, *Santiago.* Cartografía colonial chilena: mapas antiguos de Chile. Legajo I. Santiago, 1973. Facsim. 5 maps. ea. on sheets. 41 x 55 cm.

Limited ed. of 1000 copies prepared for publication by Mario Rodríguez Altamirano and José Miguel Barros Franco, both functionaries in the Ministerio de Relaciones Exteriores de Chile. The maps reproduced, which cover the period 1597 to 1646, are from the personal collections of the two individuals mentioned above. The maps are handsome facsimiles of original maps by Wytfliet, Ogilby, Mercator-Hondius and Sanson that show Chile. A descriptive text by Mario Rodríguez and an introductory statement by Mario Correa Saavedra enhance the reproductions.

COLOMBIA

7272. Colombia. Federación Nacional de Cafeteros. Mapa de utilización actual de la tierra en la zona cafetera de Colombia. Bogotá, 1971. Colored. 127 x 92 cm. Scale 1:1,500,000.

The map is part of a study conducted, *Investigaciones Económicas de la Federación Nacional de Cafeteros de Colombia,* from 1967 to 1970. Locations of coffee and other crop cultivations are indicated on this base map.

7273. _____. **Instituto Geográfico Agustín Codazzi.** Departamento de Antioquia. Bogotá, 1973. Colored. 96 x 75 cm. Scale 1:500,000. Inset: Location map.

Map shows municipal boundaries, towns, streams, roads, and rail lines. Altitude is shown by hipsometric tints and by contour lines of undetermined intervals.

7274. _____. _____. República de Colombia: mapa vial. Bogotá, 1973. Colored. 98 x 65 cm. Scale 1:1,500,000.

General physical map of the country with roads, streams, towns, historic sites and department boundaries. On the verso is general tourist information to various sections of the country. The title on the cover of the map reads, *Colombia: vial y turística.*

7275. _____. **Servicio Colombiano de Meteorología e Hidrología.** Mapa preliminar de isotermas mínimas anuales promedias, 1951-1970, en Colombia. Elaborado por S. Stanescu y J.R. Díaz. Bogotá, 1970. 130 x 92 cm. Scale 1:1,500,000. Insets: 1) Colombia-zonas de variación de la temperatura del aire mínima anual promedia, 1951-1970, con la altitud en °C. 2) Variación de la temperatura del aire mínima anual· promedia, 1951-1970.

Average temperature variation by area and by altitude are given in this map.

7276. Heliógrafo de la Costa, *Barranquilla, Colo.* Barranquilla '72. Barranquilla, Colo., 1972. 88 x 121 cm.

General map of the city with a letter and number keyed index.

7277. Ortiz, Luis Carlos. CAR: carta geográfica de la Corporación Autónoma Regional de la sabana de Bogotá y de los valles de Ubate y Chiquinquira. Bogotá, 1973. 3 sheets, ea. 94 x 62 cm. Scale 1:100,000.

Map of Bogotá and vicinity with Corp. Autónoma Regional boundary plus departmental and municipal limits.

COSTA RICA

7278. Costa Rica. Instituto Costarricense de Turismo. Ciudad de San José. [en mapas de Costa Rica y San José]. San José, 1972. Colored. 42 x 63 cm. Scale 1:10,000. On verso: Map of Costa Rica, 1:800,000. Vicinity of San José, 1:287,000.

City plan with 109 sites identified. On verso is a general map of the country and a good vicinity map of San José.

7279. _____. Instituto Geográfico Nacional. Ciudad de Puntarenas. San José, 1974. Colored. 55 x 80 cm. Scale 1:10,000.

The map is part of the Costa Rican IGN's 1:10,000 city series and it is divided into two parts, Puntarenas Oeste and Puntarenas Este. A detailed key to 144 institutions, buildings and sites of public interest is included.

7280. _____. _____. Mapa histórico-geográfico, Costa Rica. San José, 1972. Colored. 54 x 73 cm. Scale 1:700,000.

Map shows explorers routes inland and along the coast, towns and their dates of formation, Indian groups, and boundaries of Alcaldia Mayor de Nicoya and Ducado de Veragua in the country. Accompanied by a guide.

7281. _____. _____. Three maps of the city of Cartago showing land ownership for the periods 1801-1821; 1821-1841; and 1851. San José, 1967. 3 maps, 2 are 52 x 52 cm; 1 is in 2 pts, ea. 52 x 52 cm.

The 1851 map is a facsimile of Nicolas Gallegos 1851 "Plano que representa el interior de la ciudad de San José, capital de la República de Costa Rica." The earlier maps were compiled by José María Figueroa Oriamuno of the National Library in 1967. Streets, non-settled lands, streams and land owners appear in the three maps. Dimensions of the lots are indicated in the 1851 map.

7282. Tosi, Joseph A., Jr. República de Costa Rica: mapa ecológico según la clasificación de zonas de vida del mundo de L.R. Holdridge. Dibujo por José Andrés Masís. Litografiado por el Instituto Geográfico Nacional. San José, Central Científico Tropical, 1969. Colored. 50 x 53 cm. Scale 1:750,000. Inset: Isla del Coco. Inset diagram: Diagrama para la clasificación de zonas de vida o formaciones vegetales del mundo.

Map shows 19 life zones (which includes climate, vegetation, and altitude) following Holdridge's format which combines elements of latitude, altitude and humidity in a triangular mix to create life zones.

CUBA

7283. Cuba. Instituto Cubano de Geodesia y Cartografía. Mapa turístico de Cuba. La Habana, 1972. 65 x 95 cm. Scale 1:1,300,000. Insets: La Habana and vicinity. On verso: Central Habana, La Habana, Pinar del Río, Santa Clara, Varadero, Matanzas, Cienfuegos, Cárdenas, Santiago de Cuba, Camagüey, and Trinidad-Casilda.

Tha map is indexed and provides a table of distances between a number of Cuban communities. An extensive tourist guide provides information on the availability of motels, beaches, restaurants, museums and other facilities in a large number of towns.

7284. United States. Central Intelligence Agency. Cuba. Washington, 1972. 22 x 53 cm. Scale 1:2,450,000. Inset maps: Economic activity, sugar, population, land utilization.

General map with relief shown and spot heights given. Roads, railroads, provincial boundaries and major towns are shown.

DOMINICAN REPUBLIC

7285. Dominican Republic. Instituto Geográfico Universitario. Planos de ciudades, República Dominicana. Santo Domingo, 1972. Sheets: Bonao y Cercanías; Hato Mayor y Cercanías. ea. 58 x 84 cm. Scale 1:5,000.

Map of cities and vicinity in the Dominican Republic in which roads, extent of urbanization, and agricultural land use in the immediate vicinity are shown. A keyed index to buildings and streets is included.

7286. Rand McNally and Co. (firm), *Chicago, Ill.* República Dominicana. Chicago, Ill., 1974. Colored. 39 x 63 cm. Scale 1:696,960. On verso: Plans of Santo Domingo and Santiago.

General road map of the country with inset, keyed plans of the two major cities. A short historical text and several illustrations of tourist interest appear with the map. The map is distributed by Texaco.

7287. Universidad Autónoma de Santo Domingo, Santo Domingo. **Instituto Geográfico Universitario.** República Dominicana: mapa topográfico general. Santo Domingo, 1972. Blue line print. 107 x 175 cm. Scale 1:250,000.

Topographic map of the country with shaded relief and contour lines of 20 m. intervals. The map is based on five US Defense Mapping Agency 1:250,000 sheets of the country prepared in 1970.

ECUADOR

7288. Ecuador. Instituto Geográfico Militar. Ecuador: mapa político. Quito, 1972. Colored. 42 x 56 cm. Scale 1:2,000,000. Inset: Map of Archipélago de Colón. Map of the Continental Sea and island territory (200 mi. limit)

Provincial boundaries, roads, towns, and streams are indicated. A list of provinces and cantons appears below the map. Boundary or treaty claims are included.

7289. _____. _____. Dirección General de Obras Públicas. Red fundamental de carreteras. Quito, 1973. Colored. 42 x 56 cm. Scale 1:2,000,000. Inset: Provincia Insular de Galápagos.

To show highway systems with roads under construction (asphalt and cement) and under study is the main purpose of the map. General information, such as towns, provinces and streams is also provided.

7290. _____. Ministerio de Obras Públicas y Comunicaciones. Mapa de carreteras y telecomunicaciones de la República del Ecuador. Carlos A. Tufiño, cartógrafo. Quito, 1972. Colored. 42 x 54 cm. Scale 1:2,000,000. Insets: Archipiélago de Colón; Location map.

Tourist map of Ecuador showing major roads, towns, rail lines and streams. The Treaty tracts of Tratado Muñoz Vernaza-Suárez de 1916, Protocolo Mosquera-Pedemonte agosto de 1830 and Protocolo de Rio de Janeiro 1942 are shown. An inset map comparing the heights of mountains in Ecuador is included.

7291. Granado G., V.M. Downtown of Quito. Quito? 1974. Colored. 27 x 57 cm. Scale ca. 1:22, 176.

General central city map with the locations of tourist services indicated.

7292. United States. Central Intelligence Agency. Ecuador. Washington, 1973. 32 x 31 cm. Scale 1:2,500,000. Inset maps: Population, economic activity, vegetation.

General map of country showing provincial boundaries, railroads, roads, airfields, and cities. Spot elevations are given in feet.

GUATEMALA

Asamblea General del Instituto Panamericano de Geografía e Historia, VIII, Guatemala, 1965. Informe nacional. See item 7024.

7293. Guatemala. Instituto Geográfico Nacional. Mapa preliminar de la República de Guatemala. Guatemala, 1973. Colored. 56 x 55 cm. Scale 1:1,000,000.

Map of the country with the roads, towns, departments and streams shown. Belice is shown as a department of Guatemala and not as an independent political body. Altitude is indicated by shaded relief.

GUYANA

7294. Guyana. Land and Surveys Department. Cartographic Division. Gazetteer of Guyana. Georgetown, 1974. 181 p., 1 map, 24 x 16 cm.

This gazetteer furnishes the descriptive (not coordinates) location of nearly 4600 geographical names in the country. A general map of the country that accompanies the gazetteer serves as an area and not specific locator of the sites. Road mileages along Guyana's roads appear in the appendix. It is stated that the geographical coordinates, latitude and longitude, were omitted in order to facilitate its early publication. It is hoped that a 2nd ed. of the gazetteer will include coordinates.

7295. _____. Ministry of Agriculture. Lands Department. Guyana. 6. ed. Georgetown, 1972. Colored. in 4 sheets, ea. 87 x 60 cm. Scale 1:500,000 (Series E491)

This is a revised ed. of Directorate of Overseas Surveys (series E491). The map includes roads, towns, boundaries and streams. Hachured relief and spot heights are given. The boundaries of the Amerindian Reservations and Land Development projects are shown.

7296. _____. _____. Survey Department. Guyana. Georgetown, 1971. Four sheets, 2 are 85 x 54 cm; 2 are 85 x 61 cm. Scale 1:500,000.

General topographic map of Guyana with specific emphasis on agricultural regions. A legend in each map lists the 14 agricultural regions and the products grown in each; the boundaries of the regions are delineated on the maps in green. The base map used by the Survey Department is DOS series E491 last revised in 1965.

HAITI

7297. Organization of American States. Bureau of Regional Development. République d'Haïti. Washington, 1972.

7 colored maps: 1, Géologie, 96 x 129 cm. Scale 1:250,000. 2, Données hydrologiques et utilisation des eaux, 96 x 129 cm. Scale 1:250,000. 3, Sols et vocation de la terre, 96 x 129 cm. Scale 1:250,000. 4, Ecologie, 48 x 64 cm. Scale 1:500,000. 5, Répartition de la population, 48 x 64 cm. Scale 1:500,000. 6, Transport, 48 x 64 cm. Scale 1:500,000. 7, Education, 48 x 64 cm. Scale 1:500,000.

Maps were prepared as part of the OAS Bureau of Regional Development's report *Haïti; Mision D'Assistance Technique Intégrée* (Washington 1972). They provide much needed current information on the country and should be useful to those interested in the various subjects covered. The report which they accompany is filled with statistical information on various subjects affecting the economy of Haiti and the report suggests remedial action necessary for economic improvement. A must reading for Caribbean specialist.

7298. Rand McNally and Co. (firm), Chicago, Ill. Haiti. Chicago, Ill., 1974. Colored. 35 x 47 cm. Scale 1:715,968. Inset maps: Portau-Prince. On verso: Map of the West Indies, 45 x 66 cm.

General highway and tourist map of the country distributed by Texaco. The map of the West Indies on the verso shows relief by hypsometric tints and shading.

HONDURAS

7299. Honduras. Instituto Geográfico Nacional. Mapa general, República de Honduras. 4. ed. Tegucigalpa, 1974. Colored. 45 x 71 cm. Scale 1:1,000,000.

General map of the country providing transportation system information, cities, departmental boundaries, and departmental and municipal centers. Relief is given in spot heights and in contour lines of variant intervals. Projection is UTM.

7300. Rand McNally and Co. (firm), Chicago, Ill. Honduras. Chicago, Ill., 1973. 45 x 72 cm. Scale 1:1,140,480. On verso: Central America.

Highway map of Honduras, with index to the country and to the Central American map on verso, distributed by Texaco. Inset plans of Tegucigalpa-Comayagüela, San Pedro Sula and La Ceiba appear with the Honduras map. A distance chart to major centers in Central America, Panama, and Mexico appears as do short descriptions of Honduras and Central America.

JAMAICA

7301. Jamaica. Survey Department. Negril sheet: souvenir sheet 13A of Jamaica 1:12,500 series. Kingston, 1973. Colored pictomap. 51 x 76 cm. Scale 1:12,500.

Colorful pictomap of the westernmost portion of Jamaica on which roads, buildings and footpaths appear on the map. Contour lines of 25 ft. vertical intervals are provided. This map is evidently an experimental example prepared by the Survey Dept. and not part of a continuing series of pictomaps of the island.

7302. Rand McNally and Co. (firm), Chicago, Ill. Jamaica. Chicago, Ill., 1974. Colored. 37 x 82 cm. Scale 1:304,128. Inset: Location map. On verso: City plans of Kingston, Mandeville, Montego Bay and Spanish Town.

General highway map of the country with town index and locations of points of interest distributed by Texaco. A street index to the Kingston map on the verso appears, with a list of points of interest in the city.

7303. West (R.T.) and Co., *London*. Jamaica road map. London, 1973. Colored. 42 x 78 cm. Scale 1:304,128. Inset: Location map, city plans of Independence City and Edgewater City. On verso: Kingston, Montego Bay, Spanish Town, Mandeville, Port Antonio, and Ocho Ríos.

General road map of Jamaica prepared for Shell Oil Co. The inset city plans list hotels, golf courses, restaurants, and other tourist facilities. A general town index and a street index to Kingston are included. Mileage guide to cities in Jamaica is included.

7304. See item 7347a.

7305. See item 7347b.

7306. See item 7347c.

MEXICO

7307. Arbingast, Stanley A. and others. Atlas of Mexico. 2. ed. Austin, Univ. of Texas, Bureau of Business Research, 1975. 165 p. 27 x 35 cm.

This second ed. updates and augments the coverage of the original 1970 ed. Prepared by a team of nine scholars from the staff of the Univ. of Texas, led by Dr. Stanley Arbingast, director of the Bureau of Business Research, this atlas is divided into six major theme divisions devoted to the physical setting, history, population, agriculture, transportation-services-and commerce, and industry. Clear, understandable thematic maps are presented to convey information derived from statistics or from historical text. Additional statistics appear in an appendix of eight pages providing columnar information of age, travel (overseas and foreign to Mexico), import and export destination and foreign trade. A bibliography accompanies the work. An institution or a scholar will find the information provided in this atlas useful in the study of Mexico, especially in the 20th century.

7308. Cerda, J. Armando. Teotihuacán, central plateau of Mexico: archaeological and topographic map, ca. 600 A.D. N.Y., Univ. of Rochester, Dept. of

Anthropology, 1972. Colored. 88 x 114 cm. Scale 1:9,500.

Contour intervals of five meters. "Map shows extent of ancient city ca. 600 A.D.; ca. 20 kms. or 8 sq. mis. Shown are 1) partially or completely excavated structures, primarily along the 'Street of the Dead' (north-south axis), and 2) reconstructions based on Teotihuacán Mapping Project Survey of surface remains of unexcavated and partially excavated structures. An undetermined number of structures in various parts of the city have been buried or levelled for agricultural purposes in modern times. Note canalization for most water courses within the ancient city." Excavated and possible locations of other buildings are shown as are the types of structures, walls, water courses. An inset map of the central area of the city is given. Well done map of the city; valuable to the archaeologist and historian.

7309. _____. Teotihuacán, central plateau of Mexico: archaeological and topographic map of the north central zone, ca. 600 A.D. N.Y., Univ. of Rochester, Dept. of Anthropology, 1972. Colored. 192 x 121 cm. Scale 1:1,900.

This is a map of the city as it appeared in 600 A.D., with key locations to 52 structures and a legend that shows location of interior rooms, room complexes, unexcavated sites, temples, walls, water courses and the location of the mapping project's excavation. This detailed city plan, which is part of the Teotihuacán Mapping Project led by René Million of the Univ. of Rochester, is drawn with contour intervals of 1 m.

7310. Editorial Cartográfica Flecha (firm), *México*. Plano de la ciudad e México. México, 1973. 93 x 63 cm. Scale 1:30,413. On verso: Plano del centro de la ciudad de México.

General map of Mexico City with street and colonia index. The location of points of interest in the central city and the existing and proposed metro lines are also given.

7311. Esparza Torres, Héctor F. (firm), *México*. República Mexicana: mapas de los estados Patria Serie. México, Librería Patria, 1973. Colored. 54 x 74 cm. Scale 1:3,801,600.

General map of the nation with major roads and cities shown. An index to the communities appears. A brief history of the Mexico and various tourist information appears on the verso of the map.

7312. General Drafting Co. (firm), *Convent Station, N.J.* Mexico. Convent Station, N.J., 1974. Colored. 60 x 84 cm. Scale 1:3,630,000. Insets: Mexico and vicinity, 18 x 19 cm. Relief map of Mexico, 14 x 19 cm. On verso: Mexico (central area), 20 x 40 cm. Mexico, 45 x 40 cm. Monterrey and vicinity, 18 x 18 cm. Downtown Monterrey, 18 x 22 cm. Plans of Acapulco, Cuernavaca, Chihuahua, Gaudalajara, Puebla, San Luis Potosí and Taxco.

General tourist map of Mexico and its cities. Mileages and travel hints (auto) are given.

7313. Guía Roji (firm), *México*. Centro de la República Mexicana. México, 1974. Colored. 92 x 63 cm. Scale 1:500,000. Inset city plans: León, 67 x 63 cm; Guanajuato, 28 x 54 cm; Queretaro, 38 x 47 cm; Aguascalientes, 26 x 34 cm; Irapuato, 26 x 32 cm; Salamanca, 21 x 25 cm; Celaya, 23 x 34 cm; Morelia, 35 x 50 cm; Zacatecas, 23 x 20 cm; San Luis Potosí, 50 x 51 cm.

General map of central Mexico showing state and municipal boundaries, roads, streams and towns. An index to towns and city streets is included.

7314. _____, _____. Plano de la ciudad de Guadalajara. México, 1974. Colored. 81 x 115 cm. Scale 1:20,000. On verso: Mapa del estado de Jalisco. Scale 1:684,288.

General map of Guadalajara and Jalisco. A street index accompanies the city plan.

7315. _____, _____. Plano de la ciudad de México. México, 1973. Colored. 116 x 81 cm. Scale 1:20,000.

This general city plan of Mexico City is accompanied by a street index and a vicinity map.

7316. _____, _____. Plano de Puerto Vallarta. México, 1973. Colored. 28 x 53 cm. Scale 1:15,206. On verso: Mazatlan, Scale 1:9,500. Location map.

General city plans for the Pacific coast communities.

7317. Mexico. Comisión de Estudios del Territorio Nacional (CETENAL). Mapa urbana-Fresnillo, Zacatecas. México, 1972. Colored. 76 x 70 cm. Scale 1:5,000.

Excellent city plan showing various public edifices, locations of hotels, post offices, gasoline stations and banks. The area of buildings and open space are graphically indicated. Relief is indicated by contour lines. A street index is included. The map is part of a series identified as *Cetenal Mapa Urbana*.

7318. _____. **Comisión Nacional de los Salarios Mínimos.** Estados Unidos Mexicanos: zonas económicas para la fijación de los salarios mínimos, 1972-1973; división municipal del censo general de población de 1970, actualizada al 31 de enero de 1971. México, 1971. 57 x 91 cm. Scale 1:3,800,000.

Lists municipal divisions and economic zones.

7319. _____. **Dirección de Agrología.** Mapa de tipos de vegetación de la República Mexicana. Cartografía y dibujo: Rubén Rodríguez Gómez [and] Fidel Galicia Santamaría. México, 1972. Colored. 106 x 151 cm. Scale 1:2,000,000.

Explicitly colored vegetation map with color and letter codes for each type. Map has towns, roads, and political subdivisions included. The map is accompanied by a 59. guide and text entitled "Memoria del Mapa de Tipos de Vegetación de la República Mexicana." Illustrations of various vegetation types are included in the work.

7320. _____. **Dirección General de Oceanografía y Señalamiento Marítimo.** Sonora. México, 1973. Colored. 56 x 43 cm. Scale 1:1,750,000. Inset: Location map.

Map shows irrigation districts, state and international boundaries, roads, trails, and lighthouses.

7321. _____. **Secretaría de la Defensa Nacional. Departamento Geográfico Militar.** Carta general de México. México, 1973. Colored. in 4 sheets. ea. 63 x 88 cm. Scale 1:2,000,000.

General map of the country showing all classes of cities and towns, roads, railroads, airports, state and national boundaries, and forests. Relief by contour lines of 500 m. intervals are given. This is a very colorful and useful addition to Mexican mapping.

7322. Millon, René; R. Bruce Drewitt; and George L. Cowgill. The Teotihuacán map. Austin, Univ. of Texas Press, 1973. 2 v. (v. 1, Text, 154 p., bibl., illus., index; v. 2, Maps, 150 maps with 147 overlays. ea. is 26 x 26 cm.)

V. 1 of René Millon's *Urbanization at Teotihuacán, Mexico* study is an impressive cartographic achievement. Taking some 13 years (since 1960) to complete, Millon, Drewitt and Cowgill have delineated the urban center of Teotihuacán in 147 1:2,000 scale map sheets with accompanying overlays (called interpretation sheets) on which are identified topographically (on the 20 sq. km. area of the ancient city ca. 600 A.D.) the visible land mass, the boundaries of the city in phases, and the ancient ruins partially or totally visible. Millon and others have supplemented their impressive work with two smaller scale maps (1:10,000 ea.) of the city (archaeological and topographical) and a 1:2,000 composite map of the north central zone of the city. The 1:2,000 scale maps of the city are clear monochromatic representatives filled with detailed information; the 147 site maps are bound together in a spiral bound hardcover book. The cartographic work is introduced by a historical sketch of the authors' involvement in Teotihuacán and an account of the development of the city through history. Black and white photographic illustrations greatly enhance this work; a bibliography and index are especially useful to the specialist. This monumental work is especially recommended for anyone interested in the history of precolumbian civilization as well as for those interested in detailed mapping of historical sites. For archaeologist's comment, see item 659.

7323. National Geographic Society, *Washington.* Mexico. Washington, 1973. Colored. 55 x 83 cm. Scale 1:3,803,000. Inset: Central America. 1:2,534,000.

Supplement to *National Geographic* (May 1973, p. 638A). Map shows depths by contours, gradient tints and soundings. General map of the country and Central America.

NICARAGUA

7324. Nicaragua. Instituto Geográfico Nacional. Fotomapa de la ciudad de Managua. Managua, 1973. Colored photographic map. 44 x 71 cm. Scale ca. 1:20,000.

Map shows the locations of the fissures in Managua created during the Dec. 1972 earthquake.

7325. _____. _____. República de Nicaragua: mapa geológico. Managua, 1973. Colored. 52 x 61 cm. Scale 1:1,000,000.

Color coded, not letter coded, map of Nicaragua; only a copy of the original map (not a photostatic or photographic copy), is useful to the researcher in this case.

PANAMA

7326. DeDiego O., Carlos A.; Jaime Jaen Mata; and Víctor M. Alvarado. Atlas descriptivo de Panamá. Colon, Pan., McGraw-Hill Latinoamericana, 1972. 48 p., 35 colored maps. 22 x 28 cm.

General thematic atlas of Panama, for secondary school use, on which physical features, political divisions, climate, land use, industry, and other subjects are given. Descriptive text accompanies the maps. Illustrations of geographic areas and diverse cultural types appear to enhance the work. The cost of the atlas is $2.25, paper.

7327. Odin (firm), *Panama.* Ciudad de Panamá. Panama, 1973. Colored. 25 x 67 cm. Scale ca. 1:20,000. Inset: Ciudad de Panamá y alrededores. On verso: Panama, mapa de carreteras.

Map includes street index and index to towns in country. These maps were prepared by Odin Rent a Car in Panama for the delegates to the United Nations Security Council meeting of 15-21 March 1973.

7328. Rand McNally and Co. (firm), *Chicago, Ill.* Panama. Chicago, Ill. 1974. Colored. 31 x 61 cm. Scale 1:1,140,480. Insets: Zona del Canal de

Panamá; Panamá (ciudad); Colón (ciudad). On verso: Central América.

Map of Panama includes general information on roads, towns, streams and national and international boundaries. An index to towns on the map, a brief history of Panama and a distance guide to places in the country are included. The map was prepared by Texaco.

PARAGUAY

7329. DaPonte, Alberto J. Plano de la ciudad de Asunción: capital de la República del Paraguay. Asunción, 1974. 35 x 54 cm.

Street plan of Asunción with a street index on the verso. An inset map of the transportation connection between Asunción and Itaenramada appears.

PERU

7330. Góngora Perea, Amadeo. Plano de la ciudad de Lima metropolitana. Lima, Cartográfica Nacional, 1974. Colored. 60 x 87 cm. Scale ca. 1:25,000.

General street guide of city with accompanying index.

7331. Peru. Instituto Geográfico Militar. República del Perú: mapa físico político. Lima, 1973. Colored. in 4 sheets, ea. 107 x 75 cm.

Beautifully presented physical-political map of the country on which contour lines and hypsometric tints provide altitude information; cities and towns, departmental boundaries, classes of roads and railroad lines, naval and air facilities are given.

7332. _____. _____. República del Perú: mapa político. 3. ed. Lima, 1971. 8 sheets, ea. 54 x 75 cm. Scale 1:1,000,000.

General map of the nation giving administrative, urban and transportation information.

7333. _____. _____. Departamento de Apurimac. Mapa físico político. Lima, 1973. Colored. 78 x 56 cm. Scale 1:350,000. Inset: Location map.

Map of the dept. showing roads, towns, streams, provincial boundaries and relief (shown by hypsometric tints).

7334. _____. _____. Departamento de Arequipa. Mapa físico político. Lima, 1972. Colored. 56 x 81 cm. Scale 1:576,000.

General map of the department showing roads, towns, administrative divisions and relief. Relief is shown by gradient tints.

7335. _____. _____. Departamento de Ayacucho. Mapa físico político. Lima, 1973. Colored. 56 x 78 cm. Scale 1:520,000.

Map of the department with same information as those of Apurimac and Arequipa. Inset: Location map.

7336. _____. _____. Departamento de Ica. Mapa físico político. Lima, 1971. Colored. 78 x 55 cm. Scale 1:370,000.

General map of the department with roads, relief, streams, towns, and provincial limits shown. Relief indicated by color tints. Same as maps of Arequipa, Apurimac, and Ayacucho.

7337. _____. _____. Departamento de Piura. Mapa físico político. Lima, 1971. Colored. 77 x 56 cm. Scale 1:500,000.

General map with roads, towns, provinces and relief shown. Relief indicated by color tints.

7338. _____. Instituto Nacional de Planificación (INP). Oficina Nacional de Evalución de Recursos Naturales (ONERN). Mapa de centros poblados, 1961 (CENSAL). [and] Mapa de centros poblados, 1990: prospectiva. Lima, Talleres Onern, 1972. Colored. ea. 44 x 32 cm. Scale 1:5,000,000.

Part of the issuance of two maps showing population of centers actual and prospective. Five grades of population increase from slow to very high are indicated as well as new population centers. The Huancayo, Chiclayo, Arequipa areas are especially singled out for growth.

7339. Touring y Automóvil Club del Perú, *Lima.* **Departamento de Cartografía y Relevamiento.** Carreteras del Perú. Lima, 1973. Colored. 82 x 58 cm. Scale 1:2,471,040.

Map shows roads and road conditions, department boundaries, capitals of departments, provinces, districts and pueblos. Kilometric distances are indicated. Included are a location map and a distance chart. Relief is shown by shading.

SURINAM

7340. Bubberman, F.C. and others. Links with the past: the history of the cartography of Suriname, 1500-1971. Edited by C. Koeman. Amsterdam, Theatrum Orbis Terrarum, 1973. 1 v. of text. 179 p., 39 maps in folio. 50 x 35 cm.

The function of the map in Surinam's discovery and development is the subject of this Dutch, English and Spanish language atlas edited by C. Koeman. The work is divided into six main chapters covering the cartographic history of the country: a historical survey of Surinam's discovery until 1667 by Dr. G. Schilder; cartography in use of agriculture by A.H. Loor; the golden age in the cartography of Surinam, 1850-1940 by F.C. Bubberman; aerial survey, 1940-present by J.B. Ch. Wekker; foto the capítol of Surinam: Paramaribo; by Drs. B. Nelemans; and hydrographic surveys by Dr. C. Koeman. All of the essays and accompanying descriptions of the maps are well researched and presented in a readable manner. The facsimile maps are distinctively reproduced, 11 of them in color. They are presented at full size or at a readable size with the original size indicated. This is a valuable scholarly contribution to the understanding of the maps of Surinam and the various nationalities involved in its mapping.

7341. Kersten, (C.) and Co., N.V., Paramaribo, Surinam. Suriname. Paramaribo, Surinam, 1974. Colored. 63 x 52 cm. Scale 1:1,000,000. Inset: Location map.

Physiographic map of Surinam with terrain type, locations of minerals, towns, information on transportation, and streams given. Cover title reads *Kaart van Suriname* by H.N. Kahlberg, C. Kersten & Co., N.V., Paramaribo.

URUGUAY

7342. United States. Central Intelligence Agency. Uruguay. Washington, 1974. 42 x 37 cm. Scale 1:1,490,000. Insets: Population and administrative divisions, vegetation, economic activity.

General map with relief, spot heights, roads, railroad lines, town and departmental boundaries given.

Uruguay. Ministerio de Hacienda. Dirección General de Estadística y Censos. Mapas demográficos. See item 7020.

7343. _____. Ministerio de Transporte, Comunicaciones, y Turismo. Rutas de la República Oriental del Uruguay y plano de la ciudad de Montevideo. Montevideo, 1974. Colored. 58 x 50 cm. Scale ca. 1:950,400. Inset: Mapa de la zona balnearia. On verso: Maps of Montevideo and 18 other towns in Uruguay.

General map of country with helpful town plans inserted in the verso of the map. An index to streets in Montevideo is also provided. This is a standard tourist map of the country.

7344. _____. Servicio Geográfico Militar. República Oriental del Uruguay: carta geográfica. 2. ed. Montevideo, 1974. Colored. in 2 sheets. ea. 68 x 112 cm. Scale 1:500,000.

General map of the country with departmental and international boundaries, various classes of roads and classes of towns shown.

VENEZUELA

Drenikoff, Ivan. Mapas antiguos de Venezuela grabados e impresos antes de 1800 con la reproducción del primer mapa impreso en Venezuela y de mapas antiguos. See item 7029.

7345. Nectário María, hermano. Mapas y planos de Maracaibo y su región, 1499-1820. Prólogo de Tomás Polanco Alcántara. Madrid, Embajada de Venezuela, 1973. 157 p., illus., 73 map reproductions. 34 cm.

Contains an alternative title *Mapas y Planos Antiguos de la Región de Maracaibo*. This illustrated cartobibliography was published to commemorate the 150th anniversary of the naval battle of Capitán Chico before Maracaibo 24 July 1823. Maps relating to Maracaibo and region contained in the Spanish Archivo Histórico Nacional, Archivo de la Marina, Servicio Histórico Militar, Archivo del Ministerio del Ejército, Archivo General de Indias (Sevilla), Archivo de la Real Academia de la Historia and Biblioteca Nacional were used in the black and white illustrated bibliography. Nectário Maria lists the location of the maps, author, date, dimensions, and distinguishing particulars/annotations. This volume serves as a useful guide to the colonial mapping of the Maracaibo region.

7346. Venezuela. Dirección de Cartografía Nacional. Mérida. Caracas, 1973. Colored. 64 x 94 cm. Scale 1:15,000. Inset map: Location map.

Map of the town of Mérida showing street names, sites and buildings of interest (234 such locations) and extent of site occupation. Areas of green space, under cultivation and forests are given. Relief is shown by use of contour lines of 20 m. intervals.

7347. _____. Ministerio de Minas e Hidrocarburos. Dirección de Geología. Atlas geológico de Venezuela. Caracas, 1970. Colored. 44 x 63 cm. Scale 1:133,000.

Only one sheet to this proposed atlas has been issued—Estado Nueva Esparta (Edición 1-DG 1970). This colorful first map of the atlas is accompanied by explanatory legend. The latest word from Venezuela concerning the atlas was that the field work and compilation had been completed but funding to complete the atlas was lacking.

WEST INDIES

7347a. Great Britain. Directorate of Overseas Surveys. Anguilla, Lesser Antilles. Ed I-D.O.S. London? 1973. Colored. 44 x 81 cm on sheet 64 x 86 cm. Scale 1:50,000 (Series E803 [D.O.S. 443])

Topographic map of Anguilla on which roads, foot paths, vegetation, and buildings are indicated. Contour lines of 25 ft. intervals are given. A useful detailed map of the island.

7347b. _____. _____. Saint Vincent, Lesser Antilles. Ed. 3-D.O.S. London? 1973. In 2 sheets. ea. 70 x 82 cm. Scale 1:25,000 (Series E803 [D.O.S. 317])

Topographical map of the island which includes contour lines, roads, towns, vegetation and streams.

7347c. _____. _____. Tortola, Lesser Antilles. Ed. 3-D.O.S. London? 1973. Sheet B.V.I. Colored. 66 x 78 cm. Scale 1:25,000 (Series E803 [D.O.S. 346])

Survey map sheet two of six sheets that cover all of the British Virgin Islands. Roads, trails, streams, vegetation, towns and named geographical locations appear. Map is available from the Chief Secretary. Administration Bldg. Road Town, Tortola, for 11.50.

7348. Trayectoria de huracanes y de perturbaciones ciclónicas del Océano Atlántico, del Mar Caribe y del Golfo de México, 1919-1969. La Habana, Instituto Cubano del Libro, 1973. 56 l. 21 x 31 cm.

An annual record of hurricanes in the area by period and season. Excellent statistical material found in this useful atlas.

7349. Trinidad and Tobago. Surveys Division. Trinidad. 3. ed. Port-of-Spain, 1973. Colored. 63 x 79 cm. Scale 1:150,000.

General map of Trinidad with administrative boundaries, transportation systems and tourist information given.

7350. United Nations. Development Programme. Physical Planning Project, St. John's, Antigua. Montserrat: land ownership. St. John's, Antigua, 1973. 43 x 59 cm. Scale ca. 1:50,000.

Land ownership on the island—crown land, private land held in large estates, private land leased by crown, village settlement mainly on private land and real estate subdivisions on Montserrat company's land—are given.

7351. _____. **Physical Planning Office.** Grenada: population change, 1960-1970 by Enumeration District. Grenada? 1972. Blue line print. 72 x 47 cm. Scale 1:50,688 (Dwg. No. G. 2504)

This preliminary map reveals seven categories of population change on the island.

JOURNAL ABBREVIATIONS

AAAS/D	Daedalus. Journal of the American Academy of Arts and Sciences. Harvard Univ. Cambridge, Mass.
AAAS/S	Science. American Association for the Advancement of Science. Washington.
AAFH/TAM	The Americas. A quarterly publication of inter-American cultural history. Academy of American Franciscan History. Washington.
AAG/A	Annals of the Association of American Geographers. Lawrence, Kan.
AAG/PG	Professional Geographer. Journal of the Association of American Geographers. Washington.
ACCEFN/R	Revista de la Academia Colombiana de Ciencias Exactas, Físicas y Naturales. Bogotá.
AGB/BPG	Boletim Paulista de Geografia. Associação dos Geógrafos Brasileiros, Secção Regional de São Paulo. São Paulo.
AGF/B	Bulletin de l'Association de Géographes Français. Paris.
AGS/GR	The Geographical Review. American Geographical Society. N.Y.
AMNH/NH	Natural History. American Museum of Natural History. N.Y.
ANH/B	Boletín de la Academia Nacional de Historia. B.A.
APCG/Y	Yearbook. Association of Pacific Coast Geographers. Corvallis, Ore.
ATI/E	Ekistics. Rural housing in an urbanizing world. Athens Center of Ekistics of the Athens Technological Institute. Athens.
CAG/CG	Canadian Geographer. Le Géographe Canadien. Canadian Association of Geographers. Toronto, Canada.
CU/EG	Economic Geography. Clark Univ. Worcester, Mass.
ECA	E[studios] C[entro] A[mericanos]. Revista de orientación y cultura, dirigida por los PP. Jesuitas de C.A. San Salvador.
EJ	Explorers Journal. N.Y.
GDRMK/ZE	Zeitschrift für den Erdkundeunterricht. Ministerium da Kultur. East Berlin.
GH	Geographica Helvetica. Schweizerische Zeitschrift für Länder- und Völkerkunde. Kümmerly & Frey, Geographischer Verlag. Bern.
GM	The Geographical Magazine. London.
GR	Geographische Rundschau. Zeitschrift für Schulgeographie. Georg Westermann Verlag. Braunschweig, FRG.

GV/GR	Geologische Rundschau. Internationale Zeitschrift für Geologie. Geologische Vereinigung. Ferdinand Enke Verlag. Stuttgart, FRG.
GZ	Geographische Zeitschrift. Franz Steiner Verlag. Wiesbaden, FRG.
IBGE/B	Boletim Geográfico. Conselho Nacional de Geografia, Instituto Brasileiro de Geografia e Estatística. Rio.
IBGE/R	Revista Brasileira de Geografia. Conselho Nacional de Geografia, Instituto Brasileiro de Geografia e Estatística. Rio.
IBGE/RBE	Revista Brasileira de Estadística. Ministério do Planejamento e Coordenação Geral, Instituto Brasileiro de Geografia e Estatística. Rio.
IDES/DE	Desarrollo Económico. Instituto de Desarrollo Económico y Social. B.A.
IG	Information Geographique. Paris.
IGAC/CG	Colombia Geográfica. Revista del Instituto Geográfico Agustín Codazzi. Bogotá.
IGM/U	L'Universo. Rivista bimestrale dell'Istituto Geografico Militare. Firenze, Italy.
ISSQ	The Indiana Social Studies Quarterly. Official organ of the Indiana Council for Social Studies. Ball State Univ. Muncie, Ind.
JDA	Journal of Developing Areas. Western Illinois Univ. Press. Macomb, Ill.
KO	Kollasuyo. Revista de estudios bolivianos. Univ. Mayor de San Andrés. La Paz.
LSE/PS	Population Studies. A journal of demography. London School of Economics. The Population Investigation Committee. London.
MH	Mundo Hispánico. Madrid.
NGS/NGM	National Geographic Magazine. National Geographic Society. Washington.
NWJS	Nature. A weekly journal of science. Macmillan & Co. London.
OAS/AM	Américas. Organization of American States. Washington.
OAS/CI	Ciencia Interamericana. Organization of American States, Dept. of Scientific Affairs. Washington.
PAIGH/G	Revista Geográfica. Instituto Panamericano de Geografia e História, Comissão de Geografia. Rio.
PUJ/U	Universitas. Ciencias jurídicas y socioeconómicas. Pontificia Univ. Javeriana, Facultad de Derecho y Ciencias Socioeconómicas. Bogotá.
RCGS/CGJ	Canadian Geographical Journal. Royal Canadian Geographical Society. Ottawa.
RGS/GJ	The Geographical Journal. The Royal Geographical Society. London.
RMSSA/J	The Rocky Mountain Social Science Journal. The Rocky Mountain Social Science Association. [Colorado State Univ.] Fort Collins, Colo.
RU/SCID	Studies in Comparative International Development. Rutgers Univ. New Brunswick, N.J.
SBPC/CC	Ciência e Cultura. Sociedade Brasileira para o Progresso da Ciência. São Paulo.
SGB/COM	Les Cahiers d'Outre-Mer. Publiée par l'Institut de Géographie de la Faculté des Lettres de Bordeaux, par l'Institut de la France d'Outre-Mer, par la Société de Géographie de Bordeaux avec le concours du Centre National de la Recherche Scientifique et de la VIiéme section de l'École Pratique des Hautes Études. Bordeaux, France.
SGC/B	Boletín de la Sociedad Geográfica de Colombia. Academia de Ciencias Geográficas. Bogotá.
SGI/B	Bollettino della Società Geografica Italiana. Pubblicazione mensile. Roma.
SGL/B	Boletín de la Sociedad Geográfica de Lima. Lima.
SOCIOL	Sociologus. Zeitschrift für empirische Soziologie, sozialpsychologische und ethnologische Forschung (A journal for empirical sociology, social psychology and ethnic research). Berlin.
SRA/A	Anales de la Sociedad Rural Argentina. Revista pastoril y agrícola. B.A.
SSG/RGI	Rivista Geografica Italiana. Società di Studi Geografici e Coloniali. Firenze, Italy.
UA/U	Universidad. Univ. de Antioquia. Medellín, Colo.
UCE/A	Anales. Univ. Central del Ecuador. Quito.
UCEIA/H	Humanitas. Boletín ecuatoriano de antropología. Univ. Central del Ecuador, Instituto de Antropología. Quito.

UCIG/IG	Informaciones Geográficas. Organo oficial del Instituto de Geografía de la Univ. de Chile, Facultad de Filosofía y Educación. Santiago.
UES/U	La Universidad. Univ. de El Salvador. San Salvador.
UH/U	Universidad de La Habana. La Habana.
ULA/RG	Revista Geográfica. Univ. de Los Andes. Mérida, Ven.
UM/JIAS	Journal of Inter-American Studies and World Affairs. Univ. of Miami Press *for the* Center for Advanced International Studies. Coral Gables, Fla.
UNAM/RMS	Revista Mexicana de Sociología. Univ. Nacional Autónoma de México, Instituto de Investigaciones Sociales. México.
UNAMCG/A	Anuario de Geografía. Univ. Nacional Autónoma de México, Colegio de Geografía. México.
UNCP/AC	Anales Científicos de la Universidad del Centro del Perú. Univ. Nacional del Centro del Perú. Huancayo, Perú.
UNECLA/B	Economic Bulletin for Latin America. United Nations, Economic Commission for Latin America. N.Y.
UNS/EE	Estudios Económicos. Univ. Nacional del Sur, Instituto de Economía. Bahía Blanca, Arg.
UNT/H	Humanitas. Revista de la Facultad de Filosofía y Letras. Univ. Nacional de Tucumán. Tucumán, Arg.
USC/U	Universidad de San Carlos de Guatemala. Guatemala.
UW/LE	Land Economics. A quarterly journal of planning, housing and public utilities. Univ. of Wisconsin. Madison, Wis.
UWI/SES	Social and Economic Studies. Univ. of the West Indies, Institute of Social and Economic Research. Mona, Jam.
WZHUB	Wissenschaftliche Zeitschrift der Humboldt-Univ. zu Berlin, Gesellschafts- und Sprachwissenschaftliche Reihe. Berlin.
ZG	Zeitschrift für Geomorphologie. Gebrüder Borntraeger. Berlin.

Government and Politics

GENERAL

JOHN J. BAILEY
*Assistant Professor
of Government
Georgetown University*

ANDRES SUAREZ
*Professor of
Political Science
Center for
Latin American Studies
University of Florida*

PHILIP B. TAYLOR, JR.
*Professor of
Political Science
Director
Latin American
Studies Center
University of Houston*

THAT LATIN AMERICA, AS WELL AS THE LITERATURE discussing it, is in constant change is axiomatic. The topics addressed by both politics and the literature are hardly new, but the sophistication of treatment is generally reflective of rising standards of professionalism and care by authors, and of expectations by readers, if not always of skill and commitment by the decision makers who are discussed. In preparing this section on government and politics materials for the *HLAS,* the reviewers generally have been impressed that the tests applied to the topics by authors and scholars increasingly tend toward three-dimensional quality, even when the product reflects the implicit (and occasionally expressed) *a priori* predilections of the authors. The result is a body of material that in increasing measure warrants the attention of social science scholars of all regional cultures. The declaration would not necessarily have been warranted only a few years ago.

The comment can be carried too far, to be sure, and the consequences of sociopolitical conditions for scholarship are important in the Latin American setting. Under certain circumstances local publication within countries can be just as ephemeral as it ever was; or, granted that in some countries no change has ever occurred, there may be scant publication of any kind. Paraguay, Bolivia, Haiti and some other countries remain difficult places from which to write, it seems. The return to Argentina of Perón from exile produced a flood of trash, as almost every would-be exploiter of this second coming sought to link his newfound vocation to that of the old master. Who can say that several of the morally insecure tyrannies newly-populating the hemisphere, cultivating the sycophancy of advantage-seeking authors, have not recorrupted their country's outputs? The pattern of the age of *caudillaje* thus perpetuates itself. "Certain circumstances" includes the variables of the sense of proportion and of pride of a country's intellectual community, however; it is worth noting that the exquisite Uruguayan embarrassment over its present government has yet to produce anything but obdurate criticism from sources worth our consideration.

The topics that have received continued treatment include many that are traditional as well as some that have gained attention in the past decade. Problems of the political involvement of the armed forces, religion, labor and the urban poor, and the land and the people who work it, appear again in profusion. Especially notable is the more frequent appearance, within the past half dozen years, of military-inspired journals that deal with both technical and philosophical matters; the semi-official periodical publications of the Argentine and Brazilian armed forces are in all probability superior in quality and range of interest to a majority of those published elsewhere in the world. The inner turmoil of the Roman Catholic Church within the hemisphere is more than adequately examined in the book and journal pieces that appear; while many are by laymen, some of the best are by clerics—and on various sides of current issues.

On the other hand topics have received less attention than their importance warrants. The politics of education have commanded relatively little attention, despite the socializing and presumed value-changing effects of the learning process and its product for the recruitment process for participation in problem solving. A few works have apeared, to be sure, by both foreign and national scholars and observers, and they are reported in the country sections. The increasing awareness by thoughtful Latin American development-oriented decision makers that there can be little sustained institutional improvement, whether public or private, without creative administrative reform. has led to some literature; but this is also a thinly-treated topic.

To an increasing degree in the past decade there has been examination of the role of private enterprise in the developing areas. The majority of pieces reported in this section discuss foreign company effects rather than national cases, since internal business problems are normally treated in the context of economics and business administration discussions. There has of course been an explosive flowering of work dealing with the multinational companies as the result of the modishness of the "dependency" school of discussion. Still to be examined, however, is the question of economic growth within the newly-developing mode—which will inevitably gain force and utility as the result of Decision 24 of the Andean Group—of mixed public/private or mixed foreign/national capital formations and managements.

The most difficult materials to comment upon, from the point of scholarly integrity, tend to range around the questions subsumed within the currently rising political criticism of the role of the US in Latin America. They accompany a rising level of official Latin American criticism and nationalism, lodged through political channels; but whether they have preceded or postdated the criticism is uncertain. There can be little doubt that some Latin American dependency specialists find favor in the items they produce. Continued critical examination of the American role and actions is always in order, of course. The bibliographies of past critical works are huge, and grow almost daily; yet the American government and American based corporations persist in sending their overt or covert agents to (to offer examples) Cuba, Chile or Bolivia. These errands seem to occur for primarily ethnocentric reasons, although they may also be for the egocentric redemption of beleaguered bureaucrats. (Who is to say that ITT, Gulf and the fruit companies do not have their bureaucrats, too?). And unfortunately we can be certain that interventions, only marginally related to the issue of US national security as defined by the Monroe Doctrine, and interpreted by J. Reuben Clark, will continue.

It must be emphasized that it is not the critical literature in itself that is difficult to accept. There are many individual scholars, and groups of them as well, working with methodological bases demonstrative of research integrity; while their analyses are often harsh they are also fair in terms of facts and scholarship. Many of these people have found institutional backing in both Latin America and the US that assures them independence of the market-place pressures that might affect their judgment. But intermingled with them are a chaff of pseudo-intellectuals whose stale and borrowed jargon conceals bigotry and a poverty (often, even a rejection) of research. It hardly seems, even to be charitable, that some of these are concerned for offering insight or remedy. Instead, the pejorative violence of their language begs critical issues, ignores fact, and indulges in the most obvious deductive reasoning.

The significant issue broached by the critical literature is one of standards of evaluation. Numerous examples from traditional and behavioral analysis may be found which incorporate pronounced normative biases which adversely affect conceptualization and reasoning; so too are these pitfalls to be encountered in examples from dependency and varieties of Marxian analysis. While we recognize the legitimacy of advocacy in scholarship, we insist nevertheless that the conventional standards of scholarship, attention to conceptualization and rigor of analysis, must apply. The test of scholarly worth, then, is not the zeal of commitment or the felt righteousness of cause, but rather the persuasiveness of evidence and reasoning. These are criteria which the "better" of both the established and recently emerging schools of thought amply fulfill. Given the flux and at times heated dialog among contending theoretical positions, our point must be established that there can be no double standard of evaluation.

The specialist on research and teaching of Latin American Studies, at both the secondary and higher levels, will be concerned with the quality of text materials now available for classroom use. In general the thinness of secondary materials is evident. In Aug. 1975 the Consortium of Latin American Studies Program (CLASP), the institutional affiliate and partial supporter of the Latin American Studies Association (LASA) offered a national seminar designed to develop closer communication between state school systems and the higher education community of the US; if appropriate funding is achieved this will become a regular affair. The product should also include more useful and reliable texts. At the college level, however, a number of texts are now available; many new ones have appeared in this biennium, some of them general in nature and others confined to a few countries or to specialized topics. This college level phenomenon, concerning both courses and the texts, is reported briefly in the spring 1975 issue of the *Latin American Research Review*. It is in this respect that the concern for intellectual integrity that has been discussed in this introduction becomes more important, for not all of the materials offered for college text use by American publishers can be accepted uncritically on the strength of the promotional material.

On the whole the biennium therefore has produced much interesting material and a few outstanding works. The editors of this section have been able to reject, in good conscience, a larger percentage of the publications than ever before. The rising level of independent nationalism in inter-American politics, and of autonomous criticism of the US by Latin American governments, have been matched in intellectual circles by Latin American scholars. This strengthened attitude, and the discipline of mind and method needed to justify it, can only be applauded.

GENERAL

8000. Acerca de la revolución en Latino América. Córdoba, Arg., Editorial Michelor, 1970. 80 p.

Another argumentation favoring revolution in Latin America, this time, apparently, a kind of Christian revolution following the concepts of Mons. Helder Câmara. [AS]

8001. Adie, Robert F. and **Guy E. Poitras.** Latin America: the politics of immobility. Englewood Cliffs, N.J., Prentice-Hall, 1974. 278 p.

A college text structured around interest groups in national political systems, with only passing references to political parties, exogenous influencers (private and official), and other traditional topics of textbook discussions. The entire region is handled, with varying gradations of success (country-by-country), but so extended a treatment in this sort of format is not common. See possibly, for comparison, Lipset and Solari's *Elites in Latin America (HLAS 29:6144)*. [PBT]

8002. Alba, Víctor. The Latin Americans. N.Y., Frederick A. Praeger Publishers, 1969. 392 p., bibl.

An introductory college text to the region. A peculiarly personal volume, largely unembarrassed by footnotes save in explanatory passages, a lack which is appropriate in this particular case. Alba seeks to point out the unique nature of Latin American culture, and its necessary products in economic, social and political behavior. Its criticism of US involvement is well-balanced. The student is unlikely to emerge with the notion that Latin America is—or ever was about to become—Elysian. On the other hand, he will know *why* it is not, which is essential. [PBT]

Alexander, Robert J. Trotskyism in Latin America. See *HLAS 36:1452*.

8003. Ander-Egg, Ezequiel. Hacia la revolución socialista en América Latina. Córdoba, Arg., Editorial del Centro de Estudios Políticos, 1972. 245 p., bibl., tables.

Based on a series of lectures in 1969 at the Centro de Estudios Políticos of B.A., elaborates the bases of a sociology of revolution. Dependency themes dominate. [JJB]

8004. Archetti, Eduardo; Egil Fossum; and Per Olav Reinton. Agrarian structure and peasant autonomy (JPR, 3, 1970, p. 185-195, tables)

Seeking an explanation of the beginnings of peasant unrest, the authors seek to redefine the structural conditions of peasant groups in terms of autonomy. Autonomy is considered to have three dimensions, security of tenancy, market accessibility, and self-management of the plot. Previous literature concerning peasant unrest and autonomy is examined in the early pages of the paper. [PBT]

8005. Areces, Nidia R. Campesinado y reforma agraria en América Latina. B.A., Centro Editor de América Latina, 1972. 143 p., tables (Biblioteca fundamental del hombre moderno)

Brief statement concerning the problems that generally grow from land ownership and use patterns in Latin America in general is followed by individual chapters on Colombia, Peru, Guatemala, Bolivia and Cuba. The material is generally a retelling of known material, but with focus on the landworkers themselves. [PBT]

8006. Artana, Néstor. La auténtica rebelión. Santa Fe, Arg., Librería y Editorial Castellví, 1973. 176 p.

Very vague essay, part philosophy and part sociology, advocating a pacific, conservative, law-and-order revolution of the "honest" people against the "dishonest," which is called the "authentic rebellion." Not especially important. [AS]

8007. Aspectos de la realidad latinoamericana. Santiago, Editora Nacional Quimantú, 1973. 206 p., tables (Col. Camino abierto. Serie Análisis, 15)

Three papers on: dependency and foreign investment in Chile (O. Caputo and R. Pizarro); foreign investment and Latin American underdevelopment (A.G. Frank); and contemporary peasant movements in Latin America (A. Quijano). Radical approaches to the study of Latin American underdevelopment. [AS]

8008. Astiz, Carlos Alberto and Mary F. McCarthy eds. Latin American international politics: ambitions, capabilities and the national interest of Mexico, Brazil, and Argentina. Notre Dame, Ind., Univ. of Notre Dame Press, 1969. 343 p.

Although some of these articles are as much as a decade old (the research data at times are thus quite dated) the attitudes expressed concerning the three major countries are only partially out-of-date. The OAS continues in decline, Brazil's ambition continues to rise, and Argentina continues relatively mute through its own disunity. Only Mexico, here described as reluctant to develop a course of influence, has changed its views. The editor introduces each of four sections with brief essays. [PBT]

8009. *Bank of London and South America Review.* Bank of London and South America. Vol. 8, No. 4, May 1974- . London.

This monthly publication of the Bank, in its newest incarnation, carries both brief financial/economic notes on countries of the region, and its international economic groups as well as short analytical-reportorial articles. For an excellent example, see item 0000. [PBT]

Beare, Adolfo and José Gabriel. Empresa multinacional y dependencia tecnológica: el imperialismo en América Latina hoy. See item 8872.

8010. Bernard, Jean-Pierre and others. Guide to the political parties of South America. Harmondsworth, England, Penguin Books, 1973. 574 p., map, tables.

Short text-like and country-by-country treatment of parties of the ten South American nations. Although it includes recent statistics and many names, it skimps in almost every respect. An updated translation of *HLAS 31:7014a*. [PBT]

8011. Bidart Campos, Germán J. Lecciones elementales de política. B.A., Sociedad Anónima Editora Comercial, Industrial y Financiera (EDIAR), 1973. 430 p.

Introductory survey in political theory from quite traditional (formal-legal) approach. [JJB]

8012. Buntig, Aldo and Argentino Moyano C. Esta hora del cambio, ¿La Iglesia va hacia socialismo? B.A., Editorial Guadalupe, 1971. 238 p.

A detailed discussion of the Apostolic Letter "Octogésima Adveniens" by Pope Paul VI, on the 80th anniversary of "Rerum Novarum," and its possible interpretation as a basis for a Catholic movement toward socialism. A highly useful piece for researchers on the role and position of the Church in Latin America. An appendix contains short text selections from clerical documents in Latin America since 1963. [PBT]

8013. Byars, Robert S. and Joseph L. Love eds. Quantitative social science research on Latin America. Urbana, Univ. of Illinois Press, 1973. 272 p., bibl., tables.

Papers growing from a 1971 seminar on quantitative data as a method for social science research in Latin America. The six individual papers generally attack questions such as: 1) Can Latin America be viewed as an appropriate region for quantitative analysis? 2) What has been accomplished thus far by quantified research? 3) What data are presently available? and 4)

What problems have been confronted in the operationalization of concepts for quantified research? The pieces together offer useful methodological insights, and specific examples of work thus far completed (and occasionally published). Individual papers are by Peter H. Smith (history), Robert C. Hunt (social anthropology), George L. Cowgill (archaeology), Howard L. Gauthier (geography), Clifford Kauffman (political science), and Alejandro Portes (sociology and the use of secondary data). A particularly useful appendix lists data banks in the hemisphere that hold Latin American material. Includes charts. [PBT]

8014. Caldera, Rafael Tomás. Ideario: la Democracia Cristiana en América Latina. Prólogo de Alceu Amoroso Lima. Selección, introducciones y notas por . . . Barcelona, Ediciones Ariel, 1970. 308 p. (Col. DEMOS, 19)

A rather long collection of prior statements and publications by Caldera, grouped under five chapter headings, with short added forenotes by him. Chapters' topics are: overview of the continent, the challenge of development, the Latin American bloc (the reference is to viewpoint and values, not to political power), youth and the university, and the essence of the Christian message. The book is justified by the publisher on ground that Caldera is one of the Western Hemisphere's most significant Christian thinkers and political actors, rather than on his having been President of Venezuela at the time. [PBT]

8015. Calvez, Jean-Yves. Politics and society in the Third World. Translated by M.J. O'Connell. Maryknoll, N.Y., Orbis Books, 1973. 327 p.

Proceeds from incorrect assumption that analyses of politics and society in developing areas are "relatively rare" to a topical descriptive survey of Asia, Africa, and Latin America. Directed toward nonspecialist reader, this is a rather impressive attempt at encyclopedic comprehensiveness. [PBT]

8016. Cavilliotti, Marta *comp.* Cristianismo: doctrina social y revolución; antología. B.A., Centro Editor de América Latina, 1972. 176 p. (Biblioteca fundamental del hombre moderno, 79)

Reprints documents (largely from early 1970s) by reformist or radical elements of clergy in Brazil, Argentina, Colombia, Peru, and Cuba. [JJB]

8017. Centro di Azione e Documentazione sull'America Latina, *Milano, Italy.* Dossier sul Brasile. Milano, Italy, Sapere Edizioni, 1970. 406 p., bibl.

The title is valid: this is a dossier on Brazil, presenting, for the most part, materials derived from other sources, often in textual reproduction. It also is correct in that all aspects (the negative, that is) of the military government in Brazil are represented. Unlike most Italian publications on Latin America this is an exceedingly comprehensive treatment. [PBT]

8018. Centro Internacional de Estudios Superiores de Periodismo para América Latina (CIESPAL), *Quito.* Dos semanas en la prensa de América Latina. Quito, 1967. 121 p., tables.

An extraordinary examination of 29 representative capital and provincial newspapers of Latin America, compared with four major outside papers: quantity and quality analysis, sources (domestic and international), lineage, etc. This is a bible on the subject. Includes appendix with different paginations. [PBT]

8019. Chalmers, Douglas A. Parties and society in Latin America (RU/SCID, 7:2, Summer 1972, p. 102-128)

Analyzes how the distinctive socioeconomic setting in Latin America affects the structure and behavior of political parties and the functions which parties perform in the political system, e.g., elite-recruitment and policy-making. Useful middle-range speculation which provides a rather systematic inventory of testable propositions. [JJB]

8020. Cockcroft, James D.; André Gunder Frank; and **Dale L. Johnson.** Dependence and underdevelopment: Latin America's political economy. Garden City, N.Y., Anchor Books, 1972. 448 p., tables.

Consists of new and previously-published pieces by the three authors and other individuals in a combination of purposes. Essentially a major work in the radical commentary on Latin American problems, the volume challenges past interpretations and offers its own. For historian's comment, see *HLAS 36:1465.* [PBT]

8021. Comisión Episcopal Francesa del Mundo Obrero, *Paris?* Obispos, militantes y socialismo. Lima, Centro de Estudios y Publicaciones (CEP), 1972. 26 p. (Serie Cristianos y socialismo, 3)

Declaration of French Episcopal Commission on Working Life about the areas of compatibility between socialism and Catholic faith. Progressive (liberal) statement. [JJB]

8022. Congresso Latino Americano dos Secretariados Nacionais de Opinião Pública, *Lima, 1966.* Igreja e meios de comunicação social na América Latina. Tradução do espanhol de Rose Marie Muraro. Petrópolis, Bra., Conselho de cooperação dos Secretariados Católicos Latino-Americanos de Meios de Comunicação Social (CODECO) [and] Editôra Vozes, 1969. 79 p. (Col. Igreja hoje, 16)

How is the religious and personal behavior of Latin Americans affected by the media? A clerical analysis, with five chapters by individual authors, presented at the conference. The conclusions offer ideas and approaches for the use of the media for the achievement of Church goals—which are themselves subjected to examination and criticism. [Q. Jenkins]

8023. Conselho Episcopal Latino-Americano (CELAM), *Bogotá.* América Latina: ação e pastoral sociais: conclusões de Mar del Plata. Petrópolis, Bra., Editôra Vozes, 1968. 45 p.

This publication is a commentary on the Mar del Plata document, and includes statements produced by a Meeting of Chairmen of Episcopal Committees for Social Action held at Itapôa, Bahia, Bra., in May 1968. The topic is the Church's role in contribution to development and integration in Latin America; much attention is paid to agrarian reform. [PBT]

8024. Consuegra Higgins, José. El control de la natalidad como arma del imperialismo. 4. ed. Barranquilla, Colo., Univ. del Atlántico, 1972. 239 p., bibl.

Designed to refute neomalthusian pessimism of orthodox developmentalism as diverting attention from real problems (economic imperialism and structural dependency). Thesis is important due to widespread acceptance among nationalist intellectuals. [JJB]

8025. Corbett, Charles D. Politics and professionalism: the South American military (UP/O, 16:4, Winter 1973, p. 927-951)

Discusses intensity of professionalization of army combat line officers (those most likely to be involved in politics) and expansion of mission of armed forces to include development-related tasks. Capsule summaries of recent developments in Brazil, Argentina, Bolivia, and Peru. [JJB]

Cotler, Julio and **Richard R. Fagen** eds. Latin America and the United States: the changing political realities. See item 8716.

8026. *Cristianismo y Sociedad.* Junta Latino Americana de Iglesia y Sociedad. Año 10, No. 31, Entrega 2, 1972- . Montevideo.

Although many of the documents in the last half of the issue relate to Church news and events of the Roman Catholic Church, some articles and events relate to Protestant church groups as well. Thus, ecumenical in interests. The board of editors includes mostly left-inclined sociologists. Articles relate the churches to changing social events and to the changes in doctrine the churches should adopt. [PBT]

8027. Cristianos por el socialismo. B.A., Mundo Nuevo, 1973? 40 p., bibl.

Three short statements of radical Christian belief, including a popular version of the final document of the I Latin American Congress of Christians for Socialism, Santiago, April 1972. [PBT]

8028. Cuadros, Carlos. Lateinamerika im Kampf um die Befreiung seiner Volker (EAZ, 11:2, 1970, p. 233-260)

Author analyzes causes and consequences of underdevelopment in Latin America from an economic, cultural and political-ideological viewpoint. He demonstrates that the underdevelopment has its roots in the period of conquest. It is only today with the strengthening of the communist and socialist parties that a change is becoming apparent. A signpost for the future is the Cuban Revolution. All previous agrarian reforms have not been able to change the production relations on the land. In evaluating the various possible solutions the author subjects social-reformist aspirations to a critical analysis and comes to the conclusion that only by way of a thoroughgoing revolution will it be possible to overcome the deep-rooted contradictions. [H.J. Hoyer]

8029. Degregori, Pedro M. La "No Violencia" violenta. B.A. Editorial Paidós, 1973? 135 p., bibl.

After a biographical sketch of Mahatma Ghandi, the author summarizes in a few pages the doctrine of "aggressive pacifism" inspired, he says, by Ghandi's teachings. He gives no suggestion for implementing the doctrine in countries where the new converts will face Latin American soldiers and police instead of British imperialists. [AS]

8030. Di Tella, Torcuato S. Hacia una política latino-americana. Montevideo, Editorial Arca, 1970. 207 p.

Latin Americans should look objectively at where they have been and where they should go, states this scholar. Several chapters have appeared previously as articles in Latin American social science journals. It is suggested that political forces and leaders can be used for more constructive purposes than those which please the crowd. [PBT]

8031. Dickson, Thomas I., Jr. An approach to the study of the Latin American military (UM/JIAS, 14:4, Nov. 1972, p. 455-468, bibl.)

The author holds that existing analyses of the characteristics of military regimes in Latin American countries have been weak and unperceptive because essentially nonobjective. He suggests a quasi-model for examination based on three hypotheses that are stated, explicitly and unstartingly, and applied to data from Argentina, Bolivia, Brazil, and Peru. A very brief and suggestive article. [PBT]

8032. Dix, Robert H. Latin America: opposition and development (*in* Dahl, Robert A. ed. Regimes and oppositions. New Haven, Conn., Yale Univ. Press, 1973, p. 261-303, tables)

Within a volume about the role of oppositions in political systems of varying sizes this chapter offers a number of specifics and many generalizations concerning Latin American systems. The author argues the case for and against opposition parties and groups within the various Latin American types and concludes that opposition parties contribute to sociopolitical development. [PBT]

8033. Dörig, J.A. ¿Por qué son izquierdistas los intelectuales latinoamericanos? (FH, 6:66, junio 1968, p. 523-537)

A European Catholic writer argues that Latin American intellectuals are usually self-conscious, hypercritical in far too many instances, lacking in both rigor and humor; and leftist as well. [PBT]

8034. Edelstein, Joel C. Latin American studies: the need for dialogue (JDA, 6:3, April 1972, p. 319-322)

Entering the polemic initiated in 1971 in the Journal of Developing Areas in (HLAS 35:6006, 6067, 6068) Edelstein offers excerpts from the 1970 position statement entitled "A Critique on the Diffusion Theory of Development" and adopted by the Union of Radical Latin Americanists. The specialist in the social sciences today needs to be aware that URLA speaks for the radical position which is, to say the least, fashionable. [PBT]

8035. Einaudi, Luigi R. The revolutionary tradition in perspective (*in* Einaudi, Luigi R. *ed.* Beyond Cuba: Latin America takes charge of its future. N.Y., Crane, Russak, 1974, p. 13-33)

"Why has the Cuban example, which aroused such expectations, not been emulated elsewhere?" Analyzes revolutionary nature of generations of 1930 and 1950 and stresses changes in Latin American political context which affected adversely the attractiveness of the Cuban experience. [JJB]

———; **Hans Heymann, Jr.; David Rondfeldt;** and **Cesar Sereseres.** Arms transfers to Latin America: toward a policy of mutual respect. See item 8724.

8036. ———; **Michael Fleet; Richard L. Maullin;** and **Alfred C. Stepan.** The changing Catholic Church (*in* Einaudi, Luigi R. Beyond Cuba: Latin America takes charge of its future. N.Y., Crane, Russak, 1974, p. 75-96)

Useful brief introduction to recent trends in political orientations of sectors of Church. Relates internal factors (organization, finance, staffing) to external patterns to account for present diversity within Catholicism. [JJB]

8037. Encuentro Continental de Misiones en América Latina, *II, Melgar, Colo., 1968.* La pastoral en las misiones de América Latina. Bogotá, Consejo Episcopal Latinoamericano (CELAM), Depto. de Misiones, 1968. 46 p. (Documento CELAM, 5)

Working document on missionary role of Catholic Church prepared for II General Conference of Latin American bishops by CELAM's Dept. of Missions. [JJB]

8038. Errandonea, Alfredo. Explotación y dominación: el problema de la categoría definitoria de las clases sociales. Montevideo, Editorial Acción Directa, 1972. 71 p. (Col. Concepto y realidad, 3)

Analysis of the categories of exploitation and domination in Marx from "perspectivas libertarias." The author, although unfamiliar with the "Grundrisse," nevertheless mentions in his footnotes most of the recent discussions of Marx. He points out the limitations of the category of exploitation to explain the social aspects of life but interrupts his work just before elaborating upon how the category of domination complements the shortcomings of the former. [AS]

8039. Escola Interanericana de Administração Pública, *Rio.* Reforma administrativa: bibliografia selecionada. Rio, 1973. 81 1.

Bibliography compiled as a result of the I Seminário Interamericano de Reforma Administrativa, held in Rio in 1973, with the participation of Fundação Getúlio Vargas, Ministério do Planejamento e Coordenação Geral, and the Secretaria de Modernização e Reforma Administrativa. Includes some 250 items, principally from the 1960s, on administrative reform and related topics in Latin America, generally, and 16 selected countries. Provides brief author and subject index. Useful reference. [JJB]

Fagen, Richard R. and **Wayne A. Cornelius, Jr.** *eds.* Political power in Latin America: seven confrontations. See *HLAS 36:1691.*

8040. Faleroni, Alberto Daniel. La guerra de la cuarta dimensión. B.A. Luis Lasserre, 1970. 147 p., bibl.

An anti-communist, "know-your-enemy" sort of book which examines the techniques of Marxist subversion (the "war of the fourth dimension") and proposes a strategy for combating it. Hardly worth the attention of serious scholars. [AS]

8041. Fallah, Skaidrite Maliks *comp.* A selected bibliography on urban insurgency and urban unrest in Latin America and other areas. Washington, The American University, Center for Research in Social Systems, 1966. 46 p., bibl.

A short annotated bibliography. Unfortunately, the Latin America items are collected rather indiscriminantly, so are of varied quality. The major portion of the volume is of "other areas" (i.e., Africa and Asia primarily), and consists almost entirely of scholarly journal entries and books. [PBT]

8042. Fals Borda, Orlando. Subversión y desarrollo en América Latina (Sociología del Desarrollo [Barranquilla, Colo.] 1:1 oct. 1971, p. 45-56)

An introduction exploring in some detail the legal/moral meaning of "subversion" is followed by an immediate defense of it as the only way in which to free Latin America from the tentacles of US influence. Cuba under Castro, with Guevara's major influence at work, is seen as a prime example of moral subversion of/attack on the "establishment." University students of the more developed countries today follow a "Latin" script. This may be radical philosophizing, but it is assuredly not sociology. [PBT]

Fitzgibbon, Russell H. Latin America: a panorama of contemporary politics. See *HLAS 36:1692.*

8043. Floridi, Alexis and **Annette Stiefold.** The uncertain alliance: the Catholic Church and labor in Latin America. Miami, Fla., Univ. of Miami, Center for Advanced International Studies, 1973. 108 p., table (Monograph in international affairs)

Surveys three principal trends in Church-supported labor activities ("centrist-reformist," "leftist-reformist," and radical) in an attempt to discern dominant patterns in Latin America. Rather loosely organized and densely written, but useful detail for students of Church and labor. [JJB]

8044. Gonzalez, Edward and **Luigi R. Einaudi.** New patterns of leadership (*in* Einaudi, Luigi R. ed. Beyond Cuba: Latin America takes charge of its future. N.Y., Crane, Russak, 1974, p. 45-57)

Focusing on Allende's Chile and the Peruvian Junta, this interpretative essay strives to identify the principal characteristics of Latin America's emerging leadership. Assertive nationalism, leaning toward experimentation, and a gradual estrangement from the US are proffered as the salient traits of the new leadership. [AS]

8045. González Casanova, Pablo. América y el socialismo: algunas fuentes de error en la predicción política (Sociología del Desarrollo [Barranquilla, Colo.] 1:1, oct. 1971, p. 23-30)

Neomarxian critique by a leading Mexican political scientist of US imperialism and social science. Decries ideological rigidity and calls for reorientation and intensification of research on structural limitations of neoimperialism, which has shown a greater flexibility and adaptive capacity than suggested by Lenin. [JJB]

8046. González Lapeyre, Edison. Aspectos jurídicos del terrorismo. Montevideo, Amalio M. Fernández, 1972. 125 p.

A legal commentary and collection of documents on the subject. Texts of international documents, statements in international forums, and legal opinions make up 60 percent of the volume. While there is some discussion of the Latin American experience in recent years, the framework is worldwide. [PBT]

8047. Guevara, Ernesto. La revolución latinoamericana. Rosario, Arg., Editorial Encuadre, 1973. 188 p.

Reprints of some of Guevara's well-known articles and speeches on the subject of revolution in Latin America. [AS]

8048. Gunder Frank, Andre. Lumpenburguesía: lumpendesarrollo; dependencia, clase y política en Latinoamérica. B.A., Ediciones Periferia, 1973. 196 p., bibl. (Col. Estados Unidos y América Latina)

Frank has been under heavy criticism from radical, intellectual followers of dependency theory. This is his answer: Dependency finally has lost any concrete meaning and the present task is to elaborate what Frank calls "an operational definition" of the concept. It is actually a historical analysis of the linkage between different structures of economic dependency and domestic social groups profiting from such situations. Frank's ego is perhaps too obvious, but his contributions should not be slighted. [AS]

8049. Hablan los jóvenes de América Latina: recientes documentos producidos por la juventud latinoamericana. B.A., Ediciones Búsqueda-Celadec, 1973. 238 p.

Documents reflecting the interpretations given by the youth of 17 Latin American nations to their environment. Interpretations by Christian youth organizations predominate. [AS]

8050. Harris, Louis K. and **Víctor Alba.** The political culture and behavior of Latin America. Kent, Ohio, Kent State Univ. Press, 1974. 221 p., maps, tables.

A useful and somewhat more disciplined attempt by Mr. Alba, with (one supposes) the guidance of Mr. Harris, to recast his critical and insightful views of Latin American political culture in a book designed for college classroom use. See Alba's widely used *The Latin Americans* (item 8002). [PBT]

8051. Hawkins, Carroll. Two democratic labor leaders in conflict: the Latin American revolution and the role of the workers. Lexington, Mass., D.C. Heath, 1973. 140 p., bibl. (Lexington books)

Discussion of problems and prospects of noncommunist labor confederations in Latin America through a comparison of two distinctive leaders: Arturo Jáuregui, Organización Regional Inter-Americana de Trabajadores (ORIT), the pragmatist organizer; and Emilio Máspero, Central Latino Americana de Trabajadores (CLAT), the more radical ideologue. Stresses dysfunctions of external influences on Latin American unions from sources such as AFL-CIO. For historian's comment, see *HLAS 36:1699.* [JJB]

8052. Hoadley, J. Stephen. Social complexity, economic development, and military coups d'etat in Latin America and Asia (JPR, 1/2, 1973, p. 119-120, tables)

Replicates in Asian context procedures employed in

study of military intervention in Latin America. Concludes that hypotheses on Latin America are useful in the Asian case. Interesting cross-cultural comparison. [JJB]

8053. Hodges, Donald C. ed. Philosophy of the urban guerilla: the revolutionary writings of Abraham Guillén. N.Y., William Morrow, 1973. 305 p., bibl.

The reader here confronts the cosmogony of the anarcho-marxist theoretician and activist, an articulate advocate of guerilla violence (by preference) against all that resist. Hodges offers a lengthy quasi-biographical introduction, but the bulk is a selection of Guillen's writings ranked by topic. A useful contribution to the literature; a fascinating adventure into a distinct kind of universe. [PBT]

8054. Hopkins, Jack W. Contemporary research on public administration and bureaucracies in Latin America (LARR, 9:1, Spring 1974, p. 109-139, bibl.)

Surveys major English-language publications on Latin American administration. Useful bibliography and required preliminary reading for research on bureaucracy and public policy. For historian's comment, see *HLAS 36:1701*. [JJB]

8055. El imperialismo. B.A., Editorial Anteo, 1973. 219 p., tables (Pequeña biblioteca marxista leninista)

Four studies previously published by the *World Marxist Review* in which pro-Soviet Marxists validate all of Lenin's predictions. [AS]

8056. Jaguaribe, Helio. Crisis y alternativas de América Latina: reforma o revolución [and] Desarrollo político: una investigación en teoría social y política y un estudio del caso latinoamericano. B.A., Editorial Paidós, 1972. 211 p., bibl., tables (Biblioteca de economía, política, sociedad. Serie mayor, 2)

The third of a three-volume Spanish edition of the author's work in English: *Political development: general theory and a Latin American case study* (one volume). This one concentrates on the explanation of Latin American development and present trends and alternatives. An ambitious undertaking that cannot be underestimated although the denial of viability to Central American and Caribbean countries, the persistence of the dualistic model, and the emphasis on the socio-structural explanations, among others, will probably be debated. [AS]

8057. Jaquette, Jane S. Women in revolutionary movements in Latin America (WRU/JMF, 35:2, May 1973, p. 344-354)

Hypothesizes that feminist concerns in revolutionary movements are related to degree of participation by females, leadership awareness of international currents, and orientation toward peasantry. Reviews historical patterns of Latin America with capsule descriptions of several recent guerrilla movements. [JJB]

8058. Jiménez Castro, Wilburg. Administración pública para el desarrollo integral. México, Fondo de Cultura Económica, 1971. 419 p.

Extensive textbook by experienced scholar-practitioner on details of development administration. Well-grounded in Latin American literature, a useful reference. [JJB]

8059. Jordan, David C. Perón's return, Allende's fall and communism in Latin America (CIDG/O, 17:3, Fall 1973, p. 1025-1052)

Analyzes recent events from perspective of Soviet interests in eroding land base of US sea power while expanding Soviet land bases for worldwide sea power. Emphasizes linkages between Soviet Union, Cuba, and communist parties and marxist factions in Argentina and Chile. [JJB]

Jorrín, Miguel and **John D. Martz.** Latin American political thought and ideology. See *HLAS 36:1493*.

Journal of Inter-American Studies and World Affairs. See *HLAS 36:1494*.

8060. Kaplan, Marcos. Aspectos políticos de la planificación en América Latina. Caracas, Comisión de Administración Pública (CAP), Oficina de Información Administrativa, 1971. 49 p. (Cuadernos para la reforma administrativa, 3)

A primer on the subject, with special references to the peculiarities of planning within the political culture of the region. A very general work, but suggestive. [PBT]

8061. Kenski, Henry C. Teaching Latin American politics at American universities: a survey (LARR, 10:1, Spring 1975, p. 89-104, tables)

A brief examination of responses from teachers of the material which covers teaching techniques, books assigned for purchase, identification of countries discussed, and current level of student interest in Latin America. Also reports personal data concerning individual teachers. [PBT]

8062. Kohl, James and **John Litt** eds. Urban guerrilla warfare in Latin America. Cambridge, Mass., The MIT Press, 1974. 425 p., bibl., maps.

A highly partisan volume, composed of materials on Brazil, Uruguay and Argentina. An introductory essay seeks to justify and to structure out the techniques and approaches to guerrilla warfare in Latin America (making clear the region is representative of victimized countries around the world). Each portion also is introduced by long essays, followed by collections of documents and of selected chronologies. The work is marred by its openly one-sided and deliberately unbalanced introductory approach. While the documents are interesting and useful in themselves, one will have to verify the references in the introductions independently—if they are of any importance to the reader, that is. [PBT]

8063. Kossok, Manfred. The armed forces in Latin America: potential for changes in political and social functions (UM/JIAS, 14:4, Nov. 1972, p. 375-398)

Rejecting Western hypotheses advanced thus far on the behavior of the military in Latin America, the Marxist interpretation of this East German historian suggests the utility of dialectic method within the frame of class analysis. East German bibliographical citations support the interest the article should hold for scholars. [PBT]

8064. ———. Historische Gemeinsamkeiten und Besonderheiten in Lateinamerika von der Unabhängigkeitsrevolution bis zur Gegenwart (Zeitschrift für Geschichtswissenschaft [Berlin, GDR] 20:8, 1972, p. 925-953)

Optimistic analysis of the struggle for liberation and changing social structures of Latin American societies. [H.J. Hoyer]

8065. Lamberg, Robert F. Die Guerilla in Lateinamerika: Theorie und Praxis eines revolutionären Modells. München, FRG, Deutscher Taschenbuch Verlag, 1972. 235 p., bibl., map, tables.

Excellent discussion of guerrilla movements throughout Latin America. Explores how the Latin American guerrilla relates to international communist activities. Case studies of various Latin American countries. [H.J. Hoyer]

Landsberger, Henry A. *ed.* The Church and social change in Latin America. See *HLAS 36:1498.*

8066. Lanning, Eldon. A typology of Latin American political systems (CUNY/CP, 6:3, April 1974, p. 367-394, tables)

Classifies political systems (1960-72) according to: 1) power relations between central authority and politically relevant groups, and 2) dominant organizational basis of political activity. Useful for understanding logic and methodology of typologizing. [JJB]

8067. *Latin American Perspectives.* Vol. 1, No. 1, Spring 1974- . Riverside, Calif.

"Dependency Theory: a Reassessment" is the title of the first issue of this new journal, under the direction of Ronald H. Chilcote. It will focus on theoretical questions of capitalism and socialism not simply to clarify nature of socioeconomic structures but also to investigate political strategies that could transform Latin America. Orientation is clearly put: "We explicitly declare that nothing academic can ever be neutral and that all scholarship has a political function." Participating editors include Latin Americans (e.g., Aníbal Quijano and Fernando Henrique Cardoso) and non-Latin Americans (e.g., James Cockcroft and Dale Johnson). Issues will be devoted to specific topics and countries, with the forthcoming ones on Chile, Mexico, Peronism, and Cuba. [JJB]

8068. López Silva, Claudio. América Latina y sus fuerzas armadas (IAEERI/E, 2:11, mayo/junio 1971, p. 27-50, tables)

Reprints portion of a longer study which holds that the armed forces have both latent and manifest roles. The latter are relatively obvious: security, order, social support in catastrophes, education, and contribution to development. The former include patriotic symbolism, cohesion and national integration through influence over those who serve in the ranks, continuity of traditions and of formal democracy, and solidarity with the bloc of western nations. But in recent years they also have appeared as promoters of social change. The tone of the paper is textbook in nature, and it is based on a fairly broad citation of conventional middle-road literature. [PBT]

Lowenthal, Abraham F. United States policy toward Latin America: liberal, radical, and bureaucratic perspectives. See item 8754.

8069. Lumsden, Ian. Dependency, revolution, and development in Latin America (CIIA/IJ, 28:3, Summer 1973, p. 525-551)

Critically assesses development accomplishments of revolutionary regimes in Cuba, Peru, and Chile (pre-1973) in context of weakening or breaking ties of dependency with developed countries. Sees a revolutionary potential in lower classes (in contrast to new orthodoxy of nonrevolutionary proletariat) and is critical of development potential of state capitalism. [JJB]

8070. Lussu, Emilio. Teoría de los procesos insurreccionales contemporáneos. B.A., Editorial Tiempo Contemporáneo, 1972. 272 p. (Col. Crítica ideológica, 1)

Spanish translation of the Italian 2. ed. of an insurrectional manual originally published in 1936. The author, probably a Communist Party member, shows a high level of familiarity with the art as developed since Blanqui and Mazzini. For the present reviewer, it is much more knowledgeable and instructive than the contemporary tracts by Guevara or Debray. [AS]

8071. McNall, Scott. Military and paramilitary forces in Latin America: an analysis of the socioeconomic factors contributing to their dominance. Tempe, Arizona State Univ., Center for

Latin American Studies, 1973. 39 1., bibl., (Special study, 11)

Discusses intercorrelations among 26 variables concerning socioeconomic characteristics and military behavior in 17 countries. Rather crude empiricism somewhat offset by attempts to relate findings to propositions drawn from the literature. [JJB]

8072. Mariátegui, José Carlos and others. El marxismo en América Latina. B.A., Centro Editor de América Latina, 1972. 140 p. (Biblioteca fundamental del hombre moderno, 58)

Introductory notes by Chilean Socialist leader, Carlos Altamirano, summarize evolution of Marxian thought in Latin America. Contents are:
José Carlos Mariátegui "El Problema de la Tierra" p. 13-48
Julio Antonio Mella "La Lucha Revolucionaria contra el Imperialismo" p. 49-72
"Tesis de Pulacayo" p. 73-88
Ernesto Che Guevara "Excepción Histórica o Vanguardia en la Lucha Anticolonialista?" p. 89-100
Carlos Romero "Las Clases Sociales en América Latina" p. 101-124
Ruy Mauro Marini "Subdesarrollo y Revolución" p. 125-140. [JJB]

8073. Marxistas y cristianos en la construcción del socialismo. Bogotá, Centro de Investigación y Acción Social (CIAS), 1971. 79 p. (Documento de trabajo, 8)

Reprints documents and essays (e.g., by Paul VI and Chilean Bishops) from continuing dialogue on proper relationship between Marxists and Catholics. [JJB]

8074. Matos Mar, José comp. La dominación de América Latina. B.A., Amorrortu Editores, 1972. 181 p.

Contributions by leading dependency theorists:
Helio Jaguaribe "La Asistencia Técnica Extranjera y el Desarrollo Nacional" p. 7-28
Celso Furtado "La Hegemonía de Estados Unidos y el Futuro de América Latina" p. 29-52
Torcuato S. Di Tella "Tensiones Sociales en los Países de la Periferia" p. 53-68
Espartaco "La 'Crisis Latinoamericana' y su Marco Externo" p. 69-103
Osvaldo Sunkel "Política Nacional de Desarrollo y Dependencia Externa" p. 104-142
Fernando H. Cardoso and Enzo Faletto "Dependencia y Desarrollo en América Latina" p. 143-180. [JJB]

8075. Maullin, Richard L. and **Luigi R. Einaudi.** Elections and the populist challenge (*in* Einaudi, Luigi R. *ed.* Beyond Cuba: Latin America takes charge of its future. N.Y., Crane, Russak, 1974, p. 59-72)

Elections serve functions other than selection between competing elites and policies. Suggests alternative functions of elections (e.g., demonstrations of support) and assesses future impacts of urbanization and communications technology for parties and elections. [JJB]

8076. May, William F. Terrorism as strategy and ecstasy (NSSR/SR, 41:2, Summer 1974, p. 277-298)

Brilliant and wide-ranging analysis of the *weltanschauung* and metaphysics of terrorism, as well as of terrorism as a political tool. Stresses how modern technology has favored the development of the latter and how the technological environment in which we live has fostered the anomie and isolation in which nihilism (the celebration of destruction) thrives. In addition to discussing individual terrorists such as the Russian Nechaev and terrorist organizations such as the IRA Provisionals, the Algerian FLN, the Latin American guerrillas, the author further illuminates his point with the writings of Dostoievski, Mishima, Malraux, and Hannah Arendt's classic *On violence*. [Asst. Ed.]

8077. Miguens, José Enrique. Una nueva metodología para el estudio de los golpes militares en Latinoamérica. (IAEERI/E, 2, julio/agosto 1969, p. 153-166)

Very useful and systematic examination of golpes, as written up and analyzed by specialists in the US and elsewhere, with reference to Latin America. After stating that the methodology used in general has been defective (and citing instances of each typology of errors) author offers his own suggested method: the armed forces should be considered a collectivity, with its own subculture. [PBT]

Milenky, Edward S. The politics of regional organization in Latin America: the Latin American Free Trade Association. See *HLAS 36:1709*.

8078. Monroe, Elizabeth and **Robert Mabro** *eds*. Oil producers and consumers: conflict or cooperation. Roma, Center for Mediterranean Studies, 1974. 76 p., map, tables.

Synthesis of an International Seminar held in Rome, 24-28 June 1974 at the Center for Mediterranean Studies. With the participation of 26 other persons (none of them Latin American) oil problems through 1980 are discussed. Although the focus is on the Middle East, insofar as producers are concerned, the world's many problems growing out of quantities of supplies, and price levels, are presented succinctly and usefully. A sophisticated piece of extraordinary value. [PBT]

8079. Moss, Robert. La guerrilla urbana. Traducción [por] Natividad Martín Moro. Madrid, Editora Nacional, 1973. 309 p., bibl. (Serie Ciencias sociales. Mundos abiertos)

A spanish translation of this informative work covering urban guerrillas and terrorism from the Narodnaya Volya to the Tupamaros. It tries to explain the limits and possibilities of this type of revolutionary warfare.

A chapter each on Brazil and Uruguay. A good overview. [AS]

8080. Needler, Martin. Detente: impetus for change in Latin America? (CU/JIA, 28:2, 1974, p. 219-228)

A modest article that does not address itself to its title. Rather, it is a brief overview of happenings to communist and left-of-communist parties and groups in the past few years. Of some interest for neophyte students, but hardly for specialists. [PBT]

8081. Nieuwenhove, J. van. Libération et théologie en Amérique Latine (UCL/CD, 6:3, 1974, p. 615-630)

This is essentially a review article of "theologies" of liberation proposed for Latin America, in which a large number of writers suggest questions and approaches considered critical. [PBT]

8082. Ochoa Campos, Moisés. La revolución de la juventud. B.A., Plus Ultra, 1973. 144 p.

A confusing book. It opens with an image of the hippies in Piccadilly, followed with some remarks on the Cordoba student movement of 1918, and then wanders through the most diverse topics. There is also a cryptic reference to the first survey among world youth. Apparently, the author is reserving his data for another volume. [AS]

8083. O'Donnell, Guillermo A. Modernization and bureaucratic-authoritarianism: studies in South American politics. Berkeley, Univ. of California, Institute of International Studies, 1973. 219 p., bibl., tables (Politics of modernization series, 9)

Challenging conventional development theory, which assumes a linear relationship between modernization and pluralism, explores alternative hypothesis that bureaucratic-authoritarianism may be outcome of modernization in Latin American context. Particular emphasis on Brazil and Argentina; a first-rate contribution to comparative literature on political modernization. [JJB]

8084. Payne, James L. Incentive theory and political process. Lexington, Mass., D.C. Heath, 1972. 164 p., tables (Lexington books)

The prolific and incisive Dr. Payne continues to apply and expand methodology and technique first undertaken in his graduate period books, on Peru and (especially) Colombia. Arguing that politicians also have needs (incentives), he analyzes data derived from an extended interview schedule with 37 respondents. Payne's work here, as elsewhere, is marked by succinct, explicit and literate premises and writing style. The book contains many reconstructed quotations from respondents as well as sharp analysis. [PBT]

8085. Petras, James. Clases sociales y política en América Latina (Ruedo Ibérico [Paris] 22/24, dic. 1968/mayo 1969, p. 3-24)

Surveys literature on intra- and inter-class political behavior to account for general patterns of conformity and exceptional cases of revolution. Summary of literature is useful source of testable generalizations but speculation on potential future revolutionary activity is sketchy. [JJB]

8086. Pike, Fredrick B. and Thomas Stritch eds. The new corporatism: social-political structures in the Iberian world. South Bend, Ind., Notre Dame Univ., 1974. 218 p.

Reprints essays from *The Review of Politics* (36:1, Jan. 1974) with additions of Stritch's introduction and Pike's essay on Spain. A valuable collection, with a particularly interesting dialog between Schmitter and Wiarda on origins and nature of Latin American corporatism. Includes index. Contents:
Thomas Stritch "Introduction" p. xiii-xxii
Howard J. Wiarda "Corporatism and Development in the Iberic-Latin World: Persistent Strains and New Variations" p. 3-33
James M. Malloy "Authoritarianism, Corporatism and Mobilization in Peru" p. 34-51
Philippe C. Schmitter "Still the Century of Corporatism?" p. 85-131
Fredrick B. Pike "Corporatism and Latin American-United States Relations" p. 132-170
Fredrick B. Pike "The New Corporatism in Franco's Spain and some Latin American Perspectives" p. 171-210. [JJB]

8087. Poitras, Guy E. Change and Latin American politics (The Political Science Reviewer [Hampden-Sydney, Va.] 4, Fall 1974, p. 229-264)

Based upon a review of 15 books (from period 1971-73), asserts that none of the contributions substantially boost the general comprehension of change. [JJB]

8088. Political violence: Latin America; violence and urban growth, kidnapping and coups (NGIZ/IS, 26:8, 22 April 1972, p. 756-759, tables)

Reports interesting cross-cultural data on incidence of kidnappings and coups (and attempted coups) for 1971. [JJB]

8089. Puhle, Hans-Jürgen ed. Perspectivas del progreso: algunas consideraciones sobre las tendencias actuales de las ciencias sociales. Hannover, FRG, Verlag für Literatur und Zeitgeschehen [and] Fundación Friedrich Ebert-Stiftung [Bonn, FRG] [and] Instituto Latinoamericano de Investigaciones Sociales (ILDIS) [Santiago], 1969. 120 p.

Includes two papers by Carlos Fortún and Marcos Kaplan on "Comparative Politics" and "State and Development," both on Latin America. The former, on an introductory level, shows the usual dissatisfaction with the state of the discipline. The latter has been expanded since it was published here. [AS]

8090. Radiografía de un arsenal (Visión [México] 15 marzo 1975, p. 10-15, illus.)

Useful short review of weapons strengths of the armed forces of the countries of Latin America, together with some overview of weapons producing capabilities. The article concludes with suggestions about how these new weapons might be used, implying that they will not be used for internal pacification. [PBT]

8091. Rankin, Richard C. The expanding institutional concerns of the Latin American military establishments: a review article (LARR, 9:1, Spring 1974, p. 81-108)

Critical analysis of a large number of books and articles on Latin American military-political role players, most of them by US specialists. Rankin is much impressed by the recent pieces by José Nun and José Miguens, and he sets them as criteria in his generally adverse comments on the work of others. A useful conceptual starting point for students. For historian's comment, see HLAS 36:1518. [PBT]

Ratliff, William E. ed. Yearbook on Latin American communist affairs, 1971. See HLAS 36:1718.

8092. Ray, David. The dependency model of Latin American underdevelopment: three basic fallacies (UM/JIAS, 15:1, Feb. 1973, p. 4-20, bibl.)

Constructive criticism which points to: 1) limiting dependency to capitalist relationships, 2) viewing all foreign investment as detrimental, and 3) dichotomizing the dependency/nondependency variable as important flaws in dependency theory. Trenchantly argued. [JJB]

8093. *Revista del Centro de Investigación y Acción Social.* Año 22, No. 221, abril 1973- . B.A.

Think of CIAS, in the Latin American context, as a Jesuit Brookings. Principal article of this number is a discussion of liberation theology. [JJB]

8094. Ronfeldt, David F. Patterns of civil-military rule (*in* Einaudi, Luigi R. ed. Beyond Cuba: Latin America takes charge of its future. N.Y., Crane, Russak, 1974, p. 107-126)

Distinctions between military and civilian regimes have become misleading for understanding Latin American politics, since virtually all countries are governed by civil-military coalitions. The government's form depends upon the nature of the elite coalition as well as its policies and institutional bases. A typology of civil-military regimes in the 1970s is developed, and the perspectives for "new civil-military clerical oligarchies" are discussed in this insightful and highly recommended article. [AS]

8095. ———— and **Luigi R. Einaudi.** Prospects for violence (*in* Einaudi, Luigi R. ed. Beyond Cuba: Latin America takes charge of its future. N.Y., Crane, Russak, 1974, p. 35-43)

Prospects for political violence in Latin America during the 1970s are analyzed, presupposing the continuation of present Cuban inaction in supporting insurgency. Violence will probably persist, but as an ever-increasing threat to the established order, which will most likely co-opt the leftist position. [AS]

Ronning, C. Neale. Human rights and humanitarian laws in the Western Hemisphere. See item 8782a.

8096. Rosenbaum, H. Jon. Arms and security in Latin America: recent developments. Washington, The Smithsonian Institution, Woodrow Wilson Center for Scholars, 1971. 30 p., maps, tables (International affairs series, 101)

An unfortunately diminutive study of the subject, whose purpose is stated as the provision of current data toward understanding Latin American military developments. Pt. 1 sketches possible areas and causes of disputes and threats, together with mechanisms for political handling of these questions. Pt. 2 discusses materiel procurement, by purchase and by local manufacture; the emphasis in this portion is on Argentina and Brazil. Includes 12 somewhat suggestive tables whose data cutoff date was 1 Jan. 1971. [PBT]

8097. Ruddle, Kenneth and **Philip Gillette** eds. Latin American political statistics: supplement to the *Statistical Abstract of Latin America.* Introduction by Luigi Einaudi. Los Angeles, Univ. of California, Latin American Center, 1972. 128 p.

Encyclopedic coverage of political personalities, parties, elections statistics for 24 countries of the Americas (the conventional 20 plus Barbados, Trinidad and Tobago, Guyana, and Jamaica). Data are not complete in all cases (and the preface does much complaining about the problems of data collecting), but it is a most useful reference volume. [PBT]

8098. Ruiz García, Enrique. Subdesarrollo y liberación. Madrid, Alianza Editorial, 1972. 365 p. (El libro de bolsillo. Sección: humanidades)

In a thoughtful volume that attempts to discuss nearly all of the subcategories of the "Third World" the author argues that relations between the developed countries on the one hand and the underdeveloped on the other cannot be resolved through ideological hostility but through reformation of both values and operations in social, political and economic areas. [PBT]

8099. Russell, Charles A.; James A.

Miller; and **Robert E. Hildner.** The urban guerrilla in Latin America: a select bibliography (LARR, 9:1, Spring 1974, p. 37-39)

A short survey of viewpoints about guerrilla activities and purposes in Latin America, together with an annotated bibliography of 261 items. [PBT]

8100. Sacchi, Hugo M. El movimiento obrero en América Latina. B.A., Centro Editor de América Latina, 1972. 109 p., tables (Biblioteca fundamental del hombre moderno)

A short history of the labor movement. An introductory chapter scans the hemisphere, with emphasis on the countries covered in individual chapters: Argentina, Chile, Brazil and Bolivia. [PBT]

8101. Santos, Theotonio dos. Socialismo o fascismo: el nuevo carácter de la dependencia y el dilema latinoamericano. B.A. Ediciones Periferia, 1972. 342 p., tables (Col. Estados Unidos y América Latina)

The continent is undergoing radical polarization, states the author; capitalism will survive only under fascist conditions. The text is highly detailed and implemented by extended discussion of Brazil in particular (but not exclusively). Dos Santos argues that socialism is virtually inevitable. [PBT]

8102. Schmitter, Philippe C. *ed.* Military rule in Latin America: function, consequences and perspectives. Beverly Hills, Calif., Sage Publications *in cooperation with* The Univ. of Chicago, 1973. 322 p., tables (Sage research progress series on war, revolution and peacekeeping, 3)

Five papers (of seven) presented at a special conference on arms control and foreign policy in 1972 at the Univ. of Chicago are here assembled. One by Rouquie (see *HLAS 35:7466*) has been abridged and also reprinted. The other four appear for the first time. Schmitter (who prepared one of the papers) implements the collection with a literate and useful summation of them all, and advances a thesis of his own about the future of military entrepreneurship in the hemisphere. At a time in which radical posturing about the military is still the vogue, this is a calming and useful volume. [PBT]

8103. Schteingart, Martha *ed. and comp.* Urbanización y dependencia en América Latina. B.A., Ediciones Siap, 1973. 372 p., tables (Programa editorial de la Sociedad Interamericana de Planificación)

A distinguished collection of papers on urbanization by 15 writers (14 of them Latin Americans) with long records of research and publication in their professional fields. Eight general papers, only a few of which make much of an issue of dependency, are followed by case studies of six countries. [PBT]

8104. Seminário sobre Indicadores Sociais do Desenvolvimento Nacional na América Latina, *Rio, 1972.* Crise e mudança social. Organização e introdução de Cândido Mendes. Rio, Livraria Eldorado Tijuca, 1974. 306 p., tables (Col. América Latina)

Ten political sociologists contribute individual papers to a 1972 Seminar on Social Indicators of National Development in Latin America, Rio. The material is technically and conceptually sophisticated, and concerned with concepts and values shared by contemporary social scientists throughout the world. The majority of the papers concern Brazil, but since several writers are not Brazilian, other parts of Latin America also are discussed. [PBT]

8105. Sepúlveda, Alberto. El militarismo desarrollista en América Latina (CM/FI, 13:1, julio/sept. 1972, p. 45-65)

Granted new military regimes with clearly defined developmentalist goals, the need is to determine what their purposes are and what variables affect the achievement of those goals. The paper seeks to establish some predictive principles, and thus incorporates several hypotheses. The author describes it as a step toward theory, and thus deals with a substantial amount of fact. In conclusion some useful generalizations concerning Brazil's possible fragility (under military leadership) are offered. [PBT]

8106. Signos de liberación: testimonios de la iglesia en América Latina, 1969-1973. Lima, Centro de Estudios y Publicaciones, 1973. 294 p., plates.

Compilation of Church documents growing out of progressive trends since 1968 CELAM meeting of Medellín, Colo. Organized along lines of country diagnoses and prescriptions for change. Useful collection. [JJB]

8107. Smith, David Horton. Latin American student activism: participation in formal volunteer organizations by university students in six Latin cultures. Lexington, Mass., Lexington Books, 1973. 169 p., tables (Voluntary action research series)

Comparative study of student activism, empirically operationalized as membership in formal volunteer organizations of many kinds and leadership in formal student volunteer groups. It is based on data collected for the Comparative National Development Project derived from surveys made in 1964-65 among university students from Colombia, Mexico, Panama, Paraguay, Puerto Rico, and Uruguay. Considerable use of sophisticated methods of statistical analysis. Companion to the previous volume in the same series: Arthur Liebmann; Kenneth N. Walker; and Myron Glazer *Latin American university students: a six nation study* (Cambridge, Mass., Harvard Univ. Press, 1972). [AS]

8108. Solaún, Mauricio and **Michael A.**

Quinn. Sinners and heretics: the politics of military intervention in Latin America. Urbana, Univ. of Illinois Press, 1973. 228 p., bibl., tables (Illinois studies in the social sciences, 58)

A sociologist and a political scientist offer an explanatory framework for comparing 30 successful military coups in Latin America between 1943-67. They differentiate between precipitating and predisposing causes and use eight descriptive indicators to operationalize explanatory variables found in the literature. Since the bulk of what they call "primary data" comes exclusively from English-language sources, among them *Time Magazine,* and operationalization procedures are not made explicit here, the final results of the study are mixed. For historian's comment, see *HLAS 36:1723.* [AS]

8109. Stevens, Evelyn P. *Marianismo:* the other face of *machismo* in Latin America (*in* Pescatello, Ann ed. Female and male in Latin America: essays. Pittsburgh, Pa., Univ. of Pittsburgh Press, 1973, p. 89-101)

Traces historical origins of cult of feminity and the complementary dynamic between machismo and marianismo in Latin America. Speculates that role satisfaction inherent in marianismo will promote continuity in this cultural pattern. [JJB]

8110. ——————. The prospects for a women's liberation movement in Latin America (WRU/JMF, 35:2, May 1973, p. 313-321)

Compares sources of women's liberation movements in North Atlantic countries with prevailing situation in Latin America. Suggests that attitudinal factors (marianismo) and sociopolitical conditions (labor surplus and excluded marginal groups) will hinder similar liberation movements in the short run. [JJB]

8111. Strickon, Arnold and **Sidney M. Greenfield** eds. Structure and process in Latin America: patronage, clientage, and power systems. Albuquerque, Univ. of New Mexico Press, 1972. 256 p., bibl., tables (School of American research books. Advanced seminar series)

Papers prepared for 1969 seminar of this title held at Santa Fe, and followed by a panel at the LXXI Annual Meeting of the American Anthropological Association. Carefully prepared through several years of consultations. The product is a carefully-conceived set of papers that crosscut the phenomenon of social and political power at various levels (from that of local government to international relations) and in societies at various stages of development (from Argentina to Bolivia or Colombia). The first two chapters examine in detail the functional and methodological tasks that must be undertaken in patronage studies and set the criteria for the works that follow. Contents: Arnold Strickon and Sidney M. Greenfield "The Analysis of Patron-Client Relationships: an Introduction" p. 1-17
William T. Stuart "The Explanation of Patron-Client Systems: some Structural and Ecological Perspectives" p. 19-42
Arnold Strickon and Carlos Felipe "Kinsman, Patron, and Friend" p. 43-69
Sidney M. Greenfield "Charwomen, Cesspools, and Road Building: an Examination of Patronage, Clientage, and Political Power in Southeastern Minas Gerais" p. 71-100
Dwight B. Heath "New Patrons for Old: Changing Patron-Client Relationships in the Bolivian Yungas" p. 101-137
Robert W. Shirley "Patronage and Cooperation: an Analysis from São Paulo State" p. 139-157
Esther Hermitte "Ponchos, Weaving, and Patron-Client Relations in Northwest Argentina" p. 159-177
Nancie L. González "Patron-Client Relationships at the International Level" p. 178-209
William T. Stuart "On the Nonrecurrence of Patronage in San Miguel de Sema" p. 211-236. [PBT]

8112. Suárez, Pablo. Cuando la clase obrera está en el poder. B.A., Editorial Anteo, 1973. 31 p., tables.

When the working class is in power (i.e., when marxism-leninism are the guidelines of power, under the guidance of the government in Moscow) this is what occurs in the way of economic growth, says this party tract. Although this work is more a matter of praise of the USSR than guideline for Latin America, it has some interesting recapitulatory and flatly primer-like views for the generalist. [PBT]

8113. Taufic, Camilo. Periodismo y lucha de clases: la información como forma del poder político. B.A., Ediciones de la Flor, 1974. 215 p.

Published originally in Chile in 1973 (and destroyed in the coup aftermath) this is a marxian analysis of the role of the press as a phenomenon of superstructure in both the socialist and capitalist countries, as well as in developed and developing ones. [JJB]

8114. Thesing, Josef. Política y desarrollo. Bogotá, Instituto Nacional de Estudios Sociales (INES), 1973. 113 p., bibl.

Argues for greater priority to normative dimensions, such as liberty and dignity, in study of development. Economic development requires prior reforms in political structures. [JJB]

8115. Thomas, Dani B. and **Richard B. Craig.** Student dissent in Latin America: toward a comparative analysis (LARR, 8:1, Spring 1973, p. 71-93)

A specific effort to define comparatively forms and styles of student behavior, in contrast to the mere historical chronicling of the fact of dissent. Data are drawn from the period 1961-66; mathematical analysis is employed to develop correlations of student actions with a range of independent variables. For historian's comment, see *HLAS 36:1727.* [PBT]

8116. Tierra Nueva. Estudios socio-teológicos en América Latina. Centro de Estudios para el Desarrollo e Integración de América Latina. Vol. 1, No. 1, abril 1972-   . Bogotá.

New journal seeks to draw upon social sciences to achieve a kind of applied theology relevant to contemporary Latin American conditions. Articles: "La Justicia en el Mundo: Comentario y Crítica" p. 27-36
"La Violencia y el Cristiano con Selección Bibliográfica" p. 37-50
"¿Agonía o Resurgimiento? Reflexiones Teológicas acerca de la 'Contestación en la Iglesia, con Selección Bibliográfica" p. 51-59
"El Desarrollo y sus Distintas Acepciones Básicas, con Selección Bibliográfica" p. 60-69
"Estructura, Cultura y Educación" p. 70-76. [JJB]

8117. Torres, James F. Concentration of political power and levels of economic development in Latin American countries (JDA, 7:3, April 1973, p. 397-410, tables)

The relationship between the two variables is reexamined for causality in this very short piece. The author hopes to provoke rethinking by his readers. [PBT]

8118. _____. A new—and partial—approach to measurement of political power in Latin American countries (UU/WPQ, 26:2, June 1973, p. 302-313, tables)

Torres applies his theoretical analysis concerning correlation of political power with economic development (see item 8117) to data collected by written survey of the views of Latin American specialists among social scientists. [PBT]

8119. Troncoso, Oscar. La rebelión estudiantil en la sociedad de posguerra. B.A., Centro Editor de América Latina, 1973. 142 p. (Biblioteca fundamental del hombre moderno, 106)

Traces the student rebellion from the Argentine University Reform of 1918 through the Cuban Revolution to the student unrest of the 1960s in Europe, the US and the Third World. The common factor shared by the disturbances in Europe and Latin America is idealization of Castro's Cuba. The road has led from reform, which destroyed the vestiges of the 19th century, to revolution, which is the anticipation of the 21st century. [AS]

8120. Turner, Frederick C. Catholicism and nationalism in Latina America (ICISR/S, 18:4, 1971, p. 593-607, tables)

Attempts to correlate indicators of nationalism and Catholicism to explore causal interrelationships. This is a rather rough research note on work in progress. Also published in *American Behavioral Scientist* (17:6, July/Aug. 1974, p. 845-864, bibl., tables). [JJB]

8121. United States. Department of State. Arms Control and Disarmament Agency. World military expenditures and arms trade: 1963-1973. Washington, GPO, 1975. 123 p., tables.

A short introduction indicates the types of data presented. Tables comprise most of the study (p. 14-123) and include both raw data of various types and adjusted data for all countries of the world. This is an essential volume for specialists as well as generalists. [PBT]

8122. _____. _____. Bureau of Public Affairs. Arms sales in Latin America. Washington, 1973. 31 p., tables (News release)

Short study by the Bureau of Intelligence and Research from unclassified documents. The period covered, 1967-72, witnessed a sharp momentary increase in sales by European suppliers, and some increase by US public and private suppliers. The material is indicative but sparse enough to frustrate the seeking of solid data. [PBT]

8123. Vega Carballo, José Luis. La crisis de los partidos políticos tradicionales. Ciudad Universitaria Rodrigo Facio, C.R., Univ. de Costa Rica, Facultad de Ciencias y Letras, Depto. Ciencias del Hombre, 1973. 17 p.

Originally published as newspaper articles, this short, orthodox marxist approach to the topic holds that parties reflect the social structure and this is tied to the productive forces. Merely generalizations; total lack of empirical references. [AS]

8124. Verner, Joel G. Los sistemas de selección de presidentes en América Latina, 1930-1970 (CM/FI, 13[52]:4, abril/junio 1973, p. 490-512, tables)

How have presidents been selected in the 20 Latin American countries in the indicated period? What have been their career characteristics, their durability in office, and their prior political activities? This is an interesting exercise in sketching out raw data but hardly a hypothesis about leaders or political systems. [PBT]

8125. Vernon, Raymond. Sovereignty at bay: the multinational spread of U.S. enterprises. N.Y., Basic Books, 1971. 326 p., tables (Harvard multinational enterprise series)

The author foresees troubled relations between multinational companies and national governments unless the nature and function of these forms of management and developmental ownership are understood more adequately and appropriate national (official) policies are formulated. On the other hand, he rejects the notion of their unmanageability and, surely, of their invidiousness in the world's changing circumstances. While the book is concerned with worldwide facts, Vernon's prior work on Latin America is evident and in balance. [PBT]

8126. Walton, John. Political development and economic development: a regional assessment of contemporary theories (RU/SCID, 7:1, Spring 1972, p. 39-63, tables)

Theoretically interesting and methodologically imaginative essay which attempts to operationalize and explore interrelationships between political and economic development as conceptualized in contemporary development theory. Employs standardized case comparison of four subnational regions (Monterrey and Guadalajara in Mexico; Medellín and Cali in Colombia). Finds no patterned relationship among equality, capacity, and differentiation and indicators of economic development. Suggests a more fruitful direction for research is "structural factors related to comprehensive and coordinated organizational forms which, in turn, are explicitly related to varieties of economic development." [JJB]

8127. Ward, Douglas S. Needed: effective educational assistance to Latin America (JDA, 6:1, Oct. 1971, p. 3-8)

Short but pungent critical treatment of past and current US AID policies toward aid to schools and public education in Latin America. The paper is both provocative and suggestive of useful changes. [PBT]

8128. Williams, Edward J. and Freeman J. Wright. Latin American politics: a developmental approach. Palo Alto, Calif., Mayfield, 1975. 480 p., bibl., maps, plates, tables.

A college text. Material is handled on a functional, conceptual, or problem approach, rather than on a country-by-country style. [PBT]

8129. Williams, J. Earl. The role of research in Latin American labor organizations (AIFLD/R, 3:2, 1971, p. 19-29)

Short suggestive statement of the advantages labor unions might gain by seeking more exact information concerning management and investor practices through research. [PBT]

8130. Wöhlcke, Manfred. Lateinamerika in der Presse: Inhaltsanalytische Untersuchung der Lateinamerika-Berichterstattung in folgenden Presseorganen: Die Welt, Frankfurter Allgemeine, Neue Zürcher Zeitung, Handelsblatt, Le Monde, Neues Deutschland und Der Spiegel. Hamburg, FRG, Institut für Iberoamerika-Kunde [and] Ernst Kelett Verlag [Stuttgart, FRG] 1973. 159 p., illus., tables. (Schriftenreihe des Instituts für Iberoamerika-Kunde, 18)

Analysis of Latin American coverage found in major German, Swiss, and French newspapers and magazines, including *Die Welt, Frankfurter Allgemeinde, Neue Zuricher Zeitung, Handelsblatt, Le Monde, Neues Deutschland* and *Der Spiegel.* Work analyzes: 1) proportion of coverage devoted to Latin America; 2) countries which have been given most/least coverage; 3) problems of objective reporting, and 4) theoretical considerations. [H.J. Hoyer]

8131. Wolfe, Marshall. Development: images, conceptions, criteria, agents, choices (UNECLA/B, 18:1/2, 1973, p. 1-12)

Surveys dominant images of "development" current in political and academic discourse. Argues that "development" must be based upon national societal values conditioned by that which is situationally feasible. Task of social scientist is to aid political leadership in structuring choices which contribute toward attainment of goals. Essentially reformist-incremental in tone, a lucidly argued statement. [JJB]

8132. World Peace Council, *Helsinki.* Information Centre. The World Peace Council and Latin America: documents, 1969-1972. Helsinki, 1972. 32 p.

Declarations, appeals, messages of solidarity, etc., by this well-known pro-Soviet organization. [AS]

8133. Yager, Joseph A. and others. Energy and U.S. foreign policy: a report to the Energy Policy Project of the Ford Foundation. Cambridge, Mass., Ballinger, 1974. 473 p., maps, tables.

General survey of world energy problems with emphasis on US policy. Philip Musgrove discusses Latin American petroleum production in Ch. 5 (p. 69-88); Robert M. Dunn, Jr., lumps together the less-developed petroleum importing countries in Ch. 10 (p. 163-181); and Jerome Kahan discusses nuclear energy and its growth as well as safety problems in Pt. 6 (p. 331-382). Although the book's focus is worldwide, the material on Latin America is useful. [PBT]

MEXICO, CENTRAL AMERICA, THE CARIBBEAN AND THE GUIANAS

ANDRES SUAREZ
Professor of Political Science
Center for Latin American Studies
University of Florida

THE GREAT EXPECTATIONS RAISED BY COMPARATIVE POLITICS have not been fulfilled. One of the outstanding practitioners of the art, Gabriel Almond, recently acknowledged: "A mood of disillusionment appears to be sweeping the field of comparative politics . . ." Since these words were published (1969), the situation has not improved. Joseph LaPalombara suggested a way out of the present crisis: instead of the initial pretension, comparing political systems as totalities, we should restrict our concern to such political components as parties, elites, etc. One example in this direction within our geographic area is item 8205. But it is doubtful whether following this advice will allow the discipline to regain its vigor and appeal. Two other research strategy decisions are needed to restore comparative politics to its original purposes. First, to concentrate our attention on small units where significant similarities have been observed frequently. Second, to favor areas where the cooperation of qualified native scholars can be expected. The region meets both conditions. Not only are commonalities plentiful among the Caribbean islands as well as in Central America, but the emergence of a growing generation of area scholars is attested by items 8201 and 8203-8204.

The contribution by Cubans should add a new incentive to the common effort, since creative Marxism does offer original perspectives for the study of neo-colonialism, dependency, class struggle, etc., all problems of relevance to the area. Unfortunately after Guevara's death and the closing of *Pensamiento Crítico,* Cuban intellectuals have returned to the dry formulas of the Soviet manuals, increasingly limiting their interest to the domestic scene. An example of this nation-centered preoccupation is apparent in item 8236 which claims to have used documentation from the nationalized foreign firms.

Examples of comparativeness are few in this *HLAS* section. Cuba continues to inspire much interest with some significant contributions (see items 8208, 8219 and 8239). Although many of the other works reviewed attest to the professionalism of the authors and occasionally offer some deep insight, neither originality nor methodological sophistication are particularly noticeable.

MEXICO

8134. Alisky, Marvin. CONASUPO: a Mexican agency which makes low-income workers feel their government cares (IAMEA, 27:3, Winter 1973/1974, p. 47-59)

A study examining the significance of the Compañia Nacional de Subsistencias Populares (CONASUPO) as a symbol of the institutionalized reform of the Revolution. This government corporation, which provides the Mexican poor with cheap markets and assists them in selling their products, has recently begun a program of intergovernmental cooperation to upgrade farm production skills. With only one percent of Mexico's total retail food sales, CONASUPO does not threaten private retailing, but has served to combat inflation and to prepare campesinos to help themselves.

8135. ———. Mexico versus Malthus: national trends (CUH, 66/67:393, May 1974, p. 200-203, 227-230)

An examination of Mexican national trends in work, consumption, transportation, and communications with special emphasis on the problems created by the population explosion.

8136. Alvear Acevedo, Carlos. Corrientes sociales y políticas. México, Editorial Tradición, 1973. 141 p. (Col. de Estudios políticos, 3)

General overview of modern social trends since the Industrial Revolution from the viewpoint of social catholicism. The purpose: to stop communism and "Liberal corrosion."

8137. Anda, Gustavo de. ¿Hacia donde lleva Echeverría a México? México, n.p., 1972. 1 v. (Unpaged) illus.

Journalistic articles criticizing Mexican President Echeverría from the viewpoint of private enterprise and anticommunism. The intellectual level of the publication can be surmised from the title of one of the articles: "Echeverría, ¿Es Marxista-Leninista?"

8138. Bataillon, Claude. Mexique: le Président Echeverría a la moitié du chemin (FDD/NED [Problèmes d'Amérique Latine, 32] 1974, p. 7-58, tables)

A survey of the first three years of the Echeverría term in the presidency: political and administrative style, political practices, development policy, economic research, and foreign policy. The short paper is supported by detailed annexes, and a chronology for 1972 and (in much greater detail) 1973. The piece supports the generally high quality of the Latin American series of the French journal *Notes et Etudes Documentaires.* [PBT]

8139. Brading, David A. Los orígenes del nacionalismo mexicano. Traducción de Soledad Loaeza Grave. México, Secretaría de Educación Pública, 1973. 223 p. (SepSetentas, 82)

Traces the development of "creole patriotism" from its beginning in the colonial period, through its maturation in the independence struggle, to its transformation into Mexican nationalism. This evolution is seen as largely the result of the works of Carlos María de Bustamante and Father Servando Teresa de Mier, who used *indigenismo* to deny Spain the right to rule Mexico. The analysis is based primarily on the works of these two men as well as other published sources.

8140. Cárdenas ante el mundo: defensor de la República Española, Etiopía, Finlandia, Africa, luchas populares de Asia. México, La Prensa, División Comercial, 1973. 268 p., plates.

A laudatory biography of the Mexican leader written by the former chief of his presidential staff.

8141. Carrillo Castro, Alejandro. La reforma administrativa en México. México, Instituto de Administración Pública, 1973. 155 p., bibl., tables (Publicación, 3)

A systematic approach to the study of Mexican public administration. Valuable chapters on the evolution of administrative and political capabilities since 1917, as well as the reforms suggested by President Echeverría. 19 graphs enhance the significance of the contribution.

8142. Colín, Mario. Hablo de mi tierra. México, Editorial Libros de México, 1972. 192 p.

Speeches, messages, and harangues by a Mexican deputy in the best tradition of Castelar and the "torrential" Spanish and Latin American speakers of the 19th century and beyond.

8143. ———. Notas de prensa. México, Testimonios de Atlacomulco, 1972. 176 p.

Another book by this prolific writer.

8144. ———. Notas editoriales. México, Cuadernos del Estado de México, 1972. 219 p.

Editorials on the most diverse topics. Apparently previously published in the press, but no reference to the original publications.

8145. ———. Semblanzas de personajes del Estado de México. México, Cuadernos del Estado de México, 1972. 259 p., plates.

Sketches of writers, politicians, and diplomats, all of them born in the state of Mexico, written by a native of the *patria chica*.

8146. ———. Vocación al servicio del pueblo: papeles de acción política. México, Cuadernos del Estado de México, 1972. 263 p.

Speeches and other miscellaneous documents by a five-times elected deputy representing the state of Mexico.

8147. Cosío Villegas, Daniel. El sistema político mexicano: las posibilidades de cambio. 2. ed., corregida y aumentada. México, Editorial Joaquín Mortiz, 1972. 116 p. (Cuadernos de Joaquín Mortiz)

El maestro Cosío utilizes his well-known expertise in Mexican history to introduce some ironic remarks about the contributions by foreign "politólogos." The "two essential pieces" of the system, the Presidency and the Party, as well as the economy are examined in this short essay, which strongly criticizes both, especially President Echeverría. A resemblance is found between the Mexican President and Castro. According to Cosío, Echeverría, like the Cuban leader, "uses words as the preferential instrumentality to govern." Perhaps ingenious, but certainly not illuminating.

8148. Cremoux, Raúl. ¿Televisión o prisión electrónica? México, Fondo de Cultura Económica, 1974. 124 p. (Archivo del Fondo, 12)

An analysis of television's first 23 years in Mexico, which sees it as essentially controlled by US economic interests and, therefore, useless as a means for the democratic social development of the Mexican people. Calls for a social definition of mass communications and for some degree of state coordination in favor of the viewers.

Fagen, Patricia W. Exiles and citizens: Spanish Republicans in México. See item 8809.

8149. Fagen, Richard R. and **William S. Tuohy.** Aspects of the Mexican political system (RU/SCID, 7:2, Summer 1972, p. 208-220)

Previous research in Oaxaca is the basis for this brief but insightful study which closely scrutinizes the centralized, hierarchical political apparatus and the government of the Revolutionary Family.

8150. Fuentes Díaz, Vicente. La Democracia Cristiana en México: ¿un intento fallido? México, Editorial Altiplano, 1972. 125 p.

A student of Mexican political parties gives a very critical interpretation of the origins and frustrations of Christian Democracy in his country. Some interesting data on the role of Venezuelan leader Rafael Caldera and COPEI in the vicissitudes of their Mexican associates.

8151. Furtak, Robert K. El Partido Revolucionario Institucional: integración nacional y movilización electoral (CM/FI, 9:4, abril/junio 1969, p. 339-353, tables)

Drawing on a dissertation, a European specialist discusses the role of the PRI in organizing consent within the Mexican system. [P.B. Taylor, Jr.]

8152. García Cantú, Gastón. Javier Barros Sierra, 1968: conversaciones con Gastón García Cantú. 2. ed. México, Siglo XXI Editores, 1972. 214 p., plates (El hombre y su obra)

Recorded conversations between the author and the late Rector of UNAM during 1966-70. Important for those interested in Mexican education and particularly the tragic student demonstration of 1968.

8153. ———. Política mexicana. México, UNAM, Facultad de Ciencias Políticas y Sociales, Depto. de Ciencias de la Información, 1974. 421 p. (Serie: Estudios, 40)

Articles previously published in *Excelsior* by this well-known university professor on Mexican politics and society under President Echeverría. Critical of the regime, but "within the Revolution." American foreign policy towards Latin America is submitted to severe scrutiny.

8154. **González Morfín, Efraín.** Discursos de su campaña presidencial. t. 1, 1970. México, Editorial Jus, 1973. 354 p.

The first of several proposed volumes of selected campaign speeches made by the 1970 presidential candidate of the Partido de Acción Nacional (PAN).

8155. **González Pineda, Francisco** and **Antonio Delhumeau.** Los mexicanos frente al poder: participación y cultura política de los mexicanos. México, Instituto Mexicano de Estudios Políticos, 1973. 324 p., bibl.

This book, introduced by the authors as "an essay about political participation in Mexico," is really a long, verbose discourse stimulated by the conflict, which the authors believe they perceive, between the Mexicans' fascination with power and their rejection of politics as an open, legitimate way to obtain it. Elements of history, sociology, and psychoanalysis are put together for that purpose. Admittedly, there are some perceptive observations scattered through the text, but its contribution to the understanding of the Mexican political system is doubtful.

8156. **Hank González, Carlos.** Discursos: 1969-1970. Mexico, Talleres Gráficos de la Nación, 1973. 208 p.

Political addresses and speeches by the Constitutional Governor of the State of Mexico.

8157. *International Review of Administrative Sciences*. International Institute of Administrative Sciences. Vol. 40, No. 1, 1974- . Brussels.

A collection of articles on public administration and administrative law in Mexico written by high officials in the government, including Secretaries (Ministers). A legal approach is prevalent. The contribution by Alejandro Carrillo on administrative reform stands out.

8158. **Kaufman Purcell, Susan.** Decision-making in an authoritarian regime: theoretical implications from a Mexican case study (PUCIS/WP, 26:1, Oct. 1973, p. 28-54)

A good effort at fitting the Mexican government to the model of the authoritarian regime, whose characteristics are: 1) limited political pluralism, 2) low subject mobilization, 3) patrimonial rulership, and, in this case, 4) a high degree of elite consensus. In a clear, well-argued case study of the 1961 implementation of the profit sharing provision of the Constitution of 1917, the author demonstrates that the President has a substantial degree of autonomy in the decision making process. Thus, despite increasing electoral participation, one cannot yet safely conclude that the Mexican authoritarian regime is in transition toward a competitive democratic system.

8159. **Mabry, Donald J.** Mexico's Acción Nacional: a Catholic alternative to revolution. N.Y., Syracuse Univ. Press, 1973. 269 p., bibl., tables.

The first book-length history of The Partido de Acción Nacional (PAN) to be published in English. Based on party files and interviews with more than 100 party leaders and members. Author shows an excellent knowledge of the sources. He timidly suggests that PAN can be related to progressive Latin American political Catholicism.

8160. ———. Mexico's party deputy system: the first decade (UM/JIAS, 16:2, May 1974, p. 221-233, bibl., tables)

After analyzing the results of four Federal Deputy elections since 1964, the author concludes "that the party deputy system was a simulation from its very beginning."

8161. **Magaña Contreras, Manuel.** Troya juvenil. México, The Author, 1971. 315 p., bibl., plates.

A rambling book written by a Mexican Catholic to protect youth from Communism, especially from those "sinners" who have infiltrated the Church. On p. 47, Mons. Ivan Illich is called: "a man handling large sums of money in CIDOC to prepare *saboteadores marxists de sotana.*"

8162. **Manzanilla Schaffer, Víctor.** México: la entrega de la tierra y la reforma agraria integral (UPR/RCS, 16:2, junio 1972, p. 187-211)

Critical interpretation of Mexican Agrarian Reform in its development from the stage of simple redistribution of land—"peripheric agrarianism"—to present stage of "integral agrarianism." Latter is a four-stage process: 1) land redistribution, 2) social and economic organization of peasants receiving land, 3) increased production, 4) industrialization. Designed to raise peasants to level of rural middle class by raising level of consumption. This will strengthen national economy and further social and economic development of the country. Views Mexican agrarian reform as incomplete but as generally beneficial for all Mexicans.

8163. Martínez de la Vega, Francisco. En la esquina. Selección prólogo de Edmundo Domínguez Aragonés. México, Editorial Samo, 1972. 449 p.

Journalistic comments on contemporary Mexican politics and society. Too extensive. Hardly original or insightful.

Mateo, Eligio de. México y el Pacto Andino. See item 8814a.

8164. Mendieta y Núñez, Lucio. Las desviaciones de la Reforma Agraria. México, Academia de Derecho Agrario de la Asociación de Abogados, 1972. 45 p. (Monografías agrarias, 8)

Short and poignant criticism of the Mexican agrarian reform legislation by a veteran sociologist. He praises the new Federal Law of Agrarian Reform enacted under Echeverría.

8165. Mexico (state), *Mex.* **Gobierno del Estado de México. Dirección de Prensa y Relaciones Públicas.** Tercer informe de gobierno. Toluca, Mex., 1973. 206 p., plates.

A report by the government of the State of Mexico on various aspects of its 1972 program. Contains information on the administration, the economy, education, culture, community development, human resources, etc.

8166. Monroy Rivera, Oscar. México y su vivencia dramática en el pensamiento vasconcelista. México, B. Costa-Amic Editor, 1972. 133 p., bibl.

Literary pieces suggested by selections from the works of the late Mexican pensador. Vasconcelos' ideas are seen as relevant for the present integrity and moral soundness of Mexicanism.

8167. Mouroz, Jean Revel. Les politiques agricole et agraire du gouvernement Echeverría (FDD/NED [Problèmes d'Amérique Latine, 32] 1974, p. 59-80, tables, map)

A sharply critical analysis of agricultural and land distribution policies, which offers selected historical data as a basis for discussion of the past three years. Policy and administrative changes under Echeverría are discussed, and the effects on campesinos are treated. [P.B. Taylor, Jr.]

Ochoa, Guillermo. Reportaje en Chile. See item 8487.

8168. Ortiz Wadgymar, Arturo. El centralismo en México: problema estructural que se agrava (UNAM/PDD, 4:13, nov. 1972/enero 1973, p. 115-140, tables)

Viewing centralism as the growing concentration of population and industry in Mexico City, the author expresses his own preference for regionalism in this descriptive article, which shows failure to consult the available literature in public administration.

8169. Pare, Louise. Diseño teórico para el estudio del caciquismo actual en México (UNAM/RMS, 34:2, abril/junio 1972, p. 335-354, bibl.)

A good discussion of a "theoretical design" for the study of *caciquismo* in Mexico from the point of view of political anthropology. Only tangentially does the author try to apply his analytical framework to Mexican reality.

8170. Raby, David L. La contribución del cardenismo al desarrollo del México actual (Economía Política [Instituto Politécnico Nacional, México] 9:4, 1972, p. 5-42)

Regards Cárdenas as more radical in socioeconomic tendencies than his successors. Was his regime a stage in continuity or discontinuity, however? The former would imply a stage in the recapture of Mexico by former holders of power, by which workers and revolutionaries would be entrapped and co-opted. In any case, author concludes that the national bourgeoisie are in control. [P.B. Taylor, Jr.]

8171. Rangel Gaspar, Eliseo. El desarrollo democrático de México. México, B. Costa-Amic Editor, 1973. 237 p., bibl.

This conservative, yet critical, analysis of the Mexican political system in the 1970s chides the government for not being as democratic as it might be. The treatment is solidly optimistic. A promising future is foreseen if only the Mexican people can be encouraged to greater political participation.

8172. Rivanuva R., Gastón. El PRI: el gran mito mexicano. México, Editorial Tradición, 1974. 221 p., illus.

Strong criticism of the PRI for emphasizing "political stability," i.e., maintaining itself in power, rather than effective democracy. Calls for the suppression of the PRI and the establishment of genuine, independent, nationalistic political parties while recommending the proscription of marxist and other anti-Mexican groups.

8173. Romero Flores, Jesús. Lazaro Cárdenas: biografía de un gran mexicano. México, B. Costa-Amic Editor, 1971. 170 p., plates.

A rather superficial "popular" biography eulogizing Cardenas, by one of the late president's close collaborators.

Ronfeldt, David F. Atencingo: the politics of agrarian struggle in a Mexican ejido. See item 9744.

8174. ———. The Mexican army and political order since 1940. Santa Monica, Calif., The Rand Corporation, 1973. 24 p. (Rand study, P-5089)

The customary view is that the Mexican army has, for many years, played an entirely reinforcing role, supporting a decisive and legitimate government, without asserting its own partisan or preferential attitudes. Ronfeldt suggests this may well not be so, but rather that Mexico is like most other Latin American countries where one finds influential armies, save for stylistic degrees of difference. [P. B. Taylor, Jr.]

8175. Sayeg Helú, Jorge. El constitucionalismo social mexicano: la integración constitucional de México, 1808-1853. Prólogo de Jorge Gabriel García Rojas. México, Cultura y Ciencia Política, 1972. 371 p., bibl.

The first of two proposed volumes tracing the constitutional development of Mexico to 1917. This volume begins with the precolumbian and colonial antecedents and ends with the anarchy of the 1840s and early 1850s. The constitutions are seen as attempts to deal with Mexico's social problems.

8176. Silva Herzog, Jesús. Mis últimas andanzas: 1947-1972. México, Siglo XXI Editores, 1973. 350 p.

Don Jesús Silva Herzog adds a new title to his long and valuable autobiography, v. 2 of his memoirs (*Una vida en la vida de México*) covering the period 1947-72. Not only enjoyable, but indispensable reading for everyone interested in contemporary Mexico by this veteran writer and exemplary case of intellectual integrity.

Smith, Robert Freeman. The United States and revolutionary nationalism in Mexico: 1916-1932. See item 8817b.

Spota, Luis. El viaje. See item 8817c.

8177. Stevens, Evelyn P. Protest and response in Mexico. Cambridge, Mass., The MIT Press, 1974. 372 p., bibl.

An investigation of protest movements based on open-ended interviews and participant observations. Three case studies—the railroad workers, doctors, and student strikes—plus a perceptive chapter on communications, allow the author to advance generalizations that are relevant for understanding the repressive and cooptation techniques of an authoritarian regime. An interesting book.

8178. Testimonio en la muerte de Manuel Gómez Morin. México, Editorial Jus, 1973. 140 p., plates.

Manuel Gómez Morin, a co-founder of the famous Sociedad de Conferencias (1916) and founder of Acción Nacional, serving as president of the party from 1939 to 1949, died in Mexico three years ago. Introduced by a brief biographical note, this collection of eulogies rendered by his admirers and political colleagues pays homage to one of the Mexican Right's most prominent leaders.

8179. Tuohy, William S. and David F. Ronfeldt. Political control and the recruitment of middle-level elites in Mexico: an example from agrarian politics (UU/WPQ, 22:2, June 1969, p. 365-374)

Focuses on the means used by the Revolutionary Family to keep a tight control on the press and to elect only those people who are "incondicionales" in the state of Veracruz. It is unclear why the authors, after presenting such data, contend that the Mexican government is going through a transition "from a predominantly hierarchical system to a more polyarchal one."

8180. Una voz del Tercer Mundo. México, Editorial Mexicano, 1974. 479 p.

A collection of speeches, interviews, and official documents coming out of President Echeverría's state visit to six nations of Europe, Asia, and America in 1973.

8181. Warwam, Arturo. Los campesinos: hijos predilectos del régimen. México, Editorial Nuestro Tiempo, 1972? 138 p. (Col. Los grandes problemas nacionales)

An anthropologist, highly familiar with agrarian institutions and the countryside, offers a brief impressionistic report of the present situation of Mexican peasants, defined as "holders of land for the purpose of cultivation." The chapter on the control mechanism used to preserve peasant oppression is commendable.

CENTRAL AMERICA
GENERAL

8182. Galindo Pohl, Reynaldo. Condicionamiento sociopolítico de la integración (Boletín del Instituto Centroamericano de Derecho Comparado [Tegucigalpa] 9, 1968/69, p. 147-171)

Despite the title, an extensive elaboration on the legal aspects of Central American integration.

8183. Schmitter, Philippe C. Autonomy or dependence as regional integration outcomes: Central America. Berkeley, Univ. of California, Institute of International Studies, 1972. 87 p., bibl., tables.

An extension of a paper that originally appeared in the *Journal of Common Market Studies*. With his usual thoroughness and sophistication, Professor Schmitter examines here the major paradox faced by the CACM: "a process which appears to have no overt opponents, yet which seems to be locked into a hopeless political stalemate." The role of external actors is duly emphasized. A significant contribution.

COSTA RICA

8184. Suñol, Julio. Robert Vesco compra una república. San José, Talleres Gráficos de Trejos, 1974. 315 p.

A strong denunciation of American millionaire Robert Vesco's adventures in Costa Rica, written by a Costa

Rican journalist. Exposes President José Figueres' confusion between his personal fortune and the national treasury and provides valuable information on the financial policies of the third Figueres Administration which, according to this author, were disastrous.

8185. Vega Carballo, José Luis. Etapas y procesos de la evolución sociopolítica de Costa Rica (Estudios Sociales Centroamericanos [San José] 1:1, enero/abril 1972, p. 45-72, tables)

A short overview in terms of dependency and social classes. The author sees an emerging "burguesía gerencial," strongly tied to foreign capital, which is challenging the hegemony of the traditional oligarchy.

EL SALVADOR

8186. Centro Nacional de Información. Reportajes y comentarios de las elecciones: los comicios del 8 de marzo de 1970 constituyeron un voto de confianza para el gobierno. San Salvador, Imprenta Nacional, 1970? 43 p., plates, tables.

The government of General Fidel Sánchez offers information and comments on this "exemplary civic lesson," i.e., the municipal and legislative elections of 1970. Many photos and some electoral data.

8187. La Universidad. Revista bimestral de la Universidad de El Salvador. Año 95, No. 1, enero/feb. 1970- . San Salvador.

A very informative and valuable collection of papers and resolutions adopted by the First Congress for National Agrarian Reform held at the Univ. of El Salvador, 5-10 Jan. 1970, following a special resolution of the Legislative Assembly. It is revealing to note that the representatives of the entrepreneurial sector, without exception, walked out of the congress on the day of its inauguration.

GUATEMALA

8188. Díaz Castillo, Roberto. En torno a la política económica de la reforma liberal de Guatemala (Estudios [Guatemala] 4, 1971, p. 35-44)

Views the economic policy of the Barrios government as a true reform designed to modernize Guatemala's economy. Despite its principal failure to diversify agriculture, the Liberal Reform signaled the decline of the landowning aristocracy and the advent of agrarian reforms.

8189. The LASA committee report on Guatemala terror: U.S. complicity in 20 years of repression there (LADOC, 42 [Document 4, no. 14] Nov. 1973, p. 1-8)

8190. North American Congress on Latin America (NACLA), *New York*. Guatemala. Edited by Susanne Jonas and David Tobis. N.Y., NACLA, 1974. 264 p., bibl., illus., maps, plates, tables.

A useful collection covering Guatemalan political events from 1954 to 1974. The usual strong militancy of NACLA publications, but also the usual excellent level of familiarity with the sources and the resourceful attempt to avoid cliches are present. Special mention is deserved by one appendix, which tries to identify Guatemala's top bourgeoisie by economic groups and families.

8191. Tortolani, Paul. Political participation of native and foreign Catholic clergy in Guatemala (BU/JCS, 15:3, Autumn 1973, p. 407-418)

Interpretative essay examining the political dichotomy existing between an active, reform-oriented foreign clergy and their outnumbered (4:1), aloof native counterparts. The Church must assume a more active role in confronting Guatemala's pressing socioeconomic problems to avoid reappearance of the guerrilla priest phenomenon, as represented in the Melville affair, and a new outbreak of revolutionary violence.

8192. Turcios Lima. La Habana, Tricontinental, 1968. 190 p. (Col. Los hombres)

A brief biography of Turcios Lima, the brilliant guerrilla leader and genuine hero to many Guatemalans, together with a collection of documents and eulogies rendered by his comrades following his death in a car accident in 1966. Indispensable for a study of the man and his times, especially his disagreements with the Guatemalan Party of Labor (Communist).

8193. Verner, Joel Gordon. Heterogeneidad de distrito electoral y competencia entre partidos: el caso de Guatemala (UNAM/RMS, 34:1, enero/marzo 1972, p. 133-153, tables)

Sixteen hypotheses collected from the literature on party competition in the American political system are verified in the context of ecological and electoral data coming from the Congressional elections of 1966. Unfortunately, the Spanish is so poor—this is probably a translation—that the text is practically unintelligible.

HONDURAS

8194. Partido Nacional de Honduras. Comité Central. Elecciones municipales: estilo "Partido Liberal," 1962. Tegucigalpa, 1968. 41 l.

An enumeration, *municipio* by *municipio*, of the many irregularities committed by the Liberal Party in the elections of 1968, as seen by the defeated Nationals.

NICARAGUA

8195. Somoza García, Anastasio. Somoza, el líder de Nicaragua. Managua, n.p., 1969. 100 p.

Laudatory homages to that "figura cimera, General Anastasio Somoza Garcia, leader and conductor of the Nicaraguan liberal masses."

PANAMA

8196. Camargo, Edilia. La panameñidad como estilo (LNB/L, 203, oct./nov. 1972, p. 37-47)

A rhetorical essay on *panameñidad* in the literary style of the late teacher, poet, and philosopher, Isaías García Aponte.

8197. Miró G., Rodrigo. Una década crítica del periodismo nacional: del Estado del Istmo al Estado Federal (LNB/L, 201, agosto 1972, p. 8-27, facsims.)

An informative analysis of Panamanian journalism and its reflection of change in the isthmus from 1843-53.

8198. *Notes et Etudes Documentaires.* La Documentation Française. Vol. 29, No. 4043/4044, Nov. 1973- . Paris.

Introductory papers on American-Panamanian relations, 1967-1973; the Torrijos government; and the Jamaican economy.

8199. Torrijos Herrera, Omar. La batalla de Panamá. B.A., EUDEBA, 1973. 122 p.

Speeches by the self-proclaimed leader of the Panamanian October Revolution introduced by Torrijos' own account of his return from Mexico after being deposed by a new military coup. Absolutely required reading for those interested in the man and his political style.

THE CARIBBEAN
GENERAL

8200. Ameringer, Charles D. The Democratic Left in exile: the antidictatorial struggle in the Caribbean, 1945-1959. Coral Gables, Fla., Univ. of Miami Press, 1974. 352 p., bibl., maps.

Essentially a chronicle of events rather than an analysis of them, this book is a useful bringing together of materials that have been neglected because of complex political examinations. The democratic left, within a restricted geographic region, is treated in great detail as to characteristics, goals, and activities. In some degree it is a monument to a political generation that finally came to power just as the next, embodied by Fidel Castro, was arriving on stage. The book will appeal to historians and will serve as useful source material for specialists looking for detail. [P.B. Taylor, Jr.]

8201. Greene, J.E. A review of political science research in the English speaking Caribbean: toward a methodology (UWI/SES, 23:1, March 1974, p. 1-47, bibl.)

In the last few years significant political research has been coming from the different campuses at the Univ. of the West Indies. Although the strong methodological concern of Professor Greene makes him, perhaps, too punctilious in the review of the work done by his colleagues, this is, nevertheless, an excellent survey by a well-qualified scholar on the present state of political science in the area.

Oxaal, Ivar. The dependency economist as grass-roots politician in the Caribbean. See item 1279.

8202. Singham, A.W. and N.L. Singham. Cultural domination and political subordination: notes towards a theory of the Caribbean political system (CSSH, 15:3, June 1973, p. 258-288)

The underlying assumptions and ideologies of Western social science are exposed and assailed in this provocative essay tying together, primarily, recent elaborations by West Indian scholars. Using dependency theory, the authors view the growing obsolescence of the nation-state as a result of the new mercantilism advanced by the multinational corporations. Suggestive comments on the mechanisms of dependency, the social structure, and the role of the bureaucracy, among others, add to the value of this contribution.

8203. *Social and Economic Studies.* Univ. of the West Indies, Institute of Social and Economic Research. Vol. 19, No. 1, March 1970- . Mona, Jam.

A collection of excellent papers on "problems of Administrative Change" in the Commonwealth Caribbean written by scholars from the area. It is hoped that the two issues reviewed in this volume of *HLAS* will generate some publication in book-form on this vital and unexplored aspect of Caribbean politics.

8204. _____. _____, _____. Vol. 23, No. 2, June 1974- . Mona, Jam.

A high-quality collection of articles on public policy and administration in the Commonwealth Caribbean, all of which were written by scholars from the area. Another significant contribution by this prestigious journal.

8205. Verner, Joel Gordon. The recruitment of cabinet ministers in the former British Caribbean: a five-country study (JDA, 7:4, July 1973, p. 635-652, tables)

Author uses information gathered from published sources as well as from correspondence with US embassies in the five countries and with cabinet members and administrators in several, to produce some useful and occasionally surprising statistics for the manner of recruitment and the characteristics of people recruited for cabinet positions in the Bahamas, Barbados, Guyana, Jamaica, and Trinidad-Tobago. Makes no attempt to correlate the data with executive performance or behavior.

8206. Williams, Eric. A new federation for the Commonwealth Caribbean? (PQ, 44:3, July/Sept. 1973, p. 242-256)

An intelligent discussion of the problems and possibilities involved in the establishment of a Commonwealth Caribbean federation in light of past failures and of new developments, such as the move toward economic integration by the creation of a Caribbean Community. A good synthesis by the noted historian and Prime Minister of Trinidad and Tobago, who sees any new federal grouping of the Commonwealth Caribbean as a major step toward economic integration of the entire Caribbean.

CUBA

8207. Acosta, Maruja and **Jorge E. Hardoy.** Urban reform in revolutionary Cuba. Translated by Mal Bochner. New Haven, Conn., Yale Univ., 1973. 11 p., bibl., tables. (Antilles research program occasional papers, 1)

Original published in 1971 as Reforma Urbana en Cuba Revolucionaria, Caracas, Ven., Dosmil, 1971. A descriptive study based on intensive interviews conducted by Hardoy during a three-week visit to the island in Aug. 1970. The authors recognize the persistence of urban problems—housing shortages, minimal housing transfers, deterioration of cities (especially Havana), etc. Nevertheless, given the "enormous external pressures," they consider the Cuban experience successful. For annotation of the Spanish original, see *HLAS 36:443.*

8208. Bonachea, Ramón L. and **Marta San Martín.** The Cuban insurrection: 1952-1959. New Brunswick, N.J., Transaction Books, 1974. 451 p., bibl., illus., maps, plates, tables.

A very detailed narrative, beginning with the Moncada attack and centering upon the activities of the M-26-7 and the Directorio Revolucionario. The book draws upon the personal experience of one of the authors, who was a member of a DR cell. It is based upon interviews with participants now in exile (none of whom was a top insurrection leader) and demonstrates a thorough knowledge of Cuban published sources. A valuable contribution, although the judgment exercised in evaluating the sources is somewhat questionable. The annotated bibliography is excellent, but Appendix I (leadership positions held by insurrection militants in the Cuban Revolutionary Government) should be used with care, since it has some serious mistakes.

8209. Bonachea, Rolando E. and **Nelson P. Valdés** *eds.* Revolutionary struggle: 1947-1958. v. 1, Selected works of Fidel Castro. Cambridge, Mass., The MIT Press, 1972. 471 p., plates.

The first of a proposed nine-volume collection of selected writings of Fidel Castro, which should be particularly helpful to English-readers. Apparently, the editors have included everything they could track down pertaining to the Cuban leader, even a manifesto that he did not write and a version of the speech he supposedly made immediately before the Moncada attack, which was unpublished until 1964. The long introduction is useful, but the editors do not try to come to grips with the complex personality behind the writings.

Butterworth, Douglas. Grass-roots political organization in Cuba: a case of the Committees for the Defense of the Revolution. See item 9786.

8210. Cantón Navarro, José. Algunas ideas de José Martí en relación con la clase obrera y el socialismo. La Habana, Instituto Cubano del Libro, 1970. 158 p., bibl.

A brief examination of José Martí's sparse reflections on socialism and his consistent identification with the "humildes." A modest contribution, but a fair treatment of the topic.

8211. Cardenal, Ernesto. In Cuba. Translated by Donald Walsh. N.Y., New Directions, 1974. 340 p., tables (A new directions book)

Translation of Spanish original reviewed in *HLAS 35:7569.*

Casal, Lourdes *ed.* and *comp.* El caso Padilla: literatura y revolución. See *HLAS 36:4226.*

8212. Casaus, Víctor. Girón en la memoria. La Habana, Casa de las Américas, 1970. 308 p., plate (Col. Premio)

A literary reconstruction of the days of the Bay of Pigs using interviews with some of the participants, especially the aviators of the Fuerzas Armadas Revolucionarias (FAR), clippings and other documentary evidence. Apparently an example of the new Cuban "socialist realism."

8213. Castro, Fidel. Fidel Castro. La Habana, Instituto del Libro, 1968. 208 p.

Several speeches by the Cuban leader from 1965 to 1968. A useful collection, especially for those interested in Castro's pronouncements during the most radical period of the Cuban Revolution, from the second half of 1966 to 1968.

8214. _____. El proceso revolucionario. 2. ed. B.A., Aquarius, 1973? 247 p.

A collection of Fidel Castro's speeches delivered during his 1971 visit to Chile.

8215. _____. La Revolución Cubana: una confirmación de la fuerza del marxismo-leninismo, discurso pronunciado por . . . . en la Universidad Carolina de Praga, Checoslovaquia, con motivo de concedérsele el título de Doctor en Ciencias Jurídicas Honoris Causa el 22 de junio de 1972 (UC/IAP, 6, 1972, p. 7-14)

Castro explains to the Czechs how a socialist revolution was made in Cuba without marxists, but cites himself as an exception who had studied "the fundamental works of Marx, Engels, and Lenin." Previously he had always qualified his own Marxism.

8216. ———. El socialismo en Cuba. B.A., Editorial Anteo, 1973. 47 p.

A speech by Fidel Castro to the XIII Congress of the Central de Trabajadores de Cuba in Nov. 1973. Emphasizes conservation of energy and resources and increased production.

8217. Congreso Nacional Campesino de la Asociación Nacional de Agricultores Pequeños (ANAP), *IV, La Habana, 1972?* Discursos, acuerdos, reglamento, comunicado. La Habana, Comité Central del Partido, Comisión de Orientación Revolucionaria, 1972. 104 p.

The IV National Congress of ANAP was held in Havana 25-31 Dec. 1971. Among the documents published here is the speech by Fidel Castro at the closing session.

8218. Corten, André. Cuba: críticas y autocríticas (UNAM/RMS, 34:1, enero/marzo 1972, p. 95-114)

An unconvincing, and poorly documented, answer to recent books, by René Dumont and K.S. Karol, criticizing the Cuban Revolution.

8219. Domínguez, Jorge I. The civic soldier in Cuba (*in* Kelleher, Catherine McArdle *ed.* Political-military systems: comparative perspectives. Beverly Hills, Calif., Sage Publications, 1974. p. 209-238, tables (Sage research progress series on war, revolution and peacekeeping, 4)

Cuba is governed by civic soldiers—i.e., guerrilla leaders who were socialized into the fusion of civilian and military roles. They have continued as the top government elite and "have turned the civic soldier concept into a dominant norm in civilian organization." A highly recommended contribution by a young scholar who has a strong command of both the Cuban sources and the most recent literature on civilian-military relations. The question arises as to whether the role of the civic soldier has not been declining since this paper was written.

8220. Dorticós Torrado, Osvaldo. Discurso en el acto de presentación de los militantes del Partido del Instituto de Economía. La Habana, Instituto del Libro [and] Editorial de Ciencias Sociales, 1969. 39 p.

The Cuban President elaborates on the requirements to be fulfilled by the Institute's graduates. The first and most important: ideological identification with the Revolution.

8221. Edwards, Jorge. Persona non grata. Barcelona, Seix Barral Editores, 1983. 478 p. (Hispanica nova)

The first Charge d'Affaires appointed by President Allende in 1970 was declared, confidentially, persona non grata by the Cuban Government in less than three months, apparently because he was too friendly toward Heberto Padilla and the other intellectuals accused by the government of being counterrevolutionaries. Although the author, a distinguished writer, gives more attention to those relationships, there are throughout the book many perceptive observations, which help to understand Cuban life under Castro.

8222. Gambini, Hugo. El Che Guevara. Colaboradores: Julio Algañaraz [and] Leda Orellano. 5. ed. B.A., Editorial Paidós, 1973. 549 p., bibl., maps, plates (Mundo moderno, 29)

A popular biography of Guevara by an Argentine journalist. The basic facts of guerrilla life are here although embellished most of the time by dialogues and confidential bits of improbable authenticity. On the crucial period from Guevara's return to Havana in March, 1965, to his departure for Bolivia, the author sees a quarrel with the old communists and long argumentations with Fidel. He contends that Guevara stayed at Córdoba, Argentina, for 20 days in 1966 and even includes his photo, clean-shaven and blonde, taken in Córdoba.

8223. García-Calzadilla, Miguel A. The Fidel Castro I knew: biographical fragments on the Cuban Revolution. N.Y., Vantage Press, 1971. 80 p.

A Cuban exile tells the story of his meeting with Fidel in Mexico before the Granma expedition, and his disenchantment with the leader once he took power. His recollections add little, if anything, to our knowledge of the man or his times.

8224. Gardiner, C. Harvey. The Japanese and Cuba (UPR/CS, 12:2, July 1972, p. 52-73, tables)

A survey of relations between the two countries since the founding of the Cuban Republic in 1902. Trade, which was increasing in the late 1960s, has been the primary factor in those relations. Some data is shown concerning US pressures to get Japanese cooperation with the American blockade imposed on Cuba. For historian's comment, see *HLAS 36:2321*.

8225. González, Edward. The United States and Castro: breaking the deadlock (CFR/FA, 50:4, July, 1972, p. 722-737)

A judicious discussion of the conflictive interactions between Havana and Washington. The author's prediction of the virtual isolation of the US in hemispheric politics is now dangerously approaching reality with Washington policy makers giving no indication of seriously considering the recommendation for flexibility made here two years ago.

8226. Guevara, Ernesto. El hombre y el socialismo en Cuba. B.A., Ediciones Síntesis, 1973? 215 p.

A new selection of Guevara's writings: reminiscences

of the Revolutionary War, advice to the combatant, and man and socialism in Cuba.

8227. _____. La planificación socialista y su significado. B.A., El Túnel, 1973. 151 p.

A new edition of some economic papers by Guevara from the volume published by Casa de las Américas in 1970. The short introduction reflects more admiration than understanding of Guevara's economic thought.

8228. Hunt, Howard. Give us this day. New Rochelle, N.Y., Arlington House, 1973. 235 p., plates.

If Mr. Hunt can still be believed, he was the Chief of Political Action for the Exile Invasion Force defeated at the Bay of Pigs despite his total ignorance of Cuban politics, as this book proves. This is a sordid story of the mismanagement of foreign policy making, CIA blundering, and the exile leaders' *entreguismo*. The mendacity of the author is particularly obvious when he libels the few Cuban participants who mistrusted his incompetence and exceedingly reactionary views.

8229. Imágenes de Cuba, 1953-73: pasado y presente, tránsito hacia un presente definitivo. La Habana, Casa de las Américas, 1973. 1 v. (Unpaged) illus.

A booklet introducing an art exhibition on the 20th anniversary of the Moncada attack.

8230. Mallin, Jay. Phases of subversion: the Castro drive on Latin America (AF/AUR, Nov./Dec. 1973, p. 54-62, plates)

In this study, based on revelations by Cuban defectors, American official sources, and one intriguing reference to the Uruguayan Army's intelligence department, the author finds a consistency in Cuban subversive policies that is difficult to match with the facts. It never occurs to him that Cuban guerrilla warfare strategy might be correlated with American policies toward the Caribbean island.

8231. Mesa-Lago, Carmelo. Castro's domestic course (USIA/PC, 22:5, Sept./Oct. 1973, p. 27-38, plates)

An appraisal of the failure of the Cuban government to carry out promises of democratization and decentralization made in 1970. Conclusion is that the most critical factor in Castro's change in course has been the increasing Soviet influence in Cuban affairs.

8232. Nikiforov, Boris Sergeevich. Kuba: krakh burzhuaznykh politicheskikh partii, 1945-1958 (Cuba: the collapse of the bourgeois political parties, 1945-1958). Moskva, Nauka, 1973. 415 p.

A standard Soviet account of post-World War II Cuba, prior to Castro. Of interest chiefly because of the contrast with Western interpretations of the anti-Batista movement. [T.S. Cheston]

Olesen, Virginia. Context and posture: notes on socio-cultural aspects of women's roles and family policy in contemporary Cuba. See item 9808.

8233. Paulson, Rolland G. La educación rural en Cuba: una estrategia para el desarrollo revolucionario (UNAM/PDD, 4:13, nov. 1972/enero 1973, p. 45-76, bibl., tables)

Author uses primary and secondary sources as well as personal observations made on a visit to Cuba in 1970 to examine improvements in rurual education in the post-revolution period and the proposed plan of work-study as the future course of education. Despite expressed sympathy with Castro's revolution, provides a fairly objective treatment. Analysis of present situation is that efforts have been highly successful in a quantitative sense but qualitatively speaking there is little difference from other, poor Latin American nations.

8234. Peattie, Lisa. Cuban notes (MR, 10:4, Autumn 1969, p. 652-674)

An account of a 25-day visit by seven academics in 1968. The purpose was to study urban planning; the effect was to get a rather informal view of Cuba under Castro. The article has its utterly ingenuous aspects, but is also raises some difficult questions. This short piece seems a nice supplement to other accounts of the contemporary folk of Cuba. [P.B. Taylor, Jr.]

8235. Pérez, Louis A., Jr. *comp.* Women in the Cuban Revolutionary War, 1953-1958: a bibliography (SS, 39:1, Spring 1975, p. 104-108)

A supplement to Nelson P. Valdés' bibliography, see item 8246.

8236. Pino-Santos, Oscar. El asalto a Cuba por la oligarquía financiera yanqui. La Habana, Casa de las Américas, 1973. 234 p., bibl., tables.

Partially based on documentary evidence collected with the help of American members of NACLA including, supposedly, documents of the American companies nationalized in Cuba. Among other findings the author contends that in the sugar industry before 1924 "the principal development effort was not the result of American investment." Although the bibliography is too selective and disregards some important works published in this country, nevertheless an interesting contribution.

8238. Purcell, Susan Kaufman. Modernizing women for a modern society: the Cuban case (*in* Pescatello, Ann *ed.* Female and male in Latin America: essays. Pittsburgh, Pa., Univ. of Pittsburgh Press, 1973, p. 257-271)

An interpretative essay evaluating the governmentally controlled and directed women's liberation movement and its position in the overall revolutionary program. Good synthesis of available published materials.

8239. Ritter, Archibald R.M. The economic development of revolutionary Cuba: strategy and performance. N.Y., Praeger Publishers, 1974. 372 p., bibl., tables (Praeger special studies in international economics and development)

A balanced and objective study of the development strategy and economic performance of the Revolutionary Government up to 1972. The chapter on the socioeconomic problems of pre-revolutionary Cuba is excellent. Probably the best introduction available to the study of revolutionary political economy. Well-organized, well-written, and free of jargon. A welcome addition.

8240. Rivière d'Arc, Hélène. Aménagement rural a Cuba: le plan Ceiba (CDAL, 8, 1973, p. 65-89, maps, tables)

A description of Plan Ceiba to produce vegetables and bananas in the municipality by the same name in Havana province. The plan includes the building of new towns and ten high schools in the area. Interesting data and observations by a visitor to the region.

8241. Ruiz, Leovigildo. Diario de una traición: Cuba 1961. Miami, Fla., Lorie Book Stores, 1972. 311 p., illus., map.

This is the third volume of an annual series projected by a Cuban exile, giving special attention to the coercive measures used by the Castro government since 1959. The reasons why the deaths of Ty Cobb and other baseball players appear in this volume are unclear.

8242. Sabourin, Jesús. Marti en el Che (CDLA, 13:73, julio/agosto 1972, p. 5-15)

A purely literary article in which the author tries to show "essential similarities" between Marti and Che by comparing a few paragraphs from the voluminous works of the former with the scanty writings left by the guerrilla leader.

Salinas, Fernando and others. La Habana metropolitana: un instrumento para el desarrollo socialista. See *HLAS 36:449*.

8242a. Sátira contra el imperialismo yanqui de la caricatura cubana actual (UCLV/I, 10:3, julio/sept. 1968, p. 95-159, illus.)

The cartoons of 10 young visual polemicists as published in the weekly cartoon supplement to the newspaper *La Calle* in 1960-61. The group in large part came from the staff of the semi-official publication *Revolución*. These are amusing enough although the assemblage of them in one publication tends to sap their individual meanings. [P.B. Taylor, Jr.]

8243. Silverman, Bertram. Labor and revolution in Cuba (CUH, 64:378, Feb. 1973, p. 66-71, 87)

An overview of the different economic strategies followed by the Cuban regime from 1960 to 1972, written by a professional economist deeply interested in Cuban socialism.

8244. Sweezy, Paul M. Fifteenth and twentieth anniversaries for Cuba (MR, 25:4, Sept. 1973, p. 23-27)

A short interview with Mr. Sweezy, who appeals to his lack of "the necessary knowledge of the current situation in Cuba" to avoid any comment that might be construed by Castro as "ultra-leftism."

8245. Tutino, Saverio. Gli anni di Cuba. Milano, Italy, Gabriele Mzazzotta Editore, 1973. 371 p., bibl.

Concentrating almost entirely on the period 1964-70, this attempts to be an analytical chronicle of events. The writer, a correspondent for the Italian communist party newspaper, has published other work on Cuba. [P.B. Taylor, Jr.]

8246. Valdés, Nelson P. *ed.* and *comp.* A bibliography on Cuban women in the twentieth century. Pittsburgh, Pa., Univ. of Pittsburgh, Center for International Studies, 1974. 31 p. (Cuban Studies Newsletter, 4:2/74)

A welcomed first attempt in a topic of growing interest. Emphasis is on the revolutionary period since 1959.

8247. Volsky, George. Cuba: propaganda as an instrument of power and socio-economic development (SECOLAS/A, 4, March 1973, p. 5-10)

A hasty, superficial account of a generally overlooked aspect of the Cuban Revolution.

8248. Zeitlin, Maurice. The Cuban Revolution (*in* Kaplan, Lawrence *ed.* Revolutions: a comparative study. N.Y., Random House, 1973, p. 419-429)

Originally published in *TransActions* (June, 1969), this article really is about the Cuban social structure before the Revolution. According to the author Cuba was a capitalist country with a weak bourgeoisie, lacking legitimacy and a strong working class with a "durable revolutionary and socialist political culture." The supportive data for this highly controversial interpretation are minimal.

DOMINICAN REPUBLIC

8249. Dominican Republic. Oficina Nacional de Administración y Personal. Manual de organización del gobierno. Santo Domingo, 1972. 1 v. (Various pagings) tables (Publicación, 35)

An official outline of the Dominican government's nature, composition and scope, giving the legal base principal functions, organic structure, regimen of authority, and method of financing for every public institution. Reflects the changes introduced since the publication of the first manual in 1969.

8250. Franco, Franklin J. Vida, pasión y muerte del PCD. Santo Domingo, Editora Nacional, 1973? 78 p.

In 1965, the old Partido Socialista Popular (PSP) changed its name to the Dominican Communist Party, a new addition to the several varieties of Dominican Marxism. The present tract, written by a professor and participant in revolutionary politics, offers interesting information about the ideological evolution of the PCD, condemns it, and finally decrees its death.

8251. Galíndez, Jesús de. The era of Trujillo: Dominican dictator. Edited by Russell H. Fitzgibbon. Tucson, The Univ. of Arizona Press, 1973. 298 p., bibl., maps, plates.

Edited, abridged version of Galíndez' original doctoral dissertation submitted to Columbia Univ. in 1956. Author's formal-legalistic analysis presents the Dominican tyranny as a "prototype of a continental species" demonstrating the identifying characteristic of all Latin American dictatorships, i.e., a constitutional, democratic façade totally corrupted underneath. Slightly outdated by more recent research, the English language edition perhaps constitutes more of a tribute to the martyred Spanish Basque exile than a real contribution to the field.

8252. Gall, Norman. The only logical answer. Hanover, N.H., American Universities Field Staff Reports, 1971. 14 p. (Mexico & Caribbean area series, 6:1)

A mother's tragic and painful account of her son's assassination as told to an American journalist. One more in the endless series of senseless killings that have taken place in this unfortunate republic under the "democratic" and thrice "elected" administration of President Balaguer.

8253. Gómez Cerda, José. La vida sindical: del 1ro. de julio de 1970 al 30 de junio del 1971. Santo Domingo, Talleres de la Editorial Mundo Moderno, 1973. 168 p.

V. 2 of a diary by a leader of the Dominican Confederación Autónoma de Sindicatos Cristianos, affiliated with CLASC. Recommended in the preface as helpful for introducing good reading habits among the workers, or "our social class." The diary's contents and quality are such as to suggest the possibility that this purpose might backfire.

8254. Jiménez Grullón, Juan Isidro. El camilismo y la revolución dominicana. Santo Domingo? n.p., 1974? 169 p., bibl.

A veteran *litterato* and political activist expends a lot of effort, and pages, in exposing the reformism of a new and minimal Social Revolutionary Christian Party in the Dominican Republic. He sees there the influence of "Camilism"—from the guerrilla-priest killed in Colombia—and citing Marx and Engels, Lenin, and Mao, assails Camilo and his Dominican disciples as lacking intellectual rigor and political clarity. He obviously enjoys his job.

8255. Lowenthal, Abraham F. The political role of the Dominican Armed Forces: a note on the 1963 overthrow of Juan Bosch and on the 1965 Dominican "Revolution" (UM/JIAS, 15:3, Aug. 1973, p. 355-361, bibl., tables)

Using data on the 25 military officers who signed the comminique after Bosch's overthrow in 1964, Mr. Lowenthal persists in arguing that factional rivalries, not institutional or ideological considerations, played the principal role in the 1965 Dominican revolution.

8256. Rodríguez R., Víctor Melitón. Administración en la República Dominicana (Revista de Ciencias Económicas [Univ. Autónoma de Santo Domingo] 1:1, marzo/junio 1972, p. 107-115)

A brief description of the public administration in the Dominican Republic. Of no particular merit.

HAITI

8257. Casimir, Jean. Los marcos de la radicalización política en Haití (CLAPCS/AL, 14:3, julho/dez. 1971, p. 70-89)

Author identifies three periods of Haitian revolutionary struggle: independence, post-independence anarchy led by peasant guerrillas, and resistance to US occupation. He concludes that political radicalization is only possible in Haiti when the following conditions are met: 1) the existence of leaders who are capable of resisting and who fulfill their promises, 2) a strategy that accepts the possibility of retreat linked to effective political independence, 3) solidarity with all oppressed peoples, and 4) a power base in the peasantry.

8258. Pauyo, Nicolás L. and Pierre Edouard Domond. Où est allée la paix? Port-au-Prince, Presses Nationales d'Haïti, 1973? 119 p., plates.

Rhetorical exercises on the problem of peace, introduced by the image of François Duvalier.

8259. Rotberg, Robert I. and Christopher K. Clague. Haiti: the politics of squalor. Boston, Mass., Houghton Mifflin, 1971. 456 p., bibl., tables.

A pessimistic study of Papa Doc's Haiti, which is described as a predatory state where brigandage is the predominant form of power, wielded by praetorian specialists in violence who insure the safety of and respect for the all-powerful dictator. Rotberg emphasizes that this situation can only be understood in the light of Haiti's national psychology and in its historical context. Research for the study was conducted in the island, although many Haitian sources go uncited for fear of reprisals against them by the Duvalier regime. A large selective bibliography is included.

JAMAICA

8260. Foner, Nancy. Party politics in a Jamaican community (UPR/CS, 13:2, July 1973, p. 51-64)

In this study, based on research conducted in a Jamaican rural community from July 1968 through Sept. 1969, the author found that "parties do not provide the villagers with opportunities to achieve prestige, power, or significant economic gain." Although disenchanted with parties, villagers do not turn to non-electoral politics because of continuing systemic legitimacy, expression of dissatisfaction through magic and religion, and expansion of the educational system, which opens up channels of upward mobility. For supportive data the author refers to a recently-published book.

8261. Jacobs, W. Richard. Appeals by Jamaican political parties: a study of newspaper advertisements in the 1972 Jamaican general election campaign (UPR/CS, 13:2, July 1973, p. 19-50)

Newspaper advertisements by the two major parties sought to project images that allow the analyst to gain some insight into the perceptions of the Jamaican polity held by the two principal contenders. Basic similarities of approach, but differences in style and content are found in this interesting article.

8262. Senior, Olive. The message is change: a perspective on the 1972 general elections. Kingston, Kingston Publishers, 1972. 98 p.

A journalistic account of the 1972 national elections in Jamaica by a former Public Relations Officer for the Jamaican Chamber of Commerce.

Stone, Carl. Class, race and political behaviour in urban Jamaica. See item 1296.

LESSER ANTILLES

8263. Giacottino, Jean-Claude. Les possessions néerlandaises de la Caraïbe: Antilles Hollandaises et Surinam (FDD/NED [Séries Problèmes d'Amérique Latine, 25] 3935/3936, 25 Oct. 1972, p. 45-54, map)

A useful short survey of the topic, with good maps)

8264. Poncet, Edmont. Martinique, Guadeloupe, Réunion: le pillage (EP, 240, Juillet 1974, p. 60-74)

An informative paper on worsening economic conditions in the Départments d'Outre Mer as the outcome of the policies followed by the Metropolis.

8265. Rodes, Félix. Liberté pour La Guadeloupe: 169 jours de prison. Paris, Editions du Temoignage Chrétien, 1972. 316 p.

Contains the diary of a lawyer who was imprisoned for 169 days after the popular demonstrations of 1967 and several other papers related to the struggle for the independence of Guadalupe.

PUERTO RICO

8266. Anderson, Robert W. Gobierno y partidos políticos en Puerto Rico. Madrid, Editorial Tecnos, 1973. 293 p., bibl. (Semilla y surco. Col. de ciencias sociales. Serie de ciencia política)

The Spanish translation of the best available text for the study of Puerto Rican political parties. The author has added a perceptive appendix on the 1967 plebiscite and the elections of 1968.

8267. ———. Puerto Rican politics: at the crossroads or in a rut? Reflections on the elections of 1972 (UPR/CS, 13:2, July 1973, p. 5-18)

Definitely not an empirical study, but a brilliant attempt to place the Puerto Rican elections of 1972 in a historical and theoretical context. The author, a political scientist familiar with his topic, points out the possibility "that the political system in Puerto Rico has so developed that it is incapable of generating effective internal resistances to its condition of colonial inferiority and that such pressures must originate from the outside."

8268. Buitrago Ortiz, Carlos. Ideología y conservadurismo en el Puerto Rico de hoy. Río Piedras, P.R., Ediciones Bayoan, 1972. 214 p., bibl.

Based on 117 contemporary documents (speeches, editorials, etc.) for which the selection criteria are not clear. Central tendencies are found and analyzed in successive chapters. Author concludes that such tendencies are products of three elements: history, reaction to change, and relation to external influence, i.e., colonialism, both Spanish and American.

8269. Cordasco, Francesco and **Eugene Bucchioni.** The Puerto Rican experience: a sociological sourcebook. Totowa, N.J., Rowman and Littlefield, 1973. 370 p., bibl., map.

Intended as a college sociology text, this collection of interpretative essays is designed to fill the need for a convenient sourcebook affording an overview of the Puerto Rican mainland experience. The work is organized into four parts: the island background; migration, both to the US and back to the island; mainland life; and education. The general conclusion is that no past experiences of other groups furnish a model adequate to its comprehension.

8270. Geigel Polanco, Vicente. La farsa del Estado Libre Asociado. Río Piedras, P.R., Editorial Edil, 1972. 207 p., bibl.

Articles and papers written in the last 20 years against Puerto Rico's Commonwealth status from the pro-independence point of view. The author takes a rather legalistic approach. Strongly critical of Luis Muñoz Marín.

8271. López, Alfredo. The Puerto Rican papers: notes on the re-emergence of a nation. Indianapolis, Ind., The Bobbs-Merrill, 1973. 383 p.

The first 85 p. of this book, which the author describes as a "study of Puerto Ricans in New York" (p. 89), present an overview of the Caribbean island's history from a nationalist standpoint. The remainder deals with the search by a New York-born Puerto Rican for some kind of identity as a Puerto Rican nationalist and revolutionary. More valuable as personal testimony than scholarly contribution.

8272. Maldonado-Denis, Manuel. Martí y Fanon (CDLA, 13:73, julio/agosto 1972, p. 17-27)

Another literary exercise, written by a well-known Puerto Rican intellectual and supporter of independence for the island, suggesting revolutionary affinities between the compassionate Cuban patriot and the angry author of *The wretched of the earth.*

8273. Mori, Roberto. La legitimadad política en Puerto Rico: un análisis cultural (UCPR/H, 14:28, abril 1971, p. 135-155)

According to the author, the study of political culture implies familiarity with the historical background of the political system and the process through which members are socialized into the system. Obviously, it is difficult to fulfill successfully both purposes in only 20 p.

8274. Muñoz Marín, Luis. Los gobernadores electos de Puerto Rico. v. 1, 1949-1952. Río Piedras, P.R., Corporación de Servicios Bibliotecarios, (COSEBI), 1973. 528 p., bibl.

V. 1 of a series of collections of the public documents of the elected governors of Puerto Rico deals with the first governmental period of Luis Muñoz Marín, 1949-52. Includes the texts of speeches delivered in an official capacity. All material of a partisan nature has been omitted. There is a summary of political, economic, social and cultural information and another of statistics taken from the speeches as well as a useful comprehensive index. This work is a valuable primary source for the contemporary history of Puerto Rico.

8275. Quesada, Carlos. Puerto Rico: la proletarización de una economía. Madrid, Editorial ZYX, 1972. 38 p., tables (Col. Lee y discute. Serie, 5:33)

A popular denunciation of American economic exploitation in Puerto Rico.

8276. Raynal, Vicente and **Roberto Lugo.** Manual del Gobierno Civil de Puerto Rico: 1493-1972. Río Piedras, P.R., Editorial Edil, 1972. 153 p., bibl., tables.

A guide to the structure and functioning of the political system and the public administration of Puerto Rico. Designed to meet the needs of secondary schools and universities. Good use of tables.

8277. Sánchez Tarniella, Andrés. El dilema puertorriqueño: lenguaje de libertad o lenguaje de dominación; una tesis sobre la liberación de Puerto Rico. San Juan, Ediciones Bayoan, 1973. 124 p., bibl.

Paradoxically, liberation is seen here as depoliticization. It is assumed that there is a Puerto Rican identity, which is both valuable and researchable. Once that entity has been disclosed and articulated, it would be so imperative as to make domestic squabbles insignificant. Another expression of intellectual anguish over national destiny.

8278. _____. Nuevo enfoque sobre el desarrollo político de Puerto Rico. 3. ed. rev. Río Piedras, P.R., Ediciones Bayoán, 1973. 189 p.

The new approach emphasizes the autonomist tradition and finds special merits in the constitution granted by Spain at the end of 1897. Although that constitution only applied a few months, and under exceptional circumstances, the author believes that such a short period is enough to conclude that Spain had radically changed her secular colonial policies.

8279. _____. Significados: del proceso político, del Grito de Lares, de la función electoral, de la democracia, del problema económico. Madrid, Afrodisio Aguado, 1972. 215 p.

A collection of exhortative essays favoring independence by this prolific author.

8280. Silén, Juan Angel. Hacia una visión positiva del puertorriqueño. Río Piedras, P.R., Editorial Edil, 1973. 246 p., bibl.

Essentially a polemic against the literature of "docility" implicit in Pedreira and set forth formally by Marqués. After a short historical overview, Silén concentrates on the contemporary scene to understand "the struggle for independence." Silén is not always original, but he knows how to convey a kind of authenticity that makes his work valuable and credible.

8281. Varo, Carlos. Puerto Rico: radiografía de un pueblo asediado. Río Piedras, P.R., Ediciones Puerto, 1973. 479 p.

A book-length essay which can serve as a good introduction, for the non-specialist, to the problems of Puerto Rico as a US possession. In the author's view, the only remedy to the serious social ills created by colonialism is the complete independence of the island.

8282. Williams, Byron. Puerto Rico:

commonwealth, state, or nation? N.Y., Parent's Magazine Press, 1972. 249 p.

An elementary and sympathetic history of Puerto Rico by a writer of short stories and plays.

TRINIDAD AND TOBAGO

Conference on the Implications of Independence for Grenada, *St. Augustine, T. and T., 1974.* Independence for Grenada: myth or reality? Proceedings. See item 1222.

8283. Millette, James. The politics of succession: a topical analysis of the political situation in Trinidad and Tobago. Port-of-Spain, Moko Enterprises, 1972? 12 p.

A reprint of three newspaper articles, written by a prestigious Caribbean social scientist and political leader, attacking the People's National Movement (PNM) and giving a partisan analysis of the political situation in Trinidad and Tobago. The United National Independence Party advocates a program of "Black Reconstruction," which consists of rehabilitation of blacks and Indians, better organization of the socioeconomic system, Caribbean integration, popular local participation in all industries, and establishment of new links with the Third World.

8284. Robinson, A.N.R. The mechanics of independence: patterns of political and economic transformation in Trinidad and Tobago. Cambridge, Mass., The MIT Press, 1971. 200 p., bibl.

The title seems too ambitious for this rather descriptive study, heavy on official documents and speeches, but lacking any unifying framework attempting to explain "the mechanics of independence." The book, by a distinguished scholar and politician from Trinidad, is informative, but reveals nothing of the author's personal experience in the government of his country.

8285. Trinidad and Tobago. Constitution Commission. Thinking things through. Port-of-Spain, Government Printery, 1972. 112 p.

A review of the present constitution with the purpose of eliciting suggestions and advice from the people which will help the Commission to write a new constitutional proposal for Trinidad and Tobago.

THE GUIANAS

GUYANA

8286. Congress of the People's Progressive Party, *XVI, Anna Regina Estequiro, Guyana, 1970.* Report of the General Council approved by the . . . . Georgetown, 1970. 20 p. (mimeo)

A report approved by the Congress of the PPP, reorganized since 1969, according to the documents, "into a disciplined, Marxist-Leninist type party." Strongly criticizes the government of the People's National Congress (PNC). The new "line" recommends "a resolute united action on the part of all who cherish democracy and freedom."

8287. Grant, C.H. Political sequence to ALCAN nationalization in Guyana: the international aspects (UWI/SES, 22:2, June 1973, p. 249-271, bibl.)

The Demerra Bauxite Company, a subsidiary of the Aluminum Company of Canada (ALCAN) was nationalized on 15 July 1971. The strategies adopted by Alcan, the commercial banks, and the World Bank during the conflict are analyzed in this perceptive paper. The author suggests that the dependency model "should give more recognition to the fact that pressures upon the government are also generated by the international corporation either directly or in such a way that they bring the protective function of the international political groupings into play."

8288. Griffith, Cecil C. Within four walls. Lacytown, Guyana, n.p., 1971. 76 p., illus., plates.

An account of Guyana's penal system based on the author's experience during 17 years as a prison official. A comparison is made between the situation in the prisons in 1940 and that of 1971. He calls for a "new approach" to crime deterrence and penology.

Hanley, Eric R. Rice, politics and development in Guyana. See item 1241.

8289. Hazard, John. Guyana's alternative to socialist and capitalist legal models (AJCL, 16:4, 1968, p. 507-523)

Beginning with a short description of the three principal political tendencies in the new country, the article then discusses legal models and patterns that have come into force. Raises provocative questions concerning the nature and the future of the law in a new state seeking eclectic solutions. The ideological and value tendencies implicit in these solutions are at sharp variance with those that prevailed historically in the making of English common law. [P.B. Taylor, Jr.]

8290. Hope, Kempe R. The role of government expenditure in the economic development in Guyana: 1960-1970 (American Economist [Cambridge, Mass] 16:2, Fall 1972, p. 166-174, bibl., tables)

The two Development Programs, 1960-64 and 1966-72, are compared, and the role of the government is criticized in this paper written by a graduate student and statistician.

8291. Irving, Brian *ed.* Guyana: a composite monograph. Hato Rey, P.R., Inter American Univ. Press, 1972. 87 p., map.

A collection of articles by scholars with excellent reputations and considerable knowledge in the area. Designed as a follow-up to an earlier study (1964). Tries to determine progress made since independence by focusing on history, politics, economic development, race, and ecology. The central problem emerging from the study is one of creating unity in a land of racial and religious diversity. Recommended as a good introduction to present-day Guyana.

8292. Jagan, Cheddi. A West Indian state: pro-imperialist or anti-imperialist. Lacytown, Guyana, New Guyana Co., 1972. 72 p.

The Guyanese leader analyzes the failure of the Caribbean Federation in the 1960s and shows skepticism toward a new attempt in the 1970s, since the Grenada Declaration of 1971 does not offer an anti-imperialist program. Articles originally published in the *Sunday Mirror* of London.

8293. Jagan, Janet. Army intervention in the 1973 elections in Guyana. Georgetown, People's Progressive Party, Education Committee, 1973. 93 p., plates.

The accusation that numerous frauds were committed by the party in power during the 1973 elections is substantiated in this tract by Mrs. Cheddi Jagan, but the data does not seem to support the statement made in the title.

Kramer, Jane. Letter from Guyana. See item 1250.

8294. People's Progressive Party. People's Progressive Party: 1950-1971, 21 years. Lacytown, Guyana, New Guyana Co., 1972. 55 p., illus., plates.

Major events in the life of the Party, with photos.

8295. Premdas, Ralph R. Competitive party organizations and political integration in a racially fragmented state: the case of Guyana (UPR/CS, 12:4, Jan. 1973, p. 5-35)

Although the two major parties pretend to project a multiracial image, cross-sectional voting is virtually absent, and what party competition has really done is to exacerbate the ethnic conflict already present before the 1950s. Party documentation, interviews and participant observations in 1968-69 have been used for this perceptive study.

SOUTH AMERICA: WEST COAST

(Colombia, Ecuador, Peru, Bolivia, Chile)

JOHN J. BAILEY
*Assistant Professor of Government
Director, Latin American Studies Program
Georgetown University*

CHILE, OF COURSE, CONTINUES TO DOMINATE the literature on the West Coast countries, as it has in previous volumes of the *Handbook*. The substantial writing on the novelty of the "peaceful way to socialism" has been swamped by the outpouring of denunciations, justifications and (a few) explanations of the Sept. 1973 coup d'etat and subsequent military government. The literature on the overthrow of President Allende's government may equal or surpass in quantity the writing on guerrilla movements in Latin America, since the Chilean case was viewed from diverse quarters as a significant test of a democratic means to socialism and a potentially important innovation in marxian theory. Now is still the emotion-laden stage of extracting immediate political lessons, and the conclusions drawn vary according to ideological perspective. So rapid and extensive has been the reaction to the Chilean coup that the items reviewed here constitute an incomplete sampling, and so controversial is this case that perhaps more than usual the reviewer's bias must perforce affect judgments of merit. Roughly considered, the items on the coup may be grouped in terms of variations on two general themes: 1) A conspiracy of US imperialism, allied with a reactionary oligarchy and military, effected the overthrow in order to forestall a genuine popular revolution (items 8422a, 8433, 8441, 8458, 8474, 8485, 8491, 8495, 8500, and 8504); and 2) the coup was the tragic consequence of Popular Unity's administrative incompetence and Allende's political miscalculation and mismanagement (items 8423, 8435, 8484, and 8494). A definitive account is not to be found here, although significant efforts are to be expected in the next biennium.

Dependency theory has achieved almost the status of orthodoxy among Latin American scholars as the explanation for the region's underdevelopment, and applications of the theory range widely from a kind of fundamentalist cant to subtle and interesting analyses (items 8335 and 8344). There is growing interest in dependency theory among North American scholars as well, and the contributions in this section by Theodore Moran (item 8482) and Charles Goodsell (item 8372) merit particular attention. Striking in the literature on Colombia is the sense of frustration with and alienation from the controlled democracy and incremental development of the National Front experiment (items 8307, 8313, and 8323), while some fascination with the Peruvian regime continues (items 8369, 8379-8380, and 8384). In terms of research in the behavioral tradition, the contributions by John Magill (item 8412), Howard Handleman (item 8373), and Genaro Arriagada (item 8425) are particularly interesting in that all systematically ground their case studies in the relevant literature and theories. For similar reasons, Peter Cleaves' study of administrative policymaking in Chile will be of considerable interest to students of bureaucracy and development policy glly (item 8444).

The standard criticism that too little of the literature in the field is structured in a systematic and comparative fashion applies here. Also, the lack of current and substantial country surveys is a notable gap. It may be useful to remind the reader, however, that much of the political analysis reviewed here reflects efforts by scholars in and of the region to diagnose and act upon concrete problems encountered in national political life. Greater worth, then, attaches to relevance to ongoing political concerns than to methodological rigor or theoretical innovation.

COLOMBIA

8296. Acerca de la estrategia revolucionaria en Colombia. Bogotá? 1974? 247 p. (Cuadernos socialistas)

Four essays on Colombian politics from 1971-72 by Trotskyite faction of Left, originally published in *Prensa Obrera* and *Espártaco*.

8297. Arango Jaramillo, Mario. Ancestro afroindígena de las instituciones colombianas: bases para una revolución nacional. Bogotá, Ediciones Bochica, 1972. 289 p., bibl.

The causes of Colombian crisis are found in the adoption of Liberalism after Independence, while neglecting a secular past that is rooted in "the great empires of pre-Columbian America, Western Africa, and Medieval Spain." The author, a "student leader, lawyer, journalist, and traveler," according to the preface, digs in with more zeal than scholarship. [A. Suárez]

8298. Araújo Merlano, Alberto. Las cartas sobre la mesa: ¿por qué proliferan los peculados? intimidades de mis denuncias en Colpuertos. Bogotá, Ediciones Tercer Mundo, 1973. 105 p.

Series of documents, letters, and interviews concerning charges of corruption and conflict of interest in an important decentralized agency brought by a former director of the agency. Useful materials for research on administrative policymaking.

8299. Arenas, Jacobo. Diario de la resistencia de Marquetalia. 2. ed. Bogotá? Ediciones Abejón Mono, 1972. 138 p. (Serie Historia y testimonio)

Interesting memoir by guerrilla leader and Communist party member of the defense of Marquetalia (southern Tolima) against Colombian government troops during 1964-65.

8300. Arizmendi Posada, Octavio. Parlamento y subdesarrollo en América Latina. Bogotá, Ediciones Tercer Mundo, 1972. 80 p., tables (Cuadernitos. Que despierte el leñador. Serie púrpura: temas colombianos, 13)

Former member of Colombian Congress and Minister of Education speculates on institutional reforms necessary to link parliaments functionally to development decision-making. Prescriptive emphasis.

8300a. ———. Políticas contra el desempleo. Bogotá, Editorial Revista Colombiana, 1973. 185 p. (Populibro, 54)

Former Minister of Education in Colombia critiques conventional measures of economic development (industrialization, GNP) and stresses unemployment as the central problem in developing countries. Straightforward, systematic analysis of causes of unemployment in agriculture, industry, and services, with numerous specific recommendations on technology, fiscal policy, and government regulation for alleviating high levels of unemployment.

8301. Avila, Rafael. Teología evangelización y liberación. Bogotá, Ediciones Paulinas [and] Indo-American Press Service, 1973. 111 p., illus., tables (Col. Iglesia liberadora, 3)

Essays (some published previously) on evolution of theology of liberation in Latin America, with emphasis on Colombia. Attempts to integrate social sciences and theology; domination, dependency, alienation themes stressed.

8302. Bases mínimas para el programa del

Frente de Oposición Democrática. Bogotá, Congreso del Partido Comunista de Colombia, 1971. 58 p.

Colombian Communist Party's assessment of world situation and domestic Colombian politics as of late 1971.

8303. Broderick, Walter J. Camilo Torres: a biography of the priest-guerrillero. Garden City. N.Y., Doubleday, 1975. 370 p., bibl., map, plates.

Wholly sympathetic and somewhat superficial treatment of Torres written for general audience.

8304. Caballero, Enrique. El Mesías de Handel. Bogotá, Tipografía Hispana, 1972. 146 p.

A "pre-campaign" piece, revives charges of alleged unethical business activities on part of Alfonso López Michelsen in early 1940s. The scandal contributed to downfall of President Alfonso López Pumarejo in 1945.

8305. Calibán [pseud. for Enrique Santos Montejo]. Danza de las horas. Bogotá, Instituto Colombiano de Cultura, 1972. 156 p. (Biblioteca colombiana de cultura. Col. popular, 25)

Thirty-five selections, majority from 1930s-40s, from the *El Tiempo* column by the Liberal party activist.

8306. Camargo, Pedro Pablo and Angelina de Coral. La violación de derechos humanos en Colombia: el problema indígena, la justicia militar o de excepción, el trato a los presos políticos, el Concordato. Bogotá, Ediciones Libro Abierto, 1974. 49 p.

Protests assimilationist policies vis-à-vis Indian communities, violations of political rights, and treatment of political prisoners.

8307. Castello Salazar, Jorge Daniel. Crisis: el dedo en la llaga de las instituciones políticas, religiosas y civiles. Bogotá, Ediciones Tercer Mundo, 1974. 145 p., illus.

Brief commentaries on politics, religion, divorce, and a variety of other things by a solid member of Colombia's middle class. Heavily laced with skepticism and cynicism, these essays are a noteworthy indicator of the disintegrating legitimacy of established institutions.

8308. Castrillón R., Alberto. 120 [i.e., Ciento veinte] días bajo el terror militar. Bogotá, Ediciones Tupac-Amarú, 1974. 133 p.

Reprints the Army's charges against Castrillón, who was a labor leader involved in the United Fruit strike and massacre of 1928, and his speech in self-defense before the Colombian Congress in 1929.

8309. Chiappe, C. and J. Uribe. Iglesia y aspiraciones del pueblo colombiano. Bogotá, Centro de Investigaciones y Acción Social (CIAS) [and] Instituto de Doctrina y Estudios Sociales (IDES) 1971. 37 l. (Documentos de trabajo, 6)

Liberal critique of Colombian Bishops' statement of 5 March 1971 in response to civic disorder. Discussion of private property and reform programs in agriculture, industry, and urban areas.

8310. Child, Jorge. López y el pensamiento liberal: introducción a la conciencia nacional. Bogotá, Ediciones Tercer Mundo, 1974. 82 p. (Col. Tribuna libre)

Sympathetic interpretation of López and MRL (Movimiento Revolucionario Liberal) ideology by former activist in Movement. Dependency, populist, and state interventionist themes predominate.

8311. Concientizar y organizar a las masas. Bogotá, Editorial América Latina, 1974. 395 p.

An interesting study and discussion guide for group leaders in consciousness-raising, prepared in terms of radical Christian ethics. Offers 42 lesson plans, together with suggestions for tactics, further readings, etc., as to how to overcome the oppression of the US and its agents in Colombian life. [P.B. Taylor, Jr.]

8312. Consuegra Higgins, José. Como se reprime la universidad en Colombia: informe a la comunidad de la Universidad del Atlántico. Bogotá, Editorial Mejoras, 1972? 40 p.

1971-72 were difficult years for Colombian universities. Case of Atlántico illustrates national-departmental interests in conflict with ideal of university autonomy.

8313. Delgado, Oscar *comp.* Ideologías políticas y agrarias en Colombia. t. 1, La burguesía conservadora: burguesía dependiente, patriciado político, tecnoburocracia desarrollista. Selección y prefacio de . . . Bogotá, Ediciones Tercer Mundo, 1973. 176 p.

Series devoted to demonstrating ideological exhaustion and irrelevance of traditional Colombian political groups vis-à-vis challenges of development and justice. V. 1 devoted to significant speeches and writings on agrarian reform by party leaders (principally Conservative) and technicians. Future volumes projected on Liberal Party, ANAPO, and marxists.

8314. Dent, David W. Oligarchy and power structure in urban Colombia: the case of Cali (JLAS, 6:1, May 1974, p. 113-133, tables)

Based on 1966 survey data (N=65) assesses utility of concept "oligarchy" as descriptive of Cali elite behavior. Stresses perceived separation of political and economic elites and relatively greater power attributed to latter group.

8315. Desarrollo político del movimiento estudiantil. Cali, Colo., Univ. del Valle, Federación de Estudiantes, 1973. 443 p.

Documents by student groups pertaining to the extensive conflicts and strikes at the Univ. del Valle during 1970-73.

8316. Drake, George F. Elites and voluntary associations: a study of community power in Manizales. Madison, Univ. of Wisconsin, Land Tenure Center, 1973. 58 p., tables (Research paper, 52)

Summary of author's dissertation, contains useful data and analysis of voluntary associations at local level.

8317. Fals Borda, Orlando. Reflexiones sobre la aplicación del método de estudio-acción en Colombia (UNAM/RMS, 35:1, enero/marzo 1973, p. 49-62)

Reports on emergence of a science-action methodology by Rosca de Investigación Social of Colombia. Underlying premise is marxian conflict model and logic is to combine analysis with strategic activity to foment revolutionary change.

8318. Gall, Norman. Los indocumentados colombianos. Hanover, N.H., American Universities Field Staff Reports, 1972. 19 p., maps, plates (East coast South American series, 16:2)

Analyzes the sharp disparities in national wealth which have triggered what "appears to have become the largest human migration in South America's history." Discusses conflict over the Gulf of Venezuela which has exacerbated the illegal migration problem of Colombians to Venezuela.

8319. Groves, Roderick T. The Colombian National Front and administrative reform (Administration and Society [Beverly Hills, Calif.] 6:3, Nov. 1974, p. 316-336)

Identifies political stability and elite commitment as significant factors accounting for reform progress in reorganization, personnel, budgeting, and planning. Stresses limited impact of administrative reform on creating legitimacy.

8320. Guillén Martínez, Fernando. El poder: los modelos estructurales del poder político en Colombia. Bogotá, Univ. Nacional de Colombia, Centro de Investigaciones para el Desarrollo (CID), 1973. 391 p., bibl. (mimeo)

In the tradition of Toqueville, explores relationships between nature of economy and society, nature of political associations, and nature of government. Indicates discrete historical periods, whose patterns of relationships are analyzed as distinct models. Emphasis on 19th and early 20th centuries. This is a working draft in mimeo form, with troublesome stylistic problems (references in the texts do not correspond to end notes), but one of substantial scholarly worth, which suggests a significant contribution in the near future.

8321. Hoskin, Gary and Gerald Swanson. Political party leadership in Colombia: a spatial analysis (CUNY/CP, 6:3, April 1974, p. 395-423, tables)

Based on survey of Colombian political leaders, argues that party system impedes structural change. Perceptions of internal cohesion and inter-party relations are biased by leaders' organizational position, which accounts for weak class awareness and lack of structural revolution.

8322. Kline, Harvey F. Interest groups in the Colombian Congress: group behavior in a centralized, patrimonial political system (UM/JIAS, 16:3, Aug. 1974, p. 274-300, bibl., tables)

Based on survey of 70 percent of Colombian congressmen (1969?) analyzes both perceptions of strength of interest groups and frequency of their contacts with congressmen. Emphasizes patrimonial and cooptive nature of elitist politics to account for findings.

8323. Lagos, Félix. Explotación y liberación. Bogotá, Editorial Margen Izquierdo, 1974. 250 p.

Simplified and simplistic marxian analysis of imperialism and nature of Colombian polity.

8324. Lleras Restrepo, Carlos. El Liberalismo colombiano: 1972. Bogotá, Ediciones Tercer Mundo, 1973. 77 p. (Col. Tribuna libre. Serie menor, 2)

The former president remains active in national politics. An extensive overview of Liberal party ideology and review of principal policy problems both foreign and domestic.

8325. Lloreda Caicedo, Rodrigo. La juventud en el gobierno: conferencias y discursos durante su administración. Cali, Colo., Imprenta Deptal, 1969. 142 p.

Speeches by Governor of Valle del Cauca from period Sept. 1968-Aug. 1969. Insights on subnational governance.

8326. López Michelsen, Alfonso. Un mandato claro. Bogotá, Canal Ramírez-Antares, 1973. 159 p.

Fragments of speeches from López' 1972-73 presidential campaign, which led to his election in 1974 by a substantial margin.

8326a. ———; Alvaro Gómez Hurtado; María Eugenia Rojas; and Hernando Echeverry Mejía. Plataformas económicas de los candidatos presidenciales: 1974-1978. Bogotá, Sociedad Colombiana de Economistas, 1973. 69 p., tables (Revista de la SCE, 22)

Special issue of the Society's magazine with economic analyses by principal presidential candidates in 1974. Useful reference.

8327. Losada, Rodrigo. Incidencia de factores sociales personales en las opiniones políticas del congresista colombiano. Bogotá, Univ. de los Andes, Facultad de Artes y Ciencias, Depto. de Ciencia Política, 1972. 83 l.

Sequel to author's *Perfil socio-político del congresista colombiano* (see *HLAS 35:7661*) which, based upon same data, explores interrelationships between socialization factors and political opinions.

8328. Lozano Simonelli, Fabio. El eclipse del Liberalismo. Bogotá, Ediciones Tercer Mundo, 1971. 86 p. (Cuadernitos. Que despierte el leñador. Serie púrpura, 7)

Whither the Colombian Liberal Party? Speeches, letters, and essays from 1969-71 by one of the younger party leaders.

8329. Lucha obrera. 2. ed. n.p., n.p., 1972. 106 p., illus.

A pamphlet for the education of the Colombian working class. Although written with obvious revolutionary intentions, it is free—rara avis—of clichés or dogmatisms. [A. Suárez]

8330. Manual de práctica sindical. Bogotá? n.p., 1972? 154 p.

Published during early 1970s either by or on behalf of Communist-affiliated CSTC (Confederación Sindical de Trabajadores Colombianos) this is a working manual on details of founding and running labor unions.

8331. Marin Vargas, Ramón. Sus mejores páginas. Manizales, Colo., Gobierno Departamental de Caldas, 1973. 560 p. (Biblioteca de autores caldenses, 6:37)

Editorials, speeches, letters, and essays from early 1940s to mid-1960s by leader in Caldas Liberal Party. Useful compilation for contemporary regional history.

8332. Martínez, Juan Pablo and María Isabel Izquierdo. ANAPO: oposición o revolución. Bogotá, Ediciones Camilo, 1972. 103 p.

Marxian critique of ANAPO as influenced by conservative and latifundist interests and hindering the development of revolutionary forces.

8333. Maullin, Richard L. Soldiers, guerrillas, and politics in Colombia. Lexington, Mass., D.C. Heath, 1973. 168 p., bibl., tables (Lexington books)

"This study focuses on the concept of military professionalization as it relates to internal political violence in Colombia and as a factor in the Colombian military's political behavior." Clearly focused and well-executed middle-range analysis of domestic and international factors affecting internal guerrilla activity and the military's adaptations. Concentrating principally on 1960s, skillfully grounds analysis in a variety of aggregate data sources.

8334. Mejía Maya, Ignacio. Guía administrativa. Medellín, Colo., Editorial Granamérica, 1971. 181 p.

Handbook for Colombian local government, with sections on municipal council, budget, and public employees.

8335. Mendoza, Alberto and Germán Castillo. Colombia ¿auténtica o enajenada? Bogotá, Ediciones Tercer Mundo, 1973. 129 p. (Col. Tribuna libre. Serie menor, 3)

Based on a series of meetings in late 1971 of outstanding young professionals, businessmen, government officials, and Church leaders, a diagnosis of national reality. Dependency themes predominate.

8336. Operación Cacique: tácticas de intrusión de los Estados Unidos en la universidad colombiana. Bogotá, Ediciones Camilo, 1972. 102 p.

Bitter indictment of the imposition of foreign (largely US) norms and procedures in Colombian higher education. Criticism revolves around the 1967 Basic Plan for Higher Education in which an advisory group from Berkeley played an important role. Study prepared by members of the science faculty of the Univ. Nacional.

8337. Palacios, Marco. El populismo en Colombia. Bogotá, Editorial Siuasinza, 1971. 130 p. (Ediciones el tigre de papel, 1)

Interprets historical origins and characteristics of protest movements in Colombia, with special attention to National Popular Alliance (ANAPO) of ex-President Rojas Pinilla. Analyzes ideology and social composition of ANAPO to speculate on future directions of movement.

8338. Pécaut, Daniel; Ivon LeBot; and Pierre Gilhodes. Colombie, 1971-74. Paris, La Documentation Française, 1974. 110 p., maps, tables (Notes et Etudes Documentaires, 4139/4141. Problèmes d'Amérique latine, 34)

Broad and exhaustive documentary coverage of Colombia. Topics are: politics at the end of the National Front; economic strategy; student movements (1958-74); modernization of agriculture; the 1974 election; political stabilization; and peasant movements. Includes detailed chronology. [P.B. Taylor, Jr.]

8339. La política revolucionaria en Colombia: una aproximación crítica. [Material publicado en] *Crítica Marxista*. Bogotá, Editorial Latina, 1972? 154 p.

Eight essays on class struggle, student movement, art, dependency, and revisionism in a Colombian context, reprinted from the pro-Cuban *Crítica Marxista* (Cali, Colo., 1971-72).

8340. Ramírez Díaz, Luis Jorge. El sindicalismo en el mundo moderno. Bogotá, Pontificia Univ. Javeriana, Facultad de Ciencias Jurídicas y Socio-Económicas, 1972. 204 p.

Comparative study of labor movements in developed and developing countries, with emphasis on Colombia and from a legal-historical viewpoint. Of interest to students of sindicalism and corporatism, since author attempts to clarify these concepts. A law degree thesis.

8341. Ramírez Moreno, Augusto. Dialéctica anticomunista. Bogotá, Ediciones Tercer Mundo, 1973. 121 p. (Col. Tribuna libre. Serie menor, 1)

Series of brief critiques of marxian tenets (e.g., surplus value) aimed at mass audience.

8342. Restrepo A., Ignacio. Reflexiones sobre la abstención electoral en Colombia (PUJ/U, 43, Nov. 1972, p. 333-354)

Electoral abstention under National Front has generated considerable commentary. Reviews principal causes of voluntary and involuntary nonvoting, and emphasizes illiteracy as perhaps most significant factor.

8343. Restrepo Uribe, Jorge. La República de Antioquia. Medellín, Colo., Editorial Bedout, 1972. 336 p., tables.

As Colombia's second-ranking department in terms of production and population, Antioquia chafes under the centralization of decison-making in Bogotá. Documents and articles (majority from Medellín's *El Colombiano*) on themes of decentralization and federalism.

8343a. ———; **J. Emilio Duque Echeverri;** and **Samuel Syro Giraldo.** Federalismo moderno. Medellín, Colo., Editorial Bedout, 1974. 290 p.

Centralism-federalism, long a source of controversy in Colombia, is revived due to increased assumption of economic controls by central government. Federalist position, largely based in Antioquia, prefers greater decentralization. See also item 8343.

8344. Roa Suárez, Hernando. Colombia: dependiente y no participante; aspectos económicos, sociales, culturales y políticos de la participación; aproximación a un análisis crítico. Bogotá, Ediciones Tercer Mundo, 1973. 143 p., bibl., tables (Col. Tribuna libre)

Within dependency framework, attempts analysis of factors promoting and inhibiting individual and class participation in social, political, and economic life of Colombia. Systematic attempt to mobilize data to support analysis.

8345. Rodríguez Mariño, Tomás. El proceso de las decisiones públicas. Bogotá, Editextos, 1973. 150 p., illus.

Sketches principal historical periods to demonstrate interrelations of technology, economy and decision-making processes. Point of argument is to counter claims of universal applicability of political institutions as proffered by great powers. Quite ambitious exercise in historical interpretation and advocacy.

8346. Rojas, Humberto and **Alvaro Camacho.** El Frente Nacional: ideología y realidad. Bogotá, Punta de Lanza, 1973? 187 p., tables.

Humberto Rojas "El Frente Nacional: Ideología y Realidad," explores basic discrepancy between claims made and results accomplished under National Front, while Alvaro Camacho, "La Encrucijada del Frente Nacional," employs marxian analysis to reach similar conclusions on failure of bipartisan experiment.

8347. Roux López, Rodolfo de and others. Socialismo y Cristianismo. Bogotá, Centro de Investigación y Acción Social (CIAS) [and] Instituto de Doctrina y Estudios Sociales (IDES), 1971. 48 l. (Documento de trabajo, 4)

Moves from Pope Paul VI's call for analysis of relationship between Christian and socialist thought within context of individual nations to examine nature and prospects of capitalism and socialism in Colombia. Advocates "communitarian society."

8348. Sandoval Aguayo, Alberto. Revolución o subdesarrollo. Cali, Colo., Editorial Pacífico, 1973. 104 p., bibl.

Analyzes and critiques Latin American political economy from dependency perspective.

8349. Santa, Eduardo. Realidad y futuro del municipio colombiano. Bogotá, Univ. Nacional de Colombia, Dirección de Divulgación Cultural, 1969. 79 p., bibl.

Brief survey of historical evolution of municipality in Latin America and prescriptive discussion of reforms needed to reinvigorate Colombian municipio. Author is distinguished sociologist at National University.

8350. Schmidt, Steffen W. Bureaucrats as modernizing brokers?: clientelism in Colombia (CUNY/CP, 6:3, April 1974, p. 425-450, table)

Discusses relationship between partisan conflict and

patronage in context of increasingly technical bureaucracy and termination of National Front. Speculates on likelihood of greater brokerage role for bureaucrats in post-Front system.

8350a. _____. **La violencia revisited: the clientelist bases of political violence in Colombia** (JLAS, 6:1, May 1974, p. 97-111, tables)

La violencia activated and strengthened patron-client linkages along partisan lines. Relates vignettes on consequences of violence for townspeople of Salado, Nariño state.

8351. Schoultz, Lars. The Roman Catholic Church in Colombia: revolution, reform, and reaction (CLAPCS/AL, 14:3, julho/dez. 1971, p. 90-108)

Based on secondary sources, an impressionistic survey of historical development and contemporary characteristics of Colombian Church.

8352. Sherman, Gail Richardson. Colombian political bases of the Andean Pact statute on foreign capitals: national influences on international regulation of foreign investment (UM/JIAS, 15:1, Feb. 1973, p. 102-121, bibl.)

When an elite-based government manipulates nationalism to create mass support for public policy, tensions and inconsistencies result. Discusses problems inherent in Colombian government's 1971 strategy for adoption of Andean Pact accords. Useful addition to literature on domestic determinants of foreign policy.

Silva Gotay, Samuel. Teoría de la revolución de Camilo Torres: su contexto y sus consecuencias continentales. See *HLAS 36:5232.*

8353. Solaún, Mauricio and Fernando Cepeda. Political and legal challenges to foreign direct private investment in Colombia (UM/JIAS, 15:1, Feb. 1973, p. 77-101, bibl.)

Describes recent Colombian law on private foreign investment. Identifies ANAPO, traditional parties, marxist groups, and the military as primary contenders in the short-run, and assesses likely impacts on investment policy given various possible scenarios.

8354. Torres, M. ¿Democracia burguesa o democracia revolucionaria? Medellín, Colo., Editorial La Pulga, 1974. 167 p.

Marxian analysis of tactical errors committed during 1960s by Movimiento Obrero Estudiantil Campesino, Movimiento Obrero Independiente y Revolucionario, Movimiento Revolucionaria Liberal and ANAPO, in mobilizing electoral masses to achieve "revolutionary democracy."

8355. Torres Restrepo, Camilo. Revolutionary writings. Introduction by Maurice Zeitlin. N.Y., Harper & Row, 1972. 371 p.

Revision and amplification of Camilo Torres, *Revolutionary Writings* (N.Y., Herder & Herder, 1969 see *HLAS 33:7916*) translated by Robert Olsen and Linda Day. Reprints major sociological and political writings and speeches by Camilo Torres during 1956-66. Introduction is scathing critique of Colombian social conditions and US policy.

8356. Velásquez M., Luis Guillermo. De la posdata al mandato: la política de ingresos, precios y salarios. Bogotá, Editorial Publicaciones Educativas, 1974. 300 p.

Culls some 100 policy commitments from campaign speeches by López. Reviews earlier essays, statements, etc., by López to characterize president's positions on partisan and policy questions.

8357. Vieira, Gilberto; Francisco Mosquera; and Ricardo Sánchez. Colombia: tres vías a la revolución; Partido Comunista, MOIR [Movimiento Obrero Independiente Revolucionario], tendencia socialista. Entrevistas preparadas y realizadas por Oscar Collazos y Umberto Valverde. Bogotá, Círculo Rojo Editores, 1973. 208 p.

Interviews with three leaders of Colombia's marxist left (mid-1972) are useful in delineating principal lines of analysis (and strategy) and understanding sources of dissention in this camp.

8358. Villaveces, Jorge. Vida y pasión de Alianza Nacional Popular. Bogotá, Talleres de la Imprenta de Eduardo Salazar F., 1974. 267 p.

Documents, letters, and speeches by ANAPO activist from 1957-73. Contains ANAPO's detailed allegations of official fraud in 1970 presidential elections.

8359. Zuluaga, Francisco. Estructuras eclesiásticas de Colombia. 2. ed. actualizada y aumentada. Bogotá, Centro de Investigación y Acción Social (CIAS), 1971. 65 p., maps, tables (Col. Monografías y documentos, 1)

Quite useful collection of data on variety of Church-related topics: characteristics of priests and orders, parish organization, nature of hierarchy. Good historical base, with emphasis on 1950s to 1969-70.

ECUADOR

Brownrigg, Leslie Ann. Interest groups in regime changes in Ecuador. See item 1436.

8360. Filosofía y plan de gobierno en el Ecuador (IAEERI/E, 3:15, marzo/abril 1972, p. 57-60)

Military government of Feb. 1972, defines itself as revolutionary, nationalistic, social humanist, and disciplined. Criticizes past stagnation and inertia and stresses greater state intervention for development, welfare, and redistribution of wealth.

8361. Grecic, Vladimir. Trasfondos del golpe de estado en el Ecuador (IAEERI/E, 3:15, marzo/abril 1972, p. 53-56)

Brief note on events leading to Feb. 1972 coup d'etat.

8362. Larrea Alba, L. La defensa del estado en los cuatro frentes: el frente exterior, político-diplomático, el frente económico, el frente bélico, el frente interno. Quito, Editorial Casa de la Cultura Ecuatoriana, 1972. 346 p.

General treatise on political, economic, and military factors which condition the formulation of foreign policy. Written from Ecuadorean perspective but with greater emphasis on theory.

PERU

Alonso, Enrique. Fuerzas armadas y revolución nacional en Bolivia y Perú. See item 8392.

8363. Benavides Correa, Alfonso. True freedom of press. Lima, Oficina Nacional de Información, 1970. 157 p.

Reprints decree-law of 1969 and implementing decree of 1970 which regulate Peruvian press. Bulk of text devoted to defense of government's action. Important document as it relates to Peruvian case specifically and the exercise of justice in an authoritarian regime generally.

8364. *Beseda s General'nym sekretarem Tsk Peruanskoi Kompartii Khorkle del' Prado* (Interview with the General Secretary of the Peruvian Communist Party Jorge del Prado) (Latinskaia Amerika [Latin American Institute, USSR Academy of Sciences, Moscow] 4, July/Aug. 1974, p. 50-58)

Prado discusses the attitudes of the Peruvian Communist Party toward the Velasco government for a Soviet audience. Rejects the idea that junta is plying a road between capitalism and socialism—says Peru is definitely moving toward socialism. While substantial reforms had been made by nationalization and land reform, Prado felt in summer of 1974 that oligarch influence was still strong in the press, radio, TV and banking enterprises. Calls for the Peruvian Communist Party to lead in forming a united front of unions and other groups to support the government.

8365. Bobbio Centurión, Carlos. Contratos de petróleo: modelo peruano (CEHMP/R, 19:20, 1972, p. 148-158)

Outlines principal criteria of "Peruvian Model" of petroleum contracts. Evaluates comparable policies in other oil producing countries and argues the advantages of the Peruvian instrument. Useful glimpse into regime's development thinking.

Campbell, Leon G. The historiography of the Peruvian guerrilla movement, 1960-1965. See *HLAS 36:2895*.

8366. Chaney, Elsa M. Old and new feminists in Latin America: the case of Peru and Chile (WRU/JMF, 35:2, May 1973, p. 331-343)

Traces historical evolution of feminist movements since latter 19th century. Suggests that traditional role prescriptions for appropriate female behavior have persisted, tend to be accepted by both male and female, and will likely result in a distinctively conservative women's movement in these countries.

8366a. ———. Women in Latin American politics: the case of Chile and Peru (*in* Pescatello, Ann *ed.* Female and male in Latin America: essays. Pittsburgh, Pa., Univ. of Pittsburgh Press, 1973, p. 103-139, tables)

Draws on author's field work in latter 1960s to discuss historical, structural and attitudinal determinants of female political participation, primarily in voting and party activity, although with some attention to the very few female officeholders. Descriptive emphasis. For historian's comment see *HLAS 36:2897*.

8367. Chirinos Soto, Enrique. En dos análisis: golpe de estado, habeas corpus. Lima, Librería Editorial Minerva, 1974? 96 p.

Transcripts of lectures on constitutional aspects of coup d'etat and legal status of habeas corpus, especially as latter applies to case of Catholic Univ. of Peru. Historical and prescriptive emphases.

8368. Collin-Delavaud, Claude. Trois années de Révolution militaire au Pérou (FDD/NED [Problèmes d'Amérique latine, 22] 3847/3848, 27 déc. 1971, p. 33-80, bibl.)

Useful general examination of the events of 1969-71, under the supervision of the military government established in Oct. 1968. The competent text is supported by a chronology of events during the three-year period. [P.B. Taylor, Jr.]

8369. Delgado Olivera, Carlos. Significado político y social del proceso revolucionario peruano (Libre [Paris] 3, marzo/mayo 1972, p. 35-43)

Critiques marxist and behavioralist misunderstanding of Peruvian revolution. Emphasizes institutional transformation of armed forces and conservatism of traditional parties to account for 1968 coup d'etat and suggests that new political forms will emerge spontaneously from the course of the revolution.

8369a. _____. Testimonio de lucha. Lima, Ediciones Peisa, 1973. 267 p. (Biblioteca peruana, 9)

Published as part of government's educational program, this is an expanded version of *El proceso revolucionario peruano: testimonio de lucha* (Mexico, Siglo XXI, 1972). Includes 32 short essays on various aspects on junta's philosophy and programs.

8370. DeWind, Adrian. From peasants to miners: the background to strikes in the mines of Peru (SS, 39:1, Spring 1975, p. 44-72)

Describes forces (mechanization of production and commercialization of peasant economy) which, since the 1920s, have led to class consciousness and militancy among miners in large-scale enterprises. Predicts continued miner-government conflicts based upon 1970-71 strikes.

8371. Frías, Ismael. Nacionalismo y autogestión. Lima, Ediciones Inkarrí, 1971. 275 p.

Short essays on a wide variety of political, social, and economic subjects by regime's leading marxist defender. Reprinted from Lima press, 1969-70.

8372. Goodsell, Charles T. American corporations and Peruvian politics. Cambridge, Mass., Harvard Univ. Press, 1974. 272 p., bibl., tables.

Based upon three orienting hypotheses, derived from "economic imperialism" as well as development literature, analyzes consequences of large US corporations for Peruvian domestic politics. Finds generally that US companies have participated actively in Peruvian politics, utilizing their economic power and national backing, to win policies favorable (or at least acceptable) to company interests. Finds as well that Velasco government (1968-present) has severely limited influence on US companies. Calls for greater awareness of diverse forms and consequences of foreign investment in developing countries. Solid book.

Giusti, Jorge. Participación y organización de los sectores populares en América Latina: los casos de Chile y Peru. See item 8460.

8375. Henderson, Gregory; S.W. Barton; Johannes A. Binnendijk; and Carolyn E. Setlow eds. Public diplomacy and political change: four case studies, Okinawa, Peru, Czechoslovakia, Guinea. N.Y., Praeger, 1973. 339 p., bibl., maps, plates (Praeger special studies in international politics and government)

Role of communications and propaganda in international relations is unifying theme of the case studies. In Carolyn E. Setlow's "The International Petroleum Company in Peru" (p. 191-243) this orientation may have led to 1) too great a stress on the influence of newspapers (particularly *El Comercio*) in the seizure of IPC and 2) a slightly distorted understanding of the domestic perception of the IPC issue. Provides, nevertheless, useful data on development of mass communications in Peru.

8376. Jiménez, Luis F. Propiedad social: el debate. Lima, Centro de Estudios y Promoción del Desarrollo (DESCO), 1974. 165 p. (Cuadernos DESCO)

Describes public positions taken by political parties, interest associations, principal newspapers, and government on preliminary draft of Law of Social Property, which is a major aspect of the Junta's revolutionary program.

8377. Lineamientos de la política económica-social del Gobierno Revolucionario. Lima, Oficina Nacional de Información [and] Editora del *Diario Oficial El Peruano*, 1973? 46 p.

Useful quick reference on key decrees from 1968 and general overview of Junta policy as outlined in a speech (n.d.) by the Premier.

8378. Lorenz, Günter W. Zum Beispiel Peru . . . (*Zeitschrift für Kulturaustausch* [Stuttgart, FRG] 24:1, 1974, p. 68-72)

Critical analysis of the present Peruvian military regime. Author argues that although the regime is all but democratic, one cannot expect a country such as Peru to have a democratic type of government. He raises the question as to the possible applicability of the Peruvian model to other Latin American countries. [H.J. Hoyer]

8379. Lowenthal, Abraham F. Peru's "Revolutionary Government of the Armed Forces:" background and context (*in* Kelleher, Catherine McArdle ed. Political-military systems: comparative perspectives. Beverly Hills, Calif., Sage Publications, 1974, p. 147-159 [Sage research progress series on war, revolution and peacekeeping])

Rather than the social origins of military officers or advanced career training, the explanation for the revolutionary government stems more basically from Peru's comparative lag prior to 1968 in strengthening the central government to undertake development programs.

8380. Malloy, James M. Peru before and after the coup of 1968 (UM/JIAS, 14:4, Nov. 1972, p. 437-454)

Contrasts the pre-1968 interpretation of Peru by José Carlos Mariátegui (*HLAS: 34:2620-2621*) with the post-1968 analysis by Aníbal Quijano (*HLAS 35:7700*). While both analyzed Peru from a marxian perspective, Mariátegui confronted more adequately the question of national identity and the role of the Indian. Author elaborates model of national corporatism as pertinent to the Peruvian case and speculates on its likely success in generating development.

8381. Mejía Scarneo, Julio. Teoría y práctica de la revolución peruana: un reto al desarrollo económico y progreso social acelerados por el sistema nacional de planificación. Lima, Ediciones Cooperativismo y Reforma Agraria Peruana, 1970. 121 p. (Folleto, 1)

Educational pamphlet for use in officially recognized cooperatives. Summarizes and simplifies national planning processes and recent reform laws.

8382. Molina, Alfonso *comp.* Ensayos revolucionarios del Perú: antología. Lima, Ediciones Peisa, 1969? 220 p.

Eclectic potpourri of selections from prominent essayists: Manuel González Prada "La Revolución" p. 13-30
José Antonio Encinas "El Maestro" p. 31-112
Luis E. Valcárcel "Túpac Amaru Caudillo Antiespañol" p. 113-136
Raúl Porras Barrenechea "José Faustino Sánchez Carrión, el Tribuno de la República Peruana" p. 165-220.

8383. Monteforte Toledo, Mario. La solución militar a la peruana: 1968-1970. México, UNAM, Instituto de Investigaciones Sociales, 1973. 182 p., bibl.

Mexican sociologist probes distinctiveness of the Peruvian experiment. Summarizes recent policy innovations in areas such as petroleum, agriculture, and foreign affairs. Describes status of traditional political forces (e.g., labor, parties) under military rule. Chapters on military leadership and composition of government provide interesting detail. Neither rigorous nor thorough in design and execution.

8384. Palmer, David Scott. "Revolution from above:" military government and popular participation in Peru, 1968-1972. Ithaca, N.Y., Cornell Univ., Latin American Studies Program, 1973. 307 p., bibl., illus., tables (Dissertation series, 47)

Probes one of the central questions of the Peruvian experiment: how might structures and beliefs be fashioned to permit popular participation, including the previously marginalized Indians, while maintaining order? Explores corporatism as framework for participation through "communities" and cooperatives. Useful monograph.

8385. Paredes Macedo, Saturnino. Situación política y tareas del P[artido] C[omunista] Peruano. Montevideo, Nativa Libros, 1972. 146 p. (Col., Bandera roja, 29)

Fourth ed. of the political report by Secretary General of Peruvian Communist Party to the V National Conference of 1965. Anti-Soviet and anti-Cuban commentary demonstrates consequences of Soviet-Chinese dispute.

8386. Quijano, Aníbal. Nationalism and capitalism in Peru: a study in neo-imperialism. Translated by Helen R. Lane. N.Y., Monthly Review Press, 1971. 122 p.

An initial analysis of the Peruvian Military Junta's economic policies from Oct. 1968 to March 1971. Author concludes that the Junta is guided by an ideology of class reconciliation and "limited nationalism within the imperialist order." An insightful study written from the standpoint of consistent radicalism. [A. Suárez]

8387. Sonntag, Heinz Rudolf. Discusión con Héctor Béjar (Libre [Paris] 3, marzo/mayo 1972, p. 44-52)

How will the masses be integrated politically into the Peruvian revolution? Sonntag hammers at the question, and Béjar (socialist, former guerrillero, and present defender of the regime) has no firm answers.

8388. Truchis, Manuel. Problémes agraires et développement au Pérou (IRFDH/DC, 51, janvier/mars 1973, p. 10-20, tables)

A brief examination of: 1) agriculture's importance within the total Peruvian economy, 2) plans of the military government for agrarian development and land use, 3) the administrative difficulties and inefficiencies experienced, and 4) possible outcomes. The 13 short tables offer a wide variety of statistical data, although at a rather simplistic level. [P.B. Taylor, Jr.]

8389. Velasco Alvarado, Juan. Velasco, la Voz de la Revolución: discursos del Presidente de la República General de División Juan Velasco Alvarado. t. 1, 1968/70, Lima, Oficina Nacional de Difusión del SINAMOS, 1972. 288 p. (Col. Documentos revolucionarios)

Reprints 23 major addresses by Peruvian president given between Oct. 1968 and Oct. 1970. Contains index.

8390. Wagner de Reyna, Alberto. El modelo peruano. Bogotá, Publicaciones de la Univ. Externado de Colombia, 1974. 146 p., bibl.

Based principally on speeches, laws, and decrees, a rather formalistic summary by Peru's Ambassador to Colombia of public policy under the junta. Sections on finance, agriculture, industry, mining, and social mobilization.

8391. Zimmermann Zavala, Augusto. El Plan Inca, objetivo: revolución peruana. Lima, Editora del Diario Oficial *El Peruano,* 1974? 242 p.

Semi-official compilation of newspaper stories, official documents (both US and Peruvian) and conversations relating primarily to IPC case and negotiations involving such US officials as Sol Linowitz and John Irwin. Emphasizes last six months of Belaúnde's government and first six months of military rule. Valuable, though biased, account.

BOLIVIA

8392. Alonso, Enrique. Fuerzas armadas y revolución nacional en Bolivia y Perú (IAEERI/E, 2:9, enero/feb. 1971, p. 15-26)

Journalistic piece which traces evolution (to 1970) of Peruvian and Bolivian armed forces toward nationalism and social revolution. Uses lengthy quotes from Torres and Velasco to characterize regime ideologies.

Aron-Schaar, Adrianne. Local government in Bolivia: public administration and popular participation. See item 1426.

8393. Baptista Gumucio, Mariano. Este país tan solo en su agonía. La Paz, Editorial Los Amigos del Libro, 1972. 282 p.

Some 60 critical vignettes on Bolivian politics, education, and society, written in 1971 by an expatriot journalist and educator.

8394. Bolivia. Ministerio de Información y Deportes. Banzer: Presidente de los Trabajadores. La Paz?, 1972. 48 p. (Política obrera del gobierno nacionalista, 10)

The Banzer government's evaluation of union activities prior to 1971 (generally negative) and trends under the new administration (generally positive).

8395. Convención Nacional del Movimiento Nacionalista Revolucionario (MNR), *XI, La Paz, 1973.* Estatuto orgánico del M.N.R. La Paz, Movimiento Nacionalista Revolucionario (MNR), 1973. 109 p. (Documentos políticos, 9)

Specifies internal organization and procedures of the MNR. Useful document.

8396. Corbett, Charles D. The Latin American military as a socio-political force: case studies of Bolivia and Argentina. Coral Gables, Fla., Univ. of Miami, Center for International Studies, 1972. 143 p., bibl., tables (Monographs in international affairs)

While bulk of book is case studies with emphasis on historical narrative, contains interesting orienting chapters. Particularly useful is Ch. 3, "The Career System and the Formation of Political Values." Solid addition to growing literature on military.

8396a. _____. Military institutional development and sociopolitical change: the Bolivian case (UM/JIAS, 14:4, Nov. 1972, p. 399-435)

Interesting overview analysis of development of the army, particularly since 1952. Provides insights on intrainstitutional sources of cleavages and political orientations of officers. Stresses personal ambition as central dynamic.

8397. Córdova-Claure, Ted. Made in U.S.A.: crónicas. B.A., Ediciones de la Flor, 1973. 125 p.

A Bolivian intellectual relates his experiences and observations while working as a correspondent in this country. He finds very much to criticize. [A. Suárez]

8398. Debray, Régis. Declaration at the Court Martial: Camiri, Bolivia. Camiri, Bol., n.p., 1969? 39 p.

In Nov. 1967, Debray stated his self-defense in Spanish. If this is the bona fide version, it is an articulate description of his role in the guerrilla during its last days and a strong critique of Bolivian legal processes. See *HLAS 33:7525.*

8398a. _____. Prison writings. Translated by Rosemary Sheed. London, Allen Lane, 1973. 207 p.

Essays, letters, and fragments from 1969-70 on marxian theory in general and the Bolivian situation in particular. "Some Literary Reflections" is a fascinating recollection of Debray's student youth.

8399. Falange Socialista Boliviana, *La Paz.* Conozca a la Falange Socialista Boliviana. Cochabamba, Bol., Editorial Universitaria, 1972. 173 p.

Propaganda piece containing speeches and documents on FSB ideology and internal organization. Printed during brief life of Frente Popular Nacionalista (1971-74), in which the FSB participated.

8400. Frente Popular Nacionalista, *Cochabamba, Bol.* Comando Departamental Cochabamba. Desarrollo de Cochabamba. Cochabamba, Bol., 1972. 38 p. (Memorial, 1)

Letter, dated 21 June 1972, from the Frente Popular Nacionalista of the Comando Departamental of Cochabamba addressed to Col. Hugo Banzer Súarez, President of Bolivia.

8401. Frontaura Argahdoña, Manuel. La trascendencia económica, política y social de la Revolución Nacional del 9 de abril de 1952. La Paz, M.N.R., 1973. 55 p.

Quite favorable assessment of MNR accomplishments.

8402. Gallardo Lozada, Jorge. De Torres A Banzer: diez meses de emergencia en Bolivia. B.A., Ediciones Periferia,

1972. 499 p. (Col. Estados Unidos y América Latina)

An impassioned and personal view of Bolivian political events in a ten-month period of 1970 and 1971. The author was private secretary to Gen. Alfredo Ovando and Minister of Interior for Gen. Juan José Torres. [P.B. Taylor, Jr.]

8403. Gensler, Martin D. Cuba's "Second Vietnam:" Bolivia (YU/YR, 60:3, March 1971, p. 342-365)

Written in 1968, this remains a useful assessment of the significance of Guevara's Bolivian expedition for Castro's revolutionary theory and practice in the context of Soviet foreign policy and Latin American nationalism.

8404. Gómez, Juan Carlos. Las traiciones en el M.N.R. La Paz, Ediciones Verdad, 1972. 64 p.

Bitter criticism of opportunism of MNR leadership in coming to terms with military governments in post-1974 period.

8405. Guevara, Ernesto. El diario del Che en Bolivia: el proceso de Camiri. Editor: Régis Debray. B.A., Ediciones Sintesis, 1973. 269 p., facsims., plates (Co . Presente político)

Reprints Che's Bolivian diary along with documents from Debray's trial. For other versions of the diary see *HLAS 31:7254* and *HLAS 33:7719*, as well as item 8405a.

8405a. ———. El diario del Che en Bolivia: noviembre 7, 1966 a octubre 7, 1967. Cochabamba, Bol., Editorial Serrano, 1968. 264 p., plates.

Reprints, along with the Cuban version of the diary, Castro's "Introduction" and other documents, the most important being Mario Monje's defense of the Bolivian Communist Party's actions toward the guerrilla.

8406. Gussoni, Enrique Oscar. Bolivia encaminada hacia el desarrollo y la autodeterminación (IAEERI/E, 1:4, nov./dic. 1969, p. 18-24)

Describes radical nationalist response by Bolivian junta of Sept. 1969 to reorientation of US policy by former President Nixon.

8407. Holtey, Joseph. The Movimiento Nacionalista Revolucionario: Bolivia's National Revolutionary Party. Tempe, Arizona State Univ., Center for Latin American Studies, 1973. 32 l., bibl., (Special study, 12)

Narrates origins, early successes, and subsequent internal schisms of MNR.

8408. Hugo Banzer Suárez y el destino de un pueblo. La Paz, Sociedad Patria y Nacionalismo, 1973. 52 p., plates.

Propaganda pamphlet but with useful biographical data on Banzer.

8409. Ibarra, Pablo. El largo drama de la revolución boliviana (IAEERI/E, 2:12, sept./oct. 1971, p. 42-48)

Economic development and income redistribution are both necessary for successful revolution. They have not been accomplished in Bolivia due to heightened expectations of newly politicized groups and an inability to consolidate political power.

8410. Jemio Ergueta, Angel. La reforma agraria en Bolivia. La Paz, Movimiento Nacionalista Revolucionario (MNR), 1973. 110 p., tables (Documentos políticos, 8)

Pocketbook compendium of information on the agrarian reform in Bolivia by a former official in the National Council on Agrarian Reform. Includes essential points of the law as well as data on its application. [P.B. Taylor, Jr.]

8411. Jickling, David J. Municipal development in Bolivia (Studies in Comparative Local Government [International Union of Local Authorities, The Hague] 8:1, Summer 1974, p. 35-42)

Reports on post-1972 initiatives in Bolivia to strengthen local public institutions, principally through creation of National Urban Development Service (SENDU).

8412. Magill, John H. Labor unions and political socialization: a case study of Bolivian workers. N.Y., Praeger Publishers, 1974. 291 p., bibl., tables (Praeger special studies in international economics and development)

Based on 1968 survey of 365 members of mining, petroleum, factory, and *campesino* unions, finds support for hypothesis that differential experience in types of unions is related to differences in political attitudes. Study is significant in: 1) demonstrating the importance of adult socialization in secondary associations, and 2) as a solid case study of Bolivian organized workers, who have played a central role in politics since the 1952 Revolution. Thorough analysis of survey findings, systematically complemented with historical and institutional data. Quite useful contribution.

8413. Marín E., Carlos. Bolivia: una revolución traicionada: proceso y sentencia contra el MNR. La Paz, Movimiento Nacionalista Revolucionario, 1972. 1 v. (Unpaged)

Argues that, by incorporating into government the erstwhile oligarchs and beneficiaries of imperialism, the MNR abandoned its revolutionary ideals soon after 1952.

8414. Montesinos Hurtado, Augusto. Las Fuerzas Armadas de Bolivia y la caída de Torres (IAEERI/E, 2:12, sept./oct. 1971, p. 49-59, tables)

Argues that political demise of Gen. Torres was due to provocative tactics of "infantile" left, which justified a conservative coup.

8415. Paz Estenssoro, Víctor. Un nuevo modelo político en la vida institucional de Bolivia. La Paz, Movimiento Nacionalista Revolucionario (MNR), 1972. 43 p. (Cuadernos de cultura y capacitación política, 2)

Former president of Bolivia and actual leader of Movimiento Nacionalista Revolucionario justifies coalition of his party with Falange Socialista Boliviana and the armed forces in the new Frente Popular Nacionalista.

8416. Roberts Barragán, Hugo. La Revolución del 9 de abril. La Paz, Cooperativa de Artes Gráficas E. Burillo, 1971. 291 p.

Author participated in Chaco War, held leadership posts in Bolivian Nationalist Falange and subsequently in Nationalist Revolutionary Movement, and played a key role in April 1952 revolution. As critic of MNR accommodation to US interests was soon exiled and later imprisoned. Valuable memoir.

8417. Rolando Pombo, Braulio. compañeros del Che: diarios de Bolivia. Caracas, Ediciones Bárbara, 1970. 163 p. (Serie Negra: ensayos y documentos, 8)

Another pirate edition of the previous publication of these diaries by Stein and Day. See *HLAS 33:7719.*

8418. Surcou Macedo, Rodolfo. Nacionalismo y revolución integral. La Paz, The Author, 1972. 114 p.

Elaborates ideological themes of Falange Socialista Boliviana, founded in 1937 and recently allied with military and MNR in Frente Popular Nacionalista.

8419. Torres, Juan José. El General Torres habla a Bolivia. B.A., Ediciones de Crisis, 1973. 300 p. (Col. Política)

Speeches from Torres' brief administration (1970-71) and subsequent exile.

8420. Valencia Vega, Alipio. El pensamiento político en Bolivia. La Paz, Liberería Editorial Juventud, 1973. 275 p., bibl.

More an essay on social and political history than a treatise on Bolivian political thought. Chapters on preconquest society, colonial and independence periods (with discussion of Liberal-Conservative then es), and Chaco War. Good bibliography.

CHILE

8421. Alcaino Barros, Alfredo and others. Participación para una nueva sociedad. Santiago, Ediciones Portada, 1973? 222 p.

Sixteen essays on forms of participation in national politics by municipalities, interest associations, armed forces, parties, women, and youth. Emphasis on Chilean case; generally legal-institutional approaches.

8422. Allende, Salvador. Chile's road to socialism. Edited by Joan E. Garcés. Translated by J. Darling. Introduction by Richard Gott. Baltimore, Md., Penguin Books, 1973. 208 p.

Reprints "The Programme of Unidad Popular" and 22 speeches by Allende from the first six months of his administration. Includes index.

8422a. _____ La conspiración contra Chile. B.A., Ediciones Corregidor, 1973. 412 p.

Speeches from 1971-72 on general theme of imperialist threat to UP experiment in "peaceful road to socialism."

8422b. _____. Salvador Allende: su pensamiento político. B.A., Granica Editor, 1973. 427 p.

Twenty-six speeches by Allende, unannotated and unedited, from period Sept. 1970-Dec. 1972.

8423. Angell, Alan. The Chilean road to militarism (CIIA/IJ, 29:3, Summer 1974, p. 393-411)

Informed and balanced analysis of factors leading to Sept. 1973 coup. While US influenced events, much more important was domestic opposition to Allende. Insightful preliminary assessment of new military government.

8424. Arguedas, Sol. Chile: hacia el socialismo. México, Cuadernos Americanos, 1973. 179 p., plates.

Reporting on the elections of 1964 and the Allende period by a journalist strongly sympathetic to Unidad Popular, especially the Communists, and critical of the MIR. She overrates Chilean loyalty to democracy and underestimates the military threat. The role of women is emphasized. [A. Suárez]

8425. Arriagada, Genaro. La oligarquia patronal chilena. Santiago, Ediciones Nueva Universidad [and] Univ. Católica de Chile, Vicerrectoría de Comunicaciones, 1970. 174 p., tables.

Analyzes leadership selection processes and composition of principal financial, industrial and business associations over 1930-65. Finds considerable evidence of concentration of officeholding to support interpretation of oligarchy. Well-grounded in pertinent literature and supported by empirical data. Solid contribution in middle-range analysis.

8426. Baeza Flores, Alberto. Radiografía política de Chile. México, B. Costa-Amic Editor, 1972. 412 p.

Combines a highly personal literary style with solid research and balanced analysis in an extensive historical narrative of Chile from the latter 19th century to the Allende government. Fascinating vignettes and thumbnail biographical sketches of leading figures. Useful complement to conventional historical analysis.

8427. Baklanoff, Eric N. The expropriation of Anaconda in Chile: a perspective on an export "enclave" (SECOLAS/A, 4, March 1973, p. 16-38, tables)

Evaluates legal, economic, and technical issues surrounding nationalization of Anaconda by Allende government. Supports Anaconda's position in the dispute.

8428. Baraona Urzúa, Pablo and others. Fuerzas armadas y seguridad nacional. Santiago, Ediciones Portada, 1973. 310 p., tables.

Essays from the anti-Allende Institute of General Studies:
Gonzalo Ibañez S.M. "Naturaleza y Legitimidad de la Vocación Militar" p. 11-33
Sergio Miranda C. "Las Fuerzas Armadas en el Ordenamiento Jurídico Chileno" p. 34-72
Ricardo Cox "Defensa Social Interna" p. 73-121
Tomás P. MacHale "Las Relaciones Internacionales bajo el Gobierno de la Unidad Popular" p. 122-139
Pablo Baraona U. "Economía y Seguridad Nacional" p. 140-159
José Garrido Rojas "Origen y Alcances de la Crisis Alimenticia" p. 160-235
Juraj Domic K. "Destrucción de las Fuerzas Armadas por el Partido Comunista" p. 237-269
Juraj Domic K. "Modelo Indonesio de Golpe de Estado Comunista" p. 270-388
Héctor Riesle C. "La Legitimidad de la Junta de Gobierno" p. 289-308.

8429. Barraclough, Solon and others. Chile: reforma agraria y gobierno popular. B.A., Ediciones Periferia, 1973. 244 p.

Essays on agrarian policy under UP government from *dependencia* perspective:
Solon Barraclough and Almino Affonso "Diagnóstico de la Reforma Agraria Chilena: noviembre 1970-junio 1972" p. 9-92
Silvia Hernández "El Desarrollo Capitalista del Campo Chileno" p. 93-146
Hugo Zemelman "La Reforma Agraria y las Clases Dominantes" p. 147-178
Sergio Gómez "El Rol del Sector Agrícola y la Estructura de Clases" 179-218
José Bengoa "Movilización Campesina: Análisis y Perspectivas" p. 219-244.

8430. Bernauer, Ursula and **Elisabeth**

Freitag. *Poder Popular en Chile:* am Beispiel Gesundheit. Nürnberg, FRG, Laetare-Verlag [and] Imba-Verlag, Freiburg, Switzerland, 1974. 168 p. (Stichwörter, 39: Zu Lateinamerika)

Documentary history of the health care system in Chile under Allende. Discussion focuses on the conflict between members of the medical profession representing the left and the right. Documents include very moving personal accounts of the human sufferings in the callampas. [H.J. Hoyer]

8431. Birns, Laurence *ed.* The end of Chilean democracy: au IDOC dossier on the coup and its aftermath. N.Y., The Seabury Press, 1973. 219 p. (A Continuum book)

Includes 35 newspaper and magazine articles and documents pertaining to the Sept. 1973 coup, subsequent reactions of political rroups, and ensuing debate over what actually took place and extent of US involvement. Weighted toward pro-Allende, anti-US position but includes some opposing views.

8432. Blakemore, Harold. Chile: the critical juncture? (*in* The Year Book of World Affairs 1973. London, Stevens 1973, p. 39-61)

Traces development of economic and political trends under Allende government to March 1973. Competent summary.

8433. Blanco, Hugo and others. La tragedia chilena. B.A., Ediciones Pluma, 1973. 163 p.

First of a projected series on Chile by revolutionary leftists:
Silvia Díaz and Andrés Méndez "El Golpe de la Oligarquía y el Imperialismo" p. 9-40
"Entrevista con Hugo Blanco: Lo Acompañan Creus y Jura" p. 41-56
"Biografía de Hugo Blanco, Creus y Jura" p. 57-61
Ernesto González "¿A dónde va Chile?" p. 65-109
"Artículos Seleccionados de *La Verdad* y *Avanzada Socialista,* 1970-73" p. 111-163.

8434. Boizard, Ricardo. El último día de Allende. Santiago, Editorial del Pacífico, 1973. 136 p. (Alta mar)

Strongly anti-Allende journalistic account of the coup and assessment of Unidad Popular.

8435. Bourricaud, François. Chile: why Allende fell (DIS, Summer 1974, p. 402-414)

Recognizes impact of international factors but emphasizes nature of Allende's coalition (particularly the MIR) and policies pursued to explain overthrow.

8436. Campa, Riccardo. Il riformismo rivoluzionario cileno. Roma, Marsilio Editori, 1970. 415 p., bibl.

Scholarly survey of Chile down to the late 1960s. Written from a sharply-defined base which assumes the existence of class struggle within the country and nationalist interest in international relations. The book offers American specialists a viewpoint at sharp variance with most works published in this country. [P.B. Taylor, Jr.]

8437. Canihuante Toro, Gustavo. La realidad chilena y el actual proceso de cambio. Santiago, Editorial Nascimento, 1971. 176 p., tables.

A simplified and applied marxian interpretation of the Chilean situation under Popular Unity. Intended for teachers and opinion leaders for the ". . . formation of consciousness of the process . . ."

8438. Cárdenas Barrios, René. Día 11: asesinar a Allende; fascismo en Chile — ¡Alerta, Bolivia! México, Editorial Diana, 1974. 300 p., bibl.

Quite stylized denunciation of Chilean coup and military regime from perspective of Mexican Left.

8439. Castro, Fidel. The highest example of heroism. La Habana, Instituto Cubano del Libro, Editorial de Ciencias Social Sociales, 1973. 103 p., plates (Ediciones políticas)

English translation of item 8439a.

8439a. _____ . Beatriz Allende; and Raúl Roa. Allende: combatiente y soldado de la revolución. Lima, Editorial Causachun, 1973. 108 p., plates (Col. Testimonio)

Speeches by Fidel Castro and Beatriz Allende (President's daughter) on 28 Sept. 1973 and Raúl Roa (Cuban Foreign Minister) on 10 Oct. 1973 on circumstances surrounding coup d'etat and death of Allende. For English translation, see item 8439. See also by Castro and Beatriz Allende *Homenaje a Salvador Allende*. (B.A., Editorial Galerna, 1973, 105 p., plates).

8440. Centro de Estudios de la Revolución (CER). Año 3, No. 9, enero/feb. 1973- . Santiago.

Political-economic news magazine of limited circulation and critical of Allende's government. Party affiliation not indicated (PDC or National Party?). Interesting details on progress of nationalization of enterprises and political violence.

8441. Cerda, Carlos. Chile: la traición de los generales. Bogotá, Ediciones Suramérica, 1973. 102 p., plates (Col. Política)

Personal recollections of Sept. 1973 coup and aftermath of journalist and member of Chilean Communist Party Central Committee. Reprints Communist Party's Oct. 1973 declaration.

8442. Chamudes, Marcos. Chile: una advertencia americana; semimemorias de un periodista chileno que durante 40 años fue actor y testigo de la vida política de su país. Santiago, Ediciones Política, Económica, Cultura, 1972. 279 p.

As a militant communist during 1929-40 and an equally militant anti-communist thereafter, Chamudes' somewhat rambling recollections provize a unique activist perspective on Chilean politics and an interesting interpretation of Allende's government.

Chaney, Elsa M. Old and new feminists in Latin America: the case of Peru and Chile. See item 8366.

_____ . Women in Latin American politics: the case of Chile and Peru. See item 8366a.

8443. Chile. Declaración de Principios del Gobierno de Chile. Santiago, Editora Nacional Gabriela Mistral, 1974. 37 p., plates.

Important document which sets outlines of military thinking. Dominant corporatist themes: natural law, common good, principle of subsidiarity, syndicalism and guild organization. Brief reference to civic-military movement to be formed.

8443a. _____ . Presidente. Segundo mensaje del Presidente Allende ante el Congreso pleno: la lucha por la democracia económica y las libertades sociales; 21 de mayo de 1972. Santiago, 1972. 998 p., tables.

State of nation address following president Allende's first 18 months in office, accompaniez by official data and documentation on domestic planning, economic, financial, and social policies as well as foreign policy. Essential document for any rigorous assessment of the Popular Unity Government.

8444. Cleaves, Peter S. Bureaucratic politics and administration in Chile. Berkeley, Univ. of Calif. Press, 1974. 352 p., bibl., tables.

Analyzes Chilean bureaucracy and policy-making in theoretical context of organizational sociology and political economy (rather than in development administration approach hitherto dominant in the field). Temporal focus is Frei administration, with lesser consideration of Allende government. Chapters on planning, budgeting, housing, and public works. This is a first-rate contribution to comparative administration and the literature on Chilean politics.

8445. Córdova-Claure, Ted. ¿Chile sí?: los primeros 800 días. B.A., Ediciones de la Flor, 1973. 158 p.

Somewhat rambling and expansive journalistic account of UP government to Dec. 1972 by exiled Bolivian correspondent. Provides, however, interesting interviews with and observations on important personalities (e.g., Joan Garcés).

8446. Crise et réforme des structures agraires: le cas chilien et ses applications méthodologiques (IRFDH/DC, 51, janvier/mars 1973, p. 52-55)

Can the Chilean effort at agrarian reform offer pointers to specialists working in other underdeveloped countries? A very brief but useful examination.

8447. Cuéllar, Oscar. Un esquema para el análisis de los aspectos políticos de la reforma agraria. Asunción, Centro Paraguayo de Estudios Sociológicos, 1971. 26 p. (Col. de Reimpresiones, 44)

Short suggested typology for the analysis of the political effects of agrarian reform, using as a model the Frei reforms in Chile. The work is theoretical rather than factual. [P.B. Taylor, Jr.]

8448. Delano, Luis Enrique. Galo González y la construcción del partido: reportaje. Santiago?, n.p., 1968. 57 p.

Sympathetic biographical sketch of the Valparíso labor activist and subsequent General Secretary of the Chilean Communist Party during 1949-58.

8449. Evans, Les ed. Disaster in Chile: Allende's strategy and why it failed. Edited with an introduction by... N.Y., Pathfinder Press, 1974. 271 p., plates, tables (Latin America, political science)

More than 40 short articles, mainly from the Trotskyist magazine *Interpontinental Press*, on Unidad Popular and the coup. Several contributions by Hugo Blanco.

8450. Feinberg, Richard E. The triumph of Allende: Chile's legal revolution. N.Y., The New American Library, 1972. 276 p., bibl., tables.

This is a kind of "sleeper:" a former Peace Corps volunteer writes with enthusiasm about the elections of 1970 and of Allende's first nine months in power. The material is detailed, anecdotal, and has much charm. [P.B. Taylor, Jr.]

8451. Figueiredo, Jorge Mario Quinzio. Sistema electoral chileno (IEP/REP, 186, nov./dic. 1972, p. 297-378)

Devoid of analysis, a textual exegesis of Chilean electoral law.

8452. Foxley, Alejandro and others. Chile: búsqueda de un nuevo socialismo. Santiago, Univ. Católica de Chile, Centro de Estudios de Planificación Nacional (CEPLAN), 1971. 266 p.

Papers from a seminar held in Dec. 1970, at the Catholic Univ., with participants from government and academic community. Theme is relationship between socialism and democracy:
Oscar Muñoz G. "El Concepto de la Organización Económica Nacional y Elementos para su Transformación" p. 12-43
Bosco Parra A. "Socialismo, Democracia y Descentralización" p. 44-65
Eduardo García D. "Viabilidad Económica del Sistema de Autogestión" p. 66-77
Crisóstomo Pizarro C. "Participación y Desarrollo Económico en la Sociedad Socialista" p. 78-103
José Alvarez M. "Descentralización en el Socialismo y el Sistema Industrial" p. 104-127
Andrzej Wrobel K. "Descentralización en la Planificación y Manejo de la Economía Socialista" p. 128-137
Alejandro Foxley R. "Alternativas de Descentralización en el Proceso de Transformación de la Economía Nacional" p. 138-169
Jacques Chonchol Ch. "Elementos para una Discusión Sobre el Camino Chileno Hacia el Socialismo" p. 170-193
Julio Silva S. "Pluralidad de Fuerzas e Ideologías en la Construcción del Socialismo en Chile. Colaboración de Marxistas y Cristianos" p. 204-232
Mario Zañartu U. "Análisis de Costos Sociales en el Caso de Implantación de la Autogestión en Algunos Sectores de la Economía Chilena" p. 232-251
Guillermo Geisse G. "Descentralización a Partir de la Actual Concentración Urbana y Regional" p. 252-266
Luis Figueroa M. "Gestión Obrera en la Construcción del Socialismo en Chile" p. 194-204.

8453. Francis, Michael J. The Allende victory: an analysis of the 1970 Chilean presidential election. Tucson, The Univ. of Arizona Press, The Institute of Government Research, 1973. 76 p., tables (Comparative government studies, 4)

Based on an eight-month stay in Chile during 1970, provides an overview description of candidates, issues, and campaign. Last chapter is interesting critique of journalistic reporting of election.

8454. Gaitán, Gloria. El compañero presidente. Bogotá, Alfonso Renteria Mantilla, 1974. 392 p.

Personal memoir of Allende and Chilean politics during Feb.-Sept. 1973 by Colombian economist who worked in ODEPLAN (Oficina de Planificación de la Presidencia de la República). Interesting sketches of the private side of the President.

8455. Gall, Norman. Copper is the wage of Chile. Hanover, N.H., American Universities Field Staff Reports, 1972. 18 p., map, plates (West coast South America series, 19:3)

Penetrating description of production difficulties encountered in the aftermath of nationalizing in 1971 the major copper mines. Political conflict and inefficiency have been the legacy of "premature" nationalization.

8456. Galtung, Johan. Después del

Proyecto Camelot (UNAM/RMS, 30:1, enero/marzo 1968, p. 115-141)

A calm and critical reexamination of Camelot by the Norwegian social scientist who, in effect, blew the whistle on the project in Chile. The author argues that the real lessons of the breakup of Camelot have not yet been understood by a great many American social scientists as well as by agencies of the US government, even though there was an obvious and painful public relations flap over it. [P.B. Taylor, Jr.]

8457. García, Pío. Las fuerzas armadas y el golpe de estado de Chile. Prólogo y selección de textos de la revista *Chile Hoy* por . . . México, Siglo XXI Editores, 1974. 489 p.

Reprints some 120 articles from leftist weekly *Chile Hoy*, which was published during June 1972-Sept. 1973. Perception of military is loose integrating theme. Useful collection.

8458. Gayango, Ignacio. Chile: el largo camino al golpe. Barcelona, Editorial Dirosa, 1974. 257 p., plates.

Rather detailed account of Allende years by Chilean now exiled in Spain. Obviously sympathetic to UP government, with emphasis on theme of external aggression (e.g., US "Invisible blockade"), but also critical of internal fragmentation of UP.

8459. Gelbel, George. Elementos de un modelo de desarrollo (UCC/CE, 6:19, dic. 1969, p. 32-41)

Speculation by a professor of political science, on the role in development of urbanization and the middle class. No empirical data. Interesting only in view of how crucial this class turned out to be in the overthrow of President Allende — which is not foreseen at all in this essay. [J. Strasma]

8460. Giusti, Jorge. Participación y organización de los sectores populares en América Latina: los casos de Chile y Peru (UNAM/RMS, 34:1, enero/marzo 1972, p. 39-63)

Elaborates typology of participation and discusses Chilean case at length. Little attention to Peru and virtually no attempt to state comparative conclusions.

8461. Goldberg, Boris. Lateinamerika nach Chile . . . (MDZED, 27:11, Nov. 1973, p. 997-1007)

Brief and perceptive analysis of contemporary political situation in Chile, Argentina, Peru, Brazil and Cuba. Especially valuable is the discussion of the difficulties encountered by the Allende regime. Author argues that it was not the military that caused his downfall but the nature of the Allende experiment itself. [H.J. Hoyer]

8462. González Aguayo, Leopoldo. Chile: el inicio de una revolución (UNAM/RMCP, 16:63, enero/marzo 1971, p. 87-98)

Assessment by Mexican social scientist of 1) aspirations and probable difficulties of UP government and 2) US policy vis-à-vis Allende. Interesting perspective.

8463. Hansen, Roy A. Public orientations to the military in Chile (PSS/PSR, 16:2, April 1973, p. 192-208, tables)

Based on 1964-65 survey of Santiago residents (N=142), finds clear public support for military defense role, with support for secondary roles (civic action, internal order) related to legitimacy of defense function.

8464. Hareige, Dag *ed.* Chile: pa vej til sosialismen. Oslo, Pax Forlag, 1973. 207 p., tables.

Political essays by six Norwegian authors of leftist persuasion. They discuss the following facets of Chilean life in the 1970s: 1) mass organizations, women's struggles, Unidad Popular and its goals, 2) socialization of industries and land reform. 3) imperialist economic programs and their effect on Chile, and 4) the role of the Church and the media in the political struggle. The book concludes with poems of Neruda translated into Norwegian. [Renata V. Shaw]

8465. Horne, Alistair. Small earthquake in Chile: Allende's South America. N.Y., The Viking Press, 1972. 349 p., bibl., plates.

Report on a 1971 tour of the Andean countries. Well-written travelogue whose principal interest consists of vignettes and insights from interviews with leading personalities in the area.

8466. Huneeus Cox, Pablo and others. Chile: el costo social de la independencia ideológica. Santiago, Editorial del Pacífica [and] Instituto de Estudios Políticos, 1973. 255 p.

Sophisticated polemical essays on 1) appropriateness of marxian analysis in Chilean setting, and 2) (mis)applications of marxian theory by UP government:
Claudio Orrego V. "Los Fundamentos Ideológicos de la Estrategia UP" p. 13-68
Andrés Sanfuentes "El Papel de los Mitos en la Estrategia Económico-Social de la Unidad Popular" p. 69-124
Pablo Huneeus Cox "Resultados Sociales del Gran Experimento" p. 125-150
Sebastián Piñera Echeñique "El Costo Social del Gran Experimento" p. 151-186
Eduardo Palma "La Unidad Popular en el Sistema Politico Chileno" p. 185-255.

8467. International Labour Organization, *Geneva.* The settlement of labour disputes in Chile (AIFLD/R, 3:3, 1971. p. 59-81, table)

A useful general description of labor relations under the Frei government. [P.B. Taylor, Jr.]

8468. Johnson, Dale L. *ed.* The Chilean

road to socialism. Garden City, N.Y., Anchor Books, 1973. 546 p., tables.

Some 62 articles (including several original pieces), documents, and press accounts covering a broad range of political, economic, and social topics. Sympathetic to Allende government and critical of US policy toward Chile.

8469. Kay, Cristóbal. Chile: the making of a coup d'etat (SS, 39:1, Spring 1975, p. 3-25)

Draws two lessons from overthrow of Allende: 1) It is impossible to transform a society within a bourgeois institutional framework, and 2) threats from the proletariat during periods of economic crisis lead Right to seek corporate solutions.

8470. Kudachkin, Mikhail Fedorovich. Chili: bor'ba za edinstvo i pobedu Levykh sil (The struggle for unity and the victory of Left strength). Moskva, Izdatel'stvo, 1973. 213 p.

Traces the development of the Left in Chile since World War II and describes the Chilean Communist Party's struggles with the Christian Democrats under Frei. Published prior to Allende's overthrow, the book ends by arguing strongly for Communist Party cooperation with other leftist groups as the way for revolution. [T.S. Cheston]

8471. Latorre Cabal, Hugo. El pensamiento Salvador Allende. México, Fondo de Cultura Económica, 1974. 294 p.

Useful compilation of Allende's commentaries on a variety of subjects during 1969-73, organized in 27 brief sections.

8472. Lehmann, David and Hugo Zemelman. El campesinado: clase y conciencia de clase. B.A., Ediciones Nueva Visión, 1972. 113 p. (Col. Fichas, 8)

Zemelman interprets evolution of Chilean peasantry in sociological-historical terms, while Lehmann approaches same topic from linguistic-anthropological perspective (see HLAS 35:7764). Useful complementary studies.

8473. Libertà per el Cile. Roma, Partito Comunista Italiano (PCI), 1973. 1 v. (Unpaged) plates.

A folio of 42 poster-sized black-and-white photographs, with often mordant and clearly party-line text, depicts events in Chile up to and shortly after the fall of Allende. Produced specifically for wall displas, this is an interesting and well-organized way to get the message across, but it has more interest for the PR type than for a scholar. [P.B. Taylor, Jr.]

8474. MacEoin, Gary. No peaceful way: Chile's struggle for dignity. N.Y., Shved and Ward, 1974. 230 p., bibl.

Written for general audience, strongly pro-Allende, anti-US indictment of military overthrow in Sept. 1973. Develops theme that political participation by previously marginal strata during 1970-73 has changed that system to a degree which the military cannot reverse. Reports as fact much hearsay and innuendo.

8475. MacHale, Tomas P. El frente de la libertad de expresión, 1970-1972. Prólogo de Alfredo Silva Carvallo. Santiago, Ediciones Portada, 1972. 230 p., illus.

Critiques UP policies and tactics to extend political control over Chilean communications media during 1970-72. Thorough discussion of important and controversial topic.

8476. Maira, Luis. Chile: dos años de Unidad Popular. Santiago, Empresa Editora Nacional Quimantú, 1973. 295 p. (Serie Análisis. Col. Camino abierto, 22)

Some 70 journalistic essays on Chilean politics during 1971-72. Author's point of view as UP deputy is evident, but commentary maintains some objectivity.

8477. Manns, Patricio. Breve síntesis del movimiento obrero. Santiago, Empresa Editora Nacional Quimantú, 1972. 94 p., plates. (Col. Nosotros los chilenos, 27)

Describes principal leaders, organizations, and phases of development of Chilean organized labor from early 1800s to creation of Central Unica de Trabajadores in 1953. Good collection of photos; author is Socialist by tone of narrative.

8478. Mauro Marini, Ruy; Pío García; Darcy Ribeiro; and Carlos Rossi. ¿Por qué cayó Allende? Autopsia del gobierno popular chileno. B.A., Rodolfo Alonso, 1974. 84 p.

Ribeiro's essay, written *after* the coup, is a particularly interesting discussion of the democratic road to socialism. Contents:
Carlos Rossi "Notas sobre la Política Económica de la Unidad Popular en Chile" p. 9-18
Ruy Mauro Marini "La Política Económica del Gobierno de la Unidad Popular o la Expresión de la Hegemonía Pequeño-Burguesa en el Proceso Chileno" p. 21-32
Pío Garcia "La Política Económica del Gobierno Popular" p. 35-66
Darcy Ribeiro "Salvador Allende y la Izquierda Desvariada" p. 69-84.

8479. Medhurst, Kenneth. Allende's Chile. N.Y., St. Martin's Press, 1972. 202 p.

A "pre-coup" collection by supporters of Allende government published in association with *Government and Opposition*, a journal of comparative politics. Interesting concluding essay explores implications of Chilean experience for Latin Europe.
Kenneth Medhurst "Why Chile?" p. 1-9
Kenneth Medhurst "The Chilean Background" p. 9-26

Joan E. Garcés "Chile 1971: A Revolutionary Government within a Welfare State" p. 27-50
J. Biehl del Río and Gonzalo Fernández R. "The Political Pre-Requisites for a Chilean Way" p. 51-72
H. Zemelman and Patricio León "Political Opposition to the Government of Allende" p. 73-96
H.E. Bicheno "Anti-Parliamentary Themes in Chilean History: 1920-1970" p. 97-134
Gonzalo Martner "The Economic Aspects of Allende's Government: Problems and Prospects" p. 135-147
Luis Quirós Varela "Chile: Agrarian Reform and Political Processes" p. 148-175
"Chile, France and Italy: a Discussion" p. 176-195.

8480. Merkur. Deutsche Zeitschrift für europäisches Denken. Heft 9, No. 316, Jahrgang 28, Sept. 1974- . Stuttgart, FRG.

This issue of *Merkur* includes a dramatic essay written by a Colombian which describes the program of the Allende regime, his assassination, and attempts to link several Chilean military officers with the Pentagon, [H.J. Hoyer]

8481. Millas, Orlando. La clase obrera en las condiciones del gobierno popular (IAEERI/E, 3:16, mayo/junio 1972, p. 36-48)

Mid-1972 critique by Chilean Communist Party leader of economic tactics of Unidad Popular government. Calls for stricter adherence to UP's "Basic Program" and closer cooperation between coalition members.

8482. Moran, Theodore H. Multinational corporations and the politics of dependence: copper in Chile. Princeton, N.J., Princeton Univ. Press *under the auspices of the* Center for International Affairs, Harvard Univ., 1974. 286 p., bibl., tables.

Explores factors affecting behavior of multinational corporations and national governments in regard to interactive decisions on investments, controls, prices and production in primary products. Copper in Chile is the extended case study, and the analysis moves nicely between ideographic detail and middle-range generalization to construct a simplified model of host country-corporation conflict. Stresses properly limitations of static analysis and attempts consistently to incorporate a time dimension in model. Case study is skillfully developed, and the generalizations constitute a solid contribution to the literature on international relations and economic development.

8483. Morris, David J. We must make haste slowly: the process of revolution in Chile. N.Y., Random House, 1973. 307 p., bibl.

Written for general public, a sympathetic account of the origins and first 17 months of Allende's government. Rather sanguine assessment written in early 1972 is offset by a postscript from Nov. 1972 which correctly stresses the immense problems then facing the UP government.

8484. Moss, Robert. Chile's marxist experiment. Devon, England, David & Charles Newton Abbot, 1973. 225 p., bibl., (World realities series)

Among the books on Chile written for general public, this is distinctive for its negative assessment of Allende's government, which probes beyond rhetoric, and its firm grasp of detail and personalities in Chilean politics. Author's judgment of loss of democracy in 1973 as simply "temporary" may be optimistic.

8485. Mujica, Héctor. Allende y Chile: crimen y agresión fascista. Caracas, Ediciones Centauro, 1973. 158 p.

Biographical notes on Allende and political analysis by Venezuelan communist, exiled to Chile during mid-1950s. Reprints documents by elements of Popular Unity from period just prior to Sept. 1973 coup.

8486. North American Congress on Latin America (NACLA) *New York.* New Chile. N.Y., 1972. 176 p., plates, tables.

Intended by radical NACLA as introductory reader for nonspecialist on significance of UP government toward which it is quite favorably disposed. Articles on politics, art, education, status of women, etc.

8487. Ochoa, Guillermo. Reportaje en Chile. 2. ed. México, Centro de Información Política, 1972. 204 p., plates.

Interesting observations by Mexican journalist covering official visit by Luis Echeverría to Chile in April 1972. Reprints pictures, news conferences, and speeches from that occasion.

8488. Onofre Jarpa, Sergio. Creo en Chile. Santiago, Sociedad Impresora Chile, 1973. 272 p.

Essays on Chilean politics reprinted from 1956-72 by president of National Party, which was created through the union of Liberal and Conservative Parties. These writings may have significance due to alleged influence of National Party in present Junta.

8489. Orrillo, Winston ed. La verdad sobre Chile. Lima, Editorial Causachún, 1973. 181 p., illus., plates (Col. Testimonio)

Some 50 poems, letters, speeches, interviews, and articles of protest voiced in the immediate aftermath of the Sept. 1973 coup.

8490. Ossa, Juan Luis. Nacionalismo hoy. Prólogo: Sergio O. Jarpa. Santiago, The Author, 1973. 61 p.

Brief presentation of "humanist nationalism" with interpretation of Chilean history and discussion of UP government by president of National Youth, affiliated with National Party.

8491. Peña, Alcira de la. Chile: el pueblo

vencerá. B.A., Editorial Fundamentos, 1974. 92 p.

Interprets Chilean coup as outcome of global yankee imperialist plot, whose earlier victims include Brazil, Argentina, Bolivia, and Uruguay.

8492. Pérez de Arce, Hermógenes. Comentarios escogidos. Prólogo de Gonzalo Vial. Santiago, Ediciones Portada, 1973. 432 p.

Some 90 selections from Pérez's daily commentaries over Radio Agricultura during 1971-72. Advocates free enterprise perspective quite critical of Allene's nationalization policies.

8493. Petras, James F. Chile after Allende: a tale of two coups (MR, 25:7, Dec. 1973, p. 12-20)

Describes a post-coup alliance of military, National Party, and Fatherland and Liberty in a ruling coalition and demise of Christian Democratic Party. Combines subtle analysis with calculated hyperbole.

8493a. _____. Chile after the elections (MR, 25:1, May 1973, p. 15-23)

Economic problems of early 1973 were due to external-internal political opposition which was exacerbated by the overpermissiveness of the Allende government.

8493b. _____. The Chilean road to socialism: socioeconomic change and economic dislocation (Development Dialogue [Dag Hammarskjöld Foundation, Uppsala, Sweden] 1, 1973, p. 23-28)

Chilean economic problems of 1972 were due more to political opposition than government policy. Situation was exacerbated by government's timidity.

8494. Powelson, John P. What went wrong in Chile? (UCL/CD, 6:3, 1974, p. 483-500)

Places miscalculation and economic-political incompetence of UP government over foreign intervention to explain Sept. 1973 coup.

8495. Prieto, Helios. Chile: los gorilas estaban entre nosotros. B.A., Editorial Tiempo Contemporáneo, 1973. 87 p. (Col. Mundo Actual)

Written in Oct. 1973, this is a strong critique of reformist communist parties (in this case the Argentine) and denunciation of the "peaceful road to socialism" attempted by UP which sought to form an alliance with a nonexistent national bourgeoisie.

8496. Reiman, Elisabeth. La lucha por la tierra. Santiago, Empresa Editora Nacional Quimantú, 1971. 97 p., illus. (Col. Nosotros los chilenos, 3. Serie: Hoy contamos)

Simplified and richly illustrated history of peasant's status in Chile from early 19th century to 1971. With large distribution (50,000 copies) and strongly pro-UP line, interesting as propaganda piece.

8497. Sanders, Thomas G. Allende's first months. Hanover, N.H., American Universities Field Staff Reports, 1971. 9 p. (West coast South America series, 18:2)

A balanced analysis of the first months of the Allende regime, which views the UP's gains in the 1971 municipal elections as a result of Allende's personal image and the populist measures undertaken by his government. However, as is common in the Chilean political process, continuing economic problems could eradicate this "symbolic" political support. In the aftermath of Allende's downfall, the discussion of developing tensions between Chile and the US seems especially ominous. The author concludes that the Chilean "model" is not necessarily applicable within the differing contexts of other Latin American nations.

8497a. _____. The process of partisanship in Chile. Hanover, N.H., American Universities Field Staff Reports, 1973. 10 p., plates (West coast South America series, 20:1)

Develops thesis that the Allende "administration failed an opportunity to experiment with a peaceful and legal transition to socialism by unnecessarily provoking and underestimating the forces ranged against it."

8498. Sigmund, Paul E. The "invisible blockade" and the overthrow of Allende (CFR/FA, 52:2, Jan. 1974, p. 322-340)

Was there an "invisible blockade" and did this blockade contribute significantly to the overthrow of Allende? Article reviews lending policies of US government and multilateral agencies and finds the evidence on these questions to be "not persuasive." Fairly 'r not, this essay will likely be labeled the "establishment liberal" position and will certainly be a point of reference in the continuing debate on the US role in the overthrow of Allende.

8499. Sweezy, Paul M. Chile: the question of power (MR, 25:7, Dec. 1973, p. 1-11)

From the political vacillation of the Popular Unity leadership in 1971-72, draws the lesson that "gaining full state power must be the overriding objective of a serious socialist movement which achieves office through electoral means."

8500. Taufic, Camilo. Chile en la hoguera: crónica de la represión militar. B.A., Ediciones Corregidor, 1974. 269 p.

More sophisticated variation on theme of fascist-military-*cum*-US imperialism as explanation of coup and repression. Reports interesting letters and documents.

8501. La tragedia chilena: testimonios. B.A., Merayo Editor, 1973. 385 p.

Some 50 pro-UP interviews, essays, and short journalistic pieces on personalities and events surrounding the Sept. 1973 coup. Useful compilation.

8502. United States. Senate. Committee on the Judiciary. Subcommittee to Investigate Problems Connected with Refugees and Escapees. Refugee and humanitarian problems in Chile: pts. 1/2. Washington, GPO, 1974. 2 v. (117, 304 p.) tables (93rd Congress, 2d Session)

Testimony and evidence presented before Senator Kennedy's Subcommittee on the post-coup situation in Chile. Essential document.

8503. Valdés, Pablo. Chile in search of a new destiny (SECOLAS/A, 4, March 1973, p. 71-79)

Chilean envoy's interpretation of Allende's government six months before the 1973 coup.

8504. Vidales, Carlos. Contra revolución y dictadura en Chile. Bogotá, Ediciones Tierra Americana (ETA), 1974. 381 p., tables.

Mobilizes copious data to support thesis that Allende fell as victim to counterrevolutionary international bourgeoisie and its counterpart class in Chile.

8505. Villegas, Sergio. Chile: el estadio; los crímenes de la Junta Militar. B.A., Editorial Cartago, 1974. 157 p., plates.

Purports to report interviews and on-site impressions of those arrested, tortured, or mistreated by military during and after Sept. 1973 coup.

8506. White book of the change of government in Chile: 11th of September 1973. Santiago, Empresa Editora Nacional Gabriela Mistral, 1973. 257 p., illus., plates.

The military's case for overthrowing the Allende government. Extensive documentation (letters, memoranda, notes, depositions, photographs) to justify coup. Essential document.

8507. Zammit, J. Ann *ed.* The Chilean road to socialism: proceedings of an ODEPLAN-IDS Round Table, March 1972. With cooperation from Gabriel Palma. Austin, Univ. of Texas Press [and] Institute of Development Studies at the Univ. of Sussex, England, 1973. 465 p., map, tables.

Possibly the most significant compilation on pre-coup Chile. Reprints papers, documents, and senses of discussions of a ten-day conference held in March 1972 and attended by more than 60 scholars from Chile, Latin America, the US, Europe and the USSR. Includes presentations by president Allende and leading government and opposition figures. Major topics are economic, agrarian, and foreign policy, and prospects for the Chilean road to socialism. Essential reference.

8508. Zanfrognini, Giancarlo. Il comunismo in nomine partis: la Repúbblica Conciliare Cilena. Bologna, Italy, Edizione Calderini, 1973. 45 p., plates.

An extremely short and pointedly critical report of the Allende government, for general reading in Italy. Perhaps through design, its brevity robs the piece of perspective. [P. B. Taylor, Jr.]

8509. Zimbalist, Andy and Barbara Stallings. Showdown in Chile (MR, 25:5, Oct. 1973, p. 1-24)

Written vight days before the 11 Sept. 1973 coup, this article accurately assesses imminence of crisis. Quite critical of Allende government's lack of overall strategy and its attempts to create socialism without necessary seizure of state power and economic sacrifice.

SOUTH AMERICA: EAST COAST

(Venezuela, Brazil, Paraguay, Uruguay, Argentina)

PHILIP B. TAYLOR, JR.
Professor of Political Science
Director, Latin American Studies Center
University of Houston

THE PROPORTIONAL DIFFERENCES AMONG THE FIVE COUNTRIES here reported have not changed greatly during this biennium. Argentina and Brazil remain the most prolific publishers, with quality differences that span an extraordinary range. Venezuela places increasing emphasis on professional quality in political analysis in its better pieces and produces sycophantic personality adulation at its worst. Uruguay, not a prolific publisher in recent years, has suffered obvious distress at the degeneration of its constitutional order at the hands of the country's first real authoritarian regime in a century, and the literature demonstrates this. And Paraguay remains virtually mute, so far as publication is concerned: a reminder of how bad things can really be in a true dictatorship.

This is not to say that everything worthwhile about the individual countries is published within their borders. Some notable US scholars are publishing works that range from useful and interesting to challenging and even provocative on the basis of their field research; so much for the dire predictions of the Camelot era, that effective research would no longer be possible for scholars! There are increasingly competent Brazilians writing and publishing from outside their country; a few do so from within, but their materials are guardedly academic in nature. There is obviously greater freedom to publish in Argentina, even for the most extreme ideologies, during the period reviewed. Some of the materials developed with the support of the Di Tella Institute of B.A. are a match for sophistication and method of the best in the hemisphere. And the scant offerings about Uruguay have been published in that country, as has always been the case; but it must be observed that none of their publication dates occur after early 1974, when control was imposed on top of earlier censorship of the press, and conditions have changed in 1975 for the worse.

Brazilian federalism commands the attention of a good many scholars. Some regional historical treatments emphasize personal politics; others discuss population distribution and migration patterns, state level public administration, and questions of economic competition. Little is said of the two official political parties as such from within the country, but exiles have a good deal to say of the changed mood of politics since 1964—for the military government has obviously not stamped out partisanship despite its harsh attitudes. Possibly the most interesting material, from the viewpoint of possible future Brazilian national behavior, relates to the armed forces. The army's assurance that it will be in power for as long as it wishes, and that its peculiar interpretations of national interest will govern policy, is shown in the candor of its semiofficial publications. The navy is no less assured, if not so much represented in this section.

The Argentine materials are dominated, in numbers at least, by the flood of trivia by (one must suppose) seekers for gain from the return of Perón. The majority of this is simple trash. Yet a number of thoughtful works, by individuals writing from the distinct sectors of *peronismo*, explore the implications of developmental change in the country from their various viewpoints. Despite the structural and bureaucratic incompetence of this unhappy country (or, possibly, because of it), it is possible to find in the literature a range from the products of pseudo-neo-positivism (which has always had its devotees in the three east coast countries) to the plotting, planning and propaganda documents of the most extreme and violence-oriented left. Some of the work is very good indeed, reflective of the most responsible of journalistic or scholarly writing.

The topic that cuts most frequently across the publications from the five countries is the role of the Church in politics. Venezuelan Christian Social party COPEI material asks questions of papal doctrine and its interpretations for political action and decision making. The topic is an obvious one since COPEI's leader, Rafael Caldera, who authored several cited pieces, was the country's president for one term. Troubled Brazilian clerics ask the same kinds of questions, and also explore the variables composing the equations of power at state and national levels within a military-dominated regime that seems capable at times of obdurate foolishness toward social change. Argentine clerics also deal with these questions, but from a less power-conscious position. In two of these national instances, American scholars have also addressed the question of Church institutional and political power, and their works are cited.

A second topic that has been treated by both Latin American and foreign observers, including (surprisingly) a few soldiers, is the role of the military on both national and cross-national bases. Granted the Brazilian future, as well as the possible Argentine and Uruguayan futures, the topic is useful both factually and conceptually, and both approaches appear in this section.

On the whole, the materials offer more solid insights into the nature and exercise of power in the four countries (Paraguay excluded, of course, save by implication) than has been true at any time in this reviewer's memory. The generalist and specialist alike will find much of use.

VENEZUELA

8510. Acedo Mendoza, Carlos. Reforma urbana. Caracas, Fondo Editorial Común, 1974. 362 p., tables.

Quick analysis of the nature of urban problems in the country followed by a prescriptive discussion of possible reforms and improvements. The latter two-thirds of the volume consists of documents, draft laws for congressional enactment on the legal role and rights of local governments, and a highly detailed blueprint of activities and procedures of Venezuela's FUNDACOMUN (Fundación para el Desarrollo de la Comunidad y Fomento Municipal).

8511. Acedo Mendoza, Manuel. ¿Porqué Eugenio Mendoza? Presentación por Augusto Mijares. Caracas, The Author, 1973. 148 p.

To attack Eugenio Mendoza is to attack private enterprise; Mijares considers both a form of indoor sport. Fortunately, the book is less concerned with counterpolemic than with compilation of facts about the man and his multitude of enterprises and good works. On the whole, very worthwhile for the specialist.

8512. Alvarez, Federico and others. La izquierda venezolana y las elecciones del 73. Caracas, Síntesis Dosmil, 1974. 249 p.

Essays by six political activists—some members of the Communist Party, others of more moderate positions, including journalists and academics, on the meaning of the 1973 elections for the left. This is a useful and provocative volume for the specialist.

8513. Baloyra, Enrique A. Oil policies and budgets in Venezuela: 1938-1968 (LARR, 9:2, Summer 1974, p. 28-72, tables)

Using Wilkie's study on Mexican budgeting (see *HLAS 31:3355*) as a model Baloyra undertakes an interesting theoretical, as well as practical, examination of the utility of budget analysis for determining the intent and outcomes of government program priorities. The survey of comparative literature is, in some respects, more important than the detailed examination of Venezuelan experience for its provocative insights. The Venezuelan sections offer detail only in support of generalizations already abundantly (and obviously) available in other places. Read in conjunction with Tugwell's work on petroleum policy, see item 8539b.

8513a. Blanco Muñoz, Agustín. Elementos para una discusión sobre los modelos de violencia en Venezuela. Caracas, Ediciones Desorden, 1974. 257 p.

Violence for political and social purposes has been used by both the upper and lower classes. Chiefly drawing on Venezuela's experience, the writer seeks to develop a model of political violence in Latin America. He argues that if the model (and phenomena) are correctly understood, Latin America's apparently endless cycle of violence and underdevelopment can be ended.

8514. Boza, Guillermo and **Antonio Juan Sosa.** U.C.A.B.: la crisis de octubre, un estudio de sociología del conflicto. Valencia, Ven., Ediciones Vadell, 1974. 209 p., tables.

Chronology, detailed presentation of positions, and data bank drawn from behavioral observations, declarations, and university files, concerning a clash between some students and faculty and administration of the Univ. Católica Andrés Bello, Caracas. A solid piece for specialists.

8514a. Burelli, Miguel Angel. Afirmación de Venezuela: itinerario de una inquietud. Caracas, Editorial Arte, 1971. 354 p.

Collected short newspaper and magazine articles by the author, grouped in chapters on education, constitutional institutions, politics, regional needs and interests, economics, social problems, foreign policy, national traditions, and famous Venezuelans. The writer was presidential candidate in 1969, and later Ambassador to the US.

8515. Caldera Rodríguez, Rafael. Especificidad de la Democracia Cristiana. Caracas, Comité Organizador Pro Elecciones Independientes (COPEI), 1972. 145 p., bibl.

A COPEI party publication based on notes from a short course given in 1966-67 by Caldera at the Institute for Formation of party leaders. A comprehensive bibliography relating to party views and doctrine is appended.

8515a. Cannon, Mark W.; R. Scott Fosler; and **Robert Witherspoon.** Urban government for Valencia, Venezuela. Foreword by Lyle C. Fitch. N.Y., Praeger *in cooperation with the Institute of Public Administration*, 1973. 152 p., bibl., tables (Praeger special studies in international politics and government)

A depiction of one of the country's middle-sized cities, this volume focuses on administrative and decision-making processes during a period of change caused by both internal forces and outside influences. Specific attention is directed to transport, education, water/sewerage, public housing, and the role of planning for development. One of a series of highly professional and eminently worthwhile case studies, this is a book for intent specialists.

8515b. Centro de Investigaciones Sociales y Socio-Religiosas (CISOR), *Caracas.* Anuario de la Iglesia Católica en Venezuela. Caracas, 1969. 386 p.

A name-by-name listing of every office, division, parish, and diocese, etc., of the Catholic Church in the country, with its personnel. Includes alphabetical listing of all priests with corresponding dates of service.

8516. Chen, J. Chi-Yi. Développement et

animation communautaire à Vénézuela (IRFDH/DC, 21, mars 1965, p. 32-40, tables)

A specialist on internal migration in Venezuela links data concerning industrialization and economic growth to programs for community development. Assuming the growth of political-administrative stability and competence in the country in the past few years, the author expresses hope that a link between resources and community development can be forged.

8516a. ———— and **Ramón Martín Mateo.** Aspectos administrativos de la planificación: el sistema venezolano. Caracas, Univ. Católica Andrés Bello, Instituto de Investigaciones Económicas y Sociales, 1973. 203 p., bibl., map, tables.

A textbookish and detailed examination of the planning process in Venezuela, within the national planning agency, CORDIPLAN, and other official agencies. Recent developments in planning technique and conception are examined in detail, including the decision to establish eight planning regions for distinct treatment.

8517. Cross, Benedict. Marxism in Venezuela (USIA/PC, 22:6, Nov./Dec. 1973, p. 51-70, plates)

A useful and effective history of the marxist left which begins with a detailed discussion of the Communist Party. Emphasizes the period after 1958, including its involvement in guerrilla violence, its legal revival, and its division with the formation of the Movimiento al Socialismo. Electoral politics in the 1970s receives substantial attention.

8518. Diez, Julio. Notas y notables. Caracas, Talleres Gráficos de Mersifrica, 1972. 243 p.

A collection of the author's statements, some anecdotal or biographic of others, both honored and otherwise, in the country's history. Others include his interpellation, as Minister of Labor and Communications in 1970.

8519. Fonseca Fiol, Jaime. El militar: pensamiento y acción. Caracas, The Author, 1973. 345 p., plates.

The memoirs of a retired Venezuelan army officer and former ambassador to Bolivia. Strongly criticizes the Pérez Jiménez regime. Not of tremendous importance. [A. Suárez]

8519a. Gilhodes, Pierre. Venezuela: trois ans de Démocratie Chrétienne: le gouvernement de M. Rafael Caldera (FDD/NED [Séries Problèmes d'Amérique Latine, 25] 3935/3936, 25 oct. 1972, p. 5-44, tables)

A periodic report on events in Venezuela, supplemented by a number of statistical annexes plus a chronology for the 30 months to the end of 1971. Chapters deal with economic growth, domestic and foreign policies, and political groups and parties. This is highly valuable material for both students and specialists.

8520. Guevara, Angel Raúl. Los cachorros del Pentágono. 2. ed. Caracas, Fondo Editorial Salvador de la Plaza, 1973. 195 p. (Rocinante)

An attack on the Leoni government (1964-69) for its tactics in the putting down of guerrilla forces and antigovernment groups in the state of Falcón, Ven. The author claims no difference exists between the "constitutional democracy" of the post-Pérez Jiménez period and that dictatorship.

8520a. Imber, Sofía. Yo, la intrasigente. Caracas, Editorial Tiempo Nuevo, 1971. 212 p.

A collection of the author's columns for *El Nacional* of Caracas. They deal with a variety of colloquial topics and have much use for the student of contemporary Venezuelan society and values.

8521. Karst, Kenneth L. Rights in land and housing in an informal legal system: the barrios of Caracas (AJCL, 19:3, Summer 1971, p. 550-574)

The title is fully descriptive of a highly useful article. This is a short report of selected aspects of a 1967 opinion and behavioral study. While a portion of the paper is narrative and physically descriptive in nature, the conclusions suggest how law and right are developed de facto in a society whose formal legal system contains no norms.

8521a. ————; **Murray L. Schwartz,** and **Audrey J. Schwartz.** The evolution of law in the barrios of Caracas. Los Angeles, Univ. of California, Latin American Center, 1973. 125 p., plates, tables.

Amply implemented by excellent photographs, this study is based on both a behavioral and attitudinal sample survey and intensive reports from summer 1967 residence by three participant observers. The 12 barrios examined (10 responded in the survey) ranged from a few months to many years in age. Although there is a wealth of anthropological data implicit in the emphasis of this report is on the establishment of institutions, legitimacy and law.

8522. Kolb, Glen L. Democracy and dictatorship in Venezuela, 1945-1958. New London, Connecticut College, 1974. 228 p., bibl. (Connecticut College monograph, 10)

In a book that appears to place as much emphasis on style as on represented fact, the details abound. The emphasis of the work is on the period from 1948 (fall of the first AD government) to 1958 (the fall of Pérez Jiménez). On the whole, documentation tends toward the spotty in a work that is pure descriptive narrative.

8523. Lazar, Arpad von and **Vi Ann**

Beadle. National integration and insurgency in Venezuela: an exercise in causation (UU/WPQ, 24:1, March 1971, p. 136-145, tables)

The suggestion that guerrilla action is keyed by a lack of national integration is tested by use of several simple and rather obvious statistical measures. Using these measures, the authors compare Venezuelan states against known levels of illegal activity and conclude that other, more sophisticated, measures are needed. The data are used in a simple and noncorrelative way.

8524. Leonardo Ruiz Pineda: guerrillero de la libertad. Caracas, Ediciones Centauro, 1973. 216 p.

Unlike the majority of this small pocket-sized series on significant political actors of the left in recent Venezuelan partisan history, this deals with a political moderate who was killed in 1952 by the Pérez Jiménez dictatorship. Consists of elegies by 16 writers of renown in the country, plus newspaper comments at the time of his death.

8524a. Lynch, Edward. Propositions for planning new towns in Venezuela (JDA, 7:4, July 1973, p. 549-570, maps, plates)

Drawing on the experience of three planned city constructions (Ciudad Guayana, Tuy, and El Tablazo) advances propositions for city planning. These deal with usage of existing facilities in place prior to new construction, integration of on-site peoples, employment of existing (as vs. new) law, etc.

8525. Maduro, Otto. Revelación y revolución: notas sobre el Mensaje de Cristo y sus implicaciones frente a la necesitada liberación de los pueblos de América del imperialismo y de los capitalistas. Mérida, Ven., Talleres Gráficos Universitarios, 1970. 133 p. (Col. Actual serie ideas)

A Catholic university instructor in philosophy, the author also is a foundling member of the Christian Left movement in Venezuela. Within this context the book has substantial authority.

8526. Magallanes, Manuel Vicente. Cuatro partidos nacionales: Acción Democrática, COPEI, Partido Comunista de Venezuela, Unión Repúblicana Democrática. Caracas, n.p., 1973. 157 p., bibl.

A short handbook-type history and presentation of the four major continuing parties of the country. For general information only.

8526a. Márquez, Pompeyo. Socialismo en tiempo presente. Caracas, José Agustín Catala, 1973. 252 p.

The longtime Venezuelan communist leader here is presented, in large part, through his public pronouncements, selected by his editor and adulator.

8526b. Martínez C., Ildemaro. Instituciones para el desarrollo: análisis de FUNDACOMUN en Venezuela. Caracas, Instituto de Estudios Superiores de Administración, 1974. 35 p. (Ediciones IESA, 1)

An academic model for analysis of administrative institutions is applied to FUNDACOMUN, an official agency intended to improve linkages and the quality of transactions between national and local governments in Venezuela. Can such an agency reaph maturity in the Venezuelan *ambiente?* Does the model work in this application? The author's Ph.D. dissertation is here distilled.

8527. Maza Zavala, D.F. and others. Venezuela; crecimiento sin desarrollo. México, Editorial Nuestro Tiempo, 1974. 441 p., tables.

Six essays, of varying length, originality and quality, deal with the general theme of Venezuela's physical growth without qualitative social and psychological development despite the country's enormous wealth and possibilities. All Venezuelans, the authors also teach at the Central Univ. of Caracas. This is a serious work demanding the attention of the specialist. Authors are Maza, Héctor Malavé Mata, Celio S. Orta, Orlando Araujo, Miguel J. Bolívar Chollet, and Alfredo Chacón.

8528. Mikdashi, Zuhayr. The community of oil exporting countries: a study in governmental cooperation. Ithaca, N.Y., Cornell Univ. Press, 1972. 239 p. tables.

While the bulk of this rather dense work deals with the Middle Eastern countries, Venezuela is shown and discussed as an integral part of the OPEC and the world oil industry.

8528a. _____. Cooperation among oil-exporting countries with special reference to Arab countries: a political economy analysis (WPF/IO, 28:1, Winter 1974, p. 1-30, tables)

Self-explanatory title. Paper includes useful facts concerning Venezuela's role in OPEC.

8529. Myers, David J. Democratic campaigning in Venezuela: Caldera's victory. Foreword by Hermano Ginés. Caracas, Fundación La Salle de Ciencias Naturales, Instituto Caribe de Antropología y Sociología, 1973. 255 p., maps, tables (Monografía, 17)

Dr. Myers' dissertation, implemented by added materials drawn from intensive midcampaign interviews with political leaders, is a solid descriptive and analytical piece of considerable depth.

8529a. _____. Toma de decisiones sobre la renovación urbana en El Conde. Caracas, Instituto de Estudios

Superiores de Administración, 1974. 51 p., map, tables.

Short examination of the decision process, and its political and social context, in the renewal plans for a major section in the heart of Caracas. The paper is detailed and specific and useful for both specialists and a more general reader.

8530. Nott, David. Venezuela: the oil bonanza and the new government (Bank of London and South America Review [London] 8:4, May 1974, p. 196-204)

Excellent précis of Carlos Andrés Pérez' program plans which describes their background in admirably succinct style.

8531. Núñez Ecarri, Carlos. El Congreso de la República: origen y funciones del Parlamento en Venezuela. Caracas, Imprenta del Congreso de la República de Venezuela, 1971. 46 p., tables.

A primer-like explanation of the way the Venezuelan Congress works. Much too short, but very valuable contribution.

8532. Partido Social Cristiano, Comité Organizadol Pro Elecciones Independientes (COPEI), *Caracas*. Fracción Parlamentaria. La sociedad por hacer: principios fundamentales e introduccidn del Programa de Gobierno de Rafael Caldera. Caracas, 1972. 40 p. (Col. Ideología y doctrina, 1)

The platform of the party for the 1972 elections campaign, adopted by the party's 1972 convention.

8532a. Paz Galarraga, Jesús Angel. Por siempre "defensa del petróleo venezolano" (POLIT, 8:73/74, junio/julio 1969, p. 99-112)

A now somewhat dated speech by the then Vice President of the Movimiento Electoral del Pueblo in a Senate debate concerning oil policy. It is nationalist, sharply critical of existing politico-commercial relations with the US, and calls for a policy that only now (1975) is being implemented by the government.

8533. Pedro Fernández, Antonio de. El funcionario público venezolano. Caracas, Ministerio de Sanidad y Asistencia Social, Dirección de Malariología y Saneamiento Ambiental, 1973. 147 p.

Although it takes the writer an extraordinarily long time to get to the point, this small volume is useful for examining the legal status and rights of Venezuelan civil servants, both career and short or part-time. The volume includes lengthy cuttings from the writing of legal specialists, and also of relevant laws.

8533a. Petkoff, Teodoro. Razón y pasión del socialismo: el tema socialista en Venezuela. Caracas, Ediciones Centauro, 1973. 382 p.

Short newspaper articles, essays, speeches, and interviews with Petkoff, who has been a political activist for the Left for some 25 years. Now a founding leader of the Movimiento al Socialismo, earlier he was a student militant against the Pérez Jiménez military government, Communist Party leader, and guerrilla fighter.

8534. Plaza, Salvador de la and **Jacques Zuclos.** Antecedentes del revisionismo en Venezuela. Caracas, Fondo Editorial Salvador de la I laza, 1973. 187 p. (Col. Ideología)

A collection of a few major pieces by the late Salvador de la Plaza, intended by his defenders to prove that he was in fact the most certain and dedicated advocate of marxism-leninism in Venezuela while he lived. The Duclos piece deals with the dissolution of the Communist Party of the US as a horrid example of what lies in wait for the party if revisionists capture it.

8535. Rangel, Domingo Alberto. Elecciones 1973: el gran negocio. Caracas, Talleres Gráficos de Servicios Venezolanos de Publicidad, 1974. 173 p.

A detailed presentation of Rangel's (and the left's) claim that the 1973 election was bought by the Acción Democrática, with US help and funding.

8535a. Rangel, José Vicente. Tiempo de verdades. Caracas, Ediciones Centauro, 1973. 298 p.

One of a series of pocket-sized collections of statements and short comments by leading partisan leftists of Venezuela. A short statement by way of introduction by Manuel Caballero seeks to put them (and the man) in perspective.

8536. Ravell, Carola. Le programme d'action communautaire rattaché à la Présidence de la Republique du Vénézuela (IRFDH/DC, 21, mars 1965, p. 41-45)

Short informative article concerning the objectives and methodology of community development, and their contribution to the national goal of socioeconomic integration. The author was then Chief, Dept. of Community Development, in the General Secretariat of the Presidency.

8537. Ray, Talton F. The politics of the barrios of Venezuela. Berkeley, Univ. of California Press, 1969. 211 p., bibl., map, plates.

Based on author's experience of three years (1961-64) as a community development worker and Field Operations Director for Acción en Venezuela, this is a down-to-earth and solid study of the demographic, behavioral and political aspects of barrios in 16 Venezuelan cities and towns. Thus it is in some respects a useful antidote to overly ideological versions of Venezuelan lower-class political attitudes.

8538. Rouhani, Fuad. A history of O.P.E.C. N.Y., Praeger Publishers, 1971. 281 p., tables.

In effect, this is a primer on OPEC. It contains details concerning the organization's early structure, operations, and concepts. Updated to 1970 in a prefatory chapter, the work essentially dates from about 1968. The author was OPEC's first Secretary General.

8539. Tinoco, Pedro. El estado eficaz. Caracas, Italgráfica, 1974? 162 p., tables.

Former Treasury Minister under Caldera assesses administrative performance and reform efforts of COPEI government. Prescriptive emphasis. [J.J. Bailey]

8539a. Tugwell, Franklin. Petroleum policy in Venezuela: lessons in the politics of dependence management (RU/SCID, 9:1, Spring 1974, p. 84-120, table)

A tightly knit review of the clash, over time, between the Venezuelan government and the international oil companies for relative advantage. The sense of continuous conflict, discretely defined by time periods, is the keynote of the paper. The dependency-theory ideologue of the left cannot find comfort in this paper. Tugwell says in effect that Venezuela gained when she helped herself by perceptive and innovative policy in the past and will so now and in the future.

8540. Venezuela. Comisión de Administración Pública (CAP). Informe sobre la reforma de la administración pública nacional. t. 1/2. Caracas, 1972. 2 v. (645, 621 p.) tables.

Efhaustive treatment of the material, essential for specialists.

8540a. ⸻. Congreso. Comisión Redactora del Proyecto. La Constitución de 1961 y la evolución constitucional de Venezuela. t. 1, v. 2, Actas de la Comisión Redactora del Proyecto. t. 2, v. 2, Forma de estado: el Organo Deliberante Nacional [por] J.M. Casal Montbrun. Caracas, Ediciones del Congreso de la República, 1972. 2 v. (413, 448 p.)

Stenographic text of proceedings of the Editorial Committee of the Congress on the Constitution.

8540b. ⸻. Presidencia. Mensajes presidenciales. Notas e introducción por Antonio Arellano Moreno. v. 1, 1819-1875. v. 2, 1876-1890. v. 3, 1891-1909. v. 4, 1910-1939. v. 7, 1959. Caracas, 1970/1972. 7 v. (418, 422, 418, 423, 363, 591, 170 p.)

Collected papers and major addresses of the Presidents of Venezuela. V. 1 is introduced by an overview essay of presidential roles in Venezuelan history, taken individually. Bolívar's Angostura Message of 1819 leads off v. 1. The remaining items are presidential messages to the Congress, through Leoni's of 1969.

8540c. ⸻. ⸻. Comisión de Administración Pública. Administración para el Desarrollo. La reforma administrativa en Venezuela: 1969-1971. Caracas, 1971. 160 p.

An essential text for specialists, this was prepared for the Interregional Seminar of the UN on large scale administrative reform in London, Oct. 1971. Philosophy, goals, and machinery for reform are indicated.

BRAZIL

8541. Aleixo, José Carlos Brandi. Migrações internacionais de pessoal qualificado: "Brain Drain" (UMG/RBEP, 39, julho 1974, p.p. 31-81, bibl.)

Examination of the international phenomenon in both theory and fact. There is some emphasis given to the resulting problems in Latin America, and in Brazil specifically, but this is not a research piece presenting new data.

8542. Alexander, Robert J. The Brazilian Tenentes after the Revolution of 1930 (UM/JIAS, 15:2, May 1973, p. 221-248, bibl.)

What happened to the *Tenentes*, the young officers who rebelled at Fort Copacabana in 1922, and in 1924 in São Paulo, in later life? This short narrative and descriptive piece examines the histories of several dozen individuals, largely in terms of anecdotes.

8543. Alves, Marcio Moreira. A grain of mustard seed: the awakening of the Brazilian revolution. Garden City, N.Y., Doubleday Anchor Books, 1973. 194 p.

When the Brazilian Congress refused to waive Alves' parliamentary immunity in 1968, the Executive closed it down. Alves, who has spoken persistently and pungently against the regime's excesses, states his case here *in extenso* and in vigorous terms. The book has also been translated into Spanish and published simultaneously in Mexico and Havana as *El despertar de la revolución brasileña* (México, Editorial Diógenes, 1972, 251 p.). For historian's comment, see *HLAS 36:3545*.

8543a. Andrade, Manuel Correia de Oliveira. Paisagens e problemas do Brasil: aspectos da vida rural brasileira frente a industrialização e ao crescimento econômico. 4. ed. rev. São Paulo, Editôra Brasilense, 1973. 277 p., bibl., maps, plates, tables.

Essentially an economic geography of Brazil with a substantial number of tables offering recent data on production, growth of the economy, etc. The emphasis is indicated in the title.

8544. Antoine, Charles. Church and power in Brazil. Translated by Peter Nelson. Maryknoll, N.Y., Orbis Books, 1973. 275 p.

The tragedy of a trusted major social institution that did not face courageously the challenge of fascism is recounted in a treatment that focuses on the first six years of the dictatorship, 1964-69. The tone is balanced but critical and sorrowfully worthwhile for both public and students.

8544a. Aragão, José Campos de. A intentona comunista de 1935. Rio, Biblioteca do Exército Editôra, 1973. 151 p., bibl., plates (Col. General Benício, 433:110)

A major general writes of the uprising led by Luis Carlos Prestes.

8545. Arraes, Miguel. Brazil: the people and the power. Introduction by Yves Goussault. Translated by Lancelot Sheppard. London, Penguin Books, 1972. 232 p. (The Pelican Latin American library)

Popular version of where Brazil was and where it is now, by a populist governor from Pernambuco deposed from his elected office in the golpe of 1964. Although bristling with the political swear words of the leftist and nationalist, the book may be of value to the general reader.

8546. Bahia (state), *Bra*. **Secretaria de Planejamento, Ciência e Tecnologia.** Programa de governo: 1972-1974. Salvador, Bra., Impressão Pinheiro, 1974. 352 p., plates, tables.

Development plan in comprehensive detail for years 1972-74.

8547. Balan, Jorge and others. Centro e periferia no desenvolvimento brasileiro. São Paulo, Difusão Européia do Livro (DIFEL), 1974. 251 p., tables (Corpo e alma do Brasil)

Five Brazilian social scientists offer perspectives of national development with demographic considerations foremost in the analysis (but hardly excluding other treatments). This work has exceptional value for the specialist.

8547a. Barata, Júlio de Carvalho. A política social da revolução. Brasília, Ministério do Trabalho e Previdência Social, 1972. 173 p.

Speeches by the Minister of Labor and Social Welfare in the Médici government, 1970-72.

8548. Beiguelman, Paula. Pequenos estudos de ciência política. 2. ed. rev. São Paulo, Livraria Pioneira Editôra, 1973. 225 p., bibl. (Biblioteca pioneira de ciências sociais. Política)

A collection of four case studies. Three deal with slavery and racial problems, the fourth, with partisan politics during the Empire. An appendix recounts the first republic (1891-1909) in terms of political leadership and policies.

8548a. Berger, Peter L. Pyramids of sacrifice: political ethics and social change. N.Y., Basic Books, 1974. 242 p.

This is an interesting book by treatment, a significant book by scholarship, and a vitally important book for its questioning of "conventional wisdoms." The theme is development, but the author suggests that in pursuit of it ideological systems have lost sight of humane values throughout history. The case studies, both formal/academic and creative/impressionistic, are based on Latin American and Chinese data for the most part, with Brazil featured.

8548b. Bittencourt, Gustavo Francisco Feijó. Conotações do poder marítimo necessárias ao processo de engrandecimento no Brasil (BMM/RMB, 91:10/12, out./dez. 1971, p. 108-121)

A rather loose and freewheeling view of maritime doctrine concerning Brazilian needs for the future, when greatness is upon it. The author is a Captain of the Navy; his piece is hardly rigorous, but it is a useful view of one man's understanding of the national ambition.

8549. Brasileiro, Ana Maria. O federalismo cooperativo (UMG/RBEP, 39, julho 1974, p. 83-128, table)

Following a brief introduction dealing with the theory of federalism, the specific case of Brazil is discussed in some depth. What are the theoretically "correct" relations among the federal, state, and local governments, and what are the practices? Several criteria are employed, including services, tax income, de facto allocations of authority, and integration of programs.

8549a. _____. O município como sistema político. Rio, Fundação Getúlio Vargas, 1973. 124 p., bibl., tables.

A brief text on the municipality in Brazilian government and administration. Following an introductory chapter on the legal status of municípios in Brazilian law, the volume discusses the municípios of the state of Rio de Janeiro as well as some efforts at model building.

8550. Brayner, Floriano de Lima. Luzes sobre memórias. Rio, Livraria São José, 1973. 242 p., illus.

Memoirs and self-explanation of a retired Chairman of the Joint Chiefs of the Brazilian Armed Forces.

8551. Brazil. Banco Nacional da Habitação. BNH: solução brasileira de problemas brasileiros. Rio? 1972? 34 p.

A short official statement of the housing policies of the Bank.

8551a. _____. **Comissão de Coordenação**

e **Implementação de Técnicas Financeiras.** 1 [i.e., Primeiro] ciclo de palestras. Rio, Depto. de Imprensa Nacional, 1974. 224 p., tables.

Eight lectures delivered in 1973 for the benefit of the following government agencies: the Ministry of the Treasury; the Ministry of Planning and General Coordination; the Central Bank; and the Bank of Brazil. The lectures were prepared by specialists from other government agencies for purposes of information and coordination. The lecture texts are followed by transcripts of the question-and-answer periods.

8551b. ———. **Exército. Centro de Relações Públicas.** O seu exército. Rio, n.d. 1 v. (Unpaged) plates.

A glossy public relations presentation of the Brazilian Army. The focus is on training and on doctrine, but there is some useful public relations-type information on general goals of the army. A useful self-image.

8551c. ———. **Ministério do Planejamento e Coordenação Geral.** O desafio brasileiro e o programa estratégico. Rio, Fundação IBGE, 1968? 74 p., plates, tables.

National problems, and national plans to meet them, for public information — with a maximum of (highly attractive) graphics.

8551d. ———. **Presidência.** Metas e bases do plano de ação do govêrno. Brasília, 1971. 247 p., maps, plates, tables.

An exhaustive and essential document concerning state government planning for 1972: resources, means, instruments, goals. More than 75 percent of the volume is comprised of tabular and graphic presentations of intricate detail.

8552. Brazil: 1969, an unedited compilation of articles from the newsweekly *Latin America*. N.Y., Center for Inter-American Relations, 1970. 152 p.

Unfortunately, the subtitle is exact; there is neither index nor table of contents. Thus, this is like reading an undated, undiscriminating, headlineless stack of newspapers, even though of acceptable journalistic quality. The general quality of *Latin America*, the little British digest, is by now known to specialists, but the general reader may be confused by this unedited compilation.

8552a. Le Brésil en 1971 (FDD/NED [Problèmes d'Amerique Latine, 24] 3913/3914, 28 juillet 1972, p. 53-81)

Review of Brazilian governmental-political events, and of foreign policy, in 1971. A useful short section examines Brazil's pretentions to leadership and hegemonic power in South America.

8552b. Brésil 1972-1973: les deux dernières années de la Presidence Médici (FDD/NED [Problèmes d'Amérique Latine, 31] 1974, p. 1-71, map)

Médici's last two years are surveyed in some detail for political atmosphere and style, social and economic policies he promoted to have distributive and ameliorative effects throughout the country, and the "diplomatic offensive" toward neighbors and overseas countries. Annexes include biographical details concerning Ernesto Geisel's new government, the Higher School of War, legislation regulating political parties, general energy policy, and a detailed chronology.

8553. Bruneau, Thomas C. Obstacles to change in the Church: lessons from four Brazilian dioceses (UM/JIAS, 15:4, Nov. 1973, p. 395-414, bibl., tables)

The paper notes that the Church in Latin America is anything but united in its attitudes and responses to pressure for change. He suggests one must study individual dioceses to attain valid explanations, and examines four in Brazil. He indicates that factors relevant to success are the personal qualities of the bishops, the history of each individual diocese, the political climate, and the kinds of programs locally attempted. He concludes the political climate is of primary importance in authoritarian regimes, and can easily lead to nullity.

8553a. ———. The political transformation of the Brazilian Catholic Church. London, Cambridge Univ. Press, 1974. 270 p., bibl., map, tables (Perspectives on development)

That the Catholic Church in Latin America is changing, and doing so with specific political results, is axiomatic in the author's view. He seeks to explain and analyze this change. A series of solid and useful historical chapters introduces the topic of a Church that confronted with great reluctance the need to take the lead in fomenting social and political change— even against the will of the government. How the nature of the regime frustrates the will of the Church is perceived by Bruneau as its chief problem. The frustration is the greater because the Church's experience has been predicated on political power, its device for maintenance of the clerical institution, which is presently affected by the conflict. A large number of tables implements this provocative study.

8553b. ———. Power and influence: analysis of the Church in Latin America and the case of Brazil (LARR, 8:2, Summer 1973, p. 25-51)

A systematic examination of existing literature on the topic—the writer notes a marked increase as of 1965— underlies a model for analysis and use in future research.

8554. Calasans, José Adão de. O papel do município no desenvolvimento (Revista de Administração Municipal [Rio] 19:113, julho/agosto 1972, p. 30-44)

A brief overview of the município as a governmental

agency for management of the problems of urbanization. A final section refers to the possibility of inter-municipal cooperation for joint resolution of problems. A rather slim piece and not especially informative or analytical.

Câmara, Helder. Structures of injustice. See *HLAS 36:3567.*

8555. Campos, Domar and others. Paz, seu nome é desenvolvimento. Rio, Editôra Fundo de Cultura, 1968. 218 p., tables.

Six economists, five of whom have held ambassadorial rank in missions for Brazil, discuss questions less of peace than of development for Brazil. The focus is largely internal, but the mission of Brazil to motivate continental change through economic influence is made clear. Further, the collection, presented in 1967 series of addresses, also demonstrates where economics was at the official level at the time of writing, as a discipline and as a device for examining national power.

8555a. Carneiro, Nelson Souza. Palavras, leva-as o vento . . . v. 1. Brasília, Senado Federal, 1973. 271 p.

Selections from speeches and bills (1969-72) by the leader of the MDB (Movimento Democrático Brasileiro). Typical example of many such "vanity" volumes published by congressmen.

8556. Carvalho, Paulo Pinto de. Caminhos de democracia. Pôrto Alegre, Bra., Edições Flama, 1973. 128 p.

Views of life, society, ethics and politics by a leading lawyer and former government official of the state of Rio Grande do Sul.

8556a. Carvalho Neto, Joviniano Soares de. Nacionalismo em fato novo: perspectiva do nacionalismo autoritário no Brasil. Salvador, Bra., Centro de Estudos e Ação Social [and] Edições Loyola, São Paulo, 1973. 77 p. (Cadernos do CEAS, 25)

How nationalism is used by authoritarians. General review of the matter as applied to other countries of Latin America is extended in detail to Brazil.

8557. Celson, José da Silva. Marchas e contramarchas do mandonismo local: Caeté, um estudo de caso. Belo Horizonte, Bra., Univ. Federal de Minas Gerais, 1973. 156 p., tables.

A detailed study of the phenomenon of *mandonismo* (often called *coronelismo* in other regions of Brazil) in Caeté, Minas Gerais, a mining city dating from 1701. The study traces the present structure of municipal power from its founding in 1891 by the owner of a ceramics plant in the city through the 1970 election. The work explores the criteria locally accepted for elites, as well as attitudes concerning leadership, power, etc. The book includes the questionnaire used, as well as some of the computation of the data.

8558. Constituição da República Federativa do Brasil: emenda constitucional No. 1, de 17 de outubro de 1969. Belo Horizonte, Bra. Editôra Legislação Mineira, 1969? 1 v. (Various pagings)

8559. Coronel . . . el Ejército del Brasil: sus problemas y políticas (IAEERI/E, 2, julio/agosto 1969, p. 62-77, tables)

Valuable examination of the Brazilian Army by (presumably) a foreign military specialist which includes structural history and changes in the country's armed forces, current budget, doctrine, development plans, and response doctrine. The casual interest of the reader is heightened by its appearance in this journal, *Estrategia*, a quasi-official publication of the Argentine Army.

8559a. Cortés, Carlos E. Gaúcho politics in Brazil: the politics of Rio Grande do Sul, 1930-1964. Photographs by Atelier O. Dutra. Albuquerque, Univ. of New Mexico Press, 1974. 252 p., bibl., maps, plates.

The title is an unfortunately adequate description of the major portion of this book, *politiquería* in Rio Grande, and in Brazil as the result of politicking and violence by Gaúchos. The book reports virtually every personalist group, plot, movement, and leader from the fall of the Empire. What it does not do, in even a minimal way, is suggest causations or results, with one principal exception. The reader is informed that the state was driven economically to the wall by vengeful national presidents who were not Gaúchos, but this material is fragmented and highly unsatisfying. Rio Grande has enjoyed a revival since 1964 because Gaúchos are the largest element of the national army. A journalistic, narrow book.

8560. Costa, Marcelo Caetano da. Evolução política do Brasil República. Goiânia, Bra., Univ. Federal de Goiás, 1968. 74 p., bibl., illus., tables.

A somewhat quaint presentation of the thesis that radicals and communists have gained strength in Brazil because of the influx of foreign ideas and the foolishness of the ingenuous. Based on a lecture delivered under the auspices of the Commander of the Federal Garrison of Goiânia in which the armed forces are given points for their defense of the country.

Dulles, John W.F. The Brazilian Left: efforts at recovery, 1964-1970. See *HLAS 36:3582*

8561. Encontro Latino-Americano de Justiça e Paz, *IV, Rio, 1971.* Anais. Rio, Comissão Pontifícia Justiça e Paz, Seção Brasileira, 1971. 1 v. (Various pagings) tables.

Reports of 11 subject panels, rapporteurs, plus the speeches and other presentations to plenary sessions, of the conference. The reports in some instances concern only the discussions of topic panels. In a few instances the "reports" are in fact monographic pieces of substantial length. Paulo Singer's paper on the labor force and employment figures, 1920-69; Helio Jaguaribe's on recent events in inter-American relations and the crisis of the 1960s; Edmar L. Bacha's on underemployment and the social cost of hand-labor in development; and Cândido Mendes' on power elites; are all major pieces.

8561a. Estudo de problemas brasileiros. 2. ed. Recife, Bra., Univ. Federal de Pernambuco, 1971. 526 p.

The syllabus of a one-semester course on "Brazilian Problems" (i.e., Brazilian history and society) designed for teaching at the university level. Consists of papers by 17 faculty members on content, direction and purpose of the course. The semester's work became the topic of discussion during the summer among faculty and government representatives. Some of the proceedings are included.

8561b. Evans, Peter B. The military, the multinationals and the "miracle:" the political economy of the "Brazilian model" of development (RU/SCID, 9:3, Fall 1974. p. 26-45, table)

Brazil's developmental model (which is here described in narrative language rather than in difficult jargon, praise be) is economic growth and concentration imposed from above under conditions of modernization coupled with symbiosis of the military with foreign multinational interests. The rather sensible and useful article is still sharp and critical, for all its nonideological language.

8562. Flynn, Peter. Brazil: authoritarianism and class control (JLAS, 6:2, Nov. 1974, p. 315-333)

An extended and rather relaxed review article of recent publications on Brazil in the comparative politics field. Flynn pulls no punches on some pieces but is uncritical of others and concludes with the observation that American work demonstrates a wide gap between mature method (which is relatively well-handled) and general theory (which is sadly absent). A useful overview, full of nice comments for superficially sophisticated graduate students.

8563. Forman, Shepard. Disunity and discontent: a study of peasant political movements in Brazil (JLAS, 3:1, May 1971, p. 3-24)

An essentially sociological study which seeks the circumstances under which peasant protest of a local nature can be mobilized into mass movements able to organize major inputs at the national level. How has the mass peasant movement in Brazil developed, and what forms has it taken? Specialists will find this a careful and provocative piece with detail on Julião and other movements as well.

8564. Foucher, Michel. La mise en valeur de las Amazonie brésilienne; les routes transamazoniennes (FDD/NED [Problèmes d'Amérique Latine, 33] 4110/4111, 15 Sept. 1974, p. 71-96, bilb., map)

A useful historical survey of Brazilian thoughts and policies concerning occupation and exploitation of the Amazon basin. The latter part of the paper discusses its potentialities for future growth, as well as obstacles to be surmounted.

8565. Fragoso, Antônio ed. Brasil ¿milagro o engaño?: dos graves denuncios. Lima, Centro de Estudios y Publicaciones, 1973, 121 p.

Consists of two rather long statements critical of the nature of governmental policies and techniques in Brazil signed by the Bishops of the Northeast and by the Bishops of the Center-West, respectively. Proscribed in Brazil, as is noted in the introductory note by the Bishop of Crateús, they conclude that the Brazilian miracle has been a social horror from the viewpoint of the people.

8565a. Fragoso, Augusto. A Escola Superior de Guerra (Problemas Brasileiros [São Paulo] 8:88, dez. 1970, p. 19-34, map, plates)

The Commandant of the ESG explains what the school is, how it came to be established, and who played significant roles. Examines in some detail current school doctrine, including its role in examining the country's problems, its role in the formation of new elites, and prospects for its future development. A useful article for specialists.

8566. Garrastazu Médici, Emílio. Mensagem ao Congresso Nacional. Brasília, Presidencia da República, 1974. 236 p.

The State of the Union Message, 1 March 1974.

8566a. Gasparian, Marcos. O industrial. São Paulo, Livraria Martins Editôra, 1973. 231 p.

A critical examination of Brazilian industrialists, their attitudes and lifestyles, their use of power, and their role in the support of the current military government. An industrialist himself, the author is writing from direct experience.

8567. Ghioldi, Rodolfo and others. El "modelo" brasileño. B.A., Ediciones Centro de Estudios, 1972. 144 p.

Five essays by marxists on Brazilian events in a marxist framework and from a nationalist Argentine perspective. Although a highly partial view of events, this *can* be called a rather important little volume.

8568. Gregory, Afonso ed. Comunidades eclesiais de base: Utopia ou realidade. Rio, Editôra Vozes, 1973. 189 p., bibl.

Seven writers contribute to a primer-like volume on the role of the Church in community building and development.

8569. Guske, Hubertus. Helder Câmara: Katholiken Lateinamerikas suchen neue Wege. Berlin, FRG, Union-Verlag, 1973. 85 p., illus.

Short and somewhat superficial account of the life of Helder Câmara. [H.J. Hoyer]

8570. Hilton, Stanley E. Military influence on Brazilian economic policy, 1930-1945: a different view (HAHR, 53:1, Feb. 1973, p. 71-94)

Using two specific policy case studies as the basis of his paper, the author challenges interpretations of military influence and preference in national economic and development policy. The Brazilian Army emerges (tentatively) as narrowly and parochially interested in pushing for its own aggrandizement on the grounds of a national peril apparently not perceived by others. Thus it encouraged steps strengthening itself.

8571. Instituto Brasileiro de Administração Municipal, Rio. Centro de Pesquisas Urbanas. Assistência técnica e treinamento: pesquisa a nível municipal. Rio, 1972. 170 1., tables.

The write-up, complete with supporting data and questionnaire, of a Ford-supported field study on whether technical assistance in training of municipal employees has been perceived as appropriate and helpful.

8572. Jaguaribe, Hélio. Brasil: crise e alternativas. Rio, Zahar Editôres, 1974. 157 p., tables (Biblioteca de ciências sociais)

Under the present focus of governmental economic growth policies, with their emphasis on capitalism encouraged by foreign participation in critical areas, Brazil is fast approaching a practical termination of salutary change. This impending crisis should evoke alternatives, and the author offers several. A pointed and thoughtful piece by one of the country's most perceptive writers.

8572a. Jordão, Haryberto de Miranda. Esbôço de organização nacional. Rio, Editôra Civilização Brasileira, 1973. 315 p. (Col. Retratos do Brasil, 85)

A proposed constitution for a reformed Brazil, with the justifications therefor.

8573. Lambert, Denis-Clair. La croissance économique au Brésil, 1920-1970: atténuations et mutations de la dualité de structures (FDD/NED [Problèmes d'Amerique Latine, 27] 3973/3974, 23 mars 1973, p. 67-96, map, tables)

Critical examination of developmental problems in Brazil with close comment and attention to economic information, knowledge, and the state of the art in developmental economics. The paper is built around a set of hypotheses which suggest that there is insufficient exact knowledge of phenomena. The misconception of the nature of growth in Brazil is due to the fact that a dualistic Brazil has not been adequately conceived and also the widespread tendency to generalize on the basis of other country studies.

8573a. Lapagesse, Eugênio. Filosofia, objetivos, ações da reforma administrativa do estado na ação catarinense de desenvolvimento do Governador Colombo Machado Salles. Florianópolis, Bra., Imprensa Oficial do Estado, 1972. 52 p.

Proposals for administrative reform of the state of Santa Catarina as aids to its development. Essentially a theoretical document which suggests the substance of state policy.

8574. Leloup, Yves. Circonscriptions administratives actuelles au Brésil (CDAL, 7, 1973, p. 115-124, map, table)

A primer-like recounting of the historical growth and changes in the system of local government of Brazil. This is largely encyclopedia material in quality but a good starting point for the inquisitive.

8574a. _____. Croissance démographique, urbanisation, et déséquilibres régionaux au Brésil (FDD/NED [Problèmes d'Amérique Latine, 24] 3913/3914, 28 juillet 1972, p. 82-91, map, tables)

Short but extremely valuable report on the subject with some emphasis on the states of São Paulo, Guanabara, Maranhão, and brief examination of several others.

8575. Leonhart, William Kahn ed. Estrutura militar brasileira. Rio, n.p., 1972. 1 v. (Unpaged)

Three informative lectures by Col. Brasílio Marques dos Santos Sobrinho, Capt. (Navy) Munir Nagib Hanna Alzuguir, and Lt. Col. (Air) Antônio Carlos de Paiva Pessôa. The lectures were delivered in April 1972 at the Escola Superior de Guerra and addressed to a contingent from the US National War College.

8576. Levine, Robert M. Brazil at the crossroads (CUH, 64:378, Feb. 1973, p. 53-56, 86)

A useful general review of Brazil's situation at the end of 1972; what are the plans of the armed forces is the point of focus, although there is some attention to economic change amidst social stasis.

A linha revolucionária do Partido Comunista do Brazil. See *HLAS 36:3601.*

Marini, Ruy Mauro. Contradições e conflictos no Brasil contemporâneo. See *HLAS 36:3611.*

Mattos, Adherbal Meira. A Declaração de Santo Domingo e o Dereito do Mar. See item 8903a.

8577. Mayer, Antonio de Castro; Geraldo de Proença Sigaud; Plínio Correa de Oliveira; and **Luis Mendonça da Freitas.** Reforma agraria: cuestión de conciencia. Bogotá? Asociación

Colombiano para la Defensa del Derecho Natural *según autorización de* Editôra Vera Cruz, São Paulo, 1971. 224 p.

Conservative Catholic argument against agrarian reform as proposed in the middle 1960s in the Brazilian state of São Paulo. It leans heavily on Church and papal materials and doctrine. Three of the authors are clerics.

8578. Médici, Emilio Garrastazu. Objetivos, políticas y estrategias del tercer gobierno de la revolución (IAEERI/E, 1:5, enero/feb. 1970. p. 58-71)

The then-seated Brazilian President states the objectives of his government in a speech delivered in Rio but (significantly) published in a journal devoted to strategic studies and international relations in B.A. Quotes Médici as arguing that the principal objective of national development is the creation of social justice, equality, and class/race integration.

8578a. Medina, Carlos Alberto de and **Dimas Furtado.** Participação e Igreja: estudo dos movimentos e associações de leigos. Cuernavaca, Mex., Centro Intercultural de Documentação (CIDOC), 1971. 1 v. (Various pagings) tables (Sondeos, 83)

An attitude survey of 396 activists in Church-sponsored organizations and agencies, located in seven major cities. The information is presented in single variable tables. The study team incorporated 48 persons in all.

8579. Mesquita, Luciano. A política brasileira atual: alguns estudos. Brasília, Senado Federal, Serviço Gráfico, 1972. 102 p.

A series of short commentaries concerning current governmental and administrative characteristics and problems growing from a lecture series by the author, apparently for the Escola Superior da Guerra.

8580. Moreira, Hilton Beruttie Augusto. Transportes marítimos, desenvolvimento e segurança nacional (BMM/RMB, 91:10/12, out./dez. 1971, p. 44-62, tables)

A Brazilian Vice Admiral offers a straightforward, national interest-oriented, cost-benefits-based examination of Brazil's need for an increased merchant marine. He claims Brazil requires more and bigger ships and port facilities, as well as the development of an inward-oriented security sense among its merchant ship officers. Granted: in contemporary Brazilian armed forces planning, development equals national security.

8580a. Movimento Democrático Brasileiro (MDB). Diretório Nacional. MDB em ação nos comícos, rádio e televisão: democracia com desenvolvimento e justiça social. Brasília? Senado Federal, 1972. 59 p.

The platform of the party which also lists members of party bodies and of the Congress.

8581. Nery, Sebastião. Folclore político: 350 histórias da política brasileira. Rio, Edições Politika, 1973. 103 p., illus.

Includes 350 political jokes and anecdotes, carefully numbered and assorted by states. Good for cocktail party or academic footnotes.

8582. Oliven, Ruben George. A integração sócio-cultural dos moradores da Vila Farrapos na cidade de Pôrto Alegre (UMG/RBEP, 38, jan. 1974, p. 181-191, table)

Short research note on behavioral research and methods course in the department of Social Sciences at the Federal Univ. of Rio Grande do Sul.

8582a. Orlandini, Edmundo. O óbvio ululante na indústria. Rio, Alcalis, 1973? 330 p.

The rise and fall of a quasi-mythical firm, told with irony and mordant humor, taken from short pieces written for a company house organ during a period of five years, 1967-72.

8583. Pebayle, Raymond. Le Brésil méridional: Paraná, Santa Catarina, Rio Grande do Sul (FDD/NED [Problèmes d'Amérique Latine, 27] 3973/3974, 23 mars 1973, p. 51-65, maps, tables)

Detailed examination of developmental and growth problems in the named region of Brazil. Chapters deal with agriculture, resources, urban growth, etc. An essential resource piece for students of the region.

8584. Pinto, Rogerio Feital S. La ecología política del Banco Nacional de Desarrollo Económico del Brasil (BNDE): una tesis presentada al Departamento de Ciencias Políticas de la Universidad de Carolina del Norte. Washington, Organization of American states, Dept. of Economic Affairs, Cooperative Program of University Research [and] Unidad de Administración Pública 1969. 87 p., bibl.

Master's thesis in political science. A useful academic study of the establishment, activity, and effectiveness of Brazil's Development Bank.

8585. Poppino, Rollie E. Brasil: novo modelo para o desenvolvimento nacional (UMG/RBEP, 36, julho 1973, p. 105-114)

Education, intensively supported at secondary and post-secondary levels, is the solution to underdevelopment in Brazil. While some regions (São Paulo, etc.) have achieved substantial growth, others (the Northeast) are substantially retarded. The educational solution involves political risks the government is willing to take. A descriptive piece for beginners. For historian's comment, see HLAS 36:3628.

———. Brazil after a decade of revolution. See HLAS 36:3627.

8585a. Prado, João Fernando de Almeida. A política no Brasil. São Paulo, Companhia Editôra Nacional, 1973. 223 p.

A political history of Brazil to 1930.

8586. Quagliani, Antonio. L'umanesimo rivoluzionario della Chiesa brasiliana (MULINO, 18:7/8, luglio/agosto 1969, p. 800-806)

The attitudes of the Brazilian Church on a number of significant issues are reported in a popular journal: questions of social structure, change and conflict, students, education, continental integration, and the established order since 1964. Useful but hardly penetrating.

8587. Reis, Fábio Wanderley. Solidaridad, intereses y desarrollo político: un marco teórico y el caso brasileño (IDES/DE, 14:54, julio/set. 1974, p. 227-268)

Is the notion of "political development" useful? The author raises the question at length in a long and critical examination of notions of theory and typology. After 30 p. of this, Brazil is raised as a case of authoritarian power-formation. The reader will find the article relies heavily on social and political theory rather than on empirical research.

8587a. Resende, Maria Efigenia Lage de. Uma interpretação sobre a fundação de Belo Horizonte (UMG/RBEP, 39, julho 1974, p. 129-161, bibl., tables)

Historical examination of the treatment, in the state legislature, of the question of location and utility of relocation of the state capital in a new city. Data are drawn primarily from legislative actions in the period 1891-93.

8588. *Revista Brasileira de Estudos Políticos.* Univ. Federal de Minas Gerais. No. 37, set. 1973- . Belo Horizonte, Bra.

This issue devoted to six short articles by members of the Brazilian Foreign Ministry:
Joaquim Ignacio MacDowell "A Política do Brasil no Contexto do Tratado da Bacia do Prata" p. 9-22
José Ferreira Lopes "Algumas Considerações sobre o Comércio Internacional no Desenvolvimento Econômico do Brasil" p. 23-40
José Botafogo Gonçalves "Problemas Financeiros Internacionais" p. 41-50
Marcelo Raffaelli "Mar Territorial e Problemas Correlatos" p. 51-68
João Frank da Costa "Política Exterior Científica e Tecnológica" p. 69-94
Regis Novaes de Oliveira "A Evolução da Política Exterior do Brasil, em Face das Transformações do Equilibrio de Forcas" p. 95-106)

8588a. ———. ———. No. 40, jan. 1975- . Belo Horizonte, Bra.

Five articles deal with the concept of the Metropolitan Region, a post-1964 functional agency designed to meet and administer the developmental needs of a region or a project. Five short articles sketch the phenomenon:
Raul Machado Horta "Dereito Constitucional Brasileiro e as Regiões Metropolitanas" p. 9-24
Eros Roberto Grau "Análise, Crítica e Implementação da Legislação Metropolitana" p. 25-48
Mauro Barcelos Filho "O Controle do Uso do Solo Metropolitano" p. 49-68
Sérgio Tostes "Problemas Tributários da Região Metropolitana" p. 69-80
Gilson de Assis Dayrell "Problemas Institucionais na Implantação da Região Metropolitana de Belo Horizonte" p. 81-94.

8589. Ribeiro, Darcy. Teoria do Brasil. Rio, Editôra Paz e Terra, 1972. 146 p., bibl. (Série Estudos sobre o Brasil e a América Latina, 21)

One man's Brazil.

8589a. Richardson, Ivan L. Urban government in Rio de Janeiro. N.Y., Praeger Publishers, 1973. 184 p., bibl., tables (International urban studies of the Institute of Public Amministration, N.Y., 8) (Praeger special studies in international politics and government)

A descriptive and exhaustively analytical study of the subject, largely covering the period 1959-71.

Rodrigues, Eduardo Celestino. Problemas do Brasil potência. See item 8923.

8590. Rodrigues, Luiz. Evolução das normas constitucionais relativas ao funcionário público, de 1946 a 1969 (BDASP/R, 106:3, set./dez. 1971, p. 67-88)

The consitutional and legal status of public career employees in Brazil has changed substantially since 1946 through both constitutional revision and legal/political action. This is in fact a short catalogue of provisions and of clear utility for specialists.

8590a. Rosenn, Keith S. The *jeito*: Brazil's institutional bypass of the formal legal system and its development implications (AJCL, 19:3, Summer 1971, p. 514-549)

What is *jeito*; under what circumstances is it invoked (used?); and what are the customary effects? This is an exhaustive examination of its legal and social characteristics, historic and current causes, and the costs to the country's ethical, legal and social system. Reports specific (and compelling) instances. A substantial article.

8591. Sá, Maria Auxiliadora Ferraz de.

Dos velhos aos novos coronéis: um estudo das redefinições de coronelismo. Recife, Bra., Univ. Federal de Pernambuco (PIMES), 1974. 137 p., bibl.

A careful and impressive Master's paper in sociology which emphasizes the Northeast with implications as to the strength of the person (coronel) and the institution (coronelismo).

Saint-Jean, Iberico Manuel. Los ejércitos de Argentina y Brasil: algunos aspectos comparativos. See item 8689.

8592. Santos, Wanderley Guilherme dos. Coalizãos parlamentares e instabilidade governmental, a experiencia brasileira: 1961-1964 (UNAM/RMS, 35:3, julio/sept. 1973, p. 493-510, tables)

A mathematical analysis of voting patterns in the Brazilian Congress prior to the 1964 *golpe*, drawn from the author's Ph.D. dissertation (Stanford). The material is supported by a useful narrative overview of party information and disintegration up to and including the period of the title.

8592a. _____. Estrátegias de descompressão política. Brasília, Congresso Federal, Instituto de Pesquisas, Estudos e Assessoria, 1973. 78 l., tables.

Prof. dos Santos' invited lecture to the Chamber of Deputies is followed by questions/answers from the floor. An interesting and innovative presentation about how a society "decompresses" from revolutionary and authoritarian practices.

8593. Schwartzman, Simon. Empresarios y política en el proceso de industrialización: Argentina, Brasil, Australia (IDES/DE, 13:49, abril/junio 1973, p. 67-89, tables)

A comparative economic/historical paper which explores the incentives, national policies, and outcomes of empresarial activity in three countries. A model of change is introduced and employed in the analysis; the major portion is on Brazil, however, and the author has essentially scratched the surface of the topic.

8593a. _____. Representación y cooptación política en el Brasil (IDES/DE, 11:41, abril/junio 1971, p. 15-53, tables)

Author suggests the most interesting analysis of political participation is to be found neither in equal participation nor in cooptation but rather in a mixed or intermediate type. The analysis is based on much material, both theoretical (borrowing heavily from American and Brazilian authors) and empirical. A rather dense but challenging article.

8594. Skidmore, Thomas E. Black into white: race and nationality in Brazilian thought. N.Y., Oxford Univ. Press, 1974. 299 p.

Highly selective examination of the evolution of Brazilian thought on the subject of black slavery. Includes comments by Brazilians on the institution itself, its elimination, and the subsequent adjustments of Brazilian thinkers to the black's new status. Skidmore's examination is not only meticulous and enlightening but makes available material which until now was found only in fugitive sources.

8595. Smith, Peter Seaborn. Petrobrás: the politicizing of a state company, 1953-1964 (HU/BHR, 46:2, Summer 1972, p. 182-201)

A short history of Petrobrás which views it as a case in the area of national (state) companies. Petrobrás was founded for certain goals which are defined here; but politics, and the hard luck of events and resources combined to preclude its operation on efficient bases. Nevertheless it heightened nationalism and encouraged both pride and industrialization so that in the scale of overall national outcomes the author is in Petrobrás' favor.

8595a. Soares, Glaucio Ary Dillon. Alianzas electorales en el Brasil (UNAM/RMS, 35:3, julio/sept. 1973, p. 457-492, tables)

Beginning with a statistical statement of the increase in voting strength of coalitions and alliances (from 1945-62) this paper seeks reasons in terms of party identity, image, strength, etc. In what circumstances were parties likely to enter alliances? What was the effect of each type of election (federal, state, local; majority or proportional)? The goal of the paper is typologies rather than policy effects.

8595b. Souza Sobrinho. A importância de Minas na política nacional. Rio, Laemmert, 1973. 343 p.

A history of the state (and region) from colonial times to the golpe of 1964 with notable regionalist (if not chauvinistic) overtones.

8596. Stepan, Alfred ed. Authoritiarian Brazil: origins, policies, and future. New Haven, Conn., Yale Univ. Press, 1973. 265 p., tables.

Eight social scientists who previously had published work on Brazil (save one, Juan Linz) participated in a seminar on contemporary Brazil in 1971. This volume contains their papers revised in light of discussion among themselves and 12 additional invited participants. The product should command the interest and attention of Latin American specialists for the quality of the papers and the nature of the questions addressed. Linz' participation assured an element of generalization although the intellectual experience and maturity of other participants equally supported this probability.

8597. *SUDENE Informa.* Superintendência do Desenvolvimento do Nordeste. Nos. 1/2, jan./fev. 1972- . Rio.

The effects of SUDENE initiatives in the Northeast are reported in a number of short illustrated articles in this house organ. Appropriate attention is given to education, agriculture, industrialization, etc.

8597a. Syrvud, Donald E. Foundations of Brazilian economic growth. Stanford, Calif., Stanford Univ., Hoover Institution Press [and] American Enterprise Institute for Public Policy Research, Washington, 1974. 295 p., bibl., tables (AEI-Hoover research publications)

Brazilian economic growth in recent years (surely, up to the writing of this book) has been steady and almost spectacular — after a long period of inflation, social damage, and uneven growth. The changed circumstance is less miracle than strategy and a will to mobilize resources within pragmatic possibilities. The author was US Treasury Dept. representative in the Embassy in Brazil for nearly five years, which gave him access to enormous amounts of information that few persons ever obtain. It also gave him a direct and sustained policy focus. The unique combination of circumstances is reported with great objectivity. The book is not value-free, to be sure, but is sound and highly defensible in its judgments. Thought-provoking about lessons of a comparative nature, both for Latin American and for other specialists.

8597b. Szilvassy, Arpad. A participação dos alemães e seus descendentes na vida política brasileira (IRSISP/RH, 6:16/17, abril/agôsto 1963, p. 19-35, bibl.)

Historical survey of German activities in southern Brazil with particular reference to Rio Grande do Sul, Paraná, and Santa Catarina states. Their contributions to all aspects of public life are reported briefly, and the final few pages refer to political attitudes and candidacies. The author states he made use of personal studies and interviews of community leaders although the evidence is hardly visible. A useful short article on a generally little-discussed subject. A short bibliography is appended.

8598. Tavares, José Antônio Giusti. A problemática do poder e a determinação do conteúdo da análise política (UMG/RBEP, 38, jan. 1974, p. 97-141, tables)

The question of power in the State is examined comparatively on the basis of analysis of work by theoreticians from various western political systems. The view from the US (Deutsch, Dahl, Schermerhorn, Madison, Burnham, et al.) is compared with that of Europeans (Michels, Sartori, Sombart, Scheler, Tawney, to name a few). The destabilizing effects of change/development and of interest group action are introduced. A useful and provocative article.

8598a. Terra, Adamastor. Brasil: la guerrilla de Araguaia. B.A., Nativa Libros, 1973. 77 p. (Bandera roja, 35)

A reporting of guerrilla warfare and tactics in Pará state during 1972-73.

8599. Todaro Williams, Margaret. The politization of the Brazilian Catholic Church: the Catholic Electoral League (UM/JIAS, 16:3, Aug. 1974, p. 301-325, bibl.)

Active between 1932 and 1937, the League sought to reestablish the Church in Brazilian life as a political and social force. It operated as a pressure group for selected goals. The paper offers a useful narrative and descriptive statement of tactics and successes. Its concluding pages report, possibly with too much facility, its demise.

8600. Trinidade, Hélgio Henrique C. El facismo brasileño en la década del 30: orígenes históricos y base social del integral integralismo: 1932-37 (IDES/DE, 12:48, enero/marzo 1973, p. p. 687-723, tables.)

Drawn from the author's landmark dissertation at the Univ. of Paris, this article incorporates some of the narrative as well as the descriptive material concerning socioeconomic backgrounds and behavior of Integralista leadership groups.

8600a. ———. Plínio Salgado e a Revolução de Octubro de 30: antecedentes da A.I.B. (UMG/RBEP, 38, jan. 1974, p. 9-65)

A valuable piece that seeks to place Integralismo in the context of its time and to explore the views of the far right. Salgado is shown as one of a number of writers and actors. This is not a chronicling of the party's political action but rather of its ideas.

8601. Tullis, F. LaMond. Modernization in Brazil: a story of political dueling among politicians, charismatic leaders, and military guardians. Provo, Utah, Brigham Young Univ., 1973. 120 p., map, tables (The Charles E. Merrill monograph series in the humanities and social sciences, 7)

Expansion and reworking of material previously published in item 8601a. The politics of the fall of João Goulart, and of the succeeding military governments, are handled in a somewhat popular style that offers some useful chronicling.

8601a. ———. Modernization in Brazil, or the story of political dueling among politicians, charismatic leaders, and military guardians (*in* Tullis, F. LaMond *ed.* Politics and social change in Third World countries. N.Y., John Wiley, 1973, p. 107-182, bibl.)

The chapter on Brazil (which was later developed into a book, see item 8601) concentrates on national questions (see *HLAS 35:7703*) and is handled in terms of case studies. Tullis draws effectively on Samuel P. Huntington's theory in *Political order in changing societies* (New Haven, Conn., Yale Univ. Press, 1968).

8602. Universidade Federal da Bahia, *Salvador, Bra.* Escola de Administração. Centro de Administração Pública. Reforma administrativa: leituras selecionadas. Salvador, Bra., 1972. 195 p. (mimeo)

A book of readings for students in public administration. While some of the authors are American or European, the great majority are Brazilians writing case studies on reforms undertaken in Brazil.

8603. Valente, Murillo Gurgel. A política de transportes marítimos no Brasil: crônica de uma batalha. 2. ed. rev., Rio, Ministério dos Transportes, Serviço de Documentação, 1972. 112 p., tables.

A discussion of Brazil's problems and goals in the matter of ocean transport written with some passion by a longtime participant in the "battle," as government official at home and abroad. What does adequate facility mean to Brazil's national economic and sovereign interests? What have been the effects of inadequacy for growth?

8603a. Vasconcelos, Justino. Desenvolvimento com democracia. Pôrto Alegre, Bra., Livraria do Advogado [and] Instituto dos Advogados do Rio Grande do Sul, 1974. 95 p.

Seven addresses by the President of the Bar Association of the state of Rio Grande do Sul. Offers some interesting insights into the lawyer's role in Brazil, together with observations concerning land distribution, the 200-mile territorial waters limit, and penal reform.

PARAGUAY

8604. *Acción.* Revista paraguaya de reflexión y diálogo. Año 3, Epoca 3, No. 12, oct. 1971- . Asunción.

A feature magazine with clerical backing. Articles focus on the Church as a political as well as moral actor in some cases and on agricultural, familial, and health problems in other cases. This issue also includes an article on tourism.

8604a. 18 [i.e., Dieciocho] años de progreso con el Presidente Stroessner. Asunción, Ministerio de Hacienda, 1972. 164 p., plates.

A document which briefly reports on government operations under the Treasury, Colorado Party statutes and platform, and the national constitution.

8604b. Epifanio: el mago de las finanzas [por] Veritas. Asunción, n.p., 1970. 84 p., plates, tables.

A vigorous attack on Epifanio Méndez which originally appeared in *Patria*, the official paper of the Colorado Party, under the pseudonym Veritas. Méndez was President of the Central Bank of Paraguay for a period in the 1950s and was expelled from the party in 1958. An interesting bit of political history.

8604c. González Viera, Mauro. Paraguay frente al futuro. Asunción, Escuela Técnica Salesiana, 1972. 149 p., bibl.

A party-line discussion in which the author seems determined to score points for personal advantage. But at the same time an indication that (apparently) Paraguayan political-party thinking has remained where most of the region was in the last century.

8604d. Instituto de Desarrollo Integral y Armónico (IDIA), *Asunción?* Actitudes y opiniones de los líderes paraguayos acerca de las políticas poblacionales y familiares. Asunción? n.d. 148 p., tables.

Survey of opinions on population and family problems in Paraguay conducted by the Instituto de Desarrollo Integral y Armónico, with funds from the Agency for International Development (US). In order to obtain comparative data, the study is based on guidelines of the Centro Latinoamericano de Población y Familia.

8604e. Pérez Moreno, Sindulfo and **Carlos Meo.** Stroessner. t. 1. Asunción, Offsett Gráfica Asunceña, 1972. 320 p.

The first author is a retired general and now Professor of National Security Policy and Geopolitics at the Catholic Univ. of Asunción. The second author, a naturalized Italian, is professor in the Command and General Staff School of the Army. The text is prefaced by laudatory letters from the Chairman of the Executive Committee of the Colorado Party and the Ministers of National Defense and Public Works. Authenticity is thus suggested.

8604f. Romero Bastos, Raúl. El Paraguay: entre el terror y la revolución (CAM, 170:3, mayo/junio 1970, p. 29-44)

The dictatorship of Stroessner and of his Colorado Party has made Paraguay a near-totalitarian tyranny, says this writer, and its only salvation will come through revolution. If it happened in Peru (which he accepts as a possible model), it could happen there. The article discusses affected interests and social sectors but is undocumented and somewhat tautological. For historian's comment, see *HLAS 36:3377.*

8604g. Sánchez Quell, Hipólito. Alfredo Stroessner, el Programa Colorado y el desarrollo paraguayo. Asunción, Partido Colorado, 1972. 23 p.

A short party document concerning program and policy.

URUGUAY

8605. Altesor, Alberto. Algunas consideraciones sobre el Plan de Desarrollo del Partido en Montevideo durante 1968 (PCU/E, 49, enero/feb. 1969, p. 54-60, illus.)

What should be done within the Uruguayan Communist Party in the period 1968-70? A speech given by a member of the party's Executive Committee and party official in Montevideo to the National Organizational Conference in Jan. 1968, examines needs and alternatives. *Estudios* is the party's official publication.

8606. Aranegui, Manuel de. Un curioso sistema electoral (IEP/REP, 183/184, mayo/agosto 1972, p. 305-322)

A short paper on the Uruguayan election law, principally the version of 1966, including provisions of the constitution of that year that were in force for the 1971 election. The article broadly covers the legal provisions concerning parties and the rights of voters. The author seems bemused by its complexity but gives the system high marks for its ability, to the time of writing, to preclude *golpes* against the government.

8607. Arismendi, Rodney. Insurgencia juvenil. Prólogo de José Luis Massera. 3. ed. Montevideo, Ediciones Pueblos Unidos, 1972. 325 p.

The cover includes the subtitle: *¿Revuelta o revolución?* Includes several long pieces (speeches, dialogues, articles) by Arismendi, an old and experienced leader of the Uruguayan Communist Party, together with a 60-page presentation by Massera. This volume contains, in effect, the official thoughts of the party about university youth.

———. Uruguay y América Latina en los años setenta: experiencias y balance de una revolución. See item 8868.

8608. Arlas, José A. and **Jaime Teitelbaum.** Estudios sobre la Ley de Seguridad del Estado y el Orden Interno, texto completo de la Ley 14.068. Montevideo, Fundación de Cultura Universitaria, 1972. 125 p. (Col. Jus, 3)

A faculty study of the procedural and legal points involved in the Law of 1972, a major step by the Bordaberry regime toward the authoritarian military government that became a reality in 1973.

8609. Benedetti, Mario. Terremoto y después. Montevideo, Arca Editorial, 1973. 276 p. (Bolsilibros Arca, 94)

Short interpretive essays and newspaper articles written during the 18-month period ending in Aug. 1973.

8609a. Bordaberry, Juan María. Bases para un acuerdo nacional. Montevideo, Presidencia de la República, 1972. 22 p.

Four short statements by Bordaberry, in Feb.-May 1972, at the beginning of his term as constitutional president.

8610. Câmara, Helder. La América Latina y la opción de la no-violencia (Comunidad [Univ. Iberoamericana, México] 8:45, oct. 1973, p. 567-575)

The case for nonviolence for social change stated in a paper by the Archbishop of Olinda and Recife in Montevideo in Feb. 1973. Dom Helder argues that the time for Church-led redemption on a basis of social justice and community action has come, especially since the violent way has failed.

8611. Democracia Cristiana del Uruguay y Formatión del Frente Amplio. Heverlee-Louvain, Belgium, Information Documental de América Latina (INDAL), 1973, 242 p. (Dossier, 3)

Texts of 35 items, mostly party documents, explaining the viewpoints, training methods, attitudes, and organizational details of the Christian Democratic Party of Uruguay. While some materials are in-house documents, others are public materials. A useful dossier of topics on the party.

8611a. Dotta, Mario; Duaner Freire; and **Nelson Rodríguez.** El Uruguay ganadero: de la explotación primitiva a la crisis actual. Montevideo, Ediciónes de la Banda Oriental, 1972. 169 p., maps, tables.

Detailed and useful history to about 1963 written for a competition sponsored by Banco de Crédito of Montevideo on the centennial of the Asociación Rural, the estancieros' interest organization. Although the authors are university students and the book, a bit of a primer, is intended for secondary school use, the quantity of detail is highly useful.

8612. Fá Robaina, Juan Carlos. Cartas a un diputado. Montevideo, Editorial Alfa, 1972. 141 p.

Consists of 148 letters and other documents sent to a deputy in the national legislature and grouped under five general titles. They are, as he states in a modest introduction, ". . . the authentic voice of the people . . ."

8612a. Fariña, Fernando. Lo que tal vez no se sepa. B.A., The Author, 1972. 183 p., facisms.

A onetime Minister of Industry and Labor under Luis Battle Berres writes political memoirs of his youth and middle age up to 1950. An entirely personal account which helps to fill some gaps for this period.

8612b. Fuidio, Walter. Un Uruguay nuevo. Montevideo, n.p., 1973. 126 p.

A young sociologist and priest, whose viewpoint is conditioned by his teaching position in a provincial town, debates the role of Christians in a country in process of drastic change.

8613. Martínez Moreno, Carlos. Los días que vivimos: dieciséis ensayos inmediatos. Montevideo, Editorial Girón, 1973. 155 p.

Short articles commenting on the contemporary scene, March 1972-March 1973, which appeared in *Marcha* of Montevideo. The period covered saw the accelerated disappearance of constitutional freedoms in Uruguay. The length of the individual pieces (several thousand words each) justifies the attention of specialists.

8614. Movimiento de Liberación Nacional, *Montevideo.* Los Tupamaros en acción. Prólogo de Régis Debray. México, Editorial Diógenes, 1972. 241 p. (Actas Tupamaras)

Debray adds an introduction (38 p.) to a text which is the same as that annotated in *HLAS 35:7914*.

8615. Musso Ambrosi, Luis Alberto ed. and *comp*. Anales del Senado del Uruguay: cronología sistematizada; Legislatura I al XL, 1830-1971. 2. ed. rev. Montevideo, Senado de la República Oriental del Uruguay, 1971. 457 p., bibl., facsims., tables.

A listing of memberships of the Senate, persons who served as presiding officer (president), dates of service if short term, with *suplentes*, etc. A gold mine of detail.

8616. Participación del Movimiento Sindical en la Formación Profesional, Montevideo, 1972. Participación del Movimiento Sindical en la formación profesional. Montevideo, Centro Interamericano de Investigación y Documentación sobre Formación Profesional (CINTERFOR), 1972. 123 p. (Proyecto 079)

A five-day meeting in April 1972 is here reported. While the proceedings are summarized, annexes contain several texts of reports and papers presented to the meeting.

8617. Partidos políticos y clases sociales en el Uruguay: aspectos ideológicos. Montevideo, Instituto de Ciencias Sociales [and] Fundación de Cultura Universitaria, 1972. 376 p. (Papeles sociales, 3)

Gerónimo de Sierra, research director of an Institute team, explains in a brief preface that this is the basic documentation of what will become a full-scale evaluative study of the topic. This is to be hoped. For the most part the materials date from 1968 to 1972 and are cuttings of speeches, debate positions, flyers, platform statements, etc., of all parties and political groups active since 1964. This is an absolutely essential piece for the specialist on Uruguayan parties and political groups.

8618. Porzecanski, Arturo C. Uruguay's Tupamaros: the urban guerrilla. N.Y., Praeger Publishers, 1973. 80 p., bibl., tables (Praeger special studies in international politics and government)

Within its extremely limited size this book ranges broadly, with portions devoted to ideology, tactics, strategy, organization, behavior, and downfall (as of 1972). There is solid material on the membership and structure of the movement. Unfortunately a *book* on this topic is yet to be written. The length is so scanty that it does little more than whet appetites.

8619. Rouquié, Alain. L'Uruguay de M. Pacheco Areco à M. Bordaberry: les élections de novembre 1971 et les débuts de la Présidence Bordaberry (FDD/NED) [Problèmes d'Amérique Latine, 27] 3973/3974, 23 mars 1973, p. 7-50, map, tables)

Highly detailed and valuable reporting of the events and problems of the period beginning in 1970. Implemented by chronology and documents.

8620. Trías, Vivian. Uruguay hoy: crisis económica, crisis política. Montevideo, Ediciones de la Banda Oriental, 1973. 95 p., tables.

The articulate leftist political leader and journalist offers his thought about the country in the period 1965-72. The work is colloquial and thus useful to the specialist.

8620a. ———. Uruguay y sus claves geopolíticas. Montevideo, Ediciones de la Banda Oriental, 1972. 171 p., tables. (Uruguay en controversia)

Trías undertakes a period update and reconsideration of earlier writing. What factors, internal and external, condition Uruguay's economic position? The interpretation is essentially confined to a marxist and dependency-defined orientation. Trías saw the Frente Amplio as his country's salvation; Bordaberry has taken care of that assumption, in the short run at least. Book also discusses similar aspects of six hemisphere countries.

8621. Uruguay. Ministerio del Interior. 7 [i.e., Siete] meses de lucha subversiva: acción del Estado frente a la sedición desde el 1º de marzo al 30 de setiembre de 1972. Montevideo, 1972. 385 p.

A chronology of the action during the indicated period: maps of locations of attacks and counterattacks, numbers and names of the arrested, including sentences assessed, arms siezed, etc.

8622. Vasconcelos, Amílcar. Febrero amargo. 3 ed. La Paz, Uru., n.p., 1973. 152 p.

A Senator writes with much despair and bitterness of the events of the first of a series of *golpes* against the constitution in recent years, staged by the military with the collaboration of the executive branch. By the end of 1973 constitutional government had disappeared in the country, and Vasconcelos' book details the process.

8623. Wilson, Carlos. The Tupamaros: the unmentionables. Boston, Mass., Branden Press, 1974. 171 p.

This work is described as a reporting of "the controversial urban guerrillas of Uruguay." While much detail is presented, the book itself is highly partisan and subject to factual challenge in some detail. Since the cutoff date is 1972, the reader is left without insight as to what happened after the army *golpe* of 1973 and claimed eradication of the Tupamaros.

8624. Yáñez, Rubén. El fascismo y el pueblo. Montevideo, Ediciones Pueblos Unidos, 1972. 171 p.

The outcome of talks delivered at several meetings called by *seccionales* of the Uruguayan Communist Party. The author knows how to tie the European fascist experience to contemporary developments in his own country. Nothing really new, but clear and well-written. [A. Suárez]

ARGENTINA

8625. Altamirano, Carlos. Acuerdo y elecciones: el discurso del GAN (Los Libros [B.A.] 29, marzo/abril 1973, p. 12-14)

Analysis of the March 1971 announcement of a *Gran Acuerdo Nacional* at the time of the resumption of power in Argentina by the Armed Forces under Alejandro Lanusse. This short piece is essentially an exercise in semantics.

8626. Ander-Egg, Ezequiel. Hacia la revolución socialista en América Latina. Córdoba, Arg., Editorial del Centro de Estudios Políticos (CEP), 1972. 245 p., bibl., maps, plates.

A detailed argument concerning need for and tactics of socialist revolution in Latin America. The basic information concerning US intelligence/domination policy in the region is superficially impressive.

8627. Arévalo, Oscar. Breve introducción al socialismo científico: siete temas básicos. B.A., Ediciones Centro de Estudios, 1973. 235 p. (Serie Introducciones, 3)

Introductory discussion of major themes from Marx, Engels, and Lenin (e.g., surplus value, class struggle, imperialism) with only brief references to Argentine case. [J.J. Bailey]

8627a. Arnedo Alvarez, Gerónimo. ¡Unidos por una nueva Argentina liberada! B.A., Editorial Anteo, 1973. 46 p.

Report by the Secretary General of the Argentine Communist Party to the XIV Communist Party Congress, 20-24 Aug. 1973.

8627b. Astesano, Eduardo B. Manual de la militancia política. B.A., Editorial Relevo, 1973. 153 p., bibl.

The title is fully descriptive. This is not a book about militancy in Argentina, except that some of the illustrative material is drawn from this country's experience. The author is developing a theory about strategy and tactics of political militancy in developing societies.

8628. Balve, Beba and others. Lucha de calles, lucha de clases: elementos para su análisis; Córdoba 1969-1971. B.A., Ediciones La Rosa Blindada, 1973. 200 p., tables (Cuadernos latinoamericanos)

The product of a team of sociologists examining street violence and demonstrations in 1969 and 1971 (with comparative analysis offered in considerable detail concerning participants and their purposes), this is an extraordinary if not unique work. Street violence long has been an institutionalized form of action, the writers premise, and it should be studied if one is to understand the Argentine political style.

Barbé, Carlos. Il peronismo e la crisis argentina. See *HLAS 36:3031*.

8629. Belloni Ravest, Hugo. Antecedentes y perspectivas de la educación sindical en Argentina (ESC, 6:24, oct./dic. 1972, p. 226-242)

Historically, training of union leaders never loomed large in the planning of labor growth and development. But the 1939 I Regular Congress of the General Confederation of Labor voted to reverse this view. The 1947 Special CGT Congress accepted rather detailed plans and curriculum. The article then traces in detail this plan and its development through the latter 1960s. A useful and detailed piece.

8629a. Bortnik, Rubén. Peronismo, gobierno y poder: de la crisis del sistema al socialismo nacional. B.A., Ediciones Corregidor, 1973. 183 p.

Statement of the peronista view of Argentina's need for fundamental changes of social institutions and styles of behavior. The viewpoint represents the main body of thought of one segment of the peronista movement of the mid-1970s.

8630. Botana, Natalio R.; Rafael Braun; and Carlos A. Floria. El régimen militar, 1966-1973. B.A., Ediciones La Bastilla, 1973. 522 p.

The book is a collection of several dozen political editorials from *Criterio*, a B.A. journal, by authors and others whose names are cited in footnotes. Organized in four massive cluster-chapters, each is dated, and the judgments are contemporary with events or conditions discussed. A short introductory statement describes the process of creation for the journal (working through an editorial board) and the criteria generally observed in the writing process. Using a collector's technique all too common for preparing quick-and-dirty partisan commentaries, these writers have produced a volume useful for specialists.

8630a. Brignardello, Luisa A. El movimiento estudiantil argentino: corrientes ideológicas y opiniones de sus dirigentes. B.A., Ediciones Macchi, 1972. 362 p., tables.

A comprehensive examination of university student movements in Argentina based on interview material with 52 leaders of various groups of different ideological tendencies. The work is a thorough, scholarly, and valuable one for specialists.

8630b. Bustos Fierro, Raúl. 15 [i.e., Quince] notas políticas de actualidad. B.A., Editorial Plus Ultra, 1973. 94 p.

An active member of the Movimiento Nacional Justicialista from 1945, the author here collects a series of weekly pieces representing his view of his group's position from Sept. 1972 to Jan. 1973. Originally published in *La Opinión* of B.A.

8631. Cámpora, Héctor J. La revolución peronista. B.A., EUDEBA, 1973? 205 p.

Short collection of public statements and speeches by Cámpora, while "stand-in" President prior to the inauguration of Perón in July 1973. Includes his messages to the Congress (p. 76-190) where he attempts to establish a framework for the development of the peronista government which succeeded him.

8631a. Cantón, Darío. Elecciones y partidos políticos en la Argentina: historia, interpretación y balance, 1910-1966. B.A., Siglo XXI Argentina Editores, 1973. 277 p., tables.

A valuable scholarly work which demonstrates careful attention to data collection, analysis, and theory.

8632. Carpani, Ricardo. Nacionalismo, peronismo y socialismo nacional. 2. ed. B.A., Editorial Centro de Estudios Políticos, 1973. 141 p.

A left, labor-oriented, nationalist examination of Argentine political and social needs. The work is thoughtful and didactic in tone and seeks to define national socialism rather carefully in regard to the roles of both the middle class and the working class.

8632a. Carri, Roberto. Poder imperialista y liberación nacional: las luchas del peronismo contra la dependencia. B.A., Efece Ediciones, 1973. 412 p.

Drawing together materials written between 1968 and 1973, this is partially a critical examination of foreign involvement in Argentina, of the country's internal class-economic structure, and of the ways in which peronismo ought (but may well not) resolve things for the better. There is a good deal of redundancy here.

8633. Castex, Mariano N. Un año de Lanusse: del acuerdo increíble al retorno imposible. B.A., Achával Solo Fabricante de Libros, 1973. 91 p. (Col. Punto por punto)

A collection of short editorial articles by the author which appeared in newspapers and magazines during 1972.

8633a. Centro Naval, *B.A.* **Instituto Naval de Conferencias y de Publicaciones Navales.** Principios políticos universales [por] Ambrosio Romero Carranza. Patagonia: frontera y seguridad [por] Idalberto Raúl Mallo. Las fuerzas armadas y la policía frente a las alteraciones del orden público [por] Recaredo E. Vázquez. B.A., 1972. 61 p.

Three speeches on international relations and internal security delivered at B.A.'s Naval Officers Club, in June, Aug., and Sept. 1971, respectively.

8634. Ceresole, Norberto. Argentina y América Latina: doce ensayos políticos. B.A., Editorial Pleamar, 1972. 360 p. (Ciencias políticas y sociales. Itinerario americano)

A leading young peronista author and theorist writes on a variety of topics some of which are concerned with freeing Argentina from US influence with views and suggestions on this point. But the mood is implied by the short opening essay entitled "Argentina: the Necessary Violence."

8634a. _____ and **Carlos P. Mastrorilli.** Peronismo: teoría e historia del socialismo nacional. B.A., Editorial Corregidor, 1973. 431 p., maps.

Combining discrete halves by the two authors, this book examines the need and possibility for socialism of a nationalist format in Argentina. The introduction suggests that the historic resolution of constitutional/political issues is in its deathbed and that courageous efforts must be made to turn the country around. The work represents a major statement concerning peronista thought in the 1970s.

8634b. _____ ; **Miguel Gazzera;** and **Carlos P. Mastrorilli.** Peronismo: de la reforma a la revolución. B.A., A. Peña Lillo, 1972. 194 p.

An effort to define the meaning for and the possible contributions of peronismo in the 1970s to the reform of Argentine society. The writers are peronista leaders in the movement to define national socialism.

8635. Cerrutti Costa, Luis B. Socialismo y Tercer Mundo. B.A., Ediciones Rancagua, 1973. 97 p. (Biblioteca de historia y política)

Peron's overthrow in 1955 meant the exhaustion of the "national capitalist revolution." His return to power in 1973 opened the possibility of the socialist alternative. This is popular elaboration of socialist ideas by one author who seems to be unaware of the differences between the Soviet and Chinese varieties of the model. [A. Suárez]

8636. Cirigliano, Gustavo F.J. Universidad y pueblo: planteos y textos. Prólogo de Juan Emilio Cassani. B.A., Librería del Colegio, 1973. 145 p., bibl. (Biblioteca nueva pedagogía)

A serious book concerning the universities of Argentina: who, from where, and for what purpose are students? What does the faculty want and have, and what is the teaching atmosphere? What is the experience of some other countries of Latin America?

8636a. Codovilla, Victorio. 20 [i.e., Veinte] años de la vida política argentina. v. 2, Trabajos escogidos. B.A., Editorial Anteo, 1973. 191 p.

Collected works of the longtime Argentine Communist Party leader.

8637. Concatti, Rolando. Nuestra opción por el peronismo. 2. ed. Mendoza, Arg., Sacerdotes para el Tercer Mundo, 1972. 172 p.

The Movement of Priests for the Third World announces in detail its reasons for support of peronismo, not as a political party but as a social movement among the alternatives open in the country.

8638. Construir Comités de Fábrica por la independencia obrera: resoluciones de los Comités de Base por el Frente Electoral Clasista. B.A.?, n.p., 1973. 16 p.

A rather classic Communist Party tactical pamphlet from Argentina.

8638a. Cooke, John W. Apuntes para la militancia: peronismo crítico. B.A., Schapire Editor, 1972. 115 p. (Col. Mira)

The longtime peronista leader offers a personal view of his country. Some of the material is based on public speeches. The method incorporates an examination of selected political events of the past and their applications to the present.

Corbett, Charles D. The Latin American military as a socio-political force: case studies of Bolivia and Argentina. See item 8396.

8639. Corradi, Juan E. Argentina: dependency and political crisis (MR, 25:7, Dec. 1973, p. 28-42, bibl.)

An "analysis [of] the political offensive of imperialism after 1955, the mass resistance to its projects, and the temporary political defeat of those projects in 1973." Author perceives that Peronism's two major and discrete wings alternate between proposing future true development or reestablishing imperialist dependency, in a currently fragile balance.

8639a. *Cuadernos de Educación Popular.* 1-   . Córdoba, Arg. Centro de Estudios Políticos (CEP), Escuela de Capacitación Sindical, 1971-   .

New series of popular marxist manuals for the socialist education of workers written by militants of Revolutionary Peronism and published in Córdoba. Most of them are about 50 p. long. Some examples:
Ezequiel Ander-Egg "Explotación Capitalista"
Marta Harnecker and Gabriela Uribe "Monopolios y Miseria."

8640. Dana Montaño, Salvador M. Las estructuras del poder y de la representatividad en el estado moderno en función de la realidad argentina (Boletín de la Facultad de Derecho y Ciencias Sociales [Univ. Nacional de Córdoba, Arg.] 36:1/5, enero/dic. 1972, p. 183-189)

A modest reconsideration of some aspects of theory of the state in the light of recent Argentine events. The author is a professor of political theory in Argentina.

8641. Deheza, José A. Argentina: ¿país sin destino nacional? B.A., A. Peña Lillo Editor, 1972. 128 p., tables.

What is the effect of foreign investment in Argentina, and especially of the new multinational corporations? A onetime economic advisor to Argentine private enterprise offers his views.

8642. Díaz Araujo, Enrique. El G. O. U. en la revolución de 1943: una experiencia militarista en la Argentina. Mendoza, Arg., Univ. Nacional de Cuyo, Facultad de Ciencias Políticas y Sociales, Instituto de Ciencias Políticas, Centro de Investigaciones, 1970. 292 p., tables (Serie Cuadernos, 19) (mimeo)

A useful examination of the GOU (Grupo de Oficiales Unidos or Grupo Obra de Unificación) as a society and revolutionary group. A substantial amount of rather scarce material about the organization is incorporated.

8643. Dressl, Klaus. Argentinien: Politik und Parteien, 1955-1972 (Vierteljahresberichte [Bonn] 49, Sept. 1972, p. 247-272)

Good article concerning Argentine politics since the fall of Perón's first administration. Author discredits the military's role and is cautiously optimistic about that of political parties.[H.J. Hoyer]

8643a. Duejo, Gerardo. El capital monopolista y las contradicciones secundarias en la sociedad argentina. 2. ed. Córdoba, Arg., Siglo XXI Argentina Editores, 1973. 159 p., tables (La Historia inmediata)

Six short articles prepared for the Christian left periodical *Cristianismo y Revolución* (the latter interdicted by the government in 1971), together with a new introductory statement by the author. A useful series of pieces, informative, analytical and calm.

8644. Eggers Lan, Conrad. Peronismo y liberación nacional. B.A., Ediciones Búsqueda, 1973. 270 p.

A useful Christian Democratic-oriented and academic study of Argentine political positions and attitudes.

8645. Eichelbaum, Horacio. De nuevo el parlamento. B.A., Ediciones La Bastilla, 180 p., tables (Las riendas del poder)

Congress was reelected in 1973. What is it good for? The writer suggests several possible roles, in light of the return of Perón and of the recent past in which parliament was manipulated by those who felt little commitment to its constitutional-theoretical role.

8646. *Estrategia.* Instituto Argentina de Estudios Estratégicos y de las Relaciones Internacionales. Vol. 1, No. 2, julio/agosto 1969- . B.A.

A novel and worthwhile journal, many of whose contributors are military officers. Other articles in this issue consist of: a translated item from the *New York Times Magazine* on the US military industrial complex; three very useful pieces on the Brazilian armed forces, two of them by Brazilians; and items on Peru, Chile, and Paraguay. Researchers and specialists on any aspect of the military (in politics, the economy, or in its own self-judgements) must be aware of this journal, particularly if Argentina is the research focus. One is inclined to assume that the journal is a quasi-official publication of the Argentine Armed Forces.

8646a. Evers, Tilman Tönnies. Militärregierung in Argentinien: das politische System der "Argentinischen Revolution." Hamburg, FRG, Alfred Metzner Verlag, 1972. 288 p., tables.

Solid monograph concerning the military government in Argentina. Author argues that the country's systemic crisis has forced its military to shed the fictitious "apolitical" guise and to openly assume its political role of institutionalized violence, opting for various reasons almost always against change. Author evaluates the causes of the coup of 1966, the political ideology and institutions of the Onganía government, and the fall of Onganía. It concludes by stating that Argentina's problems are prognostic elements for the majority of other Latin American nations. However, outdated techniques have been applied to solve these problems. In brief, Argentine politics are not concerned with overcoming the status quo but with the distribution of profits. [H.J. Hoyer]

8647. Fernández, Julio A. Crisis in Argentina (CUH, 64:378, Feb. 1973, p. 49-52, 85)

A useful overview article of forces and changing areas of influence in Argentina prior to Perón's return. What is the state of mind of the military, with its apparent vocation for governing power, is the principal point addressed by the author.

8647a. _____. The political elite in Argentina. With a foreword by Russell H. Fitzgibbon. N.Y., New York Univ. Press, 1970. 132 p., bibl., tables.

A very brief report of a questionnaire-based study of political elites in Argentina. The data are not correlated and measures are quite simple. Ch. 5 itemizes the classificatory plan involving 782 members (total population) of the elites for 1958 and 1963. While all are included in descriptive tables, some 80 responses to attitudinal questions are recorded.

8648. Fernández Alvariño, Próspero Germán. Z - Argentina, el crimen del siglo: Teniente General Pedro Eugenio Aramburu. Introducción de Aldo Luis Molinari. B.A., The Author, 1973. 323 p., illus.

The kidnapping and murder of Gen. Aramburu, told in terms sympathetic to him. A worthwhile study for the specialist.

8649. Fornieles, Salvador. Mensaje al Presidente. B.A., A. Peña Lillo Editor, 1972. 217 p., illus., table.

To paraphrase the introductory note which addresses the President: you have said the country is going to be developed. Well, here is your agenda, just in case you follow the steps of your predecessors of the last 15 years and do nothing but talk. A conservative viewpoint on the whole.

8649a. Foro de Buenos Aires por la Vigencia de los Derechos Humanos, *B.A.* Proceso a la explotación y a la represión en la Argentina: mayo de 1973. B.A.? 1973. 222 p., illus.

A highly detailed (two-columned descriptive passages, lengthy three-columned verbatim quotations from witnesses) account of official misconduct of all kinds under the military governments of Argentina in 1972-73. While there is much of simple torture, there is also much of official misuse and abuse of power for private gain, authoritarian practices, etc.

8650. Gaignard, Romain. L'Argentine: une nation agricole en crise (FDD/NED [Problèmes d'Amérique Latine, 31] 4085/4086, 30 avril 1974, p. 73-104, maps, tables)

Highly detailed critical analysis of the agricultural problems of Argentina, noted by overmechanization, underproduction, and lacking in commercial infrastructure. A wealth of tables and maps supports a very useful piece.

8650a. _____. L'evolution de la politique argentine en 1970 et 1971: du Président Onganía au Président Lanusse (FDD/NED [Problèmes d'Amérique Latine, 24] 3913/3914, 28 juillet 1972, p. 7-51)

The customary annual review of Argentine affairs by the Institute of French Documentation. Specific attention is paid in this article to the period including the fall of Onganía, the short-lived government of Levingston, and the first stages of the Lanusse regime. Foreign policy questions are examined, and some texts of internal documents appear. The article closes with a detailed chronology of events.

8651. Galasso, Norberto. ¿Qué es el socialismo nacional? B.A., Ediciones Ayacucho, 1973. 105 p.

A discussion and analysis of marxian socialism, in both Argentine and world terms. Useful effort to relate the position of theoretical and active socialism with the country's Communist Party.

8652. Gándara, Horacio F. Yo espero. B.A., A. Peña Lillo Editor, 1972. 250 p.

A detailed report and assessment of a scandal in the Argentine Navy concerning the construction of cargo vessels. The writer was (he feels) trapped by the politics of the matter.

8652a. García Costa, Víctor. Alfredo Palacios. B.A., Centro Editor de América Latina, 1971. 114 p., plates (Vida y milagros de nuestro pueblo. La historia popular, 70)

A political biography of the noted Socialist Party leader, in this continuing series on Argentine history, see *HLAS 34:2896.*

8653. Gastiazoro, Eugenio. Argentina hoy: capitalismo dependiente y estructura de clases. 2. ed. B.A., Editorial Emecé, 1973. 239 p., tables.

A radical/nationalist economist discusses his country's problem of capitalism based on foreign investment, with the resultant distortion of Argentina's class structure. A useful and not especially ideological book, yet also a determined presentation of the nationalist viewpoint.

8653a. Gazzoli, Luis. Cuando los militares tenemos razón. B.A., Editorial Plus Ultra, 1973. 436 p. (Col. Esquemas políticos, 1)

Subtitled *From Frondizi to Levingston,* this is a very long exposition of military views concerning the outcomes of periods of civilian political control. Documents, as well as analyses, present the military view concerning each of the army's interventions or seizures of power as of 1930.

8654. Germani, Gino. El surgimiento del peronismo: el rol de los obreros y de los migrantes internos (IDES/DE, 13:51, oct./dic. 1973, p. 435-488, tables)

What was the social circumstance in which peronismo could develop and gain control of the country? A lengthy examination of some (but not all) variables yields some insights. The author concludes that additional research is needed in certain areas of social history, and these are demarcated. A provocative article with useful suggestions for comparative work.

8655. Giudici, Ernesto. Carta a mis camaradas: el poder y la revolución. B.A., Granica Editor, 1973. 218 p. (Nuevo poder)

An old marxist activist tells why he joined the Communist Party, what he felt was accomplished while he was one of its leaders, and why he left it. He continues as a freelance leftist, so to speak, and now declares his views on and attitudes toward his present role.

8656. Godio, Julio. La caída de Perón: de junio a setiembre de 1955. B.A., Granica Editor, 1973. 255 p. (Col. Nuestra América)

A detailed coverage of the period, including some official statements and documents of the leaders. The author demonstrates how the fall of Perón and its aftermath were a tragedy that precluded logically any success to the Lonardi regime that followed him.

8656a. Gori, Gastón. La tierra ajena: drama de la juventud agraria argentina. B.A., Ediciones La Bastilla, 1972. 165 p., tables (Serie Borrón y cuenta nueva)

Rural youth face a condition of effective landlessness. Economic and social effects are discussed in some detail. Is there an agrarian reform in fact? What is needed in national policy? Efforts by nonofficial groups to influence policy are discussed.

8657. Graham-Yooll, Andrew. Tiempo de violencia: cronología del "Gran Acuerdo Nacional." Prólogo de Gregorio Selser. B.A., Granica Editor, 1973. 159 p.

Armed Forces involvement in public life has implied a rising level of political violence, claim the introducer and the author. The book is actually a short essay plus a good deal of chronology to prove the point.

8657a. Grassi, Alfredo. Me tenés podrido, Argentina. B.A., Ediciones de la Flor, 1971. 186 p., tables.

A roman à clef about Argentina. So the reader will not miss the point, each short chapter is interspersed with real data about the subject from Argentine life.

8658. Grondona, Mariano. Los dos poderes. B.A., Emecé Editores, 1973. 294 p.

Two essays on the nature and use of power deal with the presidency (the man and his sources and uses of power) and the city of B.A. as the locale of the country's economic and constitutional-political power, historically. The two are linked by the author in a short final note in this innovative examination of his subject.

8659. Ibarra, Raquel; Alejandro Leloir; and Carlos Mastrorilli. Política y fuerzas armadas en la República Argentina (IAEERI/E, 3:15, marzo/abril 1972, p. 116-131)

Review article of books received by the semiofficial journal of the Argentine Institute for Strategic Studies and International Relations. A forenote states that the authors, all sociologists, wrote with complete academic freedom. Books reviewed in considerable detail are:
Carlos Fayt *El político armado: dinámica del proceso político argentino* (B.A., Editorial Pannedille, 1969)
Darío Cantón *La política de los militares argentinos, 1900-1971* (B.A., Siglo XXI Argentina Editores, 1971)

Enrique Díaz Araujo *La conspiración del 43: el G. O. U., una experiencia militarista en la Argentina* (B.A., Editorial La Bastilla, 1971, for comment on this work, see item 8642)
Robert A. Potash *El ejército y la política en la Argentina* (B.A., Editorial Sudamericana, 1971)
Juan V. Orona *La dictadura de Perón* (B.A., 1970)
Eduardo Cuenca *El militarismo en la Argentina* (B.A., Editorial Independencia, 1971).

8660. Interacción entre el Estado, las empresas y el movimiento sindical en la formación profesional. Montevideo, Centro Interamericano de Investigación y Documentación sobre Formación Profesional (CINTERFOR), 1973. 177 p., illus., tables (Informes, 51)

Proceedings of a conference 5-9 June 1972, held in B.A., concerning the training of professionals for industry (vocational advanced education), labor-management relations in industry, labor organizations, collective bargaining, etc. The 22 participants presented 15 papers on: Argentina (primarily), Brazil, Chile, and Venezuela. CINTERFOR is an affiliate of the International Labor Organization. Several papers were concerned with the details of oeprations, while others were narrative or descriptive of organizations or policy. Primarily of value to the Argentine specialist.

8660a. International Labour Organization, *Geneva.* The settlement of labour disputes in Argentina (AIFLD/R, 3:3, 1971, p. 7-31, table)

The history of collective bargaining, law, procedures, and some case instances. Compulsory arbitration procedures are discussed and conditions imposed for legal strikes. The article is very brief but useful.

8660b. Iscaro, Rubens. Diálogos sindicales entre peronistas y comunistas. B.A., Editorial Fundamentos, 1974. 122 p.

Useful and informative discussion of the communist viewpoint on current political, social, and economic issues by a labor leader who also is a longtime party leader and executive committee member. Although much of the material is cast in form of a dialogue with "workers," it is probably a narrative-style presentation of the party's views.

8661. Kaplan, Marcos. La naturaleza del gobierno peronista: 1943-1955 (*Problemas del Desarrollo* [México] 3:11, mayo/julio 1972, p. 77-94, bibl.)

A rather straightforward historical treatment of the rise and fall of the military government controlled (after 1944) by Perón. The author apportions blame for its collapse to several factors: the regime's own corruption and incompetence and US and British greed, rigging of markets, and pressure.

8661a. Kvaternik, Eugenio. ¿Fórmula o fórmulas? algo más sobre nuestro sistema de partidos (*IDES/DE*, 12:47, oct./dic. 1972, p. 613-622)

Can Argentine political stability be found in a "magic" formula based on the foundation of one or more new political parties? Some authors (especially Torcuato Di Tella) feel a center-mass conservative party such as the French Gaullist would be the answer. Although this author admits that it is an interesting model, he does not regard it as either appropriate as well represented by its proponents.

8662. Laborde, Julio and others. El llamado socialismo nacional ¿es socialismo? B.A., Ediciones Centro de Estudios, 1974. 233 p.

A series of critical essays, based on the authors' lectures, all member of the Communist Party of Argentina. Book's title is rhetorical and authors' answer is no. Lectures were delivered in 1973 at the Marxist-Leninist Study Center Victorio Codovilla, B.A. In effect, an interesting updated reinterpretation of doctrine in the current Argentine context.

8662a. La Pampa, (province) *Arg.* 4[i.e. Cuatro] años de gobierno en La Pampa: 1966-30 de junio-1970. Santa Rosa de Toay, Arg., Consejo Provincial de Difusión, 1970? 113 p., illus., maps, plates, tables.

The accomplishments of the provincial government during the time period indicated. Eleven chapters are devoted to an equal number of specific government functions, from legislation to agricultural production and progress.

8663. Lastiri, Raúl A. 67 [i.e., Sesenta y siete] días de gobierno del pueblo. B.A., Secretaría de Prensa y Difusión, 1973. 24 p.

This review of the short period of interim government by Acting President Lastiri, while also serving as President of the Chamber of Deputies, is an interesting short piece as much for what it leaves out as for what it suggests of a governmental program. The presidential message was delivered on 30 July 1973.

8663a. Latin American Perspectives. Vol. 1, No. 3, Fall 1974- . Riverside, Calif.

A newly-established radical journal's special issue on Argentina entitled "Peronism and Crisis." Contents: Juan Eugenio Corradi "Argentina and Peronism: Fragments of the Puzzle;" Alberto Ciria "Peronism Yesterday and Today;" Nancy Caro Hollander "Si Evita Viviera;" Michael Dodson "Priests and Peronism: Radical Clergy in Argentine Politics;" Juan Carlos Torre "Workers' Struggle and Consciousness;" Monica Peralta Ramos "Peronism and Dependency: Liberation or Dependency?;" and Juan C. Portantiero "Class Conflict: Dominant Classes and Political crisis."

8664. Lebedinsky, Mauricio. Marxismo-leninismo frente al revisionismo de izquierda y de derecha: en general y en la Argentina. B.A., Ediciones Centro de Estudios, 1973. 235 p.

An effort to reinterpret the role of the "left" under contemporary circumstances, in Argentina as well as in the more general world scene, by an experienced communist leader.

8664a. Little, Walter. Electoral aspects of peronism, 1946-1954 (UM/JIAS, 15:3, Aug. 1973, p. 267-284, map, bibl., tables)

Although the two peronista regimes went to great pains to seek legitimation through the electoral process, little has been known of the nature of the voting groups that supported Perón. This author offers a portion of a major study analyzing known electoral data, discussing the support base for the regimes, and its relationship to prevailing patterns of social stratification.

8665. Luna, Félix. De Perón a Lanusse: 1943-1973. B.A., Editorial Planeta Argentina, 1972. 226 p. (Biblioteca universal planeta. Panorama, 8)

Political history of the period indicated.

8665a. _____ and others. ¿Qué Argentina queremos los argentinos? B.A., Ediciones La Bastilla, 1973. 458 p. (Serie Borrón y cuenta nueva)

Fifteen Argentine writers address the question. The volume grows out of a meeting held sometime between Aug. and Dec. 1972 and convened by the Instituto para el Desarrollo de Ejecutivos en la Arngetina. From a moderate and institutional position, it explores innovations needed by the country in light of the imminent return of open political action.

8666. Marsal, J.F. *ed.* Argentina conflictiva: seis estudios sobre problemas sociales argentinos. Introducción por Juan Francisco Marsal. B.A., Editorial Paidós, 1972. 190 p. (Biblioteca de economía, política, sociedad. Serie mayor, 7)

The individual pieces in this distinguished collection are fully able to stand alone. None but one (and that marginally) are adversely affected by delays in publication and (this) reporting, since all date from the late 1960s:
Ana María Eichelbaum de Babina "La desigualdad Educacional en Argentina" p. 19-57
Francisco José Delich "Estructura Agraria y Tipos de Organización y Acción Campesina" p. 58-85
Gino Germani "La Estratificación Social y su Evolución História en Argentina" p. 86-113
Juan Francisco Marsal "Los Conflictos Políticos de la Argentina Post-Peronista" p. 136-169
José Enrique Carlos Miguens "Morfología y Comportamiento de la Opinión Pública Urbana Argentina" p. 170-190.

8666a. Martínez Nogueira, Roberto. Participación social y reforma administrativa en la Argentina: bases para una estrategia (IDES/DE, 13:50, julio/sept. 1973, p. 347-367)

The complexity of modern society requires that there be participation in the establishment and execution of delivery systems for services. This article establishes and applies a theoretical model to the Argentine example. Thus, it maintains, administration will become a force for democratization.

8667. Méndez Acébal, Ramón. Enfoques de la realidad argentina. B.A., Ediciones Lumen, 1971. 44 p.

Thirteen short pieces of modest but cynical achievement about how the Argentine political system *really* works.

8668. Mora y Araujo, Manuel. Comentarios sobre la búsqueda de la fórmula política argentina (IDES/DE, 12:47, oct./dic. 1972, p. 623-629)

A critique of Torcuato Di Tella's suggestion that a mass-center party based on the working class might be the necessary answer to Argentina's lack of political stability. For more on this subject, see item 8661a.

8669. Mugica, Carlos. Peronismo y cristianismo. B.A., Editorial Merlin, 1973. 100 p.

A jesuit priest, professor and clerical progressive asks and deals with questions of Christianity, its values in the face of need for change, its demands of the priest, and peronismo.

8670. Nadra, Fernando. Socialismo nacional. 2. ed. B.A., Ediciones Sílaba, 1973. 235 p.

A Communist Party response, supported by party documents, to the peronista claim of national socialism in the 1970s.

8670a. *Nuestra Palabra.* Partido Comunista. Año 1, No. 1, Epoca 2, junio 1973-   . B.A.

Communist Party popular publication. Although the major portion concerns Argentina, Soviet leaders and interests are also cared for.

8671. O'Donnell, Guillermo A. Un juego imposible: competición y coaliciones entre partidos políticos en Argentina, 1955-1966. B.A., Instituto Torcuato Di Tella, Centro de Investigaciones en Administración Pública, 1972. 53 p., bibl. (Documento de trabajo)

A graduate paper in political science originally written at Yale. The author concludes that in the period indicated the parties were able not to "win" but only to aggravate tensions and restrictions previously existing in competition.

8671a. Orellano, Jerónimo. La conciencia social justicialista. B.A., Ediciones Trasvasamiento, 1974. 135 p.

A catechism for the faithful; short essays, each prefaced by a quote from Perón, Eva, or from party documents of the first peronista era.

8672. Pandolfi, Rodolfo. La caída de Lanusse (Confirmado [B.A.] 19:394, 12/28, junio 1973, p. 31-39)

A detailed recounting of the politics of the termination of the Lanusse government in March 1973.

8673. Perón, Eva. La palabra, el pensamiento y la acción de Eva Perón. B.A., Editorial Freeland, 1973. 159 p.

Short excerpts under 12 chapter headings.

8674. Perón, Juan Domingo. Coloquios con ... [Edited by] Enrique Pavón Pereyra. Madrid, Editores Internacionales Técnicos Reunidos, 1973. 239 p., plates.

Dialogues with Perón by the editor in the period 1961-63. They offer a view of the great man in exile, incorporating his views and conclusions about his experiences as head of government, and the reasons for his fall.

8674a. _____. Conducción política. B.A., Presidencia de la Nación, Secretaría Política, 1974. 325 p.

The elements of political leadership and of peronismo in an official publication offering the aphorisms of the caudillo. A short appendix contains notes on two public appearances in 1973.

8674b. _____. Del poder al exilio. B.A., Ediciones Argentinas, 1973. 98 p.

Peron blames a lot of people and institutions.

8674c. _____. Dialogo entre Perón y las fuerzas armadas. B.A., Ediciones Jorge Mar [and] Centro de Documentación Justicialista, 1973. 381 p.

Documents, principally of the period 1943-55, while Perón was rising to and holding power. Also includes some materials of the Lonardi regime and a few statements as late as 1966, not all of them of peronista origin.

8674d. _____. Doctrina revolucionaria: filosófica, política, social. Prólogo de Plácido J. Vilas López. B.A., Editorial Freeland, 1973. 296 p.

Reprints a doctrinal statement of 1946, shortly after Perón's first-term inauguration. It is supplemented by a chronological listing of speeches by Perón, 1943-46, from which (presumably) the materials have been collated.

8674e. _____. La fuerza es el derecho de las bestias. B.A., Ediciones Síntesis, 1973. 196 p.

Perón's now-classic 1956 defense of his regime in reissue at the time of his return to B.A.

8674f. _____. Gobernar es persuadir. B.A., n.p., 1973. 1 v. (Unpaged) (Mensaje, 3)

A short speech by the president to provincial governors at Olivos, the presidential residence, on 2 Aug. 1973. This is typical of dozens of such pamphlet statements by Perón issued in the brief period before his death. The statement is important, however, for its moderate tone — both in delivery and in partisan tone. Perón discusses social and political problems briefly. Possibly the keynote is his statement, "to govern is not to command ... *to govern is to persuade*" (italics in the original). He has already said, earlier, in the speech, "Juvenile delinquency has flourished spectacularly .... Ideological deviations and the flowering of the ultraleft are not tolerated even in the ultraleft .... This ultraleft, even for the communist countries, is for exportation but not for importation."

8674g. _____. Juan Perón en la Argentina 1973: sus discursos, sus diálogos, sus conferencias, Plan Trienal 1974-77. B.A., Vespa Ediciones, 1974. 395 p., plates.

A comprehensive collection of Perón's public statements from his return to the country 20 June 1973 through the end of the year. Some short prefatory notes place the speeches, press conferences, interviews, and other statements in context.

8674h. _____. El libro rojo de Perón: citas. B.A., A. Peña Lillo, 1973. 205 p.

The editor leaves nothing to the imagination. Not only is the book red, but it also is little. And it is all done for cash, since he (unnamed) says it is intended to be impartial and didactic. Like Mao's piece, it offers selected concepts in a series of (31) chapters. Presumably this says less of Perón than of his public.

8674i. _____. Perón-Cooke correspondencia. B.A., Ediciones Papiro, 1972. 334 p. (Col. Política)

Exchange covering the period June 1956 to Nov. 1957 in which the two shared hopes of subversion and return to power. Perón designates Cooke his heir in case of his assassination; Cooke prepares complex plans for overthrow of the military government. Persons and interests are discussed in much detail. An essential piece for the researcher of the period, the personalities or the movement.

8674j. _____. Perón habla al país: Pacto Social, convenio colectivo de alto nivel. B.A., n.p., 1974. 11 p.

A radio-and-television speech to the nation on 14 Jan. 1974. Perón points to the problems confronting the country and suggests a new spirit of trust and good will which would lessen factional or partisan-inspired opposition with overtones of violence. He refers not to an overt "pact" as such, but rather to the need for an implicit one. This pamphlet is one of many public statements by the late President, a rather different Perón who, in contrast with the earlier one, speaks in terms of social pacification, understanding, and the national unity of all classes. This one even discusses weekend traffic accidents!

8674k. _____. Perón y el imperativo nacional: actuar dentro de la ley. B.A., Presidencia de la Nación, Secretaría Prensa y Difusión, 1974. 16 p.

A dialogue, in question/answer form, between the President and members of the Chamber of Deputies elected by the Juventud Peronista in which they discuss a Penal Code reform bill. Another look at a different man who argues for social responsibility and mutual respect for all. In this case he also appeals for observance of party discipline during the legislative process.

8674l. _____. El pueblo quiere saber de que se trata. B.A., Editorial Freeland, 1973. 240 p.

A collection of speeches and public statements of views and policy proposals by Perón dating from 1943 and 1944. The material now falls into the category of documentation for specialists.

8675. Petras, James F. and **Thomas C. Cook.** Componentes de la acción política: el ejecutivo industrial argentino (IDES/DE, 12:46, julio/sept. 1972, p. 387-396, tables)

Based on 112 interviews with company executives, conducted in the first six months of 1971, the paper presumably summarizes a major work to appear. What are the political attitudes of industrial executives (their perceptions of regimes and of forms of political action)? The paper concludes that the level of pragmatism of executives is substantially higher than previously argued by other writers.

8676. Portes, Alejandro. Perón and the national elections. Austin, Univ. of Texas at Austin, Institute of Latin American Studies, 1973. 18 p. (Special publication)

The emphasis of this short paper is principally on the political activities of the armed forces, which eventually led them into self-defeat. Therefore, the peronista return can be seen as a calm among storms in which some working class reentry to national politics may occur.

8677. Posadas, J. La renuncia de Cámpora y el fracaso del intento contrarrevolucionario de la CIA y de la derecha peronista. B.A., Ediciones Revista Marxista Latinoamericana, 1973. 62 p.

A trotskyist version of the Cámpora resignation.

8678. Prontuario: técnica del interrogatorio, la represión y el asesinato. Santiago, Empresa Editora Nacional Quimantu, 1973. 96 p., plates.

A Montonero publication transcribes lengthy interviews by interrogators of a kidnapped prison psychiatrist involved in handling the antigovernment left. Includes a section on the Trelew incident and on torture techniques.

8679. Puiggrós, Rodolfo. Adónde vamos, argentinos. B.A., Ediciones Corregidor, 1972. 214 p. (Biblioteca de las cuestiones, 2)

Puiggrós again reviews the state of Argentine politics in a rather sweeping look at historical-political tendencies of the past. Each chapter offers conclusions for the present. The final one sketches the military relationship with politics and asks where are Argentines going now.

8680. Ramil Cepeda, Carlos. Crisis de una burguesía dependiente: balance económico de la "Revolución Argentina," 1966-1971. B.A., Ediciones La Rosa Blindada, 1972. 112 p., tables.

A serious and very useful semipolemic work in which the author argues that the military government's conception of economic/political realities was faulty from its inception. As a government of and by the bourgeoisie it sought to separate politics from economics and the Argentine economy from the world economy. From this basis it sought to resolve isolated complaints unsystematically. Arguing from a socialist viewpoint, the author regards this as foolish.

8681. Rattenbach, Benjamín. El sistema social-militar en la sociedad moderna. B.A., Editorial Pleamar, 1972. 152 p., bibl.

An intriguing and presumably candidly revealing view of the military career in Argentina by a lieutenant general of the Argentine Army. Not merely a memoir, the work offers a useful base of sociological literature.

8682. Replanteo. Año 1, No. 1, agosto 1973- . B.A.

A potentially useful biweekly journal of political comment and opinion, without apparent party line in this first issue.

8683. Rivanera Carlés, Federico. Los partidos políticos ¿ representantes del pueblo o de la burguesía? B.A., Ediciones La Bastilla, 1973. 137 p., bibl. (Serie Borrón y cuenta neuva)

A short text-type piece on comparative political parties which incorporates literature from the US and Europe on party systems in these regions while also discussing Argentine parties. Of more interest to the specialist in comparative education than politics although the uses of Argentine data are interesting.

8684. Rocchetti, Tito L. El convenio multilateral en el sistema tributario argentino (Revista de la Facultad de Ciencias de la Administración [Univ. Nacional del Litoral, Sante Fé, Arg.] 1:1, 1969, p. 71-92, tables)

A technical discussion of the problem of double taxation in Argentina, in which the national and provincial governments enter into understandings concerning apportionment and collection of taxes on interprovincial business operations.

8685. Rodríguez Signes, Tulio F. El caso Lechiguanas. Paraná, Arg., Talleres Gráficos de Nueva Impresora, 1972. 93 p., illus.

Details of a land scandal involving corruption in the provincial government of Entre Ríos.

8686. Romero, César Enrique. Las creencias constitucionales y políticas: ideología de la Constitución Argentina (IEP/REP, 183/184, mayo/agosto 1972, p. 323-356)

Following a rather brief discussion of legal philosophy on points of legitimacy and constitutionality, the author explores in some detail the philosophy and ideology underlying the Argentine Constitution. Jurisprudential principles in force, principally since 1955, are examined in the light of leading cases.

8687. Rouquié, Alain. Argentine: la fin du régime militaire et le retour du Général Perón au pouvoir (FDD/NED [Problèmes d'Amérique Latine, 33] 4110/4111, 15 sept. 1974, p. 1-70, maps, tables)

Focused entirely on the political process of 1973 and on preceding partisan events of 1972, this rather long paper is a mine of information. It is supported by several biographical notes, political documents, and a listing of Ministers in cabinets of the two-year period. A chronology completes the package as is customary with this series.

8688. Rubinstein, Juan Carlos. Estrategia y táctica para el cambio. B.A., Ediciones La Bastilla, 1972. 203 p. (Serie Borrón y cuenta nueva)

A serious academic effort to examine Argentine society and its possibilities for change. Concludes that socialism is best suited for so schismatic a structure.

8689. Saint-Jean, Iberico Manuel. Los ejércitos de Argentina y Brasil: algunos aspectos comparativos (IAEERI/E, 1:5, enero/feb. 1970, p. 97-107, tables)

A short piece by an Argentine brigadier general, which emphasizes the physical differences: weapons, personnel, budgets, etc. An extremely short section is devoted to differences of doctrine.

Schwartzman, Simon. Empresarios y política en el proceso de industrialización: Argentina, Brasil, Australia. See item 8593.

8690. Selser, Gregorio. El Onganiato: la llamaban revolución argentina. v. 2. B.A., Carlos Samonta, 1973. 394 p.

A collection of the author's critical pieces on Juan Carlos Ongania published previously (and contemporaneously with his regime, 1966-67) in B.A. journals and newspapers. Their length and detail make them worth the attention of specialists.

8691. Sigal, Silvia. Acción obrera en una situación de crisis: Tucumán 1966-1968. B.A., Instituto Torcuato Di Tella, Centro de Investigaciones Sociales, 1973. 93 1., tables (Documento de trabajo, 86)

Focusing primarily on the sugar workers' union in Tucumán province, this short research article discusses the causes and effects of social decomposition in that region.

8692. Smith, Peter H. Argentina and the failure of democracy: conflict among political elites, 1904-1955. Madison, The Univ. of Wisconsin Press, 1974. 215 p., bibl., tables.

Democracy was overthrown in 1930 after a lifespan of about 18 years. This short essay (which takes up only half of the book) is supported by an equal number of pages of intensive quantitative analysis of rollcall votes in the Argentine Congress. The thesis that emerges is that the constitutional democratic process failed to serve the interests of major groups and political elites. A rather controversial work both in technique and conclusions.

Sociedad Argentina de Defensa de la Tradición, Familia y Propiedad. Comisión de Estudios. El nacionalismo: una incógnita en constante evolución. See *HLAS 36:3317.*

8693. _____. _____. **Consejo Nacional.** Los "Kerenskys" argentinos: Manifiesto de la . . . . sobre la situación actual. B.A., 1972. 192 p.

How can a conservative, intelligent, Catholic country fall into the hands of communism? In this book peronism and organized labor are only fronts or "bluffs" (sic, in English) for communism. Obviously, a highly conservative view.

8694. Taccone, Juan J. Crisis . . . repuesta sindical. B.A., Artes Gráficas Delta, 1971. 123 p.

Initial chapters are broad and shallow overviews of "crisis"; the latter half of the book is highly detailed reporting of facts and institutional goals of organized labor in Argentina.

8695. Terrera, Guillermo Alfredo. Política social con la estructura de la democracia funcional argentina. B.A., Editorial Patria Vieja, 1971. 111 p.

The author proposes "functional democracy" and "integral humanism" as the critical elements of a "Social Policy" that will ameliorate Argentine life and eliminate the need for coercive government and politics. An interesting adventure into a rather special and private view of the world.

8695a. _____. El proceso de cambio en el grupo humano argentino. B.A., Instituto de Ciencias del Hombre (ICH), 1973. 155 p.

The founder and principal theoretician of an interesting movement concerned with "social democracy" for Argentina here presents a summary of his thoughts on governmental and social reorganization of the country. Some of the materials are structural and documentary, others prescriptive.

8696. Toryho, Jacinto. Aramburu: confidencias, actitudes, propósitos. B.A., Ediciones Líbera, 1973. 257 p. (Historia política argentina)

A rather lengthy examination of the author's interpretation of Aramburu's attitudes, based on short excerpts of discussions with the then-President.

8697. Trevignani, Henry Horacio; Carlos Alberto Bertone; and **Roberto Carri.** Análisis económico y político de la dependencia. B.A., Editorial Guadalupe, 1973. 106 p. (Col. La dependencia argentina en el contexto latinoamericano, 4)

Two pre-Peronista essays, couched in marxist terminology, analyze the economic and political aspects of Argentina's dependency status and its relationship to that of the Third World. Peronism, as the leader of the anti-imperialist struggle, has become synonymous with "popular" power and working-class hegemony, in other words, "national socialism." But Perón is still faced with imperialist counterrevolution supported by the armed forces and the allies of imperialism within the government bureaucracy. [A. Suárez]

8697a. Treviño, Pepe. La carne podrida: crónica en torno de la quiebra Switt-Deltec. B.A., Ediciones del Salto, 1972. 197 p.

A case study of the bankruptcy of the Swift de La Plata frigorífica and of the aftermath in which it became a property of Deltec International, a multinational firm.

8698. Urondo, Francisco *ed.* La patria fusilada: entrevistas, testimonios de María Antonia Berger, Alberto Miguel Camps, Ricardo René Haidar. 2. ed. B.A., Ediciones de Crisis, 1973. 143 p.

Extremely long interviews (with three survivors of the Trelew massacre) followed by a short transcription of another held at the Trelew airport by spokesmen of the escapees from the prison, prior to their deaths.

8699. Vigo, Juan M. ¡La vida por Perón! Memorias de un combatiente de la resistencia. B.A., A. Peña Lillo Editor, 1973. 207 p. (Crónicas de la resistencia)

A convinced and militant peronista writes of the period after the 1955 overthrow of Perón. Much of the material was, he says in his introduction, written clandestinely while he was in jail.

JOURNAL ABBREVIATIONS

AF/AUR   Air University Review. The professional journal of the United States Air Force. Maxwell Air Force Base, Ala.

AIFLD/R	A.I.F.L.D. Review. American Institute for Free Labor Development. Washington.
AJCL	The American Journal of Comparative Law. American Association for the Comparative Study of Law. Univ. of California. Berkeley, Calif.
BDASP/R	Revista do Serviço Público. Departamento Administrativo do Serviço Público. Rio.
BMM/RMB	Revista Marítima Brasileira. Ministério de Marinha. Rio.
BU/JCS	A Journal of Church and State. Published by the J.M. Dawson Studies in Church and State of Baylor Univ. Waco., Tex.
CAM	Cuadernos Americanos. México.
CDAL	Cahiers des Amériques Latines. Paris.
CDLA	Casa de las Américas. La Habana.
CEHMP/R	Revista del Centro de Estudios Histórico-Militares del Perú. Lima.
CFR/FA	Foreign Affairs. An American quarterly review. Council on Foreign Relations, Inc. N.Y.
CIDG/O	Orbis. Bulletin international de documentation linguistique. Centre International de Dialectologie Générale. Louvain, Belgium.
CIIA/IJ	International Journal. Canadian Institute of International Affairs. Toronto, Canada.
CLAPCS/AL	América Latina. Centro Latino-Americano de Pesquisas em Ciências Sociais. Rio.
CM/FI	Foro Internacional. El Colegio de México. México.
CSSH	Comparative in Society and History. Society for the Comparative Study of Society and History. The Hague.
CU/JIA	Journal of International Affairs. Columbia Univ., School of International Affairs. N.Y.
CUH	Current History. A monthly magazine of world affairs. Philadelphia, Pa.
CUNY/CP	Comparative Politics. The City Univ. of New York, Political Science Program. N.Y.
DIS Dissent.	Published quarterly by Dissent Publishing Association. N.Y.
EAZ	Ethnographisch-Archäologische Zeitschrift. Deutscher Verlag Wissenschaften. Berlin/DDR.
EP	Economie et Politique. Revue marxiste d'économie. Paris.
ESC	Estudios Sindicales y Cooperativos. Instituto de Estudios Sindicales, Sociales y Cooperativos de Madrid. Madrid.
FDD/NED	Notes et Etudes Documentaires. France, Direction de la Documentation. Paris.
FH	Folia Humanistica. Ciencias, artes, letras. Editorial Glarma. Barcelona.
HAHR	Hispanic American Historical Review. Conference on Latin American History of the American Historical Association. Duke Univ. Press. Durham, N.C.
HU/BHR	Business History Review. Harvard Univ., Graduate School of Business Administration. Boston, Mass.
IAEERI/E	Estrategia. Instituto Argentino de Estudios Estratégicos y de las Relaciones Internacionales. B.A.
IAMEA	Inter-American Economic Affairs. Washington.
ICISR/S	Social Compass. The International Catholic Institute for Social-Ecclesiastical Research. The Hague.
IDES/DE	Desarrollo Económico. Instituto de Desarrollo Económico y Social. B.A.
IEP/REP	Revista de Estudios Políticos. Instituto de Estudios Políticos. Madrid.
IRFDH/DC	Développement et Civilisations. Institut de Recherche et de Formation en vue du Développement Harmonisé. Paris.
IRSISP/RH	Relações Humanas. Instituto de Relações Sociais e Industrias de São Paulo. São Paulo.
JDA	The Journal of Developing Areas. Western Illinois Univ. Press. Macomb, Ill.
JLAS	Journal of Latin American Studies. Centers of institutes of Latin American studies at the universities of Cambridge, Glasgow, Liverpool, London and Oxford. Cambridge University Press. London.

JPR	Journal of Peace Research. Edited at the International Peace Research Institute. Universitetforlaget. Oslo.
LADOC	Latin American Documentation. U.S. Catholic Conference. Washington.
LARR	Latin American Research Review. Latin American Studies Association. Univ. of Texas Press. Austin, Tex.
LNB/L	Lotería. Organo de la Lotería Nacional de Beneficencia. Panamá.
MDZED	Merkur. Deutsche Zeitschrift für Europäisches Denken. Deutsche Verlags-Anstalt. Stuttgart, FRG.
MR	Monthly Review. An independent Socialist magazine. N.Y.
NGIZ/IS	Internationale Spectator. Tijdschrift voor internationale politiek. Het Nederlandsch Genootschap voor Internationale Zaken. The Hague.
NSSR/SR	Social Research. An international quarterly of political and social science. Graduate Faculty of Political and Social Science, New School for Social Research. N.Y.
PCU/E	Estudios. Organo del Comite Ejecutivo del Partido Comunista. Montevideo.
POLIT	Política. Ideas para una América nueva. Caracas.
PQ	The Political Quarterly. London.
PSS/PSR	Pacific Sociological Review. Pacific Sociological Society. Univ. of Oregon. Eugene, Oreg.
PUCIS/WP	World Politics. A quarterly journal of international relations. Princeton Univ., Center of International Studies. Princeton, N.J.
PUJ/U	Universitas. Ciencias jurídicas y socioeconómicas. Pontificia Univ. Javeriana, Facultad de Derecho y Ciencias Socioeconómicas. Bogotá.
RU/SCID	Studies in Comparative International Development. Rutgers Univ. New Brunswick, N.J.
SECOLAS/A	Annals of the Southern Conference on Latin American Studies. West Georgia College. Carrollton, Ga.
SS	Science and Society. An independent journal of Marxism. N.Y.
UCC/CE	Cuadernos de Economía. Univ. Católica de Chile. Santiago.
UCL/CD	Cultures et Développement. Revue internationale des sciences du développement. Fondation Universitaire de Belgique. Louvain, Belgium.
UCLV/I	Islas. Revista de la Univ. Central de las Villas. Santa Clara, Cuba.
UCP/IAP	Ibero-Americana Pragensia. Univ. Carolina de Praga, Centro de Estudios Ibero-Americanos. Prague.
UCPR/H	Horizontes. Revista de la Univ. Católica de Puerto Rico. Ponce, P.R.
UM/JIAS	Journal of Inter-American Studies and World Affairs. Univ. of Miami Press *for the* Center for Advanced International Studies. Coral Gables, Fla.
UMG/RBEP	Revista Brasileira de Estudos Políticos. Univ. de Minas Gerais. Belo Horizonte, Bra.
UNAM/PDD	Problemas del Desarrollo. Revista latinoamericana de economía. Univ. Nacional Autónoma de México, Instituto de Investigaciones Económicas. México.
UNAM/RMS	Revista Mexicana de Sociología. Univ. Nacional Autónoma de México, Instituto de Investigaciones Sociales. México.
UNECLA/B	Economic Bulletin for Latin America. United Nations, Economic Commission for Latin America. N.Y.
UP/O	Orbis. A quarterly journal of world affairs. Univ. of Pennsylvania, Foreign Policy Research Institute. Philadelphia, Pa.
UPR/CS	Caribbean Studies. Univ. of Puerto Rico, Institute of Caribbean Studies. Río Piedras, P.R.
UPR/RCS	Revista de Ciencias Sociales. Univ. de Puerto Rico, Colegio de Ciencias Sociales. Río Piedras, P.R.
USIA/PC	Problemas of Communism. United States Information Agency. Washington.
UU/WPQ	Western Political Quarterly. Official journal of the Western Political Science Association; Pacific Northwest Political Science Association; and Southern California Political Science Association. Univ. of Utah, Institute of Government. Salt Lake City, Utah.
UWI/SES	Social and Economic Studies. Univ. of the West Indies, Institute of Social and Economic Research. Mona, Jam.

WPF/IO	International Organization. World Peace Foundation. Boston, Mass.
WRU/JMF	Journal of Marriage and the Family. Western Reserve Univ. Cleveland, Ohio.
YU/YR	The Yale Review. Yale Univ. New Haven. Conn.

International Relations

YALE H. FERGUSON
Associate Professor of Political Science
Rutgers University-Newark

C. NEALE RONNING
Professor of Political Science
New School for Social Research

SURVEYING THE LITERATURE OVER a two-year period, we once again can report an increase in sophisticated analyses of the international relations of Latin America. To be sure, there have been many items of a highly legalistic or strictly polemical character, but these are now perhaps the exception rather than the rule.

Historians have continued to be preoccupied with the record of US Manifest Destiny and imperialism from the mid-19th century to the Good Neighbor Policy. Of particular note in this category is Linderman's (item 8701) work on the social psychology behind US involvement in the Spanish American War (item 8852). Also, Abrams (item 8701) has produced a major review-essay attacking the "new orthodoxy" of "revisionist" historians, who have argued that US imperialism never differed fundamentally from that of the other principal world powers. Perhaps now that the literature is becoming so extensive, the materials may at last be at hand for a definitive resolution of the perennial controversy between traditionalists and revisionists. We should highlight, as well, the extensive publications of Czech historian Nálevka, based on official archives, on Czechoslovakian relations with Latin American governments from 1939 to the close of World War II.

As for the contemporary era, most commentators have stressed the steady deterioration in US-Latin American relations, despite Henry Kissinger's call for a "new dialogue" and his proclamation of a "Good Partner" policy at OAS meetings in 1973-74. Einaudi (item 8722), Ferguson (item 8731), and others have observed that what little remained of the "Western Hemisphere Idea" now appears to have disintegrated entirely and no "new vision" has arisen to replace it. The Cuban issue (item 8859) has to some extent receded into the background in recent years. However, several authors have probed the disquieting implications of US economic pressures and covert activities against the Allende government in Chile (item 8925 and item 8926; item 8880 and item 8879). Still others have traced the evolution of the Panama Canal question, which currently seems headed either for some sort of settlement or an explosive impasse. Also controversial has been Washington's relaxation of a longstanding curb on arms transfers to the Latin American military (item 8724) which some have seen as likely to contribute via a "contagion effect" to a renewed arms race in the area (item 8803).

In addition, there has emerged an interesting debate about the relevance of particular models of foreign-policy-making to an understanding of the fundamental content of US-Latin American policies (item 8754; item 8716; and item 8772). Some scholars have extolled the utility of a "bureaucratic" model, which views policy as essentially the outcome of a struggle between competing subunits of the national administration. Others have opted for a concept of "rational" policy—emphasizing the unity imposed by values, images, etc., shared by the entire foreign policy "establishment"—although there is no consensus among these analysts as to the exact nature of what might be termed the "rational whole." "Liberals" have tended to take administration pronouncements about the goals of US policy largely at face value and have criticized both some of the goals and the way that others have been perverted or frustrated in the process of implementation. Packenham has seized upon the "Liberal" label as a description of several underlying "assumptions" inherent in US policies toward the Third World, with which many "liberals" would doubtless not wish to be identified. Finally, "radical" scholars have advanced their own interpretation of a "rational" US orientation toward the defense of private interests abroad.

As Cotler and Fagen have pointed out, the conception of US policy held by most Latin American proponents of "dependence" theory is closer to the "rational" than the "bureaucratic" model—specifically, to the views of "radical" commentators. The literature on dependence has continued to grow, to the point where it represents perhaps the dominant trend in Latin American writings on hemisphere relations. Nevertheless, dependence theorists differ among themselves both as to the degree of attention given to political or economic forms of dependence and to the usefulness of traditional Marxist "class struggle" or Leninist "imperialism" conceptions in explaining the patterns observed.

Another subject of prominence in the literature, treated within and without a dependence framework, has been the multinational corporation. Among numerous important studies are those by two North American scholars, Berhman (item 8709) and Vernon (item 8800). The challenge the multinationals present to the nation-state, especially but not exclusively to those with a less-developed economy, has now been extensively explored, and analysts are turning increasingly to an examination of various policy options available to Latin American governments.

The steady divergence of the US and Latin America and the rise of Latin American nationalism in the 1970s has prompted interest in the emergence of a network of "subsystem" relationships in the region (item 8702 and *HLAS 35:7355*). Milenky has detailed the declining fortunes of the Latin American Free Trade Association (LAFTA), which has been largely eclipsed by the more promising and innovative Andean Common Market (ANCOM). Although political shifts in, for example, Chile and Argentina have made much more complex the task of hammering out joint Latin American positions like the 1969 consensus of Viña del Mar on key international issues, Latin American governments have been to a remarkable degree united on questions of trade with the developed countries and the need for some modification of the traditional law of the sea. Recent UN conferences have occasioned a host of useful publications on territorial waters, the exploitation of the seabed, and related matters.

Also generating substantial literature have been the policies of extra-regional powers, especially the Soviet Union (item 8747; item 8862; and item 8739), toward Latin America and the unilateral policies of leading Latin American governments. In the latter category, numerous excellent analyses of Mexican foreign policy have continued to emanate from the Colegio de México, and there have appeared several noteworthy books and articles documenting the state visits that Mexican President Echevarría has been making around the world. Moreover, Schmitt (item 8816) has produced perhaps the best historical survey of US-Mexican relations.

GENERAL

8700. Abellán, Victoria. Las N.U. y el tercer mundo: la cooperación internacional para el desarrollo. Prólogo de Manuel Diez de Velasco. Barcelona, Ediciones Japizúa, 1971. 661 p., illus., tables.

This volume is a compilation of the working papers, documents, and proceedings of two sessions of the "seminar on International Cooperation for Development Within the United Nations System," held at the Univ. of Barcelona in 1967-68 and 1969-70. The appendix includes such useful material as the text of the most important UN resolutions regarding development, a list of relevant UN studies, and a list of treaties governing the protection of private investment. [Y. Ferguson]

8701. Abrams, Richard M. United States intervention abroad: the first quarter century (AHA/R, 79:1, Feb. 1974, p. 72-102, bibl.)

Provocative review-essay reassessing US interventions, primarily in the Caribbean, in the first quarter of the 20th century. Abrams challenges what he terms the "new orthodoxy" of the "revisionists," "wherein the imperialist expansion of the United States appears indistinguishable from that of any other Western power." In fact, he contends, US imperialism generally proceeded from higher motives, and when it did not or when good intentions bore bad fruit in the day-to-day course of specific interventions, we should see these "contradictions" as "the collision of unimpeachable principle with certain inescapable realities." Among these, Abrams asserts, is the fact that without world government "there is little but good will and countervailing power to minimize the exploitation some nations are forced to endure for their deficiencies." He maintains that US decision-makers would have been less hypocritical had they frankly admitted that the right of self-determination had to be suspended when "lesser republics" were patently unable to govern themselves. [Y. Ferguson]

Agor, Weston H. Latin American interstate politics: patterns of cooperation and conflict. See *HLAS 36:1678.*

8702. ———. Nuevos modelos de relaciones interamericanas (USIA/PI, 19:6, nov./dic. 1972, p. 1-10, illus., plates)

Agor reviews recent developments in intra-Latin American multilateral diplomacy and bilateral relations, heralding (he believes) the emergence of a regional international subsystem that is increasingly independent of the US. [Y. Ferguson]

8703. Alvarado Garaieva, Teodoro. El mar territorial y el mar patrimonial. Guayaquil, Ecua., Univ. de Guayaquil, Depto. de Publicaciones, 1973. 173 p., bibl.

A distinguished Equadoran jurist presents a basic discussion of the law of the sea and the justification for a 200-mile limit. [C.N. Ronning]

8703a. Arnold, Hans. Kulturelle zusammenarbeit mit Lateinamerika (AZIF, 25:1, 1974, p. 73-79)

A high-level German government representative explores the possible areas for increased cultural exchange programs between the Federal Republic of Germany and Latin America. [H.J. Hoyer]

8704. Astiz, Carlos. As eleições norte-americanas e seus reflexos sobre a política exterior para a América Latina. Brasília, Câmara dos Deputados, Directoria Legislativa, Centro de Documentação e Informação, Divisão de Publicações, 1972. 37 p.

A US professor of political science offers some brief but thoughtful observations on the then forthcoming presidential elections of 1972. After some general comments about the US election, Prof. Astiz discusses the importance of such issues as campaign finances, crime, Vietnam, and taxes in the forthcoming elections. Useful for Latin Americans wishing to gain insight into the US electoral process. [C.N. Ronning]

8705. Baines, John M. U. S. military assistance to Latin America: an assessment (UM/JIAS, 14:4, Nov. 1972, p. 469-487, tables)

Friendly assessment of the US military-aid program in Latin America. Baines holds that such aid has not been a significant factor in causing coups or promoting the growth of military establishments in the area. He does not deal directly with another major criticism of military aid, that it identifies the US too closely with repressive regimes; however, he urges Washington to encourage the Latin American military to broaden their support "among the non-Communist elements of the left." [Y. Ferguson]

8706. Bath, C. Richard. Latin American claims on living resources of the sea (IAMEA, 27:4, Spring 1974, p. 59-85)

First-rate discussion of the principal positions of the US and Latin American countries on the complex issues in the continuing debate over the law of the sea. [Y. Ferguson]

8707. Bazarian, Jacob. Mito e realidade sobre a União Soviética: análize imparcial do regime soviético por um ex-membro do Partido Comunista. 2. ed. rev. e ampliada. São Paulo, Escolas Profissionais Salesianas, 1973. 158 p.

A former Communist (it is not clear what he is now) writes of his disillusionment with the Soviet Union and with Communism. His reasons for renouncing Communism seem to be much the same as those for embracing it in the first place—confusion. [C.N. Ronning]

8708. Bedregal, Guillermo. Integración defensiva de América Latina: algunos aspectos. La Paz, Editorial Los Amigos del Libro, 1972. 62 p.

Gives the reasons why economic integration is essential for Latin America but no indication of how it is to be carried out. [C.N. Ronning]

8709. Behrman, Jack N. Conflicting constraints on the multinational enterprise: potential for resolution. N.Y., Council of the Americas *in cooperation with the fund for Multinational Management Education,* 1974. 109 p.

Exceptionally lucid discussion of the actual and potential home-state and host-state constraints on multinational enterprises. Behrman suggests that the multinationals can justify themselves best by addressing problems that are not resolvable at the national level—coproduction activities, regional development programs, increasing the mobility of industries, introducing new products tailored to an LDC environment, etc. [Y. Ferguson]

8710. Bosc, Robert. América Latina y la política internacional. Bogotá, Centro de Investigación y Acción Social (CIAS) [and] Instituto de Doctrina y Estudios Sociales, 1971. 56 1. (Col. Documento de trabajo, 7)

A Jesuit examines several contemporary doctrines relating to war, peace, and national development. The work is of interest both from the point of view of analysis and as an example of the position of Catholic churchmen. [C.N. Ronning]

8711. Branco, Miguel do Rio. Pan-Americanismo: alguns marcos de sua evolução (IHGB/R, 292, julho/set. 1971, p. 190-200)

Rather romantic interpretation of Pan-Americanism and the Monroe Doctrine. [C.N. Ronning]

8712. Carrère, Bernard. Le développement du Tiers Monde: *partnership* ou guérilla? (UP/TM, 13:51, juillet/sept. 1972, p. 519-530)

Carrère views the energy crisis as just one of several indications that confrontation rather than "partnership" will characterize the relations between the developed and less-developed countries in the years ahead. As he sees it, this is basically an inevitable and "healthy" trend. [Y. Ferguson]

8712a. Cheston, T. Stephen and **Bernard Loeffke.** Aspects of Soviet policy toward Latin America. N.Y., MSS Information Corporation, 1974. 147 p., bibl., illus., maps, plates, tables.

Introduces student and specialist to many questions concerning relations between the Soviet Union and Latin America. Includes, among other topics, aspects of communist theory and practice as applied to Latin America; characteristics of the revolutionary process; a survey of communist parties; and factors in Soviet policy formulation. This is a welcome and much needed contribution to the field of Soviet-Latin American relations. Also contains an interesting appendix of biographical sketches of major Soviet figures who determine the USSR's foreign policy. [G.M. Dorn]

8713. Cobbledick, James R. Choice in American foreign policy: options for the future. N.Y., Thomas Y. Crowell, 1973. 282 p., bibl.

The final chapter is devoted to Latin America and presents four options for US policy in that area. They are: 1) to make Latin America a firm sphere of US influence; 2) pursue security in this area by working for the establishment of democracy in the area; 3) keep Latin America in the Security Zone but not prescribe solutions for internal problems; and 4) nonintervention and cooperation. The arguments for each option are given, and the reader is apparently left to select his choice. [C.N. Ronning]

Cochrane, James D. U. S. policy toward recognition of governments and promotion of democracy in Latin America since 1963. See *HLAS 36:1685.*

8714. Combs, Jerald A. Nationalist, realist, and radical: three views of American diplomacy. N.Y., Harper & Row, 1972. 526 p.

Highly interesting and provocative juxtaposition of readings showing the way in which a number of writers, characterized as realists, radicals or nationalists, have interpreted general and specific aspects of US foreign policy. All of the selections are indirectly relevant to the study of US-Latin American relations, and a number of them are directly related—such as those dealing with the Monroe Doctrine, the Mexican War, the Spanish American War, and Manifest Destiny. [C.N. Ronning]

8715. Conference on the Western Hemisphere, *N.Y., 1971.* Issues for the 1970's. N.Y., Center for Inter-American Relations, 1971. 138 p.

Papers presented at a conference convened at the Center for Inter-American Relations in 1971. Of particular interest are the following:
Fernando Henrique Cardoso "Political Systems and Social Pressures in Latin America in the 1970 Decade" p. 29-53
Colin I. Bradford, Jr. "Employment, Growth and Industrialization in Future Development Strategies" p. 67-83
Sergio Bitar "The Multinational Corporation and Relations Between Latin America and the United States" p. 85-104
David Bronheim "Relations among the Countries of the Western Hemisphere in the 1970's" p. 107-121.
[Y. Ferguson]

8716. Cotler, Julio and **Richard R. Fagen** *eds.* Latin America and the United States: the changing political realities. Stanford, Calif., Stanford Univ. Press, 1974. 417 p., tables.

Important collection of essays and commentaries deriving from a conference held in 1972 at the Institute of Peruvian Studies in Lima, jointly sponsored by the Social Science Research Council (SSRC) and the American Council of Learned Societies (ACLS). Contributors include many of the major scholars in the field from both Latin America and the US, although (not surprisingly) the selections are of varying quality. More significant, as Cotler and Fagen recognize in their perceptive introduction (alone worth the price of the book), is the fact that what emerges from the collection is far from a unified view. Two macro-models of US-Latin American relations completed at Lima: a Latin American "dependency" model and a North American "liberal" paradigm. At issue here were nothing less than "conflicting perspectives on the meaning of knowledge, understanding, and explanation in the social sciences" and on "the meaning of change in concrete policies." North Americans felt most comfortable with case studies of "bureaucratic politics," and they discerned significant changes in US policies over time. Latin Americans, in contrast, tended to view US policies as all-of-a-piece, evidencing great continuity. [Y. Ferguson]

8717. Dexter, Byron *ed.* and *comp.* The foreign-affairs 50-year bibliography: new evaluations of significant books in international relations, 1920-1970. With the assistance of Elizabeth H. Bryant and Janice L. Murray. N.Y., R.R. Bowker *for the* Council on Foreign Relations, 1972. 936 p.

Includes new brief reviews of circa 100 basic books on inter-American relations, Latin America in general, and particular countries in the region. Regrettably, a number of the included titles have not borne well the test of time, and articles were outside the scope of the bibliography. [Y. Ferguson]

8718. Diniz, Arthur J. Almeida. A ONU e a realidade internacional (UMG/RBEP, 36, julho 1973, p. 83-103, bibl.)

The real significance of the UN must be evaluated not in terms of its power to crush any attempt against peace but in its search for techniques for dynamic development. [C.N. Ronning]

8719. Dos Santos, Theotonio. La crisis norteamericana y América Latina. Bogotá, Ediciones El Tigre de Papel, 1972. 186 p.

Significant work by a leading "Marxist" theorist of "dependence." Although Dos Santos is clearly skeptical of "reformist" governments and desirous of socialist revolutions to shatter the old order decisively, he concludes that what can be accomplished in practice will depend upon the balance of political forces in individual countries. [Y. Ferguson]

8720. _____. Imperialismo y empresas multinacionales. B.A., Editorial Galerna, 1973. 138 p.

Highly critical and sophisticated—if somewhat doctrinaire—analysis of the multinationals. Dos Santos argues that what he terms the "new international division of labor" created by these enterprises, far from saving capitalism from its "final crisis," in fact makes the crisis more profound. [Y. Ferguson]

Douglas, William O. Holocaust of hemispheric co-op: cross currents in Latin America. See *HLAS 36:1688*.

Dozer, Donald Marquand. Are we good neighbors?: three decades of inter-American relations, 1930-1960. See *HLAS 36:1689*.

8721. _____. The challenge to Pan Americanism. Tempe, Arizona State Univ., Center for Latin American Studies, 1972. 24 p., plate (Alberdi-Sarmiento award lecture series)

So far as inter-American relations are concerned the US "will do enough if it will only cease to do the wrong things. It can do more than it is now doing for Latin America by doing less." So far as Latin America is concerned, its ills "can only be cured and its problems solved by the establishment there of open societies." [C.N. Ronning]

8722. Einaudi, Luigi R. Latin America's development and the United States (*in* Einaudi, Luigi R. *ed.* Beyond Cuba: Latin America takes charge of its future. N.Y., Crane, Russak, 1974, p. 209-228)

Einaudi points to "increased institutional development and sophistication" in Latin America today, which has contributed to something of a decline in traditional dictatorships, oligarchies, and political instability; and he reviews recent US policies toward the region. He laments the fact that, although "the decline of the 'Western Hemisphere ideal' is complete," no "new vision" has evolved to replace it. Without such a vision, he warns, "we shall... simply stumble along together in interdependent—but separate—ways." [Y. Ferguson]

8723. _____. A note on U.S. government exchange programs (*in* Einaudi, Luigi R. *ed.* Beyond Cuba: Latin America takes charge of its future. N.Y., Crane, Russak, 1974, p. 201-206)

Noting the changing environment in which exchange must take place, the author argues for professional and nonpartisan programs that will go beyond the traditional foci of the arts to encourage a "dialogue" between the "modern sectors and institutions of Latin America and the United States." [Y. Ferguson]

8724. _____; **Hans Heymann, Jr.; David Ronfeldt; and Cesar Sereseres.** Arms transfers to Latin America: toward a policy of mutual respect. A report prepared for Department of State. Santa Monica, Calif., Rand, 1973. 79 p., tables.

From the summary: "This report documents recent changes in arms transfer patterns; explores the political, economic, and military forces of international supply and Latin American demand that bear on U.S. competitiveness; focuses on the relationship between arms transfers and U.S. interests; and suggests some possible guidelines for future arms transfers in the changing international environment." The authors propose a new US policy of unrestricted but also unsubsidized military sales. The report contains a great deal of hard-to-find information, including (in the appendices) a list of principal legislative restrictions and procedures governing foreign military sales. For political scientist's comment see item   . [Y. Ferguson]

8725. Las empresas multinacionales y la política social. B.A., Librería Hachette, 1974. 198 p.

Background study and report, emanating from an International Labor Organization conference held in Geneva in late 1972, focuses on the implications of the multinational corporation for labor. [Y. Ferguson]

8726. Espinosa García, Manuel. La política económica de los Estados Unidos hacia América Latina entre 1945 y 1961. La Habana, Casa de las Américas, 1971. 194 p., bibl., tables.

A Peruvian writer sets out to show that between 1945 and 1961 Latin American dependence on the US became institutionalized, that is, it pervaded all aspects of life and was duly sanctioned and ratified by international treaties. The domestic forces which conditioned US policy are emphasized. [C.N. Ronning]

8727. *Estudios Internacionales.* Asociación Latinoamericana de Ex-Alumnos de la Academia de Derecho Internacional de La Haya. No. 1, 1971- Bogotá.

A new journal initiated by the Latin American Association of the Hague Academy of International Law. Articles in this issue focus on various legal questions concerning the OAS, the UN, LAFTA, and the Andean Pact. The constitution of the Association is reprinted. [Y. Ferguson]

8728. Fagen, Richard R. The "New Dialogue" on Latin America (SO. 11:6, Sept/Oct. 1974, p. 17, 24-26, 28, 30)

Skeptical analysis of Kissinger's "new" policies unveiled in the context of OAS foreign ministers meetings in 1974, followed by the author's own eminently sensible proposals for a *real* reorientation in US relations with Latin America. [Y. Ferguson]

8729. Fajnzyller, Fernando and others. Corporaciones multinacionales en América Latina. B.A., Ediciones Periferia, 1973. 246 p., bibl. (Col. Estados Unidos y América Latina)

Collection of five essays on the "dependence" theme. Perhaps the most interesting is Susanne Jonas (Bodenheimer), "The Design and Manipulation of the Central American Common Market" (p. 177-246) translated into Spanish from the NACLA's *Latin America and Empire Report* (May/June 1973 issue). [Y. Ferguson]

8730. Fann, K.T. and **Donald C. Hodges** *eds*. Readings in U.S. imperialism. Boston, Mass., Porter Sargent Publisher, 1971. 397 p., bibl.

Well-chosen collection of readings drawn primarily from what might be loosely termed "Marxist" literature on "imperialism," "militarism," "dependence," etc. An excellent introduction to this school of thought, although less doctrinaire writings would be of more analytical value. Numerous selections of direct or indirect relevance to Latin America. [Y. Ferguson]

8730a. Ferguson, Yale H. An end to the "special relationship:" the United States and Latin America (Revista/Review/Interamericana [Hato Rey, P.R.) 2:3, Fall 1972, p. 352-387)

Examines closely the proclaimed "benign neglect" of the Nixon policies toward Latin America and finds variation in treatment of radical regimes (acceptance of Peru as opposed to hostility toward Chile and Cuba) and a preference for conservative military governments. Useful in characterizing overall design as well as details of US policy during 1968-72. Concluding prescriptive section advocates an "activist alternative" to present official passivity. [Ed.]

8731. ———. United States policy and political development in Latin America (RU/SCID, 7:2, Summer 1972, p. 156-180)

Author discusses a number of "cycles" in US policy relating to domestic politics in Latin America over the past four decades. He finds that, in spite of lip service to democracy and the nonintervention norm, policy makers have viewed the promotion of democracy as largely contrary to the security interests of the US. [C.N. Ronning]

8732. Foro internacional sobre la vigencia de los derechos humanos en América Latina. Montevideo, Univ. de la República, 1972. 195 p. (Col. Historia y cultura, 22)

These discussions were held prior to the military coups in Chile and Uruguay. They are interesting in several respects, especially in the attempt to discuss the problem of human rights in the broader framework of underdevelopment. The objectivity of most discussions, however, leaves much to be desired. One notes that only in socialist Cuba and Chile are there no problems of rights of labor. [C.N. Ronning]

8733. Frazão, Sergio Armando. La búsqueda del orden internacional: las relaciones del poder y los cambios que se vislumbran en el mundo de hoy (CM/FI, 13[52]:4, abril/junio 1973, p. 442-454)

Author sees the creation of international institutions and mechanisms that will promote development as the objective towards which emergent powers in the international system are working. [C.N. Ronning]

8734. Freitas, José João de Oliveira. Carta da Organização dos Estados Americanos. Pôrto Alegre, Bra., Livraria Sulina Editôra, 1973. 89 p., bibl. (Col. Manuais Sulina, 34)

Descriptive outline of the structure of the Organization of American States according to the revised (1967) charter. [C.N. Ronning]

Garcés, Juan E. Investigación social y logística político-militar en Iberoamérica. See *HLAS 36:1694.*

8735. García Velutini, Oscar. El asilo, lugar de protección. Caracas, n.p., 1972. 131 p., bibl.

Somewhat sketchy and anecdotal treatment of diplomatic asylum. [C.N. Ronning]

8736. Gardner, Lloyd C. *ed.* American foreign policy, present to past: a narrative with readings and documents. N.Y., The Free Press *a division of* Macmillan, 1974. 366 p., tables (Urgent issues in American society series)

A prominent Rutgers historian offers a historical narrative, interspersed with readings and documents, of US foreign policy since World War II. His narrative proceeds from present to past, in an attempt to emphasize the Cold War roots of current policies. Watershed events in US-Latin America relations are included, although—because of the broad scope of the study—they are treated rather superficially. [Y. Ferguson]

8737. Gebhardt, Hermann P. Machtverlagerungen in Lateinamerika (AZIF, 22:12, Dez. 1971, p. 746-753)

Overview of recent political developments ("shifting forces") in South America and Latin American relations with Western Europe, Washington, Moscow, and Peking. [Y. Ferguson]

8738. González, Heliodoro. Public safety in Latin America: "State of Siege" (IAMEA, 27:3, Winter 1973, p. 87-96)

A defender of the US public-safety assistance program draws rather unconvincingly on excerpts from congressional hearings, in an attempt to make his point that "professional liberals" have based their negative assessment of the program on "foreign propaganda." [Y. Ferguson]

8739. Goure, Leon and Morris Rothenberg. Soviet penetration of Latin America. Coral Gables, Fla., Univ. of Miami, Center for Advanced International Studies, 1975. 204 p., tables (Monographs in international affairs)

Soviet images of contemporary Latin America, gleaned by the authors mainly from official pronouncements. Discussions of the USSR's relations with Cuba (continued strains likely); Soviet views on "progressive" military regimes (largely favorable and on the rise and fall of Allende (Allende erred by alienating the middle strata); and Soviet activities in Latin America generally. According to the authors, "Moscow's current prognosis for Latin America continues to be optimistic," despite the resurgence of conservative militarism in the region and differences between Soviet and Latin policies on matters like the law of the sea. The Soviets expect that the present economic crisis confronting the West will "sharpen the contradictions and rivalries between capitalist states and between them and the less-developed countries, as well as intensify the class struggle within the particular countries and on a global scale." [Y. Ferguson]

Gray, Richard B. *ed.* and *comp.* Latin America and the United States in the 1970's. See *HLAS 36:1698.*

8740. Green, María del Rosario. Las relaciones de Estados Unidos y América Latina en el marco de la dependencia (CM/FI, 13:3, enero/marzo 1973, p. 327-347)

"Panorama" of current relations between the US and Latin America in the context of "dependence." The author maintains that—aside from Cuba, Chile (under Allende), and Peru—most Latin American governments are doing little to change the prevailing pattern. There is no mention of (albeit somewhat less dramatic) rising economic nationalism in such countries as Venezuela and Mexico. [Y. Ferguson]

8741. Gurtov, Melvin. The United States against the Third World: antinationalism and intervention. N.Y., Praeger Publishers, 1974. 260 p., bibl.

Gurtov asserts that "there exists a consensus about America's role in the world that amounts to an ideology"—the "doctrine of national interest" that links "domestic tranquility" with a US "mission" to maintain "security and stability" abroad, if necessary by military intervention. He presents four case studies drawn from successive administrations (Eisenhower through Nixon), including one on "Johnson and Latin America." This reviewer would question his interpretation that the "assertion of Dominican nationalism, not communism, was Washington's first concern" in the 1965 crisis. His distinction between fear of "extremists" and of "communists" was one that Johnson policy-makers simply did not make at the time. Gurtov advocates a policy of strict nonintervention for the US in his concluding chapter. The reader might have a query, which the author does not attempt to answer: has the consensus supporting interventions been significantly eroded since Vietnam? [Y. Ferguson]

8742. Hagan, Kenneth J. American gunboat diplomacy and the old Navy: 1877-1889. Westport, Conn., Greenwood Press, 1973. 262 p., bibl., map (Contributions in military history, 4)

Hagan, a naval historian, makes an effective case that "gunboat diplomacy" attitudes, which most associate with the post-Mahan era, were present even in an earlier, supposedly "isolationist" period in US history. There are two chapters on US involvement in Panama; however, chapters on other regions suggest that policies in the Western Hemisphere were part of an evolving conception of US strategic and commercial interests worldwide. [Y. Ferguson]

Hawkins, Carroll. Two democratic labor leaders in conflict: the Latin American Revolution and the role of the workers. See *HLAS 36:1699.*

8743. Herman, Donald L. *ed.* The communist tide in Latin America: a selected treatment. Austin, The Univ. of Texas at Austin, 1973. 215 p., illus., plates.

Despite a title that might have graced either a John Birch Society or a Marxist publication, this is a useful collection of scholarly essays on various aspects of Communism in Latin America. Accounts are primarily factual rather than theoretical in orientation—for example, J.W.F. Dulles traces the activities of the Brazilian left from 1964-70. The editor advances a proposition with which few could quarrel, that the "alternatives" to "Communism" in the area seem to be more varied than many would have predicted some years ago. [Y. Ferguson]

8744. Ianni, Octávio. Diplomacia e imperialismo na América Latina. São Paulo, Centro Brasileiro de Análise e Planejamento, 1973. 98 p. (Cadernos CEBRAP, 12)

Discussion of US imperialism and Latin American dependence that is a curious cross between a sophisticated analysis and an old-fashioned polemic. Subtle and heavy-handed by turns. A slightly abbreviated, English version of this monograph appears in item 8716, p. 23-51. [Y. Ferguson]

8745. _____. Imperialismo na América Latina. Rio, Editôra Civilização Brasileira, 1972. 181 p. (Col. Documentos da história contemporânea, 58)

In the preface the author states that his purpose is to study the relationships between internal and external conditions in the Latin American countries. It might better be stated as a study of the instruments and techniques with which the US influences the internal affairs of Latin American countries. [C.N. Ronning]

8746. Iglesia A., Juan F. de la. Breves anotaciones histórico-políticas sobre la intervención militar en América Latina. Bogotá, Univ. Javeriana, Facultad de Ciencias Jurídicas y Socio Económicas, 1973. 91 p., bibl.

Brief historical summary of military interventions in Latin American politics and of the reasons usually given to explain this. Does not offer any new insights. [C.N. Ronning]

Jordan, David C. Perón's return, Allende's fall and communism in Latin America. See item 8059.

Journal of Inter-American Studies and World Affairs. See *HLAS 36:1494.*

Kane, William Everett. Civil strife in Latin America: a legal history of U.S. involvement. See *HLAS 36:1702.*

8747. Kanet, Roger E. *ed.* The Soviet Union and the developing nations. Baltimore, Md., The Johns Hopkins Univ. Press, 1974. 302 p., tables.

A generally excellent collection of scholarly essays. Of most direct relevance to Latin America is Roger Hamburg's "The Soviet Union and Latin America" (p. 179-213). Hamburg's is a well-documented survey of Soviet policies in the late 1960s and early 1970s, including the Kremlin's assessment of Allende's electoral victory in Chile and the emergence of a "leftist" military-government in Peru. [Y. Ferguson]

8747a. Kannapin, Klaus. Zur politik der BRD gegenüber Südamerika (GDRMK/ZE, 24:8/9, 1972, p. 324-330, tables)

Marxian critique of West Germany's imperialistic foreign policy vis-à-vis Latin America. [H.J. Hoyer]

8748. Kissinger, Henry A. "Good Partner" policy for the Americas (SO, 11:6, Sept./Oct. 1974, p. 16-18, 21-22)

Text of the address delivered by the Secretary of State to the General Assembly of the OAS, Atlanta, Ga., April 20, 1974. [Y. Ferguson]

8749. Krause, Walter. The implications of UNCTAD III for multinational enterprise (UM/JIAS, 15:1, Feb. 1973, p. 46-59)

Author discusses the nature of criticism against multinational enterprises at UNCTAD III and suggests a possible course of action in the light of these criticisms and other factors. [C.N. Ronning]

8749a. Kumanev, Georgii Aleksandrovich. Amerikanskaia politika "Novykh Rubezhei" v Latinskoi Amerike: 1961-1971 (The American policy of the "New Frontier" in Latin America: 1961-1971). Moskva, Nauka, 1972. 196 p., bibl.

Describes the Alliance for Progress goal of preventive revolution as a technique of imperialism to stop genuine "national liberation." The success of Cuba and the election of Allende are pointed to as symbols of the failure of New Frontier policies. [T.S. Cheston]

8750. Lebedinsky, Mauricio. América Latina en la encrucijada de la década del 70. B.A., Ediciones Centro de Estudios, 1971. 198 p., tables.

Writing before the fall of the Allende government in Chile, the author surveys current-day Latin America and concludes from the vigor of the left in several countries that the region is on the brink of its "second revolution." [Y. Ferguson]

8751. Lentin, Albert-Paul. Punta del Este y Boinas Verdes (UES/U, 93:5, sept./oct. 1968, p. 81-99)

Argues that relations between Latin America and the US as well as the situation of inequality and dominance has actually worsened since the first conference at Punta del Este in 1961. There are many factual errors in the article. [C.N. Ronning]

8752. Lima, Francisco Roberto. El principio de no intervención en el derecho internacional de América Latina (UES/U, 93:5, sept./oct. 1968, p. 27-39)

Reviews the major steps and documents in the establishment of the doctrine of nonintervention. Sees *detante* and the establishment of spheres of influence by the USSR and the US as a major threat to the doctrine. [C.N. Ronning]

8753. Lineberry, William P. The Americas: Left and Right take center state (*in* Lineberry, William P. The United States in world affairs: 1970. N.Y., Simon & Schuster *for the* Council on Foreign Relations, 1972, p. 181-207, map)

A not-particularly profound survey of developments in Latin America and US policy in 1970, which is useful mainly as a reference source for names and dates. [Y. Ferguson]

8754. Lowenthal, Abraham F. United States policy toward Latin America: liberal, radical, and bureaucratic perspectives (LARR, 8:3, Fall 1973, p. 3-25)

Lowenthal outlines three views purporting to explain the "failure" of the Alliance for Progress: 1) the "liberal" view, that stresses the "supposed discontinuities and contradictions between the aims of American policy, specific American actions, and their consequences; 2) the "radical" view, that also sees the US Government as acting "rationally," but in singleminded support of the interests of American business; and 3) the "bureaucratic politics" view, that argues goals originally conceived rationally were ultimately perverted in the process of implementation by various sub-units of the government. He argues the utility of the bureaucratic model. Nevertheless, he recognizes: "Generally accepted values, images, and premises set some of the parameters for United States foreign policy, and explication of all these should be central for foreign policy analysis." The difference in perspectives calls to mind the Introduction to the Cotler and Fagen collection (see item 8716), which, in fact, includes the Lowenthal essay. [Y. Ferguson]

8755. Luna Tobar, Alfredo. La doctrina marítima latinoamericana. Quito, Industrias Gráficas CYMA, 1972. 157 p.

Survey of the legal history of the 200-mile doctrine. Appended are the major Latin American resolutions and national laws regarding territorial waters. [Y. Ferguson]

8756. McGrath, Marcos G. ¿Ariel or Caliban? (CFR/FA, 52:1, Oct. 1973, p. 75-95)

The Archbishop of Panama reflects on change in rural Panama, the contemporary role of the Church in Latin America, and US Latin American policies. He states: "If [US] business interests, rather than the demands of justice and peace between peoples, continue to determine the relations of the entire nation toward Latin America, there are much darker days ahead." [Y. Ferguson]

8757. Mader, Julius. Los nuevos conquistadores: penetración imperialista germanooccidental en América Latina. 2. ed. Bogotá, Editorial Colombia Nueva, 1971. 145 p., plate, tables.

The book is supposedly intended to show West German economic penetration of Latin America since World War II. In fact, however, it presents a curious mixture of pre- and post-World War II penetration, no doubt to show that West Germany is continuing in the tradition of capitalist and Nazi Germany. The reader is reminded, however, that there is also a Democratic German Republic which helps to assure peace and pursues friendship among peoples. [C.N. Ronning]

8758. Mastrorilli, Carlos P. Dinámica del poder en el mundo moderno. B.A., Editorial Pleamar, 1973. 211 p.

A treatise which is the "Marxist" equivalent of an introduction to a political science text. [Y. Ferguson]

8759. Murray, D.R. Canada's first diplomatic missions in Latin America (UM/JIAS, 16:2, May 1974, p. 153-172, bibl.)

When Canada entered World War II, that country established diplomatic missions in the ABC states; a Canadian trade delegation successfully toured several South American countries in 1941; and that same year Canada made an abortive application to join the Pan American Union (which the US opposed). Murray's contention is that these initiatives were very much the product of special circumstances prevailing at the time and that Canada's interest in the inter-American system proved to be largely an "illusion." After the war Canada again looked back to Western Europe and the Commonwealth. [Y. Ferguson]

8760. Nálevka, Vladimír. El Acuerdo de Munich y la América Latina (UCP/IAP, 6, 1972, p. 111-126)

A leading Czech historian examines the reception of the fall of Czechoslovakia in Latin America, concluding that it served to harden anti-Nazi sentiment at a critical juncture in the evolution of an inter-American posture toward the European war. [Y. Ferguson]

8761. _____. Ceskoslovensko a Latinská Amerika v letech druhé svetové války. Praha, Univ. Karlova, 1972. 160 p. (Acta Universitatis Carolinae. Philosophica et historica monographia, 40/1971)

Another version of an earlier article (see item 8763). Nálevka concludes: "Full diplomatic recognition of the Czechoslovak Government in Exile not only thwarted on an international scale the plans of the nazis, who intended to liquidate Czechoslovak independence, but was directed also against post-Munich conceptions which regarded the revival of the Czechoslovak state merely as one of the alternatives in the post-war arrangement of Central Europe." [Y. Ferguson]

8762. _____. El Consorcio de Bata en América Latina durante la Segunda Guerra Mundial (UCP/IAP, 5, 1971, p. 183-191)

A fascinating footnote to history: the World War II machinations of Czech entrepreneur Jan A. Bata, who owned a network of companies in Latin America and cooperated with the Germans. [Y. Ferguson]

8763. _____. Restablecimientos de relaciones diplomáticas entre el gobierno checoslovaco en el exilio y los países de América Latina (UCP/IAP, 2, 1968, p. 93-113)

Interesting account, based on Czech archival materials, of the relations between the Czech government in exile and Latin American governments during the Second World War. [Y. Ferguson]

8764. Needler, Martin C. New directions for our Latin American policy (YU/YR, 60:3, March 1971, p. 333-341)

Needler urges US policy-makers to abandon their traditional fears of Communism/Castroism and their optimism about the "modernizing military" in Latin America. Instead, Needler maintains, Washington should support "political development" in the region, which he defines as "the growth in the capacity of institutions" to encourage popular participation "in keeping with liberal and democratic values." [Y. Ferguson]

8765. Nelson, Michael A. Soviet policy in Latin America (AF/AUR, 24:1, Nov./Dec. 1972, p. 26-33)

Brief discussion of Soviet policies in the region since the Castro Revolution, of interest principally because the article derived from a paper prepared by a US Air Force major as part of his work at the Air Command and Staff College. Echoing other observers, Nelson concludes that the Soviets' main objective now is to encourage Latin American autonomy from the US and that they are increasingly pragmatic in pursuit of this end. [Y. Ferguson]

8766. Nieto Navia, Rafael. La doctrina de Monroe. Bogotá, Ediciones Americanas, 1962. 93 p., bibl.

A curiosity indeed—a Latin American polemic extolling the virtues of the Monroe Doctrine! The author is a professor of international law at the Univ. Javeriana de Bogotá. [Y. Ferguson]

8767. Organization of American States. Asamblea General. Actas y Documentos. v. 1, Textos certificados de las resoluciones y otros documentos; v. 2, Actas de las sesiones. Washington, 1970. 2 v. (143, 1086 p.) (OEA/Ser. P/1-E. 1/2)

V. 1 contains the texts of the resolutions and other documents, and v. 2, the full text of the acts of the First Special Session of the OAS General Assembly meeting, under the revised OAS charter in Washington, D.C., June 25 to July 8, 1970. [C.N. Ronning]

8768. ———. Secretaría General. Informe de progreso de los programas y proyectos en ejecución por la Secretaría General en ejercicio 1970/71 al 31 de marzo de 1971, Washington, 1971. 1 v. (Various pagings) tables (AG/RES. 18, I-E/70)

These volumes of detailed information are perhaps the best index of the nature and extent of the economic, social, juridical and technical activities of the OAS. [C.N. Ronning]

8769. ———. Secretaria Geral. Comissão Interamericana de Direitos Humanos. Relatório sobre o trabalho realizado pela Comissão Interamericana de Direitos Humanos no vigésimo sétimo período de Sessões. Washington, 1972. 67 p. (OEA/Ser. L/V/II.27 doc. 42 rev. 1)

Contains information on several cases of violation of human rights pending against a number of governments. [C.N. Ronning]

8770. Ornstein, Roberto M. La desnuclearización de América Latina (IAEERI/E, 2:9, enero/feb. 1971, p. 81-92, map)

Brief but competent analysis of the Nuclear Non-Proliferation Treaty for Latin America (the Treaty of Tlatelolco). Emphases are on the provisions rather than on their implications and consequences. [C.N. Ronning]

8771. Orrego Vicuña, Francisco. El control de las empresas multinacionales (CM/FI, 14[53]:1, julio/sept. 1973, p. 106-128)

Sketching the challenge presented by the multinational corporation to autonomous national development, the author proceeds to examine the potential and limitations of various unilateral, regional, and global mechanisms of control. [Y. Ferguson]

8772. Packenham, Robert A. Liberal America and the Third World: political development ideas in foreign aid and social science. Princeton, N.J., Princeton Univ. Press, 1973. 395 p. bibl.

A major work that should be required reading for all students of US Latin American policies. Packenham (following Louis Hartz) finds a "coherent liberal tradition" implicit in the political development "doctrines" and "theories" advanced in US official policies and by academics, respectively. However, the four assumptions that he identifies as the essence of "Liberalism" are to some extent internally inconsistent, and his analysis does not entirely explain why some of these assumptions (rather than others of the same) have been dominant over time nor the significant policy variations between administrations. If one is stressing similarities rather than differences, this reviewer would argue, an excessive preoccupation with security coupled with "pragmatism" is a better characterization of the orientation of US policy-makers. Nevertheless, Packenham's is a very thought-provoking thesis, and he presents it persuasively. Considering the diversity in the Third World and what he believes are the ambiguous dictates of morality, Packenham prescribes, the US ought "to worry more about how to avoid mistakes of commission than about how to correct those of omission." [Y. Ferguson]

8773. Parkinson, F. Latin America, the Cold War and the world powers: 1945-1973, a study in diplomatic history. Beverly Hills, Calif., Sage Publications, 1974. 288 p., bibl. (Sage library of social research)

A relatively straightforward diplomatic history of the postwar era, with emphasis on the Latin American side of international relationships, written by an English scholar. Better for reference than notable for its analysis; also, some curious gaps in research. For example, despite a plethora of footnotes in his chapters on the Bay of Pigs, the Cuban Missile Crisis, and the

1965 Dominican case, Parkinson never once cites most of the major works on these subjects. [Y. Ferguson]

8774. Pérez Concha, Jorge. Política internacional contemporánea. Guayaquil, Ecua., Univ. de Guayaquil, 1972. 224 p.

Historical survey of international politics, beginning with an analysis of the causes of World War I and concluding with the Japanese invasion of China in 1931. [C.N. Ronning]

8775. Perusse, Roland I. *ed.* Contemporary issues in inter-American relations. San Juan, P.R., North-South Press, 1972. 60 p.

Collection of nine speeches on Latin American affairs made in 1971—seven which were delivered at the Panel on Inter-American Understanding at the LXIII US National Governors Conference in San Juan, P.R.; and others by US State Dept. officials Nathaniel Samuels and Charles A. Meyer. Perhaps the most interesting is Claudio Veliz' assessment of the events that brought Allende to power in Chile and the internal policies of the Allende government. [Y. Ferguson]

8776. Petersen, Gustav H. Latin America: benign neglect is not enough (CFR/FA, 51:3, April 1973, p. 598-607)

The US should throw its full support behind an independent, united Latin America. We need a new direction and policy that can lead us out of the aimlessness of our present Latin American policy. [C.N. Ronning]

8777. Plan de trabajo para la elaboración de un modelo mundial. B.A.? Fundación Bariloche, 1971, 13 l.

The starting point is a model by an MIT group for projecting an image of the world 50 to 200 years from now. This brief outline merely sets up a "work plan" to elaborate an alternative model. Of interest as an example of work being done along these lines, apparently in Argentina. [C.N. Ronning]

8778. Quihillalt, Oscar A. Políticas extranjeras en centrales nucleares. B.A., Comisión Nacional de Energía Atómica, 1971. 28 p. (CNEA, 298)

General discussion of the history and importance of nuclear energy is followed by a country-by-country review of the number and size of nuclear reactors and some projections into the future. Surprisingly little attention is given to Argentina considering the fact that the author is an Argentine naval officer. [C.N. Ronning]

8779. Rancaño, Mario Ramírez. Imperialismo y sectores empresariales (UNAM/RMS, 35:3, julio/sept. 1973, p. 527-567, tables)

Argues that in order to explain the exploitation of Latin American countries we must move from an analysis of contradictions among countries to an analysis of associations or alliances among classes. Imperialism in Latin America is then analyzed in this way. [C.N. Ronning]

8780. Reunión de Consulta de la Organización Continental Latinoamericana de Estudiantes (OCLAE), *II, La Habana, 1971.* Documentos. La Habana. OCLAE, 1971? 31 p.

The II meeting of the Latin American Continental Organization of Students was held in Havana in Dec. 1971. This document contains the resolutions of that conference, most of them relating to events and conditions in other countries and expressing solidarity with revolutionary forces there. It tells us little about the meeting itself, what countries were represented or how many students were in attendance. [C.N. Ronning]

8781. The role of Japan in Latin America. N.Y., Council of the Americas, 1973. 19 l.

Brief essays discussing the Japanese commercial strategy and presence in Latin America, including the unique forms that Japanese investments have taken. [Y. Ferguson]

8782. Ronfeldt, David F. and **Luigi R. Einaudi.** Conflict and cooperation among Latin American states (*in* Einaudi, Luigi R., *ed.* Beyond Cuba: Latin America takes charge of its future. N.Y., Crane, Russak, 1974, p. 185-200)

Ronfeldt finds a "striking change in the world context of the Latin American countries," including a shift in the region's "value" to the US away from security toward energy and other economic considerations. The results, he projects, are likely to be increased cooperation as well as conflict between the Latin American states and a new flexibility in their dealings both with the outside world and among themselves. [Y. Ferguson]

8782a. Ronning, C. Neale. Human rights and humanitarian laws in the Western Hemisphere (NSSR/SR, 38:2, Summer 1971, p. 320-336)

Reviews principal legal attempts in Western Hemisphere to ensure humane treatment in civil strife. Targets for priority research: territorial asylum, guerrilla warfare, and personal responsibility of officials for government acts. [J.J. Bailey]

8783. Rosen, Steven J. Rightist regimes and American interests (SO, 11:6, Sept./Oct. 1974, p. 50-61, tables)

Rosen takes another look at the debate between "liberals" and "radicals" over the relative influence of economic factors in the pattern of US support for rightist regimes in the Third World. He concludes that such factors have not always been dominant but that they are likely to increase with future increases in multinational investment, since those governments pursuing basic social change also tend—with some exceptions—to be those least receptive to the multinationals.

However, this "liberal" reviewer remains unconvinced, partly because Rosen fails to perceive the full implications of one of his "ambivalent" cases, Peru—the possibility that new rules of the game may yet be found that are acceptable to both foreign companies and reformist governments. Moreover, he neglects an argument that might have strengthened his thesis, that a gradual downgrading of security considerations by US policy-makers now allows more attention to other concerns like protection of private interests. [Y. Ferguson]

8784. Ruiz-Eldredge, Alberto. El nuevo derecho del mar. Lima, Editorial Atenas, 1973. 70 p.

This little volume is essentially the text of the author's oral presentation (as a Peruvian member) before the Inter-American Juridical Committee on the territorial waters question. With some reservations, he approved the Comité Jurídico Interamericano's (CJI) declaration of Feb. 15, 1973, which is reprinted herein. [Y. Ferguson]

8785. Rupieper, Hermann J. John F. Dulles als Kritiker der Lateinamerikapolitik der USA (JGSWGL, 10, 1973, p. 365-374)

Tracing John Foster Dulles back to his participation in the US delegation to the Versailles peace conference in 1919, Rupieper maintains that Dulles always saw Latin America as essentially a backwater region for the US compared with Europe. [Y. Ferguson]

8786. Sampay, Arturo Enrique and others. Empresas multinacionales. B.A., Cuenca Ediciones, 1973. 262 p.

Collection of essays by various Argentine academics on the multinational corporation. Of most interest is Carlos M. Vilas' "Monopolies, Multinational Corporations and the Externalization of Society and the State in Argentina" (p. 21-119). [Y. Ferguson]

8787. Sanford, Charles L. ed. Manifest Destiny and the imperialism question. N.Y., John Wiley, 1974. 159 p., bibl. (Problems in American history)

Thoughtfully edited collection of readings focusing mainly on the 19th and early 20th centuries (there are three selections on the post-World War II era). Sanford allows prominent writers and public figures from each period to speak for themselves. [Y. Ferguson]

8788. Schiff, Bennett. The Inter-American Foundation's first three years: 1971-1973. Rosslyn, Va., Inter-American Foundation, 1973? 96 p., plates.

An attractive brochure summarizing the first three years of the program and grants of the Inter-American Foundation, a semi-private US Government corporation. The Foundation's mission has been to identify and assist local organizations in Latin America whose "experimental" programs may result in meaningful social change at the grass roots level. [Y. Ferguson]

8789. Seara Vázquez, Modesto. Zones of influence (*in* The Year Book of World Affairs 1973. London, Stevens, 1973, p. 301-315)

A modest attempt to develop a theory of "zones of influence," which in concrete terms (not surprisingly) assigns the Western Hemisphere to the US. [Y. Ferguson]

8790. Selser, Gregorio. Los cuatro viajes de Cristóbal Rockefeller con su informe al Presidente Nixon. B.A., Hernández Editor, 1971. 447 p., tables.

A bitter indictment of the Nixon Administration, Governor Rockefeller, and US policies generally. Selser is particularly incensed that Rockefeller seemed oblivious to the political repression in many of the countries he visited. Day-by-day excerpts from press accounts of the visits are reprinted, as well as the Rockefeller Report. [Y. Ferguson]

8791. ———. De la CECLA a la MECLA o la diplomacia panamericana de la zanahoria. B.A., Carlos Samonta Editor, 1972. 222 p.

A Latin American tract of the old school, which argues—it must be said, with considerable justification—that little has changed despite years of rhetoric about improving US-Latin American relations. Selser points to John Plank's "memorandum" (discussed by the Council on Foreign Relations in 1971 and subsequently leaked to the Press) as evidence that, if anything, the Nixon administration was even less interested in Latin America than its predecessors. Considering that Washington simply doesn't care, Selser insists, initiatives such as the Latin American Declaration of Viña del Mar are likely to fall on deaf ears. [Y. Ferguson]

8792. Seminario de la Integración Cultural de América Latina, *Guadalajara, Mex., 1970.* La integración cultural de América Latina [por] Antonio Leaño Alverez del Castillo and others. Guadalajara, Mex., Folio Universitario, 1970. 149 p., illus. (Folia universitaria, 10)

Papers presented at a Seminar on Cultural Integration of Latin America that was held at the Univ. Autónoma de Guadalajara, Mex. [Y. Ferguson]

8793. Sepúlveda, César. El sistema interamericano: mudanza y transición. Valladolid, Spain, Univ. de Valladolid, 1973. 129 p. (Cuadernos de la Cátedra J.B. Scott)

Written by a well-known Mexican professor of international law, a short history of the evolution of inter-American institutions from 1810 to the present. It is interesting mainly because its conclusions offer a contrast to those of a multitude of past studies of this type. Sepúlveda sees the regional system in a state of profound crisis, suffering—ever since the 1965 Dominican intervention—from "a lack of enthusiasm, incomprehension, Realpolitik, and myopia." [Y. Ferguson]

8794. Smetherman, Robert M. and **Bobbie B. Smetherman.** High visibility foreign aid: The Alliance for Progress (UU/WPQ, 24:1, March 1971, p. 52-54)

"High visibility projects exact a tremendous, and often unpredicted or ignored, cost in the national unity and resolve they give to developing areas. Such assistance is likely to be censured, both as the rhetoric inevitably fails to line up to its billing, and as we become more aware of the effects of modern technology on natural ecological balances." [C.N. Ronning]

8794a. Strany Sotsializma i Latinskai Amerika (The socialist countries and Latin America) (SSSR/LA, 2, marzo/abril 1975, p. 210-217)

A report of a conference of Latin American specialists from the Soviet Union and Eastern Europe held in Moscow on Latin America and the Socialist world. Reviews a wide range of subjects: 1) Latin America's trade with the Socialist countries and its "liberation" from "imperialist monopolies;" 2) attempts of Western companies to stifle this trade; 3) the growing importance of Latin America as a source of raw materials for Eastern Europe; and 4) competition among Eastern European countries for Latin American trade. [T.S. Cheston]

8795. Szymanski, Albert. Las fundaciones internacionales y América Latina (UNAM/RMS, 35:4, oct./dic. 1973, p. 801-817)

The author examines the programs of the Ford and Rockefeller foundations in Latin America. He alleges that—contrary to stated goals—the purpose of these private activities has been to maintain the countries involved in a state of underdevelopment. [Y. Ferguson]

8796. Testa, Víctor *comp.* Empresas multinacionales e imperialismo. B.A., Siglo XXI Argentina Editores, 1973. 210 p. (Historia inmediata)

Collection of essays that adds little to our knowledge about the multinationals but is worthy of note as yet another addition to the burgeoning Latin American literature on this subject. [Y. Ferguson]

8796a. Theberge, James D. The Soviet presence in Latin America. N.Y., Crane & Russak, 1974. 107 p., bibl., tables.

Condensed review of Soviet diplomacy in Latin America in the 1960s and 1970s, especially regarding developments in aid, trade, and espionage activities. Also discusses Soviet relations with Latin American communist parties and revolutionary movements and Soviet naval presence in the Caribbean. Special attention is given to Cuba, Chile, and Peru. [T.S. Cheston]

8797. United States. Congress. House of Representatives. Committee on Foreign Affairs. Inter-American relations: a collection of documents, legislation, descriptions of inter-American organizations, and other material pertaining to inter-American affairs. Washington, GPO, 1973. 778 p., facsims., tables (93d Congress, 1st Session)

An extremely valuable reference document—edited by Barry Sklar and Virginia Hagen of the Library of Congress' Congressional Research Service for the House Committee on Foreign Affairs—which supercedes another of the same title dated Oct. 10, 1972. Contains brief descriptions of inter-American organizations and agencies; texts of their charters; resolutions and declarations concerning key regional issues; US legislation on Latin American affairs (including sections devoted specifically to Mexico, Panama, and Cuba); and a list of treaties in force (as of Jan. 1, 1972) between the US and Latin American countries. [Y. Ferguson]

8798. ―――. Department of State. Office of Media Services. Bureau of Public Affairs. The inter-American relationship. Washington, GPO, 1974. 34 p. (Dept. of State publication, 8770. Inter-American series, 107)

Collection of US statements on hemisphere policy (Oct. 1973-April 1974). Includes (among other things) texts of the "principles" accepted for a new Panama Canal treaty and Kissinger's speeches at the Conference of Tlatelolco and the Atlanta OAS General Assembly. [Y. Ferguson]

8799. Vargas Carreño, Edmundo. América Latina y los problemas contemporáneos del derecho del mar. Santiago, Editorial Andrés Bello, 1973. 159 p., tables.

An extremely useful analysis by a well-known Chilean professor and jurist of the current legal controversies surrounding the law of the sea. The appendix includes the texts of the main resolutions emanating from various international meetings, as well as tables listing the claims of each Latin American state and its subscription (and non-subscription) to specific resolutions. [Y. Ferguson]

8800. Vernon, Raymond. Restrictive business practices: the operations of multinational United States enterprises in developing countries, their role in trade and development. N.Y., United Nations Conference on Trade and Development (UNCTAD), 1972. 26 p., tables (TD/B/399)

Study prepared for the UNCTAD Secretariat. Vernon surveys the pros and cons of multinational investment in the developing countries, with special attention to the probable consequences of alternative policies available to host governments. [Y. Ferguson]

8801. Villaverde, Juan. A year of meditation: the OAS General Assembly (OAS/AM, 25:5, May 1973, p. 10-16, plates)

A highly perceptive review and analysis of the issues

faced by the Third General Assembly of the OAS. Included are such issues as "plurality of ideologies," the Charter, the formation of an organization of Latin American States and the nature and character of Latin America's relations with the US. [C.N. Ronning]

8802. Wang, Chien-hsün. Changes in relations between Peiping and Latin American countries. Taipei, Republic of China, World Anti-Communist League, China Chapter [and] Asian Peoples' Anti-Communist League, 1973. 1 v. (Various pagings)

Although the publisher is the China Chapter of the World Anti-Communist League, this little pamphlet is a reasonably objective account of evolving relations between the People's Republic of China and Latin America. The author notes that, following a period of withdrawal during the Cultural Revolution, the Chinese Communists are again active in Latin America. However, this time they are less overtly "revolutionary" and (like the Soviets) more pragmatic in their efforts to establish ties with nationalist governments in the area. [Y. Ferguson]

8803. Weaver, Jerry L. Arms transfers to Latin America: a note on the contagion effect (JPR, 11:3, 1974, p. 213-219), bibl., tables)

Taking concurrent increases in defense expenditures between six pairs of rival South American states as the indicator, Weaver finds considerable evidence for the "contagion effect." In passing, he discusses current US arms policy and speculates about likely future patterns of arms transfers. [Y. Ferguson]

8803a. Wöhlcke, Manfred. Die Beziehungen zwischen Japan und Lateinamerika. Hamburg, FRG, Institut für Ibero-Amerika-Kunde, 1972. 129 p., tables.

Focuses on the economic relations of Japan and Latin America. While Latin American nations are increasingly looking toward closer trade relations with Japan, cultural contact has been limited. Most Japanese immigration to the area took place between 1900 and the beginning of World War II. Although they arrived in significant numbers and had important economic impact in various countries, Japanese have not been assimilated by Latin American culture. [H.J. Hoyer]

Yager, Joseph A. and others. Energy and U.S. foreign policy: a report to the Energy Policy Project of the Ford Foundation. See item 8133.

MEXICO

8804. Alcalá Quintero, Francisco. México y su relación con el Mercado Común Centroamericano (CM/FI, 14:2, oct./dic. 1973, p. 175-203, tables)

Careful examination of Mexico's relations with the Central American Common Market from its inception to the present. Author believes that the CACM is "irreversible" and that Mexican-CACM ties should and probably will expand over time. Interesting tables detailing Mexico's trade with the CACM and Mexican exports as a share of the CACM's imports of specific goods. [Y. Ferguson]

8805. Braun, Elisabeth. México y la 27a. sesión de la Asamblea General de las Naciones Unidas: desarrollos y respuestas (CM/FI, 14:2, oct./dic. 1973, p. 235-244)

As the title indicates, a survey of Mexican positions in the XXVII UN General Assembly held in the Fall of 1972. [Y. Ferguson]

8806. Documentos y comentarios en torno al viaje del Presidente Echeverría, marzo-abril de 1973 (CM/FI, 14[53]: 1, julio/sept. 1973, p. 1-53)

Brief accounts of the state visits which President Echeverría paid to Canada, the United Kingdom, Belgium, France, the Soviet Union, and the People's Republic of China in March-April, 1973. Includes joint communiques issued and treaties/protocols concluded enroute. Useful documents for those seeking to trace the diplomatic footsteps of this well-traveled head of state. [Y. Ferguson]

8807. Duque, Oliverio. Visita a cuatro países europeos: viajes del Presidente Luis Echeverría. Miniprólogo de Bernardo Ponce. México, Complejo Editorial Mexicano, 1973. 159 p., plates. (Col. Metropolitana)

A journalist's account of President Echeverría's 1973 trip to Austria, West Germany, Italy, and Yugoslavia and of the speeches he made enroute. [Y. Ferguson]

8808. *Estudios Internacionales.* UNAM, Centro de Relaciones Internacionales. Vol. 3, No. 1 (Nueva época) 1973- . México.

This issue is notable for two articles: Leticia V. Juárez González, "Foreign Investment in Mexico" (p. 9-29); and Carmen Piñera Hernández, "International Responsibility and the Case of the Salinity of the Colorado River" (p. 87-105). [Y. Ferguson]

8809. Fagen, Patricia W. Exiles and citizens: Spanish Republicans in México. Austin, Univ. of Texas Press *for* the Institute of Latin American Studies, 1973. 250 p., bibl.

This excellent study focuses especially on Spanish exiles who might be called professionals and intellectuals. Their adjustment to Mexico, their impact on that country's development, and their cultural relationship to Spain are the author's major concerns. In many ways, these exiles found Mexico ideal—or rather, a country that shared many of their ideals. They were, accordingly, able to incorporate themselves into most aspects of Mexican life. Yet, because they were not native-born Mexicans, they played little or no creative part in Mexican politics. [C.N. Ronning]

8810. Foro Internacional. El Colegio de México. Vol. 14, No. 4 [56] abril/junio 1974- . México.

An excellent example of the sophisticated work on international affairs being done at El Colegio de México, this "special issue" includes several articles on the recent foreign policy of Mexico:
Mario Ojeda Gómez "Introduction: the New Policies of Mexico toward Latin America" p. 433-437
Ramón Medina Luna "The Projection of Mexico into Central America" p. 438-473
Mario Ojeda Gómez "The Relations of Mexico with the Revolutionary Cuban Regime" p. 474-506
Carlos Arriola "The Mexican-Chilean Rapprochement" p. 507-547
Wolfgang König "Mexican Policies toward LAFTA and the Other Latin American Institutions of Economic Integration" p. 548-578
Romeo Flores Caballero "Mexico and the Andean Pact" p. 579-617. [Y. Ferguson]

8811. Foro International. El Colegio de México. Vol. 15, No. 1 [57] 1974- . México.

Of particular interest in this issue:
Jorge Castañeda "The Future World and Changes in International Political Institutions" p. 1-12
Manuel Tello "Some of the Problems That Will Have to be Resolved at the Upcoming Conference on the Law of the Sea" p. 53-71
Carlos Arriola "President Echeverría in Latin America" p. 103-115. [Y. Ferguson]

8812. García Robles, Alfonso. México en las Naciones Unidas. México, UNAM, Facultad de Ciencias Políticas y Sociales, 1970. 2 v. (302, 289 p.) (Serie: Estudios, 18/19)

Mexican legal positions on a variety of questions in the UN from 1945-70, discussed by a diplomat who had a leading role in formulating and articulating many of those positions. Texts of numerous proposed resolutions and the Treaty of Tlatelolco are appended. [Y. Ferguson]

Gilderhus, Mark T. Senator Albert B. Fall and "The Plot Against Mexico." See *HLAS 36:2117*.

———. The United States and Carranza, 1917: the question of de jure recognition. See *HLAS 36:2118*.

8813. Hill, Larry D. Emissaries to a revolution: Woodrow Wilson's executive agents in Mexico. Baton Rouge, Louisiana State Univ. Press, 1973. 394 p., bibl.

Well-documented account of the activities of 11 "executive agents" of President Wilson in Mexico "and the influence they exerted on Wilson's foreign policy and on the course of the Mexican Revolution" prior to the *de facto* recognition of Carranza's government in Oct. 1915. [Y. Ferguson]

8814. Horn, James J. Did the United States plan an invasion of Mexico in 1927? (UM/JIAS, 15:4, Nov. 1973, p. 454-471, bibl.)

Despite pressures for US intervention because of Mexican economic nationalism, Church-State conflict, and support for the Liberals in Nicaragua, Horn maintains that "circumstantial evidence and logic combine to suggest that the administration of Calvin Coolidge never seriously considered such a move and that rumors of intervention were founded more upon Mexican suspicion and mistrust than upon realities in Washington." [Y. Ferguson]

Ignasias, C. Dennis. Propaganda and public opinion in Harding's foreign affairs: the case for Mexican recognition. See *HLAS 36:2123*.

8814a. Mateo, Eligio de. México y el Pacto Andino (Economía Política [Instituto Politécnico Nacional, México] 9:4, 1972, p. 109-114)

Very brief recapitulation of events up to 1972 leading to the establishment of the Andean Group, and later negotiations and efforts to bring Mexico and Venezuela into closer trading and contractual linkage with the Group. [P.B. Taylor, Jr.]

8815. Mexico for Americans (*in* Lens, Sidney. The forging of the American empire. N.Y., Thomas Y. Crowell, 1971, p. 99-110)

Lens focuses on the background of the struggle for Texas independence from Mexico. He speculates, with others, that President Jackson might well have intervened had the Texans lost the battle of San Jacinto. But Lens closes with the observation that there would not have been a "Texas problem" without the spillover of population from the US, nor would annexation have taken place without the additional surge of expansionism under Tyler and Polk. [Y. Ferguson]

Meyer, Michael C. The arms of the *Ypiranga*. See *HLAS 36:2133*.

8816. Schmitt, Karl M. Mexico and the United States, 1821-1973: conflict and coexistence. N.Y., John Wiley, 1974. 288 p. (America and the world)

Short, well-documented, and eminently readable history of US-Mexican relations 1822-1973—the best general work on this subject currently available. [Y. Ferguson]

8817. Sepúlveda, César. México y el Club de Roma: hacia los nuevos horizontes internacionales. México, Complejo Editorial Mexicano, 1974. 141 p. (Col. Metropolitana, 26)

Discussion of Mexico's proposal for a UN-approved Charter of the Economic Rights and Duties of States and President Echeverría's address on this subject (text appended) before the Club of Rome, meeting in Salzburg in 1974. [Y. Ferguson]

8817a. Sizonenko, A.I. Sovetskii Soiuz I Meksika: 50 Let (The Soviet Union and Mexico: 50 years). Moskva, Mezhdurarodnye Otnosheniia, 1974. 90 p.

Written by the leading Soviet researcher on Soviet-Latin American relations, this useful work was commissioned to celebrate the golden anniversary of the establishment of relations between the USSR and Mexico. This is of special importance to Moscow as Mexico was the first Latin American country to recognize the Soviet Union. The book reviews the whole panorama of relations, emphasizing the points of unity in the foreign policies of the two countries such as "anti-imperialism" and tends to gloss over problem areas such as the break in relations in 1930 and the exposure of KGB activities in 1971. [T.S. Cheston]

8817b. Smith, Robert Freeman. The United States and revolutionary nationalism in Mexico: 1916-1932. Chicago, Ill., The Univ. of Chicago Press, 1972. 288 p., bibl.

A well-researched book based on documentary evidence found both in the US National and Mexican Archives; although in the latter case, the author says: "the records were screened before they were delivered to me." Not diplomatic history, but an analysis of the "confrontation between Mexican revolutionary nationalism and the national interests of the United States as they were defined by U.S. political and business leaders." The author concludes that financial, not oil, interests fared better during the confrontation. [A. Suárez]

8817c. Spota, Luis. El viaje. México, Editorial Joaquín Mortiz, 1973. 301 p., plates.

A Mexican journalist's account of President Echeverría's trip to Canada, England, Belgium, France, the USSR, and China in early 1973. Avoids details on the much publicized official acts in favor of an effort to place these in a broader context of the trip and to relate his own personal experiences and observations. Contains some interesting but poorly-reproduced photographs. [A. Suárez]

8818. Tello, Manuel. México: una posición internacional México, Joaquín Mortiz Editor, 1972. 205 p. (Cuadernos de Joaquín Mortiz)

The unfinished memoirs of a prominent Mexican who was his country's foreign minister from 1958-64, dictated in the last year of his life (1970-71). Even uncompleted, the book offers insights into the background of Mexican positions in the OAS from 1951-62 and several fragments of personal reminiscenses dating back to 1924. [Y. Ferguson]

CENTRAL AMERICA

8819. Aberastury, Marcelo and **Edith Sosa.** Análisis de un caso internacional: el conflicto entre El Salvador y Honduras (IAEERI/E, 2:10, marzo/abril 1971, p. 16-32, tables)

An examination of the various sources of tension between El Salvador and Honduras and the 1969 "Soccer War." [Y. Ferguson]

8820. Arroyo C., Dulio. El proyecto de tratado con los Estados Unidos de América concerniente a la construcción de un canal a nivel por territorio panameño (LNB/L, 182, enero 1971, p. 45-57)

Analysis of a draft treaty under negotiation that would provide for a new canal on Panamanian territory. The author suggests that consideration of this treaty should be suspended until it has been determined that both Panama and the US are firmly committed to the construction of such a canal. [Y. Ferguson]

8821. Blanco, Boris. El Canal de Panamá en la economía norteamericana (Anales de Ciencias Humanas [Univ. de Panama] 1, 1971, p. 17-28)

Blanco, affiliated with the Ministry of Foreign Relations in Panama, attempts to calculate "the economic benefits received by the United States from its privileged position in the Panama Canal." He concludes that—even ignoring military and strategic benefits—the original US investment in the Canal was amortized with interest by 1954. [Y. Ferguson]

8822. Busey, James L. Political aspects of the Panama Canal: the problem of location. Tucson, Univ. of Arizona, Institute of Government Research, 1974. 55 p., bibl., maps (Comparative government studies, 5)

Good survey of the Panama Canal problem to date, including recent negotiations and a discussion of possible alternative routes. Busey favors a canal across the Tehuantepec Isthmus in Mexico. [Y. Ferguson]

8823. Castillero Calvo, Alfredo. Transitismo y dependencia: el caso del Istmo de Panamá (LNB/L, 210, julio 1973, p. 17-40)

Brief "economic history" of Panama to show that its development since the time of Spanish domination has been different from that of other Latin American countries. Its productive activity, from the outset, has been selectively specialized in the sector of services for transit activities. [C.N. Ronning]

8824. Ferro, Carlos A. El caso de las islas Santanilla. 2. ed. Tegucigalpa, Oficina de Relaciones Públicas, 1972. 159 p.

Publication of the Government of Honduras, this volume offers a brief historical background and various documents and statements concerning the transfer by treaty of the Santanilla Islands (Islas del Cisne) from the US to Honduras in Nov. 1971. The treaty settled a longstanding "colonial" question. [Y. Ferguson]

8825. Fortín Magaña, Rene. El federalismo en Centroamérica (UES/U, 93:5, sept./oct. 1968, p. 41-52)

Useful for someone who wants a very brief outline of the most important steps in attempts at political and economic integration in Central America. [C.N. Ronning]

8826. Gardiner, C. Harvey. The Japanese and Central America (UM/JIAS, 14:1, Feb. 1972, p. 15-47, tables)

Comprehensive outline of Japanese-Central American relations from the early part of the century. Contacts have been almost totally economic in nature but might be going beyond this in the 1970s. For historian's comment, see *HLAS 36:2172*. [C.N. Ronning]

8827. González Sibrián, José Luis. Las 100 [i.e., cien] horas: la guerra de legítima defensa de la República de El Salvador. Prólogo del Ramón López Jiménez. San Salvador, Tipografía Offset Central, 1973? 404 p., maps, plates.

Detailed account of the 1969 "Soccer War" as seen from the El Salvador perspective, profusely illustrated and including several maps of the fighting. The narrative also incorporates diplomatic messages exchanged by the two sides and with the OAS. A very useful, though hardly "objective," source. [Y. Ferguson]

Grieb, Kenneth J. The United States and the rise of General Maximiliano Hernández Martínez. See *HLAS 36:2173*.

Huck, Eugene R. and **Edward H. Moseley** *eds*. Militarists, merchants and missionaries: United States expansion in Middle America. See *HLAS 36:2177*.

8828. Leonard, Thomas M. The commissary issue in American-Panamanian relations, 1900-1936 (AAFH/TAM, 30:1, July 1973, p. 83-109)

In a carefully documented article, Leonard reviews the lengthy dispute between the Panamanian government and Washington over the operations of the US commissary in the Canal Zone. As part of the Good Neighbor Policy, the Roosevelt Administration resolved the issue by treaty in 1936. [Y. Ferguson]

8828a. Leonov, Nikolai Sergeevich. Nekotorye problemy politicheskoi istorii Tsentral'noi Ameriki XX Stolettiia (Some problems in the political history of Central America in the twentieth century). Moskva, Izdatel'stvo Nauka, 1972. 253 p.

Discusses US interventions in Nicaragua from 1910-26; the activities of US banana companies in Central America; the impact of the Russian Revolution on the area's revolutionary movements; the Sandino revolt in Nicaragua in 1927-34; the military dictatorships of the 1930s and 1940s; and the "bourgeois-democratic" revolution in Guatemala, 1944-54. [T.S. Cheston]

8829. *Lotería*. Lotería Nacional de Beneficencia. No. 196, marzo 1972- . Panamá.

This issue contains several articles by Panamanian jurists on the subject of the ongoing negotiations over the status of the Canal. [Y. Ferguson]

8830. Pérez Venero, A., Jr. La posición de Panamá ante las Naciones Unidas (LNB/L, 202, sept. 1972, p. 24-40, bibl.)

Review of Panama's role in the founding of the UN and its positions in the world organization to 1959. [Y. Ferguson]

8831. *Revista de la Asociación Guatemalteca de Derecho Internacional*. Vol. 2, No. 1, enero 1971- Guatemala.

The annual publication of the Guatemalan Association of International Law. Articles are of something less than compelling interest. [Y. Ferguson]

8832. Ruiz-Eldredge, Alberto. La cuestión de Panamá. Lima, Ediciones Atenas, 1973. 98 p.

Brief legal history of the Panama Canal controversy. Half the book is devoted to reprinting major treaties and UN resolutions concerning the Canal. [Y. Ferguson]

8833. Souza, Rubén Darío; César A. de León; Hugo A. Víctor; and **Carlos F. Changmarin.** Panamá: 1903-1970; nación-imperialismo, fuerzas populares-oligarquía, crisis y camino revolucionario. Santiago, Talleres de la Sociedad Impresora Horizonte, 1970. 126 p.

Tract published in Chile by Panamanian communists, in homage to Lenin on the 100th anniversary of his birth. [Y. Ferguson]

8834. Testimonio de un diálogo universitario sobre la soberanía. Panamá, Ediciones Universitarias, 1971. 44 p., plates.

The proceedings of a "dialogue" conference held at the Univ. of Panama in 1971 on the subject of the negotiations between the US and Panama concerning a new Canal treaty. [Y. Ferguson]

8835. United States. Department of State. Office of Media Services. Bureau of Public Affairs. U.S. policy toward Panama: 1903-present; questions of recognition and diplomatic relations and instances of U.S. intervention. Washington, GPO, 1974. 12 p. (Dept. of State publication, 8763. Inter-American series, 106)

Brief chronology ("tabular summary") of the Panama Canal question 1903-72. Reprint from the *Department of State Bulletin,* April 22, 1974. [Y. Ferguson]

8836. Vallejo, Antonio R. Réplica al Dr. Santiago I. Barberena: la República de El Salvador no tiene ni nunca ha tenido documentos justificativos de poseer territorio hondureño. Comayagüela, Hon., Imprenta Cultura, 1970? 20 p.

An attempt to refute—as a means of bolstering the Honduran claim—the documentary evidence advanced by one Dr. Santiago I. Barberena in El Salvador, that El Salvador has legal title to a group of disputed islands in the Gulf of Fonseca. [Y. Ferguson]

8837. Vaughn, Jack Hood. A Latin American Vietnam (The Washington Monthly [Washington] 5:8, Oct. 1973, p. 30-38)

A former US Ambassador to Panama and Assistant Secretary of State warns that failure to resolve the "colonial" status of the Panama Canal is likely to have disastrous consequences. Especially interesting is Vaughn's discussion of some of the bureaucratic barriers to a settlement within the US Government. [Y. Ferguson]

CARIBBEAN

8838. Acosta Garrido, Mercedes and **Carlos María Vilas.** Santo Domingo y Checoslovaquia en la política de bloques (UPR/RCS, 16:2, junio 1972, p. 249-261, table)

The authors explore some of the resemblances between the 1965 Dominican intervention and the Soviet intervention in Czechoslovakia. [Y. Ferguson]

8839. Bender, Lynn Darrell. Guantánamo: its political, military and legal status (UWI/CQ, 19:1, March 1973, p. 80-86)

Bender sees Guantánamo's significance to the US as essentially political and utilitarian (as a training base) rather than strategic. In his view, some eventual modification of the base's status is probable, but only in the context of a general new US relationship with the Cuban government. [Y. Ferguson]

8840. Bhana, Surendra. The United States and the development of the Puerto Rican status question: 1936-1968. Lawrence, Univ. of Kansas Press, 1975. 290 p., bibl., tables.

Scholarly history of the status controversy from 1936-68. Bhana is obviously impressed by the ingenuity of Muñoz Marín's Commonwealth "solution," which the author believes can last if Puerto Rico is made completely self-governing. [Y. Ferguson]

8841. Bonsal, Philip W. Cuba, Castro and the United States. Pittsburgh, Pa., Univ. of Pittsburgh Press, 1971. 318 p., bibl., plates.

An analysis of the Cuban Revolution and of US-Cuba relations 1959-62 by the US Ambassador to Cuba (1959-60). Bonsal criticizes the "overreaction" of Washington, including the suspension of the sugar quota in 1960, as unnecessarily widening the rift between the two countries and driving Castro decisively into the Soviet camp. He foresees no real possibility of normalizing relations with Cuba as long as Castro remains in power. [Y. Ferguson]

Callahan, James Morton. Cuba and international relations: a historical study in American diplomacy. See *HLAS 36:2287.*

8842. Challener, Richard D. Admirals, generals, and American foreign policy: 1898-1914. Princeton, N.J., Princeton Univ. Press, 1973. 433 p.

A Princeton historian examines the contributions of military elites to the upsurge in US imperial designs in the Caribbean and the Far East from 1898-1914. From his research of hitherto underutilized primary sources, Challener concludes that generals and admirals were influential but that the "military mind" seemed to exist independently among civilian leaders as well. Incidentally, the author maintains that the record gives only partial support to "realist" and "New Left" interpretations of the period. [Y. Ferguson]

8843. Chayes, Abram. The Cuban Missile Crisis: international crises and the role of law. N.Y., Oxford Univ. Press, 1974. 157 p.

A case study of the role of law in decision-making under crisis conditions, by a principal architect of the US legal position in the 1962 crisis. Chayes concludes that, although law was not a dominant factor affecting decisions in this case, it definitely "played a part in defining and shaping" the options available to Kennedy and his advisers. [Y. Ferguson]

8843a. Ferguson, Yale H. The Dominican intervention of 1965: recent interpretations (WPF/IO, 27:4, Autumn 1973, p. 517-548)

State-of-the-literature piece based on eight articles and books by principal writers on Dominican case. Attention to factual interpretation is useful to chroniclers of event; consideration of theory-relevance of case is interesting to general scholars. [Ed.]

Foner, Philip S. The Spanish-Cuban-American War and the birth of American imperialism: 1895-1902. See *HLAS 36:2292.*

8844. Franco, Franklin J. La rehabilitación (Revista de Ciencias Económicas [Univ. Autónoma de Santo Domingo] 1:1, marzo/junio 1972, p. 44-63)

Franco advances the thesis that the return of Balaguer to power in the Dominican Republic after 1966 represents, in essence, a "rehabilitation" of *Trujillismo* that has proceeded with the blessings of the US. [Y. Ferguson]

8845. Fulbright's role in the Cuban Missile Crisis (IAMEA, 27:4, Spring 1974, p. 86-94)

An excerpt from the *Congressional Record* in which Senator Fulbright responds to a statement by former Secretary of State Rusk, that the Senator had advocated "all-out bombing of Cuba" during the 1962 crisis. Fulbright maintains that he advocated an invasion (not all-out bombing) of Cuba by American forces as less risky than direct confrontation with Soviet ships at sea. He stresses, however, that he was asked for his opinion by the White House only after the quarantine option had been chosen and that he had not participated in the days of deliberations preceding the presidential decision, which he feels might have led him to a different recommendation. Fulbright sees the experience as yet another example of inadequate consultation with Congress on key foreign policy matters. [Y. Ferguson]

8846. García, Angel and **Pedro Mirón Chuk.** Antecedentes de las relaciones comerciales entre Cuba y la U.R.S.S. en los siglos XIX y XX (Economía y Desarrollo [Univ. de La Habana] 17, mayo/junio 1973, p. 87-107, bibl., tables)

A Cuban and a Soviet historian at the Institute of History of the Cuban Academy of Sciences trace the record of Russian-Cuban commercial ties prior to the Castro Revolution. [Y. Ferguson]

Gardiner, C. Harvey. The Japanese and Cuba. See *HLAS 36:2321*.

8847. Gaviria Liévano, Enrique. Roncador, Quitasueño y Serrana: análisis histórico y jurídico. Bogotá, Editorial Temis, 1973. 63 p., bibl., map.

Traces the legal issues concerning three small "islands" in the Caribbean. Colombia, Panama, Costa Rica, Nicaragua, and the US have been involved at one time or another. [C.N. Ronning]

Gensler, Martin D. Cuba's "Second Vietnam:" Bolivia. See item 8403.

8848. Goff, Fred and **Michael Locker.** La violencia de la dominación: el poder de los Estados Unidos en la República Dominicana (Revista de Ciencias Económicas [Univ. Autónoma de Santo Domingo] 1:1, marzo/junio 1972, p. 3-43)

A vitriolic analysis of US policies in the Dominican Republic from Trujillo through the 1965 civil war and beyond, by two scholar-members of the North American Congress on Latin America (NACLA). Of particular interest is Goff and Locker's attempt to explain the Johnson Administration's intervention in the 1965 crisis by linking key decision-makers to the "East Coast sugar complex." [Y. Ferguson]

8849. Halajczuk, Bohdan T. Autodefensa preventiva a la luz de la cuarantena de Cuba en 1962 (IEP/REP, 186, nov./dic. 1972, p. 277-295)

Legal analysis of the concept of "anticipatory self-defense" as manifested in the 1962 Cuban Missile Crisis. Halajczuk comments that the inter-American system to which Kennedy to some extent deferred has been undermined by the policies of the Nixon Administration, but he believes that the concept in question remains significant in a world which has not evolved centralized institutions to guarantee security. [Y. Ferguson]

8850. León, Carlos V. de. Casos y cosas de ayer. Santo Domingo, Imprenta Núñez, 1972. 356 p., plates.

A personal account of conditions under the first US military occupation of the Dominican Republic, 1916-1924. The author, 84 years of age, was a young public official at the time. [Y. Ferguson]

8851. Lewis, Vaughan A. The Bahamas in international politics: issues arising for an archipelago state (UM/JIAS, 16:2, May 1974, p. 131-152, bibl.)

Interesting application of James N. Rosenau's model of "linkages" between domestic and international systems to an analysis of several key issues facing the newly independent Bahamas. [Y. Ferguson]

8852. Linderman, Gerald F. The mirror of war: American society and the Spanish American War. Ann Arbor, Univ. of Michigan Press, 1974. 227 p., plates.

An excellent series of essays by a Univ. of Michigan historian examining the social psychology of the Spanish American War, in part by focusing on the motivations of key individuals. Includes numerous photographs of the period. [Y. Ferguson]

8853. Londoño, Julio. Geopolítica del Caribe. Bogotá, Imprenta y Litografía de las Fuerzas Militares, 1973. 192 p., bibl. (Col. De oro del militar colombiano, 6)

Brief, historical geopolitical survey of the area which is notable mainly because its publisher is the Colombian Armed Forces press. The author is a retired Colombian general. [Y. Ferguson]

8854. Mitchell, David I. *ed.* With eyes wide open: a collection of papers by Caribbean scholars on Caribbean Christian concerns. La Penitence, Guyana, CADEC, 1973. 202 p.

According to the introduction these are "theological reflections on Caribbean concerns of today." They should be of interest to the student who wishes to assess the role of religious groups in contemporary affairs of the Caribbean. [C.N. Ronning]

8855. Molineu, Harold. The concept of the Caribbean in the Latin American policy of the United States (UM/JIAS, 15:3, Aug. 1973, p. 285-307, bibl., tables)

Molineu reports on his content analysis of various scholarly sources and statements of public officials, to test the salience of "the Caribbean" as a concept in US policy. Although it is undeniable that US armed intervention in the Western Hemisphere has been confined to the Caribbean, he argues, Washington has tended to adopt an "all-inclusive policy that defines all of the Western Hemisphere as a distinct region of special interest" rather than to differentiate between countries and subregions. One wishes that Molineu had done a special survey of the post-1968 period, since Kissinger has assigned a low priority to Latin America generally and has extolled the virtues of a country-by-country approach. [Y. Ferguson]

Morales Lezcano, Víctor. Ideología y estrategia estadounidense: 1898. See *HLAS 36:2307.*

8856. Ochoa, Miguel. El último aldabonazo: análisis de las relaciones de Estados Unidos con América Latina y su reflejo en la Revolución Cubana. Bogotá, Ediciones Tercer Mundo, 1973. 204 p. (Col. Tribuna libre)

Seeking "the lesson of Cuba," Ochoa finds an explanation for the Castro Revolution in the "ineptitude" and corruption of the former ruling class and socioeconomic conditions on the island, and he attributes the radicalization of the Castro regime primarily to Washington's negative reaction to change. He concludes that the "orthodox free enterprise system" will not produce development and industrialization in Latin America. This familiar line of argument is notable only because Ochoa is a Cuban exile now living in the US. [Y. Ferguson]

8857. Paolino, Ernest N. The foundations of the American Empire: William Henry Seward and U.S. Foreign Policy. Ithaca, N.Y., Cornell Univ. Press, 1973. 235 p., bibl.

Ch. 5 establishes a link between Secretary of State William Seward's Alaska purchase in the 1860s and US interest in the West Indies and the Panama Canal. In Paolino's view, there was little difference between Seward's "expansionism" and turn-of-the-century US "imperialism": both involved a desire for commerce and way stations on established trade routes. [Y. Ferguson]

8858. Paterson, Thomas G. *ed.* American imperialism & anti-imperialism. N.Y., Thomas Y. Crowell, 1973. 149 p., bibl., map (Problem studies in American history)

Pt. 1 contains nine essays on the factors that brought the US into war with Spain in 1898. The essays do not provide a simple answer but do provide much insight. [C.N. Ronning]

8859. Petras, James. The U.S.-Cuban policy debate (MR, 26:9, Feb. 1975, p. 22-33)

Perceptive analysis of the reasons for Kissinger's reluctance to normalize relations with Cuba, as well as for the more conciliatory position on this question adopted by "liberals." In Petras' view, both positions are to some extent a response to Latin American nationalism. He sees Latin America no longer rigidly divided between revolutionary and conservative governments, rather between those whose foreign policy is or is not calculatedly "independent" of Washington. [Y. Ferguson]

Santos, Ralph G. Brazilian foreign policy and the Dominican crisis: the impact of history on events. See *HLAS 36:3641.*

Schmidt, Hans. The United States occupation of Haiti: 1915-1934. See *HLAS 36:2372.*

8860. Ruiz Bergés, Humberto. La política mundial y su incidencia en la República Dominicana (Aula [Santo Domingo] 1:2/3, julio/dic. 1972, p. 129-141, bibl.)

The author finds a trend toward greater interdependence and pragmatism in world politics, replacing the ideological conflicts of the past. In this new global context, he maintains, the Dominican Republic should strive for a position of "relative" dependence rather than "radical" dependence. [Y. Ferguson]

8861. Schreiber, Anna P. Economic coercion as an instrument of foreign policy: U.S. economic measures against Cuba and the Dominican Republic (PUCIS/WP, 25:3, April 1973, p. 387-413)

Schreiber concludes that "the experience of US economic coercion against Cuba and the Dominican Republic suggests the limits of this type of activity." In these two cases it served primarily the "symbolic function" of declaring a "position to internal and external publics." [Y. Ferguson]

8862. Theberge, James D. Russia in the Caribbean; pt. 2, A special report. Washington, Georgetown Univ., The Center for Strategic and International Studies, 1973. 166 p., bibl., maps, tables (Special report series, 13)

Special report produced by the Center for Strategic and International Studies at Georgetown Univ. There are better studies elsewhere of such topics as Soviet policies generally and Cuban "subversion," but Ch. 9 through 11 offer hard-to-find information about Soviet shipping, oceanographic activities, fishing, and naval presence in the Caribbean. Excellent maps are provided in these chapters, and the appendix includes some useful documents and a table on the "Status of Caribbean Communist and Far Left Parties, 1972." [Y. Ferguson]

8863. Tomasek, Robert D. Caribbean exile invasions: a special regional type of conflict (CIDG/O, 17:4, Winter 1974, p. 1354-1382, tables)

Tomasek meticulously compares all the postwar Caribbean exile invasions from a variety of perspectives: the degree of government support and number of governments involved, number of exiles, composition of exiles, strategy of exiles, and outcomes. A very useful piece of research, which is summarized in a single table at the conclusion of the article. [Y. Ferguson]

Williams, Byron. Puerto Rico: commonwealth, state, or nation? See *HLAS 36:2413.*

Wolpin, Miles D. The transnational appeal of the Cuban Revolution: Chile, 1958-1970. See item 8940.

8864. Young, Marilyn Blatt *ed.* American expansionism: the critical issues. Boston, Mass., Little, Brown, 1973. 184 p. (Critical issues in American history series)

Short collection of historical essays on US imperialism which "meet no single ideological or political test." There are four selections on the Spanish American War and US-Cuba relationships in the period that followed. [Y. Ferguson]

SOUTH AMERICA

8865. Arce, Daniel Valois. Reseña histórica sobre los límites de Colombia y Venezuela. Bogotá, Editorial Bedout, 1970. 128 p., maps, plates.

Very useful historical analysis of dispute between Colombia and Venezuela over the so-called Gulf of Venezuela. Contains much historical material not easily available elsewhere. [C.N. Ronning]

8866. Argentina. Presidencia. Entrevistas de los presidentes de la Argentina y Peru; la Argentina y Venezuela; la Argentina y Colombia; la Argentina y Paraguay. B.A., 1972. 4 v. (50, 36, 48, 25 p.)

Includes a number of speeches and press conferences of Gen. Lanusse (then President of Argentina) in connection with his visits abroad. They contain important comments on Argentine foreign and domestic policy during this period. [C.N. Ronning]

8867. Argentina y Brasil: estudio comparativo de algunos de sus aspectos fundamehtales (IAEERI/E, 1:5, enero/feb. 1970, p. 72-96, tables)

Statistical comparisons between Argentina and Brazil in a number of areas—population, agriculture, industry, iron and steel, merchant marine, energy, foreign trade, telecommunications, and others. Few conclusions are reached. [C.N. Ronning]

8868. Arismendi, Rodney. Uruguay y América Latina en los años setenta: experiencias y balance de una revolución. 3. ed. Montevideo, Ediciones Pueblos Unidos, 1973. 114 p.

The work was originally a preface to the Soviet edition of the author's Lenin, *revolution and Latin America*. It is not, as the title might suggest, about relations between Uruguay and Latin America but, rather, essays on political conditions and methods of social transformation in these areas. Of particular interest is the qualified criticism of leftist extremists, including the Tupamaros, and discussion of the possibility of the institutional (peaceful?) road to socialism. This was written and published before the fall of Allende in Chile and before the *coup* in Uruguay. [C.N. Ronning]

8869. Bailey, Norman A. and **Ronald M. Schneider.** Brazil's foreign policy: a case study in upward mobility (IAMEA, 27:4, Spring 1974, p. 3-25)

The authors note that little attention has been given to "the strategies and tactics used by [third rank] regional powers to elevate themselves to a position of secondary eminence on the world scene." Using Brazil as a case study they find that "supremacy, dominance, and even paramountcy may well be within Brazil's reach by the 1980s, although its position is likely to stop short of hegemony." [C.N. Ronning]

8870. Bandeira, Moniz. Presença dos Estados Unidos no Brasil: dois séculos de história. Rio, Editôra Civilização Brasileira, 1973. 497 p., bibl. (Col. Retratos do Brasil, 87)

Well-documented and highly useful interpretation of US-Brazilian relations. The work also contains much on Brazil's relations with other countries. Approximately one half of the book deals with the period from 1930 to the fall of Goulart. [C.N. Ronning]

8871. Barbosa Mutis, David. Relaciones entre el Tratado de Montevideo y el Acuerdo de Cartagena (PUJ/U, 41, junio 1971, p. 223-239)

Primarily a separate analysis of each of the agreements rather than an analysis of the relationships between them. [C.N. Ronning]

8872. Beare, Adolfo and **José Gabriel.** Empresa multinacional y dependencia tecnológica: el imperialismo en América Latina hoy. B.A., Editorial

Granica, 1974. 42 p. (Col. Cuadernos de la realidad, 8)

Short monograph examining the role of the multinationals in contemporary Argentina. A serious study, despite the rather polemical title. [Y. Ferguson]

Benítez, Luis G. Historia diplomática del Paraguay. See *HLAS 36:3355.*

Bittencourt, Gustavo Francisco Feijó. Conotações do poder marítimo necessárias ao processo de engrandecimento no Brasil. See item 8548b.

Boelcke, Willi A. Die Waffengeschäfte des Dritten Reiches mit Brasilien: Teils 1/2. See *HLAS 36:3558.*

8873. Brazil. Ministério da Marinha. Mar territorial. Brasília, Senado Federal, Servico Gráfico, 1972? 2 v. (849 p.) (Continuous pagination) tables.

V. 1 contains a brief introduction concerning the nature and importance of the oceans. The remainder of v. 1 and all of v. 2 contain the important international documents relating to the law of the sea (bilateral and multilateral agreements, resolutions, declarations, and speeches). It probably has the best collection of Brazilian decrees, legislation and declarations available. Those of several other countries are also included. V. 2 also contains several articles by Brazilian writers dealing with Brazilian claims over the territorial sea. [C.N. Ronning]

8874. ———. Ministério das Relações Exteriores. Secretaria Geral Adjunta para o Planejamento Político. Documentos de política externa. v. 1, De 15 de março a 15 de outubro de 1967; v. 2, De 28 de outubro de 1967 a 3 de mayo de 1968; v. 3, De 20 de mayo de 1968 a 11 de outubro de 1969; v. 4, De 31 de outubro de 1969 a 21 de dezembro de 1970. Brasilia, Senado Federal, 1968?-1971. 4 v. (122, 104, 272, 362 p.)

8875. Briano, Justo P. Geopolítica y geoestrategia americana. B.A., Círculo Militar, 1972. 399 p., bibl., maps (Col. Ciencias políticas y sociales)

Written by an Argentine colonel and published by the Argentine Círculo Militar, this volume is in the nature of a textbook of geopolitics with emphasis on South America. Numerous maps and tables supplement the analysis. [Y. Ferguson]

Cárcano, Miguel Angel. La política internacional en la historia argentina. See *HLAS 36:3068.*

8876. Carvajal Pérez del Castillo, Jorge. La doctrina del no alineamiento y sus proyecciones futuras. La Paz, Empresa Editora Universo, 1971. 37 p.

A Bolivian diplomat writes on the theory, justification, and objectives of non-alignment. The origins of the doctrine are also outlined. [C.N. Ronning]

8877. Cavalcanti, Themístocles Brandão and others. As Nações Unidas e os problemas internacionais. Rio, Fundação Getúlio Vargas, Instituto de Documentação, Serviço de Publicações, 1974. 229 p.

The work is a collection of essays, all by Brazilian writers, on several questions in contemporary international law. In some essays the role of the UN is stressed. Topics range from generally traditional ones such as the Law of the Sea and Disarmament to "Hijacking aned iternal war." [C.N. Ronning]

8878. Ciria, Alberto. Estados Unidos nos mira. B.A., Ediciones La Bastilla, 1973. 258 p. (Serie: Sin límites)

Interesting survey and critique of North American literature on Argentina and US-Argentine relations. For historian's comment, see *HLAS 36:3083.* [Y. Ferguson]

Conil Paz, Alberto and **Gustavo Ferrari.** Política exterior argentina. See *HLAS 36:3087.*

Duarte, Paulo de Querioz. O Nordeste na II Guerra Mundial: antecedentes e ocupação. See *HLAS 36:3580.*

8878a. Ebel, Arnold. Das Dritte Reich und Argentinien: die diplomatischen Beziehungen unter besonderer Berücksichtigung der Handelspolitik, 1933-1939. Köln, FRG, Böhlau-Verlag, 1971. 472 p., bibl. (Lateinamerikanischen Forschungen, 3)

Analysis of the diplomatic relations between the Third Reich and Argentina until 1939. Author argues that they were based on trade. [H.J. Hoyer]

8879. Fagen, Richard R. The United States and Chile: roots and branches (CFR/FA, 53:2, Jan. 1975, p. 297-313)

Vitally important, profound analysis of the background of the US political intervention against Allende in Chile, which—we now know—went far beyond the ITT affair. As Fagen suggests, the reasons for a Nixon-Kissinger concern that belied public statements of a desire for "cool but correct" relations were complex, but are depressingly familiar—maintenance of a US sphere of influence in the Western Hemisphere, the "domino theory" as applied to both Europe and Latin America, and chagrin at what had happened to a "showcase" country. Fagen declares: "only when the election of a Salvador Allende is seen by U.S. policymakers as the legitimate manifestation of a historic struggle for social justice by a people long exploited both domestically and internationally—a struggle with which the United States ought to be associated—will it be possible to say that a truly new era in foreign policy has dawned." [Y. Ferguson]

8880. Farnsworth, Elizabeth. Chile: what was the U.S. role? More than admitted (Foreign Policy [National Affairs Inc., N.Y.] 16, Fall 1974, p. 127-141)

Farnsworth attacks Paul Sigmund's assessment in his *Foreign Affairs* article of the US "invisible blockade" of the Allende government in Chile (see items 8925 and 8926). Sigmund, she insists, grossly underestimated the extent of the "economic warfare" waged against Allende and the impact of this campaign on the Chilean economy, as well as the fact that it was "part of a larger strategy, aimed at getting rid of the Allende government." [Y. Ferguson]

8881. Ferrari, Gustavo. Bibliografía de base sobre política exterior argentina (IHADER/B, 14/15:24/25 [2. serie] 1970/1971 [i.e. 1973] p. 74-97)

This is much more than a bibliography on Argentine foreign policy. Not only are the basic works analyzed in some detail, but the effort amounts to something of a bibliographical essay on Argentine foreign policy. Essential for anyone studying the subject. For historian's comment see *HLAS 36:3126*. [C.N. Ronning]

8882. Flores, Mario Cesar. Panorama do poder marítimo brasileiro. Rio, Biblioteca de Exército, Serviço de Documentação Geral de Marinha Editores, 1972. 445 p., illus., plates, tables (Publicação, 429. Col. General Benício, 105)

A theoretical and factual study of Brazilian sea power including such factors as the merchant marine, ocean resources and the juridical regime of the territorial sea. Naval officers and civilians are the authors of the several essays. [C.N. Ronning]

8883. Francis, Michael J. The United States at Rio, 1942: the strains of Pan-Americanism (JLAS, 6:1, May 1974, p. 77-95)

At the Rio meeting of 1942 there "was a clash of the foreign policies of Brazil, Chile, Argentina, and the United States which both typified and shaped inter-American relations well into the 1950s." This discussion, which is largely based on US government documents, examines the intermeshing of these foreign policies at the Rio meeting and the immediate aftermath of that conference. [C.N. Ronning]

8883a. Friedl Zapata, José A. Erscheinungsformen deutscher auswärtiger Kulturpolitik in Argentinien (Zeitschrift für Kulturaustausch [Stuttgart, FRG] 23:1, 1973, p. 34-38)

Brief but unbalanced essay concerning West Germany's cultural programs in Argentina. The author, an elitist, points to the "special relationship" between the two countries. [H.J. Hoyer]

Gall, Norman. Los indocumentados colombianos. See item 8318.

8884. García Lupo, Rogelio. La Argentina en la selva mundial. B.A., Ediciones Corregidor, 1973. 257 p.

A successful Argentine foreign policy requires a government with popular support at home. Peronism is the vehicle through which this can be accomplished. Recent Argentine relations with Bolivia are discussed as an example of what Argentina ought not to do in its foreign relations. [C.N. Ronning]

8885. Gil, Federico G. Socialist Chile and the United States (IAMEA, 27:2, Autumn 1973, p. 29-47)

Written prior to the 1973 coup, this article discusses the issues between the two governments, the reasons for the position of each, and the problems each would face in trying to resolve the issues. [C.N. Ronning]

8886. González Madariaga, Exequiel. Nuestras relaciones con Argentina: una historia deprimente. t. 2, Del Tratado de Límites a la entrega de la Puna de Atacama y al Protocolo Concha-Alcorta de 1900. Santiago, Editorial Andrés Bello, 1972. 530 p.

Title is misleading. This is really a study of Argentine-Chilean border questions between 1881 and 1900 written from a strong Chilean point of view. Contains a wealth of documentary materials. [C.N. Ronning]

8887. Government documents: the British government position on Chile, the British decision on armament orders, the U.S. response to the Chilean coup (IAMEA, 28:1, Summer 1974, p. 73-85)

Questions put to the British Secretary of State for Foreign and Commonwealth Affairs (on March 27 and 21, 1974) concerning Britain's attitude toward the military junta in Chile. The replies indicate that the British government, unlike that of the US, did not look with pleasure on the military junta and would discontinue military aid. [C.N. Ronning]

8888. Guachalla, Luis Fernando. Mision en el Paraguay: mayo, 1930-julio, 1931. La Paz, Univ. Mayor de San Andres, 1971. 287 p.

Memoirs of a Bolivian negotiator in the Chaco dispute with Paraguay. It is of interest with respect to aspects of that conflict and subsequent diplomatic efforts. Beyond that it is introspective with respect to conflict and diplomacy in general. It also contains interesting observations on Paraguay of that time. [C.N. Ronning]

8889. Gualco, Jorge Nelson. Cono sur: elección de un destino. B.A., Compañía

General Fabril Editora, 1972. 300 p., bibl., maps, tables.

A pragmatic and "humanistic" argument for the integration of the countries of the southern part of South America — Chile, Peru, Bolivia, Paraguay, Uruguay, and Argentina. An important consideration in all of this is that of thwarting the expansive ambitions of Brazil, the latter being a close ally of the US. [C.N. Ronning]

8890. Gutiérrez Gutiérrez, Mario R. La nueva imagen de Bolivia en la ONU y en los "77." La Paz, Ministerio de Relaciones Exteriores y Culto, Depto. de Prensa, 1971. 58 p., plate.

Speeches by the Bolivian Minister of Foreign Affairs delivered at the UN and in San Francisco. They offer some insight into the Bolivian position (under the government of Gen. Banzer) concerning a number of international questions including the Third World, US-Soviet relations and Bolivia's claim to coastal areas. See also by the same author: item 8891, as well as *La palabra de Bolivia en la Asamblea de Naciones Unidas* (La Paz, Ministerio de Información y Deportes, 1971. 31 p., plates) and *Bolivia, el mar y la ONU* (La Paz, Ministerio de Relaciones Exteriores y Culto, Depto. de Prensa, 1971. 33 p., plate). [C.N. Ronning]

8891. _____. Presencia internacional de la República de Bolivia. La Paz, Ministerio de Relaciones Exteriores y Culto, 1972. 159 p.

Speeches given by the Bolivian Minister of Foreign Affairs during late 1971 and 1972. Most of them contain the usual generalities, but they do offer some insights into Bolivian foreign policy and will be of interest to the student of developing nations in world affairs. See also item 8890. [C.N. Ronning]

8891a. Härtling, Pater. Allende und Dubček (NR, 84:4, 1973, p. 760-762)

Perceptive essay compares the ideals and accomplishments of Allende and Dubcek while stressing those of the Allende regime. [H.J. Hoyer]

8892. Hanson, Simon G. Kissinger on the Chilean coup (IAMEA, 27:3, Winter 1973, p. 61-85, tables)

"During the initial sessions on the nomination of Henry A. Kissinger to be Secretary of State, the Senate Foreign Relations Committee showed little interest in Latin America. No one on the Committee had more than a schoolboy's knowledge of our Latin American policy, and interest in the area was even less developed." [C.N. Ronning]

Harms-Baltzer, Kate. Die Nationalisierung der deutschen Einwanderer und ihrer Nachkommen in Brasilien als Problem der deutsch-brasilianischen Beziehunge, 1930-1938. See *HLAS 36:3593*.

8893. Henderson, Gregory; S.W. Barton; **Johannes A. Binnendijk; and Carolyn E. Setlow.** Public diplomacy and political change: four case studies; Okinawa, Peru, Czechoslovakia, Guinea. N.Y., Praeger, 1973. 339 p., bibl., tables.

Pt. 2 of this study is a useful and interesting study of the International Petroleum Company in Peru. The study concentrates on political and sociological aspects of this expropriation case and is, therefore, a highly useful complement to existing legal studies. [C.N. Ronning]

8894. Hendrickson, Embert J. Roosevelt's second Venezuelan controversy (HAHR, 50:3, Aug. 1970, p. 482-498)

The author argues that this episode shows how a great power may apply its pressures and resources to resolve a diplomatic conflict without a show of force. "Patience, dispatch, and vigilance for opportunities guided the diplomatic course of Roosevelt and his two Secretaries of State." [C.N. Ronning]

Hilton, Stanley E. Ação Integralista Brasileira. See *HLAS 36:3594*.

8895. Holguín Peláez, Hernand fascism in Brazil, 1932-1938. Proyecciones de un límite marítimo entre Colombia y Venezuela: primer ensayo sobre el tema controversia de límites Colombia-Venezuela. Bogotá. Editores y Distribuidores Asociados, 1971. 123 p., bibl., maps (Publicaciones Técnicas y económicas)

A good treatment of the background and the issues in the conflict between Colombia and Venezuela in the so-called Gulf of Venezuela. Since the issues are juridical and since discussions are stalemated, the author suggests that the parties utilize the available juridical instruments. [C.N. Ronning]

Iiams, Thomas M., Jr. Prolegoma to the study of Brazilian foreign relations from the Court-in-Rio period to the U.S. trade agreement of 1891. See *HLAS 36:3596*.

8896. Kaplan, Stephen S. and Norman C. Bonsor. Did United States aid really help Brazilian development? The prespective of a quarter-century (IAMEA, 27:3, Winter 1973, p. 25-46, tables)

The authors find that the US aid to Brazil has not led to a major redistribution of wealth nor has it significantly upgraded the standard of living for the masses of the populace but that it has been important for economic growth. [C.N. Ronning]

8897. Lafer y Félix Peña, Celso. Argentina y Brasil en el sistema de relaciones internacionales. B.A., Ediciones Nueva Visión, 1973. 117 p. (Col. Fichas, 17)

An Argentine and a Brazilian political scientist have each contributed a very brief but useful essay on the foreign policy of their respective countries. A third (joint) essay deals with the relations between Latin America and the rest of the world with emphasis on Argentina and Brazil. [C.N. Ronning]

8898. Larrea Alba, L. La defensa del estado en los cuatro frentes: el frente exterior, político-diplomático, el frente económico, el frente bélico, el frente interno. Quito, Editorial Casa de la Cultura Ecuatoriana, 1972. 346 p.

An Ecuadoran general writes about what might be called an integral concept of national defense. It involves four fronts: political-diplomatic (exterior), economic, interior, and war (military). An interesting example of the thinking of a military man concerning the role of the military. [C.N. Ronning]

Londoño Paredes, Julio. Derecho territorial de Colombia. See *HLAS 36:2817.*

8899. Loring, David C. The United States-Peruvian "fisheries" dispute (Stanford Law Review [Palo Alto, Calif.] 23:3, Feb. 1971, p. 391-453)

Traces the background and growth of the dispute, the legal arguments advanced by both parties, the interests each side believes are at stake, the policies the parties have adopted to further their interests, and discusses the paths the US might take to reduce tension and find an acceptable resolution. [C.N. Ronning]

8900. McCann, Frank D., Jr. The Brazilian-American Alliance: 1937-1945. Princeton, N.J., The Princeton Univ. Press, 1973. 527 p., bibl., maps, tables.

A comprehensive, scholarly treatment of events and conditions during the last part of the first Vargas administration which brought about a close alliance between Brazil and the US and resulted in Brazil's economic, political, and military dependence on the US. Certainly of interest to students of foreign policy and international politics as well as diplomatic history. [C.N. Ronning]

8901. Machicote, Eduardo. La expansión brasileña: notas para un estudio geohistórico. B.A., Editorial Ciencia Nueva, 1973. 65 p., maps.

An historical account and analysis of Brazilian expansionism from colonial times, written by a concerned Argentine. Much of it is an examination and analysis of the book by Gen. Goldberg do Couto e Silva, *Geopolítica do Brasil*—Rio, José Olympio Editôra, 1967, 275 p., bibl., illus., maps (Col. Documentos brasileiros, 126)—the last chapter of which analyzes some of the internal forces behind contemporary Brazilian policy. [C.N. Ronning]

8902. Mansholt, Sicco. La Argentina y el Mercado Común Europeo (SRA/A, 106:10/11, oct./dic. 1972, p. 16-19)

The president of the Commission of the European Economic Community offers some general observations concerning Argentina's relations with countries in the European Economic Community. He refers to trade, not to political ties. [C.N. Ronning]

8903. Matsushita, Hiroshi. A historical view of Argentine neutrality during World War II (IAEA/DE, 11:3, Sept. 1973, p. 272-296, bibl.)

Approaching the question within the framework of Argentine relations with Great Britain, the author finds that Argentine neutrality during World War II was conditioned primarily by pro-British and anti-American tendencies. [C.N. Ronning]

8903a. Mattos, Adherbal Meira. A Declaração de Santo Domingo e o Dereito do Mar (UMG/RBEP, 39, julho 1974, p. 171-191, bibl.)

Short note on the 1972 meeting on maritime law, territorial waters, and the submarine platform. Emphasizes Latin American views of the subject and provides a useful synthesis of them. [P.B. Taylor, Jr.]

8904. Milenky, Edward S. The politics of regional organization in Latin America: the Latin American Free Trade Association. N.Y., Praeger, 1973. 289 p., bibl., tables. (Praeger special studies in international politics and government)

A definitive study of the emergence and decline of LAFTA to 1972 based in part on 70 interviews with nationals of all the member states. Pinpointing what he believes to be the "critical relationships of integration," Milenky maintains that LAFTA "as presently organized ... lacks many of the elements necessary for a successful strategy." [Y. Ferguson]

8905. Moneta, Carlos Juan. Argentina y Australia: esquemas para la cooperación (IAEERI/E, 2:11, mayo/junio 1971, p. 51-65, table)

After a brief outline of Argentine-Australian relations, the author discusses the need for coordination of commercial policies since both export the same products. Calls for an organization of Asian and Latin American countries for these purposes. [C.N. Ronning]

8906. Montes, Elvira. Chile y la política exterior argentina (IAEERI/E, 1:4, nov./dic. 1969, p. 36-39)

The author argues that it is vital that border disputes with Chile be settled immediately since they have been the major cause of conflict between the two countries. Unfortunately, it is argued, Argentina has no general policy with respect to the settlement of these issues. [C.N. Ronning]

Moran, Theodore H. Multinational corporations and the politics of dependence: copper in Chile. See item 8482.

8907. Moreno, Juan Carlos. La recuperación de las Malvinas. B.A., Editorial Plus Ultra, 1973. 313 p., bibl. (Col. Esquemas políticos, 4)

A detailed history of the Islas Malvinas (Falkland Islands) controversy in Argentine-British relations, concluding on the optimistic note that greater contact between island residents and the mainland may soon pave the way for a transfer of sovereignty to Argentina. [Y. Ferguson]

8908. Morris, Michael. Trends in U.S.-Brazilian maritime relations (IAMEA, 27:3, Winter 1973, p. 3-24)

Despite certain differences in principle where both sides have refused to compromise (to 200-mile limit of the territorial sea, for example) a legacy of cooperation and willingness to compromise has characterized US-Brazilian relations. [C.N. Ronning]

8909. Moyano Bonilla, César. Los Monjes: valor jurídico de las notas diplomáticas colombo-venezolanas de 1952 (PUJ/U, 40, junio 1971, p. 283-367).

In 1952 Colombia, by an exchange of notes with Venezuela recognized the latter's sovereignty over Los Monjes islands. The author of this article, after an extensive discussion of treaties, concludes that the notes constitute a "treaty" under international law. This "treaty" is not valid, however, not having been made in conformity with the Colombian constitution which requires the consent of the National Congress for any alteration of the national territory. [C.N. Ronning]

8910. Nálecka, Vladimir. Tratado Antibélico Argentino: contribución a las relaciones argentino-checoslovacas en los años 1933-1935 (UCP/IAP, 1, 1967, p. 133-155)

Some interesting observations on the background and motives of the Argentine Anti-War Pact (first proposed in 1932). It is seen as, above all, a measure to secure Argentine independence. [C.N. Ronning]

8911. Nweihed, Kaldone G. La vigencia del mar: una investigación acerca de la soberanía marítima y la plataforma continental de Venezuela dentro del marco internacional del derecho del mar. t. 1. Caracas, Univ. Simón Bolivar [and] Ediciones Equinoccio, 1973. 612 p., map.

The major part of the book is a historical and jurídical study of the evolution of the law of the sea. Venezuela's position with regard to most aspects of this law are discussed within this framework. The author is a professor at the Univ. Simón Bolivar. A useful book. [C.N. Ronning]

8912. Olivares, Augusto ed. Fidel Castro, Salvador Allende: el diálogo de América. B.A., Ediciones del Centro de Artes y Ciencias, 1973? 36 p., plates (Cuadernos, 2)

Interesting illustrated pamphlet published in Argentina after the coup that overthrew the Allende government in Chile. Contents include: an interview with Castro and Allende, conducted by journalist Olivares (who later "committed suicide" with Allende in the Moneda Palace) upon the occasion of Castro's visit to Chile, and a discussion and chronology of major events in Chile (1970-73), the coup, and its aftermath. [Y. Ferguson]

8913. Orrego Vicuña, Francisco. Some international law problems posed by the nationalization of the copper industry in Chile (ASIL/J, 67:4, Oct. 1973, p. 711-727)

Examination of several questions and claims in the light of well-established precedents and contemporary doctrines of the international law of expropriation. Both parties to the dispute (the US and Chile) have invoked relevant principles and practices, all of which indicate a lack of consensus regarding the requirements of international law on the expropriation of property. [C.N. Ronning]

8914. Pelliza, Mariano A. La cuestión del Estrecho de Magallanes: cuadros históricos. B.A., Editorial Universitaria de Buenos Aires (EUDEBA), 1969. 305 p. (Col. América: temas)

The title is misleading. The work is actually a chronological study of Argentine-Chilean boundary litigation from independence to 1881 with two chapters on relevant historical antecedents. It contains, in addition to historical narrative and interpretation, many useful documents probably not readily available elsewhere. The author, an Argentine, was a historian, biographer, and Argentine Undersecretary of Foreign Affairs from 1880-1902. It is not clear when or if the work has been previously published, but the prologue notes that the author died in 1902. [C.N. Ronning]

8915. Pillet, Gastón. La cuestión del Canal de Beagle (IAEERI/E, 2:12, sept./oct. 1971, p. 34-41)

Discusses the background to the arbitral agreement with Chile (1971), the agreement itself and the reasons why an agreement was possible. [C.N. Ronning]

8916. Pontes, Élio Monnerat Solon de. Brasil: 200 milhas. Com prefácio de Álvaro Dias. Niterói, Bra., Casa do Homen de Amanhã, 1972. 306 p., plates, tables.

A Brazilian Professor of International Law argues that international law has evolved to a point where Brazil may justifiably claim jurisdiction over a 200 mile territorial sea. [C.N. Ronning]

8917. Puig, Juan Carlos; Carlos Juan Moneta; Carlos Pérez Llana; and **Alfredo J.L. Carella.** De la dependencia a la liberación: política exterior de

América Latina. B.A., Ediciones La Bastilla, 1973. 309 p. (Serie Sin límites)

Collection of scholarly essays on "dependence." These are historical case studies of Peru's regional role, the International Petroleum Co. dispute, and the foreign relations (respectively) of Brazil and Uruguay. [Y. Ferguson]

8917a. Quevedo, Numa. La meta posible: visión continental. Prólogo de Agustín Rodríguez Garavito. Bogotá, Editorial Kelly, 1970. 475 p.

Collected writings of Venezuela's Ambassador to Colombia during the Caldera period, roughly 1964-70. [P.B. Taylor, Jr.]

Randall, Stephen James. Colombia, the United States and inter-American aviation rivalry, 1927-1940. See *HLAS 36:2827*.

8918. Rangel, Domingo Alberto. El imperio y la faja bituminosa del Orinoco. Caracas, Univ. Central de Venezuela, Facultad de Ciencias Económicas y Sociales, División de Publicaciones, 1973. 45 p. (Col. Salvador de la plaza)

Discusses the importance of the oil deposits in the Orinoco area, the international implications of these rich deposits, and policy options for Venezuela. [C.N. Ronning]

8919. Relaciones argentino-brasileñas (IAERRI/E, 1:5, enero/feb. 1970, p. 48-57)

Relations with Brazil are a key factor in Argentine foreign policy. Brazil is potentially a security threat to Argentina unless the latter maintains an equilibrium through development. On the other hand a common objective of development opens up possibilities for cooperation. [C.N. Ronning]

8920. Relaciones argentino-chilenas (IAEERI/E, 1:3, sept./oct. 1969, p. 55-130, maps, table)

The second section of this volume is devoted to Argentine-Chilean relations. Most of the articles are concerned with territorial disputes, especially the Beagle Canal question. They all present useful historical and juridical information, and the discussions are often placed in a framework of broader political considerations. The article on Argentine-Chilean relations during the first Perón administration, within the framework of Perón's continental and global policies, makes a useful contribution to a much-mentioned but little-studied aspect of international relations. All-in-all, the articles in this volume are useful for the study of a number of aspects of Argentine foreign policy. [C.N. Ronning]

8921. *Revista Brasileira de Estudos Políticos.* Univ. Federal de Minas Gerais. No. 37, set. 1973- . Belo Horizonte, Bra.

The entire issue is devoted to international questions of concern to Brazil. All authors are government officials who delivered this series of papers at a conference on "Aspects of Brazilian Foreign Policy" at the Univ. of Minas Gerais. Topics deal with the territorial sea, Brazil and the La Plata Basin, the evolution of Brazilian foreign policy in the context of a changing balance of power, and scientific and technological questions in foreign policy. Papers are useful as indications of official Brazilian thinking. [C.N. Ronning]

8922. *Revista de la Academia Diplomática del Perú.* No. 8, enero/junio 1973- . Lima.

This issue contains a very brief but good summary and analysis of the meeting of the UN Security Council in Panama in March 1973 and of the meeting of the Special Commission to study the Inter-American System which met in Lima the same year. [C.N. Ronning]

Rizzo Romano, Alfredo H. Las relaciones argentino-chilenas en los últimos 70 años. See *HLAS 36:3281*.

8923. Rodrigues, Eduardo Celestino. Problemas do Brasil potência. 3. ed. rev. e atualizada. São Paulo, Editôras Unidas, 1973. 538 p., illus., maps, plates, tables.

A highly technical study of the factors considered most important in Brazilian development and national power: education, energy, resources, industry, transportation, and engineering. These factors are obviously key to Brazil's development, and the key to the development of these factors is the present military regime: "to the Armed Forces we make an appeal: remain in *control of the Revolution.*" [C.N. Ronning]

Rout, Leslie B., Jr. Politics of the Chaco Peace Conference: 1935-1939. See *HLAS 36:2960*.

8924. Ruda, José María. La posición argentina en cuanto al Tratado sobre la No Proliferación de las Armas Nucleares (IAEERI/E, 2:9, enero/feb. 1971, p. 75-80)

The article is principally a discussion of Argentina's reservations on the Treaty on Nonproliferation of Nuclear Weapons. These reservations relate primarily to provisions which might inhibit technological development. [C.N. Ronning]

Salum-Flecha, Antonio. Historia diplomática del Paraguay de 1869 a 1938. See *HLAS 36:3378*.

Santos, Ralph G. Brazilian foreign policy and the Dominican crisis: the impact of history on events. See *HLAS 36:3641*.

Scenna, Miguel Angel. ¿Cómo fueron las relaciones argentino-norteamericanas? See *HLAS 36:3303*.

Schiff, Warren. The influence of the German Armed Forces and war industry on Argentina, 1880-1914. See *HLAS 36:3306.*

8925. Sigmund, Paul E. Chile: what was the U.S. role? Less than charged (Foreign Policy, 16, Fall 1974, p. 142-156)

Sigmund replies to Farnsworth's salvo (see item 8880) against his *Foreign Affairs* article. Despite revelations which had appeared since his initial article about the covert CIA role in undermining the Allende regime, he remains convinced that Washington's actions can best be interpreted as a "misguided policy of pressure on behalf of expropriated private interests," and he argues that there were indeed genuine reasons to doubt the "creditworthiness" of the Chilean government which at least partially justified the near-cutoff of bilateral and multilateral aid. Furthermore, Sigmund contends, the overthrow of Allende should be attributed primarily to an internal political crisis in Chile rather than to external pressures. [Y. Ferguson]

8926. ———. The "invisible blockade" and the overthrow of Allende (CFR/FA, 52:2, Jan. 1974, p. 322-340)

Sigmund examines the widespread allegations that the US waged an "undeclared economic war" against the Allende government and that US policies were largely responsible for Allende's downfall. Both of these allegations, he concludes, are oversimplifications. He declares: "The lesson, if there is one, in the relations between the United States and the Allende government is that a government which is determined to nationalize U.S. companies without compensation and to carry out an internal program which effectively destroys its ability to earn foreign exchange cannot expect to receive a subsidy to do so from either the U.S. government or from U.S. private banks." Moreover, "the economic and political policies of the Allende government were a failure, in and of themselves." See also items 8880 and 8925. [Y. Ferguson]

Siles Guevara, Juan. La primera misión diplomática boliviana en Asia. See *HLAS 36:2964.*

8927. Silva, Hélio and Maria Cecília Ribas Carneiro. O ciclo de Vargas. v. 12, 1942 Guerra no Continente. Rio, Editôra Civilização Brasileira, 1972. 448 p., plates (Col. Documentos da história contemporánea, 11-K)

This is v. 12 in the very important series on the Vargas era (for other vols. see *HLAS 36:3643).* Essentially a diplomatic history of Brazil during the crucial year 1942, it is, like previous volumes, largely a collection of documents including letters, speeches and diplomatic exchanges. A very important volume in inter-American as well as international relations. [C.N. Ronning]

Soares, Alvaro Teixeira. Um desafio diplomático no século passado: navegação e limites na Amazônia; missão de nascentes de Azambuja a Bogotá, 1840-1928. See *HLAS 36:3648.*

8928. Soberanía marítima: fundamentos de la posición peruana (CM/FI, 13[52]:4, abril/junio 1973, p. 513-526)

The Peruvian Minister of Foreign Affairs makes a concise statement of: 1) the socio-economic bases for Peru's claims over adjacent waters, 2) the extent and nature of those claims, and 3) their legal justification. [C.N. Ronning]

8929. Stefanich, Juan. La Guerra del Chaco: su significación rioplatense y americana. B.A., Talleres Gráficos Lucania, 1973. 20 p.

A Paraguayan diplomat who was Minister of Foreign Relations during the Chaco War offers some interesting and perceptive observations on the war's international and regional implications. [C.N. Ronning]

8930. Storrs, Keith Larry. Brazil's independent foreign policy, 1961-1964: background, tenets, linkage to domestic politics, and aftermath. Ithaca, N.Y., Cornell Univ., 1973. 485 p. (Dissertation series, 44)

The most complete study of Brazil's "Independent Foreign Policy" that has come to the attention of this reader. It offers a particularly good example of linkages between foreign and domestic policy and discusses Brazil's relations with the US in the context of Brazil's global and regional policies. [C.N. Ronning]

8931. Tjarks, Alícia V. As primeiras relações dos Estados Unidos com o Brasil (UMG/RBEP, 36, julho 1973, p. 115-159)

Most of the article is devoted to an account of US-Portuguese relations beginning with the transfer of the Portuguese court to Brazil. There is also a brief account of the establishment of relations with the new Brazilian government following its declaration of independence. Based largely on the dispatches of the US representatives in Brazil. [C.N. Ronning]

8932. Trotman, Donald A.B. Guyana and the world: commentaries on national and international affairs, 1968-1973. Georgetown, United Nations Association of Guyana, 1973? 100 p.

Collection of short articles and speeches by a member of Guyana's delegation to the UN General Assembly between 1968-73. Guyana's Prime Minister, Forbes Burnham, wrote the foreword. [Y. Ferguson]

8933. United Nations. Development Program. Acción de las Naciones Unidas en Argentina: 1959-1972. B.A., 1972. 156 p., map, tables.

A summary of United Nations development programs in Argentina for the years cited. [C.N. Ronning]

8934. United States. Department of State. Bureau of Public Affairs. Office of Media Services. U.S. policy toward governments of Brazil: 1821-present. Washington, 1973. 11 p. (News release)

Brief annotated outline (dated Aug. 1973) of changes of government in Brazil and incidents of serious friction involving the US and Brazil which posed possible questions of recognition or changes in the status of diplomatic relations. The developments leading to each incident and the US response are briefly stated. [C.N. Ronning]

8935. The U.S. response to the Chilean coup (IAMEA, 28:1, Summer 1974, p. 87-91)

The presentation to the Congress by the Agency for International Development of its plans for Chile for fiscal 1975. It shows that the US was launching a program to assist the new regime financially. [C.N. Ronning]

8936. Uruguay. Presidencia. Secretaría. América Latina y la extensión del mar territorial: regimen jurídico. Montevideo, 1971. 440 p., fold. maps.

This excellent collection contains virtually all the relevant documents relating to Latin America's claims to the territorial sea. Inter-American, international and national documents are included. One chapter is devoted to Uruguay's position. [C.N. Ronning]

8937. Valla, Victor. Os Estados Unidos e a influencia estrangeira na economia brasileira; um período de transição, 1904-1928: pt. 3 (USP/RH, 44:89, jan./março 1972, p. 173-195)

Traces the evolution of US and other foreign influence in the Brazilian economy during World War I. At the end of the war the US had not replaced Great Britain as the principal force in the Brazilian economy but the increase of US influence had been so rapid that Brazil had begun to depend more on New York than London. For pts. 1/2 of this study, see *HLAS 34:3013*. [C.N. Ronning]

8938. Vera Villalobos, Enrique. Realidad y ficción en la política exterior: las entrevistas Lanusse-Allende (IAEERI/E, 2:12, sept./oct. 1971, p. 5-12)

The author comments on some events of the Lanusse administration which might suggest new directions in Argentine foreign policy—interviews with the Presidents of Chile and Peru, an arbitral agreement on the Beagle Canal, and the establishment of contacts with Communist China. These are greeted with approval, but it is argued that they will be meaningless unless there are also basic changes in Argentina's domestic policy. [C.N. Ronning]

8939. Villegas, Osiris Guillermo. América del Sur: geopolítica de integración y desarrollo (IAEERI/E, 2:10, marzo/abril 1971, p. 5-16)

Regional integration must be the goal of South American nations but must be preceded by national integration. This does not mean, however, that efforts toward regional integration should not continue. [C.N. Ronning]

8940. Wolpin, Miles D. The transnational appeal of the Cuban Revolution: Chile, 1958-1970 (UWI/CQ, 19:1, March 1973, p. 8-48)

A somewhat mistitled article, since Wolpin discusses mainly the *lack* of appeal of the Cuban model in Chile. Despite the contribution of the Cuban experience to thinking in some quarters on the Chilean left, he argues, other political sectors worried more about Allende than they might otherwise have done because of the Cuban precedent. A sophisticated analysis which includes a review of Chilean political coalitions 1958-70. [Y. Ferguson]

Wright, Antônio Fernanda Pacca de Almeida. Desafio americano à preponderância britânica no Brasil: 1808-1850. See *HLAS 36:3506*.

8941. Zuleta Angel, Eduardo. El llamado Golfo de Venezuela. Bogotá, n.p., 1971. 153 p., maps.

The author presents international conventions and opinions of authorities on international law to show that Colombia has only to ask for application of these treaties and the interpretation of authorities to justify its claims with respect to the so-called Gulf of Venezuela. [C.N. Ronning]

8942. Zúñiga G., Carlos Iván. Consideraciones histórico-políticas sobre el Tratado Urrutia-Thompson (LNB/L, 210, julio 1973, p. 1-16)

Analysis of the 1914 treaty between Colombia and the US which, among other things, gave Colombia special transit rights across Panama and fixed the border between the two countries. Since Panama was not a party to the treaty, she is not bound by these or other provisions. [C.N. Ronning]

JOURNAL ABBREVIATIONS

AAFH/TAM	The Americas. A quarterly journal of inter-American cultural history. Academy of American Franciscan History. Washington.
AF/AUR	Air University Review. The professional journal of the United States Air Force. Maxwell Air Force Base, Ala.

AHA/R	American Historical Review. American Historical Association. Washington.
ASIL/J	American Journal of International Law. American Society of International Law. Washington.
AZIF	Aussenpolitik. Zeitschrift für Internationale Fragen. Deutsche Verlags-Austalt. Hamburg, FRG.
CFR/FA	Foreign Affairs. An American quarterly review. Council on Foreign Relations. N.Y.
CIDG/O	Orbis. Bulletin international de documentation linguistique. Centre International de Dialectologia Générale. Louvain, Belgium.
CM/FI	Foro Internacional. El Colegio de México. México.
HAHR	Hispanic American Historical Review. Conference on Latin American History of the American Historical Association. Duke Univ. Press. Durham, N.C.
IAEA/DE	The Developing Economies. The journal of the Institute of Asian Economic Affairs. Tokyo.
IAEERI/E	Estrategia. Instituto Argentino de Estudios Estratégicos y de las Relaciones Internacionales. B.A.
IAMEA	Inter-American Economic Affairs. Washington.
IEP/REP	Revista de Estudios Políticos. Instituto de Estudios Políticos. Madrid.
IHADER/B	Boletín del Instituto de Historia Argentina Doctor Emilio Ravignani. B.A.
IHGB/R	Revista Trimestral do Instituto Histórico e Geográfico Brasileiro. Rio.
JGSWGL	Jahrbuch für Geschichte von Staat, Wirtschaft und Gesellschaft Lateinamerikas. Köln, FRG.
JLAS	Journal of Latin American Studies. Centers or institutes of Latin American studies at the universities of Cambridge, Glasgow, Liverpool, London and Oxford. Cambridge Univ. Press. London.
JPR	Journal of Peace Research. International Peace Research Institute. Universitetforlaget. Oslo.
LARR	Latin American Research Review. Latin American Studies Association. Univ. of Texas Press. Austin, Tex.
LNB/L	Loteria. Lotería Nacional de Beneficencia. Panamá.
MR	Monthly Review. An independent Socialist magazine. N.Y.
OAS/AM	Américas. Organization of American States. Washington.
PUCIS/WP	World Politics. A quarterly journal of international relations. Princeton Univ., Center of International Studies. Princeton, N.J.
PUJ/U	Universitas. Ciencias jurídicas y socioeconómicas. Pontificia Univ. Javeriana, Facultad de Derecho y Ciencias Socioeconómicas. Bogotá.
RU/SCID	Studies in Comparative International Development. Rutgers Univ. New Brunswick, N.J.
SO	Society. Social science and modern society. Transaction, Rutgers-The State Univ. New Brunswick, N.J.
SRA/A	Anales de la Sociedad Rural Argentina. Revista pastoril y agrícola. B.A.
UCP/IAP	Ibero-Americana Pragensia. Univ. Carolina de Praga, Centro de Estudios Ibero-Americanos. Prague.
UES/U	La Universidad. Univ. de El Salvador. San Salvador.
UM/JIAS	Journal of Inter-American Studies and World Affairs. Univ. of Miami Press *for the* Center for Advanced International Studies. Coral Gables, Fla.
UMG/RBEP	Revista Brasileira de Estudos Políticos. Univ. de Minas Gerais. Belo Horizonte, Bra.
UNAM/RMS	Revista Mexicana de Sociología. Univ. Nacional Autónoma de México, Instituto de Investigaciones Sociales. México.
UP/TM	Tiers Monde. Problémes des pays sous-développés. Univ. de Paris, Institut d'Étude du Développement Economique et Social. Paris.
UPR/RCS	Revista de Ciencias Sociales. Univ. de Puerto Rico, Colegio de Ciencias Sociales. Río Piedras, P.R.
USIA/PI	Problemas Internacionales. United States Information Agency. Washington.
USP/RH	Revista de História. Univ. de São Paulo, Faculdade de Filosofia, Ciências e

	Letras, Depto. de História [and] Sociedade de Estudos Históricos. São Paulo.
UU/WPQ	Western Political Quarterly. Official journal of the Western Political Science Association; Pacific Northwest Political Science Association; and Southern California Political Science Association. Univ. of Utah, Institute of Government. Salt Lake City, Utah.
UWI/CQ	Caribbean Quarterly. Univ. of the West Indies. Mona, Jam.
WPF/IO	International organization. World Peace Foundation. Boston, Mass.
YU/YR	The Yale Review. Yale Univ. New Haven, Conn.

Sociology
Latin America

(Except Brazil)

QUENTIN JENKINS
Professor of Sociology
Louisiana State University

LISANDRO PEREZ
Assistant Professor of Sociology
Louisiana State University

IN MAKING ANNUAL ASSESSMENTS OF THE SOCIOLOGICAL literature on Hispanic America, it would be beneficial if periodically we stood back and examined the current year's crop of scholarly activity in a much broader time perspective in order to determine how the field has changed in, say, the past two or three decades.

Although it can be faulted on several points, perhaps the best benchmark of the state of sociological endeavors in Latin America after World War II is L.L. Bernard's essay in *An introduction to the history of sociology,* edited by Harry Elmer Barnes (Univ. of Chicago Press, 1948). Using Mariano H. Cornejo's works as a case in point, Bernard indicates several deficiencies in the development of sociology in Hispanic America up to 1948: 1) the scarcity of sociology departments and professorships in the universities of the region; 2) largely as a consequence of the foregoing, sociologists lacked originality, borrowing indiscriminately from European social thought; and 3) the predominance of a speculative and philosophical perspective rather than an empirical approach.

The works which we had opportunity to review during this past year are evidence that significant changes have taken place since Bernard made his observations. Perhaps the major change has been the growing influence of North American sociology. Although the number of US sociologists who before the post-war period took an abiding interest in Latin America did not exceed a dozen, there are now probably hundreds who have done research in the area. This is obvious from even a cursory look at the works annotated in this section. At the same time, more than a few Latin Americans went to the US for their training. Sociology became more established in the Latin American universities, and research centers sprung up in various areas.

The most significant consequence of these developments is the growing importance of empiricism. By far the majority of the sociologists whose works were reviewed this year utilize either surveys, official statistics and enumerations, or case studies. The rise of empiricism, however, should not be interpreted to mean that Hispanic American sociologists have simply copied from their North American colleagues in the same manner that, according to Bernard, they emulated European sociologists decades ago. At present, Hispanic American sociology (for a moment we are excluding the works of North Americans) demonstrates a character all its own that is the result of the fusion of the new empiricism and the old tendencies noted by Bernard. A great number of contemporary empirical studies by Latin Americans are couched in a broad and speculative socio-philosophical frame work which usually, although not always, is heavily influenced by the Marxist dialectic. Abel Avila's *Sociología del hambre* (item 9828) is an excellent illustration (for other examples see items 9696, 9843, 9855 and 9873). The crux of this work is a commendable community survey of levels of living. Avila, however, goes further and relates his findings to questions such as man's nature, man's inhumanity, and the pervasiveness of exploitation in dependent capitalist economies.

Another distinctive feature of contemporary Hispanic American sociology is the emphasis placed on research questions related to national development. Population, rural development, modernization, social inequality and its implications for development, and urbanization are the areas that receive the most attention. Only a few of the works reviewed are in other fields of sociology such as criminology and deviance (items 9837-9838, 9850 and 9870), marriage and family relationships (items 9614, 9822, 9831, and 9839), and complex organizations (item 9643).

The literature on Hispanic America by US sociologists also exhibits this emphasis on development-related areas (see especially items 9644, 9647, 9655, 9659, 9687, 9864 and 9874). It is noteworthy that *Demography* and *Rural Sociology* continue to be the North American sociological journals that every year include an article or two dealing with Latin America (items 9613, 9660 and 9842). Among US entities that have been very productive in the area of Hispanic American sociology, it is appropriate to single out this year the Land Tenure Center at the Univ. of Wisconsin (items 9840, 9847, and 9856), and the Population Council (items 9632 and 9835).

GENERAL

9600. Alonso A., Máximo. Un continente frustrado. Santiago, Ediciones de la *Revista Técnica del Trabajo y Previsión Social,* 1970? 150 p., plates.

General treatise on Latin America in which each chapter is devoted to a major social problem: population, nutrition, education, health, continuity in government, agriculture, and militarism. Emphasis is placed on the great social injustices and inequalities that foster widespread misery and social unrest.

9601. Ander Egg, Ezequiel and others. Opresión y marginalidad de la mujer en el orden social machista. B.A., Humanitas, 1972. 206 p. (Col. Desarrollo social, 14)

Collection of papers dealing with social and historical condition of women—outgrowth of seminars and conferences given by the Instituto de Acción Social y Familiar. Mainly theoretical papers with no empirical studies. Rehash of US women's liberation literature dealing with oppression of women. Would be a good reference for courses on women taught in Spanish. [N.S. Kinzer]

9602. Araujo, Manuel Mora y. Ciência e tecnologia: indicadores sociais (*in* O outro desenvolvimento. Rio, Editôra Artenova, 1972, p. 17-60 [Biblioteca Universitária Candido Mendes, 1])

Paper presented at the Seminário sobre Indicadores Sociais de Desenvolvimento Nacional na América Latina. Discusses: 1) the scientific-technological system; 2) its mode of integration; and 3) politics and science. The framework is meta-theoretical attempting to indicate the restrictive parameters of a technocratic science (á-la-Frankfurt critical sociology). An interesting work with good insights. [J.F.B. Dasilva]

Arriaga, Eduardo E. Mortality decline and its demographic effects in Latin America. See item 2022.

9603. _____. The nature and effects of Latin America's non-western trend in fertility (PAA/D, 7:4, Nov. 1970, p. 483-501, bibl., tables)

In spite of rapid mortality decline, rapid city growth, a greater proportion of literates and higher rates of female labor force participation, Latin America did not repeat the European mortality-fertility pattern of Europe 1930-60, where all these factors contributed to population decline. Comparing Latin American and European data, Arriaga shows that Europe had a reduction in mortality over 90 years, while in Latin America mortality declined faster over 30 years. [N.S. Kinzer]

9604. Aubey, Robert; John Syle; and **Arnold Strickon.** Investment behavior and elite social structures in Latin America (UM/JIAS, 16:1, Feb. 1974, p. 73-95)

This theoretical paper develops a model which incorporates variables of kinship, friendship and reciprocity among members of the investors' elites of Latin America. Concrete references to national societies in particular are not discussed here. [P.F. Hernández]

9605. Aznar, Luis. Dependencia, crecimiento económico y conflicto sociopolítico en América Latina. 1955-1965 (IDES/DE, 12:47, oct./dic. 1972, p. 581-600, bibl., tables)

Analyzes the positive relationship between economic growth in Latin America and the incidence of social and political conflicts, postulating as an explanation the internal contradictions generated by dependent capitalist economies.

9606. Badina, Ovidiu. La correlación entre las transformaciones socio-profesionales de la juventud y las modificaciones sociales globales en la perspectiva del desarrollo planificado (UNAM/RMS, 35:4, oct./dic. 1973, p. 833-843)

The author presents a summary of reflections (there is

no bibliographical foundation) on the topic of structural (social) changes and the aspirations and expectations of youth. [P.F. Hernández]

9607. Barba, Melitón. El control de la natalidad en América Latina (UES/U, 95:5/6, sept./dic. 1970, p. 101-115)

Virulent yet interesting attack on family planning programs and on the entire neo-Malthusian viewpoint. Sees food shortages and poverty as the results of social injustices, not of high fertility.

9608. Barrios Rivas, María I. La marginalidad psicológica en la marginalidad social. B.A., Editorial Galerna, 1973. 165 p., bibl., tables (Serie Síntesis dos mil)

As a brief text-book on the subject, the book has the mark of clarity and good survey of relevant literature: most of it still not available in Spanish. [P.F. Hernández]

9609. Bastide, Roger. Contributions à une sociologie des religiones en Amérique Latine (CNRS/ASR, 18:35, jan./juin- 1973, p. 139-150)

The author surveys some of the most important pieces of research published by CIDOC (Cuernavaca, Mex.) and Dr. Ivan Illich in the "Sondeos" series: his survey, however, goes beyond the descriptive into the sociological and historical criticism of Latin America Catholicism and helps the scholar to grasp the dimensions of the "Sondeos" in a time perspective. Like Catholicism, the evolution of Protestant churches in Latin America is also surveyed, in light of the overall process of socio-economic development. [P.F. Hernández]

9610. Belcher, John C. and Pablo B. Vázquez Calcerrada. El desarrollo de una escala para medir niveles de vida entre culturas (UPR/CS, 12:1, April 1972, p. 79-88, tables)

The article is only a brief introduction (descriptive rather than theoretical) to preliminary tests of a cross-cultural scale of living standards. Although its merits and handicaps are still to be determined, its novelty makes the effort worthy of further study. [P.F. Hernández]

9611. Benítez, Wilfredo. Contribución del juguete en al formación del niño (Santiago [Santiago, Cuba] 7, junio 1972, p. 57-64)

Merely a brief account of some of Piaget's (*L'enfant et la formation du symbol*) ideas. [P.F. Hernández]

9612. *Boletín Documental sobre la Mujer.* Coordinación de Iniciativas para el Desarrollo de América Latina (CIDAL). Vol. 1, 1970- . Cuernavaca, Mex.

This issue includes a paper where a serious effort is made to define the roles of women from a socio-theological viewpoint and a Christian perspective. [P.F. Hernández]

9613. Boyd, Monica. Occupational mobility and fertility in metropolitan Latin America (PAA/D, 10:1, Feb. 1973, p. 1-17, bibl., tables)

Utilizing the results of CELADE's fertility surveys of Bogotá, San José, Mexico City, Panama City, and Caracas, the author focuses on the possible relationship between the reproductive behavior of women who have been married for at least ten years and their husband's post-marital career mobility.

9614. Cafferata, José Ignacio and others. La familia. Córdoba, Arg., Univ. Nacional de Córdoba (TEUCO), 1973. 532 p.

Interesante compilación de 22 conferencias dictadas por numerosas autoridades en torno al tema de la familia. La familia se analiza como grupo e institución social y varias ponencias examinan las relaciones entre la familia, el estado, el derecho, la fuerza laboral, y el desarrollo.

9615. Carroll, Thomas. Peasant cooperation in Latin America (*in* A review of rural cooperation in developing areas. v. 1, Rural institutions as agents of planned change. Geneva, United Nations Research Institute for Social Development [UNRISD], 1969, p. 3-94, bibl.)

These papers reflect various areas of concern in rural cooperative movements, most of them of institutional character and their relation to the planning of social change. [P.F. Hernández]

9616. Castellanos, Rosario. Mujer que sabe latín . . . México, Secretaría de Educación Pública, 1973. 213 p., plate.

Using the saying "Una mujer que sabe latín . . . ni tiene marido ni tiene buen fin," Castellanos offers autobiographical sketches of famous women authors: Dinesen, de Beauvoir, Agatha Christie and Virginia Woolf. However, the value of this slim volume is found in the discussion of Latin American women: María Luisa Bombal, Silvina Ocampo, Ulalume, María Luisa Mendoza and others. The major fault is the author's assumption that the reader is basically familiar with the author's works. [N.S. Kinzer]

9617. Centro de Estudos e Ação Social, Salvador, Bra. Dependência e marginalização: nova fase do capitalismo americano. São Paulo, Edições Loyola, 1972. 71 p., illus., tables (Cadernos do CEAS, 18)

A theoretical essay discussing the character of the new state of interrelation between developed and developing nations, that of dependence and its associated character of marginalization. Interesting but sometimes superficial and lacking fuller grasp of the present literature on the topic. [J.F.B. Dasilva]

9618. Clair, Dean J. Hospitalización de pacientes mentales en Suramérica (Revista Latinoamericana de Psicología [Bogotá] 4:1, 1972, p. 117-128, tables)

Author divides article into two parts: 1) the statistics on hospitalizations in mental hospitals in seven South American nations, and 2) impressions gained by the author upon visiting five mental hospitals in Brazil, Chile, and Peru.

9619. Cohn, Gabriel. Sociologia da comunicação: teoria e ideologia. São Paulo, Livraria Pioneira Editôra, 1973. 170 p., bibl. (Biblioteca pioneira de arte e comunicação)

A well-thought and critical analysis of the growing role of communication as: 1) a key element in modernization and development, and 2) as an ideological manifestation linked to structural attributes of the society and to political strategies of power groups. Scholarly and worth considering. [J.F.B. Dasilva]

9620. Colonnese, Louis M. Conscientization for liberation. Washington, United States Catholic Conference, Division for Latin America, 1971. 302 p.

A collection of the papers presented at the 1970 Catholic Interamerican Cooperation Program Conference. Presumably, the papers are centered around the theme of conscientization as a means to achieve the liberation of Latin America, but many depart from that theme and the book is in reality a very general reader on Latin America.

9621. Conferencia Interamericana de Seguridad Social, *IX, Quito, 1971.* Por el robustecimiento de la seguridad social. Quito, Instituto Ecuatoriano de Seguridad Social, Depto. de Asuntos Internacionales y Relaciones Públicas, 1972? 127 p.

Presents conference's highlights and most important addresses. Participating countries included Argentina, Bolivia, Brazil, Canada, Colombia, Costa Rica, Chile, Ecuador, El Salvador, US, Guatemala, Honduras, Mexico, Nicaragua, Panama, Paraguay, Dominican Republic, Venezuela and Uruguay. [G.M. Dorn]

9622. Congreso Interamericano de Psicología, *XI, México, 1967.* Memorias: la contribución de las ciencias psicológicas y del comportamiento al desarrollo social y económico de los pueblos. México, Sociedad Interamericana de Psicología [and] UNAM, 1969. 2 v. (Various pagings) bibl., tables.

Basic personality problems in Latin American societies (Kelman, Malgrath) as well as dimensions of cross-cultural research, acculturation and social mobility (Díaz Guerrero, Stenning, Holtzman, Schwartz) do constitute an excellent scholarly contribution to the socio-psychological definition of Latin American cultures. Most of the proceedings are related to more technical topics of psychological correcting scales, assessment of some areas of psychological research, etc. The two volumes are an indispensable tool for research on contemporary developments in Latin American psychology. [P.F. Hernández]

9623. Congreso Sul-Americano da Mulher em Defesa de Democracia, *I, Rio, 1967.* Anais. Rio, Campanha da Mulher pela Democracia (CAMDE), 1967? 150 p.

Report, including papers presented at the South American Congress of Women in Defense of Democracy. Texts are mainly political when not ideological and popularistic. Interesting as a social document for studies in political sociology in the area. [J.F.B. Dasilva]

9624. Cornblit, Oscar and **Jorge García-Bouza.** Report on data inventories in Chile, Argentina and Venezuela (ISSC/SSI, 9:2, April 1970, p. 69-73, tables)

A useful indicator of the types and amounts of data available and where they may be located.

9625. Cornelius, Wayne A. and **Felicity M. Trueblood** eds. Anthropological perspectives on Latin American urbanization. Beverly Hills, Calif., Sage Publications, 1974. 296 p., bibl., tables. (Latin American urban research, 4)

This current vol. in the Sage Publication Series on Latin American Urban Research is an exciting and highly scholarly addition to the field of urbanism. Refreshing perspective opposed to the concepts of anomie, alienation and the "culture of poverty." Contents are:
Robert V. Kemper "Family and Household Organization among Tzintzuntzan Migrants in Mexico City" (see item 1154)
Jack R. Rollwagen "Mediation and Rural-urban Migration in Mexico: a Proposal and a Case Study" (see item 1178)
Anthony Leeds "Housing Settlement Types, Arrangements for Living, Proletarianization, and the Social Structure of the City" (see item 1499)
Lisa R. Peattie "The Concept of 'Marginality' as Applied to Squatter Settlements in Lima" (see item 1546)
Larissa Lomnitz "The Social and Economic Organization of a Mexican Shantytown" (see item 1158)
Michael B. Whiteford "Neighbors at a Distance: Life in a Low-Income Colombian Barrio" (see item 1554)
Douglas Butterworth "Grass-Roots Political Organization in Cuba: a Case of the Committees for the Defense of the Revolution" (see item 9786)
Bryan R. Roberts "The Interrelationships of City and Provinces in Peru and Guatemala" (see item 1176)
Billie Jean Isbell "The Influence of Migrants upon Traditional Social and Political Concepts: a Peruvian Case Study" (see item 1495)
"Select Bibliography: 1972-1974" p. 263-296. [N.S. Kinzer]

9626. Cré, Gerard de. Realignments of class attitudes in the military and bourgeoisie in developing countries: Egypt, Peru and Cuba (YU/IJCS, 15:1/2, March/June 1974, p. 35-46, bibl.)

In areas which were formerly hinterland to the centers of industrialization, development (secondary) implies drastic changes in social awareness (values, attitudes, etc.) relative to the modernization of social structures (in this case imposed by the military "revolutionary" regimes). In this paper, the comparison between Egypt, Peru and Cuba proves that the struggle for reforms is more a differentiation of class ideologies (within the bourgeoisie) rather than a true inter-class conflict. [P.F. Hernández]

9627. Curso Regional Interamericano sobre Colocación Familiar, Adopción y Libertad Vigilada, *I, Montevideo, 1970.* [Actas]. Montevideo, O.E.A., Instituto del Niño, 1972. 310 p., tables.

Resumé of laws and general social work philosophy regarding adoption in Uruguay, Argentina, Peru and Chile. Useful only to social workers. [N.S. Kinzer]

9628. D'Andréa, Flávio Fortes. A realidade interna: psicodrama aplicado. São Paulo, Difel, 1974. 157 p., tables.

An attempt to present and discuss Moreno's theory and methodology of psychodrama and its possible application in a number of sociocultural conflictive settings. Interesting discussion and often good critical evaluation of potentials of such technique. [J.F.B. Dasilva]

Davidson, Maria. A comparative study of fertility in Mexico City and Caracas. See item 2026.

Desarrollo Económico. See item 2027.

9629. Dixon, James C. The effect of social desirability on two dimensions of self-evaluation in two cultures (JSP, 92:2, April 1974, p. 167-171, bibl., tables)

The paper relates an experiment of modest range concerning the self-concept measurements in three different universities (one US, one Central American, and one South American). No significant cross-cultural differences were found and only—as it could have been predicted—a higher self-reported neuroticism in all cases; perhaps more attributable to a better perception of the factors needed to alter the subjects' social set. [P.F. Hernández]

9630. _____ and others. Perceived locus of self in two cultures (SIP/RIP, 6:3/4, 1972, p. 201-211, tables)

Is there any likelihood of relation between self-perception and other aspects of the personality system? The article does not support evidence, but makes interesting inroads. The research subjects were students from three universities: Florida, US; Costa Rica; and del Valle, Colo.

9631. Dow, James. Models of middlemen: issues concerning the economic exploitation of modern peasants (SAA/HO, 32:4, Winter 1973, p. 397-406, bibl., illus.)

The exploitation of peasant strata by economic intermediaries is analyzed here with rather simple mathematical instruments. The study shows that the definite tendency of peasant and national economies to merge has not been achieved because of structural factors (many peasants remain in subsistence agriculture). [P.F. Hernández]

9632. *Estudios de Planificación Familiar.* Consejo de Población [and] Asociación Colombiana de Facultades de Medicina, División de Estudios de Población. Vol. 3, No. 3, marzo 1972- Bogotá.

Los autores presentan un gran número de cuadros y gráficos con el propósito de documentar la distribución mundial de métodos anticonceptivos y el efecto que han logrado en el control de la fecundidad.

9633. Flora, Cornelia Butler. The passive female and social change: a cross-cultural comparison of women's magazine fiction (*in* Pescatello, Ann *ed.* Female and male in Latin America [see item 9665] p. 59-85, bibl., tables)

Findings in Colombia and Mexico are compared with US life through the examples of 202 short stories. Although general views of female passivity and traditional roles hold true, it is clear that the Latin American female is undergoing rapid transformation and that many a generalization in the area is really due to Western (industrialized societies) preconceptions. Areas such as initiative, intellectual careers, independence, and social mobility were also studied. [P.F. Hernández]

9634. Geithman, David T. Middle class growth and economic development in Latin America (AJES, 33:1, Jan. 1974, p. 45-58)

This sober review of a considerable volume of literature on the topic points out the danger of generalizations which are based upon the experience of Western industrial nations: in Latin America, as Bonilla says (see *Ciencias Sociales*, v. 7., p. 150), "The gains have been superficial, precarious and slow." [P.F. Hernández]

9635. Germani, Gino. El concepto de marginalidad: significado, raíces históricas y cuestiones teóricas, con particular referencia a la marginalidad urbana. B.A., Ediciones Nueva Visión, 1973. 110 p., tables.

The clear vision and analysis of an insightful sociologist helps to clarify the concept of marginality (from the urban to the cultural sense) and to put it in a perspective which can be most helpful for applied research, namely along the lines of descriptive and causal inquiries. The book contains also a good overview of rural marginality in Latin America. [P.F. Hernández]

9636. ———. O professor e a cátedra (CLAPCS/AL, 13:1, jan./março 1970, p. 83-103)

General discussion of factors contributing to instability of the Latin American university. Exogenous factors include: political instability, fragmentation in society and the intervention of political parties. Germani contends that internal factors such as politicized professors, student intervention and a lack of an internal labor market to absorb unemployed university professors are more salient items. [N.S. Kinzer]

9637. Giraldo, Octavio. El machismo como fenómeno psicocultural (Revista Latinoamericana de Psicología [Bogotá] 4:3, 1972, p. 295-309, table)

Good general essay on the *machismo* complex. Emphasis is on its characteristics, psycho-social origins, and cultural supports.

9638. Godoy, Horacio H. El desarrollo de las ciencias sociales en América Latina en la década de 1970 (FLACSO/RLCP, 1:1, abril 1970, p. 7-19)

General outline of methodological principles for social science research in Latin America. Rather tired rehash. [N.S. Kinzer]

Goldsmith, Alfredo; Rona Goldberg; and Gilda Echeverría. An in-depth study of vasectomized men in Latin America: a preliminary report. See item 2034.

9639. Gräbener, Jürgen. Klassenbewusstsein and Rassenideologie in Lateinamerika: Überlegungen zu einer Typologie von Entlastungskonflikten (*in* Gräbener, Jürgen *comp.* Kassengesellschaft und Rassismus [see *HLAS 35:8268*] p. 131-147, table)

General treatise on social class and race relations in Latin America, with special attention to the cases of Guyana, Haiti, and Brazil.

9640. Graña, César. Cultural identity as an intellectual invention: some Spanish American examples. B.A., Instituto Torcuato Di Tella, Centro de Investigaciones Sociales, 1967. 13 p.

Paper given during the symposium on siology of the Intellectuals, B.A., 3-5 July 1967. Some reflections on the ideological currents in the sociology of knowledge in Latin America. [P.F. Hernández]

9641. Hammer, Henry B. A cross-cultural investigation of Foster's image of limited good (SIP/RIP, 6:3/4, 1972, p. 255-264, bibl., tables)

Working with Foster's hypothesis of "limited good" (Tinzuntzan, 1967), the author confirms that the more deprived children tend to see their own world as one in which there is very little room for hope of better living standards. [P.F. Hernández]

9642. Henríquez de Paredes, Querubina. Consideraciones sociológicas sobre la sexualidad (UJSC/ECA, 27:285, julio 1972, p. 465-470)

Only a journalistic overview; not relevant for research. [P.F. Hernández]

9643. Hopkins, Jack W. Contemporary research on public administration and bureaucracies in Latin America (LARR, 9:1, Spring 1974, p. 109-139, bibl.)

Very useful review of the scanty literature related to the study of complex organizations in Latin America.

9644. Horowitz, Irving Louis. Research priorities for the second development decade (RU/SCID, 7:2, Summer 1972, p. 181-186)

From a thorough review of the available literature, the author concludes that there has been too much emphasis placed on the nation-state as the unit of analysis in development research. Calls for investigations into the relationships between key sectors at an international level, as well as for analyses of socio-psychological factors in development.

9645. Ianni, Octávio. Sociologie e dépendance scientifique en Amérique Latine (ISSC/SSI, 9:4, août 1970, p. 95-110)

An interesting discussion of the impact of European and North American social thought on the analysis of "development" In Latin America.

9646. Illich, Ivan. De como aventajar a los países "desarrollados" (IDES/DE, 12:47, oct./dic. 1972, p. 601-611)

Author criticizes the imposition and acceptance in developing countries of "prefabricated" solutions to social problems elaborated in more advanced nations. Calls for research that will uncover alternatives that are more compatible with the economic realities of the Third World nations.

International Journal of Comparative Sociology. See item 1494.

The International Migration Review. See item 2043.

9647. Jaffe, A.J. Notes on family income distribution in developing countries in relation to population and economic changes (IASI/E, 26:104, sept. 1969, p. 361-376, bibl.)

Author explains and documents (with data from Argentina, Mexico, Panama, Puerto Rico, Iran, and the US) how it is possible for a country to experience rapid economic growth and at the same time fail to redistribute income more equitably.

9648. Kaplan, Lawrence ed. Revolutions: a comparative study. N.Y., Random House, 1973. 482 p., bibl.

A compilation of some of the best writings on revolutions, from the English Revolution of the 17th century to the present. Includes selections by Cosío Villegas and Zeitlin which place the revolutions of Mexico and Cuba, respectively, in a comparative and historical perspective.

9649. Kaplan, Marcos. La reforma urbana en América Latina (BNCE/CE, 22:7, julio 1972, p. 635-642)

Analyzes the relative effectiveness of the urban reform programs of Colombia, Bolivia, and Cuba.

Kemper, Robert V. Rural-urban migration in Latin America: a framework for the comparative analysis of geographic and temporal patterns. See item 2044.

9650. Kepecs, Joseph G. Psychological problems in working in developing countries (IJSP, 19:1/2, Spring/Summer 1973, p. 66-69, bibl.)

An interesting analysis of some examples of "culture shock" from a psychiatric point of view.

Kiser, Clyde V. Unresolved issues in research and fertility in Latin America. See item 2046.

9651. Lalive D'Espinay, Christian. Religión e ideología en una perspectiva sociológica. Río Piedras, P.R., Ediciones del Seminario Evangélico de Puerto Rico, 1973. 62 p.

A brief and coherent insight into the dichotomies (social reality vs. evangelical mission) of Latin American Pentecostalism. [P.F. Hernández]

9652. Lobo, Roberto Jorge Haddock. Psicologia dos desportes. Com apêndice de Roberto Simões. Con um capítulo do Luiz Carlos Agostini. São Paulo, Editôra Atlas, 1973. 202 p., bibl., illus.

A rather detailed attempt to apply theoretical and research materials from psychology (and some from social psychology and sociology) for group dynamics and individual development in sports. Interesting work in an area still highly heterogeneous. See also item 9654. [J.F.B. Dasilva]

9653. Lombardi, Miguel C. Fundamentos de sociología. B.A., Ediciones Centro de Estudios, 1973. 300 p. (Serie Introducciones, 2)

An introductory text-book with a traditional approach and a certain disdain for empirical studies; it has nevertheless some innovative views of Marxian analysis and some references to Latin American studies which are less known in the sociological milieu. [P.F. Hernández]

9654. Lyra Filho, João. Introducão à sociologia dos desportos. Rio, Bloch Editores *em convênio com o* Instituto Nacional do Livro, Ministério da Educação e Cultura, 1973. 390 p., bibl. (Col. Univ. do Estado da Guanabara, 1)

A good general introduction to the "sociology of sports" through a number of essays and attempting to bring together a variety of theoretical viewpoints. Much of the material is descriptive but covers a series of areas, and can be viewed as an "ethnology" of sports. Interesting for the general public as well as the specialist. See also item 9652. [J.F.B. Dasilva]

9655. Mathiason, John R. Patterns of powerlessness among urban poor: toward the use of mass communications for rapid social change (RU/SCID, 7:1, Spring 1972, p. 64-84, tables)

An incisive article which divides the sources of powerlessness into three categories. It was found that, "inability to adequately discriminate among objects" was the major factor in "powerlessness."

9656. Melo, José Marques de. Reflexões sôbre temas de comunicação. São Paulo, Univ. de São Paulo, Escola de Comunicações e Artes, 1972. 128 p. (Série Comunicações. Série Z, texto 1. "Especial")

Thoughts on the character and role of mass communication systems in modern life. Its relation with propaganda, its possible impact on education and economic as well as cultural life in general are examined briefly among other issues. General and essayistic. [J.F.B. Dasilva]

9657. Miller, John and **Ralph A. Gakenheimer** eds. Latin American urban policies and the social sciences. Beverly Hills, Calif., Sage Publications, 1971. 398 p., maps, tables.

Presents the papers read at the Jahuel Seminar on the Social Sciences and Urban Development in Latin America, held 22-25 April 1968. The participants, most of them North Americans, focused primarily on national urban policies and urbanization. For geographer's comment, see item 6531.

9658. Morales Vergara, Julio. Latinoamericanos en Europa, aspectos demográficos examinados a la luz de antecedentes censales de algunos países seleccionados (ICEM/IM, 12:1/2, 1974, p. 14-32, tables)

Given the extreme scarcity of sources and reports in

the field, the article constitutes an important piece of research. It clearly shows the big increase of Latin American migration to France, Italy, Belgium and Sweden, in particular during the 1970s. Most affected countries in Latin America are: Brazil, Peru, Colombia and the southern cone. Undoubtedly, the recent case of Chile completes the picture. [P.F. Hernández]

9659. Morse, Richard M. Primacía, regionalización, dependencia: enfoques sobre las ciudades latinoamericanas en el desarrollo nacional (IDES/DE, 11:41, abril/junio 1971, p. 55-85, bibl., tables)

Critical evaluation of what the author considers to be the principal foci of studies on the role of cities in national development: primacy, regionalism, and dependency.

9660. Moxley, Robert L. Social solidarity, ethnic rigidity and differentiation in Latin American communities: a structural approach (RSS/RS, 38:4, Winter 1973, p. 439-461, bibl., tables)

Precollected data from 39 Latin American community studies are analyzed in order to test the hypothesis that there is an inverse relationship between social solidarity and ethnic rigidity. The findings are probably not as significant as the author's operationalization of solidarity and rigidity, which are both measured by Guttman scales.

9661. Nun, José; Miguel Murmis; and Juan Carlos Marín. La marginalidad en América Latina: informe preliminar. B.A., Instituto Torcuato Di Tella, Centro de Investigaciones Sociales, 1968. 78 p. (Documento de trabajo, 53)

As noted this publication is an "informe preliminar" or in essence a review of the literature dealing with marginality and dependency. [N.S. Kinzer]

9662. Parrés, Ramón. Visión dinámica del disentir de la juventud (CAM, 170:3, mayo/junio 1970, p. 61-67)

Literary reflections on the topic: a journalistic editorial of very minor interest. [P.F. Hernández]

9663. Parrilla-Bonilla, Antulio. Cooperativismo: teoría y práctica. San Juan, Univ. de Puerto Rico, 1971. 352 p., bibl.

An excellent manual on the subject: it combines American and Latin American perspectives. Possibly among the best of its kind in Spanish. [P.F. Hernández]

9664. Peruzzolo, Adair Caetano. Comunicação e cultura. Pôrto Alegre, Bra., Livraria Sulina Editôra, 1972. 384 p., bibl. (Col. SERPAL, 1)

A collection of essays on the relationships and impact of communication processes and systems on the sphere of culture. Some of the contemporary developments in communication systems and their potential in education and development are also discussed. More for information than for technical use. [J.F.B. Dasilva]

9665. Pescatello, Ann ed. Female and male in Latin America: essays. Pittsburgh, Pa., Univ. of Pittsburgh Press, 1973. 342 p.

The essays included here were presented at the III Biennial Meeting of the Latin American Studies Association, Austin, Tex., Dec. 1971. Seven of the 12 essays deal with women in South America, specifically: Argentina (two of these), Colombia, Peru (two), Chile, Brazil. Especially worthy of note are Evelyn Stevens' "Marianismo: the Other Face of Machismo in Latin America," and Nancy Hollander's "Women: the Forgotten Half of Argentine History." A well-chosen collection of important essays. Highly recommended. [G.M. Dorn]

――――. The female in Ibero-America: an essay on research bibliography and research directions. See *HLAS 36:1513*.

Portes, Alejandro. The factorial structure of modernity: empirical replications and a critique. See item 9769.

9666. ――――. Sociology and the use of secondary data. Austin, Univ. of Texas Press, Institute of Latin American Studies, 1973. 56 p., bibl., tables (Offprint series, 150)

An excellent discussion of methodological problems inherent in using secondary data from Latin America. Portes focuses on four main parameters of data: availability, reliability, validity, and representativeness. Originally published in Robert S. Byars and Joseph L. Love eds. *Quantitative social science research on Latin America* (Urbana, Univ. of Illinois Press, 1973). [N.S. Kinzer]

9667. Poyares, Walter Ramos. Megacomunicação: uma nova dimensão da sociedade contemporânea. Rio, Livraria Agir Editôra, 1973. 150 p.

An essay, sometimes polemic, on the increasing importance of complex systems of communication in modern society and its relation to the process of mass culture. Discussion draws upon a variety of fields, including sociology, but more for argumentation than for technical concerns. Of limited interest as sociological material. [J.F.B. Dasilva]

9668. Psicopatología de los vicios: vistos por los más capacitados expertos. México, Organización Editorial, 1971. 125 p.

Eight brief literary essays on the topics of gambling, alcohol, tobacco and prostitution: not of scientific interest. [P.F. Hernández]

9669. Quintero Rodríguez, Alvaro. Así

son . . . Bogotá, Canal Ramírez—Antares, 1973. 121 p., plates.

Literary essays on contemporary youth in Latin America. Of limited interest for research. [P.F. Hernández]

9670. Rascovsky, Arnaldo and others. Niveles profundos del psiquismo. B.A., Editorial Sudamericana, 1971. 343 p., bibl. (Biblioteca de psicología)

Classical Freudian analysts report case histories illustrating how foetal and neonatal experiences affect development of the psyche. The intellectual contribution and cultural level of this collection is best judged by the chapter title, *"Tabaquismo y Coprofilia."* [N.S. Kinzer]

9671. Redclift, M.R. Squatter settlements in Latin American cities: the response from government (JDS, 10:1, Oct. 1973, p. 92-109, bibl.)

A brief overview of most relevant literature on the topic shows that there is an inverse relation between the increase in bureaucratic official intervention on behalf of squatter population and the effectiveness of their help. [P.F. Hernández]

9672. Ribeiro, Darcy. Cultura y alienación (Difusión Económica [Guayaquil, Ecua.] 10:3, dic. 1972, p. 49-66)

This is a reprint from a chapter in the book by the same author of *Propuestas acerca del subdesarrollo* (1969). The main theme is that consciousness is closely related to conjunctural circumstances (structural underpinnings of the social situation) and changes in spite of the possible manipulation and constraints through propaganda and repression. An interesting theoretical formulation by a well knows scholar. [J.F.B. Dasilva]

9673. Ribeiro de Oliveria, Pedro A. Le catholicisme populaire en Amérique Latine (FERES/SC, 19:4, 1972, p. 567-584, bibl.)

This work is really a critical note on a brief but most relevant bibliography on the topic. The author shows that the various typologies of Latin-American religiosity do not justify a question of pluralistic Catholicism but of different styles. His analysis of practices and their cultural "constellations" is worth reading. [P.F. Hernández]

9674. Richardson, Miles; Marta Eugenia Pardo; and **Barbara Bode.** The image of Christ in Spanish America as a model for suffering (UM/JIAS, 13:2, April 1971, p. 246-257, tables)

The "fatalism" of Latin Americans has been an important topic to such authors as George Foster and Huizer. Major contention has been that "fatalism" inhibits economic development. Article opens the above hypothesis to serious question.

9675. Roberts, Bryan R. The interrelationships of city and provinces in Peru and Guatemala (*in* Cornelius, Wayne A. and Felicity M. Trueblood *eds.* Anthropological perspectives on Latin American urbanization [see item 9625] p. 207-235, bibl.)

A very good study of cases in comparative analysis of urban behavior: it shows the greater strength of Peru's organization of urban immigrants. Fiesta systems and other important facts are studied in light of many variables. For ethnologist's comment, see item 1176. [P.F. Hernández]

9676. Rofman, Alejandro B. Strutturazione dello spazio in una società dipendente: il caso latino-americano (IFSNC/CD, 27/28, Summer 1972, p. 185-215)

An essay on the impact of a dependent capitalist economy, such as that which predominates through Latin America, on the spatial distribution of the population.

9677. Ross, John A.; Adrienne Germain; Jacqueline Forrest; and **Jeroen van Ginneken.** Hallazgos de la investigación sobre planificación familiar. Bogota, Consejo de Población [and] Univ. de Colombia, Instituto Internacional para el Estudio de la Reproducción Humana, 1972. 92 p., bibl. (Informe sobre poblacion/planificación familiar, 12)

Con la intencion de que este boletín sirva de referencia a investigadores, los autores han producido una valiosa y concisa síntesis de las principales conclusiones formuladas por numerosos estudios con respecto a la planificación familiar. Excelente bibliografia.

9678. Ruiz Ortiz, Ernesto. A mis amigos de la locura. Río Piedras, P.R., Ediciones Puerto, 1973. 68 p. (Aguja para mareantes, 5. Narrativa)

Short, incisive reflection on the topic of sanity vs. psychiatry. [P.F. Hernández]

9679. Russell, D.E.H. Rebellion, revolution, and armed force: a comparative study of fifteen countries with special emphasis on Cuba and South Africa. N.Y., Academic Press, 1974. 210 p., bibl.

Unlike the Kaplan book (see item 9648), this work has an overall purpose: the discovery of why some rebellions fail while others succeed. The principal contrasting cases examined are South Africa and Cuba, but the author also describes 13 other successful and unsuccessful rebellions, including six in Latin America.

9680. Sanders, Thomas G. Population planning and belief systems: the Catholic Church in Latin America (*in* Brown, Harrison and Edward Hutchings, Jr. *eds.* Are our descendants doomed? Technological change and population growth. N.Y., The Viking Press, 1972, p. 306-329, bibl.)

Cogent discussion of schism amongst Latin American Roman Catholic hierarchy regarding issue of contraception. Excellent synthesis of Sanders' research for *American University Field Staff Reports* on: abortion, contraception, folk Catholicism and liberal vs. conservative clergy. [N.S. Kinzer]

9681. Santos, Theotonio dos. Concepto de clases sociales. B.A., Editorial Galerna, 1973. 107 p.

Author attempts to clarify and defend Marx's concept of social classes over the objections raised by Gurvitch and Ossowsky.

9682. Segal, Sheldon J. and **Christopher Tietze.** Tecnología anticonceptiva: métodos actuales y prospectivos. Bogotá, Consejo de Población [and] Univ. Nacional de Colombia, Instituto Internacional para el Estudio de la Reproducción Humana, 1974? 35 p., bibl. (Informe sobre población/planificación familiar)

Boletín elemental pero informativo sobre las ventajas, desventajas, y eficiencia de cada uno de los actuales métodos anticonceptivos. Tambien indica posibles fronteras para la tecnología anticonceptiva. Excelente bibliografía.

9683. Silvacolmenares, Julio. ¡No...más...hijos! Genocidio preventivo en los países subdesarrollados. Bogotá, Ediciones Paulinas, 11 p., tables (Col. Defendamos la vida, 4)

This work is an excellent (also well written) exposé of that biased symbiosis of Catholic views and classic Marxist interpretation of the over-population problem. While expressing many points on behalf of the working classes, such a symbiosis fails to consider the real dimensions of the problem for the family of man.

Simmons, Alan B. Ambivalence towards small families in rural Latin America. See item 2062.

9684. Singelmann, Peter. Campesino movements and class conflict in Latin America: the functions of exchange and power (UM/JIAS, 16:1, Feb. 1974, p. 39-72, bibl.)

Using exchange theory, Singlemann focuses on transactions and exchanges campesinos engage in both horizontally (with peers) and vertically (with landlords and other patrons). Good review of the literature on campesino movements. Interesting theoretical framework. [N.S. Kinzer]

9685. Sito, Nilda. Estructura ocupacional: desarrollo y sindicalismo en los países latinoamericanos (ITT/RLS, 7:1, 1971, p. 6-36, tables)

Combines official statistics from various Latin American countries in order to analyze the impact of organized labor movements on the occupational and economic structures and on the redistribution of property and income. The relationships were regarded as very complex, confounded primarily by the inflation variable.

9686. Smith, T. Lynn. Los impedimentos a la reforma agraria en la América Latina (USIA/PI, 19:6, nov./dic. 1972, p. 23-30, plates)

Broad general overview of barriers to agricultural reform in Latin America. Smith delineates three areas: 1) the hacienda system; 2) inefficient crop rotation and planting; and 3) inefficient harvesting methods. [N.S. Kinzer]

9687. _____. The sociology of agricultural development. Leiden, The Netherlands, E.J. Brill, 1972. 103 p., bibl. (Monographs and theoretical studies in sociology and anthropology in honour of Nels Anderson, 2)

The author's life-long dedication to the study of rural life in Latin America and the US provides the basis for this excellent and concise treatise on the problems of agricultural development. Of interest not only to Latinamericanists, but also to those in rural sociology and the sociology of development.

9688. *Social and Economic Studies.* Univ. of the West Indies, Institute of Social and Economic Research. Vol. 22, No. 4, Dec. 1973- . Kingston.

This issue includes an article by Andrew Sanders "Amerindians," a superb anthropological work on family structure and its repercussions in today's life. [P.F. Hernández]

9689. La sociologie du développement latino-américain: pt. 1 (Current Sociology/La Sociologie Contemporaine [UNESCO, Paris] 18:1, 1970, p. 6-96, bibl.)

This paper, an introduction to item 9690, presents a good overview of the pioneer and free-lance sociologists who opened-up the professional and academic areas of the discipline in Latin America. [P.F. Hernández]

9690. La sociologie du développement latino-américain: pt. 2 (Current Sociology/La Sociologie Contemporaine [UNESCO, Paris] 19:1, 1971, p. 4-128, bibl.)

An excellent overview of major scholars, schools and ideologies in Latin American sociology. Of uppermost value for the assessment of current research in most sociological areas, except demography. [P.F. Hernández]

9691. Telecommunicações: alguns temas. Rio, Empresa Brasileria de Telecomunicações, 1972. 312 p., tables.

A collection of essays on communication including discussion on its role and potential in modern society, its impact on regionalism and social relations, its relation to economic development, etc. Non-technical presentation addressed to the general reader. [J.F.B. Dasilva]

9692. Temas. Teoria e prática do psiquiatra. Hospital do Servidor Público Estadual, Grupo de Estudos Psiquiátricos. Año 1, No. 2, dez. 1971- . São Paulo.

Although mainly a journal dedicated to professional communication of research and studies in psychiatry some of the papers are of interest for the sociologists and social-psychologist. Topics are: the "other" in art and psychiatry; theories in psychiatry: frigidity, confusion and pessimism; methods in psychiatry; and occupational therapy. [J.F.B. Dasilva]

9693. Tendencias demográficas y opciones para políticas de población en América Latina (UNECLA/B, 16:1, 1. semestre 1971, p. 63-96, tables)

Good overall view of population question. Includes pros and cons of family planning, governmental policies, socio-demographic factors associated with birth control and family planning. A resumé with no new information. [N.S. Kinzer]

9694. Vapñarsky, César A: Información deficiente en la investigación social para el planeamieto: algunos problemas que presenta en América Latina (Difusión Económica [Guayaquil, Ecua.] 10:2, agosto 1972, p. 177-189)

Ensayo sobre las dificultades que enfrenta el científico social en América Latina cuando intenta obtener datos confiables. El nivel del ensayo es algo elemental: es una buena sintesis, pero carece de nuevas perspectivas.

9695. Victoria, Marcos. Psicología del fútbol. B.A., Emecé Editores, 1971. 96 p. (Cuadernos de ensayos)

Supposedly a phenomenological analysis of football's (soccer) existential meaning. Written with well-larded amounts of French phrases and loaded with impressive references, this book contributes little to our understanding of a world-wide, well enjoyed spectator sport. [N.S. Kinzer]

9696. Villalba, Alfonso. Juventud, autoridad, violencia (PUC/V, 17:66, junho 1972, p. 157-169)

A more traditional discussion of the problems of the "generation gap" and "violence."

9697. Weil, Pierre and **Roland Tompakow.** O corpo fala: a linguagem silenciosa da comunicação não-verbal. Petrópolis, Bra., Editôra Vozes, 1973. 291 p., illus.

A presentation for the general public of the main ideas and referents in non-verbal communication. Outlines the general framework for a system of rules to "read" the symbolic communication of body movements. Of little sociological interest unless used as a document of cultural expression. [J.F.B. Dasilva]

9698. Weller, Robert; John J. Macisco, Jr.; and **George R. Martine.** The relative growth and importance of the components of urban growth in Latin America (PAA/D, 8:2, May 1971, p. 225-232, bibl., tables)

Authors point out that it is popular but fallacious to ascribe a single factor cause to Latin America's explosive urban growth rate—i.e. rural to urban migration. Based on data from several cities they show that urban growth rate is due to: in-migration to large cities, growth of localities previously too small to be classified as urban and extremely high birthrates of in-migrants after arrival in the city. [N.S. Kinzer]

9699. Wilson, Samuel. Occupational mobility and social stratification in Latin American cities. Ithaca, N.Y., Cornell Univ., 1972. 123 p., bibl., illus. (Dissertation series, 43)

Four capital cities of South America (Rio, B.A., Santiago and Montevideo) were selected for this thesis on social stratification. Its most relevant feature is a series of dynamic models of the variables most affecting social mobility in the various urban settings. [P.F. Hernández]

MEXICO, CENTRAL AMERICA, THE CARIBBEAN AND THE GUIANAS

PEDRO F. HERNANDEZ
Associate Professor of Sociology
Loyola University

FOR THOSE INTERESTED IN A GENERAL OVERVIEW of sociology in Latin America, the following serial publications are of value: *Boletín de Estudios Latinoamericanos,* published since 1965 by CEDLA (Centro de Estudios y Documentación Latinoamericana, Amsterdam) and *Bulletin Signalétique, Séction 21: Sociologie, Ethnologie,* published by CNRS (Centre National de la Recherche Scientifique, Paris), both of which have complemented the aims of *HLAS* during the past decade. A project funded by UNESCO and directed by P. González Casanova offers a glimpse of the history of Latin American sociology, its pioneers as well as major research trends since World War II. We hope that bibliographies on the development of sociology in each country will be compiled in the future.

Demography is prominent among the topics under review (see items 9711, 9718-9719, 9721, 9731, 9737, 9749, 9755-9757, 9759, 9763-9764 and 9768) and includes population projections and other instruments of population analysis, following the publication of the censuses of the 1970s. Rural poverty is another popular topic (see items 9703, 9705 and 9735) as is neo-colonialism (see item 9708). One cannot detect other major topics and even less attempts to rank them with objectivity. There is, however, quite a number of socio-psychological studies and literary works on the subject of national character and social "stereotypes" which if not scientific are of relevance to the sociologist. The lack of theoretical works is as noticeable now as it was two years ago.

An area synthesis of trends and topics in contemporary Latin American sociology is long overdue: UNESCO among other research agencies has been most sensitive to this issue. Every year, however, the same obstacles arise: lack of an effective system of coordination and publication of basic materials, i.e. complete annotated bibliographies, by countries and disciplines. There is also need of a research team that could devote itself entirely to compiling and evaluating sociological research in Latin America. This should be one of the first priorities of a future University of the United Nations, an ideal institution with the manpower and resources required for a task of this magnitude.

MEXICO

9700. Acosta, Helia D'. Veinte hombres y yo. México, Editores Asociados, 1972. 326 p. (Col. México vivo)

A series of Mexican personalities, from politics and literature to theater and entertainment (like Tito Guizar) are portrayed in a gifted array of memoirs from personal interviews.

9701. Alegría, Juana Armanda. Psicología de las mexicanas. México, Editorial Samo, 1974. 187 p. (Serie Cuarta dimensión)

An interesting literary essay on ancient and contemporary topics of women roles in Mexican society, lacking, though, a real psychological treatment.

9702. Amara, Giuseppe and others. 5,000 [i.e. Cinco mil] años de fracaso: actualidad del hombre. Mexico, Editorial Samo, 1971. 326 p., plates (Col. Hoy, el hombre. Serie Temática moderna)

Eight Mexican psycho-analysts present a good survey of contemporary literature around major existential topics of modern life in industrial societies: alienation, anxiety, promiscuity, violence, overpopulation and crowdedness, love, maturity, religion, youth and authority.

9703. Araud, Christian. Una experiencia de "Advocacy planning" en México (UNAM/RMS, 35:4, oct./dic. 1973, p. 773-782).

This case study shows that bureaucracies are handicapped in dealing effectively with the problem of housing in poverty areas and that the technician turned advocate will fail when the essential groups of community organization are lacking.

9704. Balán, Jorge; Harley L. Browning; Elizabeth Jelin; and Waltraut Feindt. Men in developing society: geographic and social mobility in Monterrey, Mexico. Austin, Univ. of Texas Press *for the* Institute of Latin American Studies, 1973. 348 p., bibl., maps, tables.

A model monographic work (and a thorough one) and a "must" among research tools for any future research on socio-economic problems of the area.

Brown, Jane Cowan. Patterns of intra-urban settlement in Mexico City: an examination of the Turner Theory. See item 6662.

9705. Bussey, Ellen M. The flight from rural poverty—how nations cope. Lexington, Mass., D.C. Heath, 1973. 132 p., maps, tables (Lexington books)

An interesting monograph comparing the processes of rural migration and urbanization in Mexico, Italy and the Netherlands. Provides new insights into the general area of poverty and man's struggle against it.

9706. Chance, John K. Parentesco y residencia urbana: grupo familiar y sus organización en un suburbio de Oaxaca, México (III/AI, 33:1, 1. trimestre 1973, p. 187-212, bibl., tables)

Study with high standards of scholarship, offers anthropological insight into the phenomenon of kinship and residence in a "squatter settlement" of the province. Shows that the term "squatter settlement" involves a series of family arrangements of great complexity.

9707. Cone, Cynthia A. Perceptions of occupation in a newly industrializing region of Mexico (SAA/HO, 32:2, Summer 1973, p. 143-151, bibl., illus.)

This study is part of a large project related to the impact of modernization in Ciudad Sahagin. It shows that while the labor force still prefers rural work, there has been a growing acceptance of factory employment, especially noticeable in attitudes concerning future occupations of children.

Davidson, Maria. A comparative study of fertility in Mexico City and Caracas. See item 2026.

9708. Di Tella, Torcuato S. Las clases peligrosas a comienzos del siglo XIX en México (IDES/DE, 12:48, enero/marzo 1973, p. 761-791, tables)

On the basis of scattered information and following the inspirations of Oscar Cornbilt (on the mass revolts in Peru and Bolivia in the 18th century) the author conducts a historical analysis of the lower classes which comes close to their definition in "ideal type" terms.

9709. Díaz-Guerrero, Rogelio. Una escala factorial de premisas histórico-socioculturales de la familia mexicana (SIP/RIP, 6:3/4, 1972, p. 235-244, tables)

Consistent with previous thesis of his research, the author looks for the real causes of normal behavior in the cultural setting of the actor. Here, 190 secondary school students in Mexico City answer 22 very select questions on family background whose factor analysis explains more than 2/3 of the variances.

9710. _____ and **Luis Lara Tapia.** Diferencias sexuales en el desarrollo de la personalidad del escolar mexicano (Revista Latinoamericana de Psicología [Bogotá] 4:3, 1972, p. 345-351, tables)

The application of the Holtzman Inkblot Technique (HIT) to a very adequate sample of Mexican children of various school systems (public and private, in different class milieus) apparently supports the fact that Mexican males are more active than their female counterparts when measured by the same coefficient as American (US) males.

9711. Echanove Trujillo, Carlos A. Sociología mexicana: superficie y fondo México. 4. ed. México, Editorial Porrúa, 1972. 569 p., illus., plates, tables.

The author's work has been already surveyed and extensively criticized in professional journals: the novelty of his 4. ed. and the up-dating of data (1970 census figures) and literary sources make it worthy of special mention. It is one of the most interesting attempts at analyzing major sociological traits of Mexican society. Written in an indigenous and scholarly vein, in spite of redundancies and long descriptions.

Escamilla, Mercedes. Investigación socioeconómica directa de los ejidos de Aguascaliente. See item 6668.

9712. García Ramírez, Sergio. El centro penitenciario del estado de México: significado, funcionamiento y proyecciones (UD/ED, 19:43, mayo/agosto 1971, p. 351-357, bibl.)

An excellent and documented description of the Penitentiary Center of the Capital: brief indications also of important bibliography on the topic.

9713. Gaxiola, Manuel J. La serpiente y la paloma: análisis del crecimiento de la Iglesia Apostólica de la fe en Cristo Jesús de México. South Pasedena, Calif., Christian Mission Books, 1970. 177 p., bibl., map, plates (William Carey Library)

A very interesting report—with some historical research—concerning the origins and progress of evangelism in Mexico.

9714. Gibaja, Regina E. Religión y secularización entre-campesinos y obreros (UNAM/RMS, abril/junio 1972, p. 193-244, tables)

This study is based upon functionalist premises (theoretical): the concept of secularization is geared toward the discovery of conflict between material, worldly value premises, and ideas of God inasmuch as they relate to social action. Although it is 10 years old (1964), the research points to some significant differences. However, there exists a close similarity in the maintenance of moral codes in almost all cases (with more autonomy from Church in the urban setting).

9715. González Cossio, Arturo. México: cuatro ensayos de sociología política. México, UNAM, Facultad de Ciencias Políticas y Sociales, 1972. 177 p., bibl., tables (Serie estudios, 28)

Among the papers hereby presented, only the essay on "The Mexican State" was not previously published elsewhere. They all are, however, still timely and relevant (particularly the article on "Mexican Social Classes and Strata") for any student of the Mexican society.

9716. González Salazar, Gloria. Crecimiento económico y desigualdad social en México: una visión esquemática (UNAM/RMS, 33:3, julio/sept. 1971, p. 541-562, bibl.)

Offers an overview (with very adequate bibliography) of the structural (social) handicaps of Mexican development. Aptly presented with insightful criticism.

9717. _____. Estabilidad política, crecimiento económico y clases sociales en México: 1940-1970; los antecedentes, algunas hipótesis iniciales (Problemas del Desarrollo [México], 4:13, nov. 1972/enero 1973, p. 77-114)

Internal and external circumstances lend Mexican class development (nationalistic and populistic) a peculiar character. Its traits remained the same even after the nation underwent the phase of "dependency" on outside imperial powers. State capitalism plays a leading role in Mexican development which is also tied to the Revolution of 1910 and its consequences. Although good, the article leaves many questions unanswered and lacks an adequate bibliography.

9718. Hicks, W. Whitney. Economic development and fertility change in Mexico, 1950-1970 (PAA/D, 11:3, Aug. 1974, p. 407-421, bibl.)

Two of the important indicators of industrialization (namely agricultural employment and the percentage of population in rural areas that speaks indigenous dialects) are shown here to have direct relationship to declining fertility. The study has an excellent bibliography. For physical anthropologist's comment, see item 2039.

Higgins, Cheleen Mahar. Integrative aspects of folk and western medicine among the urban poor of Oaxaca. See item 1143.

9719. Holt Buttner, Elizabeth. Composición por edad y sexo e índices de dependencia de la población en la República Mexicana. México, UNAM, 1973. 48 p., bibl., plates.

This paper represents a good analysis of the topic on the bases of 1960 and 1970s censuses: an excellent tool for further explorations.

9720. Holtzman, Wayne H. and others. Personality development in two cultures: a cross-cultural longitudinal study of school children in Mexico and the United States. Austin, Univ. of Texas Press, 1975. 427 p., bibl., tables.

Perhaps more than half of the conclusions of this study are obvious given our present knowledge of national character through literature and folklore. For instance: that Americans tend to be more complex and differentiated in their cognitive structures, more competitive, less pessimistic and less-family-oriented than Mexicans! However, well beyond the range and depth of such findings, this thoroughly scholarly team-effort has a profound relevance for the future of cross-cultural personality development research. It is here that for the first time a thorough work produces evaluation and complementarity of a whole battery of psychological tests in two different national cultures and exposes a generation or two of Mexican and American children (both in urban settings) to follow-up encounters which were never before systematically pursued. The central chapter on methodology is very illuminating in that it offers the appropriate nuances of results.

9721. Isbister, John. Birth control, income redistribution, and the rate of saving: the case of Mexico (PAA/D, 10:1, Feb. 1973, p. 85-98, bibl., tables)

A simulated growth model of the Mexican economy allows the author to predict higher levels of saving among lower classes when a decrease in fertility takes place, while the opposite occurs when the same people enjoy higher standard of living.

9722. Jonquieres C., Guido. ¿Bienaventurados los pobres? Estudio socioteológico basado en *Los hijos de Sánchez* de Oscar Lewis. México, Editorial Jus, 1973. 267 p., bibl.

Modern sociological and anthropological theory can help Catholic theology in understanding many a human phenomenon. It seems though, that in this case there may be some risks involved in taking O. Lewis' work almost too rigorously and perhaps too literally especially when he himself presented his anthropological research in a quasi-literary context.

Kemper, Robert V. Family and household organization among Tzintzuntzan migrants in Mexico City. See item 1154.

9723. Lampe, Philip E. Algunos datos empíricos sobre las clases sociales de Morelia (UPR/RCS, 16:2, junio 1972, p. 213-220)

Following the insights of Mendieta y Núñez, (predominance of cultural over economic factors), in the definition of class, the author exposes the results of a survey of 20 "barrios" of Morelia. Interesting differences in education, family size, "urban" style and a few others, contribute to a better understanding of the provincial life in Mexico.

9724. Langgulung, Hasan and **E. Paul Torrance.** A cross-cultural study of children's conceptions of situational causality in India, Western Samoa, Mexico, and the United States (JSP, 89:2, p. 175-183, bibl., tables)

A rigorous cross-cultural sample of primary school children of four nations helps us to better understand the nature and constraints of culture assimilation in view of the wide range of responses regarding physical causality of certain phenomena.

Lebowitz, Michael D. Influence of urbanization and industrialization on birth and death rates. See item 2048.

9725. Lombardo Toledano, Vicente. El problema del indio. Selección de textos de Marcela Lombardo. Introducción de Gonzalo Aguirre Beltrán. México, Secretaría de Educación Pública, 1973. 207 p., bibl., plates (SepSetentas, 114)

An important selection of speeches and journal articles (some editorials) exemplifies the "indigenista" doctrine of the famous Mexican leader: one of decisive "acculturation" through the use of Spanish and of economic liberation, in the Marxist tradition. The introductory chapter by anthropologist Aguirre Beltrán is essential to understand the work of Lombardo. The bibliographical material is very important.

9726. Lomnitz, Larissa. The social and economic organization of a Mexican shantytown (*in* Cornelius, Wayne A. and Felicity M. Trueblood *eds.* Anthropological perspectives on Latin American urbanization [see item 9625] p. 135-155, bibl., tables)

An excellent description of a slum in Mexico City in the best anthropological tradition: its views on reciprocity and kinship linkage are inspirational. For ethnologist comment, see item 1158.

9727. Mac-Lean y Estenós, Roberto. Status socio cultural de los indios de Mexico. México, UNAM, Instituto de Investigaciones Sociales, Biblioteca de Ensayos Sociológicos, 1960. 192 p., bibl. (Cuadernos de sociología)

The author merely surveys major sources of Mexican ethnology and summarizes them in a very intelligent way. Unfortunately, the bibliography lacks the rigor expected in a scientific paper.

9728. Muñoz, Humberto and Orlandina de Oliveira. Migración interna y movilidad ocupacional en la Ciudad de México (CM/DE, 7:2, 1973, p. 135-148, tables)

In spite of the methodological difficulties and the total lack of representativeness of the data, the tendencies show a clear path of ascendance in occupational mobility for all different cohorts. Interestingly enough, the upward mobility of higher social strata coexists with the marginality of an important sector of the city's population. The article complements the work of C. Stern (see *El perfil de México en 1980*, v. 3, México, Siglo XXI, 1972).

9729. Navarrete, Ifigenia M. de. Bienestar campesino y desarrollo económico. México, Fondo de Cultura Económica, 1971. 336 p., tables.

Seven scholars of the UNAM, among the best qualified in the area of rural development (all of them economists, except former Minister of Irrigation, Orive de Alba), wrote a series of essays on the spectrum of agrarian policies, facts, trends and future in the developmental perspective.

9730. _____. La mujer y los derechos sociales. México, Ediciones Oasis, 1969. 204 p., plates, tables.

As an economist and scholar the author approaches the topic from a factual viewpoint taking into consideration the Mexican economy and labor legislation affecting women. Also includes a useful list of women's organizations in Mexico.

9731. Nolasco Armas, Margarita. La reforma agraria en cuatro situaciones culturales distintas de México (INAH/A, 2,7 época, 1969 [i.e. 1971] p. 309-313, bibl.)

The difficult balance between economic-growth practices and social structures and the disastrous consequences of Mexico's agrarian reform are hereby described in a summary report of four case studies: the Yaquis, Cholula, Valley of Mexico and Tlahualillo (Durango). The author's anthropological perspective adds another dimension to the criticism of the agrarian reform.

9732. Orellana S., Carlos L. Mixtec migrants in Mexico City: a case study of urbanization (SAA/HO, 32:3, Fall 1973, p. 273-283, bibl., map, tables)

This conscientious study proves that the seemingly complex process of urbanization has universal features: migrants from rural areas tend to develop similar strategies of adaptation to cities. In this case, the old "village association" is launched in an urban setting with great success.

9733. Paulín, Georgina *comp.* Monolingües y bilingües en la población de México en 1960: estadísticas del Proyecto Sociolingüístico. México, UNAM, Instituto de Investigaciones Sociales, 1971. 253 p., maps, tables.

Statistics and corresponding maps—only part of a wider ethnographic project—are presented in this complete overview of the present situation of Mexican sociolinguistics.

9734. Peñalosa, Joaquín Antonio. El mexicano y los 7 pecados capitales. México, Ediciones Paulinas, 1972. 195 p.

Half sociologist and half psychologist, although a full-size journalist with a poetical mind, the author has produced one of the fairest, more common-sensical descriptions of the Mexican personality and national character.

9735. Poitras, Guy E. Welfare bureaucracy and clientele politics in Mexico (CU/ASQ, 18:1, March 1973, p. 18-26, bibl., tables)

In this fine work the question of political stability is recognized as dominant for the National Institute of Social Security(NISS). Insofar as Mexican social welfare is concerned, the government and labor elites slice and eat the pie at the expense of the poor and needy, especially in rural areas.

9736. Portes, Alejandro. Return of the wetback (RU/T, 11:3, March/April 1974, p. 40-46)

Popular overview analyzing continual legal and illegal Mexican migration to the US, since cancellation of the *bracero* program. Portes outlines the structural pressures leading to illegal migration including kinship and friendship ties between illegal immigrant and "native" (i.e. chicano) worker. Portes predicts that the flow of illegal immigrants from Mexico will continue unabated until unionization of agricultural and urban skilled workers in the US changes present power arrangements. [N.S. Kinzer]

Quigley, Carroll. Mexican national character and circum-Mediterranean personality structure. See item 1173.

9737. Ramos G., Sergio. Urbanización y servicios públicos en México. México, UNAM, Instituto de Investigaciones Sociales, 1972. 192 p., tables.

In this very good study of municipal services in Mexico the author has combined the most important variables of the 1960 census data (on population, housing, labor and communications) in his research.

9738. Rangel Contla, José Calixto. La pequeña burguesía en la sociedad mexicana: 1895 a 1960. Mexico, UNAM, 1972. 239 p., tables.

Although the book is somehow restricted in its theoretical (neo-Marxian) approach to new delimitation of concepts related to middle classes, the work is still very impressive and the first to provide a more coherent, complete and historical picture of the emergence of the Mexican bourgeoisie.

9739. *Revista Mexicana de Sociología.* UNAM, Instituto de Investigaciones Sociales. Vol. 32, No. 5, sept./oct. 1970-México.

This issue represents a good combination of theoretical (Mendieta y Núñez, Veros and Uribe Villegas) and empirical papers all related to Mexican sociology. Alvarado's projects of Mexican population constitute an important tool of research.

9740. _____. _____. Vol. 33, No. 3, julio/dept. 1971-México.

A particular article (González Salazar) on Mexican socio-economic inequality deserves to be mentioned here as a good introduction to major works such as the ones by Navarrete, Stavenhagen, Solis and Uniquel. Article's bibliographical references are solid.

9741. _____. _____. Vol. 34, Nos. 3/4 julio/dic. 1972-México.

Among several important papers of the X Latin American Congress of Sociology, (this issue includes only Mexican sociologists) the contributions of Pierre-Charles and Charles W. Johnson of Latin American society, dependency and revolution constitute a worthwhile search for new theoretical insights. J. Labastida posits some new looks into the political strategies of the Echeverría regime and J. Martínez Ríos (prematurely deceased) offers a superb analysis of agrarian squatters and social marginality.

9742. *Revista Mexicana del Trabajo.* Secretaría del Trabajo y Previsión Social. Tomo 2, No. 2/3, Epoca 7, abril/sept. 1972- . México.

Issue devoted to the history of the government's housing program for Mexican workers, including legislation and implementation. Includes texts of some laws (e.g. Reform of Article 123 of the Constitution) and of congressional debates on the subject compiled by IN-FONAVIT (Mexican Housing Authority).

Roberts, Robert F. Modernization and infant mortality in Mexico. See item 2058.

9743. Rollwagen, Jack R. Mediation and rural-urban migration in Mexico: a proposal and case study (*in* Cornelius Wayne A. and Felicity M. Trueblood *eds.* Anthropological perspectives on Latin American urbanization [see item 9625] p. 47-63, bibl.)

A particularly important aspect of the functions of "mediation" between groups within community and nation-oriented groups. Rural-urban migration is examined in this article in conjunction with a set of entrepreneurs of Mexticacan (a village in Jalisco.) Work opens up new perspectives in modern urban migration.

9744. Ronfeldt, David. Atencingo: the politics of agrarian struggle in a Mexican ejido. Standord, Calif., Stanford Univ., 1973. 283 p., maps, tables.

A most interesting analysis (a case study) of the ejido struggle in the state of Puebla (and in the oldest ejidos) followed by an insightful review of Mexican agrarian politics and their present dilemma: the reform of the Agrarian Reform.

9745. Sánchez Azcona, Jorge. Familia y sociedad. México, Editorial Joaquín Mortiz, 1974. 98 p. (Cuadernos de Joaquín Mortiz)

This work represents a brief review of literature on the topic: it posits the subject from the point of view of contrasting theories, namely functionalist and marxist, as they can be applied (with a few references) to Mexican urban middle classes.

Sanders, Thomas G. Mexico, 1974: demographic patterns and population policy. See item 2060.

9746. Sinaloa: desarrollo urbano. México? Comisión para el Desarrollo de Centros Poblados, 1970. 77 p., illus., maps, tables.

Mazatlán, Los Mochis and Culiacán are described in

terms of present urban conditions and development plans, together with maps and most relevant indicators of urban living.

9747. Siverts, Henning ed. Drinking patterns in highland Chiapas: a teamwork approach to the study of semantics through ethnography. Bergen, Norway, Universitetsforlaget, 1973. 187 p., bibl., illus., tables.

This anthropological study of cases—a real model for team-work in participant observation—stirred up controversy among some lower Mexican officials. The findings and presentation are as impressive as the methodology.

9748. Suárez, Luis. México: imagen de la ciudad. México, Fondo de Cultura Económica, 1974. 110 p.

The author, a very talented reporter and well-known writer, draws a series of psycho-social sketches of Mexicans and their customs in a journalistic but tasteful manner.

Thompson, Richard A. and **Michael C. Robbins.** Seasonal variation in conception in rural Uganda and Mexico. See item 1190.

9749. Trejo Reyes, Saul. Desempleo y subocupación en México (BNCE/CE, 22:5, mayo 1972, p. 411-416, tables)

The article includes major unemployment data and trends but the figures for the 1970s are based on projections and do not reflect what was discovered in the 1970 census.

9750. Ugalde, Antonio; Leslie Olson; David Schers; and **Miguel Von Hoegen.** The urbanization process of a poor Mexican neighborhood. Austin, The Univ. of Texas at Austin, Institute of Latin American Studies, 1974. 68 p., bibl., tables.

This monograph shows in a comprehensive way the most relevant features of the urban settlement process in a poor section of Ciudad Juárez, northern Mexico.

9751. Valles, Jorge. Alcoholismo: el alcohólico y su familia. México, B. Costa-Amic Editor, 1973. 174 p.

This study—a socio-psychological one—is based upon a very questionable premise, namely that alcoholics are not psychic patients. Nevertheless, it provides some interesting sociological insights into aspects of Mexican family life.

CENTRAL AMERICA

9752. Adams, Richard N. Brokers and career mobility systems in the structure of complex societies (UNM/SWJA, 26:4, Winter 1970, p. 315-327, bibl.)

A good and insightful monograph on the stratification dynamics of a national society (Guatemala).

9753. Antonini, Gustavo A. ed. Public policy and urbanization in the Dominican Republic and Costa Rica: proceedings of the XXII Annual Latin American Conference. Gainesville, Univ. of Florida, Center for Latin American Studies, 1972. 235 p., plate, tables.

This collection of papers involves such a variety of topics and thoroughness of treatment that it is difficult to make a general judgment on the book. However, the essays by Hardoy on comparative urban politics and Yujnovsky on holistic models of urban growth are among the most relevant in contemporary research on these topics.

Argueta Cordón, Antonio. El problema demográfico en El Salvador: una perspectiva cultural y una hipótesis sobre desarrollo psicológico. See item 6620.

9754. Arosemena, Jorge. Dirigentes campesinos y desarrollo rural en Guatemala (Anales de Ciencias Humanas [Editorial Universitaria, Panamá] 1, 1971, p. 71-85)

A good descriptive analysis of the leadership development program for rural Guatemala (carried by R. Landivar Univ.) and its major components: institutional and community fieldwork.

Bortner, R.W.; Claudia J. Bohn; and **David F. Hultsch.** A cross-cultural study of the effects of children on parental assessment of past, present and future. See item 9781.

Brunn, Stanley D. and **Robert N. Thomas.** Socio-economic environments and internal migration: the case of Tegucigalpa, Honduras. See item 6632.

9755. Castillo Barrantes, J. Enrique. El Instituto de Pericia Criminológica y Patología Social. San José? Univ. de Costa Rica, 1972. 134 p., bibl., plates (Publicaciones. Serie tesis de grado, 20)

An interesting piece of information with some statistical data on major activities of the past years.

9756. Censos nacionales de 1970: séptimo censo de población, tercer censo de vivienda. v. 1, Lugares poblados de la República. Panamá, Dirección de Estadística y Censo, 1970. 542 p., tables.

The presentation of this volume constitutes a great step in Panamanian statistics: housing, housing variables and related population are systematically presented. Indispensable for demographic and urban research.

9757. Cuarto censo nacional de población. San Salvador, Dirección General de Estadística y Censos, 1971. 20 l., tables.

Although only concerned with part of the material, the presentation is relevant as a research tool.

9758. Díaz Chávez, Filander. Sociología de la desintegración regional. Tegucigalpa, Univ. Nacional Autónoma de Honduras, Dirección de Extensión Universitaria, 1972. 593 p., plates (Col. Investigación y teoría, 1)

This book is a combination of literary, historical and socio-economic approaches to the topic of Honduren development. Important as a source of data but lacking bibliographical rigor.

9759. Early, John D. Revision of ladino and maya census populations of Guatemala, 1950 and 1964. (PAA/D, 11:1, Feb. 1974, p. 105-117, bibl., tables)

A sober, technically sound study of inconsistencies in responses about ethnicity, with the corresponding misclassifications of Maya people.

9760. *Estadística Panameña.* Contraloría General de la República, Dirección de Estadística y Censo, 30, 1970-Panamá.

An indispensable tool for research in Panamanian public health.

9761. Ghidinelli, Azzo. Aspectos económicos de la cultura de los caribes negros del municipio de Livingston (GIIN/GI, 7:4, oct./dic. 1972, p. 71-152)

This work (an anthropological study of cases) is only introductory to further research. Nevertheless, it constitutes a relevant description of several settlements of black Caribbeans in Guatemala (around Puerto Barrios) and of their major economic activities within family and village structures.

9762. Henríquez de Paredes, Querubina. Un dilema: la educación sexual. San Salvador, Asociación Demográfica Salvadoreña, 1970? 137 p., plates, tables.

A conscientious study of sex education, its problems and consequences among high-school students (on the basis of a national sample). The author appears very aware of the social conditions of this problem and relates her findings to such relevant areas as illegitimacy and child-bearing.

Hinshaw, Robert; P. Pyeatt; and Jean-Pierre Habicht. Environmental effects of child-spacing and population increase in highland Guatemala. See item 2041.

9763. Jaen Suárez, Omar. Desarraigo y migración de poblacines en Panamá: 1950-1960 (Anales de Ciencias Humanas [Editorial Universitaria, Panamá] 1, 1971, p. 29-58)

In spite of information lags and some methodological problems, this study is an excellent piece of research. It encompasses only the decade of the 50s and shows the relevance of agricultural correlates (density, minifundia, latifundia, etc.) to internal migration.

Logan, Michael H. Humoral medicine in Guatemala and peasant acceptance of modern medicine. See item 2236.

9764. Maccio, Guillermo A. Ajuste e interpolación de tasas de fecundidad por edad: aplicación a los países de América Central. San José, Centro Latinoamericano de Demografía, 1970. 40 p., tables (Serie AS, 6)

Another important monograph with a rigorous treatment of the subject: an indispensable tool for a more correct interpretation of population censuses in Central America.

Massajoli, Pierleone. Popoli e civiltá dell'America Centrale: i Caribi neri. See item 1260.

9765. Michielutte, Robert; Carl M. Cochrane; Clark E. Vincent; and C. Allen Haney. Consensual and legal marital unions in Costa Rica (YU/IJCS, 14:1/2, March/June 1973, p. 119-128, bibl., tables)

More specifically (than the title would suggest) the article focuses on women's reproductive behavior and confirms in more than one sense the findings of previous studies.

9766. Micklin, Michael. Urbanization, technology, and traditional values in Guatemala: some consequences of a changing social structure (SF, 47:4, June 1969, p. 438-446, tables)

A sample of male population of Guatemala City enables the author to look into the relations between structural changes and major psychological variables. Traditionalism in this study appears to decrease more rapidly than has been expected, with several variations affecting socio-economic status.

9767. Molina Chocano, Guillermo. Dependencia y cambio social en la sociedad hondureña (Estudios Sociales Centroamericanos [San José] 1:1, enero/abril 1972, p. 11-26, tables)

The author reviews only some of the major variables of

the problem and the data at hand (as far as 1968). Most relevant traits of economic dependency are well detected together with important social correlates.

9768. Montes, Segundo. El factor demográfico en la problemática salvadoreña (UJSC/ECA, 27:285, julio 1972, p. 457-464, tables)

Although the title is broader than the article's content, it includes a good account of family planning in the country.

Mundigo, Axel I. Elites, economic development and population in Honduras. See item 6634.

Onaka, Alvin T. and D.Yaukey. Reproductive time lost due to sexual union dissolution in San José, Costa Rica. See item 2052.

9769. Portes, Alejandro. The factorial structure of modernity: empirical replications and a critique (UC/AJS, 79:1, July 1973, p. 15-44, bibl., tables)

Test of modernity as an empirically identifiable syndrome based on three Guatemalan samples (both male and female): urban (n=1160), white rural (n=468) and native Indian (n=122). Factor analysis shows definite dimensionality of modernity. Hypotheses linking education, urban residence and other socialization factors are noted. Far-reaching theoretical critique of assumptions underlying the hypothesis of modernity. Modernity as a consequence of Western structural transformations may have little to do with or be detrimental to causes of development in Third World Nations. Interrelationships between empirical findings and critical analyses of these assumptions are discussed. [N.S. Kinzer]

9770. Rath, Ferdinand. América Central: tendencias pasadas y perspectivas de su población. San José, Centro Latinoamericano de Demografía, 1970. 33 p., tables (Serie AS, 1)

An excellent monograph and a necessary tool for further research on the subject.

9771. *Revista Mexicana de Sociología.* UNAM, Instituto de Investigaciones Sociales. Vol. 32, No. 1, enero/feb. 1970-México.

Of special interest to the student of Central-American sociology is J.L. Herbert's article on a Guatemalan community, a very good study of cases exemplifying a neo-Marxian interpretation of traditional vs. neo-colonial ways of life. Of moderate interest for psychologists is Rodríguez Sala's article on Mexican adolescents' view of the scientific "intelligentsia" of their country.

Sandoval V., Leopoldo R. and Fernando Cruz. Cambios en la estructura agraria de Guatemala y metas de reforma. See item 6631.

Schwartz, Norman B. Dreaming and managing the future: notes on a Guatemalan Ladino (non-Indian) theorie [sic] of dreams. See item 1181.

9772. Seligson, Mitchell A. The "dual society" thesis in Latin America: a reexamination of the Costa Rican case (SF, 51:1, Sept. 1972, p. 91-98, tables)

An elaborate treatment of several variables shows that the assumption that value differences parallel economic ones constitutes a shaky basis on which to test the so-called "Dual Society" thesis in the Latin American context.

9773. Tak, Jean van der and Murray Gendell. The size and structure of residential families, Guatemala City, 1964 (LSE/PS, 27:2, July 1973, p. 305-322, tables)

The fact that families are larger in urban than in rural areas suggests the need for a reconsideration of stages and traits of development in lesser industrialized societies. Here the data are based upon a 1964 census sample. For anthropologists comment see item 2065.

Teller, Charles H. Internal migration, socio-economic status and health: access to medical care in a Honduran city. See item 6635.

9774. Torres Rivas, Edelberto. Interpretación del desarrollo social centroamericano: procesos y estructuras de una sociedad dependiente. 2. ed. San Jose, Editorial Universitaria Centroamericana (EDUCA), 1971. 317 p., bibl., tables (Col. Seis)

D. Slutzky ably summarizes the book by noting that it describes the dynamics of the socio-economic process of Central America, its development into agro-exporting societies and their internal problems. A worthwhile example of scholarly research in the sociological literature inspired by CEPAL efforts and by the study of "dependency" theories. For political scientist's comment, see *HLAS 35:7542.*

9775. ———. Notas sobre la estructura social del campo centroamericano. Asunción, Centro Paraguayo de Estudios Sociológicos, 1972. 25 p. (Col. de Reimpresiones, 53)

A preliminary overview of rural population and land tenure structure in Central America.

Vega Carballo, José Luis. Etapas y procesos de la evolución sociopolítica de Costa Rica. See item 8185.

9776. Wi Holden, David E. Interviewer and situational bias in field surveys in Costa Rica (CLAPCS/AL, 14:3/4, julho/dez. 1971, p. 61-69, tables)

Well conducted, but of limited interest: it fails to show how the complexity and diversity of topics could also bias possible interviews.

9777. Yandle, Carolyn D. and Jeffrey W. Stone. La población de Panamá: estimaciones y proyecciones, 1961-2001. Washington, U.S. Dept. of Commerce, Bureau of the Census, 1970. 73 p., tables (Estudios demográficos para los países extranjeros. Serie P-96, 2)

Very important high quality monograph of use for further research. However, does not include the necessary corrections from the 1970s census.

THE CARIBBEAN AND THE GUIANAS

9778. Acosta, Mercedes; André Corten; Isis Duarte; and Carlos María Vilas. Imperialismo y clases sociales en el Caribe. B.A., Cuenca Ediciones, 1973. 234 p., tables.

Four essays on socio-economic problems in the sugarcane industry and political domination in Santo Domingo accompany a long and insightful analysis of race relations and racism in Haiti.

Alers, M.H. Taalproblemen van Surinaamse kinderen in Nederland. See item 1205.

9779. Altieri de Barreto, Carmen G. El lexico de la delincuencia en Puerto Rico. San Juan? Univ. de Puerto Rico, Editorial Universitaria, 1973. 230 p., bibl. (Col. UPREX, 18. Serie ciencias sociales)

This work reveals profound insights into the deviant sub-cultures of Puerto Rico. It constitutes a very useful research tool for socio-linguistics studies of the area.

Antonini, Gustavo A. ed. Public policy and urbanization in the Dominican Republic and Costa Rica: proceedings of the XXII Annual Latin American Conference. See item 9753.

Balakrishnan, T.R. A cost-benefit analysis of the Barbados Family Planning Programme. See item 2023.

9780. Blanco Lázaro, Enrique T. Proceso a la sociedad de consumo. San Juan, Editorial Edil, 1973. 156 p.

A literary analysis with a few sociological insights of consumerism and its impact on Puerto Rican society (a mirror for many Latin American societies).

9781. Bortner, R.W.; Claudia J. Bohn; and David F. Hultsch. A cross-cultural study of the effects of children on parental assessment of past, present and future (WRU/AMF, 36:2, May 1974, p. 370-378, bibl.)

An analysis of surveys from Dominican Republic, Panama and Yugoslavia strongly suggests that children do have a very positive effect on paternal assessment of their own fulfillment in terms of present and future. On the other hand, women without children also have a higher assessment. Perhaps indicative of perceived higher status without children for women. The data, however, do not prove any definite conclusions.

Bovenkerk, Frank. Emigratie uit Suriname. See item 1212.

9782. Brau, Salvador. Ensayos: disquisiciones sociológicas. Río Piedras, P.R., Editorial Edil, 1972. 294 p., tables.

A journalist with a definite penchant for sociology describes Puerto Rican life from a historical and literary perspective.

9783. Brisson, Gerald. Les relations agraires dans l'Haiti contemporaine. Port-au-Prince, n.p., 1968. 79 p.

An excellent overview of and introduction to topic: a subject in desperate need of scientific research and one in which Haiti lags behind other areas of the Caribbean.

9784. Brody, Eugene B. Psychocultural aspects of contraceptive behavior in Jamaica: individual fertility control in developing a country (UM/JNMD, 159:2, Aug. 1974, p. 108-119, bibl.)

Data from this Caribbean country suggest that family traditions and household systems, poor communication between sexual partners, strictness in child rearing and high status and role of mothers are other variables negatively influencing the regulation of fertility and thus blocking the official family-planning programs.

9785. Buitrago Ortiz, Carlos. Esperanza: an ethnographic study of a peasant community in Puerto Rico. Tucson, The Univ. of Arizona Press *for the* Wenner-Gren Foundation for Anthropological Research, 1973. 217 p., bibl., maps, plates (Viking fund publications in anthropology, 50)

Methodology and thoroughness make this a very relevant study. The situation of this Puerto Rican community offers many insights into the general patterns of rural life in the country.

9786. Butterworth, Douglas. Grass-roots political organization in Cuba: a case of the Committees for the Defense of the Revolution (*in* Cornelius, Wayne A. and Felicity M. Trueblood *eds.* Anthropological perspectives on Latin

American urbanization [see item 9625] p. 183-203, bibl.)

Initial success and subsequent decline of the committees (CDR), particularly in rural Cuba, are attributed to zeal and suspicion concerning some structural roles (spying, vigilance, etc.) and to the lack of education in community organization.

9787. Calderón González, Jorge. Amparo: Millo y azucenas. La Habana, Casa de las Américas, 1970. 234 p., bibl., plates.

This novel awarded a prize by Casa de las Americas—has valuable insights into the social life of Cuba at the beginning of the 20th century.

9788. Castro G., Carlos D. Notas para una sociología del negro antillano (LNB/L, 202, sept. 1972, p. 6-23)

Without empirical data and first-hand materials, the theoretical expression of a black sociology for the Antilles is only a heuristic desire. However, the basic hypothesis of a quasi "ghetto" social structure for the black Antilles seem to hold true in literature, observation and in the phenomenon of double marginalization among blacks.

9789. Clausner, Marlin D. Rural Santo Domingo: settled, unsettled, and resettled. Philadelphia, Pa., Temple Univ. Press, 1973. 323 p., bibl., tables.

A combination of historical and sociological analysis produced this interesting monograph: the best on the subject of land tenure, settlement patterns, distribution, rural life, etc., in Santo Domingo. The bibliography is among the best available.

Conference on the Family in the Caribbean, *II, Aruba, Netherlands Antilles, 1969.* The family in the Caribbean: proceedings. See item 1221.

Cordasco, Francesco and **Eugene Bucchioni.** The Puerto Rican experience: a sociological sourcebook. See item 8269.

9790. Cruz Díaz, Rigoberto. Muy buenos noches, Señoras y Señores . . . La Habana, Casa de las Américas, 1972. 305 p., plates.

Although a literary work (theater), this offers many socio-phychological insight into circus life in Latin American societies. It is an excellent comedy. For drama critic's comment, see *HLAS 36:6821.*

9791. Depestre, Réné. Problems of identity for the black man in Caribbean literatures (UWI/CQ, 19:3, Sept. 1973, p. 51-61)

A brief journalistic review of the complexity of issues which lie at the roots of black literature and social consciousness in the Caribbean. The poetical voice of Lalea epitomized it when he wrote: "conquer with French words this heart I received from Senegal!"

9792. Díaz, Juanita. Cuba: ante los ojos de una mujer (Vistazo de la Actualidad [Lima] *3:30, 1973, p. 34-36, plates)*

Unscholarly, journalistic impressions.

Early, John D. Revision of Ladino and Maya census populations of Guatemala, 1950 and 1964. See item 2029.

Ehrlich, Allen S. Ecological perception and economic adaptation in Jamaica. See item 1229.

Evelyn, Shirley *ed.* and *comp.* West Indian social sciences index: an index to *Moko, New World Quarterly, Savacou, Tapia,* 1963-1972. See item 1230a.

9793. Every child matters: the child in Trinidad and Tobago. Port-of-Spain, Soroptimist International Association of Port-of-Spain, 1970. 51 p.

Of some use as an introduction to child care and child welfare in Trinidad and Tobago.

Eyre, L. Alan. The shantytowns of Montego Bay, Jamaica. See item 6595.

9794. Fox, Geoffrey E. Honor, shame, and women's liberation in Cuba: views of working-class emigré men (*in* Pescatello, Ann *ed.* Female and male in Latin America [see item 9665] p. 273-290)

Based on a survey of Cuban immigrants to Chicago, the author reports on phenomena which were peripheral to his major goal (reasons for migration). In spite of some lessening of former opposition to socialism (with corresponding changes in women's roles) the older and younger generations of Cubans still adhere to values closely related to Spain and to Spanish Catholic tradition.

Fraser, Thomas M., Jr. Class and the changing bases of elite support in St. Vincent, West Indies. See item 1234.

9795. González, Alfonso. The population of Cuba (UPR/CS, 11:2, July 1971, p. 75-84, bibl., tables)

Brief, superficial overview.

Guyana. Ministry of Information and Culture. Amerindian integration: a brief outline of the progress of integration in Guyana. See item 1238.

9796. Haiti: status of Christianity. Monrovia, Calif., Missions Advanced Research & Communication Center, 1971. 27 p., illus., maps, tables (MARC country file)

An informative pamphlet on the subject of Protestant denominations, their activities, membership and related interest in the country.

9797. Hendricks, Glenn. The Dominican diaspora: from the Dominican Republic to New York City, villagers in transition. N.Y., Columbia Univ., Teachers College Press, 1974. 171 p., bibl., tables (Publications of the Center for Education in Latin America)

Complementing other views of Latin American subcultures in N.Y.C. (like Fitzpatrick and Poblete) this monograph analyzes major institutional variables in the process of acculturation. For ethnologist's comment, see item 1243.

Herzog, J.D. Father-absence and boys' school performance in Barbados. See item 1245.

9798. Hoetink, Harry. Pluralismus und Assimilation in den Kariben (*in* Gräbener, Jürgen *comp.* Kassengesellschaft und Rassismus [see *HLAS 35:8268*] p. 38-50)

Describes the complexity of societal composition in the Caribbean region in an attempt at identification which comes close to ideological "propaganda" for the similarities between Caribbean black culture and US black intellectual consciousness. The final discussion is most important.

Irving, Brian *ed.* Guyana: a composite monograph. See item 1247.

Jha, Jagdish Chandra. Indian heritage in Trinidad, West Indies. See item 1248.

9799. Kahl, Joseph A. La paradoja cubana: igualdad estratificada (UNAM/RMS, 33:4, oct./dic. 1971, p. 679-698)

Tradition, education, technical know-how and party affiliation make for a very complex and paradoxical "equality," the new form of societal stratification in a socialist regime. This is a case study based on detailed observation.

Krimpen, A. van. Een onderzoek onder werknemers van een in Suriname gevestigd energiebedrijf, de OGEM. See item 1251.

9800. Laguerre, M. The place of Voodoo in the social structure of Haiti (UWI/CQ, 19:3, Sept. 1973, p. 36-50, bibl.)

The transformation of voodoo from a messianic cult into a t
Rose Printing - Latin American Book - 27280 - joyce, Sect. 10, tp. 15, pgype of religion which fosters village solidarity is related to both the process of national independence and aspects of social stratification and communal life.

Landis, Joseph B. Racial attitudes of Africans and Indians in Guyana. See item 1254.

9801. LaRuffa, Anthony L. San Cipriano: life in a Puerto Rican community. N.Y., Gordon and Breach Science Publishers, 1971. 149 p., bibl., map, plates.

Very interesting and highly comprehensive anthropological study of cases based on participant observation.

9802. Latorre, Eduardo and others. Bonao: una ciudad dominicana. Santiago de los Caballeros, R.D., Univ. Católica Madre y Maestra, 1972. 2 v. (441, 499 p.) bibl., illus., tables (Col. Estudios, 11)

In contrast to relevant models of studies of city life in Latin America (such as Redfield's *Tepoztlán*, Lewis' *Children of Sánchez*, Whiteford's *Two cities*, etc.) this work constitutes a most ambitious attempt at exploring with scientific rigor 14 major variables (social and economic) in a medium-size Caribbean city. The questionnaires were administered to almost two percent of the total population. V. 1 is merely descriptive of five major variables (demographic, health, etc.) but v. 2 is a remarkable contribution to Caribbean and Latin American ethnology.

León, Argeliers. Presencia del africano en la cultura cubana. See item 1255.

9803. Maldonado Denis, Manuel. Puerto Rico: sociedad colonial en el Caribe (Libre [Paris] 3, marzo/mayo 1972, p. 53-69)

An excellent analysis of historical and critical sources of Puerto Rican society and its major structural aspects since colonial times. The study examines the meaning of independence vs. secondary alternatives of dependency and their impact upon the fabric of a nation.

9804. Martínez-Alier, Verena. Jungfräulichkeit und Machismo: die Rolle der Fray in Kuba in 19. Jarhundert (*in* Gräbener, Jürgen *comp.* Kassengesellschaft und Rassismus [see *HLAS 35:8268*] p. 171-197)

An excellent document of historical sociology, this article analyzes the role of honor and machismo from a perspective of class, societal structures and religious life which increases our understanding of women's roles in the Cuban society towards the end of Spanish rule.

9805. Mathurin, Agustín. Assistance sociale en Haiti: 1804-1972. Port-au-Prince, Imprimerie des Antilles, 1972. 478 p., illus., plates.

A plain, uncritical enumeration of dates and foundations concerning all forms of social welfare. Of some use to the student of Haitian public welfare.

Mevis, René *comp.* Inventory of Caribbean studies: an overview of social research on the Caribbean conducted by Antillean, Dutch and Surinamese scholars in the period 1945-1973. See item 1262.

Mijs, A.A. Onderwijs en ontwikkeling van Suriname. See item 1263.

Mintz, Sidney W. Afroamerikaner auf den Antillen. See item 1265.

———. Indiens de l'Inde aux Antilles. See item 1268.

9806. *Mujeres.* Año 13, No. 3 [through] 8, marzo [through] agosto 1973- La Habana.

Although of limited interest for the scholar, these issues contain interesting information on lower-income strata in modern Cuba.

9807. Okraku, Ishmael O. The family life-cycle and residential mobility in Puerto Rico (USC/SSR, 55:3, April 1971, p. 324-340, tables)

The concept of Life-Cycles proves valuable for research in housing needs and residential mobility. Article draws useful comparison between American (US) and Puerto Rican societies.

9808. Olesen, Virginia. Context and posture: notes on socio-cultural aspects of women's roles and family policy in contemporary Cuba (WRU/JMF, 33:3, Aug. 1971, p. 548-56)

Article discusses women's roles and public policy towards the family, as they appear in an index survey of Cuba's official newspaper *Gramma*. Although women's participation in the labor force, unions, education and politics have expanded the range of female roles, an array of emerging institutions (such as child care, etc.) tend to preserve those family linkages which are peculiar to Cuban culture. Excellent bibliography.

9809. Paniagua Rodríguez, Alejandro. Los dominicanos: sexo, otros ensayos. Santo Domingo, Editora El Médico Dominicano, 1971. 183 p., plate.

A psychiatrist depicts some relevant traints of the Dominican way of life stressing their social aspects. A couple of essays include some original historical interpretations.

9810. Parrilla Bonilla, Antulio. Puerto Rico: iglesia y sociedad 1969-1971. Cuernavaca, Mex., Centro Intercultural de Documentación (CIDOC), 1971. 1 v. (Various pagings) bibl. (SONDEOS, 84)

Monograph based on much bibliographical research concerns the ideological currents among the Catholic hierarchies of Puerto Rico and their views on major national problems.

9811. Pierre-Charles, Gérard. Der Neger in den abhängigen und unterentwickelten Gesellschaften: der Fall Haiti (*in* Gräbener, Jürgen *comp.* Kassengesellschaft und Rassismus [see *HLAS 35:8268]* p. 115-129)

Short but comprehensive overview of factors and variables of neocolonialism and underdevelopment in Haitian society. Author emphasizes some of the difficulties of societal integration in Haiti (political) and in Latin America as well as the causes of alienation in some classes.

Presser, Harriet B. Sterilization and fertility decline in Puerto Rico. See item 2055.

Ram, Bali and **G.E. Ebanks.** Stability of unions and fertility in Barbados. See item 2057.

9812. Randall, Margaret. La mujer cubana ahora. La Habana, Instituto Cubano del Libro, Editorial de Ciencias Sociales, 1972. 471 p., plates (Col. De sociología)

A combination of literary essays and case studies, this book has valuable information on the societal transformation of socialist Cuba.

9813. Religion in Jamaica. Kingston? Jamaica Information Service, 1972. 1 v. (Unpaged) plates (Facts on Jamaica series, 7)

Brief pamphlet of tourist interest.

Remy, Anselme. The unholy trinity. See item 1285.

9814. Rodríguez R., Víctor Melitón. Sindicalismo y administración de personal: dos factores de desarrollo; estudio referido a Puerto Rico y la República Dominicana. Santo Domingo, Univ. Autónoma de Santo Domingo, 1972. 179 p., bibl. (Publicaciones, 157)

In this combination handbook/textbook for labor union seminars, the synthesis of literature is more important than topical organization.

9815. Rogler, Lloyd H. The changing role of a political boss in a Puerto Rican migrant community (ASS/ASR, 39:1, Feb. 1974, p. 57-67)

Very interesting study of cases (39 months of research

in Puerto Rican community in an Eastern city) explains the persistence of the old-style ethnic-based boss, who attains power through charisma and personal favors and maintaining it in spite of the change in social structures and the gradual assimilation of the Puerto Rican community into the welfare state society (which according to this study does not imply a decline in ethnic group identity).

9816. Safa, Helen Icken. The urban poor of Puerto Rico: a study in development and inequality. N.Y., Holt, Rinehart and Winston, 1974. 116 p., bibl., plates, tables.

Landmark study with wide impact for political sociologists, urbanists, demographers and anthropologists Safa interviewed 200 San Juan, P.R., slum-dweller families in 1959-60, the slum was destroyed in 1962, but she was able, through extensive kin network systems to locate all 200 families for re-interviews in 1969. Her interviews with 15 adults—who had been young children 15 years earlier—presents an interesting time perspective. She analyzes reasons why some of the relocated families were upwardly mobile and the constraining factors on those who remained behind in the status race. Her discussion of political and social motives is insightful and refreshing. [N.S. Kinzer]

Sanders, Andrew. Family structure and domestic organization among coastal Amerindians in Guyana. See item 1290.

Sanford, Margaret. A socialization in ambiguity: child-lending in a British West Indian society. See item 1292.

Simpson, Joy M. A demographic analysis of internal migration in Trinidad and Tabago: a descriptive and theoretical orientation. See item 1293.

Smith, M.G. Race and stratification in the Caribbean. See item 1294.

Souffrant, Claude. La religion du paysan haitien: de l'anathéme au dialogue. See item 1295.

9817. Tancer, Shoshana B. *La quisqueyana:* the Dominican woman, 1940-1970 (*in* Pescatello, Ann *ed.* Female and male in Latin America [see item 9665] p. 209-229, bibl.)

A combination of African and Spanish traditions determine the role of mulatto women in the Dominican Republic, two thirds of whom are out of the market economy despite industrialization and substantial changes in the laws. These traditions are: the double standard due to the "macho" mystique, discrimination in job opportunities, emphasis on home and family as well as passivity and submissiveness. Very useful bibliography.

Vuijsje, H. Ontwikkelingsfunkties van religieuze organisaties in Suriname. See item 1300.

Watson, G. Llewellyn. Social structure and social movements: the Black Muslims in the U.S.A. and the Ras-Tafarians in Jamaica. See item 1302.

Wengen, G.D. van. De Javanen in de Surinaamse samenleving. See item 1304.

Wooding, Charles J. Winti: een Afroamerikaanse godsdienst in Suriname. See item 1307.

SOUTH AMERICA: ANDEAN COUNTRIES

(Venezuela, Colombia, Ecuador, Peru, Bolivia, Chile)

Quentin Jenkins
Professor of Sociology
Louisiana State University

Lisandro Pérez
Assistant Professor of Sociology
Louisiana State University

GENERAL

9818. Pugh, R. and others. Estudios de la realidad campesina: cooperación y cambio, informes y materiales de campo recogidos en Venezuela, Ecuador y Colombia. v. 2, Instituciones rurales y cambio dirigido. Geneva, United Nations Research Institute for Social Development (UNRISD), 1970. 421 p. (Serie UNRISD)

The papers of this volume are all case studies of individual cooperatives. Of particular importance is the description and analysis of the role of the priest (Catholic) in the cooperative movement. [P.F. Hernández]

9819. Rotondo, Humberto. Estudios sobre la familia en su relación con la salud. Lima, Univ. Nacional Mayor de San Marcos, 1970. 117 p.

Una serie de estudios realizados por el autor y sus colaboradores en torno a los valores y normas de la institución familiar y el empleo de recursos médicos. Enfocan a la población pobre y mestiza de la costa y sierra peruanas. Intrigantes ideas, pero la base empírica del trabajo es débil.

Whitten, Norman E., Jr. Ritual enactment of sex roles in the Pacific lowlands of Ecuador-Colombia. See *HLAS* 36:4596.

VENEZUELA

Abelson, Andrew E.; T.S. Baker; and Paul T. Baker. Altitude, migration, and fertility in the Andes. See item 2192.

Bartra, Roger. La estructura de clases en el agro andino venezolano. See item 7025.

9820. Bunimov-Parra, Boris. Introducción a la sociología electoral venezolana. Caracas, Editorial Arte, 1969. 374 p., bibl., maps, tables.

El autor detalladamente examina las elecciones venezolanas del período de 1946 a 1963 con énfasis en los aspectos sociales y geográficos del comportamiento electoral. Excelente uso de gráficos.

9821. Calello, Hugo. Subdesarrollo y estructura de clases en Venezuela (Ruedo Ibérico [Paris] 22/24, dic. 1968/mayo 1969, p. 113-136)

Ensayo teórico e histórico del desarrollo de las clases sociales en Venezuela. La tesis de los autores es que ese desarrollo refleja los cambios en la estructura económica.

9822. Casanova, Ramón Vicente and **Omaida Carrillo León.** La incidencia del divorcio en Los Andes. Mérida, Ven., Univ. de Los Andes, Facultad de Derecho, Centro de Jurisprudencia, 1968. 70 p., bibl., tables (Col. Justitia et jus. Sección investigaciones, 3)

Estudio de la incidencia y causas del divorcio en la población andina venezolana. Aunque se presentan numerosas cifras, el análisis anlítico de las mismas es muy limitado.

Dipolo, Mario and **María Matilde Suárez.** History, patterns, and migration: a case study in the Venezuelan Andes. See items 1461 and 2028.

9823. López, José Eliseo. Tendencias recientes de la población venezolana: estudio geográfico de la población de un país subdesarrollado. Mérida, Ven., Univ. de Los Andes, Instituto de Georgrafía, Facultad de Ciencias Forestales, 1968. 187 p., maps, tables.

Excellent demographic study of changes underway in the population of Venezuela since mid-century. Utilizing primarily the results of the 1961 enumeration as well as vital statistics, the author traces recent shifts in the age and sex structure, rural-urban distribution, economic activity, fertility, mortality, and migration. Effective use of mapping techniques and tabular presentations.

9824. Plaza, Salvador de la. Dependencia del exterior y clases sociales en Venezuela (UNAM/PDD, 1:3, abril/junio 1970, p. 31-64, tables)

Following the scheme of Marx (*Critique,* 1859) the author analyzes some historical material relative to class emergence and class structure at the national level. Some of the variables explored, particularly in the colonial period, seem more interesting than the concluding paragraphs.

Pollak-Eltz, Angelina. María Lionza: mito y culto venezolano. See item 1380.

9825. Rojas, Rubén. Hombre y vivienda. Caracas, Fondo Editorial Común, 1971? 60 p., bibl., tables.

Partiendo de la base que los programas de vivienda que solamente prestan atención al aspecto físico e ignoran las condiciones sociales están destinados a fracasar, el autor presenta el papel que debe desempeñar el Servicio Social en el mejoramiento de la vivienda, especialmente en Caracas. Interesante manual práctico de intervención social.

9826. Venezuela. Ministerio de Obras Públicas. Dirección de Planeamiento. División de Planeamiento Regional. San Juan de los Morros: estudio socioeconómico y demográfico. Caracas, 1969? 56 p., tables.

Detailed study conducted by the Division of Regional Planning of Venezuela on the demographic, health, housing, educational, and economic conditions of the medium-sized city of San Juan de los Morros.

COLOMBIA

9827. Ashton, Guy T. Rehousing and increased working-class in Cali, Colombia (CLAPSC/AL, 14:1/2, jan./junho 1971, p. 70-82)

An intensive study of class identity in a working-class housing project in Cali, Col. Author found that the residents were content with their working-class self-perceptions and sought only to improve their working-class status, largely through the accumulation of wealth.

9828. Avila, Abel. Sociología del hambre. Barranquilla, Colo., Ediciones Univ. del Atlántico, 1971. 245 p., bibl., tables.

El tema es menos amplio que lo que indica el título. El autor presenta los resultados de un estudio de la comunidad rural de La Lata en el norte de Colombia con el propósito de entender más a fondo la realidad agraria colombiana y latino-americana. Encuentra en el sistema de explotación capitalista las causas fundaentales de la miseria del sector agropecuario.

9829. Características socio-demográficas de las mujeres colombianas: encuesta nacional de fecundidad: parte urbana. Bogotá, Asociación Colombiana de Facultades de Medicina, División de Medicina Social y Población, 1973. 85 p., tables (Encuesta nacional de fecundidad)

También basada en la Encuesta Nacional de Fecundidad (see item 9833) esta obra recoje una serie de estudios realizados por varios autores en torno a la fecundidad de las mujeres urbanas de Colombia, sus características socio-demográficas, y el uso de métodos anticonceptivos.

9830. Cohen, Lucy M. Las colombianas ante la renovación universitaria. Bogotá, Ediciones Tercer Mundo, 1971. 149 p., bibl., tables (Col. Tribuna Libre, 4)

Excellent fieldwork study using questionnaire data obtained from personal interviews with 30 percent sample (n = 100) of women graduates from Colombian universities in dentistry, medicine, law and pharmacy. Cohen outlines the history of women's education in Colombia. She examines specific roles such as: woman student, woman professional and the single, married, divorced woman and the mother. Good for cross-cultural family studies, elites, sociology of education and anthropology. [N.S. Kinzer]

——. Women's entry to the professions in Colombia: selected characteristics. See item 1453.

9831. Conferencia Nacional sobre Familia, Infancia y Juventud, *I, Bogotá, 1970.* Primera Conferencia Nacional sobre Familia, Infancia y Juventud. Bogotá, Ministerio de Salud Pública, Instituto Colombiano de Bienestar Familiar, Depto. Nacional de Planeación *patrocinado por* Fondo de las Naciones Unidos para la Infancia (UNICEF), 1970. 575 p., plates, tables.

Massive volume that presents highlights of most of the 52 papers presented at the I National Conference on Family, Infancy, and Youth held in Bogotá under the auspices of UNICEF. Policy recommendations are made on such topics as housing, health, sex and procreation, socialization, and economic cooperation within the family.

9832. Correa, Patricia; Isa de Jaramillo; and Anamaría Ucrós. Influencia de la educación sexual en el nivel de información y en las actitudes hacia la sexualidad (Revista Latinoamericana de Psicología [Bogotá] 4:3, 1972, p. 323-334)

Authors conducted a survey of 2,000 high school students in Bogotá designed to measure the impact of sex education classes on the students' knowledge of biological functioning, family planning methods, the dynamics of sexual behavior, and on their attitudes towards sex.

9833. Cruz Betancourt, Carmen Inés. La apertura al cambio en la población rural. Bogotá, Asociación Colombiana de Facultades de Medicina, División de Medicina Social y Población, 1973. 84 p., bibl., tables (Encuesta nacional de fecundidad, 3)

Utilizando datos de la Encuesta Nacional de Fecundidad, se analizó la predisposición de la población rural de Colombia a incorporar patrones no-tradicionales (modernos) de comportamiento. Los resultados se analizan con respecto al uso de métodos anti-conceptivos.

Dent, David W. Oligarchy and power structure in urban Colombia: the case of Cali. See item 8314.

Drake, George F. Elites and voluntary associations: a study of community power in Manizales. See item 8316.

9834. Es, J.C. van and **William L. Flinn.** A note on the determinants of satisfaction among urban migrants in Bogotá, Colombia (IAMEA, 27:2, Autumn 1973, p. 15-28, bibl.)

Analysis of a survey of 120 household-heads in the slums of Bogota pays particular attention to "satisfactions with past attainment" (after migrating to the city). The major components of socio-economic status serve as independent variables of this search. The findings show that contrary to what people think, the crisis of expectations is far from revolutionary. [P.F. Hernández]

9835. *Estudios de Planificación Familiar.* Consejo de Población [and] Asociación Colombiana de Facultades de Medicina, División de Estudios de Población. Vol. 6, No. 2, feb. 1971- Bogotá.

Los autores estiman que los programas de salud-maternoinfantil, que incluyen el suministro sistemático de servicios de planificación familiar, constituyen una gran vía para lograr el control mundial de la natalidad. Presentan una guía para la introducción de tales programas.

Fals Borda, Orlando. Reflexiones sobre la aplicación del método de estudio-acción en Colombia. See item 8317.

9836. Flinn, William L. Family life of Latin American urban migrants: three case studies in Bogotá (UM/JIAS, 16:3, Aug. 1974, p. 326-349, bibl., tables)

The latest in a long series of valuable articles by Flinn on the residents of three peripheral shanty-towns in Bogotá. This one is devoted to household characteristics (marital status, income, occupation, education, tenure status, and value systems), particularly in comparison with rural dwellers.

──────. Rural and intra-urban migration in Colombia: two case studies in Bogotá. See item 1470.

Goldsmith, Alfredo; Gilda Echeverría; and **Rona Goldberg.** Vasectomy in Colombia: a pilot study. See item 2033.

9837. Granados Téllez, Marcos F. and others. Gamines. Bogotá, Ediciones Tercer Mundo [and] Pontificia Univ. Javeriana, Depto. de Ciencias Religiosas, 1974. 95 p., bibl., plates, tables.

Excellent study of one of Bogotá's most pressing social problems: the *gamines* (street urchins). Author and associates questioned 110 *gamines* about their reasons for leaving home, their parents, group dynamics within the gang, attitudes, socioeconomic status, and other variables. A comprehensive pioneer study.

9838. Gutiérrez, José. Gamín: un ser olvidado. México, Libros McGraw-Hill de México, 1972. 350 p.

An excellent complement to item 9837, the work of Granados Téllez. It focuses on the same subject, but with a psychological perspective. Instead of a survey, it utilized the case-study approach, examining in detail the lives of a handful of *gamines* living in Bogotá.

9839. Harkness, Shirley J. The pursuit of an ideal: migration, social class, and women's roles in Bogotá, Colombia (*in* Pescatello, Ann ed. Female and male in Latin America [see item 9665] p. 231-234, bibl.)

Harkness studied two barrios, one a working-class neighborhood, the other a poor and destitute one to compare the effects of contact with life in the capital city. Her data may indicate that the "modernization of women is a multifaceted process distinct from that of men." For ethnologist's comment, see item 1484.

9840. James, William Russell. Domestic group organization and processes in a rural Colombian town. Madison, Univ. of Wisconsin, Land Tenure Center, 1973. 45 p., bibl., illus., tables (LTC reprint, 55) (mimeo)

Interesting and rare analysis of the household group in a Latin American rural community. The author intensively studied a town in Antioquia, Colo. Special attention is paid to household characteristics, economic activities, and the phases of the developmental cycle.

9841. Lipman, Aaron. The Colombian entrepreneur in Bogotá. Coral Gables, Fla., Univ. of Miami Press, 1969. 144 p., bibl. (Hispanic-American studies, 22)

Unsophisticated, common-sensical survey of entrepreneurial circles in Bogota proves their elitist recruitment and some of its consequences for socioeconomic development. For historian's comment, see *HLAS 36:2816*. [P.F. Hernández]

Losada, Rodrigo. Incidencia de factores sociales personales en las opiniones políticas del congresista colombiana. See item 8327.

9842. Martine, George. Volume, characteristics and consequences of internal migration in Colombia (PAA/D, 12:2, May 1975, p. 193-208, bibl., tables)

Although internal migration in Colombia has been the focus of numerous studies, in this article the author presents the most succinct statement yet available on the volume and selectivity of internal movements in that country. Data are derived from the most recent census available (1964).

Micklin, Michael; Marshall Durbin; and **Carlos A. León.** The lexicon for madness in a Colombian city: an exploration in semantic space. See item 1512.

9843. Ocampo T., José Fernando. Dominio de clases en la ciudad colombiana. Medellín, Colo., Editorial La Oveja Negra, 1972. 221 p., bibl., tables.

Acerbic criticism of sociological conceptions of modernization that equate political and economic development with the rise of liberal democracy. Examines the social structure of Manizales, Colo., and concludes that the dominance of the bourgeoisie, supported by imperialism, is the real culprit in underdevelopment.

9844. *Revista de Planeación y Desarrollo.* Depto. Nacional de Planeación. Vol. 4, No. 1. enero/marzo 1972-   . Bogotá.

The entire issue is devoted to the processes of internal migration and urbanization in Colombia and to the implications of those phenomena for planners. It is divided into four articles: Ramiro Cardona G. "Mejoramiento de Tugurios y Asentamientos no Controlados: los Aspectos Sociales;" Wilfred Owen "Urbanización Planeada: Fin a la Ciudad Accidental;" "Predicción de la Población Colombiana por Departmentos;" "Movimiento Migratorio Interno en Colombia durante el Período Intercensal 1951-1964." The last two are reports of AID-sponsored projects headed by Eduardo E. Arriaga.

9845. Sanders, Thomas G. Family planning in Colombia. Hanover N.H., American Universities Field Staff Reports, 1970. 6 p. (West Coast South American series, 17:3)

Brief account of the development of family planning programs in Colombia, with emphasis on the manner in which political and religious obstacles were surmounted.

9846. La sociedad y el universitario: un análisis del conflicto estudiantil y de la educación superior en Columbia. Bucaramanga, Col., Univ. Industrial de Santander (UIS), 1971. 98 p., illus. (La universidad y el sistema social, 1)

This set of articles is devoted exclusively to the role of the university in Colombian society, particularly as it relates to the etiology of student disorders. It brings together the views of individuals that represent diverse sectors of Colombian social and political life. Included is an article by Gen. Alvaro Valencia Tovar on confrontations between students and the military.

9847. Soles, Roger E. Rural land invasions in Colombia. Madison, Univ. of Wisconsin, Land Tenure Center, 1974. 66 p., illus., tables (LTC reprint, 59) (mimeo)

Extensive analysis into the relationship between the incidence of rural land invasions in Colombia and the variables of population density, land tenure system, and capital distribution.

Villegas Moreno, Luis Alberto. Aspectos de la política social y económica de los tugurios y asentamientos no controlados. See item 6915.

———. Vivienda y desarrollo urbano en Columbia. See item 6916.

Whiteford, Andrew H. Aristocracy, oligarchy and cultural change in Colombia. See item 1552.

Whiteford, Michael B. Barrio Tulcan: fieldwork in a Colombian city. See item 1553.

———. Neighbors at a distance: life in a low income Colombian barrio. See item 1554.

EDUADOR

Arias Bazantes, Manuel. Análisis de la estructura agraria del Ecuador. See item 6924.

9848. Bride, Anne. Migrations, colonisations et modifications des structures agraires sur la côte equatorienne (UNAM/RMS, 33:4, oct./dic. 1971, p. 803-829, tables)

A rare look at the demographic processes and agrarian structure of the coast of Ecuador, with special attention to the contrasts with the Sierra.

Brownrigg, Leslie Ann. Interest groups in regime changes in Ecuador. See item 1436.

Nett, Emily M. The servant class in a developing country: Ecuador. See item 1520.

PERU

Alberti, Giorgio. The breakdown of provincial urban power structure and the rise of peasant movements. See item 1416.

Berthelot, Jean; Jean Louis Christinat; and **Olivier François Maillard.** Approaches sociologiques des communautés indiennes des Andes. See item 1430.

9849. Bresani, Jorge Bravo; Francisco Sagasti; and **Augusto Salazar Bondy.** El reto del Perú en la perspectiva del tercer mundo. Lima, Moncloa-Campodonico Editores, 1972. 118 p. (Col. Todo la realidad)

This book is a synopsis of papers presented at a colloquium in the Waston School of Business at the Univ. of Pennsylvania; the authors reflect in topics of alternatives to development and analyze the chances of the Peruvian nationalistic formula as a case in point. [P.F. Hernández]

Collier, David. Los pueblos jóvenes y la adaptación de los migrantes al ambiente urbano limeño. See item 1454.

9850. Cooper, H.H.A. The law relating to sexual offenses in Peru (AJCL, 21:1, Winter 1973, p. 86-123)

A detailed description of all Peruvian legal processes that relate to sexual offenses. Excellent legal discussion, although its sociological introduction is very weak.

Cotler, Julio. Actuales pautas de cambio en la sociedad rural del Perú. See item 1457.

———. Alternativas de cambio en dos haciendas algodoneras. See item 1458.

Escobar, Gabriel. Sicaya: cambios culturales en una comunidad mestiza andina. See item 1469.

Hargous-Vogel, Sabine. Urban problems, Peruvian style. See item 1483.

Leeds, Anthony. Political, economic and social effects of producer and consumer orientations toward housing in Brazil and Peru: a systems analysis. See item 1500.

Mangin, William. Autobiographical notes on a rural migrant to Lima, Peru. See item 6979.

9851. Marckwardt, Albert M. Evaluation of an experimental short interview form designed to collect fertility data: the case of Peru (PAA/D, 10:4, Nov. 1973, p. 639-657, bibl., tables)

The contributions of this short article are strictly methodological. It compares an experimental short interview form with the in-depth KAP interview in order to ascertain the relative strengths and weaknesses of each instrument. The samples were drawn from the population of Peru.

9852. Matos Mar, José *comp.* La obligarquía en el Perú. B.A., Amorrortu Editores, 1972. 192 p.

Interesante obra que recoje los puntos de vista de Bourricaud, Favre y Bravo Bresani con respecto a la existencia e impacto de una verdadera obligarquía en el Peru. Los tres no coinciden en la cuestion de la distribución y control del poder económico en ese país, y el resultado es una estimulante controversia con implicaciones para el estudio de clases sociales en Latinoamérica.

Moxley, Robert L. Family solidarity and quality of life in an agricultural Peruvian community. See item 1517.

9853. Myers, Sara K. Language shift among migrants to Lima, Peru. Chicago, Ill., Univ. of Chicago, Dept. of Geography, 1973. 203 p., bibl., maps, tables (Research paper, 147)

Very interesting study in sociolinguistics which analyzes the extent to which Quechua-speaking migrants from the highlands to Lima utilize Spanish in the city. Findings based on a survey of two squatter settlements in the Lima-Callao Metropolitan Area.

Orlove, Benjamin S. Abigeato: la organizacion social de una actividad ilegal. See item 1524.

⸻. Urban and rural artisans in southern Peru. See item 1525.

9854. Rodríguez, Alfredo; Gustavo Riofrío; and Eileen Welsh. De invasores a invadidos. Lima, Centro de Estudios y Promoción del Desarrollo (DESCO), 1973. 137 p.

Otro trabajo sobre la vivienda y las barriadas, pero con una perspectiva muy diferente a la de Rojas. Basándose en la situación limeña, los autores arguyen que las instituciones benefactoras que operan en las barriadas sirven para neutralizar pelíticamente a los habitantes de las mismas, canalizando las inquietudes de esos sectores hacia el consumo burgúes y el mito de la cooperación entre las clases.

Smith, Margo L. Domestic service as a channel of upward mobility for the lower-class woman: the Lima case. See item 1536.

Stein, William W. Countrymen and townsmen in the Callejón de Huaylas, Peru: two views of Andean social structure. See item 1539.

Uzzell, Douglas. Cholos and bureaus in Lima: case history and analysis. See item 1545.

⸻. The interaction of population and locality in the development of squatter settlements in Lima. See item 1546.

BOLIVIA

Aron-Schaar, Adrianne. Local government in Bolivia: public administration and popular participation. See item 1426.

Buechler, Hans C. The reorganization of counties in the Bolivian highlands: an analysis of rural-urban networks and hierarchies. See item 1439.

9855. Gerace, Frank and Hernando Lázaro. Comunicación horizontal. Lima, Librería Studium, 1973. 137 p.

The authors base this work on their experiences as organizer of Bolivian radio schools. They discuss the uses and abuses of the great improvements in the means of communication and present their proposals for a liberating and not oppressing communications network.

9856. Graeff, Peter. The effects of continued landlord presence in the Bolivian countryside during the post-reform era: lessons to be learned. Madison, Univ. of Wisconsin, Land Tenure Center, 1974. 36 p. bibl., tables (LTC reprint, 103) (mimeo)

Exactly the same research issue as in item 9857: an examination of the consequences of the remnants of the traditional agrarian structure for the success of Bolivia's agrarian reform. For ethnologist's comment, see item 1478.

Guillet, David. Integración sociopolítica de las poblaciones nuevas en Bolivia: descripcion de un caso y discusión. See item 1480.

Guzmán Arze, Humberto. Diagrama sociológico de Cochabamba. See item 1481.

Havet, José. Estructura del poder en una zona rural boliviana. See item 1485.

9857. Heyduk, Daniel. The hacienda

system and agrarian reform in highland Bolivia: a re-evaluation (UP/E, 13:1, Jan. 1974, p. 1-11, bibl.)

Regional variations in the extent to which the goals of the Bolivian agrarian reform have been achieved are seen as a result of the type of hacienda system that still predominates in different areas. According to the author, certain local adaptations of the hacienda system are antagonistic to the national integration of the peasantry.

9858. Iriarte, Gregorio. Galerías de muerte: vida de los mineros bolivianos. Montevideo, Tierra Nueva, 1972. 212 p., tables.

Serious monograph which attempts to expose the deplorable living and working conditions of Bolivian miners.

9859. Menanteau-Horta, Darío. Cambio social y orientaciones de valores culturales de la juventud en Bolivia (UPR/RCS, 16:2, junio 1972, p. 221-248, tables)

Presents the results of a survey of 1,110 Bolivian high-school students designed to ascertain their attitudes towards social change and the extent of feelings of alienation.

Montaño Aragón, Mario. El hombre del suburbio: estudio de las areas periféricas de Oruro. See item 1515.

9860. Pereira Fiorilo, Juan. Socio-política de los países subdesarrollados: ensayo sobre la realidad boliviana. Cochabamba, Bol., Editorial Canelas, 1971. 280 p.

Este largo ensayo, que innecesariamente abarca un grueso tomo, presenta los problemas sociales más importantes de Bolivia. El autor, quien se considera de centro-izquierda, ataca a la oligarquía, pero al mismo tiempo rechaza las soluciones marxistas a favor de una "revolución democrática-social."

9861. Rutte García, Alberto. Simplemente explotadas: el mundo de las empleadas domésticas de Lima. Lima, Centro de Estudios y Promoción del Desarrollo (DESCO), 1973. 164 p., bibl., tables.

Esta pequeña monografía, cuyo título está obviamente inspirado en la popular telenovela peruana 'Simplemente María,' examina las condiciones de trabajo de cinco empleadas domésticas entrevistadas por el autor. Utilizando el método biográfico, el autor describe como dichas condiciones afectan el desarrollo psíquico de las empleadas.

CHILE

9862. Ceballos Tapia, Hernán and Juan S. Gumucio Rivas. Los trabajadores independientes frente a la seguridad social. Santiago, Univ. de Chile, Facultad de Ciencias Jurídicas y Sociales, Escuela de Derecho de Santiago [and] Editorial Andrés Bello, 1972. 138 p., bibl.

This short monograph is divided into two parts: 1) a general treatise on Social Security and the self-employed worker, and 2) a description and analysis of the specifics of the Chilean Social Security system.

9863. Domínguez, Oscar. Aspiraciones de los inquilinos de la provincia de Santiago. Santiago, Instituto de Capacitación e Investigación en Reforma Agraria, 1966. 70 p. (ICIRA: estudios de reforma agraria, 2)

El autor realizó una encuesta de los inquilinos de fundos residentes en cinco comunas de la provincia de Santiago (Chile) con el propósito de indagar acerca de sus aspiraciones y condiciones de vida. Buena metodología, aunque los resultados no son muy sorprendentes.

9864. Fuchs, Claudio J. and Henry A. Landsberger. Revolution or rising expectations" or traditional life ways? A study of income aspirations in a developing country (UC/EDCC, 21:2, Jan. 1973, p. 212-226, tables)

Presents the result of a survey of 120 presidents of labor unions in Santiago and Concepcion (Chile) designed to ascertain the level of desired wages for members. The responses were compared to actual incomes in an attempt to resolve contradictory theories of income aspirations.

9865. García, César. Educación y estratificación social en Bella Vista, Santiago (Eme-Eme [Santiago, R. D.] 1:1, junio/julio 1972, p. 82-98)

Of limited interest as a study of cases from a point of view of routine functionalistic premises. [P. F. Hernández]

9866. Godoy Urzúa Hernan. El oficio de las letras: estudio sociológico de la vida literaria. Santiago, Editorial Universitaria, 1970. 257 p., bibl., tables (Col. Manuales y monografías, 8)

A unique study in the sociology of literature. The author conducted a survey of Chilean writers to determine their attitudes, aspirations, social origins, social class, their perceived role in society, the development of their careers, social contacts among them, and many other factors. Sound survey methodology.

Hall, M. Francoise. Male sexual behavior and use of contraceptives in Santiago, Chile. See item 2037.

9867. Huizer, Gerrit. The utilization of conflict in community development and peasant organization: a case from Chile (IFSNC/CD, 27/28, Summer 1972, p. 133-148)

Criticizing the view that community development is particularly enhanced by cooperation, the author presents the view that conflict within peasant communities can have positive functions and can be utilized to promote development. Provocative essay which presents a fresh perspective based on the author's firsthand experience.

Inkeles, Alex and **David H. Smith.** Becoming modern: individual change in six developing countries. See item 9892.

Plank, Stephen J. and **M. L. Milanesi.** Fertility in rural Chile. See item 2054.

9868. Porteous, J. Douglas. Urban transplantation in Chile (AGS/GR, 62:4, Oct. 1972, p. 455-478, maps, plates, tables)

A detailed study of how a company-controlled coppermining town in the Central Andes of Chile was phased out and its inhabitants resettled in larger towns. The author examines the patterns of resettlement, the attitudes of the resettled, and the directives of the planners.

9869. Portes, Alejandro. On the interpretation of class consciousness (UC/AJS, 77:2, Sept. 1971, p. 228-244, bibl., tables)

Data were obtained from two lower class samples drawn in 1962 (n=360) and 1968 (n=382) in Santiago. Based on an "index of frustration," Portes contends that the emergence of revolutionary (here equal to leftists) orientations in the lower classes is affected only by frustration and discontent (àx -la-Marx) but also by whether individuals place blame for their suffering on the existing social order or on structurally irrelevant factors. [N.S. Kinzer]

9870. Reiher, Oswin Guillermo Zbinden. El trabejo en las prisiones. Santiago, Editorial Jurídica de Chile [and] Univ. de Concepcion, Facultad de Ciencias Jurídicas y Sociales, Escuela de Derecho, 1973? 83 p., tables.

A rare look at a Latin American penal system, this brief monograph presents the results of a survey of prisoners in various institutions in the province of Concepcion (Chile).

9871. Thiesenhusen, William C. Chile's experiments in agrarian reform: four colonization projects revisited (American Journal of Agricultural Economics [American Agricultural Economic Association, Menasha, Wis.] 56, May 1974, p. 323-330, bibl., tables)

Interesting study which explores possible explanations for differences in income among beneficiaries of agrarian reform programs. The author documents the inequality in income distribution among four colonization projects and concludes that type of farming is related to such income differences.

9872. Urrutia, Cecilia. Historia de las poblaciones callampas. Santiago, Empresa Editora Nacional Quimantú, 1972. 98 p., illus., plates (Col. Nosotros los chilenos, 11. Serie Hoy contamos)

Published during the Allende period, this booklet aims to convince the reader, through photographs and personal testimonials, of the social injustices of the Frei government. It reconstructs a violent incident in 1969 when government troops stormed a squatter settlement.

9873. Urzúa, Raúl. La demanda campesina. Santiago, Univ. Católica de Chile, 1969. 257 p., bibl., tables (Ediciones nueva universidad. Comunicaciones)

Analyzes the differences among land-holding classes in their predisposition to act on behalf of agrarian reform. Proposed the thesis that those differences are rooted in the contrasting nature of the power relationships with *latifundistas*. Supporting data were gathered from rural Cile.

9874. Williamson, Robert C. Social class, mobility, and modernism: Chileans and social change (USC/SSR, 56:2, Jan. 1972, p. 149-163, tables)

The author interviewed 329 Chileans in order to ascertain certain aspects of mobility and orientations towards change. Conducted in the early Allende period, it is an interesting study in light of subsequent developments in Chile.

9875. Zeitlin, Maurice; Lynda Ann Ewen; and **Richard Earl Ratcliff.** "New princes" for old? The large corporation and the capitalist class in Chile (UC/AJS, 80:1, July 1974, p. 87-123, bibl. tables)

Detailed study of ownership and control of the 37 largest corporations in Chile 1964-66. All but one of the 15 ostensible 'management controlled' corporations were actually controlled by specific interlocking proprietary interests based on kinship ties. In spite of eight-year old data, authors update their conclusions in relation to Allende regime and its subsequent overthrow. [N. S. Kinzer]

Zúñiga, Ricardo B. The experimenting society and radical social reform: the role of the social scientist in Chile's Unidad Popular experience. See item 1559.

9876. Zúñiga Ide, Jorge. La emigracion rural en la provincia de Coquimbo: Chile. Santiago, Instituto Latinoamericano de Investigaciones

Sociales (ILDIS), 1972. 95 p., bibl., tables (Estudios y documentos, 16)

The author studies the process of urbanization by focusing on rural out-migration. The result is an excellent empirical study in which the rural areas of the province of Coquimbo (Chile) are surveyed in order to ascertain the out-migrants' characteristics and places of destination.

SOUTH AMERICA: THE RIVER PLATE

(Argentina, Paraguay, Uruguay)

NORA SCOTT KINZER
Assistant Professor of Sociology
Purdue North Central University

ARGENTINA

9877. Abadi, Mauricio and others. La fascinación de la muerte: panorama, dinamismo y prevención del suicidio. B.A., Editorial Paidós, 1973. 216 p., bibl. (Biblioteca de psicologia profunda, 38)

Series of papers by six B.A. psychoanalysts on suicide. The introduction, containing longitudinal data on B.A.'s suicide rates, if of greatest value.

Biró de Stern, Ana. El medio social del altiplano juleño. See item 1431.

9878. Büntig, Aldo J. El catolicismo popular en la Argentina. B.A., Editorial Bonum, 1969. 198 p., illus. (Cuaderno sociológico, 1)

Questionnaire results from a survey of popular or "folk" Catholicism in Argentina. Questions concerned: cult of the Virgin(s), popular saints, pilgrimages, superstitions, cult of the dead, concept of a "good" Catholic and a "good" priest. Total N=339, n=127 B.A. and n=212 from Interior. Although a poorly organized book with little cross-classification other than two-by-two tables, there is a wealth of information for anthropologists and researchers in sociology of religion.

9879. ———. Religión-enajenación en una sociedad dependiente: análisis interdisciplinar de grupos de católicos normales agentinos. B.A., Editorial Guadalupe, 1973. 121 p., bibl., tables (Col. La dependencia argentina en el contexto latinoamericano, 3)

Based on a sample of 169 respondents from four parishes: urban middle class (B.A.), urban upper middle class (B.A.), urban slum (City of Santa Fe) and partial rural (province of Santa Fe), this study investigates attitudes and psychological characteristics of church members. Focusing on alienation and dependency this very interesting and provocative study is a distinct contribution to the study of the post-conciliar Roman Catholic Church.

9880. Cabello, Plácido and **Susana Spektor.** Estructura demográfica y socio-ocupacional de la provincia de Santiago del Estero. B.A., Edición del Consejo Federal de Inversiones, 1973. 211 p., tables (Serie Técnica, 21)

Census data analyzing socio-occupational characteristics of the Province of Santiago del Estero. Longitudinal comparisons using data from 1869, 1895, 1914, 1947 and 1960. Well organized and good reference.

9881. Cárdenas, Rodolfo Marcelo. Los porteños, su tiempo, su vivir. B.A., Editorial Sudamericana, 1973. 233 p., tables.

This book contains a wealth of data concerning porteño leisure-time activity: reading, watching T.V., attending sports events, sleeping, playing with children, summer vacations and much more. Unfortunately, we are never told how these 2,530 "interviews" were obtained.

9882. Casadevall, Domingo F. El carácter porteño. B.A. Centro Editor de América Latina, 1970. 114 p. illus. (La historia popular. Vida y milagros de nuestro pueblo, 3)

Incisive psychosocial study of the *porteña* (person from B.A.) that peculiar blend of The *criollo*, European Spanish, Italian, or Middle Easterner. Attitudes, values, linguistic peculiarities, work ethic, and other topics are treated within a cultural and historical context. [G. M. Dorn]

9883. Cicourel, Aaron V. Theory and method in a study of Argentine fertility. N.Y., John Wiley and Sons, 1974. 212 p., bibl., tables.

Refreshingly honest self-evaluation of Cicourel's experience directing a fertility study in B.A. Only a scholar of Cicourel's caliber could freely discuss the sociology of failure. Recommended for methodology courses. For physical anthropologist's comment, see item 2024.

9884. Comité Judío Americano, *B.A.* Oficina Latinoamericano. Instituto de

Relaciones Humanas. Comunidades judías de Latinoamérica. B.A., Editorial Candelabro, 1970. 294 p., bibl.

Broad overall picture of Jewish communities throughout Latin America. Major focus is on large Jewish community of Argentina. Also includes directory of Jewish organizations in various countries. Although sketchy, the statistical data may be of interest to historians or sociologists.

9885. Conferencia Interamericana Especializada sobre Educación Integral de la Mujer, *B.A., 1972.* Referencias bibliográficas. B.A., Ministerio de Cultura y Educación, Centro Nacional de Documentación e Información Educativa, 1972. 1 v. (Unpaged)

Incomplete bibliography pertaining to women's social status in Argentina.

Fernández, Julio. The political elite in Argentina. See item 8647a.

9886. Form, William H. Automobile workers in four countries: the relevance of system participation for working-class movements (BJS, 25:4, Dec. 1974, p. 442-460, tables)

Review of a cross-culture comparative study of automobile workers in four countries: Olds (Lansing, Mich.), Industrias Kaiser Argentina (Cordoba, Arg.), FIAT (Turin, Italy), and Premier Automobile Limited (Bombay, India). Shows varying degrees of changes wrought in lives of industrialized workers. Similarities on certain scales (e.g., family-centered activities) are more interesting than the differences.

9887. Formosa (province), *Arg.* **Asesoría de Desarrollo.** Censo nacional de población, familias y viviendas, 1970. Formosa; datos provisorios. Formosa, Arg., 1971? 1 v. (Unpaged) maps, plates.

Comparative data on Province of Formosa. Interesting longitudinal data comparing 1947, 1960 and 1970 census data. Confusing maps in last portion of booklet.

9888. Guibourdenche de Cabezas, Marta. Problemas de la minoridad. Mendoza, Arg., Univ. Nacional de Cuyo, Facultad de Ciencias Políticas y Sociales, Centro de Investigaciones, Instituto de Sociología, 1970. 44 p., tables (Serie Cuadernos, 20)

Brief overview of problems associated with minors in Argentina. Most useful section is outline of laws dealing with *patria potestas,* adoption, juvenile delinquency and mental illness.

9889. Henault, Mirta; Peggy Morton; and Isabel Larguía. Las mujeres dicen basta. B.A., Ediciones Nueva Mujer, 1972. 130 p.

Rehash of 1960s US women's liberationist writings. Written from a leftist or Marxian point-of-view this book adds nothing to sex-role critiques but is interesting as example of consciousness-raising in a Latin American country.

9890. Horowitz, Irving Louis. Israeli ecstasies/Jewish agonies. N.Y., Oxford Univ. Press, 1974. 224 p., bibl.

Chap. 7, "Jewish Ethnicity and Latin American Nationalism," and Chap. 8, "Organization and Ideology of the Jewish Community of Argentina," are must readings for the Argentine specialist. Horowitz' research and insight into B.A.'s Jewish community provide interesting contrast to studies on North American Jews.

9891. Iñigo Carrera, Héctor. La mujer argentina. B.A., Centro Editor de América Latina, 1972. 116 p., plates (La historia popular. Vida y milagros de nuestro pueblo, 91)

A very interesting literary essay with a collection of sketches of historical value. [P. F. Hernández]

9892. Inkeles, Alex and **David H. Smith.** Becoming modern: individual change in six developing countries. Cambridge, Mass., Harvard Univ. Press, 1974. 437 p., bibl., tables.

Based on four hour face-to-face interviews with nearly 6,000 men in Argentina, Chile, Israel, Nigeria, India and East Pakistan. The authors focus on "the process whereby people move from being traditional to becoming modern personalities."

9893. Kinzer, Nora Scott. Women professionals in Buenos Aires (*in* Pescatello, Ann ed. Female and male in Latin America (see item 9665] p. 159-190)

Data obtained from 125 female subjects in "male' professions (law, medicine, pharmacy, biochemistry, architecture, agronomy and engineering). Using face-to-face interviews and a semi-structured questionnaire, the author examines stresses and strains of being a wife, mother and female professional resident in B.A. Analyzing the laws and history of women's education in Argentina, author concludes that there are decided advantages that accrue to the porteña compared to the US female professional. [Asst. Ed.]

9894. Lattes, Alfredo E. and **Raúl Poczter.** Muestra del censo de población de la ciudad de Buenos Aires de 1855. B.A., Instituto Torcuato Di Tella, Centro de Investigaciones Sociales, 1968. 78 p., facsims., maps, plate, tables (Documento de trabajo. Serie Población y sociedad, 54)

Excellent monograph for historians, demographers and sociologists. Well illustrated and anecdotal.

9895. Lineamientos de un nuevo proyecto nacional. Tucumán, Arg., Univ. Nacional de Tucumán, 1971. 254 p.

Written by an inter-disciplinary group of Argentine intellectuals, this book attempts to define reasons for Argentine economic, political and social instability. No new historical or sociological data are presented. The reader is advised to stay with McGann, Germani and Scobie.

Los Libros. See item 2232.

9896. MacEwen, Alison M. Kinship and mobility on the Argentine pampa (UP/E, 12:2, April 1973, p. 135-151, bibl., illus.)

Fifty percent sample survey (total number never indicated) of three shanty towns surrounding San Pedro, a town near Parana. Examines kinship structure and networks showing importance of network in migration and daily life. Kin ties must be cut for upward social mobility. Good reference for anthropology, urbanization, demography.

9897. Migliorini, Inés Candelaria. Los derechos civiles de la mujer en la República Argentina. B.A., Centro Nacional de Documentación e Información Educativa, 1972. 34.

Brief and incomplete outline of civil rights of women according to Argentine legal code. Emphasis placed on property and inheritance law. No discussion of separation or divorce law. Paper prepared by the Argentine Ministry of Culture and Education for the Conferencia Interamericana Especializada sobre Educación Integral de la Mujer, held in B.A., 21-25 Aug. 1972.

9898. Mirelman, Victor A. Note on Jewish settlement in Argentina, 1881-1892 (Jewish Social Studies [Conference on Jewish Social Studies, N.Y.] 33:1, Jan. 1971, p. 3-12)

Outlines Argentine government's encouraging immigration of Jews from Czarist Russia to populate pampa. Tells of problems encountered by first immigrants ranging from being refused permission to land, to inability to obtain kosher food to fraudulent land sales. Little or no attention given to importance of Baron Hirsch and the Jewish Colonization Association of London.

9899. Moffatt, Alfredo. Psicoterapía del oprimido: ideología y técnica de la psiquiatría popular. B.A., Editorial Librería ECRO, 1974. 279 p.

The book does not intend to treat the subject in a scientific manner. Nevertheless, it reports valuable psychiatric insights and experiences in group therapy among patients of big mental hospitals in B.A. [P.F. Hernández]

9900. Mora y Araujo, Manuel. La sociedad y la praxis sociológica. San Carlos de Bariloche, Arg., Fundación Bariloche, Depto. de Sociología, 1970. 30 l.

Review of ferment over use and misuse of sociology. Points out shortcomings of Latin American sociology and, in particular, Argentine sociologists. Interesting addition to comparative sociology of knowledge.

9901. Ranis, Peter. Peronistas without Perón (RU/T, 10:3, March/April 1973, p. 53-59)

Popular historical and sociological outline of present-day (1970s) Peronism. Explains why Peronism has continued legitimacy, influence and lasting impact on Argentina's workers. Shows that Perón's followers are anti-American, anti-Cuban, anti-Soviet, anti-foreign and pro-Catholic.

9902. Reina, Rubén E. Paraná: social boundaries in an Argentine city. Austin, Tex., Univ. of Texas Press *for the* Institute of Latin American Studies, 1973. 390 p., bibl., maps, plates, tables (Latin American monographs, 31)

An overly long history and participant observer reportage of the rigidly stratified society of the City of Paraná. Judicious editing would improve the book immensely. Reina never adequately describes his methodology, his sample, or his fieldwork experiences except that "the approach to the study of Paraná was not different from that used in my study of the Mayan Indians in Guatemala." Nevertheless, there is a wealth of data for the patient reader. For historian's comment, see *HLAS 36:3277.*

9903. *Revista de la Universidad.* Univ. de La Plata. No. 23, 1971- . La Plata, Arg.

This issue is devoted to "La Juventud Actual en una Sociedad de Cambio." The section on psycho-biological characteristics of the juvenile is heavily Freudian and most of the sociological articles add nothing to our understanding of Argentine youth. For those interested in sociology of literature the article by Olivera," Los Jóvenes Frente a la Literatura" is well-worth reading.

9904. Rothman, Ana María. Evolución de la fecundidad en Argentina y Uruguay. B.A., Instituto Torcuato Di Tella, Centro de Investigaciones Sociales, 1970. 30 p., bibl., tables (Serie Población y sociedad. Documento de trabajo, 69)

Fertility rates for Argentina, 1895, 1947, 1954 and 1960; 1936, 1947, 1960 and 1964; and, Uruguay, 1948, 1943, 1957 and 1963. Excellent graphs and tables.

9905. San Juan (province), *Arg.* **Secretaría Técnica de la Gobernación. Instituto de Investigaciones Económicas y Estadísticas.** Encuesta de empleo y desempleo en áreas urbanas del Gran San Juan. San Juan, Arg. 1971. 23 l., tables (mimeo)

Brief mimeographed report on employment and unemployment in San Juan area. Unfortunately, only raw data are reported and not percentages. May be of some use to demographer or economist dealing with San Juan.

9906. _____, _____. _____. Encuesta de empleo y desempleo en el departamento de Jachal. San Juan, Arg., 1971. 22 1., tables.

Raw data only on sample of families. No percentages reported. Of minor interest to economist or demographer.

9907. Schufer de Paikin, Marta L. El modelo de rol profesional del médico. B.A., Centro Interdisciplinario de Investigaciones en Psicología Matemática y Experimental (CIIPME), 1971. 50 l., tables (Publicación, 21)

Study based on questionnaires distributed to 100 physicians in five B.A. hospitals. Surprising amount of information concerning career choice and social class background. Of most interest are replies to questions concerning the practice of medicine in B.A. Excellent reference for comparative studies on sociology of medicine or occupation.

9908. Scobie, James R. Buenos Aires: plaza to suburb, 1870-1910. N.Y., Oxford Univ. Press, 1974. 323 p., bibl., maps, plates.

Written with flair and verve, illustrated by superb photographs and maps, Scobie's work in a *tour de force* not only for urban studies but sociology and anthropology. Describing the growth of B.A. from 1870 to 1910, Scobie ranges from the aristocratic Anchorenas to tenement houses and the beggars on garbage dumps. Using every available source from expansion of streetcar lines to architectural designs, Scobie's work is a shining example of creative scholarship.

9909. Somoza, Jorge L. Algunos efectos sociales y económicos derivados de la baja de la mortalidad en la República Argentina entre 1900 y 1960 (IDES/DE, 11:41, abril/junio 1971, p. 113-123, bibl., tables.)

The decline in Argentine mortality in the 20th century is analyzed in terms of its effects on various demographic variables such as the number of orphans, the proportion of surviving children, and the dependency ratio. For historian's comment see *HLAS* 36:3323. [Q. Jenkins]

_____. La mortalidad en la Argentina entre 1869 y 1960. See *HLAS 36:3324*.

9910. Ulloa, Fernando and others. Psicología argentina hoy. B.A., Ediciones Búsqueda, 1973. 158 p., bibl.

For the reader willing to wade through excess verbiage with little or no supporting data, there are interesting sidelights to the practice of psychology in a "colonized" or "underdeveloped" nation.

9911. Verón, Eliseo and **Carlos E. Sluzki.** Comunicación y neurosis. B.A., Editorial del Instituto, 1970. 334 p., bibl., plates (Comunicación y neurosis. Serie naranja: sociología)

Over a four year period, 52 taped interviews of 15-20 minutes each were obtained from patients diagnosed as neurotic (hysterical, phobic and obsessive) in three B.A. psychiatric clinics. Psycholinguistic analysis revealed markedly different speech patterns between the three groups. In spite of myriad tables and detailed statistical analysis, severe methodological problems flaw this study. Males and females are lumped together (80 percent of the sample is female). Although speech patterns vary by social class and education, all social classes are lumped as are illiterates and college graduates. The most serious problem is that there is no control group of non-hospitalized non-neurotic B.A. residents. Veron and Sluzki offer the cliché excuse that "there is the problem of defining normality."

PARAGUAY

9912. Flores Colombino, Andrés. La fuga de intelectuales: emigración paraguaya. Prólogo de Carlos Pastore. Montevideo, Talleres Gráficos de la Comunidad del Sur, 1972. 255 p., bibl.

Good review of historical literature on the topic precedes this sophisticated study of modern migration from Paraguay to neighboring countries. Valuable monograph for further research in many fields.

URUGUAY

9913. *Boletín Uruguayo de Sociología.* Año 10, Nos. 19/20, feb. 1972- . Montevideo.

Uneven collection of articles in honour of 10th anniversary of journal. The frank editorial dealing with Uruguay's past ten years is well worth reading. Also of note is the article by Renée Lescop Baudoin (Univ. of Montreal) "La Guerra de Guerrillas en América Latina entre 1960 y 1969: el Refuerzo de una Ideología y el Debilitamiento de un Movimiento."

9914. Solari, Aldo E. and **Rolando Franco.** La familia en el Uruguay (CLAPCS/AL, 14:3/4, julho/dez. 1971, p. 3-33, tables)

Impressionistic outline of Uruguayan family based on outmoded 1950s sociology. Interesting section on divorce and birth rate. Unfortunately, little or no hard data to support sweeping statements.

9915. Suanes, Héctor. *El milagro de los Andes:* diario de uno de los sobrevivientes del avión caído en la cordillera aquel día de octubre . . . B.A., Emecé Editores, 1973. 296 p.

Diary written by a member of the Uruguayan soccer team who survived an Andean plane crash by eating the flesh of those who died in the accident. Not well written, but chillingly explicit.

BRAZIL

JOSE FABIO BARBOSA DASILVA
Associate Professor of Sociology
University of Notre Dame

SEVERAL DEVELOPMENTS ARE APPARENT in the sociology studies discussed here. First, social scientists, planners, administrators, and the general public in Brazil are paying increasing attention to communications. This is apparent in the vast number of recent publications on the subject: some for the general public, some for the training of students in the new Institutos de Communicação in Brazilian universities, some the result of research carried on in these centers, and others by non-specialists in the form of commentaries on the field and its developments. All of these materials are proof of the extent of a developing consciousness of the potential of mass-communication systems in Brazil. They also serve as adjuncts to development and planning programs by presenting a "social reality" which supports and provides a socio-psychological basis for these programs. Some of the works, however, are critical of the uses of communication, whether as ideological manipulation, as an elitistic organization of processes, or as a significant (and negative) phenomena in mass society.

A second interesting development is the proliferation of counseling manuals for the general public which popularize ideas, constructs, and techniques developed in psychiatry, psychology, and social psychology for the management of self, interactional, or group problems. A number of these deal with sexual behaviour from a growth psychology perspective (i.e. problems in childhood, youth, pre and post-marriage; and others more specialized which deal with sexual problems in religious communities). These publications are quite heterogeneous: some are based on special disciplines, some are rooted in pastoral concerns (usually Catholic but including one "Espírita") and others that deal specifically with social problems and the social worker's professional role. The proliferation of these works is proof of the transformation of modern Brazilian culture, the "modernization" of the urban population, and the growing demand for publications of this nature.

A third important development is the proliferation of research reports and studies issuing from official or semi-official institutions and linked to the multiple social, community-action, regional and national planning programs. A substantial number of these studies are put out by social science graduates, often under the supervision of well qualified specialists and well established professionals. These university teams are increasingly concerned with sophisticated methodology. Moreover, the career pattern for social scientists in Brazil has altered significantly. The older academic tradition of scholarly pursuits and teaching at universities and teacher colleges has changed into one of employment outside the university, especially in government agencies and/or industry. José de Souza Martins' paper comments briefly on these changes and points out some of the problems involved. There are now centers of major significance in Brazil such as CEBRAP (Brazilian Research Center of São Paulo), which includes some renowned Brazilian scholars retired from the university system and involved with theoretical-critical studies, and the IJNPS (Instituto Joaquim Nabuco de Pesquisas Sociais of Recife) concerned with basic community and regional research chiefly the socio-economic characteristics of the area's population. In addition to these centers, there are many other institutions and government programs whose work is proof of a greater technical and methodological sophistication (see some of the reports of surveys on housing, labor force, and family budgets in this section).

A fourth development is the increasing number of publications directly linked with government policy, which propose, debate, and support official programs. These range from the "grass-roots" seminars of the Escola Superior de Guerra to position papers by government officials, all of great documentary value for students of recent changes in Brazil.

Finally there are three types of works of more immediate sociological concern. The first category includes materials on sociology per se which cover texts for professional training (largely based on classics in the field) as well as scholarly research and theoretical analyses. One must point out that at present there is a greater emphasis on training than on scholarly work. Nevertheless, serious research underway in centers other than those in São Paulo promises some valuable contributions in the future. Our second category concerns research in demography, an established tradition in Brazilian scholarship, which is well represented in this section. The last category consists of research of recently trained professionals (MA's, PhD's and other investigators) which reveals a strong but not undue concern with methodology, a familiarity with recent developments in the field (e.g., the use of Goffman's contributions by appeals to symbolic interactionism, structuralism, and phenomenology), and an innovative use of sociological theory in the study of contemporary Brazilian issues. Examples of this are the volumes edited by Gilberto Velho (item 10063) and the study of Sergio Miceli (item 10014).

The radical process undergone by Brazilian universities is evident in published studies which show what are their concerns, professional positions, academic training, creativity, and critical ability. These indicate that some major shifts are underway in the social sciences of Brazil. One of the most critical is the change of professional locus from older university settings to government and industry both of which propose and support more immediate and pragmatic objectives for the specialists. Only time will show the wisdom of this shift towards applied research. In the meantime, it will result in further division of intellectual labor and a stricter scholastic hierarchy. Nevertheless, it is encouraging to note that a few young scholars, of great intellectual potential, are still involved in basic research.

9916. Abreu, João Theodoro de Salles. A prostituição no Distrito Federal. n.p., n.p., n.d. 120 l., tables.

An exploratory survey requested by the Dept. of Justice and carried on by a social worker in various areas of the Federal District. The report is given by area, and uses mostly observation and informal interviews for description of the materials. Illustrative but not sufficiently systematic.

9917. Altenfelder, Mário. Aspectos da política do bem-estar no Brasil. Rio, Fundação Nacional do Bem-Estar do Menor, Setor de Relações Públicas, 1968. 128 p., tables.

A brief survey of welfare policy in Brazil. Good description of governmental programs and some discussion of other institutional activities. Informative although little evaluation of the topic.

9918. ———. Política nacional do bem-estar do menor. Rio? Fundação Nacional do Bem-Estar do Menor, Setor de Relações Públicas, 1970. 1 v. (Unpaged)

Similar formulation as found in the more extensive discussion by the same author in item 9917.

9919. Amazonas (state), *Bra.* **Secretaria de Planejamento e Coordenação Geral (SEPLAN). Comissão de Desenvolvimento do Estado do Amazonas (CODEAMA).** Cidade de Manaus, III pesquisa sócio-econômica, novembro de 1971. Manaus, Bra., 1972. 130 p., tables (Estudos específicos, 41)

This special report for the city of Manaus publishes results from a continuing research project directed by the local planning board. Materials include survey and census data on housing, population, education, labor, income, and various socio-economic indexes used for purpose of analysis and evaluation.

9920. Andrade, José Maria Tavares de. Recherches at débats—research and debate (FERES/SC, 19:4, 1972, p. 599-611, bibl.)

Subtitle: "The Field of Religiosity: Research Project for the Study of Popular Religiosity in Brazil." Basically this is a discussion of a research project including the selection of a theoretical frame (Weber and Bourdieu's epistemological contributions), and the reformulation of these into a more dynamic model. The paper then briefly analyzes vis-à-vis such framework the multiplicity of religious structures found in Brazil either as world religions or as popular formations and others derived from African, Amerindian, or primitive and pagan cults.

9921. Angelini, Arrigo Leonardo. Applied psychology and problems of Brazil as a developing country (SIP/RIP, 7:1/2, 1973, p. 65-75, bibl.)

In this invited paper to the Symposium entitled "Psychological Studies of Problems of Developing Countries" (XVII International Congress of Applied Psychology, 1971) the author reviews major research projects carried on by the Psychology Center in São Paulo and various local, state, and national organizations, mainly connected with government development programs. Informative but rather brief and descriptive.

9922. ———. Motivação humana: o motivo de realização. Rio, Livraria José Olympio Editôra, 1973. 216 p., bibl., plates, tables (Col. Psicologia contemporânea)

An extensive research report on the application of the studies on motivation and achievement by MacClelland and others to Brazilian populations (mostly students in the educational system of São Paulo). Includes research design, methodology and instruments, statistical analysis and discussion.

9923. Aresi, Ricardo. Noivos preparados, casais ajustados. Pôrto Alegre, Bra., Edições Paulinas, 1971. 279 p. (Col. Juventude presença)

This work is mainly a manual for preparation for marriage heavily influenced by Catholic ethics. Discussions are less dependent on technical information or counselling than on re-stating accepted and traditional views. Of documentary interest only.

9924. Arns, Paulo Evaristo. Cumunidades: união e ação. São Paulo, Edições Paulinas, 1972. 355 p. (Col. Sinal)

A discussion on the social potential of community organization for the development of collective action to solve local problems and to elaborate networks for handling or contributing to the solution of wider problems. Good presentation based on much first hand information and work. Mainly for persons associated with community action programs in Brazil.

9925. Avila, Fernando Bastos de. Introdução à sociologia. 5. ed. Rio, Livraria Agir Editôra, 1973. 359 p.

A text for courses in Introduction to Sociology following the general format of American texts. Includes some materials dealing with Brazil mainly for illustration and discussion.

9926. Azevêdo, Carlos Alberto and R. Parry Scott. Sociologia de arte na América Latina: ensaios. Recife, Bra., Edicordel, 1972. 28 p.

This pamphlet includes two very short essays on the sociology of art, mainly reinstating well known ideas by specialists in the field. One essay deals briefly with the status of sociology of art in Brazil (the contributions of Bastide, Freire, etc.), the other with the problem of art in the tropics influenced by the well known theories of Gilberto Freire. Too general for the specialist.

9927. _____; Rachel Caldas; and Vamireh Chacon. Situação sócioeconômica em áreas da zona canavieira de Pernambuco e Alagôas. Recife, Bra., Grupo Especial para Racionalização da Agroindústria Canavieira do Nordeste (GERAN), Instituto Joaquim Nabuço de Pesquisas Sociais (IJNPS), 1972. 207 p., fold. maps, tables.

Research report from a detailed monographic study of the sugar region of the states of Pernambuco and Alagoas. Description and preliminary analysis of a variety of socio-economic topics.

9928. Bahia (state), *Bra.* **Departamento de Mão-de-Obra. Divisão de Estudos e Pesquisas.** Mão-de-obra no setor primário; cultura do arroz. Salvador, Bra.? 1971. 161 l., tables.

Report on a government survey. Includes materials on land and property, production techniques used in the area, the impact of the government and its financing policy, characteristics of the local labor force, attitudes of workers toward social mobility, available training alternatives, and character and action of local associations.

9929. Baracho, José Alfredo de Oliveira. Participação nos lucros e integração social—PIS. Belo Horizonte, Bra., Edições da *Revista Brasileira de Estudos Políticos,* 1972. 121 p., bibl. (Estudos sociais e políticos, 31)

Socio-economic study of the government program for "Social Integration," its rationale, and preliminary results: workers participation in enterprise gains is viewed as an avenue for integration in complex modern groups and in general for contributing to the process of modernization.

9930. Bárbara Virgínia. A mulher na sociedade: manual prático e ilustrado de charme e etiqueta. São Paulo, Edições Paulinas, 1972. 148 p., plates.

This is one of the recent books on modern etiquette, mainly for housewives, and appealing to upward mobile females. Very interesting as a cultural document only; this is not a sociological text.

9931. Bastide, Roger. Estudos afro-brasileiros. São Paulo, Editôra Perspectiva, 1973. 384 p., illus. (Col. Estudos, 18)

This is a new edition of a number of excellent papers written by Bastide during the years he lived and taught in Brazil, most of them out of print. At the time they were published, they made a major impact on Brazilian scholarship and research. Worth rereading for their sharp observations and thoughtful analyses.

9932. Belo Horizonte (city), *Bra.* **Escola Superior de Guerra. Associação dos Diplomados. Delegacia de Minas Gerais.** A família, seu valor e seus problemas, na sociedade contemporânea. Belo Horizonte, Bra., 1972. 1 v. (Unpaged) (Trabalho do grupo, 10)

A slim volume written by non professionals taking stock of the discussions that took place during a working session of the educational program of the War College in Belo Horizonte. Interesting as a document on the character and possible results of such training program.

9933. Beltrão, Luiz. Sociedade de massa: comunicação e literatura. Petrópolis, Bra., Editôra Vozes, 1972. 110 p., bibl. (Col. Meios de comunicação social, 7. Série ensaios, 2)

Essays discussing the role of mass communication in contemporary society and their relations to literature. A main theme posits mass communication and literature as functionally congruent with two types (or stages) of societal development. More interesting for some of the insights than for substantive data.

9934. Bittencourt, Agnello. O homem amazonense e o espaço. Rio, Edições Fundação Cultural do Amazonas [and] Editôra Artenova, 1969. 46 p.

A short essay on the ecological bases of the Amazon region and its influence on society and culture as represented through human regional types and through the characteristics of the general population. Non technical and slim on the use of available sources.

9935. Brazil. Escritório de Análise Econômica e Política Agrícola. Aspectos sócio-econômicos da cultura de algodão arbóreo: primeiro relatório. Brasília, 1972. 80 1., bibl., tables.

A committee report (from the Office of Economic Analysis and Agricultural Policy) presenting socioeconomic materials in cotton agriculture (specifically for the *serido* "tree" cotton). Regional statistical data is included and briefly discussed although mostly are taken from official published sources.

9936. _____. Ministério da Agricultura. Instituto Nacional de Colonização e Reforma Agraria (INCRA). O INCRA e o cooperativismo. Brasília, 1971. 47 p., plates.

Short essay discusses the ideal rôle that cooperatives can play in the national program for colonization and agrarian reform. Brief information on a variety of coop programs supports the argumentation.

9937. _____. Serviço Nacional de Aprendizagem Comercial (SENAC). Departmento Regional de Pernambuco. Divisão de Formação Profissional. Setor de Pesquisas. Levantamento ocupacional dos menores no comêncio do Recife. Recife, Bra., 1969. 1 v. (Unpaged) tables.

Technical report of a survey research mainly for institutional use on present occupation of youngsters in the commercial enterprises of the city of Recife. Data collection from questionnaires and interviews. Descriptive statistical analysis. Good information on the character of the labor market in the area.

9938. _____. _____. _____. _____. _____. Razões de matrícula nos cursos senaqueanos e as aspirações profissionais dos seus alunos. Recife, Bra., 1969. 43 1., tables.

A research report mainly for institutional use studies reasons for enrollment and aspirations for professional careers among students of professional (technical-SENAC) schools. Data from questionnaires and interviews. Descriptive statistical analysis. Main variables are social and economic.

9939. _____. _____. _____. _____. _____. Razões do não comparecimento de comerciários aos cursos de secretário auxiliar e pessoal de crediário, sugeridos por algumas empresas do Recife para realização pelo SENAC en 1969. Recife, Bra., 1969. 1 v. (Various pagings) tables.

A research report mainly for institutional use to study evasion and non-attendance at classes in professional (technical) schools. Use of questionnaire and interviews. Main variables are social and economic.

9940. _____. Serviço Nacional de Aprendizagem Industrial (SENAI). Departamento Regional de Minas Gerais. Pesquisa de mercado de trabalho e necessidades de treinamento em Belo Horizonte e Cidade Industrial de Contagem. Belo Horizonte, Bra.? 1969. 96 1., tables.

Technical report of a survey research mainly for institutional use and planning. Data compiled from questionnaires and interviews. Descriptive statistical analysis. Informative studies of regional labor market, useful materials for comparative analysis.

9941. Calligaris, Rodolfo. A vida em família. Prefácio e notas de Elias Barbosa. São Paulo, Instituto de Difusão Espíritu, 1974. 223 p.

A work for the general public on the character, problems, crises, and solutions of family life written by and from the perspective of a "spiritualist" (*espírita*). Interesting as a document in the diffusion of popular mores.

9942. Camurça, Zélia Sá V. A presença de mulher, a educação da mulher. Fortaleza, Bra., Univ. Federal do Ceará, 1970. 47 p., bibl.

Following the recent trends of feminism this short work underlines the importance of women for modern society, criticizes the character of education as limiting feminine potentials, and discusses new possibilities for the fuller participation of women in life. Interesting document on the Brazilian manifestation of an international cultural movement.

9943. Cardoso, Fernando Henrique. Associated-dependent development: theoretical and practical implications (*in* Stepan, Alfred *ed.* Authoritarian Brazil: origins, policies, and future [see item 8596] p. 142-176, tables)

The author argues that the new-bureaucratic-authoritarian political regime in Brazil is closely related to the changes in the pattern of economic development. He notes the stability of the current model and believes that in the near future full political participation will be blocked. Regards this as detrimental since mass manipulation, increases income differentials and economic development does not favor the majority. An interesting contribution by a well known author.

9944. _____; Cândido Procopio Ferreira de Camargo; Lúcio Kowarick; and **Odon Pereira da Silva.** Cultura e participação na cidade de São Paulo. São Paulo, CEBRAP, 1973. 99 p., tables (Caderno, 14)

A collection of papers by well known scholars. Although mostly theoretical they discuss the interrelations and impact of culture on the structural elements of São Paulo (community).

9945. Carneiro, José Fernando. Psicologia do brasileiro e outros estudos. Prefácio de Erico Veríssimo. Rio, Livraria Agir *em convênio com o* Instituto Nacional do Livro (MEC), 1971. 393 p.

A series of essays (almost in the form of short stories) on Brazilian social and psychological facets. Attractive reading material but of passing professional interest. There is a sharp grasp of Brazilian characteristics in Verissimo's preface.

9946. Carvalho, Lourdes de Freitas. Serviço de arquivo médico e estatística de mu hospital. São Paulo, Edições LTr, Editôra da Univ. de São Paulo, 1973. 257 p., bibl., illus., tables.

This report describes the organization and procedures used in a hospital archive for medical and statistical information. Detailed and informative.

9947. Castro, Luiz Paiva de. A psicanálise e a realidade brasileira. Rio, Editôra Bonde, 1971. 66 p.

Essays present a critical view of psychoanalytic theory as it applies to Brazilian society and its socio-cultural specificities. Too brief and general to make a real contribution from a theoretical or methodological viewpoint.

9948. Catunda, Omar. Aspectos psicosociais do subdesenvolvimento (SBPC/CC, 25:7, julho 1973, p. 617-626)

Paper based on personal observations discusses the impact of underdevelopment on the socio-psychological world of members of various social groups including the intellectual elite, students, government personnel, etc. Useful for its insights and as a documentary source rather than a technical contribution.

9949. Centro das Indústrias das Cidades Industriais de Minas Gerais. Programa de Integração Social (PIS): manual. Contagem, Bra., 1972. 22 p., tables.

This is a manual used for purposes of diffusion of information on the government program for social integration (Programa de Integração Social). Useful information about the program its goals and procedures.

9950. Centro de Estudos e Ação Social, *Salvador, Bra.* Amazônia. São Paulo, Edições Loyola, 1973. 86 p., plates, tables (Cadernos do CEAS, 28)

This work presents a number of specialized studies dealing with important issues for the Amazon region. They include: the relationships between the Amazon and the Northeastern region; the role of the SUDAM in the process of development of the Amazon, its potentials and problems; colonization; the use of community development as basis for social participation in established programs; changes in the role of the Church in development; and the political meaning of the Trans-Amazon. Critical and perceptive.

9951. _____, _____. médio São Francisco: confins do Sertão Baiano. São Paulo, Edições Loyola, 1973. 71 p. (Cadernos do CEAS, 26)

Survey presenting socio-economic materials for a subregion of the middle São Francisco river area (westernmost Bahia) as bases for the development of regional planning and community action programs.

9952. César, Waldo A. Para uma sociologia do protestantismo brasileiro. v. 2. Petrópolis, Bra., Editôra Vozes, 1973. 48 p. (Col. Trilhas)

A brief and overall presentation of the "sociology" of Protestantism in Brazil. Includes little of the more systematic research accumulated on the topic.

9953. Coelho, Ernesto Bandeira. A Amazônia legal e a atuação da SUDAM. Rio, Escola Superior de Guerra, Depto. de Estudos, 1970. 26 p.

Very interesting description of areas and activities under the Superintendency of the Amazônia. Introductory, not scientific. [P.F. Hernández]

9954. Cogels, Gabrielle. A integração da Amazônia e a racionalização do extrativismo. Prefácio de Artur César Ferreira Reis. São Paulo, Edições Loyola, 1972, 171 p., bibl., plates, tables (Temas brasileiros, 1)

Discusses the possibilities of expanding rational planning to the area of extractive and agricultural activities in the Amazon to foster further regional and national integration. Argumentative, descriptive, but including a variety of interesting materials related to the various products extracted and crops in cultivation.

9955. Congresso Nacional de Comunicação, *I, Rio, 1971.* Anais do . . . Rio, Associação Brasileira de Imprensa, 1971. 179 p., plates.

Includes papers and discussions that took place at the I National Congress of Communication. Materials are arranged by main panels, and these include: newspapers and the legal system; integration of means of communication: newspapers-radio-TV-movies; problems and situation of small and medium newspaper enterprises in the interior of Brazil; possibilities for costs reduction in the process of production; commercial propaganda; TV news; and the crises affecting newspapers in Brazil. Although the reports are brief, they and the following discussions are illustrative of the problems affecting the means of communication in Brazil.

9956. Costa, Bolivar. O drama da classe média. Rio, Editôra Paz e Terra, 1973. 165 p., bibl. (Série Rumos da cultura moderna, 51)

Essays discussing the tensions of the middle classes in contemporary society and their significance for the present situation in Brazil. Descriptive and argumentative presentation of views held by the urban middle classes.

9957. Costa, Rovílio. Psicologia da fraternidade religiosa. Pôrto Alegre, Livraria Sulina Editôra, 1973. 63 p., bibl. (Col. Temas religiosos, 1)

A short study attempting to discuss the social-psychological climate present in a religious (Catholic) community. Too brief to allow for a systematic treatment, slim on the use of data, but occasionally insightful.

9958. Costa, Rubens Vaz da. Os bancos e a solução dos problemas do desenvolvimento urbano. Rio, Banco Nacional da Habitação, Secretaria de Divulgação, 1972. 21 p.

A short essay examining the role of the banking system in the solution of problems of urban development. The main issues are problems of financing urban development of infrastructural needs, relations with public programs and with other organizations.

9959. _____. Crescimento urbano: base do desenvolvimento econômico. Rio, Banco Nacional da Habitação, Secretaria de Divulgação, 1972. 50 p., tables.

A pamphlet discussing urban growth as a major variable supporting economic development. The case of Brazil serves as an illustration and tables including demographic and economic data are used in support of the argument.

9960. _____. Crescimento urbano do Brasil: desafio e oportunidades. Rio, Banco Nacional da Habitação, Secretaria de Divulgação, 1972. 60 p., tables.

A sketch of the recent trends in urban growth in Brazil. Presents statistical data and briefly discusses the impact of such growth on the urban infra-structure and current needs for dealing with such process.

9961. _____. Desenvolvimento e crescimento e urbano no Brasil. Rio, Banco Nacional da Habitação, Secretaria de Divulgação, 1972. 60 p., tables.

General socio-economic and demographic survey or urbanization and development in Brazil, including discussions of statistical data available. Intended as a contribution to the planning of government programs for regional and national development.

9962. _____. Notas sôbre a formulação de uma política eficiente de emprego. Rio, Banco Nacional da Habitação, Secretaria de Divulgação, 1972. 20 p.

A short essay on employment policy and increased potential productivity. The general dynamics of the labor market and the various changes in labor legislation are considered as is their potential for future change.

9963. A criança o adolescente, a cidade: estudo sociológico sôbre marginalidade... São Paulo, Gráfica Municipal, 1973. 307 p., tables.

A series of essays written for institutional purposes (evaluation and social welfare planning, the city of São Paulo) dealing with aspects of problem youth. Themes include: discussion and conceptualization of phenomena as social problems, the question of "marginality," deviance, and treatments available and in use. Informative of ideas and programs sponsored by the government.

9964. Dantas, José Lucena. O desenvolvimento de comunidade em Brasília: uma estratégia de participação social. Brasília, Fundação do Serviço Social, 1971. 60 l., tables.

A project report by the Foundation for Social Welfare (Federal District) describes the general plan (and associated theory) underlying community action programs.

9965. Delinqüência juvenil na Guanabara: introdução à teoria e pesquisa sociológicas da delinqüência juvenil na cidade do Rio de Janeiro. Rio, Tribunal de Justiça do Estado da Guanabara, Juizado de Menores, 1973. 141 p., bibl., tables.

A brief introduction to the theory and research on juvenile delinquency using the state of Guanabara as a case study. Although the emphasis is sociological there is some consideration of legal characteristics and economic underpinnings of juvenile delinquency. Materials on Guanabara are of particular interest.

9966. Delorenzo Neto, Antônio. Sociologia aplicada à educação: precedida de noções de sociologia geral. São Paulo, Livraria Duas Cidades, 1974. 328 p., bibl.

General textbook on sociology of education applying principles of general sociology and specialized research on the educational system for the development of a treatise on education. Mostly for use of students of sociology in teachers colleges.

9967. Diógenes, Luciano. Os 7 [i.e. sete] pecados da capital: Fortaleza; passado, presente, futuro. Fortaleza, Bra., n.p., 1971. 37 p., facism., maps.

This work intends to present and evaluate the main socio-economic problems of Fortaleza (capital of Ceará) most of which are persistent and related to planning difficulties as well as to scarcity of economic resources, and nature of bureaucratic organizations.

9968. Dotti, Sotero. Psicologia da adolescencia: uma psicologia do desenvolvimento. Pôrto Algre, Bra., Livraria Sulina Editôra, 1973. 487 p., tables.

A book for courses in the Psychology of Adolescense at the college level. Reviews general psychological theories and uses research results for purposes of discussion. Includes contributions from the US, Europe and Brazil.

9969. Estudo de problemas brasileiros. Recife, Bra., Univ. Federal de Pernambuco, 1971. 526 p.

Work to be used as a text in the new courses on "Brazilian Problems" included in Brazilian educational system since 1964. From a political-developmental perspective covers a number of issues (social, economic, and political as well as specialized subjects such as health and housing) all of which are considered the bottlenecks of the modernization process.

Faissol, Speridião. Migrações internas no Brasil e suas repercussões no crescimento urbano e desenvolvimento econômico. See item 7107.

9970. Faria, Luiz de Castro. O homem brasileiro: formação étnica e cultural; situação demográfica (UFG/CEB, 5, 1972, p. 35-59, tables)

A general essay discussing racial, cultural, and demographic bases of the Brazilian population with brief presentations on the Amerindian and the African. Too brief for a technical contribution the study nevertheless incorporates materials (i.e. research on the genetics of isolates) found only in highly specialized studies.

9971. Faria, Vilmar. Dépendance et idéologie des dirigeants industriels brésiliens (ADST/SDT, 13:3, juillet/sept. 1971, p. 264-281, tables)

Various studies have shown the crisis of the ideology of autonomous national development and the increasing dependence of Brazilian industry on foreign capital and technology. The study analyzes such crises by examining the attitudes of Brazilian executives. In general they tend towards a conflict-ridden political relation with the working class rather than on a united front with all classes. Moreover, the workers themselves respond according to older class formulations, i.e. a master-servant relation.

9972. Farina, Modesto. A psicodinâmica das côres em publicidade. 2. ed. São Paulo, Univ. de São Paulo, Escola de Comunicações e Artes, 1971. 38 1., bibl. (Série 1, Propaganda. Textos, 2)

Basically a series of essays directed to the general public and to persons working in the area of propaganda. Attempts to survey the theory of psychodynamic impact of colors in propaganda as well as materials involved.

9973. Farris, George F. and D. Anthony Butterfield. Control theory in Brazilian organization (CU/ASQ, 17:4, Dec. 1972, p. 574-585, tables)

Distribution of control is examined in 16 Brazilian development banks using Tannenbaum's control graph model. Contrary to common assumptions that Latin American organizations are authoritarian, control in these banks is distributed among hierarchical levels, and control by the national bank in the state-federal systems are all associated with bank effectiveness. A competency hypothesis viewing effective development banks as technocracies is suggested to explain these findings.

9974. ———— and ————. Goal congruence in Brazilian organizations (SIP/RIP, 6:3/4, 1972, p. 225-233, tables)

A study of 189 professionals in 13 Brazilian financial institutions sought to apply US derived organization theory and methodology concerning congruence between individual and organization goals. A substantial lack of congruence was found with congruence greater for higher organization levels. Results of the study indicate that questionnaire methodology is suitable for studying professionals in Brazilian organizations, and that goal congruence theory holds in Brazil as it does in the US.

9975. Fernandes, Florestan. Comunidade e sociedade: leituras sôbre problemas conceituais, metodológicos e de aplicaç ão. São Paulo, Companhia Editôra Nacional, Editôra da Univ. de São Paulo, 1973. 579 p., bibl. (Biblioteca universitária. Série 2. Ciências sociais, 34)

This is basically a reader of major theoretical formulations in the field of sociology for use by students of social sciences at the university level. Includes translations from Weber and Park to Parsons and Merton.

9976. Ferreira-Santos, Célia Almeida. A enfermagem como profissão: estudo num hospital-escola. São Paulo, Livraria Pioneira Editôra, Editôra da Univ. de São Paulo, 1973. 176 p., bibl., tables (Biblioteca pioneira de ciências sociais. Sociologia)

Research monograph of a case study of nursing in a teaching hospital carried on by a social-science trained nurse working in that hospital. Detailed information on organization, status heirarchy, role complexes and networks, formal and informal channels, socialization and interaction, values, goals, and attitudes. Informative, detailed, worth the attention of the specialist.

9977. Fonseca, Edson Nery da. Problemas de communicação da informação científica. São Paulo, Thesaurus Editôra, 1973. 132 p., illus.

A collection of essays dealing with contemporary themes on communication and distribution of scientific information. Non-technical presentation attempts to clarify some of the key problems in the area, for the general public in Brazil. Of little sociological interest.

9978. Fonseca, Mário. Sexo e casamento: problemas médicos do matrimônio. Recife, Bra., Companhia Editôra de Pernambuco, 1974. 154 p., bibl., illus., plates.

Basically a work on public health and social hygiene which discusses common medical sexual problems in marriage. Addressed to the general public and to health related personnel. Of little sociological interest beyond the identification of current problems.

Fontes, Eduardo. O Lagamar que eu conheci. See item 7112.

9979. Foracchi, Marialice Mencarini. A juventude na sociedade moderna. São Paulo, Livraria Pioneira Editôra, 1972. 168 p., bibl. (Biblioteca pioneira de ciências sociais. Sociologia)

An excellent work by a well regarded late scholar from São Paulo on the relationships between youth and the changing character of society. In two major sections she discusses the transformations in the role of youth. From being simply a "generation" (age category) it became a "revolt" group (leaders of social action) after which the group adopts an "imaginative" stance (and here lies the seedbed for innovative and critical thinking about the future and its potentials). Excellent reading, insightful and scholarly.

9980. Freire-Maia, Newton. Brasil: laboratório racial. Petrópolis, Bra., Editôra Vozes, 1973. 72 p., illus., plates.

A very general and brief collection of essays on the traditional topic of Brazil as a "melting-pot." Sporadic use of extensive research in existence.

9981. Fundação Getúlio Vargas, *Rio.* **Instituto Brasileiro de Economia. Centro de Estudos Agrícolas.** Estado de São Paulo: orçamentos familiares rurais. Rio, 1971. 275 p., tables.

A good study based on detailed and professional field research on the budget of rural families in São Paulo state. Economic analysis and some of the most critical social and cultural correlates are included and discussed.

9982. Gaiarsa, José Angelo. O espelho Mágico: um fenómeno social chamado corpo e alma. Petrópolis, Bra., Editôra Vozes, 1973. 69 p., illus., plates (Cosmovisão, 3)

An experimental graphic presentation of the socio-psychology of self. Sometimes insightful, sometimes critical, mostly for the general public.

9983. Galvão, Hélio. Novas cartas da Praia. Rio, Edições do Val, 1973? 135 p., illus., map.

An often charming series of 45 "letters" written in the first three months of 1968 from the beaches of a coastal municipio of Rio Grande do Norte. The effort is to report, in anecdotal pieces of about 500 words each, incidents, persons, conditions witnessed by a social scientist and humanist who also is a Professor of Sociology. [P. B. Taylor, Jr.]

9984. Guerreiro Ramos, Alberto. Latent functions of formalism in Brazil (USC/SSR, 56:1, Oct. 1971, p. 62-82, tables)

The study considers that formalism is not a bizarre characteristic of a trait of social pathology in peripheral societies, but a normal reaction which reflects the global strategy of such societies as they emerge from their present stage of development. Formalism in such societies is a strategy of social change, imposed by thedual character of their historical formation and by the particular way in which these societies relate to others in the world.

9985. Haller, Archibald O. and Helcio Ulhoa Saraiva. Status measurement and the variable discrimination hypothesis in an isolated Brazilian region (RSS/RS, 37:3, Sept. 1972, p. 325-351, tables)

Instruments to measure status in rural Brazil are presented and evaluated. "Component" indexes for measuring wealth, education, power, and prestige are analyzed for stability and concurrent validity. A new technique for measuring a person's prestige in the community is presented and its validity tested. An eight-item level-of-living scale is shown to be reliable and valid, and economic indicators of the SES factor measured by all of the stratification instruments are discussed.

9986. Heredia, Beatriz Alasia de and Afrânio R. Garcia, Jr. Trabalho familiar e campesinato (CLAPSC/AL, 14:1/2, jan./junho 1971, p. 10-20)

Paper based on research conducted at the Zona da Mata region of Pernambuco. The research is a study of some fundamental categories of peasant family's economic organization. Representations were disclosed through ethnographic analysis. The author shows the importance of the distinction between 1) production-unity in agricultural work and 2) consumption-unity at the household. Various types of the first are discussed. The authors then show how a similar logic underlies the classification and hierarchy of husbandry animals, and finally they discuss the division of economic activities by sex, explaining the principles that underlie such classification.

9987. Hugon, Paul. Demografia brasileira: ensaio de demoeconomia brasileira. São Paulo, Editôra Atlas [and] Editôra da Univ. de São Paulo, 1973. 342 p., tables.

A quasi-Brasilian textbook on demography by a well known economist. Good presentation, extensive use of demographic and economic data from Brazilian sources.

9988. Instituto Social Morumbi. Entorpecentes: estudio sôbre tóxicos e toxicomania. São Paulo, Edições Loyola, 1971. 182 p., bibl.

A monograph on medical as well as social characteristics of each of the major perception-distortion drugs in use. Of interest mainly for social work students (its target population).

9989. Jorge, Fernando. Chacrinha, Sílvio Santos, Ibrahim Sued, Houaiss e Cia.: um documentário para a história da televisão brasileira. São Paulo, Editôra Obelisco, 1974. 194 p.

In order to discuss the character of mass culture in Brazil, the author singles out four of the most popular live TV figures. The objective of the study is to provide materials for more detailed studies on the place and role of TV in modern Brazilian life. Interesting and informative documentation.

9990. *Jornal de Psicanálise.* Sociedade Brasileira de Psicanálise, Instituto de Psicanálise. Año 5, Nos. 13/14, maio/set. 1970- . São Paulo.

In this particular issue all the papers deal with technical questions of general psychoanalitic theory; none refers specifically to psychoanalysis or its application and use in Brazil. Of possible interest for the specialist and for studies of the character of such orientation in Brazil.

9991. Kolck, Odette Lourenção Van. Técnicas de exame psicológico e suas aplicações no Brasil: testes de aptidões. Petrópolis, Bra., Editôra Vozes, 1974. 432 p., bibl. (Col. Nova psicologia, 4)

A general presentation of the characteristics, means, and goals of aptitude tests, their technical use and possible application in Brazil. Although directed to professionals that might use such tests the discussion is general enough for the layman.

9992. Kowarick, Lucio. Estrategias do planejamento social no Brasil. São Paulo, Centro Brasileiro de Análise e Planejamento (CEBRAP), 1971? 137 l., bibl., tables (Caderno, 2)

Basically a critique of the usual techniques of social planning, particularly in their elitistic and regimentary bases, but also in their positivistic underpinnings. Theoretical analysis worth reading.

9993. Lagenest, J. B. Barruel de. Mulheres em leilão: um estudo da prostituição no Brasil. Petrópolis, Bra., Editôra Vozes, 1973. 86 p.

A very general and slim discussion of prostitution in Brazil. Little research data, some discussion from the legal and economic perspectives, and much concern from a "social-problems" viewpoint.

9994. Leeds, Anthony. Housing-settlement types, arrangements for living, proletarianization, and the social structure of the city (*in* Cornelius, Wayne A. and Felicity M. Trueblood eds. Anthropological perspectives on Latin American urbanization [see item 9625] p. 67-99, bibl.)

In his discussion of the limitations of urban planning, the author contends that any plan foresees such a small range of possibilities that when put into effect it incorporates only current knowledge without allowing for the dialectics of change. To the author the social process is also the planning process. For ethnologist's comment, see item 1499.

—————. Political, economic and social effects of producer and consumer orientations toward housing in Brazil and Peru: a systems analysis. See item 1500.

9995. ————— and **Elizabeth Leeds.** El mito de la ruralidad urbana: experiencia urbana, trabajo y valores de los "ranchos" de Rio de Janeiro y Lima (*in* Funes, Julio César ed. La ciudad y la región para el desarrollo. Caracas, Comisión de Administración Pública de Venezuela, 1972, p. 102-175, tables)

This study reports on the investigation of the popular idea in Brazil and Peru that most inhabitants of *favelas barriadas* are rural migrants who cling to their rural modes of social organization and values, because of cultural differentials which reinforce their marginality in the urban environment. The detailed analysis indicates that favelas as much as barriadas are essentially urban products not only ecologically but socially and culturally. This work was translated from the original English version.

9996. Leite, Celso Barroso. A proteção social no Brasil. Com a colaboração do Centro de Estudos de Previdência Social. São Paulo, Edições LTr, 1972. 117 p.

Study of the social welfare programs in Brazil, presents a brief history of its establishment and transformations including changes since 1964. Discusses coverage, programs and benefits, some of the persisting problems and their impact particularly among the lower strata of society. General yet informative discussion of the topic.

9997. Leite, Valerie da Motta. Avaliação da qualidade dos dados censitários. Rio, Fundação IBGE, Instituto Brasileiro de Estatística, Centro Brasileiro de Estudos Demográficos, 1970. 35 p., tables (Estudos e análises, 8)

A technical monograph on the methodology of census data collection and organization and the sources of errors in such data along with an evaluation of data quality.

9998. Lins, Rachel Caldas; Renato Carneiro Campos; and **Sergio Guerra.** Levantamento sócioeconômico em áreas do Baixo e Médio São Francisco. v. 1, Baixo São Francisco. Recife, Bra., SUVALE/Instituto Joaquim Nabuco de Pesquisas Sociais, 1972. 445 p., maps, tables.

Report of a socio-economic survey of the middle and lower São Francisco Valley regions carried out by the staff of a well known research institute. Includes a wealth of detailed information for the area, from topography and geography to more specific social, cultural, and economic materials. Informative and excellent data source.

9999. Luz, A. Cerqueira. Nordeste. Rio, Gráfica Editôra Laemmert, 1974. 76 p., fold., map, illus., plates.

A very general work including essays on issues perenial to the Northeast: potential, poverty, problems, and recent development programs. Some of the more recent information may be of interest to follow present trends in the area.

10000. Macedo, Gilberto de. Ciências do comportamento e medicina. Maceió, Bra., Univ. Federal de Alagoas, Instituto de Filosofia e Ciências Humanas, 1970. 100 p., bibl.

A brief attempt to discuss the potential contributions of the various behavioral sciences to medicine. Specific sections are dedicated to sociology and anthropology where a review of work in medical sociology and anthropology is combined with a brief discussion of further possibilities. Interesting for purposes of diffusion of information in Brazil, but too general for the specialist.

10001. Maceió (city), *Bra.* **Escola** comportamento e medicina. Maceió, Bra., Univ. Federal de Alagoas, Instituto de Filosofia e Ciências Humanas, 1970. 100 p., bibl.

A brief attempt to discuss the potential contributions of the various behavioral sciences to medicine. Specific sections are dedicated to sociology and anthropology where a review of work in medical sociology and anthropology is combined with a brief discussion of further possibilities. Interesting for purposes of diffusion of information in Brazil, but too general for the specialist.

10002. Machado, Eurico Serzedello. Sexo, amor, casamento. Rio, Companhia Editôra Americana, 1974. 95 p.

The three themes in this booklet are explored in three essays using highly heterogenous materials (from astrology to romantic poetry and techniques for sexual intercourse). Definitely a cultural more than a scientific document.

10003. Madeira, João Lyra. O IBGE e os estudos da fecundidade no Brasil: histórico e perspectivas da fecundidade (IBGE/RBE, 33:130, abril/junho 1972, p. 211-266, maps, tables)

A good study tracing the role of the IBGE in the study of fecundity in Brazil which also includes an historical analysis and possible projections on the status of fecundity in the country. Data from official publications are in some cases reorganized; materials are analysed and discussed in some detail, and some of the major problems are taken into consideration.

10004. Magalhães Júnior, Raymundo. Como você se chama? estudo sóciopsicológico dos prenomes e cognomes brasileiros. Rio, Editôra Documentário, 1974. 279 p. (Documenta/homem, 3)

A curious study in psycho-linguistics on socio-psychological underpinnings of personal names and nicknames in Brazil. Wide coverage, good technical level, and interesting analysis.

10005. Marques, Mário Osório and **Argemiro J. Brum.** Uma comunidade em busca de seu caminho. Pôrto Alegre, Bra., Livraria Sulina Editôra, 1972. 85 p. (Col. Temas filosóficos e sociais)

Report discusses a provisional evaluation of a community development program in the state of Rio Grande do Sul. Brief, descriptive and qualitative in its evaluative procedures.

10006. Martins, José de Souza. Há uma crise no ensino das ciências sociais? (SBPC/CC j25:10, Oct. 1973, p. 935-939, bibl.)

Brief discussion of the status of sociology in the secondary, teachers' training and university levels in São Paulo presented as a paper in a Seminar on the Social Sciences held at the Univ. of São Paulo. Illuminating on the current professional status of sociologists in the educational system and the increasing proliferation of technical positions in industry and bureaucracy.

10007. Mata, Milton da; Eduardo Werneck R. de Carvalho; and **Maria Thereza L.L. Castro e Silva.** Migrações internas no Brasil: aspectos econômicos e demográficos. Rio, Instituto de Planejameto Econômico e Social, Instituto de Pesquisas (IPEA/INPES), 1973. 217 p., bibl., tables (Col. Relatórios de pesquisa, 19)

Descriptive demographic study of internal migration in Brazil and their socio-economic correlates. Combines census data with results from more specialized research and extends previous studies to include materials up to 1970.

10008. Medeiros, Laudelino T. O peão de estância: um tipo de trabalhador rural. Pôrto Alegre, Bra., Univ. Federal do Rio Grande do Sul, Faculdade de Ciências Econômicas, Instituto de Estudos e Pesquisas Ecoñmicas, 1969. 42 l., tables (Estudos e trabalhos mimeografados, 8)

Report of a survey on a regional social type, the southern cowboy (peão). Materials describe and discuss the character of their place of work, the southern cattle farm (*estancia*), the hierarchy of jobs for this occupational type and their economic correlates. Informative.

10009. Medina, Carlos Alberto de. Família e mudança: o familismo numa sociedade arcaica em transformação. Petrópolis, Bra., Editôra Vozes [and] CERIS, Rio, 1974. 149 p., bibl., illus.

Interesting work on the links between family and change in Brazil. The main contention is that the ideology of the family and its associated cultural patterns of "familism" are characteristic of an archaic society now in the process of cultural change. Substantive materials (descriptive) are included and might be of interest to the specialist.

10010. _____ and **Pedro A. Ribeiro de Oliveira.** Autoridade e participação: estudo sociógico de Igreja Católica. Petrópolis, Bra., Editôra Vozes [and] Centro de Estatística Religiosa e Investigações Sociais (CERIS), Rio, 1973. 191 p., bibl. (Publicações Centro de Investigação e Divulgação [CID]. Sociologia religiosa, 2)

A sociological monograph on stratification, leadership, and participation in the Catholic church. A pionneer work of its kind in Brazil which deserves the attention of specialist.

10011. Melo, José Marques de. Estudos de jornalismo comparado. São Paulo, Livraria Pioneira Editôra, 1972. 260 p., bibl., facsims., illus., plates, tables (Biblioteca pioneira de arte e comunicação)

A series of essays and analyses on comparative communication (based on news reporting). Has a stronger technical background than most of the recent titles in communication. Interesting as an indication of the present research orientation in that field in Brazil.

10012. Melo, Veríssimo de. Informação sobre messianismo no Nordeste (PMEH/RE, 14:2, julho 1970, p. 333-348, bibl.)

This is a short essay sketching the general attributes of "messianismo" and some notes on the major movements in the Northeast of Brazil. For a fuller technical discussion see among others, Maria Isaura Pereira de Queiroz *O messianismo no Brasil e no mundo* (São Paulo, Editora de Univ. de Sãa Paulo, 1965).

10013. Menezes, José Rafael de. Afirmações e comunicações. João Pessoa, Bra., Imprensa Universitária da Paraíba, 1973. 42 p.

A short and personal critique on the distortive role played by TV analyses on communication. Interesting documentary of the times.

10014. Miceli, Sergio. A noite da madrinha. São Paulo, Editôra Perspectiva, 1972. 293 p., bibl., facsims., plates, tables (Col. Debates, 66)

An attractive study of live TV shows (in this case that of Hebe Camargo-São Paulo and the central south region) as a stepping-stone towards understanding the character of the cultural industry in an underdeveloped society. Basically a study of ideology in mass culture.

10015. Miranda, Heloísa de Resende Pires. Nossos filhos e seus problemas. Belo Horizonte, Interlivros, 1974. 240 p., bibl. (Estante de psicologia)

A presentation for the general public on the socio-psychological crises of youngsters from infancy to early adulthood and the interpretative ways developed by psychology to help parents in coping with such situations (from early sexual behavior to the crisis of generations). Of little interest to the specialist except as a cultural document.

10016. Miranda, Nicanor. 200 [i.e. Duzentos] jogos infantis. 4. ed. São Paulo, Martins, 1972. 294 p., bibl., plates, tables.

Codification and detailed presentation of 200 children games played at care centers and schools in São Paulo. Includes the discussion of reactions from teachers and students to the games. This section might be attractive to professionals interested in various formal modes of social interaction in game-playing.

10017. Mitchel, Simon. The influence of kinship in the social organization of northeast Brazilian fishermen: a contrast in case studies (JLAS, 6:2, Nov. 1974, p. 301-313)

Paper concerned with the interpretation of kinship and its significance in peasant communities. Discusses conflicting data (and interpretations) for two northeastern coastal communities in Brazil. Conclusions suggest that underlying, non-stated assumption did much to produce the conflicting differences reported.

10018. Mohana, João. A vida sexual dos solteiros e casados. 15. ed. Pôrto Alegre, Bra., Editôra Globo, 1974. 252 p., illus.

A book from a pastoral (Catholic) perspective on issues and problems in the sex life of singles and married (to a certain extent directed mainly to males). Illustrative of cultural vales and present orientations; valuable as a document not as a technical text.

10019. Montenegro, João Alfredo de Sousa. Evolução do catolicismo no Brasil. Petrópolis, Bra., Editôra Vozes, 1972. 188 p., bibl.

Socio-historical analysis of the evolution of the Catholic church and religion in Brazil from colonial times to the present; a general survey based on secondary sources for the past and some primary data for the contemporary period.

10020. Morais, José Xavier Pessoa de. Tradição e transformação no Brasil: análise sociológica, antropológica e psicoanalítica. 2. ed. Rio, Civilização Brasileira *em convênio com o* Instituto Nacional do Livro - MEC, 1973. 350 p. (Col. Retratos do Brasil, 86)

An overall study of the theme of stability and change in Brazil, whose conceptual schemes are derived from sociology, anthropology and psychoanalysis. The work is mostly descriptive, including much historical materials which illuminate current attributes of Brazilian society and culture. Nevertheless too general for the specialist.

10021. Morin, Edgar and others. Cultura e comunicação de massa. Tradução de C.N. Coutinho. Rio, Fundação Getúlio Vargas, Instituto de Documentação, Serviço de Publicações, 1972. 166 p. (Série Informação & comunicação, 5)

A collection of essays by international authors on cummunication systems and mass society, translated for use by students in schools of cummunication. Of no major interest for the sociology of Brazil but worthwhile for a general audience.

10022. Moura, Iraci Afonso de. Um ano e meio á frente do Departamento de Ação Comunitária da Fundação do Serviço Social do Distrito Federal. Brasília, Fundação do Serviço Social, Depto. de Ação Comunitária, 1972. 1 v. (Unpaged) tables.

A report on programs of the Department of Community Action of the Social Welfare Office in the Federal District. Describes goals and character of each program. Informative.

10023. Moura Castro, Cláudio de. O ortodoxia metodológica nas ciencias sociais (IBGE/B, 31:231, nov./dez. 1972, p. 99-108).

The author finds that questions of no immediate relevance as well as those that can be displaced according to context persist in the development of studies and research in the social sciences. He also regards as negative for the development of the discipline the tendency toward ritualism and excessive concern with rigor in methodology, particularly when it concerns beginning research students.

10024. Murtinho, Hélber F. O rapto de Sérgio Haziot. Com prefácio do João Claudino de Oliveira e Cruz. Rio, The Author, 1974. 235 p., facsims., illus., plates (Col. Vinte crimes e três farsas, 2)

Journalistic report of a famous crime committee in Rio based on published sources and eyewitness accounts of the "natural history" of the incident. Of literary rather than sociological interest.

10025. Neotti, Ana. A mulher no mundo em conflito. Ponta Grossa, Bra., Univ. Estadual de Ponta Grossa, 1973. 104 p., bibl. (Cadernos universitários, 7)

This discussion of the role of women in today's conflict-ridden world adds to the growing bibliography on women studies in Brazil. It examines and illustrates the impact of various women in different social settings. Mostly descriptive and argumentative it is nevertheless a good document on the status of women in modern Brazil.

10026. Neves, José Adolfo Pereira. Desenvolvimento e população. São Paulo, Editôra Atlas, 1973. 248 p., bibl., tables (Série Demografia)

A general demographic review of the relationships between population attributes and socio-economic change. Written from a global perspective it includes mostly data on world population. Designed for the training of demographers in Brazil.

10027. Nunes, Mário Ritter. O estilo na comunicação. Rio, Livraria Agir Editôra, 1973. 137 p., bibl.

This work addressed to students in schools of communication is mainly concerned with the presentation and discussion of style, its specificity in various contexts and for various purposes. Of little sociological interest.

10028. Olivan, Ruben George. Metabolismo social da cidade e outros ensaios. Pôrto Alegra, Bra., Univ. Federal do Rio Grande do Sul, Editôra da URGS, 1974. 78 p., bibl.

This brief study uses demography and ecology to trace some of the main social processes in the city. Just a sketch, not of much interest for the specialist.

10029. Oliveira, José Carlos de Araújo e. Seus filho serão robôs. Rio, Companhia Editôra Americana, 1973. 93 p., illus., plates (Série Informação contemporânea, 1)

A presentation for the general public on developments in electronics, artificial intelligence, bio-engineering, etc., and their possible impact on society.

10030. Oliveira Neto, Olinto José ed. Metodologia da pesquisa científica. t. 1, Fundamento metodológico da pesquisa científica. Pôrto Alegra, Bra., Pontifícia Univ. Católica do Rio Grande do Sul, Instituto de Psicologia [and] Bauru, Bra., Faculdade de Filosofia, Ciências e Letras do Sagrado Coração de Jesus, 1972. 112 l., tables.

The last essay in this collection, written by the editor, discusses multivariate analysis and its use in social research. The others focus on relations of theory and data, on the character of research propositions, and on hypotheses and their use in investigations. Used for training university students in the methodology of social research.

10031. Pereira, João Baptista Borges. Italianos no mundo rural paulista. São Paulo, Univ. de São Paulo, Institute de Estudos Brasileiros, 1974. 192 p., bibl., tables (Biblioteca Pioneira de Estudos Brasileiros)

An attractive monograph on the Italians (migrants and descendents) in the rural area of the state of São Paulo. In the usual monographic framework, the study includes a last section which discusses the social construction of reality among these Italians. Interesting and insightful.

10032. Pereira, Luiz Carlos Bresser. Empresários e administradores no Brasil. São Paulo, Editôra Brasiliense, 1974. 239 p., bibl., tables.

Interesting sociological study of entrepreneurs and administrators in Brazil. The author has conducted similar but more in-depth and thorough surveys of the state of São Paulo. They serve as the framework for the present study of the country as a whole, although in this case he uses more of the available statistical materials.

10033. Pereira, Maria da Luz Valente. Problemática dos inquéritos à habitação urbana. São Paulo, Univ. de São Paulo, Faculdade de Arquitectura e Urbanismo, n.d. 92 p.

An attempt at a critical evaluation of urban housing studies in Brazil. Presents a methodological framework (quite detailed) for possible studies and field research on the topic. Interesting description of the state of research methodology in this field in Brazil.

10034. Pinto, Edson. Escola para fazer ricos. Ituiutaba, Bra., Gráfica Editôra Zardo, 1970. 199 p.

Addressed to the general public, especially the aspiring lower middle classes, the work discusses potentials and avenues for social mobility, from a general perspective. Interesting cultural document rather than a scholarly work.

10035. Pinto, Luiz de Aguiar Costa. Las clases sociales. B.A., Editorial Paidós, 1973. 28 p. (Textos universitarios. Sociología y política, 9)

A text on the theory of and research in social stratification by a well known Brazilian sociologist. Good coverage of standard materials including results of studies on Brazil and Latin America.

10036. ———. Desarrollo y movilidad social. B.A., Editorial Paidós, 1973. 19 p. (Textos universitarios. Sociología y política, 10)

A theoretical analysis including observations on the Brazilian and Latin American experiences in social mobility and development. Theoretical potentials as well as structural and socio-political determinations are considered.

10037. Pontes, Hildebrando. História do futbol em Uberaba. Uberaba, Bra., Academia de Letras do Triângulo Mineiro, Bolsa de Publicações do Município de Uberaba, 1972. 195 p., plates, tables (Obras de Hildebrando Pontes publicadas, 2)

A well researched socio-historical monograph on soccer (a "case study") in the community of Uberaba (state of Minas Gerais). Contains a wealth of information that may be used for a more systematic sociology of sports in Brazil.

10038. Reis, Arthur Cézar Ferreira. A valorização da cultura no Brasil: conferência pronunciada em Florianópolis a 25 de agosto de 1972. Florianópolis, Bra., Secretaria do Governo, Depto. de Cultura, 1972. 47 p. (Col. Diniz Júnior, 1)

Transcription of a conference by the author given at the Academy of Letters of Santa Catarina on the regional character and historical roots of culture in the state. Literary, dispersive; use possibly as a cultural document only.

10039. *Revista da Universidade Federal do Pará*. Ministério da Educação e Cultura. Ano 2, No. 2, Série 1, 1. semestre, 1972- . Belém, Bra.

Includes a series of papers dealing with the region. Those of interest are: Nelson de Figuereido Ribeiro "Planning and the Use of Human Resources in the Process of Development;" José Montenegro Bacca "Exclusions from the Protection of Job Stability;" José Marcelino Monteiro da Costa "Tourism and Regional Growth;" and Catharina Vergolino Dias "Content and Limits in the Regionalization of the Amazon."

10040. Rios, José Arthur. Estruturas sociais do Brasil (UFG/CEB, 5, 1972, p. 61-80)

A description of the main attributes of the Brazilian social structure based on historical data with a discussion of changes through time. Non-technical, general overview.

10041. Róiz, José. Sexo tem nexo: problemas sexuais da juventude. Belo Horizonte, Bra., Edições Júpiter, 1974. 140 p.

A work primarily concerned with socio-psychological counseling of parents and youngsters on sex related problems and crises during adolescense. Not for specialists but offers illustration of present cultural mores.

10042. Rosen, Bernard C. Social change, migration and family interaction in Brazil (ASS/ASR, 38:2, April 1973, p. 198-212, tables)

The impact of an industrial city on rural migrant family structure and the socialization of boys is analyzed in an observational study of family interaction in 167 lower-class Brazilian families. The study revealed that after longer periods of city residence migrant families become more egalitarian, family relations more open and responsive, that parents place higher emphasis on achievement and grant more independence to their sons.

10043. Sá, Maria Auxiliadora Ferraz de. Dos velhos aos novos coronéis: um estudo das redefinições do coronelismo. Recife, Bra., Univ. Federal de Pernambuco, PIMES, 1974. 137 p., bibl.

Socio-political study of "coronelismo" in Brazil which attempts to review and critically re-elaborate the classical literature on the theme (e.g. Vitor Nunes Leal *Coronelismo, enxada, e voto: o municipio e o regime representativo no Brasil*) through contemporary manifestations of the phenomena.

10044. Saito, Hiroshi comp. A comunicação e alguns problemas rurais. Organização e introdução de . . . São Paulo, Com-Arte, 1973. 88 p., bibl. (Série Comunicação rural, 5)

The editor of this collection of papers on communication issues in the rural areas, spent years researching this subject in Brazil, particularly among Japanese and other immigrant groups.

10045. ———— and **Takashi Maeyama.** Assimilação e integração dos japoneses no Brasil. Petrópolis, Bra., Editôra Vozes [and] São Paulo, Editôra Univ. de São Paulo, 1973. 558 p., bibl., tables (Col. Estudos brasileiros, 4)

Excellent monograph on the assimilation and integration of Japanese immigrants in Brazil. The author has spent a lifetime researching Japanese immigrants and his thorough knowledge and experience enhances the scholarly quality of this work.

10046. São Paulo (state), *Bra*. **Secretaria de Economia e Planejamento. Coordenadoria de Ação Regional.** Aspectos do problema migratório no Estado de São Paulo. São Paulo, 1972. 1 v. (Various pagings) tables.

A monograph on problems related to internal migration to the state of São Paulo and prepared for the Office of Economics and Planning. Selects and compares census statistical data for the years 1950-60-70 to identify migration trends. Inferences are established through comparison of projected growth and enumerated population.

10047. Segurança & Desenvolvimento. Associação dos Diplomados da Escola Superior de Guerra (ADESG). Ano 20, Nos. 142/143, 1971- . Rio.

This is the journal of War College alumni. Includes studies of topics taken up during the training program such as: the organization of the Army High Council; the Navy and Army as instruments for national policy; the role of the Air Force in development; presidentialism in Brazil to 1930; characteristics of the new Code of Industrial Property; foreign affairs—Yugoslavia, Portugal, and Africa; population policy for Brazil; the federal government and the problem of minors; labor justice; national power: evaluation, preparation and application.

10048. Semana de Estudos do Problema de Menores, X, *São Paulo, 1970*. Estudos sôbre problema de menores: anais do . . . São Paulo, 1971. 500 p., tables.

A series of papers presented at a conference on juvenile problems. Main themes include: child desertion; delinquent youth; exceptional children; youth education and labor; social marginalization; use of host families for deserted children; and legislation on minors. Good for taking stock on the recent views on the area in the central-south among active specialists.

10049. Serviço Social da Indústria. Departamento Nacional. Manual de orçamento-programa. Rio, 1970. 63 1.

This is a technical report mainly for institutional use describing the research project and associated methodology used in the elaboration and application of a manual for study of program budgets. Informative for data specification and evaluation.

10050. Silva, Maria Lúcia Carvalho da. Algumas considerações sôbre e emancipação da mulher. São Paulo, Administração Regional no Estado de São Paulo, Serviço Social do Comércio, 1970? 22 p.

A pamphlet which discusses the problems and potentials in the changing role of women in Brazilian society. Not of much interest beyond its documentary value on contemporary perceptions of traditional sex-related roles.

10051. Silva, Nalcir S. Estudo sócio-econômico das comunidades de pesca. Florianópolis, Bra., Associação de Crédito e Assistencia Rural do Estado de Santa Catarina (ACARESC), Serviço de Extensão de Pesca de Santa Catarina, 1972. 35 p., tables.

Brief survey of fishing communities in the Camboriu coastal area of Santa Catarina conducted by students in social sciences at the state university. Descriptive materials are useful for preliminary comparisons with data derived from northeastern fishing communities that have been more systematically studied. See item 10017.

10052. Silva, Regina Nazaré e; Joanna Luzia da Silva Mota; Getúlio de Carvalho Galvão and **Malô Simões Lopes Ligocki.** Informe sobre bem-estar social. Belém, Bra., Associação de Crédito e Assistência Rural do Estado do Pará (ACAR-PARÁ), 1973. 27 1.

A brief description of the state of social welfare in the state of Pará. Little report of data, more on characteristics of programs and their possible impact.

10053. Singer, Paul Israel and **Fernando H. Cardoso.** A cidade e o campo. São Paulo, Centro Brasileiro de Análise e Planejamento (CEBRAP), 1972. 63 p., bibl. (Caderno, 7)

Two long essays by each author, one on structural linkages of dependence between rural and urban areas, the other on economic and political structures and ideology. Both are theoretical, including detailed analyses and valuable insights.

10054. Smith, T. Lynn. The role of internal migration in population redistribution in Brazil (CSIC/RIS, 29:115, enero/abril 1971, p. 109-114)

This study presents the following types of analyses for establishing inferences on the role of internal migration in the process of population redistribution: 1) those derived from a study of the 1940 and 1950 materials on state of birth cross-classified according to the state of residence, and 2) inferences of net migration between 1950 and 1960 based upon the counts of population made in the national censuses for these two years. Most of the data also appears in the author's *Brazil: people and institutions* (3. ed., Baton Rouge, Louisiana State Univ. Press, 1963).

10055. ———. Sociology and sociologists in Brazil and the United States: some aspects of their inter-relationships (CLAPCS/AL, 14:1/2, jan./junho 1971, p. 83-97)

Brief discussion of ways in which the work of sociologists in Brazil and the U.S. has been intertwined, using a simple chronological schema for organizing the presentation. Starting with the influence of Auguste Comte in both countries the author leads to present trends and finds that with the exception of Canada, in the field of sociology, Brazil and the US share similar goals and more exchange than any other American country.

10056. Souto, Cláudio. Teoria sociológica geral. Pôrto Alegre, Bra., Editôra Globo, 1974. 225 p., bibl.

Basically a textbook on general sociological theory for use in classes on theory at the graduate level. Covers classical and key modern contributors in the field in a compendia framework.

10057. Spindel, Cheywa Rojza. Evolução e aproveitamento da força de trabalho na área da Grande São Paulo (FGV/RAE, 12:3, set. 1972, p. 27-)

This paper presents an overview of a research project on labor force in metropolitan São Paulo included in the report *Recursos humanos da Grande São Paulo* (by the Grupo Executivo da Grande São Paulo, Secretaria de Economia e Planejamento, São Paulo, 1971). Main aspects deal with potential population and the actual labor force, its structure and character. Includes data from survey research and official sources.

10058. Stanfield, J. David and **Gordon C. Whiting.** Economic strata and opportunity structure as determinants of innovativeness and productivity in rural Brazil (RSS/RS, 37:3, Sept. 1972, p. 401-416, tables)

This study deals with the nature of the relationships among status, innovation, and productivity in two types of communities in Brazil (concentrated ownership and dispersed). Results suggest that innovation is related to social status and wealth regardless of community type although farmers in areas of dispersed ownership are more prone to innovate.

10059. Staniford, Philip. Pioneers in the tropics: the political organization of Japanese in an immigrant community in Brazil. N.Y., Humanities Press [and] Univ. of London, The Athlone Press, 1973. 201 p.

An excellent research monograph in the tradition of social anthropology (with contributions from the sociological theory of social networks) on the life and adaptation of Japanese immigrants in the Amazon region, where the cultivation of pepper is the main economic activity.

10060. Torres, Livingstone Belo and **Wagner Carneiro Anderi.** Leopoldina: levantamento industrial e sócioeconômico. Belo Horizonte, Bra., Serviço Social da Indústria, Depto. Regional de Minas Gerais, Serviço de Pesquisas e Estatística, 1971. 39 p., tables.

Research report of a community survey of the city of Leopoldina. Includes materials on industry and socioeconomic variables. Useful mostly as a source of data.

10061. Valente Martins, José. Brasil tem meios de controlar explosão demográfica (Economia Paulista [São Paulo] 3:30/31, març)/abril 1972, p. 22-24)

Mainly a popular, and very brief, article on the potential for control of Brazilian population growth. Of no interest to the specialist.

10062. Velho, Gilberto. Estigma e comportamento desviante em Copacabana (CLAPCS/AL, 14:1/2, jan./junho 1971, p. 3-9)

Paper based on research materials published in book form as *A utopia urbana* (Rio, ZAHAR Editores, 1973). It relates the concept of stigma to deviant behaviour in the district of Copacabana (RIo). In particular the study discusses how residence in two apartment complexes was rated as socially inferior by the population at large. This stigmatized the dwellers of these buildings irrespectively of their actual social position and character. The question of social prestige seems to be crucial for members of this community.

10063. _____ *ed.* Desvio e divergência: uma crítica da patologia social. Rio, Zahar Editores, 1974. 144 p., bibl. (Col. Antropologia social)

This book of essays by several authors includes studies on social marginality from Goffman's perspective of stigma. Cases include exceptional children, imputed homosexuality, and cultural differences. Interesting papers, based on field research (mainly Rio) and leading to insightful analyses.

10064. Velloso, João Paulo dos Reis. Brasil: emergência da nova sociedade. Rio, Ministério do Planejamento e Coordenação Geral, 1972. 19 p.

Publication of a talk by the author (Minister of State) discusses from an official viewpoint the characteristics of change in modern Brazil and its future potentials. Good document.

10065. Vieira, José Paulo Carneiro. Ritual Patropi: algumas considerações em torno da corrente prafrente (FGV/RAE, 12:3, set. 9175, p. 44—55)

As indicated by the author his goal was to discuss very freely Brazilian *futebol* (soccer) and its myths. The study focuses on the followers of the game. The analysis is based mainly on unsystematic data collection, personal reflection and knowledge. He concludes that at a time of sport-as-mass-spectable specialized journalism is the key agency for the formation and control of sport followers. Interesting insights for a sociology of sports in Brazil.

10066. Vieira, R.A. Amaral. O futuro da comunicação. Rio, Livros/Cadernos, 1974. 339 p., bibl., facsims., illus., plates (Série Cadernos didáticos)

Essays on the place and role of communication in contemporary society discusses the importance of complex communication systems for further development. Surveys some of the contemporary trends in communication in the US and Europe and examines their state in Brazil.

10067. Vinhas, M. Problemas agrário-camponeses do Brasil. 2. ed. Rio, Civilização Brasileira, 1972. 335 p., bibl., (Col. Retratos do Brasil, 65)

Designed for students in courses on "Brazilian Problems." The author discusses a variety of topical issues regarding contemporary problems in Brazilian agriculture (regional differentiation, variable productivity, dependence, rural-urban linkages, communication and transportation, etc.) and rural workers. Interesting general survey and coverage of present issues.

10068. *Workshop:* problemas de uma sociedade em mudança. Rio? Ministério da Educação e Cultura [and] Univ. Federal do Rio de Janeiro, 1971? 1 v. (Various pagings)

A series of papers presented at the meeting on "Problems of a Changing Society" at the Federal Rural Univ. (Rio) dealing with various correlated themes including the role of women, ethnics, economic change, etc. Also includes debates that followed the presentations. Papers vary in quality but are generally concerned with background information, most of it brief.

10069. Xavier, Jesuan de Paula. O instituto da pena na ressocialização do delinqüente. Brasília, Depto. de Polícia Federal, 1968. 102 p.

Legalistic and action oriented essays discussing the role of sentencing in the process of social rehabilitation of delinquents. Taking into account the particular attributes of the country's penal system, presents its arguments in a philosophical context.

JOURNAL ABBREVIATIONS

ADST/SDT	Sociologie du Travail. Association pour le Développement de la Sociologie du Travail. Paris.
AGS/GR	The Geographical Review. American Geographical Society. N.Y.
AJCL	The American Journal of Comparative Law. American Association for the Comparative Study of Law. Univ. of California. Berkeley, Calif.
AJES	The American Journal of Economics and Sociology. Published quarterly under grants from the Francis Neilson Fund and the Robert Schalkenbach Foundation. N.Y.
ASS/ASR	American Sociological Review. American Sociological Society. Manasha, Wis.
BJS	British Journal of Sociology. Published quarterly for the London School of Economics and Political Science. London.

BNCE/CE	Comercio Exterior. Banco Exterior de Comercio Exterior. México.
	CAM Cuadernos Americanos. México.
CLAPCS/AL	América Latina. Centro Latino-Americano de Pesquisas em Ciências Sociais. Rio.
CM/DE	Demografía y Economía. El Colegio de México. México.
CNRS,ASR	Archives de Sociologie des Religions. Centre Nationale de la Recherche Scientifique. Paris.
CSIC/RIS	Revista Internacional de Sociología. Consejo Superior de Investigaciones Científicas. Instituto Balmes de Sociología. Madrid.
CU/ASQ	Administrative Science Quarterly. Cornell Univ. Graduate School of Business and Public Administration. Ithaca, N.Y.
FERES/SC	Social Compass. International review of socio-religious studies (Revue internationale des études socio-religieuses). International Federation of Institutes for Social and Socio-Religious Research (Fédération Internationale des Instituts de Recherches Sociales et Socio-Religieuses (FERES). The Hague.
FGV/RAE	Revista de Administração de Empresas. Fundação Getúlio Vargas, Instituto de Documentação. São Paulo.
FLACSO/RLCP	Revista Latinoamericana de Ciencia Política. Facultad Latinoamericana de Ciencias Sociales, Escuela Latinoamericana de Ciencia Política y Administración Pública. Santiago.
GIIN/GI	Guatemala Indígena. Instituto Indigenista Nacional. Guatemala.
IAMEA	Inter-American Economic Affairs. Washington.
IASI/E	Estadística. Journal of the Inter American Statistical Institute. Washington.
IBGE/B	Boletim Geográfico. Conselho Nacional de Geografia, Instituto Brasileiro de Geografia e Estatística. Rio.
IBGE/RBE	Revista Brasileira de Estatística. Ministério do Planejamento e Coordenação Geral, Instituto Brasileiro de Geografia e Estatística. Rio.
ICEM/IM	International Migration [Migrations Internationales] [Migraciones Internacionales]. Quarterly Review of the Intergovernmental Committee for European Migration and the Research Group for European Migration Problems. This is the continuation of Migration (ICEM) and the REMP-Bulletin (REMP) a quarterly review on the role of migration movements in the contemporary world. ICEM and REMP have combined efforts. This publication edited in the Hague, Netherlands and published in Geneva, Switzerland. The pre-1974 acronym (INM).
IDES/DE	Desarrollo Económico. Instituto de Desarrollo Económico y Social. B.A.
IFSNC/CD	Community Development. International Federation of Settlements and Neighborhood Centres. Rome.
III/AI	América Indígena. Instituto Indigenista Interamericano. México.
IJSP	International Journal of Social Psychiatry. London.
ISSC/SSI	Social Sciences Information (Information sur les Sciences Sociales). International Social Science Council (Conseil International des Sciences Sociales). Paris.
ITT/RLS	Revista Latinoamericana de Sociología. Instituto Torcuato di Tella, Centro de Sociología Comparada. B.A.
JDS	The Journal of Development Studies. A quarterly journal devoted to economics, politics and social development. London.
JLAS	Journal of Latin American Studies. Centers or institutes of Latin American studies at the universities of Cambridge, Glasgow, Liverpool, London and Oxford. Cambridge Univ. Press. London.
JSP	Journal of Social Psychology. The Journal Press. Provincetown, Mass.
LARR	Latin American Research Review. Latin American Studies Association. Univ. of Texas Press. Austin, Tex.
LNB/L	Lotería. Lotería Nacional de Beneficencia. Panamá.
PAA/D	Demography. Population Association of America. Washington.
PMEH/RE	Revista de Etnografia. Museu de Etnografia e História. Porto, Portugal.
PUC/V	Veritas. Revista. Pontifícia Univ. Católica do Rio Grande do Sul. Pôrto Alegre, Bra.

RSS/RS	Rural Sociology. Rural Sociological Society. New York State College of Agriculture. Ithaca, N.Y.
RU/SCID	Studies in Comparative International Development. Rutgers Univ. New Brunswick, N.J.
RU/T	Trans-action. Social Science and Modern Society. Rutgers Univ. New Brunswick, N.J.
SAA/HO	Human Organization. Society for Applied Anthropology. N.Y.
SBPC/CC	Ciência e Cultura. Sociedade Brasileira para o Progresso da Ciência. São Paulo.
SF	Social Forces. *Published for the* Univ. of North Carolina Press *by the* Williams & Wilkins Co. Baltimore, Md.
SIP/RIP	Revista Interamericana de Psicología (Interamerican Journal of Psychology). Sociedad Interamericana de Psicología. (Interamerican Society of Psychology). Univ. of Texas. Austin, Tex.
UC/AJS	American Journal of Sociology. Univ. of Chicago. Chicago, Ill.
UC/EDCC	Economic Development and Cultural Change. Univ. of Chicago, Research Center in Economic Development and Cultural Change. Chicago, Ill.
UD/ED	Estudios de Deusto. Univ. de Deusto. Bilbao, Spain.
UES/U	La Universidad. Univ. de El Salvador. San Salvador.
UFG/CEB	Cadernos Estudos Brasileiros. Centro de Estudos Brasileiros da Univ. Federal de Goiás. Goiânia, Bra.
UJSC/ECA	Estudios Centro-Americanos. Revista de extensión cultural. Univ. José Simeón Cañas. San Salvador.
UM/JIAS	Journal of Inter-American Studies and World Affairs. Univ. of Miami Press *for the* Center for Advanced International Studies. Coral Gables, Fla.
UM/JNMD	Journal of Nervous and Mental Disease. Univ. of Maryland, Psychiatric Institute. Baltimore, Md.
UNAM/PDD	Problemas del Desarrollo. Revista latinoamericana de economía. Univ. Nacional Autónoma de México, Instituto de Investigaciones Económicas. México.
UNAM/RMS	Revista Mexicana de Sociología. Univ. Nacional Autónoma de México, Instituto de Investigaciones Sociales. México.
UNECLA/B	Economic Bulletin for Latin America. United Nations, Economic Commission for Latin America. N.Y.
UNM/SWJA	Southwestern Journal of Anthropology. Univ. of New Mexico. Albuquerque, N.M.
UP/E	Ethnology. An international journal of cultural and social anthropology. Univ. of Pittsburgh. Pittsburgh, Pa.
UPR/CS	Carribean Studies. Univ. of Puerto Rico, Institute of Caribbean Studies. Río Piedras, P.R.
UPR/RCS	Revista de Ciencias Sociales. Univ. de Puerto Rico, Colegio de Ciencias Sociales. Río Piedras, P.R.
USC/SSR	Sociology and Social Research. An international journal. Univ. of Southern California. University Park, Calif.
USIA/PI	Problemas Internacionales. United States Information Agency. Washington.
UWI/CQ	Caribbean Quarterly. Univ. of the West Indies. Mona, Jam.
WRU/JMF	Journal of Marriage and the Family. Western Reserve Univ. Cleveland, Ohio.
YU/IJCS	International Journal of Comparative Sociology. York Univ., Dept. of Sociology and Anthropology. Toronto, Canada.

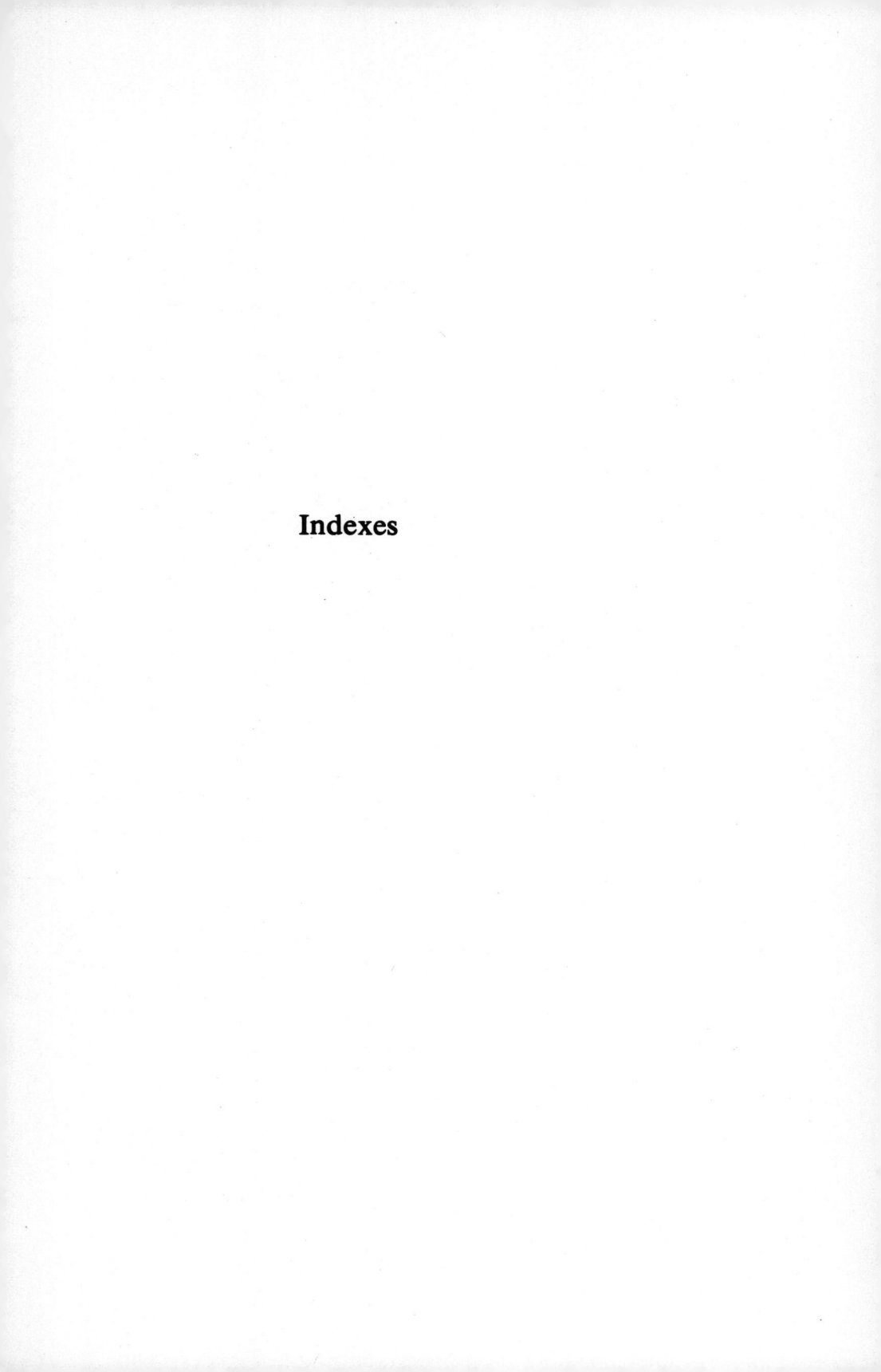

Indexes

Abbreviations and Acronyms*

*Except for journal acronyms which are listed at: a) the end of each major disciplinary section (e.g. Anthropology, Economics, etc.); and b) after each serial title in the *Title List of Journals* Indexed, p. 616.

a.	annual
ABC	Argentina, Brazil, Chile
a.C.	antes de Cristo
ACAR	Associação de Crédito e Assistência Rural, Brazil
AD	Anno Domini
A.D.	Acción Democrática, Venezuela
ADESG	Associação dos Diplomados de Escola Superior de Guerra, Brazil
AGI	Archivo General de Indias, Sevilla
AGN	Archivo General de la Nación
AID	Agency for International Development
Ala.	Alabama
ALALC	Asociación Latinoamericana de Libre Comercio
ANAPO	Alianza Nacional Popular, Colombia
ANCARSE	Associação Nordestina de Crédito e Assistência Rural de Sergipe, Brazil
APRA	Alianza Popular Revolucionaria Americana
Arg.	Argentina
Ariz.	Arizona
Ark.	Arkansas
AUFS	American Universities Field Staff Reports, Hanover, N.H.
Aug.	August, Augustan
b.	born
B.A.	Buenos Aires
BBE	Bibliografia Brasileira de Educação
BC	Before Christ
bibl.	bibliography
BID	Banco Interamericano de Desarrollo
Bol.	Bolivia
BP	before present
Bra.	Brazil
ca.	circa
C.A.	Centro América
CACM	Central American Common Market
CADE	Conferencia Anual de Ejecutivos de Empresas, Peru
CAEM	Centro de Altos Estudios Militares, Peru
Calif.	California
CARC	Centro de Arte y Comunicación
CEBRAP	Centro Brasileiro de Pesquisas, São Paulo
CEDAL	Centro de Estudios Democráticos de América Latina, Chile
CEDE	Centro de Estudios sobre Desarrollo Económico, Univ. de los Andes, Bogotá.
CEDEPLAR	Centro de Desenvolvimento e Planejamento Regional, Belo Horizonte, Brazil
CELADE	Centro Latinoamericano de Demografía
CEMLA	Centro de Estudios Monetarios Latinoamericanos, México
CENDES	Centro de Estudios del Desarrollo, Venezuela

CEPADE	Centro Paraguayo de Estudios de Desarrollo Económico y Social
CEPA-SE	Comissão Estadual de Planejamento Agrícola, Sergipe, Brazil
CEPAL	*See* ECLA.
cf.	compare
CGE	Confederación General Económica, Argentina
ch.	chapter
CHEAR	Council on Higher Education in the American Republics
cía.	compañía
CIE	Centro de Investigaciones Económicas, Buenos Aires
CLASC	Confederación Latinoamericana Sindical Cristiana
CLE	Comunidad Latinoamericana de Escritores, México
cm	centimeter
CNI	Confederação Nacional Industrial, Brazil
Co.	Company
COBAL	Companhia Brasileira de Alimentos
Col.	collection, colección, coleção
Colo.	Colombia
COMCORDE	Comisión Coordinadora para el Desarrollo Económico, Uruguay
comp.	compiler
CONDESE	Conselho de Desenvolvimento Econômico de Sergipe, Brazil
Conn.	Connecticut
COPEI	Comité Organizador Pro-Elecciones Independientes, Venezuela
CORFO	Corporación de Fomento de la Producción, Chile
Corp.	Corporation
CORP	Corporación para el Fomento de Investigaciones Económicas, Columbia
C.R.	Costa Rica
CVG	Corporación Venezolana de Guyana
d.	died
DANE	Departmento Nacional de Estadística, Colombia
d.C.	después de Cristo
Dec.	December, décembre
Del.	Deleware
dept.	department
depto.	departamento
dez.	dezembro
dic.	diciembre
DNOCS	Departamento Nacional de Obras Contra as Sêcas, Brazil
ECLA	Economic Commission for Latin America
Ecua.	Ecuador
ed(s).	edition(s), edición(es), editor(s)
EDEME	Editôra Emprendimentos Educacionais Florianópolis, Brazil
Edo.	Estado
EEC	European Economic Community
e.g.	exemplo gratia [for example]
El Sal.	El Salvador
ELN	Ejército de Liberación Nacional, Colombia
estr.	estrenado
et al.	et alia [and others]
ETENE	Escritório Técnico de Estudios Econômicos do Nordeste, Brazil
ETEPE	Escritório Técnico de Planejamento, Brazil
EUDEBA	Editorial Universitaria de Buenos Aires
facsim.	facsimile
FAO	Food and Agriculture Organization of the United Nations
feb.	February, febrero
fev.	fevreiro, février
FGV	Fundação Getúlio Vargas
FIEL	Fundación de Investigaciones Económicas Latinoamericanas, Argentina
Fla.	Florida
fold. map	folded map
fols.	folios

FRG	Federal Republic of Germany
ft.	foot, feet
Ga.	Georgia
GAO	General Accounting Office, Washington
GATT	General Agreement on Tariffs and Trade
GDR	German Democratic Republic
Gen.	General
GMT	Greenwich Meridian Time
GPO	Government Printing Office
Guat.	Guatemala
h.	hijo
HLAS	*Handbook of Latin American Studies*
HMAI	*Handbook of Middle American Indians*
Hond.	Honduras
IBBD	Instituto Brasileiro de Bibliografia e Documentação
IBRD	International Bank of Reconstruction and Development
IDB	Inter-American Development Bank
i.e.	id est [that is]
IEL	Instituto Euvaldo Lodi, Brazil
IEP	Instituto de Estudios Peruanos
IERAC	Instituto Ecuatoriana de Reforma Agraria y Colonización
III	Instituto Indigenista Interamericano, Mexico
Ill.	Illinois
IIN	Instituto Indigenista Nacional, Guatemala
illus.	illustrations
ILO	International Labour Organization, Geneva
IMES	Instituto Mexicano de Estudios Sociales
in.	inches
INAH	Instituto Nacional de Antropología e Historia, México
Inc.	incorporated
INCORA	Instituto Colombiano de Reforma Agraria
Ind.	Indiana
INEP	Instituto Nacional de Estudos Pedagógicos, Brazil
IPA	Instituto de Pastoral Andina, Univ. de San Antonio de Abad, Seminario de Antropología, Cuzco, Peru
IPEA	Instituto de Pesquisa Econômico-Social Aplicada, Brazil
IPES/GB	Instituto de Pesquisas e Estudos Sociais, Guanabara, Brazil
ir.	irregular
Jam.	Jamaica
jan.	January, janeiro, Janvier
JLP	Jamaican Labour Party
JUCEPLAN	Junta Central de Planificación, Cuba
Jul.	Juli
Jun.	Juni
Kans.	Kansas
km.	kilometers, kilómetros
Ky.	Kentucky
l.	leaves, hojas (páginas impresas por una sola cara)
La.	Louisiana
LARR	*Latin American Research Review*
LASA	Latin American Studies Associacion
LDC	Less developed country
M.	mille, mil, thousand
m.	meters, metros, monthly
Mass.	Massachusetts
Md.	Maryland
MEC	Ministério de Educação e Cultura, Brazil
Mex.	Mexico
Mich.	Michigan
mimeo	mimeographed, mimeografiado

min.	minutes, minutos
Minn.	Minnesota
MIR	Movimiento de Izquierda Revolucionaria, Chile
Miss.	Mississippi
MIT	Massachusetts Institute of Technology
mm.	milimeter
MNR	Movimiento Nacionalista Revolucionario, Bolivia
Mo.	Missouri
MRL	Movimiento Revolucionario Liberal, Colombia
ms.	manuscript
msl	mean sea level
N.C.	North Carolina
n.d.	no date
N. Dak.	North Dakota
Nebr.	Nebraska
Nev.	Nevada
n.	nacido
n.f.	neue Folge
N.H.	New Hampshire
Nic.	Nicaragua
N.J.	New Jersey
N. Mex.	New Mexico
no(s).	number(s), número(s)
NOSALF	Scandinavian Committee for Research in Latin America
Nov.	noviembre, November, novembre, novembro
n.p.	no place, no publisher
NY	New York
NYC	New York City
OAS	Organization of American States
OEA	Organización de los Estados Americanos
oct.	October, octubre
Okla.	Oklahoma
Okt.	Oktober
out.	outubro
OPEC	Organization of Petroleum Exporting Countries
OPEP	Organización de Países Exportadores de Petróleo
Oreg.	Oregon
ORIT	Organización Regional Interamericana del Trabajo
p.	page
Pa.	Pennsylvania
Pan.	Panama
Par.	Paraguay
PCV	Partido Comunista de Venezuela
PEMEX	Petróleos Mexicanos
PLANAVE	Engenharia e Planejamento Limitada, Brazil
PLANO	Planejamento e Assesoria Limitada, Brazil
PLN	Partido Liberación Nacional, Costa Rica
PNM	People's National Movement, Trinidad and Tobago
PNP	People's National Party, Jamaica
pop.	population
P.R.	Puerto Rico
PRI	Partido Revolucionario Institucional, Mexico
PROABRIL	Centro de Projetos Industriais, Brazil
Prof.	Professor
PRONAPA	Programa Nacional de Pesquisas Arqueológicas, Brazil
prov.	province, provincia
PETROBRAS	Petróleo Brasileiro
PS	Partido Socialista, Chile
pseud.	pseudonym, pseudónimo
pt(s).	part(s), parte(s)

PUC	Pontificia Universidade Católica, Rio
PURSC	Partido Unido de la Revolución Socialista de Cuba
q.	quarterly
R.D.	República Dominicana
rev.	revisada, revista, revised
R.I.	Rhode Island
Rio	Rio de Janeiro
S.a.	semiannual
SALALM	Seminar on the Acquisition of Latin American Library Materials
S.C.	South Carolina
sd.	sound
sec.	section
SENAC	Serviço Nacional de Aprendizagem Comercial, Rio
SENAI	Serviço Nacional de Aprendizagem Industrial, São Paulo
SES	socio-economic status
SESI	Serviço Social da Industria, Brazil
S. Dak.	South Dakota
Sept.	September, septiembre, septembre
set.	setembre
SIL	Summer Institute of Linguistics
SINAMOS	Sistema Nacional de Apoyo a la Movilización Social, Peru
S.J.	Society of Jesus
SNA	Sociedad Nacional de Agricultura, Chile
SPVEA	Superintendência do Plano de Valorização Econômica da Amazônia, Brazil
sq.	square
SUDAM	Superintendência do Desenvolvimento da Amazônia, Brazil
SUDENE	Superintendência do Desenvolvimento do Nordeste, Brazil
SUNY	State Universities of New York
t.	tomo, tome
TAT	Thematic Apperception Test
T. and T.	Trinidad & Tobago
Tenn.	Tennessee
Tex.	Texas
TL	Thermoluminescent
TNP	Tratado de No Proliferación
trans.	translator
UN	United Nations
UNAM	Universidad Nacional Autónoma de México
UNCTAD	United Nations Conference on Trade and Development
UNEAC	Unión de Escritores y Artistas de Cuba
UNESCO	United Nations Educational, Scientific and Cultural Organization
univ.	university, universidad, universidade, universite, universität
uniw.	uniwersytet
UP	Unidad Popular, Chile
URD	Unidad Revolucionaria Democrática
Uru.	Uruguay
US	United States of America
USIA	United States Information Agency, Washington
USSR	Union of Soviet Socialist Republics, Unión de Repúblicas Soviéticas Socialistas
UTM	Universal Transverse Mercator
v.; vol.	volume, volumen
Va.	Virginia
Ven.	Venezuela
vs.	versus
Vt.	Vermont
Wis.	Wisconsin
Wyo.	Wyoming
yr.	the younger, el joven

Title List of Journals Indexed*

Aconcagua. Iberoamérica-Europa Zeitschrift für Politik, Kultur und Wirtschaft für die Länder iberisher und deutscher Sprache. Vaduz, Lichtenstein. (ZPKW/A)

Acta Científica Venezolana. Asociación Venezolana para el Avance de la Ciencia. Caracas. (AVAC/ACV)

Acta Geneticae Medicae et Gemellologiae. Instituto Gregorio Mendel. Roma. (IGM/AGMG)

Acta Haematologica. International Journal of Haematology. S. Karger. Basel, Switzerland. (AHIJH)

Acta Prehistorica. Centro Argentino de Estudios Prehistoricos. B.A. (CAEP/AP)

Actualidad Antropológica. Suplemento de Etnía. Museo Etnográfico Municipal Dámaso Arce. Olavarría, Arg.

L'Actualité Économique. l'Institut d'Économie Appliquée. Montréal, Canada.

Administration and Society. Beverly Hills, Calif.

Administrative Science Quarterly. Cornell Univ. Graduate School of Business and Public Administration. Ithaca, N.Y. (CU/ASQ)

Ahora. Publicaciones Ahora. Santo Domingo.

A.I.F.L.D. Review. American Institute for Free Labor Development. Washington. (AIFLD/R)

Air University Review. The professional journal of the United States Air Force. Maxwell Air Force Base, Ala. (AF/AUR)

Akwesasne Notes. Kanienkahake—Mohawk Nation. Middleton, Conn.

Allpanchis Phuturinqa. Univ. de San Antonio de Abad, Seminario de Antropología, Instituto de Pastoral Andina. Cuzco, Peru. (IPA/AP)

América Indígena. Instituto Indigenista Interamericano. México. (III/AI)

América Latina. Academia de Ciencias de la URSS [Unión de Repúblicas Soviéticas Socialistas]. Moscú. (URSS/AL)

América Latina. Centro Latino-Americano de Pesquisas em Ciências Sociais. Rio. (CLAPCS/AL)

American Anthropologist. American Anthropological Association. Washington. (AAA/AA)

American Antiquity. The Society for American Archaeology. Menasha, Wis. (SAA/AA)

American Economic Review. Journal of the American Economic Association. Evanston, Ill. (AEA/AER)

American Economist. Cambridge, Mass.

American Ethnologist. American Anthropological Association. Washington. (AAA/AE)

American Historical Review. American Historical Association. Washington. (AHA/R)

American Journal of Agricultural Economics. American Agricultural Economic Association. Menasha, Wis.

American Journal of Clinical Nutrition. American Society for Clinical Nutrition. N.Y. (ASCN/J)

The American Journal of Comparative Law. American Association for the Comparative Study of Law. Univ. of California. Berkeley, Calif. (AJCL)

American Journal of Digestive Diseases. Plenum Publishing Corp., N.Y.

American Journal of Diseases of Children. Chicago American Medical Association. Chicago, Ill.

The American Journal of Economics and Sociology. Published quarterly under grants from the Francis Neilson Fund and the Robert Schalkenbach Foundation. N.Y. (AJES)

American Journal of Epidemiology. Johns

---

*Journals which have been included in the *Handbook* as individual items are listed alphabetically by title in the Author Index.

Hopkins Univ., School of Hygiene. Baltimore, Md. (JHU/AJE)
American Journal of Human Genetics. The American Society of Human Genetics. Baltimore, Md. (ASHG/J)
American Journal of International Law. American Society of International Law. Washington. (ASIL/J)
American Journal of Physical Anthropology. The official organ of the American Association of Physical Anthropologists [and] The Wistar Institute of Anatomy and Biology. Philadelphia, Pa. (AJPA)
American Journal of Public Health. American Public Health Association. N.Y.
American Journal of Sociology. Univ. of Chicago. Chicago, Ill. (UC/AJS)
American Journal of Tropical Medicine and Hygiene. American Society of Tropical Medicine and Hygiene. Waverly Press, Inc. Baltimore, Md. (ASTMH/J)
American Naturalist. Essex Institute. Lancaster, Pa.
The American Psychologist. American Psychological Association. Washington.
The American Review of Respiratory Diseases. Official Journal of the American Thoracic Society, Medical Section of the National Tuberculosis Association. N.Y. (ATS/ARRD)
American Sociological Review. American Sociological Society. Manasha, Wis. (ASS/ASR)
The Americas. A quarterly journal of inter-American cultural history. Academy of American Franciscan History. Washington. (AAFH/TAM)
Américas. Organization of American States. Washington. (OAS/AM)
Anais do Museu de Antropologia. Univ. Federal do Santa Catarina. Florianópolis, Bra.
Anales. Univ. Central del Ecuador. Quito, Ecuador. (UCE/A)
Anales Científicos de la Universidad del Centro del Perú. Nacional del Centro del Perú. Huancayo, Perú. (UNCP/AC)
Anales de Antropología. Univ. Nacional Autónoma de México, Instituto de Investigaciones Históricas. México. (UNAM/AA)
Anales de Arqueología y Etnología. Univ. Nacional de Cuyo, Facultad de Filosofía y Letras. Mendoza, Arg. (UNC/AAE)
Anales de Ciencias Humanas. Univ. de Panama. Panamá.
Anales de la Sociedad Rural Argentina. Revista pastoril y agrícola. B.A. (SRA/A)
Anales de la Univ. de Cuenca. Cuenca, Ecua. (UC/A)
Anales del Instituto de la Patagonia. Punta Arenas, Chile.
Anales del Instituto de Lingüística. Univ. Nacional de Cuyo, Facultad de Filosofía y Letras. Mendoza, Arg. (UNC/AIL)
Anales del Instituto Nacional de Antropología e Historia. Secretaría de Educación Pública. México. (INAH/A)
Anales del Museo Nacional David J. Guzmán. San Salvador. (MNDJG/A)
Andean Air Mail and Peruvian Times. Lima.
Annals of Human Biology. Taylor & Francis. London.
Annals of Human Genetics (Annals of Eugenics). University College, Galton Laboratory. London. (UCGL/AHG)
Annals of the Association of American Geographers. Lawrence, Kan. (AAG/A)
Annals of the New York Academy of Sciences. N.Y. (NYAS/A)
Annals of the Southern Conference on Latin American Studies. West Georgia College. Carrollton, Ga. (SECOLAS/A)
Annual Review of Anthropology. Annual Review Inc. Palo Alto, Calif.
Anthropological Journal of Canada. Quarterly Bulletin of the Anthropological Association of Canada. Quebec, Canada (AAC/AJ)
Anthropological Linguistics. A publication of the Archives of the Languages of the World. Indiana Univ., Anthropology Dept. Bloomington, Ind. (IU/AL)
Anthropological Quarterly. Catholic Univ. of America, Catholic Anthropological Conference. Washington. (CUA/AQ)
Anthropos. International review of ethnology and linguistics. Anthropos-Institut. Posieux, Switzerland. (AI/A)
Antike Welf: Zeitschrift für Archäeologie und Urgeschichte. Zürich, Switzerland.
Antiquitas. B.A.
Antiquity. A quarterly review of archaeology. The Antiquity Trust. Cambridge, England. (AT/A)
Antropologia. Museu do Colegio Mauá, Santa Cruz do Sul, Bra.
Antropológica. Fundación La Salle de Ciencias Naturales, Instituto Caribe de Antropología y Sociología. Caracas. (FSCN/A)
Antropológica. Sociedad de Ciencias Naturales La Salle. Caracas. (SCNLS/A)

Anuário de Divulgação Científica. Goiânia, Bra.
Anuario de Epidemiología y Estadística Vital. Ministerio de Sanidad y Asistencia Social. Caracas.
Anuario de Geografía. Univ. Nacional Autónoma de México, Colegio de Geografía. México. (UNAMCG/A)
Anuario Indigenista. Instituto Indigenista Interamericano. México. (III/A)
Arbor. Revista General de Investigación y Cultura. Madrid. (ARBOR)
Archeologia. L'archeologie dans le monde et tout ce qui concerne les recherches historiques, artistiques et scientifiques sur terre et dans les mers. Paris. (ARCHEO)
Archaeology. Archaeological Institute of America. N.Y. (AIA/A)
Archiv für Völkerkunde. Museum für Völkerkunde in Wien und von Verein Freude der Völkerkunde. Wien. (MVW/AV)
Archives de Sociologie des Religions. Centre Nationale de la Recherche Scientifique. Paris. (CNRS/ASR)
Archives of Diseases in Childhood. British Medical Association. London.
Archives of Oral Biology. Pergamon Press. London.
Archivos Latinoamericanos de Nutrición. Órgano oficial de la Sociedad Latinoamericana de Nutrición. Caracas. (SLN/ALN)
Arquivos do Museu Paranaense. Curitiba, Bra. (MP/A)
ºArstryck. Etnografiska Museum. Göteborg, Sweden. (EM/A)
Artes de México. México. (ARMEX)
Aula. Univ. Nacional Pedro Henriquez Ureña. Santo Domingo.
Aussenpolitik. Zeitschrift für Internationale Fragen. Deutsch Verlags-Austalt. Hamburg, FGR. (AZIF)
Baessler-Archiv. Beitrage zur Völkerkunde. Museums für Völkerkunde. Berlin. (MV/BA)
Bank of London and South America Review. London.
Bijdragen tot de Taal-, Land- en Volkenrunde. Koninklijk Instituut voor Taal-, Land- en Volkenrunde. Leiden, The Netherlands. (KITLV/B)
Blood. Grume & Stratton. N.Y.
Boletim Bibliográfico. Serviço Social do Comércio, Divisão de Documentação e Intercâmbio, Seção de Documentação. Rio.
Boletim do Instituto de Arqueologia Brasileira. Centro de Estudos Arqueológicos. Rio.
Boletim do Museu Paraense Emílio Goeldi. Conselho Nacional de Pesquisas, Instituto Nacional de Pesquisas da Amazônia. Belém, Bra. (MPEG/B)
Boletim Geográfico. Conselho Nacional de Geografia, Instituto Brasileiro de Geografia e Estatística. Rio. (IBGE/B)
Boletim Paranaense de Geociências. Univ. Federal do Paraná, Instituto de Geociências, Curitiba, Bra.
Boletim Paulista de Geografia. Associação dos geógrafos Brasileiros, Secção Regional de São Paulo. (AGB/BPG)
Boletín. Instituto de Antropología e Historia del Estado de Carabobo, Museo de Arte e Historia. Valencia, Ven.
Boletín. Museo Arqueológico de La Serena, Chile.
Boletín Bibliográfico de Antropología Americana. Instituto Panamericano de Geografía e Historia, Comisión de Historia. México. (BBAA)
Boletín de Estudios Latinoamericanos. Univ. of Amsterdam, Centro de Estudios y Documentación Latinoamericanos (CEDLA). Amsterdam.
Boletín de Higiene y Epidemiología. Centro Nacional de Información de Ciencias Médicas. La Habana.
Boletín de Informaciones Científicas Nacionales. Casa de la Cultura Ecuatoriana. Quito.
Boletín de la Academia de Ciencias Políticas y Sociales. Caracas. (ACPS/B)
Boletín de la Academia Nacional de Ciencias. Córdoba, Arg. (ANC/B)
Boletín de la Academia Nacional de Historia. B.A. (ANH/B)
Boletín de la Academia Nacional de Historia. Quito. (EANH/B)
Boletín de la Facultad de Derecho y Ciencias Sociales. Univ. Nacional de Córdoba, Arg.
Boletín de la Oficina Sanitaria Panamericana. Washington. (OSP/B)
Boletín de la Sociedad Geográfica de Colombia. Academia de Ciencias Geográficas. Bogotá. (SGC/B)
Boletín de la Sociedad Geográfica de Lima. Lima. (SGL/B)
Boletín de la Sociedad Geológica del Perú. Lima. (SGP/B)
Boletín de la Universidad de Chile. Santiago.
Boletín de Prehistoria de Chile. Univ. de Chile, Facultad de Filosofía y Educa-

ción, Depto. de Historia. Santiago. (UC/BPC)
Boletín del Instituto Centroamericano de Derecho Comparado. Tegucigalpa.
Boletín del Instituto de Historia Argentina Doctor Emilio Ravignani. B.A. (IHADER/B)
Boletín del Instituto Nacional de Antropología e Historia. Secretaría de Educación Pública. México. (INAH/B)
Boletín del Seminario de Arqueología. Pontificia Univ. Católica del Perú, Instituto Riva Agüero. Lima. (PUCIRA/BSA)
Boletín Histórico. Fundación John Boulton. Caracas. (FJB/BH)
Boletín Informativo. Fundación Arqueológica, Antropológica e Histórica de Puerto Rico. San Juan.
Boletín Técnico. Caracas.
Bollettino della Societá Geografica Italiana. Pubblicazione mensile. Roma. (SGI/B)
British Journal of Radiology. Allen and Son. London.
British Journal of Sociology. Published quarterly for the London School of Economics and Political Science. London. (BJS)
British Medical Journal. British Medical Association. London. (BMA/J)
Brookings Papers on Economic Activity. The Brookings Institution. Washington.
El Búho. Colegio Regional de Humacao. Humacao, P.R.
Bulletin. Sociéte Suisse des Américanistes. Geneva. (SSA/B)
Bulletin. World Health Organization. Geneva. (WHO/B)
Bulletin de la Société d'histoire de la Guadeloupe. Point-à-Pitre. (SHG/B)
Bulletin de l'Association de Géographes Français. Paris. (AGF/B)
Bulletin de l'Institut Français d'Etudes Andines. Lima. (IFEA/B)
Bulletin of the Cleveland Museum of Art. Cleveland, Ohio.
Bulletin of the Pan American Health Organization. Washington. (PAHO/B)
Bulletin of the Texas Archeological Society. Austin, Tex. (TAS/B)
Bulletin Signalétique. Centre National de la Recherche Scientifique. Paris.
Bulletins et Mémoires de la Société d'Anthropologie de Paris. Paris. (SAP/BM)
Business History Review. Harvard University Graduate School of Business Administration. Boston, Mass. (HU/BHR)
Cadernos Estudos Brasileiros. Centro de Estudos Brasileiros da Univ. Federal de Goiás. Goiânia, Bra. (UFG/CEB)
Cahiers des Amériques Latines. Paris. (CDAL)
Les Cahiers d'Outre-Mer. Publiée par l'Institut de Géographie de la Faculté des Lettres de Bordeaux, par l'Institut de la France d'Outre-Mer, par la Société de Géographie de Bordeaux *avec le concours du* Centre National de la Recherche Scientifique et de la VIiéme section de l'École Pratique des Hautes Études. Bordeaux, France. (SGB/COM)
Canadian Geographer. Le Géographe Canadien. Canadian Association of Geographers. Toronto, Canada. (CAG/CG)
Canadian Geographical Journal. Royal Canadian Geographical Society. Ottawa. (RCGS/CGJ)
Caribbean Journal of Science. Univ. of Puerto Rico, Institute of Caribbean Science. Mayagüez, P.R. (ICS/CJS)
Caribbean Quarterly. Univ. of the West Indies. Mona, Jam. (UWI/CQ)
Caribbean Review. Hato Rey, P.R.
Caribbean Studies. Univ. of Puerto Rico, Institute of Caribbean Studies. Río Piedras, P.R. (UPR/CS)
Carta Mensal. Rio.
Casa de las Américas. La Habana. (CDLA)
Challenge. New York Univ., Institute of Economic Affairs. N.Y.
Ciencia. Editora Cultural Dominicana. Santo Domingo.
Ciência e Cultura. Sociedade Brasileira para o Progresso da Ciência. São Paulo. (SBPC/CC)
Ciencia Interamericana. Organization of American States, Dept. of Scientific Affairs. Washington. (OAS/CI)
Circulation. American Heart Association. N.Y.
Colombia Geográfica. Revista del Instituto Geográfico Agustín Codazzi. Bogotá. (IGAC/CG)
Comercio Exterior. Banco Exterior de Comercio Exterior. México. (BNCE/CE)
Communautés. Entente Communautaire. Paris.
IFSNC/CD Community Development. International Federation of Settlements and Neighborhood Centres. Rome. (IFSNC/CD)
Comparative Education Review. Comparative Education Society. N.Y. (CES/CER)
Comparative Politics. The City University

of New York, Political Science Program. N.Y. (CUNY/CP)
Comparative Studies in Society and History. Society for the Comparative Study of Society and History. The Hague. (CSSH)
Comunidad. Univ. Iberoamericana. México.
Comunidades. Instituto de Estudios Sindicales, Sociales y Cooperativos, Centro de Prospección Social. Madrid (IESSC/C)
Conjuntura Econômica. Fundação Getúlio Vargas, Instituto Brasileiro de Economia. Rio. (FGV/CE)
Contraception. Geron-X, Inc. Los Altos, Calif.
Contributions of the University of California Archaeological Research Facility. Berkeley, Calif. (UCARF/C)
Cristianismo y Sociedad. Junta Latino Americana de Iglesia y Sociedad. Montevideo.
Critica d'Arte. Studio Italiano de Storia dell'Arte. Vallecchi Editore. Firenze, Italy. (CA)
Cuadernos Americanos. México. (CAM)
Cuadernos Culturales de la Industria Textil Peruana. Lima.
Cuadernos de Economía. Univ. Católica de Chile. Santiago. (UCC/CE)
Cuadernos de Historia y Arqueología. Casa de la Cultura Ecuatoriana, Núcleo del Guayas. Guayaquil, Ecua. (CCE/CHA)
Cuadernos de la C[orporación] V[enezolana] [de] F[omento]. Caracas. (CVF/C)
Cuadernos de Psicología. Univ. de Chile, Depto. de Psicología. Santiago.
Cuadernos del Instituto Nacional de Antropología. Secretaría de Estado de Cultura y Educación, Dirección General de Institutos de Investigación. B.A. (AINA/C)
Cultures et Développement. Revue internationale des sciences du développement. Fondation Universitaire de Belgique. Louvain, Belgium. (UCL/CD)
Current Anthropology. Univ. of Chicago. Chicago, Ill. (UC/CA)
Current History. A monthly magazine of world affairs. Daniel G. Redmond, Jr. Philadelphia, Pa. (CUH)
Current Sociology/La Sociologie Contemporaine. UNESCO. Paris.
Dados. Publicação semestral do Instituto Universitário de Pesquisas do Rio de Janeiro. Rio. (IUP/D)
Daedalus. Journal of the American Academy of Arts and Sciences. Harvard Univ. Cambridge, Mass. (AAAS/D)
Dédalo. Revista de arqueologia e etnologia. Univ. de São Paulo, Museu de Arqueologia e Etnologia. São Paulo. (USPMAE/D)
Demografía y Economía. El Colegio de México. México. (CM/DE)
Demography. Population Association of America. Chicago, Ill. (PAA/D)
Desarrollo Económico. Instituto de Desarrollo Económico y Social. B.A. (IDES/DE)
Desarrollo Rural en las Américas. Instituto Interamericano de Ciencias Agrícolas. Bogotá.
Deutsche Bauzeitung. Stuttgart, FRG.
The Developing Economies. The journal of the Institute of Asian Economic Affairs. Tokyo. (IAEA/DE)
Development Dialogue. Dag Hammarskjöld Foundation, Uppsala, Sweden.
Développement et Civilisations. Institut de Recherche et de Formation en vue du Développement Harmonisé. Paris. (IRFDH/DC)
Difusión Económica. Guayaquil, Ecua.
Dissent. Published quarterly by Dissent Publishing Association. N.Y. (DIS)
Docencia. Univ. Autónoma de Guadalajara, Comunidad Académica. Guadalajara, Mex.
Ecology of Food and Nutrition. Gordon and Breach. N.Y.
Economia Internazionale. Rivista dell'Istituto di Economia Internazionale. Genova, Italy. (IEI/EI)
Economia Paulista. São Paulo.
Economía. Instituto Politécnico Nacional. México.
Economía y Desarrollo. Univ. de La Habana, Instituto de Economía. La Habana.
Economic Botany. Devoted to applied botany and plant utilization. Publication of The Society for Economic Botany. *Published for the* Society *by the* New York Botanical Garden. N.Y. (SEB/EB)
Economic Bulletin for Latin America. United Nations, Economic Commission for Latin America. N.Y. (UNECLA/B)
Economic Development and Cultural Change. Univ. of Chicago, Research Center in Economic Development and Cultural Change. Chicago, Ill. (UC/EDCC)
Economic Geography. Clark Univ. Worcester, Mass. (CU/EG)
Economic Journal. Quarterly journal of

the Royal Economic Society. London. (RES/EJ)
Económica. Univ. Nacional de La Plata, Facultad de Ciencias Económicas, Instituto de Investigaciones Económicas. La Plata, Arg.
Économie et Politique. Revue marxiste d'économie. Paris. (EP)
La Educación. Organization of American States, Division of Education. Washington.
Educación. Ministerio de Educación. La Habana.
Educación Popular para el Desarrollo. Instituto de Investigación Cultural para Educación Popular. Oruro, Bol.
EDUPLAN Informa. Ministerio de Educación, Centro de Documentación e Información, Dirección de Planeamiento. Caracas.
Ekistics. Rural housing in an urbanizing world. Athens Center of Ekistics of the Athens Technological Institute. Athens. (ATI/E)
Eme-Eme. Santiago, R.D.
Encuentro. Univ. Centroamericana. Managua, Nic.
Espiral. Revista mensual de artes y letras. Editorial Iqueima. Bogotá. (ESP)
Estadística. Journal of the Inter American Statistical Institute. Washington. (IASI/E)
Estadísticas Vitales de la Salud. Ministerio de Bienestar Social, Depto. de Estadísticas y Salud. B.A.
Estrategia. Instituto Argentino de Estudios Estratégicos y de las Relaciones Internacionales. B.A. (IAEERI/E)
Estudios. Asociación José Joaquín Pardo. Guatemala.
Estudios. Órgano del Comite Ejecutivo del Partido Comunista. Montevideo. (PCU/E)
Estudios. Univ. de San Carlos de Guatemala, Facultad de Humanidades, Depto. de Historia. Guatemala. (USCG/ES)
Estudios Andinos. Instituto Boliviano de Estudio y Acción Social. La Paz. (IBEAS/EA)
Estudios Atacameños. Univ. del Norte, Museo de Arqueología. San Pedro de Atacama, Chile.
Estudios Centro-Americanos. Revista de extensión cultural. Univ. José Simeón Cañas. San Salvador. (UJSC/ECA)
E[studios] C[entro] A[mericanos]. Revista de orientación y cultura, dirigida por los PP. Jesuitas de C.A. San Salvador. (ECA)

Estudios de Deusto. Univ. de Deusto. Bilbao, Spain. (UD/ED)
Estudios Económicos. Univ. Nacional del Sur, Instituto de Economía. Bahía Blanca, Arg. (UNS/EE)
Estudios Internacionales. Asociación Latinoamericana de Ex-Alumnos de la Academia de Derecho Internacional de La Haya. Bogotá.
Estudios Internacionales. Univ. Nacional Autónoma de México, Centro de Relaciones Internacionales. México.
Estudios Latinoamericanos. Wroclaw, Poland.
Estudios Sindicales y Cooperativos. Instituto de Estudios Sindicales, Sociales y Cooperativos de Madrid. Madrid. (ESC)
Estudios Sociales Centroamericanos. Programa Centroamericano de Desarrollo de las Ciencias Sociales. San José.
Estudos CEBRAP. Centro Brasileiro de Análise e Planejamento. São Paulo.
Estudos Econômicos. Univ. de São Paulo, Instituto de Pesquisas Econômicas. São Paulo (IPE/EE)
Estudos Econômicos. Univ. de São Paulo, Instituto de Pesquisas Econômicas. São Paulo (USP/EE)
Ethnia. Centro Colombiano Antropológico de Misiones. Bogotá.
Ethnographisch-Archäologische Zeitschrift. Deutscher Verlag Wissenschaften. Berlin, GDR. (EAZ)
Ethnology. An international journal of cultural and social anthropology. Univ. of Pittsburgh. Pittsburgh, Pa. (UP/E)
Ethnos. Statens Etnografiska Museu. Stockholm. (SEM/E)
Etnía. Museo Etnográfico Municipal Dámaso Arce. Municipalidad de Olavarría, Provincia de Buenos Aires, Arg. (MEMDA/E)
Etudes Rurales. Revue trimestrielle publiée par l'Ecole Pratique des Hautes Etudes, Sorbonne, Sixième Section: Sciences économiques et sociales, *avec le concours du* Centre Nationale de la Recherche Scientifique. The Hague. (SEPHE/ER)
Evolutionary Biology. Appleton-Century-Crofts. N.Y.
Expedition. The bulletin of the University Museum of the Univ. of Pennsylvania. Philadelphia, Pa. (UMUP/E)
Explorers Journal. N.Y. (EJ)
Fénix. Biblioteca Nacional. Lima. (FENIX)
Finanças Públicas. Ministerio da Fazenda, Subsecretaria de Economia e Finanças. Brasília.

Folia Humanística. Ciencias, artes, letras. Editorial Glarma. Barcelona. (FH)
Foreign Affairs. An American quarterly review. Council on Foreign Relations, Inc. N.Y. (CFR/FA)
Foreign Policy. National Affairs, Inc. N.Y.
Foro Internacional. El Colegio de México. México. (CM/FI)
Genetics. Genetics, Inc. Univ. of Texas. Austin, Tex. (UT/G)
Geoforum. Oxford, England.
Geographica Helvetica. Schweizerische Zeitschrift für Länder- und Völkerkunde. Kümmerly & Frey, Geographischer Verlag. Bern. (GH)
The Geographical Journal. The Royal Geographical Society. London. (RGS/GJ)
The Geographical Magazine. London. (GM)
The Geographical Review. American Geographical Society. N.Y. (AGS/GR)
Geographische Rundschau. Zeitschrift für Schulgeographie. Georg Westermann Verlag. Braunschweig, FRG (GR)
Geographische Zeitschrift. Franz Steiner Verlag. Wiesbaden, FRG (GZ)
Geography. Journal of the Geographical Association. London (GA/G)
Geologie en Mijnbouw. Koninklijk Nederlands Geologisch Minjnbouwkundig Genootschap. The Hague. (KMGMG/GM)
Geologische Rundschau. Internationale Zeitschrift für Geologie. Geologische Vereinigung. Ferdinand Enke Verlag. Stuttgart, FRG. (GV/GR)
Growth and Change. Univ. of Kentucky. Lexington, Ky.
Guatemala Indígena. Instituto Indigenista Nacional. Guatemala. (GIIN/GI)
Hispanic American Historical Review. Conference on Latin American History of the American Historical Association. Duke Univ. Press. Durham, N.C. (HAHR)
Hoja Informativa. Centro de Documentación e Información Educativas. Villa María, Arg.
Hombre y Cultura. Revista del Centro de Investigaciones Antropológicas de la Univ. Nacional. Panamá. (UNCIA/HC)
L'Homme. Revue française d'anthropologie. La Sorbonne, L'École Pratique des Hautes Études. Paris. (EPHE/H)
Horizontes. Revista de la Univ. Católica de Puerto Rico. Ponce, P.R. (UCPR/H)
Hormones. S. Karger. Basel, Switzerland.
Human Biology. Official publication of the Human Biology Council. Wayne State Univ., School of Medicine. Detroit, Mich. (WSU/HB)
Human Development. S. Karger. Basel, Switzerland.
Human Ecology. Plenum Publishing Corp., N.Y.
Humangenetik. Springer-Verlag. Berlin, FRG.
The Human Geography. Association of Human Geography. Kyoto, Japan.
Human Heredity. Helbing and Lichtenhahn. Basel, Switzerland. (HH)
Human Organization. Society for Applied Anthropology. N.Y. (SAA/HO)
Humanitas. Anuario del Centro de Estudios Humanísticos. Univ. de Nuevo León. Monterrey, Mex. (UNL/H)
Humanitas. Boletín ecuatoriano de antropología. Univ. Central del Ecuador, Instituto de Antropología. Quito. (UCEIA/H)
Humanitas. Revista de la Facultad de Filosofía y Letras. Univ. Nacional de Tucumán. Tucumán, Arg. (UNT/H)
Ibero-Americana Pragensia. Univ. Carolina de Praga, Centro de Estudios Ibero-Americanos. Prague. (UCP/IAP)
Icach. Organo de divulgación cultural del Instituto de Ciencias y Artes de Chiapas. Tuxtla Gutiérrez, Mex. (ICACH)
Iheringia. Antropologia. Pôrto Alegre, Bra.
Ijyu Kenkyu. Kaigai Ijyu Jigyodan. Tokyo.
Illustrated London News. London. (ILN)
Indian Notes. Museum of the American Indian. N.Y.
Indiana. Ibero-Americanisches Institut. Berlin, FRG.
The Indiana Social Studies Quarterly. Official organ of the Indiana Council for Social Studies. Ball State Univ. Muncie, Ind. (ISSQ)
Industrial Relations. Univ. of California, Institute of Industrial Relations, Berkeley, Calif.
Informaciones Geográficas. Organo oficial del Instituto de Geografía de la Univ. de Chile, Facultad de Filosofía y Educación. Santiago. (UCIG/IG)
Information Geographique. Paris. (IG)
Inter-American Economic Affairs. Washington (IAMEA)
International Development Review. The Society for International Development. Washington. (SID/IDR)
International Economic Review. Kansai Keizai Rengokai. Osaka, Japan.

International Journal. Canadian Institute of International Affairs. Toronto, Canada. (CIIA/IJ)
International Journal of American Linguistics. Published by Indiana University under the auspices of Linguistic Society of America, American Anthropological Association, *with the cooperation of* the Joint Committee on American Native Languages. Waverly Press, Inc. Baltimore, Md. (IU/IJAL)
International Journal of Biometeorology. Swets and Zeitlinger. Amsterdam.
International Journal of Comparative Sociology. Karnatak Univ., Dept. of Social Anthropology. Dharwar, India. (KU/IJCS)
International Journal of Comparative Sociology. York Univ., Dept. of Sociology and Anthropology. Toronto, Canada. (YU/IJCS)
International Journal of Social Psychiatry. London. (IJSP)
International Labour Review. International Labour Office. Geneva. (ILO/R)
International Migration [Migrations Internationales] [Migraciones Internacionales]. Quarterly Review of the Intergovernmental Committee for European Migration and the Research Group for European Migration Problems. This is the continuation of Migration (ICEM) and the REMP-Bulletin (REMP) a quarterly review on the role of migration movements in the contemporary world. ICEM and REMP have combined efforts. This publication edited in the Hague, Netherlands and published in Geneva, Switzerland. The pre-1974 acronym (INM). (ICEM/IM)
The International Migration Review. Center for Migration Studies. N.Y. (CMS/IMR)
International Organization. World Peace Foundation. Boston, Mass. (WPF/IO)
International Review of Education. United Nations, Educational, Scientific and Cultural Organization, Institute for Education. Hamburg, FRG. (UNESCO/IRE)
Internationale Spectator. Tijdschrift voor internationale politiek. Het Nederlandsch Genootschap voor Internationale Zaken. The Hague. (NGIZ/IS)
Islas. Revista de la Univ. Central de las Villas. Santa Clara, Cuba. (UCLV/I)
Israel Journal of Medical Sciences. Weizmann Institute. Jerusalem.

Istmo. Revista del Centro de América. México. (ISTMO)
ITA-Humanidades. Ministério de Aeronáutica, Instituto Tecnológico de Aeronáutica. São José dos Campos, Bra. (ITA/H)
Jahrbuch des Museums für Völkerkunde zu Leipzig. Berlin. (MVL/J)
Jahrbuch für Geschichte von Staat, Wirtschaft und Gesellschaft Lateinamerikas. Köln, FRG. (JGSWGL)
Jewish Social Studies. Conference on Jewish Social Studies. N.Y.
Johns Hopkins Medical Journal. Johns Hopkins Univ. Press. Baltimore, Md.
Journal de la Société des Américanistes. Paris. (SA/J)
Journal of American Folklore. American Folklore Society. Austin, Tex. (AFS/JAF)
Journal of American Medical Association. Chicago, Ill.
Journal of Anthropological Research. Univ. of New Mexico. Laboratory of Anthropology, Sante Fe. Albuquerque, N. Mex. (UNM/JAR)
Journal of Applied Physiology. American Physiological Society. Washington.
Journal of Belizean Affairs. Belize City.
Journal of Biosocial Science. Blackwell Scientific Publications. Oxford, England.
A Journal of Church and State. Published by the J.M. Dawson Studies in Church and State of Baylor Univ. Waco., Tex. (BU/JCS)
Journal of Common Market Studies. Oxford, England. (JCMS)
The Journal of Developing Areas. Western Illinois Univ. Press. Macomb, Ill. (JDH)
The Journal of Development Studies. A quarterly journal devoted to economics, politics and social development. London. (JDS)
Journal of Economic History. New York Univ., Graduate School of Business Administration *for* The Economic History Association. Rensselaer, N.Y. (EHA/J)
Journal of Economic Studies. Oxford Univ. Oxford, England.
Journal of Field Archaeology. Boston Univ. Boston, Mass.
Journal of Inter-American Studies and World Affairs. Univ. of Miami Press *for the* Center for Advanced International Studies. Coral Gables, Fla. (UM/JIAS)
Journal of International Affairs. Columbia Univ., School of International Affairs. N.Y. (CU/JIA)
Journal of Latin American Studies. Cen-

ters or institutes of Latin American studies at the universities of Cambridge, Glasgow, Liverpool, London and Oxford. Cambridge Univ. Press. London (JLAS)

Journal of Marriage and the Family. Western Reserve Univ. Cleveland, Ohio. (WRU/JMF)

Journal of Nervous and Mental Disease. Univ. of Maryland, Psychiatric Institute. Baltimore, Md. (UM/JNMD)

Journal of Peace Research. Edited at the International Peace Research Institute. Universitetforlaget. Oslo. (JPR)

Journal of Physiology. Physiological Society. London.

Journal of Political Economy. Univ. of Chicago, Chicago, Ill. (JPE)

Journal of Reproductive Medicine. American Academy of Reproductive Medicine. Chicago, Ill.

Journal of Social Psychology. The Journal Press. Provincetown, Mass. (JSP)

Journal of the Barbados Museum and Historical Society. Barbados, W.I. (BMHS/J)

Journal of the Steward Anthropological Society. Urbana, Ill.

The Journal of Tropical Geography. Univ. Singapore and Univ. of Malaya. Departments of Geography. Singapore. (USM/JTG)

Journal of Tropical Pediatrics and Environmental Child Health. Staples & Staples. London.

Katunob. Southern State College. Magnolia, Ark. (SSC/K)

Kollasuyo. Revista de estudios bolivianos. Univ. Mayor de San Andrés. La Paz. (KO)

Kroeber Anthropological Society Papers. Univ. of California. Berkeley, Calif. (KAS/P)

Kurtziana. Córdoba, Arg.

Lancet. London. (LANCET)

Land Economics. A quarterly journal of planning, housing and public utilities. Univ. of Wisconsin. Madison, Wis. (UW/LE)

Latin American Documentation. U.S. Catholic Conference. Washington (LADOC)

Latin American Research Review. Latin American Studies Association. Univ. of Texas Press. Austin, Tex. (LARR)

Latinskaia Amerika. Latin American Institute, USSR Academy of Sciences. Moscow.

Lenguaje. Univ. del Valle, División de Humanidades. Cali, Colo.

Letras. Univ. Nacional Mayor de San Marcos. Lima. (UNMSM/L)

Libre. Paris.

Los Libros. Editorial Galerna. B.A.

Limen. Revista de orientación didáctica. Kapelusz Revistas. B.A.

Linguistics. An international review. Mouton. The Hague. (LING)

Logos. Bogotá.

Loteria. Organo de la Lotería Nacional de Beneficencia. Panamá. (LNB/L)

LTC Newsletter. Univ. of Wisconsin at Madison, Land Tenure Center.

Man. A monthly record of anthropological science. The Royal Anthropological Institute. London. (RAI/M)

The Massachusetts Review. A quarterly of literature, the arts and public affairs. Published independently with the support and cooperation of Amherst College, Mount Holyoke College, Smith College, and the Univ. of Massachusetts. Amherst, Mass. (TMR)

The Masterkey. Southwest Museum. Los Angeles, Calif. (SM/M)

Medical Anthropology Newsletter. South Birmingham, Ala.

Memoria de El Colegio Nacional. México. (CN/M)

Merkur. Deutsche Zeitschrift für Europäisches Denken. Deutsche Verlags-Anstalt. Stuttgart, FRG. (MDZED)

Middle American Research Institute Publication. Tulane University. New Orleans, La. (TUMARI/P)

Milbank Memorial Fund Quarterly. N.Y.

Mitteilungen der Berliner Gesellschaft für Anthropologie, Ethnologie und Urgeschichte. Berlin, FRG (BGAEU/M)

Montalban. Univ. Católica Andrés Bello, Facultad de Humanidades y Educación, Institutos Humanísticos de Investigación. Caracas. (UCAB/M)

Monthly Review. An independent Socialist magazine. N.Y. (MR)

Mundo Hispánico. Madrid. (MH)

Museum. Museum of Science. Miami, Fla.

The Museum Quarterly. The West Texas Museum Association. Lubbock, Tex.

National Geographic Magazine. National Geographic Society. Washington. (NGS/NGM)

Natural History. American Museum of Natural History. N.Y. (AMNH/NH)

Nature. A weekly journal of science. Macmillan. London (NWJS)

Newsletter of Lithic Technology. Washington State Univ., Laboratory of

TITLE LIST OF JOURNALS INDEXED

Anthropology. Pullman, Wash.
Newsletter of the Land Tenure Center. Univ. of Wisconsin, Land Tenure Center. Madison, Wis.
The New Yorker. N.Y.
Nieuwe West-Indische Gids. Martins Nijhoff. The Hague. (NWIG)
Notes et Études Documentaires. France, Direction de la Documentation. Paris. (FDD/NED)
Noticiario Mensual. Museo Nacional de Historia Natural. Santiago.
Noticias del CSUCA. Consejo Superior Universitario Centroamericano, Secretaría Permanente. San José.
Objets et Mondes. Revue trimestrielle. Musée de l'Homme. Paris (MH/OM)
Oceans. San Diego, Calif.
Orbis. Bulletin international de documentation linguistique. Centre International de Dialectologie Générale. Louvain, Belgium. (CIDG/O)
Orbis. A quarterly journal of world affairs. Univ. of Pennsylvania, Foreign Policy Research Institute. Philadelphia, Pa. (UP/O)
Oxford Economic Papers. Oxford Univ. Press. London. (OUP/OEP)
Pacific Sociological Review. Pacific Sociological Society. Univ. of Oregon. Eugene, Oreg. (PSS/PSR)
Partisans. Paris.
Pediatric Research. Helbing. Basel, Switzerland.
Pediatrics. American Academy of Pediatrics. Springfield, Ill.
El Pequeño Universo. Univ. Autónoma de Santo Domingo, Facultad de Humanidades. Santo Domingo.
Pesquisa e Planejamento. Instituto de Planejamento Econômico e Social. Rio. (IPEA/PP)
Pesquisa e Planejamento Econômico. Instituto de Planejamento Econômico e Social. Rio. (IPEA/PPE)
Plana. Oficina de Educación Iberoamericana. Madrid.
Planificación. México.
Política. Ideas para una América nueva. Caracas. (POLIT)
The Political Quarterly. London. (PQ)
The Political Science Reviewer. Hampden-Sydney, Va.
Population Studies. A journal of demography. London School of Economics, The Population Investigation Committee. London. (LSE/PS)
Prede Actualidades. Organización de los Estados Americanos, Secretaría General, Depto. de Asuntos Educativos. Washington.
Problemas Brasileiros. São Paulo.
Problemas del Desarrollo. Revista latinoamericana de economía. Univ. Nacional Autónoma de México, Instituto de Investigaciones Económicas. México. (UNAM/PDD)
Problemas Internacionales. United States Information Agency. Washington. (USIA/PI)
Problems of Communism. United States Information Agency. Washington. (USIA/PC)
Proceedings of the American Philosophical Society. Philadelphia, Pa. (APS/P)
Proceedings of the Department of Humanities. Univ. of Tokyo, College of General Education, Series of Cultural Anthropology. Tokyo.
Proceedings of the National Academy of Sciences. Washington. (NAS/P)
Professional Geographer. Journal of the Association of American Geographers. Washington. (AAG/PG)
Publicações Avulsas. Museu Paraense Emílio Goeldi. Belém, Bra. (MPEG/PA)
Quarterly. Pacific Coast Archaeological Society. Costa Mesa, Calif.
Quarterly Journal of Economics. Harvard Univ. Cambridge, Mass.
Quarterly Review. Banca Nazionale del Lavoro. Rome. (BNL/QR)
Quatenary Research. Academic Press. N.Y.
Race. The Journal of the Institute of Race Relations. London. (IRR/R)
Recursos Hidraúlicos. México.
Rehue. Univ. de Concepción, Instituto de Antropología. Concepción, Chile. (UCIA/R)
Relaciones de la Sociedad Argentina de Antropología. B.A. (SAA/R)
Relações Humanas. Instituto de Relações Sociais e Industrias de São Paulo. São Paulo. (IRSISP/RH)
Research Reports: 1967 projects. National Geographic Society. Washington.
Review of Radical Political Economics. Union of Radical Political Economists. Ann Arbor, Mich.
Revista. Comisión Municipal de Cultura, Depto. de Antropología y Folklore, Concordia, Arg.
Revista Bancária Brasileira. Rio.
Revista Brasileira de Economia. Fundação Getúlio Vargas, Instituto Brasileiro de Economia. Rio. (IBE/RBE)
Revista Brasileira de Estadística.

Ministério do Planejamento e Coordenação Geral, Instituto Brasileiro de Geografia e Estatística. Rio. (IBGE/RBE)
Revista Brasileira de Estudos Políticos. Univ. de Minas Gerais. Belo Horizonte, Bra. (UMG/RBEP)
Revista Brasileira de Geografia. Conselho Nacional de Geografia, Instituto Brasileiro de Geografia e Estadística. Rio. (IBGE/R)
Revista Cámara de Comercio de Bogotá. Bogotá.
Revista Chungara. Univ. del Norte, Depto. de Antropología. Arica, Chile.
Revista Colombiana de Antropología. Ministerio de Educación Nacional, Instituto Colombiano de Antropología. Bogotá. (ICA/RCA)
Revista de Administração de Empresas. Fundação Getúlio Vargas, Instituto de Documentação. São Paulo (FGV/RAE)
Revista de Administração Municipal. Rio.
Revista de Antropología. Casa de la Cultura Ecuatoriana, Núcleo del Azuay. Cuenca, Ecua. (CCE/RA)
Revista de Antropologia. Univ. de São Paulo, Faculdade de Filosofia, Ciências e Letras. São Paulo. (USP/RA)
Revista de Biblioteconomia de Brasília. Brasília.
Revista de Ciencias Económicas. B.A.
Revista de Ciencias Económicas. Univ. Autónoma de Santo Domingo. Santo Domingo.
Revista de Ciencias Sociales. Univ. de Puerto Rico, Colegio de Ciencias Sociales. Río Piedras, P.R. (UPR/RCS)
Revista de Economía Latinoamericana. Banco Central de Venezuela. Caracas. (BCV/REL)
Revista de Educación. Ministerio de Educación. Santiago.
Revista de Estudios Agro-Sociales. Instituto de Estudios Agro-Sociales, Madrid.
Revista de Estudios Políticos. Instituto de Estudios Políticos. Madrid. (IEP/REP)
Revista de Etnografia. Museu de Etnografia e História. Porto, Portugal. (PMEH/RE)
Revista de História. Univ. de São Paulo, Faculdade de Filosofia, Ciências e Letras, Depto. de História [and] Sociedade de Estudos Históricos. São Paulo. (USP/RH)
Revista de Indias. Consejo Superior de Investigaciones Científicas, Instituto Gonzalo Fernández de Oviedo. Madrid. (IGFO/RI)
Revista de la Academia Colombiana de Ciencias Exactas, Físicas y Naturales. Bogotá. (ACCEFN/R)
Revista de la Academia Diplomática del Perú. Lima.
Revista de la Asociación Guatemalteca de Derecho Internacional. Guatemala.
Revista de la Biblioteca Nacional José Martí. La Habana. (BNJM/R)
Revista de la Dirección de Divulgación Cultural. Bogotá.
Revista de la Facultad de Ciencias de la Administración. Univ. Nacional del Litoral. Santa Fe, Arg.
Revista de la Facultad de Ciencias Económicas y Comerciales. Univ. Nacional Mayor de San Marcos. Lima. (USM/RCEC)
Revista de la Integración. Economía, política, sociología. Banco Interamericano de Desarrollo, Instituto para la Integración de América Latina. B.A. (INTAL/RI)
Revista de la Universidad de Yucatán. Mérida, Mex. (VY/R)
Revista de Planeación y Desarrollo. Departamento Nacional de Planeación. Bogotá. (DNP/RPD)
Revista del Banco Central de Venezuela. Caracas.
Revista del Centro de Estudios Histórico-Militares del Perú. Lima. (CEHMP/R)
Revista del Centro de Investigación y Acción Social. Univ. de la Patria Nueva. B.A.
Revista del Colegio Interamericano de Defensa. Colegio Interamericano de Defensa. Washington.
Revista del Museo de La Plata. Univ. Nacional de La Plata, Facultad de Ciencias Naturales y Museo. La Plata, Arg. (UNLPM/R)
Revista del Museo Nacional. Casa de la Cultura del Perú, Museo Nacional de la Cultura Peruana. Lima. (PEMN/R)
Revista do Museu Paulista. São Paulo, Bra. (MP/R)
Revista do Serviço Público. Rio. (BDASP/R)
Revista Dominicana de Arqueología y Antropología. Univ. Autónoma de Santo Domingo, Facultad de Humanidades, Depto. de Historia y Antropología, Instituto de Investigaciones Antropológicas. Santo Domingo. (UASD/R)
Revista Econômica do Nordeste (REN). Banco do Nordeste do Brasil, Depto. de Estudos Econômicos do Nordeste (ETENE). Fortaleza, Bra. (BNB/REN)
Revista Ecuatoriana de Educación. Casa

de la Cultura Ecuatoriana. Quito.
Revista Española de Antropología Americana [Trabajos y Conferencias]. Univ. de Madrid, Facultad de Filosofía y Letras, Depto. de Antropología y Etnología de América. Madrid. (UM/REAA)
Revista Geográfica. Instituto Panamericano de Geografia e História, Comissão de Geografia. Rio. (PAIGH/G)
Revista Geográfica. Univ. de Los Andes. Mérida, Ven. (ULA/RG)
Revista ICA. Instituto Colombiano Agropecuario. Bogotá.
Revista Interamericana de Bibliografía [Inter-American Review of Bibliography]. Organization of American States. Washington. (RIB)
Revista Interamericana de Psicología (Interamerican Journal of Psychology). Sociedad Interamericana de Psicología. (Interamerican Society of Psychology). Univ. of Texas. Austin. (SIP/RIP)
Revista Internacional de Sociología. Consejo Superior de Investigaciones Científicas. Instituto Balmes de Sociología. Madrid. (CSIC/RIS)
Revista Latinoamericana de Ciencia Política. Facultad Latinoamericana de Ciencias Sociales, Escuela Latinoamericana de Ciencia Política y Administración Pública. Santiago. (FLACSO/RLCP)
Revista Latinoamericana de Psicología. Editorial Ruben Ardila. Bogotá.
Revista Latinoamericana de Sociología. Instituto Torcuato di Tella, Centro de Sociología Comparada. B.A. (ITT/RLS)
Revista Marítima Brasileira. Ministério de Marinha. Rio. (BMM/RMB)
Revista Médica de Chile. Sociedad Médica de Santiago. Santiago. (SMS/RMC)
Revista Mexicana de Sociología. Univ. Nacional Autónoma de México, Instituto de Investigaciones Sociales. México. (UNAM/RMS)
Revista Mexicana del Trabajo. Órgano oficial de la Secretaría del Trabajo y Previsión Social. México. (MSTPS/R)
Revista Nacional de Agricultura. Sociedad de Agricultores de Colombia. Bogotá.
Revista Paraguaya de Sociología. Centro Paraguayo de Estudios Sociológicos. Asunción. (CPES/RPS)
Revista Trimestral do Instituto Histórico e Geográfico Brasileiro. Rio. (IHGB/R)
Revista Uruguaya de Geografía. Univ. de la República, Facultad de Humanidades y Ciencias, Depto. de Geografía. Montevideo. (UR/RUG)
Revista Venezolana de Sanidad y Asistencia Social. Ministerio de Sanidad y Asistencia Social. Caracas.
Revista Villarreal. Univ. Nacional Federico Villarreal. Lima.
Revue des Deux Mondes. Paris.
Revue Française de Science Politique. Fondation Nationale des Sciences Politiques, l'Association Française de Science Politique, *avec le concours du* Centre National de la Recherche Scientifique. Paris. (FNSP/RFSP)
Rivista Geografica Italiana. Società di Studi Geografici e Coloniali. Firenze, Italy. (SSG/RGI)
The Rocky Mountain Social Science Journal. The Rocky Mountain Social Science Association. [Colorado State Univ.] Fort Collins, Colo. (RMSSA/J)
Ruedo Ibérico. Paris.
Runa. Archivo para las Ciencias del Hombre. Univ. de Buenos Aires, Facultad de Filosofía y Letras, Instituto de Antropología. B.A. (UBAIA/R)
Rural Sociology. Official organ of the Rural Sociological Society. New York State College of Agriculture. Ithaca, N.Y. (RSS/RS)
Rutgers Alumni Magazine. Rutgers Univ. New Brunswick, N.J.
Santiago. Univ. de Oriente. Santiago de Cuba.
Saturday Review of Education. San Francisco, Calif.
Science. American Association for the Advancement of Science. Washington. (AAAS/S)
Science and Society. An independent journal of Marxism. N.Y. (SS)
Série Lingüística. Summer Institute of Linguistics. Brasília.
Science. American Association for the Advancement of Science. Washington. (AAAS/S)
Social and Economic Studies. Univ. of the West Indies, Institute of Social and Economic Research. Mona, Jam. (UWI/SES)
Social Biology. American Eugenics Society. N.Y.
Social Compass. The International Catholic Institute for Social-Ecclesiastical Research. The Hague. (ICISR/S)
Social Compass. International review of socio-religious studies (Revue internationale des études socio-religieuses). International Federation of Institutes for Social and Socio-Religious Research

(Fédération Internationale des Instituts de Recherches Sociales et Socio-Religieuses (FERES). The Hague. (FERES/SC)
Social Forces. Published for the Univ. of North Carolina Press by the Williams & Wilkins Co. Baltimore, Md (SF)
Social Research. An international quarterly of political and social science. Graduate Faculty of Political and Social Science, New School for Social Research. N.Y. (NSSR/SR)
Social Sciences Information (Information sur les Sciences Sociales). International Social Science Council (Conseil International des Sciences Sociales). Paris. (ISSC/SSI)
La Sociedad y el Universitario. Univ. Industrial de Santander. Bucaramanga, Colo.
Sociedad y Política. Lima.
Society. Social science and modern society. Transaction, Rutgers Univ. New Brunswick, N.J. (SO)
Sociología del Desarrollo. Barranquilla, Colo.
Sociologie du Travail. Association pour le Développement de la Sociologie du Travail. Paris. (ADST/SDT)
Sociologus. Zeitschrift für empirische Soziologie, sozialpsychologische und ethnologische Forschung (A journal for empirical sociology, social psychology and ethnic research) Berlin, FRG. (SOCIOL)
Sociology and Social Research. An international journal. Univ. of Southern California. University Park, Calif. (USC/SSR)
Sociometry. American Sociological Association. N.Y. (ASA/S)
South Eastern Latin Americanist. Florida State Univ. Tallahassee, Fla.
The Southern Anthropologist. Newsletter of the Southern Anthropological Association. Univ. of New Orleans, La.
Southern Economic Journal. Chapel Hill, N.C.
Southern Medical Journal. Southern Medical Association. Birmingham, Ala.
Southwestern Journal of Anthropology. Univ. of New Mexico. Albuquerque, N.Mex. (UNM/SWJA)
Sovetskaia Etnografiia. Moskva.
Staff Papers. International Monetary Fund. Washington. (IMF/SP)
Stanford Law Review. Stanford Univ. Palo Alto, Calif.
Studia Linguistica. Revue de linguistique générale et comparée. C.W.K. Gleerup. Lund, Sweden. (SL)
Studies in Comparative International Development. Rutgers Univ. New Brunswick, N.J. (RU/SCID)
Studies in Comparative Local Government. International Union of Local Authorities. The Hague.
Suplemento Antropológico. Univ. Católica. Asunción.
Symposium. Univ. Católica de Pernambuco. Recife, Bra.
Technology and Culture. Society for the History of Technology. Detroit, Mich.
Técnicas Financieras. Centro de Estudios Monetarios Latinoamericanos. México. (CEML/TF)
Tiers Monde. Problémes des pays sous-développés. Univ. de Paris, Institut d'Etude du Développement Economique et Social. Paris. (UP/TM)
Tijdschrift voor Economische en Sociale Geographie. Netherlands Journal of Economic and Social Geography. Rotterdam, The Netherlands. (TESG)
Tissue Antigens. Munksgaard. Copenhagen.
Tools and Tillage. G.E.C. Gad. Copenhagen.
La Torre. Revista General de la Univ. de Puerto Rico. Río Piedras, P.R. (UPR/LT)
Trans-action. Social Science and Modern Society. Rutgers Univ. New Brunswick, N.J. (RU/T)
Transactions of the Royal Society of Tropical Medicine and Hygiene. London. (RSTMH/T)
Tribus. Veröfferntlichungen des Linden-Museums. Museum für Länder- und Völkerkunde. Stuttgart, FRG. (MLV/T)
El Trimestre Económico. Fondo de Cultura Económica. México. (FCE/TE)
Tropical and Geographical Medicine. Foundation Documenta de Medicina Geographica et Tropica. Haarlem, The Netherlands. (TGM)
Unesco Bulletin for Libraries. United Nations Education, Scientific and Cultural Organization. Paris. (UNESCO/BL)
UNESCO en Chile. Boletín de la Comisión Nacional. Santiago.
Uninorte. Univ. del Norte. Barranquilla, Colo.
Universidad. Univ. de Antioquia. Medellín, Colo. (UA/U)
La Universidad. Univ. de El Salvador. San Salvador. (UES/U)
Universidad de La Habana. La Habana. (UH/U)

Universidad de San Carlos de Guatemala. Guatemala. (USC/U)

Universidades. Unión de Universidades de América Latina. México.

Universitas. Ciencias jurídicas y socioeconómicas. Pontificia Univ. Javeriana, Facultad de Derecho y Ciencias Socioeconómicas. Bogotá. (PUJ/U)

Subject Index

Bibliography and General Works (1-151)
Anthropology (500-2264)
Economics (4000-4990)
Education (6000-6381)
Geography (6500-7351)
Government and Politics (8000-8699)
International Relations (8700-8942)
Sociology (9600-10,069)

Abigeato, 1524
Acagchemem Indians, 1922
Acción Democrática, Venezuela, 8526
Aché Indians, 1370
Adaptation, *Cardiopulmonary,* 1161. *Heat,* 1161. *Humans,* 1161. *Language,* 1838
Adoption. See Children and Family Relationships.
Afroamerican Studies, 503, 508, 854, 1215, 1230, 1254, 1257-8, 1265, 1276, 1280-1, 1302, 1555, 2049, 9761, 9788, 9791, 9798
Agrarian Reform, *General,* 4024, 4062, 4088-9, 4192, 4552, 6502, 6517, 6520, 6545, 6557, 8004-5, 8023, 9686. *Argentina,* 8656a. *Bolivia,* 1442, 1478, 1480, 1488-9, 4584-5, 4587, 4589, 6755, 6816, 8005, 8410, 9856, 9857. *Brazil,* 4821, 7104, 7119, 8577. *Chile,* 1451, 1459, 4596, 4601, 4615, 4621, 4626, 4634, 6838, 6852, 6861, 6868, 6871, 8429, 8446-7, 8464, 8479, 8496, 9871. *Colombia,* 4514, 6881-3, 6904, 6127, 8005, 8313, 9847. *Cuba,* 8005. *Ecuador,* 6924, 6934. *El Salvador,* 8187. *Essequibo Islands,* 6941. *Guatemala,* 6630-1, 8005, 8188. *Honduras,* 4387. *Martinique,* 1227. *Mexico,* 1149, 1165, 4267, 4299, 6149, 6695, 6712, 8162, 8164, 8167, 9731, 9744. *Peru,* 1492-3, 4644, 4653, 4655, 4667, 6968, 8005, 8373. *St. Vincent,* 1233. *Venezuela,* 4565, 4573, 6755
Agriculture, *General,* 4044, 4162, 6516, 6518, 6524, 6528, 9687. *Argentina,* 889, 4688, 4702, 4719, 4726-9, 4733, 4735, 4738, 4753, 4755, 4757-9, 6760, 6763-4, 6774-5, 6796, 6812-3, 8650, 8666. *Bolivia,* 4581, 4593, 6817, 6820, 6822, 6829, 6833. *Brazil,* 4773, 4777, 4794, 4799, 4801, 4803, 4812-3, 4819, 4821, 4827, 4836, 4849, 4851, 4867, 4873, 4882, 4897, 4902-3, 4906, 4908, 4912, 4915-6, 4925, 4929, 4942, 4944, 4961-2, 4966, 4970, 7045-6, 7055-6, 7058-9, 7063, 7074-5, 7085, 7090-1, 7132, 7135, 7138-9, 7157, 7159, 7161, 7164, 7172, 7174, 7183, 7185, 7188, 7190, 7192, 7194, 7199-200. *Cacao,* 7183, 7190. *Cañihua,* 1474, 6822. *Caribbean,* 6563. *Cattle,* 4680, 4733, 4801, 4803, 4897, 6775, 7192, 8611a. *Central America,* 4395. *Chile,* 4609. *Coffee,* 4482, 4812, 4825, 4858, 4889, 6599, 6679, 6696, 7138, 7157. *Colombia,* 4468-9, 4482, 4493, 4495, 4510, 6889, 6892, 6895, 6901-2, 8300a, 9828. *Costa Rica,* 1112, 4373, 6614. *Cotton,* 6717, 6889, 7056. *Cuba,* 6580, 6583, 8240. *Diary,* 1149, 4906. *Dominican Republic,* 6588. *Ecuador,* 973. *El Salvador,* 4389, 6622. *Fertilizers,* 4819, 7136. *Folklore,* 1419. *Guatemala,* 1128, 4400, 4405, 6630-1, 8188. *Guyana,* 1241, 6947. *Haiti,* 9783. *Hispaniola,* 833. *Honduras,* 4373, 6633. *Incas,* 1476. *Indigenous Communal,* 1141, 1149, 1165. *Irrigation,* 645, 665, 889, 973, 1000, 1149, 4190, 4277, 6666, 6674, 6680, 6695. *Jamaica,* 4341, 6598-9. *Maize,* 618, 6613. *Mesoamerica,* 618, 664. *Mexico,* 1115, 1149, 4256, 4264, 4270, 4274-5, 4290, 4298, 4308, 4310, 4312, 6666, 6668, 6674, 6679, 6695, 6706, 6709, 6713-5, 6719, 8134. *Nicaragua,* 6641. *Panama,* 4377, 4393. *Peru,* 1435, 1456, 1458, 1517, 4648, 6961, 6996. *Pimento,* 6598. *Poultry,* 6769. *Precolumbian,* 676, 678, 773, 889, 942, 973, 976, 994a, 1006-6b, 1011, 1017a, 1036, 1044, 1047-8. *Productivity,* 6502. *Quinua,* 6822: *Rice,* 4908. *Rural Development,* 6031-4. *Sesame,* 7055. *Sisal,* 7159. *Soils,* 6550, 6554, 6736, 6891, 6902, 7174. *Sugar,* 4547, 4648, 4655, 4702, 4983, 6580,

6713, 7070. *Surinam,* 1286, 1304. *Tropical,* 4146, 4191. *Uruguay,* 4680, 7016, 8611a. *Venezuela,* 1065a, 4547, 4550, 4553, 4564, 4573, 6194, 7021, 7025, 7027. *Wheat,* 1149, 4836, 7016
Agua Hedionda Site, 874
Aguaruna Indians, 1535
Aguas Verdes Site, 835, 839
Aid. *See* Economic Assistance.
Alamito Cultures, 885
Alcohol and Alcoholism, 1502, 9747, 9751
Alianza Nacional Popular, *Colombia,* 8332, 8337, 8353, 8358
Alianza Popular Revolucionaria Americana, Peru, 8374
Allende, Salvador. *See* Chile and Allende.
Alliance for Progress, 4058, 4142, 4540, 8749a, 8754, 8794
Alloalbuminemia, 2067, 2118
Almeyda Arroyo, Elías, 6866
Alto Araguaia Project, 923b
Alto Tocantins Project, 923c
Aluminum Industry, 4010
Amahuaca Indians, 6970
Amahuaca Language. *See* Panoan Languages.
Amazon River Basin, 6726
Amazonia, Bolivia, 6818
Amazônia, Brazil, 523, 911, 915, 924-5, 1432, 4904, 4969, 6749, 7060-1, 7079, 7099, 7105, 7123, 7132, 7137, 7141, 7157-8, 8564
Amazonia, Colombia, 6917
Amerindians, 1238, 1246-7, 1290, 1357, 9688
Amuesha Indians, 1537
Ancash, Peru, 1882, 1947
Ancón, Peru, 1033a
Andean Language, 1816
Andean Pact Nations, 4015-6, 4046, 4243, 4248, 4586, 4611, 4642, 8352
Andes, 937
Andido People, 2014
Anhaptoglobinemia, 2068
Anthropometric Studies, 1155, 2079-81, 2096, 2123-4, 2138, 2146, 2150, 2165
Antibodies, 2097-8, 2113
Antigua, British West Indies, 841
Antioquia, Colombia, 8343
Antiquities Traffic. *See* Illegal Antiquities Traffic.
Apalaí Language. *See* Carib Languages.
Apurlec Site, 1049a
Aramburu, Pedro Eugenio, 8648, 8696
Araucanian Indians, 946, 1490, 1532
Arawak Indians, 841-1a, 1396
Arawakan Languages, 1805, 1816, 1917, 1927, 1929, 1936, 1950, 1960
Architecture, *Argentina,* 885. *Brazil,*

6218. *Chile,* 948c. *Mesoamerica,* 602, 623-4, 634, 651, 653, 659, 669, 673, 715, 726, 754, 780. *Peru,* 1012, 1017b, 1019-9a, 1028, 1031c, 1048a-8b, 1049a
Argentina and Australia, 8905
Argentina and Brazil, 8919
Argentina and Chile, 8906, 8914-5, 8920, 8938
Argentina and Czechoslovakia, 8910
Argentina and Germany, 8878a
Argentina and International Relations, 8008
Argentina and Latin America, 8634
Argentina and the European Economic Community, 8902
Argentina and the Federal Republic of Germany, 8883a
Argentina and the UK, 8903, 8907
Argentina and the UN, 8933
Argentina and the US, 8634, 8878
Argentina and World War II, 8903
Arhuaco Indians, 1932
Arhuaco (Ica) Language. *See* Chibchan Languages.
Arid Zones. *See* Ecology.
Aripaktsa Language. *See* Rikbaktsa Language.
Armed Forces, *General,* 8025, 8031, 8052, 8063, 8068, 8071, 8077, 8090-1, 8094, 8646, 8705, 8724, 8746, 8803, 8853. *Argentina,* 8025, 8031, 8396, 8630, 8642, 8653a, 8659, 8674c, 8689. *Arms and Security,* 8096, 8121-2. *Aztecs,* 514. *Barbados,* 1240. *Bolivia,* 8025, 8031, 8392, 8396-96a, 8414. *Brazil,* 6252, 7137, 8017, 8025, 8031, 8542, 8551b, 8559, 8561b, 8565a, 8570, 8575-6, 8689. *Chavante,* 1340. *Chile,* 8423, 8428, 8463, 8500, 8506. *Colombia,* 8333. *Dominican Republic,* 8255. *Ecuador,* 8898. *Expenditures,* 4022. *Guahibos,* 1369. *Incas,* 514. *Mexico,* 8174. *Mochica,* 999. *Peru,* 4638, 8025, 8031, 8369, 8373, 8378-9, 8383, 8392. *Politics,* 8025, 8031, 8094, 8102, 8443, 8630, 8653a, 8659, 8687. *Venezuela,* 8519, 8520
Arms. *See* Armed Forces.
Art, *Afroamerican,* 1283. *Colombia,* 957. *Baja California,* 769. *Cliff Paintings,* 684. *Ecuador,* 983. *Geoglyphs,* 1025. *Mayas,* 673. *Mesoamerica,* 761. *Mochica,* 992a. *Painters/Argentina,* 891. *Painters/Aztec,* 1831. *Painters/Tlaxcala,* 748. *Panama,* 827. *Peru,* 987-997. *Petroglyphs,* 862, 883a, 922a-2c, 1008b, 1025, 1063, 1271. *Pictographs,* 862, 888, 896, 901, 928a, 935a, 941a, 1025, 1057, 1063, 1271.

Precolumbian, 827. *Puna,* 862. *South America,* 851
Art and Artifacts. This section has been discontinued. Items formerly included under this heading now appear in their proper alphabetical sequence.
Artifacts, *General,* 721, *Basalt,* 1058. *Lithic,* 747, 770, 772, 839, 862a, 864, 873, 890, 892, 901, 937, 945c-5d, 948b, 948d, 950, 955, 978c, 1008b, 1021, 1025, 1055-6. *Mesoamerica,* 717, 727, 733, 752, 754, 767, 791, 1146. *Zoomorphic,* 920
Asociación Latinoamericana de Ex-Alumnos de la Academia de Derecho Internacional de La Haya, 8727
Aspero Site, 1031d
Asto Sites, 1023
Atacama, *Puna,* 875
Atacama Desert, 6722
Atasta, Mexico, 689
Ataura, Paeru, 1027
Atchalán, Guatemala, 1168
Atlases. *See* Maps.
Atlihuetzían, Mexico, 748
Attitudinal Surveys, 8521a
Auca Indians, 1406
Auca Language. *See* Zaparoan Languages.
Automobile Industry, 4154, 4764, 6501
Axé Language. *See* Guayakí Language.
Ayahuasca. *See* Hallucinogens.
Ayampitín Complex, 875a
Aymara Languages, 1816, 1904
Ayoré Indians, 2072
Ayoré Language, 1818
Aypate Site, 1037
Ayutla Language. *See* Otomanguean Languages.
Bacairi Indians, 1957
Bacairi Language. *See* Carib Languages.
Baeza de los Quijos, Ecuador, 978a
Balance of Payments, 4091, 4176, 4347, 4470, 4694, 4721, 4818
Banco Nacional de Desenvolvimento Económico, Brazil, 8584
Banking and Commerce, *General,* 4027, 4056, 4135, 4152, 4183, 4218, *Argentina,* 4683, 4693, 4695. *Bolivia,* 4588. *Chile,* 4600, 4617, 4624. *Colombia,* 4478, 4486, 4502, 4507. *Brazil,* 4770, 4891, 4933, 4937, 4940, 4964, 4987. *Panama,* 4375. *Mexico,* 4288. *Venezuela,* 4534, 4554, 4563, 4567-8
Banzer, Hugo, 8394, 8402, 8408
Barasano (Southern) Indians, 1932
Barasano (Southern) Language. *See* Tucanoan Languages.
Barros Sierra, Javier, 8152
Basket Weaving, *Mesoamerica,* 714, *Paraguay,* 1345

Bata, Jan A., 8762
Baure. *See* Arawakan Languages.
Bayano Cuna Language, 1804, 1806
Beagle Channel, 8920, 8938
Becan, Mexico, 688
Behavioral Studies, 8521-21a
Béjar, Héctor, 8387
Belize River Valley, 1210
Belo Horizonte, Brazil, 8587a
Birth Control. *See* Family Planning.
Black Power, 1211, 1247, 1302
Bocono, Venezuela, 1064c
Bocotá Language, 1804, 1862
Boleadora, 847
Bolivia and the UN, 8890
Bonampak, Mexico, 621, 1163
Bororo Indians, 1834
Bororo Language, 1834
Boscana, Gerónimo, 1922
Bosch, Juan, 8255
Boundary Disputes, *Argentina/Chile,* 8886, 8906, 8914-5. *Bolivia/Paraguay,* 8888. *Colombia/US,* 8847. *Colombia/Venezuela,* 8865, 8895, 8941. *El Salvador/Honduras,* 8819, 8827, 8836
Brachmesophalangia, 2070
Brain Drain, *Brazil,* 8541. *Paraguay,* 9912. *Peru,* 6172
Brazil and International Relations, 8008
Brazil and the US, 8870, 8896, 8900, 8908, 8930-1, 8934, 8937
Bribri Language, 1801
Bribris, 1203
Brunka Language, 1801
Budget, *Brazil,* 4842-3, *Colombia,* 4497. *Guyana,* 4528
Caballo Muerto Complex, 1031e
Cabécar Indians, 1159
Cabecar Language, 1801
Cacao-Chiriquí Site, 824
Caciques, 8169
Cacua Indians, 1932
Caingua Indians, 1346
Cajamarquilla Site, 995, 1046
Calendrics, 794, 796, 798, 805-7, 809
Caleta Huelen-42 Site, 942b
Cali, Colombia, 8315
Câmara, Helder, 8000
Camelot, Project, 8456
Campa Indians, 1321, 1327, 1329, 1335, 1411-2, 1432
Campoma Site, 1064a
Cámpora, Héctor, 8677
Canada in Latin America, 8759
Canals, *Panama,* 6646, 8820-3, 8829, 8832, 8834-5, 8837
Cancha-Cancha Site, 1042
Cannabis, 1531
Canoero Indians, 883
Canoinhas Site, 919

SUBJECT INDEX

Caño Caroni Site, 1065c
Caño Grande Phase, 1062.
Capanahua Language. See Panoan Languages.
Cape Horn Sites, 945e
Capital Markets, 4013, 4016, 4039, 4050, 4066, 4114, 4128, 4244, 4646, 4840-1, 4875, 4900, 4988
Carache, Venezuela, 1064b
Carajá Indians, 1336
Carapana Indians, 1932
Carapana Language. See Tucanoan Languages.
Cárdenas, Lázaro, 8140, 8170, 8173
Carib Blacks, 1260, 1291
Carib Indians, 828, 1270, 1396, 2216
Carib Languages, 1816, 1861, 1936, 1957-8
The Caribbean and Canada, 4332
The Caribbean and the US, 8855
The Caribbean and the USSR, 8862
Caribbean Federation, 8292
Caribbean Free Trade Area, 4330-1
Cariña Indians, 2165
Carnivals, 1114
Cartagena, Acuerdo de, 8871
Carvings, *Mesoamerica*, 693-4, 710, 727, 753
Casas Grandes, Mexico, 613
Cashibo Language. See Panoan Language.
Cashinahua Indians, 2231
Cashinahua Language. See Panoan Languages.
Castro, Fidel, 8213-7, 8229, 8439a, 8841, 8912
Catholic Church, *General*, 8036, 8120, 9673. *Argentina*, 8016, 9878. *Brazil*, 8016, 8544, 8553-53b, 8561, 8568-9, 8577, 8578a, 8586, 8599. *Chile*, 8464. *Colombia*, 8016, 8309, 8351, 8359. *Communications Media*, 8022. *Contraception*, 2020. *Cuba*, 8016. *Doctrine and Reform*, 8012, 8016, 8021, 8026, 8106, 8116, 8136, 8351, 9680. *Education*, 6053, 6101, 6154, 6204. *Guatemala*, 8191. *Labor*, 8043. *Mexico*, 9713. *Organization*, 8036. *Paraguay*, 8604. *Peru*, 1508, 8016. *Puerto Rico*, 9810. *Socialism*, 8021, 8026. *Venezuela* 8515b
Catío Language. See Chocó Languages.
Caverna de Huargo Site, 994
Cenotes, 762
Census, *Agricultural*, 1165, 6774, 6817, *Argentina*, 9887, 9894. *Brazil*, 4849, 7084. *Chile*, 4603, 6847. *Colombia*, 6874. *Census*, 4677. *Ecuador*, 6931. *El Salvador*, 9757. *Guatemala*, 9759. *Jamaica*, 6597. *Language*, 1953. *Mexico*, 9719. *Panama*, 4377, 6648, 9756,

9760. *University*, 6004, 6139. *Uruguay*, 4677. See also Demography.
Central American Common Market, 4003, 4378, 4381, 4383, 4386, 4392, 4396, 4398-9, 8804, 8183
Central Latino Americana de Trabajadores, 8051
Ceramics, *Argentina*, 890, 906b. *Colombia*, 958. *Ecuador*, 965, 978b, 978d-9. *Martinique*, 830a. *Mayas*, 606, 619, 632, 738, 741-2, 766, 776. *Mesoamerica*, 712, 736, 751, 754, 772, 786. *Mixtec*, 696. *Peru*, 987-9, 1001, 1004, 1007, 1013, 1042, 1050. *Tupiguarani*, 902. *Uruguay*, 1053-4. *Venezuela*, 1061 See also Pottery.
Cerrito Vizcaíno Site, 1059
Cerro El Toro Site, 849
The Chaco War, 8888, 8929
Chagas Foundation, Carlos, 6359
Chakillo Site, 1008a
Chalcatzingo, Mexico, 719
Chalchuapa, Mexico, 776
Chambers of Commerce, 4488, 4500, 4536
Chamula, Mexico, 1114, 1114a, 1200, 1202a
Chamula Indians. See Mayas.
Chanchán, Peru, 1000, 1017a-7b, 1031, 1031c
Chan Kom, Mexico, 1129, 1137
Charrúa Language, 1928
Chavante Indians, 1340-1
Chavin Culture, 1006a, 1011, 1013, 1022, 1026, 1027, 1043
El Chayal, Guatemala, 745, 777
Chenalhó, Mexico, 1114
Chenes Site, Mexico, 704, 739, 754
Cherán, Mexico, 1104
Chiaraqe, Peru, 1427
Chibcha Indians, 953
Chibchan Language, 1801, 1804, 1817, 1854-6, 1879-80, 1907, 1951
Chicanel, Mexico, 686
Chichén Itzá, Mexico, 762, 1959
Chicomoztoc, 734
Children, 9611, 9627, 9641, 9720, 9724, 9793, 9837-8, 9888
Chile and Allende, 8059, 8422-22b, 8443a, 8449-50, 8453-4, 8471, 8478, 8485, 8879-80, 8885, 8887, 8891a, 8912, 8926
Chile and Cuba, 8940
Chile and Czechoslovakia, 8891a
Chile and the UK, 8887
Chile and the US, 8427, 8457, 8498, 8879-80, 8885, 8892, 8913, 8925-6, 8935
Chiloé, Chile, 936
Chimu Indians, 1017, 1017b

Chinantecan Languages, 1847
Chinchero Site, 985, 1042
Chinchiloma Site, 980
Chinchín. See Chinchiloma.
Chipaya Language, 1823
Chiquitano Indians, 1387
Chivateros Site, 1008b, 1039
Chocó Indians, 1424
Chocó Language, 1804, 1811, 1856, 1926
Chol Language. See Mayan Languages.
Cholula, Mexico, 750-1, 765, 2121
Chomsky, Noam, 1800, 1822, 1835, 1887
Chon Language, 1943
Chontal Indians, 1194
Chontal Language. See Mayan Languages.
Chorrera Culture, 969-9a
Chorti Language. See Mayan Languages.
Christian Democratic Parties, 4625, 8014, 8150, 8515, 8519a, 8611
Chuapaychu Indians, 1030
Churajón Culture, 1026b
Class Structure, *General,* 1176, 8019, 8038, 8052, 8056, 8085, 8111, 8123, 8779, 9622, 9626, 9629, 9634, 9639, 9681. *Argentina,* 4756, 8653, 8666, 8681, 9896, 9902. *Armed Forces,* 9626. *Aztecs,* 814. *Bolivia,* 1440-1, 1481, 1486, 1515. *Brazil,* 6167, 7176. *Caribbean,* 4361, 8202. *Central America,* 9775. *Chile,* 4614, 8425, 8459, 9865, 9869, 9874-5. *Colombia,* 1465, 1484, 1552, 4477, 8314, 8316, 9843. *Costa Rica,* 1159, 8185. *Cuba,* 8248, 9799. *Dominican Republic,* 4368, 9778. *Ecuador,* 1436-7, 1520. *Honduras,* 6634, 9767. *Jamaica,* 1264, 1296, 1302. *Martinique,* 1285. *Mayas,* 1103, 1134, 1151, 1154, 1158, 1168, 1172-3, 1182, 1186-7, 1189, 4265, 6160, 9708, 9715, 9717, 9723, 9738. *Nengre,* 1378. *Peru,* 1457, 1494, 1524-5, 1536, 1539. *Peru,* 6167, 9852, 9854. *Puerto Rico,* 9803. *St. Vincent,* 1234. *Trinidad and Tobago,* 8283. *Urban,* 1499. *Uruguay,* 8617. *Venezuela,* 9821, 9824
Climate. See Ecology.
Coatzospan Language. See Mixtec Language.
Coca Leaf, 1482, 1506, 2201, 2235, 2242
Cocama Language. See Tupí-Guaraní Languages.
Cochabamba, Bolivia, 1481
Coconuco, Colombia, 1445
Codex Dresden, 795
Codex Laud, 794
Codices, *Aztec,* 1831. *Maya,* 794-5, 800, 802, 1844
Cofradía, 1131
Cogui Indians, 1932
Colombia and the US, 8847, 8942

Colombia and Venezuela, 8909
Colorado Language. See Chibchan Languages.
Communications, *General,* 6248, 8075, 9656, 9691, 9697. *Argentina,* 9911. *Chile,* 8464. *Colombia,* 6909. *Mexico,* 8148, 8177. *Peru,* 6986, 8375, 9855. *Sociology,* 9619, 9655, 9664, 9667, 9691. *Surinam,* 1303.
Communism, 8341, 8707, 8743
Communist Party, *General,* 8028, 8059, 8080, 8495. *Argentina,* 8627a, 8636a, 8638, 8655, 8660b-61, 8662, 8664, 8670-70a. *Chile,* 8448, 8470, 8508. *Colombia,* 8299, 8302. *Dominican Republic,* 8250. *Peru,* 8364, 8385. *Uruguay,* 8605, 8624. *Venezuela,* 8517, 8526, 8534, 8537
Community Development, 8510, 8516, 8524a, 8536-7, 9657
Compadrazgo, 1113, 1116, 1118, 1123-4, 1145, 1188. See also Kinship.
Compañía Nacional de Subsistencias Populares, Mexico, 8134
Congress. See Parliaments and Congresses.
Conscientization, 9620
Consejo Episcopal Latinoamericano, 8037
Constitutional History and Constitutionalism, *Argentina,* 8686. *Brazil,* 6263, 8572a, 8590. *Mexico,* 8175. *Uruguay,* 8613
Construction Industry, 4278
Contacts, *Prehispanic,* 856
Continental Drift, 6721, 6846
Contraceptives. See Family Planning and Catholic Church.
Copala, Mexico, 1145
Copala Trique Language. See Otomanguean Languages.
Copan, Honduras, 669
COPEI, Venezuela, 8526
Copper Industry, 4609, 4627, 4632, 8455, 8488
Cora Indians, 1108
Cornell-Peru Project, 1463, 1491, 1540-1
Coroico, Bolivia, 1426, 1504
Corozal Project, Belize, 632, 723-4
Corporatism/Corporativism. See Dictatorships.
Cosanga Phase, 978c
Cosmology, 663, 1411, 1495
Costumes, *Mesoamerica,* 695
Coups d'etat, *General,* 4057, 8052, 8077, 8088, 8108. *Brazil,* 8544a. *Chile,* 8732, 8912, 8431, 8433-5, 8438, 8441, 8458-9, 8469, 8474, 8491, 8493, 8501-3, 8506. *Ecuador,* 8361. *Panama,* 8199. *Peru,* 8367, 8369. *Uruguay,* 8622, 8732
Coxcatlan Project, 780

Coya Indians, 1431
Cozumel, Isla, 771
Credit. See Fiscal Policy.
Creole Culture, 1216
Creole Languages, 1838
Crime and Delinquency, 1214, 1524, 9755, 9779, 9850, 9888
Cross Cultural Studies, 1137, 9781
Cuba and the US, 8225, 8236-7, 8839, 8841, 8843, 8845, 8849, 8858-9, 8861, 8864
Cuba and the USSR, 8231, 8848, 8862
Cuban Missile Crisis, 8843, 8845, 8849, 8856
The Cuban Revolution, 8035, 8207-9, 8215, 8219-20, 8229, 8233, 8235, 8234, 8248, 8940
Cubeo Indians, 1377, 1932
Cueva 3 de Los Toldos Site, 868
Cuiba Indians, 1932, 1425
Cuiba/Cuiva Language. See Guajiban Languages.
Cuillurguna (Quichua Indians), 1911
Cults, various. See Religion.
Cultural Development and Evolution, 503, 522, 526, 993, 1P62a-2b, 1102, 1121, 1142, 1301, 6053, 6100, 6149-51, 6153, 6163, 6183, 6187, 6198, 6228, 6249, 6265, 6354, 6693, 6845, 8163, 8792
Cuna Indians, 1160, 1191, 1197, 2224
Cura Indians. See Bacairi Indians.
Curanderos, 1477, 2219
Curaray Indians, 978e-9
Cusichaca, Peru, 1019-9a
Cuyamel, Honduras, 730
Czechoslovakia in Latin America, 8760-3
Darien Gap. See Pan-American Highway.
Darien Indians, 6644
Data Banks, 9624
Decapitation, *Mesoamerica,* 662, *Peru,* 1032
Demography, *General,* 505, 2038, O693. *Agricultural,* 6764. *Andean,* 1437, 6729, 6746. *Argentina,* 885, 887, 2025, 2027, 6762, 6772, 6779, 6790, 6801, 9880. *Bolivia,* 1538, 6826-9. *Brazil,* 906, 1342-3, 1375, W032, 2042, 2053, 2061, 4822, 7083-4, 7098, 7110, 7127, 7133, 7144, 7151-2, 8547, 8574-4a. *Census,* 1816, 2029, 6597, 6617, 6623, 6648. *Colombia,* 4472, 4483, 6137, 6874, 6877, 6886, 68O5, 6907-8, 9847. *Costa Rica,* 1159, 6616-7. *Cuba,* 2035, 9795. *Disease Patterns,* 2018, 2245. *Dominican Republic,* 1243, 6590. *Ecuador,* 4522, 6931. *El Salvador,* 6620, 6623, 9768. *Guahibos,* 1368. *Guatemala,* 2029. *Haiti,* 1288a. *Honduras,* 2025, 6635. *Human Adaptation,* 2192-4, 2198-2200, 2203-8, 2213-4, 6041. *Jamaica,* 2031. *Mayas,* 763. *Mexico,* 2036, 2048, 2060, 6656, 6662, 8135. *Nahuas,* 1103. *Occupational Mobility,* 8318, 9613, 9699, 9728. *Panama,* 9763, 9777. *Paraguay,* 6950, 6959. *Peru,* 1450, 1518, 1546, 6979, 6990* *Population Studies* 4029, 4522, 6503, 6505-6, 6510-2, 6519, 6524, 6537, 6540, 6542, 6555, 6616, 6632, 6635, 6667, 6702, 6752, 6772, 6790, 6801, 6827, 6827, 6834, 6839, 6875, 6907-8, 6979, 7030-1, 7041, 9659, 9675-6, 9683, 9702, 9763, 9773, 9777, 9797, 9801, 9802, 9815-6, 9823. *Precolumbian,* 505, 631, 697, 699, 881, 902, 1006b, 1031b, 2017. *Rural-Urban Mobility,* 1116, 1176, 1178, 1470, 2028, 2044, 4008, 4192, 4511, 8516, 9732, 9743. *St. Vincent,* 1233. *Trinidad and Tobago,* 1293. *Uruguay,* 4678, 7020. *Venezuela,* 1461, 2021, 2028, 2082, 7022-3, 9826
Dependence and Dependency, 1279, 4033, 4079, 4083, 4089, 4X31, 4139, 4143, 4155-6, 4166, 4213, 4343, 4363, 4394, 4498, 4613, 4744, 4751, 8003, 8007, 8020, 8048, 8067, 8069, 8074, 8092, 8101, 8103, 8183, 8185, 8202, 8287, 8301, 8310, 8335, 8339, 8344, 8348, 8484, 8639, 8697, 8716, 8719, 8726, 8729-30, 8740, 8744, 8872, 8900, 8917, 9605, 9617, 9660, 9676, 9767, 9774
Dermatoglyphic Patterns, 2069, 2088, 2110, 2112, 2114, 2116, 2121-2
Desano Indians, 1932
Desert Regions. See Arid Zones.
Devaluation, 4641
Diaguita Culture, 926, 941
Dictatorships, 8086, 8200, 8251, 8522, 8556a, 8604f, 8608
Dictionary, *Biographic,* 6651, *Geographical,* 6568, 6651, 6884, 7032. *Historical,* 6651. See also Language.
Dieties, *Cayman,* 1022. *Chac,* 622. *Ehecatl,* 790. *Ix Chel,* 708. *Soq'a Machu,* 1472. *Surinam,* 1306-7. *Tezcatlipoca,* 765. *Tlaloc,* 622, 759
Disarmament, 8770, 8877, 8924
Disease, *General,* 2217, 2243, 2262-3. *Boraceia Virus,* 2237. *Carrion,* 2002. *Chagas,* 2250. *Coronary,* 2225. *Dengue Fever,* 2233, 2240. *Encephalitis,* 2239. *Harris' Lines,* 2001. *Hemorrhagic Exanthem,* 2244, 2251. *Hepatitis,* 2252-3, 2263-4. *Hookworm,* 2003. *Hydatid,* 2257. *Malaria,* 2209. *Mental Health,* 2232, 9618, 9678, 9692, 9888, 9899. *Onchoceriasis,* 2241. *Osteophytosis,*

2004-5. *Polio,* 2W49. *Polyradiculoneuropathy,* 2238. *Smallpox,* 2215. *Streptococcal,* 2258. *Treatment,* 2248, 2261. *Tuberculosis,* 2000. *Umbilical Tetanus,* 2111. *Venereal,* 2234
Divorce. *See* Family Relationships.
Doctrine of National Interest, 8741
Doctrine of Non-alignment, 8876
Doctrine of Non-Intervention. *See* International Law.
The Dominican Republic and the US, 8838, 8848, 8850, 8861
El Dorado, 951, 954, 961
Dreams, *Ladino,* 1181
Dulles, John F., 8785
Dzibilchaltun, Mexico, 643, 672, 685
Dzibilnohac, Mexico, 704, 754
Easter Island, Chile. *See* Rape Nui.
Eastern Tucanoan Language. *See* Tucanoan Languages.
Echeverría, Luis, 8137-8, 8806-7, 8811, 8817c
Ecology, *Amazonia,* 6737. *Antarctic,* 6757. *Argentina,* 885-5a, 887. *Arid Zones,* 6969. *Brazil,* 6737, 7100, 7187. *Chile.* 938b, 942a, 947, 948c, 6849. *Climate,* 871a, 4867, 6581, 6586, 6605, 6766, 6898, 6920, 7033-4, 7100, 7124, 7126, 7160. *Colombia,* 6897, 6903, 6917. *Cultural,* 1446. *Development,* 6513, 6515, 6528-9. *Ecosystems,* 889a, 6745. *Ecuador,* 982a, 6920. *Fish and Wildlife,* 6974. *Forests,* 4658, 6761, 6811, 6872, 7078, 7123, 7125, 7190. *Geoecology,* 943, 1329. *Guyana,* 1247* *Human,* 1003, 1161. *Jamaica,* 1229. *Malvinas,* 6808. *Mexico,* 614, 641, 678, 1103, 1147, 6682, 6701. *Microenvironment,* 1003. *Nicaragua* 6642. *Panama,* 6650. *Paraguay,* 6952. *Peru,* 998, 1006a, 1036. *Pollution,* 6501, 6508-9, 6551, 6554, 6784, 7173. *Puerto Rico,* 6605. *Sabana,* 7033, 7037. *Swidden Cultivation,* 1159. *Tropical,* 6559, 6745, 7186. *Venezuela,* 7033-4. *Zoos,* 6536.
Econometric Model, 4261, 4268, 4282, 4289, 4305, 4598, 4612-3, 4692, 4819, 4867, 4892, 4898, 4934, 4951, 4989
Economic Assistance, 4346, 4484, 4501, 4584, 4659, 8074, 8127, 8725, 8749a, 8772, 8794
Economic Development, *General,* 4012, 4019, 4025, 4031, 4036, 4048-9, 4053, 4055, 4072, 4082, 4084, 4086-7, 4093, 4095-6, 4098, 4101, 4112-3, 4121, 4123-4, 4130, 4133, 4141, 4159, 4162, 4162, 4166, 4170-1, 4174-5, 4184, 4186, 4188, 4203, 4198, 4203, 4208-10, 4214, 4216, 4223, 4229, 4249, 4251, 4401, 4479, 6513, 6534, 6539, 6542-3, 6548-9, 6552, 8020, 8023, 8028, 8052, 8069, 8092, 8114, 8117-8, 8126, 8131, 8700, 8709, 8715, 8722, 8749, 8904, 9602, 9634, 9685, 9689. *Argentina,* 4686, 4689, 4691, 4696, 4707, 4714, 4716, 4730, 4740, 4746, 4749, 4754, 5788, 6794, 8643a. *Armed Forces,* 4638, 4649, 8105. *Belize,* 1207. *Bolivia,* 4591-2, 8409. *Brazil,* 4763, 4766-8, 4774-5, 4784-6, 4788, 4790, 4796, 4809, 4813-4, 4828-30, 4838, 4850, 4854-6, 4859-60, 4863, 4872, 4876, 4879, 4884-6, 4889-90, 4893, 4895, 4899-900, 4905-6, 4909-10, 4918, 4920-¿, 4928, 4930, 4931, 4933, 4941, 4943, 4945, 4945, 4947, 4952, 4955, 4958, 4966, 4968, 4971, 4973, 4980, 4982, 4984, 4990, 6284, 6294, 6378, 7044, 7051, 7054, 7064, 7066, 7072, 7076, 7106, 7132, 7140, 7145-6, 7169-70, 7179-81, 7199, 8543a, 8547, 8548a, 8551c-51d, 8555, 8572, 8573, 8583, 8585, 8588, 8593, 8593, 85971, 8923. *Caribbean,* 4326, 4336. *Chile,* 4595, 4602, 4612-4, 6870, 8432, 8452, 8478-9, 8484, 8493b, 9867-8. *Colombia,* 4466-7, 4475, 4505, 4508-9, 4512, 4513, 6873, 6877, 6894, 6899, 6914, 8300. *Costa Rica,* 4369, 4371, 4382. *Cuba,* 6582, 6584, 8227, 8239. *Dominican Republic,* 4327-9, 4355. *French Guiana,* 6942. *Guatemala,* 6628. *Guyana,* 1241, 1247, 1250, 4525-6, 6287, 8290-1. *Honduras,* 6634. *Jamaica,* 4342. *Mexico,* 2039, 4257, 4272, 4295, 4297, 4313, 4315-6, 6656-7, 6661, 6690, 6695, 6699, 8817, 9716, 9718, 9729. *Middle America,* 1101. *Panama,* 4393. *Paraguay,* 4635, 6960. *Peru,* 4645, 4652, 4656, 8377, 8381, 8386, 9849. *Poverty,* 4085. *Structural Problems,* 4002-3, 4025, 4032, 4076, 4259, 4548. *Surinam,* 1263, 1269, 1478, 1298. *Trinidad and Tobago,* 8283. *Uruguay,* 8620. *Venezuela,* 4545, 4548-9, 4562, 4566, 4570, 4578, 4580, 7P39, 8527, 8918, 9826
Economic Integration, 4030, 4036, 4036, 4048, 4054, 4064, 4087, 4094, 4099, 4100, 4112, 4116, 4118-20, 4129, 4134, 4177, 4179, 4200-1, 4207, 4228, 4234, 4236, 4242, 4247, 4287, 4330-1, 4356, 4358, 4364, 4370, 4374, 4379, 4381, 4383, 4386, 4388, 4392, 4396, 4398, 4402-3, 4518, 4539, 4672, 8708-9, 8825, 8939
Ecosystems. *See* Ecology.
Education and Developing Countries, 6025-8, 6042, 6047-8, 6050-2, 6064,

6067, 6987, 8127, 8233, 8666, 9846, 9865
Education and Politics, 6001-1
Education and Social Change, 1128, 6282, 6294, 6312-3, 6317, 6335-6, 6353, 6356
Education and Technology, 6005-7, 6009, 6312-3
Education Programs, 6226, 6227-9, 6236, 6256, 6258, 6259, 6274, 6285, 6311, 6321, 6324, 6327, 6357, 6363, 6373
Education Systems, 6008-9a, 6245, 6288-9, 6300, 6303
Educators and Students, 6208, 6260, 6270, 6284, 6296, 6298, 6301, 6305, 6326, 6328, 6356
Ejidos, 4274-5, 4283, 6668, 6714, 9744
El Encanto Site, 978
El Inga Site, 980, 1021
Elections and Electoral Traditions, 8075, 8097, 8124, 8160, 8186, 8193, 8194, 8262, 8342, 8354, 8356, 8424, 8451, 8512, 8529, 8532, 8435, 8580a, 8595, 8606, 8619, 8625, 8631a, 8676, 9820
Emberá Indians, 1932
Employment. *See* Labor.
Energy Sources, *General*, 4187, 8133. *Argentina*, 4706. *Brazil*, 4810, 4907. *Jamaica*, 4348. *Mexico*, 4281, 4296, 6661, 6666. *Nuclear*, 6522, 8778. *Peru*, 6988. *Venezuela*, 4538
Entrepreneurship, *Colombia*, 9841, *Mexico*, 1178
Esmeraldas, Ecuador, 964
Estancia La Moderna Site, 886
Ethnic Studies, 1236, 1285
Ethnography, 666, 915, 1001, 1110, 1136, 1155, 1170-1, 1189, 1191, 1202a, 1230, 1236, 1259, 1428, 1435, 1479, 1498, 1536, 1555, 1821, 1930, 1932, 1942, 1955
Exiles, *Spanish Republicans*, 8809
Explorers and Exploration, 6825, 6921, 6966
Exports. *See* Imports.
Eyiguayegi Language. *See* Guaycurú Languages.
Falange Socialista Boliviana, 8399
Falkland Islands. *See* Malvinas, Islas.
Family Planning, 2020, 2023, 2026, 2033-4, 2037, 2041, 2045-6, 2048, 2050-1, 2054-5, 2057, 2063-4, 4081, 6851, 8024, 9603, 9607, 9613, 9632, 9677, 9680, 9682, 9721, 9764, 9784, 9833, 9835, 9851, 9883, 9904
Family Relationships, 1145, 1159, 1184, 1187, 1221, 1235, 1245, 1256, 1275, 1290, 1410, 1420-1, 1517, 2052, 2057, 2062, 2065, 9614, 9627, 9709, 9745, 9765, 9819, 9822, 9831, 9836, 9840, 9845, 9914
Fanon, Frantz, 1261
Fascism, 8101
Fase Guayaquil Site, 975
Favela. *See* Slums.
Federal Republic of Germany in Latin America, 8703a, 8757
Federalism, *Brazil*, 8549. *Central America*, 8825
Fertility. *See* Family Planning.
Film Industry, 6247
Fiscal Policy, *General*, 4009, 4065, 4135, 4197, *Argentina*, 4009, 4683, 4691, 4694, 4698-700, 4723
Fish and Wildlife. *See* Ecology and Fisheries and Fishing Industry.
Fisheries and Fishing Industry, *Brazil*, 4817, 7071, 7087. *Guatemala*, 6627. *Mexico*, 6678, 6681. *Nicaragua*, 6641. *Peru*, 6964, 6999. *Uruguay*, 7013
Flora and Fauna, *Antarctic*, 6757, 6791. *Argentina*, 871, 879, 886. *Bolivia*, 897. *Brazil*, 901, 1328, 2261, 7050, 7134, 7156, 7175, 7201. *Chile*, 6853. *Ecuador*, 981, 6919, 6921-2, 6935, 6937. *Galapagos*, 6940. *Guatemala*, 6626. *Jamaica*, 6593, 6598. *Marine*, 6785. *Mexico*, 2221, 6700. *Nicaragua*, 6642. *Peru*, 4658, 6963, 6997, 7004. *South America*, 6754. *Tropics*, 6743. *Uruguay*, 7015. *Venezuela*, 1330, 7035
Folklore, *Brazil*, 7060, 8581. *Chile*, 6865. *Chontal*, 1194. *Nahua*, 1858. *Paraguay*, 6953
Food Supply. *See* Nutrition.
The Ford Foundation, 8795
Foreign Aid. *See* Economic Assistance.
Foreign Investment, *General*, 4018, 4020, 4034-5, 4037-8, 4046, 4066-7, 4075, 4077, 4093, 4107, 4109, 4155, 4158, 4160, 4184, 4279, 8007. *Argentina*, 4704, 4715, 4717. *Bolivia*, 4590. *Brazil*, 4869, 4920. *Colombia*, 4457-8, 4517, 4519, 8353. *Mexico*, 4314, 4325. *Panama*, 4397, 4404. *Peru*, 8372
Forests. *See* Ecology.
Frente Popular Nacionalista, Bolivia, 8400
Freyre, Gilberto, 6246
Galapagos Island, 6925, 6928, 6939-40
Gamio, Manuel, 652, 1102
Ganja. *See* Hallucinogens.
García Aponte, Isaías, 8196
Ge Indians, 1396
Genetics, *Animal*, 2115. *Anthropological*, 2077. *Autosomal Polymorphic Markers*, 2087. *Blood Types*, 2066, 2068, 2072, 2075, 2078, 2084-5, 2090-2, 2094, 2103, 2106, 2119, 2129. *Dental*

Morphology, 2071, 2153. *Distance,* 2081, 2095, 2108-9. *Diversity,* 2105. *Group Specific Component,* 2076. *Human Serum Albumin,* 2131-2. *Morphological Characteristics,* 2081. *Plant* 2115. *Polydactyly,* 2074. *Variability,* 2079
Geoecology. *See* Ecology.
Geography, *Natural Resources,* 6525, 6660, 6787, 6819, 6862, 6910, 6985, 6991, 6993, 7116, 7143, 7158
Geology, *General,* 6750. *Andes,* 6727. *Argentina,* 6742, 6767, 6792-3, 6810. *Bolivia,* 6814. *Brazil,* 6728, 6740, 7073, 7113. *Central America,* 6611. *Chile,* 6841, 6843-4, 6846, 6854, 6856-8, 6862. *Colombia,* 6888, 6913. *Cuba,* 6578. *Guyana,* 6943. *Mexico,* 6694, 6710, 6720. *Peru,* 6962, 6975, 7001, 7006, 7008. *Venezuela,* 6571. *Volcanoes,* 656, 6701, 6740, 6782, 7001
Geomorphology, 7197
Geophysics, *Venezuela,* 6571
Geopolitics, *General,* 8939. *Caribbean,* 8853. *Pre-Inca,* 963. *South America,* 8939
German Democratic Republic, 8757
German. *See* Federal Republic of Germany or German Democratic Republic.
Ghandi, Mahatma, 8029
Gold Market, 4491
Gómez Morin, Manuel, 8178
Good Partner Policy, 8748
Grammar. *See* Language.
Gran Acuerdo Nacional, Argentina, 8625, 8657
Grand Pajonal, Peru, 1329, 1335
Grupo de Oficiales Unidos, Argentina, 8642
Gruta del Indio Rincón del Atuel Site, 879
Guahiban/Guajiban Language, 1808, 1856, 1874
Guahibo Indians, 1368-9, 1932
Guaicuruan Languages, 1899
Guaiúba Site, 906b
Guajiro Indians, 1407-10, 1932
Guambiano Indians, 1932
Guambiano Language. *See* Chibchan Language.
Guanano Indians, 1932
Guandacol Site, 873a
Guangala Culture, 984
Guantanamo, Cuba, 8839
Guaraní Indians, 505
Guaraní Language, 1829-30, 1853, 1912, 1930 *See also* Tupí-Guaraní Languages.
Guatín, Chile, 948c-8d
Guayabo de Turrialba Site, 816
Guayakí Indians, 1331, 1345, 1405, 2072

Guayakí Language. *See* Tupí-Guaraní Languages.
Guaycurú Languages, 1930. *See also* Guaraní Languages.
Guaymí Indians, 1112, 1155
Guaymí Language. *See* Chibchan Languages.
Guerilla Warfare and Movements, 8065, 8070, 8191-2, 8230, 8299, 8333, 8398, 8520, 8523-4, 6598a, 8614, 8621
Guerillas, *Urban,* 8041, 8053, 8062, 8079, 8099, 8618, 8623
Guevara, Ernesto *Che,* 8047, 8222, 8226-7, 8242, 8403, 8405-5a
Guila Naquitz, Cueva de, 773
Guillén, Abraham, 8053
Gunboat Diplomacy, 8742
Guyana and the UN, 8932
Hacienda Grande Site, 830
Haldas Complex, 1006a
Hallucinogens, 1288, 1385, 1389, 1399, 1462, 2219-22, 2230-1, 6546, 7182
Hato de la Calzada Site, 1065a
Health Care, 1143-4, 2218, 2247, 2256, 2260, 6225, 6263, 6319. *See also* Public Health.
Highways, Mexico, 6669
History, *Archaeology,* 506. *Economic,* 4108, 4293-4, 4709, 4722. *Ethnology,* 519. *Maize,* 618. *Precolumbian,* 514
Hixkaryana Language. *See* Carib Languages.
Hokan Language. *See* Mayan Languages.
Horqueta Complex, 958
Housing, *General,* 4182, 6526. *Brazil,* 1500, 4788, 7122, 8551. *Chile,* 4620. *Colombia,* 4521, 6916. *Mexico,* 4254, 4263, 9742. *Puerto Rico,* 9807. *Uruguay,* 4679. *Venezuela,* 9825, 9827
Huaca de la Luna Site, 1014
Huaca de las Estacas Site, 1049a
Huaca de los Reyes, 1031e
Huaca del Sol Site, 1049a
Huaca El Mirador Site, 1049a
Huacjlasmarca, Peru, 1035
Huaraz Language. *See* Quechua Languages.
Huasca, Mexico, 6712
Huastec Language. *See* Mayan Languages.
Huatakame, Myth of, 1109
Huave Language, 1925, *See also* Otomanguean Languages.
Hueyepan, Mexico, 1134
Huichol Indians, 1109, 1169
Huitoto Indians, 1909, 1932
Huitotoan Languages, 1816, 1820, 1909
Human Adaptation. *See* Demography.
Human Resources, 4086, 4102, 4101, 4260, 4608
Human Rights, 6059, 8732, 8768-9

Humboldt, Alexander von, 6504, 6523, 6574-5, 6577, 6896, 6936
Hunting, *Mesoamerica,* 769
Ica Indians. See Arhuaco Indians.
Ica Language. See Chibchan Languages.
Iconography, 636, 638, 656-7, 735, 759, 762, 810, 813, 826
Ikat Painting, 891
Illegal Antiquities Traffic, 655, 667, 819, 823, 990
Im 11 Site, 965
Imperialism, 4073-4, 4111, 4143, 4149, 4206, 4212, 4661, 8045, 8055, 8323, 8336, 8372, 8386, 8701, 8720, 8730, 8742, 8744-6, 8747a, 8749a, 8757, 8779, 8787, 8857-8, 8864, 8872, 8901, 9778
Import Substitution, 4030, 4529, 4846, 4873, 4967, 4977
Imports and Exports, 4070, 4105, 4117, 4125, 4211, 4271, 4460-2, 4471, 4490, 4520, 4579, 4674, 4684-5, 4710, 4724, 4733, 4763, 4818, 4834-5, 4865, 4866, 4924, 4975-7, 4979
Incas, 872, 895, 1026a, 1530
Income, 4097
Income Distribution, 4034, 4077a, 4194, 4225, 4240, 4309, 4319, 4334, 4338, 4494, 4515-6, 4543, 4574, 4594, 4597, 4602, 4606, 4610, 4614, 4622, 4643, 4650, 4665, 4697, 4711, 4741, 4743, 4752, 4769, 4805, 4811, 4844, 4871, 4878, 4880, 4896, 4914, 4945, 4953, 4963, 4971, 9647, 9721
Independence Movements, *Puerto Rico,* 8277, 8279-81, *Trinidad and Tobago,* 8284
Indian Creek Site, 841,
Indian Policy, *Brazil,* 1314, 1326, 1349, 1379, 1392, *Peru,* 1548
Indians. See specific groups.
Indians and Integration, 516g, 1102, 1106-7, 1166-7, 1188-9, 1384, 1396, 1400, 1402, 1447, 1460, 9727
Indigenismo, 9725
Indigenous Civilizations, 500, 514, 521, 857, 860, 875a, 893, 956, 1023a, 1026b, 1062a, 1309, 1361, 1549
Industry and Industrialization, *General,* 2048, 4012, 4020-1, 4033, 4036, 4043, 4087, 4116, 4124, 4124, 4139, 4179, 4181, 4228, 4248, 8715. *Argentina,* 4690, 4720, 4744-5, *Bolivia,* 4583. *Brazil,* 4761-2, 4764-5, 4772, 4774-5, 4782, 4789, 4793, 4797-8, 4804, 4816, 4820, 4822-4, 4828, 4837, 4853, 4861, 4864, 4866, 4870, 4904, 4909, 4917, 4919, 4932, 4935, 4946, 4959, 4964-5, 4972, 4974, 4981, 4985, 4986, 7081, 7092, 7094, 7096, 7120. *Caribbean,*
4363. *Chile,* 4599, 4604, 9875. *Colombia,* 4462, 4481, 4489, 4506, 8300a. *Cuba,* 6582. *Diversification,* 6582. *Dominican, Republic,* 4344, 4367. *Education,* 6376. *El Salvador,* 4372. *Guatemala,* 6628-9. *Haiti,* 4345. *Honduras,* 4380. *Indians,* 1102, 1121. *Mexico,* 4273, 4284, 4286, 4301, 4315, 4318, 4321, 4324, 6695. *Nationalization,* 8287. *Peru,* 4654, 6989. *Uruguay,* 4668, 4670-1, 4677. *Venezuela,* 4539, 4545, 4555, 4570, 4574, 4576
Inflation, *General,* 4076, 4157, 4171, 4199, 4238. *Argentina,* 4700, 4713, 4730, 4734, 4742-3. *Brazil,* 4776, 4806, 4826, 4845, 4874, 4881, 4911, 4934, 4954, 4958, 4989-90. *Chile,* 4606, 4630. *Colombia,* 4485. *Peru,* 4641. *Venezuela,* 4559
Inga Indians, 1932
Inga Language. See Quechua Languages.
Instituto Indigenista Interamericano, 516
Instituto Nacional Indigenista, Mexico, 1183
Integralismo, Brazil, 8600-8600a
Intellectuals, 8033, 9640
Inter American Development Bank, 4173, 4182
The Inter-American Foundation, 8788
International Law, 8751
International Organizations, 8733, 8749, 8922
International Petroleum Company, Peru, 8893, 8917
Iron and Steel Industry, *Brazil,* 4781, 4862, *Mexico,* 4303
Iruya Complex, 894
Iscoconga Site, 1011
Isnos Complex, 958
Itonama Language, 1889
Iuko Indians, 1362, 1414
Ixcatlán, Mexico, 1162
Ixil Indians, 1119
Ixil Language. See Mayan Languages.
Ixtepeji, Mexico, 1152
Jade, *Mayas,* 707, 762
Jaina Figurines, 708
Japan in Latin America, *General,* 4153, 8781, 8803a, *Brazil,* 1366. *Central America,* 8826. *Cuba,* 82
Jáuregui, Arturo, 8051
Jê Languages, 1848, 1859, 1900-1, 1936, 1940-1, 1948
The *Jeito,* Brazil, 8590a
Jews in Latin America, 9884, 9890, 9898
Jíbaro Language, 1816
Jurúna Indians, 1373
Justicialismo. See Peron and Peronism.
Kaborí Indians, 1371
Kalapalo Indians, 1320

Kaminaljuyu, Guatemala, 670
Kammbá, 1283
Karacaô Indians, 1315
Karajá Language. *See* Jê Languages.
Kariri Indians, 1319
Kaxarirí Language. *See* Arawakan and Panoan Languages.
Kayabí Language. *See* Tupí-Guaraní Languages.
Kayapó Indians, 1359, 2117, 2216
Kayapó Language. *See* Jê Languages.
Kaykay, Peru, 1471
Kekchi Language. *See* Mayan Languages.
Keros, *Chile*, 932a. *Ecuador*, 968
Kinship, *General*, 8111, *Argentina*, 9896. *Chontal*, 1194. *Grenada*, 1256. *Huastec*, 1819. *Jujuy*, 1431. *Kayapó*, 1318. *Makiritare*, 2095. *Mayas*, 1189. *Mexico*, 9706, 9726. *Nahuas*, 1103, 1116, 1124. *Nengre*, 1378. *Nomatsiguenga Campa*, 1960. *Quechua*, 1468. *Shantytowns*, 1158. *Surinam*, 1216. *Trique*, 1145. *Winikina Warao*, 1351. *Zapotec*, 1182
Kohunlich, Pirámide, 774
Kreen-Akrore Indians, 1334
Kuyo Chico, Peru, 1521
Kwinti Bush Tribe, 1230
La Aguada Site, 878
La Betina Site, 1065
La Chimba Site, 965
La Gruta del Inca Site, 875a
Las Haldas Site, 1028
La Herraura Site, 926
La Iguana Site, 1061
La Maza Site, 869
La Pampa Site, 1034
La Venta Site, 719, 731
Labor, *General*, 4068, 8043, 8051, 8100, 8112, *Argentina*, 4701, 4703, 8100, 8629, 9639a, 8660, 8691, 8694, 9886, 9905-6. *Barbados*, 1240. *Bolivia*, 8100, 8394, 8412, 9858. *Brazil*, 4778, 4783, 4805, 4815, 4888, 4913, 4936, 4938, 4950, 4953, 4957, 7053, 8100. *Caribbean*, 1266-7, 4362. *Chile*, 4605, 6848, 8100, 8452, 8467, 8477-81, 9862, 9864. *Colombia*, 4473, 4476, 4483, 4489, 4501, 6879, 8329-30, 8340, 9827. *Commonwealth Caribbean*, 6565. *Cuba*, 8243. *Dominican Republic*, 8253, 9814. *Employment*, 4008, 4043, 4080, 4086, 4092, 4103, 4132, 4260, 4263, 4473, 4476, 4489, 4538, 4549, 4650, 4666, 4703, 4783, 4888, 4890, 4913, 6879, 7053, 8300a, 8715, 9707, 9749, 9752, 9905-6. *Guatemala*, 4384-5. *Honduras*, 4390. *Jamaica*, 4349. *Management*, 4004, 4544, 4558, 4664, 4701, 4868, 8660, 8675, 9752. *Mexico*, 1121, 4309, 4322, 4666, 8177, 9707. *Peru*, 4664, 4666, 8370, 9861. *Precolumbian*, 1031a. *Puerto Rico*, 9814. *Surinam*, 1213, 1251. *Unions*, 4558, 8129, 8412, 8660a-60b, 9685, 9864. *Uruguay*, 4669. *Venezuela*, 4537, 4549, 4558
Lacandon Indians, 1163, 1201
Lambityeco, Mexico, 726
Lampián, Peru, 1450
Land Reform. *See* Agrarian Reform.
Land Tenure. *See* Agrarian Reform.
Land Tenure, *Indians. See* Agriculture, Indigenous Communal.
Language, *Archaeology*, 859. *Argentina*, 1899, 1943. *Barbados*, 1220. *Bolivia*, 1805, 1818, 1875, 1889, 1894, 1904, 1944. *Brazil*, 1812-4, 1833-4, 1837, 1848, 1859, 1861, 1876, 1900-1, 1912, 1924, 1927, 1929, 1936-7, 1940-1, 1944, 1948, 1950, 1954, 1957-8. *Colombia*, 1512, 1808, 1811, 1817, 1854-6, 1874, 1876, 1903, 1906-7, 1909, 1927, 1932, 1939, 1951, 1955. *Costa Rica*, 1801. *Creole*, 1225, 1249. *Dictionaries*, 1802, 1904, 1912, 1916, 1923, 1946-7, 6568, 6651, 6884, 7032. *Ecuador*, 1911, 1916. *Grammar*, 1803, 1807-8, 1822, 1832, 1835, 1840, 1845, 1848, 1850, 1852, 1861, 1864-5, 1870, 1881-2, 1887-8, 1890, 1893, 1896, 1912, 1915-6, 1923, 1936, 1939, 1946-7, 1949. *Guatemala*, 1843, 1850, 1902. *Guyana*, 1950. *Haiti*, 1232, 1288a. *Hindi*, 1228. *Isoglosses*, 1925. *Linguistics*, 1185, 1800, 1832, 1842, 1845, 1887-8, 1924, 1952, 1954-5. *Maya*, 795, 797, 800-2, 805, 810. *Mexico*, 1802, 1809-10, 1815, 1819, 1828, 1832, 1843-4, 1847, 1852, 1857-8, 1860, 1866-9, 1872-3, 1883-5, 1890, 1898, 1916, 1919-20, 1923, 1925, 1931, 1933, 1935, 1942, 1945-6, 1952-3, 1956, 1959, 9733. *Morphology*, 1840, 1859, 1950. *Morphonemics*, 1933, 1937. *Nahuatl*, 6654. *Orthography*, 1809-10, 1864, 1904, 1916. *Olmec*, 804. *Panama*, 1804, 1806, 1811, 1862, 1879-80. *Paraguay*, 1829-30, 1853, 1912, 1928, 1930. *Peru*, 1816, 1836, 1851, 1875, 1877, 1881-2, 1886, 1892-6, 1904-5, 1910, 1914, 1921, 1934, 1938, 1944, 1947, 1960, 9853. *Philosophy*, 1800, 1842, 1888. *Phonemes*, 795, 1805-6, 1810-1, 1817, 1833, 1847, 1852, 1855-7, 1862, 1874, 1879-80, 1889, 1900-1, 1903, 1907, 1919-20, 1926, 1936, 1940, 1944-5, 1951. *Phonology*, 1804, 1806, 1809, 1817, 1827, 1830, 1832, 1844, 1850, 1852, 1854, 1856-7, 1859, 1862-3, 1876, 1879-81, 1890, 1903, 1907, 1926, 1933, 1945-7, 1952.

Pidgin, 1225. Semantics, 1803, 1812, 1819, 1863, 1875, 1893, 1896, 1905. Spanish, 1841, 1871, 1875. Surinam, 1205, 1878. Tagmemic Model, 1808, 1820, 1832-3, 1837, 1864, 1882, 1915, 1950. Transformational Analysis, 1803, 1807, 1822, 1835, 1842, 1848-9, 1851, 1865, 1871, 1887-8, 1892, 1894, 1934, 1936, 1948. Trinidad, 1838. Velars, 1826. Vocabulary, 1805-6, 1811, 1823, 1852, 1859, 1889-90, 1901, 1930, 1933. Vowel Elision, 1805
Lanusse, Alejandro, 8672, 8866
Las Marías Site, 1052a
Latin American Free Trade Area, 4001, 4003, 4006, 4010-11, 4040, 4042, 4071, 4154, 4195, 8810, 8904 Latin American Nuclear Free Zone, 8770
Latin American relations, 8702, 8706, 8708, 8710-11, 8715, 8717, 8737, 8755, 8760, 8772-3, 8782-3, 8785, 8793, 8797, 8799, 8847, 8866-70, 8883, 8889, 8897, 8917, 8927, 8930
Law of the Sea. See Territorial Waters.
Legends. See Mythology.
Leninism, 8112, 8664
Liberal Party, Colombia, 8324, 8328, 8331
Liberation Movements. See Revolutionary Movements.
Licensing Agreements. See Trademarks.
Lima, Turcois, 8192
Linguistics. See Language.
Literacy and Illiteracy, 1128, 1288a, 1466, 6099, 6102, 6209, 6222, 6274, 6331, 6338
Literature, Oral, 1186, 1942. Precolumbian, 1885
Living Standard, General, 4019, Cross Cultural, 9610, 9641
Llanganatis Mountains, Ecuador, 6926
Loa Oeste 3 Site, 944
López Michelsen, Alfonso, 8304
Los Angeles, Nicaragua, 822
Los Cerritos Site, 1061
Los Naranjos, Honduras, 690
Loxicha, Mexico, 1180
Lucumí. See Religion.
Lymphocytes, 2086
Machismo, 8109, 9601, 9637, 9804
Machu Picchu, 986, 7003
Maclasinca Language. See Otopamean Languages.
Macro Carib Languages. See Carib Languages.
Macro Tucanoan Language. See Tucanoan Languages.
Macuxí Indians, 1384
Mahekodotedi, Venezuela, 1415
Makiritare Indians. See Yekuana Indians.

Makuxí Indians, 1337-8, 1401
Malayo Indians, 1932
Malvinas, Islas, 6781, 8907
Mamean Language. See Mayan Languages.
Mamuel Choique Rock, 877
Man, Ancient, 852, 1006, 1041, 2017. Brazil, 855. Panama, 2017. Venezuela, 1065a
Management. See Labor.
Manifest Destiny, 8714, 8787
Manizales, Colombia, 1465
Manteño Culture, 984
Maps, Acquisitions, 7203. Agricultural, 675, 7239, 7272, 7285. Archaeological, 670, 7236. Atlases, 510, 6500, 7204, 7219, 7221, 7229-30, 7234, 7243, 7249-50, 7260, 7307, 7347. Brazil, 7062, 7109, 7178, 7275, 7348. Demographic, 7243, 7260, 7338, 7351. Ecology, 7282. Historical, 6533, 6535, 6663-4, 6860, 7029, 7271, 7280-1, 7322, 7340, 7345. Patagonia, 6836. Political, 7205-6, 7217, 7227-8, 7288, 7331-2, 7336-7. Road, 7212-6, 7224, 7233, 7237-8, 7240, 7242, 7246-8, 7254, 7256, 7258-9, 7285-6, 7289-90, 7292, 7293-5, 7298-303, 7311, 7313, 7328, 7334, 7336-7, 7339, 7344. Tectonic, 7225, 7244-5, 7260. Topographic, 7211, 7223, 7284, 7287, 7296, 7304-5, 7308, 7323. Venezuela, 7024, 7029
Mapuche Indians, 1451, 1464, 1502, 1513, 1543
Maracá Indians, 1391
Marajoara Culture, 924
Marginality, General, 4147, 4213, 9635, 9661. Economic, 9617. Psychological, 9608. Social, 9608
Marianismo, 8109-10
Marihuana. See Hallucinogens.
Marinahua Language. See Sharanahua Language.
Maripaston, Surinam, 1249
Maritime Policy, Brazil, 7162, 8548b, 8603. Mexico, 6696
Marketing and Product Distribution, General, 4041, 4222, 4227. Argentina, 4747. Chile, 4629. Costa Rica, 4335. Mexico, 4313. Peru, 4638
Maroon Societies, 1282, 6594
Marquetalia, Colombia, 8299
Marriage, 1336, 1348, 1351, 1408, 1428, 1433, 1819, 2096
Martí, Jose, 8210, 8242
Marxism, 6142, 8038, 8059, 8072-3, 8112, 8466, 8517, 8651, 8664
Máspero, Emilio, 8051
Mataco Indians, 1312
Maternity, Precolumbian, 507

Matlatzinca Language. *See* Otopamean Languages.
Mayan Languages, 1110, 1147, 1166, 1186, 1819, 1823-7, 1839, 1850, 1852, 1873, 1933, 1942, 1946, 1952, 1959
Mayapan, Mexico, 770
Mayas, *Ancient,* 600-4, 610-2, 626, 636-7, 643, 650, 1210
Mayas, *Living,* 1128, 1136, 1138, 1177, 1189, 1200, 1202a
Mayo Indians, 1106
Mayoruna Language. *See* Panoan Languages.
Mazahua Indians. *See* Otomí Indians.
Mazatec Indians, 1162
Mazatec Language, 1956
Meat Industry, *Argentina,* 8697a
Medicine, *Argentina,* 9907. *Brazil,* 7130. *Colombia,* 6906. *Education,* 6021, 6290. *Folk,* 1108, 1143-4, 1148, 1152, 1156, 1196, 2228. *Humoral,* 1157, 2236. *Lactose Studies,* 2101-2, 2223
Méndez, Epifanio, 8604b
Mendoza, Eugenio, 8511
Mennonites, 1872
Merchant Marines, 4675, 8580, 8882
Mestizos and Mestizoization, 1224, 2202
Metalworking, 514, 851, 853, 1004, 1013, 1024, 1051, 4226
Methodology, *General,* 8013, 8089. *Anthropology,* 1137, 8013. *Archaeology,* 668, 677, 766, 871, 917, 932, 947-7a, 8013. *Demography,* 8013. *Economics,* 4026, 4098, 4329, 4545. *Education,* 6009a, 6037, 6042, 6050, 6056, 6063, 6068, 6081, 6105, 6147, 6169, 6181, 6184, 6189, 6207, 6214, 6216, 6227, 6239, 6285-6, 6293, 6300, 6303, 6308, 6347, 6350-1, 6379. *Ethnology,* 1130. *Fertility Studies,* 2024. *Genetics,* 2077, 2079. *Geography,* 6570, 7150, 8013. *History,* 8013. *Language,* 1841, 1845, 1860. *Nutrition,* 2161. *Political Science,* 8066, 8077, 8084, 8201, 8317. *Psychodrama,* 9628. *Social Sciences,* 9638. *Sociology,* 8013, 9666
The Mexican Revolution, 6150-1, 8813
Mexican War, 8714
Mexico and Central America, 8804, 8810
Mexico and Chile, 8810
Mexico and Cuba, 8810
Mexico and International Relations, 8008
Mexico and the Andean Pact, 8810
Mexico and the Soviet Union, 8817a
Mexico and the UN, 8805, 8812
Mexico and the US, 8813-5, 8816
Mexticacan, Mexico, 1178
Mezquital Otomí Language. *See* Otomí Language.

Miahuatlan, Mexico, 696
Middle Grijalva Site, 741-2
Migrant Workers, 9736
Migration, *General,* 2043. *Andean,* 2192. *Brazil,* 2050, 2061, 4980, 7107, 7110. *Colombia,* 4511, 9834, 9836, 9842, 9848. *Costa Rica,* 4376. *Internal,* 4008. *Peru,* 9853. *Surinam,* 1212. *Transoceanic,* 671, 854, 858, 2007
Military and Militarism. *See* Armed Forces.
Minas Gerais, Brazil, 8595a
Mining Industry, *General,* 4140. *Bolivia,* 4582. *Brazil,* 4847, 7076. *Chile,* 4609, 4618, 4627, 4632. *Jamaica,* 4350, 4359, 6596. *Peru,* 4637, 4639-40, 4647, 4663, 6993. *Surinam,* 1269
Miskito Indians, 6641,
Missionaries, 1406, 8037
Mitla, Mexico, 726
Mixco, Guatemala, 1113
Mixe, Western, 1105
Mixtec Language. *See* Otomanguean Languages.
Moche Culture, 1032
Mochica Culture, 991-2a
Mollo Culture, 1026b
Money, *Precolumbian,* 969b
Money and Banking. *See* Banking and Commerce.
The Monroe Doctrine, 8711, 8714, 8766
Monte Alban, Mexico, 634, 687, 792
Monte Mór, Brazil, 914
Montevideo, Treaty of, 8871
Moon-children, *Cuna Indians,* 1197
Morbidity and Mortality Patterns, 2022, 2030, 2039, 2048, 2056, 2058, 2111, 2176, 2257, 9909
Morphology. *See* Language.
Morro de Guacara Site, 1061
Moseten Language, 1944
Movimiento Nacionalista Revolucionario, Bolivia, 8395, 8401, 8404, 8407, 8413, 8415
Muchuchíes Phase, 1064, 1064b
Muisca Culture, 962
Multinational Corporations, 4017, 4067, 4074, 4104-5, 4206, 4332, 4465, 4640, 4661, 4771, 4939, 8125, 8202, 8488, 8561b, 8641, 8697a, 8709, 8715, 8720, 8725, 8729, 8749, 8771, 8786, 8796, 8800, 8872
Muna, Mexico, 685,
Munduruku Language. *See* Tupí-Guaraní Languages.
Mura-Pirahã Language, 1937
Murals, *Precolumbian,* 621, 657
Murui Language. *See* Huitotoan Languages.
Music, *Mapuche,* 1543. *Panama,* 1160.

Precolumbian, 931a
Muyu Moqo Site, 1013
Mythology, 734, 784, 983, 1020, 1109, 1119, 1164, 1180, 1186, 1191, 1202, 1203, 1882, 1931, 1960, 1312, 1325, 1333, 1336-7, 1347, 1355, 1364, 1367, 1376, 1380, 1395, 1404, 1465, 1467, 1473, 1522, 1526, 7000, 7038
Nahua Indians, 1103, 1134, 1193, 2073, 6612
Nahuat Language. See Uto-Aztecan Languages.
Nambikuara Indians, 1323
Naranjos, Los. See Los Naranjos.
National Parks, Brazil, 1333, 1927, 6738. Central America, 6608. Mexico, 6608. Peru, 1311, 7002
Nationalism, General, 8044, 8120, 8741. Argentina, 8632, 8653. Bolivia, 8392, 8406, 8418. Brazil, 8556a. Chile, 8436, 8490. Mexico, 8139. Peru, 8371, 8386, 8392. Trinidad and Tobago, 1289. Venezuela, 8532
Nengre Creoles, 1378
Nepeña Valley, Peru, 1038, 1045
Nevado Pichu Picchu Site, 849
Newspapers. See Press.
Nexpa Site, 718
Nezahualcóyotl, 1831, 1935
Nican Pehua Zacatipán, Mexico, 1103
Nicaragua and the US, 8828a
Nine Lords of the Night, Zapotecs, 1180
Nomatsiguenga Campa Language. See Arawakan Languages.
Northeast, Brazil, 2049, 4761, 4767-8, 4774, 4785, 4787, 4803-4, 4816-7, 4830, 4838, 4848, 4861, 4872, 4887, 4892-3, 4915-6, 4921, 4925, 6355, 6366, 7048, 7055-9, 7067, 7080-3, 7087-9, 7101-2, 7106, 7108, 7111-2, 7124, 7142, 7198, 8591, 8597
Nuclear Power. See Energy Sources.
Nutrition, General, 2148, 2161, 6113. Brazil, 2140, 2177, 6319, 7080, 7082, 7088, 7097, 7117, 7172. Chile, 2176, 2179, 2184, 4622-3. Colombia, 2172, 2186-7. Costa Rica, 2190. Dominican Republic, 2162, 2164, 2166, 2183. Food Supply, 1128. Growth Pattern, 2135. Guatemala, 2142, 2157, 2159-60, 2167, 2169-71, 2185, 2191. Haiti, 1288a, 2181. Iodine Deficiency, 2151, 2156. Jamaica, 2136, 2144-5, 2188, 2195. Kwashiorkor, 2149, 2159. Marasmus, 2149. Mayas, 625, 2143. Mexico, 504, 686, 2142-3, 2149, 2158, 2173. Pediatrics, 2154-5, 2159, 2166-7, 2189-71. Peru, 1443, 2155, 2168, 2174-5. Precolumbian, 608. Seafood, 686. Venezuela, 2165, 9828. Vitamins, 2137, 2148, 2178, 2185
Oaxaca Coast Project, Mexico, 696-8
Obsidian, Mesoamerica, 689, 717, 732-3, 745, 770
Occupational Mobility. See Demography.
Oceanography, Brazil, 7175, 7189. Cuba, 6579
Ocucaje, Peru, 1020
Ofaié Language. See Jê Languages.
Oil Industry. See Petroleum Industry.
Olmec Indians, 609, 635-6, 710, 740
Omereque, Bolivia, 1480
Ometepe, Isla de, 822
Ongania, Juan Carlos, 8690
Organización Continental Latinoamericana de Estudiantes, 8780
Organization of American States, 6012-7, 6046, 6066, 8734, 8767-9, 8801
Organization of Petroleum Exporting Countries, 8528-28a, 8538
Organización Regional Inter-Americana de Trabajadores, 8051
Orinoco River Basin, 6726
Orizaba, Mexico, 1857
Ornithology, 6731, 6735, 6809
Orthography. See Language.
Oruro, Bolivia, 1515
Otavalo, Ecuador, 1550
Otomanguean Languages, 1835, 1866-8, 1916, 1919-20, 1919-20, 1926
Otomí Indians, 1123, 2224
Otomí Language, 1809-10
Otopamean Languages, 1832
Padilla, Heberto, 8221
Páez Language. See Chibchan Languages.
Paiján, Peru, 1021
Palacios, Alfredo, 8652a
Palenque, Mexico, 766, 808, 813
Paleoanthropology and Osteology, Animal, 6677. Skulls and Skeletal Remains, 672, 747, 2001, 2004-6, 2008-13, 2014-6, 2019, 2139, 2141, 2210-1
Paleoenvironments, 846, 982a, 994a
Palo Gordo, Guatemala, 786
Palo Grande Site, 869
La Pampa, Argentina, 6770, 8662a
Pampa de Tamarugal, Chile, 942c
Pan-American Highway, Panama, 6644-5, 6649
Pan Americanism. See Latin American relations.
Panama and the UN, 8830
Panama and the US, 8198, 8820-3, 8828, 8837
Panoan Languages, 1816, 1836, 1846, 1851, 1863, 1871, 1877, 1892-6, 1905, 1917, 1934, 1936, 1938, 1944
Papago Indians, 1127, 1931

Papago Language. *See* Uto-aztecan Languages.
Papaloapan River Basin, 1162
Papantla, Mexico, 1802
Paraca Indians, 1005
Paracas, Peru, 1005, 1020
Paressí Language. *See* Arawakan Languages.
Parliaments and Congresses, *Argentina,* 8645. *Brazil,* 8592. *Venezuela,* 8531-2, 8540a
Parry Fiord, Chile, 945f
Partido de Acción Nacional, Mexico, 8154, 8159, 8178
Partido Revolucionario Institucional, Mexico, 8151, 8172
Pastaza River, Peru, 1881
Pastoralism, *Andes,* 6730. *Chile,* 6840
Patagonia, Argentina, 6762, 8633
Patagonia, Chile, 928-8a, 936, 945c-5d, 6837
Patents. *See* Trademarks.
Pátzcuaro, Mexico, 1167
Peasants, *General,* 8004-5, 8007, 9615, 9631, 9684. *Argentina,* 1498, 8666. *Belize,* 1207. *Bolivia,* 1485. *Brazil,* 8563. *Chile,* 8472, 8496, 9867, 9873. *Colombia,* 6127, 9818. *Ecuador,* 9818. *Guatemala,* 2236, 9754. *Mexico,* 1115, 6149, 8134, 8181, 9729. *Peru,* 1416, 1507, 1514, 1540-1, 8370, 8373. *Puerto Rico,* 9785. *Venezuela,* 7036, 9818
Pemón Indians, 1313, 1401
Penal Systems, 8288, 9712, 9870
Pentecostalism, 9651
People's Republic of China in Latin America, 8737, 8802
Pérez, Juan Bautista, 6587
Peron and Peronism, 6098, 8059, 8629a, 8630b, 8631, 8632-3, 8631, 8632, 8634a-34b, 8637, 8638a, 8639, 8644, 8654, 8656, 8660b-61, 8663a, 8664a-65, 8669-70, 8671a, 8673, 8674-74(L), 8676-7, 8699, 9901
Peru and the US, 8372, 8375, 8899
Peruvian Revolution, 8368-69a, 8376-9, 8381-2, 8384, 8391
Petén, Guatemala, 1175
Petrobrás, Brazil, 8595
Petroglyphs, *Baja California,* 684, 737, 749
Petroleum Industry, *General,* 8078. *Argentina,* 4732. *Brazil,* 4808, 4820, 4949, 8595. *Colombia,* 4499. *Mexico,* 4253, 4311. *Peru,* 8365. *Venezuela,* 4530-1, 4546, 4551, 4557, 4561, 4571-2, 4575, 4577, 8918
Philosophy, *Education,* 6017a, 6020, 6081
Phonemes. *See* Language.
Phonology. *See* Language.

Phosphoglucomutase Variants, 2089
Piaget, Jean, 6009a
Pikillacta, Peru, 1012
Pima Indians, 1931, 2248
Pimampiro, Ecuador, 6932
Piratapuyo Language. *See* Tucanoan Languages.
Piro Indians, 1317
Piro Language. *See* Tanoan Languages.
Pisagua Viejo Site, 942c
El Plan Inca, Peru, 8391
Plantations, 503, 1266-7, 1440-1, 1458, 1488-9, 1492-3, 1534, 1544, 2040, 4196, 4527
Plants and Forests. *See* Ecology, *Flora and Fauna.*
Plattdeutsch, 1872
Playa Verde Site, 1056
Pocomochi, Guatemala, 1164, 1902
Pokom Language. *See* Mayan Languages.
Poland Syndrome, 2088
Political Asylum, 8735
Political Development, 8056, 8114, 8117-8, 8126, 8731
Political Integration, 8023, 8182-3, 8825, 8889, 8939
Political Leaders, 8044, 8097, 8124, 8179, 8195, 8601-01a
Political Models, 8031-2, 8056, 8066, 1158, 8168, 8171, 8202, 8289, 8378, 8380, 8390, 8415, 8665a, 8695, 8715
Political Modernization, 8083
Political Organization, *General,* 8001, 8010-8019, 8032, 8066, 8094, 8097, 8111-2, 8114, 8117-8, 8123, 8783. *Argentina,* 8643, 8647a, 8658, 8661a, 8667-8, 8671, 8683. *Bolivia,* 1485, 1503, 8395-6, 8399-8400, 8401, 8404, 8407, 8413, 8415, 8418. *Brazil,* 6263, 8017, 8549a, 8557, 8559a. *Cayman,* 1242. *Chile,* 8421, 8452, 8464, 8468, 8475-6, 8484, 8488, 8490, 8493, 8497, 8499, 8497a, 8499, 8940. *Chimu,* 1017. *Colombia,* 8296, 8300, 8302, 8305, 8313-4, 8319-22, 8343-43a, 8346-7, 8349. *Commonwealth Caribbean,* 8205. *Dominican Republic,* 8249-50. *Ecuador,* 8360. *Guatemala,* 1131, 8193. *Guyana,* 1247, 1250, 8286, 8294-5. *Haiti,* 8257. *Incas,* 1030a, 1030c. *Indian Communities,* 1150, 1200. *Jamaica,* 1231, 1296, 8260-2. *Mexico,* 1125-6, 8147, 8149-51, 8153, 8179. *Paraguay,* 8604a. *Peru,* 8373-4, 8376, 8378, 8383. *Puerto Rico,* 8266, 8276, 8278. *Surinam,* 1299. *Uruguay,* 8617, 8620a. *Venezuela,* 1062b, 8512, 8515, 8519a, 8526. *Yekuana,* 1316
Pollution. *See* Ecology.
Popayán, Columbia, 1554, 6893

Ports and Harbors, 4763, 4856
Potiguara Indians, 1310
Pottery, *Argentina,* 864, 876, 878, 885, 888, 894. *Aztecs,* 514, 699. *Brazil,* 914. *Chile,* 931a. *Colombia,* 954, 958a. *Ecuador,* 966-7, 972, 978d-9, 981. *Hispaniola,* 832. *Incas,* 514, 1007. *Martique,* 840. *Mayas,* 688, 764. *Mesoamerica,* 639, 660, 682, 730, 754, 786, 791. *Mixtec,* 681, 696. *Mochica,* 1044. *Nasca,* 1044. *Panama,* 821. *Peru,* 995, 1015, 1040. *South America,* 851. *Tupiguarani,* 1052a. *Uruguay,* 1059. *Venezuela,* 1065b. *See also* Ceramics.
Pozuzo, Peru, 1501
The Press, 1230a, 8018, 8113, 8130, 8197, 8363
Prestes, Luis Carlos, 8544a
Primavera Complex, 958
Protest Movements, *Mexico,* 8177
Proto + Language. *See* under language name.
Psychology Studies, 6156, 6208, 6213, 6295, 6301, 6304-5, 6307, 6309, 6323, 6340, 6342, 6368, 9622
Psychotropic Plants, 897
Public Administration, *General,* 8039, 8054, 8058, 8083, 9643. *Argentina,* 866a, 4737, 4740. *Bolivia,* 1426, 1439, 8411. *Brazil,* 8571, 8573a, 8574, 8590, 8602. *Chile,* 8444. *Colombia,* 8298, 8319, 8334, 8345, 8349-50. *Commonwealth Caribbean,* 8203-4. *Dominican Republic,* 8256. *Mexico,* 6711, 8141, 8157. *Surinam,* 1299. *Venezuela,* 8510, 8515a, 8516a, 8526b, 8533, 8539a, 8540, 8540c
Public Health, *Argentina,* 4725. *Brazil,* 4809, 6225, 6344. *Chile,* 4594, 4607, 8430. *Uruguay,* 2254. *Venezuela,* 2255
Public Opinion, *Argentina,* 8666
Public Safety Programs, 8738
Pucayacu, Ecuador, 6933
Puebla, Mexico, 6675
Puebla-Tlaxcala Project, 779
Puerto Rican Status, 8840
Punta Pichalo Site, 942c
Puntun, Mexico. *See* Xicalango.
Qollana, Peru, 1511
Qotobamba, Peru, 1522
Quebrada de Inca Cueva Site, 861
Quechua Indians, 1449, 1467, 1522, 1542, 1910, 2194, 2205
Quechua Languages, 1816, 1881-2, 1913-4, 1921, 1947
Quechumaran Languages, 1897, 1911
Quelepa Site, 817
Queredo Site, 940
Quichean Language. *See* Mayan Languages.

Quichua Language. *See* Quechumaran Languages.
Quijos Indians, 978a-8b
Quintana Roo, Mexico, 725
Quitasueño, Isla, 8847
Race and Race Relations, *General,* 1287, 9630. *Aruba,* 1236. *Bermuda,* 1257-8. *Brazil,* 1224, 2049. *Caribbean,* 1294. *Cuba,* 1255. *Ecuador,* 1556. *Grand Cayman,* 1224. *Guyana,* 1238, 1250, 1254. *Haiti,* 9778. *Jamaica,* 1296. *Mexico,* 1224. *Panama,* 1223. *Trinidad and Tobago,* 1289
Radicalism, 8714, 8754
Radiocarbon Chronology, 606, 876a, 947b
Radiocarbon Dates, *Argentina,* 876a, *Ecuador,* 966a. *Peru,* 1049a. *Venezuela,* 1064a
Rapa Nui, 934, 6850
Real Alto Site, 971
Real Estate, *Pampas,* 4705
Recuay Culture, 991
Regional Planning. *See* Economic Development.
Religion, *General,* 9674. *Afroamericans,* 1280. *Argentina,* 9879. *Aztecs,* 514. *Burial Customs,* 708, 1050. *Caribbean,* 8854. *Cult of Death,* 620, 743, 787, 822, 824-5, 970, 992, 1005, 1177. *Cult of the Jaguar,* 746. *Cult of Nuestro Padre,* 1114a. *Guatemala,* 1131, 1175, 1177. *Haiti,* 1295, 9796. *Hindu,* 1275. *Huichol,* 1169. *Inca,* 514. *Lucumí,* 1218. *Mayas,* 793. *Mesoamerica,* 648. *Mexico,* 1123, 1898, 9714. *Nahuas,* 1193, 1898. *Phallic Cult,* 757. *Political and Social Change,* 8016. *Quechua,* 1542. *Sacrifices,* 2002. *Sociology,* 9609. *Surinam,* 1300. *Tehuelche,* 1398. *Umbanda,* 1381. *Uruguay,* 8612b. *Winti-Cult,* 1306-7. *Yoruba,* 1218. *Zoque,* 1198. *See also* Catholic Church.
Republicans, Spanish. *See* Exiles.
Research, *General,* 6023-4. *Anthropology,* 501, 909, 913, 1558-9. *Archaeology,* 942a. *Economic,* 4748. *Economic Development,* 9644, 9646. *Education,* 6013, 6235, 6291, 6295, 6297K/ 6300, 6381. *Futurism,* 8777. *Geography,* 6538, 6657. *Health,* 2246. *Labor,* 8129. *Public Administration,* 9643. *Social Sciences,* 4245, 9694, 9704. *Sociology,* 9689-90
Revolution and Revolutionary Movements, 4122
Revolutionary Movements, 4122, 8000, 8003, 8006, 8035, 8047, 8051, 8053, 8056-7, 8064, 8069, 8081-2, 8119, 8208-9, 8220, 8254, 8296, 8301, 8310, 8339, 8357-8, 8642, 8750, 9648, 9679

Rikbaktsa Language, 1812-4, 1936, See also Jê Languages.
Rio Bec Area, Mexico, 678, 683, 775
Rio Candelaria Basin, Mexico, 674
Rio Fresco, Brazil, 925a
Rio Jacarei, Brazil, 921
Rio Paranapanema, Brazil, 904
River Basins. See specific river.
River Plate Basin, 4005
Roca-Runciman Treaty, 4712
The Rockefeller Foundation, 8795
Rockefeller, Nelson A., 8790
Rockshelters, *Bom Jardim Velho*, 922e, *Virador I*, 922
Roncador, Isla, 8847
Roosevelt, Theodore, 8894
Royalties. See Trademarks.
Ruiz Pineda, Leonardo, 8524
Rural Development, Brazil/6265
Rural-Urban Mobility. See Demography.
Sabina, María, 1956
Sacrifices. See Religion.
Salgado, Plínio, 8600a
Salto Grande Site, 867, 890
Saltograndense Lithic Complex, 1055
Sambaquís, 908, 921
San Agustín Site, 955
Sánchez, Fidel, 8186
San Felipe Los Alzati, Mexico, 716
San Juan Capistrano, Calif., 1922
San Juan del Rio, Mexico, 6655
San Pablo, Mexico, 718
San Pedro Sochiapan, Mexico, 1847
San Simón de la Laguna, Mexico, 1123
Santa Clara del Cobre, Mexico, 1146
Santa Cruz, Panama, 821
Santa Cruz Maya Society, 1150
Santa Eulalia, Guatemala, 1199
Santa Luisa, Mexico, 791
Santanilla, Islas, 8824
Santa Rosa Xtampak, Mexico, 704
Santería. See Witchcraft.
Santiago Atitlán, Guatemala, 1128
Santo Tomás Ocotepec, Mexico, 1141
Sanumá Indians. See Yanomamo Indians.
Savings, 4081, 4237, 4501, 4619
Science and Technology, *General*, 4000, 4029, 4047, 4061, 4130, 4189, 4229, 4244, 4250, 6005-6, 6024, 6036, 6038, 6066, 6121, 8778, 9602. *Argentina*, 4687, 4717, 4738, 4751, 6079, 6089, 6094. *Brazil*, 4795, 4827, 4922, 4926, 6233, 6242, 6250-1, 6275, 6349. *Chile*, 4600. *Colombia*, 4464, 4480. *Dominican Republic*, 4357. *Mexico*, 4252, 4323. *Uruguay*, 6176. *Venezuela*, 4542, 4574, 6193
Sculpture, *Classic Veracruz*, 728. *Colombia*, 955-5a. *Ecuador*, 978b. *Mayas*, 669, 680. *Omecs*, 609, 687, 713. *Pan-mesoamerican*, 622. *South American*, 851
Sechín, Peru, 1016, 1045
Security. See Armed Forces.
Seibal, Guatemala, 606
Selva, Salomón de la, 1935
Semantics. See Language.
Serrana, Isla, 8847
Serviço Nacional de Aprendizagem Comercial, 6234
Seward, William Henry, 8857
Sex and Sexual Relations, *General*, 9642, *Colombia*, 1557, 9832. *Dominican Republic*, 9809. *Ecuador*, 1557. *El Salvador*, 9762. *Guajiro*, 1408. *Mehinacu*, 1348. *Qolla*, 1433
Shamanism. See Witchcraft.
Shanties. See Slums.
Sharanahua Indians, 1399
Sharanahua Language. See Panoan Languages.
Shell Bar, *Argentina*, 869
Shell Celts, *Mexico*, 709
Shell Middens, *Argentina*, 890. *Brazil*, 908-9, 912, 921. *Chile*, 926. *Ecuador*, 978. *Mexico*, 686. *Panamic Molluscs*, 711. *Peru*, 1040
Sherds, *British Virgin Islands*, 836. *Colombia*, 958. *Ecuador*, 966. *Mesoamerica*, 736. *Uruguay*, 1054
Ship Building Industry, 4011
Shipibo Indians, 1327, 2202
Shirishana Indians, 2053
Sicaya, Peru, 1469
Sickle-Cell Anemia, *Jamaica*, 2138-9, 2197, 2211
Sierra de Famatina Site, 849
SINAMOS (Sistema Nacional de Apoyo a la Movilizacion Social), 1456
Siona Indians, 1932
Skulls and Skeletons. See Paleoanthropology and Osteology.
Slavery and Slave Trade, *General*, 1219. *Barbados*, 1239. *Brazil*, 503, 8594. *Caribbean*, 1265-7, 1275. *Jamaica*, 2040
Slums, *General*, 9671. *Brazil*, 7112. *British West Indies*, 1204. *Chile*, 8430, 9872. *Colombia*, 1553, 6915, 9834. *Jamaica*, 6595. *Mexico*, 1158, 9726. *Peru*, 1546. *Venezuela*, 8521-21a, 8537
Soccer War, 8819, 8827, 8836,
Sochiapan Language. See Chinantecan Languages.
Social Indicators, 8104
Social Mobility, *General*, 9622. *Mexico*, 1188-9. See also Class Structure.
Social Security, 4292, 4651, 4948, 9621, 9735, 9862
Socialism, *General*, 4122, 8003, 8012,

8045, 8073, 8101, 8210, 8626-7. *Argentina,* 8632, 8634a, 8635, 8651, 8652a, 8662, 8670, 8688. *Catholic Church,* 8021, 8073. *Chile,* 8452, 8468, 8507, 8509. *Cuba,* 8216, 8226-7, 8243. *Education,* 6001. *Venezuela,* 8533a
Socialist Party, 8028
Sociology of Education, 6284
Somoza García, Anastasio, 8195
Sorata, Bolivia, 1503
Soviet-Latin American Relations, 8794a, 8796a
Spanish American War, 8714, 8852, 8858
Spanish Republicans. *See* Exiles.
Spindle Whorls, *Ecuador,* 983-4
Sports, 9652, 9654, 9695
Sports, *Precolumbian,* 782, 786
Squatters, 1423, 1546, 9671
Sranan Language, 1878
Stamp Designs, *Precolumbian,* 712
State of Siege, 8738
Statistics, 4125, 4337, 4532, 4676, 4860, 6507, 6670, 6812, 6892, 7171, 9618, 9733
Stelae, 640, 679, 701, 743
Stock Markets, 4172, 4826
Stoneworking, *Mesoamerica,* 727
Stroessner, Alfredo, 8604g
Students, *General,* 6039, 8780. *Activism,* 6010, 6018, 6111, 6152, 6164, 6188, 8082, 8107, 8115, 8119, 8315, 8339, 8607. *Argentina,* 8630a. *Brazil,* 6241, 6276, 6291-3, 6334-6. *Colombia,* 8315, 9846. *Mexico,* 6152, 6164, 9710. *Peru,* 6170, 6175. *Venezuela,* 6188-9
Subversion and Development, 8040, 8042
Sugar Industry, 503
Suiá Indians, 1342
Suicide, 9877
Superintendência do Desenvolvimento do Nordeste, Brazil, 8597
Swan Island. *See* Santanilla Islands.
Swidden Cultivation. *See* Ecology.
Tablada de Lurín, Peru, 1010, 1039
Tacanan Languages, 1944
Tagmemic Model. *See* Language.
Taima-Taima Site, 846
Tairona Culture, 952, 1062
El Tajín, Mexico, 638, 651, 715, 791
Tamazula, Mexico, 772
Tacna, Peru, 1049
Tanoan Languages, 1886
Tarahumara Language. *See* Uto-Aztecan Languages.
Tarascan Indians, 1104, 1167, 1170
Tariff and Trade Protection, 4145
Tastil, Argentina, 870, 891
Taxation, *General,* 4065, 4106, 4137, 4202, 4207. *Agriculture,* 4023, 4373. *Argentina,* 4736, 8684. *Costa Rica,* 4373, 4391. *Extractive Industries,* 4021. *Honduras,* 4373. *Mexico,* 4269, 4291, 4300
Tchaputchayna Site, 938
Teaching Techniques, 6068, 6070, 6207
Tehuacan, Valle de, 630, 780
Tehuelche Indians, 1325
Tehuelche Language, 1944
Teixeira, Anísio, 6272, 6278, 6369
Television, 6207, 6210, 6247, 8148
Tenejapa, Mexico, 1147, 1186, 1942
Tenochtitlan, 607, 627, 756
Teotenango, Mexico, 760
Teotihuacan, Mexico, 646, 657-9, 688, 734, 759, 765, 2016
Tepehua Indians, 1202
Tepoztlán, Mexico, 1174
Tequistlatec Language. *See* Chontal Language.
Teribe Language. *See* Chibchan Languages.
Terraba Language, 1801
Territorial Waters, *General,* 6756, 8703, 8706, 8755, 8784, 8799, 8811, 8877, 8908, 8911, 8936. *Brazil,* 8588, 8873, 8882, 8908, 8916, 8921. *Peru,* 8899, 8928. *Venezuela,* 8911
Terrorism, 8046, 8076, 8079, 8189
Textiles, *Brazil,* 4802. *Ecuador,* 971. *Peru,* 1008, 1020. *Precolumbian,* 851
Thermoluminescent Dating, 960
Third World, 4007, 4246, 6510, 6518, 8015, 8098, 8700, 8712, 8741, 8747, 8772
Tiahuanaco, Bolivia, 897
Tiahuanacoid Culture, 932a-3, 2002
Tikal, 604, 619, 661, 727, 763
Tila, Mexico, 1933
Tinyash, Peru, 1048c
Tiraque, Bolivia, 1544
Tiriyó Indians, 1328, 2119
Tlacotalpan, Mexico, 6665
Tlapacoya, Mexico, 782
Tlapacoya Man, 747
Tlatelolco, Treaty of, 8770, 8812, 8924, *See also* Disarmament and Latin American Nuclear Free Zone.
Tlatilco, Mexico, 757
Toba Indians, 1333, 1376
Toctiuco Site, 972
Tollan, Mexico, 705
Toltecs, 706
Toniná, Mexico, 691-2
Tools, *Precolumbian,* 685, 717, 732
Tool Industry, 4690
Toqto, Peru, 1427
Torres, Camilo, 8254, 8303, 8355
Torrijos, Herrera, Omar, 8199
Totonac Language, 1802, 1923
Tourism, *General,* 4136, 4205, 6733.

Argentina, 6773, 6778, 6780. *Brazil,* 7052, 7057, 7093. *Ecuador,* 6929, 6936. *Jamaica,* 4352, 6594. *Mexico,* 4284, 6683, 6685-6, 6692, 6695, 6705. *Paraguay,* 6954-5. *Peru,* 6972, 7007, 7009. *Uruguay,* 7017
Trade, *General,* 4151, 4180, 4193, 4239, 4248, *Argentina,* 4718, 6759, 6809. *Brazil,* 4763, 4818, 4924. *Central America,* 4378. *Ecuador,* 1523. *El Salvador,* 6622. *Guiana Highlands,* 1332. *Jamaica,* 4353. *Liberalization,* 4003, 4287. *Mexico,* 4266, 8804. *Precolumbian,* 689, 706,
Trade Card # 2. 771, 997 *Surinam,* 1217
Trademarks, 4046, 4059,
Transformational Analysis. *See* Language.
Transoceanic Migration. *See* Migration.
Transportation, *Brazil,* 4792, 4889, 4892, 4923, 4927, 4960, 7049, 7095, 7129, 7138, 7140, 7144, 7155, 7177. *Colombia,* 6912. *Honduras,* 6636. *Peru,* 6992. *Uruguay,* 7019
Travel, *General,* 6724, 6734, 6739. *Bahamas,* 6560. *Belize,* 6564. *Bolivia,* 6831. *Caribbean,* 6560, 6562, 7028. *Central America,* 6610. *Chile,* 6863, 6869. *Colombia,* 6911. *Cuba,* 6585. *Ecuador,* 6926. *Guatemala,* 6564. *Guyana,* 6948. *Jamaica,* 6594. *Mexico,* 6564, 6671-3, 6688, 6704. *Puerto Rico,* 6572. *South America,* 6751, 6753. *Venezuela,* 7028. *Windward Islands,* 6573
Trepanation, 2018
Trinidad Hindi Language. *See* Creole Languages.
Trio Indians, 2089-91, 2133
Trique Indians, 1145
Trujillo, Rafael Leónidas, 8251
Tucano Indians, 1932
Tucanoan Languages, 1816, 1856, 1876, 1903, 1939
Tucurrique, Manuel, 1111
Tuenbo Language. *See* Chibchan Languages.
Tula Archaeological Project, Mexico, 705-6, 733
Tulan Project, 938b
Tulum, Mexico, 656
Tumbes, Peru, 1455
Tunebo Indians, 1932
Tupamaros, 8614
Tupiguarani Indians, 900, 902a, 1388, 1396
Tupí-Guaraní Language, 1816, 1821, 1833, 1837, 1908, 1936
Tuxpan, Mexico, 772
Txukuhamēi Language. *See* Kayapó Language.

Tzeltal. *See* Mayan Languages.
Tzintzuntzan, Mexico, 654, 1153-4
Tzotzil. *See* Maya Languages.
Tz'utujil Indians, 1185
UNCTAD, 4026, 4052, 4060, 8749
UN-Latin American relations, 8700, 8718, 8877, 8890, 8922
US-Latin American relations, 8701, 8705-6, 8713-4, 8716, 8719, 8721-4, 8726, 8728, 8730-1, 8736-8, 8740-2, 8744-5, 8749a, 8751, 8753-4, 8756, 8764, 8775-6, 8782-3, 8785, 8789-91, 8797-98, 8801, 8803, 8856-8, 8864, 8883
US National Governors Conference, San Juan, P.R., 8775.
USSR and Latin America, 8059, 8737, 8739, 8747, 8765, 8862
Uaxactun, 601, 763, 781
Uchucmarca Site, 1048, 1430
Umbanda. *See* Religion.
Unión Republicana Democrática, Venezuela, 8526
United Fruit Company, 6629
Universidad de América, 6158
Universities, *General,* 6001-2, 6004, 6021-2, 6036, 6040, 6043, 6053, 6055-7, 6060, 6065, 9636. *Argentina,* 4750, 6076, 6082, 6092-7, 8630a, 8636. *Autonomy,* 6019, 6065, 8312. *Bolivia,* 6108. *Brazil,* 6212, 6220-1, 6231, 6235, 6237-8, 6241, 6243, 6262, 6264, 6267, 6276, 6314-5, 6329-30, 6334-6, 6343, 6367, 6371-2, 6371-2, 6374-6, 6381. *Catholic,* 6053, 6241, 6367. *Chile,* 6055, 6115, 6118, 6121. *Colombia,* 6017, 6039, 6124-5, 6132, 6134-6, 8312, 8315, 8336, 9830. *Costa Rica,* 6110. *Cuba,* 6143. *Dominican Republic,* 6198, 6200, 6206. *Ecuador,* 6147. *Mexico,* 6016, 6039, 6054, 6058, 6060, 6151-2, 6158, 6161-2. *Panama,* 6039. *Paraguay,* 6039, 6166. *Peru,* 6055, 6058, 6062, 6171, 6175. *Puerto Rico,* 6039, 6201, 6205. *Reform,* 6035, 6053, 6055, 6096, 6108, 6115, 6118, 6136, 6143, 6147, 6175, 6188, 6212, 6221, 6243, 6264, 6374-5, 6377, 8082. *Uruguay,* 6039, 6177, 8607. *Venezuela,* 6188-90, 6192, 6197, 8514. *Violence,* 6010, 8514. *Violence,* 6010, 8514
Urabá, Colombia, 6873
Urban Guerillas. *See* Guerillas.
Urbanization, *General,* 1516, 2048, 6041, 6048, 6050, 6508, 6520-1, 6526-7, 6530-2, 6534, 6541, 6543-4, 6547, 6553, 6558, 6741, 7202, 7218, 8075, 8088, 8103, 9625, 9655, 9658, 9660, 9675, 9698. *Andean,* 1437. *Argentina,* 4725, 6777, 6786, 6804, 9908. *Aztecs,*

627. *Bolivia,* 1480, 7222. *Brazil,* 4791, 4796, 4822, 4831, 4833, 4870, 4956, 4959, 4972, 6265, 6313, 7047, 7077, 7107-8, 7114, 7120, 7122, 7147, 7154, 7163, 7165, 7167-9, 7176, 7184, 7195, 8554, 8575, 8582, 8589a. *Chile,* 1499, 4616, 8459, 9876. *Colombia, 1499, 1553, 4463, 4474, 4496, 4503-4, 6900, 6916, 4474.* Costa *Rica,* 9753. *Cuba,* 8207. *Dominican Republic,* 7285, 9753. *Ecuador,* 6927, 6930. *Guajiro,* 1409. *Guatemala, 9766. Jamaica,* 1296, 4354. *Mexico,* 1116, 1121, 1153-4, 1158, 6658, 6662, 6687, 6698, 6706, 9703, 9705-6, 9737, 9746, 9750. *Peru,* 1423, 1454, 1483, 1499, 1518, 1546, 4650, 6979. *Precolumbian,* 602, 659, 870, 1017a. *Puerto Rico,* 6603-4. *Reform,* 9649. *Uruguay,* 6182a, 7011. *Venezuela,* 4541, 4569, 7026, 7030-1, 8510, 8521-21a, 8524a, 8526b, 8529a
Urcos, Peru, 1509
Urrutia-Thompson Treaty, 8942
Urus, 1497
Uto-Aztecan Languages, 1857-8, 1869, 1883-4, 1898, 1931
Valdivia Site, 966, 967, 971
Vale do Iapó, Brazil, 901
Vale do Itajai, Brazil, 906-6a
Vale do Rio Cai, Brazil, 922d-2e
Vale do Rio Doce, Brazil, 918
Valle de Abaucán Site, 866, 893
Valle de Chancay, 1510
Valle de Mexico, 717
Valle de Nochixtlan, Mexico, 783
Valle de Oaxaca, 641, 726, 782, 1122
Valle de Vinchina, 873
Valle de Xochicalco, 646-7
Valle del Urubamba, 1344
Vasconcelos, José, 8166
Vasectomy. *See* Family Planning.
Velars. *See* Language.
Venezuela, Gulf of, 8895, 8941
Venezuela and the US, 8532a, 8894
Veraguas, Panama, 818
Vertical Adaptation Theory, 889a
Vesco, Robert, 8184
Vicos, Peru, 1463, 1491, 1540-1, 2110
Vicus-Pabur, Peru, 1002
Vilama Site, 862a
Violence, 8029, 8088, 8095, 8116, 8350a, 8505, 8513a, 8628, 8649a, 8657, 8670, 9696
La Violencia, Colombia, 8350a
Vocabulary. *See* Language.
Volcanoes. *See* Geology.
Von Thünen Theory, 7014
Voodoo, 9800
Vowel elision. *See* Language.
Wages. *See* Income.

Wajana Indians, 2090-1, 2133
Wakan, Peru, 1027a
Wamalli, Peru, 1027a
Wapishana Language. *See* Arawakan Languages.
Warao Indians, 1351-3, 1413
Water Resources, *Mexico,* 641
Waunana Language. *See* Choco Language.
Waurá Indians, 1395
Waurá Language. *See* Arawakan Languages.
Western Europe in Latin America, 8737
Wetbacks. *See* Migrant Workers.
Wilson, Woodrow, 8813
Wirikuta, Mexico, 1169
Witchcraft, 508, 802, 897, 1108, 1130, 1144, 1277, 1313, 1388, 1413, 1444, 1448, 1462, 1464, 1519, 1956-7, 6546
Witoto Indians. *See* Huitoto Indians.
Witotoan Languages. *See* Huitotoan Languages.
Women, *General,* 6123a, 8057, 8109-10, 9601, 9612-3, 9616, 9623, 9633, 9665. *Argentina,* 9885, 9889, 9891, 9893, 9897. *Black,* 1209. *Brazil,* 6277. *Chile,* 8366-66a, 8464. *Colombia,* 1452-3, 1484, 9829-30, 9839. *Cuba,* 8235, 8238, 8246, 9792, 9794, 9806, 9808, 9812. *Dominican Republic,* 9817. *Guatemala,* 1179. *Mayas,* 1129. *Mexico,* 1151, 9701, 9730. *Mundurucú,* 1372. *Peru,* 1536, 6979, 8366-66a. *Precolumbian,* 502, 507
World Power, 8552a, 8869, 8882, 8921, 8923
X-Cacal Group, 1150
Xalacapan, Mexico, 1193
Xalpatlahuac, Mexico, 1125
Xavante Language. *See* Jê Languages.
Xicalango, Mexico, 689
Xicotepec, Mexico, 1923
Xingu Tribes, 1348, 2150
Xirinachs de Zent, Costa Rica, 1159
Xiuhtecutli, 735
Xoc, Mexico, 710
Xochicalco, Mexico, 651
Xokleng Indians, 906-6a, 1393
Yejé. *See* Ayahuasca.
Yalálag, Mexico, 1151
Yalbac Hills, Belize, 1210
Yanomama Indians, 1357-8, 2099, 2107-9, 2114, 2123-8, 2241
Yavi Chico Site, 880
Ye'cuana Indians. *See* Yekuana Indians.
Yekuana Indians, 1316, 1330, 1401, 2107, 2128
Youth and Society, 9606, 9662, 9696, 9859, 9903
Yucatan, Mexico, 614

Yucana, Indians, 1932
Yuko Indians. *See* Iuko Indians.
Yupa Indians, 2082
Yuracare Language, 1944
Yutoaztecan Languages. *See* Uto-Aztecan Languages.
Zacachila, Mexico, 681
Zaparoan Languages, 1915
Zapotal, Mexico, 787
Zapotec Indians, 1118, 1122, 1152, 1180, 1182, 2173
Zapotecan Language, 1815, 1945
Zapotlan, Mexico, 772
Zinacantán, Mexico, 1114, 1115, 1120, 1130, 1139, 1200
Zinacantec Indians, 2143
Zoos. *See* Ecology.
Zoque Indians, 1187, 1198

Author Index

Bibliography and General Works (1-151)
Anthropology (500-2264)
Economics (4000-4990)
Education (6000-6381)
Geography (6500-7351)
Government and Politics (8000-8699)
International Relations (8700-8942)
Sociology (9600-10,069)

Abad Arango, Darío, 4000
Abadi, Mauricio, 9877
Abellan, Victoria, 8700
Abelson, Andrew E., 2192
Aberastury, Marcelo, 8819
Abihaggle, Carlos E., 6067
Abrahams, Roger D., 1204
Abrams, Richard M., 8701
Abreu, Aurélio M.G. de, 500
Abreu, Carlos Miguel Hecker de, 4908
Abreu, João Theodoro de Salles, 9916
Abreu, Marcello de Paiva, 4760
Abreu, Roberto Gonçalves de, 7157
Abreu Sacohetta, Lia de. See Sacohette, Lia de Abreu.
Abril, Juan Carlos, 4683
Acción, 8604
Acedo Mendoza, Carlos, 8510
Acedo Mendoza, Manuel, 8511
Acerca de la estrategia revolucionaria en Colombia, 8296
Acerca de la revolución en Latino América, 8000
Achéen, René, 4339
Acheson, James M., 1101
Acholonu, Alexander D., 1247
Achura L., Manuel, 6549
Acosta, Helia D', 9700
Acosta, Jorge R., 681
Acosta, Maruja, 8207
Acosta, Mercedes, 9778
Acosta, Phyllis B., 2134
Acosta, Pilar, 671
Acosta Garrido, Mercedes, 8838
Acosta Saignes, Miguel, 1282

Acosta Solís, Misael, 6919-6922
Adamczyk, Ricardo Calderón, 4001
Adams, Charles Dennis, 6593
Adams, Richard E.W., 600-601, 612, 629, 633, 682-683
Adams, Richard N., 9752
Adie, Robert F., 8001
Adler-Karlsson, Gunnar, 4409
Adrianzen T., Blanca, 2135, 2154-2155
Affonso, Almino, 8429
Agnew of Lochnaw, C.H., yr., 6836-6837
Agor, Weston H., 8702
Agrar- und Hydrotechnik GmbH (firm), Essen, FRG, 7044
El Agricultor Venezolano, 7021
La agricultura en Potosí: desarrollo y economía, año agrícola 1973/74, 4581
Agro, Robert J., 963
Agüero, Alicia, 4684-4685
Agüero Zahnd, H.E., 513
Aguerra, Ana M., 861
Aguiar, Neuma, 4761-4762
Aguiar, Wilson A., 6207
Aguilar, Carlos H., 816
Aguilar, Enrique, 4252
Aguilar Bulgarelli, Oscar, 4369
Aguilar Monteverde, Alonso, 4002
Aguilera, Carmen, 701
Aguilera de Litvak, C., 513
Aguilera Rojas, Javier, 7202
Aguirre, Emiliano, 671
Aguirre Beltrán, Gonzalo, 1102
Ahlfeld, Federico E., 6814
Ahmad, J., 4003
Aitken, Norman D., 4370

651

Ajace, Rodrigo, 4763
Alaluf, David, 6838
Alamo Esclusa, Víctor, 4004
Alaniz Carvajal, Jaime, 926
Alba, Víctor, 8002, 8050
Alberti, Giorgio, 1416-1417
Albes, Claudio N., 2261
Albo, Javier, 1420
Albornoz, Orlando, 6183
Albuquerque, Roberto Cavalcanti de, 4861, 6275
Albuquerque, Rubens José de Castro, 7045
Albuquerque, Therezinha Lins de, 6208
Alcaino Barros, Alfredo, 8421
Alcalá Quintero, Francisco, 8804
Alcina Franch, José, 501, 671, 964, 985
Alderman, Michael H., 2136, 2188
Alegria, Agnaldo, 7242
Alegría, Juana Armanda, 9701
Aleixo, José Carlos Brandi, 8541
Alers, M.H., 1205
Alexander, Robert J., 8542
Alfabetização de adultos: orientação nova da UNESCO, 6209
Alfaro de Lanzone, Lidia C., 513, 862-862a
Algunos aspectos básicos de la integración de la Cuenca del Plata, 4005
Alhajj M., Norman, 1800
Alisky, Marvin, 8134-8135
Alladin, M.P., 1275
Allen, Guillermo, 1420
Allende, Beatriz, 8439a
Allende, Salvador, 8422-8422b
Allison, Marvin J., 2000-2003
Allpanchis Phuturinqa, 1418-1421
Almada, Carlos G., 4006
Almada, Francisco R., 6651
Almazán Cadena, Antonio, 6652
Almeida, José, 4764-4765
Almeida, Darcy F. de, 6360
Almeida, Ruy Affonso Guimarães de, 4964
Almeida, Wanderly J. Mauro de, 4766
Almeida Andrade, Thompson. *See* Andrade, Thompson Almeida.
Almeida Biato, Francisco. *See* Biato, Francisco Almeida.
Almeida Ferreira-Santos, Célia. *See* Ferreira-Santos, Célia Almeida.
Almeida Magalhães, João Paulo de. *See* Magalhães, João Paulo de Almeida.
Almeida Prado, João Fernando de. *See* Prado, João Fernando de Almeida.
Alonso, Enrique, 8392
Alonso A., Máximo, 9600
Alonso González, Francisco, 4253.
Alphandery, Jean-Jacques, 4410
Altamira G., Armando, 6653
Altamirano, Carlos, 8625

Altenfelder, Mário, 9917-9918
Altesor, Alberto, 8605
Altieri de Barreto, Carmen G., 9779
Altimir, Oscar, 4686
Alurralde Anaya, Antonio, 4582
Alvarado, Jorge, 2137
Alvarado, Luis, 6839
Alvarado, Víctor M., 7326
Alvarado Garaieva, Teodoro, 8703
Alvarenga, Reynaldo Botrel, 4908
Alvarez, Federico, 8512
Alvarez, José, 1361
Alvarez, Maria Cristina, 1946
Alvarez Barret, Luis, 6149
Alvarez de la Cruz, Inés, 29
Alvarez de Williams, Anita, 684
Alvarez Múnera, Guillermo, 6873
Alvarez Perelló, José de Jesús, 2066
Alvargonzález Cruz, Rafael, 4767
Alvear Acevedo, Carlos, 8136
Alves, Ana Rita, 1315
Alves, Marcio Moreira, 8543
Alves, Maria Thereza, 7099
Alves da Silva, Hilberto Mascarenhas. *See* Silva, Hilberto Mascarenhas Alves da.
Alves de Brito, Fausto. *See* Brito, Fausto Alves de.
Alves de Lima, Miguel. *See* Lima, Miguel Alves de.
Alves Oliveira de Melo, Acyr. *See* Melo, Acyr Alves Oliveira de.
Alvim Martins, Marseno. *See* Martins, Marseno Alvim.
Alvirez, David, 2020
Amado, Gilson, 6210
Amara, Giuseppe, 9702
Amaral, Gilberto, 6728
Amaral Vieira, R.A. *See* Vieira, R.A. Amaral.
Amarante Macedo, Vera Amália. *See* Macedo, Vera Amália Amarante.
Amazonas (state) Bra. Secretaria de Estado de Planejamento e Coordenação Geral (SEPLAN). Comissão de Desenvolvimento do Estado do Amazonas (CODEAMA), 7046
Amazonas (state), *Bra.* Secretaria de Planejamento e Coordenação Geral (SEPLAN). Comissão de Desenvolvimento do Estado do Amazonas (CODEAMA), 9919
América Indígena, 1309, 1422
American Automobile Association, Washington, 6560
The American Library Association, 46
Américas, 6815
Ameringer, Charles D., 8200
Amérique, 6500
Amiran, David H.K., 6961
Amorim, Paulo Marcos de, 1310

Ampuero Brito, Gonzálo, 927
Anda, Gustavo de, 8137
Ander-Egg, Ezequiel, 8003, 8626, 9601
Anderi, Wagner Carneiro, 10060
Anderson, Joanne, 1879
Anderson, Robert W., 8266-8267
Andic, Faut M., 4326
Andic, Suphan, 4326
Andrade, José Maria Tavares de, 9920
Andrade, Luis Dias de, 6342
Andrade, Manuel Correia de, 4768
Andrade, Manuel Correia de Oliveira, 7047-7048, 8543a
Andrade, Thompson Almeida, 4769, 4863
Andréa, Flávio Fortes D'. *See* D'Andréa, Flávio Fortes.
Andreazza, Mário David, 7049
Andressen, Rigoberto, 7022
Andrews, A.P., 513
Andrews, E. Wyllys, IV, 612, 685-686
Andrews, E. Wyllys, V, 686, 817
Andrews, Frank M., 1423
Andrews, George F., 602
Angelini, Arrigo Leonardo, 9921-9922
Angell, Alan, 8423
Angelopoulos, Angelos, 4007
Angely, João, 7050
Angles Vargas, Víctor, 986
Angulo, Jorge, V, 719
Annable, James E., Jr., 4008
El Año Ecuatoriano, 6923
d'Ans, André-Marcel. *See* D'Ans, André-Marcel.
Antezana E., Luis, 6816
Antoine, Charles, 8544
Anton, Ferdinand, 502, 987
Antonini, Gustavo A., 9753
Antropologia do açúcar: curso sobre antropologia do açúcar promovido pelo Museu do Açúcar nos meses de maio-junho de 1971, 503
Anuario de Epidemiología y Estadística Vital, 2021
Anuario Estadístico de Venezuela: 1969, 7023
Apmann, Robert P., 6166
Applegate, Michael J., 4393
Appy, Robert, 4770
Aptheker, Herbert, 1282
Aragão, Jarbas Cavalcante de, 6211
Aragão, José Campos de, 8544a
Aragón, Eliseo B., 6654
Arancibia, Ubén Gerardo, 1312
Aranda Baeza, Ximena, 6840
Aranegui, Manuel de, 8606
Aranjo, José Tavares de, Júnior, 4771
Arango Jaramillo, Mario, 8297
Arango R., Mariano, 4456
Aráoz, Alberto, 4687
Araud, Christian, 4254, 9703

Araújo, Acrísio Tôrres, 7051
Araujo, Manuel Mora y, 9602
Araujo, Orlando, 4529
Araújo e Oliveira, José Carlos de. *See* Oliveira, José Carlos de Araújo e.
Araujo Lago, Antônio Carlos de. *See* Lago, Antônio Carlos de Araujo.
Araújo Merlano, Alberto, 8298
Araúz, Reina Torres de, 1424
Araya Pochet, Carlos, 4369
Araya Vergara, José, 6841
Arbingast, Stanley A., 7307
Arcand, Bernard, 1425
Arce, Daniel Valois, 8865
Archetti, Eduardo P., 4688, 8004
Archila, Ricardo, 88
Areces, Nidia R., 8005
Arellano M., José Pablo, 4594
Arenas, Jacobo, 8299
Arends, Tulio, 2067, 2104
Aresi, Ricardo, 9923
Arévalo, Jorge, 6874
Arévalo, Oscar, 8627
Argentina. Consejo Nacional de Desarrollo [and] Consejo Nacional de Seguridad, 4689
Argentina. Dirección Nacional de Promoción Industrial. Departamento Sectoral, 4690
Argentina. Dirección Nacional de Turismo, 6757
Argentina. Instituto Geográfico Militar, 7210
Argentina. Junta de Investigaciones Científicas y Experimentales de las Fuerzas Armadas (JICEFA), 6758-6759
Argentina. Ministerio de Agricultura y Ganadería. Comisión Reguladora de la Producción y Comercio de la Yerba Mate. Comité de Propaganda del Consumo de la Yerba Mate, 6760
Argentina. Ministerio de Agricultura y Ganadería. Subsecretaría de Recursos Naturales Renovables. Servicio Nacional Forestal, 6761
Argentina. Ministerio de Cultura y Educación. Centro Nacional de Documentación e Información Educativa, 6068-6070
Argentina. Ministerio de Cultura y Educación. Departamento de Estadística Educativa, 6071
Argentina. Ministerio de Cultura y Educación. Dirección General de Administración, 6072-6075
Argentina. Ministerio de Hacienda y Finanzas. Dirección Nacional de Programación e Investigación, 4691
Argentina. Presidencia, 8866
Argentina. Servicio Nacional de Parques

Nacionales, 7211
Argentina y Brasil: estudio comparativo de algunos de sus aspectos fundamentales, 8867
Arguedas, Sol, 8424
Argueta Cordón, Antonio, 6620
Arias, J., 513
Arias Bazantes, Manuel, 6924
Arias Sánchez, Oscar, 4371
Arioti, M., 513
Arismendi, Rodney, 8607, 8868
Arizmendi Posada, Octavio, 6122, 8300-8300a
Arizpe S., Lourdes, 1103
Arlas, José A., 8608
Armellada, Cesáro de, 1313
Armendariz, Amadeo, 4457
Armitano, Oswaldo, 4570
Arnaud, Expedito, 1314-1315
Arnaudo, Aldo A., 4009, 4692-4696
Arnedo Alvarez, Gerónimo, 8627a
Arnold, Dean E., 988-988a
Arnold, Hans, 8703a
Arnove, Robert F., 6000
Arns, Paulo Evaristo, 9924
Arnt, Nilton, 2215
Aron-Schaar, Adrianne, 1426, 1487
Arosemena R., Jorge, 4404, 9754
Arozo, Maria Amália, 6212
Arqueología peruana: precursores, 989
Arquivos Brasileiros de Psicologia Aplicada, 6213
Arraes, Miguel, 8545
Arreguín, Manuel, 6549
Arriaga, Eduardo E., 2022, 9603
Arriagada, Genaro, 8425
Arrieta, Gricelda A., 4985
Arrillaga de Maffei, B.R., 7018
Arriola, Carlos, 8810-8811
Arroyave, G., 2157
Arroyo, Víctor Manuel, 1801
Arroyo C., Dulio, 8820
Arroyo Lasa, Jesús, 6001
Arruda, Orêncio Longino de, 4974
Arruda Pinto, Aloísio de. *See* Pinto, Aloísio de Arruda.
L'art olmeque: source des arts classiques du Méxique, 687
Artana, Néstor, 8006
Arvelo-Jiménez, Nelly, 1316
Asamblea General del Instituto Panamericano de Geografía e Historia, *VIII, Guatemala, 1965,* 7024
Asamblea Nacional Popular Femenina. Comité Educativo, 6123
Aschero, Carlos A., 861, 863
Aschmann, Herman Pedro, 1802
Ascuasiati, Carlos, 4327-4329
Ashcraft, Norman, 1206-1207, 6109
Ashcroft, M.T., 2138-2139

Ashton, Guy T., 9827
Asociación de Libre Comercio del Caribe: CARIFTA, 4330
Asociación Latinoamericana de Libre Comercio, 4010-4011
Asociación Nacional de Profesortes de Geografía, 7010
Asociación Salvadoreña de Industriales, 4372
Aspectos de industrialização brasileira: conferências pronunciadas durante as comemorações do 40.º aniversário do CIESP, 4772
Aspectos de la realidad latinoamericana, 8007
Aspectos específicos de la problemática patagónica, 6762
Aspinall, W.P., 6561
Asplan S.A. (firm), *Brazil,* 4773-4774
Assadourian, Carlos Sempat, 4012
Assis, Milton Pereira de, 6240
Assis Dayrell, Gilson de. *See* Dayrell, Gilson de Assis.
Associação dos Geógrafos Brasileiros, Presidente Prudente, Bra., 7052
Associação dos Munícipios da Zona Sul do Estado do Rio Grande do Sul, *Brazil,* 4775
Associação Paulista de Bibliotecários, *São Paulo,* 47-49
Association of Universities and Colleges of Canada, *Ottawa,* 89
Astesano, Eduardo B., 8627b
Astiz, Carlos Alberto, 8008, 8704
Athens, J. Stephen, 965 974
Atherton, M.P., 6962
Atividades didáticas na educação de adultos, 6214
Atley, Suzzane de. *See* De Atley, Suzzane.
Attride, Bill, 1297
Auberger, Phillippe, 4776
Aubey, R.T., 4255
Aubey, Robert, 4013, 9604
Aufdermauer, Joerg, 700
Augelli, John P., 149
Austral, Antonio Gerónimo, 864
Los automotores como fuentes contaminantes, 6501
Automóvil Club Argentino, *Buenos Aires.* División Cartografía, 7212-7216
Avalos de Matos, Rosalía, 990
Avelino, Andrés, h., 6198
Avery, William P., 4014
Avila, Abel, 9828
Avila, Fernando Bastos de, 9925
Avila, Héctor F., 6076
Avila, Rafael, 8301
Avila Bernal, Alvaro, 6875
Avilés, René, 6150

Ayala Echavarri, Rafael, 6655
Ayensu, Edward S., 6745
Aytai, Desidério, 914
Azeredo Santos, Theóphlio de. See Santos, Theóphilo de Azeredo.
Azevêdo, Carlos Alberto, 9926-9927
Azevedo, E.S., 2068
Azevedo, Fernando de, 6215
Azevedo, Oswaldo Benjamín de, 4777
Azevedo, Tania F.S. de, 2068
Azevedo Barbosa, José Maria de Azavedo.
Azevedo Cunha, Luiz Roberto. See Cunha, Luiz Roberto Azevedo.
Aznar, Luis, 9605
Bacchieri Duarte, José. See Duarte, José Bacchieri.
Bacha, Edmar Lisboa, 4778-4779, 4888
Bacic, Uros, 4697
Badina, Ovidiu, 9606
Baena Z., Luis A., 1803
Baer, Donald E., 4373
Baer, Gerhard, 1317
Baer, Werner, 4780
Baertl, J.M., 2135
Baeta, Nilton, 4781
Báez, Mauricio, 6502
Baeza, Jorge E., 1052, 1052a, 1059
Baeza Flores, Alberto, 8426
Bahamas. Ministry of Education and Culture, 6199
Bahamondes B., Raúl, 940
Bahia (state), Bra. Departamento de Mão-de-Obra. Divisão de Estudos e Pesquisas, 9928
Bahia (state), Bra. Prefeitura Municipal do Salvador, 7261
Bahia (state), Bra. Secretaria da Indústria e Comércio, 4712
Bahia (state), Bra. Secretaria de Planejamento, Ciência e Tecnologia, 8546
Bahia (state), Bra. Secretaria do Trabalho e Bem Estar Social, 7053
Bahia (state), Bra. Secretaria do Trabalho e Bem Estar Social. Departamento de Mão de Obra. Divisão de Estudos e Pesquisas, 4783
Bailey, Norman A., 8869
Baily, Samuel L., 127
Baines, John M., 8705
Baiocchi, Josephina Desounet, 6216
Baiocchi, Mari de Nazaré, 898
Baker, Eloise, 6621
Baker, Paul T., 2192, 2202
Baker, T.S., 2192
Baklanoff, Eric N., 8427
Balakrishnan, T.R., 2023
Balan, Jorge, 8547, 9704
Balassa, Bela, 4015
Balázs, Dénes, 6925

Balderrama C., Maritza, 6105
Baldus, Herbert, 1361
Balestrini C., César, 4530
Baliero Silva, Washington. See Silva, Washington Baliero.
Ball, Joseph W., 603, 683, 688-689
Ballance, R.H., 4256
Ballesteros-Gaibrois, Manuel, 513
Balout, Lionel, 671
Balow, Tom, 6637
Baloyra, Enrique A., 4531, 8513
Baltra Cortés, Alberto, 4016, 4595
Balve, Beba, 8628
Bamberger, Joan, 1318
Bán, Alzira Dornelles, 6217
Banco Central de Venezuela, Caracas, 4532-4533
Banco Central de Venezuela. Sección Integración, 4331
Banco de Desenvolvimento do Paraná, Curitiba, Bra., 7054
Banco de la República, Bogotá, 951
Banco do Desenvolvimento do Espírito Santo, Vitória, Bra., 4784
Banco do Nordeste do Brasil (BNB), Fortaleza, Bra., 4785-4787
Banco do Nordeste do Brasil, Fortaleza, Bra.: Departamento de Estudos Econômicos do Nordeste (ETENE). Divisão de Agricultura, 7055-7058
Banco do Nordeste do Brasil, Fortaleza, Bra. Setor de Investigações Agrícolas, 7059
Banco Ganadero Argentino, Buenos Aires, 6763
Banco Minero del Perú, Lima, 4637
Banco Nacional da Habitação (BNH), Rio, 4788
Banco Nacional de Comercio Exterior, México, 4257
Banco Nacional do Desenvolvimento Econômico, Rio, 4789-4790
Bandeira, Maria de Lourdes, 1319
Bandeira, Moniz, 8870
Bandeira Coelho, Ernesto. See Coelho, Ernesto Bandeira.
Bank of London and South America Review, 8009
Bankmann, Ulf, 513, 991
Baptista, Patricia, 1804
Baptista, Priscilla M., 1805-1806
Baptista-Gumucio, Mariano, 6099-6100, 8393
Baracho, José Alfredo de Oliveira, 9929
Barahuna, Epaminondas, 7060
Baraona Urzúa, Pablo, 8428
Barat, Josef, 4791-4792
Barata, Júlio de Carvalho, 8547a
Barata, Mário, 6218
Barba, Melitón, 9607

Barbalarga, Carlos L., 6764
Bárbara Virgínia, 9930
Barbería, Arturo, 821
Barbieri de Santamarina, Estela, 6801-6802
Barbosa, José Maria de Azevedo, 7061
Barbosa, Mario Gibson, 7062
Barbosa Ferreira, Ignez Costa. *See* Ferreira, Ignez Costa Barbosa.
Barbosa Mutis, David, 8871
Barbotin, Maurice, 828
Barcellos de Paula, Jardel. *See* Paula, Jardel Barcellos de.
Barceló R., Víctor Manuel, 4258
Barceló Sifontes, Lil, 17
Barcelos Filho, Mauro, 8588a
Bareiro-Saguier, Rubén, 6949
Barja Berríos, Góver, 6817
Barkin, David, 4259, 4411, 6656
Barnet, Richard, 4017
Barnoya de Asturias, Concha, 6113
Barona de la O., Miguel, 4260
Barone, José L., 1052a
Barraclough, Solon, 4596, 8429
Barraza, Luciano, 4261
Barrera Carrasquilla, Antonio, 6503
Barreto, Irma, 4534
Barrionuevo, Alfonsina, 1427-1428
Barrios Rivas, María I., 9608
Barrocas, José M.V., 7063
Barrón, Daniel, 6963
Barros, Aluízio A. de, 4796
Barros, Frederico José O., 4793
Barros, Henrique, 7063
Barros, José Roberto Mendoça de, 4794
Barros de Castro, Antônio. *See* Castro, Antônio Barros de.
Barros Laraia, Roque de, 1361
Barroso, Carmen Lúcia de Melo, 6219
Barroso, Manoel Antônio, 6220
Barroso Leite, Celso. *See* Leite, Celso Barroso.
Barruel de Lagenest, J.B. *See* Lagenest, J.B., Barruel de
Barthel, Thomas S., 794-796
Bartolomei, José A., 4684-4685, 4698
Barton, S.W., 8375, 8893
Bartra, Roger, 7025
Bartstra, H.A., 2089-2090
Baruzzi, Robert G., 7130
Basave Fernández del Valle, Agustín, 6002
Basch, Antonín, 4018
Bases da política educacional, 6221
Bases mínimas para el programa del Frente de Oposición Democrática, 8302
Basso, Ellen B., 513, 1320
Bassols Batalla, Angel, 4262, 6657
Bastarrachea, Juan R., 1946
Baster, Nancy, 4019

Bastidas C., Alfonso, 1807
Bastide, Roger, 1208, 1282, 9609, 9931
Bastien, Rémy, 1288a
Bastos, Therezinha Xavier, 7100
Bastos de Avila, Fernando. *See* Avila, Fernando Bastos de.
Bataillon, Claude, 6658, 8138
Bate, Petersen, Luis Felipe, 928-928a
Bath, C. Richard, 8706
Batista, Bolívar, 4329
Batista, Guarocuya, 6200
Baudez, Claude F., 690-692
Baulny, O., 513
Baum, Daniel Jay, 4332
Bausani, A., 513
Bayo Cosgaya, Armando, 6574-6575
Bazarian, Jacob, 8707
Bazile, Robert, 1288a
Beadle, Vi Ann, 8523
Beals, Carleton, 6659
Beals, Ralph Leon, 1104-1106
Bear, Audrey, 1429
Beare, Adolfo, 8872
Becker, Marshall Joseph, 604
Beaucage, Pierre, 1107
Becker, Bertha K., 7064
Becker, Irene Basile, 1054
Becker-Donner, Etta, 899
Becquelin, Pierre, 690-692
Bedoya M., Angel N., 6504
Bedregal, Guillermo, 8708
Beecher, Graciella, 693
Beecher, Robert, 693
Beghin, Ivan, 2140
Behrman, Jack N., 4020-4021, 8709
Behrman, Jere R., 4597-4598
Beiguelman, Paula, 8548
Beisiegel, Celso de Rui, 6222
Bejarano, Jesús A., 4458
Bejarano B., Gastón, 6818
Belcher, John C., 9610
Bell, Betty, 605
Bellomo, Harry Rodrigues, 7065
Belloni Ravest, Hugo, 8629
Belo Horizonte (city), *Bra.* Conselho Municipal de Planejamento do Desenvolvimento, 7262
Belo Horizonte (city), *Bra.*, Escola Superior de Guerra Associação dos Diplomados. Delegacia de Minas Gerais, 9932
Beltrán, Enrique, 6660
Beltrán Martínez, Antonio, 671
Beltrão, Luiz, 9933
Beltrão, Maria da Conçeição de M. Coutinho, 900
Beltrão, Pedro Calderan, 6505
Benassini, Oscar, 6661
Benavides Correa, Alfonso, 8363
Bender, Lynn Darrell, 8839

Benedetti, Mario, 8609
Benevides Fo, F.R. de Sá e, 2116
Benfer, Alice, 629, 733
Bengoa, José, 8429
Benítez, Ana M. de, 504
Benítez, Fernando, 1108
Benítez, Jaime, 6201
Benítez, Wilfredo, 9611
Benoist, Jean, 2069
Benoit, Emile, 4022
Benson, Elizabeth P., 797, 992-992a
Benton, William, 128
Benzi, Marino, 1109
Berberián, Eduardo E., 865
Beretta, Pier Luigi, 6765
Berg, Marie L., 1808, 1874
Berger, Manfredo, 6353
Berger, Peter L., 8548a
Berger, Rainer, 606
Bergholz M., Walter, 929
Bergholz W., Hans, 929
Berlin, Brent, 1110
Berlinski, Julio, 4699
Bernal, Ignacio, 607, 694
Bernal C., Fernando, 4459
Bernal Romero, Rosendo, 1054
Bernard, H. Russell, 1809-1810
Bernard, Jean-Pierre, 8010
Bernardes, Nara Maria Guazzelli, 6236
Bernardes, Nilo, 7066
Bernauer, Ursula, 8430
Berney, Henri-Maurice, 6562
Bernhart, Michael, 4460
Berroa Belén, Carlos, 1053
Berry, Paul, 1288a
Berthelot, Jean, 1430
Bertone, Carlos Alberto, 8697
Beseda s General'nym sekretarem Tsk Peruanskoi Kompartii Khorkle del' Prado (Interview with the General Secretary of the Peruvian Communist Party Jorge del Prado), 8364
Best, Robin, 7026
Beverly, Heather, 1297
Bezerra de Siqueira, Jurandir. *See* Siqueira, Jurandir Bezerra de.
Bhana, Surendra, 8840
Bianchi, Anna Maria F., 4914
Bianchi, Lois, 6842
Biato, Francisco Almeida, 4795
Bibiliografia Brasileira de Botânica: 1971/72, 108
Bibliografie van Suriname, 1209
Bibliography of selected statistical sources of the American nations (Bibliografía de fuentes estadísticas escogidas de las naciones americanas), 109
Biblioteca Nacional, *Rio*, 7067
Biblioteca Nacional José Martí, *La Habana*. Hemeroteca e Información Humanística, 21
Bibliotecas y Archivos, 50
Bicalho, Maria Dias, 110
Bicheno, H.E., 8479
Bidart Campos, Germán J., 8011
Biehl del Río, J., 8479
Bieniek, D., 2261
Bigarella, João José, 6721
Binder, Kathleen P., 1811
Binder, Ronald G., 1811
Binnendijk, Johannes A., 8375, 8893
Bird, Richard M., 4023
Birnbaum, Stephen, 6739
Birns, Laurence, 8431
Biró de Stern, Ana, 1431
Birou, Alain, 4024
Bischof, Henning, 513, 952, 966-966a
Bishop, Ruth G., 1923
Bissainthe, Max, 81
Bitar, Sergio, 4599-4600, 8715
Bittencourt, Agnello, 9934
Bittencourt, Gustavo Francisco Feijó, 8548b
Bittmann Simons, B., 513
Black, Francis L., 2216
Blackburn, Robin, 6018
Blakemore, Harold, 8432
Blanco, Boris, 8821
Blanco, Hugo, 8433
Blanco, Ricardo A., 2070-2071, 2141-2142
Blanco Lázaro, Enrique T., 9780
Blanco Muñoz, Agustín, 8513a
Blasi, Oldemar, 901
Blaut, James M., 1221
Bloch, Thomas, 51
Blume, Helmut, 6562
Blutstein, Howard I., 6576
Bobbio Centurión, Carlos, 4638, 8365
Bode, Barbara, 9674
Bodley, John H., 1321, 1432
Boggs, Stanley H., 695
Boglár, Lejos, 1322-1323
Bohn, Claudia J., 9781
Bohorquez C., José Ignacio, 22, 52
Boisier, Sergio, 4796
Boizard, Ricardo, 8434
Boletim Carioca de Geografia, 7068
Boletim da Biblioteca da Câmara dos Deputados, 23
Boletim de Intercâmbio, 6223
Boletim Informativo FUNAI, 1324
Boletim Paranaense de Geociências, 7069
Boletim UEG, 6224
Boletín de Estudios Geográficos, 6766-6768
Boletín de Higiene y Epidemiología, 2217
Boletín de la Cámara de Comercio de Caracas, 4535

Boletín de la Sociedad Geográfica de Colombia, 6876
Boletín de la Sociedad Mexicana de Geografía y Estadística, 1
Boletín de la Universidad de Chile, 6115
Boletín del Instituto del Mar del Perú, 6964
Boletín del Museo del Hombre Dominicano, 829, 829a, 829b
Boletín Documental sobre la Mujer, 9612
Boletín Nicaragüense de Bibliografía y Documentación, 82
Boletín Técnico, 6184
Boletín Uruguayo de Sociología, 9913
Bolivia. Corporación Minera de Bolivia, 6819
Bolivia. Dirección General de Desarrollo Urbano, 7222
Bolivia. Instituto Geográfico Militar, 7223
Bolivia. Instituto Nacional de Estadística, 4583
Bolivia. Ministerio de Agricultura. Departamento de Suelos, 6820
Bolivia. Ministerio de Información y Deportes, 8394
Bolivia. Servicio Nacional de Caminos, 7224
Bolland, O. Nigel, 1210
Bologna, Alfredo Bruno, 4025
Bolton, Ralph, 1421, 1433-1434
Bonachea, Ramón L., 8208
Bonachea, Rolando E., 4412, 8209
Bonamigo, Euza Maria de Rezende, 6381
Bonasera, Ilda Finzi, 6608
Bonavia, Duccio, 993
Bonelli, Regis, 4797
Bonfanti, Celestino, 2
Bonilla, Arturo, 4298
Bonilla, Heraclio, 4639
Bonilla, Víctor Daniel, 1445
Bonilla P., Janina, 1111
Bonnano, O., 2232
Bonsal, Philip W., 8841
Bonsor, Norman C., 8896
Boodhoo, Ken I., 1211
Boon, Gerard K., 4263
Bordaberry, Juan María, 8609a
Bordaz, Robert, 4026
Borden, Michael, 2160
Boretto Ovalle, René, 1053-1054
Börgel Olivares, Reynaldo, 6843-6844
Borges, A., 513
Borges, Kléber, 6225
Borges Pereira, João Baptista. *See* Pereira, João Baptista Borges.
Bório, Edith B. Lopes, 2261
Bormida, Marcelo, 1325
Borrego Pla, M.C., 513
Borrello, María Angélica, 866
Borsdorf, Axel, 6845
Bortner, R.W., 9781
Bortnik, Rubén, 8629a
Bortoluzzi da Silveira, José Celso. *See* Silveira, José Celso Bortoluzzi da.
Bosc, Robert, 8710
Bosch Millares, Juan, 671
Boschi, Renato Raul, 6226
Boswood, Joan, 1812-1814
Botafogo Gonçalves, José. *See* Gonçalves, José Botafogo.
Botana, Natalio R., 8630
Botello, Rubén, 7225
Botrel Alvarenga, Reynaldo. *See* Alvarenga, Reynaldo Botrel.
Botto, Juvenal, 2254
Bouda, K., 1815
Boulton, C., 513
Boulton, R., 513
Bourne, Roy McDonald, 6614
Bouroncle Carrión, Alfonso, 1816
Bourricaud, François, 8435
Bovenkerk, Frank, 1212-1214
Bovenkerk-Teerink, L.M., 1214
Bowditch, Charles P., 798
Bowen, J. David, 6965
Bowker Editores Argentina, *Buenos Aires,* 111
Bowman, Isaiah, 6722
Boyce, A.J., 2194
Boyd, Monica, 9613
Boza, Guillermo, 8514
Bozzoli de Wille, María E., 1112
Bradford, Collin I., Jr., 8715
Brading, David A., 8139
Braile, Pedro Márcio, 4798
Braithwaite, L.E.S., 1253
Branco, Miguel do Rio, 8711
Brandi Aleixo, José Carlos. *See* Aleixo, José Carlos Brandi.
Brandt, Sérgio Alberto, 4799, 4902
Braniff, Beatriz, 605
Branks, Judith, 1817
Branks, Thomas, 1817
Branston, Brian, 6723
Brasil Açucareiro, 7070
Brasil: operação sul (Brazil: operation south), 4800
Brasileiro, Ana Maria, 8549-8549a
Brathwaite, Edward Kamau, 1215
Brau, Salvador, 9782
Braun, Rafael, 8630
Bravo, Héctor Félix, 6077
Bravo Ahuja, Víctor, 6151
Bray, W., 960
Brayner, Floriano de Lima, 8550
Brazil. Banco Nacional da Habitação, 8551
Brazil. Comissão de Coordenação e Imple-

mentação de Técnicas Financieras, 8551a
Brazil. Congresso. Senado. Subsecretaria de Taquigrafia, 90
Brazil. Congresso Federal. Comissão Parlamentar do Inquérito, 4801
Brazil. Conselho de Desenvolvimento de Extremo Sul (CODESUL), 4802, 7071
Brazil. Directoria de Hidrografia e Navegação, 7073
Brazil. Escritório de Análise Econômica e Política Agrícola, 9935
Brazil. Exército. Centro de Relações Públicas, 8551b
Brazil. Fundação Instituto Brasileiro de Geografia e Estatística, 7227-7228
Brazil. Fundação Nacional de Material Escolar, 7229
Brazil. Instituto Brasileiro de Geografia, 7230, 7243
Brazil. Instituto Nacional de Colonização e Reforma Agrária, 7244
Brazil. Ministério da Agricultura. Instituto Nacional de Colonização e Reforma Agraria (INCRA), 9936
Brazil. Ministério da Agricultura. Instituto Nacional de Colonização e Reforma Agrária (INCRA). Comissão de Alienação de Terras Públicas, 7074
Brazil. Ministério da Agricultura. Instituto Nacional de Colonização e Reforma Agraria (INCRA). Departamento de Desenvolvimento Rural. Divisão de Cooperativismo e Sindicalismo, 7075
Brazil. Ministério da Educação e Cultura, 6227
Brazil. Ministério da Educação e Cultura. Comissão Nacional de Moral e Civismo, 6228
Brazil. Ministério da Educação e Cultura. Conselho Federal de Educação. Departamento de Documentação e Divulga-'ão, 6229
Brazil. Ministério da Educação e Cultura. Departamento de Ensino Fundamental, 6230
Brazil. Ministério da Educação e Cultura. Secretaria Geral, 6231
Brazil. Ministério da Educação e Cultura. Secretaria Geral. Serviço de Documentação, 6232
Brazil. Ministério da Marinha, 8873
Brazil. Ministério das Minas e Energia. Departamento Nacional da Produção Mineral, 7076
Brazil. Ministério das Relações Exteriores. Secretaria Geral Adjunta para o Planejamento Político, 8874
Brazil. Ministério do Interior. Fundação Nacional do Indio (FUNAI), 1326

Brazil. Ministério do Interior. Serviço Federal de Habitação e Urbanismo (SERFHAU), 7077
Brazil. Ministério de Interior. Superintêndencia do Densenvolvimento do Nordeste (SUDENE). Departamento de Agricultura e Abastecimento. Divisão de Abastecimento e Financiamento da Produção, 7080
Brazil. Ministério do Interior. Superintendência do Desenvolvimento do Nordeste (SUDENE). Departamento de Industrialização. Divisão de Pesquisas e Planejamento, 7081
Brazil. Ministério do Interior. Superintendência do Desenvolvimento da Amazônia (SUDAM). Departamento de Recursos Naturais, 7078
Brazil. Ministério do Interior. Superintêndencia do Desenvolvimento da Amazônia (SUDAM). Divisão de Documentações, 7079
Brazil. Ministério do Interior. Superintendência de Desenvolvimento do Nordeste (SUDENE), 7082
Brazil. Ministério do Interior. Superintendência do Nordeste (SUDENE). Setor de Demografia, 7083
Brazil. Ministério do Planejamento e Coordenação Geral, 8551c
Brazil. Ministério do Planejamento e Coordenação Geral. Fundação Instituto Brasileiro de Geografia e Estatística (IBGE). Superintendência de Estatísticas Primárias. Departamento de Censos, 7084
Brazil. Minsitério do Planejamento e Coordenação Geral. Instituto de Planejamento Econômico e Social. Instituto de Planejamento, 7085
Brazil. Ministério dos Transportes. Departamento Nacional de Estradas de Rodagem, 7231
Brazil. Presidência, 6233, 8551d
Brazil. Serviço Nacional de Aprendizagem Comercial (SENAC), 6234
Brazil. Serviço Nacional de Aprendizagem Comercial (SENAC). Departamento Regional de Pernambuco. Divisão de Formação Profissional. Setor de Pesquisas, 9937-9939
Brazil. Serviço Nacional de Aprendizagem Industrial (SENAI). Departamento Regional de Minas Gerais, 9940
Brazil. Superintendência do Desenvolvimento do Nordeste (SUDENE). Departamento de Agricultura e Abastecimento. Divisão de Abastecimento e Financiamento da Produção, 4803
Brazil. Superintendência do Desenvolvi-

mento do Nordeste (SUDENE). Departamento de Industrialização, 4804
Brazil. Superintendência do Vale do São Francisco (SUVALE), 7232
Brazil Development Series/Série Desenvolvimento Brasileiro, 7072
Brazil 71: cultural aspects, 129
Brazil: 1969, an unedited compilation of articles from the newsweekly *Latin America,* 8552
Brazil Universitário, 6235
Brazleton, T.B., 2143
Brcich, Juan M., 4027
Brea, Ernst T., 1288a
Breda, Judite Ivanir, 7236
Breedlove, Dennis E., 1110
Bremmé de Santos, Ida, 1113
Brenchley, P.J., 6962
Brereton, Bridget, 1253
Bresani, Jorge Bravo, 9849
Le Brésil en 1971, 8552a
Brésil 1972-1973: les deux dernières années de la Presidence Médici, 8552b
Bresser Pereira, Luiz Carlos. *See* Pereira, Luiz Carlos Bresser.
Breuer, Wilhelm M., 4413
Briano, Justo P., 8875
Brice, Max, 4028
Briceño Perozo, Mario, 24
Bricker, Victoria Reifler, 1114-1114a
Bride, Anne, 9848
Briggs, Janet R., 1818
Brignardello, Luisa A., 8630a
Brignole, M., 513
Briquet de Lemos, Antônio Agenor. *See* Lemos, Antônio Agenor Briquet de.
Brisson, Gerald, 9783
Brito, Fausto Alves de, 4805
Brito Jambeiro, Marusia de. *See* Jambeiro, Marusia de Brito.
Brizuela, Glayds C., 818
Broadbent, Sylvia M., 953
Brochado, José Proenza, 902-902a
Brockington, Donald L., 696-698
Broderick, Walter J., 8303
Brodersohn, Mario S., 4700, 4730
Brody, Eugene B., 9784
Bromley, Raymond J., 6926
Bronheim, David, 8715
Brooke, O.G., 2144-2145, 2195
Brotherston, Gordon, 633
Browman, David L., 1435
Brown, Cecil H., 1819
Brown, Harrison, 4029
Brown, Jane Cowan, 6662
Brown, Lester, 6506
Brown, Marion, 4601
Brown, Stephen M., 2072
Browning, David, 4374
Browning, Harley L., 2043, 9704

Brownrigg, Leslie Ann, 1436-1437
Brum, Argemiro J., 10005
Brundenius, Claes, 4640
Bruneau, Thomas C., 8553-8553b
Brunhouse, Robert L., 799
Bruning, Donald F., 6769
Brunn, Stanley D., 6632
Brunnschweiler, Dieter, 6877
Brush, Stephen Bourne, 1438
Bryan, Alan L., 846
Bryce-Laporte, Roy Simon, 1221
Brzezinska, Halina, 6217
Bubberman, F.C., 7340
Bucchioni, Eugene, 8269
Buck, Wilbur F., 6563
Budhoo, Davison L., 4333
Bueno, Gerardo M., 4030
Buenos Aires (province), Arg. Ministerio de Bienestar Social, 6770
Büntig, Aldo J., 9878-9879
Buescu, Mircea, 4806
El Búho, 6202
Buechler, Hans C., 1439-1441
Buechler, Judith Maria, 1441
Buffon, Alain, 4339
Buitrago Ortiz, Carlos, 8268, 9785
Bulhões, Octavio Gouvêa de, 4807
Bullard, William R., Jr., 612
Bullen, Adelaide K., 830
Bullen, Ripley P., 513, 830, 830a
Bulletin de Liaison et de Recherche Archéologique, 831
Bunimov-Parra, Boris, 9820
Buntig, Aldo, 8012
Burelli, Miguel Angel, 8514a
Burgos-Guevara, H., 513
Burguillos, Pedro, 4570
Burkart, Walter, 6724
Burke, Melvin, 1442, 4584-4585
Burland, C.A., 513
Burnett, William C., 7006
Burrus, Ernest, 6663
Burtch, Bryan, 1820
Burton, J.H., 1443
Burton, P.J.K., 6645
Buschkens, Willem F.L., 1216
Buse, Hermann, 6966
Busey, James L., 8822
Business Venezuela, 4536
Bussey, Ellen M., 9705
Bustamante, Alberto, 4654
Bustelo, Ana Margarita, 4668
Bustos Fierro, Raúl, 8630b
Butland, Gilbert J., 6507
Butt-Colson, Audrey, 1217
Butterfield, D. Anthony, 9973-9974
Butterworth, Douglas, 6548, 9625, 9786
Buttner, Elizabeth Holt. *See* Holt Buttner, Elizabeth.
Byars, Robert S., 6548, 8013

Caballero, Enrique, 8304
Cabello, Plácido, 9880
Cabral, Alvaro, 91
Cabral Mejía, Tobías E., 11
Cabrera, Orlando Molina, 4701
Cabrera Ortiz, Wenceslao, 6725
Cáceres Freyre, J., 513
Cáceres Olazo, Mariano, 1418, 1444
Cadernos de Estudos Brasileiros, 4808
Cadernos de Pesquisa, 6236
Cadogan, León, 1821
Caetano da Costa, Marcelo. *See* Costa, Marcelo Caetano da.
Cafferata, José Ignacio, 9614
Caggiano, María, 867
Caicedo A., Antonio J., 1822
Caillods, Françoise, 6137
Calasans, José Adão de, 8554
Calcagno, Alfredo Eric, 4233
Caldas, Ana María de, 954
Caldas, Rachel, 9927, 9998
Caldera, Rafael Tomás, 8014
Caldera Rodríguez, Rafael, 8515
Calderan Beltrão, Pedro. *See* Beltrão, Pedro Calderan.
Calderón, Valentín, 903
Calderón González, Jorge, 9787
Calderón Quijano, José Antonio, 6664
Calello, Hugo, 9821
Calibán [*pseud.* for Enrique Santos Montejo], 8305
Calitri, Princine, 6600
Callen, E.O., 608
Calligaris, Rodolfo, 9941
Calvet de Villagómez, Marta, 1445
Calvez, Jean-Yves, 8015
Calvo de Elcoro, Miren Zorkunde, 12
Calvo S., Haroldo, 4461-4462
Camacho, Alvaro, 8346
Câmara, Helder, 8610
Câmara Cascudo, Luís da. *See* Cascudo, Luís da Câmara.
Cámara de Comercio de Bogotá, 92
Camargo, Cândido Procopio Ferreira de, 9944
Camargo, Edilia, 8196
Camargo, Hernando, 6878
Camargo, Pedro Pablo, 8306
Camargo Engler, Joaquim J. de. *See* Engler, Joaquim J. de Camargo.
Camargo Viana, Adolpho Carlos. *See* Viana, Adolpho Carlos Camargo.
Cambre Mariño, Jesús, 6003
Camino D.C., Alejandro, 1446
Campa, Riccardo, 8436
Campal, Esteban F., 7217
Campbell, Lyle, 1823-1827
Campiglia, Néstor, 4669
El campo venezolano, 7027
Cámpora, Héctor J., 8631

Campos, Domar, 8555
Campos, Reginaldo Z. de, 4809
Campos, Renato Carneiro, 9998
Campos, Roberto de Oliveira, 4031, 4955
Campos de Aragão, José. *See* Aragão, José Campos de.
Camurça, Zélia Sá V., 9942
Canambra Engineering Consultants (firm), *Nassau, Bahamas,* 4810
The Canadian Library Association, 46
Cañas, Jorge, 6549
Cancian, Frank, 1115
Candia Navarro, René, 4586
Cañedo, Luis, 2218
Canet, Carlos, 1218
Cañibe, Juan Manuel, 6152
Canihuante Toro, Gustavo, 8437
Canitrot, Adolfo, 4702-4703
Cannon, Mark W., 8515a
Cano, Jairo, 4264
Canosa, Cipriano, 2070
Cantini, José Luis, 6078
Cantón, Darío, 8631a
Cantón Navarro, José, 8210
Capua, Constanza di, 967
Capuñay Mimbela, Carlos, 4641
Características socio-demográficas de las mujeres colombianas: encuesta nacional de fecundidad: parte urbana, 9829
Cardenal, Ernesto, 8211
Cárdenas, Rodolfo Marcelo, 9881
Cárdenas ante el mundo: defensor de la República Española, Etiopía, Finlandia, Africa, luchas populares de Asia, 8140
Cárdenas, Martín, 6821
Cárdenas Barrios, René, 8438
Cardich, Augusto, 868, 994-994a
Cardich, Lucio Adolfo, 868
Cardona Gutiérrez, Ramiro, 2043, 4463, 6508
Cardoso, Fernando Henrique, 4032-4033, 8074, 8715, 9943-9944, 10053
Cardoso Pinto, Maurício Jorge. *See* Pinto, Maurício Jorge Cardoso.
Cardozo Gonsález, Armando, 6817, 6822
Carella, Alfredo J.L., 8917
Carey, Beverly, 6594
Carlini, E.A., 2261
Carlos, Manuel L., 513, 1116
Carlson, Paul E., 1233
Carluci, María Angélica, 2146
Carmack, Robert M., 1117
Carmona, Fernando, 6153
Carneiro, David, 6237
Carneiro, José Fernando, 9945
Carneiro, Maria Cecília Ribas, 8927
Carneiro, Nelson Souza, 8555a
Carneiro, Robert L., 1361
Carneiro Anderi, Wagner. *See* Anderi, Wagner Carneiro.

Carneiro Campos, Renato. See Campos, Renato Carneiro.
Carneiro de Lacerda Filho, Murillo. See Lacerda Filho, Murillo Carneiro de.
Carneiro Leão, A. Sergio. See Leão, A. Sergio Carneiro.
Carneiro Vieira, José Paulo. See Vieira, José Paulo Carneiro.
Carnoy, Martin, 4099, 4811, 6167
Carpani, Ricardo, 8632
Carpenter, Allan, 6621, 6637
Carrera Andrade, Jorge, 130
Carrère, Bernard, 8712
Carretero, Jimena, 4034
Carri, Roberto, 8632a, 8697
Carrillo Batalla, Tomás Enrique, 4537
Carrillo Castro, Alejandro, 8141
Carrillo Flores, Antonio, 4035
Carrillo León, Omaida, 9822
Carrizosa Umaña, Julio, 6726
Carroll, Thomas, 9615
Carsten, Dietmar M., 1327
Carta Económica Mensual, 4375
Cartagena Portalatin, Aída, 832
Carvajal, Manuel J., 4376
Carvajal Pérez del Castillo, Jorge, 8876
Carvalho, Eduardo Werneck R. de, 10007
Carvalho, Guido Ivan de, 6238
Carvalho, Irene Mello, 6239
Carvalho, Lourdes de Freitas, 9946
Carvalho, Mário Helder de Oliveira, 4816
Carvalho, Paulo Pinto de, 8556
Carvalho Barata, Júlio de. See Barata Júlio de Carvalho.
Carvalho da Silva, Maria Lúcia. See Silva, Maria Lúcia Carvalho da.
Carvalho Filho, José Julianão de, 4812
Carvalho Galvão, Getúlio de. See Galvão, Getúlio de Carvalho.
Carvalho Neto, Joviniano Soares de, 8556a
Carvalho Pereira, José Eduardo de. See Pereira José Eduardo de Carvalho.
Casad, Eugene H., 1828
Casadevall, Domingo F., 9882
Casagrande, Joseph B., 1447, 1487
Casamiquela, Rodolfo, 6771
Casanova, Ramón Vicente, 9822
Casas González, Antonio, 4036, 4538-4540
Casaus, Víctor, 8212
Casaverde Rojas, Juvenal, 1418, 1448
Cascudo, Luís da Câmara, 7086
Caseita Cavalcanti, Leonardo. See Cavalcanti, Leonardo Caseita.
Casement, Susan, 4500
Casillas, Luis R., 4037-4038
Casimir, Jean, 8257
Cassano, Paul V., 1829-1830
Castañeda, Eduardo, 6185

Castañeda, Jorge, 8811
Castañeda Delgado, P., 513
Castellanos, Diego Luis, 4039
Castellanos, Rosario, 9616
Castello Salazar, Jorge Daniel, 8307
Castex, Mariano N., 6079, 8633
Castilla, Eduardo, 2074
Castillero Calvo, Alfredo, 8823
Castillo, Germán, 8335
Castillo, Luciano, 1208
Castillo Barrantes, J. Enrique, 9755
Castillo Campano, Cristiana, 6870
Castillo F., Víctor M., 1831, 4265
Castillo Tejero, Noemi, 513, 648, 702
Castrillón R., Alberto, 8308
Castro, Antônio Barros de, 4813-4814
Castro, Astréa de Moraes e, 53
Castro, Claudio de Moura, 4815, 6240, 10023
Castro, Fernando Saboya, 4040
Castro, Fidel, 8213-8216, 8439-8439a
Castro, G.A.M., 2075
Castro, Julio, 6124
Castro, Luiz Paiva de, 9947
Castro, Ormindo Viveiros de, 6241
Castro Albuquerque, Rubens José de. See Albuquerque, Rubens José de Castro.
Castro Bastos, Leónidas, 6967
Castro e Silva, Maria Thereza L.L. See Silva, Maria Thereza L.L. Castro e.
Castro Faria, Hugo Barros de. See Faria, Hugo Barros de Castro.
Castro Faria, Luiz de. See Faria, Luiz de Castro.
Castro G., Carlos D., 9788
Castro Harrison, Jorge, 6168
Castro Mayer, Antonio de. See Mayer, Antonio de Castro.
Castro Moreira da Silva, Paulo de. See Silva, Paulo de Castro Moreira da.
Castro Rodríguez, Leandro, 4041
Catunda, Omar, 9948
Cavalcanti, Clóvis de Vasconcelos, 4817
Cavalcante, Paulo B., 1328
Cavalcante, Raimundo Nonato de Fátima, 4816
Cavalcante de Aragão, Jarbas. See Aragão, Jarbas Cavalcante de.
Cavalcanti, Clóvis de Vasconcelos, 7087-7088
Cavalcanti, Jayme, 6242
Cavalcanti, Leonardo Caseita, 4834-4835
Cavalcanti, Themístocles Brandão, 8877
Cavalcanti de Albuquerque, Roberto. See Albuquerque, Roberto Cavalcanti de.
Cavatrunci, Claudio, 513, 995
Cavilliotti, Marta, 8016
Cayman Islands handbook and businessman's guide, 131
Cayón Armelia, Edgardo, 1449

Cazes, Daniel, 1832
Ceará (state), *Bra.* Convénio Governo, 7245
Ceará (state), *Bra.* Superintendência do Desenvolvimento (SUDEC). Serviço de Informações de Mercado (SIM), 7089
Ceballos Tapia, Hernán, 9862
Cecioni, Giovanni, 6846
Ceconi, Tulio, 4748
Cecy, C., 2261
Cei, José Miguel, 6727
Celestino, Olinda, 1450
Celson, José da Silva, 8557
Censo universitario latinoamericano, 1970, 6004
Censos nacionales de 1970: III censo agropecuario, 16 de mayo de 1971; cifras preliminares, 4377
Censos nacionales de 1970: séptimo censo de población, tercer censo de vivienda, 9756
Centro das Indústrias das Cidades Industriais de Minas Gerais, 9949
Centro das Indústrias do Estado de São Paulo, *São Paulo,* 4818
Centro de Estudios de la Revolución (CER), 8440
Centro de Estudios Económicos del Sector Privado, *México,* 4266
Centro de Estudos e Ação Social, *Salvador, Bra.,* 9617, 9950-9951
Centro de Investigaciones Sociales y Socio-Religiosas (CISOR), *Caracas,* 8515b
Centro di Azione e Documentazione sull'America Latina, *Milano, Italy,* 8017
Centro Internacional de Estudios Superiores de Periodismo para América Latina (CIESPAL), *Quito,* 8018
Centro Nacional de Información, 8186
Centro Naval, *B.A.* Instituto Naval de Conferencias y de Publicaciones Navales, 8633a
Cenzano Z., Carlos F., 1008b
Cepeda, Fernando, 8353
Cerda, Carlos, 8441
Cerda, J. Armando, 7308-7309
Ceresole, Norberto, 8634-8634b
Cernuschi, Félix, 6176
Ceron, Antonio Olivio, 7090-7091
Cerqueira Luz, A. *See* Luz, A. Cerqueira.
Cerrutti Costa, Luis B., 8635
Ceruti, Carlos, 869
Cervantes Acuña, Carlos F., 6614
César, J.N., 6665
César, Waldo A., 9952
Cesarino Júnior, A.F., 6243
Cesario de Melo, A., 2261
Cesarman, Fernando, 6509

Céspedes Bedregal, J. Teófilo, 6169
Chacon, Vamireh, 9927
Chagas Meirelles, Antônio. *See* Meirelles, Antônio Chagas.
Chagas Uchôa Guerra, Francisco das. *See* Guerra, Francisco das Chagas Uchôa.
Challener, Richard D., 8842
Chalmers, Douglas A., 8019
Chamudes, Marcos, 8442
Chance, John K., 9706
Chaney, Elsa M., 8366-8366a
Changmarin, Carlos F., 8833
Chaparro-Alfonso, Julio, 4042
Chapman, F.H., 2004
Chapoy Bonifaz, Alma, 6161
Charbonneau, Paul-Eugène, 6244-6245
Charlton, Thomas H., 699
Chase, D.W., 513
Chase, H. Peter, 2147
Chaves, G.M., 2241
Chaves, Milcíades, 4464
Chaves Menoza, Alvaro, 954
Chaves Vargas, Luis Fernando, 4541
Chávez, Ezequiel A., 6154
Chayes, Abram, 8843
Checura Jeria, Jorge, 930-930a
Chen, J. Chi-Yi, 8516-8516a
Chenery, Hollis B., 4043
Chenu, J., 513
Cheston, T. Stephen, 8712a
Chiappe, C., 8309
Chiara, Vilma, 1395
Chickering, Carol Rogers, 6626
Child, Jorge, 8310
Chile, 8443
Chile. Centro de Estudios de Planificación Nacional (CEPLAN), 4602
Chile. Dirección de Asuntos Indígenas. Oficina de Planificación Agrícola. Departamento de Programación, 1451
Chile. Dirección de Estadística y Censos, 6847
Chile. Instituto Nacional de Estadísticas, 4603
Chile. Presidente, 8443a
Chile: el desafío (the challenge), 4604
Chiñas, Beverly, 1118
Chirinos Soto, Enrique, 8367
Choy, E., 513
Christinat, Jean Louis, 1420, 1430
Christmann, Federico, 2005
Christou, G., 4378
Chrostowski, Marshall S., 1329
Chudnovsky, Daniel, 4465
Chumacero, Antonio, 4314
Churchill, Anthony, 6609
Chymz, Igor, 904
Ciafardini, Horacio, 4044, 4267
Cibantos, Jubert S., 4819
Cicourel, Aaron V., 2024, 9883

Ciência e Cultura, 112
La ciencia y la tecnología al servicio de los pueblos de América: programa regional de desarrollo científico y tecnológico de la OEA, 6005
La ciencia y la tecnología en América Latina, 6006
Cigliano, Eduardo M., 867, 870
Cimillo, Elsa, 4704
Ciria, Alberto, 8663a, 8878
Cirigliano, Gustavo F.J., 6080-6082, 8636
Ciski, Robert, 1233
City University of New York, *New York.* Brooklyn College. Institute of Puerto Rican Studies, 3
La ciudad de San José: 1871-1921, 6615
Civrieux, Marc de, 1330
Clague, Christopher K., 8259
Clair, Dean J., 9618
Clan S.A. (firm), *Brazil,* 4820, 7092-7093
Clarac N., G., 513
Clark, Ronald James, 4587
Clarke, John I., 6510
Clastres, Pierre, 505, 1331, 1361
Clausner, Marlin D., 9789
Cleaves, Peter S., 8444
Clegg, E. J., 2196
Clerc, Edgar, 833
Cleve, H., 2076
Clewlow, Carl William, Jr., 609
Coard, Bernard, 1222
Cobbledick, James R., 8713
Cochrane, Carl M., 9765
Cochrane, James D., 4014, 4379
Cockcroft, James D., 8020
Codovilla, Victorio, 8636a
Coe, Michael D., 644, 800
Coelho, Alzira L.N., 4828
Coelho, Ernesto Bandeira, 9953
Coêlho, Jorge, 4821
Cogels, Gabrielle, 9954
Cohen, David W., 1219
Cohen, Lucy M., 1452-1453, 9830
Cohen, Youssef, 4822
Cohn, Gabriel, 4823, 9619
Colby, B.N., 1119
Colby, L.M., 1119
Cole, Harry James, 4831
Colín, Mario, 8142-8146
Collado, Rolando, 4394
Collier, David, 1454
Collier, Donald, 996 Collier, Jane Fishburne, 1120
Collier, Maria Elisa Dias, 6246
Collin-Delavaud, Anne, 4670, 7011
Collin-Delavaud, Claude, 1455, 6968, 8368
Collins, J.M., 513
Collymore, Frank A., 1220
Colmenares, Germán, 6125

Coloda, Santos Carlos, 6247
Colombia. Departamento Administrativo Nacional de Estadística, 6879
Colombia. Federación Nacional de Cafeteros, 7272
Colombia. Fondo de Promoción de Exportaciones (PROEXPO), 6880
Colombia Geográfica, 6890
Colombia. Departamento Nacional de Planeación, 4466-4467
Colombia. Instituto Colombiano Agropecuario (ICA). Instituto Colombiano de Reforma Agraria (INCORA). Fondo Financiero Agrario, 4468
Colombia. Instituto Colombiano de la Reforma Agraria (INCORA), 6881-6882
Colombia. Instituto Colombiano de la Reforma Agraria (INCORA). Oficina de Planeación, 6883
Colombia. Instituto Geográfico Agustín Codazzi, 6884-6886, 7273-7274
Colombia. Instituto Geográfico Agustín Codazzi. Oficina de Estudios Geográficos, 6887
Colombia. Ministerio de Agricultura, 4469
Colombia. Ministerio de Agricultura. Corporación Nacional para el Desarrollo del Chocó, 6888
Colombia. Ministerio de Agricultura. Instituto de Fomento Algodonera, 6889
Colombia. Servicio Colombiano de Meteorología e Hidrología, 7275
Colombia: trayectoria de un pueblo, 132
Colombo, B., 2103

Colonización de la cuña boscosa santafesina: reseña general, 6772
Colonnese, Louis M., 9620
Coloquio de Suelos, *I, Medellín, Colo., 1970.*

Colson, Audrey Butt, 1332
Comas, Juan, 13, 2006-2008
Comas Camps, Juan, 671
Combs, Jerald A., 8714
Comercio, 4635
Comhaire, Suzanne-Sylvain, 1208
Comisión Episcopal Francesa del Mundo Obrero, *Paris?,* 8021
Comitas, Lambros, 1288
Comité Administrador del Programa Federal de Construcción de Escuelas (CAPFCE), *México,* 6155
Comité de Información y Servicio Externo (CICE), *Quito,* 4522-4523
Comité Judío Americano, *B.A.* Oficina Latinoamericano. Instituto de Relaciones Humanas, 9884

Comité Peruano de Zonas Aridas, *Lima, 6969*
Comma, Carlton N., 93
Commission on United States-Latin American Relations, *N.Y.*, 4045
Common treatment of foreign capital, trademarks, patents, licensing agreements and royalties in the Andean Common Market, 4046
Compania do Desenvolvimento do Planalto Central (CODEPLAN), *Brasília*, 7094
Companhia Vale do Rio Doce, *Rio. Centro de Informações Técnicas*, 25
Comunicaciones del Proyecto Puebla-Tlaxcala, 700-702
Comunicações e Artes, 6248
Concatti, Rolando, 8637
Concientizar y organizar a las masas, 8311
Conde Regardiz, Pedro, 4542
Cone, Bruce W., 4970
Cone, Cynthia A., 1121, 9707
Conference of Latin Americanist Geographers, *II, Boston, Mass., 1971*, 2025
Conference on Teacher Education in the Eastern Caribbean, *VI, Montserrat, Leeward Islands, 1970*, 6203
Conference on the Family in the Caribbean, *II, Aruba, Netherlands Antilles, 1969*, 1221
Conference on the Implications of Independence for Grenada, *St. Augustine, T. and T., 1974*, 1222
Conference on the Western Hemisphere, *N.Y., 1971*, 8715
Conferencia Anual de Ejecutivos (CADE), *XII, Paracas, Peru, 1973*, 4642
Conferência de Desenvolvimento Econômico do Rio Grande do Sul, *Pôrto Alegre, Bra., 1969*, 4824
Conferência de Educadores do Distrito Federal, *III, Brasília, 1968*, 6249
Conferencia Episcopal de Bolivia, *La Paz, 1971*, 6101
Conferencia Especializada sobre la Aplicación de la Ciencia y la Tecnología al Desarrollo de América Latina, *Brasília, 1972*, 4047
Conferencia Interamericana de Seguridad Social, *IX, Quito, 1971*, 9621
Conferencia Interamericana Especializada sobre Educación Integral de la Mujer, *B.A., 1972*, 9885
Conferencia Internacional sobre la Contribución de la Investigación Científica Educacional para la Reforma Escolar en los Países Andinos, *Lima, 1971*, 6007
Conferencia Nacional sobre Familia, Infancia y Juventud, *I, Bogotá, 1970*, 9831
Conferencia Regional Latinoamericana de Población, *México, 1970*, 6511
Congreso Interamericano de Planificación, *VII, Lima, 1968*, 4048
Congreso Interamericano de Psicología, *XI, México, 1967*, 9622
Congreso Nacional de Profesores de Geografía, *III, Rivera, Uru., 1971*, 7012
Congreso Sul-Americano da Mulher em Defesa de Democracia, *I, Rio, 1967*, 9623
Congress of the People's Progressive Party, *XVI, Anna Regina Estequiro, Guyana, 1970*, 8286
Congresso Latino Americano dos Secretariados Nacionais de Opinião Pública, *Lima, 1966*, 8022
Congresso Nacional Campesino de la Asociación Nacional de Agricultores Pequeños (ANAP), *IV, La Habana, 1972?*, 8217
Congresso Nacional de Comunicação, *I, Rio, 1971*, 9955
Congresso Nacional de Educação, *XIII, Rio, 1967*, 6250
Conjuntura Econômica, 6251, 7095
Conlin, Sean, 1456, 1494
Conniff, Michael L., 6532
Conning, Arthur M., 2043
Connors, Robert E., 6601
Conrad, Geoffrey W., 644
Conroy, Michael E., 4049
Conselho do Desenvolvimento Econômico (CODEC), *Rio*, 4825
Conselho Episcopal Latino-Americano (CELAM), *Bogotá*, 8023
Considera, Cláudio Monteiro, 4969
Constitução da República Federativa do Brasil: emenda constitucional No. 1 de 17 de outubro de 1969, 8558
Construir Comités de Fábrica por la independencia obrera: resoluciones de los Comités de Base por el Frente Electoral Clasista, 8638
Consuegra Higgins, José, 8024, 8312
Contador, Claudio Roberto, 4826-4827
Contreras, José del C., 819
Contreras, Víctor Nazar, 4605
Contreras Hernández, J., 513
Convención Nacional del Movimiento Nacionalista Revolucionario (MNR), *XI, La Paz, 1973*, 8395
Cook, J.D., 2148
Cook, Scott, 1122
Cook, Thomas J., 4744, 8675
Cooke, John W., 8638a
Coombs, Philip H., 6236
Cooper, H.H.A., 9850
Cooper, Richard N., 4050

Copello Faccini, Antonio, 4051
Coppens, Huub, 4052
Coral, Angelina de, 8306
Corbett, Charles D., 8025, 8396-8396a
Corbo, Vittorio, 4606
Corcino, José J., 2178, 2180
Cordani, Umberto G., 6728
Cordasco, Francesco, 8269
Cordero Michel, Emilio, 834
Cordeu, Edgardo J., 1333
Córdova-Claude, Ted, 8397, 8445
Córdova de Castillo, Nora, 54
Córdova-Ríos, Manuel, 6970
Cornblit, Oscar, 9624
Corneilus, Wayne A., 9625
Corona Núñez, José, 703
Coronel . . . el Ejército del Brasil: sus problemas y políticas, 8559
Corradi, Juan E., 8639, 8663a
Correa, Héctor, 4053
Correa, Patricia, 9832
Correa de Oliveira, Plínio. *See* Oliveira, Plínio Correa de.
Correal Urrego, Gonzalo, 2009
Correia, Ronaldo Nunes, 7096
Correia de Andrade, Manuel. *See* Andrade, Manuel Correia de.
Correia de Oliveira Andrade, Manuel. *See* Andrade, Manuel Correia de Oliveira.
Corrientes (province), *Arg.* Ministerio de Bienestar Social. Subsecretaría de Educación y Cultura. Dirección General de Planificación e Investigación Educativa, 6083
Corro, Berta Alicia, 1223
Corson, Christopher, 629
Cortázar, Pedro Felipe, 6971
Corte, Judith de la, 7097
Corten, André, 4334, 8218, 9778
Cortés, Carlos E., 8559a
Cortés Conde, Roberto, 4705
Cortés Ruiz, Efraín C., 1123
Cortez, Roberto, 1343
Corvalán, Antonio, 6848
Cosío Villegas, Daniel, 113, 8147
Cosminsky, S., 513
Cossard-Binon, Gisèle, 1208
Cossío del Pomar, Felipe, 997
Costa, Bolivar, 9956
Costa, João Frank da, 8588
Costa, Marcelo Caetano da, 8560
Costa, Maria do Carmo, 6252
Costa, Ronaldo F.N., 4828
Costa, Rovílio, 9957
Costa, Rubens Vaz da, 4829-4831, 7098, 9958-9962
Costa Barbosa Ferreira, Ignez. *See* Ferreira, Ignez Costa Barbosa.
Costa de la Torre, Arturo, 6823

Costa Jamunda, Theobaldo. *See* Jamunda, Theobaldo Costa.
Costa Pinto, Luiz de Aguiar. *See* Pinto, Luiz de Aguiar Costa.
Costa Rabello, Ricardo da. *See* Rabello, Ricardo da Costa.
Costa Ribeiro, Carlos. *See* Ribeiro, Carlos Costa.
Costa Rica. Dirección General de Estadística y Censos, 6616-6617
Costa Rica. Instituto Costarricense de Turismo, 7278
Costa Rica. Programa Integral de Mercadero Agropecuario (PIMA), 4335
Cotler, Julio, 1457-1458, 8716
Counterpoint of the Agrarian Reform: Chile, 1973. Contrapunto de la Reforma Agraria: Chile, 1973 (Motion picture), 1459
Coutinho, Bernadete Figueiredo, 6336
Coutinho dos Santos, M. *See* Santos, M. Coutinho dos.
Cova, Arabia Teresa, 2
Cowan, Florence, 1956
Cowan, George, 1956
Cowell, Adrian, 1334
Cowgill, George, 633, 7322
Cox, B., 513
Cox, Ricardo, 8428
Cox, S.C., 619
Coy, Peter, 1124
Coyner, Mary S., 6622
Cozean, Jon D., 133
Craig, Alan K., 998
Craig, Richard B., 8115
Craven, Roy C., 610
Cravioto, Joaquín, 2149
Crawford, Michael H., 2036, 2077-2078, 2093
Cré, Gerard de, 9626
Cremoux, Raúl, 8148
Crépeau, Pierre, 1224
Crespo Toral, Hernán, 968
Criança e Escola, 6253-6255
A criança o adolescente, a cidade: estudo sociológico sôbre marginalidade, 9963
Crise et réforme des structures agraires: le cas chilien et ses applications méthodologiques, 8446
Crist, Raymond E., 6729, 6893
Cristianismo y Sociedad, 6008, 8026
Cristianos por el socialismo, 8027
Crocker, William H., 1361
Crofts, Marjorie, 1833
Cross, Benedict, 8517
Cross, Cliff, 6564
Crowder, Roberto, 869
Crowell, Thomas H., 1834
Crusol, Jean, 4339
Cruz, Fernando, 6631

Cruz, J.C., 2213
Cruz Betancourt, Carmen Inés, 9833
Cruz Díaz, Rigoberto, 9790
Cruz Pereira, Maria Lúcia da. See Pereira, Maria Lúcia da Cruz.
Cuadernos de Bibliotecología y Documentación, 114
Cuadernos de Educación Popular, 8639a
Cuadernos de la Sociedad Venezolana de Planificación, 4543
Cuadernos de Psicología, 6116
Cuadra, Héctor, 4054
Cuadros, Carlos, 8028
Cuatro censo nacional de población, 9757
Cuba, 4414-4415
Cuba. Instituto Cubano de Geodesia y Cartografía, 7283
Cuéllar, Oscar, 8447
Cuenca, Humberto, 4588
Cuesta Domingo, Mariano, 513, 999
Culbert, T. Patrick, 611-612
Cummings, Leslie P., 6941
Cummings, Richard L., 6009
Cummings, Ronald G., 6666
Cunha, Alda das Mercês Moreira da, 7099
Cunha, Luiz Antônio Constant Rodrigues da, 6256
Cunha, Luiz Roberto Azevedo, 4895
Cunha, Maria Auxiliadora Versiani, 6009a
Cunha, Osvaldo Rodrigues da, 7100
Cunha Lima, Fernando. See Lima, Fernando Cunha.
Cunha Parahym, Orlando da. See Parahym, Orlando de Cunha.
Cunill Grau, Pedro, 6849
Curnee, Russell H., 6602
Currie, Jean, 4520
Currie, Lauchlin, 4055, 4470
Curso Regional Interamericano sobre Colocación Familiar, Adopción y Libertad Vigilada, I, Montevideo, 1970, 9627
Dabbs, Jack Autrey, 14
Dacal, Ramón, 835
D'Acosta, Helia. See Acosta, Helia D'.
Dagum, Camilo, 4268
Dáhbar, Juan, 6010
Dajer Chadid, Gustavo, 4056
Daland, Robert T., 6531
Dall, Aryon, 1361
Dalle, Luis, 1419
Dalmasso, E., 6927
Daly, John P., 1835
Damásio Trindade, Maria Zélia. See Trindade, Maria Zélia Damásio.
Dana Montaño, Salvador M., 8640
D'Andréa, Flávio Fortes, 9628
Daniels, Judith, 1297
D'Ans, André-Marcel, 513, 1311, 1836
Dansereau, G., 2069

Dantas, José Lucena, 9964
D'Antoni, Héctor Luis, 871-871a
D'Antonio, William V., 6512
DaPonte, Alberto J., 7329
D'Apote, Vincenzo, 7101
D'Arc, Hélène Rivière, 6658
Darlington, Charleen Arnett, 1297
Da Rocha, Fernando J., 2079-2080, 2209
Dauelsberg, Percy, 931-931a
Daus, Federico A., 6773
Dauxion Lavaysse, Jean François, 7028
David, Wilfred L., 4525
Davidson, David M., 1282
Davidson, Maria, 2026
Davies, Thomas M., Jr., 1460
Dávila, Diana, 779
Dávila, Patricio, 779
Dawson, E. Yale, 6928
Dawson, Frank Griffith, 820
Day, Kent C., 1000, 1017a-1017b
Dayrell, Gilson de Assis, 8588a
Deambrosis, María Susana, 872
Dean, Warren, 4057, 6513
De Atley, Suzzane, 606
Debbasch, Yvan, 1282
Debien, Gabriel, 1282
DeBloois, Evan I., 704
Deboer, Warren R., 1001
Debray, Régis, 8398-8398a
DeCamp, David, 1225
The Declaration of Barbados; for the liberation of the Indians, 1226
DeDiego O., Carlos A., 7326
Deffontaines, Pierre, 6730
Degregori, Pedro M., 8029
Deheza, José A., 8641
Dehouve, Danièle, 1125
De Kadt, Emanuel, 4607
De La Fuente, Nicolás R., 873-873a
Delano, Luis Enrique, 8448
Delfino, José A., 4706
Delgado, Carlos, 6531
Delgado, Oscar, 8313
Delgado Olivera, Carlos, 8369-8369a
Delhumeau, Antonio, 8155
DeLicardie, E., 2149
Delich, Francisco José, 8666
Delinqüência juvenil na Guanabara: introdução à teoria e pesquisa sociológicas da delinqüência juvenil na cidade do Rio de Janeiro, 9965
Delorenzo Neto, Antônio, 9966
Demas, William G., 4336
Democracia Cristiana del Uruguay y Formación del Frente Amplio, 8611
Denevan, William M., 1335, 1361
Dennis, Philip A., 1126
Dent, David W., 8314
De Pablo, Juan Carlos. See Pablo, Juan Carlos de.

Departamento de Puno, 6972
Depestre, Réné, 9791
Dereims, A., 6824
Desai, P., 2139
El desarrollo de América Latina y la Alianza para el Progreso, 4058
Desarrollo Económico, 2027
Desarrollo económico y planificación en la República Argentina: selección bibliográfica, 1930-1972, 4707
Desarrollo político del movimiento estudiantil, 8315
De Schauensee, Rodolphe Meyer, 6731
Desounet Baiocchi, Josephina. *See* Baiocchi, Josephina Desounet.
Desruisseaux, Jacques, 1227
De Stefano, Gian Franco, 513, 2081
DeWind, Adrian, 8370
Dexter, Byron, 8717
Dick, Vera Maria, 4771
Di Marco, Luis E., 4708
Distrito Federal, *Bra.* Companhia do Desenvolvimento do Planalto Central (CODEPLAN), 4832-4833
Di Tella, Guido, 4059, 4709
Di Tella, Torcuato S., 8030, 8074, 9708
Día de la Estadística Nacional: reseña histórica de la Cuarta Conmemoración, 1970, 4337
Días, Antonio, 1059
Dias Bicalho, Maria. *See* Bicalho, Maria Dias.
Dias Collier, Maria Elisa. *See* Collier, Maria Elisa Dias.
Dias de Andrade, Luis. *See* Andrade, Luis Dias de.
Dias Júnior, Ondemar F., 905-905a
Díaz, Hilda M., 6799
Díaz, José María, 6732
Díaz, Juanita, 9792
Díaz, Leonardo, 4624
Díaz, Silvia, 8433
Díaz Alejandro, Carlos Federico, 4471
Díaz Araujo, Enrique, 8642
Díaz Arguedas, Julio, 6825
Díaz Castillo, Roberto, 8188
Díaz Chávez, Filander, 9758
Díaz-Guerrero, Rogelio, 6156, 9709-9710
Díaz Montero, Aníbal, 6733
Díaz Morón, Juan Klunder y. *See* Klunder y Díaz Morón, Juan.
Díaz Soler, Luis M., 1287
Díaz-Trechuelo, L., 513
Díaz Ungría, Adelaide G. de, 2082
Dibble, C.E., 513
Diccionario de sinónimos, antónimos e ideas afines, 94
Dicionário de sociologia, 95
Dickinson, Joshua C., 6627
Dickson, Thomas I., Jr., 8031

Dickudt, Horst, 7005
18 [i.e., Dieciocho] años de progreso con el Presidente Stroessner, 8604a
Diéguez, Héctor L., 4710-4711
Diehl, Richard A., 705-706
Diessl, Wilhelm G., 847
Dietschy, Hans, 1336
Diez, Julio, 8518
Digby, Adrian, 513, 633, 707
Dill, Hans-Otto, 6514
Dill, James E., 2083
Dillman, C. Daniel, 6667
Dillon Soares, Glaucio Ary. *See* Soares, Glaucio Ary Dillon.
Diniz, Arthur J. Almeida, 8718
Diniz, Edson Soares, 1337-1338
Diniz, José Alexandre Felizola, 7091
Diógenes, Luciano, 7102, 9967
Di Peso, Charles C., 613
Dipolo, Mario, 1461, 2028
Disselhoff, Hans Dietrich, 1002
Dix, Robert H., 8032
Dixon, James C., 9629-9630
Dobkin de Ríos, Marlene, 1462, 2219-2222, 2230
Dobles, Margarita, 6185
Dobner E., Horst K., 4269
Dobson, Rose, 1837
Dobyns, Henry F., 1127, 1463, 1487
Docencia, 6157
Documentário, 6257
Documentos: el Tercer Mundo ante la Conferencia de las Naciones Unidas sobre Comercio y Desarrollo—UNCTAD, 4060
Documentos y comentarios en torno al viaje del Presidente Echeverría, marzo-abril de 1973, 8806
Dodson, Michael, 8663a
Doehring, Donald O., 614
Doellinger, Carlos von, 4834-4835
Dole, Gertrude E., 1361
Dörig, J.A., 8033
Dollfus, O., 1003
Domic K., Juraj, 8428
Domínguez, Jorge I., 8219
Domínguez, Oscar, 4608, 9863
Dominican Republic. Banco Central de la República Dominicana. Oficina Nacional de Estadística, 4338
Dominican Republic. Instituto Geográfico Universitario, 7285
Dominican Republic. Oficina Nacional de Administración y Personal, 8249
Domond, Pierre Edouard, 8258
Donnan, Christopher B., 1004
Dookeran, Winston, 1253
Dornelles Bán, Alzira. *See* Bán, Alzira Dornelles.
Dorsinville, Max H., 1288a

Dorticós Torrado, Osvaldo, 8220
Dos estudios sobre población en Colombia, 4472
Dos Passos, John, 6850
dos Santos, M. Coutinho. *See* Santos, M. Coutinho dos.
Dos Santos, Theotonio. *See* Santos, Theotonio dos.
Dos Santos, Wanderly Guilherme. *See* Santos, Wanderly Guilherme dos.
Dotta, Mario, 8611a
Dotti, Sotero, 9968
Dougherty, Bernardo, 874
Doughty, Paul L., 6973
Dow, James, 9631
Dowling Desmadryl, Jorge, 1464
Dozer, Donald Marquand, 8721
Drake, George F., 1465, 8316
Drenikoff, Ivan, 7029
Dressl, Klaus, 8643
Drewitt, R. Bruce, 7322
Drosdoff, Daniel, 4712
Duarte, Isis, 9778
Duarte, José Bacchieri, 7103
Duarte, Sérgio Guerra, 6258
Duarte de Acquaviva, Edelmira, 6011
Dubly, Alain, 1466
Duckworth, John, 1297
Duckworth, W. Donald, 6745
Duclos, Jacques, 8534
Duejo, Gerardo, 8643a
Dull, John E., 4061
Dupont-Gonin, Pierre, 6942
Dütting, Dieter, 801-802
Duggal, Ved P., 1247, 1287
Dumont, J.P., 513
Dumont, René, 4416
Duncan, W. Raymond, 6197
Duque, Oliverio, 8807
Duque Echeverri, J. Emilio, 8343a
Duque Gómez, Luis, 955-955a
Durán T., Marco Antonio, 4062, 4270
Durbin, Marshall, 513, 1512, 1844
Durbin, Mridula Adenwala, 1228, 1838
Dusart, Etienne R., 6603
Dutra, Dilza Délia, 6259
Dutra, Enrique Marco, 671
Dwyer, Jane Powell, 1005
Dwyer, Edward B., 1005
Earls, John, 1467-1468
Early, John D., 1128, 2029, 9759
Eastman, Jorge Mario, 6515
Eaton, Jack D., 683, 708-709
Ebanks, G.E., 2057
Ebel, Arnold, 8878a
Eble, Alroino B., 906-906b
Ebsa, 6260
Echánove Trujillo, Carlos A., 615, 803, 9711
Echavarría, A.R., 2084-2085

Echeverría, Gilda, 2033-2034
Echeverry, Carlos, 1052a
Echeverry Majía, Hernando, 8326a
Economía y Administración, 4063
Economie antillaise, 4339
Ecuador. Corporación Ecuatoriana de Turismo, 6929
Ecuador. Instituto Geográfico Militar, 7288-7289
Ecuador. Junta Nacional de Planificación y Coordinación Económica. División de Estadística y Censos, 6930-6931
Ecuador. Misión Andina del Ecuador. Oficina de Investigaciones Sociales, 6932-6933
Ecuador. Ministerio de Obras Públicas y Comunicaciones, 7290
Edelstein, Joel C., 8034
Eden, M.J., 6943
Edição Atualizada (firm), *Rio,* 7233
Editôra e Publicidade Ltda., *Rio,* 7246
Editôra Presidente Ltda. (firm), *Rio,* 7247, 7263-7264
Editorial Cartográfica Flecha (firm), *México,* 7310
Editorial Mapa (firm), *Buenos Aires,* 7218
Educação, 6261-6262
Educação e Cultura, 6263
Educación, 6141
La Educación, 15, 6012-6017
La educación ante el Congreso, 6126
Educación Popular para el Desarrollo, 6102-6103
EDUPLAN Informe, 6186
Edwards, Bryan, 1282
Edwards, Jorge, 8221
Edwards, P.A., 6204
Eggers Lan, Conrad, 8644
Egginton, Everett, 6127
Ehrenpreis, Dag, 4417
Ehrlich, Allen S., 1229
Eibl-Eibesfeldt, Irenäus, 1339
Eichelbaum, Horacio, 8645
Eichelbaum de Babini, Ana María, 8666
Eikaas, F.H., 513
Einaudi, Luigi R., 8035-8036, 8044, 8075, 8095, 8722-8724, 8782
Eisgruber, L.M., 4970
Eisleb, Dieter, 506, 616-617
Ekholm, G.F., 513
Ekholm-Miller, Susanna, 710
Elbow, Gary S., 6628
El Dorado, 848
Elfes, Alberto, 7104
Elías, Víctor J., 4713-4714
Elizaga, Juan C., 2043
Elliott, Raymond L., 1839
Ellis, Joseph A., 134
Elmendorf, Mary Lindsay, 1129

El Salvador. Dirección General de Estadística y Censos, 6623
Elson, Benjamin, 1840
Elst, Dirk H. van der, 1230
La empresa del libro en América Latina: guía seleccionada de editoriales distribuidores y librerías de América Latina, 96
Las empresas multinacionales y la política social, 8725
Encontro de Reitores de Universidades Públicas e Diretores dos Estabelecimentos Públicos Isolados de Ensino Superior, *II, Brasília, 1973,* 6264
Encontro Latino-Americano de Justiça e Paz, *IV, Rio, 1971,* 8561
Encuentro Continental de Misiones en América Latina, *II, Melgar, Colo., 1968,* 8037
Engel, Frédéric, 1006-1006b
Engel, Lyle Kenyon, 6734
Engl, T., 513
Engler, Joaquim J. de Camargo, 4836
Ennis, J.T., 2197, 2210-2211
Ensayos ECIEL, 4064
Ensayos sobre administración política y derecho tributarios, 4065
Entre Ríos (province), *Arg.* Secretaría del Consejo Provincial de Desarrollo. Dirección de Estadística y Censos, 6774
Epifanio: el mago de las finanzas [por] Veritas, 8604b
Erasmus, Charles E., 1487
Erdle, Jim, 1297
Erices, Sergio, 933
Ernst & Ernst (firm), *Rio,* 4837
Errandonea, Alfredo, 8038
Es, J.C. van, 9834
Esaá Crespo, Cecilia, 6187
Escalante, Aquiles, 1282
Escalante H., R., 513
Escalante, Rodolfo, 6735
Escamilla, Mercedes, 6668
Escamilla González, Gloria, 4
Escandell Bonet, B., 513
Escandón, José Francisco, 4461
Escobar, Alberto, 1841
Escobar, Gabriel, 1469
Escobar, Mario, 6975
Escobar C., Luis, 4066-4067
Escobar Gutiérrez, A., 2086
Escola Interamericana de Administração Pública, *Rio,* 8039
Escudero, Carlos J. Molestina, 6516
España Krauss, Emilio, 4271
Espartaco, 8074
Esparza Torres, Héctor F. (firm), *México,* 7311
Espinosa, Juan Guillermo, 4068
Espinosa García, Manuel, 4069, 8726

Espírito Santo, Antônio, 7105
Espoueys, Oscar, 932-932a
Estadística Panameña, 9760
Estadísticas Vitales y de la Salud, 2030
Estrada D., Samuel, 1842
Estrada Monroy, Agustín, 1843
Estrada Uribe, Gabriel, 6638
Estrategia, 8646
Estrella Moreira, Júlio. *See* Moreira, Júlio Estrella.
Estructura financiera de las universidades nacionales, 6084
Estudio de la industria de comercio, 4380
Estudios de Cultura Maya, 1844
Estudios de Planificación Familiar, 9632, 9835
Estudios Internacionales, 8808, 8727
Estudios y documentos sobre Cuba, 4418
Estudo de problemas brasileiros, 7106, 8561a, 9969
Etcharren, René, 6669
Euler, R.C., 513
Evans, Clifford, 907, 911
Evans, John S., 4272
Evans, Les, 8449
Evans, Peter B., 8561b
Eveleth, Phyllis B., 2150
Evelyn, Shirley, 1230a
Evers, Tilman Tönnies, 8646a
Every child matters: the child in Trinidad and Tobago, 9793
La evolución de la ganadería vacuna en el período: 1972-1973, 6775
Ewen, Lynda Ann, 9875
Ewerton Rodrigues, Tarcísio. *See* Rodrigues, Tarcísio Ewerton.
Executive compensation service: reports on international compensation, Venezuela, 4544
Exportações latinoamericanas; evolução e estrutura, 4070
Eyre, L. Alan, 2031, 6595
Fá Robaina, Juan Carlos, 8612
Fabbrica Italiana Automobili Torino (FIAT), *Buenos Aires,* 4071, 4381
Fábrega, Horacio, 1130
Fábregat, Claudio Esteva, 671
Faccini, Antonio Copello, 4237
Facio B., Rodrigo, 4382
Fadul, Maité, 4473
Fagen, Patricia W., 8809
Fagen, Richard R., 8149, 8716, 8728, 8879
Fages, Eduardo, 6670
Faissol, Speridião, 4838, 7107-7108, 7133
Fajnzyller, Fernando, 8729
Falange Socialista Boliviana, *La Paz,* 8399
Falcón Urbano, Miguel A., 4545
Faleroni, Alberto Daniel, 8040

Falesi, Italo Claudio, 7174
Faletto, Enzo, 8074
Falla, Ricardo, 1131
Fallah, Skaidrite Maliks, 8041
Fals Borda, Orlando, 8042, 8317
Fann, K.T., 8730
Fantin, Mario, 849
Faria, Edina Gabizo de, 900
Faria, Hugo Barros de Castro, 4834-4835
Faria, Luiz de Castro, 1375, 9970
Faria, Vilmar, 9971
Farias Leitão, Saphyra. See Leitão, Saphyra Farias.
Fariña, Fernando, 8612a
Farina, Modesto, 9972
Farley, Rawle, 4072
Farnsworth, Elizabeth, 8880
Faro Passos, Carlos de. See Passos, Carlos de Faro.
Ferrari, Naira Lapis, 4985
Farris, George F., 9973-9974
Faust, Norma, 1845
Febres-Cordero, Foción, 6188
Feijó Bittencourt, Gustavo Francisco. See Bittencourt, Gustavo Francisco Feijó.
Feinberg, Richard E., 8450
Feindt, Waltraut, 2043, 9704
Feital S. Pinto, Rogerio. See Pinto, Rogerio Feital S.
Feldman, Lawrence H., 605, 629, 633, 711
Felizola Diniz, José Alexandre. See Diniz, José Alexandre Felizola.
Femenias, Jorge, 1055
Fenoy, Gerard, 83
Ferguson, F.N., 513
Ferguson, Theodore, 1222
Ferguson, Yale H., 8730a-8731
Fernandes, Florestan, 4073-4074, 6265, 9975
Fernandes, Francisca Nolasco, 6266
Fernandes Tavares, Denise. See Tavares, Denise Fernandes.
Fernández, Aníbal, 6197
Fernández, Jorge, 875-875a
Fernández, Julio A., 8647-8647a
Fernández, R.A., 4273
Fernández Alvariño, Próspero Germán, 8648
Fernández Baca, Jenaro, 1007
Fernández Distel, Alicia A., 861
Fernández R., Gonzalo, 8479
Fernández Robaina, Tomás, 84
Fernández y Fernández, Ramón, 4274-4275
Ferrá, Coloma, 6067, 6189
Ferrari, Gustavo, 8881
Ferraro, Oscar Humberto, 1363, 4636
Ferraz de Sá, Maria Auxiliadora. See Sá, Maria Auxiliadora Ferraz de.

Ferreira, Edésio Fernandes, 4839-4843
Ferreira, Evaldo Osório, 7109
Ferreira, Ignez Costa Barbosa, 7110
Ferreira, Luis Pinto, 6267
Ferreira, Maria das Graças Moreira, 110, 7164
Ferreira, Nelson Braga Octaviano, 6216
Ferreira da Silva, Luiz. See Silva, Luiz Ferreira da.
Ferreira de Camargo, Cândido Procopio. See Camargo, Cândido Procopio Ferreira de.
Ferreira Lopes, José. See Lopes, José Ferreira.
Ferreira Réis, Arthur Cézar. See Réis, Arthur Cézar Ferreira.
Ferreira-Santos, Célia Almeida, 9976
Ferreira Sena, Julio F. See Sena, Julio F. Ferreira.
Ferreira Sobral, Eduardo, 6736
Ferrer, Aldo, 4715-4716
Ferri, Mário G., 7134, 7201
Ferro, Carlos A., 8824
Ffrench Davis, Ricardo, 4075, 4609-4611
Fidel, Julio, 4717
Fidente, E., 513
Field, Frederick V., 712
Field, Julia Allen, 6737
Fields, Harriet, 1846
Fierro-Benítez, Rodrigo, 2151-2152
Fierro Vignoli, Pablo, 4671
Figueiredo, J.C., 6071a
Figueiredo, Jorge Mario, 8451
Figueiredo, Maria Helena Poppe de, 4795
Figueiredo, Nice, 55
Figueiredo Coutinho, Bernadete. See Coutinho, Bernadete Figueiredo.
Figueredo, Alfredo E., 836
Figueroa, Adolfo, 4643
Figueroa, Emilio de, 4076
Figueroa, Rolando B., 2223
Fillon, P., 6927
Filosofía y plan de gobierno en el Ecuador, 8360
Financiamiento del desarrollo urbano, 4474
El financimiento externo oficial en la estrategia del desarrollo de América Latina: implicaciones para los setenta, 4077
Findley, Roger W., 6548
Finzi-Bonasera, Ilda, 6738
Fioravanti, Antoinette, 1421
Fischbach, Ziona de, 17
Fish, Louise, 605
Fisher, J., 513
Fishlow, Albert, 4844-4846
Fitzgibbon, Russell H., 135
Flangini, Tabaré, 1056
Flannery, Kent V., 618, 644

Fleet, Michael, 8036
Fleming, S.J., 960
Fletcher, L.P., 4340
Fletcher, Lehman B., 4393
Flinn, William L., 1470, 9834, 9836
Flora, Cornelia Butler, 9633
Florén Lozano, Luis, 115
Flores, Edmundo, 4644
Flores, L., 2019
Flores, Mario Cesar, 8882
Flores, Ramón, 4329
Flores Caballero, Romeo, 8810
Flores Colombino, Andrés, 9912
Flores Ochoa, Jorge A., 1421, 1471-1473, 1494
Flores Olea, Víctor, 6018
Floria, Carlos A., 8630
Floridi, Alexis, 8043
Floyd, Barry, 4341
Flynn, Peter, 8562
Focacci, Guillermo, 933
Fock, Niels, 1361
Fodor, Eugene, 6671, 6739
Fodor, Jorge G., 4718
Fogel, Gerardo, 6950
Fogel, Ramón, 6950
Foley, James W., 4110
Fonck Sieveking, Oscar, 934
Foner, Nancy, 1231, 8260
Fonseca, Edson Nery da, 9977
Fonseca, Mário, 9978
Fonseca Fiol, Jaime, 8519
Fontenelle, L.F. Raposo, 7111
Fontes, Eduardo, 7112
Fontoura, Amaral, 6268
Foracchi, Marialice Mencarini, 9979
Ford, Donald F., 6019
Ford, Norman D., 6672
Forest, J. de Durand, 513
Foris, David, 1847
Form, William H., 9886
Forman, Shepard, 8563
Formosa (province), *Arg.* Asesoría de Desarrollo, 9887
Fornieles, Salvador, 8649
Forno, Mario, 1340-1341
Foro de Buenos Aires por la Vigencia de los Derechos Humanos, *B.A.*, 8649a
Foro Internacional, 8810-8811
Foro internacional sobre la vigencia de los derechos humanos en América Latina, 8732
Forrest, Jacqueline, 9677
Fortín Magaña, Rene, 8825
Fortún, Julia Elena, 6104
Fortune, David Lee, 1848
Fosler, R. Scott, 8515a
Fossum, Egil, 8004
Foster, David William, 97
Foster, David William, 1849

Foster, George M., 1132-1133
Fouchard, Jean, 1232
Foucher, Michel, 8564
Fought, John G., 1850
Fought, Sarah G., 1850
Fox, Geoffrey E., 9794
Fox Przeworski, J., 513
Foxley, Alejandro, 4077a, 4612-4614, 8452
Fragoso, Antônio, 8565
Fragoso, Augusto, 8565a
France-Amérique Latine, 4078
Francis, Michael J., 8453, 8883
Franco, Alberto, 6517
Franco, Franklin J., 8250, 8844
Franco, José L., 1282
Franco, Oscar, 6170
Franco, Rolando, 9914
Franco Camacho, Guillermo, 6894
Franco Viedma, Pablo, 6951
Franco diálogo entre gobierno y empresarios, 4276
Frank, André Gunder, 4079
Franklin, William L., 6974
Frankman, Myron J., 4645
Frantz, Donald G., 1851, 1934
Franz, Carl, 6673
Franzen de Lima, João. *See* Lima, João Franzen de.
Franzini, Julio César, 7013
Fraser, Thomas M., 1233
Fraser, Thomas M., Jr., 1234
Frayer, W., 2188
Frazão, Sergio Armando, 8733
Frederick, Kenneth D., 4719
Freire, Duaner, 8611a
Freire, Paulo, 6269
Freire-Maia, E.A. Chautard, 2087
Freire-Maia, Newton, 2032, 2088, 2111, 9980
Freitag, Elisabeth, 8430
Freitas, José João de Oliveira, 8734
Freitas, Luis Mendonça da, 8577
Freitas Carvalho, Lourdes de. *See* Carvalho, Lourdes de Freitas.
Frente Popular Nacionalista, *Cochabamba, Bol.,* 8400
Freyssinet, Jacques, 4080
Frías, Ismael, 8371
Friedl Zapata, José A., 8883a
Friedlander, Judith, 1134
Friedmann, John, 6531
Frikel, Protásio, 1328, 1342-1343, 1361
Frisancho, A. Roberto, 2198-2200
Fritz, John M., 526
Fritz, Margaret C., 526
Fritz W. Up de Graff, 1361
Frontaura Argandoña, Manuel, 8401
Fry, R.E., 513, 619
Fucaraccio, Angel, 4081

Fuchs, Claudio J., 9864
Fuente, Beatriz de la, 620, 713
Fuente, Julio de la, 1135
Fuentes Aguilar, Luis, 6674
Fuentes Díaz, Vicente, 8150
Fuentes Mohr, Alberto, 4383
Fuidio, Walter, 8612b
Fujii, Tatsuhiko, 1034
Fukuchi, Takao, 4082
Fulbright, J. William, 8845
Fulbright's role in the Cuban Missile Crisis, 8845
Fuller, Gary, 6851
Fundação Educacional do Estado do Paraná, *Curitiba, Bra.*, 6270
Fundação Educacional do Estado do Paraná, *Curitiba, Bra.* Grupo Assessor de Planejamento, 6271
Fundação Educacional do Sul de Santa Catarina (FESSC), *Tubarão, Bra.* Departamento de Pesquisas e Desenvolvimento, 4847
Fundação Getúlio Vargas, *Rio.* Brazilian Institute of Economics. Center for Statistics and Econometric Studies, 4848
Fundação Getúlio Vargas, *Rio.* Instituto Brasileiro de Economia. Centro de Estudos Agrícolas, 9981
Fundação Getúlio Vargas, *Rio.* Serviço de Publicações, 6272
Fundação IBGE [Instituto Brasileiro de Geografia e Estatística] *Rio.* Instituto Brasileiro de Estatística. Departamento de Censos, 4849
Fundação João Pinheiro, *Belo Horizonte, Bra.*, 4850-4851
Fundación Alemana para los Países en Vías de Desarrollo, *Berlin, FRG*, 4277
Fundación para la Educación Superior y el Desarrollo (FEDESARROLLO), *Bogotá.* Biblioteca, 26
Fung Pineda, Rosa, 1008-1008b
Funtanella, Carlos, 6577
Furquim Lambert, Levindo. *See* Lambert, Levindo Furquim.
Furrazola-Bermúdez, Gustavo, 6578
Furst, Peter R., 605, 633
Furtado, Celso, 4083-4084, 4852-4854, 8074
Furtado, Dimas, 8578a
Furtado Oliveira, Sandra. *See* Oliveira, Sandra Furtado.
Furtak, Robert K., 8151
Fyfe, W.S., 7113
Gaba, Ernesto, 4747
Gabriel, José, 8872
Gade, Daniel W., 1344, 1474-1476, 6975
Gaiarsa, José Angelo, 9982
Gaignard, Romain, 4720, 8650-8650a

Gaitán, Gloria, 8454
Gakenheimer, Ralph A., 6531, 9657
Galasso, Norberto, 8651
Galbis, Ricardo, 2224
Galiana, G.R., 6020, 6147
Galíndez, Jesús de, 8251
Galindo Pohl, Reynaldo, 8182
Gall, Norman, 8252, 8318, 8455
Gallango, María L., 2067
Gallardo Lozada, Jorge, 8402
Gallez, Paul, 4085
Galtung, Johan, 4086, 8456
Galván García, J.R., 513
Galvão, Amândio, 7063
Galvão, Clara Maria, 7099
Galvão, Getúlio de Carvalho, 10052
Galvão, Hélio, 9983
Galvão, Marília Velloso, 7133
Galvêas, Ernane, 4855
Gambini, Hugo, 8222
Gancedo, Omar Antonio, 1345-1346, 1405
Gándara, Horacio F., 8652
Gandasequi, Marco A., 4404
Gann, Thomas, 1136
Garbacz, Christopher, 4087
Garcés, Joan E., 8479
Garcés, Wilson, 6549
Garcés Contreras, Guillermo, 621
García, A., 513
Garcia, Afrânio R., Jr., 9986
García, Alicia I., 6799
García, Angel, 8846
García, Antonio, 4088-4090, 4615
García, Argimiro, 1347
García, Bernardo, 4475
García, César, 9865
García, Juan César, 6021
García, Miguel Angel, 85-86
García, Norberto, 4091, 4721
García, Pío, 8457, 8478
García Báez, Carlos, 6579
García-Bárcena G., J., 513
García Bernal, M.C., 513
García-Bouza, Jorge, 9624
García Cabrera, Carmelo, 671
García-Calzadilla, Miguel A., 8223
García Cantú, Gastón, 8152-8153
García Cisneros, Florencio, 507
García Cook, Angel, 700-702
García Costa, Víctor, 8652a
García de León, Antonio, 1852
Garcia de Mello, Luzia. *See* Mello, Luzia Garcia de.
García Galló, Gaspar Jorge, 6142
García Esteve, Joel, 6205
García Gatica, Tomás, 6852
García Lupo, Rogelio, 8884
García Moll, Roberto, 714
García Mujica, Jorge, 4473, 4475a

García Palacios, Emma, 6675
García-Palmieri, Mario R., 2225-2226
García Payón, José, 622, 715
García Ramírez, Sergio, 9712
García Robles, Alfonso, 8812
García Rosell, César, 1009
García-Sazón, Diego, 4654
García Valeriano, F., 4722
García Velutini, Oscar, 8735
García y García, J. Jesús, 27
Gardiner, C. Harvey, 8224, 8826
Gardner, Lloyd C., 8736
Gardner, Mary A., 136
Garr, Thomas M., 1420
Garrastazu Médici, Emílio, 8566, 8578
Garrido-Lecca, Guillermo, 4646
Garrido Rojas, José, 8428
Garvin, Paul L., 1853
Garza Quirós, Fernando, 4092
Gasparian, Fernando, 4093
Gasparian, Marcos, 8566a
Gastiazoro, Eugenio, 8653
Gatti, Bernadette Angelina, 6236
Gau, Enno B.H.S., 4856
Gau, Liliana, 886
Gaviria G., Juan F., 4476
Gaviria Liévano, Enrique, 8847
Gaxiola, Manuel J., 9713
Gay, Carlo T.E., 804
Gayango, Ignacio, 8458
Gazzera, Miguel, 8634b
Gazzoli, Luis, 8653a
Gebhardt, Hermann P., 8737
Geerdink, Rolf A., 2089-2091, 2133
Geigel Polanco, Vicente, 8270
Geiger, Pedro Pinchas, 4857, 6549, 7114-7115
Geithman, David T., 4376, 9634
Gelb, Alan H., 4858
Gelber, George, 8459
Gelfand, Morris A., 28
Geller, Lucio, 4723
Gendell, Murray, 2065, 9773
Gendrop, Paul, 623-624, 716
General Drafting Co. (firm), *Convent Station, N.J.,* 7312
Gensler, Martin D., 8403
Geobrás (firm) *Brazil,* 7116
Geographia Ltda. (firm), *London,* 7205
Gerace, Frank, 9855
Gerber, Stanford N., 513, 1221, 1235
Gerdel, Florence, 1854-1856
Gerena, Gabriel Cirino, 6205
Geretto, Armando, 4730
Germain, Adrienne, 9677
Germani, Gino, 8654, 8666, 9635-9636
Germidis, Dimitrios A., 4278
Ghidinelli, Azzo, 513, 625, 9761
Gholdi, Rodolfo, 8567
Giacottino, Jean-Claude, 8263

Gibaja, Regina E., 9714
Giestas, Elcio, 4843
Gifford, James C., 626, 633
Gil, Federico G., 8885
Gil-Bermejo García, J., 513
Gilbert, Alan, 6128
Gilbert, Gary C., 4094
Gilbert, V.J., 513
Gilhodes, Pierre, 4546, 8338, 8519a
Gill, George W., 605, 2010
Gill, Michael E., 5
Gillette, Philip, 8097
Gillin, John, 1361
Gilmore, Betty, 4279, 6676
Gilmore, Don, 4279, 6676
Gimeno, A., 513
Ginestar, Angel, 6189
Ginneken, Jeroen van. *See* van Ginneken, Jeroen.
Gioja, Rolando I., 6776
Giraldo, Octavio, 9637
Giraldo, Samuel Syro. *See* Syro Giraldo, Samuel.
Girard, Daniel, 6777
Girard, R., 513
Girón Padilla, Marcio Téllez. *See* Téllez Girón Padilla, Marcio.
Girvan, Norman, 4342-4343
Giudici, Ernesto, 8655
Giusti, Jorge, 8460
Givogri, Carlos A., 4706, 4724
Glade, William P., 4241
Glass, R.L., 2153
Glazer, Myron, 6039
Gnerre, M., 513
Gobeil, Oliva, 1477
Gobey, C.S., 6837
Godio, Julio, 8656
Godoy, Horacio H., 9638
Godoy Urzúa, Hernán, 9866
Goes, Ivoni dos Santos, 6291
Goes de Oliveira, Francisco Tarcízio. *See* Oliveira Francisco Tarcízio Goes de.
Goes Lodi, Nilce Aparecida e. *See* Lodi, Nilce Aparecida e Goes.
Goff, Fred, 8848
Goiás (state), *Bra.* Companhia de Desenvolvimento do Estado do Goiás (CODEG), 4859
Goiás (state), *Bra.* Departamento de Industria, 7234
Goiás (state), *Bra.* Departamento do Comércio, 7117
Goiás (state), *Bra.* Governo, 4860
Goiás (state), *Bra.* Secretaria da Indústria e Comércio. Departamento da Indústria, 7118
Goiás (state), *Bra.* Secretaria do Planejamento e Coordenação. Companhia de

Desenvolvimento do Estado de Goiás (CODERG), 7119
Goldberg, Boris, 8461
Goldberg, Rona, 2033-2034
Goldfarb, Marsha, 6117
Goldkind, Victor, 1137
Goldrich, Daniel, 1487
Goldsmith, Alfredo, 2033-2034
Goldsmith, Raymond W., 4095
Goldstein, Léa, 7120
Gollás, Manuel, 4384-4385
Goller, Patricia L., 1857
Goller, Theodore R., 1857
Golte, J., 513
Golubjatnikov, Rjurik, 2092, 2227
Gomes, Felipe Tiago, 6273
Gomes, Raymundo Pimentel, 7121
Gomes Neto, J. Mobral, 6274
Gómez, Alejandro, 4616
Gómez, Francisco Javier, 4456, 4476
Gómez, Juan Carlos, 8404
Gómez, Luis, 4344
Goméz, Sergio, 8429
Gómez Campo, Fabio Hernán, 4477
Gómez Cerda, José, 8253
Gómez Fuentealba, Raúl, 6778
Gómez Hurtado, Alvaro, 6895, 8326a
Gómez Otálora, Hernando, 4478-4479
Gomez-Tabanera, J.M., 513
Gómez Tamayo, Eduardo, 4547
Gonçalves, José Botafogo, 8588
Gonçalves de Abreu, Roberto. *See* Abreu, Roberto Gonçalves de.
Góngora Perea, Amadeo
Gonzaga da Paz, Luiz. *See* Paz, Luiz Gonzaga da.
González, Alberto Rex, 876-876a
González, Alfonso, 2035, 9795
González, Edward, 8044, 8225
González, Ernesto, 8433
González, Heliodoro, 8738
González Aguayo, Leopoldo, 8462
González Aparicio, Luis, 627
González Carbajal, Ladislao, 6143
González Casanova, Pablo, 1858, 8045
González Cossio, Arturo, 9715
González del Río Concepción, 1010
González-Ferrán, Oscar, 6740
González Lapeyre, Edison, 8046
González Madariaga, Exequiel, 8886
González Morfín, Efraín, 8154
González Pineda, Francisco, 8155
González Rul, Francisco, 717
González Salazar, Gloria, 4298, 9716-9717
González Sibrián, José Luis, 8827
González Viera, Mauro, 8604c
González-Wippler, Migene, 508
Gonzalo, Roberto, 746
Goodman, David E., 4861, 6275
Goodsell, Charles T., 8372
Gorenstein, Shirley, 628
Goreux, Louis M., 4280
Gorham, J. Richard, 6952
Gori, Gastón, 8656a
Gorodezky, C., 2086
Gossen, Gary H., 633, 1138
Gotuzzo, Lorenzo, 4617
Gougain de Contreras, Catalina, 4394
Goure, Leon, 8739
Gouvêa de Bulhões, Octavio. *See* Bulhões, Octavio Gouvêa de.
Gouveia, Aparecida Joly, 6276-6277
Gouveia Neto, Hermano, 6278
Government documents: the British government position on Chile, the British decision on armament orders, the U.S.
Gow, David, 1421
Graburn, N.H.H., 513
Graça Nicoletti, Maria da. *See* Nicoletti, Maria da Graça.
Graças Moreira Ferreira, Maria das. *See* Ferreira, Maria das Graças Moreira.
Graciarena, Jorge 4096, 6177
Gradin, Carlos J., 877
Gräbener, Jürgen, 9639
Graeff, Peter, 1478, 9856
Graham, Geroge C., 2135, 2154-2155
Graham, John A., 612, 629
Graham-Yooll, Andrew, 8657
Graña, César, 9640
Granados Téllez, Marcos F., 9837
Grandado G., V.M., 7291
Grant, C.H., 8287
Grassi, Alfredo, 8657a
Grau, Eros Roberto, 8588a
Great Britain. Directorate of Overseas Surveys, 7304-7306
Greaves, Thomas C., 1479
Grecic, Vladimir, 8361
Green, J.P., 2261
Green, María del Rosario, 8740
Green, Vera M., 1221, 1236
Greene, J.E., 8201
Greene, Jack P., 1219
Greene, Lawrence S., 2156
Greenfield, Patricia Marks, 1139
Greenfield, Sidney M., 1221, 8111
Gregor, Thomas A., 1348
Gregory, Afonso, 8568
Gregory, James R., 1140
Gregory, Peter, 4097
Greiff, Jorge Arias de, 6896
Grelier, Joseph, 6580
Grennes-Ravitz, Ronald A., 633
Greslebin, Héctor, 878
Grieb, Kenneth J., 4098
Griffin, Ernst, 7014
Griffin, G.G., 813

Griffith, Cecil C., 8288
Grigg, David, 6518
Grimes, Joseph, 1889
Grobman, Alex, 1011
Grolling, Francis Xavier, 513, 1012
Grondona, Mariano, 8658
Groot, Silvia W. de, 1237, 1282
Gross, Daniel R., 850
Grossman, Joel W., 1013
Grove, David C., 633, 718-719
Groves, Roderick T., 8319
Grunwald, Joseph, 4099
Guachalla, Luis Fernando, 8888
Guadagni, Alieto Aldo, 4725
Gualco, Jorge Nelson, 4100, 8889
Guanabara (state), Bra. Comissão Estadual de Currículo, 6279
Guanabara (state), Bra. Departamento de Estradas de Rodagem, 7248
Guanabara (state), Bra. Secretaria de Planejamento e Coordenação Geral, 7122, 7249
Guardia, Roberto de la, 821
Guariglia, G., 513
Guatemala. Instituto Geográfico Nacional, 7293
Guatemala Indígena, 2228
Guazzelli Bernardes, Nara Maria. See Bernardes, Nara Maria Guazzelli.
Gudschinsky, Sarah C., 1859-1861
Guerra, Francisco das Chagas Uchôa, 7123
Guerra, Phelippe, 7124
Guerra, Sergio, 9998
Guerra, Theophilo, 7124
Guerra Duarte, Sérgio. See Duarte, Sérgio Guerra.
Guerreiro de Lucena, Vinicius. See Lucena, Vinicius Guerreiro de.
Guerreiro Ramos, Alberto, 9984
Guerrero, C.H., 513
Guerrero Ortiz, Ramón Pablo, 4197
Guevara, Angel Raúl, 8520
Guevara, Elena Ortiz de 6779
Guevara, Ernesto, 8047, 8072, 8226-8227, 8405-8405a
Guevara, Jonathan, 702
Guía Roji (firm), *México*, 7313-7316
Guía Turística de Misiones con suplemento de Corrientes, 6780
Guibert, Claude, 4908
Guibourdenche de Cabezas, Marta, 9888
Guignabaudet, Philippe, 4101
Guillén Martínez, Fernando, 8320
Guillet, David, 1480
Guimarães, Antônio Barreto, 6280
Guimarães, Archimedes Pereira, 6281
Guimarães, Eduardo Augusto A., 4795
Guimarães de Almeida, Ruy Affonso. See Almeida, Ruy Affonso Guimarães de.

Guimarães Henriques, Márcio Olympio. See Henriques Márcio Olympio Guimarães.
Gumerman, George J., 513, 630
Gumucio Rivas, Juan S., 9862
Gunder Frank, André, 8020, 8048
Gunn, Mary R., 1862
Gunn, Robert D., 1862
Gurevitz, Nélida, 7219
Gurtov, Melvin, 8741
Guske, Hubertus, 8569
Gussinyer, Jordi, 720
Gussoni, Enrique Oscar, 4647, 8406
Gutiérrez, A., 2263
Gutiérrez, José, 9838
Gutiérrez Carranza, Claudio, 6110
Gutiérrez, Mario R., 8890-8891
Gutiérrez Santos, Luis E., 4281
Guttentag Tichauer, Werner, 87
Guyana Manufacturers Association, *Georgetown*, 137
Guyana. Land and Surveys Department. Cartographic Division, 7294
Guyana. Ministry of Agriculture. Lands Department, 7295
Guyana. Ministry of Agriculture. Survey Department, 7296
Guyana. Ministry of Information and Culture, 1238
Guyana handbook: industry, tourism, commerce, 6944
Guzmán Arze, Humberto, 1481
Guzmán Bockler, Carlos, 6111
Haberland, Wolfgang, 721-722, 822
Habicht, Jean-Pierre, 2041, 2070, 2157
Hablan los jóvenes de América Latina: recientes documentos producidos por la juventud latinoamericana, 8049
Hadda, Paulo Roberto, 4862-4863, 4909
Haddock Lobo, Roberto Jorge. See Lobo, Roberto Jorge Haddock.
Haefkens, Jacobo, 6610
Haekel, Josef, 509
Haener, Donald R., 6601
Härtling, Peter, 8891a
Hanbury-Tenison, A. Robin, 6644-6645
Hagan, Kenneth J., 8742
Hagen, Virginia, 8797
Hagelberg, G.B., 4419
Hairs, J., 513
Haiti, 4345-4346
Haiti: status of Christianity, 9796
Hajduk, Adán, 868
Halajczuk, Bohdan T., 8849
Halberstein, Robert A., 2036, 2093
Hall, M. Françoise, 2037-2038, 6519
Hall, Michele, 1297
Hall de Loos, Betty, 1863

AUTHOR INDEX

Haller, Archibald O., 9985
Hallewell, Laurence, 65
Halley Mora, Gerardo, 6953
Hamburger, Ernest W., 6282
Hammer, Henry B., 9641
Hammond, Norman, 513, 629, 631-633, 723-724, 814
Hampton, Joan, 1297
Hanbury-Tenison, Robin, 1349
Hancock, Ian F., 1225
Handler, Jerome S., 1239-1240
Haney, C. Allen, 9765
Hank González, Carlos, 8156
Hanley, Eric R., 1241
Hanley, Kathleen Jane, 1297
Hanna, Joel M., 1482, 2201-2202
Hannerz, Ulf, 1242
Hans, Nicholas, 6283
Hansen, Roy A., 8463
Hanson, James A., 4548
Hanson, Mark, 6129
Hanson, Simon G., 8892
Harbison, Frederic H., 4102
Hardoy, Jorge E., 6520-6521, 6741, 8207
Hareige, Dag, 8464
Harewood, J., 6565
Hargous-Vogel, Sabine, 1483
Hargrave, Lyndon L., 6677
Harkness, Shirley J., 1484, 9839
Harner, Michael J., 1361
Harrington, Horacio Jaime, 6742
Harrington, Richard, 6781
Harris, Allan, 1275
Harris, David, 6678
Harris, Luis K., 8050
Harris, M., 2195
Harrison, G.A., 2196
Harrison, Peter D., 513, 725
Herrman, Reimer, 6898
Hartley, L.H., 2213
Hartmann, R., 513
Hartmann, Thekla, 1350
Hartung, Horst, 634, 726
Harvey, Dodd L., 147
Harwood, Alan, 2229
Hasler, Juan A., 16
Hasperué Becerra, Oscar, 6158
Hassan, Mostafa Fathy, 4103, 4549
Hastings, C. Mansfield, 1014
Haverstock, Nathan A., 6624
Havet, José, 1485
Haviland, William A., 727
Hawkes, Jacquetta, 510
Hawkins, Carroll, 8051
Hawley, Henry, 728
Hazard, John, 8289
Headland, Paul, 1864
Healan, Dan M., 729
Healy, Paul F., 730

Heath, Dwight B., 511, 823, 1486-1487, 4386
Heaton, Louis E., 4550
Hébert-Stevens, François, 851
Hecker de Abreu, Carlos Miguel. See Abreu, Carlos Miguel Hecker de.
Hefley, James, 6976
Hefley, Marti, 6976
Heijmerink, J.J.M., 1141
Heine, Klaus, 702
Heinen, H. Dieter, 1351-1353
Heinsdijk, Dammis, 7125
Heizer, Robert F., 629, 731
Helfgott, Roy B., 4104
Helbig, Carlos, 6679
Heliógrafo de la Costa, *Barranquilla, Colo.*, 7276
Hellerman, Marcia, 1221
Hellbom, A.B., 513
Helleiner, G.K., 4105
Hellmuth, Nicholas M., 635
Helms, Mary W., 1142
Henault, Mirta, 9889
Henderson, Gregory, 8375, 8893
Hendricks, Glenn, 1243, 9797
Hendrickson, Embert J., 8894
Henriques, Márcio Olympio Guimarães, 4909
Henríquez de Paredes, Querubina, 9642, 9762
Hensey, Fritz, 1865
Heredia, Beatriz Alasia de, 9986
Heredia Cano, Fabio, 6743, 6897
Herman, Donald L., 8743
Hernández, Frank Marino, 6206
Hernández, Horacio H., 6082
Hernández, Porfirio, 1208
Hernández, Silvia, 6853, 8429
Hernández Aparicio, P., 513
Hernández de Alba, Guillermo, 6130
Hernández de Caldas, Angela, 29, 4480
Hernández Terán, José, 6680
Herranz M., Julián, 6190
Herrera, Amílcar O., 6023-6024
Herrera Navarro, Ramón, 4551
Herrero, Tudela, 513
Herschel, Federico J., 4106
Herskovits, Melville J., 1244
Herzog, J.D., 1245
Hester, Thomas R., 629, 732-733, 778
Heyden, Doris, 513, 624, 734-735
Heyduk, Daniel, 1488-1489, 4589, 9857
Hexsel, Astor Eugênio, 4864
Hicks, W. Whitney, 2039, 9718
Hidalgo, Carlos P., 2158
Hiersemenzel, Uwe-Ludwig, 4865
Higgins, Benjamin, 6549
Higgins, Cheleen Mahar, 1143
Higman, B.W., 2040
Hildner, Robert E., 8099

Hilger, M. Inez, 1361, 1490
Hill, Larry D., 8813
Hills, Robert A., 1866
Hilton, Ronald, 138
Hilton, Stanley E., 8570
Himes, James, 1491
Hines, Paul, 6025
Hinous, Pascal, 955a
Hinshaw, Robert, 2041
Hinz, E., 513
Hiraoka, Mario, 6826-6828
Hirschman, Albert O., 4107
La historia económica en América Latina, 4108
Hitchcock, A., 513
Hoadley, J. Stephen, 8052
Hochleitner, Franz Joseph, 513, 805
Hodge, Merle, 1275
Hodges, Donald C., 8053, 8730
Hoeldtke, Robert D., 2159
Hoetink, Harry, 9798
Hoff, B.J., 513
Hoffmann, Randall A., 4393
Hoja Informativa, 6085
Holdridge Propaganda (firm), Belém, Bra., 7265
Holguín Peláez, Hernando, 8895
Holland, William R., 1144
Hollander, Nancy Caro, 8663a
Hollenbach, Barbara E., 1867
Hollenbach, Elena E. de, 1145, 1868
Holm, Olaf, 512, 969-969b
Holt Buttner, Elizabeth, 9719
Holtey, Joseph, 8407
Holtzman, Wayne H., 9720
Honduras. Instituto Geográfico Nacional, 7299
Honduras. Instituto Nacional Agrario, 4387
Hongimann, J.J., 513
Hooker Cabrera, Herman, 4388
Hoover, John P., 6624
Hope, Kempe R., 4525, 8290
Hopkins, Jack W., 8054, 9643
Hopkins, Joseph, 736
Hopkinson, D.A., 2089
Horcasitas, Fernando, 1869
Horcasitas de Barros, María Luisa, 1146
Hormann, Paul Karl, 6782
Horn, James J., 8814
Horne, Alistair, 8465
Horowitz, Irving Louis, 9644, 9890
Horta, Raul Machado, 8588a
Horton, Douglas E., 1492-1493
Horton, Susan Ramírez, 4648
Hoskin, Gary, 8321
Hosono, Akio, 4082
Hourihan, John J., 1233
Hoyo Briones, María del Socorro del. *See* Socorro del Hoyo Briones, María del.

Huber, Klaus, 6609
Huddle, Donald L., 4866
Hudelson, Juan E., 1911
Huezo Selva, Rafael, 4389
Hughes, Helen, 4043
Hughes, I.G., 6596
Hugo Banzer Suárez y el destino de un peublo, 8408
Hugon, Paul, 2042, 9987
Huizer, Gerrit, 9867
Hultsch, David F. 9781
Humm, Madeline, 6977
Huneeus Cox, Pablo, 8466
Huneeus Madge, Carlos, 6118
Hunn, Eugene, 1147
Hunt, Howard, 8228
Hunt, Shane J., 4109
Hunte, George, 6566
Hunter, John M., 4110
Hunziker, Armando T., 879
Hurault, Jean-Marcel, 1246
Hurt, Wesley R., 908
Hurtado, Alberto, 2203-2204
Hurtado, Juan José, 1148
Hurwitz, Edith F., 139
Hurwitz, Samuel Justin, 139
Huscher, H.A., 513
Hutchings, Edward, 4029
Huyser, A.P., 4282
Hyde, Sylvia Y., 1870
Hyman, Ronald T., 127
Hyslop, John, 737
Ianni, Octávio, 8744-8745, 9645
Ibáñez, Francisco Maximiliano, 6783
Ibañez S.M., Gonzalo, 8428
Ibarra, Pablo, 8409
Ibarra, Raquel, 8659
Ibarra Grasso, Dick Edgar, 895
Ibero-Americana, 6
Ibiza de Restrepo, Ghislaine, 4481
Icaza, Susana J., 6113
Ichon, Alain, 743
The iconography of Middle American sculpture, 636
Idrobo, James E., 1871
Igarzábal, Antonio P., 6784
Iglesia A., Juan F. de la, 8746
Illich, Ivan, 6026-6028, 9646
Image of Peru, 6978
Imagen de El Salvador, 6625
Imagen do Brasil e da América Latina: 1973, 140
Imágenes de Cuba, 1953-1973: pasado y presente, tránsito hacia un presente definitivo, 8229
Imber, Sofía, 8520a
El imperialismo, 8055
Impérialistes, socialistes, sub-impérialistes pris dans le mécanisme de la crise: une analyse de André Gunder Grank, 4111

Ince, Basil, 1222
Incer Barquero, Jaime, 6639-6640
I.N.D.I.C.E.P., 1421
Informaciones Geográficas, 6854-6855
Informe al Gobierno de la República de Honduras sobre las cooperativas sindicales, 4390
Inforzato, Hélio, 6284
Inhorn, S.L., 2227
Iñigo Carrera, Héctor, 9891
Inkeles, Alex, 9892
Instituto Brasileiro de Administração Municipal, *Rio*. Centro de Pesquisas Urbanas, 8571
Instituto Colombiano de Comercio Exterior, *Bogotá*, 4112
Instituto de Desarrollo Integral y Armónico (IDIA), *Asunción*? 8604d
Instituto de Estudios Ibero-Americanos, *Stockholm*, 30, 141
Instituto de Ingenieros de Minas, *Santiago*, 4618
Instituto de Planejamento Econômico e Social (IPEA), *Rio*. Instituto de Planejamento (IPLAN), 4867
Instituto Euvaldo Lodi, *Florianópolis, Bra*. Núcleo Regional de Santa Catarina, 4868
Instituto Gaúcho de Reforma Agraria, *Pôrto Alegre, Bra*. Divisão de Geografia e Cartografia, 7250
Instituto Iberoamericano de Derecho Agrario y Reforma Agraria, 4552
Instituto Nacional de Cooperación Educativa, 6191
Instituto Nacional del Libro Español, *Madrid*? 31
Instituto Social Morumbi, 9988
Instituto Torcuato Di Tella, *Buenos Aires*. Centro de Investigaciones en Administración Pública, 4726
Interacción entre el Estado, las empresas y el movimiento sindical en la formación profesional, 8660
Inter-American Council for Education, Science, and Culture, *IV, Mar del Plata, Arg., 1972*, 6030
Inter-American Development Bank, 4113-4115
Inter-American Development Bank. Instituto para la Integración de América Latina (INTAL), 4116-4119
Inter-American Rural Youth Leaders' Conference, *Rio and Belo Horizonte, Bra., 1966*, 6031
Inter-American Rural Youth Leaders' Conference, *San Salvador, 1968*, 6032
Inter-American Rural Youth Leaders' Conference, *Mar del Plata and B.A., Arg., 1970*, 6033

Inter-American Rural Youth Leaders' Conference, *San Juan, 1972*, 6034
International Atomic Energy Agency, *Wien*, 6522
International Conference on Education, *XXXIV, Geneva, 1973*, 6144
International Congress for the Study of the Pre-Columbian Cultures of the Lesser Antilles, *IV, St. Lucia, 1971*, 837
International Congress for the Study of the Pre-Columbian Cultures of the Lesser Antilles, *V, Antigua, 1973*, 838
International Congress of Americanists, *XL, Roma-Genova, 1972*, 513
International Journal of Comparative Sociology, 1494
International Labour Organization, *Geneva*, 125, 6131, 8467, 8660a
International Labour Organization, *Geneva*. Programa Regular de Asistencia Técnica, 6934
The International Migration Review, 2043
International Review of Administrative Sciences, 8157
International Seminar on Tropical Meterology, *Campinas, Bra., 1969*, 7126
La investigación de los recursos marinos en México, 6681
Investimentos e reinvestimentos de capitais estrangeiros, 4869
Iriarte, Gregorio, 9858
Iribarren Charlín, Jorge, 935, 935a
Irisity, Jorge, 6178
Irving, Brian, 1247, 8291
Irwin, Richard, 7127
Irwin-Williams C., 513
Isbell, Billie Jean, 1495, 9625
Isbell, Harris, 2261
Isbell, William H., 1015
Isbister, John, 9721
Iscaro, Rubens, 8660b
Ishii, Akira, 4283
Las islas del Caribe: Rep. Dominicana, Haití, Puerto Rico, Jamaica, Cuba, 6567
Isphording, Wayne C., 738
Iszaevich, Abraham, 1149
Ivanissevich de D'Angelo Rodríguez, Magda, 6086
Ivanoff, Pierre, 637
Izaguirre de Artuccio, P., 7018
Izard, Miguel, 4553
Izquierdo, María Isabel, 8332
Jaber, Tayseer A., 4120
Jack, Robert N., 629, 733
Jackson, William Vernon, 32
Jacobs, Richard, 1222
Jacobs, Sharon, 1297
Jacobs, W. Richard, 8261

Jaén Esquivel, María Teresa, 2011
Jaen Suárez, Omar, 9763
Jaffe, A.J., 9647
Jagan, Cheddi, 8292
Jagan, Janet, 8293
Jaguaribe, Hélio, 8056, 8074
Jagaribe, Helio, 4121, 8572
Jairazbhoy, R.A., 513
Jamaica. Bank of Jamaica. Research Department, 4347
Jamaica. Department of Statistics, 142, 4348-4353, 6597
Jamaica. Ministry of Finance and Planning, 4354
Jamaica. Survey Department, 7301
James, William Russell, 9840
Jamunda, Theobaldo Costa, 99
Janiger, Oscar, 2230
Janvry, Alain de, 4727, 4738
Jaquette, Jane S., 8057
Jaquith, James R., 1872
Jambeiro, Marusia de Brito, 7128
Jaramillo, Isa de, 9832
Jarvis, Lovell S., 4728-4729
Jáuregui O., Ernesto, 6682
Jeftanovic P., Pedro, 4619
Jelin, Elizabeth, 9704
Jemio Ergueta, Angel, 8410
Jenkins, Veronica, 1297
Jerez, César, 6629
Jesse, Charles, 6568
Jha, Jagdish Chandra, 1248, 1253
Jickling, David J., 8411
Jijón y Caamaño, Jacinto, 956
Jimenes-Grullón, Juan Isidro, 4122, 6035
Jiménez, Franklin, 2169
Jiménez, Luis F., 8376
Jiménez Borja, Arturo, 1016
Jiménez Castro, Wilburg, 8058
Jiménez Grullón, Juan Isidro, 8254
Jiménez Moreno, W., 513
Jiménez Núñez, Alfredo, 671
Jiménez y Coria, Laureano, 6159
Joesink-Mandeville, LeRoy V., 739
John Bartholomew and Son, Ltd. (firm), *Edinburgh, Scotland*, 7206
Johnson, Dale L., 8020, 8468
Johnson, G., 513
Johnson, Peter T., 7203
Johnson G.C., Charles W., 4649
Johnston, Francis E., 2160
Jones, Calvin P., 6523
Jones, David, 6646
Jones, Grant D., 1150
Jongkind, C.F., 1496
Jonquieres C., Guido, 9722
Jopling, Carol F., 1151
Jordan, David C., 8059
Jordão, Haryberto de Miranda, 8572a
Jorge, Fernando, 9989

Jorge, Marcelo, 4357
Jornadas de Economía, 4730
Jornadas de Economía, *IX, Códoba, Arg. 1974,* 4731
Jornal de Psicanálise, 9990
Jorrin, Maria, 698
Joworski, Helam, 6171
Juarroz, Roberto D., 6082
Jud, G. Donald, 4284
Judde, G., 513
Julien, Michèle, 1023a
Junguito, Roberto, 4482-4483
Kahl, Joseph A., 9799
Kalnins, Arvids, 4391
Kampen, Michael Edwin, 638
Kane, N.S., 4285
Kanet, Roger E., 8747
Kannapin, Klaus, 9747a
Kaplan, B.A., 2096
Kaplan, Lawrence, 9648
Kaplan, Marcos, 4123, 4732, 8060, 8661, 9649
Kaplan, Stephen S., 8896
Karam, E., Jr., 2111
Kardonsky, C.V., 2161
Karst, Kenneth L., 8521-8521a
Katsui, Yoshio, 6740
Katuji Morikawa, Ivo. *See* Morikawa, Ivo Katuji.
Katz, Bernard S., 4286
Katz, Friedrich, 514
Katz, Phillip S., 1233
Katzman, Martin T., 4870
Kaufman Purcell, Susan, 8158, 8238
Kaupmann, Kierulff & Saxild (firm), *Copenhagen,* 7129
Kawashita, Koji, 6728
Kay, Cristóbal, 4634, 8469
Kaynor, Richard S., 4124
Kearney, Micahel, 1152
Keatinge, Richard W., 1017-1017b
Kehoe, T.F., 513
Kellenbenz, H., 513
Keller, Kathryn C., 1873
Kellers, James, 1018
Kelley, David H., 633, 797, 806
Kelley, J. Charles, 605
Kelly, Isabel, 605
Kemper, Robert V., 1153-1154, 2044, 9625
Kendall, Ann, 1019-1019a
Kendall, Aubyn, 513, 639
Kenney, Nathaniel T., 6683
Kensinger, Kenneth M., 1361, 2231
Kenski, Henry C., 8061
Kent, R.K., 1282
Kentch, Sally, 1297
Kepecs, Joseph G., 9650
Kerr, Isabel J., 1808, 1874
Kerr, K. Ann, 797

Kersten, (c.) and Co., N.V., *Paramaribo, Surinam,* 7341
Kerstenetsky, Isaac, 4780
Keshishian, John M., 640
Kesseru, Esteban, 2045
Key, Mary Ritchie de, 1875
Kiev, Ari, 1288a
Kimber, Clarissa T., 6604
King, Johannes, 1249, 1282
King, K.F.S., 4526
King, Kendall W., 1288a
King, Mary Elizabeth, 513, 1020
Kingston, Jerry L., 4125
Kingston, Jorge, 4871
Kingston, Lucia Silva, 4871
Kinzer, Nora Scott, 513, 9893
Kirk, R.L., 2094
Kirkby, Anne V.T., 641
Kirke, Henry, 6945
Kiser, Clyde V., 2046
Kissinger, Henry A., 8748
Klein, Harriet E. Manelis, 1497
Klein, R.E., 2157
Kleiner, Bernardo, 6036
Kleinpenning, J.M.G., 4872
Kline, Harvey F., 8322
Klipstein, Frederick A., 2162-2164, 2181
Klohn H., Erik, 6862
Klumpp, Deloris, 1876
Klumpp, James, 1876
Klunder y Díaz Morón, Juan, 6684
Kñakal, Jan, 4167
Kneeland, Harriet, 1877
Kneip, Lina Maria, 909
Knight, Peter T., 4873
Knobloch, Franz, 1354
Knoerich, Eckart, 6829
Knorozov, Yuri V., 807
Knowles, Yereth, 1247
Köbben, A.J.F., 1282
Koefoed, G., 1878
Köhler, U., 513
König, Wolfgang, 4287, 8810
Kohl, James, 8062
Kohn de Brief, Fritzi, 2165
Kolb, Glen L., 8522
Kolck, Odette Lourenção Van, 9991
Koolage, W.W., 513
Koontz, Carol, 1879
Kopesec, Bonnie M., 1880
Kopesec, Michael F., 1880
Kornfield, Guillermo, 1021
Korte, F., 2261
Kossok, Manfred, 513, 8063-8064
Kowarick, Lúcio, 9944, 9992
Kozlowski, Janusz K., 839, 839a
Kramer, Jane, 1250
Krapovickas, Pedro, 880
Krasnow, Michael A., 1233
Krause, G., 513

Krause, Walter, 8749
Kreisel, Werner, 6830
Krickeberg, Walter, 642
Krieger, Ronald A., 4874
Krimpen, A. van, 1251-1252
Krivoy, Ruth O. de, 4554
Krotser, G. Ramón, 740
Krzanowski, A., 513
Kubler, George, 797, 808
Kudachkin, Mikhail Fedorovich, 8470
Kudlek, M., 513
Kühnemann, Oscar, 6785
Kugenev, P.V., 6903
Kula, Marcin, 4126
Kumanev, Georgii Aleksandrovich, 8749a
Kumar, Joginder, 6524
Kummerly and Frey (firm), *Berne,* 7207
Kurjack, Edward B., 643
Kvaternik, Eugenio, 8661a
Kybal, Milic, 4018
Labarca, Guillermo, 6037
Labastida, Horacio, 4288
La Belle, Thomas J., 6192
Laborde, Julio, 8662
Lacaz, Carlos da Silva, 7130
Lacerda Filho, Murillo Carneiro de, 4875
Ladenson, Mark L., 4289
Ladman, Jerry R., 4290
Lafaye, J., 513
Lafer y Félix Peña, Celso, 8897
Lafon, Ciro René, 1498
Lage de Resende, Maria Efigenia. See Resende, Maria Efigenia Lage de.
Lagenest, J.B. Barruel de, 9993
Lago, Antônio Carlos de Araujo, 4949
Lago, Armando V., 4127
Lago, Benjamin do, 6285
Lagos, Félix, 8323
Lagrange de Castillo, H., 513
LaGuerre, John, 1253
Laguerre, M., 9800
Lagunas R., Zaid, 2012
Lagunilla Iñárritu, Alfredo, 4128
Lahmeyer Lôbo, Eulalia Maria. See Lôbo, Eulalia Maria Lahmeyer.
Lalive D'Espinay, Christian, 9651
Lalouel, Jean M., 2095
Lamb, F. Bruce, 6970
Lamberg, Robert F., 8065
Lamberg-Karlovsky, C.C., 644
Lambert, Denis-Clair, 4876, 8573
Lambert, Levindo Furquim, 7131
Laming-Emperaire, Annette, 936
Lampe, Philip E., 9723
Lamur, H.E., 2047
Landerman, Peter, 1881
Landis, Joseph B., 1254
Landsberger, Henry A., 9864
Lange de Cabrera, María Zoraida, 17
Langgulung, Hasan, 9724

Langoni, Carlos Geraldo, 4877-4878
Lanning, Edward P., 937
Lanning, Eldon, 8066
Lanus, Juan Archibaldo, 4129
Lapagesse, Eugênio, 8573a
La Pampa (province), *Arg.*, 8662a
Lapassade, Georges, 6286
Lapis Ferrari, Naira. *See* Ferrari, Naira Lapis.
La Porte, Robert 4162
Lara Tapia, Luis, 9710
Laraque, Marie-Hélène, 1445
Larguía, Isabel, 9889
Laris Casillas, Jorge, 4291
Larragoiti, Luis, 6581
Larrea Alba, L., 8362, 8898
Larrick, James W., 2205
Larsen, Donald W., 4819
Larsen, Helen, 1882
Larsen, R., 2207
LaRuffa, Anthony L., 9801
The LASA committee report on Guatemala terror: U.S. complexity in 20 years of repression there, 8189
Lasker, Gabriel W., 2096
Lastiri, Raúl A., 8663
Lastra de Suárez, Yolanda, 1883
Lasuen, José Ramón, 4130, 4555
Lathrap, Donald W., 1022
Latin America: a catalog of dissertations, 33
Latin American Perspectives, 4131, 8067, 8663a
Latorre, Eduardo, 9802
Latorre Cabal, Hugo, 8471
Latortue, François, 1288a
Lattes, Alfredo E., 9894
Lauer, Wilhelm, 779
Laufer, Deborah, 1233
Laurencich de Minelli, Laura, 513, 1155
Lavagnino, César, 4674
Lavallée, Danièle, 1003, 1023-1023a
Laverde Goubert, Luis, 6899
Layrisse, M., 2098
Layrisse, Zulay, 2097-2099
Lazar, Arpad von, 8523
Lázaro, Hernando, 9855
Lázaro, Roberto Carballo, 4672
Leal de Araujo, L., 4292
Leander, Birgitta, 1884-1885
Leão, A. Sergio Carneiro, 4843
Leap, William L., 1886
Lebedinsky, Mauricio, 8664, 8750
LeBot, Ivon, 8338
Lebowitz, Michael D., 2048
Lechin, Fuad, 2100, 6038
Lechtman, Heather, 1024
Lee, Thomas A., Jr., 633, 741-742
Leeds, Anthony, 1361, 1499-1500, 9625, 9994-9995

Leeds, Elizabeth, 9995
Lees, Susan H., 645
Leff, Nathaniel H., 4879-4880
LeGates, Richard T., 4620
Legerman, Caroline J., 1288a
Lehman, David, 4621, 8472
Lehmann, Henri, 743
Leitão, Saphyra Farias, 7099
Leitch, Adelaide, 6569
Leite, Celso Barroso, 9996
Leite, Valerie da Motta, 9997
Leloir, Alejandro, 8659
Leloup, Yves, 8574-8574a
Lemgruber, Antônio Carlos, 4881
Lemke, Donald A., 6009
Lemle, Mirian, 1887
Lemos, Antônio Agenor Briquet de, 56
Lenguaje, 1888
Lentin, Albert-Paul, 8751
León, Argeliers, 1255
León, Carlos A., 1512
León, Carlos V. de, 8850
León, César A. de, 8833
León, Patricio, 8479
León S., Luis A., 6902
Leonard, Thomas M., 8828
Leonardo Ruiz Pineda: guerrillero de la libertad, 8524
Leonardos, O.H., 7113
Leonhart, William Kahn, 8575
Leonov, Nikolai Sergeevich, 8828a
Leopoldi, José Sávio, 1355
Le Paige, Gustavo, 938-938b
Le Riverend, Julio, 4420
Lester, Kip, 6831
Levi, L. Makarius, 513
Lévi-Strauss, Claude, 1356
Levine, Robert M., 2049, 8576
Levy de Nessim, Sary, 4484
Lewald, Herald Ernest, 143
Lewis, A.B., 6630
Lewis, Robert Alden, 4650
Lewis, Vaughan A., 8851
Leyenaat, T.J.J., 513
Liberman, Gloria, 948d
Libertà per el Cile, 8473
Liboreiro, Ernesto S., 4733
The Library Association, 46
Los Libros, 2232, 6087
Liccardi, Millicent, 1889
Liebman, Arthur, 6039
Ligocki, Malô Simões Lopes, 10052
Ligocki, Marcus, 7132
Likosky, William H., 2233
Lima, Fernando Cunha, 4882
Lima, Francisco Roberto, 8752
Lima, João Franzen de, 6287
Lima, Lauro de Oliveira, 6288-6289
Lima, Miguel Alves de, 7133
Lima, P.E. de, 2150

Limen, 6088
Linares, Julio, h., 6040
Linares Málaga, Eloy, 1025
Linderman, Gerald F., 8852
Lindman, Carl Axel Magnus, 7134
Lindner-Emden, Hans, 1501
Lineamientos de la política económica-social del Gobierno Revolucionario, 8377
Lineamientos de un nuevo proyecto nacional, 9895
Lineamientos para alcanzar el mayor empleo y crecimiento en América Latina, 4132
Lineberry, William P., 8753
Lingoes, J.C., 2109
Lins, Rachel Caldas. See Caldas, Rachel.
Lins de Albuquerque, Therezinha. See Albuquerque, Therezinha Lins de.
Linsey, Susan C., 1233
Lionnet, Andrés, 1890
Lipman, Aaron, 9841
Lisker, Rubén, 2101
Lisón Tolosana, Carmelo, 671
Litt, John, 8062
Little, Michael A., 2205
Little, Walter, 8664a
Litton, Gaston L., 57-62
Litvak King, Jaime, 646-648
Livros recém-adquiridos: dezembro de 1973/junho de 1974, 34
Lizana V., María Victoria, 6856
Lizot, Jacques, 1357-1358
Llanque Chana, Domingo, 1420
Llavador Mira, J., 513
Lleras Restrepo, Carlos, 8324
Llopis, Alvaro, 2234
Lloreda, José Antonio, 6132
Lloreda Caicedo, Rodrigo, 8325
Llorente, Rodrigo, 4133
Lobb, C. Gary, 2235
Lôbo, Eulalia Maria Lahmeyer, 4883
Lôbo, Francisco Bruno, 6290
Lobo, Roberto Jorge Haddock, 9652
Lobsiger, Georges, 1891
Locker, Michael, 8848
Lockward Artiles, Andrés, 4355
Lodder, Celsius Antônio, 4884, 4959
Lodi, Nilce Aparecida e Goes, 6291-6292
Loeffke, Bernard, 8712a
Logan, Michael H., 1156-1157, 2236
Loker, June, 6525
Lomas, Roger, 706
Lomax, Alan, 1288a
Lombardi, Miguel C., 9653
Lombardo, Atilio, 7015
Lombardo Toledano, Vicente, 9725
Lomnitz, Larissa, 1158, 1502, 9625, 9726
Londoño, Julio, 8853
Long, J. Robert, 697-698

Longino de Arruda, Orêncio. See Arruda, Orêncio Longino de.
Loos, Eugene E., 1863, 1892-1896
Lopes, Gildo, 1897
Lopes, José Ferreira, 8588
Lopes, Oscar Souza, 2237
Lopes Bório, Edith B. See Bório, Edith B. Lopes.
Lopes Ligocki, Malô Simões. See Ligocki, Malô Simões Lopes.
López, Alfredo, 8271
López, Alvaro, 4483
López, F., 2238
López, José Fliseo, 9823
López, Teresa, 6581
López Acosta, Antonio, 4556
López Alonso, Sergio, 2013
López Austin, Alfredo, 1898
López C., Hugo, 4476, 4485
López de Piza, Eugenia, 1159
López G., A., 513
López Michelsen, Alfonso, 6895, 8326-8326a
López Ochoa, Jorge, 4291
López Pellón, Nivio, 7030
López Rosado, Diego G., 4293-4294
López Silva, Claudio, 8068
López Yustos, R. Alfonso, 1287
Lorandi de Gieco, Ana María, 881
Lord, Rexford D., 2239
Lorente Mourelle, Rafael, 6526
Lorenz, Günter W., 8378
Lorenzi, Mónica de, 872
Loring, David C., 8899
Losada, Rodrigo, 8327
Losada Aldana, Ramón, 4557
Losada Lora, Rodrigo, 4486
Lotería, 8829
Lounsbury, Floyd G., 797
Lourenço de Oliveira, Lólio. See Oliveira, Lólio Lourenço de.
Lourenço Filho, M.B., 6293-6295
Love, Joseph, 6548, 8013
Lovera, Delia Magda, 881
Lowenthal, Abraham F., 8255, 8379, 8754
Lowenthal, David, 6570
Lowry, William R., 4370
Loy, Jane M., 6744
Lozano, E., 1899
Lozano Simonelli, Fabio, 8328
Lubensky, Earl H., 970
Lucena, Héctor R., 4558
Lucena, Vinicius Guerreiro de, 7135
Lucha obrera, 8329
Lugo, Roberto, 8276
Lugo de Rivera, C., 2166
Luisi, Héctor, 4134
Lukesch, Anton, 509, 513, 1359-1360
Lumbreras, Luis Guillermo, 1026-1026b
Lumholtz, Carl, 649

Lumsden, Ian, 8069
Luna, Félix, 8665-8665a
Luna Tobar, Alfredo, 8755
Luraghi, R., 513
Lussu, Emilio, 8070
Lutchman, Harold A., 1247
Luyken, R., 2102
Lux, William, 144
Luz, A. Cerqueira, 9999
Lynch, Edward, 7031, 8524a
Lynch, Thomas F., 852
Lyon, Patricia J., 1361
Lyra Filho, João, 9654
Lyra Madeira, João. See Madeira, João Lyra.
Mabogunje, A.L., 6527
Mabro, Robert, 8078
Mabry, Donald J., 8159-8160
McCallum, J. Douglas, 4487
McCann, Frank D., Jr., 8900
McCarthy, Mary F., 8008
Maccio, Guillermo A., 9764
McCosker, Sandra Smith, 1160
McCullough, John M., 1161, 2206
MacDonald, Judy Smith, 1256
MacDonald Escobedo, Eugenio, 6685
McDowell, Jack, 6686
MacDowell, Joaquim Ignacio, 8588
Macedo, Gilberto de, 10000
Macedo, Sérgio D. Teixeira de, 7136
Macedo, Vera Amália Amarante, 56
Maceió (city), Bra. Escola Superior de Guerra. Associação dos Diplomados. Delegacia de Alagoas, 10001
MacEoin, Gary, 8474
MacEwen, Alison M., 9896
McEwen, William, 1503-1504
McGee, T.G., 1505
McGinn, Noel F., 6041
McGlynn, Eileen A., 515
McGrath, Marcos G., 8756
McGreevey, William Paul, 6900
Macgregor, María Teresa G. de, 6687
Machado, Eurico Serzedello, 10002
Machado Horta, Raul. See Horta, Raul Machado.
MacHale, Tomás P., 8428, 8475
Machiacado S., Flavio, 4622
Machicote, Eduardo, 8901
McIntyre, Alister, 4356
Macisco, John J., Jr., 9698
McMahan, Mike, 6688
McIntosh, Curtis, 1222
Macisco, John J., Jr., 2043
MacPhail, Donald D., 6857
McKeel, Jane, 6831
McKenzie, David, 660
Mackey, Carol J., 1031c
Mac-Lean y Estenós, Roberto, 9727
McLeod, Ruth, 1900

McMahon, David F., 1162
McNall, Scott, 8071
McNeilly, Miriam, 1164, 1902
MacNeish, Richard S., 644
McQuown, Norman, 1844
MacVean, Robert B., 2160
McVicker, Donald E., 650
Madeira, João Lyra, 7127, 10003
Mader, Julius, 8757
Madrazo, Guillermo B., 882
Maduro, Otto, 8525
Maestre Alfonso, Juan, 6528
Maeyama, Takashi, 10045
Magalhães, João Paulo de Almeida, 4885
Magalhães Júnior, Raymundo, 10004
Magallanes, Manuel Vicente, 8526
Magaña Contreras, Manuel, 8161
Magill, John H., 8412
Magrassi de Sá, Jayme. See Sá, Jayme Magrassi de.
Mahar, Dennis, 4948
Maharaj, Aknath, 1275
Maher, Patric, 6901
Maia, Newton Freire. See Freire-Maia, Newton.
Maillard, Olivier François, 1430
Maira, Luis, 8476
Makoto, Simón, 6955
Malan, Pedro, 4886
Malave, Inés, 2097
Malavé Mata, Héctor, 4559
Maldonado-Denis, Manuel, 8272, 9803
Malefijt, Annemarie De Waal, 1221
Malina, R.M., 2167
Mallin, Jay, 8230
Mallmann, C.A., 6089
Malloy, James M., 8380
Malmstrom, Vincent H., 809
Malpica S.S., Carlos, 2168
Mandel, Ernest, 6018
Mandle, Jay R., 4527
Mangin, William, 1487, 6979
Manitzas, Nita R., 4411
Mańkowska, R., 513
Manne, Alan S., 4280
Manning, Frank E., 1257-1259
Manns, Patricio, 6858, 8477
Manrique C., María Irma, 4135
Mansholt, Sicco, 8902
Mantilla S., Guillermo, 6902
Mantilla Suárez, Sergio, 4488
Manual de práctica sindical, 8330
Manya, Juan Antonio, 1419
Manzanilla Schaffer, Víctor, 8162
Manzano, Alfredo, 4357
Manzini, Giorgio Mario, 1362
Manzolli, Maria Cecília, 6381
Maranca, Silvia, 910
Maranhão (state), Bra. Escola de Ad-

ministração do Estado do Maranhão. Centro de Pesquisas, 6296
Marchesi, Enrique, 7016
Marckwardt, Albert M., 9851
Marcondes de Mattos, Fernando. See Mattos, Fernando Marcondes de.
Marcos, Jorge G., 971
Marcus, Joyce, 810, 814
Marek, Frank, 6018
Mareski, Sofía, 1363,
Margain, Carlos R., 1163
Margolis, Joan, 1297
Mariátegui, José Carlos, 8072
Marín, Juan Carlos, 9661
Marín E., Carlos, 8413
Marin Vargas, Ramón, 8331
Marini, Ruy Mauro, 8072, 8478
Marks, Susan D., 1233
Marques, Mário Osório, 10005
Marques de Melo, José. See Melo, José Marques de.
Marques Pinheiro, Lúcia. See Pinheiro, Lúcia Marques.
Marques Pinheiro, Maria do Carmo. See Pinheiro, Maria do Carmo Marques.
Márquez, Pedro José, 651
Marquez, Pompeyo, 8526a
Márquez Mayaudón, Enrique, 6529
Marrero Artiles, Levi, 4421
Marroquín, Alejandro Dagoberto, 516
Marsal, Juan Francisco, 8666
Marschall, W., 513
Marshack, Alexander, 633
Martin, Richard T., 1506
Martine, George, 2043, 6540, 9698, 9842
Martínez, Alvaro M., 6786
Martínez, Claude, 7225
Martínez, Francisco A., 7032
Martínez, G., 2103
Martínez, Héctor, 1507
Martínez, Juan Pablo, 8332
Martínez, M.A.E., 513
Martínez, Manuel, 4460, 4462
Martínez-Alier, Verena, 9804
Martínez C., Ildemaro, 8526b
Martínez Cárdenas, Jaime, 4489
Martínez Carril, Manuel, 7017
Martínez de la Vega, Francisco, 8163
Martínez Domínguez, Guillermo, 4295-4297
Martínez Escamilla, Ramón, 4298
Martínez Moreno, Carlos, 8613
Martínez Nogueira, Roberto, 8666a
Martínez Robá, Manuel, 4490
Martínez Terrero, José, 4136
Martínez Vidal, Carlos, 4687
Martinic Beros, Mateo, 6859-6860
Martins, José de Souza, 10006
Martins, José Valente. See Valente Martins, José.
Martins, Joel, 6297
Martins, Manuel J., 98
Martins, Marseno Alvim, 7137
Martinson, Tom L., 6633
Martner, Gonzalo, 8479
Maruhnic, Joan, 4102
Marxistas y cristianos en la construcción del socialismo, 8073
Marzał, Manuel María, 1418, 1508-1509
Marzano, G., 513
Massajoli, Pierleone, 1260
Massera, José Luis, 4673
Masson, P., 513
Masters, Robert V., 6980
Mastrorilli, Carlos P., 8634a-8634b, 8659, 8758
Mata, Jaime Jaen, 7326
Mata, Leonardo J., 2169-2171
Mata, Milton da, 4779, 4887-4888, 10007
Mateo, Eligio de, 8814a
Mathiason, John R., 9655
Mathiot, Madeline, 1853
Mathurin, Agustín, 9805
Matos, Eduardo, 605
Matos, Odilon Nogueira de, 4889, 7138
Matos Mar, José, 1510, 8074, 9852
Matos Mendieta, Ramiro, 1027-1027a
Matos Moctezuma, Eduardo, 652
Matson, R.G., 939
Matsushita, Hiroshi, 8903
Matsuzawa, Tsugio, 1028
Matta, Roberta da, 1364
Matthiasson, J.S., 513
Mattioni, Mario, 513, 830a, 840
Mattos, Adherbal Meira, 8903a
Mattos, Fernando Marcondes de, 4890
Mattos, Rinaldo de, 1901
Maudslay, Alfred Percival, 653
Maullin, Richard L., 8036, 8075, 8333
Mauny, Raymond, 671
Mauro, Frédéric, 6530
Mauro de Almeida, Wanderly J. See Almeida, Wanderly J. Mauro de.
May, William F., 8076
Mayer, Antonio de Castro, 8577
Mayer, Enrique, 1417
Mayers, Marvin K., 1164, 1902
Maynard, G., 4199, 4734
Mayoral, L.G., 2172
Mayorga Martínez, Pedro, 1365
Mayta Medina, Faustino, 1419
Máximo Miranda, Luis, 821
Maza Zavala, D.F., 4560, 8527
Mazess, Richard B., 2207
Mazz, Addy, 4137
Mazzoleni, G., 513
McCarthy, Gavan, 63
McDowell, Robert E., 116
McElroy, A., 513
McKerna, Mrs. James F., 6954

Mechoulam, Raphael, 2261
Meco, Joaquín, 671
Medeiros, Laudelino T., 10008
Medhurst, Kenneth, 8479
Médici, Emílio Garrastazu. See Garrastazu Médici, Emílio.
Medina, Carlos Alberto de, 8578a, 10009-10010
Medina Luna, Ramón, 8810
Meeting of the Board of Governors of the Inter American Development Bank, *XIV, Kingston, 1973*, 4138
Meggers, Betty J., 907, 911, 6745
Meighan, Clement W., 605, 744
Meirelles, Antônio Chagas, 4891
Meirinho, Jali, 99
Mejía Fernández, Miguel, 1165
Mejía Maya, Ignacio, 8334
Mejía Scarneo, Julio, 8381
Mejía Xesspe, Toribio, 1029
Mejias, Nilce Pinheiro, 6298
Mejicanos, María L., 2169
Melatti, Julio Cezar, 1361
Melazzi, Gustavo, 4139
Meldau, Elke, 6609
Melém, J.B., 7235
Melém, Maria de Nazaré, 7235
Melgar, Alicia, 4674
Mella, Julio Antonio, 8072
Mello, Guiomar Namo de, 6236
Mello, José Carlos, 4892
Mello, Luzia Garcia de, 6351
Mello Carvalho, Irene. See Carvalho, Irene Mello.
Mello Moreira, Moran de. See Moreira, Moran de Mello.
Mello Souza, Alberto de. See Souza, Alberto de Mello.
Mello Souza, Júlio César de. See Souza, Júlio César de Mello.
Melo, Acyr Alves Oliveira de, 7139
Melo, Edna Luísa de, 7236
Melo, Héctor, 4491
Melo, José Marques de, 9656, 10011
Melo, Marlos Jacob de, 4893
Mélo, Veríssimo de, 1366, 10012
Melo Barroso, Carmen Lúcia de. See Barroso, Carmen Lúcia de Melo.
Melo Pereira, Sylvia L. de. See Pereira, Sylvia L. de Melo.
Memmi, Albert, 1261
Menanteau-Horta, Darío, 9859
Mencarini Foracchi, Marialice. See Foracchi, Marialice Mencarini.
Mendes, Armando D., 7140-7141
Mendes, Josúe Camargo, 912
Méndez, Andrés, 8433
Méndez, Eustorgio, 6647
Méndez Acébal, Ramón, 8667
Méndez de Pérez, Betty, 513, 2165

Méndez Nápoles, Oscar, 6689
Mendieta y Núñez, Lucio, 4299, 6674
Mendonça da Freitas, Luis. See Freitas, Luis Mendonça da.
Mendoça de Barros, José Roberto. See Barros, José Roberto Mendoça de.
Mendonça Ramos, Raimundo Nonato. See Ramos, Raimundo Nonato Mendonça.
Mendoza, Alberto, 8335
Mendoza, Angela, 654
Mendoza, D., 2000-2001
Mendoza (province), Arg. Instituto de Investigaciones de las Zonas Aridas y Semiáridas, 6787
Menéndez, René, 6581
Menezes, José Rafael de, 10013
Menghin, Osvaldo F.A., 883-883a
Mensagem Pedagógica, 6299
Mentz, Raúl P., 6076
Meo, Carlos, 8604e
El Mercado Común Centroamericano, 4392
Merino C., Leonor, 702
Merino de Zela, E.M., 513
Merino Mañón, José, 4291, 4300
Merkur, 8480
Merrick, Thomas W., 2050, 4805
Merrifield, William R., 1866
Merrill, William C., 4393
Mesa Lago, Carmelo, 4422-4423, 4651, 8231
Mesas Redondas sobre Desarrollo y Econogía, *México, 1973,* 6690
Mesquita, Alfredo, 7142
Mesquita, Luciano, 8579
Messina Matos, Milton, 4358
Metzger, Donald J., 1368
Metzger, Lois, 1903
Metzger, Ronald, 1903
Mevis, René, 1262
México for Americans, 8815
Mexico. Comisión de Estudios del Territorio Nacional (CETENAL), 7317
Mexico. Comisión Nacional de los Salarios Mínimos, 7318
Mexico. Dirección de Agrología, 7319
Mexico. Dirección General de Oceanografía y Señalamiento Marítimo, 7320
Mexico. Secretaría de la Defensa Nacional. Departamento Geográfico Militar, 7321
Mexico (state), *Mex.* Gobierno del Estado de México. Dirección de Prensa y Relaciones Públicas, 8165
Meyer, Karl E., 655
Meyer, Richard L., 4836, 4925
Meyer L., Consuelo, 4301
Miceli, Sergio, 10014
Michaels, Joseph W., 670, 745

Michaud, Andree, 1418, 1511
Michielutte, Robert, 9765
Micklin, Michael, 1512, 9766
Micotti, Maria Cecília de Oliveira, 6300
Middlemiss, H., 2197, 2210-2211
Migliazza, E.C., 2125
Migliorini, Inés Candelaria, 9897
Miguens, José Enrique Carlos, 8077, 8666
Mijs, A.A., 1263
Mikdashi, Zunayr, 8528-8528a
Mikesell, Raymond F., 4140
1973 [Mil novecientos setenta y tres] directorio nacional de profesionales, 100
Milanesi, M.L., 2054, 2176
Milenky, Edward S., 8904
Milia, José L., 6788
Millape Caniuqueo, Antonio, 1513
Millan, Silvia, 4298
Millares Carlo, Agustín, 7
Millas, Orlando, 8481
Miller, Arthur G., 513, 629, 633, 656-657
Miller, Elmer S., 1361
Miller, Errol L., 1264
Miller, Eurico Th., 913
Miller, James A., 8099
Miller, John, 6531, 9657
Miller, Nugent, 1222
Miller, Solomon, 1487, 1514
Millette, James, 4424, 8283
Millon, Clara, 658
Millon, René, 633, 659, 7322
Milton, George, 746
Minas Gerais (state), *Bra.*, 7145-7146
Minas Gerais (state), *Bra.* Conselho Estadual do Desenvolvimento. Instituto de Geo-Ciências Aplicadas. Esquema de Trabalho Integrado no Setor Mineral, 7143
Minas Gerais (state), *Bra.* Departamento de Estradas de Rodagem. Serviço de Planejamento Rodoviário, 7144
Minas Gerais (state), *Bra.* Instituto de Geo-Ciências Aplicadas, 7251-7253
Minelli, L., 513
Minervini, Estela, 6082
Minicucci, Agostinho, 6301
Minguet, C., 513
Mintz, Sidney W., 1208, 1265-1268
Miquel i Vergés, José María, 117
Mir, Adolfo, 6160
Miraglia, L., 513
Mirambell, Lorena, 747
Miranda, Heloísa de Resende Pires, 10015
Miranda, Nicanor, 10016
Miranda C., Sergio, 8428
Miranda G., Luis Máximo, 824
Miranda Jordão, Haryberto de. *See* Jordão, Haryberto de Miranda.
Miranda S., R.P. Pedro, 1904

Mirelman, Victor A., 9898
Miró G., Rodrigo, 8197
Miró Quesada, Aurelio, 6981
Mirón Chuk, Pedro, 8846
Mischan Rodrigues, Maria Magdalena E. *See* Rodrigues, Maria Magdalena E. Mischan.
Mitchel, Simon, 10017
Mitchell, David I., 8854
Mitchell, Robert W., 660, 6700
Modenesi, Rui Lyrio, 4779
Modiano, Nancy, 1166
Mörner, Magnus, 1287
Moffatt, Alfredo, 9899
Mohana, João, 10018
Mohr, Hermann J., 4492
Molano Campuzano, Joaquín, 6903
Molen, G. van der, 1269
Molestina Zaldumbide, M. Carmen, 972
Molieri, J.J., 513
Molina, Alfonso, 8382
Molina, C.V., 2084-2085
Molina Cabrera, Orlando, 4141
Molina Chocano, Guillermo, 9767
Molina Molina, Flavio, 6691
Molina Ossa, Camilo, 6904
Molineu, Harold, 8855
Molino, Domenico, 6789
Molloy, John P., 633, 661
Monasterio, Maximina, 7033, 7037
Monckeberg, Fernando, 4623
Mondloch, Margaret, 1361, 1490
Moneta, Carlos Juan, 8905, 8917
Monge, Carlos, 2208
Monroe, Elizabeth, 8078
Monroy Rivera, Oscar, 8166
Montag, Richard, 1905
Mont'Alegre, Omer, 4894
Montañé M., Julio C., 517, 940
Montaño Aragón, Mario, 1515
Monte, Francisco, 4816
Monte-Mór, Jannice, 35
Monteforte Toledo, Mario, 8394, 8383
Monteiro, Jorge Vianna, 4895
Monteiro Considera, Cláudio. *See* Considera, Cláudio Monteiro.
Monteiro Ribeiro, Clélia. *See* Ribeiro, Clélia Monteiro.
Montenegro, Abelardo F., 4142
Montenegro, João Alfredo de Sousa, 10019
Monterrey en cifras: 1970, 6692
Montes, Élvira, 8906
Montes, Segundo, 9768
Montes Giraldo, Juan Joaquín, 1906
Montes Llamas, Gabriel, 4493
Montesinos Hurtado, Augusto, 8414
Monthly Bulletin, 4652
Montoya Sánchez, Javier, 1367
Monzalvo, Carlos Andrés, 4675

Moone, Janet Ruth, 1167
Moore, Alexander, 1168
Moore, Bruce R., 1907
Moore, Richard B., 1270
Moore, Russell Martin, 4143
Mora, Niní de, 4369
Mora López, Raziel, 701-702, 748
Mora y Araujo, Manuel, 8668, 9900
Moraes, Jomar, 64
Moraes e Castro, Astréa de. *See* Castro, Astréa de Moraes e.
Moraes Souza, Eli de. *See* Souza, Eli de Moraes.
Morais, José Xavier Pessoa de, 10020
Morales, Alberto, 2240
Morales, Marcelo, 4624
Morales Padrón, Francisco, 118, 671
Morales V., Jesús María, 6905
Morales Vergara, Julio, 9659
Moran, Theodore H., 8482
Morase, Mario A.P., 2241
Morawski, Waclaw, 4425
Morbán Laucer, Fernando A., 1271
Moreira, Amélia Alba Nogueira, 7147-7148
Moreira, Hilton Beruttie Augusto, 8580
Moreira, Júlio Estrella, 7149
Moreira, Moran de Mello, 4950
Moreira, Neiva, 4653
Moreira Alves, Marcio. *See* Alves, Marcio Moreira.
Moreira da Cunha, Alda das Mercês. *See* Cunha, Alda das Mercês Moreira da.
Moreira da Silva, Paulo de Castro. *See* Silva, Paulo de Castro Moreira da.
Moreira Ferreira, Miaria das Graças. *See* Ferreira, Maria das Graças Moreira.
Moreno, Juan Carlos, 8907
Moreno, Oscar, 6521
Moreno Avendaño, José, 6042
Moreno Russo, Laura Garcia. *See* Russo, Laura Garcia Moreno.
Morey, Nancy C., 1368
Morey, Robert V., Jr., 1368, 1369
Morj, Roberto, 8273
Morikawa, Ivo Katuji, 7174
Morin, Edgar, 10021
Morin, Françoise, 1208
Morley, Samuel A., 4896
Morresi, Eldo S., 884
Morris, Craig, 1030-1030c
Morris, David J., 8483
Morris, Fred B., 7150
Morris, L., 2215
Morris, Michael, 8908
Morrissy, J. David, 4395
Morse, Richard M., 1487, 1516, 6531-6532, 9659
Morth, Grace E., 1233
Morton, N.E., 2095

Morton, Peggy, 9889
Moseley, Michael Edward, 1014, 1031-1031a
Moser, Alvino, 6302
Moser, Christopher, 662, 1032
Mosquera, Francisco, 8357
Mosquera, Juan José Mouriño, 6303-6305
Moss, Robert, 8079, 8484
Mota, A. Teixeira da, 6533
Mota, Joanna Luzia da Silva, 10052
Motta Leite, Valerie da. *See* Leite, Valerie da Motta.
Motta Ribeiro, Antônio Carlos da. *See* Ribeiro, Antônio Carlos da Motta.
Mountjoy, Joseph B., 605, 749-750
Moura, Iraci Afonso de, 10022
Moura Castro, Cláudio de. *See* Castro, Cláudio de Moura.
Mouriño Mosquera, Juan José. *See* Mosquera, Juan José Mouriño.
Mouroz, Jean Revel, 8167
Le mouvement éducatif dans 75 pays: rapports nationaux, 6306
Movimiento de Liberación Nacional, *Montevideo,* 8614
Movimento Democrático Brasileiro (MDB). Diretório Nacional, 8580a
Moxley, Robert L., 1517, 9660
Moyano Bonilla, César, 8909
Moyano C., Argentino, 8012
Muelle, Jorge C., 1033-1033a
Mueller, Charles C., 4897
Müller, María S., 6790
Müller, Ronald, 4017
Münzel, Mark, 513, 1370-1371, 1908
Mugica, Carlos, 8669
Mujeres, 9806
Mujica, Héctor, 8485
Mujica, Jorge García. *See* García Mujica, Jorge.
Mulcahy, F. David, 1233
Mulchansingh, Vernon C., 4359
Muller, Aixa, 2104
Muller, Florencia, 751, 779
Muller, Herbert J., 1287
Muller, Keith Derald, 7151
Mundigo, Axel I., 6634
Muñoz, Humberto, 9728
Muñoz, Oscar, 4614
Múñoz Marín, Luis, 8274
Muñoz Reyes, Jorge, 6832
Munroe, Trevor, 4360
Murdock, George Peter, 1361
Murillo, Miguel A., 4396
Murmis, Miguel, 9661
Muro Orejón, A., 513
Murphy, Robert F., 1361, 1372
Murphy, Yolanda, 1372
Murray, D. R., 8759
Murtinho, Hélber F., 10024

Musalem, José, 4625
Muser, Curt, 752
Musso Ambrosi, Luis Alberto, 36, 8615
Musto, Stefan A., 4144
Myazaki, Nobue, 914
Myerhoff, Barbara G., 1169
Myers, David J., 8529-8529a
Myers, Robert G., 6172
Myers, Sarah K., 1518, 9853
Myers, Thomas P., 915, 973
Nabuco, José Thomaz, 7152
Nacional Financiera, *México,* 4302-4304
Nadra, Fernando, 8670
Nagelkerke, G.A., 1272-1274
Nálevka, Vladimír, 8760-8763, 8910
Namo de Mello, Guiomar. *See* Mello, Guiomar Namo de.
Naranjo, Claudio, 1519
Naranjo, John, 4145
Naranjo, Plutarco, 2242
Narskih, R.S., 6918
Nash, J., 513
Nassef, El Sayed, 4305
Nasser, Nássaro A. de Souza, 916
National Geographic Society, *Washington,* 7208, 7323
Navarrete, Carlos, 753
Navarrete, Ifigenia M. de, 9729-9730
Navarrete N., Antonio, 1909
Navarro, Newton, 7153
Naylor, Bernard, 65
Naylor, Thomas H., 4898-4899
Nazaré e Silva, Regina. *See* Silva, Regina Nazaré e.
Nectário María, hermano, /345
Needler, Martin C., 8080, 8764
Neel, James V., 2051, 2079, 2105-2109, 2125, 2243
Neely, James A., 630
Neira, Eduardo, 6534
Nelson, Fred W., Jr., 754
Nelson, Michael, 4146, 8765
Neotti, Ana, 10025
Nérici, Imídeo Giuseppe, 6307-6309
Nery, Sebastião, 8581
Nery da Fonseca, Edson. *See* Fonseca, Edson Nery da.
Ness, Walter L., Jr., 4900, 4988
Neto, Antônio Delorenzo, 7154
Nett, Emily M., 1520
Neves, José Adolfo Pereira, 10026
Neves, Marco Flavio, 7155
A new Guyana, 6946
New Vision, 1275
The New York Public Library, *New York.* The Branch Library System. The Office of Adult Services, 8
Newman, Marshall T., 2110
Nicaragua. Instituto Geográfico Nacional, 7324-7325

Nicholson, Henry B., 605, 633
Nick, Eva, 91
Nickel, Herbert J., 677, 4147
Nicolas, M., 840
Nicoletti, Maria da Graça, 6292
Niemeyer Fernández, Hans, 941, 941a
Nieto de Negrette, María Elena, 6189
Nieto Navia, Rafael, 8766
Nietschmann, Bernard, 6641
Nieuwenhove, J. van, 8081
Nikiforov, Boris Sergeevich, 8232
Nimuendajú, Curt, 1361
Nisbet, Charles, 1487
Niskier, Arnaldo, 145, 6310
Nissly, Charles M., 6729
Niveles de atención médica para un sistema de regionalización en Colombia, 6906
Noble, John, 2244
Nóbrega, Vandick L. de, 6311
Nodal, Roberto, 1276
Noel, Pierre, 1288a
Nogueira de Matos, Odilon. *See* Matos, Odilon Nogueira de.
Nogueira Moreira, Amélia Alba. *See* Moreira, Amélia Alba Nogueira.
Noguera, Eduardo, 755-756
Nolan, Mary Lee, 1170
Nolasco Armas, Margarita, 9731
Nolen, Barbara, 6693
Nombres geográficos de Costa Rica, 6618
Nores, Gustavo A., 4735
Noriega, Carlos, 4148
Noriega, José Sotero, 4306
North American Congress on Latin America (NACLA), *New York,* 9, 4149, 8190, 8486
Norton de Stöcker, María Eugenia, 6049
Notes et Etudes Documentaires, 8198
Noticias del CSUCA, 6112
Nott, David, 8530
Novaes, Fernando C., 7156
Novaes, Paulo, 6312
Novaes de Oliveira, Regis. *See* Oliveira, Regis Novaes de.
Noval, Joaquin, 1171
Nowotny, Karl A., 663
Nuestra Palabra, 8670a
Nun, José, 9661
Nunes, Fred, 4361
Nunes, Mário Ritter, 10027
Nunes Correia, Ronaldo. *See* Correia, Ronaldo Nunes.
Núñez, Benjamín, 6535
Núñez Atencio, Lautauro, 942-942c
Núñez del Prado, Oscar, 1521
Núñez del Prado B., Daisy, 1420
Núñez del Prado B., Juan Víctor, 1361, 1522
Núñez Ecarri, Carlos, 8531

Núñez H., Patricio, 942b-942c
Núñez L., Carlos J., 4404
Núñez Miñana, Horacio, 4730, 4736-4737
Núñez Regueiro, Víctor A., 885-885a
Núñez Regueiro de De Lorenzi, Beatriz N., 885a
Nutini, Hugo G., 2036
Nweihed, Kaldone G., 8911
Oberem, Udo, 1361, 1523
La obra del Instituto Lingüístico de Verano, 1910
Obschatko, Edith S., 4738
Ocampo Londoño, Alfonso, 6043
Ocampo T., José Fernando, 9843
Ochsenius P., Claudio, 943
Ochoa, Guillermo, 8487
Ochoa, Miguel, 8856
Ochoa Campos, Moisés, 8082
Ochoa Isaza, Gabriel, 6133
Ochoa Salas, Lorenzo, 757-758
Ochoterena F., H., 6694
O'Connell, Arturo A., 4718
Octaviano Ferreira, Nelson Braga. See Ferreira, Nelson Braga Octaviano.
Odell, Peter R., 4150
Odin (firm), *Panama,* 7327
Odle, Maurice, 4362
O'Donnell, Guillermo A., 4739-4740, 8083, 8671
La Oficina Central de Estadística de Suecia, *Stockholm,* 30
Ojeda Gómez, Mario, 8810
Okpaluba, Chuks, 1222
Okraku, Ishmael O., 9807
Olden, Daniel, 4616
Olesen, Virginia, 9808
Olien, Michael D., 518
Olivan, Ruben George, 10028
Olivares, Augusto, 8912
Olivares, José, 6861
Olivares, Juan, 6907
Oliveira, Adélia Engrácia de, 1373
Oliveira, Francisco, 4901
Oliveira, Francisco Tarcízio Goes de, 4799, 4902
Oliveira, José Carlos de Araújo e, 10029
Oliveira, Lólio Lourenço de, 6219
Oliveira, Orlandina de, 9U28
Oliveira, Pedro A. Ribeiro de, 9673, 10010
Oliveira, Plínio Correa de, 8577
Oliveira, Regis Novaes de, 8588
Oliveira, Roberto Cardoso de, 1374-1375
Oliveira, Sandra Furtado, 6240
Oliveira, Waldemir Bezerra, 7266
Oliveira Andrade, Manuel Correira de. See Andrade, Manuel Correira de Oliveira.
Oliveira Baracho, José Alfredo de. See Baracho, José Alfredo de Oliveira.

Oliveira Campos, Roberto de. See Campos, Roberto de Oliveira.
Oliveira Carvalho, Mário Helder de. See Carvalho, Mário Helder de Oliveira.
Oliveira de Melo, Acyr Alves. See Melo, Acyr Alves Oliveira de.
Oliveira Lima, Lauro de. See Lima, Lauro de Oliveira.
Oliveira Micotti, Maria Cecília de See Micotti, Maria Cecília de. Oliveira.
Oliveira Neto, Olinto José, 10030
Oliveira Penna, José Eduardo de. See Penna, José Eduardo de Oliveira.
Oliven, Ruben George, 6313, 8582
Olivera, J.H.G., 4199
Oliveros, José, 605
Olsen, Fred, 841, 841a
Olshany, Anatoli, 4426
Olson, Leslie, 9750
O'Mara, Gerald T., 4646
Onaka, Alvin T., 2052
O'Neil, Charles, 6314
O'Nell, C.W., 2173
Onofre Jarpa, Sergio, 8488
Onuki, Yoshio, 1034
Operación Cacique: tácticas de intrusión de los Estados Unidos en la universidad colombiana, 8336
Orbe, Gonzalo Rubio, 1422
Orejas Miranda, Braulio, 6536
Orellana Rodríguez, Mario, 944
Orellano, Jerónimo, 8671a
Orellana S., Carlos L., 9732
Orellana Valeriano, Simeón, 1035
Organization of American States. Asamblea General, 8767
Organization of American States. Bureau of Regional Development, 7297
Organization of American States. Centro Interamericano de Promoción de Exportaciones (CIPE), 4151
Organization of American States. Centro Interamericano para la Producción de Material Educativo y Científico para la Prensa, 6043a
Organization of American States. Departamento de Asuntos Económicos, 4495
Organization of American States. Department of Social Affairs, 6537
Organization of American States. Secretaría General, 8768
Organization of American States. Secretaría General. Comité Interamericano de la Alianza para el Progreso (CIAP), 4152
Organization of American States. Secretaria Geral. Comissão Interamericana de Direitos Humanos, 8769
Orlandini, Edmundo, 8582a

Orlando, Héctor, 6791
Orlove, Benjamin S., 1421, 1494, 1524-1525
Ornstein, Roberto M., 8770
Orr D., Carolina, 1911
Orrego V., Claudio, 8466
Orrego Vicuña, Francisco, 8771, 8913
Orrillo, Winston, 8489
Orta, Celio S., 4561
Ortega, Elpidio, 845a
Ortiz, Luis Carlos, 7277
Ortiz C., Elva L., 6134
Ortiz Mayans, Antonio, 1912
Ortiz Troncoso, Omar R., 945-945f
Ortiz Wadgymar, Arturo, 8168
Ortolani, Altino Aldo, 7157
Ortolani, Mario, 6746
Osborn, Alan J., 965, 974
Osorio, Cristina, 4608
Osório Marques, Mário. See Marques, Mário Osório.
Ossa, Juan Luis, 8490
Ossio A., Juan M., 1526
Osuji, T.O., 1222
Otão, José, 6315
Otterbein, Charlotte Swanson, 1277
Otterbein, Keith F., 1277
Oud, P.J., 1278
Owen, Michael G., 1844
Owen, Wilfred, 4496
Oxaal, Ivar, 1279
Ozawa, Terutomo, 4153
Pablo, Juan Carlos de, 4741-4743, 4748
Pacheco, Bernardo, 4307
Pacini, Dante, 6316
Packenham, Robert A., 8772
Padeen, Robert Charles, 1361
Pagney, M.P., 7034
Paige, David M., 2174-2175
Paiva, Ruy Miller, 4903
Paiva, Vanilda Pereira, 6317
Paiva Abreu, Marcello de. See Abreu, Marcello de Paiva.
Paiva de Castro, Luiz. See Castro, Luiz Paiva de.
Palacios, Marco, 8337
Palacios Mejía, Hugo, 4497
Palanca, Floreal, 886
Palavecino, Enrique, 1376
Palerm, Angel, 519, 664-665
Palermo, Alfredo, 6318
Pallestrini, Luciana, 513, 917
Palm, E.W., 513
Palma, Eduardo, 8466
Palma, Néstor Homero, 887
Palmer, David Scott, 8384
Palomino, Salvador, 1527
Palomino Flores, S., 513
Pan American Health Organization (PAHO), *Washington*, 2245-2247
Pan-American Institute of Geography and History (PAIGH), *Rio*, 7209
Panama. Banco Nacional de Panamá, 4397
Panama. Dirección de Estadística y Censo, 6648
Pandolfi, Rodolfo, 8672
Pandolfo, Clara Martin, 4904, 7158
Paniagua Rodríguez, Alejandro, 9809
Pankonin, Aldo, 886
Panorama de la economía venezolana durante el período enero-junio del año 1968; enero-junio del año 1969; segundo semestre del año 1971; tercer trimestre del año 1972; cuarto trimestre del año 1972, 4562
Pantoja Revelo, Carlos, 4498
Paolino, Ernest N., 8857
Paquien, Jorge Luis, 4154
Pará (state), *Bra*. Associação de Crédito e Assistência Rural do Estado do Pará (ACARPA), 4905
Pará (state), *Bra*. Departamento de Estradas de Rodagem do Pará, 7254
Pará (state), *Bra*. Instituto do Desenvolvimento Econômico-Social do Pará (IDESP), 4906
Paraguay today: information handbook, 6956
Parahym, Orlando da Cunha, 6319
Paraíba (state), *Bra*. Comissão Estadual de Planejamento Agrícola (CEPA), 7159
Paraíba (state), *Bra*. Secretaria da Educao e Cultura. Conselho Estadual de Cultura, 146
Paraná (state), *Bra*. Coordenação de Planejamento Estadual, 4907
Paranhos, Oscar Torres, 4908
Pardo, Marta Eugenia, 9674
Parducci Z., Ibrahim, 975
Parducci Z., Resfa, 975
Pare, Louise, 8169
Paredes Macedo, Saturnino, 8385
Parizzi, Marcelo, 4909
Parker, Gary J., 1913
Parkinson, F., 8773
Parrés, Ramón, 9662
Parrilla-Bonilla, Antulio, 9663, 9810
Parsons, James J., 976, 6538
Parsons, Jeffrey R., 1036
Participación del Movimiento Sindical en la Formación Profesional, *Montevideo, 1972*, 8616
Partido Nacional de Honduras. Comité Central, 8194
Partido Revolucionario Institucional (PRI). Comisión Nacional Editorial, *México*, 6695
Partido Social Cristiano, Comité Organizador Pro Elecciones Indepen-

dientes (COPEI), *Caracas,* 8532
Partidos políticos y clases sociales en el Uruguay: aspectos ideológicos, 8617
Pasará, Luis, 4654
Paskey, T., 2227
Pasquel, Leonardo, 6696
Passos, Carlos de Faro, 4910
Passos, Wilson Vieira, 4040
Pastore, Affonso Celso, 4911-4912
Pastore, José, 4913-4914, 6320
Pasztory, Esther, 513, 759
Patch, Richard W., 1487
Paterson, Thomas G., 8858
Patman, C.R., 6539
Patrick, George F., 4915-4916
Patterson, Orlando, 1282
Patto, Maria Helena Souza, 6321
Paula, Jardel Barcellos de, 6322
Paulat Legorreta, Jorge, 1172
Paulín, Georgina, 9733
Paulini, J. (firm), *Rio,* 7237, 7255-7256, 7267
Paulsen, Allison C., 977
Paulston, Christina Bratt, 1914
Paulston, Rolland G., 6173, 8233
Paulukat, Inge, 6582
Pauyo, Nicolás L., 8258
Pavetti Morián, Justo Manuel, 6957
Paviani, Aldo, 7110
Payne, James L., 8084
Payne O., Ruth, 6105
Paz, Luiz Gonzaga da, 7160
Paz, Pedro F., 4155-4156
Paz Barnica, Edgardo, 4398
Paz Estenssoro, Víctor, 8415
Paz Galarraga, Jesús Angel, 8532a
Paz Sánchez, Fernando, 4308
Pazos, Felipe, 4157-4158
Peattie, Lisa, 8234, 9625
Pebayle, Raymond, 8583
Pécaut, Daniel, 8338
Pederneiras, M.P., 2111
Pedersen, Ashjorn, 853
Pedersen, Poul Ove, 6531
Pedro Fernández, Antonio de, 8533
Peebles L., Federico, 6862
Peeke, M. Catherine, 1915
Peixoto, Virgília Riberio, 6336
Peláez, Carlos Manuel, 4917-4918
Peláez, César, 6540
Peláez, Emilio, 1052-1052a
Peláez Castello, Emilio, 1057
Pelissero, Norberto, 888
Pellicer, Hilda Margarita, 17
Pellicer Catalán, Manuel, 671
Pelliza, Mariano A., 8914
Pelon, W., 2263
Peltzer, Ernesto, 4563
Peña, Alcira de la, 8491
Peña, Hugo, A., 6792
Peña, Sergio de la, 4159
Peñaherrera del Aguila, Carlos, 6982
Peñalosa, Joaquín Antonio, 9734
Peñalver, Luis Manuel, 6193
Peñalver Gómez, Henriqueta, 1061
Penna, Carlos Víctor, 66-67
Penna, José Eduardo de Oliveira, 4831
Pennington, Campbell W., 2248
Pensinger, Brenda J., 1916
Penteado, Antônio Rocha, 7161-7162
People's Progressive Party, 8294
Peralta Ramos, Monica, 8663a
Peralta Rivera, E.G., 513
Pereira, Gloria, 2059
Pereira, João Baptista Borges, 10031
Pereira, Jose Carlos, 4919
Pereira, José Eduardo de Carvalho, 4886, 4920, 4964
Pereira, Luiz Carlos Bresser, 10032
Pereira, Maria da Luz Valente, 10033
Pereira, Maria Lúcia da Cruz, 6323
Pereira, Odon, 7163
Pereira, Sylvia L. de Melo, 6324
Pereira da Silva, Odon. *See* Silva, Odon Pereira da.
Pereira da Silva Filho, Amilcar. *See* Silva Filho, Amilcar Pereira da.
Pereira Fiorilo, Juan, 9860
Pereira Neves, José Adolfo. *See* Neves, José Adolfo Pereira.
Pereira Paiva, Vanilda. *See* Paiva, Vanilda Pereira.
Pereira de Assis, Milton. *See* Assis, Milton Pereira de.
Perekhrest, Stephan Makarovich, 6583
Peres, Fernando C., 4925
Pérez, Louis A., Jr., 8235
Pérez, M., 513
Pérez Arbeláez, Jorge, 4160, 4499
Pérez Brignoli, Héctor, 4161
Pérez Castro, Federico, 671
Pérez Concha, Jorge, 8774
Pérez de Arce, Hermógenes, 8492
Pérez de la Riva, Francisco, 1282
Pérez-Embid, Florentino, 118
Pérez Llana, Carlos, 8917
Pérez Mera, Amiro, 2249
Pérez Moreno, Sindulfo, 8604e
Pérez Rancier, Juan Bautista Victoriano, 6587
Pérez S., Enrique, 6908
Pérez Venero, A., Jr., 8830
Pericot, Luis, 854
Perloff, Harbey S., 6983
Pernambuco (state), *Bra.* Conselho de Desenvolvimento, 4921
Peru, 6984
Peru. Oficina de Desarrollo del Norte (ORDEN), 6985-6992
Perón, Eva, 8673

Péron, Juan Domingo, 8674-86741
Perosio, B.L., 2232
Perota, Celso, 918
Perracini, Aldo, 6325
Perrakis, S., 4309
Persson, Lars, 1377
Peru. Instituto Geográfico Militar, 7331-7337
Peru. Instituto Nacional de Planificación (INP). Oficina Nacional de Evaluación de Recursos Naturales (ONERN), 7338
Peru. Ministerio de Educación, 6174
Peru. Oficina Nacional de Desarrollo Cooperativo. Biblioteca, 37
Peru. Sistema de Asesoramiento y Fiscalización de las Cooperativas Agrarias de Producción, 4655
Perú, 1968-1973: cronología política, 4656
Peru: "you are no longer Indians . . . you are now farmers," 1528
Perusse, Roland I., 8775
Peruvian Times, 4657
Peruzzolo, Adair Caetano, 9664
Pescatello, Ann, 9665
Pessoa de Morais, José Xavier. *See* Morais, José Xavier Pessoa de.
Pessôa Ramos, Dulce Helena Alvares. *See* Ramos, Dulce Helena Alvares Pessôa.
Petana, W.B., 2250
Peter, George, 6571
Peters, C.J., 2251-2253
Peters, John Fred, 2053
Petersen, David, 750
Petersen, Gustav H., 8776
Petersen, H.S., 513
Peterwerth, Reinhard, 4399
Petkoff, Teodoro, 8533a
Petras, James F., 4162, 4626, 4744, 8085, 8493-8493b, 8675, 8859
Petrecolla, Alberto, 4711
Petrei, Amalio Humberto, 4745
Petuskov, Iván, 4427
Pezzia, A., 2000-2001
Phelan, Nancy, 6863
Philalethes, Demoticus, 1282
Phillips, George W., 1423
Phillips, Winston, 1222
Pianzola, L., 2005
Piazza, Walter F., 919
Pichler, Hans, 6611, 6782
Pichon-Riviere, E., 2232
Pickering, Robert B., 605
Pickering, Wilbur, 1917
Pickett, Velma, 1840
Piedrahita P., Dora, 119
Pierce, B. Edward, 1378
Pierre-Charles, Gérard, 4363, 4394, 9811
Pierret, T., 2179
Pierson, Donald, 855
Piho, V., 513
Pike, Eunice V., 1918-1920
Pike, Fredrick B., 8086
Pillet, Gastón, 8915
Pimentel Gomes, Raymundo. *See* Gomes, Raymundo Pimentel.
Pimentel Gurmendi, Víctor, 1008a
Piña Chan, Román, 760
Pincemin, Roberto, 4163
Pinchas Geiger, Pedro. *See* Geiger, Pedro Geiger.
Pineda, Aníbal, 6909
Pinedo del Aguila, Víctor M., 4658
Piñera Echeñique, Sebastián, 8466
Pinheiro, Lúcia Marques, 6326
Pinheiro, Maria do Carmo Marques, 6326
Pinheiro Mejias, Nilce. *See* Mejias, Nilce Pinheiro.
Pinheiro Neto, J.M., 4922
Pinho, Carlos Marques, 4164
Pinilla Aguilar, José I., 120
Pino, Frank, 121
Pino Díaz, F. del, 513
Pino-Santos, Oscar, 8236
Pinto, Aloísio de Arruda, 7164
Pinto, Aníbal, 4165-4167
Pinto, Edson, 10034
Pinto, Luiz de Aguiar Costa, 10035-10036
Pinto, Maurício Jorge Cardoso, 4949
Pinto, Rogerio Feital S., 8584
Pinto de Carvalho, Paulo. *See* Carvalho, Paulo Pinto de.
Pinto Ferreira, Luis. *See* Ferreira, Luis Pinto.
Pires, Nise, 6327
Pires Miranda, Heloísa de Resende. *See* Miranda, Heloísa de Resende Pires.
Pitaud, Henri, 6958
Pittier, Henri, 7035
Plan de trabajo para la elaboración de un modelo mundial, 8777
Plana. Oficina de Educación Iberoamericana. Nos. 143/164, mayo 1970/agosto 1972- . Madrid, 6044
La planificación en Guatemala: planes y proyectos agrícolas, 4400
Plank, Stephen J., 2054, 2176
Plano diretor de Itapetinga, 7165
Plato, C.C., 2112
Plaza, Salvador de la, 4564-4565, 8534, 9824
Pletsch, Protásio, 6328
Pochintesta, Mario, 2254
Poczter, Raúl, 9894
Poitras, Guy E., 8001, 8087, 9735
Polanski, Jorge, 6793
Poletto, Dorivaldo, 4985
Polia, Mario, 513, 1037
Polišenský, Josef, 6045
Política indigenista del Brasil, 1379

La política revolucionaria en Colombia: una aproximación crítica, 8339
Political violence: Latin America; violence and urban growth, kidnapping and coups, 8088
Pollak-Eltz, Angelina, 1208, 1280-1281, 1380
Pommeret, Xavier, 6697
Pompeu Sobrinho, Thomaz, 7166
Ponce, Claudia de Amrorim, 40
Poncet, A., 2005
Poncet, Edmont, 8264
Pons Lezica, Cipriano Ambrosio Patricio, 4168
Ponsol, Bernardo, 6642
Pont, Guillermo Marco del, 4659
Pontes, Élio Monnerat Solon de, 8916
Pontes, Hildebrando, 10037
Pontifícia Universidade Católica do Rio Grande do Sul, *Pôrto Alegre, Bra.*, 6329-6330
Poppe de Figueiredo, Maria Helena. See Figueiredo, Maria Helena Poppe de.
Poppino, Rollie E., 8585
Poppovic, Ana Maria, 6331
Porras Garcés, Pedro Ignacio, 513, 978-978e
Portantiero, Juan C., 8663a
Porteous, J. Douglas, 4627, 9868
Porter, Duncan M., 6940
Porter, Richard C., 4145
Portes, Alejandro, 8676, 9666, 9736, 9769, 9869
Porto Tavares, Vania. See Tavares, Vania Porto.
Pôrto Witter, Geraldina. See Witter, Geraldina Pôrto.
Portocarrero, Felipe, 6175
Posadas, J., 8677
Potter, D.F., 683
Powell, John Duncan, 7036
Powelson, John P., 8494
Poyares, Walter Ramos, 9667
Pozzi-Escot, I., 513
Prado, Carlos, 2177
Prado, João Fernando de Almeida, 8585a
Prado, Lafayette, 4923
Prado, Marcos, 7167
Prebisch, Raúl, 4169-4170
Precolumbian art of Mexico and Central America: exhibition catalog, 761
Prede Actualidades, 6046
Prem, Hanns J., 513, 812
Premdas, Ralph R., 8295
Pressel, Esther, 1381
Presser, Harriet B., 2055
Preston, David A., 4150, 6833
Prete, Stephanie, 1297
Preuss, Konrad Theodor, 957
Price, Barbara J., 633, 666

Price, John A., 6698
Price, Richard, 1282-1283
Price, Sally, 1283
Prieto, Helios, 8495
El Primer Congreso Nacional de Educación y Cultura, 6145
Primov, George, 1494, 1529
O problema da educação no Estado do Rio Grande do Norte: proposta de sua adequação a fim de transformá-la em efetivo instrumento do desenvolvimento regional, 6332
Problemática del desarrollo patagónico, 4746
Problemas Brasileiros, 7168
Proença Filho, Domício, 6333
Proença Sigaud, Geraldo de. See Sigaud, Geraldo de Proença.
Profesorado de tiempo completo, 6090
Programa nacional de alfabetización y educación de adultos: 1970-1975, 6106
Prontuario: técnica del interrogatorio, la represión y el asesinato, 8678
Proskouriakoff, Tatiana, 762, 797
Protsch, Reiner, 606
Proulx, Paul, 1921
Proulx, Donald A., 1038
Prous-Poitier, André, 920
Prozecanski, Arturo C., 8618
Psicopatología de los vicios por los más capacitados expertos, 9668
Psuty, Norbert P., 998, 1036
Pucciarelli, Héctor M., 2014
Puente Leyva, 4310
Pütten Velloso, Tânia. See Velloso, Tânia Pütten.
Puffer, Ruth R., 2056
Pugh, R., 9818
Puhle, Hans-Jürgen, 8089
Puig, Juan Carlos, 8917
Puiggrós, Rodolfo, 8679
Puleston, Dennis E., 513, 633, 763
Pulgar Vidal, Javier, 6994
Pullen-Burry, Bessie, 1284
Purcell, Susan Kaufman. See Kaufman Purcell, Susan.
Pyeatt, P., 2041
Quagliani, Antonia, 8586
Quatro Rodas (firm), *Rio?*, 7238
Queiroz, José Maria Vilar de, 4924
Quem é quem no Pará, 101
Quesada, Carlos, 8275
Quevedo, Numa, 8917a
Quigley, Carroll, 1173
Quihillalt, Oscar A., 8778
Quijano, Aníbal, 8386
Quinn, Michael A., 8108
Quintero Rodríguez, Alvaro, 9669
Quirarte, Jacinto, 629, 764
Quiroga, L., 513

Quiroga Santa Cruz, Marcelo, 4590
Quirós, Félix Armando, 4401
Quirós Varela, Luis, 8479
Rabello, Ophelina, 6334-6335
Rabello, Ricardo da Costa, 6336
Raby, David L., 8170
Raczynski, Dagmar, 2043
Radiografía de un arsenal, 8090
Rafael, Abascal M., 700
Rafael, Georgina, 6337
Raffaelli, Marcelo, 8588
Raffino, Rodolfo A., 867, 889-889a
Ram, Bali, 2057
Rama, Germán W., 6135
Ramaya, Narsaloo, 1275
Ramazzini, Lucía, 6113
Ramil Cepeda, Carlos, 8680
Ramírez, Irma, 2178
Ramírez, Jesús Emilio, 6910
Ramírez, M.E., 2019
Ramírez Díaz, Luis Jorge, 8340
Ramírez Gómez, Ramón, 6161
Ramírez Moreno, Augusto, 8341
Ramírez S., Thaís, 4566
Ramírez S., Tulio E., 6549
Ramírez Vargas, María Teresa, 122, 4500
Ramlot, Michel Jean Paul, 6794
Ramos, Alberto Guerreiro. See Guerreiro Ramos, Alberto.
Ramos, Alcida R., 1382
Ramos, Arthur, 520, 1383
Ramos, Dulce Helena Alvares Pessõa, 102
Ramos, Luis J., 765
Ramos, Raimundo Nonato Mendonça, 4835
Ramos de Cox, Josefina, 1039
Ramos G., Sergio, 9737
Ramos Pérez, Demetrio, 51E, 671
Ramsaran, Ramesh, 4364
Rancaño, Maria Ramírez, 8779
Rand, Abby, 6572
Rand McNally and Co. (firm), *Chicago, Ill.*, 7286, 7298, 7300, 7302, 7328
Randall, Laura, 4171
Randall, Margaret, 9812
Randle, Patricio H., 7219
Rands, Robert L., 612, 633, 766, 813
Rangel, Domingo Alberto, 8535, 8918
Rangel, José Vicente, 8535a
Rangel Contla, José Calixto, 9738
Rangel Gaspar, Eliseo, 8171
Ranis, Peter, 9901
Rankin, Richard C., 8091
Raposo, Gabriel Viriato, 1384
Rascovsky, Arnaldo, 9670
Rask, Norman, 4925
Ratcliff, Richard Earl, 9875
Rath, Ferdinand, 9770
Rathje, William L., 513, 612, 633, 644, 661

Rattenbach, Benjamín, 8681
Rattner, Heinrich, 4926
Rattner, Henrique, 7169
Rauth, José Wilson, 921
Ravell, Carola, 8536
Raven, Peter H., 1110
Ravines, Rogger, 990, 993, 1011, 1033a, 1040, 1048c
Rawls, Joseph, 1530
Ray, David, 8092
Ray, Talton F., 8537
Raynal, Vicente, 8276
Rea C., Julio, 6822
Reboratti, Carlos E., 6795
Reca, Lucio G., 4747
Recommendações das classes produtoras do Amazonas, submetidas à consideração do Exmo. Snr. Presidente da República, 7170
Recursos humanos: bibliografía, 123
Recursos humanos do Rio Grande do Sul: população, Mão-de-obra, educação, 7171
Los recursos naturales del estado de Puebla y su aprovechamiento, 6699
Redclift, M.R., 9671
Reddell, James, 660, 6700
Rede de Bibliotecas de Amazônia (REBAM), *Belém, Bra.*, 38
Redfield, Robert, 1174
Reed, Irving B., 147
Rees, John D., 6701
Reeves, W.C., 2113
Regni Cassinis, G., 513
Rehovot Conference, *VI, Jerusalem and Rehovot, Israel, 1971*, 6541
Reichel-Dolmatoff, Gerardo, 958-958a, 1361, 1385
Reichel-Dolmatoff, Inès, 1208
Reichlen, Henry, 1922
Reichlen, Paule, 1922
Reid, Aileen A., 1923
Reid, P.A., 4528
Reiher, Oswin Guillermo Zbinden, 9870
Reiman, Elisabeth, 8496
Reina, Rubén, 1175, 9902
Reinhold, Robert, 667
Reinton, Per Olav, 8004
Reipert, Herman José, 68
Réis, Arthur Cézar Ferreira, 6338, 10038
Reis, Fábio Wanderley, 8587
Reis, J., 6339
Reis, Raimundo Sousa dos, 7174
Reis Velloso, João Paulo dos. See Velloso, João Paulo dos Reis.
Relaciones argentino-brasileñas, 8919
Relaciones argentino-chilenas, 8920
Relações de publicações de Lourenço Filho em psicologia, 6340
Relatório de atividades do Summer In-

stitute of Linguistics, período de 1956 a 1973, 1924
Religion in Jamaica, 9813
Remes Lenicov, Jorge L., 4730
Remusi, Carlos A., 6796
Remy, Anselme, 122X, 1285
Rensch, Calvin R., 1925
Repertorio de publicaciones periódicas de educación de América Latina y el Caribe, 6047
Repetto Milán, Francisco, 6162
Replanteo, 8682
Reseña histórica del Proyecto Tapón del Darién, 6649
Resende, Eliseu, 4927
Resende, Maria Efigenia Lage de, 8587a
Resnick, Jane R., 4102
Rest, C.P.M. van, 1286
Restrepo A., Ignacio, 8342
Restrepo Uribe, Jorge, 8343-8343a
Reunión de Bolsas y Mercados de Valores de América, *III, Rio, 1968,* 4172
Reunión de Centros de Investigación Económica, *VIII, Buenos Aires, 1972,* 4748
Reunión de Consulta de la Organización Continental Latinoamericana de Estudiantes (OCLAE), *II, La Habana, 1971,* 8780
Reunión de Publicaciones Periódicas, *I, Bogotá, 1973,* 39
Reunión de Técnicos de Bancos Centrales del Continente Americano, *X, Caracas, 1972,* 4567
Reunión Nacional de Educación Agrícola Superior, *Maracay, Ven., 1969,* 6194
Reveiz Roldán, Edgar, 4521
Revel-Mouroz, Jean, 6702
Revista Brasileira de Estudos Políticos, 8588-8588a, 8921
Revista da Administração de Empresas, 4928
Revista da Faculdade de Educação da UFF, 6341
Revista da Universidade Federal do Pará, 10039
Revista de Educación, 6119
Revista de la Academia Diplomática del Perú, 8922
Revista de la Asociación Guatemalteca de Derecho Internacional, 8831
Revista de la Dirección Nacional de Geología y Minería, 6797
Revista de la Integración, 4173
Revista de la Universidad, 9903
Revista de Planeación y Desarrollo, 4501-4503, 9844
Revista del Banco Central de Venezuela, 4568
Revista del Centro de Investigación y Acción Social, 6091, 8093
Revista Ecuatoriana de Educación, 6148
Revista Interamericana Review, 1287
Revista Mexicana de Sociología, 9739-9741, 9771
Revista Mexicana del Trabajo, 9742
Revista Venezolana de Sanidad y Asistencia Social, 2255
La Revue Française de l'Elite Européenne, 6747
Rex, Eileen, 1926
Rey, Estrella, 842
Rey Fajardo, José del, 18
Reyeros, Rafael A., 6107
Reyes, Alvaro, 4483
Reyes, Reina, 6179
Reyes Heroles, Jesús, 4311
Reymond, Jacquelin, 946
Reyna Robles, Rosa María, 767
Reyna T., Teresa, 6703
Reynolds, Clark W., 4174
Rezende Bonamigo, Euza Maria de. See Bonamigo, Euza Maria de Rezende.
Rezende da Silva, Fernando Antônio. See Silva, Fernando Antônio Rezende da.
Rho, Franco, 6995
Rhodes, Willard, 1956
Ribas Carneiro, Maria Cecília. See Carneiro, Maria Cecília Ribas.
Ribeiro, Antônio Carlos da Motta, 4949
Ribeiro, Carlos Costa, 6360
Ribeiro, Clélia Monteiro, 6342
Ribeiro, Darcy, 1361, 6343, 8478, 8589, 9672
Ribeiro, Pedro Augusto Mentz, 922-922e
Ribeiro, Sylvio Wanick, 4929
Ribeiro de Oliveira, Pedro A. See Oliveira, Pedro A. Ribeiro de.
Riberio Peixoto, Virgília. See Peixoto, Virgília Riberio.
Riccardi, Riccardo, 6748
Ricci, Susana M., 7220
Ricci, Teodoro Ricardo, 6800-6801
Rice, Don Stephen, 768
Richards, Joan, 1927
Richardson, Bonham C., 6947
Richardson, Ivan L., 8589a
Richardson, James B., 1041
Richardson, Miles, 9674
Richter, Humberto Vendelino, 7192
Ridgwell, W.M., 1386
Riese, B., 513
Riesle C., Héctor, 8428
Riester, Jürgen, 896, 1387-1388
Rifaux, Francis, 4339
Rio de Janeiro (state), *Bra.* Companhia de Desenvolvimento Econômico do Estado do Rio de Janeiro (CODERJ). Departamento Estudos e Projetos, 4930
Rio de Janeiro (state), *Bra.* Secretaria de

Saúde e Assistencia. Serviço de Educação Sanitária, 6344
Rio Grande do Norte (state), Bra. Serviço de Informações de Mercado, 7172
Rio Grande do Sul (state), Bra., 4931
Rio Grande do Sul (state), Bra. Assembléia Legislativa. Comissão de Educação e Cultura, 6345
Rio Grande do Sul (state), Bra. Assembleía Legislativa. Comissão Parlamentar para o Estudo da Poluição e Defesa do Meio Ambiente, 7173
Rio Grande do Sul (state), Bra. Central de Comandos Mecanizados de Apôio a Agricultura, 7239
Rio Grande do Sul (state), Bra. Secretaria de Educação e Cultura, 6346-6347
Rio Grande do Sul (state), Bra. Secretaria de Educação e Cultura. Departamento de Educação Média, 6348
Río Negro (province), Arg. Ministerio de Gobierno, 7221
Riofrío, Gustavo, 9854
Ríos, Jorge Martínez, 4312
Rios, José Arthur, 10040
Ríos, Roberto, 1476
Ritter, Arch R.M., 4428, 6584, 8239
Ritter, Eric W., 769
Ritter Nunes, Mário. See Nunes, Mário Ritter.
Riva Posse, C., 2257
Rivanera Carlés, Federico, 8683
Rivanuva R., Gastón, 8172
Rivarola, Domingo M., 6959
Rivas Salmón, A., 513
Rivera, C., 2189
Rivera, Mario A., 947-947b
Rivera Cambas, Manuel, 6704
Rivera Dorado, Miguel, 513, 668, 856, 1042
Rivera Marín, Guadalupe, 4313
Rivero de la Calle, Manuel, 825
Rivière, P.G., 513
Rivière d'Arc, Hélène, 8240
Roa, Raúl, 8439a
Roa Suárez, Hernando, 8344
Robbins, Michael C., 2063
Roberts, Bryan R., 1176, 9625, 9675
Roberts, Robert F., 2058
Roberts Barragán, Hugo, 8416
Robertson, F.J., 6996
Robertson, Merle Greene, 813
Robertson, O. Zeller, Jr., 4175, 6048
Robichek, E. Walter, 4176
Robicsek, Francis, 669
Robin, John P., 4504, 4569
Robinson, A.N.R., 8284
Robinson, Joyce L., 69
Robinson, Scott S., 1389
Robredo, Jaime, 40
Robson, P., 4177
Roca, Blas, 6145a
Rocchetti, Tito L., 8684
Rocha Penteado, Antônio. See Penteado, Antônio Rocha.
Roche, Eduardo, 4570
Rodes, Félix, 8265
Rodman, Selden, 6911
Rodrigues, Eduardo Celestino, 8923
Rodrigues, Luiz, 8590
Rodrigues, Maria Magdalena E. Mischan, 4932
Rodrigues, Tarcísio Ewerton, 7174
Rodrigues Bellomo, Harry. See Bellomo, Harry Rodrigues.
Rodrigues da Cunha, Luiz Antônio Constant. See Cunha, Luiz Antônio Constant Rodrigues da.
Rodrigues da Cunha, Osvaldo. See Cunha, Osvaldo Rodrigues da.
Rodríguez, Alfredo, 9854
Rodríguez, Amílcar, 890
Rodríguez, Cecilia de, 4505
Rodríguez, D.W., 6598
Rodríguez, H., 2166, 2189
Rodríguez, Héctor Luis, 6588
Rodríguez, Jorge G., 4178
Rodríguez, Nelson, 8611a
Rodríguez-Becerra, S., 513
Rodríguez de Montes, María Luisa, 1906
Rodríguez Demorizi, Emilio, 6589
Rodríguez Escalonilla, Arturo, 124
Rodríguez Lamus, Luis Raúl, 959
Rodríguez Mariño, Tomás, 8345
Rodríguez Meliton, Haydée, 4672
Rodríguez R., Víctor Melitón, 8256, 9814
Rodríguez Rouanet, Francisco, 1177
Rodríguez Saccone, Osvaldo, 1058
Rodríguez Salazar, Oscar, 4506
Rodríguez Signes, Tulio F., 8685
Roe, Peter, 1043
Roel Pineda, Virgilio, 4660-4661
Rofman, Alejandro B., 4179, 4749, 9676
Rogler, Lloyd H., 9815
Rogers, E.S., 513
Róiz, José, 10041
Rojas, Humberto, 8346
Rojas, María Eugenia, 8326a
Rojas, Rubén, 9825
Rolandi de Perrot, Diana Susana, 891
Rolando, Pombo, Braulio, compañeros del Che: diarios de Bolivia, 8417
The role of Japan in Latin America, 8781
Rollwagen, Jack R., 1178, 9625, 9743
Romanov, M.A., 814
Romero, Carlos, 8072
Romero, César Enrique, 8686
Romero, Emilio, 6997-6998
Romero, Héctor Manuel, 6705
Romero, Luis A., 4749

Romero Bastos, Raúl, 8604f
Romero Flores, Jesús, 8173
Romero Loza, José, 4591
Romero Moreno, María Eugenia, 1390
Rona, José Pedro, 1928
Rona, Roberto, 2059, 2179
Ronfeldt, David F., 8094-8095, 8174, 8179, 8782, 9744
Ronning, C. Neale, 8782a
Rosa, Carlos Nobre, 7175
Rosas, Luis Eduardo, 4507-4509
Rosen, Bernard C., 10042
Rosen, Steven J., 8783
Rosenbaum, H. Jon, 8096
Rosenblum, Jack J., 4402
Rosengurt, Bernardo, 7018
Rosenn, Keith S., 8590a
Ross, John A., 9677
Rosselot, Jorge, 2256
Rossi, Carlos, 8478
Rossini, Rosa Ester, 7120
Rostworoski de Diez Canseco, María, 1044
Rotberg, Robert I., 8259
Roth, Walter Edmund, 1361
Rothenberg, Morris, 8739
Rothhammer, Francisco, 2109, 2114
Rothman, Ana María, 9904
Rotondo, Humberto, 9819
Rotstein, Jaime, 6349
Rouco, Cristina, 1059
Rouhani, Fuad, 8538
Rouquié, Alain, 8619, 8687
Roux López, Rodolfo de, 8347
Rovner, Irwin, 683, 685, 689, 770
Rowan, Orland, 1929
Rowe, John Howland, 1361
Rowland, Mark, 660
Rozo Vidal, Antonio, 959
Rua, João, 7176
Rubin, Vera, 1288-1288a, 1531
Rubin Zamora, Lorenzo, 103
Rubinstein, Juan Carlos, 8688
Rubio, Guillermo Perry, 4499
Rubio Mañé, J. Ignacio, 41
Ruda, José María, 8924
Ruddle, Kenneth, 1353, 1391, 8097
Ruhl, J. Mark, 6127
Rui Beisiegel, Celso de. *See* Beisiegel, Celso de Rui.
Ruiz, Leovigildo, 8241
Ruiz Berges, Humberto, 8860
Ruiz-Eldredge, Alberto, 8784, 8832
Ruiz García, Enrique, 8098
Ruiz Ortiz, Ernesto, 9678
Rumeu de Armas, Antonio, 671
Rupieper, Hermann J., 8785
Russell, Charles A., 8099
Russell, D.E.H., 9679
Russo, Laura Garcia Moreno, 70

Rutte García, Alberto, 9861
Ryan, Selwyn D., 1222, 1289
Rye, Owen S., 979
Sá, Jayme Magrassi de, 4933
Sá, Maria Auxiliadora Ferraz de, 8591, 10043
Sá e Benevides F., F.R. *See* Benevides F., F.R. de Sá e.
Sá V. Camurça, Zélia. *See* Camurça, Zélia Sá V.
Sábato, Mario, 6798
Sabloff, Jeremy A., 513, 612, 633, 644, 771
Sabourin, Jésus, 8242
Saboya de Castro, Fernando. *See* Castro, Fernando Saboya de.
Sacchi, Hugo M., 8100
Sachs, Ignacy, 6542
Sacohetta, Lia de Abreu, 2237
Sader Pérez, Rubén, 4571
Sáenz, Orlando, 4628
Sáenz de Santa María, C., 513
Safa, Helen Icken, 1221, 9816
Sagasti, Francisco, 9849
Sahota, G.S., 4934-4935
Saint-Jean, Iberico Manuel, 8689
Saint-Méry, M.L.E. Moreau de, 1282
Saínz Mont, Ramón, 4429
Saito, Hiroshi, 10044-10045
Salazar, Diego, 4483
Salazar, Ernesto, 980
Salazar Bondy, Augusto, 9849
Salazar Chambers, Pedro, 6549
Salazar, Mallen, M., 2086
Salazar Recio, Inocencio, 1420
Saldanha, Louremi Ercolani, 6350-6351
Saldanha Vargas, Arete. *See* Vargas, Arete Saldanha.
Salivia, Luis A., 6605
Salles Abreu, João Theodoro de. *See* Abreu, Theodoro de Salles.
Salm, Claudio, 4936
Salomon, João, 2070
Salvosa, C.B., 2195
Salzano, Francisco M., 1392, 2068, 2115-2119, 2150, 2209
Samamé Boggio, Mario, 4663
Samaniego, Marcial, 6960
Samaniego Román, Lorenzo Alberto, 1016, 1045
Samaroo, Brinsley, 1253, 1275
Sammy, George, 1222
Sampay, Arturo Enrique, 8786
Samper Gnecco, Andrés, 6912
Sampson, E.H., 906
San Juan (province), *Arg.* Secretaría Técnica de la Gobernación. Instituto de Investigaciones Económicas y Estadísticas, 9905-9906
San Martín, Marta, 8208

San Martín Ferrari, Hernán, 1532, 6864-6865
Sánchez, Carlos E., 4750
Sánchez, Jorge, 2199
Sánchez, Ricardo, 8357
Sánchez-Arjona, Rodrigo, 1421
Sánchez Azcona, Jorge, 9745
Sánchez de Meazzi, Stella Maris, 10
Sánchez Gamarra, Mery Alinda, 1419
Sánchez Labrador, José, 1930
Sánchez Montañes, Emma, 513, 981
Sanchez Ochoa, P., 513
Sánchez-Pérez, J.M., 148
Sánchez Quell, Hipólito, 8604g
Sánchez Tarniella, Andrés, 8277-8279
Sander, H.J., 6706
Sander, P.C., 2133
Sanders, Andrew, 1290
Sanders, Thomas G., 2060, 8497-8497a, 9680, 9845
Sanders, William T., 612, 644, 670
Sandilands, Roger J., 4510
Sandoval, Clara Elsa de, 4516
Sandoval Aguayo, Alberto, 8348
Sandoval V., Leopoldo R., 6631
Sanford, Charles L., 8787
Sanford, Margaret, 1291-1292
Sanfuentes, Andrés, 8466
Sanguineti de Rey, Margarita, 6049
Sanoja Obediente, Mario, 513, 1062-1062b
Sansón, Carlos E., 4176
Santa, Eduardo, 8349
Santa Catarina (state), Bra. Departamento Estadual de Geografia e Cartografia, 7268
Santacruz Galeano, Oscar, 6950
Santamarina, Estela Barbieri de, 6799
Santayana, S. Cano de, 513
Santelices C., Rómulo, 6120
Santiago, P.J., 2178
Santillán de Andrés, Selva E., 6800-6801
Santini, Rafael, 2178, 2180
Santistevan, Jorge, 4654
Santos, Célia Almeida Ferreira. See Ferreira-Santos, Célia Almeida.
Santos, José Wilson de O., 7177
Santos, M. Coutinho dos, 4937
Santos, Milton, 6543-6544
Santos, Roberto, 4938
Santos, Sílvio Coelho dos, 1393, 1394
Santos, Theóphilo de Azeredo, 4939-4940
Santos, Theotonio dos, 8101, 8719-8720, 9681
Santos, Wanderley Guilherme dos, 8592-8592a
Santos de Morais, Clodomir, 6545
Santos Goes, Ivoni dos. See Goes, Ivoni dos Santos.
Santos Montejo, Enrique. See Calibán [pseud. for Enrique Santos Montejo].
Santos Sanz, J., 513
Sanz de Santamaría, Carlos, 4180
São Paulo (state), Bra. Departamento de Estatística, 7178
São Paulo (state), Bra. Governo. Secretaria de Economia e Planejamento, 4941-4942
São Paulo (state), Bra. Secretaria da Agricultura, 4943
São Paulo (state), Bra. Secretaria de Economia e Planejamento. Coordenadoria de Ação Regional, 10046
São Paulo (state), Bra. Secretaria de Economia e Planejamento. Departmento de Estatística. Divisão de Estatísticas Físicas, Sociais e Culturais, 6352
São Paulo (state), Bra. Secretaria de Economia e Planejamento. Superintendência do Desenvolvimento do Litoral Paulista (SUDELPA), 7179-7180
São Paulo (state), Bra. Secretaria dos Serviços e Obras Públicas. Departamento de Águas e Energia Eléctrica. Serviço do Vale do Ribeira, 7181
Saquic Calel, Rosalío, 1179
Sarabia Viejo, M.J., 513
Saraiva, Helcio Ulhoa, 9985
Sardón, José, 4572
Sargent, Charles S., 6804
Sarma, Akkaraju V.N., 982-982a
Sarmiento, Guillermo, 7037
Saul, Frank P., 612, 629
Savoie, D., 513
Sawicki, Sandra, 6619
Saxton, Dean, 1931
Saxton, Lucille, 1931
Sayeg Helú, Jorge, 8175
Schaedel, Richard P., 1288a
Schantz, P.M., 2257
Schauer, Stanley, 1932
Schempp, Hermann, 6707
Schenk, Eric A., 2181
Schers, David, 9750
Schiff, Bennett, 8788
Schindler, H., 513
Schipani, Daniel S., 6050
Schleiffer, Hedwig, 6546
Schlenther, Ursula, 513, 961
Schlesier, K.H., 513
Schlundt, Hayes C., 6708
Schmidt, Johanna, 671
Schmidt, Max, 1361
Schmidt, Peter J., 702
Schmidt, Steffen W., 8350-8350a
Schmitt, Karl M., 4241, 8816
Schmitter, Philippe C., 8102, 8183
Schmitz, Pedro Ignacio, 923-923c, 1054
Schneider, Roberto E., 2182
Schneider, Ronald M., 8869

Schneider S., Hans, 6866
Schobinger, J. 513, 671, 857, 892
Schöndube Baumbach, Otto, 605, 772
Schoenwetter, James, 773
Schöttelndreyer, Mareike, 1926
Schomburgk, Robert H., 6948
Schoop, Wolfgang, 1533, 6830
Schoultz, Lars, 8351
Schrader, Achim, 6353
Schrader, Birgit, 6353
Schreiber, Anna P., 8861
Schreider, Frank, 6749
Schreider, Helen, 6749
Schteingart, Martha, 6547, 8103
Schufer de Paikin, Marta L., 9907
Schuler-Schömig, Immina von, 962
Schull, W.J., 2051
Schultes, Richard Evans, 7182
Schultz, Harald, 1395
Schultz, Konrad F., 4124
Schulz-Friedmann, Ramón, 815, 1180
Schumann, G., Otto, 1933
Schuster, Meinhard, 1415
Schuyler, George W., 6197
Schwartz, Audrey J., 8521a
Schwartz, Murray L., 8521a
Schwartz, Norman B., 1175, 1181
Schwartz, Stuart B., 1282
Schwartzman, Jacques, 4862
Schwartzman, Simon, 8593-8593a
Schwedes, J.A., 2157
Schwerin, Karl H., 1396
Schydlowsky, Daniel M., 4181
Sciences de la terre: pt. 2, Géologie appliquée, 6750
Scioville-Samper, Henri, 4182
Scobie, James R., 9908
Scott, C.D., 4629
Scott, Eugene, 1934
Scott, R. Parry, 9926
Scott, Robert E., 6548
Scott, Stuart D., 605
Seabra, Manoel, 4944
Seara Vázquez, Modesto, 8789
Scott, Wolf, 4019
Sebess, Pedro, 4703
Sebrell, William H., Jr., 2183
Secchi, C., 4183
El sector externo y el desarrollo económico de América Latina, 4184
Sedat, David W., 629
Seele, Enno, 6709
Seers, D., 4199
Segal, Sheldon J., 9682
Segovia, Víctor, 774
Segunda Reunión del Grupo de Trabajo para el Desarrollo de los Servicios Bibliotecarios y de Información Científica y Técnica de los Países Signatorios del convenio *Andrés Bello,* 71

Segurança & Desenvolvimento, 10047
Seid-Akhavan, M., 2120
Seidel, Robert N., 4185
Seijas, Haydée, 1397
Seiler-Baldinger, A., 513
Séjourné, Laurette, 521
Selby, Henry A., 1182
Seligsohn, Otto E., 7183
Seligson, Mitchell A., 4403, 9772
Sellon, Michael, 843
Selowsky, Marcelo, 4186, 4630
Selowsky, Marcelo, 2184
Selser, Gregorio, 8690, 8790-8791
Selva, Salomón de la, 1935
Semana de Estudos do Problema de Menores, *X, São Paulo, 1970,* 10048
Semana Social do Rio Grande do Sul, *V Pôrto Alegre, Bra., 1971,* 7184
Seminar on the Acquisition of Latin American Library Materials (SALALM), *XVII, Amherst, Mass., 1972,* 72
Seminar on the Acquisition of Latin American Library Materials (SALALM), *XVIII, Port-of-Spain, 1973,* 73
Seminario Aspectos Económicos y Tecnicos de la Planificación en el Sector de la Energía, *Berlin, FRG, 1969,* 4187
Seminario de América Latina y España, *Instituto de Cultura Hispánica, Madrid, 1969,* 4188
Seminário de Avaliação do Desenvolvimento Agropecuário do Nordeste, *I João Pessoa, Bra., 1971,* 7185
Seminario de Ideas y Proyectos Específicos (SIPE), *Santa Cruz, Bol., 1972,* 4592
Seminario de la Integración Cultural de América Latina, *Guadalajara, Mex., 1970,* 8792
Seminário de Tropicología, *Recife, Bra., 1974,* 7186
Seminario Interamericano sobre la Definición de Regiones para la Planificación del Desarrollo, *I, Hamilton, Canada, 1968,* 6549
Seminario Interamericano sobre la Integración de los Servicios de Información de Archivos, Bibliotecas y Centros de Documentación en América Latina y el Caribe, *Washington, 1972,* 74
Seminario Internacional para Profesores de Suelos, *Maracay, Ven., 1969,* 6550
Seminario Nacional de Estadísticas, *I, Montevideo, 1970,* 4676
Seminario Nacional sobre Ciencia y Tecnología para el Desarrollo, *II, Paipa, Colo., 1972,* 4189
Seminario Planificación Integrada de

Proyectos de Irrigación, *Berlin, FRG, 1970,* 4190
Seminário sobre Documentação e Informática, *Rio, 1971,* 75
Seminario sobre Evaluación de la Contaminación Ambiental, *I, Atlihuetzia, Mex., 1971,* 6551
Seminario sobre Exploración Geológico-Minera, *II, México, 1970,* 6710
Seminário sobre Indicadores Sociais do Desenvolvimento Nacional na América Latina, *Rio, 1972,* 8104
Seminario sobre Problemas y Objetivos de una Política de Transporte, *Popayán, Colo., 1973,* 4511
Seminario sobre Regionalización de las Políticas de Desarrollo en América Latina, *II, Santiago, 1969,* 6552
Seminario Utilización de Bosques Tropicales en Latinoamérica, *Bogotá, 1969,* 4191
Sempe de González Llanes, María Carlota, 893
Sena, Julio F. Ferreira, 6275
Senior, Olive, 8262
Senna, Milton Câmara, 7187
Sepúlveda, Alberto, 8105
Sepúlveda, Bernardo, 4314
Sepúlveda, César, 8793, 8817
Sepúlveda Chastinet, Yone, 40
Sercovich, Francisco C., 4751
Sergipe (state), Bra. Conselho Estadual de Agricultura. Comissão Estadual de Planejamento Agrícola (CEPA), 7188
Sergipe (state), *Bra.* Secretaria de Educação e Cultura, 6354
Serie Arqueológica, 844
Série Lingüística, 1936
Serjeant, G.R., 2138-2139, 2197, 2210-2211
Serra, José, 4945, 4968
Serra Rafols, Elías, 671
Serracino Inglott, George, 938b, 948-948d
Serrano, C., 513, 2008
Serrano, Carlos V., 2056
Serrano S., Carlos, 2121
Serviço Social da Indústria. Departamento Nacional, 10049
Serzedello Machado, Eurico. *See* Machado, Eurico Serzedello.
Sestieri, Pellegrino Claudio, 513, 1046
Setlow, Carolyn E., 8375, 8893
Setti, Enrique de Jesús, 6805
Seufert, Andy, 775
Sevilla, Santiago, 4524
Shafer, Robert Jones, 4315
Sharer, Robert J., 629, 776
Sharrett, A. Richey, 2258
Shaw, R. Paul, 4192
Sheets, Payson D., 777
Shelby, Lon, 1240
Sheldon, Steven N., 1937
Shell, Olive A., 1938
Shenkel, J. Richard, 605
Shenkman, L., 2259
Shepard, Marietta Daniels, 76
Shepherd, J.B., 6561
Sherman, Gail Richardson, 8352
Shiffer, Jeanette, 2260
Shimkin, Demitri B., 612, 644
Shubik, Martin, 4898
Sideri, S., 4193
Siegel, Bernard J., 2061
Sierra, Augusto Santiago, 6163
Sierra, Carlos J., 6711
Siffredi, Alejandra, 1325, 1398
Sigal, Silvia, 8691
Sigaud, Geraldo de Proença, 8577
Sigaut, Lorenzo Juan, 4752
Sigmund, Paul E., 8498, 8926
Sigurdsson, Haraldur, 6561
Signorini, I., 513
Signos de liberación: testimonios de la iglesia en América Latina, 1969-1973, 8106
Silén, Juan Angel, 8280
Silie, Ruben, 1208
Silva, Carlos da, 7063
Silva, Edmundo de Macedo Soares e, 4946
Silva, Fernando Antônio Rezende da, 4947-4948
Silva Filho, Amilcar Pereira da, 4949
Silva, Geraldo Afonso da, 7160
Silva, Hélio, 8927
Silva, Hilberto Mascarenhas Alves da, 6355
Silva, Iná, 6356
Silva, John P., 629, 778
Silva, Luis Angel, 1060
Silva, Luiz Carlos, 6357
Silva, Luiz Ferreira da, 7139
Silva, M.A. Pereira da, 2122
Silva, Maria Lúcia Carvalho da, 10050
Silva, Maria Thereza L.L. de Castro e, 4969, 10007
Silva, Mauricio Paranhos da, 924
Silva, Nalcir S., 10051
Silva, Odon Pereira da, 9944
Silva, Paulo de Castro Moreira da, 7189
Silva, Regina Nazaré e, 10052
Silva, Víctor, 6185
Silva, Washington Baliero, 4672
Silva-Bárcenas, A., 6694
Silva Celson, José da. *See* Celson, José da Silva.
Silva Herzog, Jesúsn 8176
Silva Kingston, Lucia. *See* Kingston, Lucia Silva.
Silva Lacaz, Carlos da. *See* Lacaz, Carlos da Silva.

Silva Mota, Joanna Luzia da. *See* Mota, Joanna Luzia da Silva.
Silvacolmenares, Julio, 9683
Silveira, José Celso Bortoluzzi da, 7065
Silver, Daniel B., 1130
Silverman, Bertram, 8243
Silvers, Arthur L., 4950
Silvert, Kalman H., 6531
Sime, Francisco, 2211a
Simmons, Alan B., 2043, 2062
Simmons, M.P., 686
Simmons, Roger A., 1534
Simões, G.V., 2209
Simões, Mário F., 925-925a
Simon, Michel, 120I
Simonsen, Mário Henrique, 4951-4955
Simposio del Proyecto Puebla-Tlaxcala, *I, Puebla, Mex., 1973,* 779
Simpósio e Mesa Redonda de Plantas Medicinais do Brasil, *IV, Rio, 1973,* 2261
Simpósio Florestal na Bahia, *I, Salvador, Bra., 1973,* 7190
Simpósio International sobre Fauna Silvestre e Pesca Fluvial e Lacustre Amazônicas, *Manaus, Bra., 1973,* 7191
Simposio Internacional sobre Posibles Relaciones Transatlánticas Precolombinas, *I, Las Palmas, Spain, 1971,* 671
Simpósio sobre a Reforma do Ensino de 1° e 2° Graus, *Pôrto Alegre, 1972,* 6358
Simpósio sôbre Desenvolvimento Urbano, *Rio, 1974,* 6553
Simposio sobre el Desarrollo de la Piscicultura en el Peru, *Lima, 1973,* 6999
Simposio sobre el Uso de los Datos de Población del Censo de 1970, *Santo Domingo, 1972,* 6590
Simpósio sobre Planejamento da Educação, *São Paulo, 1972,* 6359
Simpósio sôbre Poluição Ambiental, *I, Brasília, 1971,* 6554
Simpson, Joy M., 1293jSimpson, Miles, 6051
Sinaloa: desarrollo urbano, 9746
Singelmann, Peter, 513, 9684
Singer, Paul Israel, 4956-4958, 10053
Singh, Kelvin, 1253
Singham, A.W., 8202
Singham, Archie, 1222
Singham, N.L., 8202
Siqueira, Jurandir Bezerra de, 7160
Siqueira Júnior, Waldomiro, 7130
Siskind, Janet, 1399
Sisson, Edward B., 780
Sito, Nilda, 9685
Sitton, Salomón Nahmad, 1183
La situación del indígena en América del Sur: aportes al estudio de la fricción interétnica en los indios no-andinos, 1400
Siverts, Henning, 1535, 9747
Sizonenko, A. I., 8817a
Skidmore, Thomas E., 8594
Sklar, Barry, 8797
Slighton, Robert L., 4194
Sloan, John W., 4195, 4379, 4512
Sluzki, Carlos E., 9911
Smailus, O., 513
Small, Priscilla, 1920
Smetherman, Bobbie B., 8794
Smetherman, Robert M., 8794
Smith, A. Ledyard, 781
Smith, Clifford T., 7000
Smith, David Horton, 8107, 9892
Smith, Frank R., 2185
Smith, Harvey P., Jr., 782
Smith, M.G., 1294
Smith, Margo L., 1536
Smith, Mary Elizabeth, 513, 797
Smith, Peter H., 8692
Smith, Peter Seaborn, 8595
Smith, Richard Chase, 1537
Smith, Richard D., 1939
Smith, Robert Freeman, 8817b
Smith, Stephen, 4601
Smith, T. Lynn, 9686-9687, 10054-10055
Smolka, Martin O., 4796, 4959
Snow, Sebastian, 6751
Snyder, L.M., 2075
Soares, Glaucio Ary Dillon, 8595a
Soares de Carvalho Neto, Joviniano. *See* Carvalho Neto, Joviniano Soares de.
Soares e Silva, Edmundo de Macedo. *See* Silva, Edmundo de Macedo Soares e.
Soberanía marítima: fundamentos de la posición peruana, 8928
Social and Economic Studies, 8203-8204, 9688
Sociedad Argentina de Defensa de la Tradición, Familia y Propieded (TFP), *Buenos Aires.* Consejo Nacional, 8693
Sociedad de Promoción de Valores Nacionales, *Santiago,* 7271
Sociedad Rural Argentina, Buenos Aires, 6806
La Sociedad y el Universitario, 6136
La Sociedad y el universitario: un análisis del conflicto estudiantil y de la educación superior en Columbia, 9846
Sociedade brasileira: 1974, 104
Sociedade Comercial e Representações Gráficas Ltda. (firm), *Curitiba, Bra.,* 7240, 7257-7259, 7269
La sociologie du développement latinoaméricain: pts.1/2, 9689-9690
Socorro del Hoyo Briones, María del, 77

Solanet, Manuel A., 4960
Solano, Darío, 6200
Solar, Franz, 4961
Solari, Aldo E., 9914
Solaún, Mauricio, 8108, 8353
Sole Sanroma, Nuria, 6913
Soler, Carlos Marcelino, 6807
Soles, Orlando, 825
Soles, Roger E., 9847
Solís M., Leopoldo, 4034, 4316-4317
Solon de Pontes, Élio Monnerat. See Pontes, Élio Monnerat Solon de.
Somermeyer, W.H., 4282
Sommer, Juan, 4702
Somoza, Jorge L., 2027, O909
Somoza García, Anastasio, 8195
Sonnet, Fernando H., 4684-4685
Sonntag, Heinz Rudolf, 8387
Sorensen, Arthur P., Jr., 1361
Sorensen, Soren C., 2212
Soria Galvarro R., Jorge, 6108
Sosa, Antonio Juan, 8514
Sosa, Ademar L., 6180
Sosa, Edith, 8819
Sosnowsky, Valentín, 6195
Soto, Oscar David, 4573
Souffrant, Claude, 1295
Sousa dos Reis, Raimundo. See Reis, Raimundo Sousa dos.
Sousa Montenegro, João Alfredo de. See Montenegro, João Alfredo de Sousa.
Soutar, Andrew, 7006
Souto, Cláudio, 10056
Souza, Alberto de Mello, 4815
Souza, Eli de Moraes, 4962, 7192
Souza, Heitor G. de, 6360
Souza, Júlio César de Mello, 6361-6362
Souza, Levy Xavier de, 7193
Souza, Rubén Darío, 8833
Souza Carneiro, Nelson. See Carneiro, Nelson Souza.
Souza Lopes, Oscar. See Lopes, Oscar Souza.
Souza Martins, José de. See Martins, José de Souza.
Souza Patto, Maria Helena. See Patto, Maria Helena Souza.
Souza Sobrinho, 8595b
Spektor, Susana, 9880
Spence, Michael W., 2016
Sperandio, Liliana, 78
Sperb, Dalilla C., 6363
Spielman, Richard S., 2079, 2123-2125
Spindel, Cheywa Rojza, 10057
Spores, Ronald, 783
Spota, Luis, 8817c
Spranz, Bodo, 797
Stähle, V.D., 513
Stallings, Barbara, 8509
Stamper, B. Maxwell, 6555
Stanfield, David, 4601, 10058
Staniford, Philip, 10059
Stanton, Howard R., 1221
Statement of Jamacanisation, 4365
Stavrakis Puleston, O., 513
Stea, David, 1221
Stedman, J.G., 1282
Steadman, M., 2092
Stearman, Allyn MacLean, 1538, 6834
Steel, Beverly, 1222
Steele, Colin, 65
Stefanich, Juan, 8929
Stehberg, Rubén, 948c-948d
Stein, William W., 1539-1541
Steinberg, A.G., 2117
Stenger, Carl, 6556
Stepan, Alfred C., 8036, 8596
Stephens, S.G., 1047
Stephenson, Richard W., 7204
Stern, Jean, 784
Stern, Lilo, 1184
Sternberg, Marvin J., 4196
Stevens, Evelyn P., 8109-8110, 8177
Steward, Julian H., 1361
Stewart, Robert, 2017
Stewart, T. Dale, 672, 1287, 2018
Stiefold, Annette, 8043
Stingl, Miloslav, 673
Stini, William A., 2186-2187
Stöhr, Walter, 6549
Stölen, Kristianne, 4688
Stoll, Otto, 1185
Stone, Carl, 1296
Stone, D., 513
Stone, Jeffrey W., 9777
Stone, Linda S., 1233
Stoopler, Mark, 2188
Storni, H., 513
Storrs, Keith Larry, 8930
Stouse, Pierre A.D., Jr., 6712
Stout, Mickey, 1940-1941, 1948
Strange, Ian J., 6808
Strany Sotsializma i Latinskai Amerika, 8794a
Streeter, Lanny E., 4197
Strickon, Arnold, 8111, 9604
Stringer, Hugh, 6713
Stritch, Thomas, 8086
Stross, Brian, 1186, 1942
Sturm, Alzemiro E., 7194
Sturzenegger, Adolfo C., 4753-4754
Suanes, Héctor, 9915
Suárez, Jorge A., 1943-1945
Suárez, Luis, 9748
Suárez, María Matilde, 513, 1461, 2028, 2262
Suárez, Pablo, 8112
Suárez G., Luis, 6190
Suárez Sarabia, Irene Alicia, 6714
Subercaseaux, Benjamin, 6867

Suchlicki, Jaime, 147
Sucupira, Newton, 6364
SUDENE Informa, 8597
Suivant, Louis, 4339
Sujo Volsky, Jeannine, 1063
Sullivan, T.D., 513
Súmulas biográficas de cidadãos prestantes, 105
Sunkel, Osvaldo, 4198-4199, 8074
Suñol, Julio, 8184
Superintendência do Desenvolvimento da Região Sul (SUDESUL), Pôrto Alegre, Bra. Divisão de Documentação, 6365
Superintendência do Desenvolvimento do Nordeste, Recife, Bra. Departamento de Recursos Humanos. Divisão de Educaçao, 6366
Suplicy, Eduardo M., 4963
Supplement to the Handbook of the Robert Woods Bliss Collection of Pre-Columbian Art, 785
Surcou Macedo, Rodolfo, 8418
Suzigan, Wilson, 4964-4965, 4986
Swadesh, Mauricio, 1844, 1946
Swanson, Gerald, 8321
Sweetman, Rosemary, 605
Sweezy, Paul M., 8244, 8499
Swisshelm, Germán, 1947
Syle, John, 9604
Symposium, 6367
Syro Giraldo, Samuel, 8343a
Syrquin, M., 4318
Syrvud, Donald E., 8597a
Szilvassy, Arpad, 8597b
Szymanski, Albert, 8795
Syvrud, Donald E., 4966
Ta Ngoc Châu, 6137
Taccone, Juan J., 8694
Tak, Jean van der. See van der Tak, Jean.
Talleres-Escuela Don Bosco, La Paz, 7226
Tamames Gómez, Ramón, 4200-4201
Tamayo Herrera, José, 1418, 1542
Tampeau, Valerie, 4631
Tancer, Shoshana B., 9817
Tanis, Robert J., 2126-2127
Tareas, 4404
Tata de Suárez, Gema, 6190
Taufic, Camilo, 8113, 8500
Tavares, Denise Fernandes, 79
Tavares, José Antônio Giusti, 8598
Tavares, Maria de Conceição, 4967-4968
Tavares, Vania Porto, 4969
Tavares de Andrade, José Maria. See Andrade, José Maria Tavares de.
Tavares de Aranjo, José, Júnior. See Aranjo, José Tavares de, Júnior.
Tavárez Justo, Emma, 6146
Taylor, Alice, 6752
Taylor, Duncan, 6585
Taylor, Lance, 2184

Taylor, R.E., 605
Taylor, W.W., 513
Technical Seminar on Automated Data Processing in Tax Administration, IV, Lima, 1971, 4202
Técnica Buck Ltda. (firm), Brazil, 7195
Teitel, Simón, 4203
Teitelbaum, Jaime, 8608
Teixeira da Mota, A. See Mota, A. Teixeira da.
Teixeira de Macedo, Sérgio D. See Macedo, Sérgio D. Teixeira de.
Teixeira Filho, A.L., 4970
Tekiner, Rosselle, 513, 858
Telecomunicações: alguns temas, 9691
Teller, Charles H., 6635
Téllez Girón Padilla, Marcio, 6715
Tello, Carlos, 4319
Tello, Manuel, 8811, 8818
Temas, 9692
Temas colombianos: aspectos y problemas de una política de desarrollo, 4513
Tendencias demográficas y opciones para políticas de población en América Latina, 9693
Tepfenhart, M.A., 2117
Terhal, P., 4204
Termer, Franz, 786
Terra, Adamastor, 8598a
Terrades Saborit, I., 513
Terranova, R., 513
Terrera, Guillermo Alfredo, 8695-8695a
Terrero, José Martínez, 4205
Terzo, Frederick C., 4504, 4569
Testa, Víctor, 4206, 8796
Testimonio de un diálogo universitario sobre la soberanía, 8834
Testimonio en la muerte de Manuel Gómez Morin, 8178
Testimonios sobre la formación para el trabajo: 1539-1970, 6196
Teubal, Miguel, 4755
Teves R., Néstor, 7001
Tharp, Roland G., 1144
Thayer Escalona, Carlos, 6852
Theberge, James D., 8796a, 8862
Thesing, Josef, 8114
Thieck, Frederic, 826
Thiesenhusen, William C., 9871
Thofehrn, Hans A., 7270
Thomas, Dani B., 8115
Thomas, David J., 1401
Thomas, Garry L., 1297
Thomas, Norman D., 1187
Thomas, P.M., Jr., 683
Thomas, R. Brooke, 2205
Thomas, Robert N., 6632, 6636
Thome, Joseph R., 6868
Thompson, Donald E., 513, 1030c, 1048-1048c

Thompson, J. Eric S., 629, 633, 674
Thompson, Richard A., 1188-1189, 2063
Thomson, Robert L., 6549
Thomson, Ruth, 1940-1941, 1948
Thorne, J.P., 1949
Thorp, Rosemary, 4230
Tibón, G., 513
Tichy, Franz, 702
Tierra Nueva, 8116
Tietze, Christopher, 9682
Timo, E., 513
Tilbery, Henry, 4207
Timofeeva, N.A., 6918
Tinajero, Jorge R., 6935
Tinao, Daniel E., 6050
Tinelli, Arthur Carlos, 4971
Tinker, Jon, 7002
Tinoco, Pedro, 8539
Tironi, Ernesto, 4632
Titiev, Mischa, 1361, 1543
Tjarks, Alícia V., 8931
Tobelem, Alain, 7196
Tobias, José Antonio, 6368
Tobón, Alonso, 4514
Todaro Williams, Margaret, 8599
Togo, José, 894
Tokman, Víctor E. 4203, 4574, 4756
Tolipan, Ricardo, 4971
Tolosa, Hamilton C., 4972
Tomasek, Robert D., 8863
Tomasi, Pierre, 7225
Tomasini, J.T., 2181
Tommasi de Magrelli, W., 513
Tomo, Aldo P., 6809
Tompakow, Roland, 9697
Tondini, Angelo, 4430
Torales, Ponciano, 4208
Toran, Carey D., 1233
Tord, Luis Enrique, 7003
Torloni, Hilário, 4973
Torrance, E. Paul, 9724
Torre, Juan Carlos, 8663a
Torre Barba, Joaquín Gómez de la, 983
Tôrres, Antônio Francisco, 4974
Torres, B., 513
Torres, Camilo, 1487, 8355
Torres, Horacio, 6547
Torres, James F., 4209-4210, 8117-8118
Torres, Juan José, 8419
Torres, Livingstone Belo, 10060
Torres, M., 8354
Tôrres Araújo, Acrísio. *See* Araújo, Acrísio Tôrres.
Torres de Araúz, Reina, 827, 1191-1192, 6650
Torres, Guzmán, Manuel, 787
Torres Padilla, Oscar, 6114
Torres Paranhos, Oscar. *See* Paranhos, Oscar Torres.
Torres Pinedo, R., 2166, 2189

Torres Rivas, Edelberto, 9774-9775
Torres Trueba, Henry, 1193
Torres y Torres Lara, Carlos, 4664
Torrijos Herrera, Omar, 8199
Tortolani, Paul, 8191
Tortosa, José M., 1544
Toryho, Jacinto, 8696
Tosi, Joseph A., Jr., 7282
Tostes, Sérgio, 8588a
Toto Patiño, Alfonso, 6914
Touring y Automóvil Club del Perú, Lima. Departamento de Cartografía y Relevamiento, 7339
Tovar, Oscar, 7004
Tovar Pinzón, Hermes, 522
Trabalho inédito de Anísio Teixeira sobre o brinquedo, 6369
Tracy, Francis V., 1950
Tracy, Hubert P., 1951
Tracy, Martha, 1951
La tragedia chilena: testimonios, 8501
Trautmann, Wolfgang, 675-676, 6716
Travieso, Carmen Clemente, 7038
Trejo Reyes, Saúl, 4211, 9749
Trayectoria de huracanes y de perturbaciones ciclónicas del Océano Atlántico, del Mar Caribe y del Golfo de México, 1919-1969, 7348
Trevignani, Henry Horacio, 8697
Treviñon Pepe, 8697a
Trías, Vivian, 4212, 8620-8620a
Trimborn, Hermann, 513, 1049-1049a
Trinidad and Tobago. Ministry of Finance, 4366
Trinidade, Hélgio Henrique C., 8600-8600a
Trindade, Maria Zélia Damásio, 6370
Trinidad and Tobago, Constitution Commission, 8285
Trinidad and Tobago. Surveys Division, 7349
Trivelli O., Hugo, 4600
Troncoso, Oscar, 8119
Trotman, Donald A.B., 8932
Truchis, Manuel, 8388
True, D.L., 939
Trueblood, Felicity M., 9625
Truman, Edwin M., 4050
Trusov, Ivan I., 6586
Tschohl, Peter, 677
Tugwell, Franklin, 8539a
Tull, Marc, 1297
Tullis, F. LaMond, 8601-8601a
Tuohy, William S., 8149, 8179
Turcios Lima, 8192
Turner, B.L., 678
Turner, Frederick C., 8120
Turner, Paul R., 1194, 1952
Turner, Victor, 1195
Tutino, Saverio, 8245

Tyler, William G., 4213, 4975-4978
Uchôa Guerra, Francisco das Chagas. See Guerra, Francisco das Chagas Uchôa.
Uchuya Capcha, José, 4641
Ucrós, Anamaría, 9832
Ugalde, Antonio, 9750
Uhlenberg, Peter, 2064
Uhlig, Ralf-Dieter, 7005
Ulhoa Saraiva, Helcio. See Saraiva, Helcio Ulhoa.
Ulloa, F., 2232
Ulloa, Fernando, 9910
UNESCO en Chile. Boletín de la Comisión Nacional. No. 42, mayo 1973- Santiago, 6052
Unger, Elke, 1930
United Nations. Comisión Económica para América Latina (CEPAL), 4214-4218
United Nations Conference on Transport and Development, *Geneva, 1970,* 4228
United Nations. Departamento de Asuntos Económicos y Sociales, 4219
United Nations. Development Program, 8933
United Nations. Economic Commission for Latin America (ECLA), 4220-4227
United Nations. Development Programme. Physical Planning Project, *St. John's, Antigua,* 7350
United Nations. International Labour Organization (ILO), *Geneva.* See International Labour Organization, *Geneva.*
United Nations Office of Educational, Scientific and Cultural Organization (UNESCO). Office of Statistics, 6138
United Nations. Physical Planning Office, 7351
United States. Central Intelligence Agency, 7241, 7284, 7292, 7342
United States. Congress. House of Representatives. Committee on Foreign Affairs, 8797
United States. Department of Agriculture. Economic Research Service, 4757
United States. Department of Commerce, 4979
United States. Department of State. Arms Control and Disarmament Agency, 8121
United States. Department of State. Bureau of Public Affairs, 8122
United States. Department of State. Office of Media Services. Bureau of Public Affairs, 8798, 8835, 8934
United States. Department of the Interior. Board of Geographic Names. Defense Mapping Agency. Topographic Center, 6591
United States. Senate. Committee on the Judiciary. Subcommittee to Investigate Problems Connected with Refugees and Escapees, 8502
The U.S. response to the Chilean coup, 8935
La Universidad, 8187
Universidad Autónoma de Santo Domingo, *Santo Domingo.* Instituto Geográfico Universitario, 7287
Universidad Boliviana Mayor Tomás Frías, *Potosí, Bol.* División de Extensión Universitaria, 42
Universidad de La Pampa, *Santa Rosa de Toay, Arg.,* 6092
Universidad de la República, *Montevideo,* 43
Universidad de la República, *Montevideo.* Escuela Nacional de Bellas Artes, 6181
Universidad de los Andes, *Bogotá.* Comité de Investigaciones, 44
Universidad de los Andes, *Mérida, Ven.* Facultad de Economía. Instituto de Investigaciones Económicas, 7039
Universidad de los Andes, *Mérida, Ven.* Facultad de Humanidades y Educación. Centro de Investigaciones Literarias, 19
Universidad Federal do Paraná, *Curitiba, Bra.* Instituto de Letras e Artes. Centro de Estudos Brasileiros, 45
Universidad Mayor de San Andrés, *La Paz.* Centro Nacional de Documentación Cinetífica y Tecnológica, 80
Universidad Nacional de Colombia, *Bogotá.* División de Programación Económica, 6139
Universidad Nacional de Córdoba, *Arg.* Dirección de Planeamiento, 6093-6094
Universidad Nacional de Córdoba, *Arg.* Secretaría Técnica de Planeamiento, 6095
Universidad Nacional de Cuyo, *Mendoza, Arg.* Rectorado, 6096
Universidad Nacional de Tucumán, *Arg.* Programa de Estadística Universitaria, 6097
Universidade Católica de Pelotas, *Bra.,* 6371
Universidade de Brasília, *Bra.,* 6372
Universidade de São Paulo, *Bra.* Museu de Arte Contemporânea, 6373
Universidade Federal da Bahia, *Bra.,* 7197
Universidade Federal da Bahia, *Bra.* Escola de Administração. Centro de Administração Pública, 8602
Universidade Federal da Bahia, *Salvador, Bra.* Instituto de Geociências, 7260
Universidade Federal de Minas Gerais, *Belo Horizonte, Bra.,* 6374
Universidade Federal de Minas Gerais, *Belo Horizonte, Bra.* Centro de Desen-

volvimento e Planejamento Regional (CEDEPLAR), 4980
Universidade Federal de Viçosa, Bra. Biblioteca Central. Seção de Bibliografia e Documentação, 126
Universidade Federal do Rio Grande do Norte, Natal, Bra., 6375
Universidade-Industria: uma integração que já e realidade, 6376
Universidade para o Desenvolvimento do Estado de Santa Catarina, Florianópolis, Bra. Faculdade de Educação. Centro de Estudos e Pesquisa Educacionais, 6377-6378
Universidade para o Desenvolvimento do Estado de Santa Catarina, Florianópolis, Bra. Instituto Técnico de Administração e Gerência, 4981
Universidades, 6053-6062
University of Wisconsin, *Madison.* Land Tenure Center, 6557
Urbano, Henrique O., 1420
Ure, John, 6869
Uribe, J., 8309
Uribe Ortega, Graciela, 6870
Uribe Villegas, Oscar, 1953
Urondo, Francisco, 8698
Urquidi, Víctor L., 4229-4230
Urrejola Dittborn, Carlos, 949
Urrutia, Cecilia, 9872
Urrutia Montoya, Miguel, 4515-4516
Uruguay. Administración de Ferrocarriles del Estado (AFE), 7019
Uruguay. Ministerio de Economía y Finanzas. Dirección General de Estadística y Censos, 4677-4682
Uruguay. Ministerio de Hacienda. Dirección General de Estadística y Censos, 7020
Uruguay. Ministerio de Transporte, Comunicaciones, y Turismo, 7343
Uruguay. Ministerio de Instrucción Pública y Previsión Social. Comisión Coordinadora de los Entes de Enseñanza, 6182
Uruguay. Ministerio del Interior, 8621
Uruguay. Presidencia. Secretaría, 8936
Uruguay. Servicio Geográfico Militar, 7344
Urzúa, Raúl, 9873
Usera Mata, Luis de, 1050
Utumi, Américo, 4982
Uzzell, Douglas, 1196, 1494, 1545-1546
Vaitsos, Constantine V., 4517
Valdés, Nelson P., 4412, 8209, 8246
Valdés, Pablo, 8503
Valdez, A., 513
Valdez y Palacios, Josè Manuel, 6753
Valdman, Albert, 1288a
Valencia Vega, Alipio, 8420
Valente, Murillo Gurgel, 8603
Valente Martins, José, 10061
Valente Pereira, Maria da Luz. *See* Pereira, Maria da Luz Valente.
Valenzuela, Jaime, 4569
Valenzuela, Salomón Rivas, 6835
Valenzuela Feijóo, José, 4231
Valey, E[mil']B[orisovich], 4431
Valla, Victor, 8937
Vallarino, Yolanda, 6182a
Vallejo, Antonio R., 8836
Vallejo A., Joaquin, 4518
Vallenilla, Luis, 4575
Valles, Jorge, 9751
van den Berghe, Pierre, 1421, 1494
van der Dijs, Bertha, 6038
Van der Hammen, Thomas, 6754
van der Tak, Jean, 2065, 9773
van Es, J.C. *See* Es, J.C. van.
van Ginneken, Jeroen, 9677
van Heen, J.M. Schillhorn, 2090
van Kolck, Odette Lourenção. *See* Kolck, Odette Lourenção Van.
van Rijckeghem, W., 4734
Vandendries, René, 6548
Vandervelde, Marjorie, 1197
Vapñarsky, César A., 9694
Varela, Teodosio, 4519
Varese, Stefano, 1402, 1547-1548
Vargas, Arete Saldanha, 6379
Vargas Iraida, 513, 1062a-1062b
Vargas, José María, 6936
Vargas Carreño, Edmundo, 8799
Vargas Guadarrama, Luis A., 2011, 2019
Varo, Carlos, 8281
Varsavsky, Oscar, 4232-4233
Vasconcelos, Amílcar, 8622
Vasconcelos, Jarbas, 4983
Vasconcelos, Justino, 8603a
Vasconcelos Cavalcanti, Clóvis de. *See* Calvalcanti, Clóvis de Vasconcelos.
Vasconcelos Sobrinho, J., 7198
Vassoigne, Yolène de, 1208
Vaughan, Denton R., 6558
Vaughn, Jack Hood, 8837
Vaz da Costa, Rubens. *See* Costa, Rubens Baz da.
Văzquez Calcerrada, Pablo B., 9610
Vebr, Lubomír, 6045
Veeh, H. Herbert, 7006
Veen, L.J. van der, 1298
Vega, Bernardo, 4367
Vega, J.J., 513
Vega Carballo, José Luis, 8123, 8185
Vela, Carlos, 4234
Vela, Ruth de, 6950
Velasco, Gustavo R., 4320
Velasco Alvarado, Juan, 8389
Velasco Fernández, Hugo Mauricio, 6063
Velásquez M., Luis Guillermo, 8356

Velázquez, Tulio, 2199
Velho, Gilberto, 10062-10063
Velho, Otávio Guilherme, 7199
Véliz, Claudio, 4235
Vellard, J., 1549
Velloso, Diderot M., 4984
Velloso, João Paulo dos Reis, 10064
Velloso, Tânia Pütten, 4985
Velloso Galvão, Marília. See Galvão, Marília Velloso.
Veloz Maggiolo, Marcio, 845, 845a
Venezuela. Comisión de Administración Pública (CAP), 8540
Venezuela. Comisión del Plan Nacional de Aprovechamiento de los Recursos Hidráulicos (COPLANARH), 7040
Venezuela. Congreso. Comisión Redactora del Proyecto, 8540a
Venezuela. Dirección de Cartografía Nacional, 7346
Venezuela. Ministerio de Educación, 6064
Venezuela. Ministerio de Fomento. Dirección General de Estadísticas y Censos Nacionales, 4576
Venezuela. Ministerio de Minas e Hidrocarburos. Dirección de Geología, 7347
Venezuela. Ministerio de Minas e Hidrocarburos. Dirección General. Oficina de Economía Petrolera, 4577
Venezuela. Ministerio de Obras Públicas. Dirección de Planeamiento. División de Planeamiento Regional, 9826
Venezuela. Presidencia, 8540b
Venezuela. Presidencia. Comisión de Administración Pública, 8540c
Venezuela. Presidencia. Oficina Central de Coordinación y Planificación (CORDIPLAN), 4578-4579
Vento, Ercillo, 825
Venturini, Orlando, 7041
Vera, Luis, 6549
Vera Segura, Nelson, 4641
Vera Villalobos, Enrique, 8938
Verduga Vélez, César, 4633
Verner, Joel Gordon, 8124, 8193, 8205
Vernet, Juan, 671
Vernon, Raymond, 8125, 8800
Verón, Eliseo, 9911
Versiani Cunha, Maria Auxiliadora. See Cunha, Maria Auxiliadora Versiani.
Vian, Itamar Navildo, 6247
Viana, Adolpho Carlos Camargo, 7157
Víctor, Hugo A., 8833
Victoria, Marcos, 9695
Vidal, H., 2103
Vidales, Carlos, 8504
Vieira, Gilberto, 8357
Vieira, José Paulo Carneiro, 10065
Vieira, R.A. Amaral, 10066

Vieira Passos, Wilson. See Passos, Wilson Vieira.
Viélot, Kléber, 1288a
Vieuz, Serge, 1288a
Vigas D., Nelson, 4566
Vigo, Juan M., 8699
Vila, Fernando, 6810
Vila, Marco-Aurelio, 7042-7043
Vila Vilar, E., 513
Vilaça, Antônio, 7200
Vilar de Queiroz, José Maria. See Queiroz, José Maria Vilar de.
Vilas, Carlos María, 4368, 8838, 9778
Villa, Jaime, 6643
Villa Rojas, Alfonso, 1198
Villacorta Escobar, Manuel, 4405
Villacres Moscoso, Jorge W., 6937
Villagrán Kramer, Francisco, 4236
Villalba, Alfonso, 9696
Villamizar, Marina, 954
Villanueva, Javier, 4730
Villarejos, Víctor M., 2190, 2263-2264
Villas Bôas, Orlando, 1403-1404
Villas-Bôas, Pedro, 20
Villate, Bonilla, Eduardo, 4237
Villaveces, Jorge, 8358
Villaverde, Juan, 8801
Villavicencio Rivadeneira, Gladys, 1550
Villega Moreno, Luis Alberto, 6915-6916
Villegas, Osiris Guillermo, 8939
Villegas, Sergio, 8505
Villela, Annibal, 4780, 4986
Vincent, Clark E., 9765
Vinhas, M., 10067
Virasoro, Rafael, 6811
Vírvez, Donató, 1199
Viscarra, Irma A. de, 6822
Viscaya Canales, Isidro, 4321
Viste el Perú y sus hoteles, 7007
Vital, Sebastião Marcos, 4987-4988
Viteri, Fernando E., 2182, 2191
Viteri Gamboa, Julio, 859
Vivanco, Jorge E., 6938
Vivanco Flores, Carlos A., 1419-1420
Vivante, Armando, 1405
Vivas Dorado, Raúl, 6140
Viveiros de Castro, Ormindo. See Castro, Ormindo Viveiros de.
Vivó Escoto, Jorge A., 6612
Vogel, James A., 2213-2214
Vogel, R.C., 4238
Vogeler, Ingolf, 683
Vogt, Evon Z., 1200
Vollemaere, A.L., 513
Vollers, J.L., 1299
Volsky, George, 8247
Von Borries, Edgar, 950
von Doellinger, Carlos. See Doellinger, Carlos von.
Von Hoegen, Miguel, 9750

von Winning, Hasso, 513, 788-789
Una voz del Tercer Mundo, 8180
Vuijsje, H., 1300
Wagenheim, Kaln 6606
Waggoner, George R., 6065
Wagley, Charles 523, 1361
Wagner, Erika, 513, 524-525, 1064-1064b
Wagner de Reyna, Alberto, 8390
Wahab, I., 4239
Walcott, Derek, 1301
Walker, Della, 1247
Walker, Kenneth N., 6039
Waller, Helen, 1954
Wallin, Ruth B., 1805-1806
Wallis, Ethel Emily, 1406
Walter, Heinrich, 6559
Walters, Alan, 6609
Walton, James, 1955
Walton, John, 8126
Wanderley Reis, Fábio. See Reis, Fábio Wanderley.
Wang, Chien-hsün, 8802
Wanick Ribeiro, Sylvio, 4929
Ward, Douglas S., 8127
Ward, Richard H., 2107-2108, 2128
Warman, Arturo, 8181
Warming, Eugênio, 7201
Wassén, S. Henry 897, 1051
Wasson, R. Gordon, 1956
Watanabe, Luis, 1031e
Watanabe, S., 4322
Waterhouse, Viola G., 1857
Watson, G. Llewellyn, 1302
Watson, Lawrence C., 1407-1408
Watson-Franke, Maria-Barbara, 1409-1410
Wearing, Brian, 1247
Weaver, Jerry L., 8803
Weaver, T., 513
Webb, Kempton E., 7201a
Webb, Richard, 4665
Weber, G., 513
Webster, D.L., 683
Webster, Steven S., 1551
Weeks, Morris, Jr., 6607
Weigand, Phil C., 605
Weil, Pierre, 9697
Weinstein, B. J. de, 2129
Weischet, Wolgang, 6871
Weiss, Gerald 1361, 1411-1412
Weisskoff, Richard, 4240
Weitkamp, Lowell R., 2130-2132
Weker, H.N., 1303
Weller, Robert, 9698
Welsh, Eileen, 9854
Wengen, G.D. van, 1304
Wennergren, E. Boyd, 4593
Wenzens, Gerd, 6717
Werneck R. de Carvalho, Eduardo. See Carvalho, Eduardo Werneck R. de.
West, Robert C., 149
West B.R.T.; and Co., London, 7303
Westphalen, Wilfried, 1201
Wetering, W. van, 1282
Weyl, Richard, 6611
Wheatley, James, 1957-1958
Wheeler, James O., 6636
Whitaker, Morris D., 4593
White, Jeanne, 6939
White book of the change of government in Chile: 11th of September 1973, 8506
Whiteford, Andrew H., 1552
Whiteford, Michael B., 1553-1554, 9625
Whiting, Gordon C., 10058
Whitley, Glenn R., 790
Whitten, Norman E., Jr., 1487, 1555-1557
Who's notable in Mexico, 106
Whyte, William Foote, 1487, 1521
Wi Holden, David E., 9776
Wibel, John, 6532
Wiesner, Durán, Eduardo, 4479
Wiggins, Ira L., 6940
Wikander, Stig, 1959
Wilbert, Johannes, 984, 1413
Wilensky, Julius M., 6573
Wilford, W.T., 4378
Wilkerson, S. Jeffrey K., 629, 791
Wilkes, H. Garrison, 6613
Wilkie, James W., 6755
Willey, Gordon R., 606, 612, 633, 644, 679, 860, 1031d
Williams, Barbara J., 6718
Williams, Byron, 8282
Williams, Edward J., 8128
Williams, Eric, 1287, 8206
Williams, Glyn, 633
Williams, J. Earl, 8129
Williams, J.F., 2257
Williams, Margaret Todaro. See Todaro Williams, Margaret.
Williams, R.L., 6599
Williams García, Roberto, 1202
Williamson, Jeffrey G., 4896
Williamson, Robert B., 4241
Williamson, Robert C., 9874
Wilson, Carlos, 8623
Wilson, Carter, 1202a
Wilson, Eugene M., 738
Wilson, Jack L., 1203
Wilson, Peter, J., 1305, 1558
Wilson, Samuel, 9699
Wilson de O. Santos, José. See Santos, José Wilson de O.
Wiñar, David L., 6098
Wing, E.S., 686
Wing, Juvencio, 6164
Winkelmann, Don, 4264, 6719
Winn, Peter, 4634
Winsberg, Morton D., 4758, 6812
Winter, Carlos Thomas, 948b

Winter, Marcus C., 792
Wionczek, Miguel S., 4099, 4242-4245, 4323
Wise, Mary Ruth, 513, 1820, 1960
Wistrand, Kent, 1919
Witherspoon, Robert, 8515a
Witte, Ann Dryden, 4666
Witter, Geraldina Pôrto, 6380-6381
Wöhlcke, Manfred, 8130, 8803a
Wogart, Jan Peter, 4213, 4989-4990
Wolfe, Marshall, 8131
Wolpin, Miles D., 8940
Wood, Harold A., 6549
Woodhouse, Edward J., 4246
Wooding, Charles J., 1306-1307
Workman, P.L., 2077
Workshop: problemas de uma sociedade em mudanca, 10068
World Peace Council, Helsinki, 8132
Wouters, A.E., 1308
Wright, Freeman J., 8128
Wright, W.E., 513
Wurtman, R.J., 2159
Wustmann, Erich, 1414
Wyndham-White, Eric, 4247
Wynn, Jack T., 706
Xavier, Jesuan de Paula, 10069
Yager, Joseph A., 8133
Yajuar, Rumi, 4432
Yandle, Carolyn D., 9777
Yáñez, Rubén, 8624
Yarza C., Alberto J., 4324
Yassumoto, Y., 2261
Yaukey, D., 2052
The Year Book of World Affairs: 1973, 150
Yeaton, Leander, 1297
Yepes, J.M., 6756
Young, Marilyn Blatt, 8864
Young, Roger, 4520
Yudelevich, Moisés, 6872
Yunis Ahues, Eugenio, 6121
Zaldívar, Ramón, 4667
Zamalloa González, Zulma, 1420
Zammit, J. Ann, 8507
Zanfrognini, Giancarlo, 8508

Zapata, C.I., 2084
Zapata, Fausto, 4325
Zarubezhnye Tsentry po izuchentiiu Latinskoi Ameriki, 107
Zavala, D.F., 4580
Zavaleta Figueroa, Isaías, 7008
Zavaleta G., Amaro, 1008b
Zchock, Dieter K., 6197
Zea, Leopoldo, 6165
Zeballos Barrios, Carlos O., 7009
Zegers, B.J.M., 2133
Zegers de Landa, Gerardo, 4248
Zehnder, Wiltraut, 680
Zeil, Werner, 6782
Zeitlin, Maurice, 8248, 9875
Zeitschrift für Geschichtswissenschaft, 4249
Zeitschrift für Kulturaustausch, 151
Zemborain, Saturnino M., 4759, 6813
Zemelman, Hugo, 8429, 8472, 8479
Zéndegui, Guillermo de, 4250, 6066, 6592
Zenkovich, Vselvolod Pavlovich, 6720
Zerkowski, Ralph 4898
Zerries, O., 513, 1415
Zethelius, Sven, 6917
Zimbalist, Andy, 8509
Zimmermann de Ferreyra, María Elvira, 10
Zimmermann Zavala, Augusto, 8391
Zlater, Viera, 942b-942c
Zonn, S.V., 6918
Zorro Sánchez, Carlos, 4521
Zubieta, Tomás, 7225
Zubrow, Ezra B.W., 526
Zubryn, Emil, 793
Zucchi, Alberta, 513, 1065-1065c
Zulama Guglielmone, Hilda, 10
Zuleta Angel, Eduardo, 8941
Zuluaga, Francisco, 8359
Zúñiga, G.C., 2085
Zúñiga, Ricardo B., 1559
Zúñiga G., Carlos Iván, 8942
Zúñiga Ide, Jorge, 9876
Zuvekas, Clarence, Jr., 4251
Zymelman, Manuel, 4709